INTERVENTIONS

for Academic and Behavior Problems II:

Preventive and Remedial Approaches

Edited by

Mark R. Shinn, Ph.D.
Hill M. Walker, Ph.D.
Gary Stoner, Ph.D.

From the NASP Publications Board Operations Manual
The content of this document reflects the ideas and positions of the authors. The responsibility lies solely with the authors and does not necessarily reflect the position or ideas of the National Association of School Psychologists.

Published by the National Association of School Psychologists.

Copies may be ordered from:
NASP Publications
4340 East West Highway, Suite 402
Bethesda, MD 20814
(301) 657-0270
(301) 657-0275, fax
e-mail: *publications@naspweb.org*
www.nasponline.org

ISBN 0-932955-87-8 and 978 0932955-87-6

Printed in the United States of America

Fourth Printing, Winter 2006

10 9 8 7 6 5 4

ACKNOWLEDGMENTS

Sustaining the energy to support production of 38 edited chapters, written by some of the busiest scholars and practitioners in the country, would not have been possible for Mark R. Shinn without the support of the other Dr. Shinn and partner, Michelle, and the laughter and positive approach to life of sons Peter and Dominic. Special thanks must go to the chapter authors who contributed fine work and to the field reviewers (see below for the full list) who improved the product further.

Hill Walker wishes to express appreciation to the contributors of chapters to this volume. Their willingness to carve out these superb efforts from already overburdened schedules and substantial ongoing commitments speaks to their dedication in making best practices and state-of-the-art information available to professional consumers.

Gary Stoner expresses his appreciation and gratitude to his students—past, present, and future. Individually and collectively, they have provided, and continue to provide, opportunities to learn about and develop intervention and prevention strategies and activities in efforts to improve outcomes for children. Also, the efforts and contributions of each of the chapter authors are sincerely appreciated.

Finally, the editors would like to thank Brian Gaunt for editorial assistance in getting this project going; David Van Loo for sustaining its support and communication needs, including setting up electronic file transfer; Aziz Gokdemir and Mike Schwartz for their careful copyediting; and NASP publication committee chairs Leslie Paige and George Bear and NASP staff members Marilyn Brazier and Linda Morgan for their support.

List of reviewers:

Rose Allinder, Patty Ball, Rachel Brown-Chidsey, Andrea Canter, David Chard, Ray Christner, Amy Dilworth Gabel, Robert Dixon, Susan Dungan, Kevin Feldman, Kim Gibbons, Alex Granzin, Anne Graves, Assege HaileMariam, Heather Halsey, Keith Hollenbeck, Ron Jordan, Tom Kehle, Brian Martens, J. Christopher McGinnis, Scott Methe, Mike Meyer, Margaret O'Hearn-Curran, Robin Phaneuf, Judith Plasencia-Peinado, Robert Putnam, Alicia Rahn, Katrina Rhymer, Cathy Telzrow, Robin Thurber, Lee Wilkinson, and Chris Willis.

PREFACE

There is little doubt in the opinions of this volume's editors that neither this book nor its predecessor would have been written without the career contributions of Wesley C. Becker. Wes passed away quietly in the past year after years of service and support to our fields.

Our surmise is that few graduates of school psychology, special education, general education, or clinical psychology programs of recent years are familiar with his name or his work in making psychology applicable to education. In fact, at our ever-increasing pace in the Information Age, where new seems to replace old regardless of quality, it is quite likely that most school psychology practitioners are unaware of his influence. We worry that we all will take for granted the opportunities and bodies of knowledge Wes provided us as time passes from his pioneering efforts of the late 1960s and early 1970s.

Wes Becker graduated with a Ph.D. in Clinical Psychology, Statistics, and Learning Theory from Stanford University in 1954, completing his BA, MA, and doctoral degree in 6 years. While directing the Clinical Psychology Program at the University of Illinois, he was at the forefront of bringing the experimental analysis of behavior from the laboratory to the classroom. Working with teachers who had students with challenging behaviors in urban schools, he produced a body of knowledge that served as the foundation for applied behavior analysis and the behavior management practices used in the classrooms today. Wes served as the academic advisor of a whole generation of researchers and practitioners in applied behavior analysis and classroom management, including (in alphabetical order) C. H. Madsen, Donald Meichenbaum, K. Daniel O'Leary, Susan O'Leary, and many more.

Wes' contributions were not limited to the application and understanding of behavioral principles in the classroom. He was among the first to develop and disseminate simple and scientifically supported applications of behavioral principles to parent training. His book for parents, *Parents are Teachers*, which he wrote in 1971, has sold almost 293,000 copies. Last year, 30 years after its publication, it sold more than 1,000 copies.

No less remarkable for a man who was so integral to the beginnings of systematic (a) behavioral interventions in classrooms, and (b) parent training was Wes' later influence on the field of instructional practice. Through a set of fortuitous events, Wes was paired up with Ziggy Engelmann to co-direct the Direct Instruction (DI) model in

Project Follow Through 1968–1978. This federally funded project remains the largest educational research study in this country's history with over 100,000 primary-grade subjects from low-income communities nationwide. The DI model was implemented in 20 diverse, low-income communities with over 10,000 subjects.

The Engelmann-Becker DI model broke with prevailing convention that low-income students were somehow incapacitated by their poverty to the extent that they could not attain the achievement levels of other more advantaged students. Their well-designed, carefully sequenced curriculum, delivered through explicit instructional strategies, produced the greatest achievement outcomes of all the models tested in Project Follow Through. This work evolved into *DISTAR*, *Reading Mastery*, *Spelling Mastery*, *Corrective Reading*, and numerous spin-offs. The project produced another generation of researchers and academics in instructional design, including Doug Carnine and Russell Gersten.

It is not a coincidence that the bulk of the chapters in this volume are based on the design of carefully constructed behavioral, instructional, and parental interventions, with an emphasis on changing the environment rather than focusing solely on changing within-child characteristics. This is the influence, be it direct or indirect, of Wes Becker on the chapter authors.

More personally, each of us had the opportunity to work with him in a variety of roles. For Hill Walker, Wes Becker was a dear friend, valued colleague, and mentor for the better part of 30 years. For Mark Shinn, it was Wes Becker who as Associate Dean at the University of Oregon encouraged him to leave the comfort of public schools for the challenges of building and sustaining a science-driven, educationally focused, intervention-oriented school psychology program. It was Wes who, in his inimitable timeliness, provided Mark with direct and explicit feedback on writing, scholarship, and teaching. For Gary Stoner, Wes Becker provided the professional opportunity to become a faculty member within a growing, energetic, and innovative School Psychology Training Program at the University of Oregon. Wes also provided support in many ways for Gary's early professional growth and development, and was a valued friend and colleague.

This volume begins with the introductory chapter we asked Wes Becker to contribute to our 1991 *Interventions* book. As the reader will note, the core of his remarks were delivered in 1971. We believed them to be equally true in 1991 and hold steady to that belief in 2001. We only wish that Wes had the opportunity to say so himself.

Wesley C. Becker, Ph.D.
1928–2000

FOREWORD

Wesley C. Becker
University of Oregon

In February of 1971, nearly 20 years ago, I wrote what is quoted below as an introduction to a paper presented at the Florida State University Conference on "New Roles for School Psychologists." Many of the problems described in that paper are still present in the practice of school psychology today. In the edited collection which is the body of the book, I finally see a hope that school psychologists may be trained in and apply the interventions skills needed to be the "teacher's best friend" when it comes to solving classroom problems.

I stated at that time: "Many current problems in education can be traced to practices, presumably derived from psychological research, which have had the effect of encouraging teachers to get rid of their teaching failures rather than learning to deal with them. Many of these doubtful practices center around the use of tests by school psychologists to 'diagnose problems' and make recommendations on placement in special classes, treatment programs, the grouping of slow and fast learners, or grouping on the basis of readiness tests. Historically, many of these practices were generated from the application of a medical model to problems in clinical psychology, which was subsequently transferred to educational problems. The basic idea was that if a child is failing to learn or behave appropriately in school, there is something wrong with the child ..."

I then proceeded to describe in the paper some of the ways children with problems were characterized then. "Some children have low IQ's and it is assumed that they learn at slower rates and should be taught less. [This assumption has been clearly contradicted by recent research (Gersten, Becker, Heiry, & White, 1984)] ... Another kind of practice which actively leads to not trying to solve problems is diagnosing the failure as due to a lack of readiness. Often readiness is assumed to come with maturation, so that there is little the teacher can do but wait. In the meantime, valuable instructional time is lost and the not-ready children get further behind their peers ... However, more enlightened educators today (1971) see this 'lack of readiness' as an absence of certain preskills which can be taught. In the area of reading, however, the diagnosis of what needs to be taught often misses the mark. Children are given much practice in visual discriminations ('picture reading') and training in motor skills (walking a balance beam), little of which involves the skills needed in discriminating letters or tying "saying sounds" to the letter symbols. That current readiness tests (remember 1971) miss the mark is illustrated by findings in one of our Follow Through sites. The kindergarten children pretested at the 50th percentile but now they all could read."

I went on to describe problems of poorly motivated students. "Some children are difficult to manage and motivate using traditional methods and curricula. School psychologists in the past have often supported the teacher's inclination to blame the child (or his family), by labeling the child as emotionally disturbed and recommending treatment outside of the classroom—treatment which usually was not available or which had little effect on the classroom progress when it was available. Much current research (see Becker, Thomas, & Carnine, 1969) supports the conclusion that most such problems can be handled in the classroom if the teacher is trained to use effective reinforcers to motivate learning and to provide instructional programs that do in fact teach the skills the child needs to succeed in that class."

We found in our work in the Follow Through Program that "economically disadvantaged children had commonly been given all of the above labels and more ... New labels were also coming into vogue. Psychologists came to the 'aid' of teachers with a new diagnosis for children with normal IQ's who do not learn. They are said to have specific learning disabilities, again requiring special treatment by expert ... For the most part, the children so labeled had not been taught to read (cf. Haring & Bateman, 1977) ... It is hard for us to believe that 25% of middle-class children have caught this disease ..."

In our view then and now: "There is a need for new roles for school psychologists ... Most psychologists working in the schools have not been trained to apply the knowledge of learning processes to classroom problems. They have been taught to stay out of the classroom and pretend they know nothing about instructional processes. In fact, it has only been recently that the Division of School Psychology of the APA has even suggested that the training of school psychologists include training in curriculum and instruction.

"There is an obvious need for a drastic change in the orientation and use of psychologists in the schools. They need to be trained to provide teachers with information and procedures that we know can produce effective learning conditions ... They need to use curriculum-relevant tests ... to find out what students know and what they need to learn ... and to help teachers to apply the best instructional technology available. The new school psychologist needs to be an expert in instruction and curricula, bringing to bear in the classrooms knowledge derived from research on what it takes to make learning happen."

While the problems I described in 1971 have not gone away, the collection of intervention practices for school psychologists in this volume suggest that things are changing. They constitute first a "proclamation" that school psychology is changing its focus to one of problem solving in the schools; second, they constitute clear evidence that many of the leaders in the field are working hard for that change; and third, they provide me with new hope for the viability and educational relevance of the field. This collection is potentially a valuable resource for both the trainers of school psychologists and those already "out there" desiring to upgrade their practices.

REFERENCES

Becker, W. C., Thomas, D. R., & Carnine, D. (1969). *Reducing behavior problems: An operant conditioning guide for teachers.* Urbana, IL: ERIC Clearinghouse in Early Childhood.

Gersten, R. M., Becker, W. C., Heiry, T. J., & White, W. A. T. (1984). Entry IQ and yearly academic growth of children in Direct Instruction programs: A longitudinal study of low SES children. *Educational Evaluation and Policy Analysis, 5,* 109–121.

Haring, N. G., & Bateman, B. (1977). *Teaching the learning disabled child.* Englewood Cliffs, NJ: Prentice-Hall.

CHAPTER 1

Structuring School-Based Interventions to Achieve Integrated Primary, Secondary, and Tertiary Prevention Goals for Safe and Effective Schools

Hill M. Walker
Institute on Violence and Destructive Behavior

Mark R. Shinn
University of Oregon

INTRODUCTION

In 1992, C. Everett Koop and his associates in the medical field declared interpersonal violence to be the number one public health problem in this country (See Koop & Lundberg, 1992). Little has changed within our society during the ensuing years to alter this assessment. Destructive forms of youth behavior now routinely include violent, delinquent acts, school failure and dropout, bullying and sexual harassment, and substance abuse. Gunshot wounds have replaced auto accidents as the leading cause of paralysis among young people (Centers for Disease Control, 1994). Today's youth engage in a broad range of destructive and risky forms of behavior that pose a danger to themselves, others, and the larger society (Loeber & Farrington, 1998).

Evidence suggests that the United States has evolved into the most violent developed country in the world (Grossman, 1995; Osofsky, 1997; Satcher, 2000, 2001; Zimring & Hawkins, 1995). Tragically, between 4,000 and 5,000 U.S. children and youth die from gunshot wounds each year. Although the school shooting tragedies of the mid- to late-1990s seem to have abated, there are continuing reports of student conspiracies to commit such acts that have been detected before the fact. Furthermore, U.S. males under the age of 25 die at a rate approximately 15 times higher than that of any other developed country (Osofsky, 1997). Our society seems to be caught up in an epidemic of violence, a substantial portion of which is accounted for by youth under the age of 19 who use handguns and other weapons to settle disputes (Fagan, 1996). Most of these involved youth are males although females seem to be narrowing the gender gap in the areas of juvenile crime and gang activity (Hawkins, 1996).

Grossman (1995), in his seminal book titled *On Killing*, argues persuasively that our society inadvertently desensitizes vulnerable children and youth to violence and socializes them to accept it as a means for coping with their social environs and life's challenges. He believes that this cultural shift accounts for much of the tragic youth violence that we are experiencing today. Grossman documents the remarkable increases in the aggravated assault and incarceration rates over the past 30 years that have occurred in parallel with each other. He blames the flood of media violence as a key driving force in the casual acceptance of violence among today's children and youth, especially among those who come from at-risk backgrounds.

These trends represent unfortunate societal changes in which very serious forms of interpersonal conflict, self-destructive behavior, and violations of societal codes have occurred among our children and youth. Other, unfortunate changes have occurred in less socially visible areas including the attitudes and beliefs we hold about each other, the social fragmentation that is rampant in our society, and the incivility which is routinely displayed in our daily interactions with each other. These forms of adult behavior, in particular, provide very poor models for our children and lead to unhealthy socialization practices, which are predictably reflected in our children's values, attitudes, and behavior toward others.

Equally compelling is the growing rift between the informational "haves" and "have nots" as well as the large proportion of poorly educated Americans. With respect to literacy, according to an international comparative study conducted by the government of Canada (Organisation for Economic Co-operation and Development, Statistics Canada, Literacy, Economy, and Society, 1995), the United States had a higher concentration of adults at the *lowest* of five levels of literacy (approximately 20%) than any of the major industrial countries other than Poland. Conversely, the United States had among the *highest* percentages of literacy in the two highest levels (again, approximately 20%). This diminishing "middle class" of literacy is compounded further by the high proportions of persons with an insufficient education. As reported by the National Institute for Literacy (1999), more than 40% of all American adults fall below the benchmark level on the National Adult Literacy Survey of 1993.

These high levels of illiteracy translate directly into high rates of high school dropout with dramatic consequences in life outcomes. In contrast to about 80% of adults 25 and over with bachelor's degrees and 65% of high school graduates participating in the labor force in 1998, only 43% of high school dropouts were employed (U.S. Department of Labor, 1998). The unemployment rate for high school dropouts 25 and older was almost double that of persons with 4 years of high school and almost four times higher than college graduates. With recent dropouts, the picture is even more dismal. Of the 1997–1998 dropouts, more than one in four was unemployed. Sadly, the profile of illiteracy and high school dropout falls disproportionately on individuals with low income and/or persons of color. For every year between 1972 and 1994, persons from low-income backgrounds were twice as likely to drop out than their middle-class counterparts (National Center for Educational Statistics, 1996). Differences among ethnic groups in achievement in all academic areas, including dropout, remain highly evident on nearly all measures (e.g., U.S. Department of Education, *Digest of Educational Statistics,* 1999).

To be effective in solving these unprecedented challenges now facing us, our society must first collectively own our problems and demand effective solutions. We also must make a firm commitment to addressing the front end of these massive social problems through good faith *prevention* efforts rather than continuing our reactive posture of trying to control them through incarceration, suspension, toleration of high rates of illiteracy and school dropout, and/or the routine assignment of individuals to highly segregated alternative and special education programs.

It is essential that we engage in a national dialogue that recognizes the problems of violence and academic underachievement (especially literacy); we need to acknowledge they are not separate and unrelated problems, but are interwoven. As will be shown through the ensuing content of this volume, the prevention strategies that directly target one of these problem areas tend to have indirect, positive effects on the other target area. Although many chapters herein are, indeed, presented as separate intervention strategies for specific problems (e.g., study skills), we have also attempted to include chapters that bring to bear *integrated* systems of prevention and remediation practices (see Ikeda et al., this volume).

In particular, with respect to violence and destructive behavior, we believe that as a society, we must eschew violence in all its forms as well as the attitudes and less salient, behavioral precursors that can lead to it (e.g., aggression, mean-spirited teasing and bullying, sexual harassment, endorsement of antisocial beliefs such as "fight back, ask questions later," and so forth). That is, we must (a) change the norms and expectations around aggressive attitudes and behavior and how we relate to each other interpersonally, and also (b) directly address the known risk factors associated with future violent and delinquent behavior by targeting and intervening with at-risk children and youth early in their lives—well before they become invested in these unfortunate beliefs, acts, and behavior patterns (Eddy, Reid, & Fetrow, 2000; Walker et al., 1996).

As a nation, we have undertaken some aspects of raising public awareness and behavioral expectations regarding prevention, especially with respect to school violence. However, we remain extremely concerned about the substantial and persisting investment in reactive and punitive approaches, at both societal and school levels, as a primary strategy for addressing the challenges presented by behaviorally at-risk youth. The reliance by schools on such punitive approaches as suspension, expulsion, and "zero tolerance" policies are ultimately doomed to failure, or at best maintenance of the status quo, unless they are counterbalanced with equally strong investments in comprehensive prevention efforts that can (a) divert at-risk children from a destructive life path early in their lives and school careers, and (b) teach replacement forms of behavior, skills and strategies that lead to positive interpersonal relationships, facilitate academic success, and foster attachment and bonding to the schooling process.

With respect to academic achievement, we propose similar approaches wherein we also change the norms and expectations around achievement outcomes, and directly address the known risk factors associated with illiteracy, school failure, and underachievement early in the lives of children and youth. In recent years, our country has engaged in an intensive effort to change such norms and achievement expectations through the instrument of school reform, most notably through the specification of high academic standards (Carnine, 1995, 1997). However, we also question the wisdom of this well-intentioned effort if the end product of raising the achievement expectations "bar" is another set of punitive and reactive programs for students (e.g., retention for failing high stakes tests, no social promotion) and schools (e.g., identification as a "poor quality" school, firing of staff) without equal or more intensive prevention efforts.

Prevention as a Cost-Effective Solution to Promoting Positive Development and Preventing Problems of Those At Risk

Our primary focus in this book is on *prevention*, achievable through the implementation of *evidence-based* intervention approaches. Although this book, like its first edition, describes evidence-based remedial programs, we see a developmental prevention focus as representing long overdue policy and corresponding practices that will allow effective responding to the myriad challenges confronting today's children and youth. In the professional literature and in popular usage, prevention is typically more often thought of as a "process" rather than as a "goal or outcome" that can be realized through early intervention. We believe it is more useful to think of prevention in terms of *goals and outcomes* and the application of interventions as a *means of achieving them*. Aside from the conceptual clarity that this formulation introduces, it also helps in avoiding the polarization among constituencies that so often occurs around prevention versus intervention issues.

Thus, in public health parlance, interventions designed to keep problems from emerging are said to address *primary prevention goals* and *outcomes;* in contrast, interventions designed to reverse or preclude harm from exposure to known risk factors are referred to as addressing *secondary prevention goals and outcomes.* Finally, intervention strategies that reduce, rather than reverse, harm among the most severely involved individuals are known as *tertiary prevention* approaches. Ultimately, any comprehensive and cost-effective system for delivering more positive outcomes for our children and youth must incorporate these three types of prevention efforts—which must be achieved through *coordinated* interventions that meaningfully involve at-risk individuals, parents and caregivers, and teachers and peers. Achieving this important goal will require substantial changes in current policy and practice(s).

Effective Prevention Programs Are Known

It is interesting to observe the daily frustrations expressed by teachers, school administrators, policy makers, and the general public about not knowing what to do to reduce behavioral and academic problems or prevent them in the first place. This volume is predicated on the currently available bodies of knowledge supporting the premise that it is not just a question of knowing *what* to do but, rather, of whether we are aware of what we need to do, and *whether we are willing to do it*. This premise is reflected elegantly in McGill-Franzen and Allington (1991) who, with respect to promoting positive reading outcomes, maintain that it is not a matter of knowing what to do, but having the will to do it.

Much *is* currently known about how to address prevention goals and outcomes among today's children and youth in the areas of behavioral adjustment and school achievement. For example, in the realm of social behavior, some recent compilations and syntheses of the existing knowledge base relating to the prevention of youth violence, antisocial behavior patterns, delinquency, and high-risk forms of behavior provide a useful roadmap for policy makers and leaders in this regard (see Greenberg, Domitrovich, & Bumbarger, 1999; Loeber & Farrington, 1998; Satcher, 2000, 2001). Similarly, in reading, we have seen the National Institute on Child Health and Human Development (NICHD) report from the National Reading Panel (2000) entitled *Teaching Children to Read: An Evidence-Based Assessment of the Scientific Research Literature on Reading and Its Implications for Reading Instruction.* A joint product of six major educational organizations—including the American Federation of Teachers, the National Educational Association, the American Association of School Administrators, and the Educational Research Service—has produced an evidence-based document, entitled *What Works: An Educator's Guide to Schoolwide Reform* (American Federation of Teachers, National Educational Association, the American Association of School Administrators, & Educational Research Service, 2000), which reviews the research on 24 schoolwide prevention programs.

The crux of the problem seems to be mustering the will to address the promotion of positive outcomes and prevention of destructive behavior patterns *before* they begin emerging in the lives of our growing at-risk youth population. Given the press on existing intervention resources and the natural resistance to addressing problems either early in their trajectories or early on in the lives of vulnerable, at-risk children and youth, it is not surprising that our prevention actions are anemic (i.e., "Band Aid" interventions that can be delivered quickly without necessary training and investment of financial resources). The view that prevention means "spending money you don't have on problems that do not yet exist" remains much too popular.

Prevention *works* and is well worth the investment (Barnett, 1985; Greenwood, 1999). However, for reasonable prevention goals and outcomes to be realized, resources must be freed up to create a more balanced approach among primary, secondary, and tertiary forms of prevention. We need to invest more resources and to implement effective prevention programs that may require considering the painful task of reallocating *remedial* intervention and support resources from older youth with identified and serious problems to younger children whose current risk status may be unacceptably high.

PREVENTION OF VIOLENCE AND DESTRUCTIVE BEHAVIOR

We will use the remainder of this chapter to flesh out the major themes of this book as follows:

1. We can accomplish more and produce better outcomes through systematic and comprehensive planning wherein we invest in early intervention using evidence-based treatments for purposes of prevention.

2. We should apply evidence-based and proven, remedial interventions in careful coordination with the assessment of increased risk status and subsequent identification of severe problems.

Using the problems of antisocial and destructive behavior as examples, we will make the case that attention to the above themes will prove far more cost effective in the long run than wagering that children who are pervasively exposed to adverse risk conditions will either (a) be unaffected by them, or (b) will outgrow their problems, without the need for systematic supports, services, and timely intervention. Using the knowledge base on what we know about the etiology and treatment of antisocial behavior, we will illustrate *what we need to know* and *what we need to do* to promote more positive behavioral adjustment outcomes.

As examples of what we need to know, we will describe the path that at-risk children follow from initial risk exposure to later destructive outcomes, the risk and protective factors that operate to accelerate or buffer against the development of antisocial behavior patterns, and the two most critical developmental periods for waging effective prevention efforts. With respect to what we need to do, we will illustrate the role of schools as providing an optimal context for achieving prevention goals and outcomes, and provide examples of evidence-based interventions for achieving primary, secondary and tertiary prevention goals, along with implementation guidelines and recommendations. We will conclude with a call for school psychologists to be allowed to assume a greater role as prevention specialists among the array of current roles they are currently asked to perform in schools.

What We Need to Know: The Path From Risk Exposure to Destructive Outcomes

Child development is powerfully influenced by the operation of *risk* and *protective* factors in a person's life. Table 1 provides a listing of risk factors that are associated with destructive outcomes and a parallel listing of protective factors that can buffer and offset the damaging effects of exposure to risks.

Risk factors are regarded as causal factors, or proxies for same, operating in a developing individual's life; they can lead to unfortunate outcomes and a diminished life quality. In contrast, protective factors are those protective events and influences that shape development in a positive way and/or that serve to reduce or buffer the impact of risk factors.

Owing to the unfortunate social and economic conditions experienced by a substantial portion of our society, many developing children are exposed to a broad range of risks that operate across differing contexts. These contexts commonly include the family, school and neighborhood, community, and larger society; risks within these contexts tend to operate in an overlapping fashion (Hawkins, Catalano, & Miller, 1992). As a rule, the more proximal the risk factors, the greater their influence. Thus, family-based risks are considered to have the greatest impact on the developing child while general societal risks (e.g., social conflict, media violence) are considered to have the most indirect

TABLE 1

Risk and Protective Factors Associated With Antisocial and Criminal Behavior

RISK FACTORS

Child Factors	Family Factors	School Context	Community and Cultural Factors
prematurity	**Parental characteristics:**	school failure	socioeconomic disadvantage
low birth weight	teenage mothers	normative beliefs about aggression	population density and housing conditions
disability	single parents psychiatric disorder, especially	deviant peer group	urban area
prenatal brain damage	depression substance abuse	bullying	
birth injury	criminality antisocial models	peer rejection	neighborhood violence and crime
low intelligence	**Family environment:**	poor attachment to school	cultural norms concerning violence as acceptable
difficult temperament	family violence and disharmony marital discord	inadequate behavior	response to frustration
chronic illness	disorganized negative interaction/	management	media portrayal of violence
insecure attachment	social isolation large family size		
poor problem solving	father absence long-term parental unemployment		lack of support services
beliefs about aggression	**Parenting style:**		social or cultural discrimination
attributions	poor supervision and monitoring of child discipline style (harsh		
poor social skills	or inconsistent) rejection of child		
low self-esteem	abuse lack of warmth and		
lack of empathy	affection low involvement in		
alienation	child's activities neglect		
hyperactivity/ disruptive behavior			
impulsivity			

Table 1 continued on page 8

Table 1 continued

PROTECTIVE FACTORS

Child Factors	Family Factors	School Context	Community and Cultural Factors
social competence	supportive, caring parents	positive school climate	access to support services
social skills	family harmony	prosocial peer group	community networking
above-average intelligence	more than 2 years between siblings	responsibility and required helpfulness	attachment to the community
attachment to family	responsibility for chores or required helpfulness	sense of belonging/ bonding	participation in church or other community group
empathy			
problem solving		opportunities for some success at school and recognition of achievement	community/ cultural norms against violence
optimism	secure and stable family		
school achievement	supportive relationship with other adult		a strong cultural identity and ethnic pride
easy temperament		school norms concerning violence	
internal locus of control	small family size		
moral beliefs	strong family norms and morality		
values			
self-related cognitions			
good coping style			

effects. Patterson, Reid, and Dishion (1992) argue that the quantity and duration of risks matter; that is, the *more* risks one is exposed to and the *longer* the exposure, the greater their negative impact upon the individual's well being, life status, and school-related behavior and performance (see also Loeber & Farrington, 1998).

Numerous longitudinal studies, conducted over the past three decades, have documented the progression from early risk exposure to destructive behavioral manifestations, which, in turn, set the at-risk child up for short-term, negative outcomes that predict longer-term, more serious outcomes (Loeber & Farrington, 1998; Patterson et al., 1992). Currently, thousands of at-risk children and youth are progressing along this well-traveled path. As a general rule, the earlier intervention occurs in this progression, the greater the likelihood that the child will be successfully diverted from this path and its associated damaging outcomes which play out over the long term (Eddy et al., 2000; Reid, 1993).

Some risk factors seem to operate generically and are associated with multiple and diverse negative outcomes. Others seem to be more directly associated with specific outcomes. For example, Vance, Fernandez, and Biber (1998) conducted a comprehensive analysis of 26 risk and 28 protective factors in terms of their impact on the educational progress of a sample ($N = 652$) of adolescents with very severe behavioral and achievement problems. The sample members were about 15 years old and had an average of 14 risk and 14 protective factors each operating in their lives. Only 1 of the 26 risk factors (substance abuse) was significantly related to the adolescents' educational progress in a negative sense. In contrast, 8 of the 28 protective factors were significantly related to educational progress in a facilitative sense; one additional factor, living at home, was *negatively* related to educational progress. Interestingly, only two of the eight contributing protective factors dealt with academic dimensions. In contrast, four dealt with social relationships and the remaining two were focused on social supports and mentoring.

Risk factors that appear to operate *directly* in the development of antisocial or destructive behavior include the following: (a) getting in trouble with the teacher, (b) failure to engage and bond with the process of schooling, (c) being socially rejected by teachers and peers, and (d) failing academically, especially in reading. There are a host of nonschool-based risk factors that function *indirectly* to impair school adjustment and achievement, including poverty, chaotic and dysfunctional family environs, drug and alcohol abuse by caregivers, neglect, and physical, emotional, and sexual forms of abuse (Hawkins et al., 1992). Children coming out of family situations where they are exposed to such risks are more likely to develop antisocial behavior patterns and to lack school-readiness skills (Loeber & Farrington, 1998; Patterson et al., 1992). In addition, exposure to these risks is likely to negatively impact an at-risk child or youth's life chances and overall quality of life.

Schools themselves can do very little to influence these nonschool risk factors, as their influence occurs outside the school setting and they have very likely registered their negative, destructive effects well before the child enters school. The expertise and resources of public health, including mental health systems, and social service agencies, are necessary to address these risks prior to school age. Doing so in a cost-effective manner remains a great challenge for our society, but, as shown in the chapter by Eddy, Reid, and Curry (this volume), there are effective and reasonably efficient interventions to accomplish this goal.

A key role for schools—and the goal of prevention programs—is to *enhance protective factors* in academic, social-emotional, and mentoring-support domains in order to buffer and *offset the negative effects of risk factors,* particularly in the areas of school adjustment and achievement (Hawkins, Catalano, Kosterman, Abbott, & Hill, 1999). As part of this process, we argue that it is very important for educators to include a specific analysis of the risk and protective factors potentially operating in a vulnerable child's life upon entering school, and especially for those children who early on are referred for evaluation and/or specialized assistance or placement. For more information on the evaluation and decision-making processes based upon this approach to assessing student risk status and strengths, see Walker and Sprague (1999) and Sprague et al., this volume.

What We Need to Know: Critical Developmental Periods for Waging Prevention Efforts

The following refrain is often heard in the rhetoric surrounding at-risk children and youth: "It's never too early to attempt prevention or too late to intervene." The important wisdom to be gleaned from this observation is that mounting prevention efforts as early as possible in a child's life can be a highly cost-effective strategy. Equally important, one should *never give up* on any child or youth because of age, regardless of how far along a destructive pathway he or she happens to be. At-risk children or youth should *never* be written off because they are perceived as being past the point where the investment of intervention supports and services will make a meaningful difference in their lives. In particular, at-risk youth need to stay engaged with schooling for as long as possible because of its protective influences that operate over the preadolescent and adolescent age spans (Hawkins et al., 1999).

Because of what we know about the general condition of risk associated with impaired school adjustment, we believe that the developmental periods prior to the beginning of school (0–5) and during the K–Grade 5 elementary school years represent the two most critical opportunities for mounting preventive initiatives to offset later problematic outcomes, including school failure and delinquency. These two periods have everything to do with enhancing school adjustment and academic success and set the stage for coping with the challenges of adolescence. Children who come to school free of neglect and abuse, healthy in a physical and emotional sense, vaccinated, and ready to learn are far more likely to successfully negotiate the complex demands of the schooling process than those who are not. Similarly, those who get off to a good start in school, who learn to read at grade level by the end of Grade 3, and who do not display a challenging behavior pattern are more likely to experience school success and its many protective benefits (Citizens Crime Commission, 2000; Hawkins et al., 1999).

What We Need to Do Prior to School

Because at-risk children can be identified very early in their lives before a multitude of risks are able to register their damaging effects, "home-visiting" programs can create more positive preschooling (i.e., home) environments and increase the likelihood of positive later adjustment. The Olds Nurse Home Visitation Model (Olds, Henderson, Tatelbaum, & Chamberlin, 1986; Olds et al., 1999) and the Healthy Start Program (Duggan et al., 2000) are well-known examples of home visiting programs that can be effective in preventing child abuse and neglect as well as longer-term destructive outcomes (e.g., delinquency). The OLDS and Healthy Start models begin with hospital-based screening of family risks and births to identify children who are at risk for abuse and neglect and then link families to heath and child development services including crisis intervention, referrals to medical services, advocacy, parent education and training, family violence prevention, substance abuse services, and life-skills modeling. Both of these programs are voluntary, begin services provision during the prenatal period just prior to birth, and continue to provide family and child services for up to 2 years.

The OLDS and Healthy Start programs share the following key features. They:

1. Advocate a wellness approach,

2. Identify risks to children and their families at the earliest point of detection,

3. Create a voluntary system of family support services through collaborative agency partnerships, and

4. Ensure sensitivity to diversity and delivery of culturally competent services and supports.

The OLDS model has been extensively investigated through longitudinal research and has been shown to reduce child abuse and neglect as well as parental substance abuse; it also has been proven, as noted above, to be instrumental in the prevention of delinquency in adolescence (Olds et al., 1999). The effects of Healthy Start have been less extensively evaluated and to date have been assessed primarily by pre/post comparisons, demographic analyses, and consumer satisfaction measures, all of which tend to show positive outcomes (See Duggan et al., 2000). Treatment-control group comparisons for Healthy Start are currently underway.

As potentially effective as home visiting programs are in preventing and offsetting home- and community-based risk factors, their positive effects may be reduced if they are not followed up with a continuum of services that track and support at-risk families and their children during the preschool years. It is highly recommended that such families and their children access social services, child development opportunities, and preschool education in the 0–5 age range in order to strengthen parenting skills and to prepare children for the schooling process.

What We Need to Do Upon School Entry: Enhancing School Adjustment

As we discussed earlier in the chapter, it is of paramount importance for every child to get off to the best possible start in their school careers (Walker et al., 1998). The two greatest risks for school failure are (a) the display of a very challenging behavior pattern (i.e., antisocial behavior, aggression, opposition-defiance, bullying, etc.) and (b) early school failure, especially in learning to read. A challenging behavior pattern that is allowed to elaborate over the elementary and middle school years can lead to a youth being pressured to leave school early because of the aversive nature of his or her behavioral characteristics (Patterson et al., 1992; Schorr, 1988; Walker, Colvin, & Ramsey, 1995). Reading failure ultimately contributes to early school leaving because it is so essential to academic success.

In our view, all children should be screened at the point of school entry for their status in relation to these two risks. Chapters in this volume by Feil, Walker, and Severson; by Simmons et al.; and by Shinn, Shinn, Hamilton, and Clarke describe procedures for the early identification and treatment of children at risk for challenging behavior patterns and for reading failure. Those students who are clearly identified as school-failure risks should (a) have their reading skills carefully monitored and (b) be targeted for secondary and sometimes tertiary interventions, including specialized assistance, instruction, and intervention, until they are brought up to acceptable performance levels in each domain.

What We Need to Do Over the Long Term: Creating Schools as the Context for Achieving Prevention Goals and Outcomes

In a recent review of school-based mental health services, Hoagwood and Erwin (1997) noted that 75% of mental health services for children are currently delivered within the context of schools. Angold (2000) argues that approximately 20% of today's school-age students could qualify for a psychiatric diagnosis using the American Psychiatric Association's *Diagnostic and Statistical Manual* (DSM-IV) criteria. Thus, student populations in the K–12 grade range represent a substantial demand for mental health services in the forms of screening and assessment, services and supports, and implementation of formal interventions designed to address intractable social-emotional and academic problems. However, Walker and his colleagues (Walker, Nishioka, Zeller, Severson, & Feil, in press) recently analyzed national data on the referral and service of students with emotional and behavior disorders in school and found that slightly less than 1% on average of the public school population is served annually under the auspices of the Individuals with Disabilities Education Act (I.D.E.A., 1997).

There is an obvious need for providing prevention services generally for the positive social development of students, based on the diversity and intensity of need. Equally obvious is the importance of addressing school success and achievement. It has long been recognized that schools have the relatively unique ability to access the vast majority of at-risk children and to pull together the resources and expertise necessary to address their problems in a coordinated fashion (Hoagwood & Erwin, 1997).

We see three factors that must be addressed in this context. The first is establishing, as an overarching school mission, the creation of a school environment that serves to ameliorate the effects of *known risk variables*. Too often, schools place responsibility for this problem elsewhere and do not see themselves operating as a possible protective factor to enhance an individual student's life chances. For example, in a recent study of school administrators, Allington, McGill-Franzen, and Schick (1997) reported that the school leaders they interviewed saw the problems of students as primarily stemming from outside of school factors and conditions. Allington et al. (1997) stated that "these administrators understood the problem as one of under-prepared children rather than schools unprepared to educate children with diverse backgrounds, experiences, and interests" (p. 231). Regardless of the pressure or influence of outside-the-school, known risk factors—indeed, precisely *because* of these known risk factors—the school's mission *must not* reflect a passive status quo (i.e., a "throw up one's hands" attitude) that relies on others to make a difference in the lives of our vulnerable, at-risk children and youth.

Second, schools must be able to access and implement, with solid treatment integrity, proven intervention approaches, and be supported in doing so by our society. As but one illustration of unfortunate school practices, the widespread use of the DARE (Drug and Alcohol Resistance Education) program and the continuing use of group counseling approaches with at-risk adolescents provide compelling examples of our tendency to reinvest in program approaches that either *do not work* or are actually *iatrogenic* (Dishion & Andrews, 1995).

Third, to maximize their effectiveness, schools must become better partners with families and community agencies in consortia that implement community-wide prevention initiatives. Examples of such positive partnerships are presented in the chapter herein by Paine and Kennedy Paine. As has been emphasized earlier in this chapter, it is particularly important that school-based personnel collaborate effectively with agencies and professionals who work with at-risk families and their children in the 0-to-5 developmental period. Family resource centers that are attached to and serve anywhere from 1 to 6 schools each, depending on school size, are a viable option, in this regard, and are being implemented on a trial basis in a number of states, including Kentucky, California, and Oregon. The connection with families, agencies, and professionals in this age range allows for the possibility of addressing outside of school risk factors that can severely impair school adjustment, academic performance, and overall school success. At present, however, such partnerships seem to be the exception rather than the rule.

Evidence-Based Interventions for Achieving Primary, Secondary, and Tertiary Prevention Goals

We will use the following example of a school-based approach to the prevention of antisocial, aggressive behavior patterns that (a) targets the entire school site as well as individual students for systematic screening, assessment, and intervention; (b) provides for matching the intensity and nature of interventions with the severity and intractability of students' adjustment problems; and (c) emphasizes the fostering of positive school climates and safe learning environments for all students. Examples of proven interventions designed for achieving primary, secondary, and tertiary outcomes for at-risk students within the schooling context are briefly described.

Walker and his colleagues have developed an integrated approach for school districts' use in addressing the challenges presented by students who are at risk for destructive and antisocial behavior patterns (see Sugai, Horner, & Gresham, this volume). This overall approach is based on the premise that in order to produce consistent, socially valid behavior changes, we must intervene directly and comprehensively within and across *all* school settings in which problem behaviors are observed. This integrated model incorporates interventions designed to achieve, respectively, primary, secondary, and tertiary goals and outcomes with at-risk student populations. Further, it addresses the needs of *all* students in a given school including those who are judged to be not at risk.

Walker et al. (1996) based this model on the following assumptions, observations and recommendations about school interventions:

1. Students who are at risk for developing antisocial patterns of behavior and their correlated negative outcomes are more likely to be punished and excluded than to have their problems addressed in a positive and inclusionary manner.

2. Schools typically have maintained a reactive, punishment-oriented posture in relation to at-risk students. This approach fails to recognize the need to identify students early on who show the signs of these problems, and mount comprehensive, sustained interventions that can divert them from this path at the beginning stages of their school careers.

3. The intractability and severity of student adjustment problems are rarely appropriately matched to available interventions that can remediate or ameliorate them. Too often, very simple interventions are applied in this regard in an attempt to solve complex student problems and vice versa.

4. School interventions for at-risk students from minority backgrounds are rarely contextualized in relation to the nuances of their cultural backgrounds; in addition, teacher interactions with minority at-risk students tend to be based on low-performance expectations, are critical rather than constructive, are short in duration, and also are often punishment oriented.

5. To achieve maximum efficacy, school interventions need to incorporate *universal*, schoolwide features that address the needs of all students as well as *specific* features that address the individual needs of those students who do not respond to the universal, schoolwide intervention.

6. Intervention responses to students with severe problem behaviors tend to be developed and implemented by individual teachers rather than by a team of committed staff members.

7. Efforts to improve interventions for students with severe problem behaviors must be organized into a comprehensive and strategic building- or district-level plan that ranks as one of the top three school-improvement goals for at least two years (see Sugai et al., this volume).

Prevention strategies and interventions appropriate for at-risk students should address and systematically take into account these observations about the effective delivery of evidence-based interventions in today's schools. Doing so will help make it possible for proven interventions to be adapted to the needs of target students and school site conditions for maximal impact.

Within any school setting, it is possible to identify three types of students as follows: (a) typically developing, non-at-risk students; (b) students with an elevated risk status for developing antisocial behavior problems; and (c) students who show signs of *life-course-persistent* antisocial behavior patterns and current or future involvement in delinquent acts (Larson, 1994; Moffitt, 1994; Walker et al., 1995). It should be clear that these three "types" of students are consistently observed in the academic domain as well.

Life-course-persistent, antisocial behavior refers to at-risk students who have been socialized to antisocial behavior and delinquency, within the family context, by exposure to such risk factors as incompetent and inconsistent parenting practices; poverty; unhealthy beliefs and attitudes; physical, emotional, and sexual forms of abuse; drug and alcohol involvement; and so on (Hawkins, 1996; Loeber & Farrington, 1998). As a rule, these children and youth require the most powerful services, supports, and interventions available to us in order to impact their problems, sometimes even at just minimal levels.

These three student types are ordered along a severity-of-risk continuum, which, at one extreme, predicts the emergence of negative developmental outcomes, including delinquency and adult criminality. Members of each student group, arrayed along this continuum, are candidates for differing levels or types of intervention that represent correspondingly greater specificity, complexity, comprehensiveness, expense, and intensity (Eddy et al., 2000; Reid, 1993). Figure 1, on page 16, clarifies the relationships among these intervention levels/types and degree of student risk status.

This figure illustrates the application, to school-based problems, of the public health field's taxonomy for differing types of prevention (Larson, 1994). In this conceptualization, prevention and intervention are not viewed as distinct or mutually exclusive dimensions; but rather, different types of interventions and approaches are used to achieve specific prevention goals and outcomes (e.g., primary, secondary, tertiary).

Examples of some appropriate interventions for *primary, secondary,* and *tertiary* forms of prevention are matched by student type in Figure 1.

Primary prevention strategies focus on enhancing protective factors on a school-wide basis to keep minor problems and difficulties from developing into more serious ones and preventing children from ending up at greater risk. Interventions used to achieve primary prevention goals are applied to *all* students in the same way at the same "dosage" level. An example of this strategy in the area of antisocial behavior is *Effective Behavior Support* (EBS; see Sugai et al., this volume). In the EBS model, primary prevention strategies focus on teaching *all* students and staff school-based rules and expectations, and establishing disciplinary policies and procedures that are designed to enhance the smooth operation of a school environment. Similarly, by teaching the skills for school success (e.g., being prepared, getting to class on time, asking for help, com-

FIGURE 1

Preventing Violent and Destructive Behavior in Schools: Primary, Secondary, and Tertiary Systems of Intervention

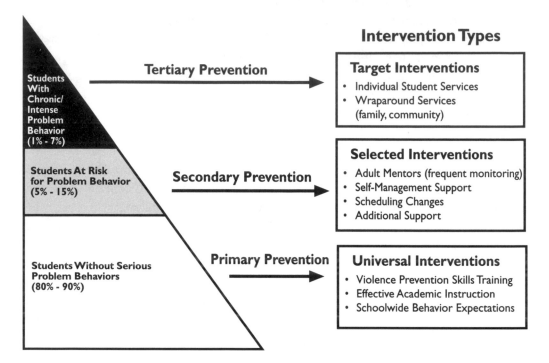

Note

Walker, H. M., Horner, R. H., Sugai, G., Bullis, M., Sprague, J. R., Bricker, D., & Kaufman, M.J. (1996). Integrated approaches to preventing antisocial behavior patterns among school-age children and youth. *Journal of Emotional and Behavioral Disorders, 4,* 194–209. Reprinted with permission.

pleting and turning in homework; see the chapter by Gleason, Archer, and Colvin, this volume), we increase the likelihood that all students will profit from instruction. These universal intervention approaches have perhaps the greatest potential for use by schools in establishing a positive school climate and as a scaffold, or support structure, for the delivery of proven techniques for diverting at-risk students from a path leading to later negative or destructive developmental outcomes. In our view, this integrated approach is greatly underutilized in the majority of today's schools where its impact could be effectively maximized.

Secondary prevention involves interventions that provide behavioral or academic support, mentoring, skill development, and assistance to more severely at-risk students. Students who do not respond to universal interventions, implemented on a schoolwide basis, become candidates for more intensive, individually tailored interventions that are more expensive. These interventions typically are applied on an individual or small group basis. Interventions for achieving secondary prevention goals are often referred to as "selected." That is, such students select themselves out as candidates for more intensive interventions by demonstrating their nonresponsiveness to schoolwide interventions, thereby indicating their need for more powerful supports and services. Examples of secondary prevention strategies include small group social skills lessons, behavioral contracting, specialized tutoring, assignment to alternative classroom placements, and the provision of Title I reading programs.

Finally, *tertiary* prevention is appropriate for severely at-risk students who are already identified as having chronic problems and who have displayed a life–course–persistent pattern of antisocial and related forms of destructive behavior. This behavior pattern may involve severe mental health problems, delinquent activities, violence, and/or vandalism (Moffitt, 1994). Successful interventions for this student population must be comprehensive, initiated early in the trajectory of risk development, be in evidence over the long term, and involve parents, teachers, and peers. As a rule, wraparound, interagency approaches to intervention that are collaborative in nature are required to impact students who fit this behavioral profile (Kukic, 1995).

School-site intervention approaches are needed that encompass *all three* of these prevention levels or types. Unfortunately, few schools implement these levels of prevention strategies within their buildings; and if they do, their efforts are rarely coordinated or interfaced with one another. To be maximally effective, prevention approaches, and the interventions comprising them, must be *directly linked* to and coordinated with each other within the context of a school site and its four systems of behavioral support (i.e., schoolwide, specific setting, classroom, and individual student). Thus, failure at one level of prevention provides an implicit assessment that the student requires a more powerful, intensive intervention at the next level of prevention. In other words, those students who do not respond to the primary-level intervention components are then referred to the more intensive one–to–one or small group strategies at the secondary prevention level. Similarly, those students who do not respond at a secondary prevention level would move to tertiary prevention, and, along with their families, teachers, and peers, receive a comprehensive, collaborative, and intensive intervention (see Walker et al., 1996). Resistance to a well-designed and implemented intervention provides a foundation for treatment-based identification of more severely involved students and allows for the most pragmatic, cost-efficient usage of intervention resources.

In a fully integrated approach of this type, it is expected that the adjustment problems of approximately 75% to 85% of a school's students can be prevented with primary prevention strategies of a universal nature. However, this figure will vary based on the overall risk status of the student population. A substantial portion of the remaining students (i.e., 10% to 15%) should respond to secondary prevention interventions of a more intensive nature. The very small number of remaining students (3% to 5%) who do not respond to secondary prevention efforts would be candidates for a complex and expensive tertiary prevention strategy.

A Sample Primary Prevention Application: Second Step

Among the most widely accepted curricular programs available for violence prevention in schools is the *Second Step* program (Committee for Children, 1992) developed and published by the Committee for Children, a nonprofit agency based in Seattle, Washington. *Second Step* is a universal intervention for preschool through Grade 8, designed to achieve primary prevention goals and outcomes. It consists of a violence prevention curriculum that teaches four essential skills to all students: (a) empathy, (b) impulse control, (c) problem solving, and (d) anger management/conflict resolution. The *Second Step* curriculum is designed to be taught at each grade level and is sequenced to take into account the developing maturity and cognitive abilities of students in the preschool through eighth-grade range. This program contains both school and parent involvement components and is being widely adopted by school districts nationally; currently, approximately 15,000 U.S. schools are implementing it. *Second Step* requires staff training for effective implementation and contains curricular materials and parent handbooks for each developmental level. The curriculum is taught by classroom teachers using the same instructional procedures as for teaching academic content with 30 key skills taught for approximately 30 minutes daily over a period of 3 to 6 months. Teaching strategies include visually presented scenarios that use modeling, problem solving, role-plays, discussion, and question answering.

Evaluation studies reported by the Committee for Children of the *Second Step* curricular program (Committee for Children, 1988, 1989, 1990, 1992) indicate that (a) perspective-taking and social problem-solving skills improved significantly following participation in the program and (b) *Second Step* students showed superior skill levels over matched control students in their responses to hypothetical social conflict situations. A third-party, independent evaluation of *Second Step* was reported in the *Journal of the American Medical Association* with positive results (Grossman et al., 1997). In a randomized controlled trial using intervention and control groups, these authors found that *Second Step* decreased rates of aggressive behavior and increased prosocial behavior for intervention students compared to control students. In January 2001, the U.S. Department of Safe and Drug Free Schools announced that *Second Step* received the highest rating of 132 intervention programs reviewed that purport to make schools safer and drug free. Information about *Second Step* can be obtained by writing to the Committee for Children, 2203 Airport Way South, Suite 500, Seattle, WA 98134-2027.

A Sample Secondary Prevention Application: First Step to Success

The *First Step to Success* home and school early intervention program is designed to address the early signs of an emerging antisocial behavior pattern (Walker et al., 1997, 1998). It consists of three modules designed to be used in concert with each other: (a) a universal, schoolwide screening procedure to detect at-risk students; (b) a school intervention involving targeted at-risk students, peers, and teachers that teaches an adaptive, prosocial pattern of school behavior; and (c) a home-intervention component that provides parent training in skills to help the child succeed in school (i.e., cooperation, listening, accepting limits, communication about school, problem solving, making friends, and developing confidence and self-esteem).

First Step has been rigorously evaluated using adult ratings of student behavior and direct behavioral observations of target students in classroom and playground settings (see Walker et al., 1998). The application of *First Step* produces high-magnitude behavior change outcomes averaging an effect size of .86 across five dependent measures (i.e., four teacher rating measures and direct behavioral observations recorded in playground and classroom settings) (see Walker et al., 1998). Four- and five-year longitudinal follow-up evaluations indicate that behavioral gains produced by the *First Step* program in kindergarten persist well into the upper elementary grades (Epstein & Walker, in press). *First Step* has been included as an exemplary best practice in six national reviews of effective interventions for addressing school safety and violence prevention priorities. Information about the *First Step* program can be obtained by contacting the publisher, Sopris West, Inc., at 4093 Specialty Place, Longmont, CO 80504 (1-800-547-6747) or by writing to the Institute on Violence and Destructive Behavior, 1265 University of Oregon, Eugene, OR 97403-1265.

A Sample Tertiary Prevention Application: Multisystemic Therapy

Multisystemic Therapy (MST) is a highly effective and widely used tertiary-level intervention designed to prevent recidivism among delinquent youth (Schoenwald, Brown, & Henggeler, 2000). It is an ecologically based, wrap-around intervention developed by Henggeler and his associates at the University of South Carolina. MST is included in the Blueprint Series of scientifically validated, violence prevention programs established by the Center for the Study and Prevention of Violence and is a thoroughly researched intervention model that works effectively for the most severely involved, at-risk adolescents (see Schoenwald et al., 2000).

The core feature of the MST program is its emphasis on changing the social ecology of these adolescent offenders and their families so that positive adjustment and functioning are enhanced and emotional difficulties and antisocial forms of behavior are attenuated. The program operates within the natural environments in which youth are involved (i.e., home, school, community) and uses a home-based, family preservation model of service delivery. One of the major goals of MST is to provide intensive, family-based supports, services, and intervention to prevent out-of-home placements for youth. In addition, intensive supervision, interagency collaboration, and consultation are key components of the MST model.

Nine principles guide the MST assessment and intervention process:

1. The primary purpose of assessment is to understand the fit between the identified problems and their broader systemic context.

2. Therapeutic contacts emphasize the positive and use systemic strengths as levers for change.

3. Interventions are designed to promote responsible behavior and decrease irresponsible behavior among family members.

4. Interventions are present focused and action oriented, targeting specified and well-defined problems.

5. Interventions target sequences of behavior within and among multiple systems that maintain the identified problems.

6. Interventions are developmentally appropriate and fit the developmental needs of the youth involved.

7. Interventions are designed to require daily or weekly effort by family members.

8. Intervention effectiveness is evaluated continuously from multiple perspectives with providers assuming accountability for overcoming barriers to successful outcomes.

9. Interventions are designed to promote treatment generalization and long-term maintenance of therapeutic change by empowering caregivers to address family members' needs across multiple systemic contexts.

The MST model is highly recommended for addressing the problems of adolescent offenders who are at high risk for recidivism, which may ultimately lead to chronic offending. Aos (1999) indicated that for each subsequent arrest prevented or avoided for a juvenile offender, approximately $30,000 is realized in long-term savings. MST is particularly appropriate for use with antisocial youth who are early starters and more likely to become recidivists (Moffitt, 1994). However, MST requires a substantial investment of personnel time and effort and those who implement it must complete an intensive course of training in the MST approach. As a result, implementation of the MST model generally achieves superior treatment integrity with correspondingly solid outcomes.

CONCLUSION

We now have available to us proven and promising prevention practices appropriate for use at primary, secondary, and tertiary levels which enable us to address the behavioral and academic needs of children and youth early on in their lives and school careers. These approaches also allow us to intervene comprehensively with them as well as with the key social agents in their lives (i.e., families, teachers, and peers). Evidence-based and highly effective intervention models, along with key support systems, are also available for use in the prenatal to age 5 developmental period that, if carefully applied, can reduce and eliminate many of the risks associated with poverty, dysfunctional families, and chaotic neighborhoods. Substantial progress has been made in synthesizing the literatures in which these innovative practices have been described and reported.

The prevention approach and supporting intervention practices described briefly in this chapter, and in the following book chapters, hold the potential to produce more positive outcomes and to redirect children and youth away from problematic lifestyles if they are implemented with integrity, scaled up, and adequately funded. We have developed this book with the idea that school psychologists working within school and community contexts are ideally positioned to take a lead role in the systematic implementation of a multitiered prevention model using evidence-based interventions. In our view, there is no higher priority than addressing the critical and growing set of needs of this country's at-risk children and youth. School psychologists are ideally positioned to assume a lead role in this effort.

REFERENCES

Allington, R. L., McGill-Franzen, A., & Schick, R. (1997). How administrators understand learning difficulties: A qualitative analysis. *Remedial and Special Education, 18,* 223-232.

American Federation of Teachers, National Educational Association, the American Association of School Administrators, & Educational Research Service. (2000). *What works: An educator's guide to schoolwide reform.* Washington, DC: American Institutes for Research.

Angold, A. (2000). *Preadolescent screening and data analysis.* Presentation to the 2nd Annual Expert Panel Meeting on Preadolescent Screening Procedures. Sponsored by the Substance Abuse and Mental Health Services Administration, National Institutes of Health, Dec. 1, Washington, DC.

Aos, S. (1999). *The comparative costs and benefits of programs to reduce crime: A review of national research with implications for Washington State.* Olympia, WA: Washington State Institute for Public Policy.

Barnett, W. S. (1985). The Perry Preschool Program and its long-term effects: A benefit-cost analysis. *High/Scope Early Childhood Policy Papers* (No. 2). Ypsilanti, MI: High/Scope.

Carnine, D. (1995). *Enhancing the education profession: Increasing the perceived and actual value of research.* Eugene, OR: National Center to Improve the Tools of Educators (NCITE).

Carnine, D. (1997). Bridging the research to practice gap. *Exceptional Children, 63,* 513-522.

Centers for Disease Control. (1994). *Report of the national center for violent injury control and prevention.* Atlanta, GA: Author.

Citizens Crime Commission. (2000). *KIIDS: Kids Intervention Investment Delinquency Solutions.* Portland, OR: Author, Portland Metropolitan Chamber of Commerce.

Committee for Children. (1988). *Second Step, grades 1-3, pilot project 1987-88, summary report.* Seattle, WA: Author.

Committee for Children. (1989). *Second Step, grades 4-5, pilot project 1988-89, summary report.* Seattle, WA: Author.

Committee for Children. (1990). *Second Step, grades 6-8, pilot project 1989-90, summary report.* Seattle, WA: Author.

Committee for Children. (1992). *Evaluation of Second Step, preschool-kindergarten: A violence prevention curriculum kit.* Seattle, WA: Author.

Dishion, T. J., & Andrews, D. W. (1995). Preventing escalation in problem behaviors with high risk young adolescents: Immediate and 1-year outcomes. *Journal of Consulting and Clinical Psychology, 63,* 538-548.

Duggan, A., Windham, A., McFarlane, E., Fuddy, L., Rohde, C., Buchbinder, S., & Sia, C. (2000). Hawaii's Healthy Start program of home visiting for at-risk families: Evaluation of family identification, family engagement, and service delivery. *Pediatrics, 105* (1, Pt. 3), 250-259.

Eddy, J. M., Reid, J. B., & Fetrow, R. A. (2000). An elementary school-based prevention program targeting modifiable antecedents of youth delinquency and violence: Linking the Interests of Families and Teachers (LIFT). *Journal of Emotional and Behavioral Disorders, 8*(3), 165-176.

Epstein, M. H., & Walker, H. M. (Eds.). (in press). Special education: Best practices and First Step to Success. In B. Burns, K. Hoagwood, & M. English (Eds.), *Community-based interventions for youth with serious emotional disorders.* Cary, NC: Oxford University Press.

Fagan, J. (1996). *Recent perspectives on youth violence.* Keynote address to the Pacific Northwest Conference on Youth Violence, May 28-30, Seattle, WA.

Greenberg, M. T., Domitrovich, C., & Bumbarger, B. (1999). *Preventing mental disorders in school-age children: A review of the effectiveness of prevention programs.* Available from the Prevention Research Center for the Promotion of Human Development, College of Health and Human Development, Pennsylvania State University, State College, PA.

Greenwood, P. W. (1999). Costs and benefits of early childhood intervention. *OJJDP Fact Sheet, 94.* U.S. Department of Justice, Office of Justice Programs, Washington, DC.

Grossman, D. (1995). *On killing.* Boston: Little Brown, Inc.

Grossman, D., Neckerman, H., Koepsell, T., Ping-Yu Liu, Asher, K., Beland, K., Frey, K., & Rivera, F. (1997). Effectiveness of a violence prevention curriculum among children in elementary school: A randomized controlled trial. *The Journal of the American Medical Association, 277,* 1605-1611.

Hawkins, D. (1996, May). *Youth violence: Reducing risk and enhancing protection.* Keynote address to the Pacific Northwest Conference on Youth Violence, Seattle, WA.

Hawkins, J. D., Catalano, R. F., Kosterman, R., Abbott, R., & Hill, K. G. (1999). Preventing adolescent health-risk behaviors by strengthening protection during childhood. *Archives of Pediatrics & Adolescent Medicine, 153,* 226-234.

Hawkins, J. D., Catalano, R. F., & Miller, J.Y. (1992). Risk and protective factors for alcohol and other drug problems in adolescence and early adulthood: Implications for substance abuse prevention. *Psychological Bulletin, 112*(1), 64-105.

Hoagwood, K., & Erwin, H. (1997). Effectiveness of school-based mental health services for children: A 10-year research review. *Journal of Child and Family Studies, 6*(4), 435-451.

I.D.E.A. (1997). *Individuals with Disabilities Education Act* (1997 reauthorization by Congress). Washington, DC: Author.

Koop, C. E., & Lundberg, G. (1992). Violence in America: A public health emergency: Time to bite the bullet back. *Journal of the American Medical Association, 267,* 3075-3076.

Kukic, S. (1995, November). *Families and communities together.* Paper presented at The Utah FACT Initiative Conference, Salt Lake City, UT.

Larson, J. (1994). Violence prevention in the schools: A review of selected programs and procedures. *School Psychology Review, 23*(2), 151-164.

Loeber, R., & Farrington, D. P. (Eds.). (1998). *Serious and violent juvenile offenders: Risk factors and successful interventions.* Thousand Oaks, CA: Sage.

McGill-Franzen, A. M., & Allington, R. L. (1991). The gridlock of low achievement: Perspectives on policy and practice. *Remedial and Special Education, 12,* 20-30.

Moffitt, T. (1994). Adolescence-limited and life-course-persistent antisocial behavior: A developmental taxonomy. *Psychological Review, 100*(4), 674-701.

National Center for Educational Statistics. (1996). *The pocket condition of education: 1996.* Washington, DC: U.S. Department of Education.

National Institute for Literacy. (1999). *Equipped for the future content standards: What adults need to know and be able to do in the 21st century.* Washington, DC: Author.

National Reading Panel (2000). *Teaching children to read: An evidence-based assessment of the scientific research literature on reading and its implications for reading instruction.* Washington, DC: National Institute on Child Health and Human Development.

Olds, D., Henderson, C. R., Kitzman, H., Eckenrode, J., Cole, R., & Tatelbaum, R. (1999). Prenatal and infancy home visitation by nurses: Recent findings. *The Future of Children, 9*(1), 44-65.

Olds, D., Henderson, C. R., Tatelbaum, R., & Chamberlin, R. (1986). Improving the delivery of prenatal care and outcomes of pregnancy: A randomized trial of nurse home visitation. *Pediatrics, 77,* 16-28.

Organization for Economic Co-operation and Development Statistics Canada, Literacy, Economy, and Society. (1995). *Results of the First International Adult Literacy Survey.* Ottawa, Canada: Author.

Osofsky, J. D. (Ed.). (1997). *Children in a violent society.* New York: Guilford.

Patterson, G. R., Reid, J. B., & Dishion, T. J. (1992). *Antisocial boys.* Eugene, OR: Castalia Press.

Reid, J. (1993). Prevention of conduct disorder before and after school entry: Relating interventions to developmental findings. *Development and Psychopathology, 5*(1/2), 243-262.

Satcher, D. (2000). *Report of the Surgeon General's conference on children's mental health: A national action agenda.* Washington, DC: Author. Available Internet: *www.surgeongeneral.gov/cmh.childreport.htm*

Satcher, D. (2001). *Youth violence: A report of the surgeon general.* Washington, DC: Author. Available Internet: *www.surgeongeneral.gov/cmh.childreport.htm*

Schoenwald, S., Brown, T. & Henggeler, S. (2000). Inside multisystemic therapy: Therapist, supervisory and program practices. *Journal of Emotional and Behavioral Disorders, 8*(2), 113-127.

Schorr, L. (1988). *Within our reach: Breaking the cycle of disadvantage.* New York: Doubleday.

U.S. Department of Education. (1999). *Digest of Educational Statistics, 1999.* Washington, DC: Author.

U.S. Department of Labor, Bureau of Labor Statistics, Office of Employment and Unemployment Statistics. (1998). *Current population survey.* Washington, DC: Author.

Vance, J., Fernandez, G., & Biber, M. (1998). Educational progress in a population of youth with aggression and emotional disturbance: The role of risk and protective factors. *Journal of Emotional and Behavioral Disorders, 6*(4), 214–221.

Walker, H. M., Colvin, G., & Ramsey, E. (1995). *Antisocial behavior in schools: Strategies and best practices.* Pacific Grove, CA: Brooks/Cole.

Walker, H. M., Horner, R. H., Sugai, G., Bullis, M., Sprague, J. R., Bricker, D., & Kaufman, M. J. (1996). Integrated approaches to preventing antisocial behavior patterns among school-age children and youth. *Journal of Emotional and Behavioral Disorders, 4,* 193–256.

Walker, H. M., Kavanagh, K., Stiller, B., Golly, A., Severson, H. H., & Feil, E. G. (1998). First Step to Success: An early intervention approach for preventing school antisocial behavior. *Journal of Emotional and Behavioral Disorders, 6*(2), 66–80.

Walker, H. M., Nishioka, V., Zeller, R., Severson, H., & Feil, E. (in press). Causal factors and potential solutions for the persistent underidentification of students having emotional or behavioral disorders in the context of schooling. *Diagnostique.*

Walker, H. M., & Sprague, J. R. (1999). The path to school failure, delinquency and violence: Causal factors and some potential solutions. *Intervention in School and Clinic, 35*(2), 67–73.

Walker, H. M., Stiller, B., Golly, A., Kavanagh, K., Severson, H. H., & Feil, E. (1997). *First Step to Success: Helping young children overcome antisocial behavior.* Longmont, CO: Sopris West.

Zimring, F., & Hawkins, D. (1995). Is American violence a crime problem? (An analysis prepared for the University of California Policy Seminar Crime Project). Santa Monica, CA: RAND Corporation.

CHAPTER 2

The Etiology of Youth Antisocial Behavior, Delinquency, and Violence and a Public Health Approach to Prevention

J. Mark Eddy and John B. Reid
Oregon Social Learning Center

Vicky Curry
University of Oregon

INTRODUCTION

In recent years, multiple-victim acts of violence have occurred in a variety of small-town and suburban schools throughout the United States. At the same time, public angst about violent crime has reached unprecedented heights (Flanagan & Longmire, 1996). The perpetrators and victims of Columbine belong to the age group of greatest public focus, teenage youth. This focus is well deserved. Across all age groups, teenagers and young adults are the most likely individuals to be charged with the commission of a violent crime. The youth victimization rate from violent crime (e.g., homicide, rape, robbery, aggravated assault) is almost three times higher than the adult rate (Sickmund, Snyder, & Poe-Yamagata, 1997), and the persons most likely to commit such crimes against youth are other youth (Snyder & Sickmund, 1995).

While it is difficult to predict a specific violent act, to the extent that violence can be predicted, it is most likely committed by youth with extensive histories of offending (Lipsey & Derzon, 1998). In turn, such histories are best predicted by the early onset of police arrest prior to midadolescence (e.g., Patterson, Capaldi, & Bank, 1991; Moffit, 1993). The most likely youth to have an early onset of police arrest are those who are already exhibiting antisocial behavior problems during their elementary school years (Capaldi & Patterson, 1996). Thus, rather than constituting a unique and separate phenomenon, violence can be viewed as simply the most horrific aspect of a larger developmental and social problem that is not new to American society: the antisocial behavior of youth.

Public concern over the misbehavior of teenagers has been a prominent feature of American urban life in particular since the Industrial Revolution (see Eddy & Swanson-Gribskov, 1997). Public attention about teenage behavior has generally focused on the most common type of antisocial behavior—property crime (e.g., burglary, theft, arson). Youth are arrested for property crimes five times more frequently than for violent crimes, a ratio that has held constant for at least the past four decades (Snyder & Sickmund, 1995). In this chapter, we discuss youth antisocial behavior in the family, school, and community context: how it is classified, how it develops, and what types of interventions have been and should be applied to prevent its occurrence in the future.

Labels for Antisocial Behavior

While youth is a time when at least some display of antisocial behavior is normative in the U.S. (Huizinga, Menard, & Elliott, 1989; Shannon, 1988), of greatest concern is the repeated display of antisocial forms of behavior over a long period of time. The label that psychiatrists and psychologists use for the persistent engagement of youth in antisocial behavior is conduct disorder (CD; APA, 1994). To receive a diagnosis of CD, a youth must exhibit a pattern of antisocial behavior over the period of a year, and at least three of the following behaviors must occur: aggression toward people or animals (e.g., "often bullies, threatens, or intimidates others"), destruction of property (e.g., "has deliberately engaged in fire setting"), deceitfulness or theft (e.g., "has broken into someone else's house, building, or car"), or serious violations of rules (e.g., "often stays out at night despite parental prohibitions"). Further, these behaviors must cause severe impairment in the day-to-day functioning of a youth either in social relationships or in academic or occupational performance. A constellation of symptoms that often precede and co-occur with CD (see Lahey & Loeber, 1997) has been labeled oppositional defiant disorder (ODD). Youth with ODD exhibit extreme levels of hostile, negative, and defiant behavior—e.g., "often loses temper," "often argues with adults," or "often actively defies or refuses to comply with adults' requests or rules"—over an extended period of time (i.e., at least six months). At any given time, researchers estimate that from 2 to 16% of youth in the United States could be diagnosed with CD or ODD (Eddy, 2001).

Within the school setting, psychiatric labels may be used as well, but more commonly, youth displaying serious and troubling behavior problems, including antisocial behaviors, are labeled Emotionally Disturbed (ED). Nationally, the prevalence of ED is probably well over 2% of the total student population, but the identification rate varies greatly from state to state and averages just under 1% (Brandenburg, Friedman, & Silver, 1990). However, researchers have estimated that over half of students with serious emotional problems are not identified as ED, but rather as Learning Disabled (LD; Bussing, Zima, Belin, & Forness, 1998). Not surprisingly, researchers consistently find that nearly half of students that are classified as ED meet criteria for either CD or ODD (Bussing, Zima, Belin, & Forness, 1998; Pelham, William, Evans, Gnagy, & Greenslade, 1992). Clearly, these various professional labels are not being given to distinct sets of behavior but rather overlapping ones. Thus, in this discussion, we define "antisocial behavior" as the persistent participation of a youth in the broad class of rule-breaking, aversive, and/or destructive behaviors covered in the CD, ODD, and ED classifications.

Business as Usual: Traditional Responses to Youth Antisocial Behavior

In the United States, the two most common responses to youth who display antisocial behavior are official sanctions and clinical treatment. These responses tend to come only after the behavior of a youth develops to the point where it is deemed a *serious* problem in family, school, and/or community contexts. In the school setting, for example, the guidelines for classifying students as ED allow for sanctions to come into play such as suspension and exclusion for youngsters deemed to be Socially Maladjusted (SM). The purpose of the SM label was to allow schools to protect themselves, if necessary, by either excluding delinquent youngsters from ED programs or by expulsion from school altogether. While expulsion seems inconsistent with the notion of "disability" as used in the ED description, expulsion is just one example of a broader societal approach to antisocial behavior that has been in vogue in the United States for several decades.

Since the 1970s, "getting tough" on antisocial and related behaviors (e.g., substance use) has been a politically popular idea, particularly in election years (e.g., Rubin, 1999). Over time, this philosophy has been translated into a variety of changes in policies and laws, not only within schools, but also within the criminal and juvenile justice systems. Many states have now lowered the age of accountability for serious crimes and have established mandatory sentences for such crimes (Eddy & Swanson-Gribskov, 1997). One key outcome of these policies is that the total number of inmates in adult correctional institutions in the United States is now at an all time high, rising from 292 per 100,000 in 1990 to over 475 per 100,000 in 1999 (U.S. Department of Justice, 2000). To accommodate this population, prison construction has become a growth industry in the U.S. In some states, the costs associated with imprisonment now rival the costs associated with public education (e.g., Greenwood, Model, Rydell, & Chiesa, 1996). Interestingly, despite the relatively high usage of sanctions, they tend to be applied inconsistently (e.g., youth are arrested for only about 5% of the crimes they commit; Dunford & Elliot, 1982). Further, there is evidence that sanctions such as imprisonment are ineffective in reducing societal rates of antisocial behavior (e.g., Ouimet & Tremblay, 1996; Biles, 1983).

A related response is the provision of services to youth who are clearly displaying clinical or dangerous levels of antisocial behavior. Such services may be applied within a clinic delivery model, or they may be provided within the juvenile justice system or the school system. For many years, about half of all referrals to child mental health clinics have involved a youth with antisocial behavior problems such as CD or ODD (e.g., Wolff, 1961; Robins, 1981). Exactly what types of treatments these children receive once they enter a system of care is less clear. While there are a variety of efficacious clinical treatments for youth antisocial behavior that have been available for several decades (Eddy, 2001), there is scant information on either how effective these treatments actually are when delivered outside of a research protocol (i.e., by practicing therapists in regular community clinics without intensive supervision) or how often these treatments actually are used in community settings.

Within the school setting, a variety of interventions have been developed and test-ed, and many of the most efficacious of these are discussed in the present volume. As in the clinical setting, however, the actual delivery of these interventions to those identi-fied as "in need" has proven difficult. For example, receiving a label such as ED legally mandates service provision under the aegis of the federal Individuals with Disabilities Education Act of 1997, yet fewer than half of students identified with ED actually receive special education services (e.g., U.S. Department of Education, 1997). Further, in recent years, it is becoming clear that the most aggressive and difficult of the students experiencing serious emotional and behavioral problems in school are excluded from, or are not helped by, current ED programs. For example, school failure is unacceptably common for students with ED, with nearly half failing to complete high school (Valdes, Williamson, & Wagner, 1990).

Regardless of how frequently either sanctions or effective clinical interventions have been applied over the past several decades, numerous official indicators of juvenile and adult crime (i.e., police detainments or arrests) have risen substantially (U.S. Department of Justice, 2000; Snyder & Sickmund, 1995). As youth crime has increased, incarceration rates (and the funds associated with them) also have increased. At the same time, funding for other public services, such as mental health or education, has tight-ened significantly. Even if adequate funds were available for clinical ser-vices for antisocial youth, the lack of a sufficient number of therapists to apply effective treat-ments to the up to 16% of youth displaying serious antisocial behavior problems suggests that it is unlikely that clinical services, alone or in concert with sanctions, will ever significantly impact the prevalence of youth antisocial behavior (Albee, 1990).

A Public Health Approach to Youth Antisocial Behavior

Sanctions and clinical services are very expensive, "short-run" responses to youth antisocial behavior. Even if applied in an effective manner, they only address the behav-ior of individuals who have already acquired extensive antisocial repertoires. They do little to address the long-run threat posed by the needs of the multiple cohorts of at-risk youth who are on their way to developing antisocial behavior problems, and who will be candidates for the short-run solutions of the future.

An alternative "public health" (Potter & Mercy, 1997) approach views sanctions and clinical services as simply end points in a set of public responses intended to decrease the prevalence and severity of the problem within the population at large. A public health approach dictates a series of steps that are intended not only to protect society (i.e., sanctions) and to mitigate current problems (i.e., clinical services), but also to decrease the need for such protection and mitigation over the long run through the *proactive* prevention of the development of youth problem behaviors (see also Moore, Prothrow-Stith, Guyer, & Spivak, 1994). Hypothetically, the longer an effective public health approach is applied, the less the need should be for end point services. Since end point services tend to be quite expensive and preventive approaches tend to be inexpensive, the public health approach appears to be a fiscally responsible approach to the problem of youth antisocial behavior (for commentary, see Moore, 1999; Rubin, 1999).

The lynchpin of the public health approach is the conceptualization of a research-based model of how a particular problem, such as youth antisocial behavior, develops and maintains over the lifespan (Mrazek & Haggerty, 1994). Such a model not only describes which factors are critical in problem development at each point in life, but also how development at one point is related to development at another point. With this model as a starting point, interventions are created to address malleable (i.e., changeable) factors in the developmental model, and studies are launched to assess whether these interventions can in fact reliably change those factors, and whether changing those factors actually results in changes in the problem of interest (see Eddy, Dishion, & Stoolmiller, 1998). Ideally, the most efficacious of these interventions are adapted to specific communities, implemented, and then rigorously evaluated; the interventions that are found to be truly effective in a community are retained, but outcomes are monitored on an ongoing basis; and, finally, the interventions that are not effective are adapted further, evaluated, and if still ineffective, discontinued.

The ultimate goal of a public health approach is to devise a continuum of effective interventions, applicable to a societal problem, that represents an integrated prevention strategy (Brown, 1991). In the case of antisocial behavior, such a continuum could range from "universal" community or school-based preventive intervention programs for the general population of children and families, to "selected" interventions for populations at high risk for the development of antisocial behaviors, to "indicated" clinical interventions for aggressive children and their families, to sanctions such as incarceration for dangerous juvenile offenders (e.g., Loeber & Farrington, 1998). Each intervention is designed to serve a different level of need, and together, the set of responses should minimize the burden of suffering that the problem creates, not only for the individuals involved (both the perpetrators and their victims), but their families, their schools, and the community at large. Clearly, this type of approach requires working within multiple systems of care, and requires coordinated planning, financing, and delivery within a given community, county, and state.

In the remainder of this chapter, we overview a development model for youth antisocial behavior, discuss an intervention strategy that is congruent with the model, Parent Management Training (PMT), and then illustrate how concepts from PMT have been incorporated into promising universal and selected preventive interventions during early and middle childhood (i.e., 3 to 11 years). These types of interventions are the most likely *not* to be conducted in schools and communities (see Eddy & Swanson-Gribskov, 1997), yet without their presence, we posit that clinical services and sanctions have little chance of decreasing the prevalence of youth antisocial behavior.

The Development of Youth Antisocial Behavior

While serious antisocial behavior is assumed to be highly stable over the course of development (e.g., Olweus, 1979), only 50% of elementary school-age children who exhibit high levels of antisocial behaviors (e.g., disobedience, fighting) continue their misbehavior into adolescence, and only 40 to 75% of adolescents who exhibit high levels (e.g., stealing, assault) continue to do so during young adulthood (see Eddy, 2001). These destructive behaviors covary with a variety of other socially problematic behaviors such as academic failure, substance use, and early sexual behavior, and several research groups have hypothesized that they constitute a "general deviance" syndrome during youth (Jessor & Jessor, 1977; Osgood, Johnston, O'Malley, & Bachman, 1988). A variety of recent studies support this notion (e.g., Ary et al., 1999). Later in life, youth who exhibit extreme forms and levels of antisocial behavior are at high risk for difficulties in almost every major area of adulthood, including their marital and family relationships, their workplace performance, and their mental and physical functioning (Eddy, 2001).

Meta-analyses of the developmental literature on youth antisocial behavior have implicated a variety of "risk" factors that, if present, increase the probability that a youth will display current or future antisocial behaviors (Lipsey & Derzon, 1998). Specifically, the "at risk" person is considered more likely to experience the negative outcome than a person randomly selected from the general population (see Mrazek & Haggerty, 1994). However, contrary to the way that risk is often discussed in the media at large, the presence of any given risk factor is usually far from a guarantee that such an outcome will actually occur.

In their analyses, Lipsey and Derzon (1998) found that during the elementary school years and during the middle to early high school years, the strongest risk factor for future antisocial behavior is past antisocial behavior. However, correlations between past and future antisocial behavior tend to hover around $r = .50$, indicating that only about 25% of future behavior is accounted for by past behavior (i.e., the square of the correlation is the percent of variance accounted for). During middle childhood, after past antisocial behavior, the following are the "strongest" predictors of serious antisocial behavior during late adolescence and young adulthood: gender ($r = .26$), socioeconomic status ($r = .24$), antisocial parents ($r = .23$), ethnicity ($r = .20$), psychological condition ($r = .15$), parent-child relations ($r = .15$), and social ties ($r = .15$). In contrast, during early adolescence, after past antisocial behavior, social ties ($r = .39$), antisocial peers ($r = .37$), school attitude/performance ($r = .19$), psychological condition ($r = .19$), parent-child relations ($r = .19$), gender ($r = .19$), and antisocial parents ($r = .16$) are the strongest predictors.

These correlations point to a variety of issues that are important to the development of antisocial behavior, including social relationships with parents and peers and differential circumstances and treatment based on individual characteristics such as gender and race. However, such information is limited without a broader context for interpretation involving the joint action of risk factors over time. Alone, any of these risk factors have little influence. However, when several risk factors interact together in the presence of other factors, the effect can be quite powerful (see Patterson, Reid, & Dishion, 1992). The tapestry that these risk factors create in concert with one another is the "developmental model" that is central to the public health approach.

The developmental model that guides our thinking about youth antisocial behavior is coercion theory (see Figure 1; Reid & Eddy, 1997). The core themes in coercion

FIGURE 1

The Coercion Model for the Development of Youth Antisocial Behavior (From Reid & Eddy, 1997)

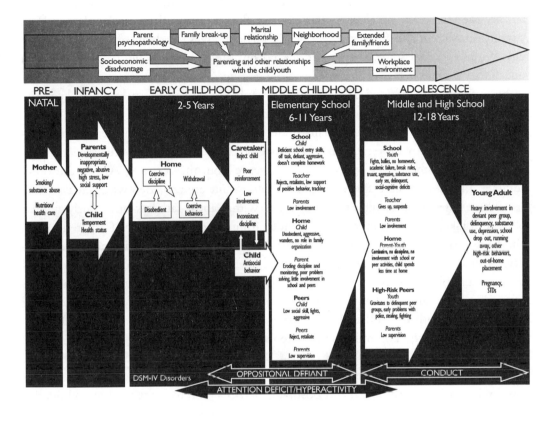

theory are popular in the development literature on youth antisocial behavior (Peplar & Rubin, 1991). Further, they are utilized in most other prominent developmental theories of antisocial behavior (Stoff, Breiling, & Maser, 1997).

Within coercion theory, the key process hypothesized to shape youth antisocial behavior is "negative reinforcement" within the youth's social relationships at home, at school, and on the playground. From the behavioral literature, negative reinforcement is the association of certain behaviors with escape from undesirable situations: the more likely a behavior effectively terminates a noxious situation, the more likely a person is to repeat the behavior under similar conditions in the future. The repeated pairing of situation and response is viewed as creating a response pattern that is usually outside of the awareness of a person—it is not that an individual is formally "choosing" to engage in the behavior each time, but rather it happens on "auto pilot" because it has worked in the past. Such a circumstance is similar to that of a track athlete who has practiced a certain move again and again. When it is time to perform, the athlete behaves in an appropriate way without having to think about it; practice has made automatic the movements required for the successful completion of the event. This level of performance is sometimes referred to as "response fluency."

Since negative reinforcement is the key factor in our developmental model of youth antisocial behavior, an illustration of how it operates is in order. For example, it is the end of a long workday and a parent and child are approaching the checkout line at the grocery store with a full cart. The parent says to the child, "I'm not going to buy any candy today, so don't ask. We'll have dinner when we get home." The line of shoppers is long and by the time they get close to the checker, the child is restless and hungry and the parent is impatient and anxious to get home. The child sees the shelves of candy near the checker and asks for some. The parent says no, but the child continues to ask. With each question, the child's voice becomes a bit more grating, until the parent perceives the child to be quite whiny and loud. The parent feels embarrassed and exasperated. To keep the child quiet, he finally backs down and buys him a candy bar.

In the end, this situation is actually quite *rewarding* for all involved. The child receives a positive reward for his escalation of negative behavior. The parent is rewarded, if only with relief from the child's demand and an escape from the accusing eyes of the other adults in the grocery store. Even the other adults in line are rewarded with quiet.

These types of difficult situations occur within most families on a fairly regular basis, and taken in isolation, can be considered innocuous. However, if a parent and a child are in many "checkout line" situations together on a *daily* basis and these situations usually turn out as above, it is very likely that aversive behavior patterns will become a staple of the interpersonal interactions between parent and child. The more often the parent and child experience these situations, the better they will get at being more aversive with each other. Further, the child will become more "skilled" at eliciting future conflicts, not only with parents, but also with siblings, peers, teachers, coaches, and others.

Unfortunately, as the rate and intensity of aversive exchanges increase in a parent-child relationship, constructive and positive behaviors tend to decrease. For a child, this means that as coercion takes over, encouragement from parents, teachers, or peers for desired behavior tends to become less frequent. The end result is that the child becomes quite adept at surviving (and "winning") in overtly aversive social situations, but at the same time, becomes quite inept at excelling in a variety of conventional settings and situations, such as academics (see Figure 2 for an example of the impact of negative reinforcement on school behavior). In the classroom, for example, the child will come to be viewed as "aggressive" or as a "fighter" and will be socially rejected and marginalized quite quickly by teachers and peers (Dodge, 1983).

As the elementary school years progress, the coercive child falls further and further behind, not only socially, but also academically. Child anxiety and depression may follow, which may result in further deleterious social and academic outcomes. Failure experiences mount. As the child becomes increasingly difficult to interact with, most children and adults may simply avoid him or her. The people who are willing to interact with the child are those under similar circumstances, including other marginalized and troubled children, as well as the marginalized and troubled adults who take advantage of them. At the same time, parental supervision of the child's friends and whereabouts may decrease until the child is "wandering" (Stoolmiller, 1994) on his own or with friends most of the time. During the early teen years, these friends coalesce into a "deviant peer" group, a

FIGURE 2

An Illustration of the Negative Reinforcement Process Central to the Coercion Model (from Patterson, Reid, & Dishion, 1992)

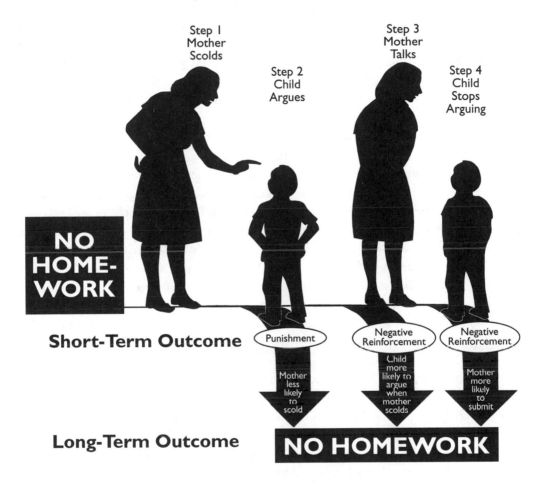

group that may have some formal designation and/or affiliation to a larger organization (i.e., a gang) but most likely is rather fluid. The combination of the deviant peer group and wandering provides the gateway to an antisocial lifestyle, including stealing, substance use, high-risk sexual behaviors, and violence (Patterson et al., 1992; Reid & Eddy, 1997; Capaldi, Crosby & Stoolmiller, 1996). A hallmark of this lifestyle includes talking about antisocial behaviors with friends and being strongly reinforced for doing such (Dishion, Eddy, Haas, Li, & Spracklen, 1997). In other words, it is generally very unlikely that this behavior is going on without the notice of others.

"Risk" and the Developmental Model

The importance of negative reinforcement in our developmental model puts a very specific spin on the meaning of "risk factor." Risk factors are important in the development of antisocial behavior to the extent that they make either a parent or a child *more likely* to be irritable, uncooperative, or aversive. In turn, such a state heightens the likelihood that the parent and child will (a) become locked into coercive interactions with each other (i.e., inept discipline and problem solving), and (b) eventually withdraw from each other (i.e., inadequate supervision, child wandering).

Thus, within the home setting, parent behaviors that might lead to a difficult child temperament at birth are viewed as risk factors, such as maternal tobacco, alcohol, or other drug use during pregnancy that might significantly and permanently alter the neural physiology of the developing fetus (Olds, Henderson & Kitzman, 1994). Further, poorly handled conflict between parents is viewed as a risk factor if it results in a parent being in an irritable, depressed mood (Patterson et al., 1992). Within the school setting, relevant risk factors are those that increase the odds of coercive exchanges between child and teacher or between child and peers.

Certainly, an important aspect of each of these risk factors is timing. If a mother uses substances during pregnancy and while nursing, the direct physiological impacts on the child can be immense (Olds, Henderson, & Tatelbaum, 1994). If substances are used and abused by parents later, the emotional and social impacts may be quite difficult, and these, in turn, may be related to physiological changes (e.g., Fisher, Gunnar, Chamberlain, & Reid, 2000), but a variety of factors can mediate, or buffer, such impacts. Given the importance of timing, probably one of the most significant risk factors for a lifetime of antisocial behavior is the age of initial onset (Dishion & Patterson, 1997). If the child is young when he or she first enters into an extensive series of coercive interactions with his parents, his teachers, and/or his peers (i.e., an "early starter"), then his development might resemble that of the hypothetical child in Figure 1, on page 33, with negative outcomes cascading upon negative outcomes during early childhood and elementary school. In contrast, if a child is an adolescent when such events first transpire (i.e., a "late starter"), she will likely have a positive repertoire of behaviors that at some point will carry her back into the conventional world and away from the deviant peer group. The more time a child has to practice coercion, the more likely he or she has an abundance of verbal and physical fighting skills and a dearth of nonviolent problem-solving skills.

An Intervention Based on the Developmental Model

Parent Management Training (PMT) is the name of the class of interventions that were developed in concert and are congruent with the developmental model in Figure 1 (see Reid, Patterson, & Snyder, in press). During PMT, parents are taught empirically based skills in positive reinforcement, discipline, monitoring, and problem solving (Forgatch & Martinez, 1999; Eddy, 2001). The consistent practice of these skills is hypothesized to lead to decreases in child antisocial behaviors and corresponding increases in child prosocial behaviors. PMT is a highly collaborative and interactive intervention: role playing of skills during treatment groups, subsequent practice at home, and the communication of the outcome of such practice in the next treatment session are critical to success. Thus, while PMT is a "behavioral" intervention, it is not

TABLE 1

Effect Sizes for Child Outcomes From Parent Management Training Studies

Reporter	Mean (SD)
Independent observer	0.85 (0.47)
Parent	0.84 (0.38)
Teacher	0.73 (0.48)

Note

From data in "The effectiveness of behavioral parent training to modify antisocial behavior in children: A meta-analysis," by W. J. Serketich & J. E. Dumas, 1996, *Behavior Therapy, 27,* 171-186.

an automated intervention. Interventionist-parent relationship factors are vital to success, and the "soft" clinical skills of the interventionist are very important (Patterson & Chamberlain, 1994; Forgatch & Patterson, 1998). In all, effective intervention with families of antisocial children requires an average of 20 to 50 hours of intensive clinical effort with both parents and other adults (e.g., teachers) to bring about long-term changes in child outcomes. Treatment procedures for a variety of populations are described in several manuals (e.g., Patterson et al., 1975; Chamberlain, 1994; Forehand & McMahon, 1981; Forgatch, 1994; Forgatch & Patterson, 1989).

There is evidence that PMT leads to positive child outcomes. In the field at large, PMT is considered one of the most promising treatments for antisocial behavior. In a review of 82 studies on psychological treatment of children and adolescents diagnosed with a conduct disorder, only two interventions were found to meet stringent criteria for "well established" treatment (Brestan & Eyberg, 1998). Both of these were variants of PMT (i.e., Patterson et al., 1975; Webster-Stratton, 1998a). Similarly, in a recent meta-analytic review, Serketich and Dumas (1996) found over 100 studies of behavioral parent-training programs (either PMT, or with primary elements of PMT) designed to target child antisocial behavior. Twenty-six of these studies included at least one comparison group (i.e., wait list control, placebo group, or another treatment). Serketich and Dumas calculated effect sizes for each of the measures in these 26 studies, and the overall means and standard deviations are listed in Table 1. These effect sizes indicate that no matter how child outcome was measured, the average child with parent(s) who received parent training had a better outcome than approximately 80% of children with parent(s) who did not receive parent training.

As predicted by our developmental model, several studies have demonstrated that the effects of PMT on child adjustment are mediated through parenting practices (Eddy & Chamberlain, 2000; Forgatch & DeGarmo, 1999; Martinez & Forgatch, in press). In their continuing study of the long-term outcomes of high-rate-offender youth who

FIGURE 3

Key Social Coercion Model Interactional Variables as Mediators of the Impact of Treatment on Youth Antisocial Behavior (From Eddy & Chamberlain, 2000)

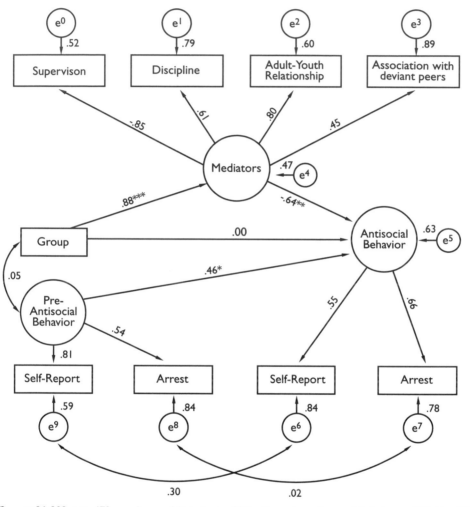

$X2_{(22)} = 21.802$, $p = .472$, goodness-of-fit index = .920, adjusted goodness-of-fit index = .837, $N = 53$

$*p < .05$, $**p < .01$, $***p < .001$

were randomly assigned to either Treatment Foster Care (Chamberlain, 1994) or services-as-usual group home care, Eddy and Chamberlain (2000) found significant relationships between the intervention and parenting (i.e., discipline, monitoring, and positive youth-adult relationship) and deviant peer association, as well as significant relationships between the intervention and subsequent youth antisocial outcomes (see also Chamberlain & Reid, 1998). However, as shown in Figure 3, when the relationships among all three factors were examined simultaneously (i.e., intervention, the mediators, and antisocial outcomes), the intervention was no longer directly related to outcomes. Rather, the impact of the intervention on the outcomes went through the hypothesized mediating variables. Based on Baron and Kenny's (1986) discussion of mediation, such a finding indicates that the effects of the intervention on antisocial behavior were attributable to the quality of parenting and related outcomes (i.e., decreased affiliation with deviant peers) present during treatment, a quality that was higher in Treatment Foster Care than group home care.

The Foundation of a Public Health Approach to Youth Antisocial Behavior: Selected and Universal Interventions

As discussed above, the most common types of interventions to address youth anti-social behavior are clinical interventions and sanctions. While these interventions often have been defined as "prevention" (see Eddy & Swanson-Gribskov, 1997), if effective, they do not decrease the number of *new* individuals displaying antisocial behavior, and thus are ultimately not preventive but curative (or punitive) in nature (see Mrazek & Haggerty, 1994). In contrast, while not often applied, there are a number of efficacious selected and universal interventions with the potential to prevent new cases. To date, the most notable among these target high-risk families during the first five years of the life of a child (i.e., selected preventive intervention), and then target all families during the elementary school years (i.e., universal preventive intervention).

Selected Preventive Interventions Prior to School Entry

Nurse Home Visitation. While a universal preventive intervention applied very early in the family lifecycle might seem like the most logical first step in preventing youth antisocial behavior, there is no system of care in the United States that reaches the majority of the population. However, there are multiple systems that could work together to identify prospective mothers who are at risk for parenting difficulties. A prominent risk factor not only for parenting difficulties but also for many other adverse physical and mental health outcomes is poverty (Anderson, 1996). Teenage, single, iso-lated, and impoverished mothers are particularly at risk for having parenting difficulties (Olds, Hill, Mihalic, & O'Brien, 1998). Prior to the birth of their child, such mothers may come in contact with the school system, the mental health system, the juvenile jus-tice system, the welfare system, and state-supported health insurance plans.

In several randomized selected prevention trials, Olds and colleagues have exam-ined the efficacy of a public health nurse home visitation program with first-time mothers, many of whom were also young, single, and impoverished (Olds, Hill, et al., 1998). One version of Olds' program includes biweekly home visits during pregnancy, weekly visits for six weeks after birth, and periodic visits through toddlerhood. During the visits, a variety of key topics are addressed, including maternal health care, maternal substance use (including the importance of not smoking during pregnancy), parenting skills, coping skills, service knowledge and utilization, and family, educational, and occupational planning. Similar to PMT, the intervention was grounded in a positive working relationship between the nurse and the mother, and focused on the day-to-day issues and social interactions the mother was facing. Most important, the issues addressed were clearly antecedents to later child problem behaviors, including antisocial behavior.

Many positive effects of the nurse home visitation program have been found (e.g., Olds, Henderson, Chamberlin, & Tatelbaum, 1986; Olds, Henderson, Tatelbaum, & Chamberlin, 1986; Olds, Hill, et al., 1998), and these benefits were particularly salient for the highest-risk mothers. Relative to mothers randomly assigned to a control group, nurse-visited mothers smoked less during pregnancy, were less likely to have a premature birth and low birth weight, were less likely to have a baby rated fussy at birth, provided more enriched and stimulating environments for their infants, and abused and neglected their children less during their early childhoods. Further, mothers in the visitation program reduced their subsequent pregnancies, and were more likely to be employed (Olds, Henderson, & Kitzman, 1994). As would be predicted from the developmental model, improvement in these outcomes had long-term effects on youth antisocial behavior. In a 15-year follow-up study, Olds found that youth whose mothers were in the nurse home visitation condition were significantly less antisocial than youth whose mothers were in the control group (Olds, Henderson, et al., 1998).

Parent Management Training. During the preschool years, a number of risk factors are important in the developmental model, including difficult child temperament, child noncompliance and aggression, parent irritability and punitiveness, and a lack of parenting skills, such as inept limit setting and low parental warmth and playfulness. Of greatest concern is when both child and parent risk factors are present in a given family. Such a situation is more likely in the families targeted in nurse home visitation. Ultimately, these parents may have their children enrolled in an early childhood program such as Head Start. Alternatively, such parents may have their children in daycare at a high school as they finish their education. Either venue would be ideal for offering a selective preventive intervention for parents.

Webster-Stratton and colleagues have developed a version of PMT that has been used with parents whose children are in Head Start (Webster-Stratton, 1998b). Webster-Stratton's parenting program is the most thoroughly investigated version of PMT, having been tested in numerous randomized efficacy trials over the past 20 years. During the program, PMT concepts such as positive reinforcement, discipline, monitoring, and problem solving are taught via short video clips of parent-child interaction, group discussion, and extensive role playing. A variety of typical situations are focused on during the program, such as how parents and children play together. Based on both parental reports and observation data, relative to control participants, Webster-Stratton has found that intervention participants demonstrate improvements in parenting skills and children's social behavior as well as decreases in child problems and aggression (e.g., Webster-Stratton, 1998b; Webster-Stratton, 1989; Webster-Stratton, Kolpacoff, & Hollingsworth, 1988). To date, all of these studies have used wait list controls, and thus the long-term impact of the program on youth antisocial behavior is not known.

Universal Prevention Programs During Elementary School

While there is wide variation across school districts, most children in the United States attend public elementary schools. When a child enters school, it is the first time that he or she joins a system of care that includes the majority of his or her birth cohort. During this period of life, the child must adapt to the demands of the peer group and teachers or face the consequences, such as peer rejection or early academic failure. In turn, these serve as risk factors for further difficulties, including youth antisocial behavior.

Several theory-driven universal interventions have been developed and tested with youngsters in elementary school (e.g., O'Donnell, Hawkins, Catalano & Abbott, 1995). Most have addressed not only the parenting factors that Olds and Webster-Stratton target (i.e., positive involvement, discipline, monitoring, problem solving), but also parental involvement in school. Further, they usually target child social skills, including anger management and problem solving. One example of this type of "multimodal" universal prevention program is Linking the Interests of Families and Teachers (LIFT; Reid, Eddy, Fetrow, & Stoolmiller, 1999).

LIFT was designed to decrease the likelihood of two major factors that put children at risk for subsequent antisocial behavior and delinquency: (1) aggressive and other socially incompetent behaviors with teachers and peers at school, and (2) inept parenting, including inconsistent and inappropriate discipline and lax supervision. LIFT has 3 main components: (1) child social skills training, (2) the playground Good Behavior Game, and (3) parent management training (see Figure 4, on page 42).

Child social skills training in the LIFT program comprises 20 sessions of one hour each conducted across a 10-week period. Sessions are held during the regular school day. Each week, the first session includes four parts: (1) classroom instruction and discussion on specific social and problem-solving skills, (2) skills practice in small and large groups, (3) free play in the context of a group cooperation game, and (4) review and presentation of daily rewards. The second session includes a formal class problem-solving session as well as free play and rewards. The curriculum is similar for all elementary school students, but delivery format, group exercises, and content emphasis are modified to address normative developmental issues depending on the grade level of the participants.

The playground Good Behavior Game takes place during the middle of the free play portion of the social skills training. A modification of the original Good Behavior Game (Barrish, Saunders, & Wolfe, 1969) is used to actively encourage positive peer relations on the playground. During the game, rewards can be earned by individual children for the demonstration of both positive problem-solving skills and other prosocial behaviors with peers as well as the inhibition of negative behaviors. These rewards are then pooled with a small group of students as well as the entire class. When a sufficient number of armbands are earned by a group or by the class, simple rewards are given (e.g., an extra recess, a pizza party). The keys to this aspect of the game are having a sufficient number of adults to roam through all parts of the playground and having these adults do a specific task (i.e., hand out colorful nylon armbands as a reward to individual students for their overtly positive behavior toward peers).

FIGURE 4

The Linking the Interests of Families and Teachers (LIFT)
Universal Prevention Program
(From Reid, Eddy, Fetrow, & Stoolmiller, 1999)

Parent Management Training in LIFT is conducted in groups of 10 to 15 parents and comprises six sessions scheduled once per week for approximately two and one half hours each. The sessions are held during the same period of time as the child social skills training. Session content focuses on positive reinforcement, discipline, monitoring, problem solving, and parent involvement in the school. Each parent session follows a common format from week to week (i.e., review of results of homework from the prior week; lecture, discussion, and role play; and presentation of homework for the coming week). The curriculum is designed to accommodate varying levels of instructor education and expertise.

A randomized prevention trial of LIFT involving over 650 youth and their families is currently underway that contrasts those assigned to the LIFT program versus those assigned to a no-treatment control group (Reid et al., 1999). Following intervention, and controlling for preintervention levels of behavior, LIFT has been found to decrease child physical aggression toward classmates on the playground, to increase teacher positive impressions of child social skills with classmates, and to decrease parent aversive behavior during family problem-solving discussions.

Beyond these statistically significant findings, the LIFT program has had "clinically significant" short- and long-term impacts on participants. For example, in the short run, observed aggressive behavior on the LIFT playgrounds decreased from a mean of 6.0 aversive physical behaviors per 30-minute recess period to only 4.8 aversive behaviors per 30-minutes; following the intervention period, the children in the control group continued to average 6.6 aversive behaviors per 30 minutes (see Stoolmiller, Eddy, & Reid, 2000). These differences translate into a relative decrease of over 1,700 physically aversive events on intervention school playgrounds during the spring quarter. Over the long run (i.e., 3 years postintervention), relative to fifth-grade youth in the LIFT group, fifth-grade youth in the control group were 2.2 times more likely to affiliate with misbehaving peers, 1.8 times more likely to be involved in patterned alcohol use, 1.5 times more likely to have tried marijuana, and 2.4 times more likely to be arrested by the age of 14 (Eddy, Reid, Stoolmiller, & Fetrow, 2001).

Discussion

The selected and universal prevention programs discussed in this chapter target specific antecedents to later youth antisocial behavior, delinquency, and violence. If these programs were delivered in concert with clinical services and sanctions, the combined package of interventions should reduce overall levels of risk of harm and failure and increase overall levels of safety and protective factors for youth in the home, school, and community. In the school setting in particular, by providing better strategies for dealing with conflict in the classroom, on the playground, and in the home, and by developing active collaboration between parents and teachers, fewer children should develop difficult patterns of aggression and noncompliance. Over the long run (e.g., 10 to 20 years), such efforts, if continuously and consistently applied, should significantly decrease the number of children in need of clinical services or sanctions. While such a time span may seem long, it is no longer than the time it takes to develop a complicated product (e.g., a new pharmaceutical) in the business world.

While prevention programs can serve the important function of diverting children from expensive endpoint services such as clinical treatment, they also can facilitate the early identification of children who do not respond to the universal interventions and who do in fact need more intensive services. As noted above, one aspect of the public health model is the continued assessment of the outcomes of programs, even after they are established within a system. Assessment of individual outcomes in the context of universal intervention could help overcome serious gaps in service within schools today. Specifically, the prevalence of students meeting criteria for ED is at least 2% (Brandenburg, et al., 1990), but only about half the children who actually meet criteria for ED receive special services nationwide (U.S. Department of Education, 1997). Of equal or greater concern is the fact that although teacher referral for special education frequently occurs in the early primary grades, the time delay between first documentation of a problem and first placement for ED services may be five years or more (Duncan, Forness, & Hartsough, 1995). Universal and repeated assessment in the context of the classroom, as well as implementation of a schoolwide program for competent behavior management (see Sugai, Horner, & Gresham, this volume), should greatly increase the ability of school system personnel to quickly and precisely determine which students need which specialized services.

Further, if an entire district were participating in a universal prevention program that included routine assessments, district administrators would be in an objective position to determine not only which schools are struggling, but also which teachers within those schools are struggling. Teachers who have difficulty with classroom organization and behavior management issues are not only placing their students at high risk for future problems, but also the future classmates of those students (Kellam, Ling, Merisca, Brown, & Ialongo, 1998). Such an assessment strategy would not only identify children who need more services, but also those teachers who need supplemental consultation, training, or support.

Research has revealed that beginning teachers are rarely completely prepared to meet core classroom requirements, including classroom management (National Commission on Teaching and America's Future, 1997). Beginning teachers continue to rate classroom management as their number one problem (Veeman, 1984). Blum (1994) surveyed all colleges and universities accredited by the National Council for Accreditation of Teacher Education to determine the percentage of teacher training programs offering specific courses in classroom discipline to their preservice teachers. Results indicated that while 51 percent of the colleges and universities offered a specific course on classroom discipline at the undergraduate level, only 43 percent of all preservice students were required to take such a course.

Since the classroom teacher is often the primary person who makes the judgment that a student requires specialized services for behavioral problems, training also could be provided in what constitutes severe emotional problems and how to identify these in the classroom setting. Teachers do not routinely get training in making these types of decisions (National Commission on Teaching and America's Future, 1997), and some teachers are probably so emotionally involved in some of their students' behavior problems that objective assessment would be quite difficult (Veeman, 1984; National Commission on Teaching and America's Future, 1997). However, if a minimal and repetitive assessment of all children were routinely conducted for *all* children, those children needing support and intervention beyond that provided in the particular intervention could be quickly identified and referred for more intensive services.

For example, within the context of universal intervention in the elementary school or selected intervention in Head Start, for those who still misbehaved in class, an individualized and more intensive program such as the First Steps early intervention (see Feil, Walker, & Severson, this volume) could be made available. In elementary schools in which a standard playground program was ineffective, more targeted interventions also could be developed and implemented (see Sugai, Horner, and Gresham, this volume). In the context of a school environment that consistently supports and assesses positive social behavior, such intensive interventions can be quickly delivered to the children they are designed to help; and when such interventions produce positive behavior changes, the universal school setting can be expected to support them. Such integrated strategies are now possible. It is time to implement and assess their joint impacts systematically in field-based studies.

REFERENCES

Albee, G. W. (1990). The futility of psychotherapy. *Journal of Mind & Behavior, 11*(3–4), 369–384.

American Psychiatric Association. (1994). *Diagnostic and statistical manual of mental disorders* (4th ed.). Washington, DC: Author.

Anderson, N. (1996, May). *Socioeconomic influences on health: A challenge to prevention researchers.* Paper presented at the Fifth Annual National Conference on Prevention Research, Washington, DC.

Ary, D. V., Duncan, T. E., Biglan, A., Metzler, C. W., Noell, J. W., & Smolkowski, K. (1999). Development of adolescent problem behavior. *Journal of Abnormal Child Psychology, 27*(2), 141–150.

Baron, R. M., & Kenny, D. A. (1986). The moderator-mediator variable distinction in social psychological research: Conceptual, strategic, and statistical considerations. *Journal of Personality and Social Psychology, 51(6),* 1173–1182.

Barrish, H. H., Saunders, M., & Wolfe, M. D. (1969). Good behavior game. Effects of individual contingencies for group consequences and disruptive behavior in a classroom. *Journal of Applied Behavior Analysis, 2,* 119–124.

Biles, D. (1983). Crime and imprisonment: A two-decade comparison between England and Wales and Australia. *British Journal of Criminology, 23*(2), 166–172.

Blum, H. (1994). *The pre-service teacher's educational training in classroom discipline: A national survey of teacher education programs.* Unpublished doctoral dissertation, Temple University Graduate Board (UMI Dissertation Service, No. 9434650).

Brandenburg, N. A., Friedman, R. M., & Silver, S. E. (1990). The epidemiology of childhood psychiatric disorders: Recent prevalence findings and methodological issues. *Journal of the American Academy of Child and Adolescent Psychiatry, 29,* 76–83.

Brestan, E. V., & Eyberg, S. M. (1998). Effective psychosocial treatments of conduct-disordered children and adolescents: 29 years, 82 studies, and 5,272 kids. *Journal of Clinical Child Psychology, 27,* 180–189.

Brown, C. H. (1991). *Principles for designing randomized preventive trials in mental health.* Paper presented at the National Conference on Prevention, Washington, DC.

Bussing, R., Zima, B. T., Belin, T. R., & Forness, S. R. (1998). Children who qualify for LD and SED programs: Do they differ in level of ADHD symptoms and comorbid psychiatric conditions? *Behavioral Disorders, 23*(2), 85–97.

Capaldi, D. M., & Patterson, G. R. (1996). Can violent offenders be distinguished from frequent offenders: Prediction from childhood to adolescence. *Journal of Research in Crime and Delinquency, 33,* 206–231.

Capaldi, D. M., Crosby, L., & Stoolmiller, M. (1996). Predicting the timing of first sexual intercourse for adolescent males. *Child Development, 67,* 344–359.

Chamberlain, P. (1994). Outcome evaluation of treatment foster care program participants. In S. Patterson (Ed.), *Family connections: A treatment foster care model for adolescents with delinquency* (Vol. 5, pp. 85–95). Eugene, OR: Castalia.

Chamberlain, P., & Reid, J. (1998). Comparison of two community alternatives to incarceration for chronic juvenile offenders. *Journal of Consulting and Clinical Psychology, 6,* 624–633.

Dishion, T. J., & Patterson, G. R. (1997). The timing and severity of antisocial behavior: Three hypotheses within an ecological framework. In D. Stoff, J. Breiling, & J. Maser (Eds.), *Handbook of antisocial behavior* (pp. 205–217). New York: Wiley.

Dishion, T. J., Eddy, J. M., Haas, E., Li, F., & Spracklen, K. (1997). Friendships and violent behavior during adolescence. *Social Development, 6*(2), 207–223.

Dodge, K. A. (1983). Behavioral antecedents of peer social status. *Child Development, 54,* 1386–1399.

Duncan, B. B., Forness, S. R., & Hartsough, C. (1995). Students identified as seriously emotionally disturbed in school-based treatment: Cognitive, psychiatric, and special educational characteristics. *Behavioral Disorders, 20,* 238–252.

Dunford, F. W., & Elliot, D. S. (1982). *Identifying career offenders with self-report data* (Grant No. MH 27552). Washington, DC: National Institute of Mental Health.

Eddy, J. M. (2001). *Aggressive and defiant behavior: The latest assessment and treatment strategies for the Conduct Disorder.* Kansas City, MO: Compact Clinicals.

Eddy, J. M., & Chamberlain, P. (2000). Family management and deviant peer association as mediators of the impact of treatment condition on youth antisocial behavior. *Journal of Consulting and Clinical Psychology, 68*(5), 857–863.

Eddy, J. M., Dishion, T. J., & Stoolmiller, M. (1998). The analysis of intervention change in children and families: Methodological and conceptual issues embedded in intervention studies. *Journal of Abnormal Child Psychology, 26,* 53–69.

Eddy, J. M., Reid, J. B., Stoolmiller, M., & Fetrow, R. A. (2001). *Three year outcomes for a preventive intervention for conduct problems.* Manuscript submitted for publication.

Eddy, J. M., & Swanson-Gribskov, L. (1997). Juvenile justice and delinquency prevention in the United States: The influence of theories and traditions on policies and practices. In T. P. Gullota, G. R. Adams, & R. Montemayor (Eds.), *Delinquent violent youth.* Thousand Oaks, CA: Sage.

Fisher, P. A., Gunnar, M. R., Chamberlain, P., & Reid, J. B. (2000). Preventive intervention for maltreated preschool children: Impact on children's behavior, neuroendocrine activity, and foster parent functioning. *Journal of the American Academy of Child and Adolescent Psychiatry, 39,* 1356–1364.

Flanagan, T. J., & Longmire, D. R. (Eds.). (1996). *Americans view crime and justice: A national public opinion survey.* Thousand Oaks, CA: Sage.

Forehand, R. L., & McMahon, R. J. (1981). *Helping the noncompliant child: A clinician's guide to parent training.* New York: Guilford Press.

Forgatch, M. S. (1994). *Parenting through change: A training manual.* Eugene, OR: Oregon Social Learning Center.

Forgatch, M. S., & DeGarmo, D. S. (1999). Parenting through change: An effective prevention program for single mothers. *Journal of Consulting and Clinical Psychology, 67*(5), 711–724.

Forgatch, M. S., & Martinez, C. R., Jr. (1999). Parent management training: A program linking basic research and practical application. *Tidsskrift for Norsk Psykologforening (Journal of the Norwegian Psychological Society), 36,* 923-937.

Forgatch, M. S., & Patterson, G. R. (1989). *Parents and adolescents living together: Vol. 2. Family problem solving* (Vol. II). Eugene, OR: Castalia.

Forgatch, M. S., & Patterson, G. R. (1998). Behavioral family therapy. In F. M. Dattilio (Ed.), *Case studies in couples and family therapy: Systematic and cognitive perspectives* (pp. 85-107). New York: Guilford Press.

Greenwood, P. W., Model, K. E., Rydell, C. P., & Chiesa, J. (1996). *Diverting children from a life of crime: Measuring costs and benefits.* Santa Monica, CA: Rand, MR699.0-UCB/RC/IF.

Huizinga, D., Menard, S., & Elliott, D. (1989). Delinquency and drug use: Temporal and developmental patterns. *Justice Quarterly, 6,* 419-455.

Jessor, R., & Jessor, S. L. (1977). *Problem behavior and psychosocial development.* New York: Academic Press.

Kellam, S. G., Ling, X., Merisca, R., Brown, C. H., & Ialongo, N. (1998). The effect of the level of aggression in the first grade classroom on the course and malleability of aggressive behavior into middle school. *Development & Psychopathology, 10*(2), 165-185.

Lahey, B. B, & Loeber, R. (1997). Attention-deficit/hyperactivity disorder, oppositional defiant disorder, conduct disorder, and adult antisocial behavior: A life span perspective. In D. M. Stoff, J. Breiling, & J. D. Maser (Eds.). *Handbook of antisocial behavior* (pp. 51-59). New York: Wiley.

Lipsey, M. W., & Derzon, J. H. (1998). Predictors of violent or serious delinquency in adolescence and early adulthood: A synthesis of longitudinal research. In R. Loeber & D. P. Farrington (Eds.), *Serious & violent juvenile offenders: Risk factors and successful interventions* (pp. 86-105). Thousand Oaks, CA: Sage.

Loeber, R., & Farrington, D. P. (1998). *Serious and violent juvenile offenders: Risk factors and successful interventions.* Thousand Oaks, CA: Sage.

Martinez, C. R., Jr., & Forgatch, M. S. (in press). Preventing problems with boys' non-compliance: Effects of a parent training intervention for divorcing mothers. *Journal of Consulting and Clinical Psychology.*

Moffitt, T. E. (1993). Adolescence-limited and life-course-persistent antisocial behavior: A developmental taxonomy. *Psychological Review, 100,* 674-701.

Moore, M. H. (1999). Early intervention: Promising path to cost-effective crime control, or primrose path to wasteful social spending? In Rubin, E. L. (Ed.), *Minimizing harm: A new crime policy for modern America* (pp. 90-100). Boulder, CO: Westview Press.

Moore, M. H., Prothrow-Stith, D., Guyer, B., & Spivak, H. (1994). Violence and intentional injuries: Criminal justice and public health perspectives on an urgent national problem. In A. J. Reiss, J. A. Roth, & National Research Council (Eds.), *Understanding and preventing violence, Vol. 4: Consequences and control* (pp. 167-216). Washington, DC: National Academy Press.

Mrazek, P. G., & Haggerty, R. J. (Eds). (1994). *Reducing risks for mental disorders: Frontiers for preventive intervention research.* Washington, DC: National Academy Press.

National Commission on Teaching and America's Future. (1997). *Doing what matters most: Investing in quality teaching.* New York: Author.

O'Donnell, J., Hawkins, J. D., Catalano, R. F., & Abbott, R. D. (1995). Preventing school failure, drug use, and delinquency among low-income children: Long-term intervention in elementary schools. *American Journal of Orthopsychiatry, 65*(1), 87-100.

Olds, D., Henderson, C. R., Jr, Cole, R., Eckenrode, J., Kitzman, H., Luckey, D., Pettitt, L., Sidora, K., Morris, P., & Powers, J. (1998). Long-term effects of nurse home visitation on children's criminal and antisocial behavior. *Journal of the American Medical Association, 280*(14), 1238-1244.

Olds, D. L., Henderson, C., Chamberlin, R., & Tatelbaum, R. (1986). Preventing child abuse and neglect: A randomized trial of nurse home visitation. *Pediatrics, 78,* 65-78.

Olds, D. L., Henderson, C. R., & Kitzman, H. (1994). Does prenatal and infancy nurse home visitation have enduring effects on qualities of parental caregiving and child health and 25 to 50 months of life? *Pediatrics, 93,* 89-98.

Olds, D. L., Henderson, C., & Tatelbaum, R. (1994). Prevention of intellectual impairment in children of women who smoke cigarettes during pregnancy. *Pediatrics, 93,* 228-233.

Olds, D. L., Henderson, C. R., Tatelbaum, R., & Chamberlin, R. (1986). Improving the delivery of prenatal care and outcomes of pregnancy: A randomized trial of nurse home visitation. *Pediatrics, 77,* 16-28.

Olds, D., Hill, P., Mihalic, S., & O'Brien, R. (1998). *Blueprints for Violence Prevention, Book Seven: Prenatal and Infancy Home Visitation by Nurses.* Boulder, CO: Center for the Study and Prevention of Violence.

Olweus, D. (1979). Stability of aggressive reaction patterns in males: A review. *Psychological Bulletin, 86,* 852-875.

Osgood, D. W., Johnston, L. D., O'Malley, P. M., & Bachman, J. G. (1988). The generality of deviance in late adolescence and early adulthood. *American Sociological Review, 53,* 81-93.

Ouimet, M., & Tremblay, P. (1996). A normative theory of the relationship between crime rates and imprisonment rates: An analysis of the penal behavior of U.S. states from 1972 to 1992. *Journal of Research in Crime & Delinquency, 33*(1) 109-125.

Patterson, G. R., & Chamberlain, P. (1994). A functional analysis of resistance during parent training therapy. *Clinical Psychology: Science and Practice, 1,* 53-70.

Patterson, G. R., Capaldi, D. M., & Bank, L. (1991). An early starter model predicting delinquency. In D. J. Pepler & K. H. Rubin (Eds.), *The development and treatment of childhood aggression* (pp. 139-168). Hillsdale, NJ: Erlbaum.

Patterson, G. R., Reid, J. B., & Dishion, T. J. (1992). *A social interactional approach: Antisocial boys* (Vol. 4). Eugene, OR: Castilia.

Patterson, G. R., Reid, J. B., Jones, R. R., & Conger, R. E. (1975). *A social learning approach to family intervention: Families with aggressive children* (Vol. 1). Eugene, OR: Castalia.

Pelham, J., William, E., Evans, S. W., Gnagy, E. M., & Greenslade, K. E. (1992). Teacher ratings of DSM-III-R symptoms for the disruptive behavior disorders: Prevalence, factor analyses, and conditional probabilities in a special education sample. *School Psychology Review, 21*(2), 285-299.

Peplar, D. J., & Rubin, K. H. (Eds.). (1991). *The development and treatment of childhood aggression.* Hillsdale, NJ: Erlbaum.

Potter, L. B., & Mercy, J. A. (1997). Public health perspective on interpersonal violence among youths in the United States. In D. M. Stoff, J. Breiling, & J. D. Maser (Eds.), *Handbook of antisocial behavior* (pp. 3-11). New York: Wiley.

Reid, J. B., & Eddy, J. M. (1997). The prevention of antisocial behavior: Some considerations in the search for effective interventions. In D. M. Stoff, J. Breiling, & J. D. Maser (Eds.), *Handbook of antisocial behavior* (pp. 343-356). New York: Wiley.

Reid, J. B., Eddy, J. M., Fetrow, R. A., & Stoolmiller, M. (1999). Description and immediate impacts of a preventative intervention for conduct problems. *American Journal of Community Psychology, 24*(4), 483-517.

Reid, J. B., Patterson, G. R., & Snyder, J. (Eds.). (in press). *The Oregon model: Understanding and altering the delinquency trajectory.* Washington, DC: American Psychological Association.

Robins, L. N. (1981). Epidemiological approaches to natural history research: Antisocial disorders in children. *Journal of the American Academy of Child Psychiatry, 20,* 566-580.

Rubin, E. L. (Ed.). (1999). *Minimizing harm: A new crime policy for modern America.* Boulder, CO: Westview Press.

Serketich, W. J., & Dumas, J. E. (1996). The effectiveness of behavioral parent training to modify antisocial behavior in children: A meta-analysis. *Behavior Therapy, 27,* 171-186.

Shannon, L. (1988). *Criminal career continuity.* New York: Human Sciences Press, Inc.

Sickmund, M., Snyder, H. N., & Poe-Yamagata, E. (1997). *Juvenile offenders and victims: 1997 update on violence.* (Statistics Summary). Pittsburgh, PA: National Center for Juvenile Justice.

Snyder, H. N., & Sickmund, N. (1995). *Juvenile offenders and victims: A national report.* Washington, DC: Office of Juvenile Justice and Delinquency Prevention, U.S. Department of Justice.

Stoff, D. M., Breiling, J., & Maser, J. D. (Eds.). (1997). *Handbook of antisocial behavior.* New York: Wiley.

Stoolmiller, M. (1994). Antisocial behavior, delinquent peer association and unsupervised wandering for boys: Growth and change from childhood to early adolescence. *Multivariate Behavioral Research, 29,* 263-288.

Stoolmiller, M., Eddy, J. M., & Reid, J. B. (2000). Detecting and describing preventative intervention effects in a universal school-based randomized trail targeting delinquent and violent behavior. *Journal of Consulting and Clinical Psychology, 68,* 296-306.

U.S. Department of Education. (1997). *Digest of education statistics* (NCES Publication 199 032). Washington, DC: National Center for Education Statistics.

U.S. Department of Justice, Bureau of Justice Statistics. (2000). *Prison statistics.* Available Internet: *www.ojp.usdoj.gov/bjs/prisons.htm*

Valdes, K., Williamson, C., & Wagner, M. (1990). *The National Longitudinal Transition Study of Special Education Students: Volume 3, Youth Categorized as Emotionally Disturbed.* Palo Alto, CA: SRI International.

Veeman, S. (1984). Perceived problems of beginning teachers. *Review of Educational Research, 54,* 143-178.

Webster-Stratton, C. (1989). Systematic comparison of consumer satisfaction of three cost-effective parent training programs for conduct problem children. *Behavior Therapy, 20*(1), 103-116.

Webster-Stratton, C. (1998a). Parent training with low-income families: Promoting parental engagement through a collaborative approach. In J. R. Lutzker (Ed)., *Handbook of child abuse research and treatment. Issues in clinical child psychology* (pp. 183-210). New York: Plenum Press.

Webster-Stratton, C. (1998b). Preventing conduct problems in Head Start children: Strengthening parenting competencies. *Journal of Consulting and Clinical Psychology, 66*(5), 715-730.

Webster-Stratton, C., Kolpacoff, M., & Hollinsworth, T. (1988). Self-administered videotape therapy for families with conduct-problem children: Comparison with two cost-effective treatments and a control group. *Journal of Consulting and Clinical Psychology, 56*(4), 558-566.

Wolff, S. (1961). Symptomatology and outcome of preschool children with behavior disorders attending a child guidance clinic. *Journal of Child Psychology and Psychiatry, 2,* 269-276.

AUTHORS' NOTES

Correspondence about this chapter should be directed to J. Mark Eddy, OSLC, 160 E. Fourth Ave., Eugene, OR 97401, *marke@oslc.org.* Support for this work was provided by Grant No. R01 MH 54248 and Grant No. P30 MH 46690 from the Prevention and Behavioral Medicine Research Branch, Division of Epidemiology and Services Research, NIMH, U.S. PHS, and Grant No. R01 MH 59127 from the Child and Adolescent Treatment and Preventive Intervention Research Branch, NIMH, U.S. PHS.

CHAPTER 3

Implementing an Intervention-Based Approach to Service Delivery: A Case Example

Martin J. Ikeda, Jeff Grimes, W. David Tilly, III,
Randy Allison, Sharon Kurns, and James Stumme
Heartland Area Education Agency 11, Johnston, Iowa

INTRODUCTION

School psychology is evolving as a profession (Ysseldyke et al., 1997; Reschly & Ysseldyke, 1995). The profession is moving from one of refer-test-place, to one of prevention, remediation, and service delivery based on educational need rather than labels (Reschly, Tilly, & Grimes, 1999). Evolution is an accepted fact in the biological sciences. In contrast, educational leaders sometimes seem surprised when conditions compel organizations to adapt to shifting societal demands, student needs, or the community's interest in accountability. Resistance to system change is often present in education (Grimes & Tilly, 1996). This chapter offers perspectives on how school districts or educational intermediate units can implement a systemic, ongoing improvement process.

We use a case example throughout this chapter to convey essential concepts in successful systems-level implementation of the intervention ideas represented within this monograph. This case example was, and continues to be, a part of the special education reform effort in Iowa that began in earnest in 1989. The Heartland Area Education Agency 11, hereafter simply identified as Heartland, is an intermediate unit in Iowa serving 56 public school districts and 34 non-public school districts, with over 350 school buildings and a general education student population of approximately 20% of the state's population. The schools in Heartland range from small (one-building schools serving K–12 populations of fewer than 250 students) to large (K–12 populations of greater than 7,500). Heartland employs 59 school psychologists with 1 full-time supervisor. The ratio of students to school psychologist is about 1500:1.

Heartland transformed from a traditional refer-test-place orientation to a problem-solving, interventions-based orientation. In the past, Heartland, like many other school systems, used a refer-test-place system that relied on norm-referenced commercial test results (e.g., the Wechsler Intelligence Scale for Children-Revised) to "diagnose" students using disability labels. After the problem was "diagnosed," individuals were placed into special classes by disability categories (Ysseldyke et al., 1997). Refer–test–place was the prevailing paradigm in the United States until the benefits of this arrangement were seriously questioned (Gresham, 1999). In a refer–test–place system, the *placement of students* in special education programs was perceived as a primary indicator of system success along with *correctly executed due process paper work* as required by the Education of All Handicapped Children Act of 1975.

Beginning in 1990 and continuing over a 3-year period, Heartland systematically replaced the refer–test–place model with a problem-solving orientation. The central purpose of a problem-solving system is improved student outcomes (Reschly, Kicklighter, & McKee, 1988). A focus on student outcomes is important, especially given the lack of outcomes reported in summaries of effectiveness of special education (Individuals with Disabilities Education Act Amendments of 1997; Kavale, 2000). A problem-solving system affects student academic and behavior success by altering (a) the processes and purposes of assessment; (b) the goals of instruction; and (c) the relationships between parents and educators, as well as school systems and the community (Ysseldyke et al., 1997). A danger in this reform was merely replacing old tests with new (Grimes & Tilly, 1996). In this monograph we articulate principles and beliefs that guide the reform process, and promote true changes in practice and in internalizing the thinking inherent in a problem-solving system.

PRINCIPLES AND BELIEFS CENTRAL TO ADOPTING A PROBLEM-SOLVING PERSPECTIVE

The process of any systemic reform begins by considering the current outcomes found in the system, and then determining whether these results are acceptable. Evidence from meta-analyses of special education effectiveness (Carlberg & Kavale, 1980; Kavale & Forness, 1985, 1987) has long cast doubt on the benefits of the refer–test–place special education system; recent analyses continue to reflect these concerns (Kavale & Forness, 1999). This finding was voiced not just by the research community, but also by practitioners across Iowa (Iowa Department of Education, 1989a). A process was implemented to explore alternative directions.

When exploring alternative directions, the first step is to identify principles representing bedrock beliefs that must be present in an improved special education service delivery system (Grimes & Tilly, 1996). When a significant discrepancy exists between expectations and how the system functions, there is the basis for an in-depth review of the service delivery system. Principles are used in this review as the reference points to define the parameter(s) of the system that must remain constant and those that must change.

In Iowa, and specifically in Heartland's reform effort, four fundamental principles were identified that formed a problem-solving system (Iowa Department of Education, 1989b):

1. Students will *benefit* from assessments that *are functional and answer specific questions* about the factors that *directly* impact the individual's learning or behavioral difficulty;

2. Students will benefit from a variety of *innovative instructional interventions;*

3. Students will benefit from direct and frequent *monitoring of progress,* and the decisions about sustaining or changing the intervention that will be made based on these data (Deno, 1986; Fuchs & Deno, 1991; Shinn 1989, 1998); and

4. An important focus is on *skill gains* demonstrated by students in response to intervention, rather than a focus on a deficit in skill due to a condition inherent to the child that is not alterable (e.g., learning disability) (Reschly et al., 1988).

Once core principles had been determined, attention shifted to garnering support of superintendents and principals within Iowa for the change, and to identifying acceptable practices that effectively and efficiently delivered needed services.

BUILDING ADMINISTRATIVE STRUCTURE FOR SUPPORTING CHANGE

Heartland is an educational service unit. As such, there are many initiatives ongoing at any one point in time. There are organizational strategic plans, state special education procedures reports, and agency mission statements to name just a few. In the area of special education, there can be multiple initiatives, as well. Functional assessment, early literacy, data-based decision making, collaboration with teachers and parents, and similar topics vie for practitioner time and are meant to improve practice. The move to problem solving had to align with the overall mission of the agency, the goals and objectives of the agency, and strategic plans put into place at an agency level. The connectedness between school psychologists, other special education staff, and others in the agency was honored and enhanced. Problem solving could not be "just another project."

Once a commitment was made to reform special education identification service delivery, procedures and operations were changed to create alignment between the problem-solving approach and everyday practice. A procedures manual for staff was developed by administrators in special education (Heartland AEA 11, 1989), which described the roles and functions of *all* staff in that changing system, including school psychologists. The manual contained forms and procedures, and described compliance monitoring, to guide all staff in their everyday practice and *educational decision making.* Professional supervision and evaluation also were aligned such that job descriptions were changed, and the factors on which staff were evaluated were linked to problem solving rather than child-find. Table 1, on page 56, highlights differences in caseloads, job description, and evaluation that have occurred since Heartland adopted a problem-solving service delivery system.

Other Area Education Agencies (AEAs) collaborated with Heartland and with the Iowa Department of Education to support the initiative called the "Renewed Service Delivery System" (RSDS). One result of RSDS was that functional assessment, collabora-

TABLE 1

Contrast in Demographics, Job Description, and Evaluation, 1991–present★

	1991	2000
General Education Population	69,662	87,759
Number of School Psychologists	32	59
Ratio of Students to School Psychologist	2,177:1	1,487:1
Major Areas of Accountability	Child find, Compliance, Counseling, Staff Development, Research, Public Awareness, Ethics, Advocacy	Consultation, Functional Assessment, Interventions, Progress Monitoring, Counseling, Staff Development, Research, Public Awareness, Ethics, Advocacy
Areas of Staff Evaluation	Timeliness of Reports, Numbers of Evaluations, Job Management	Demonstrated Knowledge and Application of: Problem Solving, Assessment, Intervention, Consultation. Job Management

Note
★ 1991 was the earliest year for which accurate data existed.

tion, and interventions were viewed as the primary roles and functions of AEA staff. Another result of RSDS was that itinerant staff, including school psychologists, worked with teachers much earlier on, before entitlement to special education was even a consideration. The intent of collaboration was to *resolve* problems in general education, or to *better define services* needed in special education. Heartland had an RSDS Core Committee, and an RSDS Steering Committee. Special education administrators worked with these two committees to understand changes that needed to occur to support the move to problem solving. State and Federal grant proposals were written to include objectives that supported problem-solving efforts. As these objectives were implemented, a functional assessment committee was developed to identify the skills staff would need to support a problem-solving model. Staff development was identified as a key component and served as a catalyst for implementing problem solving at the systems level.

An internal training cadre was developed. This cadre of 6 master's level education-al consultants, early childhood consultants, and school psychologists worked part-time carrying a caseload, and part-time in coordinating all training materials and activities. The recipients of training included AEA staff and local schools, and the original train-ing content focused on (a) building assistance teams, (b) curriculum-based measurement and its use in a problem-solving model, and (c) collaboration. The work of the training cadre had immediate and substantial impact such that, over time, the training cadre was released from carrying a caseload, and worked full-time on training the content described above, using adult learning principles. In other words, rather than relying on outside consultants to visit Heartland once or twice per year for 1 day to conduct inservices, Heartland developed *internal experts* who then were available every day, year-round to teach both Heartland and local schools the "why's" and the "what's" of problem solving.

This emphasis on building in-house expertise created the sustaining capacity need-ed to support widespread training efforts within Heartland. Problem solving was initially piloted in 10 of 56 districts for 1 year, then expanded. As procedures were refined, the *Heartland Problem-Solving Program Manual* (Heartland AEA 11, 1993) was revised (and has since been revised annually) to institutionalize procedures for *all* staff. Newsletters about Heartland's involvement in RSDS were distributed quarterly to all schools and Heartland staff. The newsletters further described the overall special edu-cation reform effort, and highlighted teachers, staff, and school buildings involved in model efforts in implementing changes in assessment and intervention practices.

CHANGES IN ASSESSMENT PRACTICES

Implementing a problem-solving approach relied on different assessment practices, which in turn required rethinking special education assessment at two levels (Grimes & Tilly, 1996). The first level was simply "educational." Assessment was redefined as a process for making a *variety* of decisions about students, not solely as testing for special education eligibility (Deno, 1995; Salvia & Ysseldyke, 1995). Heartland staff were trained to understand the assessment process not as *statically* focused on identifying stu-dent eligibility for special education services, but rather *dynamically* focused on meeting student academic and/or behavior needs.

The second level of rethinking special education assessment required a more radi-cal change in how people did business. The effort did not stop at "educating" staff by defining terms, it challenged the entire structure underlying the special education sys-tem—i.e., the disability-driven model. (For more detail see Reschly and Ysseldyke, 1995.) The structure was then realigned to broaden the scope of questions that were addressed by the system (Tilly, Reschly, & Grimes, 1999). Because the focus shifted from "disability driven" to intervention planning, different *assessment* decisions and strategies to make them were emphasized. Increased attention was allocated to assessment for screening, problem analysis, program planning, progress monitoring, and program eval-uation. The standard of assessment quality was expanded to include the concept of treatment validity (Hayes, Nelson, & Jarrett, 1987). That is, all assessment practices, in addition to being technically adequate from a psychometric perspective, needed to be *useful* for treatment planning for individual students.

As Heartland retooled to rethink how to support students, two questions arose. Given the long-standing history of assessing students primarily for entitlement/eligibility, one question related to the fiscal implications of a different identification procedure, primarily centered around numbers of students entitled. There was concern that the *wrong* children, or that *too many* children, would be identified in a problem-solving model. Given that different assessment tools were used, a second common question addressed the special education identification *process*. There was concern that, without IQ tests, children could not possibly be identified as disabled. As these questions were answered and changes occurred in service delivery, a natural progression was a shift in focus from assessment for eligibility, to assessment to identify interventions that improve the lives of students.

Will a Problem-Solving System Increase Numbers of Entitled Students?

Heartland cannot prove that the number or proportion of students identified for special education has changed as a result of implementing a problem-solving assessment system. The number and percentage of students identified have increased annually since 1977, the first year that data were kept on special education incidence in Iowa. However, the trajectory of the growth of students in special education has remained *similar* both before and after the implementation of a problem-solving system. A larger question was, were we serving *different* students in special education using problem-solving assessments, compared with what resulted through previous practice? A study conducted by Heartland documented that for students with academic difficulties, the problem-solving system could be adjusted to identify for special education (within error) roughly the *same* students as the refer-test-place system did (Tilly, Reschly, Stumme, & Burgett, 1991). Although the status quo does not necessarily represent a criterion of excellence for identification practices, these data suggest that a problem-solving system is *as* politically and professionally defensible as a refer-test-place system, and has the additional benefit of collecting information that is relevant to intervention planning for students.

What Practices Will Be Used to Identify Students With Disabilities in a Problem-Solving System?

The second question that arose as assessment practices were retooled focused on how to make the entitlement/eligibility decision. The major differences between the refer-test-place social system identification model and a problem-solving model were (a) the *assumptions* that drive the assessment and intervention process, and (b) the *levels of inference* made by assessors. In the refer-test-place model, constructs (i.e., learning disability, mental disability) targeted for assessment were primarily defined by federal and state regulatory definitions of disability categories (e.g., serious emotional disturbance, sensory impairment, etc.). That is, these constructs typically were assessed using broad, nationally normed instruments (e.g., global intelligence tests and measures of achievement) that are significantly less precise and require higher levels of inference in their interpretation (Howell & Nolet, 2000). For more detail on differences in how disability is assessed, see Grimes and Tilly (1996), or Tilly et al. (1999). Practice in Heartland found these measures to be "too far removed" from the information necessary to identify educational need *and* facilitate instructional planning.

In contrast, in a problem-solving system of assessment and intervention, the preeminent focus is on measuring educational need in *specific contexts* (e.g., a student's performance on materials used in the classroom and in relation to a district's standards and benchmarks for a given grade) and with *sufficient detail* to know what to target for intervention. The contrast boils down to specifying a learning disability versus a severe reading deficit requiring more individualized, and *potentially* special education. The presence of educational disability is inferred from the convergence of evidence from multiple sources. Entitlement criteria are based squarely on a core set of social values and assumptions regarding who should receive special education, and are informed by the best technologies measurement science has to offer at any given time (cf. Shinn, Good, & Parker, 1999).

A series of components are proposed in Figure 1, on page 60. The components represent a problem-solving model of practice serving as a structure for considering special education entitlement in a functional and noncategorical system. The problem-solving model results in defensible eligibility criteria for special education, while promoting different practices in the area of assessment, intervention, and consultation. Instead of specifying specific tests or procedures that must be completed in *every* case, a *general structure* for data collection that would be applied to every case is specified. Within this structure, general guidelines for different sources of data are specified along with performance criteria to inform decision making.

Heartland has operationalized problem solving in two ways. The first way is a four-level problem-solving approach that considers (a) the amount of resources needed to solve a problem, and (b) the severity of the problem (Figure 1). Interventive efforts at Levels I, II, and III are conducted within general education. Overall, the intensity of the problem is matched with the amount of resources necessary to improve the educational results.

Activities at Level I involve the general education classroom teacher in consultation with parents. At this level school psychologists may be involved at a very informal level, such as brief consultation in the hallway, if at all. At Level II, expertise of other teachers is used to solve problems. The vehicle used by most schools within Heartland is the building assistance team (Schrag & Henderson, 1996). For example, the guidance counselor, a Grade 2 teacher, and a Grade 4 teacher team with the chairperson (another general educator) to field problems from colleagues and create solutions. Staff from Heartland, the intermediate unit, typically do not sit on assistance teams, but can serve as ad hoc members. As problems turn more severe and/or need additional resources to

FIGURE 1

Heartland's Problem-Solving Approach and Process

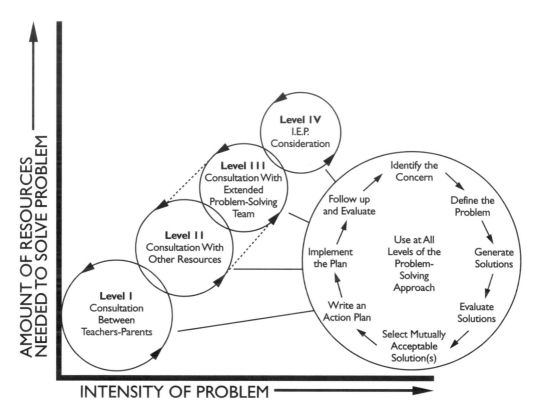

analyze the problem or support an intervention, Heartland-related service professionals become involved. This is called Level III of the problem-solving approach. For example, an assistance team may implement an intervention in which a student's seat assignment is changed, so that the student can see the chalkboard better. If the student's performance does not improve, a Heartland staff person, at Level III, helps to further analyze the problem and (a) refines, or (b) redesigns an intervention for the student. At Level III, Heartland staff coordinate the intervention efforts, and ensure that all components of an intervention are present (see Tilly & Flugum, 1995, for more information). Special education assistance and due process protections are considered at Level IV. The intent of Level IV is to *identify the conditions that enable the student to learn,* based on student outcomes with prior intervention and results of functional assessment conducted by teachers and Heartland staff.

It is noteworthy that the decisions made at all levels of the problem-solving approach are the same: teachers and Heartland staff are comparing the student's level of performance and rate of learning with what is expected in that setting. What differs is the amount of resources used to analyze problems at each level, and the technical adequacy of measures used in decision making. Multiple sources and multiple types of data are needed at all levels. As entitlement is considered, however, data sources (interviews, observations, and tests) must have demonstrated validity for *high-stakes* decision making about the performance of individual students.

The second way in which problem solving is operationalized at Heartland is the following *process:*

1. Define the problem and determine why the problem may be occurring;

2. Develop an intervention that addresses the problem;

3. Implement the intervention; and

4. Evaluate the effects of the intervention.

The process of analyzing problem behaviors requires assessors from teachers to support staff to utilize *functional* assessment procedures systematically. To move from assessments focused on eligibility to assessments focused on need and intervention, Heartland adopted a decision-making framework for (a) developing assumed causes or hypotheses, (b) validating the hypotheses, and (c) linking these assessment results to a teaching recommendation. This framework is called Curriculum-Based Evaluation (CBE) (Howell & Nolet, 2000). CBE was selected because it provides a direct link between assessment and instruction. This link is critical to support a system based on student needs and directed toward matching those needs to the appropriate instructional strategy.

As shown in Table 2, on page 62, interventive efforts must provide information about four components. Data must suggest that the learner's performance is significantly different from peer performance or an expected standard of others in the same environment. This approach from the beginning emphasizes defining a problem in relation to the least restrictive environment. The interventions must provide information about the conditions under which student outcomes will be improved. Assessment yields information upon which hypotheses can be tested. Prior to entitlement, there must be sufficient data that an intervention implemented with integrity was not powerful enough to solve the problem without additional resources. Even when interventions are not successful, however, assessments must be conducted to identify the conditions in which success will likely occur. These conditions are then tested as part of the Individualized Education Program (IEP). Finally, teams must rely on multiple methods from multiple sources and converge them to reach their decision. Accepted methods include reviews, interviews, observations, and tests, and cover areas of instruction, curriculum, environment, and within-student contributing factors.

There are many potential decisions that result from the four-level, four-step problem-solving model. Success at Level II means that the problem was resolved without needing formal involvement and coordination by Heartland staff. Data from a small sample of buildings suggest that 25% of cases are solved at Level II. Of those students who move to Level III intervention, Heartland practitioners report that about 45% have their cases solved at Level III. This means that Heartland staff were able to redefine and

TABLE 2

Major Components of Functional and Noncategorical Disability Identification Procedures

In a functional and noncategorical system, disability status is conferred by a team of individuals, including parents, who base their judgments on objective and subjective data from multiple informants and procedures. At a minimum, the following sources of data should be present:

Evidence of resistance to reasonable general education intervention efforts.

Iowa Administrative Rules of Special Education require that a general education intervention be conducted before a team considers special education. The Rules define general education interventions as a collaborative effort with the intent to improve educational performance, define components of an intervention, and introduce the concept of resistance to intervention based on data obtained through intervention.

Evidence of a severe discrepancy from peers' performance levels in the area(s) of concern.

Ecologically sensitive assessment targets are selected and an individual's performance is compared to local normative standards as to what constitutes typical performance. Specific criteria for defining the degree of discrepancy based on peers' performance are set locally and typically might be general guidelines rather than absolute cutting scores.

A data-based description of the resources necessary to improve and maintain the individual's rate of learning at an acceptable level.

Teams define the conditions under which learning is enabled. Problem analysis yields testable hypotheses regarding both problem etiology and likely problem resolution strategies. When these hypotheses are tested through interventions, the nature and amount of resources necessary to support learning can be estimated. For example, assessment must answer questions such as the following: At what level of the curriculum can the individual be instructed successfully? What environmental conditions (time of day, instructional set-up, instructional methods, physical settings, etc.) are related to student success? The list of questions is infinite, but focuses on alterable factors in instruction, curriculum, the environment, and the learner.

Convergent evidence logically and empirically supporting the teams' decisions.

This component requires that teams collect broad-based information related to the problem in addition to the targeted information collected to satisfy the initial three criteria. Information may be collected through any combination of Record Reviews, Interviews, Observations, and Specific Testing in relevant areas.

reanalyze problems, and consult with teachers in implementing intervention, to improve situations sufficiently so that special education resources were not needed as part of the solution. Although it is hoped that interventions at Level III will solve the problem, moving on to entitlement is not an "undesired" outcome. What is desired, however, is that data gathered during Levels I, II, and III of the problem-solving process *are used to determine entitlement,* and to write the IEP. Data gathered during these levels provide information about the rates of students' progress, instructional needs, and conditions in which they are *enabled* to learn, rather than simply indicating that the children are entitled to special education. Although currently Heartland does not have data examining the extent to which assessment and intervention results are used by Special Education teachers in implementing and supporting IEPs, Heartland does have data that suggests that, over time, staff evaluations are much more focused in nature. That is, only methods needed to answer specific questions are used, rather than a "shotgun" approach of the same battery of assessments used for all students.

The problem-solving approach offers a number of advantages compared to the more procedurally driven refer-test-place identification practices used earlier in Heartland. First, when teams have collected data sufficient to meet the criteria listed in Table 2, a much broader, deeper, and more relevant assessment will have been completed than has been the case in the past. This approach honors the information provided by parents and teachers to the same degree that it honors testing scores that used to serve as major criteria in the identification of educational disability. Second, lack of specific cutting scores for individual components of the system force, decisions to be made using a convergence of evidence. Third, there is little danger that scores on specific test(s) will become the *de facto* standards for entitlement, because specific, required "patterns of scores" are not the basis of entitlement decision making. Fourth, this system results in a better match between assessment methods used and the presenting problem. Indeed, there is much less "proceduralism" (i.e., the standard battery) involved in the assessment and intervention process, and far more reliance on making reasonable inferences from direct performance assessment data.

This reliance on performance data places *greater responsibility* on professionals to ensure the integrity of the assessments but, when done well, also improves the probability of the desired educational results for students. As professionals assume greater levels of responsibility, demands have emerged for more individualized professional growth opportunities. Hence, any educational system, including Heartland, will need to create a systematic, thoughtful professional development program in order to sustain effective problem solving.

PROFESSIONAL DEVELOPMENT AS A CRITICAL STEP IN CHANGING OVER TO AN INTERVENTION-FOCUSED SYSTEM

The problem-solving model relies on assessing alterable factors outside of the child—such as instruction, curriculum, and classroom arrangements—that are impacting an individual student's performance. In contrast, refer-test-place identification systems emphasize assessing less alterable constructs that exist within an individual. Heartland administration recognized that substantial staff development efforts were needed to help staff *understand* and *internalize* this conceptual shift. An alternative to staff development is simply telling people to change or to do their jobs differently. Heartland administration believed that merely telling staff to do something different would set ambiguous and ill-defined expectations at best and create a staff with varying belief systems, knowledge, and skill sets at worst. As a result of this belief system, efforts at Heartland focused on providing staff with knowledge and skills in the areas of problem-solving assessment and intervention.

There is an old folk song, "The old gray mare she ain't what she used to be" (source unknown). Staff development is not what it used to be either. Training models have changed since the days of "train and hope" strategy (National Partnership for Excellence and Accountability in Teaching, 2000). Giving people perfunctory knowledge bases and expecting them to change professional practice typically will not work (Sparks & Richardson, 1997). At Heartland, therefore, the provision of staff development needed to take on a systemic and ongoing nature. Approaching the task of training staff needs to be conceptualized and planned differently.

In essence, staff development was treated the same way as identifying the educational needs of students and developing interventions, but at a *systems level*. As RSDS evolved, Heartland school psychologists and other staff *rewrote* their job descriptions to define the expectations of the problem-solving model. Heartland staff defined the *skill expectations* against which their practice was evaluated. To understand what was needed in staff development, the performance level of staff on those skill expectations was determined. On-site observation of staff, and informal case reviews, were used to identify areas in which staff needed support. While admittedly unsystematic, these observations and case reviews established the need for a plan of action to bridge the gap between the successful adoption and implementation of a new innovation, and the existing skills of staff.

When problem solving was first implemented at Heartland, staff development focused on building skills related to (a) collaboration, (b) using curriculum-based measures in a problem-solving system, and (c) building assistance teaming. Reviews of permanent products and interviews with staff suggested that some staff could (a) explain why they analyzed a problem as they did, (b) demonstrate competence in using the "new" functional assessments, and (c) provide evidence that interventions were being collaboratively developed and implemented.

On the other hand, in the early days of problem solving at Heartland, some staff could demonstrate competence using functional assessment. The same staff, when pressed as to "why" they did not, for example, administer an IQ test, gave responses in the vein of "because this is what Heartland wants me to do." It became clear that staff needed *more* than tool training in content areas such as collaboration or building assistance teaming. Staff needed *specific training* to understand *why* problem-solving assessment in a problem-solving model was an important alternative to commercial tests and a refer-test-place model of practice.

Building a Conceptual Understanding of Problem Solving

A frequently underestimated component of staff development is the emphasis on conceptual understanding. Although an emphasis on what to do is important, why it needs to be done also needs considerable attention. Those involved in staff development may not see the immediate payoff in understanding the concepts embodied by new practices. Over the long run, however, changes in thinking are very important to improved practice and system change (Howell & Nolet, 2000). Learning different assessment techniques as "replacements" for current practices without the simultaneous understanding of the conceptual rationale and corresponding belief system restricts progress, limits personal and systemic growth, and often results in confused, unfounded practices that have little or no impact on student achievement (Hilliard, 1997). Without the foundational change in conceptual understanding of the thinking process, the prevalent result is staff knowing *what* to do under carefully prescribed conditions (e.g., to complete a form), but not being able to explain, defend, or generalize it in a way that is applicable to new problems. Hence, Heartland's staff development efforts evolved to focus not only on the tool skills needed to support a shift to intervention- focused practice (the "what"s, i.e., curriculum-based evaluation and curriculum-based measurement, functional behavioral assessment, collaboration), but also on the conceptual beliefs needed to support reform, the "why"s (Tilly et al., 1999).

THE CHALLENGE OF PERPETUAL CHANGE

In this chapter we presented a rationale for the successful move from a refer-test-place service delivery system to an intervention-oriented, problem-solving system. Creating alignment of special education policies, procedures, and practices was important in promoting change. One of the important requirements for this change, a shift in assessment practices, was described. Efforts for changing staff skill and understanding of the "why"s of problem solving were summarized. This chapter concludes with some thoughts on future directions of how related services personnel, including school psychologists, will support schools in *improving results* for *all* children.

Senge (1990) states that individuals use "mental models" to filter their understanding of life experiences. Events are perceived through the mental model and activities are aligned to one's perception. In the mid-to-late 1980s, Heartland excelled in applying a refer-test-place approach to special education. The mental model associated with a refer-test-place approach was one of "child find." However, there was little evidence that this approach led to *improved student performance* (Kavale & Forness, 1987). As a result, the mental model of the refer-test-place approach was abandoned for a problem-solving approach. The mental model of the problem-solving approach instead is solution-oriented and seeks meaningful results for students.

During Heartland's support of problem solving over the past 10 years, several things have been learned. First, staff require continuous support in refining skills. Initial staff development efforts changed practice, but not the mind-set, and consequently, problem solving was used primarily as another "child find" activity. The *form* of assessments was different, but the *functions* remained the same, to determine a student's status as eligible or not eligible for special education. After about 5 years, however, the conceptual underpinnings of problem solving started to make sense for staff, and our staff development efforts needed to change to help staff *more fully* understand what they were doing and to integrate further the mental model associated with problem solving.

Second, professional roles expanded. As Heartland staff engaged in problem solving with individual students, two things happened. Helping schools create local standards with which individual student problems were defined expanded the use of data to examine what was happening with *all* students in a school or system. Problem-solving efforts, once heavily focused on entitlement and the individual child, were applied by staff at the *systems* level. For many staff, including school psychologists, roles expanded from assessor to consultant, or from special educator to curriculum consultant and district-wide measurement consultant. As with much of the nation, Heartland staff found new roles in the realm of school improvement through prevention. As an example, several dozen of the 350-odd school buildings supported by Heartland are using Dynamic Indicators of Basic Early Literacy Skills (Good, Simmons, & Smith, 1998) to identify students who are at risk for reading failure, and are using the data to intervene in general education to assure students' maximum likelihood of becoming successful readers. This effort is called the Heartland Early Literacy Project (HELP).

Problem solving created new opportunities for all of Heartland's staff, including school psychologists. Opportunities abound in both general and special education. In general education, school psychologists are helping parents, teachers, and assistance teams implement and evaluate interventions. If an intervention needs special education resources, the assessment practices of the school psychologist are *directly relevant* for developing and evaluating the goals of individualized education programs.

The focus on school improvement is moving our agency toward the next paradigm—what we think is preventative service delivery. This is an exciting opportunity for our staff, including school psychologists, to engage the system to support all learners. This is an exciting opportunity for our system to engage with districts and assess our impact as an intermediate unit. Our work in problem solving has poised us well for this challenge. We accept this challenge and hope you work with us and learn with us as you embark on your journey to improve the lives of students in your settings.

REFERENCES

Carlberg, C., & Kavale, K. (1980). The efficacy of special versus regular class placement for exceptional children: A meta-analysis. *The Journal of Special Education, 14*(3), 295-308.

Deno, S. L. (1986). Formative evaluation of individual student programs: A new role for school psychologists. *School Psychology Review, 15,* 358-374.

Deno, S. L. (1995). School psychologist as problem solver. In A. Thomas & J. Grimes (Eds.), *Best practices in school psychology III* (pp. 471-484). Washington, DC: National Association of School Psychologists.

Education of All Handicapped Children Act of 1975, 20 U.S.C. § 1400 *et seq.*

Fuchs, L. S., & Deno, S. L. (1991). Paradigmatic distinctions between instructionally relevant measurement models. *Exceptional Children, 58,* 232-243.

Good, R. H. III, Simmons, D. C., & Smith, S. (1998). Effective academic interventions in the United States: Evaluating and enhancing the acquisition of early reading skills. *School Psychology Review, 27,* 45-56.

Gresham, F. M. (1999). Noncategorical approaches to K-12 emotional and behavioral difficulties. (1999). In D. J. Reschly, W. D. Tilly, & J. Grimes (Eds.), Functional and Noncategorical Identification in Special Education (pp. 85-108). Des Moines, IA: Iowa Department of Education.

Grimes, J. P., & Tilly W. D. (1996). Policy and process: Means to lasting educational change. *School Psychology Review, 25*(4), 431-445.

Hayes, S. C., Nelson, R. O., & Jarrett, R. B. (1987). The treatment utility of assessment: A functional approach evaluating assessment quality. *American Psychologist, 42,* 963-974.

Heartland AEA 11. (1989). *Program manual for special education (1989-1990).* Johnston, IA: Heartland AEA 11.

Heartland AEA 11. (1993). *Program manual for special education (1993-1994).* Johnston, IA: Heartland AEA 11.

Hilliard III, A. (1997). The structure of valid staff development. *Journal of Staff Development, 18,* 28-34.

Howell, K. W., & Nolet, V. (2000). *Curriculum-based evaluation: Teaching and decision making* (3rd ed.). Belmont, CA: Wadsworth.

Individuals with Disabilities Education Act Amendments of 1997, 20 U. S. C. § *1400 et seq.*

Iowa Department of Education. (1989a). *Identifying concerns with special education.* Des Moines, IA: Iowa Department of Education.

Iowa Department of Education. (1989b). *Principles for Renewal of Iowa's Special Education Service Delivery System.* Des Moines, IA: Iowa Department of Education.

Kavale, K. A. (2000). *Inclusion: Rhetoric and reality surrounding the integration of students with disabilities* (The Iowa Academy of Education Occasional Research Paper #2). Des Moines, IA: FINE Foundation.

Kavale, K. A., & Forness, S. R. (1985). *The science of learning disabilities.* San Diego, CA: College-Hill Press.

Kavale, K. A., & Forness, S. R. (1987). Substance over style: Assessing the efficacy of modality testing and teaching. *Exceptional Children, 54*(3), 228–239.

Kavale, K. A., & Forness, S. R. (1999). Effectiveness of special education. In C. R. Reynolds & T. B. Gutkin (Eds.), *The handbook of school psychology* (3rd ed.) 984–1024. New York: John Wiley.

National Partnership for Excellence and Accountability in Teaching. (2000). *Revisioning Professional Development.* Oxford, OH: National Staff Development Council.

Reschly, D. J., Kicklighter, R. H., & McKee, P. (1988). Recent placement litigation Part III: Analysis of differences in Larry P., Marshall, and S-1 and implications for future practice. *School Psychology Review, 17,* 37–48.

Reschly, D. J., Tilly III, W. D., & Grimes, J. (Eds.). (1999). *Special Education in Transition: Functional Assessment and Noncategorical Programming.* Longmont, CO: Sopris West.

Reschly, D. J. & Ysseldyke, J. (Ed.). (1995). School psychology paradigm shift. In A. Thomas & J. Grimes (Eds.), *Best practices in school psychology III* (pp. 17–31). Washington, DC: National Association of School Psychologists.

Salvia, J., & Ysseldyke, J. (1995). *Assessment* (5th ed.). Boston: Houghton Mifflin.

Schrag, J. A., & Henderson, K. (1996). *School-based interventions assistance teams and their impact on special education.* Alexandria: National Association of State Directors of Special Education.

Senge, P. M. (1990). *The fifth discipline: The art and practice of the learning organization.* New York: Currency Doubleday.

Shinn, M. R. (Ed.). (1989). *Curriculum-based measurement: Assessing special children.* New York: Guilford Press.

Shinn, M. R. (Ed.). (1998). *Advanced applications of curriculum-based measurement.* New York: Guilford.

Shinn, M. R., Good, R. H., III, & Parker, C. (1999). Noncategorical special education services with students with severe achievement deficits. In *Functional and Noncategorical Identification in Special Education* (pp. 65–84). Des Moines, IA: Iowa Department of Education.

Sparks, D., & Richardson, J. (1997). *A primer on professional development.* Oxford, OH: National Staff Development Council.

Tilly, W. D., III., & Flugum, K. R. (1995). Best practices in ensuring quality interventions. In A. Thomas and J. Grimes (Eds.), *Best practices in school psychology III* (pp. 485–500). Washington, DC: NASP Publications.

Tilly, W. D., III., Reschly, D. J., & Grimes, J. (1999). Disability determination in problem-solving systems: Conceptual foundations and critical components. In D. J. Reschly, W. D. Tilly, III, & J. Grimes (Eds.). *Special education in transition: Functional assessment and noncategorical programming* (pp. 285–321). Longmont, CO: Sopris West.

Tilly, W. D. III, Reschly, D. J., Stumme, J., & Burgett, T. (1991). [Examining rates of disability identification using traditional and problem-solving methods]. Unpublished raw data.

Ysseldyke, J., Dawson, P., Lehr, C., Reschly, D., Reynolds, M., & Telzrow, C. (1997). *School psychology: A blueprint for training and practice.* Bethesda, MD: National Association of School Psychologists.

AUTHORS' NOTES

All authors contributed equally to the development of this chapter. Address all correspondence concerning this chapter to Martin Ikeda, Heartland AEA 11, 6500 Corporate Drive, Johnston, Iowa, 50131 or e-mail *mikeda@aea11.k12.ia.us.* The authors thank and acknowledge the dedicated staff, past and present, of Heartland AEA 11, Iowa's 14 other Area Education Agencies, and Iowa's local schools; they all bring the system to life.

CHAPTER 4

What We Know About School Safety

Paul M. Kingery
Director, Hamilton Fish Institute

Hill M. Walker
Institute on Violence and Destructive Behavior

INTRODUCTION

The literature on school safety has mushroomed in the past few years. Surveys of student behavior and explanations of why schools are the scene of violent acts have proliferated. Solutions to the problem are even more numerous—from administrative and programmatic to technological and architectural. This chapter summarizes what we now know about school safety in these three areas: (1) assessing the problem, (2) studying the causes, and (3) examining interventions.

ASSESSING THE PROBLEM

We have gathered nationally representative data sets from many sources to become familiar with their methods and to scour them for information. Not content with the primary reports issued by the researchers, we have analyzed the data sets and sought points of comparisons among them. The phenomena that are collectively called school violence are best measured, at present, by self-report surveys that are administered to youth either at school or at home with strict assurances of anonymity. The degree to which fear of being discovered or false bravado leads to under- or overreporting is unknown, but we suspect that self-reports result in a net underreporting bias in part resulting from the social, familial, school, and criminal sanctions placed on a range of such behaviors. Rates of reporting are diminished in relation to laxity in assurances of anonymity. Through a procedure called "cross-survey analysis" we have found reasonable agreement on the true levels of violence, and how they have changed over the past decade or so.

Cross-survey analysis shows that weapon carrying (any type of weapon) at school is a fairly stable phenomenon. While there are some methodological differences among the various surveys, self-reports commonly stay within a relatively narrow range from year to year (Coggeshall & Kingery, in press). Despite this finding, school homicide has been viewed primarily as a recent occurrence. This is probably largely because of the media attention given to the series of school shootings in the late 1990s that involved multiple victims. Since the Littleton, Colorado, shootings in 1998, there has been a pause in media coverage. School homicides and weapon carrying at school have continued, however, and given trend data from 1990 to the present we can reasonably predict that they will continue to occur (Coggeshall & Kingery, in press; National School Safety Center, n.d.)

Episodes of weapon-facilitated youth homicide in school are largely an American phenomenon. The abundance of weapons that are freely available to youth doubtless contributes to the problem in the United States. The ready presence of guns in the United States results in many deaths among children 5–14 years of age, in comparison to other industrialized nations (National Center for Injury Prevention and Control, 1997). We do not know the effects of current or proposed gun control legislation on the problem. Although there is general agreement that guns should be kept out of the hands of unsupervised minors and definitely out of schools, the debate is so polarized around "wedge" issues on gun control that discussions of the availability of guns to minors seldom occur.

Studies of school violence have shown that the prevalence of mild to moderate school violence of the type for which few sanctions occur is fairly stable over time. Hitting, kicking, pushing, and the like are common and tolerated, and thus are hard to measure except in self-report surveys. Sexual and other forms of harassment lie even deeper beneath our field of vision. Indirect aggression eludes us almost entirely. Fighting is reportable, but generally considered "mutual," and the degree of assault or self-defense is not investigated. "Bullying" is difficult to operationalize as a precise measure, though we have clues from physical prowess ratios among children involved in fighting.

Non-weapon-related violence and other acts of aggression occur with greater frequency in schools than weapon-related violence. In 1999, 14.2% of all U.S. high school students reported that they had been involved in at least one physical fight in the preceding year (Kann et al., 2000). More than a third of elementary schools, 71.8% of middle or junior high schools, and 55.5% of high schools reported one or more incidents of physical attacks or fight, without a weapon to law enforcement (Gottfredson, Gottfredson & Czeh, 2000). In 1996, 25.9% of high school seniors reported that their property was deliberately damaged at school during the previous 12 months. More than 20% reported being threatened without a weapon in the previous 12 months, and 11.8% reported being injured without a weapon in the previous 12 months. These behaviors have been fairly stable over time (National Center for Education Statistics, 1998).

Sexual violence and aggression are also a major problem in the school setting. According to an American Association of University Women (AAUW) survey, 81% of the students sampled (grades 8–11) had experienced some form of sexual harassment at school during their academic career (AAUW, 1992). Of the 81% who reported experiencing sexual harassment, 36% of males and 65% of females had been touched, grabbed, or pinched in a sexual way; and 17% of males and 16 percent of females had had their clothes pulled at or down. A 1996 AAUW/Harris poll found that 66% of male students and 52% of female secondary school students had harassed someone at school (Lee, Croninger, Linn, & Chen, 1996). The 1994 National Crime Victimization Survey estimated that 12,057 rapes and sexual assaults had occurred at school during that year (Stein, 1999). A later report found that 4,170 incidents of rape and sexual battery had been reported by public schools to law enforcement officials during the 1996–97 academic year (Stein).

Violence and victimization in schools have very high costs and consequences for both individual students and society at large. Measuring the costs and consequences of violence in schools is as difficult as it is in the broader society. Flannery and Singer (1999) list anxiety, posttraumatic stress, low self-esteem, self-destructive behavior, anger, and aggression in children as the results of being exposed to violence. Children react differently to exposure to violence depending on their developmental stage (Osofsky, 1997), the nature of the violence, and the co-occurrence of other events in their lives (Flannery, 1997). Despite these differences, exposure to violence at any age has consequences for the individual student (Pynoos & Nader, 1998). The Youth Risk Behavior Survey reports that 5.2% of all high school students missed 1 or more days of school because they felt unsafe at school or traveling to and from school (Kann et al., 2000). In 1995, 3.7% of 8th-graders, 3.9% of 9th-graders, 3.9% of 10th-graders, 5.2% of 11th-graders, and 5.1% of 12th-graders reported that they had brought something to school to protect themselves from being attacked or harmed in the past 6 months (Bureau of Justice Statistics, 1998). In summary, school violence and aggression affect the well-being of individual students, contribute to their later problems, and create the potential for more violence in the forms of retaliation and acting out. A dollar figure for the cost of violence caused by loss of life, classroom disruption, and emotional and physical trauma is unavailable, but based on the frequency of violent, aggressive behaviors and their documented effects, we know that the cost is unacceptably high.

There are few national data on these problems for children younger than age 12, though many local studies have been completed or are underway to measure the frequency and distribution of violence, aggression, and victimization among younger students. We have fairly reliable estimates on these phenomena for children older than 12 by sex, race, and other characteristics, and readers should consult the references cited for further breakdowns.

Incidents of all types of violence in schools are vastly underreported, we think, based on evidence from people involved in all aspects of the reporting process and on the few cross-checks available (Coggeshall & Kingery, in press; Kingery & Coggeshall, in press, 2001). Students are afraid to report what they know or do not have anonymous reporting mechanisms available to them. Staff are too busy with other tasks and try to handle the more common problems themselves, resisting the burden of additional record keeping and due process in discipline. Surveillance systems that are computer-based are only now emerging, and their cost is a barrier, both in acquisition and in staff time for operation. Principals and superintendents face great risks from increasing the accuracy of their reporting, as media, parents, and others will believe that violence is increasing in the school (New York City Board of Education, 1995).

Students will accept violence among their peers that is restricted to mild to moderate forms. School officials will provide little in the way of sanctions for such actions in the school setting, unless they are particularly frustrating to a school staff member for some reason. This attitude does not reflect lack of vigilance, rather that school officials are held accountable for so many aspects of students' behavior that those aspects that are more covert are easier to ignore. Fighting, weapon-carrying, victimization, and student fears have been fairly well researched and found to be at unacceptably high levels in schools in general.

STUDYING THE CAUSES

At-risk children who end up failing in school and adopting a delinquent lifestyle in adolescence follow a well-documented pathway. It usually begins well before such children come to school and shows a characteristic progression of escalation toward ever more serious acts of deviance, school failure, delinquency, alcohol and drug involvement, and sometimes violence (see Loeber & Farrington, 1998; Patterson, Reid, & Dishion, 1992). Over the past two to three decades, longitudinal studies conducted in Australia, New Zealand, Canada, the United States, and Western Europe have documented a well-traveled destructive path that antisocial children and youth tend to follow in their childhood and youth (Loeber & Farrington, 1998; Tremblay, Pagani-Kurtz, Masse, Vitaro, & Pihl, 1995). This pathway is developmental in nature and consists of critical phases and outcomes that are highly predictable from knowledge of prior events and risk factors (Patterson et al., 1992).

Figure 1 illustrates this pathway that at-risk children by the thousands are now on (Walker & Sprague, 1999). This path begins very early in a child's life, through exposure to a host of risk factors and a lack of offsetting protective factors. These external risk factors operate at family, neighborhood, school, and societal levels and provide a fertile breeding ground for the development of antisocial, destructive behavior patterns that, if not addressed, can lead to costly outcomes later on in a child's life (e.g., delinquency; school failure; teacher, peer, and caregiver rejection; and drug and alcohol abuse).

It is important to note that identified risk factors are not necessarily the causes of violence and aggressive behavior. When discussing the causal relationship between any risk factor and the outcomes of interest it is imperative to remember that the risk factor may actually be a proxy for the real causal agent, a co-occurring factor that is not a part of the causal chain, or a mediator between the causal agent and the outcome (Baron & Kenny, 1986). Given the limited ability of the field to pinpoint causal factors we are limited to discussing risk factors. For our purposes, risk factors are those family-, neighborhood-, school-, and societal-level behaviors, attitudes, and events that can be measured, that are present in the life of an individual student before or during a violent or aggressive outcome.

FIGURE 1

The Path to Long-Term Negative Outcomes for At-Risk Children and Youth

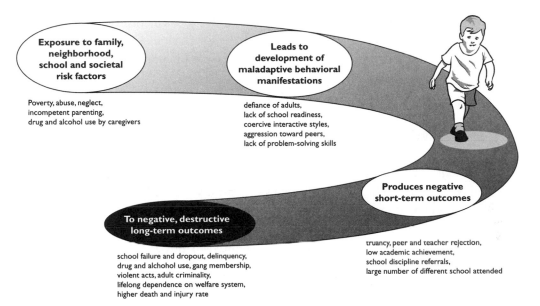

Exposure to family, neighborhood, school and societal risk factors

Poverty, abuse, neglect, incompetent parenting, drug and alcohol use by caregivers

Leads to development of maladaptive behavioral manifestations

defiance of adults, lack of school readiness, coercive interactive styles, aggression toward peers, lack of problem-solving skills

Produces negative short-term outcomes

truancy, peer and teacher rejection, low academic achievement, school discipline referrals, large number of different school attended

To negative, destructive long-term outcomes

school failure and dropout, delinquency, drug and alchohol use, gang membership, violent acts, adult criminality, lifelong dependence on welfare system, higher death and injury rate

Note

Walker, H. M., & Sprague, J. R. (1999). The path to school failure, delinquency, and violence: Causal factors and some potential solutions. *Intervention in School and Clinic, 35,* 67-73. Reprinted with permission.

Weapon Carrying at School

The best predictors of weapon carrying at school identified in nationally representative samples involve a history of various self-reported acts of extreme violence such as shooting or stabbing someone, pulling a knife or gun on someone, threatening to use a weapon to rob someone, or using a weapon in a fight (Kingery, Coggeshall, & Alford, 1999). Students who were victims or witnesses of extreme violence are also more likely to carry weapons at school (Kingery et al., 1999). In another national study, students were more likely to carry weapons if they were more often victimized and more often involved in fights (Kingery, Pruitt, Heuberger, & Brizzolara, 1995). These findings were corroborated in a regional study of Texas 8th- and 10th-graders (Kingery, Pruitt, & Heuberger, 1996), in which Texas students who carried guns at school were also more likely to have been repeatedly victimized and repeatedly involved in fights in the previous year. A study of Kentucky students found school violence to be associated with nonsexual victimization (r = .45, n = 1,374) in Grades 8 and 9 (Kingery, 1998).

Gun availability was also a factor in the Texas study (Kingery, Pruitt, & Heuberger, 1996). Guns were most commonly given to the Texas students free, although more than one-fourth were purchased. Others were obtained by borrowing, trading, or renting. The most common reasons for carrying a gun to school were being angry with intent to shoot someone or simply wanting to feel safer. Other students wanted to coerce fellow students, flaunt school rules, or gain acceptance from friends or were forced by other students to carry the gun.

Race appears to be a mixed bag. Preference for carrying handguns over knives in the community (not merely in schools) may be a more common trait of young African American males (Kingery, Biafora, & Zimmerman, 1996)—a factor that could partly explain the higher fatality rate among young African American males. The school shooting trend of recent years is more commonly a white male phenomenon, however.

Taking a Broader View of School Violence Risk Factors

Despite the growing body of research on predictors of weapon carrying in schools, we have less information about risk factors of broader violent and aggressive behaviors among students. The research has scarcely begun in the areas of predicting fighting, bullying, harassment, and other common forms of school violence. Too often research on juvenile delinquency in general is passed off as school violence information by researchers who have not specifically examined the school setting.

Even school-specific research tends to be limited to proximal or concurrent risk factors that are self-reportable. The more difficult task of examining family influences, community influences, and early life influences of all types has not yet begun. Also, the research is focused on student self-reports, which is a good starting place but lacks the greater reliability of observational research and retrospective and prospective longitudinal studies. Recent research based on the tiny samples of recent school shooters will require several years' worth of additional data to make any clear distinctions.

EXAMINING INTERVENTIONS

The material in this section describes a continuum for intervening, tracking, and monitoring at-risk children so as to maximize their life chances and illustrates an integrated approach for achieving prevention outcomes in the context of the schools.

The at-risk pathway and its consequences are not inevitable. Eddy, Reid, and Fetrow (2000) have recently argued that our best options for addressing this progressive pathway are (1) to prevent at-risk children from getting on it in the first place, or (2) failing that, to try and get them off it as early as possible in their lives and school careers. Early intervention that is comprehensive and systemic, uses evidence-based practices, and involves the most important social agents in a young child's life (i.e., parents, peers, teachers) is perhaps our most effective vehicle for accomplishing this goal (Reid, 1993; Walker, Colvin, & Ramsey, 1995; Walker & Epstein, 2000). These practices and approaches are not broadly in evidence in school, family, and community contexts, in spite of compelling evidence as to their effectiveness in preventing later destructive outcomes (see Hawkins, Catalano, Kosterman, Abbott, & Hill, 1999).

Far too often, critically important supports and services for at-risk children are sporadic and not well coordinated. This is particularly true for those up to age 5, where the potential for successfully intervening to divert children from an at-risk trajectory is greatest. For young children who are at risk, it is essential to detect conditions that foster antisocial, destructive, behavior patterns and to expose these children to evidence-based interventions that can make a difference in their lives. Such programs exist that can be applied in a continuum ranging from the prenatal period to kindergarten entry. Most importantly, these interventions can be carefully coordinated, and the at-risk children who move through them monitored and tracked continuously so that they progress smoothly from one program to another.

The Olds Nurse Home Visitation program is an exemplary, evidence-based intervention that is delivered by public health nurses who provide advocacy, support, and parent education services to expectant mothers who meet an at-risk profile (e.g., poverty, abuse, and so forth) (see Olds et al., 1999). The program contacts expectant mothers, provides support during the birth process, and also provides follow-up and support until the child reaches age 2. Twenty-year follow-up studies show that this program is highly effective in preventing delinquency and other outcomes such as child abuse. Early Head Start provides family and child supports in the form of effective child care and education in proven parenting practices. The advantage of Early Head Start is that it can be applied very early in a child's development and span the transition to preschool. Long-term follow-up studies of the Perry Preschool Project show it to be a highly effective intervention that can prevent numerous destructive outcomes over many years (e.g., delinquency, school failure, drug and alcohol involvement, and referral to special education). A number of economic analyses have shown that the Perry Preschool Project produces substantial cost savings in terms of destructive outcomes avoided and expensive supports and services not required (Barnett, 1985; Barnett & Escobar, 1992). This highly effective preschool model can bridge the gap between preschool and either regular Head Start or kindergarten.

These and similar, evidence-based programs can make a huge difference in the kind of start at-risk children have in life and in their school careers. School-readiness skills are of paramount importance in achieving school success. Full engagement with and attachment to schooling serve as powerful protective factors in offsetting a host of negative outcomes during adolescence, including delinquency (see Hawkins et al., 1999).

Walker and Severson (in press) have recently noted that the concepts of intervention and prevention seem to be confused with each other in some professional contexts. Prevention is an outcome that is realized by the application of intervention approaches. Intervention, on the other hand, is a means for achieving prevention goals and outcomes.

The U.S. Public Health Service classifies prevention as involving primary, secondary, and tertiary types. Primary prevention employs strategies to keep problems from emerging, as in teaching wellness lifestyles or mandating trigger locks. Secondary prevention, in contrast, refers to supports and interventions that deal with the problems resulting from prior exposure to risk factors. That is, attempts are made to buffer, reduce, and offset the damaging effects of such risk exposure. Teaching anger management skills would be an example of a secondary prevention technique. Finally, tertiary prevention refers to efforts to address the severe effects of long-term exposure to multiple and severe risk factors. Children who are born into chaotic or violent family conditions and who experience severe abuse and neglect early in their lives often require tertiary approaches that involve a variety of services coordinated by a case manager.

An integrated approach to prevention can be applied from birth to age 18. It is especially appropriate for the school setting and can address the needs of all types of students (i.e., students who are progressing normally [80–90%], students who are showing the early signs of prior risk exposure [10–15%], and those who require extensive services, supports, and intervention to address their myriad, severe problems and needs [1–7%]) (Walker & Sprague, 1999). Typically, universal interventions are used to achieve primary prevention goals, while selected and more expensive interventions are targeted to small groups and individuals and are used to achieve secondary prevention goals. Indicated interventions, which are very expensive and intrusive, are required for achieving tertiary prevention goals. This integrated approach is being increasingly applied within schools, with highly satisfactory results, in order to make them safer and more effective and to establish positive school climates (Eddy et al., 2000; Hawkins et al., 1999; Sprague, Sugai, & Walker, 1998; Walker & Epstein, 2000).

Figure 2 provides a schematic overview of the relationship among costs, the three types of prevention, and the intervention approaches used to address them. As a general rule, universal interventions applied to achieve primary prevention goals are the most cost-effective on a per individual basis, and indicated interventions for addressing tertiary prevention goals are the least cost-effective in this regard. A greater investment in and commitment to primary prevention approaches in schools has a number of advantages: These approaches (1) address generic problems (e.g., lack of uniform disciplinary standards across teachers and classrooms) that are not suitable for more expensive, intrusive interventions; (2) can prevent mild problems from escalating into more serious ones; (3) create a context for the effective application of secondary and tertiary prevention approaches; (4) are perceived as fair, in that all students are exposed to the universal intervention in the same manner; (5) provide for treatment-based identification of students who need more intensive and expensive secondary or tertiary prevention approaches; and, finally, (6) address the needs of *all* students who populate our public schools.

Comprehensive School Safety Interventions: Elements, Implementation, and Evidence

About a dozen universal education programs, available as stand-alone interventions for schools, fall into the top 50 percentiles of effectiveness; whereas dozens of others fall into the bottom half on effectiveness in controlled studies. In essence, most such programs are stand-alone elements in schools, most are student focused, and most are ineffective. We need to change the way schools address safety to prevent the waste of time and effort that is now common. The average school has 14 discretionary prevention programs in place (not including discipline policies and practices) (D. C.

FIGURE 2

Relationship Between Costs and Prevention Type Across the 0–18 Developmental Age Span

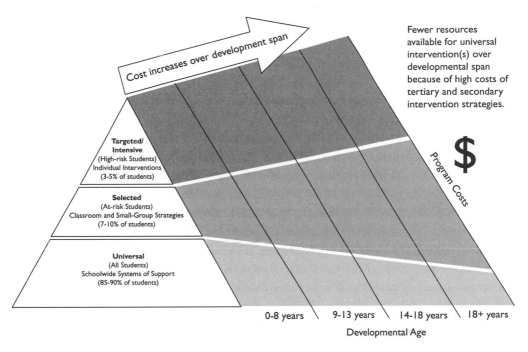

Cost increases over development span

Fewer resources available for universal intervention(s) over developmental span because of high costs of tertiary and secondary intervention strategies.

Program Costs

$

Targeted/ Intensive
(High-risk Students)
Individual Interventions
(3-5% of students)

Selected
(At-risk Students)
Classroom and Small-Group Strategies
(7-10% of students)

Universal
(All Students)
Schoolwide Systems of Support
(85-90% of students)

0-8 years 9-13 years 14-18 years 18+ years

Developmental Age

Gottfredson, personal communication, August 23, 2000), and these are generally a diverse group of interventions that are not a part of any comprehensive needs-based plan. Few, if any, interventions in schools are evaluated in accordance with minimum standards. Yet funding for school-based violence interventions has been exponential in recent years, with almost no assurance that funding is linked to quality and effectiveness.

The process of intervention is every bit as important as the choice of intervention. The involvement of key stakeholders is extremely important. The pace of the intervention in relation to other activities can have an effect. The selection of teachers or leaders for the intervention is paramount; the messenger can have nearly as strong an effect as any aspect of the curriculum or program itself. Interactive and skills-training approaches are more effective than didactic and knowledge-based approaches. Other aspects of the process are being studied but are not well researched at present.

The elements of an effective, comprehensive school safety plan might include administrative techniques, school security, universal education, counseling, alternative education, and other categories of approaches. We have not yet learned what the best practices are in each of these areas, let alone what the ideal combinations might be in one particular set of circumstances or another. Whole-school approaches are difficult to evaluate, except as an entire mix, because the multiplicity of components defies adequate comparison conditions to ferret out the portions of the overall plan that are successful. Yet the future of school safety lies in evaluating various combinations of strategies and conducting efficient evaluations that yield at least a simple comparison between two sets of strategies. Absent rigorous evaluation data, best practice information can supply guidance on the elements of a comprehensive school safety program.

Administrative Interventions

School facilities can be designed better to reduce violence (i.e., smaller, and with more visual supervision), and school climates are important in minimizing violence (i.e., gentle teaching, modeling nonviolent behavior in teacher-student interaction, etc.). Some would say it is important to implement well what we currently know about school climates while working with students to modify their behavior.

Smaller schools experience less disruptive and violent behavior than larger schools (D. C. Gottfredson, 1985; Gregory, 1992; Rutter, 1988; Stockard & Mayberry, 1992), but some evidence is conflicting (Nolin, Davies, & Chandler, 1995). Smaller schools provide opportunities for school staff and students to bond more closely to one another, thereby reducing anonymity and increasing accountability. It is unclear whether smaller schools simply have more resources per student, more parental involvement, and more cohesion-building activities than larger schools, and whether these possibly advantageous characteristics of small schools can be transplanted creatively into larger schools. Some schools have experimented with dividing large buildings into two or more smaller and totally autonomous schools with solid walls between them, but these efforts have not been evaluated.

Zero tolerance as an intervention strategy is counterproductive for dealing with weapon-carrying youth. The federal policy requiring that all states pass laws requiring that schools "consider for expulsion" all youth caught carrying firearms at school was initiated without a scientific basis for its efficacy. We have subsequently found that only 1% of youth who carry firearms to school in the U.S. are ever caught (Kingery & Coggeshall, 2001). The limited ability of present school systems to detect students who carry firearms calls into question the basis for such Draconian measures. Many have proposed that the money and effort spent in maintaining this effort would be better spent preventing youth from carrying weapons in the first place.

Security Interventions

Schools can be better designed with tighter security in mind, without making them look or feel like prisons. Visual supervision can be increased by having a "spider-shaped design" with administration in the center having full view of all corridors. Strong doors can be hidden away and pulled into action when an area of the school must be contained or cordoned off. Dark, unsupervised spaces can be designed out of the school's physical structure. Double bathroom privacy panels can be removed, as can false ceiling panels where contraband can be hidden. Lockers can be removed, and their need reduced by allowing one set of books in the classroom and another at home. Students can check bulky clothing at a secure entry room. Adequate door and window locks can be installed, and shatter-proof glass and other safety features used. The vegetation outside the building can be low and prickly, and dumpsters and other means of climbing on the school roof can be eliminated (Trump, 1998).

Security devices, other than those incorporated into the building design, may be useful but are as yet unproven. Large walk-through metal detectors are perhaps necessary in some schools, but they can slow down the start of the school day by as much as 2 hours because of long waits to enter. Small, hand-held, metal-detector devices may be more effective, especially when used in random unannounced searches. Metal detectors used for rapid searches of all students must be set so that they are not sensitive enough to pick up the metal in school binders or shoes. Banning metal altogether seems impractical, given its presence in such forms as rivets in jeans, and in notebook spines, shoes, and clothing zippers. Hand-held detectors that are used in relation to reasonable evidence of a hidden metal object on a particular student can be set to a higher level of sensitivity.

Security procedures may be as important as the design of the building itself. Security cameras can serve as a deterrent but are of little value if they are not carefully watched, particularly if students can see the security officer being less than vigilant in viewing the monitors. If they prove to be a deterrent, they should be plainly visible but protected from vandalism. Otherwise they can be hidden to prevent the aura of a "prison-like atmosphere."

Security officers are becoming more common as a result of federal funding, but their effectiveness is only now being evaluated. There are uncertainties as to exactly what their role should be, how they should be trained, and how to juggle the fact that they serve "two masters." Until a crime occurs, they serve the principal. Once a crime occurs, they outstrip the principal's authority and answer to public safety officials. Some believe they serve as a good public relations liaison between youth and law enforcement and create a sense of security. Others feel security officers make students more fearful of danger or personal injury. Traditionally, these officers are not trained to work in school settings, although they are learning from one another through involvement in school resource officer associations and other informal networks.

School officials can use a wide range of assistants in increasing the security of the school, including every member of the school staff, students, parents, volunteers, law enforcement personnel, juvenile court authorities, and probation officers. Making sure that each person has a defined and appropriate role and that the roles are complementary offers promise for maintaining school security. Knowing how to prevent violence is as important as knowing how to prevent its escalation when it breaks out.

Mental Health Interventions

School counselors, social workers, and psychologists are scarce in today's schools, and spend much of their time with guidance counseling and traffic control. (In 1997, there were approximately two counselors per 1,000 students in U.S. public schools, though the ratio varied widely by state and school [National Center for Education Statistics, 2000; calculations by the authors]). These professionals do not have the time or other resources to adequately address the mental health needs of students. Generally they rely on colleagues outside the school to assess students for their risk to others or to determine placement(s). One effective approach might be simply to recognize that problems exist with a particular student and to develop and periodically reassess the effectiveness of an intervention plan to ensure that the student's educational needs are met. Most students just need basic triage and assistance with intermittent emotional problems, stemming from concrete situations that often can be remedied with adult support. Those who are in need of more intensive services and supports will become readily apparent to school authorities.

Mental health is clearly important in any interdisciplinary effort to reduce school violence. School staff are not particularly accurate or consistent in diagnosing emotional and behavioral conditions, and their time might be better spent simply noting the problems that occur and seeking the right follow-up for each child in the educational environment. Yet the costs of even this form of assistance are probably greater than most schools are able to bear under current funding arrangements.

Behavioral Interventions

Peer mediation has its zealots, although the technique has received generally weak appraisals of its effectiveness. Youth should probably not be asked to mediate in very difficult situations and should tread lightly in negotiations between opposing individuals. Training a child as a peer mediator may be more effective as an intervention for the mediator than for the students using the mediation services.

Conflict resolution also has its devoted adherents, and the techniques are certainly promising in the right contexts, but the appraisals of its effectiveness, again, have been weak and mixed. Any such program that becomes a rallying point for nonviolence absorbs a greater portion of the explainable variance in violence over time. Peer mediation, conflict resolution, anger management, social skills training, and other techniques can be widely overlapping in their effects, as each takes a slightly different approach to achieve the same end.

Alternative Education as Intervention

Alternative education is on the rise. More than 4 million K–12 students are served today by alternative education programs and schools. Alternative education programs are required in 25 states (Civil Rights Project, 2000). In other states, local school districts retain discretion to offer alternative programs. Advocates of alternative education have formed professional associations currently in 10 states (California, Iowa, Michigan, Minnesota, Missouri, New Jersey, New York, Oklahoma, Oregon, and Washington) (D.L. White, personal communication, January 22, 2001). At the national and international levels, alternative educators are represented in two recently formed organizations:

the International Association for Learning Alternatives and the National Alternative Education Association. Raywid (1994) has developed a typology of three categories of alternative education: (1) popular innovations or choice, (2) last-chance or sentencing programs, and (3) remedial and rehabilitation or referral programs and schools. Alternative education has been practiced in the form of innovation since early in the history of U.S. schools. It has been delivered most recently, however, as remedial and rehabilitative in nature.

More complete coordination and wider applications of alternative education as a means of violence intervention are hindered by the absence of a systematic evaluation of its effectiveness, a tendency toward territoriality among alternative educators, and genuine uncertainty about the political and philosophical scope and purpose of alternative education. In the meantime, administrators apply alternative programs as acts of last resort to zero tolerance policies. Alternative education will continue to be successful in treating some symptoms of school violence (see Tobin & Sprague, this volume).

A Note on Assigning Youth to Interventions

Using risk factors haphazardly and simplistically to identify at-risk youth can produce self-fulfilling labels that unfairly stigmatize and impact the lives of at-risk youth. It appears that a single risk factor can have both a high false positive and a high false negative rate in predicting any kind of violence or antisocial behavior (Derzon, in press). Thus, rather than seizing on one observable risk factor as a basis for action, this factor should be used only as a warning sign to assess the presence of additional risk factors in relation to personal coping resources and resiliency.

Summary

Combining these interventions with those designed for more severely violent and disruptive youth in a well-coordinated plan holds the best promise for improving school safety, according to the limited best practice information currently available. As more sophisticated evaluations of whole-school approaches are undertaken, we will begin to learn the extent to which substantive improvements in school safety can be made. This will also help determine the most effective strategy mixes in particular settings.

CONCLUSION

Research findings from several disciplines have shed light on this discussion of school violence, but these outcomes do not usually address the unique aspects of the micro-environment of interest to school administrators. Clearly, children carry with them biological predispositions, learned patterns of violence, psychological vulnerabilities, and community risk factor exposure into their school environments. No effective solution to school violence can overlook the role of these factors. We must begin at the simplest level in schools to (a) assess the observable phenomena in a specific setting that can reduce school safety, (b) investigate causes that are preventable by school staff, and (c) test interventions that create the best possible learning environment, even if they do not correct deeper, underlying problems. Schools can, to a degree, be islands of greater safety within the communities they serve, just as adults can make certain that play and study areas in the community are safe for children and increase safety in transitioning from one location to another. Yet comparable processes are needed in communities, as a whole, involving coordination among different sets of players, different institutions, and different methods. Collaboration between school and community violence prevention efforts is essential to achieving sustainable change.

The empirical knowledge base on school safety is underemphasized in current federal funding priorities in the rush to implement intuitive strategies in a knee-jerk response to intense public expectations. Money is allocated in ways that are superficial but pleasing to the public. Accountability in federal and state spending has been urged but not achieved. Yet we are encouraged that federal funding for new research has recently increased. This has attracted talented social scientists, and solid training programs in universities are beginning to emerge. These are all promising signs for advancing this new field of study.

REFERENCES

American Association of University Women. (1992). *How schools shortchange girls: A study of the major findings on girls and education.* Washington, DC: Author.

Barnett, W. S. (1985). The Perry Preschool Program and its long-term effects: A benefit-cost analysis. *High/Scope Early Childhood Policy Papers* (No. 2). Ypsilanti, MI: High/Scope.

Barnett, W. S., & Escobar, C. M. (1992). Economic costs and benefits of early intervention. In S. J. Meisels & J. P. Shonkoff (Eds.), *Handbook of early childhood intervention* (1st ed., pp. 560-582). New York: Cambridge University Press.

Baron, R. M., & Kenny, D. A. (1986). The moderator-mediator variable distinction in social psychological research: Conceptual, strategic, and statistical considerations. *Journal of Personality and Social Psychology, 51,* 1173-1182.

Bureau of Justice Statistics, U.S. Department of Justice. (1998). *National crime victimization survey, 1995* [electronic data set]. Ann Arbor, MI: Author. [Inter-university Consortium for Political and Social Research (ICPSR), Producer and Distributor.]

Civil Rights Project (Harvard University), and Advancement Project. (2000). *Opportunities suspended: The devastating consequences of zero tolerance and school discipline policies.* Cambridge, MA: Authors.

Coggeshall, M. B., & Kingery, P. M. (in press). Cross-survey analysis of school violence and disorder. *Psychology in the Schools, 38*(2).

Derzon, J. H. (in press). Anti-social behavior and the prediction of violence: A meta-analysis. *Psychology in the Schools, 38*(2).

Eddy, J. M., Reid, J. B., & Fetrow, R. A. (2000). An elementary school-based prevention program targeting modifiable antecedents of youth delinquency and violence: Linking the Interests of Families and Teachers (LIFT). *Journal of Emotional and Behavioral Disorders, 8*(3), 165-176.

Flannery, D. J. (1997). School violence: Risk preventive intervention and policy. *Urban Diversity Series, No. 109.* New York: Teachers College, Institute for Urban and Minority Education and ERIC Clearinghouse on Urban Education. (ERIC Document Reproduction Service No. ED 416 272.)

Flannery, D. J., & Singer, M. I. (1999). Exposure to violence and victimization at school. *Choices Briefs, No. 4.* New York: Teachers College, Institute for Urban and Minority Education and ERIC Clearinghouse on Urban Education.

Gottfredson, D. C. (1985). *School size and school disorder.* Baltimore, MD: Center for Social Organization of Schools, Johns Hopkins University. (ERIC Reproduction Service No. ED 261 456.)

Gottfredson, D. C., Gottfredson, D. G., & Czeh, E. R. (2000). *National study of delinquency prevention in schools.* Gottfredson Associates. Final Report, Grant No. 96-MU-MU-0008. Department of Criminology, University of Maryland, College Park, MD.

Gregory, T. (1992). Small is too big: Achieving a critical anti-mass in the high school. In *Sourcebook on school and district size, cost, and quality.* Minneapolis, MN: Minnesota University, Hubert H. Humphrey Institute on Public Affairs; Oak Brook, IL: North Central Regional Educational Laboratory. (ERIC Document Reproduction Service No. ED 361 159.)

Hawkins, J. D., Catalano, R. F., Kosterman, R., Abbott, R., & Hill, K. G. (1999). Preventing adolescent health-risk behaviors by strengthening protection during childhood. *Archives of Pediatrics & Adolescent Medicine, 153,* 226-234.

Kann, L., Kichen, S. A., Williams, B. I., Ross, J. G., Lowry, R., Hill, C. V., Grun-baum, J. A., & Kolbe, L. J. (2000). Youth risk behavior surveillance—United States, 1999. *Morbidity and Mortality Weekly Report, 49*(SS-5), 1-94.

Kingery, P. M. (1998). Adolescent violence survey: A psychometric analysis. *School Psychology International, 19,* 43-59.

Kingery, P. M., Biafora, F. A., & Zimmerman, R. S. (1996). Risk factors for violent behaviors among ethnically diverse urban adolescents: Beyond race and ethnicity. *School Psychology International, 17,* 171-188.

Kingery, P. M., & Coggeshall, M. B. (in press). School-based surveillance of violence, injury and disciplinary actions. *Psychology in the Schools, 38*(2).

Kingery, P. M., & Coggeshall, M. B. (2001). School-based surveillance of violence, injury and disciplinary actions. Available Internet: *www.hamfish.org/pub/incdrept1.pdf*

Kingery, P. M., Coggeshall, M. B., & Alford, A. A. (1999). Weapon carrying by youth: Risk factors and prevention. In "Quality schools, safe schools" [Special issue], *Education and Urban Society, 31*(3), 309-333.

Kingery, P. M., Pruitt, B. E., & Heuberger, G. (1996). A profile of rural Texas adolescents who carry handguns to school. *Journal of School Health, 66*(1), 18-22.

Kingery, P. M., Pruitt, B. E., Heuberger, G. H., & Brizzolara, J. A. (1995). Violence in rural schools: An emerging problem near the United States-Mexico border. *School Psychology International, 16,* 335-344.

Lee, V. E., Croninger, R. G., Linn, E., Chen, X. (1996). The culture of sexual harassment in secondary schools. *American Educational Research Journal 33*(2), 383-417.

Loeber, R., & Farrington, D. P. (Eds.). (1998). *Serious and violent juvenile offenders: Risk factors and successful interventions.* Thousand Oaks, CA: Sage.

National Center for Education Statistics. (1998). Indicator of the month: Student victimization at school. *Indicator of the Month: November 1998.* Washington, DC: Author.

National Center for Education Statistics. (2000). *Education in brief: Public school student, staff and graduate counts by state, school year 1998-99.* NCES 2000-330. Washington, DC: Author.

National Center for Injury Prevention and Control, Division of Violence Prevention. (1997). Rates of homicide, suicide, and firearm-related death among children—26 industrialized countries. *Morbidity and Mortality Weekly Report, 46*(05), 101-105.

National School Safety Center. (n.d.). Report on school associated violent deaths. Available Internet: *www.nssc1.org/savd/savd.pdf*

New York City Board of Education. (1995). *Incident reporting systems need to be strengthened to ensure accurate reporting of school safety incidents.* (Report No. A-7-95). Albany, NY: New York Office of the Comptroller.

Nolin, M. J., Davies, E., & Chandler, K. (1995). *Student victimization at school: Statistics in brief.* National Center for Education Statistics, Report No. NCES-95-204, October 1995, table 1, p. 7, citing U.S. Department of Education, National Center for Education Statistics, *National household education survey, 1993.*

Olds, D., Henderson, C., Kirtzman, H., Eckenrode, J., Cole, R., & Tatelbaum, R. (1999). Prenatal and infancy home visitation by nurses: Recent findings. *The Future of Children, 9*(1), 44-65. Los Alto, CA: The David and Lucile Packard Foundation.

Osofsky, J. D. (Ed.). (1997). *Children in a violent society.* New York: Guilford. (ERIC Document Reproduction Service No. ED 408 056.)

Patterson, G. R., Reid, J. B., & Dishion, T. J. (1992). *Antisocial boys.* Eugene, OR: Castalia Press.

Pynoos, R. S., & Nader, K. (1998). Psychological first aid and treatment approach to children exposed to community violence: Research implications. *Journal of Traumatic Stress, I*(4), 445-473.

Raywid, M. A. (1994). Alternative schools: The state of the art. *Educational Leadership, 52,* 26-31.

Reid, J. (1993). Prevention of conduct disorder before and after school entry: Relating interventions to developmental findings. *Development and Psychopathology, 5*(1/2), 243-262.

Rutter, R. A. (1988). *Effects of school as a community.* Madison, WI: National Center on Effective Secondary Schools. (ERIC Documentation Reproduction Service No. ED 313 470.)

Sprague, J. R., Sugai, G., & Walker, H. M. (1998). Antisocial behavior in schools. In T. S. Watson & F. M. Gresham (Eds.), *Handbook of child behavior therapy* (pp. 451-474). New York: Plenum.

Stein, N. (1999) *Incidence and implications of sexual harassment and sexual violence in K-12 schools.* Available Internet: *www.hamfish.org/pub/nan.pdf*

Stockard, J., & Mayberry, M. (1992). *Effective educational environments.* Newbury Park, CA: Corwin Press.

Tremblay, R. E., Pagani-Kurtz, L., Masse, L. C., Vitaro, F., & Pihl, R. O. (1995). A bi-modal preventive intervention for disruptive kindergarten boys: Its impact through mid-adolescence. *Journal of Consulting and Clinical Psychology, 63*(4), 560-568.

Trump, T. S. (1998). *Practical school security: Basic guidelines for safe and secure schools.* Thousand Oaks, CA: Corwin Press.

Walker, H. M., Colvin, G., & Ramsey, E. (1995). *Antisocial behavior in schools: Strategies and best practices.* Pacific Grove, CA: Brooks/Cole.

Walker, H. M., & Epstein, M. (Eds.). (2000). *Making schools safer and violence free.* Austin, TX: PRO-ED.

Walker, H. M., & Severson, H. H. (in press). Developmental prevention of at-risk outcomes for vulnerable antisocial children and youth. In F. M. Gresham, K. L. Lane, & T. E. O'Shaughnessy (Eds.), *Interventions for students with or at-risk for emotional and behavioral disorders.* Boston: Allyn and Bacon.

Walker, H. M., & Sprague, J. R. (1999). The path to school failure, delinquency and violence: Causal factors and some potential solutions. *Intervention in School and Clinic, 35*(2), 67-73.

AUTHORS' NOTES

Paul M. Kingery
Director, Hamilton Fish Institute
2121 K St. NW, Suite 200
Washington, DC 20037-1830
Tel: (202) 496-2201
E-mail: *kingery@gwu.edu*

Hill M. Walker
Institute on Violence and Destructive Behavior
1265 University of Oregon
Eugene, OR 97403-1265

CHAPTER 5

Promoting Safety and Success in School by Developing Students' Strengths

Stan Paine and Cathy Kennedy Paine
Springfield School District, Springfield, Oregon

INTRODUCTION

In the wake of several sensational school shootings that have riveted the nation in recent years, a great deal of attention has been directed at the level of violence in American schools. One of those shootings occurred in our community in May 1998. Here in Springfield, Oregon, we are all too aware of the traumatic effects a violent incident can have on a school, a school district, and a community.

School violence can include "lesser" forms of intimidation such as name calling, bullying, or harassment and, as we know, can range all the way to assault and murder. Communities have pointed to everything from the popular media to the breakdown of the American family as possible causes of such violence. Many questions have been asked as to what can be done to stop these terrifying tragedies. At Centennial Elementary School in Springfield, Oregon, and at many other schools throughout the country, staff members and parents have focused on ways to work together to create a positive vision for young people that would guide them toward safety and success. Instead of concentrating only on reducing risks and problems, schools are learning ways to cultivate and enhance the qualities in young people that have long-term positive effects on their development and on the social milieu in which they live.

Researchers in education, psychology and other disciplines have explored a number of models that focus on the development of positive attributes in youth. One such model is that developed by the Search Institute of Minneapolis, Minnesota—an independent, nonprofit, nonsectarian organization whose mission is to support the healthy development of children and adolescents. In this chapter, we will use the *Developmental Assets Framework* (Scales & Leffert, 1999) as a basis for illustrating what educators can do to create safe and supportive school environments.

The Developmental Assets Framework, as shown in Table 1, on page 91, is a well-researched, strength-based approach that identifies 40 critical factors that children and adolescents need to grow up as healthy, responsible, and caring individuals. The model illustrates how families, schools, congregations, neighborhoods, youth organizations, and others in the community all play an important role in shaping young people's lives. We will describe the full model briefly, then illustrate those assets that schools, in particular, can work to develop. The Search Institute has noted that "building developmental assets is consistent with and indeed contributes toward schools' fulfilling their mission: to foster academic achievement and to provide a safe and healthy environment in which that achievement can best occur" (Starkman, Scales, & Roberts, 1999, p.3).

THE DEVELOPMENTAL ASSETS MODEL

Developmental assets are "the positive 'building blocks' (i.e., relationships, experiences, values, attitudes, and attributes) that all children and youth need for success. 'Developmental' refers to how the building blocks both emerge from and help shape how children and youth grow and develop. 'Assets' point to the fact that these building blocks are positive, that they give strength to young people" (Starkman et al., 1999, p. 2).

According to Starkman et. al. (1999), the 40 developmental assets fall into two broad categories—external and internal. External assets focus on positive experiences that youth receive from the people and organizations in their lives. They can be categorized as providing young people with (a) support, (b) empowerment, (c) boundaries and expectations, and (d) constructive use of time. Internal assets focus on the internalized qualities that encourage wise judgements, responsible choices, and genuine compassion for others. They cluster into the categories of (a) commitment to learning, (b) positive values, (c) social competencies, and (d) positive identity. These groupings are based on factors that help make young people safe, self-assured, and successful.

To develop strong *external assets,* young people need to experience the following factors:

(a) *support,* in the form of love from their families and respect and caring from others, such as friends, neighbors, and educators. They need family life, social contacts, and organizational experiences that provide positive, supportive environments for them as they grow up.

(b) *empowerment,* which comes from being respected and valued by their community. They need opportunities to contribute in positive ways to the well-being of others. This helps establish a sense of purpose.

(c) *boundaries and expectations,* which communicate what is expected of them and whether activities and behaviors are "in bounds" or "out of bounds."

(d) *constructive use of time,* which includes opportunities for growth and enrichment through creative expression (e.g., arts and music), physical activity (including

TABLE 1

Forty Developmental Assets

External Assets	
Support	Family support
	Positive family communication
	Other adult relationships
	Caring neighborhood
	Caring school climate
	Parent involvement in schooling
Empowerment	Community values youth
	Youth as resources
	Service to others
	Safety
Boundaries and Expectations	Family boundaries
	School boundaries
	Neighborhood boundaries
	Adult role models
	Positive peer influence
	High expectations
Constructive Use of Time	Creative activities
	Youth programs
	Religious community
	Time at home
Internal Assets	
Commitment to Learning	Achievement motivation
	School engagement
	Homework
	Bonding to school
	Reading for pleasure
Positive Values	Caring
	Equality and social justice
	Integrity
	Honesty
	Responsibility
	Restraint
Social Competencies	Planning and decision making
	Interpersonal competence
	Cultural competence
	Resistance skills
	Peaceful conflict resolution
Positive Identity	Personal power
	Self-esteem
	Sense of purpose
	Positive view of personal future

sports), youth programs, congregational involvement, and quality time at home with family members.

To develop strong internal assets, youth need to develop the following characteristics:

(a) *commitment to learning,* a strong belief in the importance of education and an enduring commitment to self-improvement and lifelong learning.

(b) *positive values,* including beliefs and character traits such as honesty, integrity and responsibility. These are qualities that mold their character and guide their choices through life.

(c) *social competencies,* the manners and consideration for others that equip them to make positive choices, to build relationships, and to show tolerance and respect for others.

(d) *positive identity,* a strong sense of their own power, purpose, and worth and the belief that they can make a difference in their own lives and in the lives of others.

When taken together, these external and internal assets can provide a powerful, positive influence on young people's behavior. The more assets young people experience, the more likely they are to engage in positive behaviors such as helping others and succeeding in school. The fewer assets they have, the more likely they are to engage in risk-taking behaviors such as alcohol and other drug use, antisocial behavior, and violence (Scales & Leffert, 1999).

Research Behind the Developmental Assets

Since 1989, the Search Institute has surveyed more than 350,000 6th- to 12th-graders across the United States and has conducted numerous informal discussions and focus groups. Through these efforts, the Institute has collected data to suggest that the external and internal assets make a significant difference in the lives of young people. Relations between developmental assets and adolescent behavior have been documented for all types of youth, regardless of age, gender, geographical region, town size, or race/ethnicity (Scales & Leffert, 1999).

The concept of developmental assets grew out of two types of applied research, which the Search Institute combines into one framework:

1. *Prevention research,* which focuses on the identification of protective factors that inhibit high-risk behaviors such as substance abuse, violence, sexual behavior and dropping out of school.

2. *Resiliency research,* which identifies factors that increase young people's ability to rebound in the face of adversity, such as poverty, neglect, abuse of any kind, drug/alcohol use, dangerous environments, or toxic relationships.

The current data on developmental assets are based on a sample of 99,462 6th- to 12th-graders who completed the Search Institute's *Profiles of Student Life: Attitudes and Behaviors* survey (Search Institute, 1996) during the 1996–97 school year. The sample includes responses from youth in 213 U.S. communities that surveyed their own students. Ideally, according to the Institute, all youth would possess or experience at least 31 of the 40 assets, allowing them to become strong and resilient people. The results, however, indicated that only 8% of the youth reached this criterion. In addition, fewer than half of the young people surveyed experienced as many as 25 of the 40 assets (Benson, Scales, Leffert, & Roehlkepartain, 1999).

The Search Institute has found that youth with the most assets are least likely to engage in four different patterns of high-risk behavior (alcohol use, illicit drug use, sexual activity, and violence). In addition to protecting youth from negative behaviors, having more assets increases the chances that young people will have positive attitudes and behaviors. Those youth with the most assets were more likely to succeed in school, value diversity, maintain good health, and be able to delay gratification (Scales & Leffert, 1999).

Cultivating Developmental Assets at School

If, as the research suggests, developmental assets are a good thing for young people to have, and if "more assets are better than fewer," how do we cultivate them in our students? At an empirical level, this question harbors a host of research studies. At a practical level, it asks, "What has been tried? What seems promising? What makes good sense?" It is clear to us that there are many strategies educators can employ to build and strengthen students' assets. For nearly 20 years, our day-to-day work in school administration and school psychology, respectively, has been directed, in large part, toward trying to operationalize the details of what it takes to develop the strengths of young people in active, deliberate ways.

In this section, we will illustrate the assets most readily nurtured in school settings and identify ideas for cultivating those assets within the educational environment. The strategies discussed below show some of the ways in which these variables can be developed to create a great learning and social environment for young people—one that promotes their safety and success.

Increasing and Highlighting the External Assets

We discussed earlier in this chapter how the external assets of support, empowerment, clear boundaries and expectations, and constructive use of time all contribute to the healthy development of young people. It would be easy to dismiss these assets as truisms or as factors beyond a school's control. However, some schools are rich in these qualities, while others are asset-poor. This variability is not random, but rather is a result of efforts on the part of educators to create an environment that provides young people with the best chance possible for success. For each of the four categories of external assets, we will highlight concepts and practices we have implemented that can make a positive difference for students.

Support. Strategies that enable students to experience support in schools can include enhancing the school's culture or climate and increasing the involvement of parents or other caring adults in the educational lives of the students. In addition, enabling the parents, through training or structured programs, to be a more powerful presence in their children's lives also increases support. An effective way to coordinate these services has been to provide a central location, such as a family center for volunteers and parents. Adult mentors as well as parent volunteers can be helpful in supporting students. Schools and the larger community can work together to show support for the students.

School culture has been defined as "how we do things here." School climate is "how it feels to be here." A positive valence on both concepts is essential if students are to feel comfortable and to put forth their best effort in school, both socially and academically. School staff members have a tremendous responsibility and great power to assure that the school culture and climate are positive forces for *all* students. For better or worse, staff define "how we do things here," and through their actions, outreach, tolerance, and limits, they establish "how it feels to be here." At Centennial we promote our students as "The greatest kids on planet Earth." A thorough description of the program follows in the section on Empowerment.

Another form of support comes through the direct involvement of parents and other caring adults in the lives of the students. The most common form of this involvement is volunteerism and participation in parent organizations, such as Parent-Teacher Associations (PTAs) and booster clubs.

With the increasing demands and shrinking budgets that many schools are experiencing today, there is a growing need for strong volunteer programs in the schools. Many of the roles that volunteers can play in a school can be (and usually are) filled by parents. However, when parents are unable to fill the roles needing to be filled, school staff should consider turning to other family or community members. We have recruited grandparents, aunts and uncles, teenage or adult-age brothers or sisters, senior citizens, public employees, and members of the business community as volunteers for our schools. Often, volunteers feel they get more from the relationship than they give. One 87-year-old volunteer told us, "This is the reason I get up in the morning. No, it's more than that. This is the reason I go on living." When a caring adult sees a youngster's need and steps in to fill it, that act strengthens the school's programs and empowers the young person. Volunteers can be a powerful force for helping young people succeed in school and stay out of trouble.

Many schools have strong parent organizations that conduct special events and carry out projects to create a stronger school community. These organizations provide many opportunities for parents to become actively involved in their child's school experience. Some educators are concerned that parents will "get in the way" or become easily diverted by "trivial" tasks. However, we have found that if parents and community members are informed about the goals and priorities of the school and given a role to play in them, they will become strong supporters of the vision. Toward this end, we host annual meetings for parents to discuss school goals and work plans. We conduct focus groups with the principal for parents of children at a given grade level to talk about current issues in the learning and development of their children. The principal and PTA president communicate regularly to build the PTA meeting agenda around school priorities. We also issue a quarterly school report card summarizing progress on our school goals and suggesting ways in which parents can help us meet them.

A third method of building support in schools is to offer parent training classes or workshops. One training we have offered which helps parents prevent their young people from getting into trouble is the *Second Step* parent program. The *Second Step* program (Committee for Children, 1997) is a highly rated approach for developing social skills and preventing violence in young people. The parent component *(A Family Guide to Second Step: Parenting Strategies for a Safer Tomorrow)* has been well received for assisting parents to support youth on these goals. Many similar programs exist, but few have substantive evaluation data, as *Second Step* does (Grossman et al., 1997). We offer a *Second Step* parenting series each year in both English and Spanish. This year we are also offering our first parenting series based around the Developmental Assets Model. We recently recruited several parents to attend a luncheon and training session which prepared them to step in as substitute instructional assistants in reading to ensure that lessons could go on when a regular staff member is absent. Other classes are offered as training needs are identified.

A new trend for involving parents in supporting young people's success in school is the development of family centers within schools. Most often found in elementary schools, but beginning to appear in middle schools or at a school district level, family centers offer a variety of means for promoting parent involvement in schools. Our family center provides (1) volunteer recruitment and coordination, (2) child care to enable parents with preschool-age children to volunteer in the classroom of their school-age child, (3) work parties to aid the completion of large projects, (4) materials that parents can check out to help their child with skill development at home, and (5) parent training opportunities on numerous topics. The family center also offers a comfortable place in school (e.g., with coffee and conversation) for parents whose own school experiences might have been less than comfortable, increasing the likelihood that parents will continue the connection to their child's school and the support for their child's success.

While most people agree that parents should be involved in their child's education, the participation of other caring adults can have a powerful effect. This is true in large part, we believe, because these volunteers don't have to be involved, yet they choose to get involved in the life of a young person. When an adult other than a parent demonstrates care and concern for a young person, it carries an added impetus to impress and inspire. Mentors have the power to produce greater commitment and higher achievement in young people. Mentors can serve as remedial tutors for struggling students, as enrichment enablers for high-achieving students, and as work-place connections for "career-curious" young people. Sometimes, all it takes to make mentors available for students is an invitation to get involved and a bit of time to coordinate their activities. The power of their purpose for being there and the effects of their experience are often sufficient to keep them coming back. And that has the potential to spark greater success in underachieving students.

Schools need the support of the larger community as well. Too often, there is a lack of respect and understanding between students and the rest of the community. Adults in the community look upon young people with suspicion. Young people's appearance is denigrated; their ambition is thought to be lacking; their motives are considered suspect. Furthermore, the school they attend might be considered run-down and unsafe. What is needed is more positive contact between young people and adults in the community who typically have little or no contact with youth. This can be arranged either by sending young people into the community to complete community service projects (e.g., "Good Neighbor Day," "Day of Caring") or by inviting community members into the school ("Back to School Day"). Schools can have community members read to young children, mentor older children, tutor students, serve on a task force, be interviewed by a student, speak to a class, conduct an after-school activity, or perhaps simply have lunch or attend a musical program. Each strategy can help build bridges between students and nonparent adults and can help each party begin to see the goodness and potential in the other.

Schools, in turn, have something to offer the community. Many communities do not have adequate facilities for the activities of community groups. Organizations such as scouts, sports groups, and senior citizens may be without the space they need to fulfill their purposes. That's where schools and young people can help. Many schools make their space available as community centers in the late afternoons and evenings or during summer break. If young people could be given a role in helping to make this possible—such as serving as hosts, providing child care or clean-up services, helping to coach children's sports teams or assist scout groups, there would be benefit for both older and younger students and for the adults involved. Older students benefit from the "power of purpose," younger children from involvement with a positive role model or mentor, and adults benefit from positive contact with young people.

Empowerment. Youth are empowered when young people (a) perceive that adults in the community support, respect, and value them, (b) believe that they are seen as resources rather than as a drain on resources, (c) have opportunities to be involved and to contribute to the greater good, and (d) feel safe in their own neighborhood and community.

Community support can take the form of community members or groups providing time or financial resources to their local schools. It can include community members sponsoring teams or events and attending youth events (games, concerts, plays, etc.) at school. It involves a generous community spirit in the delicate balance between managing tax rates and providing young people with good school facilities and programs. Community members show they care about youth when they give of their time, talent, and resources to support facilities and educational or recreational programs that benefit young people.

Youth are seen as resources when they are given useful roles in the school and in the community or when they are given a voice and a role to play in significant groups and events. Here in Springfield, youth at several schools wanted to do something to make a positive difference following the shooting at Thurston High School in May 1998. A group of students at Thurston High premiered the play "Bang Bang, You're Dead" to raise awareness among youth about the effects of violence. Others served on a committee to plan a memorial to those killed and injured in the shooting. At Springfield High School, students formed a group called "By Kids 4 Kids" ("BK4K") to address the tendency of youth to withhold information that might be useful to school officials in stopping violence before it happens. (See information below for more details on BK4K.) At Centennial Elementary School, three fifth-graders wrote a "Peace Pledge," which is now recited each day over the school's intercom. Allowing and encouraging young people to play leadership and advocacy roles for topics that are important to them empowers them to make a significant difference in the lives of others.

High schools and middle schools often give students a visible presence and meaningful roles to play by allowing them to spend a part of their day working in the office or cafeteria or assisting various staff members throughout the school. One middle school in our district runs a catering business in the community. Elementary schools can also find meaningful roles for students. We also have students greet visitors at school events, shelve books in the school library, recycle paper around the school, and read to and tutor younger children. A nearby elementary school has a cookie business, supplying treats for meetings around town. All of these roles can help empower students by demonstrating to them that their time and abilities are worthwhile and meaningful.

Many schools have student councils, which provide leadership experience to those who serve. However, the numbers of students who serve are often small, and schools must find ways to involve more students in lending input or playing a role in the operation of their school or the activities of their community. Student-run radio or television stations or publications, student forums, surveys, polls and elections, and student seats on the school board or city council or their subcommittees can provide a meaningful voice or a substantive role for students in the school or community.

Many high schools now require students to perform community service as a condition of graduation. Many colleges value community service when awarding scholarships. Even elementary school students are not too young to do something kind or helpful for others. These programs recognize that community service helps students develop positive values, strong character, and a sense of commitment that goes beyond one's self. Spring clean-up projects and "days of caring" give students a sample of the good feelings that come from performing community service. An ongoing service commitment, such as sustained service to a person, program, or agency, helps students begin to see service to others as a way of life.

Empowerment also comes from feeling safe and secure in school, in order to learn effectively. Schools create good learning and social environments for young people by creating safe schools. They also have a role to play in creating a sense of safety in the neighborhood and the larger community. These efforts require partnerships to prevent violence. School officials and "parents on patrol" on the school grounds or in the hallways can provide highly visible supervision before and after school and during break periods. It is even better if these supervisors are committed to interacting positively with youth as they supervise. Greeting students and calling them by name helps students feel welcome and at ease at school. Keeping a close watch over student interactions and stepping in at the first sign of conflict helps prevent larger problems from developing. For example, at Whiteaker Middle School in Keizer, Oregon, the "Mom Squad" members walk the halls of the school on a regular basis. The squad is an accepted and welcomed part of the school. The parents (some dads, but mostly moms) make themselves available to answer student questions, provide directions, prevent fights, and help at different times in the school day (Oregon Department of Education, 2000). Schools can increase people's feeling of safety by providing secure campuses with a single entry through the office, using school resource officers in middle schools and high schools, and using walkie-talkies and other communications devices to alert key staff to concerns. All of these ideas facilitate student safety.

Promoting school safety and preventing school violence is the mission of a relatively new organization called the Ribbon of Promise. The day after the shooting at Thurston High School in May 1998, community leaders created Ribbon of Promise to find a way to end school violence. Shortly after its creation, students at Springfield High School formed a spin-off group, the aforementioned "By Kids 4 Kids" (or "BK4K"), under the premise that adults cannot end school violence on their own; the effort has to involve students. The students asserted that in the culture of most schools, students do not tell adults all they know about "who did what" or "who is talking about what." To impact school violence, students must break this "code of silence" and let adults know when they have information about potential violence. We have evidence that this climate is changing in Springfield. Recently, in several schools, students have reported potentially dangerous situations to adults and these were handled efficiently. In time, the students at Springfield High hope to help start "BK4K" chapters in other high schools around the country. Founders hope that these high school leaders will influence middle school and elementary school students to also "break the code of silence" and help stop violent behavior in their schools as well.

Boundaries and expectations. Both families and schools must set clear boundaries and high expectations for young people's conduct. To assist families, educators must communicate with them about their child's behavior at school.

The school is an important partner with parents in setting guidelines for young people' conduct and in providing feedback when a youngster strays from those limits. At Centennial we notify parents in a timely manner about their child's conduct infractions at school, and advise parents to counsel their youngster constructively, rather than punish him or her harshly. This helps extend the educative and formative aspects of discipline into the home. Similarly, schools that notify parents of their child's achievements at school give parents the wonderful gift of being able to praise and celebrate the youth's success.

School boundaries are established through clear rules and consequences. These are typically set through schoolwide behavior plans and communicated to students by actively teaching the desired behaviors. Young people feel safer at school when the school culture includes the well-being and consideration of others as highly visible elements. Program developers have created effective schoolwide prevention and intervention programs in recent years that have moved the discipline of behavior management from "craft knowledge" in the repertoire of the classroom teacher to systematic, schoolwide practice involving the entire school.

One example is the Effective Behavior Support program (Sugai, 1998) developed at the University of Oregon and now in use in Springfield and in dozens of schools across the country. (See Chapters 12 and 13.) Guidelines for success, which are actively taught in class, posted throughout the school, and reviewed over the intercom or at school assemblies, define a positive culture within the school. Expectations articulated for each distinct setting in the school (classrooms, hallways, cafeteria, social areas, restrooms, etc.) are explicitly taught at the beginning of the year, then reviewed as necessary. All staff in the school are trained and empowered to follow through on these standards. Schools that provide quick, fair sanctions for violating the expectations and that provide positive feedback or extra privileges for complying with them generally prove to be safe, calm learning environments.

Another determinant of healthy youth development is positive peer influence. When a young person's friends model responsible behavior, she or he is much more likely to stay on the straight and narrow path. Educators can help cultivate positive peer influence. They can do so through seating arrangements, assignment of project partners, placement in cooperative work groups, formation of teams in physical education activities, the dynamics of class meetings, and in many other ways. This is not to say that schools should determine who a youngster's friends will be, but when coupled with the skill-development components of a program such as *Second Step,* the structure of schoolwide behavior management programs, and the parameters defined by school culture and climate, schools can have a significant positive influence on peer contacts and relations.

Perhaps the most important messages parents and schools deliver are those that communicate high expectations and belief in the young person's innate goodness and ability to do well. At Centennial School, the "Greatest Kids Campaign" delivers positive messages to kids through banners, birthday cards, award certificates, and even a school song. "I believe in you." "You have what it takes." "You can do it." These messages, though brief, are powerful words to a young person, especially when coming from a parent, teacher, or other respected adult. They communicate trust, which a young person does not want to betray, and confidence, which he or she wants to show is well-placed. Whether the challenge is trying something new or taking an advanced class, trying out for a part in a play or a spot on a team, or simply getting up and getting to school on time, these words help a young person believe that success is possible. Parents and educators must communicate their belief in their children's or students' abilities, then encourage them along the way. This simple act can unleash and spark the fulfillment of human potential.

Constructive use of time. One of the recommendations of the 1997 Presidential Youth Summit was that communities provide young people with "safe places and structured activities" to help fill their time and keep them out of trouble. Similarly, the developmental assets model cites the importance of youth using their time constructively in the arts, scouts, sports, or other interest or service groups.

Youth whose parents can afford to enroll them in private lessons or structured group activities benefit from lesson time and supplemental practice time, as well as from having a peer group with a common interest. Yet many families cannot afford this expense. It is for these young people that schools and other community agencies must provide alternatives to "hanging out." Schools can collaborate with other community agencies to provide such activities, and they can extend their programs into after-school hours and summer months.

An important role schools play is to cultivate the creative and artistic dimensions of their students' lives. Often the resources for doing so are limited, but schools can collaborate with community agencies to provide such opportunities. Schools often have the space, but not the personnel to promote participation in the arts. Community individuals or organizations often have the talent, but not the space. When each party contributes to a collaborative effort, young people are the beneficiaries, receiving opportunities where none existed previously. This partnership can open up opportunities for young people to take piano lessons, play in a band or orchestra, take the stage to act, sing, or dance, or to develop their interest and potential in the visual arts.

In recent years, more schools have started or collaborated in providing after-school or summer programs for young people. Such opportunities include both academic and recreational activities. Several schools in our community now offer after-school homework clubs or subject-specific programs to build basic skills (e.g., "Power Reading," Author's Club, Math Club) or explore topics of special interest (e.g., science camp, computer club). Youth recreation programs have long been provided at Springfield school sites in cooperation with such organizations as park and recreation districts, Young Men's Christian Association (YMCA), American Youth Soccer Organization (AYSO), Babe Ruth Leagues, Boys & Girls Clubs. These programs play an important role in providing young people with "safe places and structured activities" in which to participate during times when they are out of school, while their parents are still at work.

External assets, while essential for developing positive young people, are only half of the story. It is the internal assets that form the heart of the model and contain the ingredients for forming moral character.

Building and Enhancing Internal Assets

Internal assets are those qualities that serve as an "inner compass" to guide the young person in making wise judgments and responsible choices and to show genuine caring and concern for others. These qualities can be categorized as (a) commitment to learning, (b) positive values, (c) social competencies, and (d) positive identity. These groupings are based on what helps make young people safe, self-assured, and successful.

Commitment to learning. Young people who have a high commitment to learning have achievement motivation. Doing well is important to them. They receive and do homework, and they read independently, beyond what is assigned as homework. They feel like they have an ownership stake in their school and its activities.

Where does achievement motivation come from? What leads a young person to want to do well in school? One source is the expectations that important people in the student's life hold for him or her. Following closely is the recognition that comes from doing well. Student self-direction, in the form of goal-setting and feedback, can also play a significant role in students' success.

If schools set high, but attainable, expectations for achievement, they will increase motivation to learn for many of their students. Expectations coupled with enthusiasm—and with the academic support that enables students to succeed—can help students focus on their role in achieving success. For those students who struggle to succeed, schools can create an "academic safety net" through such programs as after school homework clubs, reading development programs, and older student or adult tutors. Our school offers homework clubs in both English and Spanish. Our "Power Reading Club" is a fluency development activity offered during the school day and after school. Our literacy lab and classwide peer tutoring programs (see Chapter 24) offer supplemental support as students develop critical reading skills.

Many schools use some form of recognition for success to motivate students to do well in school. Honor rolls, awards assemblies, announcements and public posting of successes are just some of the simple but motivating ways in which schools can recognize students for their efforts and achievements. To avoid creating an "academic elite" whose members get all the recognition, it is important that schools also recognize students who are making a strong effort or showing good progress in their academic endeavors—or in other outcomes valued by the school, such as attendance, character, or community service. At Centennial, our "Triple Crown" winners are recognized for simultaneous success in attendance, character, and effort, and anyone can be a winner.

A simple tool for motivating students to succeed in school—one that has greater potential than use in schools—is the use of self-directed goal setting and feedback (see Chapter 17). Goals, when set realistically, and feedback, especially when it is either public in nature or linked to incentives, can be an inexpensive yet effective means of motivating students to work closer to their potential.

We want students to feel connected to their school and to be actively engaged in learning, but what does it take to achieve this? Perhaps the single most significant thing schools can do to help students become successful is to provide great teaching (see

Chapters 10, 21, 22, and 23). The school administrator plays a key role here through active supervision and effective staff development. High-quality instruction, especially when it connects students with issues of genuine interest to them, will engage students' learning and help them unlock the mysteries of science, see the intrigue of math, behold the fascination of literature, and discover their voice as writers.

Commitment to learning is also developed through meaningful homework. Schools that expect students to do things at home that are related to their schoolwork are more likely to produce more successful students. Perhaps the single most important type of work younger students can do outside of school is reading (Stanovich, 1986). Out-of-school reading is important for older students as well. Homework need not duplicate the activities that students do in class. It can be tied more to the applications of a particular subject to the "real world" than might be possible in the classroom. It can also integrate goals from two different subjects or address higher-level thinking— questions that require time, thought, and writing—things for which there is not always sufficient time in a time-constrained school schedule.

Commitment to learning can be enhanced further when students engage in independent reading. Schools can do much to promote independent reading by their students. They can communicate to parents the importance of having their children read. They can coordinate programs such as "TV Turn-off Week," in which people of all ages can be encouraged to turn off the television and open up a good book. They can promote reading, especially in the summer, by forming a partnership with a local public library to give kids more exposure to libraries and books. Schools can create motivation to read with reading incentive programs or by having students set reading goals and monitor their progress. They can also encourage family reading through events such as Family Reading Night at school. Such an event might include guest readers from the community, a storyteller, computer-based reading activities, a book fair and/or a book giveaway. We have used local "civic celebrities" (police officers, firefighters, a TV weather forecaster), well-known college athletes, and international students from an area university as guest readers at our Family Reading Nights.

We want kids to care about their school. This can best be accomplished by paying close attention to the culture and climate of the school. To be most effective, a school must cultivate both culture and climate. When a school culture is made to be inclusive and empowering, school climate is high, students thrive, and they feel bonded to the school. When any part of "the way things are done" diminishes students—either intentionally or unintentionally—school climate is chilled, and bonding is eroded. Schools attending to the other variables addressed in this chapter will achieve a strong culture and a positive climate. In such an environment, students will feel more connected to the school, will be less likely to get into trouble and will be more likely to succeed.

Positive values. A second category of internal assets addresses the qualities that define who students really are—the values and ethics by which they live and the character traits they demonstrate in their daily actions.

Since the early years of the 20th century, Oregon has had a law on the books requiring schools to teach character to their students. For many years in the latter half of the

20th century, promoting character was discouraged—or even resisted—by our culture. Concerns centered around whose values were to be taught, usurping the role of the family, and whether the character traits being promoted were really religion in disguise. In the last several years (seemingly since the rash of school shootings began), it has once again become "okay," or even deemed urgent, that we promote positive values and good character in schools. Several organizations offer published programs or other support for teaching character, such as Character Counts and the Character Education Partnership. Some schools have initiated grass-roots campaigns to promote character.

At Centennial Elementary School, a fifth-grade class took on the challenge of leading the schoolwide character campaign. They identified 36 common character traits and defined each of them in children's language, made posters for each trait in English and Spanish, and then hung them throughout the school. They posted them on the school's two outdoor reader boards and announced a character word of the week and its definition over the school's intercom every day. Teachers have been discussing these traits with their students, and students have talked about how they might apply the traits at school. Staff members watch for instances of students living out the traits, and they often acknowledge students' display of the traits with a certificate to the student at the school's monthly awards assemblies. We have also developed "character cards," similar to sports trading cards, which we distribute to students as collectibles. In these ways, the school is working toward embedding the traits of good character into the culture of the school.

Social competencies. Schools are social organizations. As such, there is much that can get in the way of their primary mission of educating young people. Thus, it is important for school staff to be concerned with the social competencies of their students. Schools can address students' social competencies in the areas of interpersonal competence, cultural competence, resistance skills, and peaceful conflict resolution.

One of the most highly rated programs for actively teaching the essential social competencies of empathy, problem solving, and anger management is the Second Step program (Committee for Children, 1997). In a large-scale comparison of numerous social skills programs, Second Step emerged with high ratings and earned a strong recommendation for its effectiveness and ease of use (Grossman et al., 1997). In as little time as 20-30 minutes per week, Second Step can help children learn peaceful alternatives to fighting over their differences.

Another highly effective program for helping very young antisocial children learn to be successful in school is the First Step to Success program (Kavanagh et al., 1997). Hill Walker and his associates at the University of Oregon's Institute on Violence and Destructive Behavior (IVDB) have demonstrated that by intervening with antisocial behavior in kindergarten or first-grade youngsters, school staff can divert them from a path of disruption and failure to one of cooperation and success. We have seen very positive results as a result of using the First Step to Success program at Centennial Elementary. This program is described in detail in Chapter 8.

Class meetings (Nelsen, Lott, & Glenn, 1993) or morning meetings (Kriete, 1999) offer another way in which schools can develop social competencies. They are a natural and effective means for building a sense of community and mutual support within a class, for teaching social skills among class members, for solving problems arising among class members, and for planning class events. Teachers who hold regular class meetings report that their students show enhanced social skills and improved problem-solving abilities. (See Chapters 16 and 20 for a discussion of social skills instruction in schools.)

Schools must also develop cultural competence in their students. It is important that people have knowledge of and comfort with people of different cultural, racial, and ethnic backgrounds. To lay the groundwork for young people of all backgrounds to get along well at school, staff members must establish respect as a core value of the school. More important than saying that students must respect each other is the modeling that staff members do in their interactions with colleagues and students and the extent to which they bring the concept to life in the daily interactions within the school. Many schools incorporate the Golden Rule into their basic beliefs. Our school does so through its "Guidelines for Success": "Be H.O.T. (Here on Time), Keep Your Cool, Do Your Best, Live 'The Rule' ('Treat other people as you want them to treat you.')." These statements are posted throughout the building, announced via the intercom, and ceremoniously recited at school assemblies. Once this norm is established, we use the language of the guidelines when resolving a problem that has occurred between students. In fact, the students themselves often initiate this language when working out their differences.

Some schools have established their buildings and grounds as "racism-free," "discrimination-free," or "harassment-free" zones. Typically, this is done by involving students and other members of the school community in writing a pledge or statement of intent regarding how students and staff will treat others of different backgrounds at the school. This statement is posted, announced, recited, and woven into the fabric of the school culture. Often, special events (e.g., Martin Luther King Day celebration, Women's History Month, Native American History Month, Grandparents Day, Handicap Awareness Day) are held to highlight and reinforce the school's commitment to welcoming people of all backgrounds into the school community.

Yet another social competency in the realm of schools is resistance skills, the ability to resist negative peer pressure and dangerous situations. Schools wanting to develop students' resistance to negative influences often adopt a resistance education program, such as the D.A.R.E. (Drug Abuse Resistance Education) Program, which helps students develop the knowledge and skills to say no to drugs and violence. The D.A.R.E. program uses specially trained police officers to teach students about the effects of tobacco, alcohol, and other drugs on the human body and build student skills to resist peer pressure to use these substances or to commit acts of violence related to their use. A variety of other programs use similar approaches to transmit the knowledge and skills needed to resist peer pressure. (See Chapter 26.)

Finally, it is imperative that young people learn peaceful conflict resolution. Because of the danger in the alternative, young people must learn the value of peace and must seek to resolve conflicts nonviolently.

Following school shootings in Springfield, Oregon, and Littleton, Colorado, fifth-grade students at our school decided to take matters into their own hands. They had had enough of school violence and wanted to do something to promote peace. Without any prompting from adults, students in one fifth-grade class wrote a "peace pledge," and a girl in another class created a "peace post" for the school courtyard. The "Peace Pledge" has become a central part of the school culture and is recited over the intercom by a different student each day—always in English, and periodically also in Spanish. It is also recited by the collective student body at assemblies and is posted throughout the school in both English and Spanish. The "Peace Post" is a 4 x 4" wooden post, 36" tall with a decorative top. It is painted blue, with the word "peace" painted on each of the four sides in a different language—English, Spanish, Japanese, and Hebrew. It has become a visible symbol of the school's commitment to peaceful problem solving and peaceful interaction among all members of the school community.

In the years since the Peace Project began, one student created a peace flag, and a scout troop built benches and completed landscaping around the Peace Post to create a "Peace Plaza" where students can sit to talk out problems. Recently, students with a peace project of their own at a middle school in a nearby community learned about our peace education efforts and formed a peace partnership between their school, our school, and the local middle school, which our "founders" now attend. Through their website, they hope to spread the message of peace to other schools near and far. At Centennial, the "Peace Project," the "Guidelines for Success," and a problem-solving process based on the Second Step program are taught as a common language and as common procedures—and they are observed as core elements of the school culture.

Conflict resolution programs. As noted above, many schools use specially developed programs to teach students how to resolve conflicts peacefully. One of the most effective of these is the Second Step program. (See description above.)

Positive identity. Perhaps above all else, we want young people to see themselves as positive people—to feel that they are worthwhile human beings who have a helpful role to play in the great drama of life. Schools can help develop positive self-esteem and a sense of purpose in their students.

School staff can do a great deal to build students' self-esteem. One of the most important things they can do is to structure learning to help students achieve academic success. Success produces confidence and raises self-esteem. In addition, staff can affirm students frequently. Centennial's ongoing "Greatest Kids" campaign reminds students in many ways and on many occasions that they are "some of the greatest kids on planet Earth." Through banners hung in highly visible places, and in announcements over the intercom and in conversations held with students, this idea is reinforced. Birthday cards and award certificates given to students repeat this message, as do invitations sent to parents informing them that their child will be receiving an award at the next assembly. The message helps to create a climate in which students come to believe that they can be successful in school.

Young people also need to feel that they have a positive purpose in life, that they have some measure of control in achieving their perceived purpose, and that they have some cognitive tools for achieving that purpose.

Schools are in the business of empowerment. By its nature, education is about empowering people to know or do something they did not know or could not do previously. Reading, writing, and problem solving are obvious examples, but schools must also help young people discover their interests, talents, and aptitudes and determine how best to pursue them. School staff can help young people discern their purpose by exposing them to various vocations and models and providing them with opportunities to explore those possibilities through such means as mentoring, interviews, and job shadowing. They can show students how to imagine a positive and realistic vision for the future by identifying options and weighing the pluses and minuses of each. They can teach the cognitive tools of goal setting, action planning, and goal review via traditional vocational counseling or career awareness classes, through a group support format with peers or by an individual reflective journal-keeping process. All are likely to lead to an increased awareness on the part of the student about what she or he wants to pursue and how to go about it. The key to making the process work is to empower *all* students to view themselves as capable, to have a positive purpose and some personal power to pursue it, and to see the future as having positive possibilities for them.

CONCLUSION

In this chapter we reviewed the concept of developmental assets. We identified those assets that most readily lend themselves to development in school settings and offered many illustrations of how school leaders and support staff can cultivate the formation of developmental assets.

The words of an ancient Chinese proverb still speak to those who are in a position to be asset builders for the young people of their community:

> If there is compassion in the heart, there will be love in the home.
> If there is love in the home, there will be wholeness in the community.
> If there is wholeness in the community, there will be harmony in the nation.
> And if there is harmony in the nation, there will be peace in the world.

It is extremely important that school leaders, such as administrators, school support staff, such as counselors and psychologists—and family members—work to help build developmental assets in young people. It matters less *what* they do, but it matters a great deal that they do something. Their leadership positions and their specialized knowledge and skills can have a powerful, positive impact on the safety and success of their students, on the climate of the school, and ultimately on the livability of the community.

REFERENCES

Benson, P. L., Scales, P. C., Leffert, N., & Roehlkepartain, E. C. (1999). *A fragile foundation: The state of developmental assets among American youth.* Minneapolis: Search Institute.

Committee for Children. (1997). *Second Step.* Seattle: Author.

Grossman, D., Neckerman, H., Koepsell, T., Liu, P., Asher, K., Beland, K., Frey, K., & Rivara, F. (1997). Effectiveness of a violence prevention curriculum among children in elementary school: A randomized controlled trial. *Journal of the American Medical Association, 277,* 1605-1611.

Kavanagh, K., Golly, A., Stiller, B., Walker, H., Severson, H., & Feil, E. (1997). *First step to success.* Longmont, CO: Sopris West.

Kriete, R. (1999) *The morning meeting book.* Greenfield, MA: Northeast Foundation for Children.

Nelsen, J., Lott, L., & Glenn, S. (1993). *Positive discipline in the classroom.* Rocklin, CA: Prima Publishing.

Oregon Department of Education. (2000). *Keeping kids connected: How schools and teachers can help all students feel good about school … and why that matters.* Salem, OR: Author.

Scales, P., & Leffert, N. (1999). *Developmental assets: A synthesis of the scientific research on adolescent development.* Minneapolis: Search Institute.

Search Institute. (1996). *Profiles of student life: Attitudes and behaviors.* Minneapolis: Author.

Starkman, N., Scales, P., & Roberts, C. (1999). *Great places to learn: How asset-building schools help students succeed.* Minneapolis: Search Institute.

Stanovich, K. (1986). Matthew effects in reading: Some consequences of individual differences in the acquisition of literacy. *Reading Research Quarterly, 21,* 360-406.

Sugai, G. (1998). *Effective behavior support.* Eugene, OR: Behavior Research and Teaching, College of Education, University of Oregon.

RESOURCES

For more information on the Developmental Assets Framework or the work of the Search Institute, write to 700 South Third Street, Suite 210, Minneapolis, MN 55415-1138, call (612) 376-8955 or 1-800-888-7828 or see *www.search-institute.org.*

For more information about the Second Step Program or the work of the Committee for Children, write to 2203 Airport Way South, Suite 500, Seattle, WA 98134-2027, phone 1-800-634-4449, or see *www.cfchildren.org.*

For information on the National Resource Center for Safe Schools, write to the Northwest Regional Education Laboratory at 101 SW Main Street, Suite 500, Portland, OR 97204 or see *www.nwrel.org.*

Information about the Ribbon of Promise can be found on the Web at *www.ribbonofpromise.org* or you can contact staff at 150 Seventh Street, Springfield, OR 97477. To reach them by phone, call (541) 726-0512. Their fax number is (541) 726-0393.

For more information about the work of the Institute on Violence and Destructive Behavior (IVDB) at the University of Oregon, see *www.darkwing.uoregon.edu/~ivdb.* IVDB staff may also be reached at 1265 University of Oregon, Eugene, OR 97403-1265 or at (541) 346-3592 (phone); (541) 346-2594 (fax).

APPENDIX A

The Role of Administrators, Psychologists, and Counselors in Building Developmental Assets in School Communities

Here are 10 ways that administrators and other school support staff can promote developmental assets for young people in a school setting.

1. *Adult support.* Be a source of support. Young people benefit from the support of three or more nonparent adults. Administrators, psychologists, counselors, and other school support staff can mentor young people, read to children, or just be someone to "check in" with at school.

2. *Parent involvement.* Assist parents in developing their parenting skills. Competent and caring young people have parents who are actively involved in helping them succeed in school. Some parents need assistance in learning ways to encourage, discipline, and motivate their child. School staff can provide or support parent-training opportunities within their school.

3. *Safety.* Start or join a school safety team. In order for students to be successful they must feel safe at school. Principals, psychologists, counselors, and others can be valuable assets to a team that develops policies and procedures related to school safety.

4. *School boundaries.* Be a member of a schoolwide climate team. Competent, healthy students need a school environment that provides clear rules and consequences for both positive and negative behaviors. Psychologists and counselors are trained in schoolwide and individual management/motivation techniques.

5. *School engagement.* Work with teachers and students to ensure that all young people are actively engaged in learning. School psychologists and school counselors are important members of student support teams. They can assess the level of student engagement in the classroom and work with school staff to design academic and behavior supports for needy students.

6. *Homework.* Assist families and teachers with what to do when students fall behind in their homework. Many educators believe that adolescents are more likely to learn self-discipline, gain added practice, and succeed in school when they are assigned complete homework regularly. Counselors and psychologists can help develop daily or weekly monitoring systems, assess student strengths and weaknesses, and support families through the homework years.

Appendix A continued on page 110

Appendix A continued

7. ***Positive values.*** Be a role model and instructor in positive values. Healthy and caring young people show integrity, honesty, responsibility, and restraint in their daily lives. Counselors and psychologists can provide classroom or small group lessons that reinforce these values.

8. ***Planning and decision making.*** Teach students how to make decisions and choices. Competent young people know how to plan ahead and make choices. Model and instruct responsible decision making in daily interactions with students.

9. ***Resistance skills.*** Support school programs that teach young people resistance skills. Healthy adolescents are able to resist negative peer pressure and dangerous situations. Counselors and psychologists can support classroom or individual programs that teach these skills.

10. ***Peaceful conflict resolution.*** Be a mediator. Competent young people seek nonviolent ways to resolve conflict. Teach students the skills of negotiation, mediation, problem solving, and seeking alternative solutions to violence in their daily lives.

APPENDIX B

Ten Things Kids Can Do to Stop Violence

(This reproducible fact sheet was provided by the Connecticut Clearinghouse, a program of Wheeler Clinic, Inc., which is funded by the Department of Mental Health and Addiction Services. Found in *Peaceful Schools,* October 1998.

1. Settle arguments with words, not fists or weapons. Don't stand around and form an audience when others are arguing. A group makes a good target for violence.

2. Learn safe routes for walking in the neighborhood, and know good places to seek help.

3. Report any crimes or suspicious actions to the police, school authorities, and parents.

4. Don't open the door to anyone you don't know and trust.

5. Never go anywhere with someone you don't know and trust.

6. If someone tries to abuse you, say no, get away, and tell a trusted adult. Trust feelings, and if you sense danger, get away fast. Remember: Violence is not the victim's fault.

7. Don't use alcohol or other drugs, and stay away from places and people associated with them.

8. Stick with friends who are also against violence and drugs, and stay away from known trouble spots.

9. Get involved to make school safer and better. Hold rallies, counsel peers, settle disputes peacefully. If there's no program, help start one.

10. Help younger children learn to avoid being crime victims. Set a good example, and volunteer to help with community efforts to stop crime and prevent violence.

CHAPTER 6

Using Curriculum-Based Measurement in General Education Classrooms to Promote Reading Success

Mark R. Shinn, Michelle M. Shinn,
Chad Hamilton, and Ben Clarke
University of Oregon

INTRODUCTION

Improving the reading achievement of American school children has been a high priority goal at the local, state, and national levels since the release of *Becoming a Nation of Readers* (National Institute of Education, Commission on Reading, 1985) nearly two decades ago. Although concerns about literacy are longstanding in this country, each year it seems that (a) the problem grows more severe, and (b) the actions taken to attempt to improve literacy rates come from outside the field of education—they are high stakes in nature and potentially punitive of students, teachers, and schools alike. The solutions to the problem of literacy appear to be characterized by the use of high-stakes tests of reading at key points in time *after* students are expected to learn and demonstrate the skills tested. Students who pass these high-stakes tests can move to the next grade. Students who do not pass are proposed for retention and/or summer school.

This high-stakes testing approach that occurs after instruction is *summative evaluation*. To be certain, summative evaluation has an important role to play in improving achievement outcomes for many students, teachers, and schools. Most notably, it provides motivation for students and teachers alike to do their best work. Unfortunately, for many teachers and students, the disadvantages of summative evaluation may outweigh its benefits. In brief, summative evaluation may be too much, too late. That is, many students are tested *long after* (3–4 years) they have established a pattern of reading failure, while little systematic reading intervention has occurred to help remediate their reading difficulties. After they fail the high-stakes test(s), the students, their teachers, and their parents will be blamed.

This chapter will suggest a different assessment approach that compliments current high-stakes reading summative evaluation. The chapter will describe the use of Curriculum-Based Measurement of reading (R-CBM)—short, accurate, and easy-to-administer reading tests that can be used *formatively* throughout students' elementary education programs to help teachers and parents decide how students are progressing *during* instruction. With a lengthy and successful history of use as a formative evaluation tool with students with disabilities for writing annual Individualized Educational Program (IEP) goals and monitoring progress, R–CBM can be modified for feasibility in general education classes to help teachers identify students at risk for reading difficulty, plan initial instruction, and monitor student progress so that effective reading programs can be continued and ineffective programs changed as soon as possible.

THE NATURE OF READING AND LITERACY PROBLEMS

By now most school psychologists and educators are well aware of the state of reading skills in the United States. Statistics and task force reports abound describing the range of reading skills in the country and the difficulties with text faced by millions of Americans each day. For example, in 1993, the U.S. Department of Education conducted the National Adult Literacy Survey (NALS) to assess literacy levels in the United States. To date, the NALS is the best survey that exists about adult literacy rates in the country and is expected to be repeated in 2002. The NALS divided the U.S. population into five levels of competency with respect to reading. Results indicated that approximately 40 million U.S. citizens (21 to 23% of the adult population) would score in the *lowest* level of the test (Level 1) and another 25 to 30% of the adult population would score at Level 2. The report concluded that these 50 million adults in the two lowest levels of the NALS (U.S. Department of Education, 1993) were reading at or below a fifth-grade level, placing them at an extreme disadvantage to compete for economic success in today's marketplace.

The consequences of illiteracy can be seen directly in rates of poverty, welfare, and employment, in annual income, and in prison populations. On the NALS, 43% of Level 1 adults were living in poverty, compared to only 4% of those at Level 5. Three out of four food stamp recipients performed at Levels 1 and 2. Level 1 adults earned a median income of $240 per week and worked an average of 19 weeks per year, compared to a median income of $681 and 44 weeks per year worked for those at Level 5. Seven in 10 prisoners performed in the two lowest levels (National Institute for Literacy, 1999).

High-Stakes, Summative Evaluation of High Standards as a Solution

The national response to the problems of literacy and other academic concerns has been the explicit creation of (a) *high academic standards* to which students (and schools) will be held, and (b) the use of high-stakes achievement tests to *ensure* that the standards are being attained. Few educators and parents would argue with the idea of having high standards and holding students and schools to them. Unfortunately, as we said earlier, this high-stakes, summative approach may not work for many students.

For example, in 1993 as part of its Educational Reform Law, the state of Massachusetts set forth the task of specifying its high academic learning standards for students, schools, and school districts. The product was a set of standards entitled the *Curriculum Frameworks.* The state then developed the Massachusetts Comprehensive Assessment System (MCAS) to serve as a statewide tool to measure attainment of its high standards at Grades 4, 8, and 10. The state also set forth the condition that students are to have attained the standards assessed on the Grade 10 MCAS as one of the requirements for graduation.

Reading is assessed on the MCAS as part of its English Language Arts battery. Unfortunately, in the 3 years of reported results (Massachusetts Department of Education, 2001), few students demonstrated proficiency. Grade 4 students performing at the "Proficient" level or above were only 20%, 21%, and 20% for 1998, 1999, and 2000, respectively. Students in the "Needs Improvement" or "Failing" categories were 81%, 79%, and 80%, respectively. At Grade 10, similar low patterns of success and high frequencies of failure also were reported. "Proficiency or Above" percentages ranged from 34% to 38% with the highest percentage attained in 1998. Grade 10 failure rates ranged from 28% to 34%. If indeed meeting the high standards as measured by the Grade 10 MCAS were "enforced" as part of graduation requirements, the stakes currently would be too high for many students.

Similarly, the state of Minnesota requires that students pass a Grade 8 basic reading standards test in order to receive their high school degree. The latest reported results (Minnesota Department of Children, Families, and Learning, 2000) showed a more positive picture than the Massachusetts high-stakes testing results. Three out of every four Grade 8 students tested statewide met the standard. Of course, this meant also that one in four students failed to do so. The failure rates were very different among students from minority backgrounds and from low-income environments. More than half (61%) of eighth-grade African-American students did not attain the standards. About half (47%) of the students eligible for free/reduced-price meals also did not meet the standards.

Students alone do not face the consequences of failing to attain high standards and pass high-stakes tests—individual schools and school districts are affected as well. For example, in July 2001, schools in Colorado entered the first cycle of a school and school district accreditation process (Colorado Department of Education, 2001). To attain the status of an accredited school, one of the academic indicators is that either (a) 80% of Grade 3 students read at the "Proficient" or "Advanced" level, or (b) over a 3-year period, there is a 25% improvement over baseline in the percentage of students reading at the Proficient or Advanced level, and a 25% decrease in the number of students not on grade level. The attainment levels are determined by performance on the Colorado State Assessment of Performance (CSAP) and other third-grade literacy tests (e.g., district-developed tests).

Failure to meet these criteria results in a school or district being placed on "Academic Watch" and an approved school improvement plan being developed. If after 1 year on academic watch, failure to achieve the state standards or school improvement plan goals results in the school's being placed on "Academic Probation." Another year of failure to achieve standards results in the school/district not being accredited.

At Its Best, Summative Evaluation Is Still Not Enough

Summative evaluation, when conducted properly with valid measures, and when used to improve motivation and systemic instructional practices (e.g., curriculum choices), has the potential to improve student achievement. However, it remains to be seen whether the large-scale, high-stakes testing programs currently in use will have a significant, positive impact on the instructional practices of teachers, and consequently, the problem of illiteracy. Certainly if the emphasis remains principally on accountability, we believe we will continue to witness more of the disadvantages of high-stakes testing rather than its advantages.

Foremost among these disadvantages is summative evaluation's inability to "inform teaching" (Howell & Nolet, 1999). Assessment that informs teaching has three main objectives: (a) to identify at-risk students, (b) to help plan instruction by figuring out what needs to be taught and how to teach it, and (c) to be used in formative evaluation. Although the first two objectives are important to accomplish in improving achievement outcomes, it is this last objective, *to be used in formative evaluation,* that is of importance to teachers and parents.

Contributions of Formative Evaluation to Achieving High Standards

As stated earlier, formative evaluation is the process of assessing student achievement during instruction for the purposes of determining whether an instructional program is effective for a given individual. Effective instructional programs are sustained while ineffective instructional programs are modified in meaningful ways. Formative evaluation, then, is about measuring student growth over time; in particular, it is about measuring student growth over a *short* period such as weeks or months.

Formative evaluation is consistent with the idea of teaching and learning as a *dynamic activity;* that is, by the interaction of factors of teaching and curriculum, and student and teacher, learning or growth occurs. Formative evaluation also is consistent with the idea that the growth produced by a special combination of factors for a given individual is not necessarily the same for another. Too many instructional programs are predicated on a belief that "one size fits all," that the same combination of instructional and curricular variables will produce attainment of the same, and high, standards for all students.

Most important, the use of formative evaluation has been linked to important gains in student achievement. As described in more detail in the chapter by Deno, Espin, and Fuchs in this volume, and by a meta-analysis by L. S. Fuchs and D. Fuchs (1986), effect sizes of .5 and greater have been demonstrated when formative evaluation strategies are used in teacher decision making.

In a recent article comparing three formative methods of monitoring student reading progress, L. S. Fuchs and D. Fuchs (1999) specified six features of quality formative evaluation systems: (a) technical adequacy, (b) the capacity to model growth, (c) treatment sensitivity, (d) an independence from specific instructional techniques, (e) the capacity to inform teaching, and (f) feasibility. Of course, it seems obvious that to make accurate and valid decisions about student reading growth, the source of the data used to make the decisions needs to be technically adequate. That is, the measures must meet professional standards for reliability and validity. In the field of education, there are a number of technically adequate measures of reading achievement. Too often, these measures fail to consider L. S. Fuchs, and D. Fuchs other criteria.

The capacity to model growth, or to visually represent the "developmental reading trajectory" (Stanovich, 2000) of students, is one such criterion. To be able to accomplish this aim, it must be possible to assess student growth *continuously* with measures that avoid both floor and ceiling effects and offer parallel forms of equal difficulty.

Relatedly, reading measures must be *treatment sensitive*. Much like the use of a weight scale to evaluate the effects of a specific diet (i.e., loss or gain of pounds), performance or scores on the formative measure must change when reading skills change. If in fact there is no change in reading scores over time, it is important to be able to attribute that lack of change to no change in reading skills rather than the inability of the measure to "detect" the change.

Although some commercial reading programs include their own measures of progress, good formative evaluation measures should be *instructionally eclectic*. That is, the measure(s) should be able to demonstrate growth in reading skills, not just on the specific skills or subskills taught by specific curricula. Again, going back to the example of the weight scale, that tool is instructionally or treatment eclectic. It matters not which specific diet one is on. The weight scale can be used to evaluate *any* diet and is not tied to a belief that it is important to do just one particular diet. This instructional eclecticism facilitates teachers, making intervention changes *between* curricula as one way of modifying ineffective reading interventions for individual students. More detail is provided on this topic in the chapter by Deno, Espin, and Fuchs (this volume) and numerous other sources (e.g., L. S. Fuchs & Deno, 1991).

L. S. Fuchs and D. Fuchs (1999) also list a formative measure's *capacity to inform teaching* as a critical feature of a good formative evaluation system. This criterion implies that a formative evaluation measure should, in some way, not just signal that a reading program is working for an individual student (i.e., a "when" to change decision) but also should provide teachers with ideas as to what specific aspects of the reading program may need modification (i.e., that the measure suggests "what" to change). It is important to note the tension inherent among the other criteria and the capacity to inform teaching. For example, the *more* instructionally eclectic the formative evaluation measure, the *less* likely it may be able to inform teaching. Similarly, the greater the ability of the formative measure to model growth, the less likely it may be able to inform teaching.

Finally, L. S. Fuchs and D. Fuchs (1999) include *feasibility* as a critical feature of a good formative evaluation system. Needless to say, the best-designed formative evaluation system will not be used if it is not "doable." Among the issues that affect feasibility are the time it takes to test, score, and interpret student performance outcomes; the necessity of test construction skills; and the availability and cost of multiple forms.

CURRICULUM-BASED MEASUREMENT AS A VIABLE FORMATIVE EVALUATION SYSTEM FOR GENERAL EDUCATION

School systems need not invent or construct a formative evaluation system—nor must they undertake a massive program of research to develop assessment technology that meets the criteria set forth by L. S. Fuchs and D. Fuchs (1999). Curriculum-Based Measurement (CBM; Deno, 1985, 1986, 1989; L. S. Fuchs, 1994; Shinn, 1989, 1998; Shinn, Deno, & Fuchs, in press) has been in use for more than two decades as a tool to assess the growth of students with disabilities' basic skills and the effectiveness of their special education instructional programs. Building on this background of special education implementation, CBM increasingly has been used as a formative evaluation tool for other remedial programs such as Title I (L. S. Fuchs, D. Fuchs, Hamlett, & Ferguson, 1992) and as a general outcome indicator in general education classrooms (L. S. Fuchs & D. Fuchs, 1992; L. S. Fuchs, D. Fuchs, Hamlett, Walz, & Germann, 1993).

CBM is characterized by a set of five types of tests in the basic skill areas. In reading, the primary test (Reading-CBM or R-CBM) requires students to read connected text from their general education curriculum aloud for 1 minute and the number of words read correctly are counted. Students are tested individually. Alternately, Maze-CBM (L. S. Fuchs & D. Fuchs, 1992) has been used, typically with students at the intermediate grades. Maze-CBM requires students to read connected text silently and select one of three or four words that preserves meaning when every seventh word is replaced with a blank. For more information on the other CBM tests in the areas of spelling, written expression, and mathematics computation, see Marston (1989) or Shinn (1998).

CBM is capable of being used in formative evaluation and to inform teaching because it meets the standards set forth by L. S. Fuchs and D. Fuchs (1999). In Table 1, a sampling of research-based articles and chapters supporting each of their six criteria is presented.

Typical Special Education Practices Using CBM

When CBM has been used in formative evaluation with students with disabilities, the goals that are set and the strategies for monitoring progress are tied to students' Individualized Educational Programs (IEPs). More specifically, formative evaluation is tied to the annual goal of a student's IEP. For example, an annual IEP goal for Carlos, a fourth-grade student may be as follows:

> In 1 year, when given a randomly sampled passage from the third-grade
> HBJ series, Carlos will read 125 words correctly with 4 or fewer errors.

This annual goal is written based on Carlos' current performance in general education curriculum and is predicated on ambitious but attainable goals. For more detail on how CBM is used to write IEP goals, see L. S. Fuchs and Shinn (1989), Deno, Mirkin, and Wesson (1984), and M. R. Shinn and M. M. Shinn (2001). For formative evaluation

TABLE 1

A Sample of References on CBM Addressing the Critical Features of a Good Formative Evaluation System Presented by L. S. Fuchs and D. Fuchs (1999)

Formative Evaluation Feature	Sample References
Technical Adequacy	Deno, Mirkin, & Chiang, 1982
	L. S. Fuchs, D. Fuchs, & Maxwell, 1988
	Marston, 1989
	Shinn, Good, Knutson, Tilly, & Collins, 1992
Capacity to Model Growth	Deno, 1985
	L. S. Fuchs et al., 1993
	Marston, Lowry, Deno, & Mirkin, 1981
	Marston & Magnusson, 1985
Treatment Sensitivity	Marston, 1988
	Shinn, Good, & Stein, 1989
	Skiba, Deno, Marston, & Wesson, 1986
Instructionally Eclectic	L. S. Fuchs & Deno, 1992
	Hintze, Shapiro, & Luntz, 1994
Capacity to Inform Teaching	L. S. Fuchs, 1994
	L. S. Fuchs, D. Fuchs, & Hamlett, 1994
	Wesson, 1992
Feasibility	L. S. Fuchs, 1998
	Wesson, 1987

purposes, then, typically once or twice per week, Carlos would be tested using R–CBM by having him read a randomly selected passage from the third-grade level of his general education curriculum (Harcourt Brace Jovanovich; HBJ). The number of words read correctly would be counted and each test result would be graphed. When approximately 10 data points are obtained, it would be possible to make a judgment of Carlos' rate of progress toward his IEP annual goal. Should his rate of progress be satisfactory, his reading program would continue unmodified or perhaps his IEP goal might be raised. Should his rate of progress be unsatisfactory, his reading program would be changed in a meaningful way.

Because IEP goals are individualized, no two special education students typically have the same annual goal. Two special education students who chronologically are in the same grade (e.g., Grade 4) may have very different IEP goals. For example, whereas Carlos was expected to read 125 words correctly in 1 year, another Grade 4 student with a more severe reading performance discrepancy may be expected to read 100 words correctly per minute from the *second-grade* material in 1 year.

Because this individualized approach to formative evaluation is tied to the IEP, special education teachers must know each student's IEP goals and match their assessment materials to that goal in order to evaluate student progress properly. In addition, the special education teacher is making a commitment to collect frequent data so that decisions about student progress and IEP revisions can be made as timely as possible. Clearly, this special education commitment to formative evaluation is not trivial, but as evidenced, it certainly is important to meet the legal requirements of the Individuals with Disabilities Education Act Amendments of 1997 (IDEA '97) and to impact student achievement outcomes.

Making Use of R-CBM in General Education Feasible

In special education, issues of feasibility are less of a concern because of the legal demands for frequent progress monitoring toward individualized annual IEP goals and reporting to parents (M. R. Shinn & M. M. Shinn, 2001), and because there is an established body of knowledge as to how this formative evaluation strategy contributes to improved achievement outcomes of students with disabilities. Feasibility is enhanced by generally smaller class sizes and more personnel resources, including trained aides, than in general education. In general education, currently, there is little or no *legal mandate* for formative evaluation. Class size is larger and there are fewer personnel resources. Therefore, if R-CBM is to be used feasibly in general education classrooms, changes must be made to enable teachers to make data-based decisions about students' instructional needs and the effectiveness of their reading programs.

One of the changes to increase feasibility in general education is to use *uniform* rather than individualized R-CBM testing materials by grade. That is, when general education students are tested, they typically all read the *same* randomly selected passages from the same grade-level reader or materials that would serve as the primary instructional material for the academic year. For example, all third-graders may be tested using the 3.2 reading book in the reading series.

A second way that feasibility can be increased is to reduce the individuality of the annual goals. Unlike the use of R-CBM in special education, annual goals typically are less individualized. Using a third-grade student as an example, the annual goal may be twofold: (a) to make the same rate of progress as other third-grade students, and (b) maintain the student's "status" (e.g., be an average reader) relative to other same-grade students in that school. These two standards will be illustrated later in this chapter.

Although it would be nice to be able to have highly individualized goals and a corresponding commitment to using tailored R-CBM material for many students, feasibility would suffer. For each student in the classroom, the teacher would have to engage in individualized goal–setting activities (see L. S. Fuchs & Shinn, 19ξ

mation), and would have to keep track of which students are being testec

materials at which time.

A third way to make using R–CBM more feasible in general education is to ̲ ̲ct information *less frequently*. Again, it would be desirable to collect R–CBM information on individual students as frequently as has been shown to result in increased achievement in students with disabilities (e.g., testing on 1-2 passages per week). However, owing to the large numbers of students in general education classrooms and the limited resource support for testing individual students weekly, some trade-offs in progress monitoring frequency must be considered. As will be seen later in the chapter, the use of R–CBM in general education classrooms reduces testing to as few as between 3 and 9-10 times per year rather than a minimum of 30-36 testing times.

A fourth and final way to make the use of R–CBM in general education feasible is to change the nature of the task from one that requires students to be tested individually (i.e., measuring oral reading fluency on connected text) to one that can be group administered (e.g., a maze). L. S. Fuchs and D. Fuchs (1992) have demonstrated that a group-administered *maze task* (CBM-Maze) can serve some of the same purposes in teacher decision making, especially with respect to formative evaluation. However, the CBM-Maze task is difficult for students in the primary grades and is less effective at identifying students at risk. Finally, CBM-Maze is less sensitive to growth than the R–CBM task. For example, when students receive standard reading instruction (i.e., no special accommodations of materials, time, or techniques), they would be expected to improve an average of 1.5 words read correctly per week in Grade 2 on a R–CBM task, or about 6 words read correctly per month (L. S. Fuchs et al., 1993). In contrast, Grade 2 students would be expected to improve .39 words correctly on a CBM-Maze task per week or about 1.6 words correct per month. Only at Grade 5 are the weekly slopes of improvement equivalent for both types of CBM tasks.

In summary, although we would prefer it, we do not see the use of R–CBM the same way as it is used in special education to be feasible in general education without a considerable investment in personnel and time resources. CBM-Maze is a tool worth considering, especially for the older grades where sensitivity to reading improvement is roughly the same. It should be noted that using a group-administered CBM-Maze task comes at a loss of utility in instructional planning as teachers do not have the opportunity to "see" each individual read from their instructional materials. Additionally, the decreased sensitivity may mean that students at risk for reading failure may be detected later in their educational careers and decisions regarding rates of progress may be less timely.

Using R-CBM in General Education Classrooms: Basic Approaches

The primary purpose of using R–CBM in general education is to promote successful reading outcomes for all students by working in a *preventive* manner. That is, *all* students are tested at the beginning of the school year in an *Initial Planning Assessment* (IPA), and on a regular basis (e.g., every month, every 3 months) thereafter. Typically, the target grades are students in Grades 1 through 5. However, both Grades 1 and 5 have to consider special accommodations to what we consider "standard practice" because of potential floor effects at Grade 1 (i.e., when large numbers of students enter school not reading connected text) and potential ceiling effects at Grade 5 (i.e., students who read so well that they are using reading as a tool to learn versus learning to read). Additionally, R–CBM may be used for general education purposes in middle schools. These special accommodations will be discussed later in the chapter.

Each time general education students are tested, multiple samples of student reading performance are collected at a single testing. Because data are collected less frequently in general education use, it is extremely important that high quality (e.g., highly reliable) data be collected on those testing occasions. Usually three randomly sampled passages are sufficient for reliable decision making as this controls for the variability in difficulty among the passages (L. S. Fuchs, Tindal, & Deno, 1984). With trained personnel collecting the R–CBM data, the testing process takes approximately 5 minutes per student.

The Initial Planning Assessment (IPA) is done for three major purposes: (a) identifying as early as possible those *students at risk* for reading failure or whose skill discrepancies may require an immediate accommodation to the standard reading program in their class or school, (b) *teacher planning* so that reading instruction can be designed to match the needs of diverse groups of students, and (c) *establishing a current level of reading skill* so that an individual student's progress can be evaluated later to judge the effectiveness of the reading program. Subsequent follow-up testing for progress monitoring falls into two general approaches, *Benchmark Testing,* and *Strategic Monitoring.* These two approaches differ in the frequency with which student reading progress information is assessed throughout the school year.

In Benchmark Testing, R–CBM student progress data are collected at key intervals during the school year based on the school calendar or grading period. Most often, Benchmark Testing is completed on a trimester basis with time frames of early in the academic year (e.g., September), mid-year (e.g., early January), and a period of time 4–6 weeks before the end of the academic year (e.g., from the last week of April through early May). Other schools collect IPA and R–CBM progress monitoring data on a quarterly basis. When schools commit to a Benchmark Testing approach for assessing the growth and development of their students' reading skills, they are making a 15-minute-per-student commitment on an annual basis for initial planning and progress monitoring.

On other occasions, and in what we consider "best practices" for the primary grades, Strategic Monitoring is used. This approach is based on the need for more frequent data to ensure reading growth for emerging readers than Benchmark Testing and usually is operationalized as collecting R–CBM data *monthly.* This time commitment translates into approximately 40 to 45 minutes per year per student.

Initial Planning Assessment (IPA)

Regardless of the choice of progress monitoring approach, promoting positive reading development using R–CBM begins with an *Initial Planning Assessment* (IPA) at the beginning of the school year to help teachers (a) identify at-risk students and (b) assist in the initial stages of instructional planning. A critical use of this beginning-of-the-year testing via the IPA is to assist general education teachers in identifying students who may be at risk for reading failure, or those students whose skill deficits are so severe that some immediate modifications or problem solving around reading instruction must be considered. This same IPA information also assists teachers in making decisions about instructional planning (e.g., which books are suitable for which students, forming instructional groups) and as a beginning point for subsequent progress monitoring.

An IPA begins by having all students read three randomly selected passages from their general education reading materials for 1 minute. The number of words read correctly (WRC) is calculated for each passage and the median WRC for each student is used to summarize performance. Dropping the low and high score helps minimize the effects of the variability in reading-passage difficulty (Tilly, Shinn, & Good, in press). A simple way the results from the IPA can be summarized for individual teachers is in a class roster format where student scores are sorted from highest to lowest words read correctly and displayed in a table (Figure 1).

FIGURE 1

IPA Results for Mrs. Grady's Grade 3 Class in a Roster Format

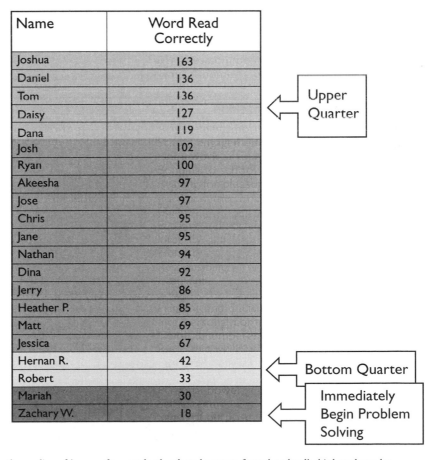

Name	Word Read Correctly	
Joshua	163	
Daniel	136	
Tom	136	Upper Quarter
Daisy	127	
Dana	119	
Josh	102	
Ryan	100	
Akeesha	97	
Jose	97	
Chris	95	
Jane	95	
Nathan	94	
Dina	92	
Jerry	86	
Heather P.	85	
Matt	69	
Jessica	67	
Hernan R.	42	Bottom Quarter
Robert	33	
Mariah	30	Immediately Begin Problem Solving
Zachary W.	18	

Note
Individual scores are the median of 3 scores from randomly selected passages from the school's third-grade reader.

FIGURE 2A

Ranges of Scores for Fall Initial Planning Assessment for Grade 3 Students at Wilson School

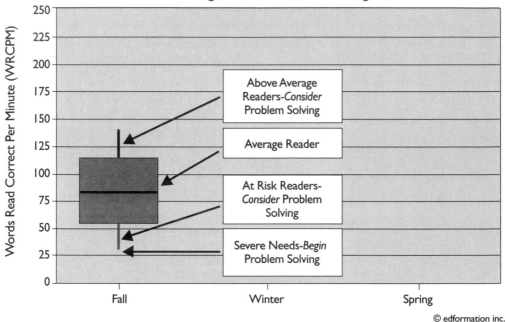

Hartford School District - Wilson Elementary
Reading - Standard Benchmark Passages

© edformation inc.

These rank-ordered rosters provide teachers with a general idea of the range of scores within a classroom, and can assist in decision making about individual students. We believe, however, that providing teachers with class roster information *alone* is not sufficient for good decision making and that teacher decision making is enhanced by providing a graph with key decision-making points identified. See for example, Figure 2A.

Identifying at-risk students or those in need of immediate problem-solving activities. Getting all students off to a good start begins with identifying the students for whom the "standard" reading program may not produce the desired outcomes. Identification early in the academic year allows teachers to plan and implement alternative reading interventions to enhance rates of reading progress. For students sufficiently discrepant in their reading skills, teachers may seek immediate assistance from problem-solving teams to consider more intensive intervention(s) such as Title I or other remedial programs.

In identifying at-risk students, there are no empirically validated standards, when using R-CBM or any other test. These standards typically are derived rationally and based on value judgments (Deno, 1989) of the persons in the school buildings or districts. For example, is *considering* students in the lowest quarter (below the 25th percentile) too high or too low a standard? Is identifying students who read at one-half the performance level of typical students sufficient for good problem-solving activities that will improve reading outcomes? We believe that these are important questions for schools, districts, teachers, and administrators to discuss to be able to meet the needs of their students. In this chapter, we will present some examples of standards that have been employed to try to improve general education reading achievement.

Identification of at-risk or significantly discrepant students can take place at two levels, within the class or within the grade. At the classroom level, teachers could identify students from their own class roster who are performing at the bottom quarter (i.e., below the 25th percentile) in the class. In Figure 1, on page 123, for example, in Mrs. G's third-grade class of 21 students, R-CBM scores range from a high score of 163 to a low score of 18 WRC with a median score of 85. The shaded areas at the bottom of the roster indicate four students who may be at risk for reading failure. It is important to note the use of the words "may be at risk." Other factors such as motivation, rapport, behavior, and health should be considered at this point. These four students also may be tested again to cross-validate the initial IPA. If the R-CBM results are accurate, at least one of the students, Zachary W., should be considered for more intensive problem solving. His reading skills are clearly the lowest and may require additional resources beyond what his classroom teacher may provide.

Identifying at-risk students or those in need of immediate problem-solving activities should not occur solely at the classroom level. Combining all the IPA information across same-grade classrooms can assist building-level teams engage in more *systematic* identification of at-risk students and those in need of immediate problem solving. By examining the instructional needs of individual students across classrooms within a grade, teams may be able to pool resources, ideas, and strategies to improve outcomes. This approach takes the sole responsibility of having to develop individual, doable, and effective solutions for each student's reading discrepancy out of the classroom teachers' hands and can allow for broader instructional decision making and interventions at the building level.

When identifying students who are at risk or in need of immediate problem solving by grade, again values-based standards need to be specified. In this school, performance of students below the 25th percentile at their grade was used to identify them as potentially at risk. Students who score below the 10th percentile may be considered in need of immediate problem solving.

Making these decisions is enhanced by giving each teacher a master graph representing the results of the grade-level IPA with key decision-making indicators specified. An example is Figure 2A, on page 124, which includes both *quantitative* (i.e., percentile rank) and *qualitative* information (i.e., reading performance "status"). The various shaded areas in Figure 2A correspond to the critical decision-making points in reading performance for all third-grade classrooms in the school, and critical percentile rank points (10th, 25th, 50th, 75th, and 90th) for decision making are labeled. The graph highlights the ranges of scores that serve as qualitative "status" descriptors. For example, in this instance, a score of reading fewer than 55 WRC, equivalent to the 25th percentile, would suggest a student being "at risk" for progressing in reading. Scores above 115 WRC (the 75th percentile) would describe the student as being "above average." As part of IPA decision making, general education teachers are instructed to plot an individual's score on WRC on a copy of the master graph and make a status decision.

FIGURE 2B

Identifying Three Third-Grade Students' Reading Status from a Fall Initial Planning Assessment at Wilson school

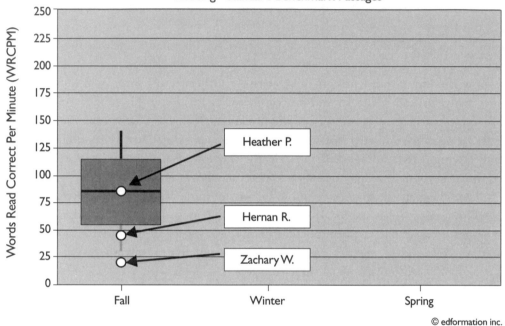

For example, the results of an IPA for three of Mrs. G's students, Heather, Hernan, and Zachary, would be plotted on individual graphs—although they are combined to save space, in Figure 2B—and a decision about each student's current reading status would be made.

Heather's IPA score of 85 WRC places her at the 50th percentile and therefore she would be considered an average third-grade reader in this school. No obvious need for modifying her *current* reading program exists. However, Hernan's and Zachary's IPA scores are below the 25th percentile when compared to other third-graders. Performance in this range suggests that both students be considered at risk for reading failure and that proactive modifications or enhancements of their read program be considered. Furthermore, Zachary's score of 18 WRC places him well below the 10th percentile, indicating a more serious problem and perhaps the need for convening a team to commence planning a more intensive and individualized reading program.

Instructional planning. In addition to identifying at-risk students, IPA results can be used as a starting point for *instructional planning*. Among the important instructional decisions for which the IPA information can be used is matching students to reading materials of *suitable difficulty*. Suitable difficulty is defined broadly as the level at which the textbook or other reading material is not too difficult to decode or understand, and at the same time not so easy that it does not provide challenging practice (Taylor, Harris, & Pearson, 1988). Material that is too difficult is considered *frustrational*-level material; material that is too easy is considered *independent*-level material (Gickling & Armstrong, 1978). *Instructional* reading level is considered to be the most difficult level of material a student can handle with assistance from a teacher (Taylor et al., 1988). The placement of students in instructional material that is too difficult has been associated with differences in instructional quality provided to those students (Allington, 1983; Berliner, 1981) and students' sense of failure (Bristow, 1985), with resulting lower reading success rates.

Therefore, to increase the likelihood of students' reading success, it seems important to be able to match current reading skills with material suitable for reading instruction. At the least, avoiding placing students in material that is at the frustrational level is highly desirable. Despite this preference, determining a suitable instructional reading level has remained an inexact procedure (Taylor et al., 1988), with no consensus on methods or standards (Kender, 1969). In fact, in recent years, this instructional variable has all but been ignored in general education and students have been placed in reading materials solely at their grade placement, regardless of their success.

The IPA data derived with R–CBM can assist in selecting suitable reading instructional materials by considering the placement standards suggested by L. S. Fuchs and Deno (1982). Their criteria suggest that suitable instructional reading material is the highest level in the curriculum at which a student reading first- or second-grade material reads at 40-60 WRC with 4 or fewer errors or 70-100 WRC with 6 or fewer errors for third- through sixth-grade material. These criteria are considered *minimum* and assume that the reading instructional program places considerable importance on *teacher-led instruction*. Should the instructional program rely primarily on student-directed instruction (e.g., sustained silent reading), student reading performance must be even higher (i.e., at the independent level).

To illustrate, in Mrs. Grady's third-grade classroom, each student's IPA score was plotted on a graph of the recommended minimum instructional placement standards, a sample of which is shown in Figure 3A, on page 128.

In looking at Robert's IPA results, shown in Figure 3B, on page 128, his score of 33 WRC on passages from the third-grade reader is clearly outside the standards. This material may be too difficult for him to make adequate progress in reading. In contrast, this material may be too easy for Joshua, who read 163 WRC from these same passages. For Akeesha, whose IPA score was 97 WRC, this reading material may be suitable, assuming that teacher-led instruction is a key component of the reading program. Finally, for those students for whom the material is too difficult or too easy, teachers may do follow-up testing using R–CBM in a process called Survey-Level Assessment (SLA). The process of SLA requires that students be tested individually reading passages from curriculum levels of reading materials that are easier (i.e., lower in the scope and sequence) or more difficult until suitable materials are identified. For more detail on SLA, see L. S. Fuchs and Shinn (1989) or Shinn and Hubbard (1992).

FIGURE 3A

Graph of Instructional Placement Standards for Instructional Planning

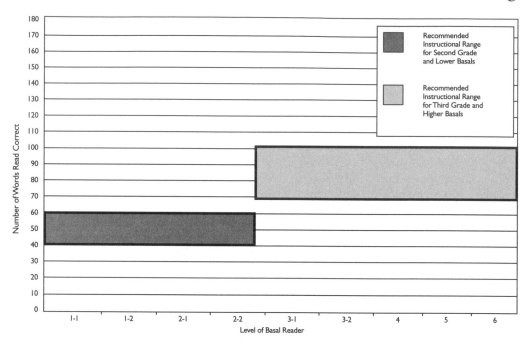

FIGURE 3B

Graph of Instructional Placement Standards for Instructional Planning

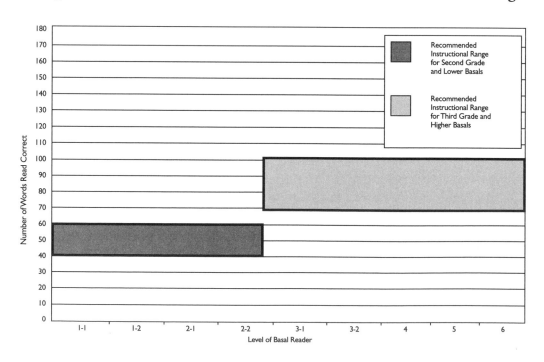

The same IPA information can be used to help teachers form their instructional groups (Wesson, 1992). Using the minimum third-grade instructional placement standards of reading 70–100 WRC with 6 for fewer errors, Mrs. Grady would look for students whose reading skills are similar, beginning with those students who perform in this range. In examining Figure 4, it appears that 12 students meet the criterion for WRC. These students could constitute a middle reading group and the third-grade book would be used. Five students perform well above this criterion, and at least one, Joshua, reads much better than the other four. At the least, Dana, Daisy, Tom, and Daniel could be formed into a reading group but more challenging instructional materials may need to be identified using SLA. Four of the students in Mrs. Grady's classroom read well below the minimum criterion of 70–100 WRC. Three of these students may be grouped together in a low reading group where easier materials would be used. Again, these materials would be identified using SLA procedures. As mentioned earlier, Zachary's reading skills seem significantly different and lower than other students' and more intensive instructional planning may be needed.

FIGURE 4

Making Instructional Grouping Decisions Based on the IPA and L.S. Fuchs and Deno (1982) Standards

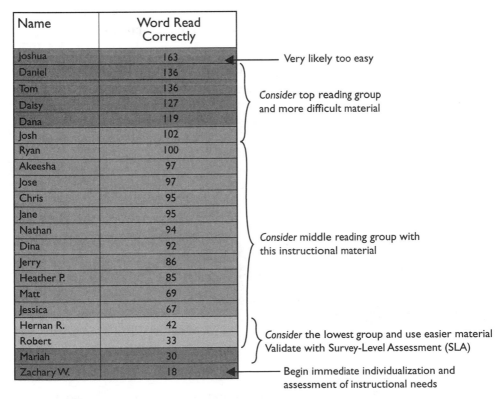

Note

Individual scores are the median of 3 scores from randomly selected passages from the school's third-grade reader.

Once the IPA has been conducted, at-risk students have been identified, and instruction has been planned, general education teachers/schools must decide which of the two options for monitoring the reading progress of the students in their classrooms—either Benchmark Testing or Strategic Monitoring—will be used.

Evaluating Reading Progress With a Benchmark Testing Approach

Benchmark Testing refers to regularly, but relatively infrequently, scheduled checks of all students' reading performance in general education. Extensive detail on how to complete Benchmark Testing is available in Shinn (2001). Benchmark Testing typically consists of an IPA at the beginning of the year followed up by two checks of student progress, typically at mid-year and near, but not at the end of, the academic year. Benchmark Testing is the most simple and feasible method of monitoring the reading growth of students with an estimated cost of about 15 minutes per student in testing time. This approach is the one that we suggest all grades begin with.

For each Benchmark Testing period, the IPA testing procedures described earlier are used. That is, students read three randomly selected passages from their general education reading series and the median WRC is used to summarize student performance.

FIGURE 5A

Results of Fall and Winter Benchmark Testing for Grade 3 Students at Wilson School

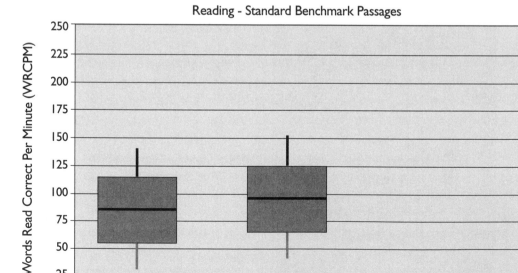

Hartford School District - Wilson Elementary

Reading - Standard Benchmark Passages

© edformation inc.

FIGURE 5B

Results of Fall, Winter, and Spring Benchmark Testing for Grade 3 Students at Wilson School

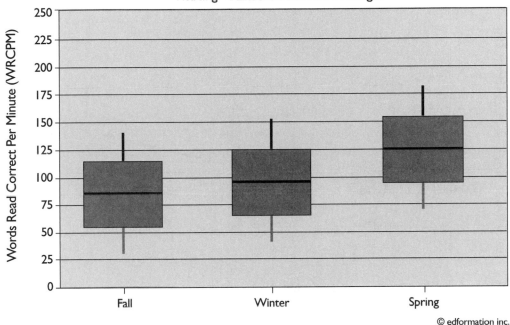

Hartford School District - Wilson Elementary
Reading - Standard Benchmark Passages

© edformation inc.

It is important to note that all passages are drawn from the *same* level of the general education curriculum each testing time. Unless students are given intensive practice on the passages used in the IPA, a practice that is not recommended, the same three passages can be used. However, it is easiest to sample randomly from a pool of passages for the appropriate level of the general education curriculum. Again, each student's scores are graphed on a chart and a decision is made regarding their risk status, instructional needs, and rate of progress.

Figures 5A and 5B show respectively, the reading growth of students in Grade 3 at Wilson School from the Fall IPA to the Winter Benchmark, and from the Fall IPA to the Winter Benchmark to the Spring Benchmark. It is noteworthy that student reading scores on R–CBM grew at about equal rates across the range of skills. That is, students performing at about the 50th percentile improved at about the same rate as students at the 25th percentile, 10th percentile, etc. This information provides validation of reading growth across the range of skills within the school and could be used for program evaluation purposes.

For formative evaluation purposes, the information provides teachers at least two opportunities to modify instructional programs for students who are at risk or who are

FIGURE 5C

Results of Benchmark Testing for Heather P. Compared to Rates of Progress of Other Grade 3 Students at Wilson School

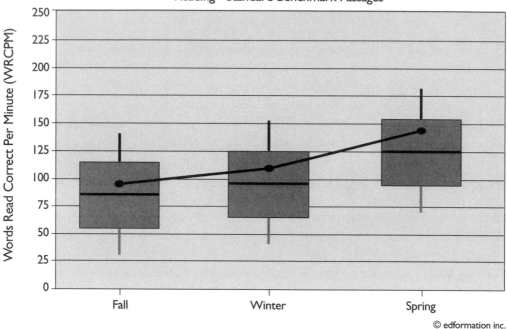

Hartford School District - Wilson Elementary
Reading - Standard Benchmark Passages

© edformation inc.

not making adequate progress. Three students' outcomes are illustrated in Figures 5C, 5D, and 5E. Figure 5C depicts Heather, a student whose Fall IPA status was as an average reading student in her school with an R–CBM score of 85 WRC, corresponding to the 50th percentile. At the Winter Benchmark, Heather's reading performance improved to 105 WRC or grew by 20 WRC over the 12-week period. This 1.7 WRC per week growth rate was about the same as the rate of typical students. Her Winter Benchmark reading status remained as an average reader. Thus, at mid-year, Mrs. Grady had two pieces of reading information—Heather's rate of growth and status relative to peers—with which to evaluate the effects of the reading program and make any necessary changes. In this instance, Heather's reading program was continued without change. By the Spring Benchmark testing period, Heather's R–CBM scores improved to 145 WRC, a score that placed her at the 66th percentile and within the average range of performance. From a summative perspective, Heather improved in her reading skills at the same rate as other students and maintained her overall status relative to other students. One could conclude that her third-grade reading program, as structured, was successful.

FIGURE 5D

Results of Benchmark Testing for Hernan R. Compared to Rates of Progress of Other Grade 3 Students at Wilson School

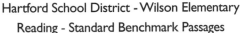

Hartford School District - Wilson Elementary
Reading - Standard Benchmark Passages

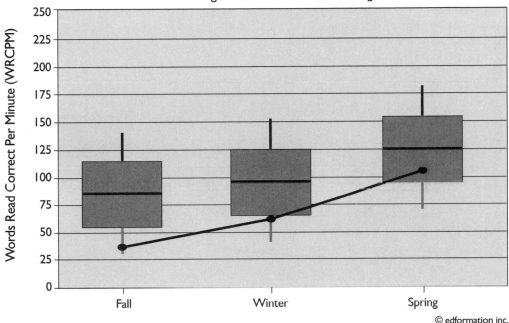

© edformation inc.

In Figures 5D and 5E the performance of two students who were considered at risk following the IPA is depicted. Hernan (Figure 5D) was performing at the 14th percentile in the Fall and Zachary (Figure 5E) was performing at the 7th percentile. Results of the Winter Benchmark testing indicated that both students were making progress in reading in comparison to their Fall performance. Although Hernan's reading performance in the Winter still placed him at risk for reading failure (i.e., below the 25th percentile), he was making progress over time, and growing at the same rate as his peers. No changes in his reading program were required. In fact, at the Spring Benchmark, Hernan was performing at the 36th percentile, or within the low average range.

In contrast, Zachary's reading program produced different outcomes. In the Fall, Zachary was identified as highly at risk and significant alterations were made to his proposed reading program. Although his R-CBM WRC improved by the Winter Benchmark testing, he was not progressing at the same rate as his peers. This information suggested that another change in his reading program was warranted. The modified reading program appeared to have a greater impact as demonstrated by a higher rate of growth from the Winter Benchmark testing to Spring testing. His rate of growth was

FIGURE 5E

Results of Benchmark Testing for Zachary W. Compared to Rates of Progress of Other Grade 3 Students at Wilson School

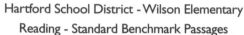

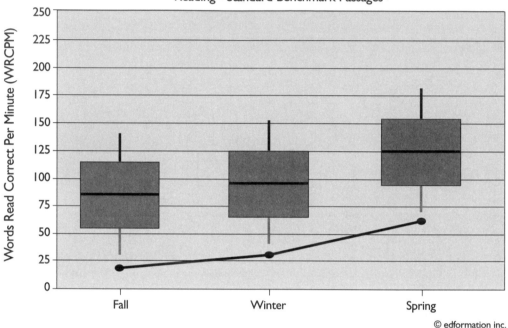

© edformation inc.

more like that of typical students, although not as rapid, and his relative status still placed him in the at–risk category. Options to improve his reading program further would be considered at that point.

Evaluating Reading Growth Using a Strategic Approach

As stated earlier, the major procedural difference between Benchmark Testing and Strategic Monitoring is the frequency with which progress is monitored and opportunities for data-based changes in reading programs are provided. These procedural differences have large potential impacts on teacher decision making and student achievement outcomes. Strategic Monitoring takes place usually on a *monthly* basis and thus allows *more* opportunities, typically eight to nine versus two, for teachers to make changes in individual reading programs. Relatedly, when students are not progressing and their programs require modification, students are in ineffective programs for less time as the duration between testing is shorter.

Because getting children off to a successful start is so important, we recommend that the reading growth of primary-grade students be supported by use of a Strategic

FIGURE 6A

Results of Strategic Monitoring of Reading for Grade 2 Students at Wilson School

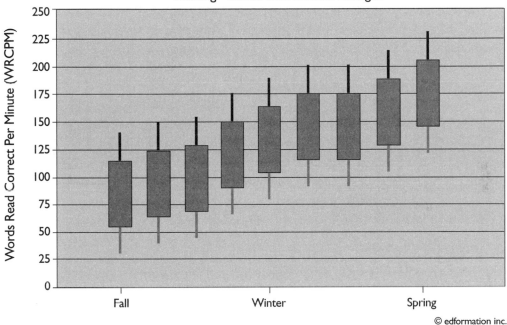

Hartford School District - Wilson Elementary
Reading - Standard Benchmark Passages

© edformation inc.

Monitoring approach. We liken Strategic Monitoring to the concept of "well checks" for young children. The younger the child, the greater the frequency of well checks, to ensure early and accurate attainment of positive developmental trajectories and, when necessary, timely problem identification.

We also recommend Strategic Monitoring for at-risk students in Grades 3–5. The increased frequency of testing allows more opportunities to change ineffective interventions and prevents older students from being maintained in ineffective programs for long periods.

The specific testing procedures for Strategic Monitoring are the same as those for Benchmark Testing. Each month, the students read three randomly selected passages from their general education curriculum and the median WRC is used to summarize their performance. In this instance, however, it is recommended that passages be drawn randomly from a larger pool of passages (e.g., 20–30) to minimize practice effects. Monthly results are added to the IPA graph as they are obtained.

The rates of reading growth of second-grade students on R-CBM over a 9-month period are shown in Figure 6A. Overall, a similar and positive reading growth rate is documented across the range of skills.

FIGURE 6B

Strategic Monitoring Results for Elizabeth Compared to Rates of Progress of Grade 2 Students at Wilson School

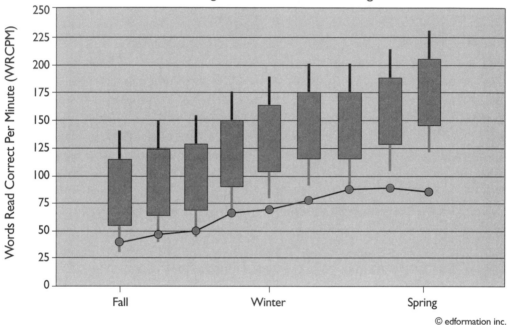

Hartford School District - Wilson Elementary
Reading - Standard Benchmark Passages

© edformation inc.

Strategic Monitoring results for two second-grade students, Elizabeth and Jackie, are shown in Figures 6B and 6C, respectively. Elizabeth began the year as an at-risk student and the standard reading program was individualized to improve her likelihood of reading success. By January, it appears that she was making the same rate of reading progress as typical students, albeit with lower overall reading skills. However, no growth was observed in February and March and her reading program was modified. These changes were ineffective, however, as Elizabeth failed to improve in subsequent testing. The need for *another* modified and likely considerably more intensive reading program was clear by the end of the year.

In Figure 6C, Jackie's Strategic Monitoring results are shown. He began the year as an at-risk student and his reading program was individualized. In contrast to Elizabeth, however, Jackie's reading program appeared to be working. With the exception of 1 month, his growth rate *exceeded* that of typical students. By the end of the year, Jackie was performing in the low average range of reading skills compared to other second-graders in his school.

FIGURE 6C

Strategic Monitoring Results for Jackie Compared to Rates of Progress of Grade 2 Students at Wilson School

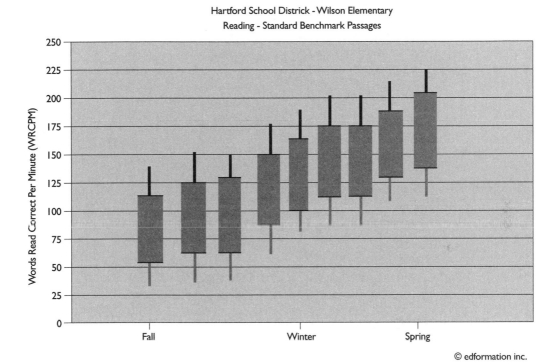

Hartford School Districk - Wilson Elementary
Reading - Standard Benchmark Passages

© edformation inc.

Specific Accommodations and Issues of Effective Implementation

Earlier in this chapter, we suggested that special issues need to be considered when R-CBM is used with students in Grades 1 and 5 and when used in middle schools. Furthermore, to enhance success, a number of features need to be attended to. We will now explore these issues briefly.

Grade 1 students. Exactly when to begin assessing the growth and development of reading using R-CBM is an issue. In many schools, typical students enter Grade 1 with reading skills that can be measured easily and accurately. In other schools, most students enter school without skills to read even one word from connected text. When the majority of students are reading at least a few words from connected text, we recommend a Strategic Monitoring approach be used to ensure that developmental reading trajectories are described and so that reading programs can be adjusted as necessary. R-CBM Strategic Monitoring can be preceded or accompanied by the continuous assessment of early literacy skills as described in the chapter by Simmons et al. in this volume. Whatever time frame or monitoring approach is used, however, we strongly recommend the use of a *discontinue rule* whereby if students read less than five words correctly on the first passage, that score is used and no additional passages are administered.

Grade 5 students and middle school entry. By Grade 5, many students have mastered basic reading skills and are employing reading as a tool for learning rather than learning to read. The cost-benefit of Benchmark testing with *all* students needs to be evaluated. We recommend conducting an IPA for the purposes of identifying at-risk students and instructional planning at these grades. We recommend using either Benchmark or Strategic Monitoring approaches only for those students who are identified as at risk. Additionally, we strongly recommend an IPA be conducted when students enter middle school for the purposes of identifying at-risk students and providing them with an intensive *general education* remedial reading program. Typically, the first year of middle school is the last and only opportunity to attend to the reading skills of students without jeopardizing attainment of necessary courses for high school graduation. Of course, students who receive this intensive program should have their improvement evaluated as frequently as possible.

Ensuring success. Over the years, we have observed a number of issues and actions that increase or decrease the likelihood of success in using CBM in general education classrooms. First and foremost, we believe that success is enhanced when assessing the growth and development of reading skills is seen as a whole school responsibility rather than that of each teacher, one by one. When *all* school staff, including school psychologists, support personnel, and school administrators participate in collecting reading outcome data, feasibility is increased as the ratio of data collectors to students is decreased.

Second, efficient and timely information management is essential. IPA data should be available for teachers to use in their *initial* instructional planning, not by receiving information months later. General education teachers should be seen as the *users* of R-CBM data, not as their organizers and disseminators. Therefore, some member(s) of the school staff with information management skills must be identified and supported in advance. We expect technological advances such as the Web-based *AIMSweb* system (Edformation, Inc., 2001) specifically designed for the purposes of IPA and Benchmark and Strategic Monitoring to be invaluable in this process of getting teachers to make decisions and "not graphs and dots."

Finally, we must recognize that knowing who is at risk and the effects (or lack thereof) of their instructional programs is not enough. We must be prepared to support general education teachers by having a range of effective reading interventions that can be provided for students in need. Other chapters in this volume are one source of things that can be done to help teachers develop more effective reading programs.

SUMMARY

In this chapter, we have tried to make the case that many of the current initiatives in reading assessment may fall short of meeting their goals of increasing reading achievement. It quite likely may be a case of "too little, too late" for the students and their teachers at best, and at worst, may provide another excuse for high stakes, negative consequences such as retention, and opportunities to blame and punish schools and our teachers. It is widely recognized that formative evaluation, the assessment of students *during* instruction, has had positive effects on achievement and teaching practices. It is proactive and can serve in a preventative capacity.

In special education, Curriculum-Based Measurement (CBM) has been validated as a tool for use in formative evaluation where students' progress is monitored on a weekly basis. Formative evaluation, specifically CBM, must be made more feasible for general education as well. With more students and fewer resources, general education teachers are not as well equipped to assess student reading growth in the same way as special education teachers. We have attempted to describe two approaches to using CBM in general education classrooms, Benchmark Testing and Strategic Monitoring. Both rely on the same initial practice of completing an Initial Performance Assessment (IPA). Through this practice and through the subsequent evaluation of student outcomes, we believe we can improve reading outcomes for *all* students.

REFERENCES

Allington, R. (1983). The reading instruction provided readers of differing reading abilities. *The Elementary School Journal, 83,* 548-559.

Berliner, D. C. (1981). Academic learning time and reading achievement. In J. Guthrie (Ed.), *Comprehension and teaching—Research reviews, Vol. 2.* New York: Academic Press.

Bristow, P. (1985). Are poor readers passive readers? Some evidence, possible solutions, and potential solutions. *The Reading Teacher,* 318-325.

Colorado Department of Education. (2001). *Colorado education accreditation indicators.* Denver, CO: Author.

Deno, S. L. (1985). Curriculum-based measurement: The emerging alternative. *Exceptional Children, 52,* 219-232.

Deno, S. L. (1986). Formative evaluation of individual student programs: A new role for school psychologists. *School Psychology Review, 15,* 358-374.

Deno, S. L. (1989). Curriculum-based measurement and alternative special education services: A fundamental and direct relationship. In M. R. Shinn (Ed.), *Curriculum-based measurement: Assessing special children* (pp. 1-17). New York: Guilford Press.

Deno, S. L., Mirkin, P., & Chiang, B. (1982). Identifying valid measures of reading. *Exceptional Children, 49,* 36-45.

Deno, S. L., Mirkin, P., & Wesson, C. (1984). How to write effective data-based IEPs. *Teaching Exceptional Children, 16,* 99-104.

Edformation, Inc. (2001). *AIMSweb information management and decision-making systems.* Eden Prairie, MN: Author.

Fuchs, L. S. (1994). *Connecting performance assessment to instruction.* Reston, VA: Council for Exceptional Children.

Fuchs, L. S. (1998). Computer applications to address implementation difficulties associated with curriculum-based measurement. In M. R. Shinn, (Ed.) *Advanced applications of curriculum-based measurement* (pp. 89-112). New York: Guilford Press.

Fuchs, L. S., & Deno, S. L. (1982). *Developing goals and objectives for educational programs.* Washington, DC: American Association of Colleges for Teacher Education.

Fuchs, L. S., & Deno, S. L. (1991). Paradigmatic distinctions between instructionally relevant measurement models. *Exceptional Children, 57,* 488-500.

Fuchs, L. S., & Deno, S. L. (1992). Effects of curriculum within curriculum-based measurement. *Exceptional Children, 58,* 232-243.

Fuchs, L. S., & Fuchs, D. (1986). Effects of systematic formative evaluation on student achievement: A meta-analysis. *Exceptional Children, 53,* 199-208.

Fuchs, L. S., & Fuchs, D. (1992). Identifying a measure for monitoring student reading progress. *School Psychology Review, 21,* 45-58.

Fuchs, L. S., & Fuchs, D. (1999). Monitoring student progress toward the development of reading competence: A review of three forms of classroom-based assessment. *School Psychology Review, 28,* 659-671.

Fuchs, L. S., Fuchs, D., & Hamlett, C. L. (1994). Strengthening the connection between assessment and instructional planning with expert systems. *Exceptional Children, 61,* 138-146.

Fuchs, L. S., Fuchs, D., Hamlett, C. L., & Ferguson, C. (1992). Effects of expert system consultation within curriculum-based measurement using a reading maze task. *Exceptional Children, 58,* 436-450.

Fuchs, L. S., Fuchs, D., Hamlett, C., Walz, L., & Germann, G. (1993). Formative evaluation of academic progress: How much growth can we expect? *School Psychology Review, 22,* 27-48.

Fuchs, L. S., Fuchs, D., & Maxwell, L. (1988). The validity of informal reading comprehension measures. *Remedial and Special Education, 9,* 20-28.

Fuchs, L. S., & Shinn, M. R. (1989). Writing CBM IEP objectives. In M. R. Shinn (Ed.), *Curriculum-based measurement: Assessing special children* (pp. 132-154). New York: Guilford Press.

Fuchs, L., Tindal, G., & Deno, S. (1984). Methodological issues in curriculum based reading assessment. *Diagnostique, 9,* 191-207.

Gickling, E. E., & Armstrong, D. L. (1978). Levels of instructional difficulty as related to on-task behavior, task completion, and comprehension. *Journal of Learning Disabilities, 11,* 559-566.

Hintze, J. M., Shapiro, E. S., & Luntz, M. (1994). The effects of curriculum on the sensitivity of curriculum-based measurement of reading. *The Journal of Special Education, 28,* 188-202.

Howell, K. W., & Nolet, V. (1999). *Curriculum-based evaluation: Teaching and decision making* (3rd ed.). Atlanta, GA: Wadsworth.

Kender, J. P. (1969). How useful are informal reading tests? In A. Beery, T. C. Barrett, & W. R. Powell (Eds.), *Elementary reading instruction.* Boston: Allyn and Bacon.

Marston, D. (1988). The effectiveness of special education: A time-series analysis of reading performance in regular and special education settings. *Journal of Special Education, 21,* 13-26.

Marston, D. (1989). Curriculum-based measurement: What is it and why do it? In M. R. Shinn (Ed.), *Curriculum-based measurement: Assessing special children* (pp. 18-78). New York: Guilford Press.

Marston, D., Lowry, L., Deno, S. L., & Mirkin, P. (1981). *An analysis of learning trends in simple measures of reading, spelling, and written expression: A longitudinal study.* Minneapolis: University of Minnesota Institute for Research on Learning Disabilities.

Marston, D., & Magnusson, D. (1985). Implementing curriculum-based measurement in special and regular education settings. *Exceptional Children, 52,* 266-276.

Massachusetts Department of Education. (2001). *Spring 2000 MCAS tests: Report of state results.* Boston: Author.

Minnesota Department of Children, Families, and Learning. (2000). *1999 Minnesota comprehensive assessment results.* St. Paul, MN: Author.

National Institute for Literacy. (1999). *Equipped for the future content standards: What adults need to know and be able to do in the 21st century.* Washington, DC: Author.

National Institute of Education, Commission on Reading. (1985). *Becoming a nation of readers: The report of the Commission on Reading.* Washington, DC: Author.

Shinn, M. R. (Ed.). (1989). *Curriculum-based measurement: Assessing special children.* New York: Guilford Press.

Shinn, M. R. (Ed.). (1998). *Advanced applications of curriculum-based measurement*. New York: Guilford Press.

Shinn, M. R. (2001). *AIMSweb Training Workbook: Organizing and implementing a school Benchmark Assessment System*. Eden Prairie, MN: Edformation, Inc.

Shinn, M. R., Deno, S. L., & Fuchs, L. S. (in press). *Curriculum-based measurement and its use in a problem-solving model*. New York: Guilford Press.

Shinn, M. R., Good, R. H., Knutson, N., Tilly, W. D., & Collins, V. (1992). Curriculum-based reading fluency: A confirmatory analysis of its relation to reading. *School Psychology Review, 21,* 458-478.

Shinn, M. R., Good, R. H., & Stein, S. (1989). Summarizing trend in student achievement: A comparison of evaluative models. *School Psychology Review, 18,* 356-370.

Shinn, M. R., & Hubbard, D. D. (1992). Curriculum-based measurement and problem-solving assessment: Basic procedures and outcomes. *FOCUS on Exceptional Children, 24,* 1-20.

Shinn, M. R., & Shinn, M. M. (2001). Writing and evaluating IEP goals and making appropriate revisions to ensure participation and progress in general curriculum. In C. F. Telzrow & M. Tankersley, *IDEA Amendments of 1997: Practice guidelines for school-based teams* (pp. 351–382). Bethesda, MD: National Association of School Psychologists.

Skiba, R. J., Deno, S. L., Marston, D., & Wesson, C. (1986). Characteristics of time-series data collected through curriculum-based reading measurement. *Diagnostique, 12,* 3-15.

Stanovich, K. E. (2001). *Progress in understanding reading*. New York: Guilford Press.

Taylor, B., Harris, L. A., & Pearson, P. D. (1988). *Reading difficulties: Instruction and assessment*. New York: Random House.

Tilly, W. D., Shinn, M. R., & Good, R. H. (in press). The effect of passage difficulty on reading curriculum-based measurement data: A generalizability theory approach. *School Psychology Review.*

U.S. Department of Education. (1993). *National Adult Literacy Survey (NALS)*. Washington, DC: Author.

Wesson, C. (1987). Facilitating the efficiency of ongoing curriculum-based measurement. *Teacher Education and Special Education, 9,* 166-172.

Wesson, C. L. (1992). Using curriculum-based measurement to create instructional groups. *Preventing School Failure, 36,* 17-20.

AUTHORS' NOTES

This chapter was supported in part by Grant No. 84.029D60057 (Leadership Training in Curriculum-Based Measurement and Its Use in a Problem-Solving Model), sponsored by the U.S. Department of Education, Office of Special Education Research. The views expressed within this paper are not necessarily those of the USDE. Most figures were produced by *AIMSweb Benchmark*, a web-based information management system designed for CBM and other general outcome measures. Address all correspondence and questions about this manuscript to Mark R. Shinn, Ph.D., (541) 346-2144, e-mail: *mshinn@oregon.uoregon.edu*.

CHAPTER 7

Early Screening and Intervention to Prevent the Development of
Aggressive, Destructive Behavior Patterns
Among At-Risk Children

Edward G. Feil, Herbert H. Severson, and Hill M. Walker
Institute on Violence and Destructive Behavior

INTRODUCTION

Professionals in the field of school psychology are well aware of the positive impact of early intervention and prevention efforts in successfully reducing later, disruptive behavior disorders among at-risk children and youth. Current NASP efforts to provide preventive interventions to young children on a universal basis are being fueled by evidence that points to the critical period of *school entry* and the need to ensure that every child has a good school beginning *(NASP 1999–2000 Annual Report)*. School bonding, engagement, attachment and success can function as powerful protective factors against later destructive outcomes; they operate much like a vaccine or inoculation in this regard. Early intervention directed toward ensuring a successful start to a child's school career is a proven method for developing this protective influence (see Hawkins, Catalano, Kosterman, Abbott, & Hill, 1999).

Well-conducted, longitudinal research suggests that much of problem behavior in adolescence has its origins in early childhood (Kazdin, 1987; Loeber & Farrington, 1998; Patterson, Reid, & Dishion, 1992; see also Eddy, Reid, & Curry, this volume). The preschool-age period (i.e., from 3 to 5 years of age) provides an opportunity to impact vulnerable children's later lives (a) by addressing risk factors, and their associated behavioral correlates, early on in the child's development; and (b) by developing the academic and social readiness skills that contribute to subsequent school success and social effectiveness. This early developmental period can be viewed as providing a pivotal window in which to intervene for preventing later potential problems, such as violence, substance abuse, educational failure, adolescent delinquency, and adult criminal involvement. Collaborative early intervention approaches, mounted within home, school, and community contexts, are perhaps one of the best hopes we have for preventing and remediating antisocial behavior patterns before they become chronic and intractable (Zigler, Taussig, & Black, 1992).

The broad and growing awareness of the importance of early intervention to the developmental prevention of later problems has changed the landscape of policy and practice regarding children's mental health (Burns & Goldman, 1998; Hoagwood, 2000). In addition, changes in the federal law that mandates and regulates delivery of services to children eligible for special education, under the aegis of Individuals with Disabilities Education Act, Amendments of 1997 (IDEA '97), have made it less difficult for professionals to accomplish early screening, identification, and intervention for children who are at risk for problems in their learning and behavioral potentials. The school psychologist can play a pivotal role in assisting vulnerable children and their families to access services, supports, and proven practices in this critically important area.

With the enactment of the Public Law (PL) 99-457 amendments to IDEA, two major changes occurred in the field of special education. First, all children needing special education and related services, from birth to 21 years, were now ruled eligible for federal and state funding for special education and related services. Second, PL 99-457 further defined and delineated the early identification and assessment requirements associated with the mandate to initiate a comprehensive child-find system. "The child find system must include the policies and procedures that the State will follow to ensure that ... *an effective method is developed and implemented to determine* which children are receiving needed services and *which children are not receiving those services"* (Federal Register, v54(119), p. 26319, 303.321, emphasis added). Each state has now begun to implement child-find systems for young children needing special education and related services— albeit often with limited tools with which to complete this child-find task.

Advances in the development of early screening and intervention approaches over the past decade have made it possible to serve the growing at-risk child populations with much greater cost effectiveness and efficiency (see Greenberg, Domitrovich, & Bumbarger, 1999; Hawkins et al., 1999; Merrell, 1999; Sprague & Walker, 2000; Walker, Colvin, & Ramsey, 1995). However, the vast majority of early childhood education programs, schools, and districts have not yet taken full advantage of these innovations and advances.

The focus of this chapter is twofold: (a) we review the literature on traditional, as well as relatively new, approaches to screening and identification and describe our own work in this regard using multiple gating approaches to assessment; and (b) we discuss some elements of effective early intervention for behaviorally at-risk children and highlight the *First Step to Success* home and school early intervention program for addressing aggressive, disruptive and bullying behavior at the point of school entry (see Walker et al., 1997, 1998). The chapter concludes with some recommendations regarding needed future developments in policy and practice(s) in serving the growing population of young children with challenging behaviors with which school professionals must now cope.

APPROACHES TO SCREENING AND IDENTIFICATION

It can be argued that the current way of identifying students with behavioral needs is failing. From the available data on current practices, it appears that both systematic identification procedures and consistency of outcomes are lacking. As a result, Behavior Disorder (BD) students are identified too late in their school careers, at which point interventions are not only less successful but also come at increasing cost. The main outcome of these practices is "too little, too late."

Central to the current student identification "process," for lack of a better term, is teacher nomination and referral. Teachers' nomination and referral of at-risk students have been the subject of considerable debate and controversy in the professional literature over the years (Gerber & Semmel, 1984; Gresham, Lane, MacMillan, & Bocian, 1999; Walker, Severson, & Feil, 1995). On the one hand, some argue that a teacher's referral of a student is primarily motivated by the desire to be rid of troublesome, difficult-to-teach students so as to create more easily managed, homogeneous classrooms. A counter argument is that teachers are driven by their good faith interest in securing assistance for students whose problems and needs exceed teachers' skill levels and accommodation capacities. We believe teacher referral practices are governed more by the latter consideration than the former. However, there are a number of problems associated with an exclusive reliance upon teacher nomination and referral of students who need specialized services including differences in behavioral tolerances among teachers, underreferral that leads to lack of service, and insensitivity to internalizing problems.

If teacher nominations are the *only* school-based avenue or approach available for meeting the needs of students with BD, then the idiosyncratic behavioral standards, tolerance levels, and judgmental biases of referring teachers are free to operate in an unconstrained fashion across classrooms and school settings. Long-established, empirical evidence shows that regular teachers vary tremendously on these dimensions (Brophy, 1986; Brophy & Evertson, 1981; Gerber & Semmel, 1984; Walker, 1986). Thus, students with identical behavioral characteristics and needs are likely to have very different probabilities of referral across individual teachers and classrooms because of this teacher variability. On the surface of it, this appears to be patently unfair to those vulnerable children and youth (i.e., internalizers) who may have serious and unmet mental health needs or problems, but who are assigned to a teacher who is unlikely to refer them. The underidentification and referral of behaviorally at-risk students continues to plague our prevention-intervention efforts and is a critical, unmet problem; yet school administrators go to what appear to be extraordinary lengths to prevent the overreferral of students with serious behavior disorders.

In traditional practice, the classroom teacher has been the primary gatekeeper who determines whether a given child is referred for evaluation and thus is afforded the possibility of accessing specialized services for learning and/or behavioral-emotional problems. Lloyd, Kauffman, Landrum, and Roe (1991) analyzed school records to investigate the context surrounding the teacher referral process. They found that regular teachers were involved in over 75% of all referrals and that students, in general, were far more likely to be referred for academic than behavioral problems. In their sample, two thirds of all school referrals occurred in the K–3 grade range and 69% involved boys. They found also that the referral rate peaked around Grade 2.

While academic problems and reading difficulties ranked first among the primary reasons for referral, social, emotional, and behavioral adjustment problems ranked a distant seventh on the list of teacher referral reasons. If this study were to be repeated today, it is possible that the results might differ somewhat, given the heightened sensitivity that many teachers now have, owing to the school shooting tragedies of the past decade, to the problems of troubled youth. In our own work with preschool teachers, staff development sessions on working with challenging forms of behavior is often the most requested.

The referral practices documented by Lloyd and his colleagues reveal teachers' legitimate concerns about the academic difficulties that many students experience in their early school careers and that hold the potential to impair their school engagement and achievement. It is laudable that regular teachers hold this level of sensitivity to the academic status of young children; however, the story is often different for students who are behaviorally at risk, and who may be equally likely to fail school. Unless a given student (a) behaves in a bizarre, atypical, or troubling fashion; (b) exhibits a behavior pattern that conflicts with teacher values (lying, stealing, cheating); and/or (c) pressures the teacher's ability to manage the classroom by being aggressive, disruptive, or defiant, teachers are generally less likely to refer and perhaps more inclined to hope that the normalizing processes of schooling will solve any emergent social-behavioral adjustment problems. The evidence shows that children who bring a well-developed pattern of challenging behavior with them to the schooling process are more likely to grow *into* rather than out of it (Lynam, 1996; Moffitt, 1994). Effectively addressing the needs of such children requires mounting a coordinated intervention, as early as possible in an at-risk child's life and school career, that involves parents and caregivers, the target child, teachers, and peers (Reid, 1993). In the absence of systematic and early identification, this becomes very difficult to do.

Walker and his colleagues (Walker, Nishioka, Zeller, Severson, & Feil, 2000) recently analyzed the referral and certification patterns for emotionally disturbed students in grades K–12 based upon the Annual Reports to Congress on progress in implementing IDEA during the 1990s. Figure 1 illustrates the replicating pattern of referral frequency by grade level across the decade for Emotionally Disturbed (ED) students.

In stark contrast to academic referrals by regular teachers, the corresponding behavioral referral and certification rates for the IDEA category of emotional disturbance tend to peak at about age 15, when students are in the tenth grade (see Figure 1). This practice severely reduces opportunities to divert behaviorally at-risk children from a destructive path early on in their school careers. Follow-up studies of students served by IDEA in different disability categories indicate that ED students fare very poorly in their postschooling adjustments and quality of life (Wagner, 1989). Early intervention that systematically addresses both school- and nonschool-based risk factors, along with their behavioral correlates, is one of the best strategies available for diverting behaviorally at-risk children and youth from such a destructive life path (Kashani, Jones, Bumby, & Thomas, 1998).

FIGURE 1

Students With Emotional Disturbance Served by Age
(1993–94, 1997–98, and 1998–99 School Years)

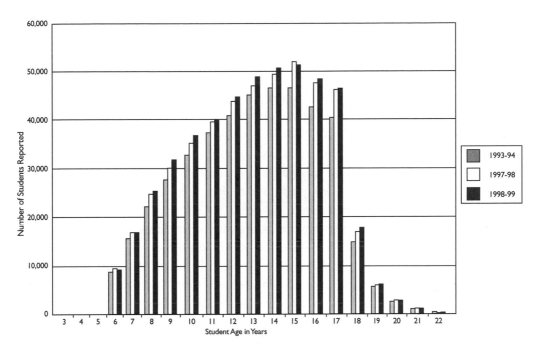

Note

Walker, H. M., Nishioka, V. M., Zeller, R., Severson, H. H., & Feil, E.G. (2000). Causal factors and potential solutions for the persistent underidentification of students having emotional or behavioral disorders in the context of schooling. *Assessment for Effective Intervention, 2*(1), 29–39. The figure is on page 31. Reprinted with permission.

While Hoagwood & Erwin (1997) and Angold (2000) indicate that approximately 20% and 22%, respectively, of the school-age population is in need of treatment for mental health problems, IDEA currently serves slightly less than 1% annually of the K–12 student population as ED. This figure is unlikely to increase substantively until school-based barriers to early identification (e.g., cost, stigma, perceived teacher incompetence) are addressed and resolved. Given the enduring nature of these obstacles, other avenues will need to be found and developed in the short run in order to address the chasm that now exists between available services and the mental health needs of the preschool and K–12 student population (Walker et al., 2000).

In the following section, we review some traditional and more recent approaches to the early screening and identification of behaviorally at-risk children and youth in the context of schooling. We also examine many of their upsides, as well as downsides, and discuss their likely cost effectiveness and practicality. Following this section, we describe our work in the multiple-gating screening and assessment of behaviorally at-risk students within the context of schooling. The screening and identification strategies reviewed below include Likert teacher ratings, critical behavioral events, archival school records, and direct behavioral observations.

Teacher Use of Likert Rating Scales

Teacher ratings of student behavior, based on Likert scales, have been a popular albeit unsystematic approach in the evaluation of students referred for social, emotional, and behavioral problems (see Merrell, 1999, 2001). Such Likert scales typically ask the rater to assess students' behavior along 3, 5, or 7 point dimensions of problem frequency or severity. Hundreds of such scales are in use and evaluations of many of these can be accessed through the *Buros Mental Measurements Yearbook,* which annually reviews newly developed scales. *The Child Behavior Checklist* (Achenbach, 1991) has become the rating scale standard for measuring child and youth psychopathology and is, by far, the most widely used instrument for this purpose. Merrell (1999) has contributed a comprehensive analysis of assessment instruments for use in social, emotional, and behavioral domains.

In addition to their unsystematic use, critics of teacher rating instruments point to their global and relatively crude assessment properties (e.g., "How many fidgets are there in pretty much?"). Others argue that teacher ratings pale in sensitivity in comparison to more direct measures such as in vivo behavioral observations. In spite of these criticisms, teacher ratings continue to be a widely used and important source of information in child screening, identification, and evaluation processes. These ratings have the advantage of defining and pinpointing the behavioral content of a student's perceived adjustment problems and can be standardized so as to enable valid social comparisons referenced to normative age and gender scores. Merrell (2001) has pointed out that Likert behavioral ratings have a number of additional advantages. They (a) are relatively inexpensive; (b) provide essential information on low-frequency behavioral events of potential importance; (c) are relatively objective and reliable, especially when compared to interview and projective assessment methods; (d) can assess individuals who are unable to contribute self-reports; (e) take into account the many observations and judgments of child behavior made by social agents within natural settings over the long term; and (f) reflect the judgments of expert social informants who are familiar with the student's behavioral characteristics (i.e., parents, teachers, peers).

Drummond (1993) has developed an intriguing matrix system, based on Likert teacher ratings, to screen entire classrooms of students for their risk status in relation to antisocial behavior patterns. *Drummond's Student Risk Screening Scale* (SRSS) is a cost efficient procedure for quickly screening whole classrooms. A matrix format is used that has seven behavioral descriptors across the top of the rating form and students' names down the left side. The classroom teacher assigns every student a Likert rating, ranging from 0 = never to 3 = frequently, for each of these seven items of the SSRS: (1) stealing; (2) lying, cheating, sneaking; (3) behavior problems; (4) peer rejection; (5) low academic achievement; (6) negative attitude; and (7) aggressive behavior. Teachers compare each student against all others in the classroom as they rate each item. The SRSS is brief, research based, easily understood, valid, and cost efficient.

The major advantages of the SRSS are that (a) all students are systematically screened and evaluated; (b) it accomplishes universal screening; and (c) normative social comparisons are facilitated by requiring the teacher to evaluate *all* students on each item at the same time rather than rating individual students on a series of items on a case-by-case basis. The SRSS thus affords every student an equal chance to be evaluated in relation to the seven SRSS items. A matrix system of this type is also ideally suited for the classwide assessment and pre-post evaluation of instruction for all students in a series of social skills. A more complete description of the SRSS and its potential applications is provided in Walker, Colvin, and Ramsey (1995). Information about the SRSS can be obtained by contacting the author of the system.

Critical Behavioral Events

Critical behavioral events refer to episodes having great intensity and social impact; they include but are not limited to assault, fire setting, self-injury, exposing oneself, stealing, cheating, bullying, and so on. The importance of critical events derives from their severity and their potential destructiveness to the individual. The impact of critical events is not dependent upon their frequency of occurrence but rather determined by the fact that they occur *at all*. These are rare occurrences in the behavioral repertoires of typically developing children and youth but are not infrequent in the lives of some behaviorally at-risk individuals.

Gresham, MacMillan, and Bocian (1996) conducted a study of the *Critical Events Index* (CEI) in their use of the SSBD screening procedure within a larger study of the social-affective status of at-risk students. The CEI was used to identify three groups of students from an elementary-aged student sample based upon the groups' total number of critical events: (a) high risk (n = 30), (b) moderate risk (n = 55), and (c) low risk (n = 30). These groups were then contrasted on a series of cognitive/achievement, social competence, externalizing behavior, and school history variables as derived from searches of archival school records of individual students. Multivariate and univariate analysis procedures showed that the three at-risk groups were differentiated primarily on social competence and externalizing behavioral measures. However, a series of cross-validated, stepwise discriminant function analyses, contrasting the high, and low, risk groups only, and using combinations of social competence, externalizing, internalizing, and school history variables, correctly identified over 85% of the high-risk group and 78% of the low-risk group. These authors recommend inclusion of critical events measures within multimethod assessments of at-risk, behavioral status and they view these events as "vital signs" or indicators of childhood psychopathology.

Blechman and Hile (in press) make the following observations regarding critical events:

1. Student involvement in critical events provides a bias-free screen for the detection of at-risk students in the general or universal student population; and

2. Systematic documentation of all critical events provides the most effective and least expensive method of screening for at-risk students.

They note further that a reliance upon readily available information from student records within screening efforts reduces costs, increases feasibility, and avoids extraordinarily adverse consequences to students. Blechman and Hile (in press) define critical events in their work as including school and criminal offenses, threats of violence or suicide, suicide attempts, and caregiver requests for assistance with behavior management and argue that these events offer a useful and inexpensive predictor of future and more serious critical events. The work of these authors reflects an increasing trend toward using critical behavioral events in screening practices, as either rated by knowledgeable informants or culled from existing archival records.

Archival School Records

If the early preschool detection of behavior problems is not possible, school records can provide an additional valuable source of screening information. Archival school records that accumulate as a natural part of the schooling process provide a rich and inexpensive information source regarding a range of school adjustment problems and also provide a record of the manner in which schools try to cope with such problems. Because these records build naturally as an ordinary part of the schooling process, they are relatively unobtrusive and far less reactive than typically recorded assessments (e.g., teacher ratings, in vivo behavioral observations, sociometric measures).

Walker and his colleagues have developed the *School Archival Records Search (SARS)* procedure (see Walker, Block-Pedego, Todis, & Severson, 1991) to accomplish the coding, analysis, and aggregation of archival school records. SARS provides for the systematic coding of 11 archival variables, which can then be analyzed individually or aggregated into domain scores that provide profiles of student status in three areas of school adjustment: *disruption, needs assistance, and low achievement.* The individual SARS variables that are coded include the following: number of different schools attended, days absent, low achievement, grades retained, academic/behavioral referrals, current Individualized Educational Program (IEP), nonregular classroom placement, Title I, referrals out of school, negative narrative comments, and school discipline referrals. In the context of schooling, archival school records are the closest proxy we have for police contacts and juvenile records that are used in evaluating delinquency prevention programs and in validating measures that purport to predict later delinquent acts.

Disciplinary referrals of students to the front office who are involved in behavioral episodes, as reflected in archival school records, have emerged as a very useful measure for assessing overall school status and for identifying student groups and individuals who are in need of behavioral supports and intervention (see Sugai, Sprague, Horner, & Walker, 2000; Walker, Stieber, Ramsey, & O'Neill, 1990). Sugai, Horner, and their colleagues have conducted extensive research on this topic in the past 5 years. Most recently, Sugai et al. (2000) reported normative data profiles on disciplinary referrals involving a sample of 11 elementary schools and 9 middle/junior high schools. These elementary schools averaged 0.5 disciplinary referrals per student per school year. At the middle/junior high school level, this level of disciplinary referrals was a *very* common occurrence. In the Sugai et al. study, the elementary schools averaged 566 students enrolled and 283 disciplinary referrals within a school year; the middle/junior high schools averaged 635 students and 1,535 disciplinary referrals within a school year.

These authors also analyzed some of the patterns that existed within this pool of disciplinary referrals. Based on this analysis, they argue that these patterns can guide the direction and focus of intervention approaches for addressing chronic behavior problems within the school setting (i.e., targeting the whole school, small groups, and/or individual students). For example, at the elementary level, Sugai et al. (2000) found that the top 5% of students with the most discipline referrals also accounted for 59% of total disciplinary referrals within the school; at the middle/junior high level, the top 5% accounted for 40% of all discipline referrals. These figures closely parallel outcomes for juvenile crime where 6–8% of juveniles typically account for 60 to 65% of all delinquent acts (Loeber & Farrington, 1998). According to Sugai et al., elementary-aged students with 5 or more disciplinary referrals within a school year are considered to be behaviorally at risk; those with 10 or more such referrals are considered to be chronic discipline problems who may be severely at risk for both in-school and out-of-school destructive outcomes.

Recording and utilizing disciplinary referrals to identify at-risk students and to guide intervention applications requires the computerization of school records. Horner and his associates have developed the *School Wide Information System (SWIS)* procedure, which is a Web-based, computer application for entering, organizing, and reporting office discipline referrals found within schools (May et al., 2001). SWIS computerizes discipline referrals and is a valuable tool for use by teachers and school administrators in collecting and analyzing discipline-related information. One of the advantages of the SWIS procedure is that it systematizes and standardizes the process of documenting, recording and reporting on disciplinary referrals.

Figure 2, on page 152, contains the *SWIS Office Referral Form,* which is completed for each disciplinary referral made by a teacher to the school office. This referral form documents each disciplinary episode for which a front office referral is initiated by the teacher. The SWIS referral form describes the location, specific problem behavior, possible motivation(s) for the behavior, the resulting administrative decision, and other persons who were involved in the incident. Parents are asked to sign and date the referral form to indicate that they have knowledge of the incident, the referral, and its disposition.

SWIS is an important advance in the computerization of archival school records that allows individual schools to profile themselves in relation to disciplinary practices and their resulting effects. It can be used also as a measure of certain aspects of school reform efforts, as a measure of the school's climate, as a pre-post measure of schoolwide interventions, and as a vehicle for guiding and targeting allocation of intervention

FIGURE 2

SWIS Office Discipline Referral Form

SWIS OFFICE DISCIPLINE REFERRAL FORM

Student(s) _____ Referring Staff _____ Grade Level _____ Date _____ Time _____

Location

• Classroom	• Cafeteria	• Bus Loading zone	• Other _____
• Playground	• Bathroom/restroom	• Parking Lot	
• Commons/common area	• Gym	• On bus	
• Hallway/breezeway	• Library	• Special event/assembly/field trip	

Problem Behaviors (check the most intrusive)

• Minor/warning	• Tardy	• Tobacco	• Bomb threat
• Abusive lang./inapprop. lang.	• Skip class/truancy	• Alcohol/drugs	• Arson
• Fighting/physical aggression	• Forgery/theft	• Combustibles	• Weapons
• Defiance/disrespect/insubordination/non-compliant	• Dress code violation	• Vandalism	• Other _____
• Harassment/tease/taunt	• Lying/cheating	• Property damage	
• Disruption			

Possible Motivation

• Obtain peer attention	• Avoid tasks/activities	• Don't know
• Obtain adult attention	• Avoid peer(s)	• Other _____
• Obtain items/activities	• Avoid adult(s)	

Others Involved

• None   • Peers   • Staff   • Teacher   • Substitute   • Unknown   • Other _____

Administrative Decision

• Time in office	• Detention	• Saturday School	• In-school suspension
• Loss of privilege	• Parent contact	• Individualized instruction	• Out-of-school suspension
• Conference with student	• Other _____		

Comments:

Follow Up Comments:

Note

The SWIS Office Discipline Referral Form is reprinted with permission from Robert Horner, Director, Educational and Community Supports, College of Education, University of Oregon.

resources to small groups and individuals. It is also recommended as a schoolwide, behavioral screening device to identify those students who are experiencing serious to chronic school adjustment problems.

Behavioral Observations

Behavioral observations recorded in natural settings (e.g., homes, classrooms, playgrounds, hallways) remain the preferred assessment method of most behavior analysts for assessing the behavior problems of students. In typical school usage, the teacher referral process requires that a school psychologist, or other related-services professional, directly observe the target student in a setting or context in which the problem behavior occurs (i.e., the referral setting). The main purpose of this observation is to confirm or disconfirm the accuracy and validity of the teacher referral. A wide range of coding systems and recording procedures are used for this purpose. However, the vast majority of them do not have adequate technical data or information to support their use(s). In addition, most of these codes lack local, state, or national norms that are appropriate for making social comparisons among students.

Teacher referrals are often based upon discrete behavioral events of high intensity or salience (e.g., insubordination, teacher defiance) that may be missed within the narrow window of *time* and *occasions* sampling that most such observations involve. Naturalistic behavioral observations are also vulnerable to observer bias and expectancy effects that can be induced by the observer's prior knowledge of the case. Further, direct observations are time-consuming and labor intensive in that they usually require considerable planning and careful monitoring if they are conducted effectively (see Merrell, 2001).

In spite of these downsides, naturalistic behavioral observations remain popular among school professionals and they do have an important role to play in the screening-identification process *if* they are incorporated into a comprehensive assessment process that involves other, less expensive measures (e.g., teacher nominations, rankings, ratings, archival records searches, etc.). We do not recommend their use in isolation; but rather that they be an important component of a multiagent, multimethod, and multisetting assessment approach to the screening-identification process (Merrell, 1999).

Herein, we have briefly reviewed a number of commonly used, and several relatively new, approaches to the screening and identification of students having behavior problems in the school setting. The choice of which approach or method to use depends upon an array of factors specific to the decision that has to be made and the amount of professional time, skills, and resources available. Many differing assessment options exist within these general approaches that have excellent psychometrics and whose power, efficacy, and precision have been greatly enhanced by recent advances in assessment and computer-based technology.

We are advocates of universal screening procedures, implemented on a regular basis, that systematize the screening-identification process, that integrate the above methods into a comprehensive system, and that avoid or buffer many of the problems attendant upon idiosyncratic teacher referrals. In the next section, we review our work in developing, validating, and standardizing multiple-gating approaches to the universal screening of students in the preschool through elementary age range to accurately identify those who are behaviorally at risk.

Screening With Multiple Gates: The SSBD & ESP Systems

Since 1985, the present authors have been engaged in a systematic program of research focused on two primary goals: 1) the proactive, universal screening of children from ages 3 through 11 who are experiencing school-related behavior disorders, and 2) coordinating school and home intervention approaches to ensure that each behaviorally at-risk child gets off to the best start possible in school. The *Systematic Screening for Behavior Disorders* (SSBD) procedure was developed and field-tested to accomplish the first goal. The *First Step to Success* early intervention program was developed and evaluated to accomplish the second goal.

Systematic Screening for Behavior Disorders (SSBD). Walker and Severson (1990) developed the *Systematic Screening for Behavior Disorders (SSBD)* screening procedure for use with elementary-age children (K–6 grades) based upon a conceptual model, and corresponding empirical findings, that children's problem behavioral characteristics can be divided reliably into "externalizing" (e.g. aggressive, hyperactive, noncompliant, antisocial, etc.) and "internalizing" (e.g. shy, phobic, depressed, anxious, isolated from peers, etc.) dimensions (see Achenbach, 1991; Ross, 1980). The *SSBD* was patterned after screening models developed and validated by Greenwood, Walker, Todd, & Hops (1979) for the preschool screening of children at risk for social withdrawal and by Loeber, Dishion, and Patterson (1984) for the screening of adolescents at risk for later delinquency. The *SSBD* is a proactive, universal screening procedure that gives each student an equal chance to be screened and identified for either externalizing or internalizing behavior disorders. The *SSBD* procedure consists of three screening stages or gates where movement through each gate is required for consideration at the next gate. Most students are screened out in the initial *SSBD* gates because they do not meet the behavioral criteria necessary to proceed to the next phase of screening.

Walker and Severson began their first trial testing of the *SSBD* in the mid-1980s and conducted extensive research, supported by a series of federal grants, on this screening system prior to its publication in 1990 (Walker, Severson, et al., 1990).

Figure 3 illustrates the three screening stages of the *SSBD*. In stage one, teachers are asked to think about all students in their class and to nominate those students whose characteristic behavior patterns most closely match either the externalizing or internalizing behavioral definitions provided for them. The three highest ranked externalizing students and the three highest ranked internalizers then move to screening stage (gate) two where their behavior is more specifically rated by the teacher on a 33-item Critical Events Index (CEI) and on both an Adaptive (11 items) and a Maladaptive (12 items) Likert rating scale that requires estimates of frequency of occurrence.

FIGURE 3

SSBD/ESP Multiple Gating Procedure

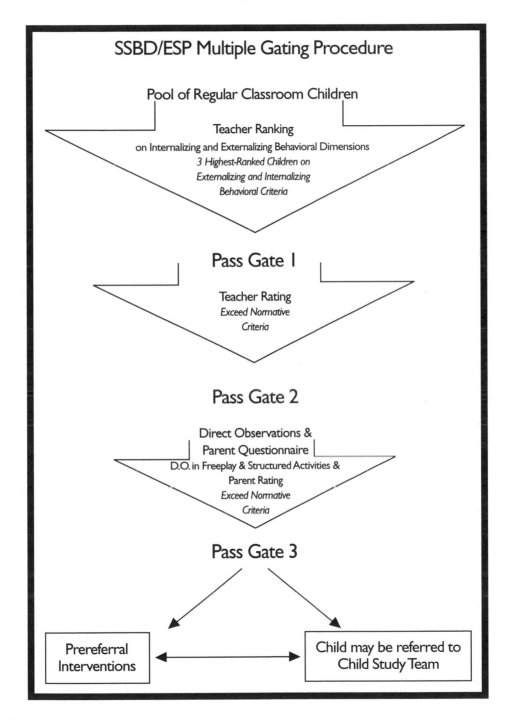

Note

Feil, E. G., Walker, H. M., & Severson, H. H. (1995). The early screening project for young children with behavior problems. *Journal of Emotional and Behavioral Disorders, 3*, 194-202, 213. Reprinted with permission.

Students who exceed national, normative cutoff scores on these measures move on to gate three where they are observed in classroom and playground settings. Using a direct observation procedure, a school professional (school psychologist, counselor, or behavioral specialist) observes and codes each target child's behavior for two 20-minute sessions in the regular classroom. A stopwatch measure of Academic Engaged Time (AET) is used for the classroom observations. A 10-second, partial interval code (*Peer Social Behavior*, or PSB) that records the level, quality, and distribution of the target student's peer-related, social behavior at recess, is used to assess the target student's playground behavior during the two 20-minute sessions. Normative data for the stage two instruments consist of over 4,000 cases representing the four U.S. census zones. The *SSBD* user's manual also provides normative observation data for the AET and PSB codes involving over 1300 cases—also collected across the four census zones.

Those students who exceed national, normative cutoff points on the AET and PSB codes are considered to have serious problems and are referred for further evaluation to specialized, school-based services. As a rule, an archival records search is conducted at this point to provide confirmation of the results of the screening-identification process and serves as a further source of information for decision making.

The first two screening stages of the *SSBD* can be completed by the classroom teacher in approximately 1 hour. This screening procedure typically identifies one externalizer in every classroom and one internalizer in every two or three classrooms. The time involved in conducting *SSBD* screening assessments increases as one moves through the screening stages; however, the number of students who are the targets of those assessments is greatly reduced from stage one to three. It is recommended that universal *SSBD* screenings be conducted twice a year (e.g., in October and February) to identify students in need of intervention supports and services and to maximize the sensitivity of school staff to initial behavior problems in the fall and to detect emerging behavior problems later in the school year. The SSBD has been extensively researched and has excellent psychometrics (see Walker & Severson, 1990).

Following publication of the *SSBD,* considerable interest was expressed by other researchers in adapting the screening system. Eisert, Walker, Severson, and Block (1989), for example, conducted a study to determine whether the *SSBD* could be successfully adapted for preschool use. These investigators found that the Peer Social Behavior (PSB) observation data were able to reliably discriminate among preschool groups of Externalizers, Internalizers, and non-behavior-problem children in free play settings at recess.

Another successful adaptation by Sinclair, Del'Homme, and Gonzalez (1993) was reported in which the *SSBD* was further tested with preschool children. In this study, Sinclair and her colleagues made the following changes to the *SSBD* procedure: (a) in stage one, the teachers were asked to nominate and rank order only seven Externalizers and seven Internalizers (out of classes of 15) rather than 10 of each; (b) the direct observation of Academic Engaged Time was eliminated; and (c) the time allocated to direct observations using the PSB code was doubled. The research by Sinclair and colleagues was encouraging in that it resulted in changes that were needed to make the *SSBD* more appropriate for the preschool population.

In 1990, Edward Feil, in collaboration with the *SSBD* authors, began work on the development of a preschool version of the *SSBD.* The adapted version of the *SSBD* is called the *Early Screening Project* (ESP) and was published in 1995. In revising the *SSBD* for use with preschoolers, these authors found it necessary to change some of the *SSBD* procedures and instruments in order to take into account developmental differences between younger and older students. These changes have been detailed elsewhere (Feil & Becker, 1993; Feil, Walker, & Severson, 1995).

Beginning in 1991, studies on the *ESP* were conducted to assess its reliability and validity (see Feil & Becker, 1993). These findings have proven promising to date; the *ESP* reliability and validity data consistently show very strong results. The interrater reliability coefficients of most *ESP* measures are at least .80, which meet Salvia and Ysseldyke's (1988) guidelines for a screening instrument. Validity studies consistently show strong relationships between the *ESP* screening measures and selected, concurrent validity measures (e.g., *Conners Teacher Rating Scales* [Conners, 1989] and *Preschool Behavior Questionnaire* [Behar & Stringfield, 1974]). Results for the *ESP* also show good sensitivity (62%) and excellent specificity (94%), suggesting that it provides accurate assessments with a minimal risk of identifying a child who exhibits developmentally appropriate behavior.

The *ESP* can be a valuable tool for early childhood educators in screening for school adjustment problems at an early age; the problems can then be addressed through developmentally appropriate early intervention(s). Preschool programs, facing increasing federal and state requirements (e.g., Child–Find), need to maximize their resources within a proactive and fair child-find system. We believe the *ESP* can minimize the time and materials costs of preschool behavioral assessments while increasing their level of accuracy over that produced by many currently used approaches.

The universal, early screening of behaviorally at-risk children can only be justified if effective early intervention supports and services are available to address the needs of those who are identified. The next section describes our work over the past decade in developing a collaborative home-school, early intervention program that addresses challenging forms of child behavior at the point of school entry.

EARLY INTERVENTION TO ADDRESS CHALLENGING BEHAVIOR

Substantial research indicates that earlier intervention is a promising strategy in diverting antisocial children from a path that leads to numerous destructive outcomes (Eddy, Reid, & Curry, this volume). Reid (1993) has noted that effective early interventions must include the three social agents who have the greatest influence in a developing child's life (i.e. parents, teachers, and peers). Greenberg et al. (1999) have developed criteria that define effective interventions, along with intervention programs matching these criteria, that address externalizing and internalizing behavior disorders.

The *First Step to Success* early intervention program was identified by Greenberg et al. (1999) as a model program in their review. This intervention program is designed to achieve secondary prevention goals and targets those at-risk children who exhibit high levels of aggressive and/or oppositional behavior and who are likely to fail school (see Walker et al., 1997). This collaborative home and school intervention involves (a) school and home activity rewards provided for appropriate school behavior, (b) group and individual reinforcement systems, (c) a school-based point system, (d) behavioral contracting procedures, (e) adult praise, and (f) a home visiting curriculum. The *First Step* intervention is implemented initially by a school professional (e.g., counselor, school psychologist, early interventionist) who serves as a behavioral coach. The classroom teacher takes over running *First Step* on a daily basis after the first five program days have been successfully completed by the coach.

First Step is initiated in classroom situations but can be extended to the playground and other school settings as needed. The home visiting component of the program, called homeBase, consists of six visits with the family (one per week) by the behavioral coach to work with the child's parents in teaching and practicing school success skills at home. HomeBase skills address the constructs of communication, cooperation, limit setting, problem solving and emotional regulation, friendship making, and self-esteem. *First Step* has three modules: (a) a proactive universal screening procedure, which provides four screening options including the *ESP* procedure described earlier, (b) a school intervention that targets the at-risk child, peers, and teachers and teaches the target child an adaptive behavior pattern at school, and (c) a parent-training component in which parents or caregivers are exposed to six lessons, as noted (over a 6-week period) that allow them to teach their child key skills for enhancing school adjustment and success. These *First Step* modular components are described below in more detail.

The classroom component of *First Step* uses a preschool adaptation of the Contingencies for Learning Academics and Social Skills (CLASS) Program (Hops & Walker, 1988) developed for remediating the behavior problems of acting-out children. The coach meets initially with the child and directly teaches him or her appropriate forms of social behavior, specific to classroom (teacher-related) and playground (peer-related) interactional contexts. Following this instruction, the school intervention program is implemented for two brief periods (20–30 minutes/day) daily during the 5-day, coach phase. On the 6th day, the regular teacher assumes control of the program. By day 10, the intervention is expanded to all settings and periods in which the child is experiencing problems. Home and school incentives are provided to support the child's attempts at behavior change and to motivate peers to participate in the intervention as special helpers and supportive agents.

In the homeBase part of *First Step,* parents are taught how to help their child get off to a good start in school. The six weekly, skills-building sessions (of approximately an hour each) are held with the parent(s) (usually in the home) and are facilitated by the *First Step* coach. During each session, (a) the activities of the past week are reviewed and discussed, (b) new skills are presented to the parent(s) to be taught and practiced with the child, and (c) practice sessions (5 minutes/day) are modeled, role-played and set up for the parent and child. A series of games and fun activities are provided to the parent(s) and child for practicing and strengthening the newly learned skills during daily parent-child interactions. The child's teacher also praises the child's reports of learning and practicing these skills at home and prompts and praises their display at school.

Effectiveness of the First Step Program

The *First Step* intervention was successfully implemented and trial-tested in the Eugene, Oregon, 4J School District during the 1993-94 and 1994-95 school years. A total of 46 kindergarten children, who were at risk for developing antisocial behavior, and their teachers, peers, and parents participated in the intervention (24 in year one and 22 in year two). Of the 46 cases, 26% were female, 33% were receiving special education services by the end of the study, 7% were children of minority status, and 37% lived in families with low incomes (i.e., children received reduced or free lunches).

A cohort design, with experimental and wait-list control groups, was used to evaluate *First Step* intervention effects and to establish a causal relationship between the intervention and resulting changes in child behavior. Cohorts 1 and 2 were divided into two equal groups with half the students receiving the *First Step* intervention in Year 1 and the other half serving as wait-list controls during the intervention. Both groups were assessed at pre- and postintervention time points. The wait-list controls were then subsequently exposed to the *First Step* intervention during Year 2. A complete description of the results of this investigation, along with pre-post and follow-up data, can be found in Walker et al. (1998). Longer-term follow-up results into Grades 4 and 5 for these same cohorts are reported in Epstein and Walker (in press).

The results of the *First Step* intervention were particularly encouraging in that they moved target students to points within the normative range on two of the most important measures used to evaluate the program (i.e., teacher ratings of child aggression on the Child Behavior Checklist and direct observations of academic engaged time). Measures of aggression are markers for later antisocial behavior patterns and for a host of social adjustment problems (Loeber & Farrington, 1998). Academic Engaged Time (AET) is a moderately strong correlate of academic performance and provides a sensitive measure of a student's ability to meet the academic demands of instructional settings. Normative levels for AET, based upon observational data, are considered to be in the range of 75% to 85% when recorded within regular classroom settings (see Rich & Ross, 1989).

At preintervention, Cohort 1 students averaged 62% AET and Cohort 2 students 59% AET; at immediate postintervention following the 3-month intervention, these percentages were 82% and 90%, respectively. Longer-term follow-up results indicated that substantial portions of the original cohorts' intervention gains were maintained across the primary and intermediate grades where cohort members had been assigned to differing teachers and peer groups within each grade level. This was especially true for the AET measure. Child aggression ratings on the Achenbach Checklist showed satisfactory maintenance from their immediate, postintervention levels.

Replication and Social Validation of the First Step Program

During the 1996–97 school year, Golly, Stiller, and Walker (1998) conducted a replication and social validation study of the *First Step* intervention program. They applied the intervention to 20 kindergartners identified as having the early signs of a developing, antisocial behavior pattern and used the same dependent measures as Walker et al. (1998). Their results were almost identical to those reported by Walker et al. (1998). As part of this replication study, Golly et al. trained 141 school district personnel in a 1-day workshop format in how to implement the *First Step* intervention. These trainees were then followed up at the end of the school year to determine how many had actually implemented *First Step* and how satisfied they were with it. Approximately half of these trainees were able to implement *First Step* during the current school year. All those who implemented it and responded to the survey reported high levels of satisfaction. The most commonly cited barriers they encountered during implementation were (a) parents who did not consistently follow through with their homeBase responsibilities, (b) lack of administrative support, and/or (c) not having the resources necessary to implement the program. Participants also reported high satisfaction levels with the workshop training.

Future Directions for the First Step Program

Currently, *First Step* is being implemented in 16 states, three Canadian provinces, and Australia and New Zealand. In the 1999 legislative session, the Oregon Legislature appropriated $500,000 to begin making *First Step* available to all school districts and schools in Oregon that wished to adopt it. In the past two years, our staff has trained teams of school professionals in *First Step* implementation in 30 of Oregon's 36 counties. We plan to continue this Oregon *First Step* replication initiative in Oregon for the foreseeable future.

A Spanish translation of *First Step* currently exists. We have spent the last two years developing the Pre-K version of the program for 3- to 5-year-olds. In March 2001 the authors received a 5-year grant from the U.S. Administration on Children, Youth, and Families to establish a Head Start Quality Research Center focused on adapting the Pre-K *First Step* program for use with Head Start children and families. We look forward to pursuing these new initiatives and expect they will further strengthen and extend the program's reach.

POLICY RECOMMENDATIONS

The ultimate goal of any behavioral intervention is to affect the incidence or prevalence of a significant recurring problem. Progress in impacting the skills of individual children and their parents via family-friendly interventions needs to result in correlated changes in the reduced prevalence of behavior disorders. In order to decrease the occurrence of antisocial behavior, it is of critical importance that validated, cost-effective home and school interventions be delivered early on in the school careers of at-risk children.

The origins of antisocial behavior patterns are in evidence at a very early age, and these behavioral signs can be prevented from escalating into more serious and intractable problems. Such effective practices should include universal screening to provide early detection, school-based interventions, training in parenting skills, and teacher inservice training, all of which have been empirically demonstrated to increase prosocial behavior and reduce aggressive behavior problems (Jensen, 2001; Reid, 1993; Walker, Colvin, & Ramsey, 1995). If we are to succeed in diverting the thousands of children who are currently on a destructive life path from long-term negative outcomes, it is imperative that we make far greater investments in prevention initiatives than is currently the case. Many of the children currently entering the schoolhouse have already been exposed to numerous, severe risks in their first years of life. The damaging effects of such exposure can easily be seen in the behavioral, emotional, and social characteristics of such children as they try to cope with the unfamiliar demands of the schooling process.

In many cases, these children come from such dysfunctional backgrounds that the normalizing and protective influences of the schooling process are insufficient to undo their background's negative impact. These children are destined to struggle in school and in many other sectors of their lives. They are candidates for secondary and tertiary prevention strategies from the moment they begin their school careers (see Eddy, Reid, & Curry, this volume). Other children are at risk, but at far less severity, and they are much more likely to have successful school experiences. Some may demonstrate the social resiliency necessary to lead productive, fulfilling lives (Katz, 1997).

We believe the risk factors that result in children coming to school suffering from such damage can be effectively addressed by nurse home-visiting programs (see Olds et al., 1999), by Head Start, by proven preschool models such as the remarkably effective Perry Preschool Project (see Barnett, 1985), and by the Regional Intervention Program developed by Strain and his colleagues (Strain & Timm, in press), which teaches families how to cope effectively with severe oppositional behavior in young children. A coordinated continuum of effective early interventions, including the above programs, that addresses the needs of severely at-risk children from ages 0–5 and their families, is a social investment that has the potential to return significant cost savings over the long term.

Similarly, we need to ensure that every child has access to the supports and resources necessary to successfully negotiate the transitions from preschool to kindergarten and first grade. Getting off to the best possible start in school is of critical importance to every child and, most especially, to an at-risk child's school career. Compelling longitudinal research by Hawkins et al. (1999) shows that comprehensive early intervention, delivered in the first three grades of school and that involves parents, teachers, and the target child, provides protection against a number of health-risk behaviors at age 18. These risks include delinquent acts, school failure and dropout, teenage pregnancy, heavy drinking, school behavior problems, and having multiple sex partners. We cannot afford to ignore the enormous policy implications of these and similar robust findings.

We currently have the knowledge and available expertise to implement these prevention initiatives with good integrity. However, as yet, we have not demonstrated the will to (a) assume ownership of them, (b) invest the resources necessary to support their implementation, and (c) provide the long-term supports that will ensure their maintenance and durability. We are hopeful that the next decade will see positive changes in the policies of schools, mental health systems, social services agencies, and legislative bodies that will allow these important goals to be realized.

REFERENCES

Achenbach, T. (1991). *The Child Behavior Checklist: Manual for the teacher's report form.* Burlington, VT: Department of Psychiatry, University of Vermont.

Angold, A. (2000). *Preadolescent screening and data analysis.* Paper presented to the 2nd Annual Expert Panel Meeting on Preadolescent Screening Procedures. Sponsored by the Substance Abuse and Mental Health Services Administration, National Institutes of Health, Dec. 1, Washington, DC.

Barnett, W. S. (1985). The Perry Preschool Program and its long-term effects: A benefit-cost analysis. *High/Scope Early Childhood Policy Papers* (No. 2). Ypsilanti, MI: High/Scope.

Behar, L., & Stringfield, S. (1974). *Manual for the preschool behavior questionnaire.* Durham, NC: Behar.

Blechman, E., & Hile, M. (in press). Broadband risk assessment. In E. Blechman, C. Fishman, & D. Fishman (Eds.), *Building a prosocial community: School-based prevention of youth violence, suicide and substance abuse.* Champaign, IL: Research Press.

Brophy, A. L. (1986). Confidence intervals for true scores and retest scores on clinical tests. *Journal of Clinical Psychology, 42*(6), 989-991.

Brophy, J., & Evertson, C. (1981). *Student characteristics and teaching.* New York: Longman.

Burns, B., & Goldman, S. K. (Eds.). (1998). *Systems of care, promising practices in children's mental health series, Vol. IV: Promising practices in wraparound for children with serious emotional disturbance and their families* [microform]. Rockville, MD: National Technical Assistance Center for Children's Mental Health, Georgetown University.

Conners, C. K. (1989). *Manual for the Conners' Rating Scales.* North Tonawanda, NY: Multi-Health Systems.

Drummond, T. (1993). *The Student Risk Screening Scale* (SRSS). Grants Pass, OR: Josephine County Mental Health Program.

Eisert, D. C., Walker, H. M., Severson, H., & Block, A. (1989). Patterns of social-behavioral competence in behavior disordered preschoolers. *Early Childhood Development and Care, 41,* 139-152.

Epstein, M. H., & Walker, H. M. (Eds.). (in press). Special education: Best practices and *First Step to Success.* In B. Burns, K. Hoagwood, & M. English (Eds.), *Community-based interventions for youth with serious emotional disorders.* Cary, NC: Oxford University Press.

Feil, E. G., & Becker, W. C. (1993). Investigation of a multiple-gated screening system for preschool behavior problems. *Behavioral Disorders, 19*(1), 44-53.

Feil, E. G., Walker, H. M., & Severson, H. H. (1995). Young children with behavior problems: Research and development of the Early Screening Project. *Journal of Emotional and Behavioral Disorders, 3*(4), 194-202.

Gerber, M. M., & Semmel, M. I. (1984). Teacher as imperfect test: Reconceptualizing the referral process. *Educational Psychologist, 19*(3), 137-148.

Golly, A., Stiller, B., & Walker, H. M. (1998). First Step to Success: Replication and social validation of an early intervention program for achieving secondary prevention goals. *Journal of Emotional and Behavioral Disorders, 6*(4), 243-250.

Greenberg, M. T., Domitrovich, C., & Bumbarger, B. (1999). *Preventing mental disorders in school-age children: A review of the effectiveness of prevention programs.* Available from the Prevention Research Center for the Promotion of Human Development, College of Health and Human Development, Pennsylvania State University, State College, PA.

Greenwood, C., Walker, H. M., Todd, N., & Hops, H. (1979). Selecting a cost-effective device for the assessment of social withdrawal. *Journal of Applied Behavior Analysis, 12,* 639-652.

Gresham, F. M., Lane, K. L., MacMillan, D. L., & Bocian, K. M. (1999). Social and academic profiles of externalizing and internalizing groups: Risk factors for emotional and behavioral disorders. *Behavioral Disorders, 24*(3), 231-245.

Gresham, F. M., MacMillan, D. L., & Bocian, K. (1996). "Behavioral earthquakes": Low frequency, salient behavioral events that differentiate students at-risk for behavioral disorders. *Behavioral Disorders, 21*(4), 277-292.

Hawkins, J. D., Catalano, R. F., Kosterman, R., Abbott, R., & Hill, K. G. (1999). Preventing adolescent health-risk behaviors by strengthening protection during childhood. *Archives of Pediatrics & Adolescent Medicine, 153,* 226-234.

Hoagwood, K. (2000). Commentary: The dose effect in children's mental health services. *Journal of the American Academy of Child and Adolescent Psychiatry, 39*(2), 172-175.

Hoagwood, K., & Erwin, H. D. (1997). Effectiveness of school-based mental health services for children: A 10-year research review. *Journal of Child and Family Studies, 6*(4), 435-451.

Hops, H., & Walker, H. M. (1988). *CLASS: Contingencies for Learning Academic and Social Skills.* Seattle, WA: Educational Achievement Systems.

Jensen, P. S. (2001). The search for evidence-based approaches to children's mental health. *Emotional & Behavioral Disorders in Youth, 1*(3), 49, 50, 65.

Kashani, J. H., Jones, M. R., Bumby, K. M., & Thomas, L. A. (1998). Youth violence: Psychosocial risk factors, treatment, prevention, and recommendations. *Journal of Emotional and Behavioral Disorders, 7*(4), 200-210.

Katz, M. (1997). *On playing a poor hand well.* New York: Norton.

Kazdin, A. (1987). Treatment of antisocial behavior in children: Current status and future directions. *Psychological Bulletin, 102,* 187-203.

Lloyd, J. W., Kauffman, J. M., Landrum, T. J., & Roe, D. L. (1991). Why do teachers refer pupils for special education? An analysis of referral records. *Exceptionality, 2*(3), 115-126.

Loeber, R., Dishion, T. J., & Patterson, G. R. (1984). Multiple gating: A multi-stage assessment procedure for identifying youths at risk for delinquency. *Journal of Research in Crime and Delinquency, 21*(1), 7-32.

Loeber, R., & Farrington, D. P. (Eds.). (1998). *Serious and violent juvenile offenders: Risk factors and successful interventions.* Thousand Oaks, CA: Sage.

Lynam, D. (1996). Early identification of chronic offenders: Who is the fledgling psychopath? *Psychological Bulletin, 120,* 209-234.

May, S., Ard, B., Todd, A., Horner, R., Glasgow, A., Sugai, G., & Sprague, J. R. (2001). *SWIS user's manual: Learning to use the school-wide information system.* Eugene: Center on Positive Behavioral Interventions and Supports, University of Oregon.

Merrell, K. W. (1999). *Behavioral, social, and emotional assessment of children and adolescents.* Mahwah, NJ: Erlbaum.

Merrell, K. W. (2001). Assessment of children's social skills: Recent developments, best practices, and new directions. *Exceptionality, 9*(1 & 2), 3-18.

Moffitt, T. (1994). Adolescence-limited and life-course-persistent antisocial behavior: A developmental taxonomy. *Psychological Review, 100*(4), 674-701.

National Association of School Psychologists. (2000). *1999-2000 annual report.* Bethesda, MD: Author.

Olds, D., Henderson, C., Kirtzman, H., Eckenrode, J., Cole, R., & Tatelbaum, R. (1999). Prenatal and infancy home visitation by nurses: Recent findings. *The Future of Children, 9*(1), 44-65. Los Alto, CA: The David and Lucile Packard Foundation.

Patterson, G. R., Reid, J. B., & Dishion, T. J. (1992). *Antisocial boys.* Eugene, OR: Castalia.

Reid, J. B. (1993). Prevention of conduct disorder before and after school entry: Relating interventions to developmental findings. *Development & Psychopathology, 5,* 311-319.

Rich, H., & Ross, S. (1989). Students' time on learning tasks in special education. *Exceptional Children, 55*(6), 508-515.

Ross, A. (1980). *Psychological disorders of children: A behavioral approach to theory, research and therapy* (2nd ed.). New York: McGraw-Hill.

Salvia, J., & Ysseldyke, J. E. (1988). Assessment in special and remedial education. Boston: Houghton Mifflin.

Sinclair, E., Del'Homme, M., & Gonzalez, M. (1993). Systematic screening for preschool behavior disorders. *Behavioral Disorders, 18*(3), 175-185.

Sprague, J. R., & Walker, H. M. (2000). Early identification and intervention for youth with antisocial and violent behavior. In R. Skiba & R. L. Peterson (Eds.), Building safe and responsive schools: Perspectives on school discipline and school violence. *Exceptional Children, 66*(3[Special issue]), 367-379.

Strain, P. S., & Timm, M. A. (in press). An evaluation of the Regional Intervention Program over a quarter century. *Behavioral Disorders.*

Sugai, G., Sprague, J. R., Horner, R. H., & Walker, H. M. (2000). Preventing school violence: The use of office discipline referrals to assess and monitor school-wide discipline interventions. *Journal of Emotional and Behavioral Disorders, 8*(2), 94-101.

Wagner, M. (1989, April). *The national transition study: Results of a national longitudinal study of transition from school to work for students with disabilities.* Paper presented at the Council for Exceptional Children's Annual Convention, San Francisco.

Walker, H. M. (1986). The Assessments for Integration into Mainstream Settings (AIMS) assessment system: Rationale, instruments, procedures, and outcomes. *Journal of Clinical Child Psychology, 15*(1), 55–63.

Walker, H. M., Block-Pedego, A., Todis, B., & Severson, H. (1991). *School archival records search (SARS): User's guide and technical manual.* Longmont, CO: Sopris West.

Walker, H. M., Colvin, G., & Ramsey, E. (1995). *Antisocial behavior in schools: Strategies and best practices.* Pacific Grove, CA: Brooks/Cole.

Walker, H. M., Kavanagh, K., Stiller, B., Golly, A., Severson, H. H., & Feil, E. G. (1997). *First step to success: Helping young children overcome antisocial behavior.* Longmont, CO: Sopris West.

Walker, H. M., Kavanagh, K., Stiller, B., Golly, A., Severson, H. H., & Feil, E. G. (1998). First step to success: An early intervention approach for preventing school antisocial behavior. *Journal of Emotional and Behavioral Disorders, 6*(2), 66–80.

Walker, H. M., Nishioka, V., Zeller, R., Severson, H. H., & Feil, E. G. (2000). Causal factors and partial solutions for the persistent under-identification of students having emotional and behavioral disorders in the context of schooling. *Assessment for Effective Intervention, 26*(1), 29–40.

Walker, H. M., & Severson, H. H. (1990). *Systematic Screening for Behavior Disorders: User's guide and administration manual.* Longmont, CO: Sopris West.

Walker, H. M., Severson, H. H., & Feil, E. G. (1995). *Early Screening Project: A proven child-find process.* Longmont, CO: Sopris West.

Walker, H. M., Severson, H. H., Todis, B. J., Block-Pedego, A., Williams, G .J., Haring, N. G., & Barckley, M. (1990). Systematic Screening for Behavior Disorders (SSBD): Further validation, replication, and normative data. *Remedial and Special Education, 11*(2), 32–46.

Walker, H. M., Stieber, S., Ramsey, E., & O'Neill, R. E. (1990). Longitudinal prediction of the school achievement, adjustment, and delinquency of antisocial versus at-risk boys. *Remedial and Special Education, 12*(4), 43–51.

Zigler, E., Taussig, C., & Black, K. (1992). Early childhood intervention: A promising preventative for juvenile delinquency. *American Psychologist, 47,* 997–1006.

AUTHORS' NOTES

Author correspondence and reprint requests should be sent to Edward Feil, Ph.D., Oregon Research Institute, 1715 Franklin Blvd., Eugene, OR 97403-1983. Ph.: (541) 484-2123; Fax: (541) 484-1108; E-mail: *edf@ori.org.*

CHAPTER 8

Tools for Building Safe, Effective Schools

Kevin P. Dwyer
American Institutes for Research

At a conference on youth violence His Holiness the Dalai Lama was asked in a loud crass voice by a past Director of the FBI, "What would you suggest to get today's disrespectful youth to be respectful of authority?" In a very soft and even voice His Holiness said, "If you listen to them they will respect you."

INTRODUCTION

In one state almost 80% of high school students surveyed reported that they felt they could not talk to an adult in their school about personal problems (Rhode Island Departments of Education & Health, 1999). A national survey of youth reports similar isolation from this adult support (Shell Oil Company, 1999). Listening and caring are critical characteristics of safe schools (Dwyer & Osher, 2000). Do schools have in place policies, procedures, and practices that enable students to be heard and to feel safe, cared for, and respected?

Building safe and effective schools for the 21st century is not an easy task. It will require far more than adding a curriculum for teaching social skills or a peer conflict resolution strategy. Social skill and problem-solving skill development is necessary but not sufficient for improving the safety and effectiveness of schools. Furthermore, adding another curriculum to the already burdened teaching demands could result in a poor application of either intervention and do harm by ineffectively using valuable teaching time and other human resources. If making schools safe and effective for *all* children required simple strategies, effective solutions already would be in place.

This chapter proposes, first, that schools must ensure that children learn psychological and behavioral skills and competencies in addition to traditional academic skills. Building safe, effective schools requires the planned, coordinated infusion of several strategies that are designed, implemented, and evaluated to make sure that all children have the academic, psychosocial, and behavioral skills that result in successful functioning. Second, it argues that schools should achieve high standards of safety and effectiveness when targeting and reducing the student behaviors that increase fear, delay or disrupt instruction, and result in teachers feeling burned-out and in children feeling unprotected and neglected. Third, it prescribes that resources and authorization for assessing, planning, training, implementing, and evaluating programs be included. Combinations of coordinated strategies that are implemented effectively will increase instructional time, academic achievement, and graduation rates as well as decrease time lost to discipline referrals, suspensions and expulsions, grade retentions, and inappropriate referrals to special education (Skiba & Peterson, 1999).

There is enough evidence that, without psychosocial behavioral skills, children are less academically successful and teachers are prevented from teaching (American Federation of Teachers, 1998; Skiba & Peterson, 1999). Incorporating psychosocial and behavioral competence into the goals of schooling is now a policy of many states, federal agencies, and the nation's educational leadership (National Education Goals Panel, 1992; Learning First Alliance, 2001) including the U.S. Departments of Education, Justice, and Health and Human Services (Dwyer & Osher, 2000). These policies, designed to address barriers to academic achievement, were catapulted into prominence by a rash of school violence in the last decade.

Violence is rare in schools; on the other hand, bullying and disrupted teaching are too common (National Education Goals Panel, 1998). However, the small number of school shootings during the last decade resulting in multiple deaths created a strong public outcry to improve school safety. In 1998, in response to this outcry and at the request of then-President Clinton, the Department of Justice under Attorney General Janet Reno and the Department of Education under Secretary Richard Riley prepared *Early Warning, Timely Response: A Guide to Safe Schools* (Dwyer, Osher, & Warger, 1998). The *Guide* was mailed to every school principal in the United States in September 1998. Between 1998 and 2001 over one million copies of the *Guide* were copied, downloaded, reprinted, and distributed to schools, agencies, organizations, and concerned individuals across the nation and the world.

Pleased by the positive feedback on the *Early Warning Guide,* these federal departments prepared *Safeguarding Our Children: An Action Guide* (Dwyer & Osher, 2000) to help schools implement the school safety principles addressed in the *Early Warning Guide.* The *Action Guide* contains many examples of model strategies and programs designed to reduce school violence and strategies to help children gain access to research-based services and supports. The *Action Guide* is grounded in evidence-based practices that have a history of several years of data supporting their efficacy. An outgrowth of these documents and the nation's concern for school safety resulted in the federal funding of numerous interagency grants awarded to local school systems to develop comprehensive school safety programs (U.S. Department of Health and Human Services, 1999c).

Implementing the *Action Guide*

This chapter will help familiarize the reader with the tools in the *Action Guide.* The reader will learn the "how to" for assessing the school community and developing and implementing a comprehensive plan that would address the psychosocial and academic goals of education in a safe school environment. A comprehensive plan for prevention through early and intensive intervention must include strategies for the following:

- Establishing a responsive school climate;

- Ensuring strategies for promoting mental health, by teaching and supporting skills that improve problem solving, and for preventing emotional and behavior problems;

- Recognizing, reporting, and using the early warning signs of psychosocial, behavioral and academic problems and the imminent warning signs of violence, in order to provide early and individualized school interventions.

- Ensuring a full array of effective interventions, including intensive interagency interventions for children and families needing those supports;

- Addressing school-community crises in a planned and effective manner; and

- Ensuring that all plans for programs, interventions, and strategies in each school are both family friendly and culturally competent.

The foundation for this approach is based upon education and public health theory using a three-level model broadly recognized as the most effective and resource-efficient approach to successfully address these goals (National Research Council & Institute of Medicine, 1999; 2000; Marx & Wooley, 1998; Nastasi, Varjas, & Bernstein, 1997). Figure 1, on page 170, illustrates this model.

THE COMPREHENSIVE THREE-LEVEL APPROACH TO PREVENTION AND INTERVENTION

A planned and aligned combination of strategies forming a comprehensive program of evidence-based interventions is critical. Piecemeal solutions either do not work or are less effective in reaching all children (U.S. Departments of Education & Justice, 1998; Dwyer, 2001). Prevention without early intervention serves those not at risk, and intensive interventions without prevention result in overuse of costly high- intensity services. It is the integration of all three that ensures all children will have maximum opportunities to learn.

Proven interventions must be used. Many violence prevention and intervention strategies are untested and unproven. According to *Youth Violence: A Report of the Surgeon General* (Satcher, 2001) metal detectors, school resource officers, zero tolerance, and television monitors all remain unproven strategies, not yet subjected to rigorous research. (Unproven programs may well be effective but at present there is insufficient information to justify that claim.) The Surgeon General's report (Satcher, 2001) also states that

FIGURE 1

Comprehensive Three-Level Approach to Prevention and Intervention

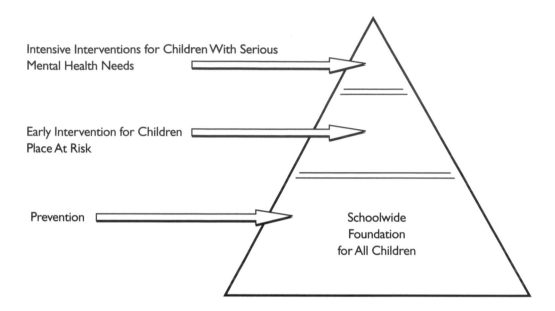

Drug Abuse Resistance Education (D.A.R.E.), peer counseling, boot camps, and residential programs are ineffective or disproved interventions in reducing delinquency and drug abuse, whereas researched strategies such as I Can Problem Solve, The Good Behavior Game, and Multisystemic Therapy can prevent problems and effectively treat problems when implemented with fidelity.

Many "programs" are designed to address one or more elements of prevention or intervention. Yet, few have demonstrated that they address the three-level approach to prevention and intervention necessary to ensure mentally healthy and safe schools. The three-level approach to school safety is an analog of the "public health" approach to illness: prevent what you can (immunization); intervene early for those most vulnerable (prenatal and infant care for teen mothers, diet to prevent diabetes and heart disease for those at higher risk); and intensively treat those who are already ill (antibiotics for bacterial infections). Similar models have been presented by the Institute of Medicine (Allensworth, Lawson, Nicholson, & Wyche, 1997). The model in the *Action Guide* is in line with Walker and Sprague's revision of this model for use in schools in addressing students' mental health (1999). The same model can be used for academics; prevent illiteracy through effective reading instruction; intervene early for those who are at risk for reading problems and those not responding to the regular instructional program; and intensively address those nonreaders with identified dyslexia early in their schooling.

A schoolwide behavior/mental health prevention program, like any effective reading program, will meet the needs of the vast majority of students and is the foundation for any effective school (see Figure 1). However, if there are no early or intensive interventions in place for those not responding to the reading program, the school will have large numbers of retentions or referrals to special education for suspected "learning disabilities." A school that does not address the needs of the students who fail to learn the skills necessary to behave appropriately will have educational "casualties," either referred for special education as emotionally disturbed or suspended, expelled and sent to juvenile detention programs as delinquents, or both. Therefore, it is critical for all schools to include, within their ongoing programs, behavioral and academic remedial intervention strategies that work. And, for those children who are entrenched in a morass of difficulties, intensive interventions must be in effect. These intensive interventions will often require wraparound services, case management, respite family services, and coordination among a range of social agencies.

The *Early Warning* and *Action Guide* recommend a plan that incorporates these three components as an integral part of the school's reform or improvement plan. Each component is not an "add-on" but an integral component of school improvement plans (Adelman & Taylor, 1998). The model is also dependent upon a schoolwide team for the planning and implementation of integrated academic and psychosocial, behavioral programming that is coordinated across the whole school community. School communities that have comprehensive prevention and response plans in place, and teams to design and implement those plans, report the following outcomes:

- Improved academic achievement;

- Reduced disciplinary actions (referrals, suspensions, expulsions);

- Improved school climate/culture that is conducive to learning;

- Improved staff morale and parent satisfaction;

- Improved use of human and financial resources; and

- Improved safety.

SYSTEMIC PLANNING

Planning Takes Time, Administrative Support, and Teaming

The *Action Guide* was designed for individuals and teams in school systems whose responsibility is to create a comprehensive school-community program that addresses the academic and behavioral needs of all children and includes violence prevention and crisis response planning.

Take time to plan. Building a comprehensive plan takes time and requires administrative authorization and input from families and the entire school community. Significant time and resources must be available to allow for effective planning (Fullen

& Stiegelbauer, 1991). Many have found that planning requires slowing down the "quick fix" advocates who may be intervention focused. All too frequently school systems "identify" an observable problem such as "student-to-student fighting" and designate a faculty member to implement a "conflict resolution program" only to realize later that the recent increase in fighting may have been a result of some institutional practice such as the overemphasis on numerous grade-level athletic or academic competitions in combination with changed demographics. Thoughtful and careful planning enables the team to examine multiple variables to better determine what is behind the observable troubling behaviors.

Although everyone wants to ensure that the school is immune from strife, aggression, and violence, no plan can guarantee that a school community will be immune to violence. However, having a plan in place and implementing that plan with fidelity can *reduce* the likelihood of violence and enable school communities to be prepared should an act of violence occur. Proposing plans with unrealistic expectations or guarantees can be as harmful as not planning. All stakeholders need to be reminded that the best-researched interventions, when properly implemented, may show outcomes of *reduced* fighting, *reduced* vandalism, *reduced* bullying, *reduced* drug use, and *reduced* office referrals. Some also show *increased* reading scores with more children reaching basic skill levels. However, no program ensures that *all* children will reach a set standard of competency. Further, few proven strategies or interventions have been tried with all racial, ethnic, cultural, language, and disability groups. Developmental appropriateness must also be considered—strategies that work with primary grade children can be inappropriate for intermediate grades. (See Hawkins, Catalano, & Associates, 1992.)

Demonstrate administrative leadership. The importance of careful planning cannot be understated. Critical to school-community planning is the administrative authority and resource support necessary to plan effectively. Systemic changes frequently require policy decisions, modifications of roles and responsibilities, and "waivers" from less productive demands that can be barriers to implementation. The school or district central office administration provides the authority and resources to initiate the planning process. The local school administrator should be an active participant on the planning team. This administrative participation models support for the plan and acknowledges its central importance in school improvement.

Include the community. Evidence suggests that some of the most promising prevention and intervention strategies involve the entire educational community—administrators, teachers, families, students, support staff, and community members—working together to form positive relationships with all children (Marx & Wooley, 1998; Nastasi et al., 1997). The inclusion of critical stakeholders in the earliest stages of planning enhances essential "buy-in" (Knoff, 1996).

Safety and responsiveness to the mental health needs of students should be a top, schoolwide priority and a key component of school improvement (Curtis & Stollar, 1995; Elias & Tobias, 1996; Knoff, 1996). When students feel safe, behaviorally competent, and cared for, they learn better (Comer, Haynes, Joyner, & Ben-Avie, 1996; Slavin, Madden, Karweit, Dolan, & Wasik, 1992).

The planning group must ask the following questions:

- Are the school improvement plans based on an effective assessment of the school community's assets and needs?

- Is the plan made up of interventions that have worked in other similar communities (rural/urban, high mobility, high poverty)?

- Is the cost of training and implementation clearly defined and understood by critical stakeholders?

- Will additional staff be needed, or will staff be reassigned and roles changed?

- Do the interventions "fit" the diversity of the school community, including use with both male and female students as well as differing ethnic, racial, and language groups? Are the plans developmentally appropriate, sequenced, and aligned?

- Can some components of the interventions be altered without losing positive effects? Are there clear and fundamental principles identified that must be maintained?

- Is there technical assistance available for the interventions? How much will the technical assistance cost?

- Is there a recommended evaluation process, including measures of fidelity?

LINKING THE SCHOOLWIDE TEAM WITH THE STUDENT SUPPORT TEAM

In most schools, specific individuals are already charged with pieces of this planning-implementation task. Existing structures should be used whenever possible to facilitate program buy-in and development. Developing another team, another coordinator, and another plan may result in fragmentation and poor coordination.

The *Action Guide* recommends that schools employ two teams: one that addresses overall school improvement and another that addresses individual student needs. A minimum of three people—the principal; a master teacher; and a mental health professional such as a counselor, school psychologist or social worker—should serve on both teams as a *core* group that coordinates the efforts of both teams, works to establish school improvement efforts, and helps to ensure that plans are aligned, implemented, and embedded in the school's foundation (Knoff, Curtis, & Batsche, 1997).

The *Action Guide* refers to the first team as the Schoolwide Team. Most schools already have such a team in place that addresses school climate, academic reform, and operational policies and procedures, as well as selecting programs to be implemented

FIGURE 2

School Teams

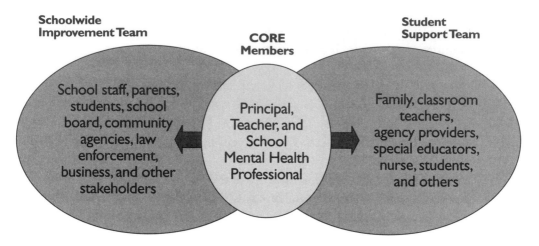

Adapted from Dwyer and Osher (2000)

throughout the school. The second team, referred to as the Student Support Team, addresses student individual needs and, in some schools, may be known as the Child Study Team or Student Assistance Team. Responsibilities of the Student Support Team include evaluating student academic and behavioral needs, consulting with teachers and families, and generating effective planned interventions.

Each team has different responsibilities but coordination is necessary to ensure their tasks' effectiveness. To facilitate coordination the teams should have the above core group members in common. Figure 2 shows how school teams work together.

Linking the Schoolwide Team with the Student Support Team enables school improvement efforts to effectively reach all children including those with specific academic and psychosocial needs and disabilities. School reform and school improvement will succeed when behavioral, mental health, and academic skills are addressed in strategic planning efforts (Adelman & Taylor, 1998).

Forming Your Schoolwide Team

As indicated earlier, most schools have an existing schoolwide team responsible for school improvement, operations, and reform. Broad community participation can make such a team more effective. The schoolwide team must be as broad based as possible. The following members are suggested:

- PTA, PTO representatives, family advocacy members, including mental health advocates;

- Students;

- Law enforcement personnel, attorneys, judges, and probation officers;

- Representatives of the faith community;

- Media representatives;

- Mental health and child welfare personnel;

- Physicians and nurses (including representatives from health maintenance organizations);

- Family agency and family resource center staff;

- Business leaders;

- Recreation, cultural, and arts organizations staff;

- Youth workers and volunteers;

- Local officials, including school board members and representatives from special commissions;

- Interest group representatives and grass-roots community organization members;

- College or university faculty;

- Members of local advisory boards; and

- Other influential community members.

Schoolwide Team Effectiveness

Once this group has been assembled, there is no assurance that its members will function as an effective team. A *core* group member should act as the team facilitator to ensure that the team functions effectively and maintains its visionary goals. Cohesiveness, a shared purpose, and other primary characteristics of effective teams will be enhanced through the following practices:

- Take time at the onset to agree on a vision;

- Ensure that each member makes a commitment to participate in all relevant team activities;

- Avoid blaming. Agencies and families cannot improve coordination in an atmosphere of blame;

- Provide team members with the necessary information and support to enable them to participate on the team as equals. Avoid the perception of a "rubber stamp" participation of members;

- Staff the team with a secretary. All team members should receive copies of meeting notes and proposed reforms in a timely fashion to prepare for the next meeting. Meeting schedules should be prepared well in advance;

- Appoint a member to be responsible for liaison functions. This includes keeping the greater school community informed, as well as linking to other school and community teams; and

- Develop a process for solving problems and making decisions. For example, the team should determine whether decisions would be made by consensus, majority, or some other clear and agreed upon process.

Building a team takes time. Over time, as members support each other and accomplish objectives, a feeling of trust and mutual respect will emerge. Additional individuals may be included at various points and this may have an impact on team dynamics and functioning. Thus, it is important that the team membership remain consistent, providing stability for planning, implementation tasks, and interpersonal processes. Every plan should begin with an assessment to determine what available resources and critical needs exist, as well as how the plan maximizes resource strengths and addresses identified needs. Further, assessments provide the team with base-rate data enabling you to evaluate your early and intensive intervention program(s).

Your Student Support Team

Safe schools each have a specialized Student Support Team of trained professionals (including core team members—the principal, master teacher, and school mental health staff) who provide consultation; use problem solving; and develop, monitor, and evaluate interventions when referred students are believed to be involved in high-risk behaviors or are experiencing academic and/or emotional stress. Most schools already have established procedures and teams to address such academic and behavior problems. In some schools, these are called the Child Study Team, Student Assistance Team, Prereferral Team, or School-Based Assistance Team. In developing your plan, avoid duplicating what already exists. In your assessment, examine the functions of the existing team(s). Does your team provide quick access to trained professionals whose responsibility includes determining what to do to assist these students? Does it use a problem-solving model that examines and evaluates environmental factors and interventions already tried? Does the team have adequately trained members to address both academic and behavioral issues? Does the team have access to in-school and agency specialists required to supplement existing team skills? Is the team adequately resourced (in terms of time, clerical staff, computers, and communication equipment) to provide the support and consultation necessary to implement effective interventions? How has the team's functioning been evaluated in the past? When team consultation is commonplace and readily available to all staff, the referral of concerns becomes a normalized process. Student Support Teams should involve the referring person, principal, master teacher, student's teacher(s), parents, the school psychologist, counselor, school nurse, and other related in-school and/or community providers as well as other persons recommended by the student's family. When the student is receiving special education services, any team meeting may require following regulations mandated by the laws and regulations of the state and be constituted as an Individualized Education Program (IEP) Team.

CONDUCTING YOUR SCHOOL ASSESSMENT FOR ASSETS AND NEEDS: DESIGNING THE IMPLEMENTATION PLAN

Research demonstrates that school communities can do a great deal to prevent emotional and behavior problems, including violence (Elliott, Hamburg, & Williams, 1998, Knoff & Batsche, 1995; Minke & Bear, 2000; U.S. Department of Health and Human Services, 2001; Resnick, 1997). Having in place a safe and responsive foundation helps all children—and it enables school communities to provide more efficient and effective services to students who need additional support.

A safe school environment begins with an examination of the foundation of the school. Is the school a caring, family-friendly learning environment? Do all the children and their families understand the school's rules of discipline? Are social skills and problem-solving skills taught and reinforced? Are there mechanisms for evaluating the levels of competence with which these skills as well as academic skills are demonstrated? Are programs and interventions theory-driven and evidence-based?

There are 13 characteristics presented in the *Early Warning* and *Action Guides* that define safe, mentally healthy, and responsive schools. Assessing your school using these 13 characteristics may help you determine where you are and what you need to do to better ensure that your school is responsive. [See Chapter 2, "Building a Schoolwide Foundation" in Dwyer and Osher (2000).] These characteristics are listed as follows:

- Focus on academic achievement;

- Involve families in meaningful ways;

- Develop links internally and to the community;

- Emphasize positive relationships among students and staff;

- Discuss safety issues openly;

- Treat students with equal respect;

- Create ways for students to share their concerns;

- Help children feel comfortable expressing their feelings;

- Have in place a system for referring children who are suspected of being abused or neglected;

- Offer extended day programs for children and youth;

- Promote good citizenship and character through psychosocial skill development;

- Identify problems and assess progress toward solutions; and

- Support students in all transitions, particularly transition to adult life.

Many of these characteristics of a safe and responsive school have been documented in several publications that deal with drug abuse prevention, school safety, and general school reform (Adelman, 1996; Dwyer & Bernstein, 1998; Lawson & Briar-Lawson, 1997; Peters & McMahon, 1996; Marx & Wooley, 1998; U.S. Departments of Education & Justice, 1999; Woodruff et al., 1999; .)

As your school team conducts the self-assessment, the initial data collection process will provide insight into the current school and community environment. How safe are your school's children? How does your school prevent and address mental health problems such as depression and anxiety? Does your school inadvertently induce frustration through poor individualized instruction? Does it teach effective coping strategies for normal developmental stress? Do students report having trusting relationships with staff? Is staff responsive when students voice concerns? This initial assessment will furnish your school with data that will be critical to the establishment of your school's mental health and violence prevention benchmarks.

Most schools are doing many things successfully. Measuring that success enables the school to validate its progress and gain resources to sustain its efforts. It is critical that each school periodically check available data sets to maintain its success and examine overlooked issues that can inadvertently harm children. Once these benchmarks are established and calculated, you can target "big picture" indices that will assist in identifying weaknesses and in measuring progress. Examples of a wide range of measurable indices might include achievement scores; school attendance; suspensions and expulsions; student drug and alcohol use; discipline referrals; health-room referrals; referrals to community agencies, parental involvement, parental satisfaction, teacher and student satisfaction, and so forth. Student safety surveys are a critical data source. With base-rate data, these indices can be continuously monitored to determine the school's progress and the effects of the strategies and interventions that make up your program reforms.

Ongoing data collection also allows your team to assess the impact of existing and additional prevention efforts. In collecting these data, the team can address three important questions: (1) What proven strategies are we implementing? (2) Can we show that we are implementing them with adequate fidelity to the researched program or strategy? (3) Are the effects positive at significant measurable levels? In other words, is the effort worth it? Such monitoring and evaluation, like curriculum-based report cards, can assist schools and your team in determining what needs to be maintained and what may need to be modified or discarded. Existing techniques should be carefully examined as to their appropriateness and cost-effectiveness. As a result, unsuccessful programs can be stopped; poorly implemented programs can be modified as necessary; and successful programs can be continued, expanded, and institutionalized.

The assessment for establishing the base-rate data may span several months. All necessary stakeholders should be included in this process. Ideally, the team will conduct its assessment over one school term. Some have used extra days in the summer to examine base-rate data. Many successful programs, like Project ACHIEVE, suggest that the first year be one of assessment, goal setting, planning, and training before implementation (Knoff, 1996). Some schools may already have this task started but most should allow a few weeks for the Schoolwide Team to examine its characteristics for a responsive and safe school. The core team members will want to schedule frequent meetings to review these plans and their implementation.

ASSESSING RESPONSIVE SCHOOL CHARACTERISTICS

Schools need to establish base-rate data to help define reasonable goals. Most needs assessments for safe schools focus on one or more of the following: (1) the numbers of discipline referrals; (2) surveys of student, teacher, and family safety concerns; or (3) an analysis of the school plant. These are important variables to measure and cannot be overlooked. However, in evaluating the responsiveness of your school, it is critical to examine what your school is doing that is effective and what school–community assets are in place for the caring of students. Evaluating each one of the above 13 characteristics individually and together is critical to determining where you are and what you need to address in your blueprint. The goals for a responsive school are extremely important to education reform and an academically successful school. For example, focusing on academic achievement requires more than mere yearly measurements for achieving high academic standards. It requires frequent measurements of each individual student's progress and having in place quality (observable) instruction—and for those who need it, effective individualized attention to ensure progress. It also requires using evidence-based instructional and behavior management methods in the early grades and plans to support developmental transitions. For example, not teaching social skills until fifth grade because "young children's language development is conceptually concrete" defies the available research evidence. I-Can-Problem-Solve (Schure &

Spivack, 1982; Schure, 1997), a well-researched program, has been shown to positively affect the behavior of preschoolers and is quite appropriate for primary-grade students. Attaching effective academic and behavioral instruction to the goal of high academic standards is the only way to reach those standards (Adelman, 1996; Dwyer, Osher, & Hoffman, 2000).

Yet some schools fail to match high standards with needed high-quality instruction. According to reports of the National Assessment of Educational Progress, 40% of all 9-year-olds score below the standard of "basic" reading level (Learning First Alliance, 1998). Academic self-image begins early and, according to the Learning First Alliance's report on reading, children define themselves academically via their reading skills as early as first grade. Therefore, we must examine whether our schools' instructional environments and activities are enabling children to reach high standards. Are schools doing the right things to enable all primary-grade children to reach "basic" reading levels and if many are failing, what action plan must we include to reach this goal? Teaching "social skills" or establishing a conflict resolution program when the school is failing to teach reading to 4 out of 10 children may not be a productive use of school resources. The leadership in education recommends providing all children "explicit, systematic instruction in phonics and exposure to rich literature, both fiction and non-fiction" (Learning First Alliance, 1998. p. 5). Is this type of reading program in place in your school? Is every child's developmental progress being monitored and are deficiencies properly remediated?

Using existing data sets effectively. Your initial task might be to assess your school in relation to each of the 13 characteristics listed above. You should first review each area and decide whether your school is particularly strong, needs work, or is lacking in each characteristic. Use your existing data sets for this purpose whenever possible. School and community agencies maintain numerous data sets that can be used in this assessment of school-community needs and assets. In schools, records are kept on academic performance by school, grade levels, classrooms, and individual students. Discipline actions such as referrals from staff, suspensions, expulsions, and other actions should be documented and assessed. The numbers of student awards, parent volunteers, workshops, and trained mentors will also be valuable information to be included in the assessment. Attendance, mobility, and reduced and free lunch eligibility may help determine needs. Referrals for special education and related services and trends in those data can inform the school in developing effective academic and behavioral prevention programs. Remember—unused data sets are valueless.

Community data are frequently available from multiple agencies. For example, if your school community has applied for a grant it may have already gathered these data—do not reinvent the wheel. Your team might discover that students report higher rates of bullying and extortion related to increased gang activity. Gang activity in the community might require increased police monitoring or the reallocation of personnel and resources in targeted neighborhoods to support families and provide effective alternatives to gang membership. Juvenile authorities can provide trend data on the numbers of children and youth in their system and their needs. An increased number of "latchkey" children and youth also may be related to gang activity and the increase in drug abuse or vandalism and other problems. Schools exist in communities and the walls do not protect students from those community problems.

The medical community can share resource data on wellness programs, prenatal care, training of primary care physicians and pediatricians, as well as illness data including injuries related to violence to self and others. Similarly, mental health service data, including, for example, information about increases in referrals for childhood depression, attention deficit hyperactivity disorder, and anxiety disorders, can be valuable. Do not forget to assess your school's services including data showing increases in the number of school psychologists, counselors, social workers, and nurses, as well as community mental health providers and children insured under the State Children's Health Insurance Program. Assets can also include other services and grants within both the school system and other agencies. Frequently, parallel grants exist in the same community; services mapping helps your team collaborate and coordinate to better serve children and families. Mapping the whole community is important to this process. The Harvard School of Public Health has provided such a community mapping of strengths and needs (Prothrow-Stith, 1987)

Data analysis helps define needs. Once you have determined the areas in which your school has significant strengths and you have also identified areas that need attention, you should look at those need areas more closely. Just knowing that your school community is weak in a particular area will not provide all the information you need to create meaningful interventions. The data may tell you *what* is causing the problem but not *why* this is taking place. Once the particular cause is uncovered, appropriate interventions will become more apparent. For example, if the team learns that many parents are not participating in school activities you may find that the primary employer is an hour's drive from the school and the employer provides no family leave for school activities. Many families may not attend because they lack literacy in English and no one on the school staff who speaks their language is communicating with them.

Teams should use their data sets to begin more detailed and exhaustive discussion about unmet needs that may require changes in services, policies, and preventive priorities. The following section will look at one of the 13 characteristics—*focus on academic achievement*—to suggest methods a school might use to determine its needs.

Focus on academic achievement. Effective schools with high academic standards convey the attitude that all children can achieve academically and behave appropriately. Successfully achieving those standards requires adequate resources and program monitoring by the school's leadership, which ensures that all students receive effective instruction and necessary academic support.

- **Review statistics.** Examine your base data. For example, take a look at the percentage of students who graduate, drop out, repeat grades, or are referred for special education. Also look at children's progress in basic skills, and look at grades, trends, and changes as children transition to middle and high school. Attendance data also are a good measure of student engagement in academics. Research has shown that children who have high attendance rates score better on achievement tests (Finn & Rock, 1997).

- **Generate potential solutions.** Data on academic success and failure provides your team with the first step for developing cost-effective interventions. Data may tell you that your school's reading program is not accomplishing your goals. Data may also tell you that your school is experiencing a large number of behavior problems that result in reduced instructional time. These data inform the team that training and consultation are needed to improve academic achievement. When such services are unavailable or inadequate, the school may require additional resources or reorganization of resources and instructional strategies.

- **Offer training and consultation for academics.** Provide teachers with the necessary training and support to implement more effective instruction. Plan for teachers and staff to receive appropriate training in how to address the needs of diverse learners, including students with disabilities. Ensure that all children feel challenged but not frustrated. Investigate the possibility of using master teachers, team teaching, or coaching. Provide ongoing instructional consultation for academic and behavioral issues that affect learning and instruction. Include student-centered instruction techniques such as curriculum-based instruction, outcomes-based measurement, direct instruction, and structured cooperative learning.

- **Provide training and consultation for behavior.** As noted, positive behavior is related to academic learning, yet most teachers report they need more support and training to manage behavior in today's classroom (American Federation of Teachers, 1998). Is in-service training that teaches positive behavioral classroom management techniques readily available? Skilled classroom management has long-term effects—even on children who show early aggression (Kellam, Rebok, Ialongo, & Mayer, 1994).

- **Ensure remedial instruction and support** to prevent students from experiencing frustration or failure. The *Early Warning Guide* and the *Action Guide* emphasize early and timely interventions for children showing academic, emotional, and behavioral risk signs so those children can get the support they need before they begin to experience frustration, failure, or peer alienation. Success for All is a comprehensive approach to elementary school early intervention (Slavin, 1995; Slavin et al., 1992). As all children are exposed to effective instruction, learning problems are immediately identified and addressed. The interventions are intensive. The result is improved achievement scores (Ross, Smith, Slavin, & Madden, 1997). Frequently, such planned service interventions require additional resources. Use your community links to seek additional support from volunteers, after-school programs, and parent support groups to reinforce teachers' instruction. Remember that intensive remedial instruction is best accomplished by a highly trained teacher. Volunteers can help free teachers from noninstructional tasks. Avoid putting the "kind and caring" but untrained volunteer with the child who has serious reading deficits and expecting that "good" will prevail. It is critical to match instructional needs with skilled professional instructors. Trained volunteers can be effective in reinforcing skills taught by qualified teachers.

Each of the 13 characteristics is seen as critical. They should be examined by the Schoolwide Team to ensure coordination within the school and among the school's partners. Many schools have access to multiple programs within their own buildings. They may have numerous symptom-driven teams, interventions, projects, and strategies in place. Planned links with the community require the school to coordinate its services and programs effectively to avoid duplication.

Partnerships require maintenance, planning, and evaluation of their effectiveness. Interagency partnerships are difficult to establish and maintain. However, they are frequently most effective when they are built on trust and on written collaborative agreements. For example, school-based health clinics have been increasing—more than doubling in the past decade. These clinics have a demonstrated positive effect in measured health and prevention outcomes. Mental health and other health services are best delivered in the schools for many of our children. Evidence shows that the number of provider-child-family contacts increases dramatically when services are offered in the school rather than in off-site clinics (U.S. Department of Health and Human Services, 1999a). Some schools have worked cooperatively with health and mental health departments to secure funding for school-based health clinics (Dryfoos, 1994). Such complex interagency agreements require clear role definitions as well as cost sharing. Some school-based clinics have failed to engage in a full partnership with health and mental health school staff. The absence of a planned partnership results in poor use of resources (Dwyer, 2001). Success achieved through integrated service planning can be well worth the effort involved (Adelman & Taylor, 2001).

After examining your own systems coordination and linkages, look at the organization of your existing school partnerships (see above list). How do they fit together? Who is responsible for maintaining and measuring their effectiveness? Looking at all the existing links, do they appear to be sufficient? Are some children left out because of age, language, culture, or disability? Is the infrastructure (space, transportation, and equipment) adequate?

Many partnerships with community organizations may not be developed because of limited space available for providing services. Schools should be ready to cost-share by keeping the school building open through the evening to provide the space while the community partner provides the staff and materials. To enhance collaboration with family services, schools may provide their pupil services staffs flex time to work in the evening with families. A good model is Strengthening Families, a parent workshop that is cotaught by pupil services and local Mental Health Association staff (Kumpfer, DeMarsh, & Child, 1989). The Parent Teacher Association (PTA) could sponsor childcare while the parents and siblings are receiving services. Such services, using community links, can be cost effective and outcome effective. The faith-based community can also participate in linking with the school. Volunteers should be recruited. Parent outreach and consultation can be carried out in houses of worship, where parents feel comfortable. Common goals can be discussed. Issues around prejudice and group conflicts can be addressed.

Successful schools have many of the *characteristics* in place. The assessment may help the school community acknowledge and build upon its strengths. Several of the characteristics speak to students and their comfort in sharing their thoughts and expressing their feelings. When examining the characteristics that address students, it is critical to engage them in planning and implementation. How do students feel about the school environment, including issues of respect and fair treatment? What do you do to provide ways for students to share their concerns about subjects such as bullying, inappropriate touching, and verbal harassment? Do students have adults they can trust to share their feelings and worries? Are there "open doors" to psychological and counseling services? You may want to survey students or conduct focus groups with students to identify their perceptions.

Michael Furlong and colleagues developed an effective questionnaire for students at all grade levels to voice their concerns about the quality of care and safety in their school. It is an excellent starting point. The instrument has been employed successfully in Ventura, California, to survey student attitudes. When children's feelings are respected, acknowledged, and addressed early, feelings of isolation, rejection, and anger are less likely to occur—reducing the chances of learning being disrupted by behavior problems (see School Safety Survey, UCSB School Climate and Safety Partnership, Furlong & Morrison, 1995).

Once your team has evaluated its school-community capacities, needs, and problems, you are ready to put together your three-tiered comprehensive plan. The *Action Guide* suggests you begin with your schoolwide foundation for prevention.

PRIMARY PREVENTION PLANS

Responsive schools provide primary prevention by strategically planning to ensure that staff are trained and supported in implementing the schoolwide plan. The core team members (noted previously) may take the responsibility to assist the staff in maintaining the plan for effective prevention. Monitoring and support ensure that the skills are consistently taught and reinforced. The *Action Guide* describes four key components for schoolwide prevention:

- Creating a caring school community in which all members feel connected, safe, and supported.

- Teaching appropriate behaviors and social problem-solving skills.

- Implementing positive behavior support systems.

- Providing appropriate academic instruction. (*Action Guide,* p. 7)

Two schoolwide programs highlighted in the *Action Guide* are Project ACHIEVE (Knoff & Batsche, 1995) and Positive Behavioral Interventions and Supports—PBIS (Sugai & Horner, 1999). Both programs incorporate many of the components that are discussed in this chapter. They require training, staff support, and effective leadership. Like most successful schoolwide prevention programs they also require reallocated or additional resources, strong school staff and administrative "buy-in," comprehensive in-service training, ongoing consultation, and the availability of technical assistance. Project ACHIEVE, like the generic *Action Guide* model, begins with strategic planning by the school-community team working together to adopt high academic standards and a schoolwide system of positive, skill-oriented behavior management. Students are taught prosocial behaviors, problem solving, and anger management skills while teachers and parents are trained and assisted in using positive and planned interventions when problems occur. Behavioral and academic remediation is in place and community agency connections are accessed to address intensive needs.

PBIS, like ACHIEVE, was developed with U.S. Department of Education grants. PBIS focuses on prevention as well as providing behavioral supports to students with chronic behavior problems. Again, teacher consultation and training are critical components. The schoolwide behavior support system focuses on where behavior problems occur, and how factors present in the environment sustain the problem behaviors. Like ACHIEVE, the model requires a skilled professional team for ongoing monitoring and support. A structured formal functional assessment component is integrated into the PBIS program.

Some differences between PBIS and ACHIEVE are more in emphasis than in critical concepts. For example, ACHIEVE uses a "stop-and-think" technique to increase reflective rather than impulsive reaction to environmental situations and places a strong emphasis on academics and on teaching social skills. PBIS provides prevention and intervention for problem behavior, focusing more on discipline, reinforcing expected behavior, and discouraging rule violations. Both address a positive, caring school environment and require ongoing consultation, monitoring, and evaluation. Both have demonstrated significant reductions in discipline problems, retention rates, and increased teacher and parent satisfaction. Achievement gains, from pre- to postprogram implementations, have been reported by ACHIEVE (Knoff & Batsche, 1995).

Other successful schoolwide programs include Success for All (Slavin, Madden, Dolan, & Wasik, 1996) and the School Development Program (Comer et al., 1996; Haynes & Comer, 1993). The Success for All program is academic in its focus. The School Development Program targets the nurturing school environment and the multiple developmental areas that must be addressed (psychological, physical, behavioral, and academic) to ensure success. All of these programs address the array of instructional and related services necessary for prevention and early intervention that can reduce the likelihood of violence.

FROM PREVENTION TO INTERVENTION: CONNECTING EARLY WARNING SIGNS TO EARLY INTERVENTIONS

Using the modified public health model outlined in the *Action Guide,* it is extremely important that the focus of the schoolwide plan be on prevention. Prevention strategies will reduce problem behaviors and academic failure for most children. A percentage (20–40%) of children may be at risk for academic, behavioral, or psychosocial problems in your school (U.S. Department of Health and Human Services, 1999b). The Early Warning Signs (see Figure 1) identify some of the risk factors that can result in personal risk, class disruptions, and even violence. Early warning signs should help drive effective assessment and interventions by your Student Support Team. Services, strategies, and interventions for the earliest signs of problems are necessary to complement your effective prevention plans.

FIGURE I

Early and Imminent Warning Signs

This not a Checklist.

Early Warning Signs

- Social withdrawal.
- Excessive feelings of isolation and being alone.
- Excessive feelings of rejection.
- Being a victim of violence.
- Feelings of being picked on and persecuted.
- Low school interest and poor academic performance.
- Expression of violence in writings and drawings.
- Uncontrolled anger.
- Patterns of impulsive and chronic hitting, intimidating, and bullying behaviors.
- History of discipline problems.
- Past history of violent and aggressive behavior.
- Intolerance for differences and prejudicial attitudes.
- Drug use and alcohol use.
- Affiliation with gangs.
- Inappropriate access to, possession of, and use of firearms.
- Serious threats of violence (also an imminent warning sign).

Imminent Warning Signs

- Serious physical fighting with peers or family members.
- Severe destruction of property.
- Severe rage for seemingly minor reasons.
- Detailed threats of lethal violence.
- Possession and/or use of firearms and other weapons (on school property).

Note

Reprinted from *Early Warning, Timely Response: A Guide to Safe Schools* by Dwyer et al. (1998).

Referral process

Once school staff, parents, and community members become familiar with the warning signs and understand the importance of being responsive to a child exhibiting signs, they need to know how and to whom to respond. Teachers and staff should feel confident that support is readily available when they share their concerns. Having quick access to trained professionals is imperative. Consequently, your school plan should provide easy access to the Student Support Team. Training should inform staff, students, and families of the referral process for seeking help when early warning signs are observed.

An open and responsive referral process frequently requires modifications of existing procedures and policies. The following policy considerations may be helpful:

- **Policies for warning sign referrals should be clearly known.** The referral process should be simple, easy to access, and enable timely feedback to the person making the referral. If the concern is determined to be serious, but not to pose a threat of imminent danger, referral should be made to the Student Support Team. (The child's family should be contacted once a concern is recognized.) The family is consulted before implementing any formal assessments or interventions with the child. In cases where school-based contextual factors (such as bullying, poor communication between school and home, untreated disability) are determined to be causing or exacerbating the child's troubling behavior, the school acts quickly to modify them.

- **Policies and procedures should ensure that staff and students use the early warning signs for referral purposes only.** Only trained professionals should make diagnoses in consultation with the child's parents or guardian. Although teachers and other non-mental health staff are highly valued informants about child behavior, they should not make these diagnostic determinations.

- **Policies should be in place to address imminent dangers.** There must also be policies and procedures that ensure immediate safety when there is a threat of imminent danger. When warning signs indicate that danger is imminent, safety must always be the first and foremost consideration. Action must be taken immediately.

  - ▲ Cooperative agreements should be in place with law enforcement authorities when firearms, lethal weapons, explosives, and other dangerous materials are involved or suspected.

  - ▲ Imminent warning signs require procedures that enable the school to secure the student(s) while the Student Support Team gathers information, contacts the student's family, and observes, interviews, evaluates, and involves significant persons, including the family and any community providers. A threat assessment is necessary to determine the level of lethality and the best immediate and possible long-term plan for the student and others. Plans for validated imminent threats will usually require interagency coordination and collaboration as well as family cooperation.

▲ In situations where students are not determined to be an imminent threat but do present serious mental or emotional problems, parents should be immediately informed of the concerns. Schools should have agreements in place with community services enabling them or the families to seek assistance from appropriate agencies, child and family services, and community mental health centers. These referral responses should reflect school board policies and be consistent with the violence prevention and response plan.

• **Procedures for students to share concerns should be provided.** The school should provide a vehicle such as a telephone "hotline" or suggestion box in the school for students who have concerns about another student to communicate those concerns without fear of reprisal. Trusted faculty can also be confidants for students to report concerns. Once students recognize the value of the reporting system and the sense of security it brings to the school and the confidentiality of the process, they will be more likely to reflect their concerns and ally with the school community, thus furthering safety efforts.

• **Policies should be established for evaluation and record keeping.** Team functioning, the immediate and long-term plans, and the referral process for responding to warning signs should be evaluated periodically. Policies for enabling this evaluation as a component of the plan are important. Confidential records may be maintained using the ethical guideline of "do no harm"— keeping records that benefit the child, family, and school in developing and evaluating interventions. Families must have knowledge and access to any records the school maintains, including interagency records as required by law or interagency agreement.

What policies and procedures does your school have in place to support children at risk of behavior problems and those in crisis? Are consequences for aggression, for example, designed to develop replacements for aggression—or merely to punish it? Some schools have put several strategies in place including conflict resolution programs (Nastasi et al., 1997). For low-level aggression, the Think Time Strategy (Nelson, 1996) has been successfully implemented in many schools to replace traditional "time-out," resulting in fewer repeat offenders. Aggression Replacement Training (U.S. Department of Health and Human Services, 2001) is another promising program for more embedded aggressive behavior patterns. Having policies and procedures that allow such responses to replace less effective suspension and expulsion procedures that do not provide appropriate interventions helps your school become a more caring, disciplined environment (Skiba & Peterson, 1999).

Part of the training of school staff, families, and stakeholders should address the sometimes hard-to-believe reality that behavioral, mental, and emotional problems in children are common, reversible, and preventable. The Surgeon General reports that epidemiological research shows that as many as 21% of children and youth (ages 9–17) have a diagnosable mental or addictive disorder and that 11%, or 4 million youth, suffer *significant* functional impairment from these disorders. For *extreme* impairment, the estimate is 5% of children or 1.81 million (U.S. Department of Health and Human Services, 1999a). According to that report, although many believe Attention-Deficit/Hyperactivity Disorder (ADHD) is the most common childhood problem, twice as many children are functionally affected by anxiety and depression (U.S. Department of Health and Human Services, 1999a). Behavioral treatments for mental and emotional problems, among others, are proven effective (Weisz, Weiss, Han, Granger, & Morton, 1995). The team should use this and other research-based information to further develop resources and adequate interventions for students with troubling behaviors.

Finally, this information can be used to make recommendations for policy and procedures that are responsive to the needs of these students. The focus of these policies should be on the following:

- Educating the school community about the early warning signs of mental and emotional problems and warning signs of violence;

- Planning for the development and implementation of interventions for troubled students; and

- Creation of policies and procedures for responding to crises.

Educators and parents—and students—can ensure that the early warning signs are utilized effectively by recognizing the following principles: (1) do no harm; (2) understand troubling behavior and aggression within a context; (3) avoid stereotypes; (4) understand signs within a developmental context; and (5) understand that children usually exhibit multiple warning signs when there is a problem (adapted from the *Early Warning Guide*). There are also single-page handouts in the *Early Warning Guide* for both parents and students to assist schools in involving them in this process. These handouts and referenced versions of the *Guides* can be downloaded from *www.air.org/cecp.*

Connecting the Early Warning Signs to Early Interventions

Teachers, administrators, and other school support staff are on the front line when it comes to observing troublesome behavior. They need to know the early warning signs, know with whom to share their concerns, and how to get help. Remember that the Student Support Team, with mental health expertise, should be responsible for addressing concerns about early warning signs. Staff should also be aware of the "conspiracy of silence" among students.

Caring school environments where students connect with teachers and staff are shown to support intergenerational problem solving. Furlong (2001) reports that schools supporting student dialogue about concerns, where teachers are permitted to make personal contact with students, and where student input about school climate is valued, build resiliency and reduce the "conspiracy of silence" by developing student trust of staff. Schools where shared information is ignored or results in automatic suspensions, expulsions, and arrests will be less likely to reduce the "conspiracy of silence" among students.

Procedures need to be in place that enable staff, students, and families to report concerns. Urgent, imminent concerns require the immediate availability of the principal and other personnel designated by the principal. In situations where there is no perceived imminent danger the procedures may allow for contact with the school psychologist or counselor who takes responsibility for organizing a response to the concerns. As with any serious issue of this type, the family should be consulted prior to conducting assessments or interventions. Family participation is invaluable in the determination of what to do.

Of equal importance are school policies that support ongoing training and consultation. An effective model should be procedurally supported in order to have in place a team problem-solving process. The Referral, Question, Consultation model is recommended in this regard (see *Action Guide*). This strategy is one of the eight components of Project ACHIEVE designed to investigate concerns of teachers, parents, or others working with an individual student. Specific hypothesis-driven referral questions are made and data-based, ongoing consultation is provided with the student, in partnership with teacher(s) and parents. Strategies are generated based on these consultations and interventions are designed and measured to alleviate the conditions causing the troubling behaviors. Everything is done within the context of the life-space environment of the child. A similar team problem-solving model is used with the PBIS program. Both involve team problem solving, consultation, and planning followed by intervention, monitoring, and evaluation of results.

The referral process enables the consultation team (Student Support Team) to establish base-rate data, to initiate a functional assessment, and to develop the structured interventions necessary to (a) replace the troubling behaviors and (b) make the environment, and the critical interactions, conducive to the child's learning and psychological well-being. Interventions must be implemented as planned and the components of an intervention should be theory driven and evidence based. Fidelity, within the context of appropriate individualization, should be maintained. When the interventions have had adequate time to effect change, systematic monitoring should help determine whether adjustments are required. An intervention that is not evaluated teaches little to the teacher, the team, or family. Data-driven evaluations are critical.

Understanding early and imminent warning signs is an essential step in ensuring a safe school. However, it can be difficult to acknowledge that a child is troubled.

Everyone—including administrators, families, teachers, school staff, students, and community members—may find it too troubling sometimes to admit that a child close to them needs help. When faced with such resistance or denial, the school team, working with others, must persist to ensure that the student gets the help he or she needs. Experience has shown that, for some families with histories of distrust of school authority or disappointments in promised interventions, rebuilding trust is the first step to an intervention (Catron, Harris, & Weiss, 1998).

By now, both the Schoolwide and Student Support teams should have a good idea of which policies, procedures, and practices need to be implemented to address troubling student behavior. It is important to have administrative support and to identify the people who will be responsible for implementation. The Student Support Team is the responsible agent in this regard. The team should be as inclusive as possible. Many others may be called to participate in designing and implementing the student's plan. The team problem-solving process should not be rigid or static but instead structured. A specific problem-solving team and the school's policies and procedures should enable the resources necessary for each situation. The team, in conjunction with the people responsible for each intervention, should also develop evaluation criteria and timelines for the implementation of each suggested change.

The *Action Guide* provides two pages of early intervention strategies including "environmental modifications" such as changing the structure of class seating in order to increase proximity control, to a "behavioral support plan" to teach a replacement behavior in multiple environments to facilitate generalization. Other recommended interventions include Positive Adolescent Choices Training (U.S. Department of Health and Human Services, 2001)—a promising secondary school curriculum for African-American youth who are demonstrating conduct problems or have histories of victimization.

Having in place trained staff and multiple strategies that can address a full complex of needs is critical. These services, related policies, and rules will provide the second level of foundation for creating a school environment that prevents many acts of violence from occurring by helping the school community to be aware of students' need for help and preparing them to provide that support. Research has shown that having this supportive environment will, in many cases, eliminate another 15–17% of student behavior problems (Walker & Sprague, 1999).

As the recent Surgeon General's report indicated, as many as 5% of students will still have significant emotional and behavioral problems (U.S. Department of Health & Human Services, 1999a). These students will need more intensive services. Supporting early intervention for at-risk early warning signs is doubly important when addressing services to students with complex, functionally disabling problems.

PROVIDING TARGETED AND INTENSIVE SUPPORT TO TROUBLED STUDENTS

In addition to effective violence prevention strategies and early interventions for children showing risk behaviors, each school-community plan must include more intense interventions for students who are extremely behaviorally or emotionally disabled. Services for these children must address the specific and complex factors that influence emotional turmoil and potentially violent behavior. To maximize success, these programs need to include coordination among multiple agencies. However, many of these services can be located in the school to best integrate community programs and services. Most mental health professionals regard schools as a primary site for the delivery of such services. These complex interventions require managed coordination to maximize success and should include:

- Classroom-based efforts to enable learning;

- An array of well-defined student and family assistance services;

- Supported transitions—including to and from out-of-school placements;

- Home involvement in schooling and interagency interventions;

- Outreach to the greater community for involvement and support; and

- Crisis prevention and intervention.

Involving families in meaningful ways includes seeking and using the wealth of information families bring to the team. Families can help not only by providing information about the child's history, services sought and used, but also by developing hypotheses, discussing patterns of behaviors, and helping identify workable interventions. Families should be partners in the process, including participating in selecting and evaluating interventions. Preplanning with the family should be considered as well. The team also should develop an awareness of and respect for the family's culture and seek to develop team competence in cultures served in the community.

The team problem-solving process may involve curriculum-based assessments, other assessments, and functional assessments of problem behaviors. An effective consultation process will identify instructional goals along with the strategies, behavioral interventions, and supports that lead to improved outcomes. Targeted environments for intervention may be identified but coordinated interventions may also be necessary across multiple settings, including the classroom, the cafeteria, the school bus, recreation center, the home, and the community. Interventions that involve multiple agencies usually require case management from a designated case manager. Successful interventions take into account all of the information gathered during the student assistance team's referral and hypotheses assessment process.

Preplanning by team members for effective problem solving is critical. Problem-solving teams do not spend their valuable time sharing long lists of data or reading reports. Reports should have been reviewed before the meeting to enable all to be prepared for problem solving, for confirming or discarding hypotheses, and generating likely strategies and interventions (Batsche, 2000). When the referrals suggest the need for urgent or imminent intervention plans the process requires a rapid response by the team to determine the need for a comprehensive threat assessment and interagency action plan. It is important to recognize that early warning signs can become a regular responsibility on the Student Support Team's schedule in a normalized manner, provided that the referral and response process is as quick as possible. Developing and designing intensive, sustained interagency interventions for children and youth with complex and severe problems will, in an inclusive educational environment, be a regular responsibility of the Student Support Team. Referrals that require an immediate response and a threat assessment will require immediate rapid response as noted above. However, these referrals will be very rare in most schools.

It is critical for all school-community staffs and families to understand the referral process, workings, and goals of the Student Support Team, and the immediate response process for those students whom the school principal and core team members believe need immediate evaluation and intervention (Dwyer & Osher, 2000).

DESIGNING INTENSIVE INTERVENTIONS

As indicated earlier, 5% of children and youth manifest mental and emotional problems that have severe effects on their functioning. This number does not include children with academic or physical disabilities who are mentally and emotionally healthy and resilient. For these children the responsive school environment, effective special education, and Section 504 supports should suffice. In all cases, schools must be vigilant to examine the school, home, and community environments that may victimize the student. In searching for what is "wrong," the team focus is on both these environments and the student. Sometimes, when the student has behavioral difficulties, it is due to other issues such as instructional methods, peer pressures, family issues, and other unrecognized needs.

As stated, be it an early risk-reduction intervention or an intensive, multiagency intervention, effective consultation and functional assessment processes will be necessary to identify instructional goals, and the strategies, behavioral interventions and supports, family services, and coordinated service plan that will lead to improved outcomes. Intensive interventions will require significant policy and resource decisions. For example, intensive services, provided by community agencies and providers within the school, are far more effective than services provided in clinical settings according to the Vanderbilt School-based Counseling Project (Catron et al., 1998). The effectiveness of "counseling" and other direct services is dependent on several factors; the Vanderbilt study showed that for some youth, academic tutoring was as effective as clinical counseling. The study did not include a combination of efforts or indications that clinical services in the school were coordinated with other staff efforts. The critical finding was that over 96% of the in-school referred group initiated services whereas only 13% of the clinic-based youth initiated services.

Although manualized counseling and intervention strategies have been shown to be effective in research settings for specific conditions such as anxiety disorders (Kendall, 1994), interventions need to be developed based on the complex academic and behavioral needs of the individual child. The Student Support Team should designate a case manager to ensure that the specifics of the plan are appropriately implemented and that the plan's success (or failure) is monitored. The case manager helps the team and family determine whether the plan should continue, be modified, or whether additional attention is needed. The case manager may request greater coordination between agency personnel and school personnel to maximize positive effects. Regardless, it is critical to ensure effective service delivery and evaluation so that the interagency team avoids pitfalls of "blaming," of using confidentiality as a barrier, and/or of denying services based on funding silos or antiquated school or agency policies that are unfriendly to families.

CHOOSING PREVENTION AND INTERVENTION STRATEGIES

Numerous programs have been developed to improve the emotional, behavioral, and social outcomes of students exhibiting troubling behavior and other mental health problems. As a group, these programs might be classified generically as counseling, therapy, behavior management, cognitive behavioral treatment, or psycho-educational interventions because they attempt to directly use social learning principles and contingency management procedures to affect behavior. Some teach new skills for coping with interpersonal difficulties. Others focus on the behavior of caregivers and school staff. An example of such proven interventions is Multisystemic Therapy (MST) (Henggeler, Mihalic, Rone, Thomas, & Timmons-Mitchell, 1998; Henggeler, Schoenwald, Borduin, Roland, & Cunningham, 1998), which has been shown to be effective with conduct-disordered, delinquent youth as well as youth with substance abuse problems and suicidal and homicidal impulses. MST relies upon an effective, ecological assessment and the use of family and other strengths within that environment. Interventions are reality-bound, here-and-now, and target sequences of youth and caregiver behaviors. Qualified professional interventionists are trained and supervised to ensure demonstrated competency and fidelity to the MST model. Evaluation is ongoing and from multiple perspectives of behavior and relationships. Treatment generalization is stressed and family empowerment enables long-term support and maintenance of outcomes.

Multidimensional Treatment Foster Care is another promising, intensive intervention when compared to residential treatment or juvenile detention (Chamberlain & Weinrott, 1990; Chamberlain & Reid, 1998). This program is an alternative to incarceration or residential treatment. Foster families are trained and supervised; youth receive behavior management, skill-focused therapy, and case management to ensure effective interagency services.

There are many behavioral and cognitive behavioral treatments that are promising in treating depression, anxiety disorders, and oppositional disorders (Horner & Sugai & Horner, 1999; Lochman, 1992). Many of these programs are evidence based and have produced positive outcomes for students with behavioral difficulties. It is very important, however, to understand that even though a program may be backed by research studies, no one program can fit the needs of all school communities. Program effectiveness is dependent on a number of things, including ease of implementation (i.e., training required to implement, qualifications of staff and time required), costs (i.e., fiscal, time), and content (i.e., appropriateness for the student's needs, and for the student's developmental level, culture, and language). There are a number of considerations that should be kept in mind when selecting appropriate programs for your particular setting. Interagency planning should include an examination of how each team member is going to demonstrate his or her own competence in using proven or promising programs.

FUNCTIONAL ASSESSMENT AND INTERAGENCY TREATMENT PLAN

Schools should be actively involved in working with other agencies and the family to measure problem behaviors and define the targeted behaviors' frequency, intensity, and functional intent of that problem behavior. Information also is gathered as to when the behavior does not occur, when appropriate behaviors are evident, and which factors facilitate the appropriate behavior. Functional behavioral assessments are quite valuable in this process and may not be a common practice of other agencies. A great deal has been written and discussed about functional behavioral assessments, particularly in the National Association of School Psychologists' *Communiqué* (December 1999, Volume 28, # 4; September 1999, Volume 28, # 1). Manuals such as the one published by the California Department of Education (Browning Wright, & Gurman, 1994) are excellent references for team training. During this problem-solving phase, a team identifies the hypothesized causes of targeted behavior and formulates interventions to replace the inappropriate forms of behavior with appropriate ones. Skills and competencies for appropriate replacements are examined. The team must determine whether the problem behavior is attributable to a skill deficit, a competency problem, or simply motivational factors. In using functional assessment procedures, we look beyond the behavior itself and focus on the stimuli, conditions, and social-behavioral and environmental contexts that prompt and maintain the problem behavior. The major objective is to promote (through contingencies) the appropriate replacement behavior that serves the same function(s) as the problem behavior.

Under the Individuals with Disabilities Education Act (IDEA; Public Law 105-12 and *Final Regulations* published in the Federal Register, March 12, 1999), an IEP team must conduct a functional behavioral assessment and an associated behavioral intervention plan for any child with a disability who has been removed from the current education placement for more than 10 school days in the same school year. If the child already has a behavioral intervention plan, the IEP team shall meet to review the plan and its implementation, and modify the plan and its implementation, as necessary, to address the behavior.

The behaviors to be addressed should be few in number. They should be mean-ingful (important to parents and teachers) and should allow the child to meet a need that was previously met by engaging in the undesirable behavior. Once the replacement behavior is defined, a plan should be developed to either teach the child how to engage in the replacement behavior or to change the environmental conditions that are caus-ing or maintaining the undesirable behavior. Each step of the plan should be carefully implemented and monitored to maintain fidelity. Consideration of generalization issues should be incorporated into the plan and strengths in the child's environment should be used to support the change process. Approximately two months should be provided to determine the success of the plan. However, plan consultants should examine the interventions for fidelity more regularly and counseling and training should be consis-tent with the manualized approach. If the plan is successful in meeting its intended goals, then a decision must be made to determine whether the intervention should be continued, and whether other problem behaviors also should be addressed. Additional support may be necessary to generalize the obtained successes. Some components of plans, such as academic tutoring, may need to be maintained over longer periods of time. Ultimately, the intervention should include a self-management and monitoring component so that the student can begin to take responsibility for his or her own behavior. If the plan does not meet its desired goals, then revisions to the intervention, or the selection of a different intervention, may be necessary.

Schools also can use other services for children whose emotional problems severe-ly disable their school functioning. Services under Section 504 of the Rehabilitation Act enable related counseling and other accommodations as well as academic tutorial support. Services also are available under the National Special Education Law (IDEA Amendments of 1997) when children manifest complex disabilities that have emotion-al components or have an emotional disturbance that functionally interferes with their learning.

Special Education and Related Services as a Component of Intensive Services

Under the Individuals with Disabilities Education Act (IDEA), children whose dis-abilities make them eligible to receive special education and related services are entitled to "positive behavioral interventions, strategies, and support" incorporated into their Individualized Educational Programs (IEPs), when their behavior impedes their own and others' learning. Among the categories of eligibility are students with emotional disturbance who, under the Federal definition, include youth who demonstrate unsat-isfactory personal relationships with peers and teachers, and have inappropriate types of behavior or feelings under normal circumstances. It is also important to point out that the positive behavioral interventions, strategies, and supports that are available under IEPs are not restricted to students with emotional disturbance, but apply to all students with disabilities whose behavior interferes with their learning or the learning of oth-ers. For the most part, these services can be provided in the regular classroom, since

IDEA specifies, under its Least Restrictive Environment (LRE) requirements, that special classes, separate schooling, or other removal of children with disabilities from the regular educational environment occurs only if the nature of severity of the disability is such that education in regular classes with the use of supplementary aids and services cannot be achieved satisfactorily.

Alternative Programs and Schools

Schools should do everything possible to enable children and youth with intensive emotional problems to remain in their home school—when that environment is helpful. If the necessary intensive services require an alternative placement, that component of the array of services should be available. Research on the positive effects of alternative placements is largely absent (Gottfredson, 1997). Many alternative placements have been unsuccessful in trying to address the complex needs of severely troubled children and youth whose behavior is unmanageable. Some alternative schools have been criticized as "dead-end dumping grounds for delinquent and pre-delinquent youth" (Dwyer & Caplan, 1996). Such programs have increased dramatically in recent years and three out of four school districts report having some form of alternative program(s) (National School Boards Association, 1999). Some alternative programs are located within neighborhood schools. Others are located in separate facilities. Boot Camp is an alternative education program that has been proven to be ineffective (U.S. Department of Health and Human Services, 2001). Some alternative programs for juveniles are promising, such as the Intensive Supervision Project (U.S. Department of Health and Human Services, 2001). Day treatment programs that provide intensive mental health and special education services may be effective but have yet to be subjected to rigorous research. Effective alternative programs are not custodial and collaborate with regular schools to facilitate reintegration. Other characteristics of effective alternative programs include the following (Dwyer, 1996):

- Intensive remedial instruction in credit-earning coursework;

- Continuation of special education services for students with IEPs;

- Positive behavioral training—including social skills and anger management/abatement;

- Psychological/mental health consultation and counseling;

- Intensive, active family involvement;

- Transition services that support the return to regular school;

- Community agency involvement (mental health, social service, and probation);

- Caring teaching staff—voluntary assigned and highly trained; and

- Voluntary participation (alternative to a less educational/punitive environment).

Systems of Care

A *system of care* has been defined by the Center for Mental Health Services, Substance Abuse and Mental Health Services Administration, U.S. Department of Health and Human Services (*www.mentalhealth.org/publications/allpubs/ca-0014/socare.htm*) as a coordinated continuum of mental health and related services and supports organized to work together to provide care. It is designed to help a child or adolescent having serious emotional disturbances, with the involvement of his or her family, get the services he or she needs in or near the family home and school community. In systems of care, local public and private organizations work in teams to plan and implement a tailored set of services for each individual child's physical, emotional, social, educational, and family needs. The child and his or her family are included in planning the ser-vices. Like Multisystemic Therapy (MST), the system of care builds upon the child's strengths rather than focusing services and supports on problems alone.

The range of services that may be included in a system of care include the following:

case management (service coordination)	legal services
community-based in-patient psychiatric care	protection and advocacy
counseling (career, individual, group, and youth)	psychiatric consultation
crisis outreach teams	recreation therapy
crisis residential care	respite care
day treatment	self-help or support groups
education/special education services	small therapeutic group care
family support	therapeutic foster care
health services	transportation
independent living supports	tutoring
intensive family-based counseling (in the home)	vocational counseling

Effective *systems of care* tailor interventions to address the strengths and needs of individual youth, who frequently require different interventions at different developmental stages and transitions through their schooling. It is critical to plan carefully for these complex interventions and strategies to ensure proper management, avoid duplication, and provide barrier-breaking funding streams and easy family access. Interagency plans must include evaluation of the progress of such service plans (and integrate with the child's IEP, when one exists), including recognition of problems and solution-focused modifications (see U.S. Department of Health and Human Services, 1999b).

Similar to systems of care is the concept of *Wraparound Services* (Burns & Goldman, 1999). The Milwaukee Wraparound program is one promising model that exists within the managed care funding environment. It furnishes an array of mental health services for children and youth with severe emotional and behavioral disorders (Stroul & Friedman, 1996). Wraparound is an *approach* to providing services for children with serious emotional and behavioral problems. The wraparound process ordinarily begins when the team, or family member, identifies the child as being at risk for residential placement or being removed from the home. Teams need to be aware that children may be "manageable" in school but remain behaviorally troubled, even dangerous to self or others at home or in the community. A fully comprehensive team, including the child and family, consisting both of professional service providers (mental health workers, educators, child welfare workers, and members of law enforcement and juvenile justice systems) and informal supports from the community (extended family members, friends, clergy—whomever the family might call to help during a crisis), may be needed to develop an effective alternative to residential treatment.

School-based mental health services are best designed and integrated into the school when roles and responsibilities are well defined and funding policies are in place. These services are best provided by mental health specialists who are traditionally employed by school systems (i.e., appropriately trained school psychologists, counselors, social workers, and behavioral specialists) and by staff from community agencies who bring their services to the school. Funding for services should be made available to all service providers for the full array of risk reduction interventions provided to children and families. Medicaid and the State Children's Health Insurance Program (SCHIP) funds as well as state and local mental health and education budgets (among others) should be examined for effective funding and service integration. Human resources are best utilized in these models when systems focus on the child and family strengths and the broadened goals of education rather than on pathology.

Recommended Proven and Promising Programs

The Center for Mental Health Services of the Substance Abuse and Mental Health Services Administration (SAMHSA) developed a matrix of evidence-based and promising "programs." The Safe and Drug-Free Schools Expert Panel has also listed over 40 "programs" that are proven or promising (2001). The Surgeon General documents cited in this chapter also have presented interventions and therapies that have proven merit for specific mental and emotional conditions including youth violence. Your team should explore these documents that may be available through the organizations' Web sites for selecting what best fits your comprehensive plan. Many more interventions and strategies will be researched and reviewed in the future. Having access to these Web sites can keep your team abreast of what works.

IMPLEMENTING YOUR SCHOOLWIDE PREVENTION AND INTERVENTION PLAN

Once your team has selected its interventions for a comprehensive plan, check it against the effectiveness principles. Seek feedback from a variety of sources by circulating drafts to stakeholders. Include in your plan how it will result in the intended educational outcomes and how it will build upon existing activities and reforms. Make sure that your team's plan addresses the interagency collaboration required to ensure the full array of service options for inclusiveness. Make sure everyone knows the steps in your planning regarding training, roles and responsibilities, and funding streams. Once you have large group consensus for the plan and the 80% staff/participant "buy-in," your team is ready to implement your plan. You have already secured top-level approval, established your baselines, secured funding, and revised policies and procedures necessary to begin broad informing and training. Your team should have methods in place for determining competencies for those trained.

Be clear in including families and other stakeholders in implementing schoolwide prevention curricula, rules, policies, and practices that may be new or previously fully shared. Families must be involved in implementing the plan and youth should be appropriately involved. Change is hard to communicate, and there should be open lines of communication throughout the process. Communicate fully how your team's plans will be evaluated. Use your base data and connect to long-term academic improvements. Authors of ACHIEVE have indicated that achievement score improvement is a third-year expectancy. Monitoring and evaluation responsibilities may remain with the team members, particularly the school psychologist, principal, and teacher specialist; however, there should be some outside oversight. If there is a possible university connection, that university's researchers may be interested in providing guidance in this process. An external evaluation may assist your team in seeing more objectively what has to be modified, scrapped, or retaught.

RESPONDING TO CRISIS

Crisis intervention plans are briefly discussed in the following sections. This topic is dealt with more extensively by S. Paine and C. Kennedy Paine in this volume.

Being Prepared

What does the school do if a youth kills himself or herself in school? What does the school do if a disturbed father is holding the first grade hostage and threatening to kill his 6-year-old daughter? What does the school do if four seniors are killed in an auto crash the night before graduation? Does the school crisis plan address all possible scenarios and is there a trained response team in place as part of your plan?

When other components of the prevention and intervention plan are in place, the likelihood of tragic violence is reduced. However, violence or dangerous threats of violence can happen at any time, anywhere. Effective and safe schools are well prepared for any potential crisis, natural disaster, or violent act. Crisis plans also help enable members of the school community to feel more secure, cared for, and safe. Everyone should be aware that the plan exists and that it is an active plan. Open information about preparedness through community awareness can be reassuring.

When Crisis Occurs

Most schools prepare for fires with "fire-drills," hoping a dangerous fire will never occur. In most communities the law requires this. Communities also must plan for the possibility of natural disasters such as earthquakes or floods. However, few schools are ready to deal with the distraught father holding a class hostage. More common to all schools are crises such as the homicide, suicide, or accidental death of family members, staff, or a child. School shootings, where many children and staff are killed or wounded, result in a trauma that can be pervasive—increasing fear and confusion for the whole community, even the whole nation. Fortunately, these types of situations are rare. A natural disaster or vehicle accident is far more likely to occur. Still, schools must be prepared.

Crisis intervention planning is a vital component of any comprehensive safe school plan. Every school community should have a crisis intervention plan in place for different kinds of situations. For example, some communities may be more vulnerable to specific natural disasters. The plan should be periodically evaluated and updated to ensure effective implementation.

The data on youth mortality provide information suggesting that a school crisis plan is necessary—73% of youth deaths are caused by accidents, homicide, and suicide (National Research Council & Institute of Medicine, 1999). Sadly, a high school with 2,000 students may expect, on average, one suicide every 3 years among its student body. Having crisis plans in place can help reduce the chances of either inappropriate denial or overreactions by students, staff, and families to deaths of a classmate, teacher, or other school-related person(s).

Defining a Crisis

Your school policy should define a "crisis." However, each state or school system may form its own definition. Most school systems have already determined this definition and it is critical that all staff and the community stakeholders in crisis response understand that definition. Some definitions include all natural disasters, fires, and the death or suicide of a student, staff member, or a student's immediate family.

Assessing Your School (Identifying the Problem)

Effective and safe schools prepare for crises in advance. They engage in a variety of activities that are designed to prevent a crisis, intervene during a crisis, and respond effectively in the aftermath of a tragedy. Carefully review current procedures and policies that are in place in your school. Compare your school's plan for preparedness with the following list. As you review, note which components are already in place, which need enhancements, and which need to be developed.

Has your school:

- Developed a plan to ensure that the staff and students know how to behave during a crisis?

- Made sure teachers and staff are trained in a range of skills including dealing with escalating classroom situations as well as responding to a serious crisis?

- Discussed and referenced district and state policies and procedures in its crisis procedures? (Many states now have recommended crisis intervention manuals available to their local education agencies and schools.)

- Involved community agencies, including police, fire, and rescue, as well as hospital, health, social welfare, and mental health services? (The faith-based community, juvenile justice, and related family support systems also have been successfully included in such team plans.)

- Provided the core team with time and resources to meet regularly to identify potentially troubled or violent students and situations that may be dangerous?

- Researched the availability of federal, state, and local resources that may be available to help during and after a crisis?

THREE NECESSARY COMPONENTS OF CRISIS RESPONSE

The three components of a crisis response plan that your team must address in your assessment are as follows:

1. Developing the crisis plan;

2. Intervening during a crisis to ensure safety; and

3. Responding in the aftermath of crisis.

1. Developing the Crisis Plan

Crisis planning requires a strong commitment from the school system's top administration and school board to provide the policies and resources for ensuring that the plan will be implemented. Policies can provide the foundation for the plan. It is critical that the school's crisis response plan be written and widely distributed. Effective school plans generally have explicit procedures for each type of possible crisis. The plan should clearly define the roles and responsibilities for all school staff as well as for the school team, the community, and district crisis response team members.

All crisis plans should include preplanned components for the following:

- **Evacuation procedures and other procedures to protect students and staff from harm.** It is critical that schools identify safe areas where students and staff should go in a crisis. It also is important that schools practice having staff and students evacuate the premises in an orderly manner. Schools should have an emergency "crisis box" that contains emergency contact cards for each student (or portable computer with critical information), a bullhorn, a cell phone, crisis team badges, and first aid equipment.

- **An effective, foolproof communication system.** Individuals must have designated roles and responsibilities to prevent confusion. Schools should have a confidential "signal" known to staff and a practiced response to that crisis signal.

- **A process for securing immediate external support from law enforcement officials and other relevant community agencies.** Police and rescue should know your building and (whenever possible) the in-school crisis team.

A crisis plan must address many complex contingencies. There should be a step-by-step procedure to use when a crisis occurs. As you review or develop your own procedural checklist, consider the necessity of including the following activities:

1. Assess life/safety issues immediately.

2. Provide immediate emergency medical care.

3. Call 911 and notify police/rescue first. Call the superintendent second.

4. Convene the crisis team to assess the situation and implement the crisis response procedures.

5. Evaluate available and needed resources.

6. Alert school staff to the situation.

7. Activate the crisis communication procedure and system of verification.

8. Secure all areas.

9. Implement evacuation and other procedures to protect students and staff from harm. Avoid dismissing students to unknown care.

10. Adjust the bell schedule to ensure safety during the crisis.

11. Alert persons in charge of various information systems to prevent confusion and misinformation. Notify parents.

12. Contact appropriate community agencies and the school district's public information office, if appropriate.

13. Implement postcrisis procedures.

2. Intervening During a Crisis to Ensure Safety

Weapons used in or around schools, bomb threats or explosions, and group (gang, racial) fights, as well as natural disasters, accidents, and suicides, call for immediate, planned action, and long-term, postcrisis intervention. Plans require both in-school procedures and procedures for law enforcement and fire/rescue. Families should be aware of your school's plans. Your specific plan for such contingencies reduces chaos and trauma.

3. Responding in the Aftermath of Crisis

Plans for immediate crisis intervention plans that are comprehensive and coordinated are critical for addressing the immediate issues of safety and trauma prevention. However, equally important are training and responsiveness to the immediate emotional trauma for students and staff as well as the long-term support needs for other individuals close to the trauma. Your plan and team must be prepared to seek help for critical counseling and support issues. If the Student Support Team or its core members do not have members with adequate knowledge of mental health and behavioral issues related to the crisis, it is important to include other community professionals with that expertise in planning at this stage. Training, time, and resources are required to ensure the following:

> **Members of the crisis team understand natural stress reactions.** They also should be familiar with how different individuals might respond to death and loss, including developmental considerations, religious beliefs, and cultural values.

> **Professionals** both within the school district and within the greater community are involved to assist individuals who are at risk for severe stress reactions. Parents understand children's reactions to violence (e.g., unrealistic fears of the future, difficulty sleeping, physical illness, and distractibility).

> **Teachers and other staff deal with their reactions to the crisis.** Debriefing and grief counseling are just as important for adults as they are for

students. Both short-term and long-term mental health counseling must be provided following a crisis.

Victims and family members of victims are helped to re-enter the school environment. Often, school friends need guidance in how to act. The school community should work with students and parents to design a plan that makes it easier for victims and their classmates to adjust.

Once the team has developed a crisis response plan, it needs to designate people to carry out the plan during emergency situations. The next section discusses how to establish a crisis response team.

ESTABLISHING A CRISIS RESPONSE TEAM

Your in-school crisis response team must be accessible at all times. It may involve some of the core members of your Schoolwide Team, such as the school psychologist, but in most cases it will need to include other staff who have specific crisis skills and roles. The individual school administrator is critical and, when possible, the team should include the school nurse and security personnel or building services staff. All team members must be trained and have proven skills required in various types of crisis situations and backup personnel should be identified to ensure that all roles are covered when critical staff members are unavailable. All persons on the in-school team and the community team should become aware of each other's roles and, when possible, carry out crisis practice sessions together.

The crisis response team should be made up of trained personnel who are part of the regular school staff. Many experts recommend that the team be composed of voluntary members, since roles can involve significant responsibilities (such as emergency first aid) and, sometimes, risk. Teams are most effective when they are relatively small (4 or 5 staff members in a small school). A roster of team members should be available to all school staff and related agencies (for example, police, fire and rescue, and the school system district office) forming the community crisis response team.

District Team

School districts should have in place a crisis team with the responsibility to assist each school within the district and to ensure that the resources are available to deal with each possible emergency. The district-level team is also responsible for supporting appropriate procedures and coordinating the policies and procedures with each in-school crisis team. Training of staff at the local school will require the district's endorsement. Coordination among the superintendent, the police chief, fire and rescue chief, hospital administrators and the related service agencies (and nongovernmental services), and parent and faith-based community leaders will be necessary.

Community Crisis Response Team

The community crisis response team associated with each school also should be defined. This team is formed by multiple agencies and generally involves law enforcement, and fire and rescue as well as health, mental health, and hospital facilities. These professionals should know and understand the roles of the in-school team, district team, and emergency personnel. The roles of all involved should be included in the school/school system's crisis plan.

CONCLUSION

The plans and steps to implementation described in this chapter follow those in the book, *Safeguarding Our Children: An Action Guide.* The planning and implementation process for fully installing the *Action Guide* model requires a minimum of 3 years of sustained effort. Our children deserve no less and without such comprehensive programs we will fail to safeguard *all children,* including those who are vulnerable, hard to teach, and troubled. This author believes that if you measure what you do and use those data to evaluate your services, your school will improve over time. The plan, outlined herein, although designed primarily for school safety, also is the plan for increasing graduation rates, reducing drug abuse, reducing teen pregnancy, and reducing the risky behaviors that result in lost potential (see Hawkins, Catalano, Abbott, & Hill, 1999). It is a plan for teaching mental health, for preventing mental and emotional problems, and for reducing the ravages of emotional and behavioral disorders.

REFERENCES

Adelman, H. S. (1996) Restructuring educational support services and integrating community resources: Beyond the full service school model. *School Psychology Review, 25,* 431–445.

Adelman, H., & Taylor, L. (1998). *Restructuring boards of education to enhance school's effectiveness in addressing barriers to student learning.* Los Angeles: Center for Mental Health in Schools, University of California Los Angeles.

Adelman, H., & Taylor, L. (2001). *From the Center's Clearinghouse: Financial strategies to aid in addressing barriers to learning.* Los Angeles: Center for Mental Health in Schools, University of California Los Angeles.

Allensworth, D., Lawson, E., Nicholson, L., & Wyche, J. (1997). Schools and health: Our nation's investment. Washington, DC: Institute of Medicine, National Academy Press.

American Federation of Teachers. (1998). *American Federation of Teachers position on school discipline and safety.* Washington, DC: Author.

American Psychological Association. (1999). *Warning signs.* Washington, DC: Author.

Batsche, G. (2000). *Advanced workshop on facilitation of problem-solving teams and site-based evaluation of team performance.* 2000 Annual Convention, National Association of School Psychologists, New Orleans, LA.

Browning-Wright, D., & Gurman, H. B. (1994). *Positive intervention for serious behavior problems: Best practices in implementing the positive behavioral intervention regulations.* Sacramento, CA: RiSE California Department of Education, Special Education Division.

Burns, B. J., & Goldman, S. K. (Eds.) (1999). Promising practices in wraparound for children with serious emotional disturbance and their families. In U.S. Department of Health and Human Services, *Systems of care: Promising practices in children's mental health, 1998 Series, Vols. I-VII.* Washington, DC: Center for Effective Collaboration and Practice, American Institutes for Research.

Catron, T., Harris, V. S., & Weiss, B. (1998). Posttreatment results after 2 years of services in the Vanderbilt School-based Counseling Project. In M. Epstein, K. Kutash, & A. Duchnowski (Eds.), *Outcomes: For children and youth with behavioral and emotional disorders and their families: Programs and evaluation best practices.* Austin, TX: Pro-Ed.

Chamberlain, P., & Reid, J. B. (1998). Comparison of two community alternatives to incarceration for chronic juvenile offenders. *Journal of Consulting and Clinical Psychology, 66,* 624–633.

Chamberlain, P., & Weinrott, M. (1990). Specialized foster care: Treating seriously emotionally disturbed children. *Child Today, 19,* 24–27.

Comer, J. P., (1998). Educating poor minority children. *Scientific American, 259,* 42–48.

Comer, J. P., Haynes, N. M., Joyner, E. T., & Ben-Avie, M. (Eds.). (1996). *Rallying the whole village: The Comer process for reforming education.* New York: Teachers College Press.

Curtis, M. J., & Stollar, S. A. (1995). System-level consultation and organizational change. In A. Thomas & J. Grimes (Eds.), *Best Practices in School Psychology III* (pp. 51-58). Washington, DC: National Association of School Psychologists.

Dryfoos, J. G. (1994). *Full service schools: A revolution in health and social services for children, youth, and families.* San Francisco: Jossey-Bass.

Dwyer, K. (1996). Building safe, effective schools. Updating school board policies. *National Educational Policy Network, Volume 27,* Number 6, 1-5.

Dwyer, K. (2001). *Coordinated school mental health services.* Alexandria, VA: National Mental Health Association.

Dwyer, K., & Bernstein, R. (1998). Mental health in the schools: Linking islands of hope in a sea of despair. *School Psychology Review, 27*(2), 277-286.

Dwyer, K., & Caplan, K. (1996). *Toward truly collaborative approaches in mental health. Grand rounds presentation.* Center for School Mental Health Assistance. Baltimore: University of Maryland School of Medicine.

Dwyer, K., & Osher, D. (2000). *Safeguarding our children: An action guide: Implementing Early Warning, Timely Response.* Washington, DC: U.S. Departments of Education and Justice, American Institutes for Research.

Dwyer, K., Osher, D., & Hoffman, C. (2000). Creating responsive schools: Contex-tualizing Early Warning, Timely Response. *Exceptional Children, 66*(3), 347-365.

Dwyer, K., Osher, D., & Warger, C. (1998). *Early Warning, Timely Response: A guide to safe schools.* Washington, DC: U.S. Department of Education.

Elias, M. J., & Tobias, S. E. (1996). *Social problem solving: Interventions in the schools.* New York: Guilford Press.

Elliott, D. S., Hamburg, B. A., & Williams, K.R. (1998). *Violence in American schools.* New York: Cambridge University Press.

Finn, J. D., & Rock, D. A. (1997). Academic success among students at risk for school failure. *Journal of Applied Psychology, 82*(2), 221-234.

Fullen, M. G., & Stiegelbauer, S. (1991). *The new meaning of educational change* (2nd ed.). New York: Columbia University Teachers College Press.

Furlong, M. (2001). *Lost opportunities and new horizons: Santa Barbara Public Health Week.* Santa Barbara, CA: UCSB, Gevirtz Graduate School of Education.

Furlong, M., & Morrison, G. (1995). School violence and safety in perspective. *School Psychology Review, 23,* 2, 139-150.

Gottfredson, D. C. (1997). School-based crime prevention. In L. W. Sherman (Ed.), *Preventing crime: What works, what doesn't, what's promising: A report to the United States Congress.* Washington, DC: U.S. Department of Justice.

Haynes, N. M., & Comer, J. P. (1993). The Yale school development program: Process outcomes and policy implications. *Urban Education, 28,* 166-199.

Hawkins, J. D., Catalano, R. F., & Associates (Eds.). (1992). *Communities that care: Action for drug abuse prevention.* San Francisco: Jossey-Bass.

Hawkins, J. D., Catalano, R. F., Abbott, R., & Hill, K. (1999). Preventing adolescent health-risk behaviors by strengthening protection during childhood. *Archives of Pediatrics and Adolescent Medicine, Vol. 153,* March, 226-234.

Henggeler, S. W., Mihalic, S. F., Rone, L., Thomas. C., & Timmons-Mitchell, J. (1998). *Multisystemic therapy.* In D. S. Elliott (Ed.), *Blueprint for violence prevention.* Boulder, CO: University of Colorado at Boulder.

Henggeler, S. W., Schoenwald, S. K., Borduin, C. M., Roland, M. D., & Cunning-ham, P. B. (1998). *Multisystemic treatment for antisocial behavior in children and adolescents.* New York: Guilford Press.

Kellam, S. G., Rebok, G. W., Ialongo, N., & Mayer, L. S. (1994). The source of mal-leability of aggressive behavior from early first grade into middle school: Results of a developmental epidemiological-based prevention trial. *Journal of Child Psychology and Psychiatry, 32,* 259-281.

Kendall, P. C. (1994). Treating anxiety disorders in children: Results of a randomized clinical trial. *Journal of Consulting and Clinical Psychology, 62,* 100-110.

Knoff, H. M. (1996). The interface of school community and health care reform: Organizational directions toward effective services for children. *School Psychology Review, 25*(4), 446-464.

Knoff, H. M., & Batsche, G. M. (1995). Project ACHIEVE: Analyzing a school reform process for at-risk and underachieving students. *School Psychology Review, 24,* 579-603.

Knoff, H. M., Curtis, M. J., & Batsche, G. M. (1997). The future of school psychology: Perspectives on effective training. *School Psychology Review, 26*(1), 93-103.

Kumpfer, K. L., DeMarsh, A. J., & Child, W. (1989). *The Strengthening Families program: Training manuals.* Salt Lake City, UT: Department of Health Education, University of Utah.

Lawson, H., & Briar-Lawson, K. (1997). *Connecting the dots: Progress toward the integration of school reform, school linked services, parent involvement and community schools.* Oxford, OH: Danforth Foundation and Institute for Educational Leadership.

Learning First Alliance. (1998). *Every child reading: An action plan of the Learning First Alliance.* Washington, DC: Author.

Learning First Alliance. (2001). *Every child learning: Safe and supportive schools.* Washing-ton, DC: Author.

Marx, E., & Wooley, S. (1998). *Health is academic.* New York: Teachers College Press.

Minke, K. M., & Bear, G. C. (2000). *Preventing school problems—Promoting school success: Strategies and programs that work.* Bethesda, MD: National Association of School Psychologists.

Nastasi, B. K., Varjas, K., & Bernstein, R. (1997). *Exemplary mental health programs: School psychologists as mental health providers.* Bethesda, MD: National Association of School Psychologists.

National Education Goals Panel. (1998). *Data volume for the National Education Goals Report.* Washington, DC: U.S. Government Printing Office.

National Research Council & Institute of Medicine. (1999). *Risk and opportunities: Synthesis of studies on adolescence.* Washington, DC: National Academy Press.

National Research Council & Institute of Medicine. (2000). From neutrons to neighborhoods: The science of early childhood development. In J. P. Shonkoff & D. A. Phillips (Eds.), *Report: Board on children, youth and families, commission on behavioral and social sciences and education*. Washington, DC: National Academy Press.

National School Boards Association. (1999). Alternative schools. *National education policy network: Updating school board policies, Vol. 30*. Alexandria, VA: Author.

Nelson, J. R. (1996). Designing schools to meet the needs of students who exhibit disruptive behavior. *Journal of Emotional and Behavioral Disorders, 4*, 147-161.

Peters, R., & McMahon, R. J. (1996). *Parent training: Foundations for research and practice*. New York: Guilford Press.

Prothrow-Stith, D. (1987). *Violence prevention curriculum for adolescents*. Newton, MA: Education Development Center.

Resnick, M. D. (1997). Protecting adolescents from harm. Findings from the National Longitudinal Study on Adolescent Health. *Journal of the American Medical Association 278*(10), 823-832.

Rhode Island Departments of Education & Health. (1999). *Fit for high achievement: Healthy schools! Healthy kids!* Providence, RI: Author.

Ross, S. M., Smith, C., Slavin, R. E., & Madden, N. A. (1997). Improving the academic success of disadvantaged children: An examination of Success for All. *Psychology in the Schools, 34*(2), 171-180.

Satcher, D. (2001). *Report of the surgeon general's conference on children's mental health: A national action agenda*. Washington, DC: U.S. Department of Health and Human Services.

Schure, M. B. (1997). Interpersonal cognitive problem solving: Primary prevention of early high-risk behaviors in the preschool and primary years. In G. W. Albee & T. P. Gullotta (Eds.), *Primary prevention works* (pp. 167-188). Thousand Oaks, CA: Sage.

Schure, M. B., & Spivack, G. (1982). Interpersonal problem-solving in young children: A cognitive approach to prevention. *American Journal of Community Psychology, 10*, 341-356.

Shell Oil Company. (1999). *Shell survey of adolescent attitudes*. New York: Author.

Skiba, R., & Peterson, R. (1999). The dark side of zero tolerance. *Phi Delta Kappan, 80*, 372-382.

Slavin, R. (1995). *Cooperative Learning*. Boston: Allyn and Bacon.

Slavin, R. E., Madden, N. A., Dolan, L., & Wasik, B. A. (1996). *Every child, every school: Success for all*. Thousand Oaks, CA: Corwin Press.

Slavin, R. E., Madden, N. A., Karweit, N. L., Dolan, L. J., & Wasik, B. A. (1992). *Success for all: A relentless approach to prevention and early intervention in elementary schools*. Arlington, VA: Educational Research Service.

Stroul, B. A., & Friedman, R. M. (1996). *A system of care for children and adolescents with severe emotional disturbance*. Washington, DC: National Technical Assistance Center for Child Mental Health, Georgetown University.

Sugai, G., & Horner, R. (1999). Discipline and behavior support: Preferred processes and practices. *Effective School Practices, 17*(4), 10–22.

U.S. Departments of Education & Justice. (1998). *1998 Annual report on school safety.* Washington DC: Author.

U.S. Departments of Education & Justice. (1999). *1999 Annual report on school safety.* Washington, DC: Author.

U.S. Department of Health and Human Services. (1999a). *Mental health: A report of the Surgeon General.* Pittsburgh, PA: Superintendent of Documents.

U.S. Department of Health and Human Services. (1999b). *Systems of care: Promising practices in children's mental health, 1998 Series, Vols. I-VII.* Washington, DC: Center for Effective Collaboration and Practice, American Institutes for Research.

U.S. Department of Health and Human Services. (1999c). *Safe Schools/Healthy Students: Request for proposals. July, 1999.* Rockville, MD: Substance Abuse and Mental Health Services Administration.

U.S. Department of Health and Human Services. (2001). *Youth violence: A report of the Surgeon General.* Washington, DC: Government Printing Office.

Walker, H. M., & Sprague, J. R. (1999). The path to school failure, delinquency and violence: Causal factors and some potential solutions. *Interventions in School and Clinic, 35*(2), 67–73.

Weisz, J. R., Weiss, B., Han, S. S., Granger, D. A., & Morton, T. (1995). Effects of psychotherapy with children and adolescents revisited: A meta-analysis of treatment outcome studies. *Psychological Bulletin, 117,* 450–468.

Woodruff, D. W., Osher, D., Hoffman, C. C., Gruner, A., King, M., Snow, S. T., & McIntire, J. C. (1999). The role of education in a system of care: Effectively serving children with emotional and behavioral disorders. *Systems of care: Promising practices in children's mental health, 1998 series, Volume III.* Washington, DC: Center for Effective Collaboration and Practices, American Institutes for Research.

AUTHORS' NOTES

Kevin P. Dwyer is Senior Advisor, Prevention & Children's Mental Health, National Mental Health Association, and Senior Education Advisor at the American Institutes for Research. He served as President of the National Association of School Psychologists, 1999–2000. He can be contacted at *ekdwyer@aol.com*

CHAPTER 9

Evaluation Strategies for Preventing and Remediating Basic Skill Deficits

Stanley L. Deno and Christine A. Espin
University of Minnesota

Lynn S. Fuchs
Peabody College of Vanderbilt University

INTRODUCTION

Effective teaching requires ongoing evaluation of student performance. Even the dialogue between Socrates and the slave boy Menos—our early exemplar of teaching—illustrates the close connection between the questions asked by Socrates and the previous answers given by Menos. Likewise, contemporary instructional models specify the close connection between student performance data and adjustments in various components of the instruction. For many years, books on teaching disabled learners have begun with the assertion that "good teaching requires assessment" (Zigmond, Vallecorsa, & Silverman, 1983, p. 1). And finally, the Individuals with Disabilities Education Act (IDEA) of 1990 requires, among other things, that each student's Individual Educational Plan (IEP) specify procedures for evaluating the special education program provided for that student.

In this chapter, our purpose is to provide school psychologists with a simple evaluation strategy that they can use not only to comply with the rules and regulations regarding the development of IEPs, but also to increase the likelihood that their efforts to intervene will result in more effective instruction. In our presentation we begin with a *conceptual rationale* for evaluating academic interventions, follow with a description of the *two primary models* applied in special and compensatory education programs (*summarizing recent research* on one of those models), and close with a *case illustration* of how an instructional evaluation model can be used to improve the instruction for students at risk of school failure.

CONCEPTUAL RATIONALE

The success of using systematic procedures for evaluating instructional interventions derives from the fact that people modify their behavior as a result of experience. For example, a child's experience in touching a hot stove is likely to decrease reaching for objects on the stove. Alternative psychological theories have been created to explain why those modifications in behavior occur. In early learning theory, Thorndike (1903) proposed the "Law of Effect"—that behavior producing "satisfying consequences" would be repeated, and conversely, that behavior leading to unsatisfying results would be less likely to reoccur. Subsequently, B. F. Skinner reformulated the Law of Effect as the "contingency of reinforcement" (Skinner, 1953). In the development of cognitive models, the mechanism proposed to account for the effects of behavioral consequences was the "feedback loop" (Miller, Galanter, & Pribram, 1960). The feedback loop, based on cybernetic principles, provided for modifications in behavior through adjustments made by cognitive processes in response to information from the environment. Subsequently, the constructs "metacognition" (Flavell, 1979) and "self-regulation" (Bandura, 1986) were proposed as "next generation" constructs that could account for behavior change as a result of experience. Regardless of whether one prefers behavioral or cognitive theory, it is clear that psychologists have long been interested in accounting for the systematic adjustments in behavior that occur during and after task engagement. As we examine the role of student performance evaluation in improving instructional intervention, we will rely on the fundamental assumption that *teacher behavior will change* as a function of environmental experience, particularly as a result of instruction.

Even though a wide variety of different experiences can be identified that influence subsequent behavior, in the case of instruction we believe that the most influential experiences altering teacher performance should be those produced by the teachers' students—particularly those student behaviors that are indicative of academic and social development. In the best of all instructional worlds, we would like to see teachers making changes in their instruction in response to observations of how well, or how poorly, their students are developing academic and social competence.

Instructional Design Models

Not surprisingly, instructional evaluation models have explicitly provided for the use of student performance data to correct or adjust instructional programs (Bloom, Madaus, & Hastings, 1981; Gagne, Briggs & Wager, 1988). In these models, a distinction is made between the uses of student performance data to accomplish either *summative* or *formative* evaluation. Summative evaluation is retrospective. Data are aggregated *after* the completion of instruction to determine whether a program, now completed, was successful. In large part, the current emphasis on "high stakes tests" as an approach to improving education is based on a summative evaluation model. The formative evaluation of instruction, in contrast, involves using student performance data *during* the course of instruction as a corrective mechanism for altering ongoing instruction in ways that ultimately increase instructional effectiveness. Thus, formative evaluation is both contemporaneous and prospective, rather than retrospective. As schools have struggled to respond to the "standards-based reform movement," other voices have emerged to argue for collecting student progress data prior to high-stakes testing in an effort to enhance learning and teaching before confronting accountability standards (Shepard, 2000). In this respect, the summative evaluation model imposed by state legislatures has prompted schools to develop formative evaluation procedures. Because the focus of this chapter is on using evaluation to improve intervention effectiveness, the emphasis of our discussion will be on evaluating formatively, rather than summatively.

Formative Evaluation

The central feature of formative evaluation is that the data important to improving program effectiveness are collected *during* rather than before or after program implementation. The reason why data collected after program implementation do not benefit the student is, of course, obvious. Data collected at the end of a school year, or even a grading period can be useful for summative evaluations of the program, but they are too late to benefit the students who have been unsuccessful.

Less obvious may be the reason why data collected prior to instruction may not suffice to improve program effectiveness. After all, the purpose of collecting data during an initial assessment includes diagnosis of problems and prescription of those instructional and intervention techniques that are most likely to benefit the student. Belief continues to be widespread, despite lack of supporting evidence, that a good initial assessment or "differential diagnosis" can somehow increase the effectiveness of program placement and planning decisions (Watkins, 2000). Ideas abound that classifying student "types" (e.g., "simultaneous" and "sequential" processors) will enable us to match them to a corresponding intervention with the presumption that the major task is done. By specifying a prior "successful" intervention, formative evaluation is not only unnecessary but also a waste of resources.

It is beyond the scope of this chapter to discuss the reasons for the continuing failure of the differential diagnosis/prescriptive treatment (DD/PT) model to produce more effective outcomes (Kavale & Forness, 1999). Suffice it to say, however, that the Aptitude-by-Treatment Interaction (ATI) model at the heart of DD/PT has not been successfully tested and efforts to establish even reliable "learner profiles" continue to founder, much less treatments that are reliably effective with those profiles (Watkins, 2000). Despite their hallowed place in the traditions of psychology and special education, diagnostic-prescriptive approaches to instruction have not been demonstrably successful (Deno, 1990; Lloyd, 1984). The present state of the art with respect to DD/PT remains as it was when Salvia and Ysseldyke described it as experimentation without consent (Salvia & Ysseldyke, 1985).

In contrast, for more than 15 years, evidence has been available that formatively evaluating instruction results in increased student achievement (L. S. Fuchs &

D. Fuchs, 1986). In their meta-analysis of 21 studies, L. S. Fuchs and D. Fuchs found that students gained approximately .70 standard deviations, or about 25 percentile points, in basic skills when their teachers used progress monitoring data as a basis for formative evaluation. A key finding in that meta-analysis, and in subsequent research (L. S. Fuchs, D. Fuchs, & Hamlett, 1989b), is that collecting student performance data during an instructional program produces greater effects if teachers deliberately use the data to make decisions to modify their instruction. For example, teachers who followed a rule to raise student performance goals when the data indicated that higher goals were attainable produced higher levels of achievement than teachers who did not revise goals upward when the data indicated that such a revision was warranted. In the third section of this chapter ("Applying Evaluation Strategies"), we provide a summary of the present state of knowledge with respect to the key components of an effective formative evaluation approach that is based on student progress monitoring.

The rationale for using evaluation to improve academic interventions is clear. Theoretical models of human behavior specify the key role that events subsequent to instrumental behavior play in future occurrence of that behavior. Instructional models typically include the use of student performance data to provide feedback to both student and teacher. And finally, research evidence indicates that real gains are made when individual student programs are evaluated continuously and the data are used to evaluate those programs formatively. The conclusion seems inescapable. We can increase the success of academic interventions if we evaluate the student performance effects of our interventions. Despite a checkered history in this area, we can learn to bring our instructional interventions under the control of student performance outcomes. The procedures outlined in this chapter are a step toward helping those of us who create academic intervention programs to use student performance data to modify our interventions in response to the data produced by student performance. As we stated at the outset, our assumption is that academic programs improve to the extent that we self-regulate our behavior, and that adults can improve in their self-regulatory skills (Watson & Tharp, 1993).

APPROACHES TO PROGRESS MONITORING

Educators are, and have been, deeply dissatisfied with traditional models of evaluating student progress. The most widely used measures—commercial, norm-referenced achievement tests—have been criticized on the grounds that they are biased regarding curriculum content (Armbruster, Stevens, & Rosenshine, 1977; Jenkins & Pany, 1978; Kohn, 2001), and that many are technically inadequate for decision making regarding individual students (Salvia & Ysseldyke, 1998) and not useful for making instructional decisions (Salmon-Cox, 1981; Thompson, 2001). While commonly used texts strongly encourage teachers to use "informal measures" in designing and evaluating instruction (cf. Taylor, 2000), the bulk of attention is given to the technical adequacy and uses of commercially available (i.e., "formal") devices. As a result, teachers typically are left to design their own data collection procedures and devices when they make instructional decisions.

Perhaps more than any other component of the schools, special education has emphasized the importance of evaluating instruction. The Individuals with Disabilities Education Act of 1990 requires collaborative teams to set long-range goals and short-term objectives for students, and to specify the method for evaluating student progress toward those goals. This emphasis in special education on goal setting and evaluation of student progress, combined with the inadequacies of the standardized norm-referenced evaluation instruments, has resulted in new, more effective technologies for measuring student progress.

Two general models used for student progress monitoring have been identified (Deno & Mirkin, 1977; L. S. Fuchs & Deno, 1991). Those approaches are *Mastery Monitoring (MM)* and *General Outcome Measurement (GOM)*. Student progress monitoring procedures derived from these models address published achievement test shortcomings by measuring student performance on tasks directly related to the curriculum and by generating information useful for instructional decision making. Both models contain three basic components: (a) precise specification of goals or objectives (i.e., *what to measure*), (b) procedures for measurement (i.e., *how to measure*), and (c) rules for data utilization (i.e., *how to use data* to make instructional decisions). In the following subsections, the models will be described in terms of the assumptions underlying each model and these basic components. A case study then will be presented to illustrate the use of the General Outcome Measurement model in three phases of educational programming for children with learning difficulties.

Mastery Monitoring

Mastery monitoring (MM) is based on a task-analytic approach to learning wherein the "whole" is reduced to its component parts for purposes of instruction. As a result of this reduction, then, the subtasks that have been identified become the basis for both teaching and testing. Inherent in the task-analytic approach is the specification of a performance standard for each task that, when attained, is the basis for inferring that task mastery has occurred. Through the process of task analysis, subtasks are specified and an interdependent hierarchical structure is created. In an interdependent structure of tasks, students must develop their performance to some established criterion level on task A before proceeding to task B, and then must meet criterion performance on task B before proceeding to task C, and so on. The interdependent task structure serves as the basis for specifying the patterns and orders in which tasks should be taught and "mastered" for learning to occur most efficiently.

It would be fair to say that the MM approach is pervasive in instructional programs for students in special education and in many other remedial programs. Indeed, the basic assumptions of the MM approach can be seen in the rules and regulations for developing Individual Education Programs (IEPs) required by IDEA. A core feature of the IEP since its inception has been the specification of Annual Goals and Short-Term Objectives. Interpretation of what is required in designing those goals and objectives has generally been that the objectives are to be "steps" along the way to achieving the long-range goals. The operating assumptions seem to be that attainment of those objectives should be a criterion-referenced act. In this interpretation, acceptable progress for students on an IEP, then, should include frequent monitoring of progress toward Annual Goals through testing for mastery on Short-Term Objectives. We hasten to add here that this prevalent interpretation is, in fact, not specified in law and regulations, and whether mastery of Short-Term Objectives will lead to attainment of Annual Goals is typically unknown.

The development of a Mastery Monitoring system can be illustrated through a task such as "writing a paragraph." A task analysis of paragraph writing might proceed by reducing the whole into large subtasks comprising "developing ideational content," "developing paragraph structure," "writing sentences," and "using formal codes." Further reduction of the task progresses by reducing each of these larger components into subtasks thought to be prerequisite to acquiring competence on the larger components of paragraph composition. A component such as "using formal codes" could be analyzed into "capitalization" and "punctuation" while "writing sentences" could be reduced to "expressing complete thoughts" and "composing sentences."

In a typical task analysis, the resulting structure is branching, and subordinate relationships among subtasks are most clearly identified *within* a branch rather than *across* branches. In paragraph writing, for example, an assumption might be made that "using formal codes" is superordinate to punctuating, but the relationship between punctuation and sentence content is unspecified. The result is that the degree of interdepen-dency among tasks within a given structure is usually incomplete or uncertain. Nevertheless, a task analysis inevitably leads to the specification of a set of related tasks that, when mastered, are thought to lay the basis for acquiring proficient performance on the global task that has been analyzed. In the example given, mastery of the component skills is thought to be necessary for acquiring proficiency at writing paragraphs.

Developing a progress monitoring system based on a task-analytic approach consists of creating tests for each of the subtasks that generate data on whether the standard or "criterion" for performance on that task has been met. Since the subtasks are qualitatively different from one another, it is common to create measurement procedures that differ from one another in terms of task stimuli, response requirements, and scoring procedures. For example, tests for measuring student skills at "punctuating sentences" are usually quite different from those used to assess skill in "expressing complete thoughts" when writing a sentence. In the former case, punctuation might be scored in terms of percentage correct, while expressing complete thoughts might be scored using a rubric. For each skill or subskill, then, tests are created and a sequence of teach, test, and decide is completed. Conceptually, students will not progress to new skills/subskills until they demonstrate mastery (i.e., "pass the test").

In general, MM involves teaching to criterion and then proceeding to the next subtask in the sequence and teaching and testing until mastery on that next task or unit of the curriculum has occurred. In the MM approach a linear sequencing of the subtasks is not necessary, but it is common to develop linear sequences for teaching and

FIGURE 1

Mastery Monitoring Progress Graphs

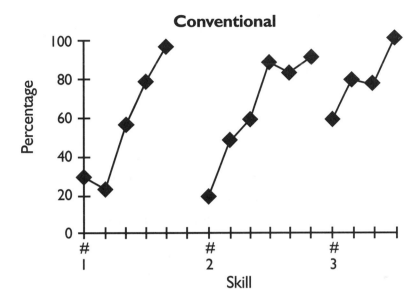

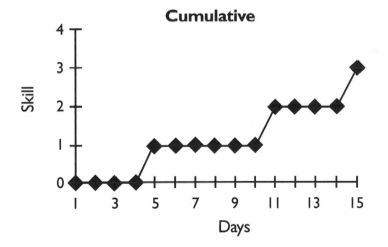

testing based on these analyses, and to track progress through those sequences. Obvious examples of this approach include unit testing in mathematics and spelling. In both cases, the content of one unit is often very different from the next, and performance requirements on one unit test differ qualitatively from the next.

An illustration of two ways to graphically display progress when using MM is provided in Figure 1. As can be seen in the figure, the *"conventional"* graph reveals the accuracy of student response on successive tests of individual skills as a student progresses through the linear sequence of tasks that has been specified. At the point where the mastery criterion for a particular skill is attained, testing on that skill ceases and testing on the next skill begins. In a conventional MM graph, performance typically drops off as each new skill is introduced and then rises to the criterion level. Although on a conventional graph it is possible to see the rate at which *individual* skills are being mastered by examining individual skill slopes, the rate of progress *through the skill sequence* is not clearly represented. In contrast, on the *"cumulative"* graph the change in accuracy on successive testing for each task or unit is not shown. Instead, each higher level on the graph indicates that the criterion on the test for the next skill in the task sequence has been met. The plot on this graph is cumulative, and the flat segments indicate a period of time (usually days) of instruction during which the student did not attain criterion on the test. In a cumulative graph, the steepness of the overall slope through any set of skills is the most relevant piece of information for progress monitoring since it is indicative of the rate of progress that a student is making through the skill sequence.

The use of the graphs used to communicate progress when doing progress monitoring is important because the pictorial representations of student progress become powerful instruments in both evaluation and communication of program effectiveness. When evaluating instructional interventions, the most useful graphs are those that enable simple and direct comparisons of differences in the rate of student progress before and after interventions. Approaches to graphing student progress that are easily understood by parents, teachers, and students are to be preferred for use in communicating the success of instructional programs.

What is measured. Mastery Monitoring (MM) rests on the assumption that students acquire general curriculum competence through the attainment of specific subordinate skills in a hierarchical skill sequence. Knowledge and skill, then, are viewed as products of learning *separate, but related, skills* that are ultimately integrated and retained as the larger goals of the curriculum. The focus of MM is on *what* is measured and when it is measured; that is, the hierarchical skill sequence serves as the basis for teaching and measurement. In the historical literature of educational psychology and instructional design, MM has much in common with Bloom's Mastery Learning model (Block, 1971; Bloom, Madaus, & Hastings, 1981).

How to measure. Because of the simplicity of testing *exactly* what you are teaching inherent in MM, historically little attention has been paid to *how* to measure progress. It is presumed that teachers prepare their own tests or they use those provided with the curriculum. The "how to measure" is not specified in a Mastery Monitoring approach to evaluation. Similarly, little attention has been paid to how to determine "mastery." A general criterion for mastery of 80-90% is often adopted; however, it is left to the individual instructor to establish procedures for evaluating whether a student has reached the 80% success rate. Furthermore, little or no empirical evidence has ever been accumulated to establish necessary and sufficient criterion levels for prerequisite skills within task hierarchies.

How to use the data collected. The data collected through MM lead to one basic instructional decision: (a) to move the student onto a new unit (when mastery is achieved), or (b) to reteach and retest the student on the current skill (when mastery is not achieved). The content of instruction for the individual student, therefore, is determined by the initial objectives specified prior to instruction and the progress of the student through those objectives. It is important to note that failure to make this decision correctly (i.e., to move the student to the next skill regardless of test performance) negates the defensibility of MM as a way of measuring progress.

Assumptions. Three assumptions form the basis for Mastery Monitoring. The first, based on Carroll's (1963) model of school learning, is that all students can learn given the appropriate amount of time and quality of instruction. The second is that complex academic tasks can be broken down into hierarchical subtasks. Finally, it is assumed that maximal learning occurs as a function of student progress through this hierarchy of subtasks. While these assumptions provide a coherent theory of mastery learning, we need to point out here that they have been criticized on the grounds that it is not practical to allocate sufficient instructional time necessary to bring *all* students to mastery, that it may not be possible to define every complex task as a hierarchy of subtasks, and that maximum learning for *all* students may not occur via progression through all subtasks in the prescribed manner (Cox & Dunn, 1979; Mueller, 1976). Another frequent criticism of this approach has been that it is "reductionist" rather than holistic and constructive (Hesushius, 1991).

General Outcome Measurement

A second approach to progress monitoring involves repeated sampling of performance on a criterion-valid task to assess change in proficiency on that task. Over the past two decades, this approach to progress monitoring has been widely applied in Curriculum-Based Measurement (CBM; Deno, 1985; Deno & Fuchs, 1987). When abstracted from the curriculum, this approach has been referred to as "General Outcome Measurement" (GOM) (L. S. Fuchs & Deno, 1991). The notion of "General Outcome" derives from the fact that the intent of measurement is to produce an empirical basis for inferring increased proficiency in a broad domain such as "reading" or "written expression" rather than simply to improve performance on a fairly narrowly defined skill. The result of this approach to measurement produces what has been called elsewhere "Dynamic Indicators of Basic Skills" (DIBS; Shinn, 1998). The results of this approach to measurement are thought to be *"dynamic"* because the data represent change (growth). The data are an *"indicator"* in that they represent significant changes in important developmental processes underlying performance in that broad domain that are not directly observed. Further, as "indicators," the data represent *"basic skills"*— in the sense that increases in the indicators enable predictions about improvements in performance on many qualitatively different tasks in that domain.

The difference between MM and GOM is quite clear and straightforward. As described earlier in the example of "writing a paragraph," the development of an MM system is based on a task analysis of that desired curriculum outcome. In contrast, GOM begins with the assumption that "paragraph writing" is a task within the broad domain of "written expression," and that "paragraph writing" needs to be measured in such a way that the resulting data are indicative of broad improvements in written expression. Where in MM the "paragraph writing" outcome is first reduced to skills thought to be subordinate to that outcome, in GOM the goal is to develop procedures for direct and repeated sampling of performance that are indicative of the desired outcome—i.e., improved written expression.

In both MM and GOM, the task of "paragraph writing" may serve as the basis for assessment. In MM, students would be expected to demonstrate "mastery" of paragraph writing as the final task—the ultimate requirement—in the skill sequence that must be mastered. In GOM, students would be asked to write a paragraph from the very outset of instruction. Assessment of paragraph writing would be structured in such a way as to provide data indicative not only of changes in "paragraph writing" but, more broadly, of improvements in "written expression." Thus, while the paragraph writing task might appear to be the same in both MM and GOM, the assumptions on which assessments are based are quite different, the task may be structured quite differently, the scoring procedures might be different, and, certainly, the timing of mea-surement on that task will differ.

Where MM and GOM intersect, it is at the level of *measuring proficiency* on the final task taught and assessed in the MM sequence. Even when MM and GOM involve measuring performance on the same task, they typically differ markedly with respect to the information that is collected regarding student progress. With MM the relevant information is the rate of progress through mastery tests of subskills, while in GOM the information is the rate of increase in performance on a task selected as indicative of the broader outcome.

In GOM, the rate of increase in task performance is always obtained by repeatedly sampling performance *on the same task* throughout the course of instruction. The operating assumption is that, although student performance on the terminal task will be low at the outset of instruction, it will increase across time if the student is learning to do the task. If the data collected are criterion valid, then the increase in performance scores on this task would enable predictions about improvement in the broad domain represented by the task. Within GOM, then, progress monitoring consists of measuring the rate of a student's growth on a task with known criterion validity. When GOMs are carefully developed, the data produced through their application are similar to those produced through growth measurements in other growth domains such as height and weight, and the growth curves developed through GOM are similar in appearance to height and weight charts (Deno, 1985).

GOM graphs. All GOM approaches have in common a focus on creating graphic records of growth in performance across time. The growth records are used to evaluate the effects of instructional interventions intended to effect improvements in performance. An example graph of the progress monitoring data collected through GOM is provided in Figure 2. The graph in Figure 2 displays the number of correct word sequences produced in repeated 3-minute writing samples (Espin, Scierka, Skare, Halverson, 1999) across 25 school days. Correct word sequences are two adjacently written words that are spelled correctly and that are semantically and syntactically acceptable in the context of the phrase in which they are written.

FIGURE 2

General Outcome Measurement Progress Graph

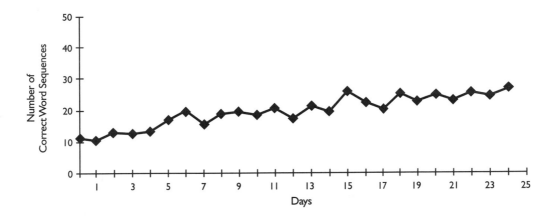

At the outset, the student was writing paragraphs with 10–15 correct word sequences. As instruction and practice at paragraph writing occurred, the performance in writing correct word sequences increased until, at the end of this series of samples, the student was writing paragraphs with nearly 30 correct word sequences. In this conventional GOM graph of the student's performance, the overall upward slope of the data represents the rate of improvement in writing proficiency. When the graph from Figure 2 is compared with the graphs in Figure 1, on page 219, the connection between MM and GOM becomes apparent. The progress monitoring graph for GOM is similar to the conventional graph in Figure 1 except that all of the data displayed on the GOM graph are derived from measurements of performance on the final integrative skill—the general outcome—in the task-analytic sequence. Another difference that is common is that the critical data in most MM represent accuracy alone (i.e., percentage correct) while the GOM data typically include not only accuracy but also speed (i.e., amount produced within a time-limited sample).

In essence, all GOM approaches share the use of single-case research designs as the method for attempting to identify environmental variables that significantly affect performance, and to improve student programs through formative evaluation. Single-case research methods are highly flexible and can be used with many types of measurement. In their most basic form, however, single-case research designs are based on a time-series data record created through repeated measurement of performance on the *same,* rather than successively different, tasks (Kratochwill & Levin, 1992). Thus, analysis of the environmental variables effecting behavioral change is more easily conducted when the data record is produced through GOM rather than MM.

What to measure. Because GOM rests on the principle of repeated measurement of performance on the same task, the value of the progress monitoring data produced through using this approach depends on the significance of the task that is measured.

Historically, what is to be measured through achievement tests has been based on the judgment of curriculum specialists and test developers. In such cases, curriculum specialists presumed to be able to identify key outcomes have been asked to identify those skills or competencies that are at the top of the hierarchy in a particular curriculum domain, and test developers have set about designing ways to test that performance. The authority of judgments about curriculum content has been so complete that it is common to find textbooks on assessment proclaiming that content validity is the most important kind of validity for achievement tests (cf. Taylor, 2000).

In the past decade emphasis in assessment has shifted to developing alternative approaches to assessment, and the emphasis in task selection has been on what is referred to as "authenticity." While the meaning of "authenticity" has not been precisely operationalized, the referent seems to be that a task should be perceived as "real and "meaningful" to the learners within the context of their lives. "Authentic" tasks are not simply contrived by a test maker who is remote from the learner's interest and experience (Shepard, 2000). From this perspective, the term "authentic" seems to refer to whether the task is something typical of what an individual might do in applying the subject matter to produce something of interest to the learner (and to those interested in making an inference about learner competence). This emphasis on the meaningful application of knowledge is accompanied by a concern for the substance content of tasks rather than simply the specific skills involved inherent in the task. Thus, writing an alternative conclusion to a story would likely be judged more "authentic" than answering comprehension questions about story content as a task for assessing a student's reading proficiency. In such a case, the focus in appraising performance will be on the quality of the alternative conclusion that has been written rather than on the mechanics of paragraph composition and grammar.

As an alternative approach to arguing about authenticity, an empirical approach to selecting critical tasks and developing valid GOMs can be found in the special education literature. Thus far, empirical investigations have focused on reading, spelling, written expression, and arithmetic in the elementary grades (cf. Deno, Marston, & Mirkin, 1982; Deno, Mirkin, & Chiang, 1982; L. S. Fuchs, D. Fuchs, & Maxwell, 1988; Germann & Tindal, 1985; Marston & Magnusson 1988; Shinn, 1989). Extensions of this research have been made to monitoring growth in early literacy (Kaminski & Good, 1996: Priest, Spicuzza, Haseth, Peterson, & McConnell, 1992), secondary reading and writing (Espin, Busch, Shin, & Kruschwitz, 2001; Espin, De La Paz, Scierka, & Roelofs, in press; Espin & Deno, 1993, 1995; Espin & Foegen, 1996; Espin et al., 2000; Espin & Tindal, 1998), and middle school math (Foegen, 1995). The validity criteria examined in research on these measures are multidimensional. They include not only criterion-related validity with respect to commercially available norm-referenced tests, but also teacher judgment of student proficiency, developmental growth and sensitivity to that growth across short and long time periods, utility in increasing instructional effectiveness, utility in instructional diagnosis, utility in evaluating program entry and exit, placement in special and compensatory educational programs, and performance on norm-referenced standardized achievement tests. Review and examination of this body of research illustrates that it is possible to use an empirical approach for selecting important tasks to create GOM procedures with known technical characteristics.

How to measure. If anything has been learned from the history of psychometrics, it is that standardization of assessment procedures is requisite for comparisons among individuals on the same occasion, and within individuals from one occasion to the next. Historically, assessment has been used to differentiate between individuals; thus, standardization has been developed to legitimate statements of individual standing within the normative population. Standardization of progress monitoring procedures in GOM is no less important. Progress monitoring data are used both to ascertain growth over baseline performance and to make judgments about goal attainment. Making these comparative judgments requires that the data produced be reliable and that the conditions for administering the progress measures be consistent. Casualness (i.e., lack of standardization) in assessing progress can only contribute to measurement error and then to erroneous conclusions regarding program success. Error will result in the continuation of programs that are not succeeding and the potential abandonment of programs that are. Furthermore, many advantages accrue when progress monitoring procedures are standardized. For example, if standardized procedures are used it becomes possible to gather normative data that can serve as a basis for establishing reasonable empirical goals for the individual. Seldom does any empirical basis exist for goal selection. As has already been mentioned with respect to specifying mastery criteria, the specification of criterion levels of performance—standards—is usually quite arbitrary. In the face of insufficient empirical information, then, we rely on specifying high levels of accuracy as if doing so somehow guarantees sufficiency.

In contrast, when progress monitoring procedures are standardized, normative peer sampling within classrooms can be conducted by teachers to assist them in making judgments about whether students might be able to function successfully in the general education classroom and about those levels of performance that are typical for students of the same age and grade (D. Fuchs, L. S. Fuchs, & Fernstrom, 1993; Shinn, Baker, Habedank, & Good, 1993). More ambitious undertakings have involved developing school and district norms for performance on standardized GOMs (cf. Marston & Magnusson, 1988). We should keep in mind, of course, that the purpose of progress monitoring is to be able to empirically determine our success in developing the individual student program. At the same time, we would be foolish if we failed to recognize the efficiency of using progress monitoring procedures that, in addition to producing data for reporting to parents and school personnel, can enable our evaluations of programs and groups as well.

How to use the data. No aspect of progress monitoring can be more important than how the data are used to improve educational outcomes for students. Indeed, the broader conception of validity articulated by Messick (1995) is based on a consideration of the social consequences of assessment. Messick's view is that for a test to be validated it is necessary to demonstrate that using the test properly results in benefits to the individual and society. Good and Jefferson (1998) have analyzed Messick's views on test validity with respect to GOM and concluded that GOM meets the broader criteria of validity that Messick has outlined.

A significant aspect of the recent research on GOM is the focus on how the data obtained through progress monitoring are used by professionals as a basis for educational decision making. This research has demonstrated the consequences of using GOM data to make decisions during prereferral screening, eligibility for services, instructional evaluation, reintegration evaluation, and program effectiveness (Marston & Magnusson, 1988; Shinn, 2002). Among these decisions, evaluating *instructional effectiveness* is most central to the purpose of progress monitoring. If progress monitoring is to function as a dynamic in the development of improved instructional programs, teachers must be able to use the information generated to determine whether, and if so when, a program is effective and when to make necessary changes in the program. Fortunately, evidence exists that teachers can use GOM to increase their effectiveness. In the next section, evidence from recent research is presented that summarizes the key variables and effects of using progress monitoring within systematic formative evaluation.

Recent Research

One well-established, long-standing research program documents how one form of GOM, Curriculum-Based Measurement (CBM), can help teachers plan better instruction and effect better student outcomes. Studies have examined the effects of data utilization strategies, as well as CBM's overall contribution to instructional planning and student learning within general and special education.

Specific effects of alternative data-utilization strategies. CBM has been shown to enhance teacher planning and student learning by helping teachers set ambitious student goals, by assisting teachers in determining when instructional adaptations are necessary to prompt better student growth, and by providing ideas for potentially effective teaching adjustments.

With respect to helping teachers *set ambitious goals,* L. S. Fuchs, D. Fuchs, and Hamlett (1989a) explored the contribution of goal-raising guidelines within CBM decision-making rules. Teachers were assigned randomly to and participated in one of three treatments for 15 weeks in mathematics: no CBM, CBM *without* a goal-raising rule, and CBM *with* a goal-raising rule. The goal-raising rule required teachers to increase goals whenever the student's actual rate of growth, represented by an ordinary least-squares regression through 7–10 CBM data points, was greater than the growth rate anticipated by the teacher. Teachers in the CBM goal-raising condition raised goals more frequently (for 15 of 30 students) than teachers in the non-goal-raising condition (for 1 of 30 students). Concurrent with teachers' goal raising was differential student achievement on pre- and poststandardized achievement tests: The effect size comparing the pre-post change of the two CBM conditions (i.e., with and without the goal-raising rule) was .52 standard deviations. Consequently, using CBM to monitor the appropriateness of instructional goals and to adjust goals upward when possible represents one means by which CBM can be used to assist teachers in their instructional planning.

A second way in which CBM can be used to enhance instructional decision making is to assess the adequacy of student progress and *determine whether, and if so when, instructional adaptation is necessary.* When the actual growth rate (ordinary least–squares regression line through 7–10 CBM scores) is less than the expected growth rate (slope of the goal line), it can be reasonably concluded that the intervention is ineffective and teachers are expected to modify the instructional program to promote stronger learning. L. S. Fuchs, D. Fuchs, and Hamlett (1989b) estimated the contribution of this CBM decision-making strategy with 29 special educators who implemented CBM for 15 school weeks with 53 students with mild/moderate disabilities. Teachers in a "CBM-measurement only" group measured students' reading growth as required but did not use the assessment information to restructure students' reading programs. Teachers in the CBM-"change the program" decision-rule group measured student performance and used the assessment information to determine when to introduce programmatic adaptations to enhance growth rates. Results indicated that although teachers in both groups measured student performance, important differences were associated with the use of the "change the program" decision rule. As indicated by student performance on the Stanford Achievement Test-Reading Comprehension Subtest, students in the "change the program" decision-rule group achieved significantly better than a no-CBM control group (ES = .72 standard deviations), whereas the "measurement only" CBM group did not (ES = .36 standard deviations). Moreover, the slopes of the two CBM treatment groups were significantly different, favoring the achievement of the "change the program" group (ES = .86 standard deviations). As suggested by these findings and results of other researchers (e.g., Stecker & Fuchs, 2000; Wesson, Skiba, Sevcik, King, & Deno, 1984), collecting CBM data, in and of itself, exerts only a small effect on student learning. To enhance student outcomes in important ways, teachers need to use the CBM data experimentally to build effective programs for difficult-to-teach students by changing ineffective programs and by raising goals for those students whose programs are effective.

As just illustrated, to help teachers determine when adjustments are required in students' programs and for identifying when goal increases are warranted, the CBM graph, which shows a student's total scores across time, is used. In addition, by inspecting the graph, the teachers may *formulate ideas for potentially effective instructional adaptations.* For example, a flat or decelerating slope may generate hypotheses about lack of maintenance of previously learned material or about motivational problems.

With GOM, performance is sampled from the annual curriculum on each assessment, thereby providing information about content previously taught and content that will be taught during the upcoming portions of the academic year. Performance on previously taught content permits conclusions about retention; performance on to-be taught material permits inferences about generalization. Also, CBM performance can be summarized beyond graphic displays to derive rich descriptions of student performance. That is, because CBM assesses performance on the year's curriculum at each testing, descriptions of strengths and weaknesses in the curriculum can be generated. The value of these diagnostic profiles, as tools with which to supplement CBM graphic displays, has been investigated in math (L. S. Fuchs, D. Fuchs, Hamlett, & Stecker, 1991), reading (L. S. Fuchs, D. Fuchs, & Hamlett, 1989c), and spelling (L. S. Fuchs, D. Fuchs, Hamlett, & Allinder, 1991). In each investigation, teachers were assigned randomly to one of three conditions: no CBM, CBM with goal-raising and change-the-program decision rules, and CBM with goal-raising and change-the-program decision rules along with CBM diagnostic profiles. In all three studies, teachers in the diagnostic profile treatment group generated instructional plans that were more varied and more responsive to individuals' learning needs. Moreover, they effected better student learning as measured on change between pre- and posttest performance on global measures of achievement. Effect sizes associated with the CBM diagnostic profile groups ranged from .65 to 1.23 standard deviations. This series of studies demonstrated how structured, well-organized CBM information about students' strengths and difficulties in the curriculum can help teachers build better programs and effect greater learning.

CBM's overall contribution to teacher planning and student achievement in regular classrooms. In addition to examining the contribution of each strategy by which CBM informs and strengthens instructional plans, research has examined CBM's overall contribution to teacher planning and student achievement in general education classrooms and in special education.

With respect to *general education,* the question is whether CBM can be used to adapt the setting to boost student performance and avoid special education referral. This process of adapting general education to preclude the need for a special education is known widely as "prereferral assessment" (e.g., Graden, Casey, & Christenson, 1985), a process we label Initial Teacher Problem Solving. Although current special education practice often incorporates efforts by general educators to improve outcomes, the nature of modifications often is insubstantial, and the effects of those adaptations frequently are evaluated unsystematically (D. Fuchs & L. S. Fuchs, 1992). With the addition of CBM, these problem-solving efforts can be formalized and systematized.

In this way, the Minneapolis Public Schools incorporated CBM prereferral assessment into its eligibility assessment process (Marston & Magnusson, 1988). Over 6 weeks, interventions were implemented, and ongoing CBM data were collected to assess the extent to which students' academic needs could be addressed in the regular classroom when instructional adaptations were introduced. Only pupils whose performance did *not* improve as a function of those adaptations were identified for special education services. Marston and Magnusson reported that 25–45% of initially referred students were deemed eligible for special education after CBM problem solving. This figure is dramatically lower than the estimate reported by Algozzine, Christenson, and Ysseldyke (1982), in which 90% of referred students were subsequently identified for special education using conventional assessment procedures.

In a similar way, L. S. Fuchs, D. Fuchs, Hamlett, Phillips, and Karns (1995) studied the viability of CBM prereferral assessment. General educators were assigned randomly to two treatments. In both treatments, teachers implemented ongoing CBM in mathematics with all students in their classes beginning in September. In addition, to facilitate the link between CBM and instruction, teachers in both conditions incorporated a structured form of peer-assisted learning (e.g., D. Fuchs, L. S. Fuchs, Mathes, & Simmons, 1997; L. S. Fuchs, D. Fuchs, Phillips, Hamlett, & Karns, 1995). This combination of CBM and peer-assisted learning strategies represented the baseline treatment in the L. S. Fuchs, D. Fuchs, Hamlett, et al. (1995) study. Unfortunately, because at least 10–33% of students fail to demonstrate persuasive progress with otherwise demonstrably effective programs, a need exists to identify and treat students who manifest unacceptable performance and growth. So, the second treatment in the L. S. Fuchs, D. Fuchs, Hamlett, et al. (1995) study focused on individual adaptations conducted in regular classrooms. Beginning in November, the bimonthly CBM class reports identified up to two students per class whose CBM progress was inadequate (i.e., low level combined with low slope, relative to classmates). For these students, teachers (a) formulated an adaptation before the next 2-week report; (b) implemented that adaptation at least four times in the upcoming 2 weeks; and (c) when CBM identified the same student multiple times over reports, modified previous adaptations to enhance progress.

Results demonstrated that when general educators were specifically prompted with CBM and supported to engage in instructional adaptation, they did so with respectable fidelity. Across three to six 2-week adaptation cycles, teachers ignored requests for adaptations only infrequently; they often implemented multiple strategies concurrently to address the problems of target students, and some teachers manifested modified student programs *repeatedly* in a variety of ways in an attempt to boost progress. Moreover, the teachers' reliance on individual adaptations appeared to prompt changes in their thinking about differentiating their instructional plans. Compared to teachers in the baseline treatment, those in the adaptations treatment reported (a) more modifications in their goals and strategies for poorly progressing students; (b) a greater variety of skills taught; (c) selective reteaching of lessons more frequently; and (d) more frequent deviation from the teacher's manual for selected students.

Findings were not, however, uniformly positive. Despite many focused, data-based attempts to enhance learning, some children proved unresponsive to regular classroom adaptations. Two brief cases illustrate students' differential responsiveness. Over a 12-week period, a fourth-grade teacher implemented a rich set of adaptations, relying on basic facts drills, motivational workcharts and contracts, and manipulatives. The target student, who exhibited a CBM slope of .21 digits per week when identified for adaptation, responded well to these modifications to the general education classroom and completed the school year with a slope of .63 digits per week—the average slope for the class. This success contrasts with the experience of a third-grade teacher who also implemented a large number and rich set of adaptations including drilling basic facts, slicing back to second-grade material, implementing a motivational workchart, and using money as a manipulative to work on conceptual underpinnings. Despite this teacher's similar level of effort to modify general education classroom instruction, her target student demonstrated little improvement in growth rate: He ended the year with a relatively low slope of .28 digits per week, which was similar to his slope at the time he was identified for adaptation and was considerably lower than his classmates' average slope of .98 digits per week.

Three of the 10 teachers effected substantial improvement for target students. This suggests that, with the assistance of rich assessment information and consultative support to formulate feasible adaptations, general education classroom teachers may be able to address the problems of some portion (in this case, 30%) of students who initially demonstrate significant learning discrepancies from classroom peers. Nevertheless, this database simultaneously indicates that some students will remain unresponsive to an adapted general education environment.

This unresponsiveness creates the need for additional resources—specifically, the individualized instruction, the small-size instructional groups, and the more highly trained teachers available through *special education*—to address the learning problems of a small portion of learners. In fact, strong evidence supports CBM's utility in helping special educators plan more effective programs. Studies (e.g., L. S. Fuchs, Deno, & Mirkin, 1984; L. S. Fuchs, D. Fuchs, Hamlett, & Allinder, 1991; L. S. Fuchs, D. Fuchs, Hamlett, & Ferguson, 1992; Jones & Krouse, 1988; Stecker & L. S. Fuchs, 2000; Wesson et al., 1984; Wesson, 1991) provide corroborating evidence of dramatic effects on student outcomes in reading, spelling, and math when special educators rely on CBM to inform instructional planning.

To illustrate this database, we briefly describe a study in reading—one that is illustrative of many—provided by L. S. Fuchs et al. (1984), who conducted a study in the New York City Public Schools. In this study, teachers participated for 18 weeks in a conventional monitoring contrast group or a CBM treatment group, where teachers measured students' reading performance at least twice weekly, scored and graphed those performances, and used prescriptive CBM decision rules for evaluating the students' reading programs. Children whose teachers employed CBM to develop reading programs achieved better than students whose teachers used conventional monitoring methods on the Passage Reading Test and on the decoding and comprehension subtests of the Stanford Diagnostic Reading Test, with respective effect sizes of 1.18, .94, and .99. This suggests that, with the focus on assessing GOM growth using CBM's passage reading fluency, teachers planned better reading programs comprehensively to include a multiple focus on fluency, decoding, and comprehension.

Thus far in this chapter we have developed a conceptual rationale for using student progress evaluations to increase intervention effectiveness, considered general approaches to student progress monitoring, and summarized recent research on variables in designing evaluation that affect student progress. In the closing section we present a case study illustrating the use of General Outcome Measurement in prevention, referral, and intervention for an individual student. In doing so, we highlight the possible functions of a school psychologist at each phase of the process. While the focus of our example is on reading, similar procedures can be used in spelling, written expression, and mathematics.

APPLYING EVALUATION STRATEGIES: A CASE EXAMPLE

In the following case study, we illustrate how General Outcome Measurement (GOM) procedures can be used to evaluate the progress of a child in general and special education. In addition, we illustrate how General Outcome Measurement can be combined with Mastery Monitoring to evaluate the progress of students receiving special education services. Our case study presents a model in which the school psychologist and classroom teachers work closely together to evaluate the effects of prereferral interventions and special education services for an individual child. We begin by describing the use of GOM to evaluate the effects of prereferral interventions on a student's performance in the general education classroom, and then demonstrate how GOM can be used to continue to monitor that child once he or she is placed in special education.

As stated earlier, one of the most important aspects of GOM is the use of the data for instructional decision making. Teachers' use of GOM data increases with the use of specified data-decision rules. Several different types of data-decision rules are possible, but two are prevalent: (a) comparing the *slope* (i.e., rate of growth) to the goal line, and (b) comparing the *level* of performance to the goal line. The type of data-decision rule chosen is less important than choosing a rule and consistently implementing it (L. S. Fuchs & D. Fuchs, 1986).

The use of slope (i.e., rate of growth) was illustrated earlier in the review of GOM research. The teacher inspects the graph and draws a slope line through the data to represent the student's growth rate. If the slope is less than the expected rate of growth, the teacher makes a change in instruction; if the slope line is greater than the expected rate, the teacher raises the goal. In the case study that follows, we illustrate the second type of data-decision rule in which the teacher compares the student's level of performance to the goal line. Using this data-decision rule, the teacher inspects the graph to determine whether consecutive data points are falling above or below the goal line. If the student's performance falls below the goal line during 3 consecutive weeks, the instruction is modified. If the student's performance is above the goal line during 6 consecutive weeks, the goal is raised.

Evaluation of Student Performance in the General Education Curriculum

The first step in implementing a GOM progress measurement system is to identify students who may be at risk for failure in general education (for more detail, see Shinn, Shinn, Hamilton, & Clarke, this volume). Once these students are identified, their performance in the general education classroom is monitored. If the students experience difficulties, prereferral interventions are implemented, and the effects of those interventions are evaluated using GOM data.

For example, consider Tyler, a third grader at South Elementary School who has been identified as a student at risk in the general education classroom. He was identified through the screening procedures implemented at South during the first month of school. In September, all students in the school were screened using General Outcome Measures in reading. The classroom teachers, paraprofessionals, Chapter 1 teachers, and school psychologists participated in the screening procedures. Students read aloud for 1 minute from 3 standard grade-level passages. The number of words read correctly on each passage was counted, and the median or middle score of the 3 recorded. The school psychologist gathered the data from each teacher, and rank-ordered the scores within each grade level to identify those students scoring in the lowest 20% of the grade-level distribution. Because Tyler scored in the lowest 20%, his teacher, Mrs. Smith, will monitor his performance once per week.

Expected rate of growth. Before beginning to monitor Tyler, Mrs. Smith and the school psychologist meet to discuss a reasonable estimate of growth for Tyler. They consider both school- and district-level data in their decision making. Schoolwide screening data indicate that the average score for third-graders is 104 words read correctly; in contrast, Tyler reads only 47 words correctly. Districtwide data reveal that the average third-grader in the district improves at a rate of 1.5 words per week. Mrs. Smith wants to be ambitious in her goal setting, so she and the school psychologist choose an increase of 2 words per week as an expected rate of growth for Tyler. Tyler's year-end goal is thus 107 words read correctly in 1 minute:

[Long Range Goal = (expected rate of growth X the number of weeks) + beginning level of performance.]

Mrs. Smith creates a graph for Tyler that displays his baseline or beginning performance, his long-range goal, and his expected rate of growth (see Figure 3).

Monitoring. On Wednesday of each week, Tyler reads aloud for 1 minute from a selected grade-level passage. Mrs. Smith records the number of words read aloud and graphs the score each week.

Data utilization. The data utilization rules used at South Elementary are as follows:

1. If a student's scores fall below the expected rate of growth for 3 consecutive weeks, change the instructional plan;

2. If after 3 interventions (i.e., a minimum of 9 weeks and no more than 12 weeks) the student's data continue to fall below the expected rate of growth, and if the student is experiencing difficulty in the general reading program, consider referral to Title 1 or special education programs.

Mrs. Smith begins her instruction, the core of which is based on the use of trade books, mixed with direct instruction on phonics and word skills. On Mondays, Mrs. Smith introduces the story or section of the story to be read that week. She introduces new words to the students, and uses the words to instruct students on decoding or word attack strategies. On Tuesdays and Wednesdays, Mrs. Smith reads part of the story aloud to the students. Students then read the same section of the story aloud as a group, and then to each other in pairs. On Thursdays, Mrs. Smith works with the students on comprehension-building activities, including creating story grammar maps, summarizing text, formulating questions, and predicting future events. On Fridays, Mrs. Smith reviews all of the skills covered that week.

FIGURE 3

Evaluation Strategies

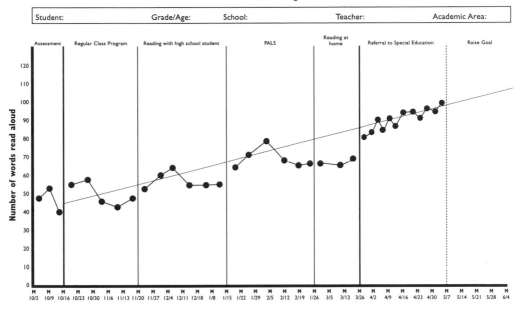

Once every 3 weeks, the classroom teachers and the school psychologist meet to inspect the graphs and discuss the progress of the at-risk students who are being monitored. Tyler's progress is illustrated in the graph in Figure 3. On Weeks 3, 4, and 5, Tyler's performance falls below the goal line, necessitating a modification of his reading program. Because his scores are only slightly below his goal line, Mrs. Smith and the psychologist believe that a minor intervention will be appropriate. Tyler has an interest in many of the books Mrs. Smith has in her classroom, especially those related to sports, but he is not skilled enough to read them independently. South Elementary has a companion program with the high school where high-school students volunteer to work with elementary school students during the school day. Mrs. Smith arranges for one of the high-school football players to come to South twice a week to read with Tyler. She picks out an autobiography of a famous football player as the first book for Tyler and the high school student to read together.

Evaluation of first instructional modification. Immediately following the first modification in his instructional program, Tyler's performance improves, indicating that the modification is effective. However, his performance levels off after this initial improvement; thus, his data points for Weeks 9, 10, and 11 once again fall below the goal line. Additionally, Tyler is experiencing increasing frustration in reading, has begun to misbehave during reading instruction, and does not complete his classwork during reading time. Given these converging factors, Mrs. Smith and the school psychologist decide that a more intensive instructional modification is in order for Tyler. At a recent in-service, Mrs. Smith learned about a program called Peer-Assisted Learning (PALS). PALS is a systematic classwide peer tutoring program in which students work in pairs to practice reading aloud, summarizing, identifying the main idea, and predicting future events (D. Fuchs et al., 1997; D. Fuchs et al., 2001; for more detail, see the chapter by Greenwood, Maheady, & Delquadri, this volume). Mrs. Smith decides to implement the PALS program into her instruction because of her concerns for Tyler and for other students like Tyler who are struggling in reading. Mrs. Smith likes the idea of PALS because it allows for intensive instruction to be given to readers at all levels of the reading-performance continuum and because it can be easily added to her existing instruction.

Evaluation of second instructional modification. On Monday, Wednesday, and Friday of each week, Mrs. Smith implements the PALS program for Tyler and all other students in the class. For 35 minutes of each class period, students are assigned a partner and work on their reading skills using three PALS techniques: (a) Partner Reading, (b) Paragraph Shrinking, and (c) Prediction Relay. Mrs. Smith finds that PALS has a positive effect on the reading performance of several of the students in the class, including Tyler. Over a period of 3 weeks, Tyler's performance keeps pace with his long-range goal; however, his performance gradually begins to level off until, during Weeks 15, 16, and 17, it once again falls below his goal line. His performance is in stark contrast to the other students who are being monitored in Mrs. Smith's classroom and who are benefiting from implementation of PALS. Mrs. Smith and the school psychologist meet once again to brainstorm about an intervention for Tyler that may help him to continue to improve in reading. Mrs. Smith reports that Tyler's frustration level in reading is increasing once again, and Mrs. Smith and the psychologist discuss the possibility that Tyler may need a more intensive reading program. However, they both agree that it is worthwhile to try one more modification in the general education classroom before referring Tyler for services in special education.

Because of Tyler's continued struggles in reading, Mrs. Smith and the psychologist decide to consult with the special education teacher, with Tyler's parents, and with Tyler. In this way, Mrs. Smith and the psychologist hope to get an idea for an effective and intensive intervention that will allow Tyler to improve his reading in the general education classroom. After consultation with all interested parties, Mrs. Smith and the psychologist decide on an intervention that involves a home-school collaborative effort. The special education teacher will supply high-interest, low-level reading materials for Tyler to read at home with his parents each evening. Tyler and his parents agree that he will read for 20 minutes each evening from these materials.

Evaluation of third instructional modification. This final modification in Tyler's program results in some improvement, but Tyler's performance remains below the goal line, and he is falling further behind his peers. And although Tyler and his parents have faithfully implemented the 20 minutes of reading each evening, his parents report that Tyler is becoming increasingly frustrated, making it more and more difficult to get him to do the reading. Mrs. Smith and the school psychologist, in consultation with Tyler's parents and the special education teacher, agree that Tyler may need a more intensive reading program than that which can be delivered in the general education classroom.

Tyler is referred for special education. The school psychologist conducts the assessment, and determines that Tyler meets the district and state eligibility criteria for placement in special education. Tyler will receive 1 hour of service in reading in the resource room in addition to the reading instruction he currently receives in the general education classroom.

Evaluating the Effects of Special Education

After Tyler is referred to special education, an IEP is developed for him in reading. The long-range goal initially developed for Tyler in Mrs. Smith's class is maintained— that of 107 words read correctly in 1 minute. Mrs. Smith, the school psychologist, and the special education teacher all believe that it is possible to move Tyler toward the initial goal set for him.

The special education teacher decides to implement an intensive reading program for Tyler. The assessment data reveal that Tyler has difficulties making many of the sound-symbol relations between the written text and the phonemes or sounds represented by that text. The special education teacher decides to use *Reading Mastery* (Engelmann & Bruner, 1995) with Tyler. She includes him in a group with four other students who are at approximately the same reading level as Tyler. *Reading Mastery* is an intensive, systematic reading program that emphasizes sound-symbol identification, left-to-right orientation, blending, word attack, reading in text, and comprehension. In *Reading Mastery,* a hierarchy of skills is identified, and students' mastery of each skill is recorded via unit tests. The special education teacher thus uses a combination of Mastery Monitoring and General Outcome Measurement. She keeps a continuous record of Tyler's performance on the skills included in the *Reading Mastery* curriculum. This record reveals whether Tyler is learning the skills presented to him each week, and whether he is successfully moving through the *Reading Mastery* curriculum. In addition, the special education teacher monitors Tyler's performance two times a week using the same reading GOMs selected from the general education curriculum materials that were used by Mrs. Smith. Tyler's performance on the general outcome measures reveals whether the use of the *Reading Mastery* curriculum is helping Tyler to become a more successful reader in general. Moreover, by comparing Tyler's performance in special education to his prior performance in the general education classroom, the teacher is able to evaluate the effectiveness of special education for Tyler.

After a period of 6 weeks, Tyler's data reveal that the *Reading Mastery* program is effective. Tyler's performance is at or above his goal line. His teacher believes that Tyler can improve even more, so she implements a minor modification in his program. Building on the reading that Tyler has continued to do at home with his parents, the special education teacher adds a monitoring component to this activity. Tyler records the number of pages he reads each evening with his parents. When he reaches 100 pages, Tyler is allowed to choose from a menu of reinforcers, including leaving school to have lunch with his Dad, going to a hockey game at the university, earning 30 minutes of computer time during the school day, and getting a sports magazine.

This minor modification in Tyler's program is effective as revealed by the steady increase in his performance. The most recent 3 weeks of data collection reveal that Tyler's performance has exceeded his goal for six consecutive data points. At this point, the special education teacher raises Tyler's goal, and continues with instruction.

CONCLUSION

In this chapter we have attempted to provide a coherent perspective on the use of evaluation to improve the effectiveness of interventions. Our view is that assessment in education has focused for too long on distinguishing among students for the purposes of classification and placement in compensatory education programs. Assessment for the purpose of evaluating individual student progress to evaluate program effectiveness has been neglected to the point where technologies for this purpose have only recently begun to develop. As interest increases in establishing accountability for student success in high-stakes testing programs, we expect to see increased interest in procedures for evaluating the effectiveness of individual instructional programs. With this increased interest in program effectiveness we should expect to see increased use of formative as well as summative evaluation. The framework we have provided in this chapter can provide a useful starting point for any professional educator who is interesting in using formative evaluation as part of an intervention strategy for increasing program effectiveness.

REFERENCES

Algozzine, B., Christenson, S., & Ysseldyke, J. E. (1982). Probabilities associated with the referral to placement process. *Teacher Education and Special Education, 5*(3), 19-23.

Armbruster, B. B., Stevens, R. G., & Rosenshine, B. (1977). *Analyzing content coverage and emphasis: A study of three curricula and two tests (Technical Representative N26).* Urbana, IL: University of Illinois, Center for Study of Reading.

Bandura, A. (1986). *Social foundations of thought and action: A social-cognitive theory.* Englewood Cliffs, NJ: Prentice-Hall.

Block, J. H. (Ed.). (1971). *Mastery learning.* New York: Holt, Rinehart, and Winston.

Bloom, B. S., Madaus, G. F., & Hastings, J. T. (1981). *Evaluation to improve learning.* New York: McGraw-Hill.

Carroll, J. B. (1963). A model of school learning. *Teachers College Record, 64,* 723-733.

Cox, W. F., Jr., & Dunn, T. G. (1979). Mastery learning: A psychological trap? *Educational Psychologist, 14,* 24-29.

Deno, S. L. (1985). Curriculum-based measurement: The emerging alternative. *Exceptional Children, 52,* 219-232.

Deno, S. L. (1990). Individual differences and individual difference: The essential difference of special education. *Journal of Special Education, 24*(2), 160-173.

Deno, S. L. (1997). "Whether" thou goest: Perspectives on progress monitoring. In E. Kame'enui, J. Lloyd, & D. Chard (Eds.), *Issues in educating students with disabilities.* Mahwah, NJ: Erlbaum.

Deno, S. L., & Fuchs, L. S. (1987). Developing curriculum-based measurement systems for databased special education problem solving. *Focus on Exceptional Children, 19*(8), 1-15.

Deno, S., Marston, D., & Mirkin, P. (1982). Valid measurement procedures for continuous evaluation of written expression. *Exceptional Children, 1982, 48*(4), 368-371.

Deno, S. L., & Mirkin, P. K. (1977). *Data based program modification: A manual.* Arling-ton, VA: Council for Exceptional Children.

Deno, S., Mirkin, P., & Chiang, B. (1982). Identifying valid measures of reading. *Exceptional Children, 49*(1), 36-45.

Engelmann, S., & Bruner, E. C. (1995). *Reading mastery.* DeSoto, TX: SRA.

Espin, C. A., Busch, T., Shin, J., & Kruschwitz, R. (2001). Curriculum-based measures in the content areas: Validity of vocabulary-matching measures as indicators of performance in social studies. *Learning Disabilities Research and Practice, 16,* 142-151.

Espin, C. A., De La Paz, S., Scierka, B. J., & Roelofs, L. (in press). Relation between curriculum-based measures in written expression and quality and completeness of expository writing for middle-school students. *Journal of Special Education.*

Espin, C. A., & Deno, S. L. (1993). Performance in reading from content-area text as an indicator of achievement. *Remedial and Special Education 14*(6), 47-59.

Espin, C. A., & Deno, S. L. (1995). Curriculum-based measures for secondary students: Utility and task specificity of text-based reading and vocabulary measures for predicting performance on content-area tasks. *Diagnostique, 20,* 121-142.

Espin, C. A., & Foegen, A. (1996). Validity of three general outcome measures for predicting secondary students' performance on content-area tasks. *Exceptional Children, 62,* 497-514.

Espin, C. A., Scierka, B. J., Skare, S., & Halverson, N. (1999). Criterion-related validity of curriculum-based measures in writing for secondary students. *Reading and Writing Quarterly, 15,* 5-27.

Espin, C. A., Skare, S., Shin, J., Deno, S. L., Robinson, S., & Brenner, B. (2000). Identifying indicators of growth in written expression for middle-school students. *Journal of Special Education, 34,* 140-153.

Espin, C. A., & Tindal, G. (1998). Curriculum-based measurement for secondary students. In M. R. Shinn (Ed.), *Advanced applications of curriculum-based measurement.* New York: Guilford Press.

Foegen, A. (1995). *Reliability and validity of three general outcome measures for low-achieving students in secondary mathematics.* Unpublished doctoral dissertation, University of Minnesota, Minneapolis.

Flavell, J. H. (1979). Metacognition and cognitive monitoring: A new area of cognitive developmental inquiry. *American Psychologist, 35,* 906-911.

Fuchs, D., & Fuchs, L. S. (1992). Limitations of a "feel-good" approach to consultation. *Journal of Educational and Psychological Consultation, 3,* 93-97.

Fuchs, D., Fuchs, L. S., & Fernstrom, P. J. (1993). A conservative approach to special education reform: Mainstreaming through transenvironmental programming and curriculum-based measurement. *American Educational Research Journal, 30,* 149-178.

Fuchs, D., Fuchs, L. S., Mathes, P. G., & Simmons, D. C. (1997). Peer-Assisted Learning Strategies: Making classrooms more responsive to diversity. *American Educational Research Journal, 34,* 174-206.

Fuchs, D., Fuchs, L. S., Thompson, A., Svenson, E., Yen, L., Otaiba, S. A., Yang, N., McMaster, K. N., Prentice, K., Kazdan, S., & Saenz, L. (2001). Peer-assisted learning strategies in reading: Extensions for kindergarten, first grade, and high school. *Remedial and Special Education, 22,* 15-21.

Fuchs, L. S., & Deno, S. L. (1991). Paradigmatic distinctions between instructionally relevant measurement models. *Exceptional Children, 57,* 488-501.

Fuchs, L. S., & Fuchs, D. (1986). Effects of systematic formative evaluation: A meta-analysis. *Exceptional Children, 53,* 199-208.

Fuchs, L. S., Fuchs, D., & Hamlett, C. L. (1989a). Effects of alternative goal structures within curriculum-based measurement. *Exceptional Children, 55,* 429-438.

Fuchs, L. S., Fuchs, D., & Hamlett, C. L. (1989b). Effects of instrumental use of curriculum-based measurement to enhance instructional programs. *Remedial and Special Education, 10*(2), 43-52.

Fuchs, L. S., Deno, S. L., & Mirkin, P. K. (1984). The effects of frequent curriculum-based measurement and evaluation on student achievement, pedagogy, and student awareness of learning. *American Educational Research Journal, 21,* 449-460.

Fuchs, L. S., Fuchs, D., & Hamlett, C. L. (1989c). Monitoring reading growth using student recalls: Effects of two teacher feedback systems. *Journal of Educational Research, 83,* 103-111.

Fuchs, L. S., Fuchs, D., Hamlett, C. L., & Ferguson, C. (1992). Effects of expert system consultation within curriculum-based measurement using a reading maze task. *Exceptional Children, 58,* 436-450.

Fuchs, L. S., Fuchs, D., Hamlett, C. L., Allinder, R. M. (1991). Effects of expert system advice within curriculum-based measurement on teacher planning and student achievement in spelling. *School Psychology Review, 20,* 49-66.

Fuchs, L. S., Fuchs, D., Hamlett, C. L., Phillips, N. B., & Karns, K. (1995). General educators' specialized adaptation for students with learning disabilities. *Exceptional Children, 61,* 440-459.

Fuchs, L. S., Fuchs, D., Hamlett, C. L., & Stecker, P. M. (1991). Effects of curriculum-based measurement and consultation on teacher planning and student achievement in mathematics operations. *American Educational Research Journal, 28,* 617-641.

Fuchs, L. S., Fuchs, D., & Maxwell, L. (1988). The validity of informal reading comprehension measures. *Remedial and Special Education, 9,* 20-28.

Fuchs, L. S., Fuchs, D., Phillips, N., Hamlett, C. L., & Karns, K. (1995). Acquisition and transfer effects of class wide peer-assisted learning strategies in mathematics for students with varying learning histories. *School Psychology Review, 24,* 604-620.

Gagne, R. M., Briggs, L., & Wager, W. (1988). *Principles of instructional design.* New York: Holt, Rinehart, and Winston.

Germann, G., & Tindal, G. (1985). An application of curriculum-based assessment: The use of direct and repeated measurement. *Exceptional Children,* 52, 244-265.

Good, R. H, & Jefferson, G. (1998). Contemporary perspectives on curriculum-based measurement validity. In M. Shinn (Ed.), *Advanced applications of curriculum-based measurement.* New York: Guilford Press.

Graden, J. L., Casey, A., & Christenson, S. L. (1985). Implementing a prereferral intervention system: Part I. The model. *Exceptional Children, 51,* 377-384.

Hesushius, L. (1991). Curriculum-based assessment and direct instruction: Critical reflections on fundamental assumptions. *Exceptional Children, 57,* 315-328.

Individuals with Disabilities Education Act of 1990. 20 U.S.C. 1400.

Jenkins, J., & Pany, D. (1978). Standardized achievement tests: How useful for special education? *Exceptional Children, 44,* 448-453.

Jones, E. D., & Krouse, J. P. (1988). The effectiveness of databased instruction by student teachers in classrooms for pupils with mild learning handicaps. *Teacher Education and Special Education, 11,* 9-19.

Kavale, K. A., & Forness, S. R. (1999). Effectiveness of special education. In C. R. Reynolds & T. B. Gutkin (Eds.), *The handbook of school psychology* (pp. 984-1024). New York: Wiley.

Kaminski, R. A., & Good, R. H. (1996). Toward a technology for assessing basic early literacy skills. *School Psychology Review, 25,* 215-227.

Kohn, A. (2001). Fighting the tests: A practical guide to rescuing our schools. *Phi Delta Kappan, 82*(5), 349-357.

Kratochwill, T. R., & Levin, J. R. (1992). *Single-case research design and analysis.* Hillsdale, NJ: Erlbaum.

Lloyd, J. W. (1984). How shall we individualize instruction—or should we? *Remedial and Special Education, 5*(1), 7-15.

Marston, D., & Magnusson, D. (1988). Curriculum-based assessment: District-level implementation. In J. Graden, J. Zins, & M. Curtis (Eds.), *Alternative educational delivery systems: Enhancing instructional options for all students* (pp. 137-172). Washington, DC: National Association of School Psychologists.

Messick, S. 1995. Validity of psychological assessment. *American Psychologist, 50,* 741-749.

Miller, G. A., Galanter, E., & Pribram, K. H. (1960). *Plans and the structure of behavior.* New York: Holt, Rinehart, and Winston.

Mueller, D. J. (1976). Mastery learning: Partly boon, partly boon doggle. *Teachers College Record, 78,* 41-52.

Priest, J., Spicuzza, R., Haseth, M., Peterson, C., & McConnell, S. (1992, December). *Developing a continuous progress monitoring tool for preschoolers with disabilities.* Poster presented at the national conference of the Division for Early Childhood, Washington, DC.

Salmon-Cox, L. (1981). Teachers and standardized achievement tests: What's really happening? *Phi Delta Kappan, 62,* 631-634.

Salvia, J., & Ysseldyke, J. (1985). *Assessment in special and remedial education.* Boston: Houghton Mifflin.

Salvia, J., & Ysseldyke, J. (1998). *Assessment* (7th ed.). Boston: Houghton Mifflin.

Shepard, L. (2000). The role of assessment in a learning culture. *Phi Delta Kappan, 29*(7), 4-14.

Shinn, M. R. (1989). *Curriculum-based measurement.* New York: Guilford Press.

Shinn, M. (Ed.). (1998). *Advanced applications of Curriculum-Based Measurement.* New York: Guilford Press.

Shinn, M. R. (2002). Best practices in curriculum-based measurement and its use in a problem-solving model. In A. Thomas & J. Grimes (Eds.), *Best practices in school psychology IV.* Bethesda, MD: National Association of School Psychologists.

Shinn, M. R., Baker, S., Habedank, L., & Good, R. H. (1993). The effects of classroom reading performance data on general education teachers' and parents' attitudes about reintegration. *Exceptionality, 4,* 205-228.

Skinner, B. F. (1953). *Science and human behavior.* New York: Macmillan.

Stecker, P. M., & Fuchs, L. S. (2000). Effecting superior achievement using curriculum-based measurement: The importance of individual progress monitoring. *Learning Disabilities Research and Practice, 15,* 128-135.

Taylor, R. L. (2000). *Assessment of Exceptional Students.* Needham Heights, MA: Allyn and Bacon.

Thompson, S. (2001). The authentic standards movement and its evil twin. *Phi Delta Kappan 82*(5), 358-362.

Thorndike, R. L. (1903). *Educational psychology.* New York: Lemcke and Buechner.

Watkins, M. (2000). Cognitive profile analysis: A shared professional myth. *School Psychology Quarterly, 15*(4), 465-479.

Watson, D. L. & Tharp, R. G. (1993). *Self-directed behavior: Self modification for personal adjustment* (6th ed.). Pacific Grove, CA: Brooks/Cole.

Wesson, C. L. (1991). Curriculum-based measurement and two models of follow-up consultation. *Exceptional Children, 57,* 246-257.

Wesson, C. L., Skiba, R., Sevcik, B., King, R., & Deno, S. (1984). The effects of technically adequate instructional data on achievement. *Remedial and Special Education, 5,* 17-22.

Zigmond, N., Vallecorsa, A., & Silverman, R. (1983). *Assessment for instructional planning in special education.* Englewood Cliffs, NJ: Prentice-Hall.

AUTHORS' NOTES

This section of the chapter is adapted from an earlier work by the first author (Deno, 1997).

CHAPTER 10

Selecting and Evaluating Classroom Interventions

Stephen N. Elliott
University of Wisconsin-Madison

Joseph C. Witt
Louisiana State University

Thomas R. Kratochwill
University of Wisconsin-Madison

Karen Callan Stoiber
University of Wisconsin-Milwaukee

INTRODUCTION

Significant challenges confront school psychologists and educators involved in selecting, implementing, and evaluating interventions for children with learning and behavior problems. The major challenge, in most cases, is not the result of a lack of potentially effective interventions. Rather, it is the result of a combination of factors emanating, in part, from (a) a limited relationship with the child and/or teachers and parents, (b) contextual factors surrounding the intervention environment, (c) a lack of a technology that clearly links assessment results to interventions, and (d) a narrow conceptualization of intervention targets.

The purposes of this chapter are to provide an overview of the problem-solving process involved in intervention selection and evaluation and a review of three constructs (intervention acceptability, teacher empowerment, and intervention integrity) that are critical to the effective use of classroom interventions. In addition to these two major goals, we discuss the evaluation of interventions in the context of the current discussions about evidence-based interventions. Readers interested in the mechanics and effects of actual interventions for children will find excellent summaries in many of the remaining chapters in this volume and in comprehensive volumes such as *Handbook of Behavior Therapy in Education* (Witt, Elliott, & Gresham, 1988), *The Practice of Child Therapy* (Morris & Kratochwill, 1998), *Handbook of Group Interventions for Children and Families* (Stoiber & Kratochwill, 1998), and *The Academic Intervention Monitoring System*

(Elliott, DiPerna, & Shapiro, 2001). Readers desiring more information on the therapeutic relationship than is covered in this chapter are referred to *Interviewing Strategies for Helpers* (Cormier & Cormier, 1985).

The Problem-Solving Process and Models of Intervention

Although this chapter focuses on interventions, it is premised on the assumption that interventions follow from an adequate assessment of the problem and conceptually are consistent with a model of psychopathology, as well as a wellness model that emphasizes development of social competencies (Kratochwill & Stoiber, 2000a; Stoiber & Kratochwill, 2000). Loosely defined, a model of psychopathology is a collection of assumptions regarding the role of biological, psychological, social, environmental, and other factors thought to contribute to the development of a person's problem(s). Numerous models for conceptualizing deviant behavior exist: the medical or biological model, the psychodynamic model, and the behavioral model have a long history (Johnson, Rasbury, & Siegel, 1986). More recent models include the family model, the limited-capacities model, and the cognitive model (Levine & Sandeen, 1985). These models range from those that emphasize the individual to those that focus on the entire family, and from those that emphasize biological factors to those that focus on social and environment causes of problem behavior. Models also vary as to whether the child's problem behavior is viewed as an overt symptom of some inferred underlying process or whether the overt symptom(s) are considered to be the problem.

Each model provides a conceptual framework to organize information about a child's problem behavior and to identify potential intervention goals or impact points. Let us examine the attributes of a behavioral model for understanding a child's problem and planning intervention strategies.

Various nuances of a behavioral model have been developed; however, Kanfer's (1973) S-O-R-K-C model (Figure 1) is useful for working with both social (Elliott & Gresham, 1991) and academic problems (Elliott, DiPerna, & Shapiro, 2001). In this characterization of behavior, the *S* stands for stimulus, the *O* for the biological state of the organism, the *R* for response, the *K* for the ratio of consequence frequency to response, and the *C* for consequence. The formula describes the smallest unit of analysis for a behavior episode and summarizes the major components acting at the time of a response that affect the probability of the occurrence of the response. Target problems in a behavioral model generally are characterized as either a deficit or excess in the client's behavior, inappropriate environmental stimulus control, inappropriate client-generated stimulus control, and/or inappropriate reinforcement contingencies. A behavioral model offers a rather substantial array of environmental (*S, K,* and *C*) and personal (*O* and *R*) components that are hypothesized to influence behavior and could become the focus of intervention. Thus, the school psychologist's goal in the problem-solving process is to assess and functionally analyze these five components *and* to select one or more components to change, with the prediction that the problem behavior and social competencies and skills will also change.

FIGURE 1

The S-O-R-K-C Model of Behavior With Treatment Impact Points

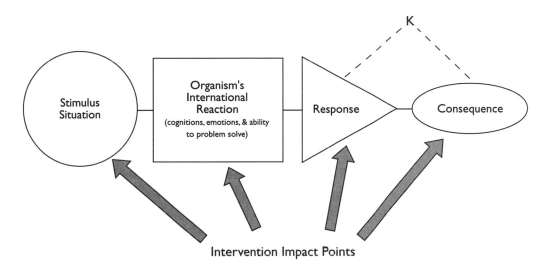

To reiterate, the value of any model, whether it is the S-O-R-K-C behavioral model or one of the several others listed earlier, is its information-organizing role. Assuming school psychologists and educators collectively have the ability and methods to assess the critical components in the model accurately, they are well on their way to generating a number of intervention alternatives if they are given reasonable resources and staff time.

Four Factors That Influence Intervention Selection and Use

Given our previous discussion about various models of human behavior, the multi-component nature of problem behavior, and the variety of potential intervention impact points, it logically follows that for the overwhelming majority of problems there are many interventions, or more likely intervention packages, available. Thus, as noted at the outset of this chapter, the major problems confronting school psychologists are the *selection* and appropriate *use* of interventions rather than a lack of appropriate interventions.

Issues of selection and use are magnified when a school psychologist works in a consultative or indirect service arrangement in which a consultee, most likely a teacher and/or a parent, actually implements the intervention with the child. Under such indirect service conditions, interventions must meet with the approval of significant adults (i.e., parents, teachers, other school officials) and be sufficiently easy to implement by individuals with varying degrees of intervention knowledge and skills. In sum, psychologists are charged with the primary responsibility of selecting an intervention for a given problem or issue. The primary factor driving this decision is that the selected intervention must be, first and foremost, likely to be effective. *Effectiveness* alone, however, is not enough. Interventions also must be socially valid, capable of being delivered as prescribed, and ideally within the resources and skills of the intervention agent. These factors, supplemental yet important to the overall effectiveness of an intervention, are referred to as *intervention acceptability, teacher/parent empowerment,* and *intervention integrity.* In the remainder of this chapter, we examine each of these selection and use factors. A brief overview and discussion of the relative importance of each of these four factors serves as an advance organizer to a detailed review of research and practical guidelines underlying them.

Intervention effectiveness. The topic of intervention effectiveness has engendered much discussion and nearly as much research (e.g., see Kratochwill & Stoiber, 2000a). Whether one is primarily a researcher or a practitioner, the first question about an intervention usually is *Does it work?* In fact, there are a growing number of books that are directly focused on this topic (e.g., Hibbs & Jensen, 1996; Nathan & Gorman, 1998). The reason for addressing this concern was captured more than 30 years ago by Baer, Wolf, and Risley (1968): "If the application of behavioral techniques does not produce large enough effects for practical value, then application has failed … Its practical value, specifically its powers in altering behavior enough to be socially important, is the essential criterion" (p. 96). This social importance criterion that Baer et al. referred to essentially amounts to a difference in performance that results in a constructive difference as perceived by significant others, measured by comparison to an objective standard, and maintained over time.

Although much has been written about intervention effectiveness, many questions and issues remain to be examined. For example, *How much change in outcomes is enough? What are the side effects of our interventions? Should a clinical judgment model, a statistical model, or both be used to make decisions about outcome effectiveness?* These questions are beyond the central focus of this chapter, but currently are influencing both research and practice. Interested readers are referred to conceptual works by Jacobson, Follette, and Revenstorf (1984) on clinical versus statistical criteria for outcome effectiveness; Yeaton (1988) and Yeaton and Sechrest (1981) on intervention-effect norms and intervention strength; and to statistical work on the use of effect size indices by Thompson (1999).

Intervention acceptability. Concern about the acceptability and use of interventions has been a persistent theme in psychology and education (Elliott, 1988; O'Leary, 1984; Reppucci & Saunders, 1974). The causes of this concern about acceptance have ranged from the real possibility that an intervention will restrict an individual's rights (U.S. Congress, 1974) to negative reaction to the use of nonhumanistic jargon (Witt, Moe, Gutkin, & Andrews, 1984). Consequently, researchers have invested substantial energy and resources to identify the features of interventions that consumers (i.e., teachers, parents, and children) like and dislike. Kazdin (1981a) gave this work on the likes and dislikes of consumers of psychological services the label *intervention acceptability,* and defined it as "judgments by laypersons, clients, and others of whether intervention procedures are appropriate, fair, and reasonable for the problem or client" (p. 493). This line of research has been the central focus of the larger domain of work on the social validity of interventions (Kazdin, 1977; Wolf, 1978) and has gained considerable interest among researchers and practitioners interested in the intervention selection and implementation phase of behavioral and organizational consultation (Elliott, 1988; Gresham & Kendall, 1987).

In addition to a scientific interest in intervention acceptability, there are strong pragmatic and legal/ethical reasons for assessing consumers' acceptance of interventions. Courts, for example, have ruled out certain procedures that might be unacceptable because they infringe on client rights. Institutional review committees, which are standard elements of practice today, routinely are used to decide whether an intervention is acceptable for a given problem. Ethics codes and research on children's involvement in intervention decisions support the involvement of children in selecting intervention procedures (Elliott, 1986; Melton, 1983). Finally, perhaps the most compelling rationale for being concerned about the acceptability of an intervention was cited by Wolf (1978):

> If the participants don't like the intervention they may avoid it, or run away, or complain loudly. And thus, society will be less likely to use our technology [behavior modification], no matter how potentially effective and efficient it might be. (p. 206)

Intervention resistance and empowerment. The fact that some apparently effective interventions are never tried or are rejected after only a day or two of use often is a sign that the intervention agent dislikes or has some objection to the procedure. Research on help-giving (Dunst & Trivette, 1988) and problem-solving consultation (Witt & Martens, 1988) has focused on the fact that many "installed" interventions simply do not fit into the routines and environments of help givers (i.e., teachers). This work has called for a reorientation to a philosophy of empowerment as a means of avoiding resistance from help givers. A philosophy of empowerment assumes that (a) the help giver already possesses many competencies to change a problem and (b) the failure to use these competencies is the result of the existing social structure and lack of resources available within that structure. Given this orientation, the role of a consultant becomes one of helping a teacher identify needs and locate resources for meeting the needs, and of linking the teacher to these resources. In the development of many interventions it seems that school psychologists do a good job of helping identify needs. Resistance from teachers, however, often occurs when psychologists may simply try to install intervention packages without consideration of the teachers' skills and the resources indigenous to their classrooms. Thus, recognizing resistance and utilizing a philosophy of empowerment in developing interventions are critical components of the implementation and continued use of an intervention.

Intervention integrity. Intervention integrity is the degree to which an intervention plan is implemented as intended. Many intervention failures probably can be attributed to the fact that intervention plans were not implemented as intended (Gresham, 1989). The reasons for poor intervention integrity are multifaceted; for example, the intervention may be too complicated, the intervention agent may lack time or skills to implement it, or the child–client may resist and deter application of the intervention. Surprisingly, few studies in the intervention literature have assessed the integrity of interventions. In summary, most research published in one of the most rigorous journals failed to demonstrate that changes in dependent or outcome variables were due to intentional changes in independent or intervention variables (Peterson, Hommer, & Wonderlich, 1982). Implementation of interventions as prescribed remains an important challenge to researchers and practitioners alike.

Guiding the Intervention Process

Clearly, we believe, the information and actions associated with acceptability, agent empowerment, and integrity are critical but often ignored in the day-to-day handling of classroom interventions. Securing information and eliciting cooperation on these issues, however, are only a few of the many features that define a successful intervention plan. As illustrated in Figure 2, the typical intervention conceptually consists of at least 13 steps driven by a series of questions, such as: *Are the intervention goals realistic? Do the data support the problem definition? Is the intervention acceptable to all parties involved? Is the integrity of the intervention maintained? Is the intervention effective? Is it cost-effective and beneficial? And finally, Is the intervention in line with societal goals?* Most of these questions can be contextualized as ethical concerns in human services.

In summary, guiding the intervention process, whether in a consultative arrangement or directly with the client, ideally requires an array of technical skills that encompass both assessment and intervention domains, a conceptual model (or models) of human behavior, and communication skills that demonstrate sensitivity and respect for others. In the following discussion we review applied research and practical guidelines about evidence-based interventions, acceptability, empowerment, integrity, and evaluation of effectiveness. We believe knowledge of these can advance one's role in guiding the intervention process.

STRATEGIES TO CONSIDER FOR SELECTING AN INTERVENTION PROGRAM

As was noted in the previous section, assessment is typically designed to accomplish several important goals, including to select target problems or challenging behaviors, identify social competencies as a focus of treatment, yield a diagnosis or classification, and, ultimately, lead to the development of an effective intervention program. In this section of the chapter we review four strategies that can be used for designing an intervention program. These approaches include diagnosis matching, identification of response classes, functional assessment, and individual case formulations based on a scientist-practitioner framework. Each of these strategies has several subdomains that further allow psychologists and other practitioners to refine an intervention program based on recent conceptual advances that have occurred in the research and scientific literature. The strategies we review build upon those identified by previous writers who

FIGURE 2

Intervention Decision-Making and Implementation

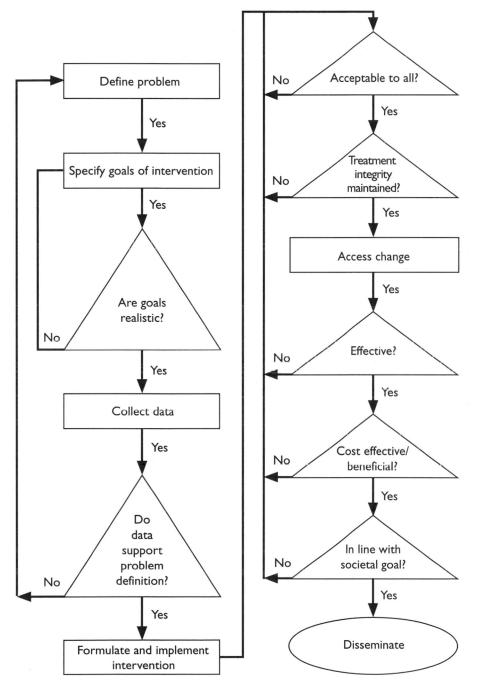

Note

Intervention flowchart. From *School Psychology: Essentials of Theory and Practice,* by C. R. Reynolds, T. Gutkin, S. N. Elliott, and J.C. Witt, 1984, New York: John Wiley. Copyright 1984 by John Wiley. Reprinted with permission.

have addressed the issue of linking assessment to intervention design and implementation (e.g., Barnett, Bell, & Carey, 1999; Hayes, Barlow, & Nelson-Gray, 1999; Kratochwill & Stoiber, 2000b; Shapiro, 1996).

Diagnostic Approach

School psychologists may design or select their intervention programs based on a formal diagnosis such as those described in the *Diagnostic and Statistical Manual of Mental Disorders* (4th ed.) (DSM-IV; 1994). Although DSM-IV is typically not used in school settings for determining an "official" categorization of children with exceptional education needs (special education categories are used instead of this system), many school psychologists rely on diagnostic formulations to help in selection of intervention programs (Kratochwill & Stoiber, 2000b). The primary reason for this reliance on DSM-IV pertains to increasing empirical support that links diagnostic formulations of childhood disorders to interventions that have been subjected to empirical evaluation, often called empirically supported interventions or evidence-based interventions (Kratochwill & Stoiber, 2000a; Stoiber & Kratochwill, 2000). Essentially, a specific diagnosis (ADHD, conduct disorder) is matched to the intervention program based on a series of research studies that support the positive outcomes for children who are diagnosed with this particular disorder.

Recently, intervention programs have been designed and evaluated based on rather strict criteria formulated by professional organizations. In fact, the effectiveness of interventions has been a major focus of task forces from organizations that stipulate intervention criteria linked to diagnostic categories based on the DSM-IV. For example, Division 12 of the American Psychological Association (APA) developed criteria for identification of evidence-based treatments for many disorders. Table 1 shows the criteria that the Division 12 Task Force has adopted for identification of interventions that meet the criteria and are subsequently linked to diagnostic categories of DSM-IV (e.g., anxiety disorder, conduct disorder). In fact, Division 12 has embraced a diagnostic "pathological" model in the linkage of interventions to child and adolescent problems. As an example of interventions in this area, Table 2, on page 252, features some programs that have been linked to empirically supported interventions for behavioral and cognitive behavioral procedures for fears and phobias in children and adolescents (Ollendick & King, 1998). The procedure of selecting intervention programs that have been identified with empirical support and linked to the DSM-IV categories should increase the probability of outcome success when used in applied settings. APA Division 53 (Child Clinical) has already made major inroads in the identification of beneficial treatments for a variety of childhood disorders. Because many of these interventions have been implemented in school settings, they are relevant for the practice of school psychologists. In addition, many of these intervention programs incorporated a treatment manual and/or implementation protocol, thereby providing a structure for replicating interventions in applied settings in a manner that is consistent with their original formulation and implementation in the clinical research trials.

TABLE 1

Criteria for Classification as an Evidence–Based Treatment

A. At least two between-group design studies, with a minimum of 30 subjects across studies receiving the same treatment for the same target problem, and with prospective design and random assignment of subjects to conditions. Findings must show the treatment to be (a) better than the control or comparison groups or (b) equivalent to an already-established evidence-based treatment (EBT).

OR

B. At least two within-group or single-case design studies, with a minimum of 30 subjects across studies receiving the same treatment for the same target problem. Findings must show the treatment to be better than the control or comparison conditions, following establishment of a reliable baseline.

OR

C. A combination of one or more between-group and one or more within-group or single-subject studies, with a minimum of 30 subjects across studies receiving the same treatment for the same target problem. Studies must meet the appropriate criteria notes in A and B.

AND

D. The majority of applicable studies must support the treatment.

E. The treatment procedures must show acceptable adherence to the treatment manual or drug protocol.

Despite the empirical advances and practical development of materials linked to a diagnostic approach to intervention design and implementation, a number of limitations can be identified (Kratochwill & Stoiber, 2000a, 2000b; Stoiber & Kratochwill, 2000; Shapiro, 1996). First, the diagnostic approach embraces a pathological model in design of intervention programs. Because formal person-centered disorders are a central feature of this approach and used as the basis for linking the intervention, a pathological focus is inherent which limits the range and scope of intervention components to this framework (Kratochwill & Stoiber, 2000b). For example, interventions designed to eliminate the symptoms of conduct disorder often do not focus on teaching social competencies to replace the problematic behavior reduced or eliminated by the traditional intervention. The DSM also has little to offer the psychologist interested in developing academic interventions (Shapiro, 1996).

Second, another major issue is that a diagnostic approach tends not to focus on prevention strategies in the design of intervention programs. Although some of the programs might be developed and implemented for this purpose, the primary focus has

TABLE 2

Summary EST Status of Behavioral and Cognitive–Behavioral Treatments for Phobias and Anxiety Disorders in Children and Adolescents

TREATMENT	EST STATUS
For Phobias	
Systematic Desensitization and its Variants	
Imaginal Desensitization	Probably Efficacious
In Vivo Desensitization	Probably Efficacious
Emotive Imagery	Experimental
Modeling and Its Variants	
Live Modeling	Probably Efficacious
Filmed Modeling	Probably Efficacious
Participant Modeling	Well-Established
Operant Procedures	
Reinforced Practice	Well-Established
Cognitive-Behavioral	
Procedures	
Cognitive-Behavior Therapy	Probably Efficacious
For Anxiety Disorders	
Cognitive-Behavioral Procedures	
Cognitive-Behavior Therapy	Probably Efficacious
Cognitive-Behavior Therapy + Family Anxiety Management	Probably Efficacious

Note
EST, empirically supported treatment

been on treating already existing disorders that are well entrenched and problematic to the client and care providers.

Third, a diagnostic approach may be extremely expensive in terms of intervention program implementation. Typically, yielding a formal diagnosis for the individual is necessary, which requires considerable assessment. It remains unclear if the cost of this diagnosis is warranted in child treatment or that it yields results that are better than those of other approaches. In addition, implementation of the intervention protocol may not be cost effective in terms of time and procedures, which may make such an approach impractical or prohibitive in many school sites. Nevertheless, the diagnostic formulation approach has yielded some very significant and innovative treatment programs for a variety of childhood disorders and must be considered.

Fourth, the categorical approach used by the Division 12 Task Force involves determining whether an intervention program meets specific criteria. A number of programs that fail to meet these stringent criteria might be overlooked and not implemented, although they may be better than the alternative (e.g., developing a piecemeal program or one that lacks a sound theoretical basis). In contrast, APA Division 16 and Society for the Study of School Psychology (SSSP) Task Force on Evidence-Based Interventions (EBIs) in School Psychology provides a "consumers report" framework for evaluating "school-based" interventions on the basis of efficacy criteria.

More specifically, the School Psychology Task Force on EBIs has recommended that several key components of the intervention should be evaluated for determining the level of empirical evidence, including: (a) a clear theoretical or empirical basis, (b) a comparison group demonstrating similar characteristics or the same target problem to test outcome differences, (c) a link between intervention components and significant outcome effects, (d) use of multi-source and/or multi-component outcome data, (e) data on the durability of intervention effects, (f) intervention procedures that incorporate an intervention manual or protocol, and (g) evidence of intervention integrity. Interventions can be scaled from "no support" to "considerable support" based on judgments about the degree to which these various methodological and conceptual criteria were addressed in the study (see Kratochwill et al., 2001).

A final limitation of the diagnostic approach pertains to the level of understanding of the nature of the problem yielded by the diagnosis. As Hayes, Barlow, and Nelson-Gray (1999) noted, the diagnosis may be insufficient to develop an intervention-problem match. Even specific anxiety disorders may not be operationalized enough through the DSM to be able to develop an intervention match. Related to this breakdown in the intervention-problem match is the issue of intervention feasibility. An intervention program may have been shown to be beneficial for a specific disorder; however, issues surrounding the typical school context do not permit its application in the typical school environment. Therefore, the school psychologist must rely on other strategies to better understand the nature of the child's problem and the design of intervention programs. Some of these other approaches to selecting effective interventions are discussed next.

Response Class/Keystone Behavior Approach

As targets for change, the response class/keystone behavior strategy focuses on those behaviors in the development of an intervention program considered to have widespread benefits for the child (Barnett et al., 1999; Hayes et al., 1999). In the response class/keystone procedure, the child may be assessed for problematic response classes within the diagnostic category, although this may not be necessary. Keystone behaviors are viewed as foundational skills or competencies that are necessary for the child's successful response to the intervention. Keystone responses can be defined as:

1. Pivotal behaviors associated with response classes of maladaptive behaviors that can have a positive effect on other responses;

2. Behaviors that result in other beneficial collateral outcomes for the individual, and/or;

3. Foundation skills necessary for adaptation to the present and future environment (such as the regular education classroom).

One example of how the keystone approach might be used can be illustrated by considering a child with some type of anxiety disorder. It is likely that the child will experience problematic arousal, cognitive difficulties in the area of self-efficacy, as well as behavioral avoidance of a feared person, object, or situation. The intervention might focus on exposure of the child to the phobic conditions to reduce arousal. Nevertheless, the child may also lack some specific skills in being able to perform adequately in an applied setting, and these deficits in social performance may be central to the anxiety. Social competencies might be identified and also targeted as a response class (considered "keystone") to the individual's anxiety problem and future success in coping with the environment (for more information, see the second point in Barnett et al., 1999).

Basically, the keystone metaphor refers to a series of responses that are correlated or linked and central to the child's problematic experiences with the disorder. Social competence is considered a keystone behavior because it contributes to the child's capacity to interact effectively, which is an essential foundation for children's success in school and in the community. When the key response is identified (e.g., interact with peers and adults), all the other responses would be hypothesized to move in a positive therapeutic direction.

Another application of the keystone approach can occur for a child with severe aggression. A diagnostic formulation might yield a finding that the child was experiencing symptoms that correspond to the DSM diagnosis of conduct disorder with one dimension being aggressive behavior. Based on the work of Patterson and his associates (e.g., Patterson, Reid, & Dishion, 1992) a series of aggressive responses that are highly correlated might be the focus of the intervention efforts. The intervention would focus on this dimension with the hope that it would be "keystone" to resolution of the child's problematic responses in classroom, playground, or home environments (see point one in Barnett et al., 1999).

Despite the potential advantages that a response class or keystone behavior strategy brings to the intervention selection and design process, there are several limitations that can be identified. First, because this strategy is often added to the diagnostic formulation, it will require even greater psychologist training, time and expense in assessment, supervision, monitoring, etc. (Hayes et al., 1999). Basically, in contrast to treatment manuals, which are designed to focus on global aspects of the disorder, the customized response class to keystone strategy will require greater assessment commitment, which could be a challenge within schools and other applied settings. Second, there is a paucity of research to support this approach over the diagnostic approach or some of the other formulations discussed later in this section.

Functional Assessment

Functional assessment is a systematic process aimed at identifying factors or "controlling variables" that contribute to a child's problem behavior. For children who display challenging academic or social behavior, it is considered important to take into account the function of the behavior based on context, intents, antecedents, consequences, etc., to formulate the intervention (see Reschly, Tilly, & Grimes, 1999). Functional assessment goes beyond identification of the topography of behavior to link responses specifically to the reasons for the challenging behavior displayed by the child. The functional assessment approach has evolved and now incorporates a broad-based focus beyond its tradition in applied behavior analysis (Stoiber & Kratochwill, in press). However, traditionally, this assessment methodology grew out of the behavior analysis field where various contingencies of reinforcement and punishment were found to be uniquely related to challenging behaviors. Some behavioral interventions can be implemented *without* an analysis of the functions of the behavior (e.g., reinforcement can be withdrawn when a challenging behavior occurs). Yet, some of the traditional behavioral interventions, such as time-out, can be improved if the procedure is *matched* to the hypothesized function of the problematic behavior.

Functional assessment has garnered some empirical support, especially in the area of development of programs based on applied behavior analysis interventions with persons with severe challenging behavior (see Neef & Iwata, 1994; Schill, Kratochwill, & Gardner, 1996). However, little research comparing the outcomes of functional assessment to other assessment options has been conducted. Functional assessment is often implemented by using a descriptive assessment approach; that is, the function is described and the intervention is selected based on this description. This approach can be extended into an experimental procedure called "functional analysis," which is typically implemented by using single-case experimental designs to test functional hypotheses from assessment procedures. Functional assessment also typically incorporates a series of steps that involve a problem-solving process much like the steps associated with consultation. For example, O'Neill and his associates (1997) suggested that a functional assessment involves (a) a description of the undesirable behaviors and operational specification of these, (b) prediction of the times and situations when the undesirable behavior occurs and will not occur during a typical daily routine, and (c) definition of the functions of maintaining conditions. Conducting a systematic functional analysis in which the various functions are manipulated experimentally to determine their controlling effect over the individuals' challenging behaviors can extend these steps. Currently, several functional assessment instruments have been created for school-based practitioners, and most are associated with the behavior analysis tradition (e.g., Gable, Quinn, Rutherford, Howell, & Hoffman, 1998; Jensen et al., 1999; Nelson, Roberts, & Smith, 1998; Witt & Beck, 1999).

Although functional assessment strategies have gained increasing attention and are now mandated as part of federal regulations, there are clear limitations evident in the approach to the design of intervention programs. First of all, until recently, few formalized protocols for conducting functional assessment were available. Many practitioners thus conduct a functional assessment without benefit of a formal protocol, making the strategy somewhat informal and of unknown reliability. It is likely that the recent development of more standardized instruments will facilitate reliable application of functional assessment in applied settings. Second, as noted previously, many of the traditional functional assessment procedures are linked to behavioral psychology and, specifically, to applied behavior analysis functions and intervention tactics. As a result, many of the functions identified relate to reinforcement strategies, which are then manipulated, without an assessment of what needs to occur to facilitate the child's development of a desirable "competing" or "replacement" behavior. In other words, a broadened range of functions, including the child's needs and intents, would provide a more comprehensive informational base and should be considered when functional assessment strategies are designed. Third, many functional assessment strategies still focus on reduction of problematic behavior and only minimally on building social competencies (Stoiber & Kratochwill, 2000). One recent protocol called the *Functional Assessment and Intervention System* (FAIS) (Stoiber & Kratochwill, 2000) is designed to focus on *both* challenging behaviors as well as social competencies in the design of intervention programs.

A fourth limitation is that despite the conceptual linkage of functional assessment and intervention, there is still a paucity of comparative research supporting the efficacy of functional assessment and its empirical basis as related to effective intervention outcomes. In two studies by Kratochwill and his associates (Beavers, Kratochwill, & Braden, 2001; Schill-Twernbold, Kratochwill, & Elliott, 1998), functional assessment has not been found to be more effective than more traditional approaches in the design and outcomes of intervention programs within a consultation framework. These findings may be due, in part, to a failure to accurately identify the true "function" underlying the problem behavior or a failure to select an intervention that is functionally linked to the behavior. Nevertheless, research on treatment validity remains limited based on the nature of the problems, use of descriptive functional assessment, and the outcome measures used in investigations. More research is needed to further test the functional assessment approach. Despite these limitations, functional analysis has demonstrated considerable efficacy over the past several years in the design of intervention programs and will likely be supported in the future.

Case Formulations/Scientist-Practitioner Approach

Hayes et al. (1999) identified an assessment strategy called "case formulation" that bears some similarity to both the response class/keystone behavior strategy and the functional assessment tactics described in the previous section. The similarity to the response class/keystone approach is the focus on central underlying problems of the child, and the similarity to the functional assessment approach is an evaluation of the functions of the behavior during the problem situation(s). As an illustration, the case approach presented by Turkat (1990) involves development of a case formulation, evaluation of the formulation, and linkage of the formulation to intervention selection. This formulation can be tested within sessions and therefore bears some similarity to an experimental functional analysis. We consider this case formulation approach as one example of a scientist-practitioner framework for designing interventions. In a scientist-practitioner framework the clinician selects a procedure for a particular individual or family and tests out the approach in a series of individual case evaluation strategies that could involve single-case research design structures (e.g., Hayes et al., 1999).

The case formulation/scientist-practitioner approach has a number of beneficial dimensions, but many of these remain to be empirically evaluated through comparative research on the approaches outlined in this section. Thus, a first limitation of this approach is the lack of empirical data comparing the efficacy of this approach with that of others. Second, traditional applications of the case formulation approach have been embedded within a pathological model, and therefore share some of the same difficulties that the more traditional diagnostic approach confronts when implemented in applied settings. Nevertheless, it is possible to extend the case formulation approach into other models of intervention selection and invoke a prosocial or social competency framework when implementing a case.

A third limitation of this approach pertains to the cost of engaging in an empirical approach to practice—a tactic discussed for years as problematic in school-based services. Although a variety of program evaluation tactics might be used to facilitate understanding the scientist-practitioner approach, it is clear that invoking single-case experimental designs to examine the efficacy of case formulation approaches within a scientist-practitioner model can be time consuming and on occasion unrealistic in many practice settings. Nevertheless, compromises in experimental outcome evaluation can be made and program evaluation based on case study models that have been suggested for practice settings could be used (Kratochwill, 1985) for a case-based scientist-practitioner model of practice—a strategy that we strongly encourage individuals to adopt in applied settings and especially in work in schools.

Perhaps one feature that has hindered the development of this and any approach to evaluation of practice is the lack of a protocol for planning and conducting the evaluation. Stoiber and Kratochwill (2000) designed a protocol for evaluation of interventions

TABLE 3

Distinctive Features of the Outcomes: PME, the Functional Assessment Planner, and the Social Competency Checklist

OUTCOMES: PME

- A unique assessment and intervention planning tool for:

  - Individual case-centered intervention outcome evaluation (specific protocol)

  - Group-oriented intervention outcome evaluation

  - System (program intervention outcome evaluation)

- 5-step problem-solving process

- Can be used with academic and/or social behavioral intervention programs

- Uses a direct outcome assessment format that involves a graphic presentation of data

- Integrates a goal attainment framework around intervention design and outcome assessment

- Theoretically embraces a scientist-practitioner model of practice

- Linked to Functional Assessment and Intervention System and Social Competency Checklist

- Can be linked to state standards for assessment to plan outcome evaluation for academic competencies

- Can be used on Palm Pilot especially with graphic functions and report format

in applied settings, called *Outcomes: Planning, Monitoring, Evaluating* (Outcomes: PME). The Outcomes: PME protocol takes the practitioner through five problem-solving steps in the design, implementation, and monitoring of an intervention for academic and/or social behavior. Table 3 presents information about Outcomes: PME and the associated tasks for its implementation in applied settings. Outcomes: PME incorporates a goal attainment framework but any type of outcome data can compliment the goal focus.

INTERVENTION ACCEPTABILITY: UNDERSTANDING AND IMPROVING INTERVENTION SELECTION

Several factors have been demonstrated empirically to influence people's judgments of intervention acceptability. These factors have been incorporated into conceptual models by Witt and Elliott (1985) and Reimers, Wacker, and Koeppl (1987) and written about more recently by Finn (2000) and others. Witt and Elliott (1985) developed a working model of intervention acceptability that stressed the interrelations among four elements: acceptability, use, integrity, and effectiveness. The hypothesized relationships among these four elements can be characterized as sequential and reciprocal. That is, *acceptability* is ultimately the initial issue in the sequence of intervention selection and use. Once an intervention is deemed generally acceptable, the probability of using the intervention is high, relative to interventions of lower rated acceptability. A central element hypothesized to link use and effectiveness is intervention *integrity*. If integrity is high, then the probability of effecting a behavioral change is enhanced. Finally, if the *effectiveness* of the intervention meets or exceeds the expectations of the service provider, then the probability of judging the intervention acceptable is enhanced. The reaction of a recipient of the intervention toward the service provider also should influence the service provider's evaluation of the intervention. To date, empirical evidence has not been amassed in a single investigation to support or refute this model; however, researchers have provided evidence about several of the interrelationships among the four elements.

Stimulated by the Witt and Elliott model, Reimers et al. (1987) developed a more complex model of intervention acceptability. These authors assumed that an intervention must be well understood before acceptability is assessed, and they therefore incorporated an intervention knowledge component into their decision-making flowchart concerning acceptability. According to the Reimers et al. model, when a proposed intervention is perceived to be low in acceptability, it is likely that low compliance will follow, thus decreasing the probability of the intervention's being effective. In this model, compliance represents a teacher's or parent's attempt to implement an intervention. Once an intervention has been attempted, maintenance is the major issue. If an intervention is rated high in acceptability, then it is likely that compliance with the recommendations will be high. However, the effects of intervention can still range from ineffective to highly effective. If the intervention is ineffective, then there will not be maintenance of intervention, and reassessment of the problem behavior, the recommended procedure, or the intervention integrity is probably warranted. If the problem is identified correctly, and if the recommended intervention was implemented as prescribed, then some modifications of the intervention may be warranted or another intervention might be proposed. At this point, then, the cycle would repeat itself. When an intervention is highly effective, it is assumed that maintenance of intervention effects will also be high, provided that a family or school routine was not significantly disrupted either by the resulting change in behavior, or by the changes brought about by implementing the procedure. Disruption can occur, for example, when unusual resources or amounts of time are needed to continue an intervention.

Neither the Witt and Elliott (1985) model nor the Reimers et al. (1987) model fully characterizes the complex array of variables that potentially interact to influence the selection and implementation of interventions. Although imperfect, these models have been heuristic guides to stimulating research questions.

Research Methods and Findings on Intervention Acceptability

With the publication of two intervention acceptability studies in 1980, Kazdin (1980a, 1980b) provided a paradigm that subsequent researchers have used to investigate the acceptability of interventions used with children. The essential elements of this paradigm have been a pencil-and-paper problem intervention vignette followed by objective evaluative ratings about the intervention. Within this paradigm, the primary independent variables manipulated have been severity of the target problem and type of intervention used. Other independent variables of interest have included an array of demographic characteristics of the rater of the interventions. For example, when teachers have been the intervention evaluators, information about years of teaching experience, type of training, and knowledge of behavioral principles and methods have been measured. In addition, some acceptability researchers (e.g., Elliott, Turco, & Gresham, 1987; Kazdin, French, & Sherick, 1981) have investigated how different consumers (i.e., parents, teachers, children, and hospital staff) evaluate interventions, thus involving the rater as an independent variable. The primary dependent variable of interest in intervention acceptability research has been consumers' evaluative reactions to interventions as operationalized by one of several rating scales: the Behavior Intervention Rating Scale (BIRS), Children's Intervention Rating Profile (CIRP), Intervention Rating Profile-20 (IRP-20), Intervention Rating Profile-15 (IRP-15), and Treatment Evaluation Inventory (TEI). Interested readers are referred to Elliott (1988) for a review of all the intervention acceptability rating scales.

An Examination of Variables That Influence Teachers' Intervention Selections

Before examining specific studies, it is important to highlight that the majority of published research on intervention acceptability has been analogue studies and, with the exception of a few studies (e.g., McMahon & Forehand, 1983; Shapiro & Goldberg, 1986), has been concerned predominantly with preintervention judgments of consultees (intervention agents) rather than clients. A rather long list of variables can be generated that can influence a teacher's selection of an intervention for a child with challenging behavior problems. In the context of a consultation service delivery model, within which a school psychologist interacts with a teacher to assess and treat a child, Table 4 was developed to characterize the variables that have been investigated by researchers interested in understanding preintervention acceptability and the effects on intervention outcomes.

TABLE 4

Variables in a Consultative Framework That Can Influence Teachers' Evaluations of Treatment Acceptability

Consultant (psychologist) —	Consultee (teacher) —	Treatment —	Client (child)
Jargon	Years of experience	Time required	Severity of problem
Involvement	Knowledge of behavior principles	Type of treatment	Type of problem
	Type of training	Reported effectiveness	
	Class management techniques used		

Note

The variables in this table have been invesitgated empirically. Many more variables, such as the race and sex of the consultant, consultee, and client, could be investigated. Most analogue research to date has been with female teachers and hypothetical male problem children because this is most representative of reality. The arrows in this table indicate direction of influence.

From "Acceptability of Behavioral Treatment: A Review of Variables that Influence Treatment Selection" by S. N. Elliott, 1988, *Professional Psychology: Research and Practice, 19,* p. 70. Copyright 1988 by the American Psychological Association. Reprinted with permission.

Psychologist-associated variables that affect intervention acceptability. Two variables, the jargon used in describing interventions and consultant involvement in interventions, are the only psychologist-associated variables that have been studied within the intervention acceptability paradigm.

Several researchers have demonstrated that people's evaluations of psychological interventions vary as a function of what the intervention is called and how it is described. For example, Woolfolk and her associates (Woolfolk & Woolfolk, 1979; Woolfolk, Woolfolk, & Wilson, 1977) presented preservice teachers a videotape of a teacher who reinforced appropriate behavior, ignored inappropriate behavior, and used a backup token economy during an elementary school class. For one group of preservice teachers, the videotape was described as illustrative of "behavior modification" and for the other group it was called "humanistic education." These investigators found that the personal qualities of the teacher and the effectiveness of the teaching method were perceived more positively when the method was labeled humanistic education as opposed to behavior modification.

As an extension of his acceptability research, Witt and several colleagues (Witt, Moe, Gutkin, & Andrews, 1984) investigated the effects that the type of language used to describe interventions had on teachers' rating of the intervention's acceptability. Specifically, these researchers manipulated three types of jargon (behavioral, pragmatic, and humanistic) used to describe an intervention that required a target child to stay in at recess for his misbehavior. The major finding with regard to the jargon variable was that the intervention described in pragmatic terms was rated significantly more acceptable than the same intervention described in either humanistic or behavioral terms.

Martens, Peterson, Witt, and Cirone (1986) investigated the intervention preferences of 2,493 regular and special education teachers from Iowa and Nebraska. By using the Classroom Intervention Profile, a 65-item questionnaire that requires the rating of 49 classroom interventions on three scales (i.e., Effectiveness, Ease of Use, and Frequency of Use), these researchers were able to deduce several significant tendencies with regard to teachers' intervention preferences. Of interest here is their finding that consultation with other personnel was rated relatively low as to effectiveness and ease of use. By comparison, interventions involving verbal redirection, manipulation of a material reward, and in-class timeout were rated consistently higher than consultation with a specialist such as a psychologist. Martens et al. attributed this poor acceptance of consultation to the relatively large time involvement required. The variable of amount of time required for an intervention has been found consistently to influence teachers' acceptability ratings of interventions (Witt, Elliott, & Martens, 1984).

This time variable, as it relates to school psychologists' involvement in intervention, requires more detailed examination and clarification. At present, we know, from self-reports, that teachers generally prefer to use interventions that can be conducted in their own classrooms and that require little time in consultation (indirect service) with specialists such as psychologists. It has yet to be established empirically, however, that teachers do not want psychologists to be highly involved in direct intervention of students within their classrooms.

Teachers' intervention preferences and variables that influence these preferences. Unlike the acceptability research with psychologist-associated variables, the research investigations with teachers are numerous and provide insights about the variables that have an impact on intervention selection and use. In this section we review research that covers child variables (e.g., severity of problem, type of problem), intervention characteristics (e.g., time involved, punishment versus reinforcement, group versus individual contingencies, strong versus weak intervention effects), and teacher background variables (e.g., years of experience, special versus regular education training, knowledge of interventions).

The severity of a child's problem has appeared as an independent variable in many studies (Elliott, Turco, & Gresham, 1987; Elliott, Witt, Galvin, & Peterson, 1984; Frentz & Kelley, 1986; Kazdin, 1980a; Martens, Witt, Elliott, & Darveaux, 1985; VonBrock & Elliott, 1987; Witt, Elliott, & Martens, 1984; Witt, Martens, & Elliott, 1984; Witt, Moe, Gutkin, & Andrews, 1984). This severity variable has been operationalized by changes in the degree to which a target child behaves inappropriately or by the number of children who are behaving inappropriately. In general, the collective results of these studies have demonstrated that the more severe a child's problem, the more acceptable any given intervention. Several specifics concerning the problem severity variable are of interest.

It appears that the severity of a target problem influences how complex an acceptable intervention can be. For example, in a two-experiment study, Elliott et al. (1984) investigated experienced teachers' acceptability ratings for behavioral interventions. In the first part of the study, general and special education teachers were asked to read one of three case descriptions of an elementary school student whose misbehaviors were of a low (daydreaming), moderate (obscene language), or severe (destruction of others' property) nature and to rate the acceptability of one of three positively oriented intervention methods that were either low in complexity (praise), of moderate complexity (home reinforcement), or highly complex (token economy). The results indicated that the least complex intervention (praise) was the most acceptable intervention for the least severe problem behavior (daydreaming). The most complex intervention (token economy) was rated the most acceptable intervention for the most severe behavior problem (destroying property) (Elliott et al., 1984).

In the second part of the Elliott et al. (1984) study, all of the variables remained the same except that teachers were asked to evaluate the acceptability of one of three reductive intervention methods that were either low (ignoring), medium (response cost lottery), or high (seclusion time-out) in complexity. The results again indicated that the least complex intervention (ignoring) was the most acceptable intervention for the least severe behavior problem (daydreaming).

An investigation by Frentz and Kelley (1986) of parents' acceptability ratings of reductive interventions provides support and generalizable evidence for the conclusion that intervention acceptability is affected significantly by the severity of the target problem. Frentz and Kelley asked 82 mothers to rate, by the Treatment Evaluation Inventory (TEI), five intervention procedures (i.e., differential attention, response cost, time-out, spanking alone, and time-out with spanking) as methods for resolving a mild or a severe child behavior problem. The results indicated that the sampled parents rated all interventions as being more acceptable when applied to the severe problem.

The type of interventions assessed on acceptability studies generally have been characterized as either positive (e.g., praise, DRO, DRL, token economy) or reductive (e.g., response cost, time-out, overcorrection). In general, researchers have found that the acceptability ratings of all varieties of consumers (teachers, parents, children) consistently have been higher for constructive than reductive intervention procedures (Elliott et al., 1984; Kazdin, 1980a, 1980b, 1981a; Martens et al., 1986; Witt et al., 1984; Witt & Robbins, 1985).

Time is a valuable asset to teachers, who often are responsible for educating 25 or more children at once. Thus, it should not be surprising to find that when teachers evaluate a behavior change procedure prior to use, they are time conscious. The research on intervention acceptability has indicated that time consumption is a very salient factor in teachers' preintervention acceptability ratings of intervention procedures (Elliott et al., 1984; Kazdin, 1982; Witt et al., 1984; and Witt & Martens, 1983).

As a means of illustrating the relationship between acceptability and time consumption, we will review one study in detail. Witt et al. (1984) directly manipulated the variables of teacher time involvement, intervention type, and behavior problem severity in a factorial design to assess how 180 teachers would evaluate interventions on the IRP-20. Descriptions of the interventions included estimates of the amount of time required to implement the intervention. An intervention was classified as requiring low amounts of teacher time if it required fewer than 30 minutes per day, as requiring moderate amounts of teacher time if it required 1–2 hours to prepare and 30-60 minutes to maintain, and as requiring high amounts of teacher time if it necessitated more than 2 hours of start-up and approximately 1 hour per day to maintain. The results of the study indicated that time in itself affected acceptability ratings, and, more importantly, time interacted significantly with both problem severity and intervention type. In summary, all other things being equal, teachers preferred interventions that were more time-efficient; however, when confronted with a severe problem, they seemed to adjust their expectations upward about the strength of intervention and consequently the time involved to change the problem behavior. Based on this and other analogue studies, it seems that teachers are time-conscious but not time-obsessed when selecting interventions.

After an intervention has been implemented, the ultimate criterion for evaluating it is effectiveness: Did the prescribed intervention change the problematic behavior and/or increase social competencies in the desired direction and to the desired extent? In the preceding argument, however, we have hypothesized that prior to selection and implementation of an intervention, acceptability is an important evaluation criterion. Given the existence of these two important intervention evaluation criteria, the relationship between them requires attention. Several researchers, in fact, have investigated the effect of intervention outcome, or effectiveness information, on consumers' ratings of intervention acceptability (Clark & Elliott, 1988; Kazdin, 1981a; Von Brock & Elliott, 1987).

VonBrock and Elliott (1987) examined the impact of outcome information on teachers' ratings of intervention acceptability. They had 216 experienced teachers rate one of three interventions (token economy, response cost, or time-out) for changing a mild or severe classroom behavior problem. One of three types of effectiveness information accompanied each problem intervention scenario. Teachers received either no effectiveness information, teacher-satisfaction effectiveness information, or researcher-supplied effectiveness information. The results suggested that effectiveness information did influence ratings when the problem severity was taken into consideration. The milder the problem, the greater the influence of information from research sources about an intervention's effectiveness on effectiveness and acceptability ratings compared with a no-information condition. This was a surprising finding. One possible explanation for this finding is that with mild problems teachers consider what researchers have to say about interventions, but with severe problems they rely more on their own judgments. This finding suggests that teachers may be more amenable to information about interventions before a problem becomes too severe. Catching problems early may give school psychologists greater freedom in choice of intervention with their consultees. Another explanation may be that teachers have preconceived notions about interventions. When presented with a mild problem, they feel there is more room for decision making about how to handle the problem, and therefore they are willing to experiment with different interventions. In such a circumstance they are more influenced by information concerning these interventions. In contrast, with severe problems, teachers may not be as comfortable about experimenting with interventions and may rely more on past practice or judgment.

In a follow-up investigation to the VonBrock and Elliott (1987) study, Clark and Elliott (1988) examined the effects of intervention effectiveness information on teachers' preintervention acceptability ratings of overcorrection and modeling coaching, procedures for social behavior deficits. The variable of intervention effectiveness had two levels, strong and weak, and was presented in an intervention description narrative accompanied by a graph illustrating the target child's behavior and a "normal" comparison of peers' behavior over a 12-week period. The results confirmed the hypothesis that intervention effectiveness information does affect teachers' preintervention rationale of acceptability. When given an intervention that was described as strong and successful, teachers rated it higher than if it had been described as weak and relatively unsuccessful.

There have been several other studies examining the influence of intervention effectiveness information on ratings of acceptability. Prior to the Clark and Elliott study, two investigators specifically studied this relationship (Kazdin, 1981a; Von Brock, 1985). In the Kazdin study, no relationship was found between the strength of therapeutic effects and ratings of preintervention acceptability. Some researchers (McMahon & Forehand, 1983; Witt et al., 1984) have questioned Kazdin's methodology and believe that his intervention strength variable had a restricted range and his sample of college students was unrepresentative of the persons usually involved in intervention decisions. The results from the Clark and Elliott (1988) study suggest that when classroom teachers clearly understand what is being presented to them, intervention effectiveness information does affect their perceptions of acceptability of an intervention.

In addition to the three preintervention analogue investigations of the effectiveness-acceptability relationship we have reviewed, Shapiro and Goldberg (1986) conducted an intervention study in which the postintervention acceptability and effectiveness relationship have been examined. Briefly, these researchers were interested in children's reactions to three types of group interventions that had been used to influence their spelling achievement. By using the CIRP to operationalize intervention acceptability, Shapiro and Goldberg reported that although no differences in effectiveness in promoting spelling were found among the three different group contingencies, the sixth graders rated the independent contingency more acceptable than either the interdependent contingency or the dependent group contingency. This naturalistic, postintervention rating of group contingencies by children is consistent with the findings of Elliott et al.'s (1987) analogue investigation of preintervention acceptability.

In the continuing search for explanations for differential acceptance of interventions, investigators have begun intentionally to measure, control, or manipulate rater variables such as technical knowledge of interventions, experience with interventions, and type of education. To date, however, only four published studies have systematically considered teachers' background information and its effect on intervention acceptability ratings.

Several research teams (e.g., Jeger & McClure, 1979; McMahon, Forehand, & Griest, 1981) have suggested that more positive attitudes toward behavioral techniques follow increases in knowledge of such techniques. On the basis of this premise, McKee (1984) set out essentially to replicate Kazdin's (1980a) investigation of the acceptability of reinforcement of incompatible behavior, positive practice, time-out from reinforcement, and medication with a group of teachers who varied in their knowledge of behavioral principles. McKee measured teachers' knowledge with a modified 16-item version of the Knowledge of Behavioral Principles as Applied to Children test (KBPAC) (O'Dell, Tarler-Benlolo, & Flynn, 1979) and was able to assign teachers to a high- or low-knowledge group by using a median-split technique. Specifically, McKee found that the teachers in the high-knowledge group generally rated all interventions more acceptable on the TEI than did the teachers in the low-knowledge group. These data are supportive of the understanding component in the Reimers et al. model of intervention acceptability in that it suggests that improved acceptability and potentially increased use of interventions may be facilitated through increased familiarity with basic behavioral intervention principles.

Another teacher background variable of interest to some researchers has been teaching experience (Witt et al., 1984; Witt & Robbins, 1985). Witt and his associates reported finding an inverse relation between years of teaching experience and intervention acceptability. Specifically, in the Witt et al. (1984) study, which was reviewed earlier, years of teaching experience was found to be a significant covariate with teachers' acceptability evaluations of behavioral, pragmatic, and humanistic interventions. In general, teachers with more experience in the field seem to find all interventions less acceptable.

Children's intervention preferences and variables that influence these preferences. Research by Foxx and Jones (1978), Ollendick, Matson, Esveldt-Dawson, and Shapiro (1980), and Krigin, Braukmann, Atwater, and Wolf (1982) provides information about children's satisfaction with an intervention. Kazdin et al. (1981) assessed children's acceptability of psychological interventions more directly using the TEI. The Kazdin et al. (1981) investigation was an analogue study of how child psychiatric inpatients, their parents, and the institutional staff rated the acceptability of four interventions (positive reinforcement of incompatible behavior, positive practice, medication, and time-out from reinforcement) for children with severe behavior problems. The relative ratings of acceptability for the four interventions were identical for children, parents, and staff, although children rated all interventions as less acceptable than did parents or staff members. Specifically, reinforcement of incompatible behavior was evaluated as the most acceptable intervention for a child displaying a severe behavior problem. Positive practice, medication, and time-out from reinforcement successively received lower ratings than reinforcement of incompatible behavior.

Elliott, Witt, Galvin, and Moe (1986) investigated typical sixth-grade children's reactions to 12 interventions for classroom misbehaviors involving a male student who either destroyed another student's property or frequently talked out of turn. The students' acceptability ratings were documented by the CIRP (Witt & Elliott, 1985). Specifically, the interventions that emphasized individual teacher-student interactions, or group reinforcement, or punitive sanctions for the misbehaving child were rated the most acceptable. Public reprimands of an individual and punitive contingencies for a group when only one child misbehaved were rated as unacceptable interventions by sixth graders. The four traditional interventions (i.e., principal's office, point system, staying in during recess, quiet room) as a group were rated the most acceptable methods when compared with the group of behavioral interventions. A final finding by Elliott et al. (1986) was that severity of the behavior problem did not significantly affect sixth-grade students' ratings of interventions except for the traditional interventions.

Given the perceived popularity of group contingency interventions among teachers' and children's differential acceptability responses to group contingency methods (Elliott et al., 1986; Turco & Elliott, 1986), a more detailed investigation of various types of group contingency methods was undertaken by Elliott, Turco, Evans, and Gresham (1984). A sample of 660 black and white, male and female, fifth graders responded on the CIRP to one of three problem severity (two children being disruptive, half a class being disruptive, a whole class being disruptive) and one of the three group contingency methods. Significant results were observed for interactions between rater's gender and problem behavior severity and between rater's race and problem behavior severity. The major new findings of this study of intervention acceptability were the following: (a) Female students rated the three forms of group contingency interventions less acceptable than did the males, the disparity increasing as the severity of the problem increased; (b) African American students, in general, rated group contingency interventions significantly more acceptable than did white students; and (c) the three forms of group contingency interventions were acceptable in an absolute sense and were not rated significantly different. These findings highlight the impact of two individual differences, race and children's acceptability judgments of interventions, and they reinforce a common perception that group contingency interventions generally are acceptable to children.

Summary of Research Findings With Recommendations for Practice

Based on the acceptability studies reviewed, four general conclusions seem warranted. First, a meaningful methodology exists for quantifying consumers' and clients' evaluations of descriptions of interventions. Second, intervention acceptability is a complex construct that is influenced by several salient child, teacher, and psychologist variables. Third, under most conditions, typical educational consumers evaluate constructive interventions relatively more acceptable than reductive interventions. Fourth, a moderate to strong positive relation exists between preintervention acceptability and perceived intervention effectiveness.

Research on consumers' acceptability of intervention procedures is relevant to successful consultation and intervention in educational settings. Although the findings do not provide a direct prescription for selecting an intervention, they do provide a conceptual organizer and sensitize a consultant and consultee to a list of variables that require consideration prior to the implementation of an intervention. At a very basic level, interventions can be evaluated on two dimensions: (a) acceptability and (b) effectiveness. Ideally, only interventions with a history of documented effectiveness should be considered, thus narrowing preintervention discussion to issues of acceptability. At this point a consultant can begin to assess the consultee's philosophy about interventions (e.g., reinforcement versus punishment; teacher-initiated versus psychologist- or parent-initiated; individual versus group), his or her intervention knowledge and skills, time and material resources, and experience with interventions. Instruments like those in the *Academic Intervention Monitoring System* (Elliott et al., 2001), where teachers directly identify instructional and behavior management tactics that they have in their repertoire and feel comfortable using with a target student, are sure to be more acceptable and likely to be implemented.

Most researchers have taken a "majority" approach to the study of intervention acceptability. With this approach, although we learn what interventions the majority of the consumers prefer, we risk overlooking a significant minority of consumers' evaluations. We have learned that consumers who vary in their knowledge of interventions differentially rate the acceptability of interventions. This finding argues for much more attention to participants' background information in our research and also for more single-case investigations.

INCREASING THE LIKELIHOOD THAT TEACHERS WILL IMPLEMENT INTERVENTIONS

It would be very convenient for school psychologists to be able to function unobstructed in the following way: A teacher has a student with a challenging academic and behavior problem; from a review of the research literature, an intervention is developed by the school psychologist for the problem and shared with the teacher, whereupon the teacher implements the intervention successfully. This process is attractive to many school psychologists because it requires very little of their time and it allows them to feel good about their expertise and a job well done.

The application of an intervention to the problem is a common process. As it typically occurs in schools, this process largely is reactive (i.e., it occurs in response to an acute need), it is problem focused (i.e., it results in the application of an intervention for a particular child), it is time-limited (i.e., it does not continue for more than two or three sessions because of time constraints on all parties), and its evaluation is short-term, child-focused, and generally subjective (e.g., a consultant may ask a teacher, "How have things been going with Susan the past couple of weeks?"). Researchers who have examined this process have provided evidence that suggests that many discrete behav-

iors that teachers consider intolerable, when clearly defined and thoroughly operationalized, can be reduced or eliminated over short periods (Lentz, 1988; Witt, Daly, &
Noell, 2000).

The goals of consultative interventions typically have two characteristics in common. First, there is a recognition that something is not functioning properly (usually
having to do with the child and/or the consultee) and that this something should be
"fixed." Second, emphasis is usually placed upon only a small part of the ecological system, usually with little recognition of the reciprocal interactions that can occur between
the many elements of a system. In a typical case, a teacher reports to a consultant that
a child is performing below expectations. After a thorough analysis, the consultant
determines that the child has a performance deficit and suggests that the teacher implement an intervention, such as a point system, to reinforce performance. Even though
attempts usually are made to involve the teacher in the design and implementation of
an intervention, the focus of such consultation is both molecular and child-centered in
that only one element of the system is singled out for intervention, that one element
typically being the child. Simply stated, the primary goal of this type of problem-cen-
tered consultation is to provide the teacher with a solution to a well-defined problem.
This solution is usually something that will address a particular narrow behavior problem the child is exhibiting.

We advocate a systems orientation in determining desired outcomes (Bergan, 1977;
Bergan & Kratochwill, 1990). This perspective can help in three ways. First, it makes it
possible to enter the multivariate world of the teacher. If the teacher had only to focus
on and "fix" the problem under consideration in a consultative interaction, then she or
he could probably do a pretty good job; but the teacher has to solve the particular problem and simultaneously consider and act upon all the other problems that are
occurring. Second, a systems orientation reminds us that "we can never do just one
thing" (Willems, 1974, p. 162), and changes in one behavior of one child can have
strong ramifications for other elements within the system (Petrie et al., 1980). Third,
when one moves away from "fixing" a problem as the sole objective of a consultative
intervention, other outcomes become important, including engendering in teachers
and students the perception that they exist in a supportive environment that is conducive to their well-being and to optimal functioning.

Some Assumptions About Working With Teachers in Classroom Management

Based on our experiences of working in schools to design and implement interventions in classrooms, we formulated three fundamental assumptions about consulting
with teachers.

Assumption 1. Most referrals for intervention are due to inappropriately arranged
antecedents rather than inappropriately arranged consequences (Gresham & Witt,
1987).

Corollary A: It is always easier to prevent behavior problems than to remediate them (i.e., it is easier to control antecedents than to control consequences).

Corollary B: Most consultative interventions ignore the complexity of the environmental context of problems (i.e., they may fix the problem, but not help the system).

The strongest evidence we can provide in support of the overall assumption is that effective and ineffective teachers do not differ much with respect to how they handle discipline problems. Instead, they differ with respect to the number of discipline problems they encounter, the effective teachers having fewer problems (Duke, 1982). In operational terms, effective teachers are likely to focus on antecedent control and establish a structure such that problems are less likely to occur. The interested reader is referred to Duke (1982) or Elliott et al. (2001) for an extensive list of skills displayed by effective teachers and to Witt et al. (2000) for a description of how to assess students within the context of the classroom.

Suffice it to say, effective teachers do a lot. The things they do prevent many discipline problems. If we approach a problem, the cause of which is some teacher or environmental antecedent, with a view to addressing and directly fixing the difficulty, as defined by the teachers, then the fix, which typically involves the application of consequences to student behavior, will probably be short-term. In conceptualizing the teacher's behavior as a set of antecedent conditions that can prevent misbehavior, it is useful to move from the abstract to the concrete. Witt and Martens (1988), for example, have used the problem of the time-efficient transitioning of students from one activity to another as a way to examine the issue of antecedent control. The literature on effective teaching is very clear that transitions in the classroom are periods when there is a high probability that students will engage in misbehavior and when valuable academic learning time is lost (Gettinger, 1988). Effective teachers set extremely high standards for student behavior during transitions. They take all the time necessary at the beginning of the year to teach children how to make the transitions, and they have well-established consequences for violations of established standards (Witt, LaFluer, Naquin & Gilbertson, 1999).

In general, good teachers establish routines and procedures that prevent most problems. Contrast this practice with the practice of a teacher who simply assumes children will know what to do during transitions, will not waste time, and will not get into trouble. There is an extremely high probability that this teacher will have problems. He or she will want these problems fixed either through the advice of a consultant or, more likely, through referral of the disturbing children to special education. It seems unwise, in the case of an ineffective teacher, to engage in case-centered consultation with the goal of reducing the amount of time wasting, talking without permission, and bothering of other children by developing techniques for applying individual consequences to children who engage in high rates of inappropriate behavior during transitions. Instead, our efforts might be more appropriately focused upon establishing antecedent conditions that involve displaying what we call good teaching behaviors and teaching social competencies that involve appropriate behavior on the part of the children. A list of activities designed for antecedent control of behavior is presented in Table 5.

TABLE 5

**Teacher–Related Antecedent Behaviors Designed to
Control Inappropriate Student Behavior**

- Teacher reminds students of the classroom rules.

- Teacher maintains eye contact with students.

- Teacher reminds students about expected behaviors that are critical to an activity before beginning the activity.

- Teacher uses nonverbal signals to redirect a student while teaching other students.

- Instructional routines for academic and nonacademic activities are understood by students.

- Pace of instructional lessons is brisk and directed by the teacher.

- Transitions from one task to another are short and organized.

- Expectations about the use of class time are communicated clearly and frequently.

According to Ysseldyke and Christenson (1987), these antecedent-oriented interventions arc synonymous with the effective teaching behaviors.

Assumption 2. Consultative activities directed toward child behaviors may not lead to decreases in teachers' complaints.

Except in rare cases, consultation does not occur proactively. The antecedent event that occasions consultation is not a system-level demand that we work to prevent problems. Because most school psychologists have more to handle than time permits, they seldom say proactively: "Teacher, I noticed you were having some difficulty with Joshua today and I would like to help you." Instead, consultation interventions most frequently are reactive, rather than proactive.

If it is correct to assume that consultation is mostly reactive, then to what stimulus events is consultation a reaction? Consultation occurs in response to problems that prove frustrating or aversive to teachers. However, to say that consultative behavior is occasioned chiefly by problems of this nature is not completely correct. A problem is a necessary, but not sufficient, condition for consultation to occur. Teachers encounter dozens of problems in a single day that are not brought to consultants. Thus, a problem situation is but the first step in a chain of circumstances that leads to consultation and intervention activities.

The critical element linking a problem with consultative intervention is a *complaint* or referral (Baer, 1987, 1988). Consultation typically originates when a problem is present and after a complaint or referral. Other factors, such as system-level expectations for consultation to occur, round out the necessary and sufficient antecedent conditions.

On the consequent side of the functional analysis equation for consultative behavior, there are pleasant and unpleasant events that maintain consultative behavior. Certainly there are positively reinforcing events that accrue to consultants assisting teachers with a problem (e.g., admiration, knowledge of a job well done); however, negative reinforcement is probably the most potent of the consequences that influence the rate of consultative behavior. Consultants are motivated to avoid or reduce pain, and the most common form of pain for school-based professionals is the complaint. Teachers are likewise motivated to reduce their frustration and the irritability associated with the problem(s) through the consultation process.

It is generally assumed that consultants and teachers want to solve the problem(s) being complained about. Furthermore, one would suppose that when the problem(s) that has motivated the complaint is resolved, then so will the complaints. Baer (1987) suggested that we have virtually no data to support the hypothesis that solving a given problem will reduce complaining. On the other hand, there is considerable evidence to suggest that the solutions generated in consultative interventions provide teachers with additional problems about which to complain (Witt, 1986; Witt & Elliott, 1985). Teachers complain about the solutions generated by problem solving, saying that such solutions (e.g., a point system) take too much time, are not realistic in a classroom of 25 children, have negative effects on other children, or will not work. When a teacher initiates an intervention through consultation, the intervention may bring with it side effects and possibly more complaining. Reaction could take the form of complaints from other children, who also want, for example, a contract because they too would like to be rewarded for their work. If the teacher spends too much time on an intervention for a particular child and neglects other areas of responsibility, then there will be complaints about the neglected areas and the teacher may complain to the consultant about these problems.

The proposition that we consult mostly in reaction to complaints also implies that the quieting of a complaint is a desired outcome of the consultation process. The quieting of a complaint remains an implicit goal because consultants are reluctant, if they ever think about it, to aspire toward the goal of reducing teachers' complaints. Instead, what are talked about during consultation are the more explicit goals of solving the stated problems; and we assume that solving the problem that has prompted the teacher's complaining will reduce the frequency or intensity of complaining.

Teachers have a difficult job because, in addition to teaching large numbers of children, they often have many forms to complete, playground duty, after-school activities, and so forth. They perform these activities with very minimal technical, clerical, or even social support and often receive a considerable amount of negative feedback (e.g., criticism and complaining) in the process. The demand characteristics of the system in which they function, including institutionalized methods for handling problems in schools (e.g., referral to special education), have the effect of limiting the kinds of problems about which teachers can legitimately complain. If they want to get raises and move up in the system, then it is difficult for them to complain (except possibly to other teachers) about too much paperwork or other manifestations of "stupidity" within a school's administration. The system does, however, establish methods by which they can complain about the worst children in their classes. These formal complaints are called referrals to special education and at a more informal level are called requests for consultation.

This context suggests a recipe for failure. Take one marginally effective teacher who is not well trained in classroom management, is overburdened with responsibilities, is feeling undervalued and perhaps even victimized by the system, and give this teacher a classroom with several unruly children. Allow this teacher only a limited number of issues about which to complain. For example, allow the teacher to complain only about children who may be "behaviorally handicapped" and in need of special services. Add to this a consultant interested only in reducing the frequency of behavior problems in the teacher's classroom and who is often unaware of the complexities and other demands under which the teacher must operate. The consultant attempts to "fix" problems identified by the teacher by asking this overburdened and ineffective teacher to do even more than he or she currently is doing. The teacher responds passively by either haphazardly doing what was asked or not doing it at all and continues to complain about the same problems as before, in addition to taking issue with the solutions offered by the consultant. Introduction by a consultant of a new intervention in a system that is not working properly appears to be relatively common, and it frequently leads to some frustration and failure for both consultant and teacher. Some relatively circumscribed problems may even be resolved along the way, but complaining may remain unchanged or even increase.

If the complaint plays such a powerful role in the consultative process, then school-based consultants may want to consider its importance as an initiator of consultative activities and as an outcome of the consultation process. Viewing the reduction of complaining as a legitimate outcome can influence how we work with teachers and cause us to monitor teacher complaints. This leads us to discuss an empowerment philosophy of teacher consultation in which the focus of consultative intervention may be more appropriately directed toward helping teachers be more effective in making the total system work and doing this in a way that simplifies rather than complicates their lives and allows for the development of a strong sense of self-efficacy.

Assumption 3. Merely talking to teachers about intervention (e.g., in collaborative consultation) may be insufficient to bring about full teacher use of an intervention.

Getting a teacher to use an intervention is usually brought about by one or more persons (i.e., a team) talking to another (i.e., the teacher) to resolve the problem of a child. *Talk* is neither a sophisticated assessment device nor is it a potent agent for consultee or child behavior change.

The self-report of the teacher plays a key role in consultation. First, it is typical for the consultant to *ask* the teacher about what the problem is and about what factors might be contributing to the problem. Second, the teacher is frequently dependent upon the consultant to *explain* what intervention plan might be put into place. Third, the consultant must rely on the teacher's report of whether the intervention was used and whether it produced desirable effects.

Witt, Noell, and their colleagues (Witt et al., 1997; Noell & Witt, in press) in a series of studies have shown that teachers rarely follow through with intervention following verbal interactions with a consultant even though teachers often do report that they follow through. That is, what teachers do and what teachers say are sometimes at odds. Wickstrom, Jones, LaFleur, and Witt (1998), for example, found that 33 out of 33 teachers reported they had implemented interventions developed during consultation with good fidelity to the intervention plan. Direct observation of the same teachers, however, revealed none of them implemented legally mandated prereferral interventions with greater than 10% integrity. These data would suggest that merely asking a teacher whether the intervention was used properly is insufficient. In a series of studies, Noell and Witt (in press) found that teachers typically implement an intervention for 2–4 days and then quit using it.

What has been found to be effective in getting teachers to follow through with intervention use is a combination of monitoring and performance feedback. Monitoring is conducted by developing interventions that leave "footprints" or permanent products. A smiley face chart, for example, produces the chart itself where a teacher has placed a smiley face here and there. A consultant can review the chart and get direct evidence if the chart was used. If the teacher cannot produce the chart, then it is assumed the intervention was not used. In addition to monitoring the intervention, several studies (e.g., Mortenson & Witt, 1998; Witt et al., 1997) have demonstrated the effectiveness of performance feedback. In using performance feedback, typically the consultant meets briefly with the teacher and reviews the teacher's implementation of the intervention. If the intervention is not being used, then the consultant and the teacher use problem solving to find ways to remove barriers to implementation. Frequently, the barrier is that the teacher is busy and has competing demands. Merely having another adult who is concerned that the intervention be implemented is sufficient to raise the priority of intervention implementation. The performance feedback sessions most frequently have been conducted daily but Mortenson and Witt (1998) conducted the review only once per week and found this was sufficient to maintain adequate levels of intervention integrity.

From this research it appears that teacher implementation of an intervention is an ordinary behavior subject to the same rules as any other behavior. Behaviors often are performed to obtain or to avoid some consequence. If a teacher is asked to use an intervention and there is no consequence (i.e., no one bothers to ask the teacher about implementation or seems to care if it is implemented), then the teacher is unlikely to continue to implement the intervention, especially when there are many other behaviors the teacher is required to do which are monitored and for which consequences are provided. The literature in this area is filled with "explanations" of "why" a teacher does not implement an intervention (e.g., resistance, theme interference). The good news is that rather than figuring out how to deal with these "deep" issues, the problem may be pretty simple when working with busy people such as teachers. If you want a teacher to use an intervention, then let the teacher know it is important and that someone will be coming around to check in and see how it is going.

INTERVENTION INTEGRITY: IMPROVING IMPLEMENTATION AND EVALUATION

Standardization, or procedural specification of an intervention, refers to the development of formal guidelines, procedural protocols, and/or manuals when the intervention is implemented. Use of a standardized format for intervention has several advantages for research (Kratochwill & Stoiber, 2000b; Kratochwill, Van Someren, & Sheridan, 1989). First, standardization of an intervention will allow replication of intervention procedures developed and empirically supported in research for dissemination in practice. Replication is important to develop the empirical efficacy of various interventions and to generate the techniques in research and practice across problem behaviors, settings, and intervention agents.

A second reason for recommending standardization of intervention in research and practice is to facilitate training in specific intervention skills. A major shortcoming of some intervention techniques is the lack of specific procedures for training individuals in their use (Matarazzo & Patterson, 1986). Some empirical work has suggested that a standardized approach focused on competency-based criteria can be used to train school psychologists in consultation (e.g., Kratochwill, Elliott, & Busse, 1995) and for preservice and in-service preparation of classroom and special education teachers (West, Idol, & Cannon, 1987). The use of standardized formats in consultation training and practice would appear to be essential in the empirical development of effective techniques that are disseminated in practice to assist consultees and clients (Kazdin, Kratochwill, & VandenBos, 1986).

Third, the development of standardized interventions may also enhance development of appropriate psychometric characteristics in research such as intervention effect norms. The issue of appropriate psychometric properties in the intervention field may be subject to debate. However, it is quite possible that the issues surrounding the appropriate choice of psychometric models cannot be resolved unless a standardized format is developed and used in research. In this way, the efficacy of traditional (e.g., classical test theory, domain-sampling model, multitrait-multimethod matrix, and latent trait theory) versus alternative measurement formats in "intervention validity" can be developed (Hayes, Nelson, & Jarrett, 1986).

Once intervention procedures have been specified or procedurally standardized in a manual, a major issue that must be addressed is implementation integrity, that is, the degree to which an intervention is being implemented as intended (see above discussion of acceptability and the role of integrity). Integrity is evaluated by comparison of an intervention as it is actually implemented with how it is intended to be implemented. Researchers have stressed that when an intervention is implemented, it must be carried out as originally intended (Peterson et al., 1982; Yeaton & Sechrest, 1981). Assessment of intervention integrity in consultation is important for several reasons. Investigators must assess the implementation of the consultation *process* to ensure that consultation actually is being practiced, that the consultant is following the four stages of consultation, and that the consultee is implementing the intervention program as developed during the problem analysis phase. In fact, some research has supported the notion that the entire consultation *process* is necessary in reducing problem behaviors of students (Fuchs & Fuchs, 1989). Failure to monitor the integrity of consultation can threaten the reliability and validity of an intervention.

Integrity can be evaluated at several levels (Kratochwill, Sheridan, & Van Someren, 1988). First, integrity of the consultation process can be assessed. It must be demonstrated that the professional consultant is following a specific consultation model or format. Typically, the integrity of this process can be checked by direct observation or by monitoring record forms of the process. Objective coding procedures of consultation could be conducted in research. For example, a verbal coding strategy called the Consultation Analysis Record (CAR) has been developed in behavioral consultation (Bergan & Tombari, 1975); it provides information regarding the source, content, and process of verbalizations of the consultant and consultee. Figure 3 displays the CAR.

Demonstrating the integrity of the consultation process is a first step. At the next level it must be demonstrated that the consultee is implementing the intervention program as intended. This is the level at which intervention integrity usually has been evaluated; and based on our rationale in the previous section, this assessment is critical. Integrity at this level can be evaluated through assessment of the consultee and through data on the client's responsiveness to the intervention. In research, data on consultee integrity can be obtained from the CAR and coded to examine topics discussed during the consultation interviews. In practice, direct observational assessment data can be gathered to determine if the consultee is implementing the intervention program as intended. Gresham (1989) also presented examples of a self-report integrity assessment (see Table 6, on page 278) and a rating scale that can be completed by the consultee or consultant or by an independent observer (see Table 7, on page 279). Both examples refer to a response cost lottery program implemented in a classroom.

Finally, if a child is involved in implementing an intervention (e.g., a self-control strategy), program implementation and its integrity can be monitored at the client level. In addition to direct observational assessment of the child, self-monitoring strategies can be used to monitor intervention integrity (Gardner & Cole, 1988). In determining the degree to which consultation integrity is maintained in research and practice, it is important to identify elements that enter into the process in addition to the usual components of intervention (Kazdin, 1986). These variables include, for example, such factors as the number of therapeutic contacts, duration of contacts, and time between visits. Such information may have bearing on successful programs and outcomes for the client.

FIGURE 3

Consultation Analysis Record

Consultant: _____ Case #: _____

Consultee: _____ Interview Type: _____

Page: _____

	Message Content		Message Content							Message Process						
	Consultee	Consultant	Background Environment	Behavior	Setting Behavior	Individual Characteristics	Observation	Plan	Other	Negative Evaluation	Positive Evaluation	Inference	Specifications	Summarization	Negative Validation	Positive Validation
1																
2																
3																
4																
5																
6																
7																
8																
9																
10																
11																
12																
13																
14																
15																
16																
17																
18																
19																
20																
21																
22																
23																
24																
25																

Note

Consultation-analysis record form. Reprinted from "The Analysis of Verbal Interactions Occurring During Consultation" by J. R. Bergan and M. L. Tombari, 1975, *Journal of School Psychology, 13,* p. 212, Copyright 1975, with permission from Elsevier Science.

In summary, we strongly encourage more attention be paid to the integrity of interventions. This attention does not require new technology. Methods such as component checklists or rating scales, or direct observation of the intervention implementation, may provide the necessary information to decide whether an inter-

TABLE 6

Example of a Self-Report Integrity Assessment

Date:_____ Teacher:_____ Day: M T W Th F

Response Cost Lottery

Directions: Please complete this form each day after the period in which the intervention has been implemented in your classroom.

	Strongly Disagree				Strongly Agree
1. I described the response cost lottery system to the class.	1	2	3	4	5
2. I displayed and described the rewards which students could receive in the lottery.	1	2	3	4	5
3. I placed a 3 x 5 inch card on top of each student's desk.	1	2	3	4	5
4. I taped the card on 3 sides with one side open.	1	2	3	4	5
5. I inserted 4 slips of colored paper inside each card using different colors for each student.	1	2	3	4	5
6. I left the lottery in effect for __ hour today.	1	2	3	4	5
7. I removed slips from each card whenever a student violated a class rule.	1	2	3	4	5
8. I restated the class rule whenever a student violated a class rule.	1	2	3	4	5
9. I placed the remaining tickets in the lottery box after lottery time concluded today.	1	2	3	4	5
10. I conducted the drawing for the winner today (Friday only).	1	2	3	4	5
11. The winner was allowed to select a reward (Friday only).	1	2	3	4	5

Note   -

From "Assessment of Treatment Integrity in School Consultation and Prereferral Intervention" by F. M. Gresham, 1989, *School Psychology Review, 18.* Copyright 1989 by *School Psychology Review.* Reprinted with permission.

TABLE 7

Example of a Behavior Rating Scale for Treatment Integrity

Consultee:_____ Date:_____ Consultant:_____

Response Cost Lottery

	Strongly Disagree			Strongly Agree	
1. Described system to students.	1	2	3	4	5
2. Displayed and described reinforcers.	1	2	3	4	5
3. Placed 3 x 5 card on students' desks.	1	2	3	4	5
4. Card taped on 3 sides.	1	2	3	4	5
5. 4 slips of colored paper inserted (different colors for each student)	1	2	3	4	5
6. Lottery in effect for __ hour.	1	2	3	4	5
7. Slips removed contingent on rule violations.	1	2	3	4	5
8. Teacher restates rule contingent on violation.	1	2	3	4	5
9. Remaining tickets placed in box.	1	2	3	4	5
10. Drawing occurs on Friday.	1	2	3	4	5
11. Winner selects reinforcer on Friday.	1	2	3	4	5

Note

From "Assessment of Treatment Integrity in School Consultation and Prereferral Intervention" by F. M. Gresham, 1989, *School Psychology Review, 18.* Copyright 1989 by *School Psychology Review.* Reprinted with permission.

vention has been implemented with integrity. Without such information, modification to interventions may be misguided.

Assessing Intervention Process and Outcomes

Questions about intervention effectiveness are relevant before, during, and after the implementation of a given intervention. Prior to selecting a specific intervention, one must identify an intervention procedure that is theoretically consistent or empirically linked with the intended approach to change, then focus on what challenges and social competencies and populations the intervention has been used with, and finally examine the relative effectiveness of the intervention in comparison with several other interventions. The effectiveness information available for a given intervention may come in the form of a case study, a single-case data-based report, a group comparison study, and/or meta-analytic review of effect sizes, or more likely by way of testimonial from an "expert" source. Generally, the more sources of information about the effectiveness of a given intervention the better. Yet prior to using any intervention in a "new" problem area or situation, past effectiveness information is imperfect. Thus, psychologists and other intervention agents ethically are bound to monitor the effects (both intended and unintended) of their intervention procedures during intervention and after termination of the intervention. Some basics of intervention evaluation are worth reviewing because of their influence on planning intervention procedures and on the establishment of accountable practices. Specifically, case study and single-subject design methodologies are emphasized. Readers interested in a more comprehensive examination of intervention evaluation are referred to Hayes et al.'s (1999) book on the scientist-practitioner and to the insightful article of Jacobson et al. (1984) on reporting variability and evaluating clinical significance.

A discussion of the dimensions of outcome change and expectations provides a context for intervention evaluation before the specific methods of case study and single-subject designs are examined. Change in some aspect of a client's functioning, whether it be directly observable or not, is always a central goal of intervention. The dimensions of client outcome of primary interest can be characterized as frequency, duration, intensity, and latency. These dimensions usually can be measured effectively through direct methods (e.g., observation or self-monitoring). However, numerous other assessment methods are often used, including rating scales completed by teachers or parents; functional assessment; role-play; and self-report inventories (Kratochwill, Sheridan, Carlson, & Lasechi, 1999). It is desirable to use several methods of assessment and several sources of information (Stoiber & Kratochwill, 2001). Ideally, the client's functioning should be measured several times within four time frames: before intervention (baseline), during intervention, immediately after intervention, and several months following termination of the intervention. By definition, at least two assessments, one preintervention and the other postintervention, of a client's functioning are essential to determine the magnitude of change. The more data points available during intervention, the more information about variability of change, from which more accurate inferences can be made about the process of change and about intervention components.

One useful strategy that is receiving increasing attention in recent years is performance or progress monitoring (Kern & Dunlap, 1999; Stoiber & Kratochwill, 2001). The notion of progress monitoring fits within the framework of determining the child's responsiveness to the intervention. Ongoing data regarding how the child is progressing toward a desired intervention goal or outcome are collected in conjunction with the implementation of the intervention. A variety of data can be collected for the purpose of monitoring intervention outcomes, including direct observations, goal attainment scaling or ratings, work samples, CBM probes, anecdotal records, parent reports and/or ratings, and child self-ratings. In addition, a multi-source approach to conducting progress monitoring is suggested so that consensus can be achieved in evaluating the child's progress across more than one evaluator. The use of multi-source data fits well within a collaborative decision-making framework for designing and evaluating interventions.

Ongoing performance or progress monitoring should contribute to a better understanding of whether and which components of an intervention, including instructional or environmental modifications, are effective. Another intent of performance/progress monitoring is that it provides a purposeful structure for guiding the development of alternative interventions if the present intervention is not successful. Progress monitoring is considered critical for documenting that the intervention was implemented with integrity and as intended. Finally, progress monitoring data are essential when a child's response to an intervention is used for making decisions about the child's psychological or educational needs, or for determining a child's disability status (see Reschly, Tilly, & Grimes, 1999).

Decisions about intervention outcomes should involve information from many sources (e.g., parents, teachers, peers, self-report) about changes in the client's problematic behavior and social competencies. Information about the trend and the magnitude of change is difficult to interpret without some comparative standard or criterion. In academic domains, outcome criteria are usually available in the form of curriculum mastery tests, lists of essential grade skills, or assigned learning objectives. In contrast, outcome criteria in social/emotional domains are less standardized and more variable across settings. Therefore, comparisons with typical peers, with intervention goals established a priori, and with behavior standards established by significant adults are the primary criteria by which behavioral changes are interpreted. Additional criteria for a successful intervention are maintenance of the change over time and generalization of the behavior across settings.

An example tool that can be used to structure the outcome evaluation process of a school-based intervention program is Outcomes: PME (Stoiber & Kratochwill, 2001). Outcomes: PME is built around a scientist-practitioner or evidence-based framework and is a general assessment instrument designed to facilitate the design, implementation, and monitoring of academic and social behavioral interventions. It can be used to plan and monitor interventions for virtually any domain of performance across traditional educational and mental health settings. Outcomes: PME embraces a goal-attainment framework but allows the assessor to integrate multiple sources of progress monitoring data for purposes of making decisions about the efficacy of interventions. The structure of Outcomes: PME lends itself to (a) prereferral activities typically performed by school-based collaborative teams (e.g., collaborative support teams, student assistance teams), (b) intervention planning and monitoring activities, and (c) special education decision making that occurs through the Individual Educational Program team process. An important characteristic of Outcomes: PME is that it can be applied both for documenting and determining the effectiveness of interventions and for determining eligibility for special programs based on a consensus-building framework called *convergent evidence scaling*. Another unique feature of Outcomes: PME is that it incorporates diverse progress monitoring components and the recording of intervention results based on multiple data sources (e.g., direct observation, goal attainment ratings, anecdotal records, work samples). In addition, it can be used in conjunction with traditional assessment and/or alternative assessment procedures, such as functional assessment of social performance (for example, with the Functional Assessment and Intervention System; Stoiber & Kratochwill, 2001) and with the assessment of academic and social competencies (for example with the Social Competency Checklist; Stoiber & Kratochwill, 2001). Table 3, on page 258, presents some of the characteristics of Outcomes: PME with a focus on its application in practice.

Evaluation and Design Frameworks

A strong case for intervention effectiveness requires repeated measurements over time of a well-defined problem and the comparison of the measurement results with an appropriate standard of performance. Procedures for accomplishing such a goal vary largely depending on the cooperation of others involved in delivering the intervention and the setting in which the client is treated. We now examine two procedures for evaluating school-based, individualized interventions, including case studies and single-case design.

Case study methods. Case studies have been a popular method for describing and documenting intervention effectiveness. There are three basic types of case studies (Kratochwill, 1985): (a) the nonintervention case study, (b) the assessment/diagnosis case study, and (c) the intervention case study. Of particular interest here is the intervention case study, which is further subdivided into uncontrolled, pre-experimental, and clinical replication cases. In all three subtypes of intervention case studies, an intervention agent is usually interested in evaluating the efficacy of some intervention for a single client or small group of clients. Usually, case studies are conducted in the absence of experimental controls; hence, various sources of internal validity may not be addressed. As a result, many rival interpretations to account for any client changes in outcome may not be ruled out.

Advocates of the case study approach (e.g., Kazdin, 1981b; Kratochwill, 1985) acknowledge its limitations for reaching valid decisions about outcome effectiveness, but also recognize that in many situations case studies provide an appropriate method for enhancing best professional practices. Kazdin (1981b) and Kratochwill (1985) identified several means by which intervention case studies can be improved: (a) collecting direct measures of behavior change to supplement traditional anecdotal descriptions of clients; (b) increasing the number of times data are collected on clients over the course of intervention in addition to the traditional preintervention and postintervention assessments; (c) involving control over some important independent intervention variables to decrease inference levels about which variables affect behavior; and (d) using standardized assessment and intervention procedures so that appropriate replication by other practitioners or researchers is possible. Information about the projected performance of the stipulated behaviors (with and without intervention) in view of the severity of the clients' problems, the number and diversity of clients, the addition of social validity measures of the behavior change, the integrity of the intervention, and reports of maintenance and generalization also are enhancements of case study methods (Kratochwill, 1985). A good example of intervention case studies that is worthy of inspection is a published report by Kazdin, Esveldt-Dawson, French, and Unis (1987) on the intervention for antisocial child behavior. Outcomes: PME (Stoiber & Kratochwill, 2001) introduced in this chapter, can be used in the context of a case study framework featuring an A/B design structure.

Single-case designs. Single-case strategies are constructed from basic design elements and are classified as within-, between-, or combined-series designs.

1. *Within-series designs: Simple and complex phase changes.* In a simple phase-change single-case design, the dependent measures are evaluated within a time series. At the point of phase change or intervention implementation, differences in levels and trends in the data series are evaluated. Several phases of the design are structured so that there is a replication of the intervention effect. A variety of single-case studies have used the simple phase-change structure in applied research. For example, Wagner and Winett (1988) used a simple within-series design structure to evaluate a program designed to promote selection of items from a low-fat, high-fiber menu (salads) in a fast food restaurant. Specifically, the authors use an A/B/A/B design, the baseline of which involved an analysis of the percentage of sales of salads by total sales for a period of 3 weeks. Following this phase, the intervention consisted of placing prompts at the entrance and near the cash register and placing 10 cards on tables for approximately 3 weeks. The authors found that the diners in the fast food restaurant in fact increased their consumption of salads during the intervention period. This effect was replicated in the second B (salad-promoting) phase, in the replication component of the design.

This common design can be extended to more complex phase changes. Basically, complex phase changes can be designed by using the same logic as the simple phase-change strategies and allowing comparison of the effects of adding or subtracting various intervention components across phases of the investigation. For example, an investigator may be interested in evaluating the effects of a component package in which the B intervention has several specific components added to it (e.g., B + C + D). A design would be developed in which the investigator uses the logic of the simple phase-change strategy to evaluate the intervention effect. This strategy would consist of the design paradigm A/B + C + D/A/B + C + D/A/B + C + D. Indeed, one of the more common applications of the complex phase-change designs is to examine interventions that consist of multi-component programs. Various single components could also be evaluated in this design strategy by systematically dropping out various components across replication series. In this way, the program evaluator or researcher can determine whether the intervention effects are additive or which optimal combinations of intervention components are contributing to the outcome.

2. *Between-series designs: Alternating intervention designs.* School psychologists using a between-series format for single-case research essentially have the option of using an alternating intervention design (ATD) or a simultaneous intervention design (STD).

The STD is used in rather rare instances where the school psychologist is interested in comparing interventions that are presented simultaneously. Although current applications of this design are rather limited, the procedure would have some application to assessing clients' preference among alternative interventions that have been presented during the same session or interval. Based on its limited use, it is not discussed here. The researcher using ATD compares different interventions with the same client, and two or more data series are compared across time, the analysis taking into account trend and variability in the dependent variable. The client is exposed to different interventions for equal periods of time, and the intervention phases are alternated within a very short period of time, such as from one session to the other or from one part of the day to the other. The researcher sequences these interventions randomly or through a counterbalancing procedure, but the client receives equal exposure to the interventions while setting and time variables are controlled across phases of the experiment.

Stern, Fowler, and Kohler (1988) used an alternating intervention design in a study in which they compared two interventions, in which the clients were assigned two different roles: peer monitor and point earner. In the study, two fifth-grade students' off-task and disruptive behaviors were decreased during an intervention in which they were appointed as either peer monitors or point earners. Children in the study worked in dyads in which one child served as a peer monitor and the other earned points for his or her monitor for performing good behavior. The points were accumulated as part of a group contingency program. The researchers introduced the two appointments in an independent math period in which they alternated these appointments across days. Specifically, the peer monitor and point earner roles were alternate every other day. The researchers found that the peer monitor and point earner roles were equally effective in reducing each student's inappropriate behavior. Moreover, the frequency of the students' target behavior declined during the intervention to a level within the range of inappropriate behavior levels exhibited by normative peers. The researchers also monitored the speed with which the students completed math problems. They found that although their speed increased during both interventions, their accuracy varied.

As can be seen from this study, the major advantage of the ATD is that the researcher can compare two or more interventions in a relatively short period. Moreover, it is not always necessary to withdraw the intervention completely in this type of design to establish an intervention's effects. The ATD unfortunately is greatly influenced by many intervention interference problems and requires rather careful monitoring during implementation.

3. *Combined-series (multiple-baseline) designs.* Combined-series designs, as the name implies, involve an integration of within- and between-series elements in a design format. Usually, combined-series designs involve straightforward application of the multiple-baseline procedure and its associated variations. In these designs, a single within-in-series element (e.g., A/B phase) is replicated across clients, settings, or behaviors. Various threats to validity are controlled by the staggered implementation across data series. Basically, this procedure is structured so that as each intervention is implemented the changes involved affect only the series in which the intervention is introduced, the other series remaining stable across phases. Although the multiple-baseline design requires a minimum of two series, it is recommended that four or more series be structured, depending on practical constraints in the setting.

In one example of a multiple-baseline design, McEvoy et al. (1988) used group affection activities to increase the interaction of three young autistic children with nondisabled peers. The authors found that peer interaction increased during free play when the affection activities were conducted, but not when similar activities were used without the affection intervention package. This interaction included initiations by both autistic and nondisabled children. Reciprocal interactions occurred more frequently with nondisabled peers who had participated in the affection activities. This application of the multiple-baseline design essentially involved the application of the affection activities across three individuals and the percentage of peer interaction served as the dependent variable.

Considerations. One major challenge confronting school psychologists involved in implementing interventions in applied settings is designing an evaluation scheme to determine if services are effective. We have placed special emphasis on case study and single-case designs because these procedures have a history of application to the evaluation of clinical problems in applied settings. Moreover, these procedures have often been recommended as the "best choice" for empirical evaluation in practice (Hayes et al., 1999). Although there is debate about whether these procedures can be implemented in the usual routine practice of a school psychologist, case study and single-case research designs have been used extensively in psychology and education to evaluate research projects. Our perspective is that for most practitioners, the methodology of *case studies* will be most compatible with the demands of practice, recognizing there will be many compromises necessary in the evaluation process.

CONCLUSIONS

We have focused on an array of interrelated intervention issues in this chapter, beginning with a discussion of problem solving and models that help link assessments to intervention and then focusing on aspects of intervention selection, implementation, integrity, and finally evaluation. Our opening premise was that the major challenge facing school psychologists and other educators who are involved in treating students' classroom problems is the identification of acceptable and effective interventions that a teacher can implement with integrity. We believe that many such interventions exist, as evidenced in the content of several other chapters in this volume. In designing interventions for implementation in the regular classroom, the major task in identifying such interventions requires knowledge of and respect for many variables associated with the teachers, such as skill, knowledge, time, and the availability of resources. This review of the intervention acceptability research and analyses of intervention integrity and teacher empowerment is intended to provide a foundation for improving the effectiveness of classroom interventions.

REFERENCES

Baer, D. M. (1987). The difference between basic and applied behavior analysis is one behavior. *Behavior Analysis, 22,* 101–106.

Baer, D. M. (1988). If you know why you're changing a behavior, you'll know when you've changed it enough. *Behavioral Assessment, 10,* 219–223.

Baer, D. M., Wolf, M., & Risley, T. (1968). Some current dimensions of applied behavior analysis. *Journal of Applied Behavior Analysis, 1,* 91–97.

Barnett, D. W., Bell, S. H., & Carey, K. T. (1999). *Designing preschool interventions: A practitioner's guide.* New York: Guilford Press.

Beavers, K. F., Kratochwill, T. R., & Braden, J. P. (2001). *Treatment utility of assessment within consultation: A functional assessment vs. an empiric approach to academic reading interventions.* Manuscript submitted for publication.

Bergan, J. R. (1977). *Behavioral consultation.* Columbus, OH: Merrill.

Bergan, J. R., & Kratochwill, T. R. (1990). *Behavioral consultation and therapy.* New York: Plenum.

Bergan, J. R., & Tombari, M. L. (1975). The analysis of verbal interactions occurring during consultation. *Journal of School Psychology, 13,* 209–226.

Clark, L., & Elliott, S. N. (1988). The influence of intervention strength information of knowledgeable teachers' preintervention evaluations of social skills training methods. *Professional School Psychology, 3,* 241–251.

Cormier, W. H., & Cormier, L. S. (1985). *Interviewing strategies for helpers* (2nd ed.). Monterey, CA: Brooks/Cole.

Duke, D. L. (1982). *Helping teachers manage classrooms.* Alexandria, VA: Association for Supervision of Curriculum and Instruction.

Dunst, C. J., & Trivette, C. M. (1988). Helping helplessness and harm. In J. C. Witt, S. N. Elliott, & F. M. Gresham (Eds.), *Handbook of behavior therapy in education* (pp. 343–376). New York: Plenum.

Elliott, S. N. (1986). Children's ratings of the acceptability of classroom interventions in misbehavior: Findings and methodological considerations. *Journal of School Psychology, 24,* 23–35.

Elliott, S. N. (1988). Acceptability of behavioral interventions in educational psychology. In J. C. Witt, S. N. Elliott, & F. M. Gresham (Eds.), *Handbook of behavior therapy in education* (pp. 121–150). New York: Plenum.

Elliott, S. N., DiPerna, J. C., & Shapiro, E. S. (2001). *The academic intervention monitoring system.* San Antonio: The Psychological Corporation.

Elliott, S. N., & Gresham, F. M. (1991). *Social skills intervention guide.* Circle Pines, MN: American Guidance Service.

Elliott, S. N., Turco, T. L., Evans, S., & Gresham, F. M. (1984, November). *Group contingency interventions: Children's acceptability ratings.* Presented at the annual convention of the Association for the Advancement of Behavior Therapy, Philadelphia, PA.

Elliott, S. N., Turco, T. L., & Gresham, F. M. (1987). Consumers' and clients' preintervention acceptability ratings of classroom-based group contingencies. *Journal of School Psychology, 25,* 145–154.

Elliott, S. N., Witt, J. C., Galvin, G. A., & Moe, G. L. (1986). Children's involvement in intervention selection: Acceptability of interventions for misbehaving peers. *Professional Psychology: Research and Practice, 17,* 235–241.

Elliott, S. N., Witt, J. C., Galvin, G., & Peterson, R. (1984). Acceptability of positive and reductive interventions: Factors that influence teachers' decisions. *Journal of School Psychology, 22,* 353–360.

Finn, C. A. (2000). *Remediating behavior problems of young children: The impact of parent treatment acceptability and the efficacy of conjoint behavioural consultation and videotape therapy.* Unpublished dissertation, McGill University, Montreal.

Foxx, R. M., & Jones, J. R. (1978). A remediation program for increasing the spelling achievement of elementary and junior high school students. *Behavior Modification, 2,* 211–230.

Frentz, C., & Kelley, M. L. (1986). Parents' acceptance of reductive intervention methods: The influence of problem severity and perception of child behavior. *Behavior Therapy, 17,* 75–81.

Fuchs, D., & Fuch, L. S. (1989). Exploring effective and efficient prereferral interventions: A component analysis of behavioral consultation. *School Psychology Review, 18,* 260–279.

Gable, R. A., Quinn, M. M., Rutherford, R. B., Howell, K. W., & Hoffman, C. C. (1998). Addressing student problem behavior—Part II: Conducting a functional behavioral assessment (3rd ed.). Washington, DC: Center for Effective Collaboration and Practice.

Gardner, W. I., & Cole, C. L. (1988). Self-monitoring procedures. In E. S. Shapiro & T. R. Kratochwill (Eds.), *Behavioral assessment in schools: Conceptual foundations and practical applications* (pp. 206–246). New York: Guilford.

Gettinger, M. (1988). Methods of proactive classroom management. *School Psychology Review, 17,* 227–242.

Gresham, F. M. (1989). Assessment of intervention integrity in school consultation and prereferral interventions. *School Psychology Review, 18,* 37–50.

Gresham, F. M., & Kendall, G. K. (1987). School consultation research: Methodological critique and future research directions. *School Psychology Review, 16,* 306–316.

Gresham, F. M., & Witt, J. C. (1987, October). *Practical considerations in the implementation of classroom interventions.* Paper presented at the annual meeting of the Oregon School Psychological Association, Eugene, OR.

Hayes, S. C., Barlow, D. H., & Nelson-Gray, R. O. (1999). *The scientist practitioner: Research and accountability in the age of managed care* (2nd ed.). Boston: Allyn and Bacon.

Hayes, S. C., Nelson, R. O., & Jarrett, R. B. (1986). Evaluating the quality of behavioral assessment. In R. O. Nelson & S. C. Hayes (Eds.), *Conceptual foundations of behavioral assessment* (pp. 463–503). New York: Guilford.

Hibbs, E. D., & Jensen, P. S. (1996). *Psychological treatments for child and adolescent disorders: Empirically based strategies for clinical practice.* Washington, DC: American Psychological Association.

Jacobson, N. S., Follette, W.C., & Revenstorf, D. (1984). Psychotherapy outcome research: Methods for reporting variability and evaluating clinical significance. *Behavior Therapy, 15,* 336–352.

Jeger, A. M., & McClure, G. (1979). Attitudinal effects of undergraduate behavioral training. *Policy Studies Review, 23,* 147–186.

Jensen, W. R., Likins, M., Althouse, R. B., Hofmeister, A. M., Morgan, D. P., Reavis, H. K., Rhode, G., & Taylor-Sweeten, M. (1999). *Functional assessment and intervention program (FAIP).* (Version 1.0). Longmont, CO: Sopris West.

Johnson, J. H., Rasbury, W. D., & Siegel, J. L. (1986). *Approaches to child intervention: Introduction to therapy, research, and practice.* New York: Pergamon.

Kanfer, F. H. (1973). Behavior modification—An overview. In C. Thoresen (Ed.), *Behavior modification in education* (pp. 10–47). Chicago: University of Chicago Press.

Kazdin, A. E. (1977). Assessing the clinical or applied significance of behavior change through social validation. *Behavior Modification, 1,* 427–452.

Kazdin, A. E. (1980a). Acceptability of alternative interventions for deviant child behavior. *Journal of Applied Behavior Analysis, 13,* 259–273.

Kazdin, A. E. (1980b). Acceptability of time-out from reinforcement procedures for disruptive child behavior. *Behavior Therapy, 11,* 329–344.

Kazdin, A. E. (1981a). Acceptability of child intervention techniques: The influence of intervention efficacy and adverse side effects. *Behavior Therapy, 12,* 493–506.

Kazdin, A. E. (1981b). Drawing valid references from case studies. *Journal of Consulting and Clinical Psychology, 49,* 183–192.

Kazdin, A. E. (1982). *Single case research designs: Methods for clinical and applied settings.* New York: Oxford University Press.

Kazdin, A. E. (1986). Comparative outcome studies of psychotherapy: Methodological issues and strategies. *Journal of Consulting and Clinical Psychology, 54,* 95–105.

Kazdin, A. E., Esveldt-Dawson, L., French, N. H., & Unis, A. S. (1987). Problem-solving skills training and relationship therapy in the intervention of antisocial child behavior. *Journal of Consulting and Clinical Psychology, 55,* 76–85.

Kazdin, A. E., French, N. H., & Sherick, R. B. (1981). Acceptability of alternative interventions for children: Evaluating of inpatient children, parents, and staff. *Journal of Consulting and Clinical Psychology, 49,* 900–907.

Kazdin, A. E., Kratochwill, T. R., & VandenBos, G. R. (1986). Beyond clinical trials: Generalizing from research to practice. *Professional Psychology: Research and Practice, 17,* 391–398.

Kern, L., & Dunlap, G. (1999). Developing effective program plans for students with disabilities. In D. J. Reschly, W. D. Tilly III, and J. P. Grimes (Eds.), Special education in transition: Functional assessment and noncategorical programming (pp. 213–232). Longmont, CO: Sopris West.

Kratochwill, T. R. (1985). Case study research in school psychology. *School Psychology Review, 14,* 204-215.

Kratochwill, T. R., Elliott, S. N., & Busse, R. T. (1995). Behavior consultation: A five-year evaluation of consultant and client outcomes. *School Psychology Quarterly, 10*(2), 87-117.

Kratochwill, T. R., Sheridan, S. M., Carlson, J., & Lasecki, K. L. (1999). Advances in behavioral assessment. In C. R. Reynolds & T. B. Gutkin (Eds.), *The handbook of school psychology* (3rd ed., pp. 350-382). New York: Wiley.

Kratochwill, T. R., Sheridan, S. M., & Van Someren, K. R. (1988). Research in behavioral consultation: Current status and future directions. In F. J. West (Ed.), *School consultation: Interdisciplinary perspectives on theory, research, training, and practice* (pp. 77-102). Austin, TX: Association of Educational and Psychological Consultants.

Kratochwill, T. R., & Stoiber, K. C. (2000a). Empirically supported interventions and school psychology: Conceptual and practice issues: Part II. *School Psychology Quarterly, 15,* 233-253.

Kratochwill, T. R., & Stoiber, K. C. (2000b). Uncovering critical research agendas for school psychology: Conceptual dimensions and future directions. *School Psychology Review, 29,* 591-603.

Kratochwill, T. R., Stoiber, K. C., Christenson, S., Durlak, J. A., Levin, J. R., Waas, G., Natasi, B., Talley, R., Schensul, S., Shernoff, E., & Lewis-Snyder, G. (2001). *Procedural and Coding Manual for Identification of Evidence-Based Interventions.* Washington, DC: Task Force on Evidence-Based Interventions in School Psychology, Division 16, American Psychological Association and Society for the Study of School Psychology.

Kratochwill, T. R., Van Someren, K. R., & Sheridan, S. M. (1989). Training behavioral consultants: A competency-based model to teach interview skills. *Professional School Psychology, 4,* 41-58.

Krigin, K. A., Braukmann, C. J., Atwater, J. D., & Wolf, M. M. (1982). An evaluation of teaching-family (Achievement Place) group homes for juvenile offenders. *Journal of Applied Behavior Analysis, 15,* 1-16.

Lentz, F. E. (1988). Reductive procedures. In J. C. Witt, S. N. Elliott, & F. M. Gresham (Eds.), *Handbook of behavior therapy in education.* New York: Plenum.

Levine, F. M., & Sandeen, E. (1985). *Conceptualization in psychotherapy: The models approach.* Hillsdale, NJ: Erlbaum.

Martens, B. K., Peterson, R. L., Witt, J. C., & Cirone, S. (1986). Teacher perceptions of school-based intervention: Ratings of intervention effectiveness, ease of use, and frequency of use. *Exceptional Children, 53,* 212-223.

Martens, B. K., Witt, J. C., Elliott, S. N., & Darveaux, D. X. (1985). Teacher judgments concerning the acceptability of school-based interventions. *Professional Psychology: Research and Practice, 16,* 78-88.

Matarazzo, R. G., & Patterson, D. (1986). Research on the teaching and learning of psychotherapeutic skills. In S. L. Garfield & A. E. Bergan (Eds.), *Handbook of psychotherapy and behavior approach* (3rd ed.; pp. 821-843). New York: Wiley.

McEvoy, M. A., Nordquist, V. M., Twardosz, S., Heckaman, K. A., Wehby, J. H., & Denny, R. K. (1988). Promoting autistic children's peer interaction in an integrated early childhood setting using affection activities. *Journal of Applied Behavior Analysis, 21,* 193-200.

McKee, W. T. (1984). *Acceptability of alternative classroom intervention strategies and factors affecting teachers' ratings.* Unpublished master's thesis, University of British Columbia, Vancouver.

McMahon, R. J., & Forehand, R. L. (1983). Consumer satisfaction in behavioral intervention for children: Types, issues, and recommendations. *Behavior Therapy, 14,* 209-225.

McMahon, R. J., Forehand, R., & Griest, D. L. (1981). Effects of knowledge of social learning principles on enhancing intervention outcome and generalization in a parent training program. *Journal of Consulting and Clinical Psychology, 49,* 526-532.

Melton, G. B. (1983). Decision making by children: Psychological risks and benefits. In G. B. Melton, G. P. Koocher, & M. J. Saks (Eds.), *Children's competence to consent* (pp. 137-159). New York: Plenum.

Morris, R. J., & Kratochwill, T. R. (Eds.). (1998). *The practice of child therapy* (3rd ed). New York: Pergamon.

Mortenson, B. P., & Witt, J. C. (1998). The use of weekly performance feedback to increase teacher implementation of an academic intervention. *School Psychology Review, 27,* 613-627.

Nathan, P. E., & Gorman, J. M. (1998). *A guide to treatments that work.* New York, New York: Oxford University Press.

Neef, N. A., & Iwata, B. A. (1994). Current research on functional analysis methodologies: An introduction. *Journal of Applied Behavior Analysis, 27,* 211-214.

Nelson, J. R., Roberts, M. L., & Smith, D. J. (1998). *Conducting functional behavioral assessments: A practical guide.* Longmont, CO: Sopris West.

Noell, G. H., & Witt, J. C. (in press). When does consultation lead to intervention implementation? Critical issues for research and practice. *Journal of Special Education.*

O'Dell, S. L., Tarler-Benlolo, L., & Flynn, J. M. (1979). An instrument to measure knowledge of behavioral principles as applied to children. *Journal of Behavior Therapy and Experimental Psychology, 10,* 29-34.

O'Leary, K. D. (1984). The image of behavior therapy: It is time to take a stand. *Behavior Therapy, 15,* 219-233.

Ollendick, T. H., & King, N. I. (1998). Empirically supported treatments for children with phobic and anxiety disorders: Current status. *Journal of Clinical Child Psychology, 27,* 156-167.

Ollendick, T. H., Matson, J. L., Esveldt-Dawson, K., & Shapiro, E. S. (1980). Increasing spelling achievement: An analysis of intervention procedures utilizing an alternative interventions design. *Journal of Applied Behavior Analysis, 15,* 477-492.

O'Neill, R. E., Horner, R. H., Albin, R. W., Sprague, J. R., Storey, K., & Newton, J. S. (1997). *Functional assessment and program development for problem behavior* (2nd ed.). Pacific Grove, CA: Brooks/Cole.

Patterson, G. R., Reid, J. B., & Dishion, T. J. (1992). *Antisocial boys.* Eugene, OR: Castalia.

Peterson, K., Hommer, A. L., & Wonderlich, S. A. (1982). The integrity of independent variables in behavior analysis. *Journal of Applied Behavior Analysis, 15,* 477-492.

Petrie, P., Brown, K. D., Piersel, W. C., Frinfrock. S. R., Schelble, M., Lablanc, C. P., & Kratochwill, T. R. (1980). The school psychologist as behavioral ecologist. *Journal of School Psychology, 18,* 222-233.

Reimers, T. M., Wacker, D. P., & Koeppl, G. (1987). Acceptability of behavioral interventions: A review of the literature. *School Psychology Review, 16,* 212-227.

Reppucci, N. D., & Saunders, J. T. (1974). The social psychology of behavior modification: Problems of implementation in natural settings. *American Psychologist, 29,* 649-660.

Reschly, D. J., Tilly, W. D., & Grimes, J. P. (Eds.). (1999). *Special education in transition: Functional assessment and noncategorical programming.* Longmont, CO: Sopris West.

Schill, M. T., Kratochwill, T. R., & Gardner, W. I. (1996). Conducting a functional analysis of behavior. In M. J. Breen & C. R. Fiedler (Eds.), *Behavioral approach to assessment of youth with emotional/behavioral disorders* (pp. 83-179). Austin, TX: PRO-ED.

Schill-Twernbold, M., Kratochwill, T. R., & Elliott, S. N. (1998). Functional assessment in behavioral consultation: A treatment utility study. *School Psychology Quarterly, 13,* 116-140.

Shapiro, E. S. (1996). *Academic skills problems: Direct assessment and intervention.* New York: Guilford.

Shapiro, E. S., & Goldberg, R. (1986). A comparison of group contingencies for increasing spelling performance among sixth grade students. *School Psychology Review, 15,* 546-667.

Stern, G. W., Fowler, S. A., & Kohler, F. W. (1988). A comparison of two intervention roles: Peer monitor and point earner. *Journal of Applied Behavior Analysis, 21,* 103-109.

Stoiber, K. C., & Kratochwill, T. R. (1998). *Handbook of group interventions for children and families.* Boston: Allyn & Bacon.

Stoiber, K. C., & Kratochwill, T. R. (2000). *Functional assessment and intervention system.* San Antonio: TX: The Psychological Corporation.

Stoiber, K. C., & Kratochwill, T. R. (2001). *Outcomes: Planning, monitoring, evaluating.* San Antonio: TX: The Psychological Corporation.

Thompson, B. (1999). Improving research clarity and usefulness with effect size indices as supplements to statistical significance tests. *Exceptional Children, 65*(3), 329-337.

Turco, T. L., & Elliott, S. N. (1986). Assessment of students' acceptability of teacher-initiated interventions for classroom misbehavior. *Journal of School Psychology, 24,* 307-313.

Turkat, I. D. (1990). *The personality disorders: A psychological approach to clinical management.* New York: Pergamon.

U.S. Congress, Senate Committee on the Judiciary, Subcommittee on Constitutional Rights. (1974). *Individual rights and the federal role in behavior modification.* 93rd Cong., 2nd session, November 1974. Washington, DC: U.S. Government Printing Office.

VonBrock, M. B. (1985). *The influence of effectiveness information on teachers' ratings of acceptability.* Unpublished master's thesis, Louisiana State University, Baton Rouge.

VonBrock, M. B., & Elliott, S. N. (1987). The influence of intervention effectiveness information on the acceptability of classroom interventions. *Journal of School Psychology, 25,* 131-144.

Wagner, J. L., & Winett, R. A. (1988). Prompting one low-fat, high-fiber selection in a fast-food restaurant. *Journal of Applied Behavior, 21,* 179-185.

West, J. G., Idol, L., & Cannon, G. (1987). *A curriculum for preservice and inservice preparation of classroom and special education teachers in collaborative consultation.* Austin: The University of Texas at Austin, Research & Training Project on School Consultation.

Wickstrom, K., Jones, K., LaFleur, L., & Witt, J. C. (1998). An analysis of intervention integrity in school-based consultation. *School Psychology Quarterly, 13,* 141-151.

Willems, E. P. (1974). Behavioral technology and behavioral ecology. *Journal of Applied Behavior Analysis, 7,* 151-165.

Witt, J. C. (1986). Teachers' resistance to the use of school-based intervention. *Journal of School Psychology, 24,* 37-44.

Witt, J. C., & Beck, R. (1999). *One minute academic functional assessment and interventions: "Can't" do it ... or "won't" do it?* Longmont, CO: Sopris West.

Witt, J. C., Daly, E., & Noell, G. (2000). *Functional assessments.* Longmont, CO: Sopris West.

Witt, J. C., & Elliott, S. N. (1985). Acceptability of classroom management strategies. In T. R. Kratochwill (Ed.), *Advances in school psychology* (Vol. 4; pp. 251-288). Hillsdale, NJ: Erlbaum.

Witt, J. C., Elliott, S. N., & Gresham, F. M. (Eds.). (1988). *Handbook of behavior therapy in education.* New York: Plenum.

Witt, J. C., Elliott, S. N., & Martens, B. K. (1984). Acceptability of behavioral interventions used in classrooms: The influence of teacher time, severity of behavior problem, and type of intervention. *Behavioral Disorders, 10,* 95-104.

Witt, J. C., LaFleur, L., Naquin, G., & Gilbertson, D. (1999). *Teaching effective classroom routines.* Longmont, CO: Sopris West.

Witt, J. C., & Martens, B. K. (1983). Assessing the acceptability of behavioral interventions used in classrooms. *Psychology in the Schools, 20,* 510-517.

Witt, J. C., & Martens, B. K. (1988). Problems with problem-solving consultation: A re-analysis of assumptions, methods, and goals. *School Psychology Review, 17,* 211-226.

Witt, J. C., Martens, B. K., & Elliott, S. N. (1984). Factors affecting teachers' judgments of the acceptability of behavioral interventions: Time involvement, behavior problem severity, and type of intervention. *Behavior Therapy, 15,* 204-209.

Witt, J. C., Moe, G., Gutkin, T. B., & Andrews, L. (1984). The effect of saying the same thing in different ways: The problem of language and jargon in school-based consultation. *Journal of School Psychology, 22,* 361-367.

Witt, J. C., Noell, G. H., LaFleur, L. H., & Mortenson, B. P. (1997). Increasing teacher usage of interventions in general education settings. *Journal of Applied Behavior Analysis, 30,* 693-696.

Witt, J. C., & Robbins, J. R. (1985). Acceptability of reductive interventions for the control of inappropriate child behavior. *Journal of Abnormal Child Psychology, 13,* 59-67.

Wolf, M. M. (1978). Social validity: The case of subjective measurement or how applied behavior analysis is findings its heart. *Journal of Applied Behavior Analysis, 11,* 203-214.

Woolfolk, R. C., & Woolfolk, A. E. (1979). Modifying the effect of the behavior modification label. *Behavior Therapy, 10,* 575-578.

Woolfolk, A. E., Woolfolk, R. C., & Wilson, G. T. (1977). A rose by any other name: Labeling bias and attitudes toward behavior modification. *Journal of Consulting and Clinical Psychology, 45,* 184-191.

Yeaton, W. H. (1988). Acceptability of behavioral interventions in educational settings. In J. C. Witt, S. N. Elliott, & F. M. Gresham (Eds.), *Handbook of behavior therapy in education* (pp. 171-188). New York: Plenum.

Yeaton, W. H., & Sechrest, L. (1981). Critical dimensions in the choice and maintenance of successful interventions: Strength, integrity, and effectiveness. *Journal of Consulting and Clinical Psychology, 49,* 156-167.

Ysseldyke, J. E., & Christenson, S. (1987). *The Instructional Environmental Scale.* Austin, TX: PRO-ED.

CHAPTER 11

Sources of Vulnerability to School Violence: Systems-Level Assessment and Strategies to Improve Safety and Climate

Jeffrey Sprague and Hill M. Walker
The University of Oregon Institute on Violence and Destructive Behavior

Susan Sowards, Clair Van Bloem, and Peter Eberhardt
Lane County Council of Governments

Brooke Marshall
Springfield, Oregon, School District

INTRODUCTION

Most schools in the U.S. are relatively safe places for children, youth, and the adults who teach and support them (U.S. Departments of Justice and Education, 1999). In fact, notwithstanding the disturbing reports of violence (e.g., mass school shootings, murder, assault) in our schools during the past decade, the schools are becoming relatively safer in light of a number of key indicators to be presented herein. However, the fears about personal safety of students, teachers, parents, and community members are real and need to be addressed. It also is true that some schools have serious crime and violence problems and many schools are having to deal with more serious problem behaviors (e.g., bullying, harassment, victimization, drug and alcohol abuse, the effects of family disruption, poverty, and so on) (Kingery, 1999). An understanding of the complex, interconnecting relations and factors affecting the safety and climate of schools is necessary for (a) identifying antisocial and violent youth early in their school careers and (b) developing and implementing effective interventions in the contexts of schools, communities, and families.

This chapter addresses the growing problem of antisocial behavior occurring within the context of schooling and describes methods to assess its impact on the dimensions of school safety, effectiveness, and ecology. We outline a model of school, neighborhood, and family assessment based on four sources of vulnerability or risk to school safety and illustrate the potential efficacy of the conceptual model using data from one community. Guidelines and recommendations are presented regarding research-based practices, tools, and approaches in both screening and intervention. An approach for coordinating integrated approaches to school-based prevention of antisocial behavior is also described, and the implications for school safety are discussed.

The Current Topography of Youth Violence and Antisocial Behavior

In this section, we discuss trends in youth violence in general and the impact on school safety and climate.

Youth violence. Nearly all scientific studies of violence in America indicate that violent crime, overall, has remained relatively stable over the past 15 to 20 years despite progressively more severe sentences given by the courts during this period (Furlong, 1994; Roth, 1994). These trends do not hold, however, for violent *juvenile* crime, which until recently had been increasing dramatically in all sectors of our society. Violent crimes among juveniles increased by 41% from 1982 to 1991. During this same period, the number of arrests for murder and aggravated assault committed by juveniles increased by 93% and 72% respectively (Wilson & Howell, 1993), and the juvenile murder rate doubled again from 1992 to 1998 (Office of Juvenile Justice and Delinquency Prevention, 1999).

These statistics suggest continuing high rates of juvenile violence unless they are offset through a coordinated plan of prevention, early intervention, and graduated sanctions (Walker, Irvin, & Sprague, 1997). Small decreases in the overall volume of juvenile violence in the past 2 years appear to confound this trend to some extent (Sickmund, Snyder, & Poe-Yamagata, 1997). These decreases may not signal the beginning of a general downward trend, however, when changes in youth and community demographics are considered. For example, the U.S. Office of Juvenile Justice and Delinquency Prevention (OJJDP) estimates that the U.S. juvenile (all children ages 10-17) population will increase substantially in the next decade and that the number of juvenile arrests for violent crime will show a similar increase.

School safety and violence. Schools often reflect the societal trends outlined earlier, and we are now beginning to see the tragedy of interpersonal violence and conflict played out in the daily lives of students and staff in settings that were once relatively safe. Statistics from recent reports on violence provide striking examples of this development:

1. Over 100,000 students bring weapons to school every day with an average of 32 students killed with these weapons annually on school campuses in the period 1992–2000 (U.S. Departments of Justice and Education, 1999);

2. Large numbers of students fear victimization (e.g., mean-spirited teasing, bullying, and sexual harassment) in school and on the way to and from school where bullies and gang members are likely to prey on them (Kaufman et al., 1999);

3. More than 6,000 teachers are threatened annually and well over 200 are physically injured by students on school grounds;

4. Schools are major sites for recruitment and related activities by organized gangs (Committee for Children, 1997; National School Safety Center, 1996; Office of Juvenile Justice and Delinquency Prevention, 1999; Walker, Colvin, & Ramsey, 1995);

5. A study by the National Institute of Education found that 40% of juvenile robberies and 36% of assaults against urban youth took place in schools (Crowe, 1991); and

6. Half of all students who admit bringing weapons to school say they do so for their own protection.

The problems outlined above compete directly with the instructional mission of schools. The result is decreased academic achievement and lower quality of life for student and staff alike. The *National Educational Goals Panel Report* (U. S. Department of Education, 1998) lists four essential areas in which national school performance has declined:

1. Reading achievement at Grade 12 has decreased (Goal 3);

2. Student drug use has increased (Goal 7);

3. Threats and injuries to public school teachers have increased (Goal 7); and

4. More teachers are reporting that disruptions in their classroom interfere with their teaching (Goal 7).

These outcomes illustrate the clear link between school climate and academic achievement. We cannot achieve national educational goals without addressing these disturbing conditions. In the next section, we address the four sources of vulnerability to school violence. These four sources provide a comprehensive map for intervention planning.

What Is a Safe School? Four Sources of Vulnerability to School Violence

Defining school safety as only or primarily the absence of serious violent behavior (e.g., school shootings) seriously limits its scope and may lead policy makers and other stakeholders to adopt expensive, narrowly focused strategies such as investing in security technology without addressing school climate. If we define our goal too narrowly—preventing school shootings—we may end up with excessive use of law

FIGURE 1

Four Major Sources of Vulnerability to the Safety of Schools

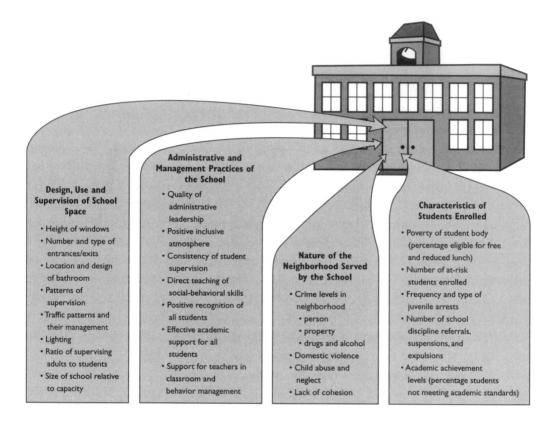

Design, Use and Supervision of School Space

- Height of windows
- Number and type of entrances/exits
- Location and design of bathroom
- Patterns of supervision
- Traffic patterns and their management
- Lighting
- Ratio of supervising adults to students
- Size of school relative to capacity

Administrative and Management Practices of the School

- Quality of administrative leadership
- Positive inclusive atmosphere
- Consistency of student supervision
- Direct teaching of social-behavioral skills
- Positive recognition of all students
- Effective academic support for all students
- Support for teachers in classroom and behavior management

Nature of the Neighborhood Served by the School

- Crime levels in neighborhood
  - person
  - property
  - drugs and alcohol
- Domestic violence
- Child abuse and neglect
- Lack of cohesion

Characteristics of Students Enrolled

- Poverty of student body (percentage eligible for free and reduced lunch)
- Number of at-risk students enrolled
- Frequency and type of juvenile arrests
- Number of school discipline referrals, suspensions, and expulsions
- Academic achievement levels (percentage students not meeting academic standards)

enforcement and/or school security technology (Green, 1999). Although necessary and appropriate, law enforcement and technological approaches need to be balanced with the overall mission of schooling, which is to promote academic excellence, socialization, citizenship, and healthy lives for our children.

Typically, in the search for school safety solutions, the lion's share of educators' attention is focused on individual student backgrounds, characteristics, attitudes, and behaviors. Clearly, students with antisocial and violent behavior patterns pose serious risks to the overall safety and climate of any school. However, the presence of substantial numbers of antisocial students in a school is not the *only* risk to its safety. Four other sources of vulnerability to the safety of school settings are illustrated in Figure 1. These include (a) the physical layout of the school building and the supervision/use of school space, (b) administrative, teaching, and management practices of the school, (c) the characteristics of the surrounding neighborhood(s) served by the school, and (d) characteristics of the students enrolled in the school. These remaining four sources of vulnerability shown in Figure 1, which are often neglected, can be very powerful in accounting for variations in the relative safety of today's schools.

Ensuring the safety and security of students and staff members in today's schools is a daunting task that requires a comprehensive approach. Our society's myriad social problems (e.g., abuse, neglect, fragmentation, rage, interpersonal violence, and so forth) are spilling over into the schooling process at an alarming rate. It is essential that school officials address each of these four sources of vulnerability systematically in order to create safe and effective schools. With proper and thorough assessment, school officials can identify, plan for, and ameliorate the risk factors that move schools in the direction of potential violence and reduced safety.

Physical layout of the school building and grounds. Perhaps the most neglected of the four sources of vulnerability displayed in Figure 1 is the architectural design of the school building and surrounding grounds (Schneider, Walker, & Sprague, 2000). School safety and security were not dominant concerns when most of our school facilities were designed, and consequently school planners did not pay much attention to it. Fortunately, the knowledge and techniques for designing safer schools are available now and must be addressed in existing schools and those to be built (Schneider et al., 2000).

School leaders can make use of time-tested principles of architecture to enhance safety and improve security in the design and retrofitting of schools, and they can employ newer technologies to monitor spaces and the individuals who inhabit them (Green, 1999). These design and monitoring techniques represent cost-effective approaches to making school buildings and grounds safer and violence-free. The goals of these approaches are to prevent interpersonal conflict; to reduce the opportunities for vandalism, violence, and victimization of others; and to facilitate the smooth operation of the school building.

This knowledge of architecture and ecology has been organized and formulated into a set of principles known as Crime Prevention Through Environmental Design (CPTED). CPTED helps us to understand how the physical environment affects human behavior. Thus, it can be used to improve the management and use of physical spaces in both school and nonschool settings. It has been used extensively in the prevention and deterrence of criminal behavior in a range of community settings. CPTED also has been applied with considerable effectiveness in making school sites safer and more secure in recent years. CPTED procedures require a thorough assessment of the school building and grounds, followed by changes in architectural features, supervision, etc.

CPTED assessment procedures are relatively straightforward (See Crowe, 1991; Schneider et al., 2000). Every school can benefit from an assessment of its environment to determine whether the school is a safe and secure place to learn and work. A school site riddled with criminal activity has an obvious need for such an assessment, but even campuses that seem at first glance to be orderly and secure may, when inspected, be found to present a multitude of risks. The assessment should begin with tools such as the National School Safety Center's School Crime Assessment Tool (Stephens, 1995) or the Oregon School Safety Survey (Sprague, Colvin, & Irvin, 1995). These tools allow stakeholders to give input on particular areas of concern to them. Following this initial assessment, it is typical to employ a CPTED expert (local law enforcement or security personnel) of the school site to do a walk-through and provide an intensive site assessment.

In the wake of recent, highly publicized school shootings, some public officials and parents have pushed for high-security architectural designs using metal detectors, locked gates, video surveillance cameras, etc. Others insist that a well-designed school should look like a place to learn—not a locked-down fortress. Prudent application of CPTED principles can satisfy *both* perspectives. Architectural features that allow school staff members natural surveillance can provide controlled access to the school and reduce violence risk while enhancing, rather than detracting from, the learning environment.

Weaknesses in the overall architectural design of a school can be difficult or expensive to overcome in older buildings. Reasonable security arrangements can reduce, but not eliminate, the risk of an armed intruder or other violent incidents (Schneider et al., 2000). These include:

1. **Closed campuses.** Closing high school campuses during school hours simplifies surveillance demands and helps prevent entry by unauthorized persons.

2. **Security cameras.** Strategically placed cameras can be a deterrent by themselves and may assist in identifying intruders.

3. **Staff and visitor identification badges.** Visitors, staff, and substitutes should be asked to check in at the office and wear identifying badges.

4. **Volunteer supervisors.** Volunteers can assist with building supervision before school and during lunch, patrolling and talking to students.

5. **Campus supervisors.** Teachers or school resource officers can be assigned each period throughout the day to walk around and monitor activity on campus.

6. **Two-way communication.** Duty teachers, monitors, and administrators can carry two-way radios to facilitate efficient communication.

7. **Child study teams.** Building administrators, school psychologists, counselors, and others can meet regularly to review any student who has generated concerns by any staff member or parent. Problem solving takes place, and action plans are developed ranging from continued monitoring to intervention.

8. **Safety committees.** A safety committee can meet monthly to review any safety concerns on campus. The committee is composed of classified staff, certified employees, and administration.

9. **Lockdown procedures.** Building emergency procedures are reviewed with staff each fall and are contained in the staff handbook.

10. ***Confidential reporting systems.*** The school can use an answering-machine system that allows individuals to leave messages for anyone during nonschool hours. The machine tape is reviewed each morning at 7:30 with messages distributed as necessary.

11. ***School resource officers.*** Schools increasingly use either sworn officers or community safety personnel to supervise students, provide training, and intervene in conflict or illegal activity.

The administrative, teaching and management practices of the school. Many school practices contribute to the development of antisocial behavior and potential for violence. Because of the overemphasis on individual child characteristics, these important variables are often overlooked. These include, among others:

1. Ineffective instruction that results in academic failure;

2. Inconsistent and punitive classroom and behavior management practices;

3. Lack of opportunity to learn and practice prosocial interpersonal and self-management skills;

4. Unclear rules and expectations regarding appropriate behavior;

5. Failure to correct rule violations and reward adherence to them;

6. Failure to individualize instruction to adapt to individual differences; and (perhaps most important)

7. Failure to assist students from at-risk backgrounds to bond with the schooling process.

For more detail on these factors see Colvin, Kame'enui, and Sugai (1993); Hawkins, Catalano, Kosterman, Abbott, and Hill (1999); Mayer (1995); Walker and Eaton-Walker (2000), and Walker et al. (1996).

These factors are *all* amenable to change in a positive, proactive manner. Schools can serve as an ideal setting to organize efforts against the increasing problems of children and youth who display antisocial behavior (Mayer, 1995; Sugai & Horner, 1994; Walker et al., 1996). Unfortunately, school personnel have a long history of focusing solutions elsewhere or applying simple and unproven solutions to complex behavior problems (e.g., office discipline referrals, suspensions). They express understandable disappointment when these attempts do not work as expected (See Walker et al., 1996). This practice is sustained by a tendency to try to eliminate the presenting problem quickly (i.e., remove the student via suspension or expulsion) rather than focus on the administrative, teaching, and management practices that either contribute to or reduce them (Tobin, Sugai, & Martin, 2000).

A solid research base exists to guide a careful analysis of the administrative, teaching, and management practices in a school and construct alternatives to ineffective approaches. Interventions must be implemented that target whole school and individual approaches. Educators in today's schools and classrooms must be supported to adopt and sustain effective, cost-efficient practices (Gottfredson, 1997; Walker et al., 1996). Effective approaches to proactive school-wide discipline and management, for example, include (a) systematic social skills instruction; (b) academic/curricular restructuring; (c) positive, behaviorally based interventions; (d) early screening and identification of antisocial behavior patterns; and (e) preventive school-wide discipline systems (Biglan, 1995; Lipsey, 1991; Mayer, 1995; Sprague, Sugai, & Walker, 1998; Sugai & Horner, 1994; Tolan & Guerra, 1994; Walker et al., 1995; Walker et al., 1996). More specific details on many of theses practices are contained in other chapters in this volume.

We recommend that intervention selection be based upon a thorough assessment of school functioning (Sugai, Lewis-Palmer, Todd, & Horner, 2000), with special attention to disciplinary referral patterns (Sugai, Sprague, Horner, & Walker, 2000), the quality and consistency of academic instruction, and so on. Thorough needs assessments can guide planning, avoid overlapping or conflicting services, and serve as the basis for evaluation of change. Accomplishing change(s) of this magnitude in schools requires an appropriate and sustained investment in staff development (Hawkins et al., 1999; Sprague et al., in press). In our work, we provide training and support to representative teams of teachers in schools over a 2- to 3-year period, providing training and technical assistance to install each of the above components. These school teams work to complete initial and ongoing needs assessment, choose interventions (e.g., school rules, social skills curriculum), and use student- and staff-level data to refine and evaluate their efforts (see Todd, Horner, Vanater, & Schneider, 2000; Sprague et al., in press for a description of this work).

The characteristics of the surrounding neighborhood. The contexts in which school-influencing risk factors are found include the family, neighborhood, community, and, finally, the larger society (Hawkins & Catalano, 1992). Across these contexts, contributing risk factors include poverty, dysfunctional and chaotic family life, drug and alcohol abuse by primary caregivers, domestic abuse, neglect, emotional, physical and sexual abuse, negative attitudes toward schooling, the modeling of physical intimidation and aggression, media violence, the growing incivility of our society, and so on. These risk factors provide a fertile breeding ground for the development of antisocial and coercive behavioral styles among the children who are pervasively exposed to them.

Assessment of neighborhood and family characteristics can be accomplished in large measure by using archival data collected, often routinely, by law enforcement, child protective services, juvenile authorities, and health departments. While many of these variables are not directly impacted by schools, knowledge of their presence can influence the choice of interventions at school, allocation of resources to include families and community members in interventions, etc. We will illustrate the constructive use of these information sources in the context of this paper.

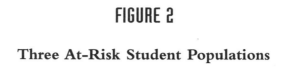

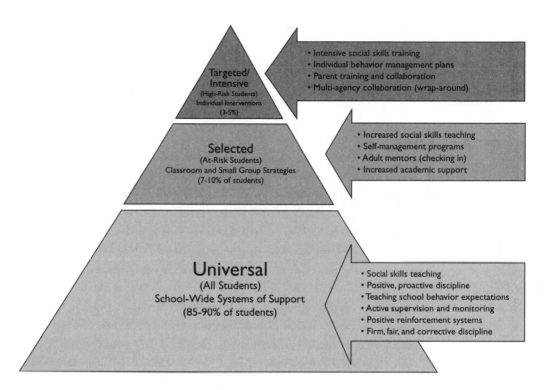

The characteristics of the students in the school. Our schools are made increasingly unsafe by the attitudes, beliefs, and dangerous behavior patterns of the increasing numbers of antisocial children and youth who attend them. These characteristics are stimulated by the risk factors listed earlier regarding family, community, and society. The task of schools, families, and communities is to increase the child's resilience, teach skills for success, and develop positive alternatives to replace the maladaptive forms of behavior the child has learned to achieve his or her social goals.

In any school, we would expect to find three relatively distinct populations of students: (a) typically developing students, (b) those *at-risk* for behavioral and academic problems, and (c) *high-risk* students who *already* manifest serious behavioral and academic difficulties (Sprague & Walker, 2000). Differing but complimentary approaches are necessary to address the needs of these three student groups in any school. A characteristic distribution of students of each type (see Figure 2) indicates the level of intervention each needs and their prevalence in the school. Identifying the characteristics of students in the school includes identifying rates of juvenile arrests or contacts with law enforcement, the frequency and severity of discipline referrals in school, proportion of students in poverty, academic achievement levels, and so forth.

PRACTICAL APPLICATION

In the remainder of this chapter we illustrate the use of three of four components of this conceptual model by using data from 15 middle schools located in a suburban community in the Pacific Northwest. We provide a description of family, neighborhood, and student characteristics, along with selected correlations between these variables. Intervention implications of this systems-level analysis are presented.

Measures

We gathered archival data from various sources as described later in this chapter. In addition, building principals from these schools provided data on one self-report assessment of school functioning related to school discipline (Sugai, Lewis-Palmer, Todd, & Horner, 2000). Each of the measures, except the principal self-report, used in this analysis was obtained from archival database records maintained by law enforcement, child protective services, juvenile justice, and local school districts. These measures included (a) the percentage of eighth-graders not meeting state academic standards for reading, math, and language; (b) percentage of students at each participating school who were eligible for free and reduced lunches; (c) family mobility, expressed as the percentage of students moving in or out of the school; (d) documented domestic violence cases occurring by zip code area (rate per 1,000 population); (e) child abuse cases by zip code (rate per 1,000 population); (f) antisocial behavior (person and property crimes) in the neighborhood measured as rate per 1,000 youth ages 10–17; and (g) alcohol- and drug-related crimes in the neighborhood measured as rate per 1,000 youth ages 10–17.

Building principals at each school were asked to complete a one-page self-report on the status of the discipline systems in their school. The survey was based on criteria developed by the Effective Behavioral Support (EBS) projects at the University of Oregon (Sugai & Horner, 1994; Sprague et al., 1998) and included items related to school-wide discipline practices, discipline data collection and analysis, school-wide rules and teaching procedures, classroom management, and individual student supports. A copy is available from the first author. Principals rated each of the listed items as "in place," "working on it," or "to do." We derived a summary score based on the relative distribution of these responses, assigning a 3, 2, or 1 score, respectively.

FINDINGS

We present herein a summary of the archival and self-report data collected on these middle schools and discuss our findings relative to the four sources of vulnerability to school safety. Table 1 provides a summary of each archival variable score, the total scores, and rank ordering of participating schools based on these total scores.

TABLE 1

Summary of Archival Data by Middle School Attendance Area

School	1998 Percentage Eligible Free and Reduced	Average Percentage Not Meeting Academic Standard	1999 Mobility	Family Violence	Child Abuse	Alcohol and Drug Crimes	ASB Rate/1000	EBS Score	Total
1	61.95	45	24.07	3.54	3.25	31.00	213.9	12	382.70
2	52.72	49	28.33	3.54	3.25	21.60	139.0	9	297.44
3	51.99	52	25.02	1.02	3.30	12.90	73.8	21	220.02
4	28.84	45	18.89	2.77	2.19	15.50	88.4	13	201.59
5	31.32	25	12.50	1.11	1.20	24.20	84.9	Missing	180.52
6	50.13	53	28.44	3.54	3.25	1.30	16.1	24	156.05
7	38.42	38	17.61	2.84	1.70	9.30	45.7	14	153.06
8	17.48	45	11.08	2.84	1.70	11.10	69.3	5	158.80
9	18.68	13	9.96	2.08	1.39	30.60	71.7	15	147.41
10	12.82	22	14.58	1.20	1.20	24.30	59.4	20	134.99
11	30.58	33	13.62	1.02	3.30	12.30	41.7	19	135.82
12	15.42	42	10.63	2.77	3.25	10.60	41.6	17	126.27
13	25.54	23	12.79	1.11	3.30	14.80	59.9	Missing	140.24
14	16.07	24	10.49	2.08	1.39	17.40	28.8	18	100.53
15	17.55	25	10.30	1.84	1.20	7.90	23.9	16	87.99

Note

ASB: Antisocal behavior.

Features of the School Buildings and Grounds

We did not conduct an analysis of the physical layout of the building and grounds. At the time of the preparation of this chapter, approximately one-third of the school buildings had conducted such an analysis and had received a summary report and recommendations. These reports identified vulnerable spaces in the buildings and recommended changes in the physical layout, changes in supervision practices, and addition of technology such as surveillance cameras. We were not able to track any environmental changes resulting from this assessment. All of the remaining middle schools in the community were scheduled to undergo a CPTED assessment.

Administrative, Academic, and Behavior Management Practices

EBS survey. Thirteen of the 15 participating schools returned the EBS self-report measure. The mean score on this rating (out of a possible 30 points) was 15 (range

5–24, SD = 5.6). To the extent that this survey accurately reflects the status of discipline systems in each school, most indicated the need for substantial improvement in their behavior management practices.

Academic achievement scores. The average percentage of eighth-graders not meeting basic state academic standards in reading, math, and language was 36% (range 13–53, SD = 12.8). This mean score was within the range of the state average for this measure.

Community and Neighborhood Assessment

Domestic and child abuse. The mean rate per thousand of documented domestic abuse was 2.22 (range 1.02–3.54, SD = .97). Mean rate per thousand of documented child abuse cases was 2.32 (range 1.20–3.30, SD = 0.95).

Mobility. Percentage of moving in and out of the school during the year averaged 16.6 percent (range 10–28.5, SD = 6.8)

Characteristics of Students Enrolled

Antisocial behavior and alcohol and drug crimes. Regarding antisocial behavior (i.e., person, property, and other crimes not including alcohol and drugs), the mean rate per thousand was 70.5 (range 16.1–213.9, SD = 50.1). Alcohol and drug crimes rate per thousand averaged 16.3 (range, 1.3–31, SD = 8.5).

"Risk Composite" Scores and Correlations

Risk scores. Each of these indices was summed, excluding the EBS score, to obtain a total "risk composite" score for each school. We then rank-ordered the schools based on this score. Risk scores for the participating schools averaged 187.31 with a range of 87.99–382.7 (SD = 75.01) (see Table 1, on page 305). Some schools clearly were more at risk for school violence.

Relationships between the risk factors. Selected correlation scores of the risk variables are presented in Table 2. Our hypothesis was that the pattern of risk factors would vary between schools, and that poverty, indicated by the proportion of students eligible for free and reduced lunch, would be highly correlated with other risk factors. It is apparent that for the highest-ranked schools, the risk factors tended to cluster together. Not surprisingly, the highest correlation scores were between free and reduced lunch (poverty indicator) by mobility and total score (.90 and .81, respectively). Poverty also was strongly correlated with academic risk (.67) and moderately correlated with antisocial behavior rates (.59). Academic risk and mobility also were highly correlated (.76), as were alcohol, drug, and antisocial behavior crimes (.69). EBS scores (principal self-report regarding school discipline systems) resulted in low or negative correlations with the risk indicators (EBS rating by overall was -.38).

TABLE 2

Selected Correlations of Risk Variables

Free and reduced by mobility	0.90
Free and reduced by total score	0.81
Academics by mobility	0.76
Alcohol and drugs by ASB	0.69
Free and reduced by academics	0.67
Academics by child abuse	0.63
Free and reduced by child abuse	0.61
Free and reduced by ASB rate	0.59
Academics by family violence	0.58
Academics by total	0.52
Free and reduced by family violence	0.41
Child abuse by ASB	0.28
Academics by ASB	0.27
Family violence by child abuse	0.23
Free and reduced by alcohol and drug crimes	0.06
Free and reduced by EBS Score	0.02
Academics by EBS	-0.12
Child abuse by A and D	-0.22
EBS by Overall	-0.38
Academics by A and D	-0.42

DISCUSSION

We presented an analysis of archival risk factor data, and one protective factor indicator to illustrate the relationship among three of the four sources of vulnerability to school safety. We found that schools with high-risk indicators in one area tended to be at high risk in all areas, and vice versa. The single protective factor indicator—that is, the self report from school principals—was not correlated with school risk status. In addition, the present analysis, as noted, did not provide a measure of CPTED issues in the schools.

The obtained correlations were consistent with our hypotheses regarding poverty and low income as a generalized indicator of risk. Of the 20 scores presented, free and reduced lunch status accounted for 5 of the top 10. These findings are consistent with other literature on school safety and youth violence that shows a strong relationship between low income and delinquency (Loeber, Green, Lahey, Frick, & McBurnett, 2000). This is not to say that poverty "causes" violence or delinquency, but rather the stresses caused by lack of income, unemployment, etc., set the stage for poor parenting, drug and alcohol use by caregivers, etc. (Patterson, Reid, & Dishion, 1992).

Of interest is the apparent weak relationship between the principal self-ranking of school discipline practices and the overall risk score. We might expect that lower risk schools might also indicate better administrative and management practices owing to decreased risk and stress presented by families and students. The present findings would not support this hypothesis and call us to study further the complex relationship between contextual "risk" and the administrative and management practices of the school. It is likely that we will find low-risk schools that operate inefficiently or that actually create conditions that promote antisocial behavior, and high-risk schools that operate very smoothly, with less than expected prevalence of problem behaviors. For example, a low-risk school that is unorganized and provides limited student supervision during lunch and recess may have high rates of bullying and harassment. Alternatively, a high-risk school that has high staff cohesion, clear behavioral expectations, and a well-run academic program may have lower than expected rates of the same behaviors.

Using the Archival Information

These findings provide a preliminary model and demonstration of the use of archival data to assess violence and other potential risks to safety in schools. Using these findings, school and community leaders would be able to reliably identify the highest-risk schools. Once this ranking has been accomplished, more detailed analysis of specific schools needs should be conducted. In addition, these rankings could be used to set priorities for resource allocation strategies regarding violence prevention and other interventions to enhance school safety. Clearly, the top-ranked middle schools in this sample showed high-risk status in all domain areas and would require additional resources to address the needs of at-risk students in their schools compared to the needs of those in lower-risk schools. These resources would be used to change discipline practices, provide additional academic support, and so on. We believe that this type of analysis would facilitate better targeting of resources compared to allocation models based on typically used, simple cost per child formulae.

We only gathered one protective factor measure, the EBS survey self-report by participating principals. This measure was poorly correlated with measures and data we collected on the risk factors we obtained. This poor correlation would be expected given that it is a measure of positive attributes of the school building while all other measures focused on negative outcomes. What is important to note here is that we have a relatively poor understanding of the true relationship between administrative and management practices of the school and their impact on risk indicators for students in the school (Hawkins et al. 1999). Much research is needed to assess the impact of multi-component, multi-environment interventions on a school's risk status and overall effectiveness (Greenberg, Domitrovich, & Bumbarger, 1999). We are at the beginning of an era, hopefully, in which solid answers to these complex questions can be developed.

CONCLUSION

The available literature on school safety clearly documents the role of each of the four sources of vulnerability in making schools less safe (U.S. Departments of Justice and Education, 1998, 1999; Hawkins et al., 1999; Stephens, 1995). Our analysis sheds light on the relationship among the four sources and indicates that schools with high levels of one risk factor generally will be high in others. We now discuss an approach to prevent school violence that has the potential to positively impact two of these sources: (a) the administrative and management practices of the school; and (b) the characteristics of the students enrolled in the school.

The U.S. Public Health Service (PHS) has developed a classification system of prevention approaches that provides for the coordinated integration of differing intervention types necessary to address the divergent needs of these three student types, present in different proportions in each of the middle schools. The three prevention approaches contained in the U.S. PHS classification system are primary, secondary, and tertiary. Primary prevention refers to the use of approaches that prevent problems from emerging; secondary prevention addresses the problems that are not yet of a chronic nature or severe magnitude; and tertiary prevention uses the most powerful intervention approaches available to address the problems of severely at-risk individuals. Walker and his colleagues have outlined an integrated prevention model, based upon this classification system, for addressing the problem of school-based antisocial behavior patterns (Walker et al., 1996).

Universal interventions, applied to everyone in the same manner and degree, are used to achieve primary prevention goals; that is, to keep problems from emerging. We would expect these interventions to benefit both high- and low-risk schools. Some good examples of such interventions are (a) developing a school-wide discipline plan, (b) the school-wide teaching of conflict resolution and violence prevention skills, (c) establishing high and consistent academic expectations for all students, and (d) using the most effective, research-based methods for teaching beginning reading at the point of school entry and in the primary grades. Many of the chapters in this book provide detailed descriptions of how these important interventions can be implemented to improve school climate.

Individualized interventions applied to one case at a time or to small groups of at-risk individuals (e.g., alternative classrooms or "schools within schools") are used to achieve secondary and tertiary prevention goals. Typically, these interventions are more labor-intensive, complex, often intrusive, costly, but can be very powerful if properly implemented. They are necessary to address the more severe problems of chronically at-risk students who "select" themselves out by not responding to primary prevention approaches and are in need of much more intensive intervention services and supports. Often, the implementation of these interventions is preceded by a functional behavioral assessment (O'Neill et al., 1997) to identify the conditions (e.g., antecedents and consequences) that sustain and motivate the problem behavior. We also recommend a comprehensive assessment of family, school, and individual *risk* (e.g., Achenbach, 1991;

Walker & McConnell, 1995; Walker & Severson, 1990) and *protective* factors (Epstein & Sharma, 1998) to guide broader ecological interventions.

This integrated model, although it has rarely been implemented fully in the context of schooling, provides an ideal means for schools to develop, implement, and monitor a comprehensive management system that addresses the needs of *all* students in the school. It is also a fair system in that typically developing students are not penalized by being denied access to potentially beneficial interventions. In addition, it has the potential to positively impact the operations, administration, and overall climate of the school. This model, through its emphasis on the use of primary prevention goals achieved through universal interventions, maximizes the efficient use of school resources and provides a supportive context for the application of necessary secondary and tertiary interventions for the more severely involved students. Finally, it provides a built-in screening and assessment process; that is, through careful monitoring of students' responses to the primary prevention interventions, it is possible to detect those who are at greater risk and in need of more intensive services and support.

Emerging public concerns regarding the safety of students in schools and communities, coupled with recent school shootings and media coverage of youth violence in general, are generating enormous pressures on educators and community leaders to take ownership of the problems presented by antisocial, delinquent, and violent youth. The production of recent public documents by the U.S. Justice and Education departments reflects the government's response to this growing public concern (Dwyer & Osher, 2000; Dwyer, Osher, & Warger, 1998; U.S. Departments of Justice and Education, 1998, 1999).

Over the next several years, an enormous amount of federal and state resources will be invested in school safety and violence prevention. It is extremely important that these precious resources be used to promote the *adoption of best professional practices* and that proven, evidence-based interventions are implemented in addressing them. These developments also create significant opportunities for school professionals (counselors, general educators, school psychologists, special educators, social workers, and so on) to collaborate more effectively and to forge new working relationships with families and community agencies. If we can implement with integrity that which we currently know regarding these problems, a major positive impact can be achieved. The stakes are high for our society and school systems. Yet the potential gains are well worth the investment and effort.

REFERENCES

Achenbach, T. (1991). *The Child Behavior Checklist: Manual for the teacher's report form.* Burlington, VT: Department of Psychiatry, University of Vermont.

Biglan, A. (1995). Translating what we know about the context of antisocial behavior into a lower prevalence of such behavior. *Journal of Applied Behavior Analysis, 28,* 479-492.

Colvin, G., Kame'enui, E. J., & Sugai, G. (1993). School-wide and classroom management: Reconceptualizing the integration and management of students with behavior problems in general education. *Education and Treatment of Children, 16,* 361-381.

Committee for Children. (1997). *Second step: Violence prevention curriculum.* Seattle, WA: Author.

Crowe, T. (1991). *Habitual offenders: Guidelines for citizen action and public responses.* Washington, DC: Office of Juvenile Justice and Delinquency Prevention, U. S. Department of Justice.

Dwyer, K., & Osher, D. (2000). *Safeguarding our children: An Action Guide.* Washington, DC: U.S. Departments of Education and Justice, American Institute for Research.

Dwyer, K., Osher, D., & Warger, C. (1998). *Early warning, timely response: A guide to safe schools.* Washington, DC: U.S. Department of Education.

Epstein, M. H., & Sharma, J. (1998). *Behavioral and emotional rating scale.* Austin, TX: PRO-ED.

Furlong, M. J. (1994). Evaluating school violence trends. *National School Safety Center News Journal, 3,* 23-27.

Gottfredson, D. C. (1997). School-based crime prevention. In L. Sherman, D. Gottfredson, D. Mackenzie, J. Eck, P. Reuter, & S. Bushway (Eds.), *Preventing crime: What works, what doesn't, what's promising.* College Park, MD: Department of Criminology and Criminal Justice.

Green, M. (1999). *The appropriate and effective use of security technologies in U.S. schools: A guide for schools and law enforcement agencies* (Sandia National Laboratories, National Institute of Justice Research Report). Washington, DC: U.S. Department of Justice.

Greenberg, M. T., Domitrovich, C., & Bumbarger, B. (1999) *Preventing mental disorders in school-age children: A review of the effectiveness of prevention programs* (Report submitted to Center for Mental Health Services, Substance Abuse Mental Health Services Administration). Washington, DC: U.S. Department of Health and Human Services.

Hawkins, J. D., & Catalano, R. F. (1992). *Communities that care.* San Francisco, CA: Jossey-Bass.

Hawkins, J. D., Catalano, R. F., Kosterman, R., Abbott, R., & Hill, K. G. (1999). Preventing adolescent health-risk behaviors by strengthening protection during childhood. *Archives of Pediatrics and Adolescent Medicine, 153,* 226-234.

Kaufman, P., Chen, X., Choy, S. P., Ruddy, S. A., Miller, A. K., Chandler, K. A., Chapman, C. D., Rand, M. R., & Klaus, P. (1999). *Indicator of school crime and safety* (NCES 1999-057/MCJ-178906). Washington, DC: U.S. Departments of Education and Justice.

Kingery, P. (1999). Suspensions and expulsions: New Directions. In The Hamilton-Fish National Institute on School and Community Violence, *Effective violence prevention programs.* Washington, DC: George Washington University.

Lipsey, M. W. (1991). The effect of treatment on juvenile delinquents: Results from meta-analysis. In F. Losel, D. Bender, & T. Bliesener (Eds.), *Psychology and law.* New York: Walter de Gruyter.

Loeber, R., Green, S. M., Lahey, B. B., Frick, P. J., & McBurnett, K. (2000). Findings on disruptive behavior disorders from the first decade of the developmental trends study. *Clinical Child and Family Psychology Review, 3,* 37-59.

Mayer, G. R. (1995). Preventing antisocial behavior in the schools. *Journal of Applied Behavior Analysis, 28*(4), 467-478.

National School Safety Center. (1996). *National School Safety Center Newsletter, March.* Malibu, CA: National School Safety Center.

O'Neill, R. E., Horner, R. H., Albin, R. W., Sprague, J. R., Newton, S., & Storey, K. (1997). *Functional assessment and program development for problem behavior: A practical handbook* (2nd ed.). Pacific Grove, CA: Brookes/Cole.

Office of Juvenile Justice and Delinquency Prevention. (1999). *Guide for implementing a comprehensive strategy for serious, violent and chronic juvenile offenders.* Washington, DC: Author.

Patterson, G. R., Reid, J. B., & Dishion, T. J. (1992). *Antisocial boys.* Eugene, OR: Castalia.

Roth, J. A. (1994). *Understanding and preventing violence: National Institute of Justice Research in Brief.* Washington, DC: U. S. Department of Justice, Office of Justice Programs, National Institute of Justice.

Schneider, T., Walker, H. M., & Sprague, J. R. (2000). *Safe school design: A handbook for educational leaders.* Eugene, OR: ERIC Clearinghouse on Educational Management, College of Education, University of Oregon.

Sickmund, M., Snyder, H. N., & Poe-Yamagata, E. (1997). *Juvenile offenders and victims: 1997 update on violence.* Washington, DC: Office of Juvenile Justice and Delinquency Prevention.

Sprague, J., Colvin, G., & Irvin, L. (1995). *The Oregon school safety survey.* Eugene: University of Oregon.

Sprague, J. R., Sugai, G., & Walker, H. (1998). Antisocial behavior in schools. In T. S. Watson & F. M. Gresham (Eds.), *Handbook of child behavior therapy* (pp. 451-474). New York: Plenum.

Sprague, J., & Walker, H. (2000). Early identification and intervention for youth with antisocial and violent behavior. *Exceptional Children, 66*(3), 367-379.

Sprague, J., Walker, H., Golly, A., White, K., Myers, D. R., & Shannon, T. (in press). Translating research into effective practice: The effects of a universal staff and student intervention on key indicators of school safety and discipline. *Education and Treatment of Children, 23.*

Stephens, R. D. (1995). *Safe schools: A handbook for violence prevention.* Bloomington, IN: National Education Service.

Sugai, G., & Horner, R. (1994). Including students with severe behavior problems in general education settings: Assumptions, challenges, and solutions. *Oregon Conference Monograph, 6,* 102-120.

Sugai, G., Lewis-Palmer, T., Todd, A., & Horner, R. (2000). *Effective Behavior Support (EBS) survey: Assessing and planning behavior support in schools.* Eugene: University of Oregon.

Sugai, G., Sprague, J. R., Horner, R. H., & Walker, H. M. (2000). Preventing school violence: The use of office discipline referrals to assess and monitor school-wide discipline interventions. *Journal of Emotional and Behavioral Disorders, 8*(2), 94-101.

Tobin, T., Sugai, G., & Martin, E. (2000). *Final report for Project CREDENTIALS: Current research on educational endeavors to increase at-risk learners' success* (Report submitted to the Office of Professional Technical Education, Oregon Department of Education). Eugene: University of Oregon, College of Education, Behavioral Research and Teaching.

Todd, A. W., Horner, R. H., Vanater, S. M., & Schneider, C. F. (2000). Working together to make change: An example of positive behavioral support for a student with traumatic brain injury. *Education and Treatment of Children, 20*(4), 425-440.

Tolan, P., & Guerra, N. (1994). *What works in reducing adolescent violence: An empirical review of the field.* Boulder, CO: Center for the Study and Prevention of Violence, University of Colorado.

U.S. Department of Education. (1998). *National Educational Goals Panel Report.* Washington, DC: Author.

U.S. Departments of Justice and Education. (1998). *First Annual Report on School Safety.* Washington, DC: Author.

U.S. Departments of Justice and Education. (1999). *Annual Report on School Safety.* Washington, DC: Author.

Walker, H. M., Colvin, G., & Ramsey, E. (1995). *Antisocial behavior in school: Strategies and best practices.* Pacific Grove, CA: Brooks/Cole.

Walker, H. M., & Eaton-Walker, J. (2000). Key questions about school safety: Critical issues and recommended solutions. *NASSP Bulletin (National Association of Secondary School Principals), March,* 46-55.

Walker, H. M., Horner, R. H., Sugai, G., Bullis, M., Sprague, J. R., Bricker, D., & Kaufman, M. J. (1996). Integrated approaches to preventing antisocial behavior patterns among school-age children and youth. *Journal of Emotional and Behavioral Disorders, 4*(4), 194-209.

Walker, H. M., Irvin, L. K., & Sprague, J. R. (1997). Violence prevention and school safety: Issues, problems, approaches, and recommended solutions. *OSSC Bulletin (Oregon School Study Council), 41*(1).

Walker, H. M., & McConnell, S. R. (1995). *The Walker-McConnell scale of social competence and school adjustment (SSCSA)*. Florence, KY: Thomson Learning.

Walker, H. M., & Severson, H. H. (1990). *Systematic screening for behavior disorders.* Longmont, CO: Sopris West.

Wilson, J., & Howell, J. (1993). *A comprehensive strategy for serious, violent, and chronic juvenile offenders.* Washington, DC: Office of Juvenile Justice and Delinquency Prevention, U. S. Department of Justice.

AUTHORS' NOTES

The development of this chapter was supported in part by grants awarded by the U.S. Office of Juvenile Justice and Delinquency Prevention, Grants No. 97-JN-FX-0022 and 97-MU-FX-K012, and the U.S. Department of Education, Safe Schools/Healthy Students, CFDA 84.184, Lane Council of Governments subcontract. Opinions expressed herein do not necessarily reflect the position of the U.S. Department of Education, and such endorsements should not be inferred.

CHAPTER 12

Behaviorally Effective School Environments

George Sugai and Robert H. Horner
University of Oregon

Frank M. Gresham
University of California, Riverside

INTRODUCTION

Calls to improve the quality of school discipline and safety have increased dramatically in response to recent school shootings, rising problem behaviors in schools, and a lack of school preparedness. Over the past 20 years, discipline, related factors (e.g., fighting, violence, vandalism, truancy, lack of discipline, drug use) have been among the top concerns of the general public and teachers (Elam, Rose, & Gallup, 1996a, 1996b). In addition, since 1975 efforts to improve educational services and opportunities for students with emotional and behavioral disorders have increased in general education settings (P. L. 94-142, Individuals with Disabilities Education Act Amendments of 1997 [IDEA 1997]; U.S. Department of Education, 1994).

The escalating concerns about students who display antisocial behavior are not new and, in fact, have been discussed regularly ever since our public school system was established. Although different in form, the immediate response then, as now, has been to tighten structural controls (e.g., lockdowns, security guards, metal detectors), exclude students with serious troubling behavior (e.g., expulsion, alternative placements), and increase punishments (e.g., corporal punishment, restrictions, in-school detention) (Elliot, Hamburg & Williams, 1998; Loeber & Farrington, 1998).

As problem behaviors escalate there is greater police presence on school campuses, installation of metal detectors, greater use of random drug tests and searches, and adoption of school uniforms. All of these responses have emotional appeal and political support, but have *not* been shown to be effective in improving discipline or safety in our schools (Elliot et al., 1998; Loeber & Farrington, 1998). Faced with a lack of viable alternatives, existing systems have answered the challenges presented by students with problem behavior by excluding them from school and by increasing the use of punishment-based strategies (Mayer, 1995; Mayer & Sulzer-Azaroff, 1990). Unfortunately, punishment-based interventions have been shown to be one of the three *least effective* responses (in addition to psychotherapy and counseling) that institutions can make to violent problem behavior (Gottfredson, 1997; Lipsey, 1991, 1992; Lipsey & Wilson, 1993; Tolan & Guerra, 1994). In fact, if punishing problem behavior is used without a system of positive behavior support, increases in aggression, vandalism, truancy, tardiness, and dropping out (Guess, Helmstetter, Turnbull, & Knowlton, 1987; Mayer, 1995; Mayer & Sulzer-Azaroff, 1990), in addition to increases in mental health problems (McCord, 1995), tend to be observed. When reactive management is overemphasized, and prevention is underemphasized, students with problem behaviors are the most likely to (a) be excluded from school (Reichle, 1990), (b) drop out (U.S. Department of Education, 1994), (c) prompt teacher requests for assistance (Horner, Diemer, & Brazeau, 1992; Sprague & Rian, 1993), and (d) become involved in antisocial lifestyles (American Psychological Association, 1993; Walker, Colvin, & Ramsey, 1995).

In a review of schooling practices related to making schools safer and less violent, Morrison, Furlong, and Morrison (1997) cite six factors that affect the academic and social development of students:

1. *Academic failure* is a strong predictor of later psychological disturbance, delinquency, substance abuse, and dropping out of school.

2. *Lack of attachment,* commitment, and bonding to school is associated with school failure.

3. *Negative expectations* for students by staff.

4. *Peer rejection,* or association with a negative peer culture, are high risk factors for school failure.

5. *Negative school climate,* teacher apathy, authoritarian leadership style, and lack of teacher student participation are not associated with effective schools.

6. *High student density* due to limited space, low capacity to avoid confrontations, and poor building design may promote violent behavior.

Fortunately, yet ironically, as incidence and prevalence rates of problem behavior have increased, so has the effectiveness of behaviorally based interventions to address deviant and destructive behavior (Carr et al., 1999). We are more effective today at responding to behavioral problems than ever before (Biglan, 1995; Larson, 1994; Mayer, 1995; Peacock Hill Working Group, 1991; Sugai & Horner, 1994, 1996; Sugai & Tindal, 1993; Walker et al., 1995; Wolery, Bailey, & Sugai, 1988). For example, we know that social skills instruction, instructional and curricular adaptations, and behaviorally based interventions are among the *most effective* interventions for reducing problem behaviors and educating students with severe problem behavior (Gottfredson, 1997; Lipsey, 1991,

FIGURE 1

Summary of Scientific Conclusions From Gottfredson (1997) of What Works, Does Not Work, and Is Promising in School–Based Prevention Programs

	To Prevent Crime and Delinquency	To Prevent Substance Use
What works?	• Programs aimed at building school capacity to initiate and sustain innovation. • Programs aimed at clarifying and communicating norms about behaviors: by establishing school rules, improving the consistency of their enforcement (particularly when they emphasize positive reinforcement of appropriate behavior), or communicating norms through school-wide campaigns (e.g., anti-bullying campaigns) or ceremonies. • Comprehensive instructional programs that focus on a range of social competency skills (e.g., developing self-control, stress-management, responsible decision making, social problem solving, and communication skills) and that are delivered over a long period to continually reinforce skills.	• Programs aimed at clarifying and communicating norms about behavior. • Comprehensive instructional programs that focus on a range of social competency skills (e.g., developing self-control, stress-management, responsible decision making, social problem solving, and communication skills) and that are delivered over a long period of time to continually reinforce skills. • Behavior modification programs and programs that teach "thinking skills" to high-risk youths.
What is promising?	• Programs that group youths into smaller "schools within schools" to create smaller units, more supportive interactions, or greater flexibility in instruction. • Behavior modification programs and programs that teach "thinking skills" to high-risk youths.	• Programs aimed at building school capacity to initiate and sustain innovation. • Programs that group youths into smaller "schools within schools" to create smaller units, more supportive interactions, or greater flexibility in instruction. • Programs that improve classroom management and that use effective instructional techniques.
What does not work	• Counseling students, particularly in a peer group context, does not reduce delinquency or substance use. • Offering youths alternative activities such as recreation and community service activities in the absence of more potent prevention programming does not reduce substance use. This conclusion is based on reviews of broadly defined alternative activities in school and community settings. Effects of these programs on other forms of delinquency are not known.	

1992; Lipsey & Wilson, 1993; Tolan & Guerra, 1994; Walker et al., 1995). Procedures such as functional assessment, social skills instruction, self-management strategies, and direct instruction have impressive empirical support (Kauffman, 1997b). In addition, Gottfredson (1997) examined 149 published studies of school-based programs designed to prevent problem behavior, especially crime, delinquency, and substance use. A summary of her scientific conclusions is shown in Figure 1. The consistent theme is that (a) investing in students through effective instruction in social skills and academics and (b) redoubling efforts to establish predictable and positive learning environments remain the most promising strategies for reversing current trends.

Unfortunately, we have been ineffective in obtaining sustained and accurate use of these practices in schools, especially for children with disabilities who present significant behavioral challenges. This failure exists not because we lack the technology or are uncaring, but because we have failed to (a) increase the capacity of educators to create and maintain environments that blend these technologies with sustainable support systems (Sugai & Horner, 1994, 1996; Sugai, Horner, Dunlap et al., 2000; Zins & Ponti, 1990) and (b) establish effective and efficient mechanisms to disseminate to educators what we know works; that is, we have not operationalized the call for "research-to-practice" (Carnine, 1997).

A major thesis of this chapter is that in our effort to build effective behavioral procedures we have paid insufficient attention to establishing effective *systems* of school-wide positive behavioral interventions and supports. More importantly, we have failed to prepare teachers and administrators to understand and implement systems that make effective and sustained use of these preferred practices (Sugai, Bullis, & Cumblad, 1997). It is not enough to identify practices that are effective. We also need to define and build systems that will support effective practices over time. Zins and Ponti (1990) addressed the need for supportive systems when they wrote, "A program consisting of potent and validly conceived mechanisms and processes may not succeed because the host environments are not able to support those processes" (p. 24).

The purpose of this chapter is to provide an overview of both the practices that have been demonstrated to improve the behavior of students in schools and the "host environment" systems that nurture and sustain these practices. Priority is given to proactive efforts that unify school, family, and community; increase the effectiveness, efficiency, and relevance of team-based problem solving; and give high priority to an agenda of primary prevention.

THE CONTENT OF SOCIALLY COMPETENT SCHOOL ENVIRONMENTS

To develop and sustain socially competent school environments and to improve school discipline, an analysis of the problem context and the use of a systems approach to school-wide discipline and positive behavior support are necessary. The basic message is that effective schools invest in systems and strategies that *prevent* behavior problems rather than relying on compelling consequences to deter problem behavior (Furlong, Morrison, Chung, Bates, & Morrison, 1997; Walker et al., 1996).

A comprehensive approach to school discipline emphasizes (a) teaching appropriate behaviors rather than just punishing unwanted behavior, (b) matching the level of intervention resources to the level of behavioral challenge presented by students, and (c) designing and integrating multiple systems that deal with the full range of discipline challenges (Walker et al., 1995). Among the most important messages for school redesign is the need to prevent behavior problems through proactive instruction rather than reactive remediation of discipline problems after they develop. Just as our business community has learned that quality products come from systems that emphasize building initial quality into the product rather than elaborate systems to check for errors after the product is built (Albin, 1992; Deming, 1986), so we must emphasize and invest in teaching appropriate behaviors before problems develop (Colvin, Kame'enui, & Sugai, 1993; Colvin, Sugai, & Patching, 1993; Gresham, 1997; Sugai, 1992). Viewing inappropriate problems as outcomes of inefficiencies of the system (Jenkins & Jenkins, 1995) is a more efficient and effective way to improve discipline in our schools.

Even proactive efforts, however, will need to be accompanied by targeted behavioral programs for those students who come to school with well-established patterns of antisocial and disruptive behavior. For these students, the key is to ensure that the resources (time, personnel, materials) assembled for behavioral intervention match the magnitude of the challenge. In this regard Travis Thompson's (1994) assessment of American education is most relevant: "We in America have for too long approached our children's futures as if we were taking a chance on the lottery. We invest very little and hope that somehow chance will bail us out." Our history suggests that low cost, get-tough efforts have had minimal value in addressing serious patterns of violent and destructive behavior.

Effective discipline efforts also move beyond the "silver bullet" approach to establish durable reform. Violence in our schools has multiple causes and will require an integration of multiple behavioral systems. To expect one package, or one tactic, to address the full spectrum of behavioral challenges underestimates the breadth of the challenges. What is needed is a constellation of procedures that are delivered within well-integrated systems.

One comprehensive approach to educational and behavioral support builds from assumptions about the distribution of behavioral challenges in our schools. This approach emphasizes that prevention of academic and behavioral failure requires attention to multiple systems of intervention: Universal Interventions, Specialized Group Interventions, and Specialized Individual Interventions (Colvin, Kame'enui, & Sugai, 1993; Sugai, 1996; Sugai & Horner, 1994, 1996, 1999; Sugai, Horner, Dunlap, et al., 2000; Walker et al., 1996). Two important principles are illustrated in this framework. First, the intensity of the intervention must be commensurate with the severity or intensity of the problem behavior. Second, the effectiveness and efficiency of the individual student system are dependent upon the effectiveness and efficiency of the school-wide system. Figure 2, on page 320, illustrates the elements of this model for both behavioral and academic problems. Each triangle represents all students in a school. For both behavioral and academic goals, the school begins with proactive, uni-

FIGURE 2

Continuum of Behavioral Support

Designing School-Wide Systems for Student Success

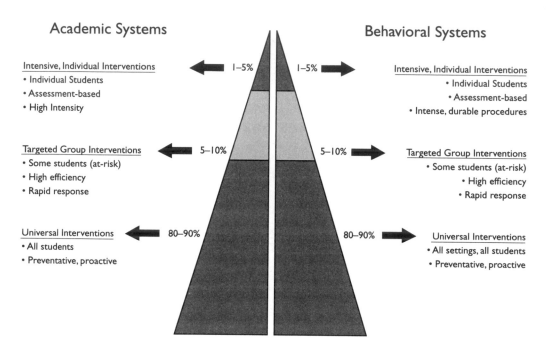

versal interventions that target instruction on appropriate skills for *all* students. All children will receive instruction in basic reading skills. All children also will receive instruction on basic social skills. The universal intervention will be effective with many, but not all, students. The large group of students in the lower part of each triangle represents those students who respond successfully to the proactive, universal intervention. Of those students who *do not* respond to the universal intervention, some will respond to efficient, specialized group interventions. Those children who do not learn reading skills from the universal intervention may succeed in a smaller group–instruction format that allows more practice. Those children who do not perform appropriate social skills after the universal intervention may respond to a simple group intervention that targets increased structure and contingent feedback. These students are represented in the middle section of each triangle. There will remain, however, a small number of students at the top of each triangle who enter schools either with significant skill deficits or learned misrules and do not respond to either universal or specialized group interventions. These students will need highly individualized and intense interventions either to learn to read or to develop social behaviors that will allow them to succeed in school.

Applying this comprehensive approach to behavioral support in schools involves attending to the behavior of all students in the school, not just those with problem behaviors. The key is to prevent students from moving toward violent and destructive behavior. Results from recent work (Colvin, Kame'enui, & Sugai, 1993; Hall, 1997; Taylor-Greene et al., 1997) suggest that a major proportion (>80%) of the total student body in many elementary or middle schools enter the schoolhouse door without major problem behaviors. These students have adequate social skills, are ready to learn and respond to universal interventions that teach social behaviors. The goal for this large group of students is to elaborate and maintain their social and academic readiness, and prevent the acquisition of norm-violating behaviors that would lead them toward anti-social lifestyles. These students also provide the foundation for a positive social culture within the school.

A second, smaller group of students (5–10%) will be "at-risk" for severe problem behaviors because they enter school from backgrounds with significant risk factors, such as poverty, disability, dysfunctional family structure, and/or deteriorating neighborhoods. These students will engage in problem behaviors beyond an acceptable level, and will be unresponsive to the basic discipline systems used for the whole student body even after they receive the universal training. These "at-risk" students require more targeted attention (e.g., small group instruction), but often are responsive to simple, individually focused interventions (e.g., token economies, behavioral contracts, self-management). The behavior support goal for this group is to decrease opportunities or situations in which high risk behaviors might be fostered and to establish effective and efficient pro-social repertoires that would increase their responsiveness to universal interventions.

A third group of students (1–5%) will display chronic patterns of violent, disruptive, or destructive behavior. These students will contribute 40–50% of the major behavioral disruptions in the school, draw 50–60% of building and classroom resources and attention, and will not demonstrate responsiveness to universal or targeted group intervention procedures. Support for these students will be intense, individualized, and often require comprehensive systems integration in which school personnel collaborate with the family, community agencies, and juvenile justice officials (i.e., multi-sector initiatives and cross-systems change) (Lawson & Sailor, 2000). The behavior support objective for this group of students is to reduce the intensity, frequency, and complexity of their problem behavior patterns, and provide suitable prosocial replacements that will compete with their more intrusive and unacceptable problem behaviors.

The organization of students into these three groups oversimplifies the dynamic of behavioral challenges in schools, but it emphasizes the different intervention systems that any school will need. Prevention of future behavior problems becomes the guiding theme of the interventions (Walker et al., 1996). To summarize, in terms of "prevention," *primary prevention* involves efforts to avert the initial acquisition of problem behaviors. Like prenatal care, early childhood vaccination, dental fluoridation, and other health enhancing efforts, the emphasis with primary prevention in schools is on procedures that can be used universally (with and by everyone), are comparatively inexpensive to administer, and avoid the development of problems. *Secondary prevention* refers to procedures that quickly remediate problems while they are still emerging. Like early medical care for a young child with asthma, secondary prevention efforts in schools involve procedures that are more intense, for example, special classes, small group interventions, and individually targeted procedures (e.g., behavioral contracts, social skills instruction, problem solving training). *Tertiary prevention* involves more intense interventions for students with ingrained, chronic patterns of problem behavior. Like insulin interventions for individuals with diabetes or medication control of high blood pressure, interventions typically must be highly individualized, incorporate wraparound services, and emphasize protection and control as well as a focus on behavior change.

Alignment of the behavioral challenges presented by the full range of students in a school with integration of the three prevention approaches provides a useful structure for organizing the multiple behavioral systems needed in a school that promotes high levels of behavioral competence.

PROMOTING BEHAVIORAL COMPETENCE: EFFECTIVE BEHAVIORAL PRACTICES IN SCHOOLS

Exciting advances are occurring in the use of behavioral procedures in schools (Gresham, Sugai, & Horner, 2001). Initial strategies and tools for responding to individual students are leading to broader classroom interventions, and more recently, to school-wide and district-wide systems for behavior change. Central examples of these changes lie in School-Wide, Classroom, and Individual Student systems as described below.

School-Wide Behavior Support Systems

The school-wide system consists of a set of universal or general strategies and processes that are intended to create an environment to which most students (i.e., 80-85%) respond predictably and prosocially (Colvin, Kame'enui, & Sugai, 1993; Colvin, Martz, DeForest & Wilt, 1995; Colvin, Sugai, & Kame'enui, 1993; Pruitt, Kelsh, & Sugai, 1989; Taylor-Greene & Kartub, 2000). For these students the goal is to maximize academic achievement, enhance peer and adult interactions, and inhibit problem behaviors. School-wide systems are designed to have primary prevention functions. The school-wide system has little impact on the behavior of those students who pre-sent the most severe and intractable behavior patterns. In fact, school-wide strategies and processes might be conceptualized as "screening" devices for identifying these students who, by definition, do not respond favorably to universal or general interventions (Taylor-Greene et al., 1997).

The school-wide system is composed of six major components: (a) a statement of purpose (or mission), (b) a list of positively stated behavioral expectations or rules, (c) procedures for directly teaching these expectations to students (Gresham, 1998), (d) a continuum of strategies for encouraging these expectations, (e) a continuum of strategies for discouraging rule violations, and (f) procedures for monitoring and record-keeping (Colvin, Kame'enui, & Sugai, 1993; Colvin, Sugai, & Kame'enui, 1993; Sulzer-Azaroff & Mayer, 1994). School-wide systems are important because they provide a foundation for enhancing consistency and prosocial behavior within and across individual classrooms and non-classroom settings (e.g., hallways, cafeterias, buses, assemblies, playgrounds) (Colvin, Sugai, Good, & Lee, 1997; Kartub, Taylor-Greene, March, & Horner, 2000; Nelson & Colvin, 1995). By increasing the efficiency with which school-wide systems function, greater attention and resources can be directed toward classroom and individual student systems.

Gottfredson and her colleagues indicate that schools which have (a) clear school expectations and rules, reward structures, and sanctions for rule violations; (b) efficient faculty communication and problem solving structures; and (c) present a caring and prosocial climate are associated with greater capacity to respond to disruption and tend to have reduced rates of problem behavior (Corcoran, 1985; Gottfredson, 1987, 1997; Gottfredson & Gottfredson, 1985; Gottfredson, Gottfredson, & Hybl, 1993). In addition, Gottfredson (1997) indicates four strategies for improving classroom and school environments:

> (1) building school capacity to manage itself; (2) setting norms or expectations for behavior and establishing and enforcing school rules, policies, or regulations; (3) changing classroom instructional and management practices to enhance classroom climate or improve educational processes; and (4) grouping students in different ways to achieve smaller, less alienating, or otherwise more suitable micro-climates within the school (pp. 5–15).

School-wide systems have process features that support and sustain the development and use of these effective practices and promote classroom and school climates. Effective school-wide behavior support systems have (a) an administrator who is an active leader and participant in quality improvement systems, (b) a team-based decision- and problem-solving structure with grade and staff representation and high status in the operation of discipline systems, (c) high commitment (>80%) from all staff (e.g., classified, certified, administrative, special), (d) a behavior support action plan that has high priority and is integrated into the school improvement plan, (e) in-house behavioral capacity (technical expertise), and (f) a long-term (3–4 years) investment in the effort (Colvin, Kame'enui, & Sugai, 1993; Lewis & Sugai, 1999; Sugai & Horner, 1996).

Classroom Behavior Support Systems

Although school-wide rules and expectations serve as foundations for classroom discipline, classroom systems possess greater variability because teachers display individualized expertise and content knowledge in curriculum, design of instruction, and behavior management. In addition, their approach to classroom management is shaped by their prior teaching experiences and pre-service and in-service training history, etc. (Smylie, 1988, 1989). Because of these differences classroom systems represent mini school-wide systems. In addition to the six components indicated for the school-wide systems, classroom management systems include strategies and processes for (a) curriculum selection and modification/accommodation, (b) design of instruction, (c) pre-sentation of curriculum and instruction, and (d) proactive classroom management.

When selecting a curriculum that increases student engagement and minimizes disruptive student behavior, the following questions should be considered: (a) Is the acquisition of misrules controlled? (b) Are skill components sequenced? (c) Is presentation content detailed? (d) Is student engagement maximized? (e) Are correction procedures given? (f) Are practice activities included? and (g) Are cumulative reviews provided? (Kame'enui & Darch, 1995). When student performance progress is inadequate, Deschenes, Ebeling, and Sprague (1994) suggest the following curriculum adaptations be used to improve the match between student skills and curriculum demands: (a) adapt amount to be learned, (b) adapt amount of time allotted and allowed, (c) increase amount of teacher assistance, (d) adapt delivery of instruction, (e) adapt skill difficulty, (f) adapt learner's response mode, (g) adapt amount of learner involvement, (h) adapt goals, or (i) provide different instruction and materials.

Although a classroom teacher might have the best curriculum and the most complete lesson plans, students still may fail to benefit because the teacher's instructional presentation skills are insufficient. The research on effective teaching behaviors is well developed and clear (e.g., Brewer, Hawkins, Catalano, & Neckerman, 1995; Cotton, 1995; Emmer, Evertson, Clements, & Worsham, 1994; Evertson, Emmer, Clements, & Worsham, 1994; Good & Brophy, 1987; Paine, Raddichi, Rosellini, Deutchman, & Darch, 1983; Rosenshine, 1986). A summary of these effective teaching behaviors is provided in Figure 3.

The goal of proactive classroom management is to increase predictability and to accommodate the individual and collective needs of students. In general, six major areas should be considered: (a) physical environment (e.g., traffic patterns, seating arrangements, unsupervisable areas), (b) student routines (e.g., transitions, starting/ending work, getting help or materials), (c) teacher routines (e.g., working with assistants and volunteers, taking attendance, dealing with visitors, scheduling), (d) behavior management (e.g., encouraging prosocial behavior, discouraging rule violations, responding to crises), (e) curriculum and materials (e.g., availability, quantity and quality), and (f) data management and evaluation (e.g., grading work, individual education plan progress, keeping track of problem behavior) (Colvin & Lazar, 1997; Good & Brophy, 1987; Kame'enui & Darch, 1995; Paine et al., 1983; Sprick, Sprick, & Garrison, 1992).

Like the approach for establishing school-wide behavior support, the process of proactive classroom management is based on an instructional approach in which the structures and functions of classrooms are taught to students with the same strategies used to teach academic skills and content knowledge (Colvin, Sugai, & Patching, 1993; Kame'enui & Darch, 1995; Sugai, 1992). This teaching approach involves four basic steps. The first is to teach the behavioral expectation, rule, or routine directly and

FIGURE 3

Summary of Effective Teaching Practices

1. Structured and scheduled opportunities to learn.

2. Curriculum aligned with desired outcomes.

3. Curriculum is delivered directly.

4. Students successfully interacting (engaged) with curriculum.

5. Brisk pacing.

6. Continuous monitoring of students and structuring of activities.

7. Specific explanations and instructions for new concepts.

8. Allocated time for guided practice.

9. Cumulative review of skills being taught.

10. Regular and varied assessments of learning of new concepts.

11. Regular and active interactions with individual students.

12. Frequent and detailed feedback.

13. Varied forms of positive reinforcement.

14. Effective and varied questioning strategies.

15. Student attention secured and maintained within and across instructional activities and environments.

16. Reinforcement for task completion.

17. Appropriate selection of examples and non-examples.

18. Clearly defined and enforced behavioral expectations.

19. Appropriate use of model/demonstration.

20. Appropriate use of behavioral rehearsal.

21. Effective, planned, and smooth transition within and between lessons.

22. High rates of correct student responding.

23. Positive, predictable, and orderly learning environment.

24. High expectations for achievement.

explicitly to all students. The teaching process consists of carefully selecting and sequencing teaching examples (positive and negative), providing demonstrations and role play (behavioral rehearsal) practice activities, testing with untrained examples, and providing informative corrections for errors and adequate positive reinforcement for correct responding (Engelmann & Carnine, 1982; Kame'enui & Simmons, 1990; Sugai, 1992; Sugai & Lewis, 1996). The second step is to arrange opportunities for the expectation, rule, or routine to be elicited in the natural environment. The third step is to monitor (active supervision) the student's performance in the natural environment by providing corrective feedback and positive reinforcement based on the student's performance. The final step is to monitor the progress being made by the student to determine the effectiveness and efficiency with which he or she displays the expectation, rule, or routine and to make appropriate modifications in the instruction. Specific, intense, and comprehensive teaching is recommended at the beginning of the school year (e.g., first day and week of school) along with regular review and practice sessions throughout the school year (Jones & Jones, 1995; Kame'enui & Darch, 1995; Paine et al., 1983; Sprick et al., 1992).

Individual Student Behavior Support Systems

Although proactive, comprehensive school-wide behavior systems may have a noticeable impact on the majority of students (e.g., 80-85%) and proactive classroom behavior support systems may promote relatively high rates of academic engagement for most students, a small proportion of students will not respond favorably and may require specially designed group or individualized interventions (Kauffman, 1997a; Walker et al., 1995). These students display high rates of problem behavior (externalizing and internalizing) that tend to be unresponsive to general or universal interventions which are effective for the largest proportion of students (primary prevention).

In general, a system for developing, implementing, and managing programming for individual students who display severe behavior problems should include the following prerequisites: (a) written policies, procedures, and formats; (b) active administrative support; (c) comprehensive, proactive school-wide system of behavior support; (d) in-building behavioral competence; (e) team-based problem-solving response (e.g., behavior support team, teacher assistance team); (f) sufficient resources (e.g., personnel, time); and (g) intact, proactive, and comprehensive school-wide system of behavior support/discipline. The general content of the specialized school-based interventions that are needed to respond to the severity of the problem behaviors displayed by these students consists of the following components: (a) early identification/intervention, (b) efficient request for assistance, (c) immediate planned response to crisis situations, (d) functional behavioral assessment, (e) competing pathways summary, (f) behavior support plan, (g) plan for implementation of behavior support plan, (h) active implementation of plan, (i) ongoing record-keeping and evaluation, and (j) wraparound processes.

Early identification/intervention. Identifying students who are at-risk for antisocial outcomes early in school is widely recommended (Walker et al., 1995; Walker &

Epstein, 2001); however, empirically validated tools are limited in number. One tool that has been shown to be reliable and valid is the Systematic Screener for Behavior Disorders (SSBD) (Walker & Severson, 1990). This three-"gate" process is used in the early elementary grades by schools to identify students with externalizing and internalizing problem behaviors. First, teachers nominate and rank order students from most to least externalizing and internalizing. Second, regular classroom teachers rate these students' behavioral status on a brief checklist and rating scales of adaptive and maladaptive behaviors. Third, behavioral observations are conducted to determine the extent to which problem behaviors are occurring in classroom and playground settings. To provide behavioral support to these students, Walker and associates have developed a program, *First Step to Success,* which includes a highly structured system for social skills training and behavior management for home and school settings (Walker et al., 1995; Walker et al., 1996). Initial research on the effectiveness of First Step to Success is promising in that participating students have maintained satisfactory levels of social behavior competence two years later (Golly, Sprague, & Walker, 2000; Golly, Stiller, & Walker, 1998; Walker et al., 1998).

Early identification also can be part of middle school programs. Preliminary work by Tobin, Sugai, and Colvin (1996) indicates that specific behavior incidents in the first term of sixth grade can predict significant behavioral problems in eighth grade and in high school. For example, if a student receives one office discipline referral for harassment or fighting in the first term of the sixth grade, the probability of that student having chronic problem behavior in eighth grade is about 70%. These findings indicate that we can identify students who are at-risk of significant behavioral difficulties early in middle school grades; however, research on the features of an early intervention strategy for these students is not decisive.

Another form of early identification and intervention involves mobilizing proactive intervention efforts immediately when the need is indicated. Students with chronic problem behavior frequently have histories of repeated office referrals, behavioral incident reports, and requests for assistance by their teachers, but without a systematic and planned response by the school. A proactive response would be to mobilize early intervention as soon as a significant kind or number of behavioral incidents has occurred; for example, when three office referrals are earned, a referral to a grade level team for behavioral contracting should be initiated.

Efficient request for assistance. When confronted by a student whose behaviors are unresponsive to available classroom strategies, teachers must have a mechanism for requesting assistance that is effective, efficient, and relevant (Sugai & Tindal, 1993). Request for assistance systems may take a variety of forms. At the informal level they can involve discussions with peers or supervisors, drop-ins at meetings, telephone or written consultations, etc. At the formal level teams can be established to provide opportunities for structured problem solving (e.g., teacher or student assistance teams, behavior support teams, discipline committees). Regardless of the format, the process of requesting assistance includes a description of (a) the problem behavior, (b) the problem context or setting, (c) previously attempted interventions and their outcomes, and

(d) the kind of assistance being requested (e.g., assessment, intervention planning) (Todd, Horner, Sugai, & Colvin, 1999).

Immediate planned response to crisis situations. When teachers present a request for assistance, they are indicating that previous intervention efforts have failed and that outside assistance is being requested. Often this request is made in response to a crisis situation. If these teachers are told that they must wait a week for a regularly scheduled meeting of the teacher assistance team or for a specialist to conduct behavioral observations before any action is taken, then they are not likely to find the process to be useful because they must "make do" until assistance can be provided.

Systems for requesting assistance must be efficient, effective, and relevant to the teacher making the request and the student. To respond to the teacher's request and to increase the probability that the student can succeed in the immediate future, behavior support specialists or teams should provide some kind of response within 24 hours. This response can be structural (e.g., change seating/classroom assignment), logistical (e.g., change schedule, teacher; shorten day), instructional/curricular (e.g., change curriculum or lesson design), social (e.g., change peer network), etc. A short-term, immediate response provides relief to the teacher-student-school system so that opportunities for effective and relevant long-term behavior support planning can occur.

Functional behavioral assessment. Functional behavioral assessment is the process of identifying the events that reliably predict and maintain problem behaviors (Horner, 1994; Horner & Carr, 1997; O'Neill, Horner, Albin, Storey, & Sprague, 1997; Sugai & Horner, 1999–2000). Functional assessment has long been a part of behavioral theory (Bijou & Baer, 1961; Bijou, Peterson, & Ault, 1968; Carr, 1977) and has grown into a practical technology for addressing severe problem behaviors over the past 15 years (Horner, 1994; Iwata, Dorsey, Slifer, Bauman, & Richman, 1982; Mace & Lalli, 1991; Northup et al., 1991; O'Neill et al., 1997; Repp, Felce, & Barton, 1988; Repp & Horner, 1999; Sugai & Tindal, 1993), but only recently has been referenced to school-based interventions (Horner, Sugai, Todd, & Lewis-Palmer, 1999–2000; Kern & Dunlap, 1999; Lewis & Sugai, 1993, 1996a, 1996b; Sugai & Horner, 1999–2000; Sugai, Horner, Dunlap, et al., 2000; Sugai, Lewis-Palmer, & Hagan-Burke, 1999–2000). The purpose for conducting a functional behavioral assessment is to improve the effectiveness and efficiency of behavioral support. The assessment is conducted by a teacher, behavioral specialist, or administrator and typically begins with interviews that both define problem behaviors and identify when, where, with whom, and with what they are most and least likely to occur. Most importantly, a functional behavioral assessment also identifies the events or conditions that appear to maintain occurrences of the problem behavior. This focus is different from determining what "causes" the problem behavior. The key issue is to understand what events reinforce (or maintain) the problem behaviors across time. The reasons why problems begin are often not the same as the reasons why a pattern of problem behavior repeats. Regardless of the complex social, emotional, biological, educational, and cultural variables that lead to the emergence of problem behaviors, they will not continue across time unless the behaviors produce some form of positive (obtain desired events) or negative (avoid/escape undesired events) reinforcement. A

FIGURE 4

Structure of Functional Assessment Hypothesis Statements

Testable Hypothesis

Setting Events ➡ Triggering Antecedents ➡ Problem Behavior ➡ Maintaining Consequences

fundamental message from research efforts is that the effectiveness of behavioral support requires attention to the events that maintain problem behaviors (*Exceptionality,* 1999–2000; *Journal of Applied Behavior Analysis,* 1994). As such, these events are a central concern for any assessment effort.

Information from functional behavioral assessment interviews is used to guide direct observation of the student in the school (or home). These observations typically are done by a behavioral specialist, teacher, or administrator, and allow confirmation and/or refinement of the hypotheses developed from initial interviews (O'Neill et al., 1997; Sugai & Tindal, 1993). The result is a set of hypothesis statements that indicate (a) the conditions/situations likely to produce problem behaviors (e.g., when asked to respond publicly in class), (b) the problem behaviors (e.g., Jason will refuse, and be verbally abusive toward his teacher), and (c) the consequence events that appear to maintain the problem behaviors (e.g., avoiding the public humiliation associated with not being able to answer correctly). This structure for functional hypothesis statements is illustrated in Figure 4.

By organizing problem behavior patterns in this form, interventions can be designed to (a) change the conditions that evoke problem behaviors, (b) teach new skills (appropriate behaviors) that will replace the problem behaviors, and (c) alter the consequences so problem behaviors are not rewarded and appropriate behaviors are rewarded. In effect, the information from a functional behavioral assessment allows identification of how the environment needs to change to produce change in the student. If no change in the environment or adult behavior is made, then change in the student's behavior is not expected.

For example, a second grader who cries, throws materials, and hits others when she is supposed to be doing seat work may pose a real challenge for her teacher. It would not be uncommon for a teacher to remove the child from the room for a short time when these behaviors occurred (time out). If a functional behavioral assessment indicated that the child found the seat work too difficult (or too boring) and was engaging in behaviors that led to escape from the seat work, then being removed actually might be reinforcing the problem behaviors rather than providing a correction. Alternatively, the exact same behaviors may be maintained by access to individualized attention (e.g., the teacher may come over and provide help with the difficult assignment). The message from these examples is that a functional behavioral assessment helps define the events that appear to maintain on going patterns of problem behavior. This information is critical to the design of behavioral support. Far too often school personnel deliver standard disciplinary consequences (e.g., detention, reprimands, extra time with the teacher during recess, referral to the office) under the assumption that these are punishing to the student when in fact these events serve to reward the problem behavior. Effective behavioral support for students with more severe problem behaviors requires use of functional behavioral assessments.

When interventions are developed without conducting a functional behavioral assessment, interventions are not only highly likely to *not* be effective, but actually may make the problem behavior worse. Consistent with 1997 amendments to the Individuals with Disabilities Education Act, schools are now expected to have the capacity to conduct functional behavioral assessments of problem behavior (Turnbull, Rainbolt & Buchele-Ash, 1997; Wilcox, Turnbull, & Turnbull, 1999–2000). Multiple approaches exist for how functional behavioral assessments may be conducted (Axelrod, 1987; Cooper, Wacker, Sasso, Reimers, & Donn, 1990; Gresham & Noell, 1999; Iwata et al., 1982; Mace & Roberts, 1993; O'Neill et al., 1997; Reed, Thomas, Sprague, & Horner, 1997; Reichle & Wacker, 1993; Repp & Horner, 1999; Sugai et al., 1999–2000).

Behavior support plans. A support plan is a description of how the elements in an individualized education plan will be developed and/or adapted to produce meaningful change in student behavior (Horner et al., 1999–2000; O'Neill et al., 1997). In many ways support plans are blueprints for how teachers, staff, and families will behave differently. Changes in student behavior will result from changes in the behavior of teachers, staff, and families (e.g., scheduling, monitoring, curriculum, instruction on social skills, consequences). Among the more daunting challenges is making an appropriate selection from among the huge array of intervention options. However, the decision can be made easier by focusing on the selection of an effective and efficient set of procedures that will be a good match with the challenges presented by the student. The procedures must be technically logical given our understanding of the problem behavior from the functional behavioral assessment, and they must be "contextually appropriate" in terms of needed resources, the skills required of implementers, the willingness of implementers to use the procedures, and the administrative support for the implementation (Albin, Lucyshyn, Horner, & Flannery, 1996).

One process that has proven useful for the design of behavioral support is the development of a "competing behavior model" that is used to organize the set of events that may be most effective for a particular student in a particular context (Horner, O'Neill, & Flannery, 1993; O'Neill et al., 1997; Sugai, Lewis-Palmer, Hagan-Burke, 1999–2000). This process is based on the assumption that problem behaviors are not some form of bacteria that can be eliminated, but a durable part of a student's way of behaving. If the student is to move beyond use of the problem behaviors, then he or she must learn new ways of dealing with problem situations. In essence, more appropriate competing "behavior paths" must be created, and the student must

FIGURE 5

Competing Behavior Model

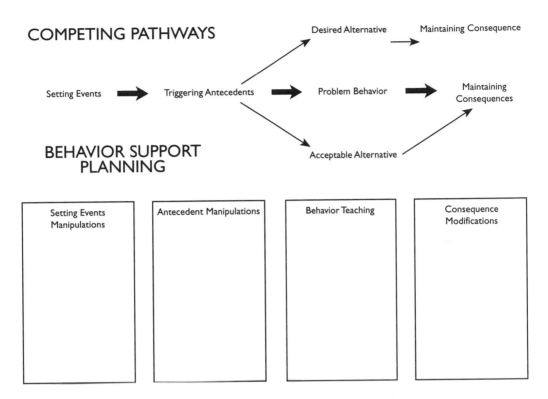

learn how to use these new paths. Figure 5 depicts the structural model for organizing a competing behavior analysis.

The competing behavior process is organized around the functional behavioral assessment hypothesis statements and involves the following steps. An example of this approach is provided in Figure 6, on page 332.

1. Write the functional behavioral assessment hypothesis statement (the setting event, controlling antecedent, problem behavior, and maintaining consequences).

2. Identify what the desired behavior should be given the problem conditions/situations.

3. Identify an alternative, appropriate behavior that the student may use to obtain the same reinforcing outcome produced by the problem behaviors.

4. Identify changes that can be made to the setting events and controlling antecedents to make the problem behavior irrelevant (e.g., changes in sleep patterns or curriculum schedule).

FIGURE 6

Example of a Behavior Support Plan

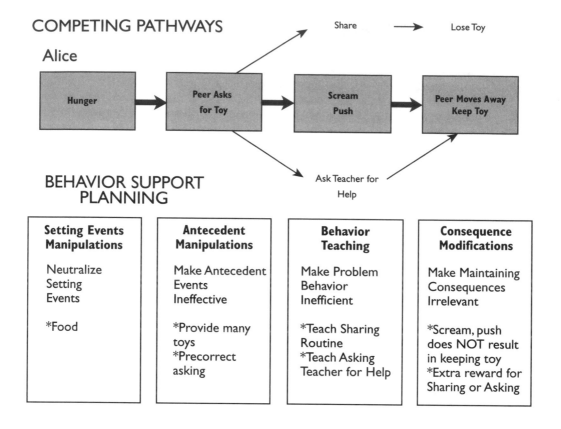

COMPETING PATHWAYS

Alice

BEHAVIOR SUPPORT PLANNING

Setting Events Manipulations	Antecedent Manipulations	Behavior Teaching	Consequence Modifications
Neutralize Setting Events	Make Antecedent Events Ineffective	Make Problem Behavior Inefficient	Make Maintaining Consequences Irrelevant
*Food	*Provide many toys *Precorrect asking	*Teach Sharing Routine *Teach Asking Teacher for Help	*Scream, push does NOT result in keeping toy *Extra reward for Sharing or Asking

5. Identify skills to be taught that would make "desired" behaviors or "alternative, appropriate" behaviors more likely.

6. Identify procedures for ensuring that (a) the problem behavior is not rewarded and (b) alternative, appropriate behavior is positively reinforced.

7. Identify procedures for ensuring that the most desired behavior results in more positive reinforcement than all other behaviors.

8. Make a list of changes that will make competing (appropriate) behaviors more likely than problem behaviors.

9. Select the most efficient and potentially effective cluster of strategies from the list that are consistent with the skills, values, and resources of the people who will be implementing the support plan.

10. Organize these strategies into a written behavior support plan.

Implementation of behavioral support. Establishing procedures for effective implementation of behavioral support is as important as taking the time to conduct a functional behavioral assessment, designing a plan that is technically sound, and ensuring good contextual fit (Albin et al., 1996; Horner et al., 1999–2000; O'Neill et al., 1997; Repp & Horner, 1999; Sugai & Tindal, 1993). At this time, we have more recommendations than empirically documented procedures about how to design behavioral interventions to achieve effective implementation; however, the most common recommendations include the following:

1. Design behavior support plans with *those* individuals who will need to implement the intervention.

2. Ensure that interventions are within the skills, resources, values, and administrative support of those who must implement the intervention.

3. Provide sufficient training (both before and during initial periods of implementation) to ensure that the implementation agents (family, teachers, etc.) are fluent in the intervention procedures.

4. Provide a system in which the implementation agents receive feedback on the fidelity with which the intervention is being implemented.

5. Include a formal system to monitor if the intervention is being successful, and a structure for modifying the intervention in response to this ongoing information.

Record keeping and evaluation. Collecting and maintaining information is a critical feature of the individual student behavior support process. This information has multiple purposes: accountability, program effectiveness, program evaluation, communications, etc. The need and importance of collecting information about the problem behavior and the environmental context (i.e., conditions under which the problem behavior is observed and maintaining consequences) have been iterated. Equally important, information on the implementation of the behavior plan must be collected. The literature is replete with the processes and methods for developing and implementing data collection procedures (e.g., Alberto & Troutman, 1995; Repp & Horner, 1999; Sugai & Tindal, 1993; Wolery et al., 1988). Common recommendations include the following:

1. Data collection activities should be simple to use, ongoing, integrated into instructional routines and activities, and consume no more than 5% of the teacher's time.

2. Measures should be calibrated to represent behaviors being examined, such as amount of behavior, type of behavior (e.g., latency, duration, frequency), and behavior definitions.

3. Data evaluation procedures should be linked to previously established behavioral objectives and prior and immediate student performance data.

Wraparound. In some cases, the individualized systems that are designed and implemented by schools are insufficient to meet the specialized needs of students with severe behavior problems. Stroul and Friedman (1986) characterize this community-based approach as a "system of care." Eber and Nelson (1997) describe a system of care as "a community-based approach to providing comprehensive, integrated ser-vices that are available through multiple agencies and professionals, in collaboration with families" (p. 387). Recent efforts have focused on an approach called "wraparound," which integrates school, family, and community resources into an efficient and focused support system (Adelman, 1996; Adelman & Taylor, in press; Eber & Nelson, 1997, VanDenBerg & Grealish, 1996). Wraparound is a "process for planning the delivery of services within a system of care. Typically, wraparound planning results in a blend of nontraditional supports (e.g., community mentors, respite providers, parent partners) with traditional services and is a tool that can be used across the full continuum of services" (Eber & Nelson, 1997, pp. 387–388). Wraparound has the following features (Eber & Nelson, 1997): (a) community-based interagency teams; (b) school-based planning teams; (c) individualized planning to address student and family needs; (d) sensitivity to cultural, social, and racial needs of student and families; (e) parental involvement at all levels; (f) flexible, non-categorized funding; (g) interagency implementation; (h) unconditional services; and (i) measured outcomes.

Although systematic empirical studies of the effectiveness of wraparound services are not widely available, initial program evaluations by Eber and her colleagues indicate promising outcomes for children and families involved in an Illinois initiative to implement the wraparound approach (Eber, 1996; Eber, Rolf, & Scheiber, 1996). They noted the following positive outcomes:

> 1) children and youth making a successful transition from residential settings to their homes, while improving at school and in the community; 2) youngsters at risk of being placed outside their homes and neighborhood schools being effectively supported to prevent such moves; and 3) families reporting significant improvements in children's adaptability and high satisfaction at being included in decisions about how services are provided (p. 390).

The wraparound approach extends the continuum of service options available to schools as they develop, implement, and sustain behavior support efforts for all students, but especially for students who have significant problem behaviors.

THE PROCESS OF ESTABLISHING AND SUSTAINING SOCIALLY COMPETENT SCHOOL ENVIRONMENTS

In summary, a significant body of knowledge about effective technologies for improving school-wide discipline for the majority of students in schools and the behavioral outcomes of individual students with significant behavioral challenges exists; however, we have not demonstrated adequately how these technologies can be incorporated and sustained in school environments. Promising work being conducted by researchers around the nation (e.g., Bierman, Greenberg, and colleagues of the Fast Track Program of the Conduct Problems Prevention Research Group; Sugai and colleagues at the University of Oregon Effective Behavior Support Project in Eugene; Knoff and colleagues at the University of South Florida; Embry and colleagues of PeaceBuilders in Arizona; Gottfredson, Gottfredson, and colleagues at the University of Maryland and Johns Hopkins University; Elliott, Guerra, and colleagues at the Center for the Prevention of Violence at the University of Colorado at Boulder) has begun to shape the critical features of the host environment that is required to support and sustain the use of effective behavior support and discipline practices. What is different today is recognition that schools are complex environments that will not be easily influenced by subtle, isolated efforts. Efforts to implement individual elements will not be effective. For example, Nelson (1996) found that a comprehensively designed school-wide program to reduce disruptive behavior that included school-wide organizational practices, school-wide classroom management, individual behavioral programs, and an advisory board was associated with improvements in social, behavioral, and academic adjustment. In addition, Gottfredson (1997) indicates that "leadership, teacher morale, teacher mastery, school climate, and resources" (p. 5-5) are required for school improvement efforts to be efficiently and effectively implemented and sustained. Gottfredson, Gottfredson, and Hybl (1993) add that a "systematic, integrated approach to discipline management that provided a mix of activities that targeted the entire school, classrooms within the school, and individuals within the school would be most beneficial" (p. 186). In reviewing the components and outcomes of such an approach they indicate the following:

> To summarize, the program had four components: (a) school discipline policy review and revision, (b) computerized behavior tracking, (c) improved classroom organization and management, and (d) positive reinforcement. All interventions were aimed ultimately at decreasing student misbehavior and increasing appropriate behavior in school by (a) decreasing punitive measures taken in response to misbehavior and increasing positive reinforcement of appropriate behavior; (b) increasing clarity of expectations for student behavior and student perceptions of the fairness of the rules governing their behavior; (c) increasing consistent following-through in response to student behavior both in school and at home; and (d) improving classroom organization and

management. All four components were expected to affect each of these intermediate outcomes. (p. 186).

An Approach to Implementation

The challenge to meeting the behavior support needs of all staff and students is not the identification of effective strategies. The real challenge is developing and maintaining "host environments" that can support the adoption and sustaining of these effective practices (Gottfredson & Gottfredson, 1996; Guerra & Williams, 1996; Lewis & Sugai, 1999; Sugai & Horner, 1994, 1999; Zins & Ponti, 1990). To take fullest advantage of the research validated tools available to us, a systems approach that reflects the features described previously must be applied. In general, the implementation of a school-wide system of behavior support consists of a six-step process: (a) establish leadership team, (b) define commitment, (c) develop an action plan, (d) implement action plan, (e) monitor effects, and (f) compare effects with current needs and revise action plan (Lewis & Sugai, 1999; Sugai & Horner, 1994, 1999; Sulzer-Azaroff & Mayer, 1994) (see Figure 7). The first two steps serve as the foundation for the effective and efficient implementation of the specific techniques and strategies associated with school-wide, specific setting, classroom, and individual student systems. The remaining four steps form a repeating cycle that allows a school to continue improvement and adaptation over time, even with shifting needs and change in personnel.

Establish leadership team. To increase the effectiveness, efficiency, and relevance of the implementation process, a leadership team should be formed and its roles and responsibilities should be clearly established (Todd, Horner, Sugai, & Colvin, 1999; Todd, Horner, Sugai, & Sprague, 1999). In general, this school-wide leadership team is charged with oversight for all three behavior support subsystems. Responsibilities include (a) assessing what is in place, (b) establishing behavior support as a priority and long-term goal for the building's school improvement plan, (c) developing and implementing professional development activities for all staff, (d) developing and implementing plans that enable building staff to achieve behavior support goals, (e) developing and operating ongoing record-keeping procedures to evaluate the implementation of behavior support, and (f) engaging in regular communications and problem solving with building staff.

Membership of this team should represent the characteristics of the school faculty and enable efficient communication between the team and faculty. At minimum, the team should have (a) grade level teaching representatives, (b) a school administrator with policy and resource decision-making authority, (c) behavior specialists (e.g., school counselor, school psychologist), (d) a special educator, (e) supervisors and educational assistants for major non-classroom settings (e.g., cafeteria, playground, hallways, bus loading), and (f) parents. Student and community representation, school nurse, custodial staff, bus drivers, etc., should be included as appropriate and possible.

If a school has existing behavior-related initiatives and teams in place (e.g., character education, school safety, drop-out prevention, school climate, etc.), then an

FIGURE 7

Behavior Support System Implementation

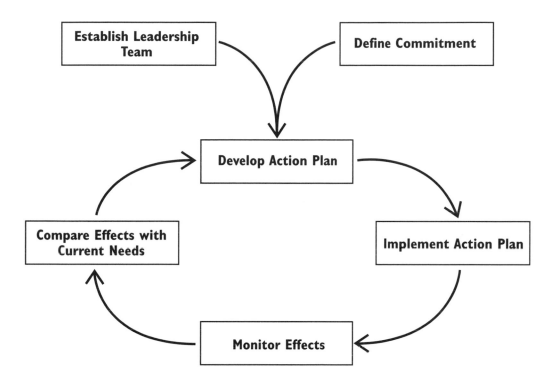

inventory should be completed to consider disbanding, consolidating, or prioritizing these groups. Elimination or consolidation of a team should be considered if the need is unjustified, outcomes are not clear, and improvements are not being achieved, etc. School staff must work to increase the efficiency and effectiveness of their efforts by prioritizing, consolidating, and emphasizing the use of evidence-based practices.

Define commitment to behavior support systems. A companion step to establishing effective school-wide behavior support is a clear definition of the commitment within the school to behavior support systems. Defining commitment includes self-assessing the need for behavior support systems, clarifying the vision of the faculty for educating children with problem behaviors, ensuring that behavior support is among the top priorities for the school, and allocation of the administrative, fiscal, time, and personnel resources needed to make durable change.

In particular, six prerequisites must be established. First, the need for addressing behavior support must be specified and clarified. A staff and/or student survey (e.g., EBS Self-Assessment Survey by Sugai, Horner, & Todd, 1996), a review of behavior incidents (e.g., office or discipline referrals, behavior incidence reports, attendance patterns) (Walker, Block-Pedego, Todis, & Severson, 1991 [SARS]), or systematic observations in common school settings (e.g., cafeteria, classrooms, hallways) can be used to clarify this need. For example, Sugai, Lewis-Palmer, Todd, and Horner (2000) have developed a tool for school staff to identify the extent to which their school uses effective behavior support practices. This survey enables staff members to review which effective practices are in place and/or are in need of improvement across school-wide, classroom, non-classroom, and individual student systems. The results are then used to build a focused action plan.

Second, the willingness and commitment of a majority (>80%) of the school staff must be secured and fostered. If this level of commitment is not present, then initial efforts should involve activities that are low effort and high impact and that result in increased staff "buy-in" (e.g., establishment of a behavior support committee, conducting a needs assessment). A direct relationship usually exists between level of participation by staff and amount and fidelity of implementation.

Third, high priority should be given to addressing behavior support needs at the school-wide level. The behavior support initiative should be established as one of the top three school improvement goals to ensure that sufficient attention, resources, and activity are available. Schools might include and formalize their behavior support effort in their annual school improvement plan, staff development activities, or budgetary investments.

Fourth, in addition to high priority, a 3–4 year commitment should be made to the high fidelity implementation of the initiative. Durable change in school systems takes time. It is common for a school to take a year to implement school-wide behavior support before being ready to address classroom or individual student strategies. Clarifying a commitment to durable implementation helps avoid the all too common result of small investments in educational reform likely to lead to disappointing outcomes and the abandonment of the intervention (Latham, 1988).

Fifth, efforts should be focused on establishing and sustaining behavioral competence or expertise in the school. If the technical knowledge of school-wide discipline, social skills instruction, active supervision, token economies, behavioral contracting, and functional behavioral assessment are not found within a school, then emphasis shifts from implementation of school-wide behavior support systems to securing outside technical knowledge. This situation creates a dependence upon the availability and scheduling of district-level expertise.

Finally, and possibly most importantly, active administrative support should be secured. Administrators can show their backing of the behavior support process by (a) actively participating in activities, (b) increasing project visibility and priority (e.g., faculty meetings agenda, newsletters), (c) securing resources (e.g., time, personnel, materials), (d) arranging professional development opportunities, (e) sustaining priority, (f) providing positive reinforcement for accomplishments, (g) addressing implementation roadblocks, (h) embedding effective procedures in the policies and operations manuals of the school, and (i) maintaining regular communications with district leadership (Colvin & Sprick, 1996; Horner, Sugai, & Horner, 2000).

These preliminaries increase the probability that implementation will be sustained at high levels of accuracy, across multiple years, with changes in teaching and administrative staff, and with shifts in student populations (Latham, 1988; Sugai & Horner, 1999; Taylor-Greene et al., 1997; Todd, Horner, Sugai, & Sprague, 1999)

Develop an evidence-based action plan. After a leadership team is established and prerequisites secured, attention can be directed to the development of an evidence-based action plan. The adoption of a curriculum or practice should not be based on its logical appeal, newness, innovation, or packaging. Instead, the determination and adoption of an action plan should be based on three decision criteria: (a) relevance, (b) effectiveness, and (c) efficiency.

First, does the plan address the needs defined through the self-assessment and review of the school's current data? A clear and direct link should be indicated between the goals of the plan and the prioritized needs of the school. The outcomes should be measurable to assess the extent of the match and the degree to which the outcomes are being achieved.

Second, does research evidence exist to support the adoption of the practices proposed in the action plan? A wealth of empirically validated procedures exists for individual student, classroom, and school-wide behavior support. Before non-validated practices are adopted, care should be taken to review alternatives, and ensure a logical fit between the resources and needs of the school, and the processes and outcomes of the practice.

Third, do the characteristics of the curriculum, intervention, or practice match the contextual-specific characteristics of the school, staff, and/or students? To the greatest extent possible, the features of the action plan should be relevant to the demographic, linguistic, and social characteristics of the school's neighborhood, students, staff, and families. School teams also should assess the degree to which the curriculum is modifiable.

Perform the action plan. Actual implementation of behavior support activities should be initiated. Implementation involves three dynamic and ongoing activities. First, a detailed action plan should include a delineation of the activities, people, resources, and schedules for implementing the action plan and achieving the teams' behavior support goals. In addition, the action plan should be incorporated into the building's school improvement plan and be endorsed by its administrative leadership team (e.g., site council, parent/teacher association, school board).

Second, the commitment and responsibilities of building staff should be defined to prepare for the implementation of behavior support activities. To increase the likelihood that staff, as a whole, will adopt and implement action plan activities, the team should assume responsibility for major administrative tasks (e.g., preparing materials, summarizing outcomes, organizing activities) so staff can focus their attention on the critical implementation activities. In addition, the team should regularly and frequently acknowledge staff contributions in and efforts toward the implementation of the action plan. Like students, staff must be positively reinforced for their efforts.

Finally, the school leadership team should arrange staff development activities to ensure that all staff are familiar with the implementation of the action plan. This may include presentations at regular faculty meetings, specific in-service events, and opportunities for faculty and staff to receive feedback on the extent to which agreed-upon activities are occurring and having an effect.

Monitor effects. School leadership teams should develop a formative (ongoing) means of monitoring the implementation of their action plan. Two levels of monitoring should be conducted. First, information should be collected on the degree to which features of the action plan are being implemented with high fidelity or accuracy and fluency, and by all designated staff members. This assessment can be accomplished by developing checklists or conducting observations that are based on the necessary steps of the implementation plan. Second, information should be collected on the impact of the action plan's implementation. This assessment can be conducted in a summative format at the end of a school year (e.g., EBS Self-assessment Survey or student achievement on standardized tests) or formatively on a weekly or monthly basis (e.g., office discipline referrals, behavioral incident reports, attendance rates) throughout the year.

Office discipline referral information can be an important source of information. However, for these types of data to be useful, school leadership teams should consider that the data are only as good as the (a) definitions and procedures that are in place for office discipline referrals, (b) degree to which staff consistently and accurately use the definitions and procedures, and (c) summarization procedures and data-decision rules that are in place to analyze the data (Lewis-Palmer, Sugai, & Larson, 1999; Tobin, Sugai, & Colvin, 2000). Based on their analysis of the data, leadership teams might agree to (a) continue implementation of an action plan as originally developed, (b) discontinue the action plan because action plan goals or outcomes have been or are not likely to be achieved, or (c) modify features of the implementation of an action plan to increase effectiveness or efficiency. Regardless of the decision, data should be used to justify the conclusion.

Another useful source of information is social validation data from students, families, staff, and/or others (Wolf, 1978). Written or interview questions should ask respondents their perceptions about the extent to which (a) features and goals of the action plan are acceptable, (b) strategies for achieving these goals are appropriate, (c) results or outcomes that are associated with these strategies are meaningful, and (d) next steps, directions, or modifications are justifiable.

A key to sustained implementation of school-wide behavior support systems is consistent and sustained feedback to faculty and staff about (a) the extent of the perceived need, (b) the specific procedures being employed in the action plan, (c) the extent to which the procedures are being conducted as planned, and (d) the effects being produced.

Compare effects with needs and revise action plan. The final step in the implementation process is to compare the results obtained against the perceived needs of the school and revise the action plan accordingly. If office discipline referrals have decreased, then have they decreased to a manageable level? If the hallways are less noisy and littered, then is the effort to maintain this effect sustainable? If individual interventions are proving effective, then how many individualized programs can the school implement? The major message is that sustained implementation of effective systems is never a static process. The foundation elements (Leadership team and Commitment) provide a starting point for the continuous cycle of planning, implementing, monitoring, comparing, and revising that results in durable systems change. By establishing sound behavioral systems with clear outcomes and measures, the cycle can become a highly efficient process.

CONCLUSION

A convergence of political will and behavioral science is emerging around the issue of violence in schools. Schools face a growing and compelling call for school-wide behavior reform. Families, school boards, communities, and national leaders are all demanding that schools be safe, effective, and constructive environments. Simultaneously, educators have available to them an array of proven procedures for improving the instructional, behavioral, and management systems that can meet these expectations. The challenge is becoming less one of identifying strategies and procedures that work than in defining the process for implementing these practices in all 110,000 schools across the nation. The message from this chapter is that while we should celebrate the gains that have brought us effective strategies for teaching reading, building independent learners, and supporting behaviorally effective settings, we must view with concern the extent to which we have defined the systems for implementing these effective procedures on a broad scale. We offer in this chapter one view of the specific content needed to create socially competent schools, the strategies for promoting behavioral competence for all children, and the systems needed to sustain socially competent environments for long periods. Schools remain complex environments. No single strategy or procedure will be appropriate or effective in all schools, but the organizational structures offered here build on a model that allows the local faculty, staff, and community to adapt procedures to fit local needs and yet achieve a consistent set of critical features that make schools safe, predictable, and constructive social settings. Children will learn best in schools with effective behavioral systems. The shift is from looking for tactics to "control" student behavior to building school-wide systems that define, teach, monitor, and acknowledge appropriate social behavior.

REFERENCES

Adelman, H. S. (1996). *Restructuring education support services: Toward the concept of an enabling component.* Kent, OH: American School Health Association.

Adelman, H. S., & Taylor, L. (in press). System reform to address barriers to learning: Beyond school-linked services and full service schools. *American Journal of Orthopsychiatry.*

Alberto, P. A., & Troutman, A. C. (1995). *Applied behavior analysis for teachers* (4th ed.). Englewood Cliffs, NJ: Merrill/Prentice-Hall.

Albin, J. M. (1992) *Quality improvement in employment and other human services.* Baltimore: Brookes.

Albin, R. W., Lucyshyn, L. M., Horner, R. H., & Flannery, K. B. (1996). Contextual fit for behavioral support plans: A model for "Goodness-of-fit." In L. K. Koegel, R. L. Koegel, & G. Dunlap (Eds.), *Positive behavior support: Including people with difficult behavior in the community* (pp. 81-89). Baltimore: Brookes.

American Psychological Association. (1993). *Violence and youth: Psychology's response.* Washington, DC: Author.

Axelrod, S. (1987). Functional and structural analyses of behavior: Approaches leading to reduced use of punishment procedures. *Research in Developmental Disabilities, 8,* 165-178.

Biglan, A. (1995). Translating what we know about the context of antisocial behavior into a lower prevalence of such behavior. *Journal of Applied Behavior Analysis, 28,* 479-492.

Bijou, S. W., & Baer, D. M. (1961). *Child development I: A systematic and empirical theory.* Englewood Cliffs, NJ: Prentice Hall.

Bijou, S. W., Peterson, R. F., & Ault, M. H. (1968). A method to integrate descriptive and experimental field studies at the level of data and empirical concepts. *Journal of Applied Behavior Analysis, 1,* 175-191.

Brewer, D. D., Hawkins, J. D., Catalano, R. F., & Neckerman, H. J. (1995). Preventing serious, violent, and chronic juvenile offending: A review of evaluations of selected strategies in childhood, adolescence, and the community. In J. D. Howell, B. Krisberg, J. J. Wilson, & J. D. Hawkins (Eds.), *Serious, violent and chronic juvenile offenders: A sourcebook (pp. 61–141).* Newbury Park, CA: Sage.

Carnine, D. (1997). Bridging the research-to-practice gap. *Exceptional Children, 63,* 513-521.

Carr, E. G. (1977). The motivation of self-injurious behavior: A review of some hypotheses. *Psychological Bulletin, 84,* 800-816.

Carr, E. G., Horner, R. H., Turnbull, A. P., Marquis, J. G., Magito McLaughlin, D., McAtee, M. L., Smith, C. E., Anderson Ryan, K., Ruef, M. B., & Doolabh, A. (1999). *Positive behavior support for people with developmental disabilities: A research synthesis.* Washington, DC: American Association on Mental Retardation.

Colvin, G., Kame'enui, E., & Sugai, G. (1993). Reconceptualizing behavior management and school-wide discipline in general education. *Education and Treatment of Children, 16,* 361-381.

Colvin, G. & Lazar, M. (1997). *The effective elementary classroom: Managing for success.* Longmont, CO: Sopris West.

Colvin, G., Martz, G., DeForest, D., & Wilt, J. (1995). Developing a school-wide discipline plan: Addressing all students, all settings and all staff. In *The Oregon Conference Monograph* (Vol. 7, pp. 169-193). Eugene, OR: University of Oregon.

Colvin, G., & Sprick, R. (1996). *Administrative support and the implementation of school-wide discipline.* Unpublished manuscript. Behavioral Research and Teaching, College of Education, University of Oregon, Eugene.

Colvin, G., Sugai, G., Good, R., & Lee, Y. (1997). Effect of active supervision and pre-correction on transition behaviors of elementary students. *School Psychology Quarterly, 12*(4), 344-363.

Colvin, G., Sugai, G., & Kame'enui, E. (1993). *Proactive school-wide discipline: Implementation manual.* Project PREPARE, Behavioral Research and Teaching, College of Education, University of Oregon, Eugene.

Colvin, G., Sugai, G., & Patching, W. (1993). Pre-correction: An instructional strategy for managing predictable behavior problems. *Intervention, 28,* 143-150.

Cooper, L. J., Wacker, D. P., Sasso, G. M., Reimers, T. M., & Donn, L. K. (1990). Using parents as therapists to evaluate appropriate behavior of their children: Application to a tertiary diagnostic clinic. *Journal of Applied Behavior Analysis, 23,* 285-296.

Corcoran, T. B. (1985). Effective secondary schools. In R. M. J. Kyle (Ed.), *Reaching excellence: An effective schools sourcebook (pp. 71-98).* Washington, D.C.: U.S. Government Printing Office.

Cotton, K. (1995). *Effective schooling practices: A research synthesis, 1995 update.* Portland, OR: Northwest Educational Laboratories.

Deming, W. F. (1986) *Out of the crisis.* Cambridge: Massachusetts Institute of Technology, Center for Advanced Engineering Study.

Deschenes, C., Ebling, D.G., & Sprague, J. (1994). *Adapting curriculum and instruction in inclusive classrooms.* The Center for School and Community Integration, Bloomington, IN.

Eber, L. (1996). Restructuring schools through wraparound planning: The LADSE experience. In R. J. Illback & C. M. Nelson (Eds.), *School-based services for students with emotional and behavioral disorders* (pp. 139-154). Binghamton, NY: Haworth.

Eber, L., & Nelson, C. M. (1997). School-based wraparound planning: Integrating services for students with emotional and behavioral needs. *American Journal of Orthopsychiatry, 67,* 385-395.

Eber, L., Rolf, K., & Scheiber, M. P. (1996). *A look at the 5 year ISBE EBD Initiative: End of year report for 1995-1996.* La Grange, IL: La Grange Area Department of Special Education.

Elam, S. M., Rose, L. C., & Gallup, A. M. (1996a). 28th annual Phi Delta Kappa/Gallup poll of the public's attitudes toward the public schools. *Phi Delta Kappan, 78*(1), 41-59.

Elam, S. M., Rose, L. C., & Gallup, A. M. (1996b). The third Phi Delta Kappa poll of teachers' attitudes toward the public schools. *Phi Delta Kappan, 78*(3), 244-250.

Elliot, D.S, Hamburg, B.A., & Williams, K.R. (1998). *Violence in American schools: A new perspective.* New York: Cambridge University Press.

Emmer, E. T., Evertson, C. M., Clements, B. S., & Worsham, M. E. (1994). *Classroom management for secondary teachers* (3rd ed.). Boston: Allyn & Bacon.

Engelmann, S., & Carnine, D. (1982). *Theory of instruction: Principles and applications.* New York: Irvington.

Evertson, C. M., Emmer, E.T., Clements, B. S., & Worsham, M. S. (1994). *Classroom management for elementary teachers* (3rd ed.). Boston: Allyn & Bacon.

Exceptionality (1999–2000). Special issue on functional behavioral assessment. *8*(3).

Furlong, M. J., Morrison, G. M., Chung, A., Bates, M., & Morrison, R. (1997). School violence: A multicomponent reduction strategy. In G. Bear, K. Minke, & A.Thomas, (Eds.), *Children's needs II: Development, problems and alternatives* (pp. 245-256). Bethesda, MD: National Association of School Psychologists.

Golly, A., Sprague, J., & Walker, H. (2000). First Step to Success Program: An analysis of outcomes with identical twins across multiple baselines. *Behavioral Disorders, 25*(3), 170-182.

Golly, A., Stiller, B., & Walker, H. (1998). The First Step to Success: Replication and social validation of an early intervention program. *Journal of Emotional and Behavioral Disorders, 6*(4), 243-250.

Good, T. L., & Brophy, J. E. (1987). *Looking in classrooms* (4th ed.). New York: Harper & Row.

Gottfredson, D. C. (1987). An evaluation of an organization development approach to reducing school disorder. *Evaluation Review, 11,* 739-763.

Gottfredson, D. C. (1997). School-based crime prevention. In L. Sherman, D. Gottfredson, Mackenzie, D. J. Eck, P. Reuter, & S. Bushway (Eds.), *Preventing crime: What works, what doesn't, what's promising* (pp. 5-1–5-74). College Park, MD: Department of Criminology and Criminal Justice, University of Maryland.

Gottfredson, G. D., & Gottfredson, D. C. (1985). *Victimization in schools.* New York: Plenum Press.

Gottfredson, G. D., & Gottfredson, D. C. (1996). *A national study of delinquency prevention in schools: Rationale for a study to describe the extensiveness and implementation of programs to prevent adolescent problem behavior in schools.* Ellicott City, MD: Gottfredson Associates.

Gottfredson, D. C., Gottfredson, G. D., & Hybl, L. G. (1993). Managing adolescent behavior: A multiyear, multischool study. *American Educational Research Journal, 30,* 179-215.

Gresham, F. M. (1997). Treatment integrity in single-subject research. In R. Franklin, D. Allison, & B. Gorman (Eds.), *Design and analysis of single case research* (pp. 93-117). Hillsdale, NJ: Erlbaum.

Gresham, F. M. (1998). Social skills training with children: Social learning and applied behavior analytic approaches. In T. S. Watson & F. M. Gresham (Eds.), *Handbook of child behavior therapy* (pp. 475-497). New York: Plenum.

Gresham, F. M. & Noell, G. H. (1999). Functional analysis assessment as a cornerstone for noncategorical special education. In D. J. Reschly, W. D. Tilly, III., & J. P. Grimes (Eds.), *Special education in transition: functional assessment and noncategorical programming* (pp. 39-64). Longmont, CO: Sopris West.

Gresham, F. M., Sugai, G., & Horner, R. H. (2001). Social competence of students with high incidence disabilities: Conceptual and methodological issues in interpreting outcomes of social skills training. *Exceptional Children, 67*(3), 331-344.

Guerra, N. G., & Williams, K. R. (1996). *A program planning guide for youth violence prevention: A risk-focused approach.* Boulder: Center for the Study and Prevention of Violence, University of Colorado.

Guess, D., Helmstetter, E., Turnbull, H. R., III, & Knowlton, S. (1987). Use of aversive procedures with persons who are disabled: An historical review and critical analysis. *In Monograph of the Association for Persons with Severe Handicaps* (Vol. 2). Washington, DC: Association for Persons with Severe Handicaps.

Hall, S. (1997). *A descriptive analysis of discipline referrals in six elementary and middle schools* (1994-1995). Unpublished Masters Thesis. Eugene, OR: University of Oregon.

Horner, R. H. (1994). Functional assessment: Contributions and future directions. *Journal of Applied Behavior Analysis, 27,* 401-404.

Horner, R. H., & Carr, E. G., (1997) Behavioral support for students with severe disabilities: Functional assessment and comprehensive intervention. *Journal of Special Education, 31*(1), 84-104.

Horner, R. H., Diemer, S. M., & Brazeau, K. C. (1992). Educational support for students with severe problem behaviors in Oregon: A descriptive analysis from the 1987-1988 school year. *Journal of the Association of Persons with Severe Handicaps, 17*(3), 154-169

Horner, R. H., O'Neill, R. E., & Flannery, K. B. (1993). Building effective behavior support plans from functional assessment information. In M. E. Snell (Ed.), *Systematic instruction of persons with severe handicaps* (4th ed.; pp. 184-214). Columbus, OH: Merrill.

Horner, R. H., Sugai, G., & Horner, H. F. (2000). A schoolwide approach to student discipline. *The School Administrator, 2*(57), 20-23.

Horner, R. H., Sugai, G., Todd, A. W., & Lewis-Palmer, T. (1999-2000). Elements of behavior support plans: A technical brief. *Exceptionality, 8*(3), 205-215.

Iwata, B. A., Dorsey, M. F., Slifer, K. J., Bauman, K. E., & Richman, G. S. (1982). Toward a functional analysis of self-injury. *Analysis and Intervention in Developmental Disabilities, 2,* 3-20.

Jenkins, K. D., & Jenkins, D. M. (1995). Total quality education: Refining the middle school concept. *Middle School Journal, 27*(2), 3-11.

Jones, V. G., & Jones, L. S. (1995). *Comprehensive classroom management: Creating positive learning environments for all students* (4th ed.). Boston: Allyn & Bacon.

Journal of Applied Behavior Analysis (1994). Special issue on functional analysis approaches to behavioral assessment and treatment. *27*(2).

Kame'enui, E. J., & Darch, C. B. (1995). *Instructional classroom management: A proactive approach to behavior management.* White Plains, NY: Longman.

Kame'enui, E. J., & Simmons, D. C. (1990). Designing classroom management strategies within the context of instruction. In *Designing instructional strategies: The prevention of academic learning problems.* Columbus, OH: Merrill.

Kartub, D. T., Taylor-Greene, S., March, R. E., & Horner, R. H. (2000). Reducing hallway noise: A systems approach. *Journal of Positive Behavior Interventions, 2*(3), 179-182.

Kauffman, J. (1997a). *Characteristics of emotional and behavioral disorders of children and youth* (6th ed.). Engelwood Cliffs, NJ: Merrill/Prentice Hall.

Kauffman, J. (1997b). *Today's special education and its messages for tomorrow.* Paper presented at the annual convention of the Council for Exceptional Children, Salt Lake City, UT.

Kern, L., & Dunlap, G. (1999). Assessment-based interventions for children with emotional and behavioral disorders. In A. Repp & R. Horner. (Eds), *Functional analysis of problem behavior: From assessment to effective support* (pp. 197-218). Belmont, CA: Wadsworth.

Larson, J. (1994). Violence prevention in schools: A review of selected programs and procedures. *School Psychology Review, 23,* 151-164.

Latham, G. (1988). The birth and death cycles of educational innovations. *Principal, 68*(1), 41-43.

Lawson, H. A., & Sailor, W. (2000). Integrating services, collaborating, and developing connections with schools. *Focus on Exceptional Children, 33*(2), 1-22. Denver, CO: Love Publishing.

Lewis, T. J., & Sugai, G. (1993). Teaching communicative alternatives to socially withdrawn behavior: An investigation in maintaining treatment effects. *Journal of Behavioral Education, 3,* 61-75.

Lewis, T. J., & Sugai, G. (1996a). Descriptive and experimental analysis of teacher and peer attention and the use of assessment-based intervention to improve the prosocial behavior of a student in a general education setting. *Journal of Behavioral Education, 6,* 7-24.

Lewis, T. J., & Sugai, G. (1996b). Functional assessment of problem behavior: A pilot investigation of the comparative and interactive effects of teacher and peer social attention on students in general education settings. *School Psychology Quarterly, 11,* 1-19.

Lewis, T. J., & Sugai, G. (1999). Effective behavior support: A systems approach to proactive school-wide management. *Focus on Exceptional Children, 31*(6), 1-24.

Lewis-Palmer, T., Sugai, G., & Larson, S. (1999). Using data to guide decisions about program implementation and effectiveness. *Effective School Practices, 17*(4), 47-53.

Lipsey, M. W. (1991). The effect of treatment on juvenile delinquents: Results from meta-analysis. In F. Losel, D. Bender, & T. Bliesener (Eds.), *Psychology and law* (pp. 131-143). New York: Walter de Gruyter.

Lipsey, M. W. (1992). Juvenile delinquency treatment: A meta-analytic inquiry into the variability of effects. In T. D. Cook, H. Cooper, D. S. Cordray, H. Hartman, L. V. Hedges, R. V. Light, T. A. Louis, & F. Mostellar (Eds.), *Meta-analysis for explanation* (pp. 8-127). Beverly Hills, CA: Sage.

Lipsey, M. W., & Wilson, D. B. (1993). The efficacy of psychological, educational, and behavioral treatment: Confirmation from meta-analysis. *American Psychologist, 48,* 1181-1209.

Loeber, R., & Farrington, D. (1998) *Serious and violent juvenile offenders: Risk factors and successful interventions.* London: Sage.

Mace, F. C., & Lalli, J. S. (1991). Linking descriptive and experimental analyses in the treatment of bizarre speech. *Journal of Applied Behavior Analysis, 24,* 553-562.

Mace, F. C. & Roberts, M. L. (1993). Factors affecting selection of behavioral interventions. In J. Reichle & D.P. Wacker (Eds.), *Communicative alternatives to challenging behavior: Integrating functional assessment and intervention strategies* (pp. 113-133). Baltimore: Brookes.

Mayer, G. R. (1995). Preventing antisocial behavior in the schools. *Journal of Applied Behavior Analysis, 28,* 467-478.

Mayer, G. R., & Sulzer-Azaroff, B. (1990). Interventions for vandalism. In G. Stoner, M. R. Shinn, & H. M. Walker (Eds.), *Interventions for achievement and behavior problems* (pp. 559-580). Washington, DC: National Association of School Psychologists.

McCord, J. (Ed.) (1995). *Coercion and punishment in long-term perspective.* New York: Cambridge University Press.

Morrison, G. M., Furlong, M. J., & Morrison, R. L. (1997). The safe school: Moving beyond crime prevention to school empowerment. In A. Goldstein & J. Conoley (Eds.), *School violence intervention: A practical handbook* (pp. 236-264). New York: Guilford.

Nelson, J. R. (1996). Designing schools to meet the needs of students who exhibit disruptive behavior. *Journal of Emotional and Behavioral Disorders, 4,* 147-161.

Nelson, R., & Colvin, G. (1995). School-wide discipline: Procedures for managing common areas. *The Oregon Conference Monograph* (Vol. 7). Eugene, OR: University of Oregon.

Northrup, J., Wacker, D., Sasso, G., Steege, M., Cigrand, K., Cook, J., & DeRaad, A. (1991). A brief functional analysis of aggressive and alternative behavior in an outclinic setting. *Journal of Applied Behavior Analysis, 24,* 509-522.

O'Neill, R. E., Horner, R. H., Albin, R. W., Storey, K., & Sprague, J. R. (1997). *Functional analysis of problem behavior: A practical assessment guide* (2nd ed.). Pacific Grove, CA: Brookes/Cole.

Paine, S. C., Radicchi, J., Rosellini, L. C., Deutchman, L., & Darch, C. B. (1983). *Structuring your classroom for academic success.* Champaign, IL: Research Press.

Peacock Hill Working Group (1991). Problems and promises in special education and related services for children and youth with emotional or behavioral disorders. *Behavioral Disorders, 16,* 299-313.

Pruitt, R., Kelsh, B., & Sugai, G. M. (1989). Pro-tickets: A positive school-wide behavior management program. In *1989 Oregon Conference Monograph.* Eugene, OR: University of Oregon.

Reed, H., Thomas, E., Sprague, J. R. & Horner, R. H. (1997). The student guided functional assessment interview: An analysis of student and teacher agreement. *Journal of Behavioral Education, 7*(1), 33-49.

Reichle, J. (1990). *National working conference on positive approaches to the management of excess behavior: Final report and recommendations.* Minneapolis, MN: Institute on Community Integration, University of Minnesota.

Reichle, J. & Wacker, D. P. (Eds.) (1993). *Communicative alternatives to challenging behavior: Integrating functional assessment and intervention strategies.* Baltimore: Brookes.

Repp, A. C., Felce, D., & Barton, L. E. (1988). Basing the treatment of stereotypic and self-injurious behaviors on hypotheses of their causes. *Journal of Applied Behavior Analysis, 21,* 281-289.

Repp, A. C., & Horner, R. H. (Eds.) (1999). *Functional analysis of problem behavior: From effective assessment to effective support.* Belmont, CA: Wadsworth.

Rosenshine, B. V. (1986). Synthesis of research on explicit teaching. *Educational Leadership, 43,* 60-69.

Smylie, M. A. (1988). The enhancement function of staff development: Organizational and psychological antecedents to individual teacher change. *American Educational Research Journal, 25,* 1-25.

Smylie, M. A. (1989). Teachers' views of the effectiveness of sources of learning to teach. *The Elementary School Journal, 89,* 543-558.

Sprague, J. R., & Rian, V. (1993). *Support systems for students with severe problem behaviors in Indiana: A descriptive analysis of school structure and student demographics.* Unpublished manuscript, Indiana University, Bloomington.

Sprick, R., Sprick, M., & Garrison, M. (1992). *Foundations: Developing positive school-wide discipline policies.* Longmont, CO: Sopris West.

Stroul, B. A., & Friedman, R. (1986). *A system of care for severely emotionally disturbed children and youth.* Washington, DC: CASSP Technical Assistance Center.

Sugai, G. M. (1992). The design of instruction and the proactive management of social behaviors. *Learning Disabilities Forum, 17*(2), 20-23.

Sugai, G. (1996). Providing effective behavior support to all students: Procedures and processes. *SAIL, 11*(1), 1-4.

Sugai, G., Bullis, M., & Cumblad, M. (1997). Skill development and support in emotional and behavioral disorders. *Journal of Emotional and Behavioral Disorders, 5,* 55-64.

Sugai, G., & Horner, R. (1994). Including students with severe behavior problems in general education settings: Assumptions, challenges, and solutions. In J. Marr, G. Sugai, & G. Tindal (Eds.), *The Oregon Conference Monograph* (Vol. 7; pp. 102-120). Eugene, OR: University of Oregon.

Sugai, G., & Horner, R. (1996). *Antisocial behavior, discipline, and behavioral support: A look from the schoolhouse door.* Unpublished manuscript. Behavioral Research and Teaching, University of Oregon, Eugene, Oregon.

Sugai, G., & Horner, R. H. (1999). Discipline and behavioral support: Preferred processes and practices. *Effective School Practices, 17*(4), 10-22.

Sugai, G., & Horner, R. H. (1999-2000). Including the functional behavioral assessment technology in schools. *Exceptionality, 8*(3), 145-148.

Sugai, G., Horner, R. H., Dunlap, G., Hieneman, M., Lewis, T. J., Nelson, C. M., Scott, T., Liaupsin, C., Sailor, W., Turnbull, A. P., Turnbull, H.R., III, Wickham, D., Wilcox, B., & Ruef, M. (2000). Applying positive behavior support and functional behavioral assessment in schools. *Journal of Positive Behavior Interventions, 2*(3), 131-143.

Sugai, G., Horner, R. H., & Todd, A. W. (1996). *EBS Self-Assessment Survey.* University of Oregon, Eugene.

Sugai, G., & Lewis, T. (1996). Preferred and promising practices for social skills instruction. *Focus on Exceptional Children, 29*(4), 1-16.

Sugai, G., Lewis-Palmer, T., & Hagan-Burke, S. (1999-2000). Overview of the FBA process. *Exceptionality, 8*(3), 149-160.

Sugai, G., Lewis-Palmer, T., Todd, A., & Horner, R. (2000). *Effective Behavior Support (EBS) survey: Assessing and planning behavior support in schools.* University of Oregon, Eugene.

Sugai, G., Sprague, J. R., Horner, R. H., & Walker, H. M. (2000). Preventing school violence: The use of office discipline referrals to assess and monitor school-wide discipline interventions. *Journal of Emotional and Behavior Disorders, 8,* 94-101.

Sugai, G. M., & Tindal, G. (1993). *Effective school consultation: An interactive approach.* Pacific Grove, CA: Brookes/Cole.

Sulzer-Azaroff, B. & Mayer, G. R. (1994). *Achieving educational excellence: Behavior analysis for achieving classroom and schoolwide behavior change.* San Marcos, CA; Western Image.

Taylor-Greene, S., Brown, D., Nelson, L., Longton, J., Gassman, Cohen, J., Swartz, J., Horner, R. H., Sugai, G., & Hall, S. (1997). School-wide behavioral support: Starting the year off right. *Journal of Behavioral Education, 7,* 99-112.

Taylor-Greene, S., & Kartub, D. (2000). Durable implementation of school-wide behavior support: The high five program. *Journal of Positive Behavior Interventions, 2*(4), 233-235.

Thompson, T. (1994). *Kennedy Center Newsletter.* Kennedy Center, Nashville, TN.

Tobin, T., Sugai, G., & Colvin, G. (1996). Patterns in middle school discipline records. *Journal of Emotional and Behavioral Disorders, 4*(2), 82-94.

Tobin, T., Sugai, G., & Colvin, G. (2000). Research brief: Using discipline referrals to make decisions. *Bulletin of the National Association of Secondary Principals, 84*(616), 106-120.

Todd, A. W., Horner, R. H., Sugai, G., & Colvin, G. (1999). Individualizing school-wide discipline for students with chronic problem behaviors: A team approach. *Effective School Practices, 17*(4), 72-82.

Todd, A. W., Horner, R. H., Sugai, G., & Sprague, J. R. (1999). Effective behavior support: Strengthening school-wide systems through a team-based approach. *Effective School Practices, 17*(4), 23-37.

Tolan, P., & Guerra, N. (1994). *What works in reducing adolescent violence: An empirical review of the field.* Center for the Study and Prevention of Violence, University of Colorado, Boulder.

Turnbull, R., Rainbolt, K., & Buchele-Ash, A. (1997). *Individuals with disabilities education act: Digest and significance of 1997 amendments.* Unpublished report.

U.S. Department of Education (1994). *Sixteenth annual report to Congress on the implementation of Public Law 94-142: The Education for All Handicapped Children Act.* Washington, DC.

VanDenBerg, J. E., & Grealish, E. M. (1996). Individualized services and supports through wraparound process: Philosophy and procedures. *Journal of Child and Family Studies, 5,* 7-21.

Walker, H. M., Block-Pedego, A., Todis, B., & Severson, H. (1991). *School archival records search (SARS): User's guide and technical manual.* Longmont, CO: Sopris West.

Walker, H. M., Colvin, G., & Ramsey, E. (1995). *Antisocial behavior in public school: Strategies and best practices.* Pacific Grove, CA: Brookes/Cole.

Walker, H. M., & Epstein, M. H. (2001). *Making schools safer and violence free: Critical issues, solutions, and recommended practices.* Austin: PRO-ED.

Walker, H. M., Horner, R. H., Sugai, G., Bullis, M. Sprague, J., Bricker, D., & Kaufman, M. J. (1996) Integrated approaches to preventing antisocial behavior patterns among school-age children and youth. *Journal of Emotional and Behavioral Disorders, 4,* 194-209.

Walker, H. M., Kavanagh, K., Golly, A., Stiller, B., Severson, H. H., & Feil, E. G. (1998). *First steps: An early intervention program for antisocial kindergartners.* Longmont, CO: Sopris West.

Walker, H. M., & Severson, H. H. (1990). *Systematic screening for behavior disorders (SSBD): User's guide and technical manual.* Longmont, CO: Sopris West.

Wilcox, B. L., Turnbull H. R., III, & Turnbull, A. P. (1999-2000). Behavioral issues and IDEA: Positive behavioral interventions and supports and the functional behavioral assessment in the disciplinary context. *Exceptionality, 8*(3), 173-187.

Wolery, M. R., Bailey, D. B., Jr., & Sugai, G. M. (1988). *Effective teaching: Principles and procedures of applied behavior analysis with exceptional students.* Boston: Allyn & Bacon.

Wolf, M. M. (1978). Social validity: The case for subjective measurement or how behavior analysis is finding its heart. *Journal of Applied Behavior Analysis, 11,* 203-214.

Zins, J. E., & Ponti, C. R. (1990). Best practices in school-based consultation. In A. Thomas and J. Grimes (eds.), *Best practices in school psychology II* (pp. 673-694). Washington, DC: National Association of School Psychologists.

CHAPTER 13

Bullying Prevention in Elementary Schools:
The Importance of Adult Leadership, Peer Group Support,
and Student Social–Emotional Skills

Jennie L. Snell and Elizabeth P. MacKenzie
Committee for Children, Seattle, Washington

Karin S. Frey
University of Washington

INTRODUCTION

Bullying is currently a serious and prevalent problem in our schools. Its negative effects are not limited to individual children who bully or those who are victimized by peers. Bullying is a systemic social problem that impacts the entire school, and has far-reaching implications for children's social and emotional adjustment. In 1993 the National Education Goals Panel (1999) outlined eight educational goals, which included improving school safety. According to the panel's follow-up report, very little progress has been made; most indicators suggested no improvements in school safety and others suggested a decline. Despite increased public concern and media attention related to school safety, research on bullying in the United States has lagged behind that in other countries. The majority of empirical research on bullying has been conducted in northern European countries (e.g., Olweus, 1973; Roland, 2000; Salmivalli, Huttunen, & Lagerspetz, 1997), the United Kingdom (e.g., Boulton & Underwood, 1992; Eslea & Smith, 1998; Smith & Sharp, 1994), Canada (e.g., Atlas & Pepler, 1998; Pepler, Craig, Ziegler, & Charach, 1994), and Australia (e.g., Rigby & Slee, 1991, 1993).

Bullying exists within a multilevel social context. Solutions to bullying problems require a coordinated social commitment on the part of both adults and children in the school. In this chapter we summarize the background research literature on bullying. Further, we examine factors that influence adult responsiveness and peer bystander behavior, as well as the social-emotional skills that enable children to form supportive social networks. Finally, we conclude with a description of *Steps to Respect,* a universal primary prevention program for elementary schools designed to reduce bullying problems.

BACKGROUND

Definition

People of all ages experience conflict in their relationships with others; hence, distinguishing bullying from other types of conflict is a crucial task for both children and adults. Verbal and physical aggression are frequently seen during conflicts among children of similar age, size, or status. On the surface, some of these behaviors overlap with those seen in bullying; however, there are several distinguishing features of bullying. Although there is no universally agreed upon definition of bullying (Harachi, Catalano, & Hawkins, 1999), most investigators in the field include the following three key elements (Atlas & Pepler, 1998; Craig & Pepler, 1999; Hazler, 1996; Olweus, 1993; Salmivalli et al., 1997): Bullying (a) involves a power imbalance in which the child doing the bullying has more power owing to such factors as age, size, support of the peer group, or higher status, (b) is carried out with an intent to harm the targeted child, and (c) is usually a repeated activity in which a particular child is singled out more than once and often in a chronic manner.

Characteristics of Bullying

Bullying behaviors encompass verbal aggression, physical aggression, and relationship-damaging behaviors. Bullying also may have sexual content, especially in the later elementary and middle school years. Bullying is often categorized as direct or indirect to differentiate behaviors that are expressed overtly from those that are expressed covertly (Olweus, 1993). Although examples of bullying do not all fall neatly into one of these two categories, they provide a useful framework for conceptualization purposes.

Direct Bullying

Direct bullying is characterized by open attacks on the targeted child, including physical and verbal aggression (Olweus, 1993). In cases of direct bullying, the child being bullied and often others in the environment know the identity of the person(s) doing the bullying. Direct physical bullying is the easiest form to recognize because the effects of the bullying are immediate and delivered directly to the targeted child. Examples of direct bullying include taunts, name calling, racial slurs, insults, physical harm, and threats.

Indirect Bullying

Indirect bullying involves covert, harmful behaviors directed toward another child (Olweus, 1993). Indirect bullying is more difficult to recognize and respond to because the person being bullied may not be present when the bullying occurs and/or may not know the identity of the child doing the bullying. There may be a delay between the occurrence of the bullying and its impact on the targeted child. Examples of indirect bullying include spreading rumors, writing graffiti about another child, and encouraging others not to play with a particular child.

Investigation of indirect bullying has been less common than for direct bullying. We have supplemented our discussion of indirect bullying with insights derived from the areas of indirect and relational aggression. The primary purpose of both forms of aggression is social exclusion or the damaging of a child's reputation or status within the peer group (Bjorkqvist, 1994; Bjorkqvist, Lagerspetz, & Kaukiainen, 1992; Crick & Grotpeter, 1995; Lagerspetz, Bjorkqvist, & Peltonen, 1988). Many of the behaviors classified as relational or indirect aggression resemble classic bullying scenarios (e.g., starting an injurious rumor, social exclusion) (Bjorkqvist, 1994; Crick & Grotpeter, 1995). However, caution is necessary since conclusions in these research literatures are based on a wider range of aggressive conflicts, only a portion of which constitute indirect bullying. Finally, in some cases, indirect bullying leads to physical harm (e.g., spreading a false rumor so that one child will fight another child; attaching a "kick me" sign to another child's back).

Prevalence

Most of the information regarding the prevalence of bullying problems is based on children's self-reports. The earliest figures were obtained in Norway as part of a nation-wide campaign to decrease bullying in schools (Olweus, 1993). About 7% of students reported regularly bullying others, while 9% reported that they were frequently victimized. Figures obtained by researchers in Europe, North America, Japan, Australia, and New Zealand have revealed rates of bullying problems comparable to or higher than the Norwegian sample (Smith et al., 1999). A survey of British adolescents indicated that those forming 21 to 27% of the sample were regularly targeted (Whitney & Smith, 1993). Canadian research has estimated the rate of bullying to be approximately 20% (Ziegler & Pepler, 1993). One of the few studies to examine chronic peer victimization problems in the United States revealed that 10% of a group of third- through sixth-graders were repeatedly victimized (Perry, Kusel, & Perry, 1988). A more recent study of U.S. fifth-graders found that 18% of those in the sample were regularly victimized by peers (Pellegrini, Bartini, & Brooks, 1999). A reasonably conservative estimate would be that 10-20% of North American schoolchildren are chronic targets of bullying.

Sex Differences

Early research in this field focused on direct bullying in exclusively male samples (e.g., Olweus, 1978). Research examining sex differences in bullying problems has been limited and has yielded mixed findings. Certainly, there is a commonly held view that girls bully less frequently than boys. When children's self-reports of direct bullying behavior are examined, girls report less frequent bullying behaviors than boys across age groups (e.g., Olweus, 1993). Furthermore, both boys (80%) and girls (60%) are more likely to report being bullied by boys than by girls. Recent observational research, however, reveals nearly equal rates of direct bullying for boys and girls (Craig & Pepler, 1995). Girls participated in both physical and verbal bullying, though they engaged in physical bullying less frequently than boys. Some evidence suggests that girls engage in indirect bullying more frequently than boys (Olweus, 1993), a finding that is consistent with research on relational and indirect aggression in elementary school (Crick & Grotpeter, 1995; Bjorkqvist et al., 1992; Lagerspetz et al., 1988). In general, research indicates that girls do engage in a wide range of aggressive behaviors and that they do so more frequently than is commonly thought.

Victimization. School-age boys consistently report being physically victimized more than do girls (e.g., Olweus, 1991; Perry et al., 1988; Rigby & Slee, 1991). This may explain why there is a stronger association between victimization and small physical size for boys than for girls (Olweus, 1993). Girls report being the target of taunts and insults more frequently than boys (Olweus, 1991) or at rates equal to that of boys (Perry et al., 1988). This verbal form of bullying does not require greater physical power in order to inflict pain.

Little is known about sex differences in victimization due to indirect bullying. In a study of relational aggression, Crick and Grotpeter (1996) found that boys and girls reported similar rates of victimization. Girls, however, report being more distressed by these events than do boys (Crick, 1995). These studies did not discriminate between bullying per se and more evenly matched bouts of relational aggression. Therefore, conclusions related to rates of indirect bullying are premature. What is clear is that children of both genders are impacted by bullying—and contrary to common myths, both boys and girls participate in a wide range of aggressive behaviors toward school mates.

Consequences of Bullying

For Children Who Bully

Criminal activity is one long-term sequela of chronic bullying. Olweus (1991) found that 60% of the boys identified as having serious bullying problems between sixth and ninth grades had at least one criminal conviction by age 24, and 40% of them had three or more arrests. Only 10% of the group of boys who did not engage in bullying behavior had criminal records as adults. These troubling results parallel those of longitudinal studies of aggressive behavior that have consistently identified childhood aggression as a significant risk factor for the development of criminal and other antisocial behaviors in adolescence and adulthood (e.g., Eron, Huesmann, Dubow, Romanoff, & Yarmel, 1987; Farrington, 1991; Loeber et al., 1993). More recently, a specific relationship between early childhood physical aggression and serious acts of delinquency and physical violence during adolescence was demonstrated (Nagin & Tremblay, 1999).

Very little is known about the specific impacts of direct bullying on children's subsequent interpersonal functioning and peer networks. However, research has consistently demonstrated a relationship between externalizing behaviors (e.g., aggression, oppositionality, and disruptiveness) and peer rejection in the elementary years (see Coie, Dodge, & Kupersmidt, 1990, for a review; Dishion, Patterson, Stoolmiller, & Skinner, 1991). Cairns and colleagues (Cairns, Cairns, Neckerman, Gest, & Gariepy, 1988; Patterson, Reid, & Dishion, 1992) have argued that some aggressive children may actually have leadership potential with peers. A reliance on coercive control strategies keeps children from developing this potential in a prosocial way. Over time, aggressive children are more likely to experience a decline in their peer group status. As they reach the upper grades of school, this can narrow their peer group to include only other children who have aggressive behavior problems, thus forming a deviant peer group that may contribute to the development of more serious patterns of antisocial behavior, including adolescent gangs.

The impact of indirect bullying on children who victimize others is not well understood. Research on relational aggression, however, suggests that relationally aggressive children are more likely to be rejected by peers (Crick & Grotpeter, 1995) and that they are at risk for the development of future social adjustment problems throughout the elementary years. This is especially true for children who are relationally aggressive and lack prosocial skills (Crick, 1996).

For Children Who Are Targets of Bullying

Peer victimization is associated with immediate and long-term negative effects on academic, social, and emotional functioning.

Academic functioning. As early as kindergarten, children who are bullied develop negative attitudes about school (Kochenderfer & Ladd, 1996). They also tend to view their school environment as less supportive than other children (Whitney & Smith, 1993). Academic problems seen in targeted children include avoidance and dislike of school, leading in later years to a greater risk of truancy and school dropout (Sharp, 1995). In a study of American teenagers, 17% reported that bullying had interfered with their academic performance (Hazler, Hoover, & Oliver, 1992). The American Association of University Women study on sexual harassment revealed that nearly 25% of students did not want to attend school, stayed home from school, or skipped class as a result of sexual bullying by peers (AAUW, 1993).

Social functioning. Bullying has negative effects on targeted children's peer relationships. Being a frequent target of bullying is positively associated with peer rejection (Hodges & Perry, 1999; Salmivalli, Lagerspetz, Bjorkqvist, Osterman, & Kaukiainen, 1996). Children tend to judge victimized children quite negatively and blame them for the bullying they endure (Oliver, Hoover, & Hazler, 1994). It should be emphasized that it is not simply the case that rejected children are bullied more, but that the experience of victimization actually leads to increases in peer rejection (Hodges & Perry, 1999). Peers apply negative labels such as "weak" and "nerdy" to victimized children (Charach, Pepler, & Ziegler, 1995) and show little empathy for them (Perry, Williard, & Perry, 1990). Furthermore, empathy for victimized children appears to diminish with increased age (Rigby & Slee, 1991). Relational aggression researchers have discovered similar findings linking victimization to increased rejection (Crick & Bigbee, 1998; Crick & Grotpeter, 1996). Taken together, these findings suggest that victimization can lead to further peer rejection and the development of an emotionally painful cycle in which the children who are most in need of support from their peers are increasingly less likely to receive it.

Being the recipient of aggression has been identified as one social learning process by which aggressive behavior may be learned (Huesmann & Eron, 1984). Indeed, research suggests that bullying and victimization are comorbid problems for a significant minority of children (Olweus, 1978, 1993). Further, observational research has revealed that when children are targets of aggression on the playground they are more likely to reciprocate with an aggressive response (Pepler, Craig, & Roberts, 1998). Longer-term relationships between victimization and aggression also have been demonstrated. For example, it has been demonstrated that behavior problems increase after children have been bullied and that these problems worsen over time (Schwartz, McFaydem-Ketchum, Dodge, Pettit, & Bates, 1998).

Emotional functioning. Children who are bullied tend to have lower self-esteem and feel more depressed, lonely, anxious, and insecure than nontargeted children (Boivin, Hymel, & Bukowski, 1995; Craig, 1998; Hodges & Perry, 1996; Olweus, 1978; Rigby & Slee, 1993; Slee, 1995). A relationship between peer victimization and emotional problems has been shown in children as young as preschool (Crick, Casas, & Ku, 1999) and kindergarten (Kochenderfer & Ladd, 1996) as well as in school-age children (Crick & Bigbee, 1998). Feelings of loneliness often persist even after the bullying stops (Boulton & Underwood, 1992).

Echoing an earlier point, it is not simply the case that children with emotional problems are bullied more. The experience of victimization itself leads to more emotional problems such as a decrease in self-esteem (Egan & Perry, 1998). Children begin to blame themselves for the bullying and may see themselves as social failures (Graham & Juvonen, 1998). These harmful emotional consequences have been found to extend into adulthood in the form of lower self-esteem and increased risk for depression (Olweus, 1993).

Finally, the experience of chronic bullying may lead to life-threatening consequences for some children. Norway's nationwide antibullying campaign was launched after the suicides of three young boys were attributed to bullying (Olweus, 1993). Similar national attention was focused on bullying in Japan following a chain of suicides by children who were bullied at school (Morita, Soeda, Soeda, and Taki, 1999). Empirical support for the link between being bullied and developing suicidal thoughts has been demonstrated in a study of Australian schoolchildren (Rigby & Slee, 1999).

BULLYING AS A SOCIAL CONTEXT AND IMPLICATIONS FOR PREVENTION

Most of the research reviewed in this chapter, up to this point, has focused on bullying from the perspective of children who bully and children who are victimized. However, when features of evidence-supported bullying prevention programs are coupled with the findings from recent research, the importance of viewing the conceptualization and prevention of bullying within a social context is strongly evident. Research related to the role of adult leadership, peer group processes, and student social-emotional skills in bullying problems is outlined below.

Adult Leadership

Schoolwide Changes

Government campaigns to reduce school bullying in countries such as Norway (e.g., Olweus, 1991) and England (e.g., Smith & Sharp, 1994) have prompted much of the research on bullying prevention program effectiveness (Smith & Brain, 2000). Previously evaluated programs emphasize a "whole school" approach to bullying with intervention targeting change at multiple levels. A particular emphasis is placed on the school level (Olweus, 1991, 1993). Examples of specific program goals common to the whole school approaches include (a) assessment of bullying problems through student surveys, (b) establishment of clear schoolwide policy and classroom rules about bullying, (c) increased staff responsiveness to bullying, and (d) improved parental awareness of and involvement in working on bullying problems.

Research has supported the effectiveness of whole school bullying prevention programs. Their use has been associated with (a) significant reductions in student reports of bullying (Olweus, 1991; Smith & Sharp, 1994), (b) improved classroom discipline and more positive student attitudes toward school (Olweus, 1991), and (c) increases in students' willingness to seek assistance to deal with bullying (Smith & Sharp, 1994). It should be noted that program effectiveness varied across schools. In general, the schools with the largest reductions in bullying were those that most thoroughly and consistently implemented the program (Eslea & Smith, 1998; Roland, 2000).

Staff awareness and intervention

A major obstacle to bullying prevention is lack of adult awareness of and/or intervention in bullying problems. Bullying is often covert as it tends to occur in less supervised areas of the school (Smith, 1991). Many students do *not* report being bullied to adults (O'Moore, Kirkham, & Smith, 1997; Ziegler & Pepler, 1993). Moreover, children report that adults rarely intervene in bullying problems (Olweus, 1993). Parents tend to be unaware of children's struggles with bullying and appear unlikely to address the issue with them (Olweus, 1993).

The often covert nature of bullying coupled with children's reluctance to request adult assistance appears to play a role in the low rate of intervention displayed by adults. Adults' misperceptions of bullying is another contributing factor. For example, Boulton (1996) found that lunchroom supervisors tended to mislabel true aggression as rough-and-tumble play (i.e., play-fighting). Moreover, adults may believe they are intervening in more bullying than is truly the case. Observational research of bullying paints an alarming picture of adult awareness and intervention. Teachers showed limited awareness of bullying incidents—even when these occurred in the classroom—and were found to intervene in only 18% of cases (Atlas & Pepler, 1998). Despite evidence that adults respond to only a small minority of bullying incidents, teachers describe themselves as intervening the majority of the time (Charach et al., 1995).

These findings indicate that effective bullying prevention efforts must increase adult responsiveness to bullying. In addition to raising awareness of the seriousness and pervasiveness of bullying, it is critical that all school personnel be taught how to correctly identify bullying, to increase monitoring of peer interactions, and to effectively intervene in bullying problems.

Peer Group Processes

Processes that occur within children's peer groups are another major contributor to the problem of bullying. The majority of children in a sample of Canadian elementary students reported that bullying is upsetting to watch. They endorsed conflicting feelings when they observed bullying, including confusion, fear of becoming the next target, and lack of knowledge regarding what to do (Pepler et al., 1994). Strong or confusing emotional reactions such as these reduce children's tendency to help others, by focusing on their own distress rather than that of the targeted child (Eisenberg, Wentzel, & Harris, 1998). There is also evidence that children look to peers for cues regarding how to respond to bullying (Salmivalli et al., 1997). Studies have demonstrated that most children report that they are sympathetic toward targets, and that they actively support children who are victimized. However, a significant minority of these children also reported that they would engage in bullying or felt a low level of sympathy for targeted children (O'Connell et al., 1997, as cited in O'Connell, Pepler, & Craig, 1999; Rigby & Slee, 1991).

Indeed, there are many ways children respond to bullying that make the situation worse. For instance, providing an audience for the behavior by standing around and watching or laughing can reinforce it (Craig & Pepler, 1995; Salmivalli et al., 1996). Moreover, observational research reveals that children's self-reports, like those of adults', overestimate the extent to which they engage in helpful bystander behavior. Live observations of bullying showed that bystanders were involved in a striking 85% of bullying episodes. In 81% of these cases, other children reinforced the bullying by providing attention or actually joining in the aggression (Craig & Pepler, 1995). They were also more respectful and friendly toward the child doing the bullying. In contrast, peers intervened to stop the bullying in only 11% of cases. Peers reinforced an equal proportion of bullying events whether the incident took place on the playground or in the classroom (Craig, Pepler, & Atlas, 2000).

Findings from observational research conducted in North America underscore the need to place bullying problems within a larger social context. Individual child characteristics such as level of social skills and aggression do not sufficiently predict bullying or other aggressive behaviors on the playground (Pepler et al., 1998; Stoolmiller, Eddy, & Reid, 2000). Rather, larger contextual factors (e.g., peers' reinforcement and modeling of aggression) are significantly related to aggression (Craig et al., 2000; Stoolmiller et al., 2000). Approaching bullying by solely trying to change the behavior of individual children does not address the role of peer processes in bullying (Craig et al. 2000; O'Connell et al., 1999; Salmivalli et al., 1997; Sutton & Smith, 1999). Consequently, many experts in the field strongly recommend that bullying prevention programs also address peer group attitudes, behaviors, and norms around bullying (Craig & Pepler, 1995; Craig et al., 2000; O'Connell et al., 1999; Salmivalli, 1999) as well as social skills training (Pepler et al., 1998).

Student Social-Emotional Skills

In addition to the monitoring and protection that adults provide, children need assistance coping with the emotional and social challenges posed by bullying. Research suggests that specific student social-emotional skills appear important in bullying prevention because they promote supportive peer networks, healthy peer relationships, and effective responses to bullying.

Promoting Supportive Peer Networks

There is a relationship among children's emotional competence, social skills, and the social goals that motivate skill use (Erdley & Asher, 1996, 1999; Parkhurst & Asher, 1985; Rose & Asher, 1999). Research shows, for example, that children are most likely to behave prosocially if they are able to empathize with the pain of others, and if they have skills that enable them to (a) regulate the negative emotions aroused by observing suffering and (b) respond assertively rather than withdraw (Eisenberg et al., 1996, 1997; Midlarsky & Hannah, 1985). It appears that empathy leads to a desire to help others as long as the level of emotional arousal is not so high that individuals become focused on alleviating their own distress rather than that of others (Hoffman, 1983; see review in Eisenberg, 2000). Empathy for others may also encourage children to choose positive rather than coercive social goals. Meta-analyses indicate that empathy is negatively related to aggression (Miller & Eisenberg, 1988), and this appears to be equally true for physical, verbal, and indirect aggression (Kaukiainen et al., 1999). A causal link is suggested by longitudinal research showing that higher levels of empathy in the preschool and elementary years predict later decreases in the severity or stability of aggressive and disruptive behavior (Hastings, Zahn-Waxler, Robinson, Usher, & Bridges, 2000).

In sum, the work of Eisenberg and her colleagues indicates that children's actions are more consistent with feelings of concern and social responsibility if they are able to manage the emotional arousal caused by empathic concern (Eisenberg et al., 1998). Thus, an approach that fosters children's empathy as well as effective emotion management may increase constructive bystander responses to bullying.

Promoting Effective Responses to Bullying on the Part of Victimized Children

Learning emotion management strategies and assertive response patterns may also assist children who are bullied. Children who cry or anger easily are increasingly likely to be rejected as the school year progresses (Maszk, Eisenberg, & Guthrie, 1999), putting them at risk for victimization (Asher, Rose, & Gabriel, in press; Ladd, Kochenderfer, & Coleman, 1997; Perry et al., 1988). In general, research shows that in comparison to nontargeted children, targeted children are more likely to reward bullying by giving in, crying easily, failing to defend themselves, and responding passively and nonassertively (Hodges, Boivin, Vitaro, & Bukowski, 1999; Olweus, 1993; Perry et al., 1990; Schwartz, Dodge, & Coie, 1993). Aggressive responses to bullying are associated with increased duration and severity of bullying incidents, increasing the risk of physical harm. Assertive self-defense, on the other hand, is associated with shorter incidents (Kochenderfer & Ladd, 1997; Wilton, Craig, & Pepler, 2000). These findings as well as those on helping behavior suggest that teaching children assertiveness and emotion management skills to use in coping with bullying may be a useful adjunct to school-wide environmental changes.

Promoting Healthy Peer Relationships

Fostering children's ability to interact skillfully with peers may provide additional benefits by buffering children from the effects of bullying. Research supports friendship as a protective factor against bullying (Boulton, Trueman, Chau, Whitehand, & Amatya, 1999). Children with at least one friend are less likely to be bullied (Hodges, Malone, & Perry, 1997). Moreover, children who were bullied but had a best friend developed fewer emotional and behavioral problems. Having a best friend also appears to reduce the likelihood that victimized children will be subject to further bullying later in the school year (Hodges et al., 1999). In addition, there is evidence that friendship moderates the positive relationship between early harsh home environment and later peer victimization (Schwartz, Dodge, Pettit, Bates, & Conduct Problems Prevention Research Group, 2000). Of course, not all friendships are supportive. Children often feel lonely and are more likely to avoid school if their friendships are nonsupportive and conflict-ridden (Ladd, Kochenderfer, & Coleman, 1996; Parker & Asher, 1993). It is important for children to learn how to respond to friends who do not treat them respectfully.

As noted previously, both aggressive behavior and peer victimization are associated with peer rejection. Rejection by peers is related to multiple negative outcomes such as school dropout, relationship difficulties later in life, and mental health problems (Cowen, Pederson, Babigian, Izzo, & Trost, 1973; Ollendick, Weist, Borden, & Greene, 1992; Parker & Asher, 1987). Teaching children skills such as successful group-joining strategies (Putallaz & Gottman, 1981; Putallaz & Wasserman, 1990), for example, may decrease the probability of social exclusion.

Interpersonal skills also appear important for children who display aggressive behavior. Training in group entry, as well as other social interaction skills, have been treatment components in school-based programs for aggressive children who were also rejected by peers (e.g., Coie, Underwood, & Lochman, 1991). Thus, providing all children with the social skills (e.g., expressing care, playing cooperatively, resolving conflicts) necessary to form and maintain friendships may contribute to bullying reduction in the long run (Asher, Parker, & Walker, 1996; Rose & Asher, 1999).

Summary and Implications

Bullying is a complex, distressing problem for school-age children and one for which they receive limited adult help. There are clear harmful effects from bullying on the development of large numbers of children. Not only are social and emotional adjustment impacted; bullying negatively affects children's academic functioning. There is a tendency to view bullying as a problem of individual children who are bullied or who bully others. However, there is evidence that individuals who observe bullying often behave in ways that maintain or exacerbate the problem. A comparison of self-report data with observational research findings indicates that not only do adults and children underestimate the degree to which they contribute to bullying problems, but they overestimate the frequency of constructive intervention attempts.

Past bullying prevention programs identified the development of effective school discipline policies and the improvement of adult responsiveness to bullying problems as key components of bullying prevention. There is also evidence that a more comprehensive approach to bullying prevention, specifically, one that addresses key peer group processes and student social-emotional skills as well as school- and adult-focused components, may enhance program efficacy. The following is a description of a recently developed bullying prevention program, Steps to Respect, that attempts to combine these elements.

Steps to Respect

Overview

Steps to Respect (Committee for Children, 2001) is an elementary school program designed to reduce bullying and promote healthy peer relationships. The program was developed by Committee for Children, a not-for-profit organization that develops, researches, and distributes school-based social-emotional learning programs. Steps to Respect is a universal primary prevention program. As is true of all universal prevention programs, some children will need additional intervention to effectively address more serious problems such as chronic bullying or chronic victimization, particularly if these problems are present in multiple settings. Other chapters in this book present intervention programs that may address the additional needs of higher-risk students.

Steps to Respect major program components consist of a program guide, staff training, an intermediate grade student curriculum, and telephone consultation ser-vices. These major components reflect schoolwide, adult, peer group, and individual-level factors related to bullying problems. The Steps to Respect program components are outlined below. Examples of specific program goals and skills are outlined in Table 1.

Development of the Steps to Respect Program

Steps to Respect was developed by an interdisciplinary team of curriculum developers, educators, trainers, and psychologists at Committee for Children. In addition, several external consultants with expertise in the areas of bullying and victimization provided input during the development process and reviewed student lessons. Lessons were field-tested in elementary schools in Canada and the United States in order to provide feedback to developers regarding lesson content and structure.

Specific attention was given during development to incorporating elements into the program that prior research has demonstrated to be important in preventing bullying. Student lessons are embedded within a focus that emphasizes the importance of adult responsiveness and schoolwide change to prevent bullying. It is strongly recommended that the schoolwide program elements (e.g., creating a bullying policy) and staff training to increase adult responsiveness be implemented before the student-level interventions. This approach ensures that adults in the environment are trained to respond effectively and promptly to bullying problems.

Steps to Respect student lessons emphasize student social-emotional skills that previous research has shown to be important, including skills for coping with bullying, general friendship skills and emotion management skills. Finally, based on research showing the critical role that bystanders play in contributing to the problem of bullying, Steps to Respect lessons teach empathy for bullied children and specific helpful ways children can respond when they witness bullying.

Program Guide and Consultation Services

The effectiveness of bullying prevention efforts has differed, in part, as a function of implementation quality (Eslea & Smith, 1998; Roland, 2000). Thus, in addition to an overview of the program content, goals, and research foundations, the Program Guide contains a schoolwide implementation manual. The implementation manual provides concrete information regarding setting up a whole school response to bullying. Specifically, it provides information, examples, and guidelines to principals and other key personnel for fostering staff support for the program, developing a schoolwide antibullying policy and reporting procedure, promoting a positive playground environment, encouraging prosocial student behaviors, monitoring program implementation, and establishing screening and referral procedures for students in need of additional assessment and intervention services. In addition to these written materials, telephone consultation is available through Committee for Children's Implementation Support Services. Implementation specialists are available to answer questions schools may have and respond to requests for assistance regarding issues such as the schoolwide policy and reporting procedure. Implementation specialists also facilitate a Web-based forum for educators to exchange implementation ideas and questions.

TABLE 1

Steps to Respect: Program Goals and Skills

Goal/skill	Example/s

Program Guide and Implementation Support Services

Goal/skill	Example/s
Policy and procedures	Develop antibullying policy and reporting procedure; develop referral procedure for students in need of additional services; adopt schoolwide positive reinforcement procedures to promote prosocial student behavior.
School structure	Increase supervision on playground and after-school bus lines; rotate use of specific playground sites (e.g., kickball diamond) by classroom.
Implementation quality	Secure staff support, clarify staff roles and responsibilities; conduct booster staff training sessions, track frequency of bullying reports.
Parent involvement	Provide information and encourage involvement through parents' night, handouts.

Staff Training

Goal/skill	Example/s
Knowledge	Understand prevalence and impact of bullying on students and school climate.
Monitoring	Identify bullying, monitor student interactions within and outside of the classroom.
Intervention	Intervene effectively in response to observations and student reports of bullying; follow school procedures for reporting and discipline, train staff to use supportive coaching techniques.

Student Curriculum

Social-emotional skills

Goal/skill	Example/s
Emotional competence	Empathy, perspective taking, emotion management.
Self-regulation skills	Risk assessment and decision making; setting and achieving prosocial goals.
Responses to bullying	Identifying bullying, responding to bullying through assertion or reporting to adults.
Peer group behavior	Bystander behavior that helps stop bullying rather than making it worse.
Positive social values	Respect for diversity, fairness, social responsibility.
Friendship skills	Joining, initiating conversation, building trust, including others, assertion, conflict resolution.

Academic skills

Goal/skill	Example/s
Language arts	Vocabulary enrichment, analysis of literary elements, text comprehension, writing.
Other subjects	Dramatic role plays; extension activities related to history, multiculturalism, geography.

Staff Training

Training goals are to achieve effective prevention and intervention in bullying problems by increasing (a) adult awareness of bullying and its impact on student development, (b) adult monitoring of student interactions as well as adult ability to correctly identify bullying, and (c) effective responses to bullying incidents through the use of a schoolwide reporting procedure. The staff training consists of a core training session and two specialty training sessions; the entire training can be presented in 1 day or spread out over 2–3 days. The core session is an all-staff training; attendance includes administrative staff, teachers, school psychologists or counselors, volunteers, custodial staff, playground monitors, bus drivers, office staff, and aides. Teachers, school psychologists, counselors, and administrators learn more in-depth coaching processes to use with children who are targeted and those who bully others. Finally, a short curriculum orientation for classroom instructors focuses on basic teaching strategies emphasized in student lessons such as role-playing techniques.

Student Curriculum

Steps to Respect contains a 12- to 14-week student curriculum to be taught by intermediate-grade elementary school teachers. The general goals of the curriculum (see Table 1 for specific skill examples) are to reduce bullying by promoting (1) the recognition of bullying, (2) safe and effective responses to bullying, (3) emotional competence, (4) supportive peer group behaviors, (5) friendship skills, (6) self-management skills, and (7) positive social values. In order to provide additional learning opportunities and encourage classroom use, the curriculum content was developed to integrate with other academic areas.

The curriculum materials consist of scripted lesson cards, handouts, overhead transparencies, and videotapes. Videotape vignettes, photo cards, and literature are used to stimulate class discussion, role-playing activities, direct instruction, games, and written assignments. The curriculum has three levels, each corresponding to a different grade. Each level contains skill lessons and a literature-based unit. Ten skill lessons focus on general and program-specific social-emotional skill development and contain extension activities with links to other academic skill areas. Literature-based lessons (8–10 in number) use existing children's literature to fully integrate social-emotional content (e.g., empathy) with language arts learning. Further, some of the literature units also address multicultural issues as well as other academic areas such as history. The inclusion of the student curriculum program component, especially its strong emphasis on friendship development and peer group contributions to bullying, is based on previously discussed research suggesting that bullying prevention may be enhanced through the use of more comprehensive programs.

Additional Program Resources

Parent resources. Steps to Respect contains a scripted parents' night program overview session, an informational brochure, and a series of handouts that suggest ways that parents can support the program at home.

Evaluation of Steps to Respect

In the fall of 2000, researchers at Committee for Children began a 3-year longitudinal study of the efficacy of the Steps to Respect program in improving bullying problems and fostering healthy peer relationships. The inclusion of a control group and use of playground observations as well as student and teacher-report survey methodology make the study unique in bullying prevention outcome research. Results of this research will be described in forthcoming reports.

CONCLUSION

Bullying is a complex problem that requires intervention on multiple levels. Information is now available to guide schools in responding sensitively and effectively to bullying. Prior research has identified schoolwide change to be a key component of effective bullying prevention (Olweus, 1991; Smith & Sharp, 1994). Active adult involvement is necessary to right the power imbalance inherent to bullying and bring about the school-level changes that have been shown to reduce it.. There is evidence that a more comprehensive approach to bullying prevention—that is, one that addresses key peer group processes and student social emotional skills as well as adult-focused components—may enhance program efficacy. Bullying prevention approaches that encourage a coordinated effort between the adults and children in a school community show the greatest promise for addressing this difficult problem. By leading such an effort, educators hope to decrease the suffering of victimized children and promote the development of a responsible, respectful school community.

Contact Information

Steps to Respect is available from Committee for Children. For more information about program components and pricing information, please contact Committee for Children at (800) 634-4449, visit our website at *www.cfchildren.org,* or write us at 568 1st Ave. S., Ste. 600, Seattle WA 98104-2804.

REFERENCES

American Association of University Women (AAUW). (1993). *Hostile hallways: The AAUW survey on sexual harassment in America's schools.* Washington, DC: Author.

Asher, S. R., Parker, J. G., & Walker, L. (1996). Distinguishing friendship from acceptance: Implications for intervention and assessment. In Bukowski et al. (Eds.), *The company they keep: Friendship in childhood and adolescence* (pp. 366-405). New York: Cambridge University Press.

Asher, S. R., Rose, A. J., & Gabriel, S. W. (in press). Peer rejection in everyday life. In M. Leary (Ed.), *Interpersonal rejection.* New York: Oxford University Press.

Atlas, R. S., & Pepler, D. J. (1998). Observations of bullying in the classroom. *The Journal of Educational Research, 92,* 86-99.

Bjorkqvist, K. (1994). Sex differences in physical, verbal, and indirect aggression: A review of recent research. *Sex Roles, 30,* 177-188.

Bjorkqvist, K., Lagerspetz, K., & Kaukiainen, A. (1992). Do girls manipulate and boys fight? Developmental trends in regard to direct and indirect aggression. *Aggressive Behavior, 18,* 117-127.

Boivin, M., Hymel, S., & Bukowksi, W. M. (1995). The roles of social withdrawal, peer rejection, and victimization by peers in predicting loneliness and depressed mood in children. *Development and Psychopathology, 7,* 765-785.

Boulton, M. J. (1996). Lunchtime supervisors' attitudes towards playful fighting, and ability to differentiate between playful and aggressive fighting: An intervention study. *British Journal of Educational Psychology, 66,* 367-381.

Boulton, M. J., Trueman, M., Chau, C., Whitehand, C., & Amatya, K. (1999). Concurrent and longitudinal links between friendship and peer victimization: Implications for befriending interventions. *Journal of Adolescence, 22,* 461-466.

Boulton, M. J., & Underwood, K. (1992). Bully victim problems among middle school children. *British Journal of Educational Psychology, 62,* 73-87.

Cairns, R. B., Cairns, B. D., Neckerman, H. J., Gest, S., & Gariepy, J. L. (1988). Peer networks and aggressive behavior: Social support or social rejection? *Developmental Psychology, 24,* 815-823.

Charach, A., Pepler, D. J., & Ziegler, S. (1995). Bullying at school: A Canadian perspective. *Education Canada, 35,* 12-18.

Coie, J. D., Dodge, K., & Kupersmidt, J. (1990). Peer group behavior and social status. In S. R. Asher & J. D. Coie (Eds.), *Peer rejection in childhood* (pp. 17-59). New York: Cambridge University Press.

Coie, J. D., Underwood, M., & Lochman, J. E. (1991). Programmatic intervention with aggressive children in the school setting. In D. J. Pepler & K. H. Rubin (Eds.), *The development and treatment of childhood aggression* (pp. 389-410). Hillsdale, NJ: Erlbaum.

Committee for Children. (2001). Steps to Respect™: A bullying prevention program. Seattle, WA: Committee for Children.

Cowen, E. L., Pederson, A., Babigian, H., Izzo, L. D., & Trost, M. A. (1973). Long-term follow-up of early detected vulnerable children. *Journal of Consulting and Clinical Psychology, 41,* 438-446.

Craig, W. M. (1998). The relationship among bullying, victimization, depression, anxiety, and aggression in elementary school children. *Personality and Individual Differences, 24,* 123-130.

Craig, W. M., & Pepler, D. J. (1995). Peer processes in bullying and victimization: An observational study. *Exceptionality Education Canada, 5,* 81-95.

Craig, W. M., & Pepler, D. J. (1999). Children who bully—Will they just grow out of it? *Orbit, 29,* 16-19.

Craig, W. M., Pepler, D. J., & Atlas, R. (2000). Observations of bullying in the classroom. *School Psychology International, 21,* 22-36.

Crick, N. R. (1995). Relational aggression: The role of intent attributions, feelings of distress, and provocation type. *Development and Psychopathology, 7,* 313-322.

Crick, N. R. (1996). The role of overt aggression, relational aggression, and prosocial behavior in the prediction of children's future social adjustment. *Child Development, 67,* 2317-2327.

Crick, N. R., & Bigbee, M. A. (1998). Relational and overt forms of peer victimization: A multi-informant approach. *Journal of Consulting and Clinical Psychology, 66,* 337-347.

Crick, N. R., Casas, J. F., & Ku, H. C. (1999). Relational and physical forms of peer victimization in preschool. *Developmental Psychology, 35,* 376-385.

Crick, N. R., & Grotpeter, J. K. (1995). Relational aggression, gender, and social-psychological adjustment. *Child Development, 66,* 710-722.

Crick, N. R., & Grotpeter, J. K. (1996). Children's treatment by peers: Victims of relational and overt aggression. *Development and Psychopathology, 8,* 367-380.

Dishion, T. J., Patterson, G. R., Stoolmiller, M., & Skinner, M. L. (1991). Family, school, and behavioral antecedents to early adolescent involvement with antisocial peers. *Developmental Psychology, 27,* 172-180.

Egan, S. K., & Perry, D. G. (1998). Does low self-regard invite victimization? *Developmental Psychology, 34,* 299-309.

Eisenberg, N. (2000). Emotion regulation and moral development. *Annual Review of Psychology, 51,* 665-697.

Eisenberg, N., Fabes, R. A., Karbon, M., Murphy, B. C., Carlo, G., & Wosinski, M. (1996). Relations of school children's comforting behavior to empathy-related reactions and shyness. *Social Development, 5,* 330-351.

Eisenberg, N., Fabes, R. A., Shepard, S. A., Murphy, B. C., Guthrie, I. K., Jones, S., Friedman, J., Poulin, R., & Maszk, P. (1997). Contemporaneous and longitudinal prediction of children's social functioning from regulation and emotionality. *Child Development, 68,* 642-664.

Eisenberg, N., Wentzel, M., & Harris, J. D. (1998). The role of emotionality and regulation in empathy-related responding. *School Psychology Review, 27,* 506-521.

Erdley, C. A., & Asher, S. R. (1996). Children's social goals and self-efficacy perceptions as influences on their responses to ambiguous provocation. *Child Development, 67,* 1329-1344.

Erdley, C. A., & Asher, S. R. (1999). A social goals perspective on children's social competence. *Journal of Emotional and Behavioral Disorders, 7,* 156-167.

Eron, L. D., Huesmann, L. R., Dubow, E., Romanoff, R., & Yarmel, P. W. (1987). Aggression and its correlates over 22 years. In D. H. Crowell, I. M. Evans, & C. R. O'Donnell (Eds.), *Childhood aggression and violence: Sources of influence, prevention, and control* (pp. 249-262). New York: Plenum.

Eslea, M., & Smith, P. K. (1998). The long-term effectiveness of anti-bullying work in primary schools. *Educational Research, 40,* 203-218.

Farrington, D. P. (1991). Childhood aggression and adult violence: Early precursors and later life outcomes. In D. J. Pepler & K. H. Rubin (Eds.), *The development and treatment of childhood aggression* (pp. 5-30). Hillsdale, NJ: Erlbaum.

Graham, S., & Juvonen, J. (1998). Self-blame and peer victimization in middle school: An attributional analysis. *Developmental Psychology, 34,* 587-599.

Harachi, T. W., Catalano, R. F., & Hawkins, J. D. (1999). U.S. and Canada. In P. K. Smith, Y. Morita, J. Junger-Tas, D. Olweus, R. Catalano, & P. Slee (Eds.), *The nature of school bullying: A cross-national perspective* (pp. 287-306). New York: Routledge.

Hastings, P. D., Zahn-Waxler, C., Robinson, J., Usher, B., & Bridges, D. (2000). The development of concern for others in children with behavior problems. *Developmental Psychology, 36,* 531-546.

Hazler, R. J. (1996). *Breaking the cycle of violence: Interventions for bullying and victimization.* Washington, DC: Accelerated Development.

Hazler, R., Hoover, J., & Oliver, R. (1992). What kids say about bullying. *The Executive Educator, 14,* 20-22.

Hodges, E. V. E., Boivin, M., Vitaro, F., & Bukowski, W. M. (1999). The power of friendship: Protection against an escalating cycle of peer victimization. *Developmental Psychology, 35,* 94-101.

Hodges, E. V. E., Malone, M. J., Jr., & Perry, D. G. (1997). Individual risk and social risk as interacting determinants of victimization in the peer group. *Developmental Psychology, 33,* 1032-1039.

Hodges, E. V. E., & Perry, D. G. (1996). Victims of peer abuse: An overview. *Reclaiming children and youth: Journal of emotional and behavioral problems, 5,* 23-28.

Hodges, E. V. E., & Perry, D. G. (1999). Personal and interpersonal antecedents and consequences of victimization by peers. *Journal of Social and Personality Psychology, 76,* 677-685.

Hoffman, M. L. (1983). Affective and cognitive processes in moral internalization. In E. T. Higgens, D. N. Ruble, & W. W. Hartup (Eds.), *Social cognition and social development: A socio-cultural perspective* (pp. 236-274). Cambridge, U.K.: Cambridge University Press.

Huesmann, L. R., & Eron, L. D. (1984). Cognitive processes and the persistence of aggressive behavior. *Aggressive Behavior, 10,* 243-251.

Kaukiainen, A., Bjorkqvist, K., Lagerspetz, K., Osterman, K., Salmivalli, C., Rothberg, S., & Ahlbom, A. (1999). The relationships between social intelligence, empathy, and three types of aggression. *Aggressive Behavior, 25,* 81–89.

Kochenderfer, B. J., & Ladd, G. W. (1996). Peer victimization: Cause or consequence of school maladjustment? *Child Development, 67,* 1305–1317.

Kochenderfer, B. J., & Ladd, G. W. (1997). Victimized children's responses to peers' aggression: Behaviors associated with reduced versus continued victimization. *Development and Psychopathology, 9,* 59–73.

Ladd, G. W., Kochenderfer, B. J., & Coleman, C. C. (1996). Friendship quality as a predictor of young children's early school adjustment. *Child Development, 67,* 1103–1118.

Ladd, G. W., Kochenderfer, B. J., & Coleman, C. C. (1997). Classroom peer acceptance, friendship, and victimization: Distinct relational systems that contribute uniquely to children's school adjustment? *Child Development, 68,* 1181–1197.

Lagerspetz, K. M., Bjorkqvist, K., & Peltonen, T. (1988). Is indirect aggression typical of females? Gender differences in aggressiveness in 1- to 12-year-old children. *Aggressive Behavior, 14,* 403–414.

Loeber, R., Wung, P., Keenan, K., Giroux, B., Stouthamer-Loeber, M., Van Kammen, W. B., & Maughan, B. (1993). Developmental pathways in disruptive child behavior. *Development and Psychopathology, 5,* 103–133.

Maszk, P., Eisenberg, N., & Guthrie, I. K. (1999). Relations of children's social status to their emotionality and regulation: A short-term longitudinal study. *Merrill-Palmer Quarterly, 45,* 468–492.

Midlarsky, E., & Hannah, M. E. (1985). Competence, reticence, and helping by children and adolescents. *Developmental Psychology, 21,* 534–541.

Miller, P., & Eisenberg, N. (1988). The relation of empathy to aggressive and externalizing/antisocial behavior. *Psychological Bulletin, 103,* 324–344.

Morita, Y., Soeda, H., Soeda, K., & Taki, M. (1999). Japan. In P. K. Smith, Y. Morita, J. Junger-Tas, D. Olweus, R. Catalano, & P. Slee (Eds.), *The nature of school bullying: A cross-national perspective* (pp. 309–323). New York: Routledge.

Nagin, D., & Tremblay, R. E. (1999). Trajectories of boys' physical aggression, opposition, and hyperactivity on the path to physically violent and nonviolent juvenile delinquency. *Child Development, 70,* 1181–1196.

National Education Goals Panel. (1999). *The National Education Goals report: Building a nation of learners, 1999.* Washington, DC: U.S. Government Printing Office.

O'Connell, P., Pepler, D., & Craig, W. (1999). Peer involvement in bullying: Insights and challenges for intervention. *Journal of Adolescence, 22,* 1–16.

O'Connell, P., Sedigndeilami, F., Pepler, D., Craig, W., Connolly, J., Atlas, R., Smith, C., & Charach, A. (1997). Prevalence of bullying and victimization among Canadian elementary and middle school children. Poster session presented at the meeting of the Society for Research in Child Development, Washington, D.C.

Oliver, R., Hoover, J. H., & Hazler, R. (1994). The perceived roles of bullying in small-town Midwestern schools. *Journal of Counseling and Development, 72,* 416–420.

Ollendick, T. H., Weist, M. D., Borden, M. C., & Greene, R. W. (1992). Sociometric status and academic, behavioral, and psychological adjustment: A five-year longitudinal study. *Journal of Consulting and Clinical Psychology, 60,* 80–87.

Olweus, D. (1973). Personality and aggression. In J. K. Cole & D. D. Jensen (Eds.), *Nebraska Symposium on Motivation 1972.* Lincoln: University of Nebraska Press.

Olweus, D. (1978). *Aggression in the schools: Bullies and whipping boys.* Washington, DC: Hemisphere Press (Wiley).

Olweus, D. (1991). Bully/victim problems among schoolchildren: Basic facts and effects of a school-based intervention program. In D. Pepler & K. Rubin (Eds.), *The development and treatment of childhood aggression* (pp. 411–448). Hillsdale, NJ: Erlbaum.

Olweus, D. (1993). *Bullying at school.* Cambridge, MA: Blackwell.

O'Moore, A. M., Kirkham, C., & Smith, M. (1997). Bullying behavior in Irish schools: A nationwide study. *The Irish Journal of Psychology, 18,* 141–169.

Parker, J. G., & Asher, S. R. (1987). Peer relations and later personal adjustment: Are low accepted children "at risk"? *Psychological Bulletin, 102,* 357–389.

Parker, J. G., & Asher, S. R. (1993). Friendship quality and middle childhood: Links with peer group acceptance and feelings of loneliness and social dissatisfaction. *Developmental Psychology, 29,* 611–621.

Parkhurst, J. T., & Asher, S. R. (1985). Goals and concerns: Implications for the study of children's social competence. In B. B. Lahey & A. E. Kazdin (Eds.), *Advances in clinical child psychology* (Vol. 8, pp. 201–228). New York: Plenum Press.

Patterson, G. R., Reid, J. B., & Dishion, T. J. (1992). *A social learning approach, volume 4: Antisocial boys.* Eugene, OR: Castalia.

Pellegrini, A. D., Bartini, M., & Brooks, F. (1999). School bullies, victims, and aggressive victims: Factors relating to group affiliation and victimization in early adolescence. *Journal of Educational Psychology, 91,* 216–224.

Pepler, D. J., Craig, W. M., & Roberts, W. (1998). Observations of aggressive and nonaggressive children on the school playground. *Merrill-Palmer Quarterly, 44,* 55–76.

Pepler, D. J., Craig, W. M., Ziegler, S., & Charach, A. (1994). An evaluation of an anti-bullying intervention in Toronto schools. *Canadian Journal of Community Mental Health, 13,* 95–110.

Perry, D. G., Kusel, S. J., & Perry, L. C. (1988). Victims of peer aggression. *Developmental Psychology, 24,* 807–814.

Perry, D. G., Williard, J., & Perry, L. C. (1990). Peers' perceptions of the consequences that victimized children provide aggressors. *Child Development, 61,* 1310–1325.

Putallaz, M., & Gottman, J. M. (1981). An interactional model of children's entry into peer groups. *Child Development, 52,* 986–994.

Putallaz, M., & Wasserman, A. (1990). Children's entry behavior. In S. R. Asher & J. D. Coie (Eds.), *Peer rejection in childhood* (pp. 60–89). New York: Cambridge University Press.

Rigby, K., & Slee, P. T. (1991). Bullying among Australian school children: Reported behavior and attitudes toward victims. *The Journal of Social Psychology, 131,* 615–627.

Rigby, K., & Slee, P. T. (1993). Dimensions of interpersonal relations among Australian school children and their implications for psychological well-being. *Journal of Social Psychology, 133,* 33–42.

Rigby K., & Slee, P. T. (1999). Suicidal ideation among adolescent schoolchildren, involvement in bully/victim problems, and perceived low social support. *Suicide and life-threatening behavior, 29,* 119–130.

Roland, E. (2000). Bullying in school: Three national innovations in Norwegian schools in 15 years. *Aggressive Behavior, 26,* 135–143.

Rose, A. J., & Asher, S. R. (1999). Children's goals and strategies in response to conflicts within a friendship. *Developmental Psychology, 35,* 69–79.

Salmivalli, C. (1999). Participant role approach to school bullying: Implications for interventions. *Journal of Adolescence, 22,* 453–459.

Salmivalli, C., Huttunen, A., & Lagerspetz, K. M. J. (1997). Peer networks and bullying in schools. *Scandinavian Journal of Psychology, 38,* 305–312.

Salmivalli, C., Lagerspetz, K. M. J., Bjorkqvist, K., Osterman, K., & Kaukiainen, A. (1996). Bullying as a group process: Participant roles and their relations to social status within the group. *Aggressive Behavior, 22,* 1–15.

Schwartz, D., Dodge, K. A., & Coie, J. D. (1993). The emergence of chronic peer victimization in boys' play groups. *Child Development, 64,* 1755–1772.

Schwartz, D., Dodge, K. A., Pettit, G. S., Bates, J. E., & Conduct Problems Prevention Research Group. (2000). Friendship as a moderating factor in the pathway between early harsh home environment and later victimization in the peer group. *Developmental Psychology, 36,* 646–662.

Schwartz, D., McFaydem-Ketchum, S., Dodge, K., Pettit, G., & Bates, J. E. (1998). Peer group victimization as a predictor of children's behavior problems at home and in school. *Development and Psychopathology, 10,* 87–99.

Sharp, S. (1995). How much does bullying hurt? The effects of bullying on the personal well-being and educational progress of secondary aged students. *Educational and Child Psychology, 12,* 81–88.

Slee, P. (1995). Peer victimization and its relationship to depression among Australian primary school students. *Personality and Individual Differences, 18,* 57–62.

Smith, P. (1991). The silent nightmare: Bullying and victimization in school peer groups. *Bulletin of the British Psychological Society, 4,* 243–248.

Smith, P., Morita, Y., Junger-Tas, J., Olweus, D., Catalano, R., & Slee, P. (1999). *The nature of school bullying: A cross-national perspective.* New York: Routledge.

Smith, P. K., & Brain, P. (2000). Bullying in schools: Lessons from two decades of research. *Aggressive Behavior, 26,* 1–9.

Smith, P., & Sharp, S. (1994). *School bullying: Insights and perspectives.* New York: Routledge.

Stoolmiller, M., Eddy, J. M., & Reid, J. B. (2000). Detecting and describing preventive intervention effects in a universal school-based randomized trial targeting delinquent and violent behavior. *Journal of Consulting and Clinical Psychology, 68,* 296–306.

Sutton, J., & Smith, P. K. (1999). Bullying as a group process: An adaptation of the participant role approach. *Aggressive Behavior, 25,* 97-111.

Whitney, I., & Smith, P. (1993). A survey of the nature and extent of bullying in junior/middle and secondary schools. *Educational Research, 35,* 3-25.

Wilton, M. M., Craig, W. M., Pepler, D. J. (2000). Emotional regulation and display in classroom victims of bullying: Characteristic expressions of affect, coping styles and relevant contextual factors. *Social Development, 9,* 226-245.

Ziegler, S., & Pepler, D. (1993). Bullying at school: Pervasive and persistent. *Orbit, 24,* 29-31.

Chapter 14

Prevention and Management of Behavior Problems in Secondary Schools

Randall S. Sprick
Teaching Strategies, Eugene, Oregon

Chris Borgmeier
University of Oregon

Victor Nolet
Western Washington University

INTRODUCTION

Secondary educators often express concerns about student discipline. Unfortunately, there is a paucity of empirically validated procedures for effective management of students' behavior in secondary classrooms. Disciplinary procedures employed at middle and high school levels seem to primarily consist of reactive administrative interventions, such as removal of problem students, rather than proactive educational and behavioral procedures.

Suspension and detention have commonly been identified as the most frequent form of discipline used in secondary schools (Skiba, Peterson, & Williams, 1997; Uchitelle, Bartz, & Hillman, 1989). Unfortunately, such exclusionary discipline methods have not been found to improve school outcomes, and may even have negative consequences on students, such as lost learning time in the classroom and increased risk of school dropout (Eckstrom, Goertz, Pollack, & Rock, 1986; Wehlage & Rutter, 1986). Also, the amendments to the Individuals with Disabilities Act (IDEA) passed in 1997 have greatly restricted the extent to which schools may use suspension or expulsion with students who have Individual Educational Plans (IEPs) (Yell, 1998). Suspension or expulsion would be viewed as a change in placement—and must be approved by an IEP team. Students on IEPs may not be out of placement for more than 10 days during an entire school year. Furthermore, the team must verify that the reason a student has been suspended or expelled is not a manifestation of the student's disability (Hartwig & Ruesch, 2000).

We believe that the use of effective instructional and classroom management practices can prevent many disciplinary problems that occur in secondary classrooms and significantly decrease the use of exclusionary discipline methods. This chapter reviews these management strategies, which can be employed by secondary classroom teachers. Some of the techniques described are documented in the research literature, some are extrapolations from research in the elementary grades, and some are based on the experiences of the authors.

Creating a Successful School Climate

There are many risk factors that may adversely affect a child's behavior in school, some of which are substance abuse, crisis situations, dysfunctional family life, and physiological problems. However, in spite of these external risk factors, school may, in fact, be a protective factor and make a difference in a child's social development. In studying high school students' perceptions of the impact of social versus school factors on their motivation to be successful, researchers at the Center for Research on the Context of Secondary School Teaching (CRC) have noted:

> Of most importance to practitioner and policy makers is the fact that many of the forces students mention are not objective constraints but factors under the control of teachers and principals. Furthermore, these young people present a view of themselves that may be surprising to those who are convinced that the plethora of social problems precludes effective responses through school improvement efforts. We find that despite negative outside influences, students from all achievement levels and sociocultural backgrounds want to succeed and want to be in an environment in which it is possible to do so. (Phelan, Davidson, & Cao, 1992, p. 696)

The overarching policies and climate of the school can serve as a powerful antecedent, prompting either responsible or irresponsible student behavior (Sprick, Garrison, & Howard, 1998; Sprick, Sprick & Garrison, 1992). Some of the factors at a schoolwide level that have an impact on student behavior include (a) clearly defined expectations for academic and social behavior, (b) direct instruction of expectations, (c) effective staff supervision of common areas, (d) clearly defined procedures for responding to misbehavior, (e) procedures for providing age-appropriate positive feedback, and (f) effective classroom organization and management (Sprick, Howard, Wise, Marcum, & Haykin, 1998; Sprick et al., 1992; Sugai & Horner, 1999). Because school personnel have more control over their own management practices than they do over the child's home life or physiology, it is our position that management of behavioral contingencies should always be one of the first interventions implemented to help a child improve his or her behavior. This position was emphasized in a recent article by the Committee on Preventative Psychiatry (1999) in which the authors stated, " . . . good schools, fostering academic success, responsibility, and self-discipline are associated with diminished risk for conduct disorders" (p. 238). This chapter will examine those classroom procedures that have a high probability of improving student behavior in secondary settings.

The Role of the School Psychologist

The procedures presented in this chapter are based on the premise that school psychologists can function (in a consultative role) as a resource to general education secondary teachers to intervene with discipline-related problems before a referral for special services becomes necessary. A major advantage that accrues when school psychologists assume a proactive role as a first step in problem solving is that teachers may be more receptive to intervention suggestions if the problem has not been occurring over a long period of time. To be most effective, the school psychologist must cultivate a relationship with teachers in which he or she is viewed as a nonthreatening resource person rather than a gatekeeper whose primary role is to facilitate removal of problem students from the classroom (Sprick & Garrison, 1993).

In developing this collaborative relationship, the psychologist may be involved in classroom observations, student progress monitoring, intervention planning with staff, and in-service teacher training. Fundamental to the relationship is the establishment of the school psychologist's credibility as someone who has skills and expertise to offer teachers in the design of secondary classroom interventions. Hence, school psychologists need to know about procedures that contribute to effective instruction and classroom management at the secondary level. The goal of this chapter is to provide school psychologists with some of this precise information. Other chapters in this volume (e.g., Schumaker, Deschler, & McKnight; Higgins, Boone, & Lovitt) offer additional critical information.

This chapter has three sections. The first section presents strategies for managing classrooms to prevent misbehavior. The second presents strategies for reducing unacceptable behaviors and increasing desired behaviors. These first two sections consist of procedures that are to be implemented by the classroom teacher; it is assumed that the psychologist is serving as a consultant in helping a teacher implement these procedures. The final section presents a variety of strategies that can be implemented by either the teacher or the psychologist in working with individual students with chronic problems.

PREVENTING MISBEHAVIOR

A key to effective behavior management at the secondary level is preventing problems before they have a chance to start. The most effective management techniques involve "not merely responding effectively when problems occur but preventing problems from occurring frequently" (Brophy & Evertson, 1983, p. 263). Effective managers know how they want each activity in the classroom to look, and they spend time teaching students to behave in appropriate ways (Darch, Miller, & Shippen, 1998; Emmer & Evertson, 1996; Jones & Jones, 1998; Sprick, 1985; Sprick, Garrison, & Howard, 1998).

Critical features of these skills include (a) rules and behavioral expectations, (b) routines and habits, (c) scanning, (d) scheduling, (e) student involvement in the lesson, and (f) effective evaluation and grading policies, which are discussed below.

Rules and Behavioral Expectations

The expectations a teacher has regarding students' possibilities for success can have a significant effect on student learning. Good (1987) summarizes two types of teacher expectations. The first is self-fulfilling prophecy: A teacher's beliefs about students' performance, in fact, influence that performance in a direction consistent with the teacher's beliefs. The second type is referred to as sustaining expectations: A teacher fails to see some students' potential and thus does not respond to those students in ways that would encourage them to fulfill their potential. Given these potential effects of teachers' expectations, teachers must strive to view every student as capable. More important, teachers must behave in a manner that clearly communicates expectations of good performance as well as behavior.

Classroom rules can effectively communicate to students that teachers have specific expectations about student behavior (Emmer & Evertson, 1996). Although high school teachers may not wish to post rules in a prominent place, as may be the practice in lower grades, rules can nevertheless be communicated in a "get acquainted" letter handed to students at the beginning of each year or quarter or through frequent class discussions or as part of a class syllabus.

In general, positively stated rules have advantages over negatively stated rules. Positively stated rules (e.g., "Arrive on time with all materials," "Stay on task") communicate a positive expectation and let students know what is important to the teacher. When presented to students, a set of positively stated rules allows teachers to conduct an invitational optimistic discussion regarding classroom behavior. Negatively stated rules (e.g., "Don't talk to your neighbor," "No cheating") insinuate an expectation of inappropriate behavior, and may even invite some of the students to challenge the rules. Also, a long list of negatively stated rules may force the teacher to spend valuable instructional time policing all the misbehaviors listed in the rules.

In most cases, the teacher can get by with three to eight rules. It is possible that a few of these may be negatively stated for the sake of clarity. For example, the rule, "No food or drink in the computer room" is clear and communicates important information.

Many people like to involve the students in the development of the rules, but this practice may be very difficult for a teacher with six different classes of students. At the secondary level, the best way to involve the students is to get them into a discussion of why the rules are important and how the rules relate to success in the subject of the class.

While positively stated rules are generally more desirable than negative ones, a disadvantage with the use of positive rules is that they are more broad and general than a list of "don'ts". For example, the positively stated rule, "Students are expected to make appropriate contributions to class discussions," is more general than the negatively stated rule, "No talking without raising your hand." Consequently, the teachers need to spend time in the first week of a semester teaching students how the positively stated rules relate to the specific procedures and routines in the classroom.

To communicate how the rules relate to specific classroom procedures, teachers first must know exactly how they expect classes of students to behave during every activity and then successfully communicate this information to their students. Teachers who are unclear about their expectations for student behavior will be inconsistent in their interactions with students (Evertson & Emmer, 1982). For example, the teacher may sometimes expect students to raise their hands to speak in class and at other times the teacher may not follow this expectation and respond to call-outs; or a teacher may sometimes allow students to talk during independent work periods and other times become angry with them for doing so. Secondary classroom teachers need to be unequivocal about (a) what students should do when they enter the room before the bell rings; (b) where students should go and what they should have with them at the beginning of class; (c) what students should be doing during the time the teacher is taking attendance or dealing with other administrative duties; and (d) how students are expected to behave in a variety of situations—such as lectures, discussions, independent work periods, films, and so on. A school psychologist working with a teacher who is experiencing difficulty managing student behavior could start by assisting the teacher in clarifying expectations for student behavior during each activity.

When teachers know how each activity and corresponding student behavior should look, they can communicate this information to students. A faulty assumption made by some teachers is that students in the secondary grades automatically know how to behave in every classroom setting. These teachers do not recognize that each teacher is slightly different in the way he or she conducts class and expects students to behave. In the absence of explicitly communicated expectations, students are forced to guess how each teacher wants them to act.

Teaching clear rules and expectations allows teachers to start their classroom off positively. Evertson and Emmer (1982) found that teacher behavior and classroom management during the first weeks of the school year are instrumental in determining the tone of a classroom for the remainder of the year. Teachers should enter the classroom on the first day of school with a clear plan so that they can quickly establish a consistent routine and a clear understanding of rules, behavioral expectations, and consequences among their students.

Teaching students to behave appropriately requires that the teacher discuss and clarify specific expectations for part of the class period throughout the entire first week of each new semester (Darch et al., 1998). Presenting all of this information only one time when going over the classroom rules on the first day may overwhelm some students. Thus, it is recommended that for the first five days of school, before beginning any new activity teachers should present information to the students on behavioral expectations for the upcoming activity. Students should be involved in discussions about how the expectations relate to the classroom rules and why the expectations are important for increasing every student's opportunity for success.

TABLE 1

Examples of Providing Specific Feedback
About Meeting Expectations

If behavior during the activity went well, the teacher might say:	"During today's lecture, whenever anyone had anything to say you remembered to raise your hand, and all the questions and comments were very pertinent to the subject of the lecture. Hand raising is important if everyone in the room is to get an opportunity to participate when they wish to."
If an activity did not go well, the teacher might say:	"During our independent work period, there were three or four times that I had to say, 'It's too loud. Please quiet down.' Getting to work together on your assignments is useful because you can learn by working together. However, if I have to keep reminding you to keep the noise down and to talk only about the assignment, I may need to say that no talking will be allowed. Tomorrow, work a little harder on managing the noise level."

Also during the first week, at the conclusion of each activity, teachers should provide students with specific feedback about how well expectations were met. Table 1 shows examples of how this information can be communicated to students.

Introducing each activity with a reminder of expectations and concluding it with feedback about how well those expectations were met allows teachers to calmly and assertively communicate to students how they want the classroom to run. The goal for teachers is to create the impression that they are confident that each student will behave appropriately when given clear information about expectations.

Routines and Habits

Many classroom behavior problems can be prevented through the use of established daily classroom routines and habits. For example, daily routines provide an efficient structure for keeping students actively engaged in academic tasks. Effective teachers use consistent routines and monitoring to establish expectations that class time will be used for classwork (Evertson & Emmer, 1982). These effective secondary teachers have routines for beginning class, assigning and collecting homework and classwork, arranging for makeup work for students who are absent, taking roll, correcting papers in class, dealing with students who do not have necessary materials, dealing with late assignments, allowing or not allowing the students to leave the classroom during class, having students clean up after labs, and excusing the class at the end of the period. These routines create an efficient, businesslike atmosphere in the classroom, where student attention is focused on academic tasks.

A crucial time for setting up effective routines is at the beginning of each class period. Without a routine for engaging students in academic tasks as soon as they enter the room, the teacher may be required to begin the period by quieting them down and getting them in their seats. An inefficient class beginning may result in 2 or 3 minutes—at best, and often more—wasted every day. If students are allowed to sit and do nothing for 2 minutes while the teacher completes administrative duties, some students will misbehave in order to have something to do. The sheer task of getting a disorganized class ready to work also provides increased opportunity for defiance and getting negative attention.

Here is an example of what a secondary teacher could say to establish a routine for getting class started and for dealing with any students who are late to class:

> Each day when you come into class, there will be a challenge problem on the overhead. Come into class, put your homework on your desk, and then get started on the challenge problem. You may work quietly with one or two other students on the problem. When the bell rings, continue to work on the problem, and I will take roll and collect your homework. If you finish the problem, you may talk quietly to your neighbor, but only after you have worked out the solution to the problem. In my class if you are not in the room with all your materials by the time the bell rings, you are considered tardy. If you are late, sign your name on the clipboard by the door. If you have a blue slip from another staff member or the office giving you permission to be late, simply attach the slip to the clipboard when you sign in. When you are late, please do not disrupt class or interrupt me, just sign the clipboard.

Notice that this teacher has students engaged in an academic task even while attendance is being taken. The teacher has outlined what students can do when they have finished the problem and has specified that until the problem is completed, students are expected to continue working. In short, the teacher has (a) communicated the expectation that students will be on time to class, and (b) provided clear information about what students should do when they are late.

Teachers also should establish and use routines during transitions between activities. A transition such as moving from a lecture/discussion format to working with the textbook requires that students use different materials and that they get their books out and open them. If this transition is handled poorly it can take too long and the attention of the class may be diverted, again increasing opportunities for defiance and attention getting. Teachers should try to conduct transitions quickly and efficiently so that students' attention is drawn to the next part of the task as soon as possible.

At the beginning of the school year, the teacher might introduce a transition in the following manner:

> Class, the next thing we are going to do is go over the assignment to answer the study questions at the end of the chapter. Before you get your books out, I want to let you know how I do things. First, I really dislike having to repeat instructions, so when I ask you to get your books open to a particular page, I will write the page number on the board, so there is no reason for anyone to ask, "What page?" In addition, I do not like to waste time each day moving from the lecture to going over the assignment, so when I ask you to get your books out and open, please do so quickly and quietly. Open your books to page 42 [while writing the page number on the board].

Efficient routines and smooth transitions help to keep students actively engaged in instructional tasks. Keeping students involved in instruction reduces behavior problems and consistently is correlated positively with academic achievement (Brophy & Evertson, 1976).

Scanning

Another tool used by effective teachers to prevent misbehavior and increase student motivation is scanning (Evertson & Emmer, 1982). Scanning is the process of frequently glancing to all parts of the room where students are located. Almost all teachers are good at scanning during teacher-directed instruction, but scanning is also critical during activities such as independent seatwork or lab activities. One of the obvious purposes for scanning is to catch minor misbehavior before it becomes a severe problem. Another reason teachers should scan is to demonstrate that they observe and are aware of the students' efforts to meet classroom expectations. Teachers who neglect to scan tend to interact only with misbehavior; however, teachers who scan are aware of and can provide feedback on both desirable and undesirable behaviors. Scanning is an important strategy for developing what Kounin (1970) referred to as "withitness"—the ability of effective teachers to be so in touch with what is happening in the classroom that they almost seem to know what students are going to do before they have a chance to do it.

Scanning is an easily observable teacher behavior that can be increased through coaching and practice. School psychologists can help teachers become better scanners by observing teachers' rates of scanning and providing feedback and modeling as needed.

Scheduling

The way teachers arrange activities within a 50-minute class period can have a significant impact on secondary students' behavior. Teachers who expect students to spend

TABLE 2

Examples of 50-Minute Class Schedules

Time	Schedule A	Schedule B
8:00	Attendance/Challenge Problem	Attendance/Challenge Problem
8:03	Lecture/discussion	Teacher-directed review
8:08		Lecture/discussion
8:18	Independent work	
8:20		Guided practice on assignment
8:25		Independent work on part of assignment
8:30		Correct problems just completed
8:35		Independent work
8:50		Questions/discussion of assignment
8:55	Class dismissed	Class dismissed

the majority of each class period engaged in paper-and-pencil tasks or who always give students a long time at the end of the class period for independent work should expect behavior problems.

Look at the two schedules shown in Table 2. Schedule A leaves lots of time for students to get off task. However, Schedule B, because it is so structured and teacher directed, does not allow as much opportunity for students to get off task. Intermixing teacher-directed instruction and student seatwork has a further advantage of giving students more guidance throughout their assigned tasks, thus reducing the chance that a student will make errors on an assignment. Some teachers are reticent about trying a sequence like Schedule B because of the number of transitions required. However, the teacher who establishes an active schedule from the beginning and runs the transitions efficiently as presented above can keep students focused on instructional tasks.

Student Involvement in the Lesson

Effective teachers do not simply lecture; they get students to participate in the lesson, and thus reduce misbehavior (Gunter & Hummel, 1998; Christenson, Ysseldyke, & Thurlow, 1989). By giving students frequent opportunities to respond and participate, the teacher can derive information on the degree to which students are mastering important concepts. On the basis of the correct and incorrect responses of students, the teacher can proceed with the lesson, or review and provide additional information and practice of key information. When giving a standard lecture without student participation, the teacher receives no information on the degree of student understanding or mastery.

One of the most obvious ways of facilitating student involvement in the lesson is for the teacher to ask questions frequently. However, care must be taken to involve all students, not just those who volunteer, because students who tend to volunteer often are those who are highly motivated by the content of the presentation.

Effective questioning, which involves virtually every member of the class, can be accomplished in three basic ways. Although rather unusual at the secondary level, one effective way to involve the class is to use whole-group choral responses. Choral responses are especially effective for the introduction of new vocabulary and for reviewing previously taught facts. However, choral responses are not feasible for responses that could be phrased in a variety of ways. Another approach is used when asking questions that have numerous correct answers: Here, the teacher should ask the question, instruct everyone to get an answer ready, and then call on an individual student. By waiting to name the student who is assigned to answer the question, the teacher increases the likelihood that all students will be thinking about the question and trying to develop an answer.

A third way to involve students in lessons via question asking and answering is to give frequent ungraded quizzes. Having each student answer three or four questions on a quiz and then correct the answers allows every student to participate, practice, and receive feedback on correct and incorrect responses. Frequent ungraded quizzes are a common feature of most mastery learning models of effective instruction (Becker, 1986).

Another important variable to consider with student participation is the extent that they understand in-class assignments or projects. Evertson and Emmer (1982) found that effective teachers clearly communicated directions and objectives of assignments. If students do not clearly understand the assignment—and, specifically, what they should be doing—they are much more likely to engage in off-task behaviors.

Structuring lessons in ways that require participation from students on a daily basis ensures that teachers receive ongoing feedback on whether students have achieved mastery on the material being taught. Teachers who rely primarily on lecturing and calling on volunteers receive insufficient feedback on mastery because students who do not understand rarely raise their hand to say, "I don't know."

Effective Evaluation and Grading Policies

One of the key ways to increase student motivation is to demonstrate to students that if they participate in class, complete assignments, and try their best, it makes a difference in whether they will succeed in passing tests and getting decent grades. In many classes a low-performing student could do everything the teacher asks—follow the rules, attempt to participate in class, try to do assignments and tests—and still fail. A student who continually experiences failure after trying to comply with a teacher's expectations has no incentive for behaving the way the teacher asks.

This section will examine ways teachers can demonstrate to students that effort pays off with passing grades. First, the evaluation procedures used to determine mastery will be examined, and then other aspects of grading systems will be explored that can help improve a student's motivation for earning a passing grade.

An effective evaluation system can make a big difference in student motivation. Teachers can increase their students' success on tests and prevent behavior problems by following three relatively simple steps:

1. When preparing unit tests, write the test first. The test should reflect the objectives the teacher has identified as being important. Thus, what is on a teacher's test should not be a surprise to students.

2. When introducing concepts in class that will be covered on the test, inform students that "this information is important" and they will be tested on it.

3. Provide students the opportunities to practice on the concepts taught until they achieve mastery.

By following these three steps, all students learn that if you pay attention in class, the lessons help prepare you for the test. Unfortunately in some classrooms the relationship between instruction and testing is not adequately clear to some students. Once students learn that passing tests is not a mysterious process, there is an increased chance that they will strive to achieve a passing grade. However, for students to be motivated toward grades, they must fully understand the teacher's grading system. The remainder of this section explores other aspects of grading systems that can affect student motivation.

Grades and their relationship to student behavior should function as a reinforcement system, not as a punishment tool. Many teachers expect students to be motivated to avoid getting bad grades. The problem with this assumption is that typically low-performing students may have become totally inured to receiving bad grades. An alternative approach is to construct grading systems so that a passing grade depends on student effort as well as mastery of material. When it is clear that effort and participation in class contribute to a student's grade, there is a good chance that the student will be more highly motivated to attend and behave in class. For more detailed information on this topic see Sprick (1985).

Another factor affecting whether students are motivated by grades is the extent to which the grading system is understood. Grading policies should be clearly stated and simple enough to be summarized on a handout. At the beginning of each new semester, the teacher should distribute and discuss this handout with students and explain the system in 5–10 minutes. In essence, the teacher will teach students that if you play by the rules, you can win the game—and winning the game means passing the course. If the system is so complex that students have trouble understanding it, some students will assume the rules are too complicated for them to possibly win the game—so why bother to play?

Another advantage in using an uncomplicated grading system is that simple and understandable policies allow students to monitor their own progress in class. Effective grading practices often involve students in keeping track of their own grades.

TABLE 3

Example of a Student Grading Record Form

Student: _____

Class: _____

Period: _____

Tests	Quizzes	Term Paper	Homework	Participation
#1 /100 points	#1 /100 points	/200 points	#1 /10 points	#1 /20 points
#2 /100 points	#2 /100 points		#2 /10 points	#2 /20 points
#3 /100 points	#3 /100 points		#3 /10 points	#3 /20 points
#4 /100 points	#4 /100 points		#4 /10 points	#4 /20 points
#5 /100 points	#5 /100 points		#5 /10 points	#5 /20 points
			#6 /10 points	#6 /20 points
			#7 /10 points	#7 /20 points
			#8 /10 points	#8 /20 points
			#9 /10 points	#9 /20 points
			#10 /10 points	#10 /20 points
Total /500 pts	Total /500 pts	Total /200 pts	Total /100 pts	Total /200 pts

FINAL SCORE   /1500 points

Sophisticated students know where they stand at any point during the grading period. Ask high-performing students what their grades are and you get responses such as, "In history I have a B but there are three more tests in the grading period so I know I can kick it up to an A if I study for those tests." Ask lower-performing students the same question and they look at you as if you are crazy. Many lower-performing students think that grades are something teachers do to them at the end of the semester. Students who do not know their current grade are unlikely to be motivated to want to get a better grade. Unless students are required to keep track of their grades, only the most motivated will do so. One way to help students track their own grades is to give them a form at the beginning of the semester that they can keep in their notebooks and that they are required to keep up to date. A sample of such a record sheet is shown in Table 3.

A sheet of this type makes it possible to have students total their points to date and determine their grades. Each week the teacher can put information on the board out-lining where student point totals are heading in terms of letter grades—an example is shown in Figure 1.

The procedure requires teachers to use a point system for determining grades. Unfortunately, some teachers will give letter grades on assignments without using a

FIGURE 1

Classroom Example of Using the Blackboard to Keep Students Updated on Their Grades

Second Period Grades as of Monday, November 3
  325 points possible so far.

    293 - 325 = A
    260 - 292 = B
    227 - 259 = C
    195 - 226 = D
    Less than 195, come and see me!

point system, making it very difficult to communicate to students the relative weight of different types of assignments. For example, a low-performing student who gets an A on a homework assignment may think that a D on a term paper has been offset. Through the use of points, the teacher can more readily communicate that the term paper is worth a possible 200 points and each homework assignment is worth 10 points. Therefore, it is expected that students should put far more time and effort into the term paper than into a homework assignment and it is clear that the term paper makes up a greater portion of a final grade than does a homework assignment.

Another point system grading technique that can increase student motivation involves establishing a percentage of the actual academic grade (and thus the total points earned) that is based on participation and effort. To incorporate this procedure the teacher must decide how many points students can earn each week for behavior and participation before the term begins. This number should be based on the approximate percentage input this behavior grade will have on the total grade. For example, in a ninth-grade science class the teacher estimates that there will be approximately 750 points for tests, labs, homework, and the final exam during the 12-week trimester. If the teacher would like behavior and effort to have a 25% impact on the grade, the grading system should have approximately 1,000 total points possible. Assigning 20 points possible per week would result in 240 points for behavior during a 12-week trimester. Thus there would be a total possible of 990 points, 240 being approximately 25% of the 990 point total.

The recommended percentage of the grade to be based on behavior and participation can range from 0 to 80 depending on the class. Percentages generally will be higher in classes of middle and junior high school students than at the high school level. That is, in middle school and junior high, one of the major objectives should be to teach students how to behave in ways that will allow them to be successful in further academic pursuits. Consequently, a greater percentage of the grade can be based on the degree to which students exhibit these behaviors.

Once the number of participation points possible each week has been determined, the teacher must decide on a system for students to earn those points. The criteria for awarding points should be made as objective as possible, and students should be told in advance how their behavior will be evaluated. In the example of the science class with 20 points possible each week, the teacher might present the plan to the class in the following manner:

> Each week, I will put a grade in the grade book based on your behavior and participation. There are 20 points possible, and each week you begin the week with 16 points. I will determine your points based on how well you use your class time and each of you will get a score between 0 and 20. Anytime I tell you that you are using your class time well, I will make a note next to your name on the class list attached to this clipboard, and that raises your score 1 point. Anytime you are wasting class time and I need to remind you to get back on target, you lose a point. Each Friday, I will post the scores on the bulletin board in the same way that I post the scores for tests. Look for your student number to find the points you earned for the week. Anytime during the week that you want to know where you are, come and look at my clipboard before or after class.

The teacher can extend this system to include consequences for tardies, late work, not having materials, and any other frequent but minor types of problems. However, the system should not be viewed as consisting predominantly of negative consequences. It is important to note that such a grading system carries with it the responsibility that the teacher must make a concerted effort to get to each student two to four times each week to acknowledge positive performance. The goal is for students to see that by using class time well they can improve their grade. Detailed information on establishing and implementing a system of this type is provided in Sprick (1985).

Teachers frequently are concerned about the legality of a system that bases a percentage of student grades on behavior. The most important consideration is that students be informed from the beginning of a course how behavior will affect their grades and how their points will be determined each week. Disputes with grading often involve a teacher who modifies a student grade at the end of the term because of misbehavior during the term.

It should be noted that some professionals have argued that a student's grade should entirely reflect the degree of mastery of course content and should not involve any aspect of student behavior (Gathercoal, 1987). However, the authors have found participation grading to be an effective tool for preventing and reducing minor misbehavior and for increasing the motivation of many students.

BEHAVIOR CHANGE

Many adolescents exhibit complex behavior patterns that have been maintained by a long history of attention from peers, teachers, or parents; escape from schoolwork; or even escape from school. Common sense suggests that if behavioral contingencies such as reprimands, time in the office, and detention or suspension were always effective, there would be few behavior problems in schools. Unfortunately these consequences often function unintentionally as either positive or negative reinforcement procedures. To further complicate matters, by the time some students get to high school, they have learned a large repertoire of disruptive behaviors that can seem impervious to change.

Use of the strategies discussed thus far can prevent a significant amount of misbehavior in secondary classrooms. However, some misbehavior probably will occur regardless of the effectiveness of prevention strategies employed. This section will present procedures that secondary teachers can use to increase desirable behaviors and address discipline problems that do occur. First, a review of some basic principles of behavior management will be presented. Table 4, on page 388, may be a useful tool to help refresh the behavior management skills of secondary teachers. For a more in-depth study of the application of behavioral principles in classroom settings encourage teachers to examine Alberto and Troutman (1986), Becker (1986), Kerr and Nelson (1998), or Sulzer-Azaroff and Mayer (1986).

These seven basic principles can be reviewed and discussed with secondary teachers. However, in working with secondary teachers, the school psychologist should be careful not to alienate teachers with unnecessary or unfamiliar vocabulary. For example, to many teachers, the word punishment means something different from the classic behavioral definition (i.e., a stimulus that follows a behavior and reduces the future occurrence of that behavior). When some teachers hear the word punishment, they assume an angry, vengeful procedure implemented by the teacher. Given these potential differences in vocabulary, it is clear that communication between psychologists and teachers has the potential to be difficult, yet this communication must be precise. Throughout the remainder of this chapter, punishment procedures will be referred to as punitive consequences.

Guidelines for Reducing Misbehavior Using Punitive Consequences

This section will examine procedures for reducing misbehavior. Guidelines will be given for effectively implementing punitive consequences and then four specific consequences will be presented. An effective secondary teacher must demonstrate an ability to act when misbehavior occurs. Thus, reprimands and sanctions are important procedures for teachers to be able to implement (Doyle, 1986). We see the need for secondary teachers to be familiar with seven major guidelines for implementing punitive consequences effectively.

TABLE 4

Review of Basic Classroom and Behavior Management Strategies

1. Interventions with individual students who have discipline problems must be aimed at reducing undesirable behaviors, increasing desirable behaviors, and maintaining acceptable behaviors.

2. Behaviors that are positively reinforced are likely to occur more often in the future.

3. Behaviors that are not reinforced will tend to occur less often in the future. The process of extinction relies on this relationship.

4. Behaviors that are punished will tend to happen less often in the future.

5. Behaviors that terminate or remove an unpleasant (aversive) stimulus are likely to occur in the future whenever that aversive stimulus reoccurs. The principle of negative reinforcement is based on this relationship.

6. One person's meat is another's poison: Events that serve as positive reinforcers, punishers, or aversive stimuli differ from one person to the next.

7. Problem behaviors should be understood and addressed according to the appropriate dimensions. Behavior can be problematic owing to intensity, duration, latency, rate, or location.

Guideline 1: Stay calm. When working with secondary-level students, this is the most important guideline. Some students derive a great sense of power from their ability to make adults angry. In working with this type of student, an emotional response from the teacher serves as a powerful positive reinforcer of inappropriate behavior. As noted earlier, behaviors that are not positively reinforced will tend to happen less often in the future. When the teacher calmly informs the student of a consequence, it communicates that the misbehavior has no power to affect the teacher, and the student's misbehavior is essentially placed on extinction. A calm implementation also communicates that the teacher's feelings have nothing to do with the fact that the consequence is being implemented. The student has been previously informed that the behavior would lead to the consequence and now the teacher is calmly following through on that arrangement.

Guideline 2: Treat students with respect. During any implementation of a consequence students should be treated with dignity and respect. Humiliation, sarcasm, and ridicule should never be used as consequences. Respect for students is evidenced by use of adult vocabulary, offering students choices about events that affect them, use of realistic timelines, and use of age-appropriate consequences for desired as well as undesired behaviors.

Guideline 3: Develop a hierarchy of consequences. The most frequent misbehaviors in classrooms are minor infractions, and yet in many classrooms the teacher's only consequences are severe, such as referral to the office. Office referral is appropriate for severe problems, but is inappropriate for behaviors such as talking in class, being off task, forgetting materials, handing assignments in late, and other minor disruptive behavior. If mild consequences are not used, the teacher must tolerate lots of these minor infractions, because office referral is too severe a consequence to reasonably fit the infraction. Each teacher needs a range of consequences to fit the range in severity of classroom rule infractions (Sprick, 1981).

For most behavior, soft reprimands and/or individual and private discussions should be the first step. In many cases, simply informing the student that a behavior is unacceptable may be sufficient to reduce the future occurrence of mild misbehavior (Darch et al., 1998; Walker, Colvin, & Ramsey, 1995). A soft reprimand can be verbal or nonverbal, and should communicate to the student what behavior is expected.

Some advantages of reprimands are that they are quick, easy, and involve no record keeping on the part of the teacher. Also, reprimands have less probability of creating adversarial relationships between the teacher and the student than more intrusive consequences, such as separating the student from his or her friends or requiring the student to stay after class. An effective reprimand communicates that the teacher fully anticipates students will be successful in meeting positive expectations in the future.

Finally, reprimands are most useful for minor classroom infractions in the early stages of a semester while the teacher is still clarifying classroom expectations. However, if the misbehavior continues after the students know and understand the expectations, reprimands may not be sufficient and another consequence (e.g., separating the student from their friends) may need to be established.

Guideline 4: Plan ahead. For consequences to be most effective, students should know which behaviors will meet with a teacher response. If reprimands have not worked, inform the student that future infractions will no longer be reprimanded but will entail a specific consequence. After reviewing with the student what the specific consequence will be, the teacher should question the student to ensure understanding. When equipped with the information that misbehavior will result in a specific consequence, the student will thus understand that to choose to engage in the behavior is to also choose to receive the consequence.

Guideline 5: Establish a concurrent plan to reinforce success. When dealing with chronic misbehavior, a punitive consequence alone has a relatively low probability of changing student behavior. Many students with problem behavior have developed a "So what?" attitude toward being kept after school or being sent to the vice-principal's office. If reprimands have not been effective and it becomes necessary to establish another consequence, the teacher also needs to think about how to motivate the student to cooperate. An intervention that applies consequences only for misbehavior is usually doomed to failure primarily because it does not teach students appropriate behavior.

The goal of the intervention is for the student to learn that inappropriate behavior results in aversive consequences, but appropriate behavior results in pleasant consequences. How to accomplish this goal in ways that are not embarrassing to the student will be covered later in the chapter.

Guideline 6: Be as consistent as possible. Students must see that, once it is made clear that a behavior will lead to a specific consequence, the teacher follows through consistently. If some days the students "get away with it," the behavior can become part of a game the students play: "Let's see if I can do it again today and not get caught."

Guideline 7: Keep the interaction short. When an infraction occurs, the teacher should simply state the misbehavior and state the consequence and then resume instruction. If the teacher spends more than 3 seconds on the problem, the flow of the lesson is lost. All too often, misbehaving students can control the pace of the instruction through their misbehavior. For example, each time an infraction occurs, the teacher may have to stop teaching and says things like: "Jason, I am getting very tired of this. We have discussed this before and you know that when this happens I keep you after school. I do not like keeping you after any more than you like being kept after, but you leave me no choice. I now fully expect you to get your act together."

If the scenario above is happening several times a week, it is easy to observe how much attention the student is receiving for the inappropriate behavior. Not only is the student getting attention from the teacher during the lecture, but every other student in the class is watching the interaction. When the teacher singles out an individual for a lecture on behavior, the student is put on display in front of peers. Some students like nothing better than being the center of attention for having been "bad."

When the chronic misbehavior occurs, the teacher should spend no more than 3 seconds with a student who has misbehaved. If the situation has previously been discussed with the student, at the time of the infraction the teacher can simply say, "Jason, that is disruptive; you owe me time after school. Now class look at Problem 3." It is important that the teacher immediately shifts the focus off the problem student and back to instruction.

Four Specific Classroom Consequences for Reducing Misbehavior

As discussed earlier in the chapter, the most common negative consequence in secondary schools seems to be office referral. Although office referral is a reasonable consequence for dangerous, illegal, or truly insubordinate behavior, it is not reasonable or even effective for typical classroom misbehavior. Secondary teachers need to understand that a mild consequence implemented calmly and consistently will tend to work better than a more severe consequence implemented emotionally or inconsistently. The following consequences are presented in order of least to most intrusive. The first employs response cost, a procedure that reduces the frequency of occurrence of a behavior through contingent removal of a previously earned reinforcer. In a general sense, the other three procedures could be thought of as forms of time-out, in which the student is denied the opportunity to receive attention or social reinforcement for a fixed period of time.

Response cost. Response cost programs offer flexibility in classrooms because they can be implemented in a variety of ways. Students earn points toward valued reinforcers; teachers commonly give each student a specific number of behavior points at the start of the week and the number of points a student earns increases with the occurrence of appropriate behaviors or decreases with the occurrence of inappropriate behavior throughout the week. For example, each time the teacher reminds a student to get back to work, the teacher records the reprimand and the student loses one point. It is important to note that these points are not deducted from points earned from other point "categories" such as tests and assignments. For programs using response cost to be effective, the students must be taught how the whole system works. The teacher must also keep an emphasis on awarding points for positive behavior rather than simply taking away points for misbehavior.

Time owed. In essence time owed involves keeping a student after class for a short period of time. This consequence can be used only in schools that have passing periods long enough to keep a student after class for a short time and still give the student time to get to the next class. For example, if a school has 4-minute passing periods and in 3 minutes a student could get to the farthest room in the school, the teacher could keep a student after class for up to 1 minute without having to give the student an excuse to get into the next class. The teacher informs students in advance that for certain infractions they may be kept after class for 30 seconds per infraction. This rule would allow the teacher to use this with any student for two infractions per class period. This consequence is very mild but it can be effective with some students, because it cuts into their time for socializing out in the school halls.

During instructional periods the goal is to have students actively engaged in the lesson. However, when time owed is used students should not be allowed to do assigned work. Assigned work should not be part of a consequence because the student may assume that it is punishment. Furthermore, allowing academic work to be completed during this time can make the time go by very quickly and reduce the aversive nature of time owed. Completing work during time owed may even inadvertently create a "study hall" for that student that frees up time during another part of their day. The student should sit and do nothing during the time owed.

Isolation area in class. This is essentially a secondary-level version of time-out. One of the major mistakes teachers make with this procedure is to isolate students for long periods of time; the isolation period should be relatively short. In this procedure a desk and chair are set off to the side of the room and students are informed that for various infractions they will be sent to this area until they are ready to participate appropriately in class. Generally this procedure is used more frequently at the middle school and junior high levels than at the high school level. While in the isolation area, the students should have nothing to do. The goal of this procedure is to impress on the students that because of their misbehavior they are not being allowed to participate for a short time.

The length of time the students remain in the isolation area can either be a standard 5-minute period, or if the teacher prefers, the students can be informed that they may rejoin the class whenever they feel ready. However, if the isolated students are permitted to choose to come out on their own, the teacher should specify a criterion such as, "You may rejoin the group when you are ready to quietly work on your math at your seat."

After-school detention. This is one of the most common consequences in use in secondary schools. Routinely, all students assigned to detention after school report to a particular room. In many schools there will be 20 or 30 students after school each day. The detention period is usually 30-60 minutes and students are usually required or allowed to do academic work during this time.

This consequence has more potential problems than any of the consequences previously described. The biggest problem is student transportation. Usually the infraction occurs on one day, the parents are notified that evening, the student stays after school the next day, and the student and/or the parents are responsible for arranging transportation. This means that there is a 24- to 31-hour delay between the infraction and the consequence. This time delay reduces the potential effectiveness of the consequence. Another problem with keeping students after school is getting the student to show up. If the student does not come to the detention area, there need to be additional consequences imposed. A final problem is that the student is now in the same room with other students with problem behaviors and these students often reinforce one another's misbehavior.

If the same students are routinely being kept after school in detention, it is important to change the consequence. Have the student spend the detention time after school with the teacher who assigned the time. In this way, the student is not in the room with other problem students and will probably find the after-school time to be more boring. Unfortunately, this procedure may be more punishing to the teacher than to the student. The teacher needs to evaluate whether keeping the student after school would be effective in changing the behavior and whether accomplishing this change is worth the time and effort required to keep the student after school.

Maintaining and Increasing Student Motivation

One useful way of thinking about student motivation is the Expectancy X Value (expectancy multiplied by value) theory (Feather, 1982). According to this theory, student effort on a task will be a product of the degree to which the student expects to be successful at the task multiplied times the degree to which the student values the rewards that accompany success. Note that the function described is multiplicative rather than additive, because if either expectancy or value is equal to zero, student effort will also be nonexistent.

If the teacher does an effective job of teaching behavioral expectations and organizing the classroom during the first weeks of the school year, as was described in the first section of this chapter, students will know exactly what is required to be success-ful. If the teacher does an exemplary job, every student will believe that it is possible to be successful if they do the things the teacher asks them to do. If the teacher follows through and implements effective instructional practices, students will experience suc-cess in their daily learning activities. To put it another way, the teacher has built the expectancy that success will be possible, and the first half of the expectancy times value theory has been accomplished. The second half of the equation—value—then needs to be addressed.

The majority of students in the typical secondary classroom already value good grades and the satisfaction associated with successful task completion. However, other students just don't seem to care. To motivate these students, secondary teachers need to do more than teach interesting classes and manage a reasonable grading system; second-ary teachers need to implement techniques that will increase student motivation in extrinsic ways. Although this can be accomplished with a variety of strategies, two major techniques will be discussed here: (a) using teacher and peer attention to reinforce desired behaviors, and (b) using more structured or tangible rewards when necessary.

Differential Teacher and Peer Attention

Some secondary students who do not seem to value success get far more attention for misbehavior than for positive behavior (Sprick & Howard, 1995; Walker, H. et al., 1995). It could be argued that the attention is, in fact, serving to reinforce the inappropriate behavior. One tool for increasing the motivation of these students is to change which cat-egories of behaviors lead to attention and recognition from the teacher and from peers.

The first step in this behavior change process is to reduce the amount of attention the student receives for negative behavior. This can be accomplished by ignoring the majority of minor misbehavior and by implementing mild and quick consequences for the more severe misbehaviors. For example, the teacher may decide to ignore a student who neglects to raise her hand or gets out of her seat; but the teacher may institute con-sequences for the same student when she uses offensive language or is physically aggressive. As was previously described, when implementing consequences the teacher should be calm and should take no more than three seconds to state the consequence. By delivering consequences in this fashion, the teacher reduces the amount of time spent with the student following the severe misbehaviors. By ignoring the minor mis-behaviors, the teacher reduces the number of times during each class period the student gets attention for misbehavior. In doing this, the teacher has also reduced the amount of peer attention the misbehaving student receives. By maintaining a focus on instruction, the teacher can keep the attention of the class focused on the task, rather than on the student who is trying to gain recognition through inappropriate behavior.

At the same time the teacher is working on reducing attention to misbehavior, effort must be put into giving time and attention to appropriate behavior. At the sec-ondary level this can be challenging, especially when the teacher perceives a long, negative history of interactions with a student. Getting past this history is important. A teacher should attempt to interact with students while they are behaving appropriately three times more frequently than while they are behaving inappropriately. This can be accomplished in two ways: first, by simply interacting with a student while that student is behaving appropriately, and second by using effective praise.

Examples of interacting with a problem student while he is behaving appropriately include saying hello to him as he enters the classroom, calling on him when he appears to be listening, looking at his work while he is on task, talking with him in the hallway, smiling at the student when he hands in the assignment, making sustained eye contact during a lecture, or asking the student to take a note to the office. Although none of the examples above involve overt praise, the interaction communicates that the student is of interest and value to the teacher and that the student does not need to misbehave in order to be acknowledged or recognized.

Praise can be another useful technique for increasing student motivation. Secondary teachers too often assume that students with a history of problem behavior are unresponsive to praise. To be effective, praise must be contingent, descriptive, and nonembarrassing. Contingent praise follows an appropriate behavior that is new or difficult for the student, or follows a behavior the individual is proud of. No one wants to be praised gratuitously.

Effective praise is descriptive rather than evaluative. In acknowledging a student's performance the teacher should state exactly what behavior the student exhibited that is important. The focus should be on what the student did, not on how much it pleases the teacher. Over time, descriptive praise will help students to learn to evaluate and reinforce their own behavior.

At the secondary level, the teacher should be careful not to put the student in the position of being embarrassed in front of peers for having done a good job. In general, praise will be less embarrassing if it is (a) distributed so that every student gets positive feedback, (b) if it is part of the flow of instruction, and (c) if it focuses on the behavior rather than on the student. Another important factor is that the positive feedback be implemented in a manner that the teacher is comfortable with. If the teacher tends to be businesslike, then positive feedback to students can be given in a very businesslike manner. If the teacher is very energetic and friendly, then positive feedback can be given in a very energetic and friendly manner. If the businesslike teacher attempts to reinforce in an overly friendly manner, the students may feel that the interaction is insincere. For more details on effective praise see Sprick (1985) and Brophy (1981).

Structured Rewards

In addition to frequent attention to positive behavior, secondary teachers can increase student motivation through the use of more structured rewards. One systematic way of delivering feedback and rewards has already been presented—designing a portion of the grading system on student behavior. In this system, when praising a positive behavior or reprimanding an inappropriate behavior the teacher records the interaction. At the end of each week, every student is given a score for that week that

TABLE 5

Intermittent Rewards Suitable for Secondary Students

- Writing a note to the student's parents
- Calling the student's parents
- Complimenting the student in front of another staff member
- Giving the student a responsibility
- Tickets to a school activity
- Coupon to rent a movie
- Privately praising the student's classroom performance in a nonclassroom setting such as in the hall after school

- Writing a note to the student
- Calling the student
- Asking one of the administrators to reward the student's behavior
- Tokens for a video arcade
- Food
- Letting the student choose an activity for the class
- Checking out a book the student might be interested in

is entered into the grade book based on the number of positive comments and negative comments. One of the goals of this procedure is for students to see that appropriate behavior can positively affect their grades.

Another way to reward appropriate performance is through a variety of intermittent rewards. Unlike structured reinforcement systems, where a contract is made that states, "If you do ..., you get ...," intermittent rewards are delivered sporadically at the discretion of the teacher. For example, when a student makes a really significant step toward success, the teacher may want to use a stronger reinforcer than praise. This is the time to provide a special reward. Intermittent rewards should give students the feeling that their behavior was truly special. If any specific reinforcer is used too much, there can be an inflationary phenomenon and the reinforcer may lose value to the student because of its overuse. This problem can be reduced if the teacher implements a variety of intermittent rewards. Table 5 shows a list of some potentially effective rewards that can be used intermittently at the secondary level.

With the students who are not intrinsically motivated, effective praise, frequent attention, and occasional intermittent rewards may fill out the value portion of the motivation equation. The eventual goal is that every student will become intrinsically motivated; however, until that occurs the school staff must demonstrate that positive behaviors lead to positive consequences.

INTERVENTIONS INSTITUTED DIRECTLY BY THE PSYCHOLOGIST

The interventions presented thus far are procedures to be implemented by the classroom teacher. There are several effective interventions that can be facilitated through the direct involvement of the school psychologist. School psychologists not only play an important role as a consultant to teachers in schools, but also in directly working with students to clarify rules and expectations, teaching students successful classroom behaviors, assessing student ability, and implementing reinforcement programs with individual students.

Clarifying Rules and Expectations

In the case of a student who is chronically misbehaving, the school psychologist may observe him or her in the classroom, review the teacher's rules with the student, and ask the student questions regarding the teacher's behavioral expectations. "What are you supposed to be doing during the time your teacher is taking attendance? If you have a question or something to say while the teacher is lecturing, how are you supposed to get the teacher to call on you?" By observing in the classroom and interviewing the student, the school psychologist can determine whether the student's misbehavior is a result of not understanding the teacher's expectations or a result of choosing to misbehave or break the rules.

If the student lacks a detailed understanding of the teacher's expectations, we recommend that the school psychologist arrange a meeting with the teacher and the student so that these expectations can be discussed in a positive manner. As a third party at this meeting, the school psychologist asks questions of both the teacher and the student to help clarify the minute-by-minute expectations for that classroom. With some students it may also be helpful to have the school psychologist and the student practice and role-play classroom situations to be sure that the student can meet the expectations (Colvin, Kame'enui, & Sugai, 1993; Colvin & Sugai, 1988).

Improving Students' Participation in Class

School psychologists can also help students who do not actively participate in class, meet with them and establish an expectation that they should be taking notes in class. To avoid overwhelming the student and to determine whether this will be a helpful intervention, the school psychologist can start by working with the student on one class period. The school psychologist can then teach the student to take notes by giving a very specific assignment, such as, "Make at least three specific notes each day in a notebook during fourth period." In addition the psychologist can help the student realize that teachers tend to flag the most important information and can encourage the student to write a note anytime the teacher says things like:

> "This is important."
> "Be sure to study pages ..."
> "You really need to know ..."
> "Pay particular attention to ..."

The psychologist and the student can then meet once a week to examine the notes the student has made. The school psychologist can reinforce the student if he or she is meeting the expectation of participating in class or can provide additional encouragement, strategies or instruction if necessary.

Assisting Students in Understanding Grading Practices

Another direct intervention strategy involves the school psychologist meeting with the student to discuss grades. A surprising number of secondary-level students do not understand grading practices. The psychologist can interview the student about one or more teachers' grading practices and, if the student is uncertain, can coach the student in how to go to the teacher to find out more. Below are some of the types of information students may need coaching in how to obtain:

> How many points they have currently,
> How many points are currently possible,
> Any assignments that they have not turned in, and
> The teacher's grading scale (e.g., 90% for an A, and so on).

After the student has gathered this information, the psychologist can teach the student to track grades and monitor progress.

It may also be useful for the school psychologist to help the student set realistic goals for improving performance. Goal setting has been demonstrated to be an effective procedure for improving student performance (Bandura & Schunk, 1981; Tollefson, Tracy, Johnsen, Farmer, & Buenning, 1984). The student may need assistance initially, because the goals should be specific, fairly immediate, and challenging but obtainable. Written contracts are also a useful tool for helping a student become more motivated to improve performance and thus improve grades. For more detailed information on goal setting and contracts see Sprick & Howard (1995).

Mediating Consequences With Teachers and Students

In some situations it is beneficial for the school psychologist to mediate a meeting between the teacher and the student. By facilitating a discussion, the psychologist can help the teacher in clarifying expectations and in helping the teacher and the student negotiate the consequences for unacceptable behavior (Sprick et al., 1993). The goal is to ensure that the student understands which behaviors will lead to negative consequences and also which acceptable behaviors the teacher wishes to see. A meeting of this type not only helps clarify expectations for the student, it can also help the teacher be more consistent. When the teacher has explained his or her procedures to the student in front of a third party, there is an increased accountability for following through on what was stated.

Implementing a Reinforcement Program

In some cases teachers may be unwilling to establish a plan to reinforce success. In this situation, a plan can be established and implemented by the psychologist. One example would be a daily report card that the teacher signs if the student has behaved appropriately. The psychologist then meets with the student weekly to debrief the student's performance, awards points for good days, sets goals, and provides reinforcers as the student accumulates enough points.

Teaching Students to Interact With Teachers

If a student behaves in ways that result in frequent negative interactions with adults, the school psychologist can teach the student to interact positively with the teacher. Training the student to do things as simple as saying hello and smiling at the teacher can go a long way toward helping improve a teacher's perception and willingness to help a student. Other strategies that can be shared include teaching the student when and how to go to the teacher and ask a question and teaching the student to appropriately reinforce the teacher's behavior.

CONCLUSIONS

Classroom management procedures implemented by secondary teachers play a major role in affecting the behavior of all students who are not intrinsically motivated. The effective secondary teacher (a) organizes the classroom and instruction in ways that communicate to students that they can be successful if they are willing to follow the rules and try; (b) develops strategies for dealing with misbehavior that are efficient and consistent and that do not allow misbehavior to interrupt the flow of instruction; (c) provides extrinsic motivation to the students who need it in the form of positive attention, praise, and intermittent rewards; and (d) uses a grading system that allows students to earn points for participation, completion of assignments, and tests, while providing frequent feedback to students regarding their performance.

The school psychologist can assist teachers and students in implementing strategies such as clarification of expectations, goal setting, and training the student in how to interact with teachers. The goal of the psychologist should be to work with teachers and students before a problem has gone on so long that the teacher only wants the student removed from the room. The strategies presented in this chapter can counter many problems before they reach crisis proportions. Effective teaching and classroom management need to be proactive processes and the psychologist can play a significant role in helping teachers incorporate these practices into their teaching repertoire.

REFERENCES

Alberto, Y. C., & Troutman, A. C. (1986). *Applied behavior analysis for teachers* (2nd ed.). Columbus, OH: Merrill.

Bandura, A., & Schunk, D. (1981). Cultivating competence, self-efficacy, and intrinsic interest through proximal self motivation. *Journal of Personality and Social Psychology, 41,* 586-598.

Becker, W. C. (1986). *Applied psychology for teachers.* Chicago: Science Research Associates.

Brophy, J. E. (1981). Teacher praise: A functional analysis. *Review of Educational Research, 51,* 5-32.

Brophy, J. E., & Evertson, C. M. (1976). *Learning from teaching: A developmental perspective.* Boston: Allyn and Bacon.

Brophy, J. E., & Evertson, C. M. (1983). Classroom organization and management. *Elementary School Journal, 83,* 265-285.

Christenson, S. L., Ysseldyke, J. E., & Thurlow, M. L. (1989). Critical instructional factors for students with mild handicaps: An integrative review. *Remedial and Special Education, 10,* 21-31.

Colvin, G., Kame'enui, E. J., & Sugai, G. (1993). Reconceptualizing behavior management and school-wide discipline in general education. *Education and Treatment of Children, 16,* 361-381.

Colvin, G., & Sugai, G. (1988). Proactive strategies for managing social behavior problems: An instructional approach. *Education and Treatment of Children, 11,* 341-348.

Committee on Preventative Psychiatry. (1999). *Journal of American Academy of Child and Adolescence Psychiatry, 28,* 235-241.

Darch, C, Miller, A., & Shippen, P. (1998). Instructional classroom management: A proactive model for managing student behavior. *Beyond Behavior, 9*(3), 18-27.

Doyle, W. (1986). Classroom organization and management. In M. C. Wittrock (Ed.), *Handbook of research on teaching* (3rd ed., pp. 392-431). New York: Macmillan.

Eckstrom, R. B., Goertz, M. E., Pollack, J. M., & Rock, D. A. (1986). Who drops out of high school and why? Findings from a national study. *Teachers College Record, 87,* 357-373.

Emmer, E., & Evertson, C. (1996). *Classroom management for secondary teachers* (4th ed.). Boston: Allyn and Bacon Walker.

Evertson, C. M., & Emmer, E. T. (1982). Effective management at the beginning of the school year in junior high classes. *Journal of Educational Psychology, 74,* 485-498.

Feather, N. T. (Ed.). (1982). *Expectations and actions.* Hillsdale, NJ: Erlbaum.

Gathercoal, F. (1987). *Judicious discipline.* Ann Arbor, MI: Prakken.

Good, T. L. (1987). Teacher expectations. In D. C. Berliner & B. V. Rosenshine (Eds.), *Talks to teachers* (pp. 159-200). New York: Random House.

Gunter, P., & Hummel, J. H. (1998). Are effective academic practices used to teach students with behavior disorders? *Beyond Behavior, 9*(3), 5-11.

Hartwig, E. P., & Ruesch, G. M. (2000). Disciplining students in special education. *Journal of Special Education, 33*(4), 240-247.

Jones, V. F., & Jones, L. S. (1998). *Comprehensive classroom management: Creating communities of support and solving problems* (5th ed.). Boston: Allyn and Bacon.

Kerr, M. M., & Nelson, C. M. (1998). *Strategies for managing behavior problems in the classroom* (2nd ed.). Columbus, OH: Merrill.

Kounin, J. S. (1970). *Discipline and group management in classrooms.* New York: Holt, Rinehart and Winston.

Phelan, P., Davidson, A., & Cao, H. (1992). Speaking up: Students' perspectives on school. *Phi Delta Kappan, 73,* 695-704.

Skiba, R. J., Peterson, R. L., & Williams, T. (1997). Office referrals and suspension: Disciplinary intervention in middle schools. *Education and Treatment of Children, 20,* 295-315.

Sprick, R. (1981). *The solution book: A guide to classroom discipline.* Chicago: Science Research Associates.

Sprick, R. (1985). *Discipline in the secondary classroom.* West Nyack, NY: Center for Applied Research in Education.

Sprick, R., Sprick, M., & Garrison, M. (1992). *Foundations: Establishing positive discipline policies.* Longmont, CO: Sopris West.

Sprick, R., & Garrison, M. (1993). *Interventions: Collaborative planning for high risk students.* Longmont, CO: Sopris West.

Sprick, R., & Howard, L. (1995). *Teacher's encyclopedia of behavior management: 100 problems/500 plans.* Longmont, CO: Sopris West.

Sprick, R., Garrison, M., & Howard, L. (1998). *CHAMPs: A proactive and positive approach to classroom management.* Longmont, CO: Sopris West.

Sprick, R., Howard, L., Wise, B., Marcum, K., & Haykin, M., (1998). *The administrator's desk reference of behavior management, volumes I, II, & III.* Longmont, CO: Sopris West.

Sugai, G., & Horner, R. (1999). Discipline and behavioral support: Practices, pitfalls and promises. *Effective School Practices, 17*(4), 10-22.

Sulzer-Azaroff, B., & Mayer, G. R. (1986). *Achieving educational excellence: Using behavioral strategies.* New York: Holt, Rinehart and Winston.

Tollefson, N., Tracy, D., Johnsen, E. Farmer, W., & Buenning, M. (1984). Goal setting and personal responsibility for LD adolescents. *Psychology in the Schools, 21,* 224-233.

Uchitelle, S., Bartz, D., & Hillman, L. (1989). Strategies for reducing suspensions. *Urban Education, 24,* 163-176.

Walker, H. (1995). *The acting out child: Coping with classroom disruption.* Longmont, CO: Sopris West.

Walker, H., Colvin, G., & Ramsey, E. (1995). *Antisocial behavior in schools: Strategies and best practices.* Pacific Grove, CA: Brookes/Cole.

Wehlage, G. G., & Rutter, R. A. (1986). Dropping out: How much do schools contribute to the problem? *Teachers College Record, 87,* 374–393.

Yell, M. (1998). Disciplining students with disabilities. In *The law and special education* (pp. 313–351). Columbus, OH: Merrill/Prentice Hall.

CHAPTER 15

Teaching Social Skills to High-Risk Children and Youth:
Preventive and Remedial Strategies

Frank M. Gresham
University of California-Riverside

INTRODUCTION

Most students who are considered to be at risk for emotional and behavioral difficulties in school settings are considered as such based on a behavior pattern that does not meet teachers' social behavior standards and that exceeds teachers' tolerance levels for classroom behavior (Gresham & Reschly, 1988; Hersh & Walker, 1983). These students exhibit a behavior pattern that creates a poor "fit" between teachers' expectations for appropriate academic and social behaviors and create substantial difficulties for high-risk students, their teachers, and peers within the context of general education settings. Many of these students enter school without being socially and emotionally ready for the demands of the school experience. They perform more poorly academically, have fewer positive social interactions, and are at risk for grade retention and future school dropout (The Child Mental Health Foundations and Agencies Network, 2000).

Research indicates that of the total student body in an elementary or middle school, approximately 80% of students *will not* exhibit major behavior problems and are open to universal guidance and instruction on social norms because of previous successful learning experiences (Gresham, Sugai, Horner, Quinn, & McInerney, 1998). A second, smaller group of students (about 10 to 15%) will be at risk for severe behavior problems. These students engage in problem behaviors beyond acceptable levels and will not respond to basic schoolwide interventions (Taylor-Greene et al., 1997). A third group of students (about 1 to 7%) display chronic patterns of violent, disruptive, and destructive behavior. These students contribute 40 to 50% of major behavioral disruptions in the school and draw 50 to 60% of building and classroom resources and attention, and will not respond to typical, schoolwide intervention (Colvin, Sugai, & Kame'enui, 1993).

Social competence deficits are characteristic of the second and third groups of students described above. These social competence deficits are often accompanied by an *externalizing behavior pattern* and are particularly critical in the development and maintenance of childhood disorders such as oppositional defiant disorder, conduct disorder, and attention deficit/hyperactivity disorder (Achenbach, 1985; Hinshaw, 1987). For example, students exhibiting an antisocial behavior pattern characterized by aggression, hostility, and violation of social norms are highly resistant to intervention, particularly if the intervention does not occur early in the child's educational career (Walker, Colvin, & Ramsey, 1995). Kazdin (1987) argued that after about age 8, an antisocial behavior pattern should be viewed as a chronic condition (similar to, for instance, diabetes) that cannot be "cured," but rather managed with appropriate interventions and supports.

Students with attention deficit/hyperactivity disorder (ADHD) also exhibit significant deficits in social competence and difficulties in interpersonal relationships (Barkley, 1990; Guevremont, 1990; Landau & Moore, 1991). Pelham and Bender (1982) estimated that over half of children with ADHD experience substantial difficulties in interpersonal relationships with other children, their parents, and their teachers. Landau and Moore suggested that these children evoke an extremely negative response from their peer group, which, in turn, leads to higher levels of peer rejection (Milich & Landau, 1989). These students are perceived by peers and teachers as annoying, boisterous, intractable, and irritating; much of which can be attributed to the core behavioral characteristics of impulsivity, inattention, and overactivity (Whalen & Henker, 1985).

EXTREME-RISK STUDENTS

Recently, researchers and practitioners have focused on another group of children who are at extremely high risk for developing a lifelong pattern of antisocial behavior. These children exhibit a behavior pattern marked by hyperactivity-impulsivity-inattention coupled with conduct problems (HIA + CP) characterized by fighting, stealing, truancy, noncompliance, and arguing (Lynam, 1996). Using the terminology of the *Diagnostic and Statistical Manual of Mental Disorders* (4th ed.) (American Psychiatric Association, 1994), these children would be considered at risk for comorbid diagnoses of ADHD and conduct disorder/oppositional defiant disorder. Lynam (1996) termed these children "fledgling psychopaths" and suggested that they are at greater risk for developing a lifelong pattern of antisocial behavior than children demonstrating HIA or conduct problems alone. Another term that might be applied is "students who exhibit antisocial behavior + hyperactivity," or ABH.

Lynam's (1996) "fledgling psychopaths" can be traced back to the work of Cleckley (1976) who described *psychopathy* as a behavior pattern marked by risk taking, sensation seeking, and involvement in a variety of criminal activities. Socially, the psychopathic individual may be described as egocentric, manipulative, grandiose, and forceful (Lynam, 1996). Psychopaths exhibit shallow emotions, lack empathy, and show little remorse for wrongdoing. In his work with violent offenders, Hare (1981) described psychopaths as among the most violent and persistent of offenders in that they commit more thefts, robberies, and assaults and escape more often than nonpsychopathic offenders (Hare, 1981; Hare & Jutai, 1983; Hare, McPherson, & Forth, 1988).

Students demonstrating the combination of ABH are likely to possess the worst features of both domains because they tend to be more physically aggressive, persist longer in antisocial behavior, display more severe achievement deficits, and have higher levels of peer rejection than children with attention problems or conduct problems alone (Farrington, Loeber, & Van Kammer 1990; Gresham, MacMillan, Bocian, Ward, & Forness, 1998; Hinshaw, 1987; Hinshaw, Lahey, & Hart, 1993). Identification of this group of children has substantial implications for assessment and intervention in schools. Bullis, Walker, and Sprague (in press) warn that there are some extremely antisocial individuals who are very socially skilled but use these skills to achieve antisocial ends. As such, these persons do not need social skills training in the same manner that is required for the majority of high-risk students.

Summary

Research has shown that the prognosis for children becomes markedly worse when comorbidity of ABH is present. Comorbid diagnoses are increasing in prevalence and significantly hinder the development and functioning of many children (Loney, 1987; McConaughy & Skiba, 1993). Children with this behavior pattern evidence a variety of delinquent acts in adolescence, more severe aggression in adolescence, and more violent offending in adulthood than those who are not comorbid for these diagnoses (Loeber, Brinthaupt, & Green, 1990; Lynam, 1996, 1997). What is particularly disturbing about this group is the *impulsive response style* coupled with the tendency to engage in severe aggression and violent behavior. Owing to the immediate and often dangerous behavior associated with such problem behavior patterns, efforts to correctly identify and subsequently intervene on these behavior patterns are crucial.

THEORETICAL AND EMPIRICAL FOUNDATIONS

Definitional Issues

A recent review of theories and definitions of social skills by Merrell and Gimpel (1998) indicated that there were 15 definitions that have been used in the literature. Gresham (1986) suggested that although there are numerous social skill definitions, three general definitions or conceptualizations could be distilled from the literature on children's social skills.

One of these can be termed the *peer acceptance* definition, which defines a person as socially skilled if peers accept him or her. This view was prominent in the earlier work of many researchers in the child development literature (Asher & Hymel, 1981; Gottman, 1977; Ladd, 1981; Oden & Asher, 1977). A major disadvantage of this definition is that it does not detail or identify the specific behaviors in specific situations that lead to peer acceptance or lack thereof.

Another definition might be termed the *behavioral definition*, which conceives social skills as situationally specific behaviors that have an increased likelihood of being reinforced and a decreased likelihood of being punished or extinguished. This definition historically has been adopted by researchers from the applied behavior analysis and behavior therapy camps (Bellack & Hersen, 1979; Foster & Ritchey, 1979; Strain, 1977; Strain, Cooke, & Apolloni, 1976). It has a major disadvantage: it does not ensure that the social behaviors identified are socially significant behaviors that result in socially important outcomes for individuals. In other words, merely increasing the frequency of certain behaviors that are identified a priori as "social skills" does not establish the social validity of those behaviors (Wolf, 1978).

A final definition of social skills based on the work of McFall (1982) has been termed the *social validity definition*. According to this definition, social skills are specific behaviors or behavior patterns that predict or otherwise result in important social outcomes for children and youth (Gresham, 1983, 1998). Social important outcomes represent outcomes that treatment consumers consider important, adaptive, and functional (Hawkins, 1991; Wolf, 1978). In short, socially important outcomes are those that make a difference in terms of an individual's functioning or adaptation to societal expectations. Socially important outcomes may include peer acceptance and friendships (McConnell & Odom, 1986; Newcomb, Bukowski, & Pattee, 1993; Parker & Asher, 1987), teacher and parental acceptance (Gresham, 1992, 1998; Gresham & Elliott, 1990; Merrell, 1993; Walker & McConnell, 1995a, 1995b), and school adjustment (Gresham & MacMillan, 1997; Hersh & Walker, 1983; Walker, Irvin, Noell, & Singer, 1992).

The social validity definition also distinguishes between the concepts of *social competence* and *social skills*. In this view, social skills are specific behaviors that an individual exhibits to perform competently on a social task. Social competence is an evaluative term based on judgments that a person has performed a social task competently. These judgments may be based on opinions of significant others (e.g., teachers, parents, peers), comparisons to explicit criteria (e.g., number of social tasks correctly performed), and/or comparisons to a normative sample. In short, this conceptualization of social competence considers social skills to be *specific behaviors* that result in *judgments* about those behaviors (McFall, 1982).

Social Competence and Social–Behavioral Expectations in School

Schools are generally accessible to all children, their parents, and teachers, thereby making them ideal settings for teaching and refining students' social behavior. Schools are a microcosm of society and represent a place where students and adults work, play, eat, and live together for 6 hours per day, 5 days per week, and at least 180 days per year. By the end of Grade 5, children will have spent a minimum total of 5,400 hours in school (Gresham, 1997). During this time, children are exposed to literally hundreds of thousands of social interactions with peers and adults. As such, schools are a major socializing institution in society. For many children, school entry represents a particularly difficult period, putting them at risk for problems in peer and teacher social interactions and relationships.

One way of conceptualizing how children are considered to be at risk for social competence difficulties is to examine the social behavior standards expected or set by significant others in environments in which children function. For example, the standards, expectations, and tolerance levels that teachers hold for students' social behavior influence teaching behaviors as well as peer interactions in the classroom (Hersh & Walker, 1983). Brophy and Good (1986) suggested that students perceived as being brighter or more competent receive more teacher attention, are given greater opportunities to respond, are praised more, and are given more verbal cues during teaching interactions than students perceived as being less competent.

In addition to academic expectations, teachers also hold certain expectations, standards, and tolerance levels for students' social behavior. Most teachers would consider a behavioral repertoire to be indicative of successful adjustment if (a) academic performance (e.g., listening to the teacher, completing tasks, complying with the teacher's directions) is facilitated, and (b) disruptive or unusual behaviors challenging the teacher's authority and disturbing the classroom ecology (e.g., cheating, stealing, defying the teacher) are absent (Gresham & Reschly, 1988; Hersh & Walker, 1983). Most students with—or at risk for—high-incidence disabilities (e.g., specific learning disabilities, emotional disturbance, mild mental retardation, and ADHD) are considered problematic based on difficulties in their "teachability." *Teachability* represents a pattern of social behavior that Hersh and Walker called a *model behavior profile* expected by most teachers. Many, if not most, students with high-incidence disabilities probably were referred originally for assessment and placement into special education based on substantial deviations from this model behavior profile that created difficulties in their "teachability."

Walker and colleagues presented a useful, empirically derived conceptual model of interpersonal social-behavioral competence for school settings (Walker et al., 1992). The adaptive teacher-related adjustment behaviors define the model behavior profile described earlier and result in teacher acceptance and school success. The maladaptive domain is characteristic of behaviors that disturb the classroom ecology and result in teacher rejection, school failure, and referral to special education.

The social behaviors in the adaptive peer-related adjustment domain are substantially different from those in the teacher-related adjustment domain. These behaviors are essential for the formation of friendships and peer acceptance (through cooperating with, supporting, and assisting peers), but have little to do with classroom success and teacher acceptance. The maladaptive behaviors in this domain are likely to result in peer rejection or neglect (e.g., disrupting the group, starting fights, and bragging), but share many similarities with the maladaptive behaviors in the teacher-related maladaptive domain. This model of social-behavioral functioning is essential for understanding the referral process, the goals and outcomes of social skills interventions, and predicting the outcomes of attempts to include all students with disabilities in general education classrooms.

Dimensions of Social Skills

There is a large body of empirical research, accumulated over the years, that has concentrated on developing a classification or taxonomy for maladaptive or problem behaviors. For example, Achenbach and colleagues have developed a reliable and valid classification or taxonomy for externalizing and internalizing behavior patterns that are reflected in teacher, parent, and student rating scales (Achenbach, 1991a, 1991b, 1991c). More recently, Reynolds and Kamphaus (1992) developed the Behavioral Assessment System for Children (BASC) that uses a dimensional approach emphasizing maladaptive behaviors in children and adolescents.

Caldarella and Merrell (1997) synthesized 21 investigations using 19 rating scales or inventories and derived a taxonomy or classification of social skills. Studies in this analysis and synthesis of factor analytic research included 22,000 students ranging from 3 to 18 years of age with equal gender representation across studies. Teacher ratings were used in about 75% of the studies, with parent and student self-report measures being used in 19%. Peer sociometrics were used in only 5% of the studies.

Table 1 presents the taxonomy developed by Caldarella and Merrell's (1997) synthesis, which includes five broad social skills domains: (a) peer relations skills, (b) self-management skills, (c) academic skills, (d) compliance skills, and (e) assertion skills. This taxonomy provides useful directions for selecting target social skills for more in-depth assessment and intervention. A number of these social skill domains have been used in published social skills curricula and interventions programs (Elias & Clabby, 1992; Elliott & Gresham, 1992; Goldstein, 1988; Walker et al., 1983).

Caldarella and Merrell (1997) emphasize that this taxonomy is useful because it (a) provides a nomenclature to refer to typical social behavior patterns, (b) identifies a profile of social skill dimensions on which students may have relative strengths and weaknesses, (c) can be used to design interventions to teach social skills, (d) can be used to measure the outcomes of social skills interventions, and (e) can facilitate theory development concerning the causes, prognosis, and responsiveness of students to social skills intervention procedures.

Classification of Social Skills Deficits

A key aspect of social skills assessment and intervention is an accurate classification of the specific type(s) of social skills deficits a student may have. Gresham (1981) distinguished between social skill *acquisition deficits* and *performance deficits*. This distinction is important because it suggests different intervention approaches in remediating social skills deficits and may indicate different settings for carrying out social skills training (e.g., pullout groups versus contextually based interventions in naturalistic settings). A third type of social skill deficit may be called a *fluency deficit,* in which a student may know how to and wants to perform a given social skill but executes it awkwardly or in an unpolished manner.

Social skill *acquisition deficits* refer to the absence of knowledge needed to execute a particular social skill—even under optimal conditions. Social *performance deficits* represent the presence of social skills in an individual's repertoire, but the failure to perform these skills at an acceptable level in particular situations. Acquisition deficits can be thought of as "Can't do" or skill deficits, whereas performance deficits are "Won't do"

TABLE 1

Most Common Dimensions of Social Skills

Domain	Frequency	Percentage of Studies
Peer Relationships (social interaction, prosocial, peer-preferred, empathy, social participation)	11 studies	52.38%
Self-Management (self-control, social convention, social independence, social responsibility, classroom compliance)	11 studies	52.38%
Academic (school adjustment, respect for social rules at school, task orientation, academic responsibility, cooperation-compliance)	10 studies	47.62%
Compliance (social cooperation, competence, cooperation-compliance)	8 studies	38.09%
Assertion (assertive social skills, social initiation, social activator)	7 studies	33.33%

Note

Based on a review by Caldarella and Merrell (1997).

or motivational deficits. Fluency deficits stem from a lack of exposure to a number of competent models for particular social behaviors, from lack of practice, or from inadequate behavioral rehearsal of newly taught or infrequently used social skills.

Gresham and Elliott (1990) expanded this social skill classification model to include the notion of *competing problem behaviors*. In this classification scheme, two dimensions of behavior—social skills and competing problem behaviors—are combined to classify

FIGURE 1

Social Skills Classification Model

Problem Behavior Dimension	Acquisition	Performance	Fluency
Present	Acquisition Deficit	Performance Deficit	Fluency Deficit
Absent	Acquisition Deficit	Performance Deficit	Fluency Deficit

social skills difficulties. Competing behaviors can include internalizing or overcontrolled behavior patterns (e.g., anxiety, depression, social withdrawal) or externalizing or undercontrolled behavior patterns (e.g., aggression, impulsivity, disruption). Figure 1 presents this social skill classification model.

The two-dimensional social skill deficit classification model presented in Figure 1 is pivotal to linking assessment results to interventions for social skills deficits. It is inappropriate to teach a social skill to children who already have that skill in their repertoires (i.e., with a performance deficit). Similarly, intervention procedures designed to increase the performance of a social skill (e.g., prompting, reinforcement) are not efficient in remediating acquisition deficits. Finally, students having fluency deficits do not require that a skill be taught—nor do they require antecedent/consequent procedures to increase the frequency of a behavioral performance. Rather, these students require more practice (i.e., opportunities to respond) and rehearsal (repetitions) of the skill for adequate and socially effective behavioral performances.

ASSESSMENT OF SOCIAL SKILLS

A number of methods have been used to assess the social skills of children and youth, and most of them can provide useful information regarding prosocial and competing problem behaviors. Social skills assessment can be conceptualized as taking place in five major stages of the assessment/intervention sequence: (a) screening, (b) classification, (c) target behavior selection, (d) functional assessment, and (e) evaluation of intervention. Gresham (1995) presented 12 major goals of social skills assessment that

TABLE 2

Goals of Social Skills Assessment

Problem Identification

- Identify Social Skills Strengths
- Identify Social Skills Acquisition Deficits
- Identify Social Skills Performance Deficits
- Identify Social Skills Fluency Deficits
- Identify Competing Problem Behaviors

Problem Analysis

- Conduct Functional Assessment
- Determine the Social Validity of Specific Social Skills for Treatment Consumers
- Select Target Behaviors for Intervention

Plan Implementation

- Develop and Implement Intervention Strategies Based on Assessment Information

Treatment Evaluation

- Select Appropriate Outcome Measures
- Evaluate Effects of Intervention
- Assess Generalization and Maintenance of Effects

can be found in Table 2. These 12 goals of social skills assessment can be classified within the four stages of a problem-solving model: (a) problem identification, (b) problem analysis, (c) plan implementation, and (d) treatment evaluation (Bergan & Kratochwill, 1990).

Social skills assessment methods can be broadly classified as being either *indirect* or *direct* (Gresham & Lambros, 1998). Indirect assessment methods assess social behavior that is removed in time and place from its actual occurrence. Examples of these methods include interviews, ratings by others, peer assessment methods, and analogue role-play measures. Direct assessment methods assess social behavior at the time and place of its actual occurrence and include naturalistic observations (e.g., classrooms or playgrounds) and self-monitoring strategies. This chapter will focus on three commonly used social skills assessment methods: functional assessment interviews, naturalistic observations, and behavioral ratings by others.

Functional Assessment Interviews

A functional assessment interview (FAI) has four goals: (a) to identify and define social skills difficulties, (b) to assist in the differentiation of social skill acquisition, performance, and fluency deficits, (c) to identify competing problem behaviors that interfere with acquisition, performance, and/or fluency, and (d) to obtain preliminary information regarding the possible functions of competing problem behaviors. A *functional assessment* seeks to identify the functions or "causes" of behavior. This information is valuable because once a behavioral function is identified, specific intervention strategies based on behavioral function can be prescribed.

Behavior serves two fundamental functions: (a) to *obtain* something desirable (e.g., social attention, preferred activities, or material objects) and (b) to *avoid, escape,* or *delay* something undesirable or aversive (e.g., difficult tasks, social activities, or interruption of preferred activities). These two functions describe the processes of positive and negative reinforcement, respectively. For example, a child's social withdrawal behavior may serve to increase the frequency of adult and/or peer prompts to join an ongoing activity (i.e., it may serve a social attention or positive reinforcement function). In contrast, social withdrawal may serve to allow a child to terminate aversive social interactions with peers (i.e., it may serve an escape or negative reinforcement function). The only way to know for sure which function social withdrawal serves is to directly test both of these hypotheses by systematically manipulating environmental events (e.g., presenting and withdrawing social attention).

Professionals conducting FAIs should engage in the following: (a) eliciting from the interviewee a specific, precise description of social skill deficits and competing problem behaviors, (b) formulating a tentative description of environmental conditions surrounding socially skilled and competing problem behaviors, and (c) evaluating the effects of social skills interventions in terms of measurable behavior change. Elements of the above sequence can be described as problem identification, problem analysis, and problem evaluation, respectively (see Bergan & Kratochwill, 1990).

Naturalistic Observations of Social Behavior

Systematic observations of behavior represent one of the most important social skills assessment methods. Observational data are very sensitive to treatment effects and should be included in *all* social skills assessment and intervention activities. Although there are a variety of elaborate coding systems available for naturalistic observation of social behavior, it is recommended that recording procedures be kept as simple as possible. Four factors should be considered in using systematic behavioral observations: (a) operational definitions of behavior, (b) dimensions of behavior being assessed, (c) number of behaviors assessed, and (d) number of observation sessions.

Operational definitions of behavior should describe the specific verbal, physical, and/or spatial parameters of behavior and environmental events (Gresham, Gansle, & Noell, 1993). Operational definitions should be clear, objective, and complete. An efficient way of formulating an operational definition of social skills is through the FAI described earlier. Recall that the primary purpose of this interview is to obtain a clear and objective definition of target behaviors. Behavior rating scales (to be described in the next section) should be used to identify general areas of concern and to establish normative levels of functioning in social skills and competing problem behaviors. The FAI should be used to operationally define behaviors of greatest concern to teachers and/or parents, and direct observations of these behaviors in naturalistic settings should be used to estimate their frequency, rate, or duration.

Social behavior can be described and assessed along the behavioral dimensions of frequency, temporality, and quality. Frequency, or how often a behavior occurs, is often used as an index of social competence. Frequency, however, sometimes can be misleading because how often a person exhibits a social behavior may not predict important social outcomes for them such as peer acceptance (Gresham, 1983). Some social skill deficits are clearly defined as problems because they either do not occur or occur at low frequencies. Examples include saying "Please," "Thank you," and "Excuse me" or asking for permission to get out of one's seat in class or before leaving home.

Some social skills may be measured using temporal dimensions of behavior such as duration, latency, or interresponse times. Examples of social skills that can be measured by durations are length of social interactions with others, amount of time engaged in cooperative play, or the ratio of positive to negative social interaction durations. One easy way of assessing the duration of social skills is to start a stopwatch whenever the child meets the definition of behavior and to stop it when the child is not engaged in the behavior. This process continues throughout the observation session. The duration is calculated by dividing the elapsed time on the stopwatch by the total time observed and multiplying by 100, thereby yielding a percentage.

Walker et al. (1995) recommend the use of duration recording of *alone* and *negative social behavior* on the playground (recess) for students demonstrating an antisocial behavior pattern. Alone can be defined as when a child is not within 10 feet of another child, is not engaged in any organized activity, and is not exchanging social signals (verbal or nonverbal) with any other children. *Negative social behavior* can be defined as displaying hostile behavior or body language toward peers; attempting to tease, bully, or otherwise intimidate others; reacting with anger or rejection of social bids of peers; or displaying aggressive behavior with the intent to harm or force the submission of peers.

Antisocial children spend more time alone and are more negative in their social interactions than are nonantisocial children. Surprisingly, antisocial and nonantisocial students *do not differ in their durations of total positive social behaviors* (Walker et al., 1995; Walker & Severson, 1992). Based on playground recording, if a target student spends between 12% and 15% of the time in solitary activity ("alone") and engages in negative social interactions 10% or more of the time, he or she is at risk for antisocial behavior (Walker et al., 1995).

Some students have social skills deficits and competing problem behaviors that are limited to one or two behaviors. Other students exhibit multiple social skills deficits and competing problem behavior excesses, thereby presenting an unmanageable number of behaviors to assess. An important decision facing assessors is determining the number of behaviors to be observed. This decision is influenced by the nature and severity of the student's social competence difficulties as well as the degree of teacher and/or parent concern with each behavioral excess or deficit.

Some teachers and parents may list 5 to 10 behaviors that they consider problematic. Although some students will display 10 or more problem behaviors and/or social skills deficits, not all of these behaviors are independent. Some behaviors are subsets of a larger class or category of behavior that share certain similarities. These larger categories, known as *response classes,* describe a class or category of behavior that share similarities (topographical response class) or are controlled by the same environmental events (functional response class).

For example, the topographical response class of *social withdrawal* might include the behaviors of sulking, standing alone on the playground, walking away from peers, and ignoring social bids from peers to join in games or activities. Although these behaviors may appear different, they may belong to the same topographical response class, and the operational definition of social withdrawal would include the behaviors listed above. In this example, it should be noted that these behaviors probably belong to the same *functional response class* because each behavior serves the same function (i.e., avoidance of peer social interactions). Practitioners should determine which behaviors are—and which are not—members of specific topographical and functional response classes for observational and intervention purposes.

Another consideration in using naturalistic observations is the number of times a student should be observed. The central issue here is the *representativeness* of observational data. That is, are the observations representative of the student's typical behavior in classroom, playground, or other settings? Based on observations of actual behavior, the observer infers that the observed behavior is representative of the student's typical behavior in that setting. Depending on the representativeness of the observation, this inference may or may not be justified.

Observers must sample the behaviors of concern to obtain reasonable estimates of the baseline rates or durations of behavior. One rule of thumb would be to collect observational data for 2–3 sessions in the setting of concern (e.g., classroom or playground). These sessions should reflect the setting(s) of greatest concern to those referring the student for social skills assessment and intervention. Also, keep in mind that social behavior observed in naturalistic settings does not have a normative database against which to judge the severity of social skills deficits and competing behavior excesses (Gresham & Lambros, 1998). To determine whether the observed behavior is a problem, one can compare the target student's behavior(s) with another nonreferred student's behavior(s) in the same classroom. This procedure allows the assessor to have a local classroom or playground norm that can be used for comparison.

Behavior Rating Scales

Ratings of social behavior by significant others such as teachers and parents represent a useful and efficient method of obtaining information in school and home settings. Behavior ratings can be used prior to FAIs to guide the direction and topics discussed in the interview. It should be noted that behavior ratings are a measure of *typical performances* across a variety of situations over time rather than the actual frequencies of behavior at any given time (e.g., via direct observations of social behavior). Raters also may have their own idiosyncratic definitions of what constitutes any given social skill or problem behavior and their own notions of the relative frequency of behavior (e.g., "Sometimes" versus "A lot").

Gresham and Elliott (1990) suggested that the following points should be kept in mind when using behavior rating scales:

One, ratings are summaries of observations of the relative frequency of specific behaviors. The precision of measurement with rating scales is relative, not exact, and needs to be supplemented with more direct methods of assessment.

Two, ratings of social behavior are evaluative judgments affected by the environment and a rater's standards for behavior. An individual's social behavior may change depending on the situation and thus might be characterized as situationally specific rather than as traits or permanent characteristics (Achenbach, McConaughy, & Howell, 1987; Kazdin, 1979).

Three, the social validity of behaviors assessed and treated should be understood. The social validity of a behavior is reflected in the importance attributed to it by significant others in a student's environment and may vary across raters and settings.

Four, multiple raters of a student's social behavior may agree only moderately and, in some cases, very little. This reality is based on three factors: (a) many social behaviors are situationally specific, (b) all measures contain some degree of error, and (c) rating scales use rather simple frequency response categories for quantifying behaviors that may range widely in their frequency, intensity, and duration.

And five, although many student characteristics may influence social behavior, the student's sex is particularly important (Gresham & Elliott, 1990). Sex is most consistently associated with differences in social behavior and therefore social skill ratings should be interpreted within a sex-relevant perspective.

Although there are a number of social skills rating scales available, four are distinguished by having large national standardization samples, adequate to excellent psychometric properties, and being easily obtainable from reputable publishing companies. These rating scales are (a) Walker–McConnell Scales of Social Competence and School Adjustment (Walker & McConnell, 1995a, 1995b), (b) School Social Behavior Scales (Merrell, 1993), (c) Preschool and Kindergarten Behavior Scales (Merrell, 1994), and (d) the Social Skills Rating System (Gresham & Elliott, 1990). Only the Social Skills Rating System utilizes ratings from three sources: teacher, parent, and student—thereby providing a more comprehensive picture of students' social competence.

TYPES OF SOCIAL SKILLS TRAINING (SST)

Social skills intervention takes place in school and home settings both informally and formally using either *universal* or *selected* intervention procedures. *Informal* social skills intervention is based on the notion of incidental learning and takes advantage of naturally occurring behavioral incidents or events to teach prosocial behavior. Most social skills instruction in home, school, and community settings can be characterized as informal or incidental. There are literally thousands of behavioral incidents that occur in home, school, and community settings, thereby creating rich opportunities for using these behavioral incidents as the basis for SST.

Formal SST can take place in a classroom setting in which the entire class is exposed to a social skills curriculum or in a small group setting removed from the classroom. Walker et al. (1995) refer to these teaching formats, respectively, as *universal* and *selected* interventions. The logic of universal interventions is similar to that behind vaccinations, schoolwide discipline plans, or school rules that are designed to affect all students under the same conditions.

Universal interventions are less expensive in terms of time, effort, and efficiency than selected interventions. Universal interventions also are designed to prevent more serious problems from developing later in a student's life and therefore represent a type of primary prevention. It should be noted that universal interventions may not be strong enough to impact those students who are at extreme risk for developing problems in their social behavior.

Selected interventions are usually conducted with students who have been identified as being at risk for behavior problems based on an individual assessment of a student's social skills deficits and competing problem behaviors. These interventions are implemented to prevent existing problems from developing into more serious behavior problems and therefore are either secondary or tertiary interventions. Compared to universal interventions, selected interventions are more expensive, more time consuming, and more intense (Walker et al., 1995). Since the focus of this chapter is on at-risk students, selected interventions will be described in some detail.

Objectives of SST

SST has four objectives: (a) promoting skill acquisition, (b) enhancing skill performance, (c) reducing or eliminating competing problem behaviors, and (d) facilitating generalization and maintenance of social skills. Typically, students have some combination of social skill acquisition and performance deficits that are accompanied by competing problem behaviors. As such, an accurate assessment and classification of a student's specific social skills deficits is critical to the success of SST efforts.

Table 3 lists specific SST and behavior reduction strategies for each of the four goals of SST. School psychologists should match appropriate intervention strategies with the particular deficits or competing problem behaviors that a student exhibits. Additionally, programming for generalization and maintenance of trained social skills should be incorporated from the very beginning of any SST program (Gresham, 1998).

TABLE 3

Social Skills Training Objectives and Strategies

I. PROMOTING SKILL ACQUISITION
   A. Modeling
   B. Coaching
   C. Behavioral Rehearsal

II. ENHANCING SKILL PERFORMANCE
   A. Manipulation of antecedents
      1. Peer initiation strategies
      2. Proactive classroom management strategies
      3. Peer tutoring
      4. Incidental teaching
   B. Manipulation of consequences
      1. Contingency contracting
      2. Group-oriented contingency systems
      3. School/home notes
      4. Verbal praise
      5. Activity reinforcers
      6. Token/point systems

III. REMOVING COMPETING PROBLEM BEHAVIORS
   A. Differential reinforcement
      1. Differential reinforcement of other behavior (DRO)
      2. Differential reinforcement of low rates of behavior (DRL)
      3. Differential reinforcement of incompatible behaviors (DRI)
   B. Overcorrection
      1. Restitution
      2. Positive practice
   C. Time-Out
      1. Nonexclusionary (contingent observation)
      2. Exclusionary
   D. Systematic desensitization (for anxiety-based competing behaviors)
   E. Flooding/Exposure (for anxiety-based competing behaviors)

IV. FACILITATING GENERALIZATION
   A. Topographical Generalization
      1. Training diversely
      2. Exploiting functional contingencies
      3. Incorporating functional mediators
   B. Functional Generalization
      1. Identifying strong competing stimuli in specific situations
      2. Identifying strong competing problem behaviors in specific situations
      3. Identifying functionally equivalent socially skilled behaviors
      4. Increasing reliability and efficiency of socially skilled behaviors (building fluency)
      5. Decreasing reliability and efficiency of competing problem behaviors

Promoting Skill Acquisition

Procedures designed to promote social skill acquisition should be used under the following circumstances: (a) when students do not have a particular social skill in their repertoire, (b) when students do not know a particular step in the performance of a social behavioral sequence, or (c) when the execution of the social skill is awkward or ineffective (i.e., a fluency deficit). Three procedures represent pathways to remediating social skill acquisition deficits: modeling, coaching, and behavioral rehearsal. A detailed presentation of how to teach social skills using these procedures can be found in the *Social Skills Intervention Guide* (Elliott & Gresham, 1992).

Modeling is the process of learning by observing another person perform a behavior (Bandura, 1977). Modeled instruction presents the entire sequence of behaviors involved in a particular social skill and teaches how to integrate specific behaviors into a composite behavior pattern. Modeling is one of the most effective and efficient ways of teaching social behavior (Elliott & Gresham, 1992; Schneider, 1992).

Coaching uses verbal instruction to teach social behavior. Unlike modeling, which emphasizes visual displays of behavioral performances, coaching utilizes a student's receptive language skills. Coaching is accomplished in three fundamental steps: (a) presenting social concepts or rules, (b) providing opportunities for practice or rehearsal, and (c) providing specific informational feedback on the quality of behavioral performances (Elliott & Gresham, 1992).

Behavioral rehearsal involves practicing a newly learned behavior in a structured, protective situation of role playing. Students can enhance their proficiency and fluency in using social skills without experiencing negative consequences. There are three forms of behavioral rehearsal: (a) covert rehearsal, (b) verbal rehearsal, and (c) overt rehearsal (Elliott & Gresham, 1992). These three procedures can be used in a number of ways and combinations to teach social behavior.

Enhancing Skill Performance

Most social skills interventions involve procedures for increasing the frequency of specific prosocial behaviors. This suggests that most social skills interventions for most students should take place in naturalistic environments such as classrooms or playgrounds rather than in small, pullout groups. Using a consultative framework for this type of SST is the most efficient use of a school psychologist's time. Failure to perform certain social skills in specific situations is attributable to two reasons: (a) inappropriately arranged antecedents, and/or (b) inappropriately arranged consequences. A number of specific procedures can be classified under the broad rubrics of antecedent and consequent strategies.

Two general strategies fall under the category of antecedent strategies: peer-mediated interventions and cueing/prompting. Peer-mediated interventions can include three techniques: peer initiations, peer tutoring, and peer modeling (Kohler & Strain, 1990). With peer initiation strategies, a student's peers are used to initiate and maintain social interactions with socially withdrawn or isolated students. This procedure is effective with students who are having performance deficits and evidencing relatively low rates of social interaction. Peer tutoring has been used primarily to enhance academic skills (Skinner, 1998), and peer modeling is used primarily to remediate social skill acquisition deficits.

A cueing and prompting procedure uses verbal and nonverbal cues or prompts to facilitate prosocial behaviors. Simple prompts or cues for some students may be all that is needed to signal them to engage in socially appropriate behavior (e.g., "Say thank you" or "Ask Mark to join your group"). Cueing and prompting is one of the easiest and most efficient social skills intervention strategies (Elliott & Gresham, 1992; Walker et al., 1995).

All interventions based on consequent control involve some form of positive reinforcement. Reinforcement-based strategies assume that the student knows how to perform a social skill, but is not doing so because of insufficient or nonexistent reinforcement for that behavior. Reinforcement procedures include attention, social praise, tokens/points, activity reinforcers, behavioral contracts, and school-home notes. More extensive descriptions can be found in other comprehensive sources (Elliott & Gresham, 1992; Walker, et al., 1995; Watson & Gresham, 1998).

Removing or Eliminating Competing Problem Behaviors

The goal of SST is clearly to develop and refine prosocial behaviors. However, the failure of some students to either acquire or perform certain social skills may be attributable to the presence of competing problem behaviors. In the case of acquisition deficits, the competing problem behavior may block social skill acquisition. For example, a student's impulsivity and defiant behavior may block the acquisition of prosocial behavior (e.g., cooperation and sharing) with peers. With performance deficits, aggressive behavior may be performed instead of a prosocial behavior because it may be more efficient and reliable in producing reinforcement. A number of techniques are effective in reducing competing problem behaviors—they are presented in Table 3. Because of the author's interest in delivering positive behavioral interventions, only differential reinforcement techniques are discussed.

Differential reinforcement is based on the principle of stimulus control in which a behavior is reinforced in the presence of one stimulus and is not reinforced in the presence of other stimuli. After a number of trials of differential reinforcement, a behavior will come under the control of the stimulus associated with reinforcement and will therefore be under *stimulus control*. Principles of stimulus control can be used to decrease rates of undesirable behavior and increase rates of prosocial behavior. Three types of differential reinforcement are used most frequently: differential reinforcement of other behavior (DRO), differential reinforcement of low rates of behavior (DRL), and differential reinforcement of incompatible behavior (DRI).

DRO refers to the delivery of a reinforcer after any behavior except the target behavior. It decreases the frequency of a target behavior and increases the frequencies of all other behaviors. Technically, *any* behavior except the target behavior is reinforced. Practically, only *appropriate* behaviors are reinforced in a DRO.

Two types of DRO are used: interval DRO and momentary DRO. Interval DRO involves the reinforcement of a behavior if the targeted behavior does not occur in a specified time interval. Thus, in an interval DRO-2-minute, the first behavior occurring after a 2-minute interval elapses in which the target behavior *did not occur* is reinforced. If the target behavior occurs at any time during the 2-minute interval, the timer is reset to the beginning of the interval. In momentary DRO, behavior is *sampled* at the end of a specified time interval. If the target behavior is not occurring at the end of an interval, the first behavior occurring *after the interval* is reinforced. In a momentary DRO 2-minute, a behavior is reinforced if the target behavior is not occurring at the end of the 2-minute sampling time.

Either DRO schedule can be used to reduce the frequency of problem behaviors in a variety of settings. The primary difficulty with interval DRO schedules is keeping up with time intervals and resetting the timer. Momentary DRO schedules are more user-friendly than interval DROs and should be adequate for most practical purposes.

DRL involves the reinforcement of reductions in the frequency of target behaviors in a specified time interval. Two variations of DRL are described: classic DRL and full session DRL. In classic DRL, the time elapsing between behaviors, called interresponse times or IRTs, is gradually lengthened. For example, if a student interrupts frequently, interruptions could be reduced in frequency by reinforcing the student for waiting 5 minutes between instances of interruptions. If the student interrupted before 5 minutes elapsed (e.g., 2 minutes or 4 minutes), the timer would be reset and the 5-minute waiting requirement would remain in effect. This would be called a classic DRL-5-minute schedule of reinforcement.

In full session DRL, reinforcement is provided when the overall frequency of a target behavior is reduced in a specified time period. The difference between a full session DRL and a classic DRL is that full session DRLs do not require longer and longer intervals between occurrences of a target behavior. Instead, the requirement is that the overall frequency of a target behavior in a specified time interval be reduced. For example, a teacher might set a criterion of five or fewer occurrences of disruptive behavior in a 25-minute reading lesson. If this criterion is met, the student would receive reinforcement. Full session DRLs are more user-friendly than classic DRLs and are easily adapted within the context of group contingency systems.

In DRI, behaviors that are incompatible with the target behavior are reinforced. Whereas DRO and DRL focus on reducing the frequencies of problem behaviors, DRI emphasizes *increasing* frequencies of prosocial behaviors. DRI reduces the frequency of competing problem behaviors because prosocial behaviors that are incompatible with problem behaviors are increased in frequency. Several examples should make this clear: sharing is incompatible with stingy behavior; complimenting others is incompatible with verbally teasing others; asking others to borrow a toy is incompatible with grabbing a toy; compromising with others is incompatible with fighting.

DRIs are not effective because of the incompatibility of behaviors, but rather because of the *relative rate of reinforcement* for each behavior (McDowell, 1982). For example, a student might "choose" to tease others or the child might "choose" to compliment others. Complimenting is incompatible with teasing; however, the child can "choose" to stop complimenting and start teasing at any time. DRI makes particular use of the *Matching Law* (Herrnstein, 1970), which states that response rate matches reinforcement rate. For instance, if complimenting is reinforced after every six occurrences and teasing is reinforced after every two occurrences, then complimenting should be three times more frequent than teasing. Based on principles of matching, a student's behavior should follow the Matching Law and incompatible problem behaviors should decrease and prosocial behaviors should increase using DRI.

Facilitating Generalization and Maintenance

There are two basic learning processes essential to all behavioral interventions: *discrimination* and *generalization* (Stokes, 1992). Discrimination and generalization represent polar opposites on the continuum of behavior change. A major problem confronting the enterprise of SST is that it is much easier to get some behaviors to occur in one place for a limited period of time than it is to get social behavior to occur in more than one place for an extended period of time. That is, teaching discriminations is easier than ensuring the generalization and maintenance of these effects across settings, behaviors, and time.

Generalization of behavior change is directly related to the phenomenon of *resistance to intervention*. If social skill deficits occur at low frequencies, competing problem behaviors occur at high frequencies, and both of these deficits and excesses are chronic (i.e., they have lasted a relatively long period of time), they will tend to show less generalization across different nontraining conditions and less maintenance over time when SST is withdrawn (Gresham, 1991). Some students relatively quickly discriminate training from nontraining conditions, particularly when training conditions are vastly different from nontraining conditions. For example, students exposed to a highly structured point system complete with a response cost component for inappropriate behavior and a reinforcement component for socially appropriate behavior will readily discriminate when the program is in effect and when it is withdrawn. Discrimination being the polar opposite of generalization, behavior will deteriorate rapidly to baseline levels when one returns to nontraining conditions.

Generalization can be viewed from two fundamental perspectives. One emphasizes behavioral *form* or *topography* and the other emphasizes behavioral *function* (Edelstein, 1989; Stokes & Osnes, 1989). The topographical description of generalization refers to the occurrence of relevant behaviors under different, nontraining conditions (Stokes & Osnes, 1989). These so-called relevant behaviors (e.g., social skills) can occur across settings or situations (setting generalization), behaviors (response generalization), and/or over time (maintenance). Three categories of topographical generalization strategies are presented in Table 3, on page 417. A more detailed treatment of these strategies can be found in Stokes and Osnes. Topographical generalization is *descriptive* or *correlational* and does not explain why generalization or maintenance occurs. What is needed is a *functional* account or explanation of these outcomes.

The functional approach to generalization consists of two types. First, *stimulus generalization* is the occurrence of the same behavior under variations of the original stimulus (the greater the difference between the training stimulus and subsequent stimuli, the less generalization). Second, *response generalization* is the control of multiple behaviors by the same stimulus, thereby creating a functional response class.

One way of understanding generalization errors, functionally, is within the context of competing behaviors. Horner and Billingsley (1988) offered the following scenario: A student has acquired a new, adaptive social skill and demonstrates excellent generalization across new situations. A new situation is encountered that contains a strong competing stimulus. This competing stimulus is likely to elicit old, undesirable behavior. The practical effect is that the new adaptive social skill does not generalize to situations containing the strong competing stimulus.

The above scenario would create no problems if the student did not have to encounter environments with the strong competing stimulus. However, it is not always possible to arrange this—such as when the strong competing stimulus is a classmate, a particular peer group, or a teacher. The notion of strong competing stimuli may explain why so many problem drinkers "fall off the wagon" (bars, alcohol, and drinking buddies are strong competing stimuli for excessive drinking behavior).

One reason, among many, that social skills fail to generalize is that the newly taught behavior is overpowered by older and stronger competing behaviors. At school, a student may behave appropriately until he or she encounters a peer group that engages in and encourages rule violations that set the occasion for the student to engage in inappropriate behaviors. This is an important concept for understanding why some behaviors generalize to new situations, but not others, and why a behavior that has been maintained well for a long time may suddenly deteriorate (Horner & Billingsley, 1988).

An important part of the SST process is to determine the *reliability* and *efficiency* of competing problem behaviors relative to socially skilled alternative behaviors. Competing problem behaviors often are performed instead of socially skilled behaviors because the competing behaviors are more efficient and more reliable than the socially skilled behavior (Horner & Billingsley, 1988). Efficient behaviors are those that (a) are easier to perform in terms of response effort and (b) produce reinforcement more rapidly. Reliable behaviors are those that produce the desired outcomes more frequently than do socially skilled alternative behaviors. For example, pushing into the lunch line may be more efficient and reliable than politely asking to cut into the lunch line.

Horner and Billingsley (1988) have referred to the above scenario as the *functional equivalence of behavior.* That is, two or more behaviors can be equal in their ability to produce reinforcement. Thus, grabbing a toy is more efficient than asking for toys, and pushing a peer out of the way is more efficient than asking a peer to move. All things being equal, preexisting behaviors lead to more powerful and immediate reinforcers; in other words, they more efficiently produce the same reinforcement yielded by the socially skilled behavior—they are more cost beneficial.

To program for functional generalization, school psychologists should (a) decrease the efficiency and reliability of competing, inappropriate behaviors, and (b) increase the efficiency and reliability of socially skilled alternative behaviors. The former can be accomplished by many procedures listed in Table 3 under "Removing Competing

Problem Behaviors." The latter can be achieved by spending more time and effort in building the fluency of trained social skills using combinations of modeling, coaching, and, most important, behavioral rehearsal with specific performance feedback.

CONCLUSIONS AND RECOMMENDATIONS

Clearly the development and maintenance of social competence is a key aspect of a child's development. The extent to which a child is successful in making friends, gaining peer acceptance, and getting along with teachers and other adults defines social competence. The National Educational Goals Panel (1999) suggested the following:

> … A solid base of *emotional security* and *social competence* enables children to participate fully in learning experiences and form good relationships with teachers and peers. In building and maintaining such relationships, key social skills are: respecting the rights of others, relating to peers without being too submissive or overbearing, being willing to give and receive support, and treating others as one would like to be treated. To the extent that children develop these social skills and attitudes, they function better in the school setting. (p. 3)

This chapter focused on empirically established intervention strategies designed to facilitate the acquisition, performance, generalization, and maintenance of social skills. It should be noted that SST is not equally effective across different populations of students encountered in school settings. For instance, Mathur and colleagues (Mathur, Kavale, Quinn, Forness, & Rutherford, 1998) analyzed 35 group and 64 single case design studies with students having emotional and behavioral disorders (EBDs). Overall, this research synthesis of 328 effect sizes showed that SST had an average effect size of .20, meaning 58% of children improved compared to controls not receiving SST. Using the percentage of nonoverlapping data points in the 64 single case design studies, Mathur et al. showed a moderate effect size of 63%. Based on these data, Mathur et al. concluded that SST has limited value in intervention programs for students with EBDs. Kavale and Forness (1995) reached a similar conclusion in a meta-analysis of studies conducted with students having learning disabilities (LD). Readers should consider several issues in evaluating the outcomes of these meta-analyses: (a) the concept of resis-tance to intervention, (b) matching interventions to types of social skills deficits, (c) treatment integrity issues, and (d) relevance and sensitivity of dependent measures.

Resistance to Intervention

It should be noted that previous meta-analyses with *non-special-education populations* have shown much larger effect sizes (Beelman, Pfingsten, & Losel, 1994; Schneider, 1992). It may be that special education populations (e.g., EBD and LD) represent groups of students whose social skills are highly resistant to intervention. Gresham (1991) used the concept of *resistance to intervention* as an approach to make eligibility determinations for students with EBDs. Resistance to intervention is defined as a lack of change in target behaviors as a function of a given intervention. Since the goal of intervention is to produce a discrepancy between baseline and postintervention levels of performance, the failure to produce such a discrepancy may be attributable to the low strength or intensity of the intervention relative to the magnitude of social skill deficits.

The meta-analyses with EBD (Mathur et al., 1998) and LD (Kavale & Forness, 1995) students showed that the average amount of SST was 30 hours. This amounted to 2.5 to 3.0 hours per week for 10–12 weeks. Moreover, the average age of students in both of these meta-analyses was approximately 12 years, which may be too late for SST interventions to effectively remediate severe social skills deficits. Kazdin (1987) suggested that the optimal age for interventions is prior to age 8 if one wants to remediate antisocial behavior patterns.

Given the long-standing nature of social skill deficits in EBD and LD groups, one should not be surprised that 30 hours of instruction may not be sufficient to remediate these students' severe social skills deficits. The weak treatment effects of SST for these groups are evidence of their resistance to intervention and suggest that SST should be more frequent and intense. Future research should systematically investigate outcomes of different levels of SST intensity, applied to high-incidence disability groups such as EBD, LD, and ADHD.

Matching Treatment to Type of Social Skill Deficit

The small effect sizes noted in previous meta-analyses with EBD and LD groups can be attributed, in part, to the failure to match specific social skills interventions to specific types of social skills deficits. This chapter noted previously that SST has four objectives—promoting skill acquisition, enhancing skill performance, removing competing problem behaviors, and facilitating generalization and maintenance. Students are likely to have some combination of acquisition and performance deficits, some of which are accompanied by competing problem behaviors and some of which are not.

Many, if not most, SST studies present the same intervention for all students without first assessing and determining the specific types of social skills deficits students may have. As reviewed earlier, social skills interventions for acquisition deficits are different from interventions for performance or fluency deficits. Recent developments in the use of functional-assessment-based behavior support planning offer a technology to increase the "fit" between social skills interventions and reductions in competing problem behaviors (Horner, 1994); Horner & Carr, 1997; Lewis & Sugai, 1996). In this approach, testable hypotheses about predictable occasioning and maintaining functions are developed and tested. Based on these hypotheses, competing replacement behaviors (i.e., social skills) are identified and specifically designed behavior support plans are developed, implemented, and monitored.

Treatment Integrity Issues

There is little evidence in the meta-analyses of the SST literature that these interventions were implemented as planned or intended. A fundamental goal of all intervention research is the unequivocal demonstration that changes in a dependent variable are related to systematic, manipulated changes in an independent (treatment) variable and not caused by extraneous variables. *Treatment integrity* refers to the degree to which a treatment is implemented as intended or planned (Gresham, 1989, 1997; Yeaton & Sechrest, 1981). Treatment integrity is concerned with the *accuracy* and *consistency* with which treatments are implemented.

Based on the absence of treatment integrity data in the SST literature, we do not know whether a SST program is ineffective because of a poor treatment or whether it would be effective if it were implemented with high integrity. This is a particularly critical issue in SST with special populations whose social skills deficits are more resistant to intervention and thus require more frequent and more intense levels of SST. Monitoring of treatment integrity should be a high priority in SST research in the future.

Relevance and Sensitivity of Dependent Measures

Another reason for the weak effects of SST may be the use of assessments that show little correspondence between the behaviors that are assessed and those behaviors that are taught. Outcome measures in SST include a number of strategies ranging from "homemade" ratings scales to performance on measures of social cognition, often with little regard to reliability and validity—particularly social validity issues (Walker et al., 1998). Based on both narrative and meta-analytic reviews of the SST literature, there is often little rhyme and much less reason in many studies' selection of particular outcome measures. This lack of order and logic may contribute to the weak effects of SST.

Gresham (1983) classified social skills measures based on a social validity criterion. *Type I* measures represent a socially valued treatment goal in the sense that social systems (e.g., schools, courts, mental health agencies) and significant others (e.g., teachers, parents) tend to refer children for evaluation and intervention based on these measures. Type I measures include peer acceptance/rejection, friendship status, teacher or parent judgments, and some types of archival data (e.g., school attendance disciplinary referrals, school suspensions, arrests).

Type I measures are inherently socially valid; however, a major disadvantage of these measures is that they are not particularly sensitive in detecting short-term treatment effects. Sechrest, McKnight, and McKnight (1996) argued for using the method of *just noticeable differences* (JNDs) to gauge treatment outcomes. In applying the JND approach to SST, the question is this: How much of a difference in social behavior is required for it to be noticed by significant others in the student's environment? Often it is the case that very large and consistent changes in social behavior over a period of time are required before they are noticed by others (Sechrest et al., 1996). For example, large and extended increases in positive social interactions with peers may be required before these changes are reflected in sociometric measures of peer acceptance and friendship ratings. A similar phenomenon may exist in using teacher and parent rating scales as outcome measures. Since most SST interventions are 30 hours or less in duration, many of these studies using Type I measures may, in part, account for the weak treatment effects.

Type II measures have demonstrated empirical relationships with Type I measures and, as such, serve as indicators of one's standing on Type I measures (Gresham, 1983). Type II measures are not socially valid in and of themselves, but they are useful because they predict important social outcomes for students. Common Type II measures are direct observations of social behavior in natural environments such as classrooms or playgrounds. These measures are used frequently in SST research, and they are used exclusively in studies employing single case experimental designs.

Type III measures represent the least socially valid measures in assessing social competence because they show little correspondence to Type I or Type II measures (Bellack, Hersen, & Turner, 1978; Bellack, Hersen, & Lamparski, 1979; Ubain & Kendall, 1980). Gresham (1983, 1986) argued that although Type III measures have some face validity, they do not predict important social outcomes for students. Examples of Type III measures include behavioral role-play tests, social problem-solving measures, and measures of social cognition.

There is little evidence that performance on Type III measures is related to (a) social behavior in naturalistic settings (Type II measures), (b) teacher or parent judgments of social competence (Type I measures), or (c) other Type I measures (Gresham, 1983, 1986). Support for this conclusion can be found in the meta-analyses by Beelman et al. (1994) and Denham and Almeida (1987), which showed that social problem-solving interventions had a relatively strong impact on social problem-solving skills, but had little impact on behavior ratings or social interaction skills measured in naturalistic settings.

REFERENCES

Achenbach, T. (1985). *Assessment and taxonomy of child and adolescent psychopathology.* Beverly Hills, CA: Sage.

Achenbach, T. (1991a). *Manual for the Child Behavior Checklist and 1991 Profile.* Burlington, VT: University of Vermont.

Achenbach, T. (1991b). *Manual for the Teacher's Report Form and 1991 Profile.* Burlington, VT: University of Vermont.

Achenbach, T. (1991c). *Manual for the Youth Self-Report and 1991 Profile.* Burlington, VT: University of Vermont.

Achenbach, T., McConaughy, S., & Howell, C. (1987). Child/adolescent behavioral and emotional problems: Implications for cross-informant correlations for situational specificity. *Psychological Bulletin, 101,* 213-232.

American Psychiatric Association (1994). *Diagnostic and statistical manual of mental disorders* (4th ed.). Washington, DC: Author.

Asher, S., & Hymel, S. (1981). Children's social competence in peer relations: Sociometric and behavioral assessment. In J. Wine & M. Syme (Eds.), *Social competence* (pp. 125-157). New York: Guilford Press.

Bandura, A. (1977). *Social learning theory.* Englewood Cliffs, NJ: Prentice-Hall.

Barkley, R. (1990). *Attention deficit-hyperactivity disorder: A handbook of diagnosis and treatment.* New York: Guilford Press.

Beelman, A., Pfingsten, U., & Losel, F. (1994). Effects of training social competence in children: A meta-analysis of recent evaluation studies. *Journal of Clinical Child Psychology, 23,* 260-271.

Bellack, A., & Hersen, M. (1979). *Research and practice in social skills training.* New York: Plenum Press.

Bellack, A., Hersen, M., & Lamparski, D. (1979). Role-play tests for assessing social skills: Are they valid? Are they useful? *Journal of Consulting and Clinical Psychology, 47,* 335-342.

Bellack, A., Hersen, M., & Turner, S. (1978). Role-play tests for assessing social skills: Are they valid? *Behavior Therapy, 9,* 448-461.

Bergan, J., & Kratochwill, T. (1990). *Behavioral consultation and therapy.* New York: Plenum Press.

Brophy, J., & Good, T. (1986). Teacher behavior and student achievement. In M. Wittrock (Ed.), *Handbook of research on teaching* (3rd ed., pp. 328-375). New York: Macmillan.

Bullis, M., Walker, H., & Sprague, J. (in press). A promise unfulfilled: Social skills training with at-risk and antisocial children and youth. *Exceptionality.*

Caldarella, P., & Merrell, K. (1997). Common dimensions of social skills of children and adolescents: A taxonomy of positive social behaviors. *School Psychology Review, 26,* 265-279.

Cleckley, H. (1976). *The mask of sanity.* St. Louis, MO: Mosby.

Colvin, G., Sugai, G., & Kame'enui, E. (1993). *Proactive school-wide discipline: Implementation manual.* Project PREPARE, Behavioral Research and Teaching, College of Education, University of Oregon, Eugene.

Denham, S., & Almeida, M. (1987). Children's social problem solving skills, behavioral adjustment, and interventions: A meta-analysis evaluating theory and practice. *Journal of Applied Developmental Psychology, 8,* 391–409.

Edelstein, B. (1989). Generalization: Terminological, methodological, and conceptual issues. *Behavior Therapy, 20,* 311–324.

Elias, M., & Clabby, J. (1992). *Building social problem solving skills: Guidelines from a school-based program.* San Francisco: Jossey-Bass.

Elliott, S. N., & Gresham, F.M. (1992). *Social skills intervention guide.* Circle Pines, MN: American Guidance Service.

Farrington, D., Loeber, R., & Van Kammer, W. (1990). Long-term criminal outcomes of hyperactivity-impulsivity-inattention deficit and conduct problems in childhood. In N. Robbins & M. Rutter (Eds.), *Straight and devious pathways from childhood to adulthood* (pp. 62–81). Cambridge, UK: Cambridge University Press.

Foster, S., & Ritchey, W. (1979). Issues in the assessment of social competence in children. *Journal of Applied Behavior Analysis, 12,* 625–638.

Goldstein, A. (1988). *The PREPARE curriculum.* Champaign, IL: Research Press.

Gottman, J. (1977). Toward a definition of social isolation in children. *Child Development, 48,* 513–517.

Gresham, F. M. (1981). Social skills training with handicapped children: A review. *Review of Educational Research, 51,* 139–176.

Gresham, F. M. (1983). Social validity in the assessment of children's social skills: Establishing standards for social competency. *Journal of Psychoeducational Assessment, 1,* 297–307.

Gresham, F. M. (1986). Conceptual issues in the assessment of social competence in children. In P. Strain, M. Guralnick, & H. Walker (Eds.), *Children's social behavior: Development, assessment, and modification* (pp. 143–179). Orlando, FL: Academic Press.

Gresham, F. M. (1989). Assessment of treatment integrity in consultation and prereferral intervention. *School Psychology Review, 18,* 37–50.

Gresham, F. M. (1991). Conceptualizing behavior disorders in terms of resistance to intervention. *School Psychology Review, 20,* 23–36.

Gresham, F. M. (1992). Social skills and learning disabilities: Causal, concomitant, or correlational? *School Psychology Review, 21,* 348–360.

Gresham, F. M. (1995). Best practices in social skills training. In A. Thomas & J. Grimes (Eds.), *Best practices in school psychology III* (pp. 1021–1031). Washington, DC: National Association of School Psychologists.

Gresham, F. M. (1997). Social skills. In G. Bear, & K. Minke, & A. Thomas (Eds.), *Children's needs II: Development, problems and alternatives* (pp. 515–526). Bethesda, MD: National Association of School Psychologists.

Gresham, F. M. (1998). Social skills training with children: Social learning and applied behavior analytic approaches. In T. S. Watson & F. M. Gresham (Eds.), *Handbook of child behavior therapy* (pp. 475-498). New York: Plenum Press.

Gresham, F. M., & Elliott, S. N. (1990). *Social skills rating system.* Circle Pines, MN: American Guidance Service.

Gresham, F. M., & Lambros, K. (1998). Behavioral and functional assessment. In T. S. Watson & F. M. Gresham (Eds.), *Handbook of child behavior therapy* (pp. 3-22). New York: Plenum Press.

Gresham, F. M., & MacMillan, D. L. (1997). Social competence and affective characteristics of students with mild disabilities. *Review of Educational Research, 67,* 377-415.

Gresham, F. M., & Reschly, D. J. (1988). Issues in the conceptualization and assessment of social skills in the mildly handicapped. In T. Kratochwill (Ed.), *Advances in school psychology* (Vol. 6, pp. 203-247). Hillsdale, NJ: Lawrence Erlbaum.

Gresham, F. M., Gansle, K., & Noell, G. (1993). Treatment integrity in applied behavior analysis with children. *Journal of Applied Behavior Analysis, 26,* 257-263.

Gresham, F. M., MacMillan, D. L., Bocian, K., Ward, S., & Forness, S. (1998). Comorbidity of hyperactivity-impulsivity-inattention and conduct problems: Risk factors in social, affective, and academic domains. *Journal of Abnormal Child Psychology, 26,* 393-406.

Gresham, F. M., Sugai, G., Horner, R., Quinn, M., & McInerney, M. (1998). *Classroom and schoolwide practices that support students' social competence: A synthesis of research.* Washington, DC: Office of Special Education Programs.

Guevremont, D. (1990). Social skills and peer relationship training. In R. Barkley (Ed.), *Attention deficit-hyperactivity disorder: A handbook of diagnosis and treatment* (pp. 540-572). New York: Guilford Press.

Hare, R. (1981). Psychopathy and violence. In J. Hayes, T. Roberts, & K. Solway (Eds.), *Violence and the violent individual* (pp. 53-74). Jamaica, NY: Spectrum.

Hare, R., & Jutai, J. (1983). Psychopathy and cerebral asymmetry in semantic processing. *Personality and Individual Differences, 9,* 329-337.

Hare, R., McPherson, L., & Forth, A. (1988). Male psychopaths and their criminal careers. *Journal of Consulting and Clinical Psychology, 56,* 741-747.

Hawkins, R. (1991). Is social validity what we are interested in? Argument for a functional approach. *Journal of Applied Behavior Analysis, 24,* 205-213.

Herrnstein, R. (1970). On the law of effect. *Journal of Experimental Analysis of Behavior, 13,* 243-266.

Hersh, R., & Walker, H. (1983). Great expectations: Making schools effective for all students. *Policy Studies Review, 2,* 147-188.

Hinshaw, S. (1987). On the distinction between attention deficit/hyperactivity and conduct problems/aggression in child psychopathology. *Psychological Bulletin, 101,* 443-463.

Hinshaw, S., Lahey, B., & Hart, E. (1993). Issues of taxonomy and comorbidity in the development of conduct disorder. *Development and Psychopathology, 5,* 31-49.

Horner, R. (1994). Functional assessment contributions and future directions. *Journal of Applied Behavior Analysis, 27,* 401-404.

Horner, R., & Billingsley, F. (1988). The effects of competing behavior on the general-ization and maintenance of adaptive behavior in applied settings. In R. Horner, G. Dunlap, & R. Koegel (Eds.), *Generalization and maintenance: Lifestyle changes in applied settings* (pp. 197–220). Baltimore: Brookes.

Horner, R., & Carr, E. (1997). Behavior support for students with severe disabilities: Functional assessment and comprehensive intervention. *The Journal of Special Education, 31,* 84–104.

Kavale, K., & Forness, S. (1995). Social skill deficits and training: A meta-analysis of the research in learning disabilities. In T. Scruggs & M. Mastropieri (Eds.), *Advances in learning and behavioral disabilities* (Vol. 9, pp. 119–160). Greenwich, CT: JAI Press.

Kazdin, A. (1979). Situational specificity: The two-edged sword of behavioral assess-ment. *Behavioral Assessment, 1,* 57–75.

Kazdin, A. (1987). Treatment of antisocial behavior in children: Current status and future directions. *Psychological Bulletin, 102,* 187–203.

Kohler, F., & Strain, P. (1990). Peer-assisted interventions: Early promises, notable achievements, and future aspirations. *Clinical Psychology Review, 10,* 441–452.

Ladd, G. (1981). Effectiveness of a social learning method for enhancing children's social interaction and peer acceptance. *Child Development, 52,* 171–178.

Landau, S., & Moore, L. (1991). Social skills deficits with attention hyperactivity disor-der. *School Psychology Review, 20,* 235–251.

Lewis, T., & Sugai, G. (1996). Functional assessment of problem behavior: A pilot inves-tigation of the comprehensive and interactive effects of teacher and peer social attention on students in general education settings. *School Psychology Quarterly, 11,* 1–19.

Loeber, R., Brinthaupt, V., & Green, S. (1990). Attention deficits, impulsivity, and hyper-activity with and without conduct problems: Relationships to delinquency and unique contextual factors. In R. McMahon & R. Peters (Eds.), *Behavior disorders of adolescence: Research intervention, and policy in clinical and school settings* (pp. 39–61). New York: Plenum Press.

Loney, J. (1987). Hyperactivity and aggression in the diagnosis of attention deficit dis-order. In B. Lahey & A. Kazdin (Eds.), *Advances in clinical child psychology* (Vol. 10, pp. 99–135). New York: Plenum Press.

Lynam, D. (1996). Early identification of chronic offenders: Who is the fledgling psy-chopath? *Psychological Bulletin, 120,* 209–234.

Lynam, D. (1997). Pursuing the psychopath: Capturing the fledgling psychopath in a nomological net. *Journal of Abnormal Psychology, 106,* 425–438.

Mathur, S., Kavale, K., Quinn, M., Forness, S., & Rutherford, R. (1998). Social skills intervention with students with emotional and behavioral problems: A quantitative synthesis of single subject research. *Behavioral Disorders, 23,* 193–201.

McConaughy, S., & Skiba, R. (1993). Comorbidity of externalizing and internalizing problems. *School Psychology Review, 22,* 421–436.

McConnell, S., & Odom, S. (1986). Sociometrics: Peer-referenced measures and assessment of social competence. In P. Strain, M. Guralnick, & H. Walker (Eds.), *Children's social behavior: Development, assessment, and modification* (pp. 215-275). Orlando, FL: Academic Press.

McDowell, J. J. (1982). The importance of Herrnstein's mathematical statement of the Law of Effect for behavior therapy. *American Psychologist, 37,* 771-779.

McFall, R. (1982). A review and reformulation of the concept of social skills. *Behavioral Assessment, 4,* 1-35.

Merrell, K. (1993). *School social behavior scales.* Austin, TX: Pro-Ed.

Merrell, K. (1994). *Preschool and kindergarten behavior scales.* Austin, TX: Pro-Ed.

Merrell, K., & Gimpel, G. (1998). *Social skills of children and adolescents: Conceptualization, assessment, and treatment.* Mahwah, NJ: Erlbaum.

Milich, R., & Landau, S. (1989). The role of social status variables in differentiating subgroups of hyperactive children. In L. Bloomingdale & J. Swanson (Eds.), *Attention deficit disorder: Current concepts and emerging trends in attentional and behavioral disorders of childhood* (Vol. 5, pp. 1-16). Elmsford, NY: Pergamon Press.

National Educational Goals Panel. (1999). *The national education goals report: Building a nation of learners.* Washington, DC: U.S. Government Printing Office.

Newcomb, A., Bukowski, W., & Pattee, L. (1993). Children's peer relations: A meta-analytic review of popular, rejected, neglected, controversial, and average sociometric status. *Psychological Bulletin, 113,* 306-347.

Oden, S., & Asher, S. (1977). Coaching children in social skills for friendship making. *Child Development, 48,* 496-506.

Parker, J., & Asher, S. (1987). Peer relations and later personal adjustment: Are low-accepted children at-risk? *Psychological Bulletin, 102,* 357-389.

Pelham, W., & Bender, M. (1982). Peer relations in hyperactive children: Description and treatment. In K. Gadow & I. Bialer (Eds.), *Advances in learning and behavioral disabilities: A research annual* (Vol. 1, pp. 365-346). Greenwich, CT: JAI Press.

Reynolds, C., & Kamphaus, R. (1992). *Behavioral assessment system for children.* Circle Pines, MN: American Guidance Service.

Schneider, B. (1992). Didactic methods for enhancing children's peer relations: A quantitative review. *Clinical Psychology Review, 12,* 363-382.

Sechrest, L., McKnight, P., & McKnight, K. (1996). Calibration of measures for psychotherapy outcome studies. *American Psychologist, 51,* 1065-1071.

Skinner, C. (1998). Preventing academic skills deficits. In T. S. Watson & F. M. Gresham (Eds.), *Handbook of child behavior therapy* (pp. 61-82). New York: Plenum Press.

Stokes, T. (1992). Discrimination and generalization. *Journal of Applied Behavior Analysis, 25,* 429-432.

Stokes, T., & Osnes, P. (1989). An operant pursuit of generalization. *Behavior Therapy, 20,* 337-355.

Strain, P. (1977). An experimental analysis of peer social initiations on the behavior of withdrawn preschool children: Some training and generalization effects. *Journal of Abnormal Child Psychology, 5,* 445-455.

Strain, P., Cooke, R., & Apolloni, T. (1976). *Teaching exceptional children: Assessing and modifying social behavior.* New York: Academic Press.

Taylor-Greene, S., Brown, D., Nelson, L., Longton, J., Gassman, C., Swartz, J., Horner, R., Sugai, G., & Hall, S. (1997). School-wide behavioral support: Starting the year off right. *Journal of Behavioral Education, 7,* 99-112.

The Child Mental Health Foundations and Agencies Network. (2000). *A good beginning: Sending America's children to school with the social and emotional competence they need to succeed.* Bethesda, MD.

Ubain, E., & Kendall, P. (1980). Review of social-cognitive problem-solving interventions with children. *Psychological Bulletin, 88,* 109-143.

Walker, H., Colvin, G., & Ramsey, E. (1995). *Antisocial behavior in school: Strategies and best practices.* Pacific Grove, CA: Brooks/Cole.

Walker, H., Forness, S., Kauffman, J., Epstein, M., Gresham, F. M., Nelson, C. M., & Strain, P. (1998). Macro-social validation: Referencing outcomes in behavioral disorders to societal issues and problems. *Behavioral Disorders, 24,* 7-18.

Walker, H., Irvin, L., Noell, J., & Singer, G. (1992). A construct score approach to the assessment of social competence: Rationale, technological considerations, and anticipated outcomes. *Behavior Modification, 16,* 448-474.

Walker, H., & McConnell, S. (1995a). *Walker-McConnell scale of social competence and school adjustment: Elementary version.* San Diego: Singular.

Walker, H., & McConnell, S. (1995b). *Walker-McConnell scale of social competence and school adjustment: Adolescent version.* San Diego: Singular.

Walker, H., McConnell, S., Holmes, D., Todis, B., Walker, J., & Golden, N. (1983). *The Walker social skills curriculum: The ACCEPTS program (A Curriculum for Children's Effective Peer and Teacher Skills).* Austin, TX: Pro-Ed.

Walker, H., & Severson, H. (1992). *Systematic screening for behavior disorders.* Longmont, CO: Sopris West.

Watson, T. S., & Gresham, F. M. (Eds.). (1998). *Handbook of child behavior therapy.* New York: Plenum Press.

Whalen, C., & Henker, B. (1985). The social worlds of hyperactive children. *Clinical Psychology Review, 5,* 1-32.

Wolf, M. (1978). Social validity: The case for subjective measurement or how applied behavior analysis is finding its heart. *Journal of Applied Behavior Analysis, 11,* 203-214.

Yeaton, W., & Sechrest, L. (1981). Critical dimensions in the choice and maintenance of effective treatments: Strength, integrity, and effectiveness. *Journal of Consulting and Clinical Psychology, 49,* 156-167.

AUTHORS' NOTES

Portions of this chapter have been previously published in "Social training with children: Social learning and applied behavior analytic approaches." by F. M. Gresham in Handbook of Child Behavior Therapy (pp. 475-497) by T. S. Watson & F. M. Gresham (Eds.) New York: Plenum Press.

CHAPTER 16

Self-Monitoring Procedures for Children and Adolescents

Edward S. Shapiro, Stacy L. Durnan, Erin E. Post,
and Tara Skibitsky Levinson
Lehigh University

INTRODUCTION

Self-Monitoring (SM) is a well-established technique that has often been used to address behavioral and academic problems in children and adolescents (e.g., Shapiro & Cole, 1994). Two processes make up the SM procedure: (a) *observation* of one's own behavior, and (b) *recording* that behavior in some way. Although these two processes have been described in the literature as separate, for practical purposes in clinical use they are linked. Certainly a student could be asked to self-assess ("Tell me if you are on-task when you hear the signal") without self-recording. Likewise, a student could self-record without self-assessing ("At the signal I will tell you if you are on-task, please record what I tell you"). However, separating these two actions in application is not logical because if you want a student to self-assess, then you want that student also to self-record.

Self-monitoring has long been recognized as both an assessment and intervention strategy (e.g., Korotitsch & Nelson-Gray, 1999; Nelson, 1977). As an assessment strategy, SM functions as a method for collecting data about an individual as reported by the individual himself or herself. Because data are collected at the time the behavior actually occurs, SM is viewed as a form of *direct* rather than *indirect* assessment on the continuum of behavioral assessment (Shapiro & Kratochwill, 2000). As an intervention strategy, SM is designed to function as a method that will alter behavior while simply collecting data. In other words, it is *reactive*. Many of us have had the experience of implementing a weight loss program where behaviors such as recording one's weight, what one eats, or the number of fat grams consumed can serve as enough of a stimulus to reduce our weight without putting a specific diet plan in place. In reality, there are few situations where SM in school settings is used as only an assessment tool (Shapiro & Cole, 1999). More typically, especially with children, SM is viewed as a strategy to impact behavior change, and not simply to monitor performance.

Applications of SM are extremely important in the process of teaching and learning. The goal of all teaching is to have students become capable of using the learning that they acquire under conditions where they are not being prompted by others (e.g., teachers) to engage in those behaviors. A student who is able to show behavior that was learned in one setting under related conditions is engaging in a form of self-management, which always includes an SM process. It is important to note that the SM process may not be visible to others. Initially, SM may start out as an overt procedure with specific cueing (e.g., a beep on a tape recorder) for assessment and evidence that behavior is being recorded (e.g., student places a check mark on a recording sheet). However, as the student acquires the desired skill or behavior, the cues and recording of behavior may become covert. We all experience covert SM when we "talk to ourselves" in a new situation, or respond and later retrospectively think about what we may have been thinking at the time we responded.

Several important behavioral principles are linked to the process of SM. Of greatest importance is the concept of *reactivity*. As indicated previously, behavior can change simply as a function of collecting data. Although some investigators suggest that reactivity of behavior is the occurrence of behavior *without* the presence of reinforcement, a more accurate statement would be that it is without the presence of overt or specified extrinsic reinforcement. For any behavior change to occur, there must be reinforcement of some form on some schedule. When reactivity of SM behavior is evident, it is likely that the lack of "reinforcement" really refers to the lack of identifiable, extrinsic rewards; there are likely intrinsic or unidentifiable rewards that are known or recognized by the individual alone. For example, if self-monitoring the number of problems done correctly on a math worksheet in class has improved math performance, this is probably an indication of the presence of intrinsic rewards—such as the importance of getting better grades, the avoidance of having to do the worksheet as homework, or anticipating praise from the teacher or parents about improved academic performance.

A second important concept that underlies SM is *accuracy*. The concern is whether the individual is accurate in the self-monitoring of his or her behavior. Interestingly, research over the years has found that accuracy is not always evident when SM reactivity is present. At times, individuals who engage in SM may show substantial behavior change, but the behavior they are self-monitoring and the recording of that behavior on the SM device are highly disparate. Although some researchers have concluded that accuracy and reactivity of SM may be independent, in truth there must be some minimal level of SM accuracy for any reactivity to occur. Unless an individual has some level of accuracy, it would be impossible to attribute the behavior change evident directly to the SM process (Nelson & Hayes, 1981).

Limitations of SM are few. Self-monitoring is a procedure that has broad applicability across ages, cognitive ability levels, types of problems, and settings. Indeed, probably the only limitation is the belief that an individual requires some minimal level of intellectual ability for SM to be effective. In its early days of development, these beliefs prohibited its use for individuals with mental retardation (e.g., Shapiro, 1981).

The countering of this concept occurred through many empirical studies showing its applicability to populations that were limited in their cognitive abilities (e.g., Litrownik, Freitas, & Franzini, 1978; Shapiro & Klein, 1980). Today, the belief of a minimal cognitive requirement for SM is no longer applicable—nor is it evident in the literature.

The purpose of this chapter is provide a review of the use and application of SM. Emphasis throughout the chapter is on the method and its application, rather than underlying conceptualization. The research used to illustrate the applications of SM is not meant to be comprehensive. Readers are encouraged to seek out resources that have undertaken a more comprehensive examination of SM and its related self-management techniques (Cone, 1999; Shapiro & Cole, 1994).

TEACHING STUDENTS TO SELF-MONITOR

Designing a procedure to teach students to self-monitor is simple, but requires several considerations. First, an understanding of the type of students doing the self-monitoring and the type of behaviors to be monitored is important. In the procedure itself, the types of prompts, recording device, schedule for SM, the need to check for accuracy, and the type of training necessary to perform the required SM all must be examined. This section will review each of these characteristics of programs focused on teaching SM.

Types of Students

A substantial base of empirical literature has demonstrated the feasibility of SM procedures in children and adolescents with a diverse range of individual differences. SM procedures have been used in general and special education settings with students who have developmental disabilities (Hughes, Korinek, & Gorman, 1991), brain injury (Selznick & Savage, 2000), learning disabilities (Dunlap & Dunlap, 1989), comorbid ADHD and learning disabilities (Shimabukuro, Prater, Jenkins, & Edelen-Smith, 1999), autism (Koegel & Koegel, 1990), emotional/behavioral disorders (Hughes, Ruhl, & Misra, 1989; Kern, Dunlap, Childs, & Clarke, 1994), as well as with students with no exceptionality (Wood, Murdock, Cronin, Dawson, & Kirby, 1998). Children of all ages, from preschool to high school, can learn to use and benefit from SM.

Although SM has typically been used by an individual child to observe and record target behaviors that occur in one or more settings (Kern, Marder, Boyajian, Elliot, & McElhattan, 1997; Peterson, Young, West, & Peterson, 1999), it can also be used successfully with groups of students or an entire class (Kern et al., 1994). Because of the unobtrusive nature of its procedures, SM can be used as an intervention for specific individuals, while at the same time providing benefits to the larger class.

Types of Behaviors

Children and adolescents can be taught to successfully monitor almost any relevant target behavior across a variety of settings. The behaviors range from those readily observable by the student and by others (e.g., calling out in class, getting out of one's seat, failing to complete seatwork completion) to more subjective behaviors that are only observable to the student (e.g., negative thoughts, levels of anxiety). For more detail on the range of behaviors that have been used in SM studies, see the review by Cole and Bambara (2000). Examples in the literature include self-monitoring of in-class transition behaviors by preschoolers with developmental delays (Connell, Carta, Lutz, Randall, & Wilson, 1993), SM of teachers' expectancies by middle school students with learning disabilities (Clees, 1994), SM spelling behavior by an elementary-age student with severe behavior disorders (McDougall & Brady, 1995), SM social skills by high school males with emotional and behavioral disorders (Moore, Cartledge, & Heckman, 1995), and SM attending behavior by elementary students with attention-deficit/hyperactivity disorder (ADHD) (Mathes & Bender, 1997).

Designing a Self-Monitoring Program

A number of factors are considered when designing a self-monitoring procedure. The ultimate goal of SM is to ensure that the students will self-monitor the targeted behavior and that the monitoring will be accurate. The first step is to define the target behavior in operational terms. The target behavior may virtually be any observable or nonobservable response that can be clearly understood by the student. The behavior should be defined concretely and explicitly to minimize the possibility of misunderstanding. Accuracy in discriminating the occurrence of the behavior for the observer can be enhanced by offering definitions that indicate not only what a behavior *is,* but also what it *is not.* For example, target behaviors such as "being good" or "staying on-task" are vague terms that can be interpreted in many ways, whereas "staying in the seat," "feet on the floor," "not talking to other students," and "raising hand to talk" are a lot more specific. Providing examples (e.g., eyes on one's work, writing answers to problems) as well as nonexamples (e.g., staring out the window, playing with one's pencil) help to provide clear discriminations that operationally define the behavior of interest.

The second step involves selecting an SM method for recording the occurrence (or nonoccurrence) of the target behavior. It is important to select a method that is appropriate for the behavior(s) being recorded and that is relatively easy to use. The procedure for using the method should also be very clear and concise for the student to understand and be adapted to the student's level of cognitive functioning (Dunlap, Dunlap, Koegel, & Koegel, 1991). For example, a procedure that requires a student to self-monitor following specified time intervals (i.e., every 15 minutes) would be appropriate for high-rate or continuous (i.e., ongoing) behaviors, such as on-task behavior. With young children and children with more severe disabilities, ongoing visual reminders of the target behaviors may be necessary (Shapiro & Cole, 1999). For example, if young students are asked to self-monitor their completion of a sorting task, a picture of the completed task may be placed on a chart, below which students need to place a check mark when they complete the task. To be feasible for school settings, SM methods should be relatively inexpensive and unobtrusive (Cole, Marder, & McCann, 2000), match the natural classroom structure and routine, and be socially acceptable to those involved. Using these guidelines, the practitioner must make a number of specific decisions regarding the type of prompting, recording device, schedule for SM, and accuracy checks that will be used.

Prompts. Several types of prompts have been used in the literature to signal students to self-monitor in the initial learning stages. In school-based settings, the most common application involves the use of external verbal or nonverbal prompts, and can be delivered by another person (e.g., teacher, aide, support person, peer) or by a mechanical device (e.g., tone from a tape recorder, timer, bell, switching the lights on and off) (Cole et al., 2000). Verbal prompting may involve a simple reminder from the teacher to self-monitor at the end of the period. This type of prompt is often effective when an entire class is engaged in a self-monitoring procedure. In a situation where only one or a few target students self-monitor, a nonverbal prompt (e.g., teacher tapping the student[s] on the shoulder) to elicit SM may be needed. A prerecorded tone is one of the most commonly used prompts in schools since it requires little time and effort on the part of the teacher and can be used with individuals or large groups (e.g., DiGangi, Maag, & Rutherford, 1991; McDougall & Brady, 1995).

SM prompts may also take the form of internal prompts. Typically referred to as self-prompting, internal prompts involve students noting on their own, from time to time during the designated SM time period, whether or not they were engaging in the target behavior (e.g., Heins, Lloyd, & Hallahan, 1986; Ollendick, 1995). Although this strategy has been used for students who have difficulty attending to task, the empirical support for the effectiveness of internal prompts is questionable. For example, Heins et al. (1986) compared externally cued and noncued (i.e., internally prompted) self-recording of attention to task for four boys with learning disabilities who were trained in both procedures. Although the students did learn to self-monitor using both procedures, their monitoring was inconsistent in the noncued condition and there were fewer reactive effects reported for this condition than for the prompted SM.

Recording devices. There are several considerations involved in selecting a recording device. First, to increase the accuracy of SM, the device should be available for recording target behaviors *when* the behavior occurs. That is, minimal time should elapse between when the behavior actually occurs and when it is recorded. Second, if the device is to be used in more than one setting, it should be portable and conve-nient. Third, the recording device should be simple and not distracting. If a child is focused on the SM device, she or he may miss other task requirements. The device should be sufficiently visible so that the child attends to and remembers to use it, but should not be so obtrusive that attention is drawn from the task. This is a particularly important concern if the SM procedure is being used in an inclusive classroom or community-based setting because a student may stop using a device if he or she feels embarrassed by peers for using the self-monitoring procedure. Finally, one of the most practical considerations in designing a recording device is cost. It is important to match the design of the recording device with the resources available in the classroom.

Given these criteria for recording devices, it is not surprising that the most popular devices in school-based settings are paper-and-pencil procedures (e.g., Harris, Graham, Reid, McElroy, & Stern Hamby, 1994). Paper-and-pencil recording forms can

FIGURE 1

Examples of Paper and Pencil Self-Monitoring Sheet

Name: _____   Date: _____

Class Preparation:

• When I hear the first beep, I will answer yes or no to questions related to my classroom preparation.

	YES	NO
Pencil on desk		
Book open to correct page		
Clean paper on desk		
All other material put away		
Sitting quietly		
Eyes on teacher		

During Class:

• When I hear the beep, I will place a check in the box if I am on-task and if I have spoken only when raising my hand.

	1	2	3	4	5
On-task					
Raised my hand to speak					

Classroom self-monitoring:

Name: _____   Date: _____

1. Worked without disturbing others.	1	2	3	4
2. Participated in class.	1	2	3	4
3. Listened and paid attention when the teacher was talking.	1	2	3	4
4. Asked for help when I needed it.	1	2	3	4
5. Completed class assignment.	1	2	3	4
6. Turned in completed assignment.	1	2	3	4

be in the form of an index card or slip of paper on which the child makes a tally mark each time the behavior occurs, a checklist the student uses to check off target behaviors at the sound of a cue, or a recording sheet on which students answer specific questions at the end of a period (see Figures 1 and 2 for examples of paper-and-pencil

FIGURE 2

Example of Self-Monitoring a Series of Activities

Name: _____   Date: _____

Assignment Checklist

	YES	NO
1. Is my name on the paper?		
2. Do all my sentences begin with a capital letter?		
3. Do my sentences end with the proper punctuation?		
4. Did I answer all the questions?		
5. Did I check my work for spelling errors?		
6. Did I turn my assigment in?		

SM recording sheets). The recording form is typically placed on the student's desk (e.g., McCarl, Svobodny, & Beare, 1991; Selznick & Savage, 2000; Wood et al., 1998), but may also be placed on the wall next to the student's desk (e.g., Workman, Helton, & Watson, 1982), or carried in a folder or notebook by an adolescent throughout the day (e.g., Clees, 1994).

Less conventional types of recording devices have also been used for SM. For example, Miller, Strain, Boyd, Jarzynka, and McFetridge (1993) had preschoolers use a "thumbs up" or "thumbs down" signal when teachers asked them to monitor their behavior following transition, free play, and small-group instruction. Davies and Witte (2000) used a large group chart with colored tokens to decrease inappropriate verbalizations in students with ADHD. Another novel interpretation of self-recording entailed teenagers with autism removing a token from a back pocket and placing it in a front pocket to self-monitor each transition to a new activity (Newman, Buffington, O'Grady, McDonald, Poulson, & Hemmes, 1995).

Schedule of self-monitoring. When and how often a student will self-monitor are other factors that need to be considered when developing SM procedures. The schedule of SM will depend on the nature of the target behaviors and the environmental setting in which SM occurs. Educators need to consider whether the SM procedures will be restricted to a particular class or be carried over throughout the school day.

One popular variation for SM is momentary time-sampling, or spot-checking (e.g., Prater, Hogan, & Miller, 1992). Using this procedure, children are signaled by an auditory tone to self-monitor several times throughout a class period (e.g., in 1- to

5-minute intervals). The length of the interval between occurrences of SM will depend on the characteristics of the children involved (e.g., age, type of disability, attentional difficulties) but are typically random periods within a set period of time (e.g., on average every 30 seconds, ranging from 10 to 60 seconds). Younger children and students with more severe cognitive and attentional disabilities should have shorter SM intervals. When they hear the tone, the children are instructed to decide whether they were attending ("mark a +") or were not attending ("mark a −") to the task at the moment they heard the tone. Results are summarized by the percentage on-task, which is calculated by dividing the number of on-task occurrences by the total number of times the signal was given, and then multiplying it by 100.

Although momentary time sampling is most commonly used for on-task behavior (McCarl et al., 1991), it has also been used to self-monitor other behaviors. For example, in one study, three elementary school students with severe behavior disorders were taught to self-monitor their use of a study strategy during a spelling study period using momentary sampling (McDougall & Brady, 1995).

Varying the length of the intervals between SM events can help to avoid having the student predict when the SM cue will be delivered (Maag, Rutherford, & DiGangi, 1992). Some students may be capable, from the onset of SM, of monitoring behaviors over lengthy intervals. Others may initially require short intervals with a gradual lengthening of intervals over time. In designing a self-monitoring system, it is important to determine the appropriate SM interval given the individual needs and capacities of children by examining the student's initial accuracy of SM. Students who show poor accuracy of SM may improve their accuracy by increasing the frequency of the SM process. Once they show evidence of high accuracy of SM, the intervals between SM events can be gradually lengthened, thus providing maintenance of behavior over time with less frequent need to engage in overt self-monitoring of responses.

Accuracy checks. A final consideration for SM is determining the accuracy of a student's self-monitoring. The most commonly used procedure is comparing recordings made by the child with those made simultaneously by another observer (Dunlap & Dunlap, 1989). The extent to which a student is able to match an observer's recordings of a target behavior determines the accuracy of SM. A minimum criterion should be established prior to beginning the SM intervention (e.g., no more than one session per week with less than 80% accuracy). If this level is not maintained, booster sessions may be needed to ensure that the student understands the definitions of the target behaviors and the steps of SM.

Training. Methods to train students in SM procedures may range from simple verbal instructions, to more complex training packages that include verbal instruction, and to modeling, behavior rehearsal, corrective performance feedback, and positive reinforcement for accurate SM. All of these training procedures may occur in a location separate from or within the natural setting where the SM will actually take place.

Verbal instructions usually set the stage for SM by giving the students a general description of the purpose and process of SM. The emphasis is on accuracy of recording behavior and discriminating occurrences from nonoccurrences. Students are given an explicit set of directions for the steps in the SM process (e.g., "When you hear the beep it will be time for you to ask yourself if you were working on your classwork. Then you will check the correct box on the self-recording sheet."). Modeling of desired and undesired examples of the target behavior in the classroom setting may also be used. Role playing also may be used to have students practice the SM process. For example, the trainer may observe students in a simulated situation. When the beep is heard, the instructor then asks the students, "Was I in my seat and was I paying attention?" Then the instructor and the students practice filling in the SM sheet. When the students clearly understand the target behaviors and the SM procedures in the teaching session, the instructor practices SM in the classroom.

Some training procedures are more complex and elaborately scripted. For example, Snyder and Bambara (1997) trained students with learning disabilities to self-monitor classroom preparedness behavior using a training model for skill acquisition (Deshler, Alley, Warner, & Schumaker, 1981). Training steps consisted of (a) an analysis of the student's current behavior pattern, (b) a description of the new SM strategy, (c) modeling, (d) verbal rehearsal, (e) student practice with sample classroom materials, and (f) student practice using actual classroom materials. In the initial intervention, the students were trained to use the SM sheets in a learning support classroom by a special education teacher. The teacher led the students through the process of problem identification, goal setting, self-monitoring, and self-evaluation. Once students were able to self-monitor and self-evaluate the target behaviors with 100% accuracy for 3 consecutive days, they were trained to generalize the self-management package to their general education social studies classroom. A similar training format was used to train the SM procedures in the general education classroom. The special education teacher continued to monitor the SM procedures and provided frequent feedback to the students to ensure accuracy. As the students independently demonstrated classroom preparedness behaviors in the general education classroom, the special education teacher faded feedback and monitoring

In sum, it is critical for the student to understand what is expected and have the skills to follow the SM procedure being taught. To increase the likelihood of accurate SM by students, all comprehensive training programs should include (a) explicit definitions of the target behavior, (b) simplified behavior counting and recording procedures, (c) specific and relatively short periods in which SM occurs, (d) teacher reliability checks and feedback, and (e) sufficient practice to ensure that fluency in SM is attained (Firth & Armstrong, 1985).

COMMON SCHOOL-BASED APPLICATIONS OF SELF-MONITORING

Self-monitoring in school-based settings has been applied to academic performance, the complex process of self-regulated learning, on-task behavior, and problem behaviors. Additionally, SM has been used as part of a procedure to promote independence and to enhance social skills.

The use of SM to measure academic performance can be divided into three different components: (a) productivity, (b) work accuracy, and (c) the strategies used in the completion of a task. The specific academic behaviors that are typically targeted for self-monitoring academic performance are productivity and accuracy of an academic task. A less common academic behavior that is monitored is the process of an academic task.

Self-monitoring academic productivity. When academic productivity is the target of the SM intervention, students record whether the required academic task was completed, regardless of its accuracy. Shimabukuro et al. (1999) had three male students with learning disabilities and ADHD self-monitor their academic productivity and accuracy. All three students scored within average range of intelligence on individual school evaluations, but demonstrated a history of academic deficits and had problems paying attention during academic periods. Students measured productivity by counting the number of items they completed and then comparing that to the number of items assigned to each academic task at the end of each independent work period. For three targeted academic areas—reading comprehension, mathematics, and written expression—students computed academic productivity scores themselves as percentages by dividing the number of items completed by the number of items assigned, and then multiplied the result by 100. This score was then recorded and graphed by the students. All three students increased their academic productivity with SM in all three academic areas. Additionally, although not specifically targeted, improvements occurred in academic accuracy and on-task behavior.

Self-monitoring academic accuracy. When academic accuracy is the target of SM, students record what they believe is the number of correct responses they have from their completed work. The procedure can also involve an actual comparison of their work to an answer sheet. For example, Lam, Cole, Shapiro, and Bambara (1994) worked with three male students classified as mildly mentally retarded with severe behavior disorders who were experiencing difficulties in mathematics. These students also had poor performance on independent work and low rates of on-task behavior. During an independent work session, the students were taught to self-monitor their academic accuracy. Students checked the accuracy of their math work by comparing their answers to an answer key after they were cued by a tone that was on a one-minute variable-interval schedule. Copies of the answer key were on their desks and covered by a sheet. To prevent cheating, the students were instructed to move the cover sheet only to the *last* problem they completed during that interval. Students then recorded the number of problems they had answered correctly. Academic accuracy, on-task behavior, and disruptive behavior were assessed. Academic accuracy substantially improved for two students during the self-monitoring of academic accuracy. Additionally, self-monitoring academic accuracy resulted in positive effects for on-task and disruptive behaviors.

Self-monitoring strategies. A less common form of self-monitoring academic performance is to record *strategy use*—in order words, to record whether essential or required steps in doing an academic task were completed. Miller, Miller, Wheeler, and Selinger (1989) taught an 11-year old student with a severe behavioral disorder who was functioning 2 years below grade level in reading, spelling, and math to self-monitor the process involved when completing 2-digit subtraction with regrouping math problems. The SM process included a step-by-step sequential checklist with 7 self-instructional steps. The student self-monitored the process by recording a check after completing each step. To fade the intervention, the 7-step SM checklists were reduced in length and then fully eliminated. Results showed that this student increased accuracy on the math problem and continued with a high accuracy rate during the fading and follow-up phase.

Self-Monitoring Within Self-Regulated Learning

Self-Monitoring has also been examined when it is part of a broader, self-regulatory, multiple-component process. This differs from the SM procedures for academic skills described previously where the student observes and records discrete behaviors (e.g., number of problems completed, number of words written). Self-regulation stresses behavior that includes personal metacognitive, motivational, behavioral, and environmental processes to enhance academic achievement (Zimmerman, 1986, 1989). Academic learning is viewed as something learners do for themselves, through the use of self-initiated goals, accuracy in their behavioral SM, and the resourcefulness of their strategic thinking (Zimmerman, 1998). Thus, SM is only *one* process within the *multiple processes* involved in the self-regulation of academic learning.

SM has been discussed as one of the most important subprocesses of self-regulated learning (Lan, 1998). When used during an academic learning experience, SM initiates a self-reflective practice that makes the learner examine all aspects of the learning process, which can lead to the detection of a discrepancy between the goals of the student and the actual performance, and allow for correction if needed (Zimmerman & Risemberg, 1997b). During self-regulation, SM serves to monitor the *process* of learning that is occurring, not just the outcome behavior.

Although self-regulation can be applied to most areas of academic learning, much work has been done with acquiring written expression, an activity that requires planning and initiation (Zimmerman & Risemberg, 1997a). Zimmerman and Kitsantas (1999) used a multilevel view of written expression skill acquisition by comparing the revision of a sentence-combining task by focusing either on (a) the process goal, (b) the outcome goal, or (c) the combination of first focusing on the process goal and then shifting to the outcome goal. Additionally, the use of self-recording was examined in the investigation. A total of 84 female high school students participated in the investigation and were assigned to one of six experimental conditions. Those assigned to the outcome-goal condition were told to focus on rewriting the sentence using a minimal number of words while producing a complete sentence. Students in the outcome-goal condition with self-recording were told to count the number of words in their sentence and record that number. Participants assigned to the process-goal condition were told to focus on properly executing three key strategy steps in every rewriting problem they attempted. Individuals assigned to the process-goal plus self-recording condition were instructed to write down the *number* of strategy steps that they completed correctly. Students assigned to the combined group were instructed to properly execute the three strategy steps during the first 15 minutes and then were instructed to focus on the outcome goal of using the minimal number of words. Those who were self-recording were instructed to record the number of strategies completed correctly and then to count the number of words in the sentence.

Results of this investigation indicated that the combined group displayed the highest level of writing skill. Additionally, self-recording conditions displayed significantly greater rewriting skills. Thus, it seems that within self-regulated learning a multilevel view of skill acquisition allows learners to have a hierarchy of specific goals, and the use of SM helps achieve mastery of each specific goal (Zimmerman & Kitsantas, 1999).

Self-Monitoring On-Task Behavior

The most widely targeted behavior of SM interventions is attention, or on-task behavior (e.g., Reid, 1996; Webber, Scheuermann, McCall, & Coleman, 1993). This SM intervention requires students to observe and record whether or not they are working on an assigned activity or paying attention.

The prototypical procedure for SM on-task behavior in the classroom uses momentary time sampling where the class period is divided into time intervals and the students are cued to self-observe and record on-task or off-task behavior (Hallahan, Lloyd, Kneedler, & Marshall, 1982). At the sound of a tone on a variable-interval schedule, students are taught to ask themselves, "Was I paying attention when I heard the tone?" and record "yes" or "no." The most commonly used recording device is a paper-and-pencil recording sheet.

Interval lengths for SM on-task behavior have varied widely in the literature from a few seconds to over an hour. Again, the length of the interval should be determined by student characteristics and environmental conditions. For example, for students with more extreme attentional difficulties, shorter interval lengths are recommended. However, if there is one particular academic task in which the student seems to be exhibiting less off-task behavior, longer intervals may be used for that specific task. After a student shows improvement on SM, interval lengths may be increased to reduce dependency on external cueing.

Using variable-length intervals—as opposed to consistent intervals, which may lead to students learning to be on-task only just prior to the cue—helps keep the student on-task during the whole interval. For example, Harris et al. (1994) conducted an SM intervention targeting attention or on-task behavior where the interval lengths had an average of 45 seconds with a range of 10–90 seconds. Four students with learning disabilities who had difficulty attending to tasks and completing classroom assignments participated in an SM on-task intervention during spelling. Students were instructed to ask themselves, immediately after hearing a tone through headphones connected to a tape player, whether they were paying attention—and record their yes/no answer on a tally sheet. The tones for cueing to self-monitor occurred at random intervals during spelling. Additionally, at the end of spelling, the students graphed the number of tallies they had for "yes." It should be noted, however, that graphing is not typically included in self-monitoring on-task behavior, but may provide possible motivation or feedback effects (Harris et al., 1994).

Self-Monitoring Problem Behaviors

Applications of SM have been extended to the broad class of disruptive and internalizing problems of children. Among the externalizing behaviors are interventions that have targeted such problems as making negative statements to others, accepting negative feedback from teachers without comment, and other challenging disruptive behaviors. Likewise, SM has been applied in more clinical, therapeutic settings to students with difficulties in the areas of anxiety, depression, or phobias.

Using self-monitoring with students with disruptive behavior problems. Interventions involving SM can be used with a variety of disruptive or aggressive behaviors exhibited by individual students or whole classes. For example, Martella, Leonard, Marchand-Martella, and Agran (1993) wanted to reduce the frequent negative statements that a 12-year-old student with mental retardation uttered in his self-contained special education classroom. To do this, they trained the student to self-monitor these types of statements. He was given an SM sheet with the heading "negative statements," examples of these comments, and 45 boxes in which to record each occurrence. Before intervention, the student participated in three training sessions to learn how to self-monitor. In the first one, the trainer stated five examples of positive comments and five examples of negative comments in random order and asked the student to identify which were positive and which were negative. Correct answers were praised and incorrect answers were modeled correctly, followed by the student correcting his mistake. The second session added a component in which the student learned to mark each negative statement. The final session added the component of giving five examples of negative statements and five examples of positive statements.

After these sessions, the intervention began. The trainer highlighted the number of boxes that indicated a maximum number of negative comments the student was allowed to make that day and still select either a small or a large reward from a reinforcer menu. If his count of the number of negative statements spoken each day was in agreement with the trainer's (80% or higher), he received the small reinforcer. If his recordings continued to match the trainer's and continued to be at or below the criterion level for four consecutive sessions, he received the large reinforcer. Additionally, the student charted his number of negative statements made each day on standard graph paper. This SM procedure was successful in reducing this student's negative statements.

Self-monitoring also has proved to be a successful intervention for reducing the disruptive behavior of multiple students. For example, Kern et al. (1994) evaluated the effects of SM on the on-task and disruptive (including aggression, property destruction, leaving the room, or excessive noncompliance) behaviors of a self-contained public school special education class for students with emotional and behavioral problems. All six students self-monitored their on-task behavior and one individualized behavior selected by the teacher as needing improvement (e.g., appropriately accepting feedback or engaging in appropriate interactions) during a 45-minute math session. Before the procedure was implemented, students were briefly asked to describe and provide examples of on- and off-task behavior and their specific target behavior. Then the trainer provided several examples and asked the students whether they would score them as on-task or off-task. The students all responded accurately to the training session.

Each student received an SM recording sheet that contained statements such as "I am on task," "I had a positive attitude," or "I had appropriate adult interactions." When a bell was sounded from a tape recorder, students recorded "yes" or "no" to each statement. Initially an adult also recorded the responses at the same time so that corrective feedback could be given. All the students reached 80% agreement by the second day. This SM procedure, which was added to a previously implemented point and time-out system, increased the percentage of intervals each student was on-task while decreasing disruptive behaviors to near 0% of the intervals observed.

Self-monitoring interventions can be specialized to fit characteristics of students or entire classrooms. For example, SM procedures can be added to existing classroom point systems or level systems (e.g., Kern et al., 1994). Cavalier, Ferretti, and Hodges (1997) reduced the high-rate verbalizations of two students with learning disabilities by teaching them to monitor their behavior. As a result, both students were able to reduce this problem behavior that had previously impeded their progression through the class-wide level system (comparable to a token economy) already in place.

Using self-monitoring with students with internalizing problems. Using SM with students with internalizing problems such as anxiety, depression, or phobias allows the student to report covert thoughts and feelings, levels of depressed or anxious feelings, and conditions surrounding the problem situations (Cole & Bambara, 2000). This information is often vital to treating the problem and often is obtained through behavioral diaries, counting devices, or checklists of predetermined behaviors. In one study, for example, four adolescents used a Panic Attack Record (PAR) to *monitor* the date, time, duration, location, circumstance, and symptoms during their panic attacks and a form to *rate* the extent to which they had avoided three agoraphobic situations (Ollendick, 1995).

Cognitive behavior therapy is often a preferred mode of treatment when working with children who present with internalizing problems such as depression. In particular, effective treatment of depression requires that children maintain cognitive awareness of internal states. SM can offer a mechanism for teaching children how to attain a connection with their own thoughts and feelings. For example, children with depression can be taught to monitor "pleasant events" as a therapeutic procedure (Reynolds & Stark, 1987). A pleasant event schedule is constructed by administering a questionnaire to all the children in the school. This questionnaire asks children to list five things they like to do and five things that make them happy. Rating each as "O.K.," "really fun," or in between, by marking the appropriate smiley face, these age-appropriate pleasant events then are listed along with blank "other" spaces in a booklet for the student participating in the intervention. Students then monitor themselves and mark a check each time they participate in an enjoyable activity or have a pleasant thought. In this way, the student focuses on positive events to help treat depressed symptoms.

Although numerous studies show positive outcomes for SM with students with internalizing problems, developmental considerations are especially important when monitoring internalizing disorders. Some younger children may not be able to understand their feelings or be able to monitor them (King, Ollendick, & Murphy, 1997). Additionally, it may be difficult to obtain accurate narrative descriptions of behavior from all children (Shapiro, 1984). Instead, as with all SM procedures, it is important to provide children and adolescents with simple procedures and clear behavioral definitions.

Self-Monitoring to Promote Independence

Besides inherently enabling students with the ability to monitor and thus control their behavior, some SM interventions have specifically targeted behaviors that increase students' ability to manage their own daily schedule of activities and thus increase their independence from adults. For example, Trammel, Schloss, and Alper (1994) used SM to increase the monitoring, by eight middle and high school students with learning disabilities, of assignments given and the completion of those assignments. Increasing independence can be accomplished through teaching students with special needs to monitor their use of a daily calendar in order to fulfill daily responsibilities (Flores, Schloss, & Alper, 1995).

Even preschoolers have been taught to self-monitor responsibilities to attain independence in monitoring their academic work schedule. Connell et al. (1993) used an SM procedure to improve problem behaviors during in-class transitional periods of three preschool classrooms of children with developmental delays. Specific transition behaviors included (a) failing to clean up after the signal to switch had been given, (b) talking too loud, (c) requiring excessive teacher prompting, (d) failing to find assigned seats, (e) the inability to independently find and put on a coat, and (f) wandering into the hallway when told to line up. Consistent with good principles of teaching SM, teachers initially provided visual prompts using posters or signs illustrating students who were engaging in the targeted behaviors. Teachers then defined the appropriate and inappropriate performance of each of these behaviors, followed by modeling and rehearsing them with the students. On the second day the students were taught to self-assess their independent behavior in three steps. First, they practiced raising their hands above their head when a required behavior had been performed, and keeping their hands in their lap when it had not been performed. Then they practiced these behaviors with clearly observable responses. Finally, they were taught to assess their own performance of specific transitional skills.

After this training, the teacher reviewed the self-assessment procedure and targeted behaviors either before free-play or prior to giving the clean-up cue. After 2 weeks this procedure was faded so that it was used only once or twice a week, and finally not at all. Results showed that those preschoolers selected for data collection improved their transitional skills and were able to independently respond as treatment was faded.

Using Self-Monitoring to Enhance Social Skills

One final area in which SM is often used is the development of social skills. As a form of self-management, social skills require that students often monitor thoughts and feelings that precede social interactions. For some children, focusing on prosocial skills helps to decrease negative behaviors (e.g., Ninness, Fuerst, Rutherford, & Glenn, 1991). Other times social skills are the direct targets of difficulties exhibited by the student. Traditionally, social skills are taught through explicit instruction, including direct practice, verbal training, modeling, role playing, and reinforcement. However, Gumpel and Golan (2000) hypothesized that not all social skill deficits are strictly skills deficits (i.e., "can't do" problems), but are performance-based deficits (i.e., "won't do" problems). To test their hypothesis, Gumpel and Golan examined the prosocial after-school game-playing behaviors of five 8- to 10-year-olds from resource or pull-out programs before and after self-recording and group-monitoring treatments.

Each of the five students possessed low levels of appropriate game-playing behavior such as following rules and turn taking. The students were trained to SM through a process whereby each participant had a different role while playing the game. One student taught the rules to the other members, one student monitored group members' behaviors explained to him by the experimenter, one student recorded appropriate group behaviors (provided by the experimenter), one student recorded the game's outcomes, and one student assisted the experimenter in distributing reinforcers before and after the game, as well as serving as a substitute.

The first treatment condition involved each player recording his or her own positive behaviors (frequency count) and then verbally answering whether or not he or she had played the game, followed the rules, and participated fully. Each group member recorded his or her points (number of behaviors plus 20% more than the mean number of positive behaviors for the baseline condition) on self-recording sheets and summarized them on "Today's Behaviors" posters. The introduction of this treatment increased and quickly improved the prosocial behaviors of all five participants. The intervention suggested that self-monitoring the frequencies of one's appropriate social interactions can have a strong mediating effect on those skills.

Self-monitoring also has been successful when used in conjunction with explicit social skills training. Shearer, Kohler, Buchan, and McCullough (1996) taught three preschoolers with autism how to initiate social interactions, respond to other children's initiations, and be persistent in social bids. At the same time, these preschoolers learned to self-monitor these behaviors by moving a bead after each social exchange. The experimenters found that as a result, they were able to increase and maintain these students' independent interactions. Similarly, Moore et al. (1995) used SM following training three male ninth-grade students with emotional or behavioral problems in appropriate game-related social skills. After the training, which involved discussions of the rationale for the training, social modeling, role playing, and homework assignments, the students tallied the number of times they had performed the learned skills during class play sessions and after gym class. Each day, the target behaviors were graphed and discussed. As a result of this treatment, appropriate game-playing behavior increased for each student.

CONCLUSIONS

Self-monitoring is a flexible intervention that has been applied to a variety of academic and nonacademic school-based problems. The procedure has been successful in helping students monitor their academic performance, as well as increase their on-task behavior. It can be applied to various externalizing and internalizing problems that can affect the classroom and its students. Applications of SM for academic problems have targeted simple concrete actions (e.g., number of problems done correctly), as well as complex, multicomponent skills such as writing and problem solving. Aggression, inappropriate verbalizations, disruptions, depression, anxiety, and phobias can all be treated effectively through SM interventions. Finally, SM is unique in that it can be used to increase students' independence by teaching them to independently monitor their daily responsibilities, to self-monitor their own behaviors throughout the day, and by enhancing their social skills.

Keys to using SM successfully include a recognition that some amount of training is needed, that target behaviors to be monitored must be well defined and clear to the student, and that the procedure for recording the behavior needs to be explicitly described. Adaptations of the procedures must also be considered based on the cognitive level and type of problem that a student presents.

There are very few cautions that need to be considered in using self-monitoring. One particular caution is that although SM can be reactive and result in behavior change simply as a function of implementation, it is not always reactive. Many times, additional external contingencies must be added to explicitly provide rewards to students for engaging in accurate SM. By itself, SM may not always be a powerful enough intervention to solve difficult, intractable problems. However, the important benefits of SM as part of a component in teaching self-management suggest that it can and should be used in combination with almost all other behavioral interventions.

In sum, SM offers an extremely valuable component for impacting almost all types of behavior difficulties shown by students. When implemented alone or as part of more involved interventions, SM can potentially serve as an important vehicle for increasing a student's behavioral self-control.

REFERENCES

Cavalier, A. R., Ferretti, R. P., & Hodges, A. E. (1997). Self-management within a classroom token economy for students with learning disabilities. *Research in Developmental Disabilities, 18*(3), 167-178.

Clees, T. J. (1994). Self-recording of students' daily schedules of teachers' expectancies: Perspectives on reactivity, stimulus control, and generalization. *Exceptionality, 5,* 113-129.

Cole, C. L., & Bambara, L. M. (2000). Self-monitoring: Theory and practice. In E. S. Shapiro & T. R. Kratochwill (Eds.), *Behavioral assessment in schools* (2nd ed., pp.202-232). New York: The Guilford Press.

Cole, C. L., Marder, T., & McCann, L. (2000). Self-monitoring. In E. S. Shapiro and T. R. Kratochwill (Eds.), *Conducting school-based assessments of child and adolescent behavior* (pp. 121-149). New York: The Guilford Press.

Cone, J. D. (1999). Introduction to the special section on self-monitoring: A major assessment method in clinical psychology. *Psychological Assessment, 11,* 411-414.

Connell, M. C., Carta, J. J., Lutz, S., Randall, C., & Wilson, J. (1993). Building independence during in-class transitions: Teaching in-class transition skills to preschoolers with developmental delays through choral-response-based self-assessment and contingent praise. *Education and Treatment of Children, 16*(2), 160-174.

Davies, S., & Witte, R. (2000). Self-management and peer-monitoring with a group contingency to decrease uncontrolled verbalizations of children with attention-deficit/hyperactivity disorder. *Psychology in the schools, 37,* 135-147.

Deshler, D. D., Alley, G. R., Warner, M. M., & Schumaker, J. B. (1981). Instructional practices for promoting skill acquisition and generalization in severely learning disabled adolescents. *Learning Disability Quarterly, 4,* 415-421.

DiGangi, S. M., Maag, J. W., & Rutherford, R. B. (1991). Self-graphing of on-task behavior: Enhancing the reactive effects of self-monitoring on on-task behavior and academic performance. *Learning Disabilities Quarterly, 14,* 221-230.

Dunlap, L. K., & Dunlap, G. (1989). A self-monitoring package for teaching subtraction with regrouping to students with learning disabilities. *Journal of Applied Behavior Analysis, 22,* 309-314.

Dunlap, L. K., Dunlap, G., Koegel, L. K., & Koegel, R. K, (1991). Using self-monitoring to increase independence. *Teaching Exceptional Children, 23,* 17-22.

Firth, G. H., & Armstrong, S. W. (1985). Self-monitoring for behavior-disordered students. *Teaching Exceptional Children, 18,* 144-148.

Flores, D. M., Schloss, P. J., & Alper, S. (1995). The use of a daily calendar to increase responsibilities fulfilled by secondary students with special needs. *Remedial and Special Education, 16*(1), 38-43.

Gumpel, T. P., & Golan, H. (2000). Teaching game-playing social skills using a self-monitoring treatment package. *Psychology in the Schools, 37*(3), 253-261.

Hallahan, D. P., Lloyd, J. W., Kneedler, R. D., & Marshall, K. J. (1982). A comparison of the effects of self- versus teacher-assessment of on-task behavior. *Behavior Therapy, 13,* 715-723.

Harris, K. R., Graham, S., Reid, R., McElroy, K., & Stern Hamby, R. (1994). Self-monitoring of attention versus self-monitoring of performance: Replication and cross-task comparison studies. *Learning Disabilities Quarterly, 17,* 121-139.

Heins, E. D., Lloyd, J. W., & Hallahan, D. (1986). Cued and noncued self-recording of attention to task. *Behavior Modification, 10,* 235-254.

Hughes, C. A., Korinek, L., & Gorman, J. (1991). Self-management for students with mental retardation in public school settings: A research review. *Education and Training in Mental Retardation, 26,* 271-291.

Hughes, C. A., Ruhl, K. L., & Misra, A. (1989). Self-management with behaviorally disordered students in school settings: A promise unfulfilled? *Behavioral Disorders, 14,* 250-262.

Kern, L., Dunlap, G., Childs, K. E., & Clarke, S. (1994). Use of a classwide self-management program to improve the behavior of students with emotional and behavioral disorders. *Education and Treatment of Children, 17*(3), 445-458.

Kern, L. K., Marder, T. J., Boyajian, A. E., Elliot, C. M., & McElhattan, D. (1997). Augmenting the independence of self-management procedures by teaching self-initiation across settings and activities. *School Psychology Quarterly, 12,* 23-32.

King, N. J., Ollendick, T. H., & Murphy, G. C. (1997). Assessment of childhood phobias. *Clinical Psychology Review, 17*(7), 667-687.

Koegel, R. L., & Koegel, L. K. (1990). Extended reductions in stereotypic behavior of students with autism through a self-management treatment package. *Journal of Applied Behavior Analysis, 23,* 119-127.

Korotitsch, W. J., & Nelson-Gray, R. O. (1999). An overview of self-monitoring research in assessment and treatment. *Psychological Assessment, 11,* 415-425.

Lam, A. L., Cole, C. L., Shapiro, E. S., & Bambara, L. M. (1994). Relative effects of self-monitoring on-task behavior, academic accuracy, and disruptive behavior in students with behavior disorders. *School Psychology Review, 23,* 44-58.

Lan, W. Y. (1998). Teaching self-monitoring skills in statistics. In D. H. Schunk & B. J. Zimmerman (Eds.), *Self-regulated learning: From teaching to self-reflective practice* (pp. 1-19). New York: The Guilford Press.

Litrownik, A. J., Freitas, J. L., & Franzini, L. R. (1978). Self-regulation in mentally retarded children: Assessment and training of self-monitoring skills. *American Journal of Mental Deficiency, 82,* 499-506.

Maag, J. W., Rutherford, A. B., & DiGangi, S. A. (1992). Effects of self-monitoring and contingent reinforcement on on-task behavior and academic productivity of learning-disabled students. A social validation study. *Psychology in the Schools, 29,* 157-172.

Martella, R. C., Leonard, I. J., Marchand-Martella, N. E., & Agran, M. (1993). Self-monitoring negative statements. *Journal of Behavioral Education, 3*(1), 77-86.

Mathes, M.Y., & Bender, W. N. (1997). The effects of self-monitoring on children with attention-deficit/hyperactivity disorder who are receiving pharmacological interventions. *Remedial and Special Education, 18,* 121-128.

McCarl, J. J., Svobodny, L., & Beare, P. L. (1991). Self-recording in a classroom for students with mild to moderate mental handicaps: Effects on productivity and on-task behavior. *Education and Training in Mental Retardation, 26,* 79-88.

McDougall, D., & Brady, M. P. (1995). Using audio-cued self-monitoring for students with severe behavior disorders. *Journal of Educational Research, 88,* 309-317.

Miller, L. J., Strain, P. S., Boyd, K., Jarzynka, J., & McFetridge, M. (1993). The effects of classwide self-assessment on preschool children's engagement in transition, free play, and small group instruction. *Early Education & Development, 4,* 162-181.

Miller, M., Miller, S. R., Wheeler, J., & Selinger, J. (1989). Can a single-classroom treatment approach change academic performance and behavioral characteristics in severely behaviorally disordered adolescents: An experimental inquiry. *Behavioral Disorders, 14,* 215-225.

Moore, R. J., Cartledge, G., & Heckman, K. (1995). The effects of social skill instruction and self-monitoring on game-related behaviors of adolescents with emotional or behavioral disorders. *Behavioral Disorders, 20,* 253-266.

Nelson, R. O. (1977). Methodological issues in assessment via self-monitoring. In J. D. Cone & R. P. Hawkins (Eds.), *Behavioral assessment: New directions in clinical psychology* (pp. 217-240). New York: Bruner/Mazel.

Nelson, R. O., & Hayes, S. C. (1981). Theoretical explanations for self-monitoring. *Behavior Modification, 5,* 3-14.

Newman, B., Buffington, D. M., O'Grady, M. A., McDonald, M. E., Poulson, C. L., & Hemmes, N. S. (1995). Self-management of schedule following in three teenagers with autism. *Behavioral Disorders, 20,* 190-196.

Ninness, H. A. C., Fuerst, J., Rutherford, R. D., & Glenn, S. S. (1991). Effects of self-management training and reinforcement on the transfer of improved conduct in the absence of supervision. *Journal of Applied Behavior Analysis, 24,* 499-508.

Ollendick, T. H. (1995). Cognitive behavioral treatment of panic disorder with agoraphobia in adolescents: A multiple baseline design analysis. *Behavior Therapy, 26,* 517-531.

Peterson, L. D., Young, K. R., West, R. P., & Peterson, M. H. (1999). Effects of self-management on generalization of student performance to regular classrooms. *Education and Treatment of Children, 22,* 357-372.

Prater, M. A., Hogan, S., & Miller, S. R. (1992). Using self-monitoring to improve on-task behavior and academic skills of an adolescent with mild handicaps across special and regular education settings. *Education and Treatment of Children, 15,* 43-55.

Reid, R. (1996). Research in self-monitoring with students with learning disabilities: The present, the prospects, the pitfalls. *Journal of learning disabilities, 29,* 317-331.

Reynolds, W. M., & Stark, K. D. (1987). School-based intervention strategies for the treatment of depression in children and adolescents. *School-Based Affective and Social Interventions, 3-4,* 69-88.

Selznick, L., & Savage, R. C. (2000). Using self-monitoring procedures to increase on-task behavior with three adolescent boys with brain injury. *Behavioral Interventions, 15,* 243-260.

Shapiro, E. S. (1981). Self-control procedures with the mentally retarded. In M. Hersen, R. M. Eisler, & P. M. Miller (Eds.), *Progress in behavior modification* (Vol. 12, pp. 265-297). New York: Academic Press.

Shapiro, E. S. (1984). Self-monitoring procedures. In T. H. Ollendick & M. Hersen (Eds.), *Child behavioral assessment: Principles and procedures* (pp. 148-165). New York: Pergamon Press.

Shapiro, E. S., & Cole, C. L. (1994). *Behavior change in the classroom: Self-management interventions.* New York: Guilford Press.

Shapiro, E. S., & Cole, C. L. (1999). Self-monitoring in assessing children's problems. *Psychological Assessment, 11,* 448-457.

Shapiro, E. S., & Klein, R. D. (1980). Self-management of classroom behavior with retarded/disturbed children. *Behavior Modification, 4,* 83-97.

Shapiro, E. S., & Kratochwill, T. R. (2000). Introduction: Conducting a multidimensional behavioral assessment. In E. S. Shapiro & T. R. Kratochwill (Eds.), *Conducting school-based assessments of child and adolescent behavior* (pp. 1-26). New York: Guilford Press.

Shearer, D. D., Kohler, F. W., Buchan, K. A., & McCullough, K. A. (1996). Promoting independent interactions between preschoolers with autism and their nondisabled peers: An analysis of self-monitoring. *Early Education and Development, 7*(3), 205-220.

Shimabukuro, S. M., Prater, M. A., Jenkins, A., & Edelen-Smith, P. (1999). The effects of self-monitoring of academic performance on students with learning disabilities and ADD/ADHD. *Education and Treatment of Children, 22,* 397-414.

Snyder, M. C., & Bambara, L. M. (1997). Teaching secondary students with learning disabilities to self-management classroom survival skills. *Journal of Learning Disabilities, 30,* 534-543.

Trammel, D. L., Schloss, P. J., & Alper, S. (1994). Using self-recording, evaluation, and graphing to increase completion of homework assignments. *Journal of Learning Disabilities, 27*(2), 75-81.

Webber, J., Scheuermann, B., McCall, C., & Coleman, M. (1993). Research on self-monitoring as a behavior management technique in special education classrooms: A descriptive review. *Remedial and Special Education, 14,* 38-56.

Wood, S. J., Murdock, J. Y., Cronin, M. E., Dawson, N. M., & Kirby, P. C. (1998). Effects of self-monitoring on on-task behaviors of at-risk middle school students. *Journal of Behavioral Education, 8,* 263-279.

Workman, E. A., Helton, G. B., & Watson, P. J. (1982). Self-monitoring effects in a four-year-old child: An ecological behavior analysis. *Journal of School Psychology, 20,* 57-64.

Zimmerman, B. J. (1986). Development of self-regulated learning: Which are the key subprocesses? *Contemporary Educational Psychologist, 16,* 307-313.

Zimmerman, B. J. (1989). A social cognitive view of self-regulated academic learning. *Journal of Educational Psychology, 81,* 329–339.

Zimmerman, B. J. (1998). Developing self-fulfilling cycles of academic regulation: An analysis of exemplary instructional models. In D. H. Schunk & B. J. Zimmerman (Eds.), *Self-regulated learning: From teaching to self-reflective practice* (pp. 1-19). New York: The Guilford Press.

Zimmerman, B. J. & Kitsantas, A. (1999). Acquiring writing revision skill: Shifting from process to outcome self-regulatory goals. *Journal of Educational Psychology, 91,* 241–250.

Zimmerman, B. J. & Risemberg, R. (1997a). Becoming a self-regulated writer: A social cognitive perspective. *Contemporary Educational Psychology, 22,* 73-101.

Zimmerman, B. J. & Risemberg, R. (1997b). Self-regulatory dimensions of academic learning and motivation. In G. D. Phye (Ed.), *Handbook of academic learning: Construction of knowledge* (pp. 105-125). San Diego: Academic Press.

CHAPTER 17

Arranging Preschool Environments to Facilitate Valued Social and Educational Outcomes

Ilene S. Schwartz
University of Washington

Ann N. Garfinkle
Vanderbilt University

Carol Davis
University of Washington

INTRODUCTION

The report, *Eager to Learn,* from the National Research Council states, "There can be no question that the environment in which a child grows up has a powerful impact on how the child develops and what the child learns" (2001, p. 1). To early childhood educators and early childhood special educators, the forcefulness of the National Academy of Sciences' statement is no surprise—both groups have long recognized that the way in which classroom environments are arranged has a direct influence on young children's participation, interaction, and learning. As such, both groups support guidelines emphasizing that classroom environments for young children must be safe, clean, and well organized.

The National Association for the Education of Young Children (NAEYC), a professional organization that advocates for early childhood education, suggests that a "high quality early childhood program provides a safe, nurturing environment that promotes the physical, social, emotional, and cognitive development of young children while responding to the needs of families" (Bredekamp & Copple, 1997, p. 17). As such, NAEYC has developed quality indicators for classroom environments, including small group size, low teacher-child ratios, developmentally appropriate curriculum, adequate teacher training, parent-teacher communication, and an environment that is safe and clean. In addition to these classroom features, a primary professional organization that advocates for early childhood special education, the Division of Early Childhood (DEC) of the Council for Exceptional Children, recommends practices that incorporate issues of scheduling, transitions, natural environments, peer interactions, and use of effective instructional strategies in defining quality early childhood special education programs. These guidelines, as a matter of course, lead us to consider not only environment-child development relationships, but also methods for the assessment of early childhood classroom environments.

A number of assessments have been developed (i.e., Infant/Toddler Environment Rating Scale [I/TERS; Harms, Cryer, & Clifford, 1990]; Early Childhood Environment Rating Scale [ECERS; Harms & Clifford, 1980]) with the aim of standardizing and quantifying these indicators of high quality classroom environments. As state legislatures enact laws that regulate the quality of child care (as is already the case in North Carolina and Tennessee) these types of assessments may become keystones in determining the overall rating of the quality of centers. These measures, however, are global measures of quality—they do not evaluate the match between an individual child's needs and the corresponding supports available in that environment. To accurately assess the environment for a child with special needs the individual child's experience in that environment must be measured (Wolery, Brashers, Pauca, & Grant, 2000) That is, what is the child doing in the classroom? What materials is she using and how is she using them? What types of interactions does he have with teachers and peers? Without this information about the *process* of early intervention, we can never evaluate the appropriateness or effectiveness of any program for any child. While early childhood special education researchers have developed tools to measure this more precise conceptualization of quality, none have been published in a form to which nonresearchers have easy access.

The discussion above may lead one to assume that to the early childhood educator and the early childhood special educator, "environment" means the physical dimensions of a child's home, child care, preschool program, and any other setting where the child spends time. Both groups, however, have expanded the term "environment" to include references to the social aspects of the environment. That is, both groups recognize that the type, amount, and affect involved between and among people are important variables and are part of the environment.

Many texts provide basic information (e.g., descriptions, checklists, inventories, etc.) about how early childhood and early childhood special educators can create a classroom environment that promotes growth, learning, and development of skills, although little of this information is research based (Wolery, Bailey, & Sugai, 1988). Most of the texts describe dimensions of the physical environment (e.g., the use of low barriers, lack of clutter, clearly defined storage places, soft and quiet areas, adequate space, etc.), the use of activities and learning environments (e.g., block areas, dramatic play areas, sensory activities, arts and crafts areas, reading and language arts areas, science areas, etc.), and instructional practices (e.g., the format of instruction as well as particular intervention strategies) (e.g., Allen & Schwartz, 2001; Bailey & Wolery, 1992). Other texts focus arranging the environment to facilitate the learning of skills within a particular domain (e.g., structuring a classroom to facilitate literacy; Dickinson & Tabors, 2001) or make suggestions so that all the materials in the environment will be selected to address a specific dimension or value that is important in children's learning (e.g., The Anti-Bias Curriculum; Derman-Sparks & the Anti-Bias Curriculum Task Force, 1989).

Collectively, these texts provide more than enough basic information to assist educators in establishing a safe, engaging, and responsive environment. To implement high-quality early education, however, the educator must move beyond the basics to ensure that each classroom environment matches the needs of the children in that classroom. That is, the educator, through the learning environment created in the classroom, must support and facilitate important outcomes for all children. Then, educators must monitor and evaluate these arrangements, use these results to make data-based changes, and be fluent in understanding and describing the choices they have made. If educators are going to look for elements in classroom environments that may facilitate specific experiences and outcomes for young children, it is important for researchers, practitioners, and families to come to a common understanding of what important outcomes are.

EXPANDING AND REDEFINING OUTCOMES FOR YOUNG CHILDREN

Implied above is a subtle point: for a child to achieve any particular outcome, the environment must facilitate that learning, achievement, or development for that child. To this end, individual children with special needs have individualized objectives, and as a group children with special needs should receive intervention that will result in their achieving important outcomes that enhance the quality of their lives. Most providers and consumers of these educational services would agree that individualized educational planning, specialized instruction, and evaluation of progress toward educational objectives are important. However, reaching consensus on what constitutes important and meaningful outcomes is more difficult.

Traditionally, special education has defined outcomes in terms of the developmental domains measured on standardized tests—for example, cognitive, communication, motor, and social. In the current educational climate, legislators are pressuring educators to define outcomes in terms of statewide test scores and objectives. In Washington State, for example, special educators are now required to link goals and objectives on students' Individualized Education Plans (IEPs) to statewide curricula and Essential Academic Learning Requirements (EALRs). These methods for describing outcomes, for young children with disabilities in particular, are not in the best interest of children, teachers, families, or quality education. This is because these types of system-generated outcomes do not consider the individual diversity of skills and behaviors young children learn, nor do they carefully consider the contexts in which much of this learning occurs.

Schwartz and her colleagues attempted to address this need to define important outcomes for young children in special education through a 5-year, federally funded longitudinal investigation of children with severe disabilities in inclusive settings (Schwartz, Staub, Gallucci, & Peck, 1995). The primary objective of that project was to find a way to describe the important outcomes that children achieved in inclusive settings. The many hours devoted to observing children in classrooms, talking to teachers and parents, and interviewing typically developing peers resulted in the development of a framework that has proved to be a useful way to describe such observed outcomes.

FIGURE 1

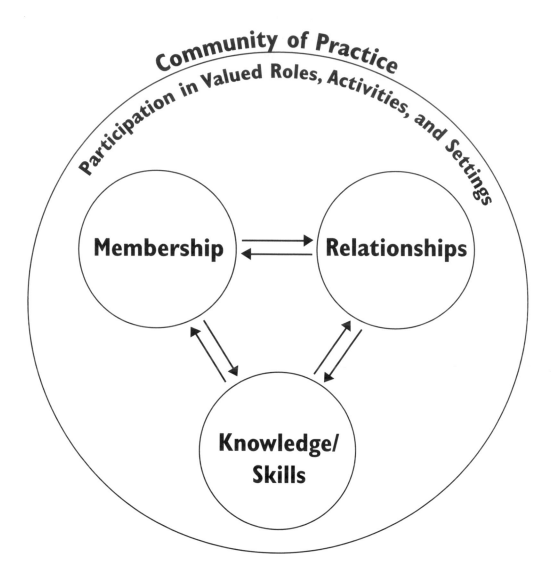

The outcome framework consists of three interrelated domains: membership, relationships, and knowledge/skills (Schwartz, 2000) (see Figure 1). The intervention and learning that take place in these domains are set in a context of valued activities and routines with an emphasis placed on active participation in meaningful, culturally relevant, interesting settings. This outcomes framework is particularly helpful because it captures the outcomes that are meaningful to educators and parents while at the same time it describes what children are learning and doing in a holistic manner, without the constraints imposed by traditional developmental and educational domains.

Further, this model suggests that each of the outcome domains (membership, relationships, and knowledge/skills) is affected by the others in a bidirectional manner. That is, changes in skills will also affect relationships and membership. While this is a fairly traditional view, the model also suggests that changes in relationships affect changes in skills and membership, and that changes in membership also affect skills and relationships. These last two interdependencies have received little thought or attention in our professional literature. This imbalance of professional attention is evident when one compares the amount of literature devoted to teaching children skills as opposed to teaching children about membership. In addition to understanding these bidirectional influences, understanding the framework also depends on understanding what is meant by "membership," "relationships," and "skills." Each is discussed below.

Membership refers to how the child is accepted into and participates in groups. Membership also is used to indicate the child's sense of belonging to the social fabric of the group. Membership can be achieved through participation in either formal (e.g., circle time) or informal (e.g., playing on the playground) activities. Direct measures of memberships are still in the development stages (Garfinkle & Schwartz, 1998); however, membership can be informally assessed by looking for any accommodations that are made to facilitate the participation of a child (e.g., changes in rules of a game on the playground to give a child with a disability an extra turn) in classroom activities and overt symbols of membership (e.g., a cubby or mailbox in a classroom). Membership also can be measured by observing teacher-designed groups in the classroom (e.g., literacy groups, snack groups); student-designed groups in and out of the classroom (e.g., play groups, student-initiated project groups); activities in which the entire class participates as one group (e.g., class meetings); activities in which the entire school participates as one group (e.g., assemblies); and activities outside of school (e.g., scouts, sports teams, activities at churches/synagogues).

Whereas the domain of membership refers to the interactions a child has with a group of peers, the area of relationships focuses attention on interactions with individual peers. Unlike traditional discussions of social interactions, where most typically the number of interactions and responses is counted, the goal of focusing on relationships is to evaluate a more complex interaction than can be described by focusing solely on initiations and responses. Thus, the domain of relationships refers to a broad range of behaviors and complex interpersonal interactions. A child may form relationships with peers in all the different environments in which she or he spends time. Further, relationships can be categorized as follows: play/companionship (e.g., children who choose to play together during free time); helper (e.g., a child who assists a peer); helpee (e.g., a child who receives help from a peer); peer (e.g., two children who may be walking next to each other during a transition and interact, but may not choose to interact given a free choice situation); and conflictual (e.g., children arguing over the rules of a game or over taking turns with a preferred material). We hypothesize that children with successful relationships have interactions with many children and that these interactions occur across the different categories of this domain.

Knowledge/skills is the most traditional of the three outcome domains and is the most familiar to school psychologists and special educators. Of the three outcome domains, it is also the easiest to quantify. As such, this domain requires less explanation than the previous domains. We conceptualize the knowledge/skills domain to include social communication skills, academic skills, cognitive skills, motor skills, adaptive skills, etc.

It is important to note that to be successful in school and society, children need to learn skills; however, while knowledge and skills are necessary for success, they are insufficient to constitute a complete set of desirable outcomes. When planning or evaluating a comprehensive program for children with disabilities, all three domains—membership, relationships, and skills—must be considered. Together, these three domains provide a holistic and community-based view of a child's educational plan. Thus, educators must be prepared to create a physical and social environment that supports growth and learning across all three domains.

In the remainder of this chapter we will describe research examining different characteristics of effective classroom environments. To relate these studies to the outcome framework introduced above, we present the literature review in terms of how the research can be linked to the desired outcome areas. For each of the three outcome areas, membership, relationships, and knowledge/skills, we highlight how the physical and social dimensions of the classroom environment can be arranged to produce these valued outcomes.

So, how will this review of the literature differ from the many other reviews of the literature on classroom environments? Let us demonstrate by discussing one of the seminal research articles in this area. In 1972, LeLaurin and Risley published an article comparing two types of staffing patterns in a child care environment, "man-to-man" and "zone." In the "man-to-man" model of supervision, staff members are assigned to specific children and those children move through activities as a group. In the "zone" model of child supervision, staff members are assigned to activities or areas of the classroom and children are free to move from area to area and activity to activity at their own pace. LeLaurin and Risley found that children were actively engaged for more time when a "zone" supervision arrangement was used. This study has become a classic in early childhood special education and is cited in almost every review of environmental arrangements we could find (e.g., Allen & Schwartz, 2001; Bailey & Wolery, 1992; Carta, Sainato, & Greenwood, 1988; Hundert, 1995). Looking at the results of this study through the lenses of the outcome framework described above can help us look at this article in a new way. More engaged time means more time interacting with planned activities that may mean better and more meaningful knowledge and skill development for children. By linking specific aspects of planning classroom environments to positive outcomes for children, we may be better able to assist teachers in designing learning environments, implementing those conditions to optimize learning, monitoring the effectiveness of teachers' choices on children's learning, and enhancing teachers' understanding of the decisions they have made. The following brief literature review is focused on making such linkages.

REVIEW OF THE LITERATURE ON CLASSROOM ENVIRONMENTS

Membership

Based on qualitative studies of membership, it is clear that the classroom ecology can facilitate or impede membership. Teachers, often unintentionally, create aspects of the classroom environment that cue the children on how to interact with one another. For example, Schnorr (1990) in her year-long observational and interview study reports that the children often described a child with Down's syndrome, Peter, as the teacher did. So, when the teacher called the child "little Peter" the other children thought of Peter as "little," not as a big child, not like the kind of children they were. The children also took cues from the way the teacher used the physical environment. So, when the teacher used Peter's desk to stack papers, the children learned that Peter did not have a real place (literally and figuratively) in their class. To prevent these types of inadvertent teaching and learning, the teacher must create a physical and social environment that systematically facilitates the membership of all of the children into the social fabric of the classroom.

Physical dimensions. Furniture, decorations, and other accessories can help to facilitate or interfere with membership in the classroom. For example, having names on cubbies or mailboxes may be a clear marker of membership. Conversely, if a child who participates in a classroom part time does not have his own mailbox, it can be a clear signal to the other classroom participants that the teacher does not consider him a member.

Class schedule. Returning to Schnorr's study (1990), it was reported that Peter's schedule did not match his classmates'—he only attended some class activities and in some of those he left early to get on the bus to go home. This difference in schedule was often cited by the typically developing children as a reason for not thinking of Peter as a member of their class. From this finding, one may conclude that class schedules are important. This is not to say that all children should be engaged in the same activity or instruction all the time. Rather, what is recommended is support and planning. If a child needs support sitting at large-group circle time, the instructional or management solution is not to excuse the child from the activity, but rather to teach the child the skills needed to successfully participate in the activity.

Number and type of materials. Facilitating classroom membership necessitates viewing the materials in the classroom with a critical eye. Teachers should provide materials that are interesting and facilitate the behaviors associated with membership. In addition, teachers may want to make rules that increase the likelihood of membership. For example, in her classroom Vivian Paley (1993) made the rule that children could not be excluded from play or from using any of the classroom toys or educational materials. This rule had a major impact on the behavior of the children and the entire climate of the social environment of the classroom.

Social dimensions. In addition to physical dimensions, there are several social dimensions of the environment that influence the membership status of individual children within the class. These dimensions include group assignment (i.e., who is in a group and how long groups stay together), skills selection and instructional methods, teacher strategies for establishing and supporting relationships, the strategies around resolving conflict, and the type of "teacher talk" the teacher uses. Garfinkle and Schwartz (1996, 1997, 1998) implemented a series of studies in which children worked in consistent small groups across an extended length of time in integrated preschool settings. Although assessments of membership were not the primary dependent variables, observations recorded systematically in field notes and in interviews with participating teachers indicated that the target children all had become more valued members of the classroom community. Although more empirical work is needed in this vein, it is clear from the results of these studies that the choices teachers made in arranging the physical and social environment were influential to the membership status of children in the classroom.

Relationships

Individual ingredients of relationships, such as social interactions, are one of the most studied aspects in preschool classrooms. For example, the type of children (e.g., those with and without disabilities), number of children, number of adults, and adult behavior all can facilitate or create barriers to interactions (e.g., Chandler, Fowler, & Lubeck, 1992; Odom & Watts, 1991). In the next section we identify studies that provide clear examples of how the classroom environment affects relationships.

Physical dimensions. The physical arrangement of classrooms affects the types and amount of student interactions. The number of play areas, the size of the play areas, and the number of chairs (or other equipment) in any area all can have an influence on peer interactions and ultimately on relationships (e.g., Brown, Fox, & Brady, 1987). For example, painting on an individual easel is a noninteractive activity; however, if easels are placed in proximity or tabletop easels are used with paints placed so that children are sharing them, the painting activity can facilitate interactions.

Class schedule. Class schedules, that is, how teachers plan for and actually allocate instructional time, can also facilitate or create barriers for children developing meaningful social relationships with their peers. Odom, Peterson, McConnell, and Ostrosky (1990) found that children were more likely to engage in social interaction during play activities than during preacademic times. However, their observations revealed that children in early childhood special education classrooms spent more time participating in preacademic activities than did typically developing children. This allocation of instruction time put children with disabilities at double jeopardy in the social domain. Since the majority of children with disabilities in preschool demonstrate problems in the area of social behavior, it is important to prioritize social skills and outcomes when planning class schedules and activities. If teachers value social interactions and ultimately positive peer relationships, more time must be spent in activities that encourage the development and formation of these relationships.

Number and type of materials. The idea that certain toys facilitate social play and other toys encourage more isolate play is well documented (Beckman & Kohl, 1984; Martin, Brady, & Williams, 1991; Rubin, 1977). When planning classroom environments to facilitate relationship development, teachers must move beyond this distinction and consider the type of individual relationships materials can promote. Do some materials tend to place some children in the role of being the helpee (i.e., having to receive assistance from peers)? For example, for children with fine motor problems, negotiating art materials (e.g., scissors, markers with tight caps) and snack materials (e.g., juice boxes, milk cartons) can be difficult. Are there activities/materials in the classroom that facilitate the independence of every child so that every child has the opportunity to be a helper? For example, do all children have the opportunity to hand out materials and rotate through class jobs (e.g., line leader)? Do some materials facilitate use by dyads only (e.g., having pairs work on projects rather than small groups)? For example, can access to some preferred computer games be limited to two players? Are some materials limited in number so that children have to share and figure out how to resolve the conflicts that may arise over a shortage of preferred materials? For example, preferred figurines and small manipulatives can be limited so that children need to play together cooperatively, rather than in a parallel manner. If helping children develop a full range of relationships is a priority to teachers, then classroom materials should be selected with the intent of promoting a wide array of peer interactions.

In summary, teacher behavior sets the stage for peer interactions and the development of meaningful relationships in preschool classrooms. Teacher behaviors can serve to either promote social interactions or interfere with them (e.g., Innocenti et al., 1986; Odom & Watts, 1991). Further, children can learn how to facilitate the interactions of their peers with disabilities and some of these peer-mediated interactions can facilitate interactions beyond the training settings and activities (e.g., Hecimovic, Fox, Shores, & Strain, 1985; Odom, Hoyson, Jamieson, & Strain, 1985). Teacher social behavior can have direct influences on the relationships children develop in and out of the classroom (Odom & Brown, 1993). If developing a wide range of relationships is a valued outcome, teachers must structure the social dimension of the classroom environment to facilitate peer interactions.

Knowledge/Skills

The domain of knowledge/skills, because it is most closely aligned with how we have traditionally described outcomes in special education, has been well documented. Many of these studies, however, focus on the relationship of teacher behavior to child outcomes. Equally important is the role of the classroom environment. For example, if independence is an important outcome for children, environments must be arranged to allow children to be independent (e.g., hanging up their own coats, walking without holding hands with an adult, carrying their own lunches or snacks).

Physical dimensions. The physical environment affects what children learn. When books are available, children read (Adams, 1990); when there are interesting things to talk about and people to talk to, children talk (Hart & Risley, 1995); when there are computers available, children use them (Closing the Gap, 2001; Wright & Shade, 1994); and when there are art materials available, children use them (Schirrmacher, 1993). There are many chapters available describing the optimal physical dimensions of early childhood classrooms (e.g., Allen & Schwartz, 2001; Bailey & Wolery, 1992; Gordon & Williams-Browne, 1995). Once again, however, these texts often provide "laundry lists" that should be viewed as starting points. They help to identify the necessary components of a quality early childhood program; yet ultimately, it is the responsibility of skilled teachers to fine tune the physical dimensions of the environment to support the development of knowledge and skills that are most important to the children in their classroom and their families.

Class schedule. A consistent, predictable schedule is an important component in every preschool classroom (Bailey & Wolery, 1992). Having a schedule posted, however, is not enough. Schedules are only effective if teachers adhere to them, and many preschool classrooms do not follow the schedules posted (Odom et al., 1990). The sequence of activities in a classroom influences child participation and outcomes. For example, Krantz and Risley (1977) found that when the classroom schedule started out with activities that promote active engagement and then progressed to more sedentary activities, disruptive behaviors in the classroom decreased as compared to allocation of instructional time that required children to begin the day with more passive forms of engagement.

Number and type of materials. As noted above, different types of materials can facilitate the acquisition of valued knowledge and skills. Hemmeter and Kaiser (1990) modified the environments of young children by adding toys that were conducive to using naturalistic language facilitation strategies. As a result of the change in the environment and support for fathers' mediation of those materials, children demonstrated increased use of spontaneous language and active engagement. Similar results have been shown with older children and play materials (e.g., Horner, 1980; Nordquist, Twardosz, & McEvoy, 1991). Therefore, it is important for teachers to consider the desired outcomes for individual children when planning what materials to include in the classroom.

Social dimensions. The teacher's interactions with students have a substantial influence on the knowledge and skills children acquire. Thus, when implementing instructional strategies, the teacher should ensure that he or she is both using an effective strategy, and doing so in a manner that also facilitates his or her relationships with the students. One example of an intervention that combines these two elements is choice-making. Choice-making has been empirically validated with children with severe disabilities, behavioral disorders, and autism. In this strategy children are not asked if they want to complete an activity, but rather are given choices about when to complete specific activities and the types of materials they want to use (e.g., "Do you want to use a marker or a pencil to write your name?") (e.g., Dunlap et al., 1994; Dyer, Dunlap, & Winterling, 1990). The use of this strategy *can* simultaneously increase a child's engagement or compliance while at the same time helping to avoid power struggles around teacher-directed activities.

There are numerous other well-documented intervention strategies, but it is beyond the scope of this chapter to review effective instructional strategies for preschool classrooms. For more information on this topic readers should refer to texts by Allen and Schwartz (2001), Bailey and Wolery, (1992), Sandall and Schwartz (2002), or Wolery and Wilbers (1994).

IMPLICATIONS FOR PRACTICE

Teaching is one of the most complex professions in our society. Not only must teachers keep track of a large number of young children and keep them safe, but they also are expected to help these children learn and develop in meaningful ways. Well-organized classrooms, with clear and predictable schedules and well-defined rules and expectations, are a hallmark of successful teachers. Based on our review of the research, our own teaching experiences, and many years of visiting and consulting in classrooms, we end this chapter with practical suggestions for putting information about quality classroom environments into practice.

- The basic structural elements of an effective classroom environment—organization, schedule, rules and expectations—are necessary but not sufficient basic components of every classroom. These elements must be present in classrooms for children with and without disabilities. If these elements are not present or not working efficiently, any consultation or changes intended to solve or prevent individual or group problems should begin with the basics.

- Once the basics of elements of effective classroom structure are in place, teachers, in consultation with the children's parents, must decide what outcomes are of highest priority. Once these decisions are made, decisions about classroom arrangement can be made to facilitate those outcomes. For example, if membership is being emphasized, certain activities can be conducted in consistent small groups; alternatively, if relationships are a high priority, reciprocal peer tutoring might provide a facilitative structure for classroom activities.

- Classroom arrangements can facilitate independent child behavior, encourage cooperative peer interaction, or promote challenging behavior. If chronic challenging behavior occurs in the classroom, teachers should first evaluate how the classroom environment might be contributing to the problem.

- Preschool teachers play a very important role in creating, adapting, and enhancing the physical and social environment of their classrooms; therefore they must consider the intended and potential unintended outcomes that the environment will facilitate.

REFERENCES

Adams, M. (1990). *Learning to read: Thinking and learning about print.* Cambridge, MA: MIT Press.

Allen, K. E., & Schwartz, I. S. (2001). *The exceptional child: Inclusion in early childhood education.* Albany, NY: Delmar.

Beckman, P. J., & Kohl, F. L. (1984). The effects of social and isolate toys on the interactions and play integrated and nonintegrated groups of preschoolers. *Education and Training of the Mentally Retarded, 19,* 169-174.

Bailey, D. B., & Wolery, M. (1992). *Teaching infants and preschoolers with disabilities.* New York: Merrill.

Bredekamp, S., & Copple, C. (1997). *Appropriate practice in early childhood programs* (rev. ed.). Washington, DC: National Association for the Education of Young Children.

Brown, W. H., Fox, J. J., & Brady, M. P. (1987). The effects of spatial density on 3- and 4-year-old children's socially directed behavior during free play: An investigation of a setting factor. *Education and Treatment of Children, 10,* 247-258.

Carta, J. J., Sainato, D. M., & Greenwood, C. R., (1988). Advances in ecological assessment of classroom instruction for young children with handicaps. In S. L. Odom & M. B. Karnes (Eds.), *Early intervention for infants and children with handicaps* (pp. 217-239). Baltimore: Brookes.

Chandler, L. K., Fowler, S. A., & Lubeck, R. C. (1992). An analysis of the effects of multiple setting events on the social behavior of preschool children with special needs. *Journal of Applied Behavior Analysis, 25,* 249-263.

Closing the Gap. (2001). Available Internet: *www.closingthegap.com.*

Derman-Sparks, L., & the Anti-Bias Curriculum Task Force. (1989). *Anti-bias curriculum: Tools for empowering young children.* Washington, DC: National Association for the Education of Young Children.

Dickinson, D. K., & Tabors, P. O. (2001). *Beginning literacy with language.* Baltimore: Brookes.

Dunlap, G., dePerczel, M., Clarke, S., Wilson, D., Wright, S., White, R., & Gomez, A. (1994). Choice making to promote adaptive behavior for students with emotional and behavioral challenges. *Journal of Applied Behavior Analysis, 27,* 505-518.

Dyer, K., Dunlap, G., & Winterling, V. (1990). Effects of choice-making on the serious problem behaviors of students with severe handicaps. *Journal of Applied Behavior Analysis, 23,* 515-524.

Garfinkle, A. N., & Schwartz, I. S. (1996, May). *PECS with peers: Increasing social interaction in an integrated preschool.* Paper presented at the Association for Behavior Analysis Annual Conference, San Francisco.

Garfinkle, A. N., & Schwartz, I. S. (1997, May). *Peer imitation: Using observational learning to increase social interaction in young children with autism.* Paper presented at the Association for Behavior Analysis Annual Conference, Chicago.

Garfinkle, A. N., & Schwartz, I. S. (1998, May). Belonging in kindergarten: Social ratings and membership of children with autism in an integrated kindergarten. Paper presented at the Association for Behavior Analysis Annual Conference, Orlando, FL.

Gordon, A., & Williams-Browne, K. (1995). *Beginnings and beyond*. Albany, NY: Delmar.

Harms, T., & Clifford, R. M. (1980). *Early childhood rating scale*. New York: Teachers College Press.

Harms, T., Cryer, D., & Clifford, R. M. (1990). *Infant/toddler environment rating scale*. New York: Teachers College Press.

Hart, B. M., & Risley, T. R. (1995). *Meaningful differences in the everyday experience of young American children*. Baltimore: Brookes.

Hecimovic, A., Fox, J. J., Shores, R. E., & Strain, P. S. (1985). An analysis of developmentally integrated and segregated free play settings and the generalization of newly-acquired social behaviors of socially withdrawn preschoolers. *Behavioral Assessment, 7*, 367–388.

Hemmeter, M. L., & Kaiser, A. P. (1990). Environmental influences on children's language: A model and case study. *Education and Treatment of Children, 13*, 331–341.

Horner, R. D. (1980). The effects of an environmental "enrichment" program on the behavior of institutionalized profoundly retarded children. *Journal of Applied Behavior Analysis, 13*, 473–491.

Hundert, J. (1995). *Enhancing social competence in young students*. Austin, TX: Pro-Ed.

Innocenti, M. S., Stowischek, J., Rule, S., Killoran, J., Striefel, S., & Boswell, C. (1986). A naturalistic study of the relationship between preschool setting events and peer interaction in four activity contexts. *Early Childhood Research Quarterly, 1*, 141–153.

Krantz, P. J., & Risley, T. R. (1977). Behavior ecology in the classroom. In K. D. O'Leary & S. G. O'Leary (Eds.), *Classroom management: The successful use of behavior modification* (pp. 349–366). New York: Pergamon Press.

LeLaurin, K., & Risley, T. R. (1972). The organization of day care environments: "Zone" to "man-to-man" staff assignments. *Journal of Applied Behavior Analysis, 5*, 225–232.

Martin, S., Brady, M., & Williams, R. (1991). Effects of toys on the social behavior of preschool children in integrated and nonintegrated groups: Investigations of a setting event. *Journal of Early Intervention, 15*(2), 153–161.

National Research Council. (2001). *Eager to learn: Educating our preschoolers*. Committee on Early Childhood Pedagogy. B. T. Bowman, M. S. Donovan, M. S. Burns (Eds.). Commission on Behavioral and Social Sciences and Education. Washington, DC: National Academy Press.

Nordquist, V. M., Twardosz, S., McEvoy, M. (1991). Effect of environmental reorganization in classrooms for children with autism. *Journal of Early Intervention, 15*, 135–152.

Odom, S. L., & Brown, W. H. (1993). Social interaction skills interventions for young children with disabilities in integrated settings. In C. A. Peck, S. L. Odom, & D. D. Bricker (Eds.), *Integrating young children with disabilities into community programs* (pp. 39–64). Baltimore: Brookes.

Odom, S. L., Hoyson, M., Jamieson, B., & Strain, P. S. (1985). Increasing handicapped preschoolers' peer social interaction: Cross-setting and component analysis. *Journal of Applied Behavior Analysis, 18,* 3-16.

Odom, S. L., Peterson, C., McConnell, S., & Ostrosky, M. (1990). Ecobehavior analysis of early education/specialized classroom settings and peer social interaction. *Education and Treatment of Children, 13,* 316-330.

Odom, S. L., & Watts, E. (1991). Reducing teacher prompts in peer mediated interventions for young children with autism. *Journal of Special Education, 25,* 26-43.

Paley, V. (1993). *You can't say you can't play.* Cambridge, MA: Harvard University Press.

Rubin, K. H. (1977). The social and cognitive value of preschool toys and activities. *Canadian Journal of Behavioral Science, 9,* 382-385.

Sandall, S. R., & Schwartz, I. S. (2002). *Building blocks: A comprehensive approach for supporting young children in inclusive placements.* Baltimore: Brookes.

Schirrmacher, R. (1993). *Art and creative development for young children.* Albany, NY. Delmar.

Schnorr, R. F. (1990). "Peter? He comes and goes…" First graders' perspectives on a part-time mainstream student. *Journal of the Association for Persons with Severe Handicaps, 15,* 231-240.

Schwartz, I. S. (2000). Standing on the shoulders of giants: Looking ahead to facilitating membership and relationships for children with disabilities. *Topics in Early Childhood Special Education, 20*(2), 123-128.

Schwartz, I. S., Staub, D., Gallucci, C., & Peck, C. A. (1995). Blending qualitative and behavior analytic research methods to evaluate outcomes in inclusive schools. *Journal of Behavioral Education, 5*(1), 93-106.

Wolery, M., Bailey, D. B., & Sugai, G. M. (1988). *Effective teaching: Principles and procedures of applied behavior analysis with exceptional students.* Boston: Allyn and Bacon.

Wolery, M., Brashers, M., Pauca, T., & Grant, S. (2000). *Quality of inclusive experiences measure.* Unpublished manuscript, Frank Porter Graham Child Development Center, University of North Carolina, Chapel Hill.

Wolery, M., & Wilbers, J. S. (1994). *Including children with special needs in early childhood programs.* Washington, DC: National Association for the Education of Young Children.

Wright, J. L., & Shade, D. D. (Eds.) (1994). *Young children: Active learners in a technological age.* Washington, DC: National Association for the Education of Young Children.

CHAPTER 18

*Promoting Communication Competence
in Preschool Age Children*

Howard Goldstein and Juliann Woods
Florida State University

INTRODUCTION

Communication and language development are among the most important areas for success in education, employment, and social relationships—or more simply stated, for life. This chapter presents approaches that are essential to interdisciplinary teams seeking to examine and improve the communicative and linguistic competence of preschool children. This will be accomplished by examining the interrelated and complex influences that affect communication and language development, the interactive nature of the multiple outcomes this development facilitates, and the diversity of effective intervention strategies for improving communicative competence.

The terms *communication, language,* and *speech* frequently are used interchangeably. However, team members need to understand the important distinctions among these systems. Communication entails sending and receiving messages, experiences, ideas, or feelings to another through a variety of modalities. Children (and adults) communicate without language or speech through facial expressions, gestures, proxemics, or variations in pitch, rate, or tone of vocalizations and cries. A message may be communicated intentionally, yet without words, when a child squeals and turns away from a plate of carrots or unintentionally when a toddler's wiggling or kicking communicates restlessness to her parent. These nonlinguistic or paralinguistic communication behaviors develop early, are useful throughout the life span, and increase in sophistication when language and speech are included (McLean & Snyder-McLean, 1999).

Language is a complex and dynamic social process that uses a shared, rule-governed code of arbitrary symbols to represent objects, events, thoughts, and ideas (Owens, 1998). Language is a body of knowledge that provides a framework for a child to think about people, objects, and experiences occurring in the present, in the past, and even in the future. Those who share and use the symbols determine the code. A cow is a "cow" because members of the social system who share the code determined that the word "cow" would represent a large milk-producing animal. Members of the social system learn the rules or conventions for putting symbols together to generate messages to serve myriad communicative functions. Language requires a modality for expression of the code such as speech, writing, or use of manual signs. Members of the social system also determine new symbols or changes to rules as the social system evolves. This can be seen in the new words added to the dictionary (e.g., "e-mail") or the acceptance of various grammatical forms over time (e.g., "ain't").

Speech, very simply, is the oral expression of language. Speech relies on precise physiological and neuromuscular coordination resulting in the production of sounds that have meaning to others familiar with the language. Speech disorders affect a child's ability to produce audible, intelligible, and fluent speech (McLean & Cripe, 1997), whereas language disorders affect rules that govern the comprehension and production of phonemes, morphemes, semantics, syntax, and morphology. Phonemes are the smallest units of sound that affect the meaning of a word, e.g., "cat" versus "cap." Morphemes affect meaning in words (e.g., cat, cats, catty). Semantics is the relationship between the word and its meaning, (e.g., one furry, four-legged animal that purrs versus more than one purring pet versus the act of being critical and petty). Syntax allows a speaker or listener to produce or understand the meaning of the sentence through the order of the words. You use your competence in syntax to respond appropriately to the following sentences: "Sock your brother," and "Get your brother's sock." Pragmatics concerns the effectiveness of language within the social setting and allows us to engage in conversations, to exchange information to accomplish goals, and to perform various actions. Disorders in pragmatic skills may affect the understanding and use of phonology, morphology, syntax, and semantics, such as when a child uses inappropriate language in a social situation (e.g., repeating words to a grandparent heard from a parent after backing the car into a tree!). Disorders in communication impact a child's ability to affect the world at the most essential levels of behavior regulation and emotional, physical, and social need (Wetherby, Prizant, & Schuler, 2000). Although each of these systems has been defined separately, it is the interrelatedness among the systems that is most intriguing and results in a comprehensive model for prevention, assessment, and intervention.

DEVELOPMENT OF COMMUNICATIVE COMPETENCE

Multiple Influences on Communication Development

How communication and language are defined relates to the beliefs about what influences a child's development of communication and language. The definitions provided emphasize the social purpose of language and communication. Language is used by, for, and between people to get things done (Austin, 1962). The factors that influence the development of communicative competence reflect a social interaction perspective that is meant to subsume transactional, ecological, developmental, and behavioral models. One might choose to outline a set of factors influential in the developmental process, but it would be woefully misleading. Again, it is in a description of the interrelatedness

FIGURE 1

Interrelated Influences on Communicative Competence

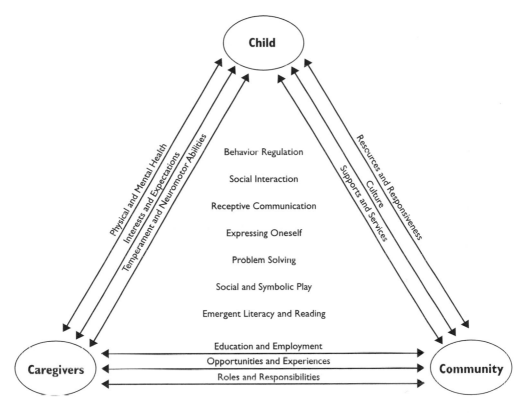

Note

This model represents the multiple factors that interact among the child, the caregivers, and the community to affect development, with many of the associated communicative outcomes listed in the middle of the triangle.

of the influences that the most accurate and meaningful picture of the child's skills and capabilities can be illustrated. Figure 1 presents a graphic depiction of these interrelated influences, with associated outcomes in the middle of the diagram.

Children present abilities that include their genetic composition, sensory and motor capacities, health status, temperament, and potential for growth. A child's development is related to the interactions with and expectations of the primary caregivers. It also is affected by the family's capacity to provide opportunities for experiences; the family's physical and mental health, income and educational levels; the community the family lives in; and the resources available to the family and within the community. Sameroff and colleagues (Sameroff & Chandler, 1975; Sameroff & Fiese, 1990) proposed a transactional model for conceptualizing development that revolutionized the way developmental researchers consider relationships among child characteristics, caregiver characteristics, and environmental influences over time. Developmental outcomes at any point result from the continuous, dynamic interplay among child behavior, caregiver responses to the child's behavior, and environmental variables that may influence both the child and the caregiver. Learning is bi-directional, which means children learn from people, places, and activities within their world and in turn affect them in the process.

Children are viewed as active participants who learn to affect the behavior and attitudes of others through active signaling of functions, such as requesting, rejecting, and commenting. Children gradually learn to use more sophisticated and conventional means to communicate through caregivers' contingent social responsiveness (Dunst, Lowe, & Bartholomew, 1990). The quality and nature of the contexts in which interaction occurs are considered to have a great influence on the successful development of cognitive and communicative competence (Clarke-Stewart, 1973). Factors affecting caregivers (e.g., psychological well-being, social support), as well as children's biological capacity to engage in social exchanges, will influence caregivers' availability and responsiveness to young children (Dunst et al., 1990). Over time, when children's social communicative behavior can be accurately interpreted by caregivers, and caregivers are able to respond to meet children's needs or to support social exchange, both caregivers and children develop a sense of efficacy. A cumulative effect of positive contingent responsiveness is that interactions become more predictable as expectancies and contingencies increase. Hence, development is influenced by children's ability to produce readable signals, caregivers' ability to respond appropriately to children's signals, and the routinization of such patterns. These patterns exist within the context of the family and the community in which the family lives. Vocabularies and even sentence structures will vary, as will rules for politeness. Each component of language is learned as it is used ... within interactions with others and the environment (McLean & Snyder-McLean, 1999).

Outcomes Associated With Communicative Competence

Recognition of the inputs to the system provides a basis for the examination of the outcomes related to communication and language development. The outcomes of communication and language provide the means for interacting with others and conducting the actions necessary to lead a successful life (without obvious consideration of the sound, word, and grammatical components of language). Language should not be viewed as the sum of the components of phonology, morphology, syntax, semantics, and pragmatics. These components interact to produce meaningful and functional outcomes, as the following example illustrates.

A kindergarten child, Josh, approaches his classroom door on the first day of school clinging tightly to his older brother's hand. He stops in his tracks, refusing to go inside or to release the safe and familiar appendage of his brother. Without words, his brother understands this behavior and responds. He turns to him and smiles, offering reassurance. He points to the "Welcome" sign and asks if Josh can read what it says. After a slight head shake "no" from his younger sibling, big brother picks him up and walks over to the sign to read it for him. Beneath the sign are pictures of the children assigned to the class with descriptions of the activities for the first day. Together they look for his picture and identify the choices available. The teacher has placed pictures of the play areas, including the blocks, books, and dramatic play areas by his picture. After careful scanning of the environment and a big sigh of relief, Josh spots a neighborhood friend driving a truckload of blocks and decides to join him. He approaches him with a friendly tug on the shoulder and says, "Hey Cody, how did you get here? My brother just dropped me off on his way to school. I don't want to play dress-up stuff with the girls but these blocks are cool. Let's build a gas station and a garage for the cars and trucks."

Until the last exchange, only the older brother in this scenario produced language. However, Josh was certainly using language to communicate his emotions and choices within the situation. Understanding and engaging one's social environment successfully, be it a new or a familiar experience, requires both knowledge and the use of language. In this scenario, Josh regulated his brother's behavior by a tight hand squeeze, refusal to walk, and a small shake of his head. In turn, his older brother's responses affected Josh's behavior by carrying him over to an opportunity for choice making that would increase his sense of control over the situation. Although Josh could not read the word "Welcome" when asked, he exhibited his early literacy skills by recognizing that the sign was meaningful and was successful at identifying the picture representations of himself and the play areas in the classroom. He predicted that the pictures represented the play choices available to him based on experiences in preschool. At last, he expressed himself using words to initiate a conversation, ask a question, share information, express an opinion, and present a proposal to a friend within the context of the actions that had just been occurring. If only Josh's words and sentences had been considered, many communicative outcomes would have been missed.

The interrelationships of language and communication with other areas of development result in a child being able to express herself or himself—to notice the world and to be able to define it. It provides vehicles (e.g., gestures, words, signs, print) for requesting, describing, rejecting, and sharing ideas and information that enable the formation and the expansion of concepts about people, objects, and events through continued experience and growth. Language, verbal and written, is the primary means used in formal educational settings for teaching and learning. The ideas and information are used in interactions that are not constrained by space or time. Conversations can be shared about what happened previously or is likely to happen in the future between people, places, or objects that may or may not be together as the events unfold. Children, like Josh, use language to share their thoughts, predictions, memories, solutions to problems, values and beliefs. Realizing Cody had not just appeared at the classroom, he inquired about his arrival. Josh shared his evaluation of the centers available (and a possible early gender bias) and proposed a cooperative play scheme. The play activity will provide additional opportunities to practice and expand language and communication outcomes in conjunction with motor, cognitive, and social skill development.

An essential outcome for a successful life is the ability to understand and use language in social situations (Guralnick, 1997). Language is a mechanism for people to identify with a group and is integral to the development and maintenance of culture. The most successful social interactions acknowledge the varying vocabularies, grammars, and formalities necessary for discussions among spiritual leaders, farmers, CEOs, gang members, golfers, and Cub Scouts. Very young children learn the variations of language appropriate to request attention from grandparents, siblings, peers, or strangers by having opportunities to observe, practice, and receive feedback from their social network. Children gain control of social environments and themselves using language and communication. They have ways to ask for attention, to share frustration, or to indicate the need for help. These important outcomes are seen most poignantly in children with challenging behaviors who do not have effective and efficient means of communication and rely on acting out toward others (e.g., hitting, spitting, biting) or toward themselves (e.g., self-injurious behavior).

Contributions of the Speech-Language Pathologist to the Team

Many team members are involved in teaching language and communication to preschoolers and identifying communication impairments. Speech-language pathologists play a primary but not exclusive role in assessing communication skills, prioritizing communication goals, and designing and implementing intervention programs. It is important to note that collaboration skills are essential for effective intervention. Responsibilities must be shared with a team composed of family members and professionals from various disciplines (e.g., school psychology, speech-language pathology, audiology, general and special education, social work, nursing, physical therapy, occupational therapy) depending on the needs of the child and family. Information regarding the child's communication status provides the foundation for making informed decisions by the family and the development of a comprehensive and coordinated intervention plan for children with delays or disorders affecting communication. Communication plays an integral role in the development of other social and preacademic skills. Early education and coordination of services with the family and teachers can enhance the child's communication skill development within daily activities and related interventions.

A variety of dynamic and convergent measurement strategies can be used to assess receptive and expressive communication and language skills, including standardized and nonstandardized methods that explore the child's abilities across the broad range of social communication forms and functions. These strategies generally involve observing how children use or respond to language in everyday environments, in structured situations, and in environments arranged to provide varying levels of communication expectations and supports to determine the child's range of skills. Children's language skills are compared to other observations or normative data that reflect typical performance of children at different ages or developmental levels to determine whether and where significant deficiencies exist. Discrepancies among communication skills are identified, such as adequate use of multiword sentences coupled with a very low frequency of social communication initiations. Prevention of future difficulties or early intervention for identified delays requires examination of each component rather than review of a global test score.

The team members engage the child's communication partners in the assessment process to identify the child's and family's strengths and interests that can be capitalized upon to enhance communication abilities. The values and expectations of the family's culture are integral to the assessment and treatment process. As the assessment is conducted, the speech–language pathologist is able to provide additional diagnostic information on language skills related to reading, challenging behaviors, and social interactions to the family and other team members who may not be fully aware of the relationships between language and other outcomes. Early education for family members who may not appreciate the impact of language for future learning is essential for recruiting their support to expand the intervention activities to include communication and language skill development as a preventative measure. The speech–language pathologist interested in coordinated services often needs to educate team members that communication and language are more than speech.

To select treatment goals, service delivery teams (including family members) consider the developmental appropriateness of possible goals as well as their usefulness in home, educational, and community settings. Consideration should be given to the potential for treatment goals to enhance participation and success in future inclusive settings as well as present settings and family life. Because individual team members do not have contact with children with language disorders in every communicative situation and environment, the team typically considers a variety of strategies for rearranging communication environments and modifying the behavior of potential communication partners (e.g., parents, teachers, peers, speech–language pathologists). The main objectives of communication intervention are to increase the frequency and quality of contexts that set the occasion for and reinforce language learning and use. As the experimental literature on child language intervention reflects, there are a myriad of ways by which these objectives have been realized. The team members are responsible for identifying intervention approaches that are likely to be effective with individual children given their particular life circumstances. They need to adapt intervention approaches to particular language objectives and to clinical, educational, caregiving, or home situations, ensuring consistent implementation across an array of possible intervention agents. They also need to monitor children's progress and facilitate prompt revisions in implementation, intervention approaches, or goals as indicated by evaluation results.

As a result of the large caseloads served by many speech–language pathologists affiliated with public school programs, typically little time is allocated for consultation with other team members. However, speech–language pathologists should coordinate with classroom teachers and other team members regarding language skill development that relates to academic and social skill development. For example, they must consult with educators when a child's language impairment includes weaknesses that place the child at risk for future reading difficulties as the demand for fluency and deep comprehension in reading increases—and also to make sure that the pace of both regular and remedial efforts is consistent (Snow, Scarborough, & Burns, 1999). To develop interventions that are appropriate to the individual child's program, information from the other team members regarding curricular goals and adaptations as well as preferred routines and activities is essential for the speech-language pathologist. This information is considered in relation to knowledge of how communication typically develops.

Prevention and Normal Development

Because communication competence encompasses so many interrelated skills, one needs to have a firm grounding in normal communication development. Indeed, the deployment of a multitude of prevention and early intervention strategies requires consideration of a number of factors. One needs to consider multiple aspects of communication that may be addressed given a child's profile of strengths and weaknesses and the family's goals and priorities. In this section, we will present an overview of normal communication development and suggest prevention strategies that stem from this knowledge base.

Newborns enter the world communicating. Their repertoires are limited but functional for caregivers who identify the child's cries as a signal of distress and eye gaze as a signal of interest. This ability expands rapidly in the first 5 years to include thousands of words used in an infinite number of combinations to accomplish an extensive array of social, cognitive, and linguistic functions. Team members who work with young children have an important role to play in improving prevention efforts. The first step in prevention is education—knowing when and how communication develops. Table 1 includes general information regarding early development in the outcome areas identified within the model presented above (see Figure 1, on page 471). It is important to understand typical development and recognize that there is a good deal of normal variation, in order to begin identifying children with developmental disabilities that affect communication.

The second step in prevention is translating the "when and how" into meaningful information for caregivers and teachers. Hart and Risley (1995, 1999) provide in-depth analysis of the language development of 42 children from a cross section of the American population including professional, working class, and low-income families. The most significant finding identified by the authors was that the amount of time families spent talking with young children is the most significant predictor of communication competence at age 3. "Optional talk" or conversations enhance the child's ability to problem solve and persuade, the size of his or her vocabulary and range of expression, and the frequency of initiations and turns taken in conversations. Children who converse more with parents in casual topics have larger vocabularies despite not developing grammatical categories earlier than other children (Hart & Risley, 1995). The conversation format provides an exchange that requires both speaking and listening, practice in selecting appropriate responses to keep the interaction moving, and spontaneous elaborations on topics of interest. Not only does the amount of talk within conversations before age 3 relates to dramatic differences in child performance at age 3, but these differences have been shown to persist into third grade (Walker, Greenwood, Hart, & Carta, 1994).

A third step in prevention is early identification. To initiate appropriate services, it is essential to identify children along the continuum from developmental delay to spe-

TABLE 1

General Communication Competence Milestones at 12 Months, 24 Months, 36 Months, and 3–5 Years

Within 1st Year					
Social Interaction/ Behavior Regulation	**Receptive Communication/ Comprehension**	**Expressive Communication**	**Problem Solving**	**Social and Symbolic Play**	**Literacy Skills**
- requests social routine - requests comfort - calls - shows off - greets - requests permission - simple actions and contingent responses between peers - maintains 1 or 2 turns	- responds to different tones in voice, facial expressions, gestures, and eye gaze - responds to own name - comprehends some word meanings dependent on environment and knowledge of prior similar experience, and knowledge of semantic relations to know how these elements go together	- nonspeech sounds that include a vowel sound and may include a consonant preceding or following the vowel - contact and distal gestures for intentional communication	- attends to objects and people - finds object after watching it disappear - uses movement as a means to attain an end - demonstrates tool use after demonstration - engages in goal-directed behavior - performs an action to produce a result - groups objects together - completes 2-step problem solving with novel toy	- early exploratory actions on objects (mouthing, banging) - manipulates toys for sensory effects - uses realistic objects conventionally (rolls cars, hugs baby) - combines toy play with vocalizations - combines related objects together (e.g., spoon in cup) - applies action scheme to self only - places objects near adult and looks for use of object (e.g., pushes cup to adult and watches for adult to drink)	- holds book - looks at pictures in books - vocalizes at pictures

By 24 Months					
- intense watchfulness of peer - imitates peer - watches, points at, takes toy of other child - can introduce topic - engages in dialog of a few turns - repetition used to remain on topic - one-half utterances on topic, extended topic maintenance in routines - initiates interactions	- comprehends action words - follows simple 1-step commands (get the book) - identifies pictures (animals, people, food, clothing, body parts) - comprehends words for absent objects - understands complex sentences - understands prepositions (in, on, under, etc.)	- slow vocabulary growth with some attrition of vocabulary; usually does not exceed 10 to 20 single words at one time - vocabulary growth from a few dozen to several hundred words - expansion of single word semantic relations (e.g., action, attribute, denial, location, possession)	- uses an adult to achieve a goal - rotates and examines 3-D aspects of an object - attends to shapes of things and uses some appropriately - groups objects together - completes 2-step problem solving with novel toy	- uses toy objects conventionally and applies action scheme to others (brushes doll's hair) - spends most group time in solitary activity, watching other children - short, isolated schema combinations (combines 2 actions or toys such as rocking doll and putting it to bed; pouring from pitcher into cup) - play themes restricted to personally experienced events	- enjoys looking at books with others - turns pages in book - may repeat words from books while being read to

By 36 Months					
- will exchange roles in dyadic games involving two clearly differentiated roles that are associated with different speaking parts (e.g., play telephone, taking pictures with toy camera) - will use polite forms (e.g., please, thank you, excuse me) - will use simple repairs (e.g., "What?")	- can carry out 2- to 3-step directions (e.g., "Go to your room, get a book, and bring it to Mom.") - understands possessives (mine, yours) - understands common verbs and adjectives - understands "wh-" questions in context (e.g., "Where is Daddy?", "What do you want to eat?")	- word combinations to encode semantic relations (e.g., action + object, agent + action, attribute + object, action + location, etc.) - imitation as a predominant strategy in language learning - begins to engage in conversation by providing new information about the previous speaker's topic, requesting information, and providing information about things in the past	- uses some foresight before acting - uses tool to obtain object - invents means to attain a goal through thought process rather than trial-and-error - operates mechanical toys - manipulates objects into small openings - can relate one experience to another using "if… then" logic	- pretends with objects dissimilar in shape to substitute for the real object (e.g., substitutes leaf for fork) - plays alongside peers, though not interactively - uses one object to stand for a different object similar in shape (uses banana for telephone) - demonstrates or verbalizes play plan before acting - uses multiple action schemes in sequence (makes cake, eats, and washes dishes) - pretend themes are restricted to personally experienced events - plays well with 2 or 3 children in a group - associative play, borrowing, encouraging	- recognizes that the pictures represent something - recognizes familiar signs and logos (e.g., McDonald's) - labels pictures in book (e.g., bear, bunny, cat, doll)

Table 1 continued on p. 478

Table 1 *continued*

3–5 Years

Social Interaction/ Behavior Regulation	Receptive Communication/ Comprehension	Expressive Communication	Problem Solving	Social and Symbolic Play	Literacy Skills
- can engage in dialog beyond a few turns - more aware of social aspects of discourse - acknowledges partner's turn, can determine how much information listener needs - modifies language when talking to younger child - increased awareness of listener's role and understanding	- comprehends sentences based on morphological and syntactic rules (uses word order strategy for agent-action-recipient relations) - will respond appropriately to "why" and "how" questions - can respond to "when" and other "wh-" questions out of context ("What did you do at the zoo?")	- develops semantic relational terms to encode spatial, dimensional, temporal, causal, quantity, color, age, and other relations - uses grammatical morphemes (prepositions, tense markers, plural endings, pronouns, articles) - uses syntax (rules of word order) to construct declarative, negative, imperative, interrogative, passive, and complex sentences - vocabulary ranges	- solves 4- to 6-step puzzle - can build vertical block structure requiring balance and coordination - can put graduated sizes in order - uses representational thinking constructions - can integrate spatial, cause-and-effect, and representational thinking into problem solving	- verbalizes play plan with roles - pretends without an object for a prop - plays spontaneously with other children in complicated verbal communication - pretend themes include events that child has observed but not experienced (policeman or fireman schemas) - increased rough-and-tumble play - begins cooperative play - engages in sociodramatic play in which the child takes on a role of someone else and elaborates on the theme in cooperation with other players (playing restaurant or doctor) - group play replaces parallel play - prefers playing with other children to playing alone, unless engrossed in a project - develops novel schemas for events child has not personally experienced or observed (astronaut builds ship, flies to strange planet, explores, eats unusual foods, talks with creatures on planet)	- can recognize alliteration (little lollipop) - can recite rhyming words and familiar nursery rhymes - can blend two sounds (m-at) - begins scribbling as writing - pretends to read books, cards, etc.

cific language impairment to pervasive communication disorder. Recent studies have sought to identify early indicators that predict persistent communication and language delay. Measures of vocabulary, while possibly enlightening, are not sufficient. The findings from these studies suggest a number of components including early social interaction behaviors that may result in earlier identification and intervention. Deficits in the ability to share attention and affective states with eye gaze and facial expression (Kasari, Sigman, Mundy, & Yirmiya, 1990) or a low rate of communication with gestures or vocalizations (Thal & Tobias, 1994, Wetherby et al., 2000) may signal an early and persistent concern. Children who have a limited range of communicative functions, especially in their ability to establish joint attention, are at risk even before words would be expected to develop. Children with a limited repertoire of gestures prior to 18 months should be considered at risk, as should children who rely on gestures and exhibit a limited use of vocalizations to communicate. A limited consonant inventory and a less complex syllabic structure in vocal communication may predict problems.

Children who exhibit a delay in both language comprehension and production are more likely to have persistent problems (Wetherby et al., 2000).

Longitudinal studies of children identified with language disorders suggest that for many of the children the disorder persists as the child grows older, but changes in how it is evidenced. Early, obvious language errors may become subtler as articulation errors are corrected and sentence structures become more complete (Aram, Ekelman, & Nation, 1984). Error-free verbal skills may hide language comprehension disorders that increase in importance as academic contexts become more diverse. Follow-up studies of children with preschool language impairments have confirmed earlier evidence that these children are at heightened risk of showing reading problems in school (Catts, Fey, Zhang, & Tomblin, 1999). Risk for academic difficulties may remain high even if children receive high-quality speech-language therapy in the preschool years and even if their early language difficulties appear to disappear or to become only mild in severity by kindergarten.

EARLY INTERVENTION STRATEGIES

In this section, an overview of recommended practices for promoting communicative competence is provided. We focus our discussion on early intervention strategies that can be implemented in the everyday life of preschool children, beginning with techniques that focus primarily on language input to more structured techniques that can be tailored to a broader array of communication skills. We also discuss specialized strategies for promoting social interaction and emergent literacy skills in preschool children.

Language Stimulation Techniques

A number of language stimulation procedures have been used to provide frequent and appropriate linguistic input or models for children with language disorders. Perhaps because of the potency of observational learning, systematic modeling of language content, form, and use has been shown to be surprisingly effective (Bandura, 1977; Browder, Schoen, & Lentz, 1986–1987; Glidden & Warner, 1982; Goldstein & Brown, 1989; Hepting & Goldstein, 1996a; LeBlanc, Etzel, & Domash, 1978). Adding to the usefulness of these procedures is the fact that language stimulation can be implemented across a child's everyday circumstances by parents, teachers, peers, siblings, and others. Stimulation approaches have been investigated with a full range of developmental disabilities and severity levels (from specific language impairment to severe mental retardation and autism) and usually have focused on teaching vocabulary, early word combinations, and simple sentences. Some of the techniques considered stimulation approaches are modeling, repeating, expanding, or recasting of children's utterances. The distinction among these approaches is the extent to which adults model language that builds upon what the child has already said.

Perhaps the most important distinction among various stimulation approaches is the comparison of focused stimulation, which targets specific language goals, versus general linguistic stimulation, which implies providing lots of language input at the child's general development level (see Leonard, 1981; Fey, Cleave, Long, & Hughes, 1993). Focused stimulation approaches have repeatedly produced learning of targeted skills, but not pervasive effects on global measures of language development (Girolametto, Pearce, & Weitzman, 1996; Goldstein & Brown, 1989; Leonard et al., 1982; McLean & Vincent, 1984; Schwartz, Chapman, Terrell, Prelock, & Rowan, 1985; Schwartz & Leonard, 1985; Wilcox, Kouri, & Caswell, 1991). General stimulation has been used to stimulate more pervasive growth in language skills, but not surprisingly, treatment effects are harder to detect (Cole & Dale, 1986; Kaiser et al., 1996; Tannock, Girolametto, & Siegel, 1992). Comparison studies provide some evidence of an advantage for stimulation approaches over imitation-based approaches (Camarata & Nelson, 1992; Connell, 1987; Courtright & Courtright, 1976, 1979). However, imitation training more fairly should be considered a component of intervention, as it no longer is recommended for exclusive use.

Studies of language development seem to support the application of stimulation approaches to communication intervention. As discussed earlier, Hart and her colleagues' striking evidence of how having large disparities in the amount of language stimulation experienced by typical children in American homes predicts differences in vocabulary growth and later school achievement is a good example (Hart & Risley, 1995, 1999; Walker et al., 1994). The language intervention literature rarely provides explicit information on the precise quality and quantity of language stimulation provided, admittedly a difficult undertaking. Nonetheless, more precise characterizations of stimulation treatments and the fidelity of these treatments over time are needed to judge the degree of short- and long-term effectiveness of these language intervention approaches. One might predict that more stimulation would produce the best results, but this is likely to be overly simplistic. Based on Vygotsky's notion of the "zone of proximal development" (cf. Olswang, Bain, & Johnson, 1992), one might expect the child's "readiness" to be an important determination of what input should be provided. Likewise, stimulation may vary in effectiveness depending on when it is provided, which may depend on the child's state of awareness and its functional relevance to the child. Indeed, the realization that language intervention should teach functions that children will be highly motivated to use has spurred the next set of developments in the field.

Teaching an Array of Communicative Functions in the Natural Milieu

If early interventionists emphasize teaching preschoolers to label objects or to respond to questions and such, then they are ignoring the full complement of language functions. For example, children with language impairments have been taught adaptive skills, such as gestural responses (Buffington, Krantz, McClannahan, & Poulson, 1998); prelinguistic and verbal requesting for desired objects, materials, and foods (Bray, Biasini, Thrasher, 1983; Halle, Marshall, & Spradlin, 1979; Koegel, Camarata, Valdez-Menchaca, & Koegel, 1998; Schussler & Spradlin, 1991); requesting clarification (Dollaghan & Kaston, 1986); requesting permission, expressing rejection, and commenting (Charlop & Trasowech, 1991; Schwartz, Anderson, & Halle, 1989); initiating and responding in conversational and sociodramatic play contexts (Goldstein & Cisar, 1992); as well as responding to questions (Ingenmey & Van Houten, 1991; Secan, Egel, & Tilley, 1989; Warren, McQuarter, & Rogers-Warren, 1984).

The research on teaching different language functions has spawned the development of techniques for teaching language incidentally in the context of children's everyday activities. Milieu language teaching is a family of procedures designed to capitalize on children's desires and interests and to embed teaching opportunities in their natural environments. A variety of intervention strategies have been empirically validated with preschool children in classroom and home settings, including incidental language teaching, enhanced milieu treatment, environmental arrangement, caregiver-child responsive interactions, response prompting and shaping, mand-model procedures, time delay, and the use of specialized materials. Incidental teaching (cf. Hart & Risley, 1975), perhaps the hallmark of milieu language teaching, requires that the child initiate an attempt to communicate, usually to make a request. Incidental teaching capitalizes on these opportunities to teach more elaborated language forms. Mand-model procedures were developed as an extension of incidental teaching to prompt children who were not initiating requests. *Mands* are questions or commands asking the child to express desires (e.g., "tell me what you want") and *models* are requests to imitate a developmentally appropriate form for communicating that message (e.g., "say, I want juice"). Likewise, time delay procedures were developed to teach children to initiate and use those communicative forms independently (e.g., pausing with an expectant look before prompting with a mand or a model).

Milieu language teaching usually is used to teach requesting, because high motivation is inherent when individuals are requesting desired items that presumably function as reinforcers. Milieu strategies often capitalize on situations in which children's attention is focused on desired objects, materials, or foods to teach language skills ranging from simple vocabulary to complex sentences. Children typically maintain and generalize their use of these language skills, because these incidental teaching procedures include the same or similar stimuli as those present in children's everyday lives. Not surprisingly, teaching children to exert control over their environment using increasingly complex language also has been shown to have general benefits in promoting language development (cf. Kaiser, Yoder, & Keetz, 1992 for a review). Milieu teaching has even been adapted for use with prelinguistic children with developmental delays to teach intentional requests in the form of gestures or vocalizations (McGee, Morrier, & Daly, 1999; Yoder, Warren, Kim, & Gazdag, 1994). Because milieu teaching is usually implemented in everyday contexts, many studies have used teachers and parents (Alpert & Kaiser, 1992; Charlop & Trasowech, 1991; Delaney & Kaiser, 2001; Hemmeter & Kaiser, 1994; Kaiser, Hancock, & Nietfeld, 2000; Laski, Charlop, & Schreibman, 1988) and peers (Goldstein & Wickstrom, 1986; McGee, Almeida, Sulzer-Azaroff, & Feldman, 1992) as intervention agents.

It is worth noting that these functional teaching approaches have been developed and applied mainly with children with mental retardation and autism. An examination of the literature demonstrates that a growing array of communicative functions are being taught to young children with disabilities using milieu teaching procedures: pre-verbal communication (eye contact, joint attention, and motor imitation, Hwang & Hughes, 2000); spontaneous productions of "I like/love you" (Charlop & Walsh, 1986); descriptions of drawings and play activities (Ingenmey & Van Houten, 1991); social amenities such as "please, thank you, excuse me, you're welcome, hello" (Matson, Sevin, Box, Francis, & Sevin, 1993); positive interactions with peers (McGee et al., 1992); answers to "Where is ____?" questions (McGee, Krantz, & McClannahan, 1985); phoneme production (Koegel, Camarata, Koegel, Ben-Tall, & Smith, 1998); and simply increased talking (Laski et al., 1988). Research on milieu language teaching procedures has been extensive and has been applied to teaching early language skills to a broad population of children (see Kaiser et al., 1992).

Other procedures that are designed for use in natural environments with a focus on following the child's lead might be considered forms of milieu language teaching. For example the Natural Language Paradigm (NLP) is a multiple component intervention that might be considered a form of milieu teaching (e.g., Koegel, O'Dell, & Koegel, 1987; Laski et al., 1988). The operational characteristics of this approach have begun to be clarified, especially when contrasted with discrete-trial training (Koegel, Koegel, & Surratt, 1992). For example, Koegel, Camarata, Koegel, et al. (1998) contrasted the procedural differences in analog (discrete-trial) vs. naturalistic (NLP) intervention approaches based on selection of stimulus items, steps in training, interaction patterns, response-reinforcer contingencies, and the types of consequences provided.

Routines-based intervention extends milieu teaching by focusing on everyday activities that are predictable, repetitive, functional, and that result in meaningful outcomes. The familiarity of the routine allows the child to attend to new or more sophisticated skill requirements and the predictable sequence helps caregivers utilize intervention strategies (Christenson, Ysseldyke, & Thurlow, 1989; Dunst et al., 1987). These teaching and learning opportunities can occur numerous times throughout the day within a variety of routines and activities, providing the early intervention team with the contexts for embedding intervention under the family's guidance (Warren & Horn, 1996). Intervention is designed to be portable and adaptable to the family's interests, needs, and responsibilities. Embedded intervention implemented by caregivers can occur at home, at childcare, in the car, at the soccer game, in the laundromat, in the yard, in the doctor's office, at playgroup, at the park, at grandma's house, at the neighbor's house, or anywhere families go (Woods-Cripe & Venn, 1997).

There is no compelling evidence that milieu teaching procedures are clearly more effective than the procedures that have developed out of discrete-trial procedures. Indeed, one might argue that there is a great deal of commonality in the procedures employed. An analysis of naturalistic language intervention procedures offered by Hepting and Goldstein (1996b) includes many of the instructional techniques found in the discrete-trial teaching literature. One can argue that milieu language teaching procedures can be more easily incorporated into everyday activities and reduce the need to program for generalization. Such comparisons of treatment approaches are not necessarily straightforward and comparison studies have yielded mixed results. Koegel, Camarata, Koegel, Ben–Tall, and Smith (1998) contrasted traditional (analog) articulation training with a naturalistic approach (NLP) in a single-subject experiment (counterbalanced reversal design) and found much greater generalization to conversational language samples for phonemes taught using the naturalistic procedures. Yoder et al. (1995) argue that teaching approaches may differ depending on the language skills being taught or the linguistic sophistication of the children. However, a careful inspection of the correlational findings used to detect aptitude-by-treatment interactions indicates that few children consistently fall into the regions of significance that are differentially predictive of outcomes (e.g., Cole, Mills, Dale, & Jenkins, 1996; Yoder et al., 1995; Yoder & Warren, 1999). Defining profiles that are predictive of differential treatment effects is thus likely to be difficult.

Relations Between Communication and Challenging Behavior

It is important to consider the role of communication and language as a means of controlling one's environment. One may consider children's tantrums and aggressive behavior as a means of controlling one's environment, although these behavior patterns are not considered appropriate forms of communication. However, the hypothesis that challenging behaviors serve a communicative function has important implications. Teaching more appropriate communication forms has the potential to prevent or ameliorate challenging behavior. Wickstrom-Kane and Goldstein (1999) have pointed out that toddlers frequently are referred for early intervention services because they demonstrate high rates of challenging behavior. One of the keys to service delivery is to help families deal with challenging behavior, and that is done by teaching children more appropriate ways of communicating and teaching family members not to reinforce inappropriate forms of communication. Investigators have developed functional assessment procedures for identifying antecedent and consequent variables that appear to motivate challenging behavior especially among individuals with severe disabilities. These individuals then are taught specific language skills to serve the same communicative function as the challenging behavior. When individuals are taught these adaptive alternatives, a reduction in challenging behavior results (Carr & Durand, 1985; Davis, Brady, Williams, & Hamilton, 1992; Durand & Carr, 1992; Koegel et al., 1992; Wacker et al., 1990).

Control over one's environment can be manifested not just on a social level but also on a personal level. Treatment approaches have included different strategies for using language skills as a means of self-control (Osnes, Guevremont, & Stokes, 1986; Sainato, Goldstein, & Strain, 1992). That is, children are taught to use language to mediate their own verbal and nonverbal actions. Examples of such actions include prompting oneself to stay in one's seat, reminding oneself to describe school day events during dinnertime conversations at home, and prompting oneself to interact socially with peers during different activities.

This is an especially important area because of the intense interest in managing problem behavior in children in school, as well as in home and community settings. In fact, this line of research may open new avenues for involving school psychologists and speech-language pathologists in the treatment of children who might not be characterized as language disordered. The replacement of challenging behaviors with appropriate and increasingly sophisticated communication skills has the potential to have far-reaching implications for academic achievement, social relationship development, vocational outcomes, and even reducing violence and crime (Cairns, Cairns, & Neckerman, 1989; Dishion, Patterson, Stoolmiller, & Skinner, 1991; Dunlap & Kern, 1997; Fey, Catts, & Larrivee, 1995; Parker & Asher, 1987; Reid & Patterson, 1991; Walker, Stieber, & O'Neill, 1990).

Teaching Peer Interaction Skills

Although peers serve as models and children naturally shape behavior in a reciprocal manner, it is up to teachers and caregivers to make conscious decisions to optimize these interactions. Peers are modeling social behavior for one another constantly and this is likely to play an important role in observational learning of communication skills and social problem solving. Teachers and caregivers should try to incorporate opportunities for observational learning into a variety of activities, such as group activities entailing show and share, word-play activities, and singing; story reading; as well as play times. Observational learning may not always result. For example, one should not expect observational learning to occur when there is a large discrepancy between modeled behavior and the existing repertoire of a child with special needs. Furthermore, modeling tends to be more robust when models are high-status peers who share many characteristics with the learner (Hosford, 1980; Rosekrans, 1967). Another systematic approach to optimizing observational learning is to start with short or no delays between modeled and imitated performance, before expecting performance long after initial observations (Goldstein & Mousetis, 1989). One needs to reinforce spontaneous, delayed imitative attempts to encourage delayed observation learning.

There also has been an increased awareness of the need for children with developmental disabilities to learn how to interact with their peers who are not disabled. One of the primary strategies used to promote peer interaction is indirect. That is, typical peers have been taught to initiate and respond to their classmates with social communication deficits. Perhaps the most effective strategy for promoting peer interaction is to promote social initiations on the part of typical peers (Odom et al., 1999). Social initiations can take a variety of forms: play organizers, offering assistance, asking questions, requesting attention, and commenting. It is worth noting that even commenting about ongoing activities, which does not obligate a response, is surprisingly effective in evoking responses and additional comments among young children. Typical peers should be encouraged to initiate often to children with special needs, but not to be bossy. This approach has been quite effective in producing improved interaction on the part of children who had been socially withdrawn or socially inappropriate. Moreover, there has been an increased emphasis on teaching peers facilitative communication strategies (e.g., talking about ongoing activities and responding to verbalizations), which in turn have produced improved social communication in children with developmental disabilities (English, Goldstein, Shafer, & Kaczmarek, 1997; Goldstein, English, Shafer, & Kaczmarek, 1997; Goldstein, Kaczmarek, Pennington, & Shafer, 1992; Goldstein & Wickstrom, 1986; Haring & Lovinger, 1989; James & Egel, 1986).

Interactions will not persist if the interaction partners are not responsive. Thus, peers should be encouraged to model the kind of responsiveness that we desire on the part of the children with social deficits. Peers can be taught to demonstrate a variety of responses, such as accepting or sharing toys and materials; complying with requests for assistance, attention, information, or objects; reciprocating affectionate behaviors; and taking turns in social exchanges.

In more structured interventions, such as when teaching sociodramatic play scripts or reciprocal peer tutoring situations, careful planning is required. Scripts have been developed to target the communication needs of individual children with autism, for example. Social scripts have been taught directly (Krantz & McClannahan, 1993) or through peer modeling (Charlop & Milstein, 1989). In inclusive preschool settings, it is important to try to balance participation among children and to avoid relegating the child with special needs to a largely passive role (Goldstein & Kaczmarek, 1992). One should be able to create variations for each role to accommodate different ability levels. For example, Goldstein and his colleagues taught sociodramatic play scripts to children with developmental disabilities and typical peers simultaneously with the scripts adaptable so that they could be tailored to the language levels of the participants (Goldstein & Cisar, 1992). The social-communicative acts could vary from gestural communication or single-word utterances to complex sentences. It is helpful to have peers model communicative acts that are slightly more sophisticated than those currently being exhibited by the child with special needs. It may be useful to impose group rather than individual contingencies and to teach peers to offer supportive comments to one another. Supportive comments could be augmented with physical or affection activities as well, such as hugs, pats on the back, shaking hands, and dancing together (Brown, Ragland, & Fox, 1988; McEvoy et al., 1988).

Although there are a number of strategies that can be used to promote socialization with peers, it may be challenging to plan for their systematic use and to implement socialization activities consistently and often enough. Kohler and Strain (1999) offer six examples of peer-mediated procedures that were incorporated across the day into an inclusive preschool program. This is a departure from the more common practice of focusing on a single peer intervention strategy. Consequently, it is up to teachers and caregivers to expand their teaching repertoires and to develop plans that incorporate many of the strategies discussed above into a variety of activities. It also is up to them to structure the environment and activities to facilitate socialization and to teach peers how to interact in productive ways. Increased social interactions can set the stage for other developments as well, e.g., generalized use of newly acquired language skills, modeling of new language skills, inclusion in more normalized educational settings, and, one hopes, the development of positive, long-lasting relationships with peers and others. Enlisting the help of peers may help teachers to deal effectively with teaching more complex communication skills, such as teaching preschoolers to select themes and topics for different contexts, how to enter into an ongoing activity gracefully, how to contribute to group discussions, and the like.

Teaching Emergent Literacy Skills

The National Research Council report on preventing reading problems in young children (Snow, Burns, & Griffin, 1998) concluded that the majority of reading problems could be prevented—primarily by reducing the number of children who enter school with low levels of emergent literacy skills. Children with more of these "emergent literacy" skills appear to profit more from reading instruction, learn to read sooner, and read better than do children with less of these skills (Torgesen & Davis, 1996; Whitehurst & Lonigan, 1998). The relevant skills include oral language, print knowledge, and phonological processing. Oral language consists of receptive and expressive vocabulary and grammar. Print knowledge refers to recognition of letters and their sounds. Phonological processing refers to children's developing sensitivity to the sound structure of oral language and the use of phonological or sound-based codes when processing language. Phonological sensitivity or the ability to manipulate the sound structure of oral language has received considerable research attention (e.g., Bryant, MacLean, Bradley, & Crossland, 1990; Wagner & Torgesen, 1987; Wagner, Torgesen, & Rashotte, 1994). Children with better phonological sensitivity are better at detecting or manipulating rhymes, syllables, or phonemes and better performance is an excellent predictor of later reading ability. This association is robust even after controlling for factors such as IQ, vocabulary, memory, and socioeconomic status (Bryant et al., 1990; Raz & Bryant, 1990; Wagner & Torgesen, 1987; Wagner et al., 1994).

Interventions to enhance emergent literacy skills have included phonological sensitivity training (e.g., Ball & Blachman, 1988; Lundberg, Frost, & Petersen, 1988; Torgesen, Morgan, & Davis, 1992; Uhry & Shepherd, 1993); whole language instruction (e.g., Adams, 1991); and shared-reading interventions (e.g., Arnold, Lonigan, Whitehurst, & Epstein, 1994; Hockenberger, Goldstein, & Haas, 1999; Huebner, 2000; Justice & Ezell, 2000; Lonigan & Whitehurst, 1998).

A small number of studies have examined phonological sensitivity in preschool children. These studies demonstrate that phonological sensitivity can be measured, even in preschoolers who have not received formal instruction (e.g., Chaney, 1992; Lonigan, Burgess, Anthony, & Barker, 1998; MacLean, Bryant, & Bradley, 1987; Raz & Bryant, 1990; Wagner et al., 1994). Furthermore, children's early emerging phonological sensitivity skills predict their early decoding skills (e.g., MacLean et al., 1987; Lonigan, Burgess, & Anthony, 2000). Studies that have provided phonological sensitivity training have yielded positive effects on children's reading and spelling skills (for reviews, see Bus & van IJzendoorn, 1999; Whitehurst & Lonigan, 1998). Most of these studies taught phonological sensitivity skills to children who were beginning reading instruction in kindergarten or first grade. However, Byrne and Fielding-Barnsley (1991) found that preschool children improved their phonological sensitivity skills after 12 weeks of their Sound Foundations program when compared to a control group exposed to a semantic categorization program. Children maintained some of these gains through first and second grade (Byrne & Fielding-Barnsley, 1993, 1995). When regular preschool teachers implemented the program, smaller effects were produced, presumably because of poorer fidelity of program implementation (Byrne & Fielding-Barnsley, 1995). In an attempt to remedy the fidelity of treatment problem, Lonigan and his colleagues (in press) implemented a Computer-Assisted Instruction (CAI) phonological sensitivity program with preschool children who were at risk for reading problems. CAI, which was effective in enhancing phonological sensitivity performance in comparison to techniques used in a control group, has the potential to minimize problems of poor implementation of phonological sensitivity training programs in childcare, preschool, and even home environments.

Shared book reading offers an advantageous routine for facilitating communication development. Whitehurst and his colleagues developed an interactive shared-reading intervention called *dialogic reading* that entails adults having a conversation and asking questions about a book while it is being read to children. Investigators have shown that dialogic reading facilitates language development in preschool children. These results have been replicated when parents, childcare workers, and teachers implement dialogic reading, with middle-class children as well as low-income children (Arnold et al., 1994; Heubner, 2000; Lonigan & Whitehurst, 1998; Valdez-Menchaca & Whitehurst, 1992; Whitehurst et al., 1988, 1994). Dale and his colleagues (1996) found that a dialogic reading intervention produced greater improvements in linguistic performance in children with language delays than did a play-oriented language facilitation intervention. Crain-Thoreson and Dale (1999) found smaller effects on vocabulary development of preschoolers with language delays, although this outcome has been affected consistently in previous studies. They suggested that more intensive or longer intervention periods might improve results with this population. Hockenberger et al. (1999) taught mothers from low-income homes to comment during shared book reading and to relate book content to the children's experiences. The changes in children's rate of conversational utterances seemed to mirror the rates demonstrated by their mothers, regardless of whether the children were identified as developmentally disabled. Shared book reading is not likely to have much affect on phonological processing skills, but it is likely to help promote print awareness, as well as facilitating oral language and conceptual development. Thus, a combination of approaches may be needed to facilitate the range of relevant emergent literacy skills and prevent reading problems.

SUMMARY AND CONCLUSION

School psychologists need to realize that preschool-aged children may demonstrate a variety of communication problems. Although communication impairments may be obvious if problems are pervasive, communication problems sometimes may be difficult to diagnose or even context specific. We have presented a model and developmental information to outline some of the important developmental outcomes reflected in competent communication in preschool-aged children, and to highlight the interaction among the multiple influences on communication development that may be inherent in children, their caregivers, and their communities. Communication is a dynamic, complex process. We have emphasized the role of communication in the social milieu and how it is essential for understanding and controlling one's environment. Furthermore, it is important to realize the role of early communication skills in relation to areas that historically have been viewed as separate areas of development, namely peer interactions and relationship development, challenging behavior, and emergent literacy skills.

Speech-language pathologists are a valuable resource for determining whether a child should be referred for speech and language services. More important, well-trained speech-language pathologists should be valuable team members when designing educational programs that will benefit preschool-aged children generally in home, childcare, and community settings. We have attempted to identify a number of therapeutic approaches that should have broad applicability beyond sole use with children with communication impairments. We have discussed strategies that may be used to design environments to improve language stimulation and help to ensure that diverse communicative functions are addressed. Although arranging the environment and providing ample opportunities to observe and use communication skills are essential components of early intervention, they may not be sufficient. For example, Filla, Wolery, and Anthony (1999) set up theme boxes in a restricted play space with two play partners in preschool classrooms but found that peer conversation rates did not improve until prompting procedures were instituted. Indeed, that is why the various milieu teaching procedures are important. They offer systematic approaches to prompting children to expand their repertoire of communicative functions and to use increasingly complex language skills. Hepting and Goldstein (1996b) reviewed 34 naturalistic language-treatment studies and found that the treatments seemed to use a limited set of basic teaching procedures. Treatments could be characterized by whether they used eight procedures that manipulated antecedents (prompting imitation, manding verbalization, requesting elaboration or clarification, waiting for initiations or responses, arranging the environment, modeling, repeating/expanding/recasting, and descriptive talking) and three procedures that manipulated consequences (delivering desired consequences, praising, minimal encouragers).

In the final sections of the chapter, we highlighted three areas that have taken on new importance to both school psychologists and speech-language pathologists. The realization that challenging behavior typically serves a communicative function has led to new approaches to evaluating the functions of such behavior. Once those functions are identified, our goal is to teach more appropriate, alternative forms of communication to serve those functions. Although the bulk of the research to date has dealt with severe aggressive and self-injurious behavior, the realization that improved communication skills may prevent the development of all kinds of socially maladaptive behavior has widespread implications for enhancing academic, social, and ultimately vocational outcomes in the general population. Likewise, the early focus on peer interaction and relationship development in preschool-aged children has profound implications in a related vein. Typical peers have been shown to be highly effective in facilitating improved social and communicative functioning, especially in children who are severely socially withdrawn (e.g., children with autism). However, the techniques used in peer-mediated intervention approaches have broad applicability and are likely to have desirable outcomes for typical peers as well as for children with disabilities. When peers are serving as intervention agents directly or indirectly they are learning more sophisticated communication skills; they also are learning to deal more effectively and perhaps empathetically with individuals who are less skilled or have special needs.

Investigators are beginning to illuminate the importance of preschool years to subsequent development of literacy skills. Knowing that phonological processing skills are necessary components to early reading ability is sure to spur further development of strategies that can be used with preschoolers to teach them to manipulate words and speech sounds and to learn about letter-sound correspondence. A myriad of possible ways to make book reading interactive and enjoyable need to be explored to discern how to maximize the effects on children's language development.

In short, we have sought to expand readers' perspectives on what communication entails in preschool-aged children and how its development is affected by a multiplicity of factors. We have introduced a wide range of effective and promising strategies for facilitating improved communication competence. Clearly, challenges remain as teams of professionals, caregivers, and parents try to identify those communication skills that would prove most functional and lead to generalized outcomes for individual children in their unique social and cultural circumstances. Further refinement is needed so that we can better tailor prevention and early intervention strategies for widespread adoption and implementation within home, school, and community contexts.

REFERENCES

Adams, M. J. (1991). Why not phonics and whole language? In W. Ellis (Ed.), *All language and the creation of literacy* (pp. 40-52). Baltimore: Orton Dyslexia Society.

Alpert, C., & Kaiser, A. (1992). Training parents as milieu language teachers. *Journal of Early Intervention, 16,* 31-52.

Aram, D., Ekelman, B., & Nation, J. (1984). Preschoolers with language disorders: 10 years later. *Journal of Speech and Hearing Research, 27,* 232-244.

Arnold, D. S., Lonigan, C. J., Whitehurst, G. J., & Epstein, J. N. (1994). Accelerating language development through picture-book reading: Replication and extension to a videotape training format. *Journal of Educational Psychology, 86,* 235-243.

Austin, J. (1962). *How to do things with words.* London: Oxford University Press.

Ball, E. W., & Blachman, B. A. (1988). Phoneme segmentation training: Effect on reading readiness. *Annals of Dyslexia, 38,* 208-225.

Bandura, A. (1977). *Social learning theory.* Englewood Cliffs, NJ: Prentice-Hall.

Bray, N. W., Biasini, F. J., & Thrasher, K. A. (1983). The effect of communicative demands on request-making in the moderately and severely mentally retarded. *Applied Research in the Mentally Retarded, 4,* 13-28.

Browder, D., Schoen, S. & Lentz, F. (1986-1987). Learning to learn through observation. *The Journal of Special Education, 20,* 447-461.

Brown, W. H., Ragland, E. U., & Fox, J. J. (1988). Effects of group socialization procedures on the social interactions of preschool children. *Research in Developmental Disabilities, 9,* 359-376.

Bryant, P. E., MacLean, M., Bradley, L. L., & Crossland, J. (1990). Rhyme and alliteration, phoneme detection, and learning to read. *Developmental Psychology, 26,* 429-438.

Buffington, D. M., Krantz, P. J., McClannahan, L. E., & Poulson, C. L. (1998). Procedures for teaching appropriate gestural communication skills to children with autism. *Journal of Autism and Developmental Disorders, 28,* 535-545.

Bus, A. G., & van IJzendoorn, M. H. (1999). Phonological awareness and early reading: A meta-analysis of experimental training studies. *Journal of Educational Psychology, 91,* 403-414.

Byrne, B., & Fielding-Barnsley, R. F. (1991). Evaluation of a program to teach phonemic awareness to young children. *Journal of Educational Psychology, 82,* 805-812.

Byrne, B., & Fielding-Barnsley, R. F. (1993). Evaluation of a program to teach phonemic awareness to young children: A one year follow-up. *Journal of Educational Psychology, 85,* 104-111.

Byrne, B., & Fielding-Barnsley, R. (1995). Evaluation of a program to teach phonemic awareness to young children: A 2- and 3-year follow-up and a new preschool trial. *Journal of Educational Psychology, 87,* 488-503.

Cairns, R. B., Cairns, B. D., & Neckerman, H. J. (1989). Early school dropout: Configurations and determinants. *Child Development, 60,* 1437-1452.

Camarata, S. M. & Nelson, K. E. (1992). Treatment efficiency as a function of target selection in the remediation of child language disorders. *Clinical Linguistics & Phonetics, 6,* 167-178.

Carr, E. G., & Durand, V. M. (1985). Reducing behavior problems through functional communication training. *Journal of Applied Behavior Analysis, 18,* 111-126.

Catts, H. W., Fey, M. E., Zhang, X., & Tomblin, B. (1999). Language basis of reading and reading disabilities: Evidence from a longitudinal investigation. *Scientific Studies of Reading, 3,* 331-361.

Chaney, C. (1992). Language development, metalinguistic skills, and print awareness in 3-year-old children. *Applied Psycholinguistics, 13,* 485-514.

Charlop, M. H., & Milstein, J. P. (1989). Teaching autistic children conversational speech using video modeling. *Journal of Applied Behavior Analysis, 22,* 275-285.

Charlop, M. H., & Trasowech, J. E. (1991). Increasing children's daily spontaneous speech. *Journal of Applied Behavioral Analysis, 24,* 747-761.

Charlop, M. H., & Walsh, M. E. (1986). Increasing autistic children's spontaneous verbalizations of affection: An assessment of time delay and peer modeling procedures. *Journal of Applied Behavior Analysis, 19,* 307-314.

Christenson, S. L., Ysseldyke, J. E., & Thurlow, M. L. (1989). Critical instructional factors for students with mild handicaps: An integrative review. *Remedial & Special Education, 10*(5), 21-31.

Clarke-Stewart, K. A. (1973). Interactions between mothers and their young children: Characteristics and consequences. *Monographs of the Society for Research in Child Development, 38*(6-7, Serial No. 153).

Cole, K. N., & Dale, P. S. (1986). Direct language instruction and interactive language instruction with language delayed preschool children: A comparison study. *Journal of Speech and Hearing Research, 29,* 206-217.

Cole, K., Mills, P. E., Dale, P. S., & Jenkins, J. R. (1996). Preschool language facilitation methods and child characteristics. *Journal of Early Intervention, 20,* 113-131.

Connell, P. J. (1987). An effect of modeling and imitation teaching procedures on children with and without specific language impairment. *Journal of Speech and Hearing Research, 30,* 105-113.

Courtright, J. A., & Courtright, I. C. (1976). Imitative modeling as a theoretical base for instructing language disordered children. *Journal of Speech and Hearing Research, 19,* 655-663.

Courtright, J. A., & Courtright, I. C. (1979). Imitative modeling as a language intervention strategy: The effects of two mediating variables. *Journal of Speech and Hearing Research, 22,* 389-402.

Crain-Thoreson, C., & Dale, P. S. (1999). Enhancing linguistic performance: Parents and teachers as book reading partners for children with language delays. *Topics in Early Childhood Special Education, 19,* 28-39.

Dale, P. S., Crain-Thoreson, C., Notari-Syverson, A., & Cole, K. (1996). Parent-child bookreading as an intervention for young children with language delays. *Topics in Early Childhood Special Education, 16,* 213-235.

Davis, C. A., Brady, M. P., Williams, R. E., & Hamilton, R. (1992). Effects of high-probability requests on the acquisition and generalization of responses to requests in young children with behavior disorders. *Journal of Applied Behavior Analysis, 25,* 905-916.

Delaney, E. M., & Kaiser, A. P. (2001). The effects of teaching parents blended communication and behavior support strategies. *Behavioral Disorders, 26,* 93-116.

Dishion, T. J., Patterson, G. R., Stoolmiller, M., & Skinner, M. L. (1991). Family, school, and behavioral antecedents to early adolescent involvement with antisocial peers. *Developmental Psychology, 27,* 172-180.

Dollaghan, C., & Kaston, N. (1986). A comprehension monitoring program for language-impaired children. *Journal of Speech and Hearing Disorders, 51,* 264-271.

Dunlap, G., & Kern, L. (1997). Modifying instructional activities to promote desirable behavior: A conceptual and practical framework. *School Psychology Quarterly, 11*(4), 297-312.

Dunst, C. J., Lesko, J., Holbert, K., Wilson, L., Sharpe, K., & Liles, R. (1987). A systematic approach to infant intervention. *Topics in Early Childhood Special Education, 7*(2), 19-37.

Dunst, C. J., Lowe, L. W., & Bartholomew, P. C. (1990). Contingent social responsiveness, family ecology, and infant communicative competence. *National Student Speech Language Hearing Association Journal, 17,* 39-49.

Durand, V. M., & Carr, E. G. (1992). An analysis of maintenance following functional communication training. *Journal of Applied Behavior Analysis, 25,* 777-794.

English, K., Goldstein, H., Shafer, K., & Kaczmarek, L. (1997). Promoting interactions among preschoolers with and without disabilities: Effects of a buddy skills-training program. *Exceptional Children, 63,* 229-243.

Fey, M. E., Catts, H. W., & Larrivee, L. S. (1995). Preparing preschoolers for the academic and social challenges of school. In M. E. Fey, J. Windsor, & S. F. Warren (Eds.), *Language intervention: Preschool through the elementary years* (pp. 3-37). Baltimore: Brookes.

Fey, M. E., Cleave, P. L., Long, S. H., & Hughes, D. L. (1993). Two approaches to the facilitation of grammar in children with language impairment: An experimental evaluation. *Journal of Speech and Hearing Research, 36,* 141-157.

Filla, A., Wolery, M., & Anthony, L. (1999). Promoting children's conversations during play with adult prompts. *Journal of Early Intervention, 22,* 93-108.

Girolametto, L., Pearce, P., & Weitzman, E. (1996). Interactive focused stimulation for toddlers with expressive vocabulary delays. *Journal of Speech and Hearing Research, 39,* 1274-1283.

Glidden, L M., & Warner, D. A. (1982). Research on imitation in mentally retarded persons: Theory-bound or ecological validity run amuck? *Applied Research in Mental Retardation, 3,* 383-395.

Goldstein, H., & Brown, W. H. (1989). Observational learning of receptive and expressive language by handicapped preschool children. *Education and Treatment of Children, 12,* 5-37.

Goldstein, H., & Cisar, C. L. (1992). Promoting interaction during sociodramatic play: Teaching scripts to typical preschoolers and classmates with handicaps. *Journal of Applied Behavior Analysis, 25,* 265-280.

Goldstein, H., English, K., Shafer, K., & Kaczmarek, L. (1997). Interaction among preschoolers with and without disabilities: Effects of across-the-day peer intervention. *Journal of Speech, Language, and Hearing Research, 40,* 33-48.

Goldstein, H., & Kaczmarek, L. (1992). Promoting communicative interaction among children in integrated intervention settings. In S. F. Warren & J. Reichle (Eds.), *Communication and language intervention series: Vol. 1. Causes and effects in communication and language intervention* (pp. 81-112). Baltimore: Brookes.

Goldstein, H., Kaczmarek, L., Pennington, R., & Shafer, K. (1992). Peer-mediated intervention: Attending to, commenting on, and acknowledging the behavior of preschoolers with autism. *Journal of Applied Behavior Analysis, 25,* 289-305.

Goldstein, H., & Mousetis, L. (1989). Generalized language learning by children with severe mental retardation: Effects of peer's expressive modeling. *Journal of Applied Behavior Analysis, 22,* 245-259.

Goldstein, H., & Wickstrom, S. (1986). Peer intervention effects on communication interaction among handicapped and nonhandicapped preschoolers. *Journal of Applied Behavior Analysis, 19,* 209-214.

Guralnick, M. J. (1997). *The effectiveness of early intervention.* Baltimore: Brookes.

Halle, J. W., Marshall, A. M., & Spradlin, J. E. (1979). Time delay: A technique to increase language use and facilitate generalization in retarded children. *Journal of Applied Behavior Analysis, 12,* 431-439.

Haring, T. G., & Lovinger, L. (1989). Promoting social interaction through teaching generalized play initiation responses to preschool children with autism. *Journal of the Association for Persons with Severe Handicaps, 14*(1), 58-67.

Hart, B. M., & Risley, T. R. (1975). Incidental teaching of language in the preschool. *Journal of Applied Behavior Analysis, 8,* 411-420.

Hart, B. M., & Risley, T. R. (1995). *Meaningful differences in the everyday experience of young American children.* Baltimore: Brookes.

Hart, B. M., & Risley, T. R. (1999). *The social world of children: Learning to talk.* Baltimore: Brookes.

Hemmeter, M. L., & Kaiser, A. P. (1994). Enhanced Milieu Teaching: Effects of parent-implemented language intervention. *Journal of Early Intervention, 18,* 269-289.

Hepting, N. H., & Goldstein, H. (1996a). Requesting by preschoolers with developmental disabilities: Videotape self-modeling and learning of new linguistic structures. *Topics in Early Childhood Special Education, 16,* 407-427.

Hepting, N., & Goldstein, H. (1996b). What's "natural" about naturalistic language intervention? *Journal of Early Intervention, 20,* 250-264.

Hockenberger, E. H., Goldstein, H., & Haas, L. S. (1999). Effects of commenting during joint book reading by mothers with low SES. *Topics in Early Childhood Special Education, 19,* 15-27.

Hosford, R. E. (1980). Self-as-model: A cognitive social learning technique. *The Counseling Psychologist, 9,* 45-62.

Huebner, C. E. (2000). Promoting toddlers' language development through community-based intervention. *Journal of Applied Developmental Psychology 21,* 513-535.

Hwang, B., & Hughes, C. (2000). Increasing early social-communicative skills of preverbal preschool children with autism through social interactive training. *Journal of the Association for Persons with Severe Handicaps, 25,* 18-28.

Ingenmey, R., & Van Houten, R. (1991). Using time delay to promote spontaneous speech in an autistic child. *Journal of Applied Behavior Analysis, 24,* 591-596.

James, S. D., & Egel, A. L. (1986). A direct prompting strategy for increasing reciprocal interactions between handicapped and nonhandicapped siblings. *Journal of Applied Behavior Analysis, 19,* 173-186.

Justice, L. M., & Ezell, H. K. (2000). Enhancing children's print and word awareness through home-based parent intervention. *American Journal of Speech-Language Pathology, 9,* 257-269.

Kaiser, A. P., Hancock, T. B., & Nietfeld, J. P. (2000). The effects of parent-implemented Enhanced Milieu Teaching on the social communication of children who have autism. *Early Education & Development, 11,* 423-446.

Kaiser, A. P., Hemmeter, M. L., Ostrosky, M., Fisher, R., Yoder, P., & Keefer, M. (1996). The effects of teaching parents to use responsive interaction strategies. *Topics in Early Childhood Special Education, 16,* 375-406.

Kaiser, A. P., Yoder, P. J., & Keetz, A. (1992). Evaluating milieu teaching. In S. F. Warren and J. Reichle (Eds.), *Causes and effects in communication and language intervention* (pp. 9-47). Baltimore: Brookes.

Kasari, C., Sigman, M., Mundy, P., & Yirmiya, N. (1990). Affective sharing in the context of joint attention interactions of normal, autistic and mentally retarded children. *Journal of Autism and Developmental Disorders, 20,* 87-100.

Koegel, R. L., Camarata, S., Koegel, L. K., Ben-Tall, A., & Smith, A. E. (1998). Increasing speech intelligibility in children with autism. *Journal of Autism and Developmental Disorders, 28,* 241-251.

Koegel, R. L., Camarata, S., Valdez-Menchaca, & Koegel, L. (1998). Setting generalization of question-asking by children with autism. *American Journal on Mental Retardation, 102,* 346-357.

Koegel, R. L., Koegel, L. K., & Surratt, A. (1992). Language intervention and disruptive behavior in preschool children with autism. *Journal of Autism and Developmental Disorders, 22,* 141-153.

Koegel, R. L., O'Dell, M. C., & Koegel, L. K. (1987). A natural language teaching paradigm for nonverbal autistic children. *Journal of Autism & Developmental Disorders, 17,* 187-200.

Kohler, F. W., & Strain, P. S. (1999) Maximizing peer-mediated resources in integrated preschool classrooms. *Topics in Early Childhood Special Education, 19,* 92-102.

Krantz, P. J., & McClannahan, L. E. (1993). Teaching children with autism to initiate to peers: Effects of a script-fading procedure. *Journal of Applied Behavior Analysis, 26,* 121-132.

Laski, K., Charlop, M., & Schreibman, L. (1988). Training parents to use the natural language paradigm to increase their autistic children's speech. *Journal of Applied Behavior Analysis, 21,* 391–400.

LeBlanc, J., Etzel, B., & Domash, M. (1978). A functional curriculum for early intervention. In K. E. Allen, V. A. Holm, & R. L. Schiefelbusch (Eds.), *Early intervention—A team approach* (pp. 331–381). Baltimore: University Park Press.

Leonard, L. B. (1981). Facilitating linguistic skills in children with specific language impairment. *Applied Psycholinguistics, 2,* 89–118.

Leonard, L. B., Schwartz, R., Chapman, K., Rowan, L., Prelock, P., Terrell, B., Weiss, A., & Messick, C. (1982). Early lexical acquisition in children with specific language impairment. *Journal of Speech and Hearing Research, 25,* 554–559.

Lonigan, C. J., Bacon, K. D., Phillips, B. M., Cantor, B. G., Anthony, J. L., & Goldstein, H. (in press). Evaluation of a computer-assisted instruction phonological sensitivity program with preschool children at-risk for reading problems. *Journal of Early Intervention.*

Lonigan, C. J., Burgess, S. R., & Anthony, J. L. (2000). Development of emergent literacy and early reading skills in preschool children: Evidence from a latent variable longitudinal study. *Developmental Psychology, 36,* 596–613.

Lonigan, C. J., Burgess, S. R., Anthony, J. L., & Barker, T. A. (1998). Development of phonological sensitivity in two- to five-year-old children. *Journal of Educational Psychology, 90,* 294–311.

Lonigan, C. J., & Whitehurst, G. J. (1998). Relative efficacy of parent and teacher involvement in a shared-reading intervention for preschool children from low-income backgrounds. *Early Childhood Research Quarterly, 17,* 265–292.

Lundberg, I., Frost, J., & Petersen, O. (1988). Effects of an extensive program for stimulating phonological awareness in preschool children. *Reading Research Quarterly, 23,* 263–284.

MacLean, M., Bryant, P., & Bradley, L. (1987). Rhymes, nursery rhymes, and reading in early childhood. *Merrill-Palmer Quarterly, 33,* 255–282.

Matson, J. L., Sevin, J. A., Box, M. L., Francis, K. L., & Sevin, B. M. (1993). An evaluation of two methods for increasing self-initiated verbalizations in autistic children. *Journal of Applied Behavior Analysis, 26,* 389–398.

McEvoy, M. A., Nordquist, V. M., Twardosz, S., Heckaman, K., Wehby, J. H., & Denny, R. K. (1988). Promoting autistic children's peer interaction in an integrated early childhood setting using affection activities. *Journal of Applied Behavior Analysis, 21,* 193–200.

McGee, G. C., Almeida, M. C., Sulzer-Azaroff, B., & Feldman, R. S. (1992). Promoting reciprocal interactions via peer incidental teaching. *Journal of Applied Behavior Analysis, 25,* 117–126.

McGee, G. G., Krantz, P. J., & McClannahan, L. E. (1985). The facilitative effects of incidental teaching on preposition use by autistic children. *Journal of Applied Behavior Analysis, 18,* 17–31.

McGee, G. G., Morrier, M. J., & Daly, T. (1999). An incidental teaching approach to early intervention for toddlers with autism. *Journal of the Association for Persons with Severe Handicaps, 24,* 133–146.

McLean, L. K., & Cripe, J. W. (1997). The effectiveness of early intervention for children with communication disorders. In M. Guralnick (Ed.), *The Effectiveness of Early Intervention.* Baltimore: Brookes.

McLean, J., & Snyder-McLean, L. (1999). *How children learn language.* San Diego: Singular.

McLean, M., & Vincent, L. (1984). The use of expansions as a language intervention technique in the natural environment. *Journal of the Division for Early Childhood, 9,* 57–66.

Odom, S. L., McConnell, S. R., McEvoy, M. A., Peterson, C., Ostrosky, M., Chandler, L. K., Spicuzza, R. J., Skellenger, A., Creighton, M., & Favazza, P. C. (1999). Relative effects of interventions supporting the social competence of young children with disabilities. *Topics in Early Childhood Special Education, 19,* 75–91.

Olswang, L. B., Bain, B. A., & Johnson, G. A. (1992). Using dynamic assessment with children with language disorders. In S. F. Warren & J. Reichle (Eds.), *Causes and effects in communication and language intervention* (pp. 187–215). Baltimore: Brookes.

Osnes, P. G., Guevremont, D. C., & Stokes, T. F. (1986). If I say I'll talk more, then I will: Correspondence training to increase peer-directed talk by socially withdrawn children. *Behavior Modification, 10,* 287–299.

Owens, R. E. (1998). *Language disorders: A functional approach to assessment and intervention* (3rd ed.). Boston: Allyn and Bacon.

Parker, J. G., & Asher, S. R. (1987). Peer relations and later personal adjustment: Are low-accepted children at risk? *Psychological Bulletin, 102,* 357–389.

Raz, I. S., & Bryant, P. (1990). Social background, phonological awareness, and children's reading. *British Journal of Developmental Psychology, 8,* 209–225.

Reid, J. B., & Patterson, G. R. (1991). Early prevention and intervention with conduct problems: A social interactional model for the integration of research and practice. In G. Stoner, M. R. Shinn, & H. M. Walker (Eds.), *Interventions for achievement and behavior problems* (pp. 715–739). Silver Spring, MD: National Association of School Psychologists.

Rosekrans, M. A. (1967). Imitation in children as a function of perceived similarity to a social model and vicarious reinforcement. *Journal of Personality and Social Psychology, 7,* 307–315.

Sainato, D. A., Goldstein, H., & Strain, P. S. (1992). Effects of self-evaluation on preschool children's use of social interaction strategies with their classmates with autism. *Journal of Applied Behavior Analysis, 25,* 127–141.

Sameroff, A., & Chandler, M. (1975). Reproductive risk and the continuum of caretaking causality. In F. Horowitz (Ed.)., *Review of Child Development Research, Vol. 4* (pp. 187–244). Chicago: University of Chicago Press.

Sameroff, A., & Fiese, B. H. (1990) Transactional regulation and early intervention. In S. J. Meisels & J. P. Shonkoff (Eds.), *Handbook of early childhood intervention* (pp. 119-149). New York: Cambridge University Press.

Schussler, N. G., & Spradlin, J. E. (1991). Assessment of stimuli controlling the requests of students with severe mental retardation during a snack routine. *Journal of Applied Behavior Analysis, 24,* 791-797.

Schwartz, I. S., Anderson, S. R., & Halle, J. W. (1989). Training teachers to use naturalistic time delay: Effects on teacher behavior and on the language use of students. *Journal of the Association for Persons with Severe Handicaps, 14,* 48-57.

Schwartz, R. G., Chapman, K., Terrell, B. Y., Prelock, P., & Rowan, L. (1985). Facilitating word combination in language-impaired children through discourse structure. *Journal of Speech and Hearing Disorders, 50,* 31-39.

Schwartz, R. G., & Leonard, L. B. (1985). Lexical imitation and acquisition in language-impaired children. *Journal of Speech and Hearing Disorders, 50,* 141-149.

Secan, K. E., Egel, A. L., & Tilley, C. S. (1989). Acquisition, generalization, and maintenance of question-answering skills in autistic children. *Journal of Applied Behavior Analysis, 22,* 181-196.

Snow, C. E., Burns, M. S., & Griffin, P. (Eds.). (1998). *Preventing reading difficulties in young children.* Washington, DC: National Academy Press.

Snow, C. E., Scarborough, H. S., & Burns, M. S. (1999). What speech-language pathologists need to know about early reading. *Topics in Language Disorders, 20,* 48-58.

Tannock, R., Girolametto, L., & Siegel, L. (1992). Language intervention with children who have developmental delays: Effects of an interactive approach. *American Journal on Mental Retardation, 97,* 145-160.

Thal, D., & Tobias, S. (1994). Relationships between language and gesture in normally-developing and late-talking toddlers. *Journal of Speech and Hearing Research, 37,* 157-170.

Torgesen, J. K., & Davis, C. (1996). Individual difference variables that predict response to training in phonological awareness. *Journal of Experimental Child Psychology, 63,* 1-21.

Torgesen, J. K., Morgan, S., & Davis, C. (1992). Effects of two types of phonological awareness training on word learning in kindergarten children. *Journal of Educational Psychology, 84,* 364-370.

Uhry, J. K. & Shepherd, M. J. (1993). Segmentation/spelling instruction as part of a first-grade reading program: Effects on several measures of reading. *Reading Research Quarterly, 28,* 218-233.

Valdez-Menchaca, M. C., & Whitehurst, G. J. (1992). Accelerating language development through picture book reading: A systematic extension to Mexican day-care. *Developmental Psychology, 28,* 1106-1114.

Wacker, D. P., Steege, M. W., Northup, J., Sasso, G., Berg, W., Reimers, T., Cooper, L., Cigrand, K., & Donn, L. (1990). A component analysis of functional communication training across three topographies of severe behavior problems. *Journal of Applied Behavior Analysis, 23,* 417-429.

Wagner, R. K. & Torgesen, J. K. (1987). The nature of phonological processing and its causal role in the acquisition of reading skills. *Psychological Bulletin, 101,* 192-212.

Wagner, R. K., Torgesen, J. K., & Rashotte, C. A. (1994). Development of reading-related phonological processing abilities: New evidence of bidirectional causality from a latent variable longitudinal study. *Developmental Psychology, 30,* 73-87.

Walker, D., Greenwood, C. R., Hart, B., & Carta, J. (1994). Prediction of school outcomes based on early language production and socioeconomic factors. *Child Development, 65,* 606-621.

Walker, H. M., Stieber, S., & O'Neill, R. (1990). Middle school behavioral profiles of antisocial and at-risk control boys: Descriptive and predictive outcomes. *Exceptionality, 2,* 61-77.

Warren, S. F., & Horn, E. M. (1996). Generalization issues in providing integrated services. In R. A. McWilliam (Ed.), *Rethinking pull-out services in early intervention* (pp. 49-69). Baltimore: Brookes.

Warren, S. F., McQuarter, R. J., & Rogers-Warren, A. K. (1984). The effects of mands and models on the speech of unresponsive language-delayed preschool children. *Journal of Speech & Hearing Disorders, 49,* 43-52.

Wetherby, A. M., Prizant, B. M., & Schuler, A. L. (2000). Understanding the nature of communication and language impairments. In A. M. Wetherby & B. M. Prizant (Eds.), *Autism spectrum disorders: A transactional developmental perspective* (pp. 109-141). Baltimore: Brookes.

Whitehurst, G. J., Arnold, D. S., Epstein, J. N., Angell, A. L., Smith, M., & Fischel, J. E. (1994). A picture book reading intervention in day care and home for children from low-income families. *Developmental Psychology, 30,* 679-689.

Whitehurst, G. J., Falco, F., Lonigan, C. J., Fischel, J. E., DeBaryshe, B. D., Valdez-Menchaca, M. C., & Caulfield, M. (1988). Accelerating language development through picture-book reading. *Developmental Psychology, 24,* 552-558.

Whitehurst, G. J., & Lonigan, C. J. (1998). Child development and emergent literacy. *Child Development, 68,* 848-872.

Wickstrom-Kane, S., & Goldstein, H. (1999). Communication assessment and intervention to address challenging behavior in toddlers. *Topics in Language Disorders, 19,* 70-89.

Wilcox, M. J., Kouri, T. A., & Caswell, S. B. (1991). Early language intervention: A comparison of classroom and individual treatment. *American Journal of Speech-Language Pathology, 1,* 49-62.

Woods-Cripe, J., & Venn, M. L. (1997). Family-guided routines for early intervention services. *Young Exceptional Children, 1*(1), 18-26.

Yoder, P. J., Kaiser, A. P., Goldstein, H., Alpert, C., Mousetis, L., Kaczmarek, L., & Fischer, R. (1995). An exploratory comparison of milieu teaching and responsive interaction in classroom applications. *Journal of Early Intervention, 19,* 218-242.

Yoder, P. J., & Warren, S. F. (1999). Facilitating self-initiated proto-declaratives and proto-imperatives in prelinguistic children with developmental disabilities. *Journal of Early Intervention, 22,* 337-354.

Yoder, P. J., Warren, S. F., Kim, K., & Gazdag, G. E. (1994). Facilitating prelinguistic communication skills in young children with developmental delay II: Systematic replication and extension. *Journal of Speech and Hearing Research, 37,* 841–851.

AUTHOR'S NOTE

Address for Correspondence: Department of Communication Disorders, 107 Regional Rehab Center, Florida State University, Tallahassee, FL 32306-1200. Phone: (850) 644-2238; E-mail: *hgoldste@garnet.acns.fsu.edu, jwoods@garnet.acns.fsu.edu*

CHAPTER 19

Promoting Social Development in Preschool Classrooms

Scott R. McConnell, Kristen N. Missall,
Benjamin Silberglitt, and Mary A. McEvoy
Early Childhood Research Institute
Center on Early Education and Development
University of Minnesota

INTRODUCTION

Social interaction is a basic foundation of human functioning. From the earliest days of a child's life, when interactions begin, centered around meeting basic human needs, social interaction sets the context for much of child development (Odom, McConnell, & McEvoy, 1992). Because of its centrality to almost all other human adaptation and behavior, there is a strong developmental and survival imperative for social interaction.

Empirically, we know that social interaction and social development begin in the earliest months of life, with behaviors and competencies continuing to elaborate and emerge over a number of years (Hartup, 1983). Further, social interaction functions as a "keystone" of development, with social behaviors setting the occasion for development in other domains like language, cognition, and motor performance (Guralnick, 1992).

The development of social interaction skills in preschool children is of central importance to teachers and parents (Odom, McConnell, & Chandler, 1994; Priest et al., in press). There is some evidence to suggest long-term negative consequences for deficits and delays in social development for preschoolers (Guralnick, 1992; Odom, McConnell, & McEvoy, 1992), and emerging evidence that social interaction interventions provided in preschool can have long-term benefit for treated children (Odom et al., 1999). As a result, there is strong and continued interest among school psychologists in assessing, identifying, and treating social interaction skill deficits and social competence problems in the preschool years.

The purpose of this chapter is to describe interventions that enhance the development of high-quality peer relations for preschool-aged children, with a special emphasis on at-risk children. We assume the primary readers of this chapter are practicing school psychologists and students training to be school psychologists who possess general background and knowledge in both child development and classroom-based intervention. We also assume readers of this chapter are interested in gaining more in-depth knowledge of social development and social interaction interventions for preschool children, including both core concepts and research on specific interventions. As a result, we intend this chapter as a scholarly review of selected factors affecting the social development of preschool children and a detailed review of intervention options (and related research) with this population.

What Is "Social Development" and Why Is It Important?

Social development is both the process and product of acquiring and elaborating behaviors and competencies that engage others in productive, reinforcing, and reciprocal interactions. Perhaps driven by its survival value, social development begins in early infancy with a baby's response to social and other stimuli from caregivers (Bell, 1968; Cairns, Green, & MacConbie, 1980). Elaboration of these initial responses occurs quickly, with young children responding to more and varied types of social behaviors from caregivers, and beginning to direct visual, vocal, and gestural behaviors to others in ways that initiate and maintain social interaction. As development continues in other domains, children's social behaviors also continue to develop; over time, preschool children initiate and respond to social bids from other children and begin to extend and elaborate their ongoing interactions with adults and children into a set of behaviors we typically call "play."

Social development in the preschool years serves as a "foundation," both for other developmental domains and for continued social development after preschool. Language, motor, and cognitive development all occur during (and may indeed be dependent upon) social interaction (Hart & Risley, 1996; Hartup, 1983). In this sense, social interaction can be seen as setting the occasion for naturally occurring opportunities to learn, refine, and expand children's repertoires across other important domains of development.

Evidence from multiple sources suggests that social development in preschool years establishes a developmental trajectory for performance and competence in later years. In other words, measures of the quality and reciprocity of interactions and relations in late infancy (often referred to as attachment) are associated with a variety of later social and behavioral outcomes (Hartup, 1983; LaFreniere & Sroufe, 1985). Social interaction rates increase over time (Greenwood, Walker, Todd, & Hops, 1981), social play increases in complexity and amount, and stable play partners and friendships emerge. Social development in preschool is instrumental in children's acquisition of other important skills and competencies. Social skills and behaviors mastered in preschool serve, both directly and indirectly, as essential elements of social functioning in home, school, and community settings. Social competence is a keystone to academic success and school adjustment in early elementary school (Ladd & Coleman, 1997; Missall, 2000), and later success in academic and vocational settings. Retrospective analyses suggest that the quality and extent of social relations and friendships in early childhood are related to a variety of long-term outcomes, including vocational and social adaptation (McConnell & Odom, 1986).

In summary, social development begins soon after a child's birth and continues beyond the preschool years. It also relates closely, in functional and reciprocal ways, to development in other domains. A large body of empirical research documents both the short- and long-term consequences of deficits and delays in social development, and a growing body of research describes components of effective intervention. The net effect is that from a prevention and early intervention perspective, monitoring and intervention for social development problems can and should start in the preschool years.

BASIC TERMS

What Is Social Competence?

Researchers and reviewers agree that attainment of competent social behaviors is essential for a child's future development and ultimate success in American education and society (Krumboltz, Ford, Nichols, & Wentzel, 1987; Saunders & Green, 1993; Wentzel, 1991). However, there is no singularly accepted definition of "social competence." Social competence has been variously defined as a complex construct of human interaction that involves the interrelationship of cognitive, social, and biological factors (Saunders & Green, 1993; Masten et al., 1995) or as a developmental construct that includes the capacity to initiate, develop, and maintain satisfying relationships with others, especially peers (Katz, 1987). Some researchers have argued that social competence is reflected in the effectiveness and appropriateness of children's interactions with others, rather than the frequency or quality of the interactions (Guralnick, 1992; Pellegrini & Glickman, 1990; Ross & Rogers, 1990; Wright, 1980), whereas others focus more closely on the frequency or rate of various components of interaction and social behavior (Greenwood et al., 1981; McEvoy, Odom, & McConnell, 1992; Tremblay, Strain, Hendrickson, & Shores, 1981). Still others have related the level of social competence to the cognitive ability of the child (Bjorkland, 1989; Bronfenbrenner, 1979).

Odom and McConnell (1985) proposed a performance-based, empirical model of social *competence* in which multiple people (e.g., teachers, parents, peers, independent observers) with a variety of perspectives evaluate a child's social behaviors. While this model has links to theoretical analyses (Hops, 1983; McFall, 1982), empirical analyses also suggest the value and validity of this approach (McConnell & Odom, 1999; Odom et al., 1999). In this performance-based model, social competence is defined as "the interpersonal social performance of children with other children or adults as judged by significant social agents in the child's environment" (Odom & McConnell, 1985, p. 9).

One might argue that "competence" literally reflects skill mastery and is only discernable by examining behavior (see Foulks & Morrow, 1989; Gilbert, 1978). In our work, we view competence and skills as not interchangeable concepts. Rather, *compe-*

tence is a general evaluative term referring to the quality or adequacy of a person's overall performance in a particular task, and *skills* are the specific abilities required to perform competently at a task (McFall, 1982). By assuming this perspective, we come to view social competence as a terminal objective that is achieved most directly by acquiring social skills.

What Is Social Interaction?

Social interaction is the foundation upon which children develop social competence (Gresham, 1997; Hartup, 1983; Odom et al., 1992; Piaget, 1926). Social interaction can be defined as the direct exchange of words, gestures, toys, or other materials between two or more children. While specific target behaviors have been identified that are associated with normative levels of social interaction (see the following section), the *amount of time* that a child spends in social interaction appears to be singularly important in determining social competence (Greenwood et al., 1981; McConnell & Odom, 1999) and may be a sensitive measure of a child's level of social development (McEvoy, Silberglitt, Novak, & Priest, 2000).

What Are Social Skills?

Social skills are discrete elements of social behavior. While there are a variety of overlapping definitions of social skills reported in the professional literature (Walker, Colvin, & Ramsey, 1995), Walker and his colleagues (Walker et al., 1983) define social skills as a set of behaviors that (a) an individual demonstrates to initiate and maintain positive social relationships, (b) contribute to peer acceptance and to a satisfactory school adjustment, and (c) are used by an individual to cope effectively and adaptively in a range of social environments.

The concept of social skills commonly fits within one of two general conceptual models: a trait model and a molecular-behavioral model (McFall, 1982). When the concept of social skill is used in a trait model, it is treated as a hypothetical construct referring to a general, underlying personality characteristic that is reasonably stable over time and relatively consistent across situations. Thus, in trait models, social skills are not directly observable but are inferred by observing children in one or more social situations. That is, the more adequately a person performs in a social situation, the higher that individual's inferred level of social skills. Two examples of trait-like social skills are attachment and social withdrawal. While specific definitions of attachment differ, the general notion is that early experiences (and, to some extent, personal characteristics) determine the extent to which a child has a "safe and secure base" for exploring new situations and participating socially (c.f., Ainsworth, Blehar, Waters, & Wall, 1978); social performance in later life is presumed to be largely a product of the child's attachment history, a stable characteristic. Similarly, social withdrawal is seen by some theorists and researchers as a stable feature, perhaps based on temperament or other person-specific characteristics, that influences much of a child's social performance (Hartup, 1983).

In the *molecular model,* social skills are defined as specific, observable units of *behavior*, which are the building blocks of the individual's overall performance in each interpersonal situation. Social skills are viewed as learned behaviors in specific situations. Thus, a person who performs skillfully today in a particular situation may not do so *tomorrow*, although there is likely to be some positive correlation in performance over time as long as the situation remains unchanged.

Empirical research has identified a variety of specific social skills, with evidence of the functional importance of each. Social skills include a variety of *initiations,* or behaviors that begin social interactions (McEvoy et al., 1992; Tremblay et al., 1981) and *social responses,* or behaviors that serve to continue social interactions after another's initiation (Greenwood et al., 1981). Additionally, molecular analyses have identified a variety of social skills that reflect relations between the behaviors of interacting children, such as the likelihood of responses to others' initiations or the degree of reciprocity between social initiations made and those initiations received (Greenwood et al., 1981; Walker, Greenwood, Hops, & Todd, 1979).

A variety of "prosocial" or desirable social skills have also been identified. For example, prosocial skills in the classroom include: cooperation and self-control (e.g., sharing materials, following classroom rules, controlling temper) (Agostin & Bain, 1997; Foulks & Morrow, 1989); assertiveness, initiative, and an absence of disruptive and hostile-aggressive behaviors (Gresham, 1997; Harper, Guidubaldi, & Kehle, 1978; Taylor & Trickett, 1989); cooperative pretend play skills (Odom, Peterson, McConnell, & Ostrosky, 1990; Taylor & Machida, 1994); and negotiation skills (Piaget, 1926).

Much of the work on specific, observable social skills for preschool children has emphasized the interactional and interpersonal nature of social interaction, and has adopted an explicit, environmental approach to assessment and intervention that might best be described as "behavioral" or "behavior analytic" (McConnell, McEvoy, & Odom, 1992; McEvoy et al., 1992; Odom & McConnell, 1992; Odom, McConnell, & McEvoy, 1992; Strain, Odom, & McConnell, 1984). In this explicit, behavioral approach, social skills that function to initiate, maintain, and produce reinforcing social interactions and relations have been identified through descriptive and experimental work. Additional research has identified instructional and ecological interventions that promote learning and using these skills by preschool children (McEvoy et al., 1992), as well as factors that influence the likelihood that intervention procedures will be implemented (Peterson & McConnell, 1996). Information about specific social skills and effective intervention tactics has then been combined into standardized intervention programs (Vanderbilt-Minnesota Social Interaction Project, 1993) that can be implemented in preschool classroom settings.

Relations Between Social Development and Other Domains

Social Competence and Communicative Competence

Social development and social competence are closely entwined with language development and communicative competence (Hazen & Black, 1989). Language skills develop in a social context and are the means by which children initiate, respond, and maintain social interactions. Indeed, the appropriate use of language skills can be seen as a social skill. Many researchers and practitioners view language development as an element of social development (Gallagher, 1991; Guralnick, 1992; Windsor, 1995).

Consequently, it should come as no surprise that children with language difficulties often experience social difficulties. The exact relations between early oral language impairment and social problems are unclear (Windsor, 1995). However, there is evidence that social problems among children with significant language impairments are well established during the preschool years (Hadley & Rice, 1991; Rice, 1993). In fact, many children with significant language impairments exhibit deficient social interaction skills, including disruptive behaviors such as hitting and biting (O'Neill & Reichle, 1993). Research suggests that these challenging behaviors serve communicative functions and decrease when more socially appropriate forms of communication are learned (Carr & Durand, 1985; Hunt, Alwell, Goetz, & Sailor, 1990).

Social Competence and Antisocial Behavior

Accumulated research demonstrates that antisocial behavior can be, to some extent, predicted (and its development might be influenced) by deficits or delays in development of social skills. Specific risk or predictive factors include social skill deficits (Patterson, Reid, & Dishion, 1992; Walker & McConnell, 1995); significantly lower levels of academic engagement (Walker, Shinn, O'Neill, & Ramsey, 1987); measured inappropriate behaviors such as noncompliance, negative verbalizations or vocalizations, and off-task behavior (Charlebois, LeBlanc, Gagnon, & Larivee, 1994); and higher rates of negative interactions than peers during free play (Walker, Hops, & Greenwood, 1993).

Children as young as age 3–4 can show early indicators, or "soft signs," of antisocial behavior patterns (Walker et al., 1995). For many children, such behavior patterns do not change over time; rather, antisocial behavior becomes more durable and resistant to treatment after the age of about 8 years (Mayer, 1995). Available data indicate approximately half of all antisocial children go on to become adolescent delinquent offenders, and one-half to three-quarters of adolescent offenders become adult criminals (Patterson, DeBaryshe, & Ramsey, 1989).

Social Competence and Academic Performance

Schools play an important role in the development of children's social competence. The literature indicates that teachers are sensitive to individual differences in classroom conduct, value socially competent behavior, and spend time teaching their students how to behave and act responsibly (Doyle, 1986; Wentzel, 1991; Walker & McConnell, 1995). Teachers are more appreciative and positive toward students they rate as cooperative and persistent. However, students rated as less competent (e.g., more off task, more disruptive) receive less one-on-one instruction than other students (Bursuck & Asher, 1986; Walker et al., 1995).

Children with early social difficulties are at a significant risk for experiencing later academic difficulties and school maladjustment (Hinshaw, 1992; Masten et al., 1995). For example, antisocial behavior is often related to reading problems and poor peer relations in elementary grades, and with academic problems later in adolescence (Loeber, 1990; Masten & Coatsworth, 1995). It is conceivable that, as early as kindergarten, poor peer relations and negative school attitudes initiate a cycle of problematic outcomes for children, including academic disengagement, low self-esteem, withdrawal from the school environment, and so on, (Ladd & Coleman, 1997).

Summary of Relations Among Developmental Domains

While experimental evidence is still sketchy, there is some reason to expect that social competence and skills serve as protective factors, both promoting development in desired domains (e.g., language) and inhibiting development in less-desired domains (e.g., antisocial behavior). In particular, children who effectively engage the social environment, emit high rates of social desirable behaviors, receive high rates of responses to these behaviors, and secure high rates of reinforcement for this participation from the social environment are expected to continue on this developmental path, acquiring new skills and competencies as opportunities (and developmental expectations) present themselves.

DESCRIPTIVE RESEARCH ON SOCIAL DEVELOPMENT

A variety of theoretical and conceptual models have been offered for describing social development of young children (e.g., Cairns et al., 1980; Guralnick, 1992; Hartup, 1983). In general, these models describe the universality of social development and its fundamental importance to the health and adaptation of an individual and its species. These models also commonly feature: (a) multi-level descriptions of skill, performance, or competence in the social domain, extending from specific behaviors, characteristics, or responses to more molar traits or competencies; (b) interactional or transactional models of *development, in which, for example* a child's change *and development* are considered to occur within the context of ongoing social interactions and social relationships; (c) a "developmental" model that describes either aggregated change over time or more stage-like transitions, but in either case assumes the form and/or frequency of child behavior changing over time; and (d) the primacy of social relationships, with adults or children, as important contributors to and outcomes of social development.

Several models of social development might be described as "ecobehavioral" (Schroeder, 1990). An ecobehavioral model of social development has four essential features. First, this model suggests that acquisition of social behaviors (and elaborated forms of social interaction and social relationships) typically occurs for all children through naturally occurring opportunities for learning. Second, this model focuses on interactions between the developing child and parents, caregivers, and other children that provide these opportunities for learning, and on ecological variables (from proximal, like materials and activities, to distal, such as program arrangements and developmental history) that affect the quality and frequency of these opportunities. Third, this model directs attention to individual and group characteristics that may interact with development, given the rate and quality of "appropriate" opportunities and consequences for social interaction over time. Specifically, it appears that social interaction and social relationship deficits are characteristic of children with a variety of disabilities, most notably autism (Odom, Chandler, Ostrovsky, McConnell, & Reaney, 1992; Sigman & Ruskin, 1999) and mental retardation (Guralnick, 1992). These characteristic differences may also interact with dominant treatment models (e.g., segregated classrooms for children with disabilities) in ways that further influence the course of social development. Also, individual characteristics (e.g., language delays or behavioral excesses such as stereotypy or aggression) may further influence the frequency and type of social interactions, and thus further compound effects on social development.

Finally, this ecobehavioral model is fundamentally "developmental," suggesting that a child's future opportunities for development are influenced or constrained by previous development. In this view, then, social skills and competencies aggregate and elaborate over opportunities and time; acquisition, generalization, or elaboration of new responses and competencies requires, in many instances, the previous acquisition of more fundamental skills (Guralnick, 1992; Odom, McConnell, & McEvoy, 1992). For instance, children who demonstrate low frequencies of social initiations to peers have lower overall rates of social interaction, and thus are likely to have fewer opportunities for encountering social conflict and acquiring skills for resolving this conflict appropriately.

The characteristics of child experiences at different stages co-mingle to create mechanisms for, and consequences of, social development. While detailed review of these age-and-stage characteristics is not possible here, an overview of these factors is summarized in Table 1.

Several common features can be drawn from the information in Table 1. First, there is continued development in rate, type, and elaboration of individual social responses across the preschool and early elementary years. For instance, social initiations begin as instances of mutual gaze or joint attention (Moore & Dunham, 1995); visual initiations never "disappear" from a child's repertoire, but rather this early skill is joined over time by gesture/motor and vocal/verbal initiations. As these new behaviors are learned, they both increase in rate and generalize across responses (i.e., adding new topographies that lead to social interaction) and settings (i.e., skills are emitted in a greater variety of situations, with new social partners). Indeed, during this age period, *social development* is marked by rapid and ongoing increases and elaborations in social responding.

Second, children's social skills develop in ways that closely track (and are likely influenced by) the social settings in which they spend their time. For instance, as children have access to same-age peers, they also begin to develop play and peer interaction

TABLE 1

Characteristics of Social Development by Age Period

	Infancy and toddlerhood	Preschool	Kindergarten/ early elementary
Social settings and opportunities	Settings limited to home or small groups	Home, community settings, with initial opportunities for interaction with agemates in stable play groups (especially in congregate care); increasing mobility and access to more varied materials and activities	Near-universal enrollment in congregate educational settings, with access to same-age peers; continued access to parents, siblings, and same-age community peers; increasing mobility and access to wider range of materials and child-directed activities
Social partners	Parents and adult caregivers	Parents and adult caregivers; siblings; same-age peers	Parents and adult caregivers; siblings; same-age and older/younger peers
Emergent skills	Social and joint attention; vocal, gestural initiations; social communication	Play and friendships; social conventions; social interaction embedded in many activities	Differentiated peer- and teacher-preferred social behaviors; social conventions; organized, rule-governed play
Characteristics of social interaction	Higher proportion of adult-initiated interaction; increasing rate of social interaction	Increasing/asymptotic rate of social interaction; approaching parity in initiations made and received	Slow/little increase in overall interaction rate; elaboration of settings and activities, with increased balance between informal and organized play
Characteristics of social competence	Increasing balance in initiations; increasing elaboration of social responses (visual, motor, vocal/verbal)	High degree of reciprocity in type, valence of social behaviors; increasing elaboration of social responses; reciprocal influence of social behaviors and other responses	High degree of reciprocity in type, valence of social behaviors; continued elaboration of social responses, including behaviors embedded in formal and informal activities.

skills. Transitions across social settings (e.g., from home to day care) provide both challenge and opportunity for the social development of individual children.

Third, social behaviors and competencies emerge and accrete over time. The earliest social interactions occur with parents, and children continue to interact with parents over this age range. At the same time, however, children add new social responses to their interactions with parents, and add new social partners in their interactions across days. In this way, social development builds later–developing skills on those developed earlier in a child's life.

Factors That May Affect Social Development Outcomes

Developmental Disability

As a group, children with developmental and other disabilities are at risk for lower rates of social interaction and delays or deficits in the development of social competencies (Odom, McConnell, & McEvoy, 1992; Odom et al., 1990). These delays and deficits are noted for children in early childhood special education generally, as well as children in particular diagnostic groups (e.g., Guralnick & Groom, 1988; Lord, 1993; Lord & Magill-Evans, 1995; Sigman & Ruskin, 1999).

Specific reasons for these delays, and the mechanisms that may be unique to children with disabilities, are not known. Some have argued that observed deficits and delays are consequences of cognitive or other characteristics associated with particular disabilities (Guralnick, 1992; Sigman, 1994), while others have argued that effects may be due (at least in part) to restricted opportunities and access to social settings (Odom, McConnell & McEvoy, 1992). While empirical or theoretical analyses of potential causes are likely to continue, a pragmatic view of available evidence suggests that children with disabilities, as a class, are at risk for social interaction and social competence deficits and are a reasonable group for further screening and possible early intervention (McEvoy et al., 1992).

Language

As we noted earlier, language delays and social skill deficits are tightly related. In fact, there is both descriptive and experimental evidence that language delay, in and of itself, contributes to social interaction deficits and social competence problems (English, Goldstein, Shafer, & Kaczmarek, 1997; Goldstein et al., 1992; Windsor, 1995). Conceptually, there is strong support for a reciprocal influence between language and social development; and language delays are likely to restrict opportunities for interaction with others, which in turn prevents age-appropriate acquisition and elaboration of social behaviors. As social delays grow, the child's opportunities for social participation decrease, thereby restricting opportunities for language learning. This cycle is likely to continue until intervention is implemented in one or both domains.

INTERVENTION PROCEDURES THAT WORK

Fox, McEvoy, Leech, and Moroney (1990) identified three major types of social interaction interventions that educators can use to promote social interaction between children with social interaction skill deficits and their peers. These procedures include ones that attempt to increase social interaction by manipulating environmental variables, procedures that rely extensively on teacher prompts and use of praise (Child-Specific Interventions), and procedures that rely primarily on peers as intervention change-agents (Peer-Mediated Interventions). These intervention types can also be combined into a more comprehensive intervention package.

These types of intervention differ procedurally and, perhaps, in effectiveness. In this section, we provide a review of the essential features of each major type of social interaction skill intervention, and the supporting research for each.

Environmental Arrangements

Of the different types of social interaction interventions, those that focus on environmental manipulations appear to be the easiest to implement and require the least amount of teacher training (McEvoy et al., 1992). In fact, DeKleyn and Odom (1989) found that effectively organized environments significantly increased peer-to-peer interaction. However, much of this environmental arrangement research has been conducted with children who have disabilities and have concomitant social interaction skills deficits or concerns. Thus, a review of this research is, by definition, a review at the intersection of research in both early *intervention* and early childhood special education.

A number of researchers have examined features of the environment that can be directly manipulated to promote social interaction. Environmental interventions range from manipulating setting factors (such as group size or selection of play materials) to incorporating specific procedures to promote interaction within the context of ongoing preschool activities. In addition, most research in this area has examined the effects of these types of interventions on children in inclusive settings, often contrasting them with the effects of intervention in segregated settings.

Group Size

Much of the research on social interaction interventions for young children has been conducted in preschool classrooms, where much of social interaction occurs in group settings. Early researchers noticed that characteristics of classroom groups appeared to influence social interaction, with special attention to group size. Most of the research on the effects of group size on social interaction has been descriptive and the results equivocal. For example, Smith and Connolly (1976) found that smaller group size correlated with higher rates of imaginative play for preschoolers. Similarly, Vandell and Mueller (1977) found that interaction increased for toddlers when they were in smaller-sized play groups. However, in a more recent evaluation, McCabe et al. (1996) and McCabe, Jenkins, Mills, Dale, and Cole (1999) examined group size effects on the amount and diversity of language and play skills used by preschool children with disabilities. Twenty-four children with disabilities and 24 children without language disabilities were observed during freeplay under differing group size and group composition activities. Results showed that group size and composition did not have significant effects on child social language or cognitive level of play. The authors suggest that variables such as age of and familiarity with peers, gender, or complexity of disability may be mitigating factors. However, it is possible that typically developing peers may not provide a more complex language environment for children with disabilities.

In summary, research on the effects of group size on social interaction produced, at best, weak and inconsistent effects. While the size of children's social play groups has important logistical and safety consequences, and while group size may interact with other aspects of classroom behavior management, there is little reason to believe that varying the size of a child's play group will, in and of itself, affect social interaction and long-term development. Rather, other aspects of the play group—particularly the group's composition—may be more important.

Group Composition

Nothing in the field of early intervention has generated more discussion than the concept of inclusion. In fact, to date, the field has not agreed upon a definition of "inclusion." However, regardless of the definition or feature of interest, a common purpose of all inclusion efforts is to bring young children with and without disabilities into contact with each other (Odom et al., 1999). So, are social interaction interventions more effective in inclusive settings? Odom and McEvoy (1988) point out that inclusive *practice* alone may benefit children with mild disabilities. However, for children with moderate or extensive disabilities, simply providing opportunities for children to play together may be a necessary but not sufficient intervention to promote social development. In fact, McCabe et al. (1999) found that the composition of a play group (segregated or integrated) alone did not affect play. It appears that for most children with disabilities, a comprehensive intervention that includes specific procedures to promote interaction is an important part of an instructional program in inclusive settings.

Types of Materials and Activities

A number of researchers have suggested that the type and quantity of play materials affect social interaction skill development. In a set of classic studies, Quillitch and Risley (1973) and Hendrickson, Strain, Tremblay, and Shores (1981) found that different types of toys promoted social, isolate, or parallel play. Similarly, McCabe et al. (1999) found that play materials significantly influenced the types of young children's play, with the greatest influences in the area of dramatic play.

With respect to the influence of activities on social interactions, Bricker (1995) has described an activity-based instructional format that may be a good setting for social interaction interventions. In short, activity-based interventions are those that adapt typical preschool classroom activities (like circle time, play in a water table, or sociodramatic activities) by (a) adding content that is matched specifically to the current developmental needs of an individual child (e.g., rhyming songs, identifying colors, or elaborating language) and (b) embedding structured and naturally occurring prompts for the child to engage this content (including teacher prompts and requests, and interactions with other children). This activity-based instructional approach allows the teacher to promote interaction during naturally occurring activities, which in turn promotes children's access to "natural" reinforcement of interactions (McConnell, 1987). In a similar vein, there has long been an emphasis on incorporating interventions to promote interaction within the context of preschool games and activities. For example, Rogers-Warren and Baer (1976) used an incidental teaching procedure to teach young children to share and praise. Incidental teaching is a set of procedures in which teachers or parents both structure the environment to elicit language (e.g., placing desired materials in sight but out of reach, or providing high-interest activities that are language-rich) and then using a hierarchical series of prompts to increase rates of child language and interaction (e.g., prompting the child to point to or ask for a preferred item, or asking open-ended questions during high-interest activities). Access to materials and activities was made contingent upon engaging in a positive social behavior. The researchers reported increases in both target behavior and generalization across contexts.

By using another activity-based approach, McEvoy and colleagues (1988) implemented group affection activities to increase the social skills of young children with autism. Prompts for social interaction were included within the context of routine preschool games and songs. For example, children were prompted to "give your friend a high five" or "smile at your friend." Results showed that children with and without disabilities began to interact more frequently during the activity when the intervention was introduced, as well as in later freeplay activities when no intervention was in place. Results similar to these also have been reported by Brown, Ragland, and Fox (1988) and Frea, Craig-Unkefer, Odom, and Johnson (1999). Both studies used variations of McEvoy and colleagues' (1988) procedures, demonstrating the effects of these interventions across other populations of children.

Summary

The early childhood research literature contains a number of effective interventions that can be used to promote social interaction skill development. In choosing an intervention, an educator must take into consideration the level of individual child need, the teacher time required to implement, and the ease of implementation. Environmental interventions represent one class of interventions that typically are easy to implement, thus assuring good fidelity of treatment. While *they* appear to be most effective with children who have mild social disabilities, it is clear that a well-orga-nized environment is a critical component of any intervention. More experimental research is needed in this area to fully understand the effects of environmental arrangements on child–child social interaction.

In short, research on the effects of environmental arrangements, and practical procedures based on this research, have shown consistent (although at times modest) improvement in social interaction and social development. Given the nature and effect of these arrangements, we consider them to be a "necessary condition" for most social development interventions. At times when these interventions are not, in and of themselves, sufficient to produce desired change in interaction and development, other types of interventions will need to be added.

Child-Specific Interventions

Child-specific interventions are designed to reduce perceived or identified deficits in a child's social repertoire. Child-specific interventions generally operate by intervening directly with a target child to increase appropriate or decrease inappropriate behaviors. These interventions usually require the involvement of at least one of the child's primary educators, and intervention strategies can be grouped into three broad categories: skills instruction, prompting, and reinforcement. Many interventions for individual children are designed in a manner that combines several strategies from across these categories. However, each of these categories will be discussed separately below.

Skills Instruction

Teaching social skills directly to an individual child or group of children is one method of child-specific intervention. This method holds many similarities to instruction of academic concepts, and includes strategies such as modeling appropriate behavior and providing opportunities to demonstrate and practice newly acquired behaviors with feedback (Elliott & Gresham, 1993). These strategies often follow a cognitive-behavioral or social learning theory approach in an attempt to overcome a skill deficit. Research with preschool children suggests that social skill instruction alone does lead to acquisition of social skills, with children able to demonstrate these skills in structured instructional and role play settings; however, social skills training alone produces little or no reliable change in the naturally occurring behavior during free play (McConnell, Sisson, Cort, & Strain, 1991). As such, skills instruction may be a necessary component of social development intervention, but is not sufficient as the sole feature of that intervention. Typically, social skills training for preschool children includes some or all of the following components: (a) modeling of desired social skills, (b) providing direct instruction in social skills, and (c) providing "coaching," or praise and corrective feedback, for the use of social skills in an instructional setting.

Modeling. Modeling is a social learning procedure (Bandura, 1977) that employs observational learning to teach children specific social behaviors. Modeling generally involves the use of a teacher or peer who demonstrates a behavior. This demonstration can be accompanied by a verbal explanation to increase the likelihood of rapid acquisition of the behavior. The target child is then prompted to imitate that behavior. Modeling has proven successful in promoting the acquisition of new social behaviors (Gresham, 1985; Wandless & Prinz, 1982), and generalization to other settings and peers has been demonstrated when used in tandem with prompting and reinforcement procedures (Belchic & Harris, 1994).

Modeling can be provided in different ways. Perhaps most indirect, children can be placed in structured play activities with other children who are presumed (and, perhaps, prompted) to behave competently (O'Connor, 1969). More directly, modeling can be embedded into a structured instructional setting, where a teacher or other adult demonstrates a particular social skill, and then prompts children in the group to demonstrate variations of this skill to other children in quasi-naturalistic play sessions (McConnell et al., 1991). Whether indirect or direct, the principal goal is to provide intervention participants with real-world examples of desired social skill performance. Modeling is a component of virtually all child-specific intervention programs, with models provided by either teachers or peers (e.g., McConnell et al., 1991; Walker et al.,

1983). While modeling may be a critical element of social interaction interventions for young children, there is little evidence that it is sufficient to produce generalized change *alone*.

Social skill instruction. Social skills can be taught directly to children, using variations of direct instruction (in which behavioral components are identified, demonstrated, and practiced explicitly) and behavioral rehearsal (where individual children perform these components and begin to integrate components in a structured instructional setting). Most existing social skills training curricula include some degree of social skills training, with some variations in both the explicitness and structure of instructional procedures and in the specific skills taught (cf. Hendrickson et al., 1993; Vanderbilt-Minnesota Social Interaction Project, 1993). While there is little research on the effects of social skill instruction alone for preschool children, available evidence suggests that this instruction improves child performance in structured role-play circumstances but produces negligible effects (without additional intervention components) for child behavior in naturalistic freeplay settings (Belchic & Harris, 1994; Elliott & Gresham, 1993; McConnell et al., 1991; Odom et al., 1999).

Coaching. "Coaching" *is* used to describe a rather broad set of procedures that introduce prompts to engage in specific social skills, and praise for using those skills, in naturalistic play settings. Coaching is a three-step process consisting of verbal instructions, skill rehearsal, and feedback or reinforcement for performance (Elliott & Gresham, 1993). Coaching procedures typically are implemented during free-play or structured play settings, where focal children are in proximity to peers and activities where social interaction is likely to occur. In this way, coaching brings "intervention" into naturalistic settings.

Research on the use of coaching to instruct social skills has involved both preschool (English et al., 1997; McConnell et al., 1991; Odom, Hoyson, Jamieson, & Strain, 1985; Odom & Strain, 1986) and elementary students (Ladd, 1981; Oden & Asher, 1977). Because of the significant verbal component of this procedure, there are concerns regarding its use with preschool children, especially those with disabilities. However, Elliott and Gresham (1993) have suggested that modeling may be incorporated into the coaching process to supplement this verbal component. Similarly, some procedures implement visual or verbal/visual cuing systems to communicate with children; one version of such a system provides the child with ongoing information about behavioral goals for an individual play session (e.g., the number of initiations or time in social interaction), as well as visual records of praise for completing specific social interactions (Vanderbilt-Minnesota Social Interaction Project, 1993). Visual systems of this sort appear ancillary to the primary functions of prompting and praising social interaction, but have facilitated strategies for systematically fading coaching procedures over time (Odom, Chandler, et al., 1992).

Prompting

Prompting usually indicates the use of a physical, verbal, or visual *cue* that indicates to a child that he or she is to engage in a specific social *behavior*, such as initiating play or sharing a toy. Prompts are assumed to be given as a *supplement* to the natural cues in the child's environment and are used when those natural cues are not followed by an appropriate response by the target child (Alberto & Troutman, 1999). For example, a peer may attempt to engage the target child in a game of catch by holding up a ball and waving it in the direction of the target child (a natural cue). If the target child fails to respond appropriately, the teacher may then prompt the child verbally by saying, "Catch the ball," visually by showing the child a picture of two children playing catch, or physically by holding the child's arms out in the direction of the peer. The level of intrusiveness of the prompt depends on the level of need demonstrated by the child.

Prompting is often used in tandem with other intervention strategies, such as modeling and reinforcement, as prompting alone *is* most effective in addressing performance deficits in children's social behavior. Prompting has consistently been empirically supported as a strategy for improving levels of social initiations and interactions among preschool children (see Belchic & Harris, 1994, and McConnell et al., 1991, for examples).

Behavioral momentum. In a variation of prompting procedures, Davis, Brady, Hamilton, McEvoy, and Williams (1994) demonstrated that "behavioral momentum" interventions, which are traditionally used to increase rates of compliance, can also increase levels of initiation to and interaction from children with disabilities to typically developing peers. This intervention is remarkably simple, requiring teachers or others to first ask the target child to complete a series of requests that are very likely to be performed ("high-probability *requests*," labeling objects, or taking materials) and then immediately asking the child to perform a task that is less likely to be performed ("low-probability requests," such as initiating social interaction). In Davis and colleagues' (1994) study, increases in social interaction were produced and maintained even after high-probability requests had been faded, and increases in interactions with other, non-participating peers in other settings were observed.

Priming. Priming, like behavioral momentum, is an "antecedent" intervention (that is, one provided prior to instances in which the target behavior is expected to occur), provided before the child is engaged in social interaction during freeplay activities. Priming involves delivery of prompts before rather than during an activity (Zanolli & Daggett, 1998). For instance, a teacher might ask a child to join a particular activity, seek out a particular peer, and produce particular initiations during an upcoming play activity.

One recent study (Zanolli and Daggett, 1998) found that priming increased the rate of social initiations by two socially withdrawn children. However, these increases were much larger when the children also were reinforced at a high, rather than a low, rate for their initiations. The need for high levels of reinforcement might contradict the advantage priming claims to hold as a less teacher-intensive procedure.

Correspondence training. Correspondence training takes advantage of relations between verbal and other behavior; in one variation of correspondence training, a child is asked to describe specific behaviors they will emit during an upcoming period. The child receives reinforcement contingent upon both the occurrence of these behaviors and the correspondence with their previous statement (Risley & Hart, 1968). In this way, correspondence training can be used to extend the effects of social skills training into a greater variety of generalization settings.

A variety of self-evaluation techniques that represent close variations of correspondence *training* (Sainato, Goldstein, & Strain, 1992). Correspondence training has been explored as a primary intervention tactic to increase social interaction skills and participation (Osnes, Guevremont, & Stokes, 1986). Correspondence training or its variations have also been used to promote generalization of social interaction interventions for both target children (Shearer, Kohler, Buchan, & McCullough, 1996; Strain, Kohler, Storey, & Danko, 1994) and peers (Odom & Watts, 1991; Sainato et al., 1992). Correspondence training and related self-evaluation tactics appear to hold special promise for extending the effects of social interaction interventions across time and settings.

Reinforcement

Reinforcement occurs when the consequence to a behavior increases the likelihood of that behavior occurring in the future. Reinforcement can be naturally occurring (e.g., when children have opportunities for preferred play after making social initiations to peers) or artificially provided (i.e., when a teacher praises a child for initiating socially to peers). In social interaction training, the typical goal for providing reinforcement is that natural reinforcers for social interaction with peers will eventually take over, precluding the need for artificial reinforcers. This concept is known as behavioral trapping (McConnell, 1987; Stokes & Baer, 1977).

Reinforcement is *often* delivered in the form of tangible signs or exchanges, such as stickers, tokens, and "happy faces." Perhaps the most appealing aspect of the use of such reinforcement is its wide range of empirical support (i.e., Wolfe, Boyd, & Wolfe, 1983; see McEvoy et al., 1992, for a review). Reinforcement is used in the majority of social skills intervention research and curricula, most often in tandem with one or more of the other intervention strategies discussed here. Several unique methods of using reinforcement to increase preschoolers' social behaviors have also been explored. These methods include verbal praise delivered to the target child alone and group-oriented contingencies for the behavior of some or all children in the target child's play group.

Praise. In a pioneering study of the effects of reinforcement on social behavior, Allen, Hart, Buell, Harris, and Wolf (1964) found the careful delivery of praise by a teacher effectively increased the amount of time a socially isolated preschool girl engaged in social interaction with her peers. This increase was maintained even after teacher praise had been faded to normal levels. While this particular study examined the effects of praise alone, many other studies have combined praise with the delivery of other methods of reinforcement.

Teacher praise is a frequent component of social interaction skills training interventions for preschool-aged children, both because it is effective and because it is easily delivered. However, some have raised concerns that teacher praise can interrupt ongoing social interaction, thus confounding the establishment of naturally occurring reinforcement contingencies (Strain, Kerr, & Ragland, 1979). Others have suggested that it may be difficult to engineer high and stable rates of teacher praise for child social interactions (McConnell et al., 1992; Peterson & McConnell, 1993). So, while frequently seen as one aspect of many interventions, teacher praise is rarely used in isolation to produce enduring changes in children's social interactions.

Group contingencies. Group contingencies involve the delivery of reinforcement to a group, dependent on the behavior of one member of the group (dependent contingency) or the entire group (interdependent contingency). Research has demonstrated some success in using group contingencies, along with other strategies, to increase levels of social interaction in integrated settings. (Kohler, Strain, Maretsky, & DeCesare, 1990; McConnell et al., 1991). These studies have suggested that group contingencies change the behavior of both target child and peers in ways that produce more, and more natural, social interaction. Specifically, in McConnell and colleagues' (1991) study, introduction of a group contingency (in which all children in a play group received praise contingent upon social interaction of an individual child), slight increases were noted in initiation rates for both target children and peers, a higher proportion of these initiations produced social interaction, and behavior between target children and peers was more reciprocal. These findings suggest that group contingencies can change the existing relations between target children and peers in ways that produce more natural, and perhaps more generalized, social interaction.

Potential Problems With Prompting and Reinforcement

Despite the effectiveness of prompting and reinforcement for improving the social interaction skills of preschoolers, the use of such procedures in a classroom setting may have deleterious effects on peers' perceptions of the subject of the intervention (Odom et al. 1999). Additionally, while the fading of prompts and reinforcement has been successfully accomplished in research (Fox, Shores, Lindeman & Strain, 1887; Odom, Chandler, Ostrosky, et al., 1992; Timm, Strain, & Eller, 1979), these fading processes have been lengthy and time-intensive, making them impractical for most classroom settings. One potential solution to these problems has been to incorporate peers in the delivery of skills instruction, prompts, and reinforcement.

Peer-Mediated Interventions

Unlike child-specific interventions, *peer-mediated interventions* teach a child's peers to support her or his social skills. By using the peer as an intervention agent, Strain and Odom (1986) argue that these interventions avoid a major pitfall of child-specific approaches: When teachers prompt and praise social behaviors, they often disrupt ongoing social interaction between a target child and peers. While prompting and reinforcement used in child-specific procedures may yield more interaction during intervention, these interactions have tended to be relatively brief (Odom & Strain, 1986) and may interrupt establishing natural reinforcers for social interaction (cf. McConnell, 1987). Peer-mediated interventions avoid this disruption because interactions during social play are exclusively with peers, rather than with peers and the teacher, using pre-specified behaviors that the peer has been taught by the teacher. The consequences for social behavior from target children are play and social responses from peers, both of which may be established as naturally occurring reinforcers.

Four major components of peer-mediated interventions have been identified (Strain and Odom, 1986): (a) selection of peer target behaviors, (b) environmental arrangement to promote interaction, (c) method of training peers, and (d) use of daily intervention sessions. A thorough discussion of environmental arrangement appears earlier in this chapter, so here we will focus on target behaviors and method of training.

Target Behaviors

Most often, peer-mediated interventions have taught peers to utilize one or more social initiations that are known to promote positive social interaction (Tremblay et al., 1981). These initiations include *play organizers* (i.e., a suggestion of an idea for play), *sharing* (i.e., offering an object or cooperatively using a toy), *providing assistance* (i.e., providing help to another child), and *physical affection* (i.e., positive physical contact). Odom and Brown (1993) extended this list, suggesting other behaviors to be targeted for intervention, including conversation, compliments, verbal and nonverbal responding, and other initiation strategies. These social skills are distinguished by their high likelihood of producing positive social responses from other children, and are thus suitable for peer-mediated intervention. By teaching these skills to socially competent children, then prompting these children to direct one of more of these social behaviors to a child selected for intervention, an intervention agent can be more certain that positive social interaction will result.

Method of Training

As with child-specific interventions, peer-mediated interventions generally involve some form of skills instruction, followed by prompting (and sometimes praise) for application of those skills in natural settings. Strain and Odom (1986) have stressed the importance of providing daily skills instruction to peers, as well as daily intervention sessions for peers with target children. These authors also provide an example of training peers that includes modeling, prompting, and reinforcement. Such a thoroughly planned and regularly delivered approach increases the number of initiations and length of interactions for target children (Strain & Odom, 1986). In a variation on traditional peer-mediated interventions, English and colleagues (1997) developed a "buddy" program, in which peers were paired with target children throughout the day, thus promoting interaction during the entire school day rather than solely during freeplay activities.

In a similar vein, Odom and colleagues (1985) reported that prompting peers may be more important than reinforcing them. In this study, when reinforcers for peer initiations were withdrawn during intervention, there was no noticeable effect on the frequency of peer's initiations. However, when verbal prompting was withdrawn, the frequency of peer initiations was greatly reduced.

Once peer initiations are occurring with some frequency, teacher prompts for these initiations can be faded. For example, Odom and Watts (1991) found that teacher's verbal prompts could be faded by providing peers a combination of correspondence training and visual feedback, in which a teacher drew a "happy face" on an index card for each successful interaction between the peer and the target child. In a subsequent study, Odom and colleagues (1992) found that verbal prompts and visual feedback could be faded to visual feedback only, which could then be faded entirely, with generally positive results for maintenance of peer initiations and interactions with target children.

Potential Problems With Peer-Mediated Interventions

Some teachers and others who have implemented peer-mediated interventions report concern for the potentially negative effect on the peers involved in the intervention. Indeed, some studies have found that interactions decreased between peer "confederates" (that is, the children engaged as peers in peer-mediated interventions) and other children not involved in the intervention (Shafer, Egel, & Neef, 1984), while other studies reviewed by Strain and Odom (1986) found no negative effects on peer confederates. While the possibility of negative effects on peer confederates are of some concern, it is likely that the frequency of interaction with non-target children will decrease somewhat, as peer confederates are now interacting with a larger number of peers. This decrease must be weighed against the many benefits of peer-mediated interventions for both target children and peer confederates.

Additionally, some researchers and practitioners have reported problems with "burnout," or decreased compliance with intervention procedures. by peers participating in these studies (McEvoy et al., 1992; Odom, et al., 1985; Peterson & McConnell, 1993). In many instances, the peers in these interventions are asked to produce high rates of initiations and responses, and to maintain engaging play, with children who have a long history of social isolation, few age-appropriate social and play skills, and (occasionally) some competing or challenging behaviors. Interventionists have reported some rate of refusal to participate in daily intervention activities, or noncompliance with teacher prompts for interaction during these activities. While little research has addressed this issue directly, applied experience suggests the great importance of both selecting socially competent and "resilient" peers, providing ongoing reinforcement for peers' participation in intervention activities, and exploring the option of multiple peers rotating their participation in ongoing intervention activities.

Comprehensive Interventions

For our purposes here, comprehensive social interaction interventions are those that include components of two or more of the intervention types discussed in the previous sections. Empirical evaluations of comprehensive interventions typically have included some form of social skills training for all participating children, some delivery of teacher prompts and reinforcement in freeplay situations, and some explicit attention to distributing training and prompts in ways that promote reciprocal interactions between and balanced effects across children with autism and their peers.

Several different investigations have shown the positive effects of treatment packages that include social skills training for children with social skill deficits and typically developing peers, along with reinforcement contingencies implemented during freeplay activities (Gonzalez-Lopez & Kamps, 1997; Kamps et al., 1992; Lefebvre & Strain, 1989). Participants in these studies have included children in preschool (Lefebvre & Strain, 1989) and early elementary school (Gonzalez-Lopez & Kamps, 1997; Kamps et al., 1992), with a focus on children with disabilities. Social skills training programs employed in these studies have varied somewhat, but typically include some teacher-led instructional group with didactic presentation and modeling. Reinforcement contingencies have been both individual (Gonzalez-Lopez & Kamps, 1997; Kamps et al., 1992) and group-oriented (Lefebvre & Strain, 1989; McConnell et al., 1991). Across all investigations, however, study results indicate that the package of social skills training and reinforcement directed at both young target children and their socially competent peers produced increases in social interaction (and its various components).

A recent study by Odom and colleagues (1999) suggests the relative contributions or effectiveness of different types of intervention. In Odom and colleagues' study, 22 classrooms serving 98 preschool children with a variety of disabilities were randomly assigned to five intervention conditions, including a control condition (in which teachers continued their pre-existing social interaction interventions) or one of four standardized interventions: environmental arrangements, child-specific intervention (including social skills training as well as prompts and praise to target children during freeplay), peer-mediated intervention (including social skills training as well as prompts and praise to peers during freeplay), and a comprehensive intervention (including social skills training as well as prompts and praise for both target children and peers during freeplay). The researchers gathered data from a variety of sources, including behavioral observation, social impact (or sociometrics), and teacher ratings, in a repeated-measures experimental design. At the end of 55–60 days of treatment, three conditions—environmental arrangement, child-specific, and peer-mediated interventions—had produced significant changes in observed social interaction rates for young children with disabilities. By the following year, only children in the peer-mediated condition continued to show improvement compared to those in the control condition for frequency of interaction, although teacher ratings of social interaction quality suggested maintained effects for both peer-mediated and comprehensive intervention conditions. Odom and colleagues speculate that the comprehensive intervention, which was logistically most challenging for teachers to implement, may have consequently not been implemented with sufficient fidelity to produce expected effects.

In the one comparison study of different social skills training programs conducted to date, results suggest that some caution be exercised in employing procedures that are logistically more demanding but not necessarily any more powerful. Further research should explore the relation between intervention complexity, immediate intervention effects, and long-term intervention outcomes, as well as procedures for helping maximize the fidelity of complex and demanding interventions.

FUTURE DIRECTIONS

Since the late 1970s a great variety of research has been conducted on the social development of preschool children, and on the effects of different intervention tactics for promoting this development. We know a great deal more about how to teach social skills in isolation, and how to promote the use of these skills in natural freeplay settings. And while there is much yet to learn about promoting broad generalization and maintenance of these skills, and about affecting long-term developmental outcomes, we have a set of research-based procedures that directly inform and define "best practices" for social skills interventions for preschool youngsters.

In spite of these remarkable advances, some significant challenges remain. In particular, researchers and practitioners still need to grapple with assessment practices that help allocate and target intervention procedures, and with program implementation practices that will bring social interaction interventions to a point where they are implemented broadly. These issues of assessment and "bringing intervention to scale" are likely to define continued success in research and practice of social interaction interventions.

Assessment

The assessment of social skills in young children is an area that is receiving a great deal of attention, particularly given the link between social skill development in a child's early years and future academic and behavioral outcomes. While traditional methods (e.g. rating scales and skill checklists) provide information about skill acquisition, or lack there of, they often do not provide enough information about growth and development or assist in designing an effective intervention.

With the recent emphasis on outcomes in general education, researchers are looking at more effective ways to both assess social skills and use that assessment information to both inform practice and monitor progress in important areas of child development. Three areas of assessment that are receiving increasing attention are the identification of contextual factors that impact social development, the direct link between assessment information and intervention, and monitoring growth and development.

Contextual Factors That Influence Social Development

As was mentioned previously, social skill development may be influenced significantly by both the proximal and distal factors that impact a child's day-to-day life. For example, the rate and quality of adult child interaction, access to socially adept peers, or community factors such as recreation opportunities will influence social development. Assessment procedures are needed that measure both the quantity and the quality of these factors. Information from these assessments could be used to increase the likelihood that factors that promote interaction are included in classroom, home, and community settings. Similarly, information about the presence of factors that inhibit social development may be used in designing effective intervention strategies. A number of ecobehavioral assessment procedures have been developed including *Code for Interactive Recording of Caregiver and Learning Environment–2 (CIRCLE-2)* (Atwater, Montagna, Creighton, Williams, & Hou, 1993); *Ecobehavioral System for Complex Assessments of Preschool Environments (ESCAPE)* (Greenwood, Carta, Kamps, & Delquadri, 1997), and *Ecobehavioral Assessment of Social Interaction (EASI)* (Richardson, McConnell, McEvoy, & Creighton, 1992). Common features of these assessment procedures include (a) direct assessment of target child behaviors of interest for intervention (e.g., social interaction), (b) direct assessment of peer and teacher behaviors that are likely to prompt and provide consequences for these target child behaviors (e.g., response to social initiations, praise for social interaction), and (c) environmental events that are likely to promote (e.g., freeplay activities) and inhibit (e.g., table-top activities) specific social behaviors. Data from these assessment procedures can be analyzed by practitioners to identify naturally occurring situations in which desired (or undesired) behaviors are likely to occur for the purposes of planning intervention. These assessment procedures can then be used subsequently to assess the extent to which the planned intervention has been implemented, and what the effects of this implementation are for the target child's behavior.

Linking Assessment and Intervention

One primary purpose of any assessment procedure is to provide critical information that can be used *to* design effective interventions. Indeed, one of the most important characteristics of assessment in early childhood education is utility for decision-making regarding early intervention (Bagnato & Neisworth, 1991). Unfortunately, most currently available assessment tools are not useful for making decisions about early intervention and education (Neisworth & Bagnato, 1996).

The Data-Based-Problem-Solving Model (Deno, 1989) is one example of a process linking assessment information with intervention selection. In this model, a problem is identified, usually through ongoing monitoring of development. A series of assessments are then conducted, including ecobehavioral observations, activity-based assessments, and parent interviews. This information is then used to design a specific intervention that addresses the needs of the child and family. Ongoing progress monitoring is used to determine intervention effectiveness.

One example of the decision-making model is the First Step program (Walker, Severson, Feil, Stiller, & Golly, 1998). This 12-week program incorporates the problem identification process through a universal screening and early detection system, involving teacher nominations, rankings and ratings, and direct observations to determine the best candidates for intervention. Identified children participate in school- and home-based intervention components, including teacher praise and direct reinforcement, as well as parent training and increased home/school communication. Throughout the intervention phase, progress monitoring of classroom performance coincides with implementation of planned reinforcement. Results of child progress are communicated between home and school, with a goal of assessing and improving intervention effectiveness. By using school- and home-based intervention procedures that are informed both by a systematic early screening process and by ongoing progress monitoring, this program is indeed a first step toward bridging the present gap between assessment and intervention in early childhood social development.

More research is needed to assist educators and parents in making decisions about how to use assessment information to generate effective interventions. Future research should look more toward computerized models that generate potential interventions based on reliable assessment information from multiple sources.

Ongoing Progress Monitoring

Research in child development has indicated clearly the links between acquisition of social skills in early childhood and later academic and behavioral competencies. Unfortunately, assessment procedures are not available currently that would let families and educators know if a child's early developmental trajectory is on target to produce later desirable academic and behavioral outcomes. This information would allow educators to implement an intervention, if necessary, early in a child's development and evaluate the effectiveness of the intervention on the developmental trajectory. Continuous Progress Monitoring is an example of formative evaluation, an assessment practice that informs intervention during, rather than after, its implementation (Fuchs & Deno, 1991; Deno, 1997).

For an assessment tool to be useful for continually monitoring progress, it must possess characteristics such as sensitivity to small increments of change, inexpensiveness, and efficiency, while maintaining standards of reliability and validity (Fuchs & Deno, 1991; Deno, 1997). These qualities of sensitivity and efficiency are especially important for a progress-monitoring tool because of the need for frequent administration so that one can maximize the effectiveness of intervention practices (Deno, Mirkin, Robinson, *and* Evans, 1980). In addition, these measures allow for repeatable, reliable, inexpensive, and sensitive monitoring of children's growth toward long-term developmental goals (McConnell, 2000).

Recently, McEvoy et al. (2000) have developed and evaluated an assessment for monitoring the growth and development of preschool social skills. By using an Individual Growth and Development Indicator (IGDI) assessment, educators and parents observe children playing for 5 minutes and record the number of social turns observed. Preliminary analysis indicate that these very brief assessments correlate with standardized assessments of social development, show growth over time, and can be repeated frequently to monitor both general social development and intervention effectiveness. While the development of such tools for monitoring preschooler's social growth is in the early stages (Early Childhood Research Institute on Measuring Growth and Development, 2000), this line of research holds the potential for improving the link between early education and later school outcomes.

Bringing Interventions to Scale

Research in social skills intervention since the 1970s has tracked closely to public and professional concern in this area: Much of the work has focused on children with developmental and other disabilities receiving special education and related services in segregated or integrated/inclusive classrooms, much of the work has taken place in school or day care settings, and much of the work has been implemented (or intended to be implemented) by skilled classroom teachers. To some extent, the compilation of research in this area has been criticized for too narrow a focus, and for too little attention to scaling intervention procedures to the resources and capacity found in typical preschool settings (McConnell et al., 1992). Indeed, recent findings from a comparison of several "state of the art" social interaction interventions suggested that logistical demands placed on teachers for implementation may interact directly with intervention outcomes (Odom et al., 1999).

In recent years, research in social interaction interventions has begun to migrate in ways that are especially important for classroom interventionists and the professionals who consult with these teachers. Research has occurred more often in typical classroom settings, and researchers have begun to pay explicit attention to development of procedures that are easy and efficient to implement (Fox et al., 1990; Goldstein, Kaczmarek, & Hepting, 1994; Peterson & McConnell, 1993; Odom & McConnell, 1992).

From these recent developments in social interaction intervention research have emerged both theoretical analysis and review of the effects of different factors on intervention integrity (McConnell et al., 1992; Peterson & McConnell, 1993) and research on components that affect this integrity (Peterson & McConnell, 1996). While this line of research is still rather new, and further developments are needed to make definitive statements, we can conclude, at least tentatively, some broad principles about social interaction interventions with preschool children.. First, social interaction interventions are often demanding of time and energy from teachers, peers, and target children; further, to be maximally effective, it appears that these interventions should last for long periods of time (e.g., 100 days or more). Thus, it seems clear that teachers, support personnel, and program administrators considering implementation of systematic efforts to affect social interaction skills must consider long-term commitments to these interventions.

Second, it appears that implementation of interventions varies somewhat across settings and, perhaps, time. While a few studies have specifically explored training, support and consultation strategies for teachers and other classroom personnel (Hendrickson et al., 1993; Peterson & McConnell, 1996), to date there are no specific investigations that inform potential users and support personnel about effective procedures for maintaining high degrees of intervention fidelity over long periods of time.

Third, specific strategies for tailoring intervention to individual children are still emerging. While some research has been conducted on "response-dependent fading" (or reducing intervention components and supports as child performance improves) and these procedures have been implemented in several social interaction curricula (e.g., Vanderbilt-Minnesota Social Interaction Project, 1993), further research and development is needed in this area. It is quite likely that developments in dynamic, ongoing assessment of social interaction skills (e.g., McEvoy et al., 2000) will greatly assist practitioners in tailoring individual interventions and in mounting significant efforts to monitor and prevent early social problems among preschool children.

CONCLUSION

The past decades have seen tremendous growth in both our declarative knowledge of both social development and its determinants, as well as in procedural knowledge of how to affect the short- and medium-term social performance of preschool children. Indeed, we now know enough to support broad and universal attention: In our reading, extant research supports both the importance of monitoring social development and interactive competence for all young children and an affirmative obligation to introduce interventions that promote that development when needed. While we do not know "everything" about social development, its determinants, and its promotion, we do know enough to act with confidence.

This chapter has reviewed a range of theoretical and conceptual issues and arguments, descriptive research of social development and factors that affect that development, individual tactics and procedures that increase components of social interaction under at least some conditions, and constellations of interventions that can be implemented in a wide variety of settings. With information such as this, professionals working with young children and the programs that serve them can select and implement individual components, tailoring assessment and intervention to the perceived needs and resources of a particular program. Alternatively, professionals can select one of several standardized interventions, then work in collaborative ways to implement the selected package across an extended period of time. In either approach, ongoing assessment of child progress, intervention implementation and fidelity, and individual child goals and objectives will be needed and will contribute to ongoing refinement of the scope and direction of intervention.

While we still have much to learn about long-term effects of social interaction interventions for preschool children, we can assert that our ultimate goals of promoting healthy social development among young children are more likely to be reached by starting intervention early and making that intervention effective. Taken together, the research literature and practical applications of that research literature provide a broad set of tools for carrying out this effort.

REFERENCES

Agostin, T. M., & Bain, S. K. (1997). Predicting early school success with developmental and social skills screeners. *Psychology in the Schools, 34*(3), 219-228.

Ainsworth, M. D. S., Blehar, M. C., Waters, E., & Wall, S. (1978). *Patterns of attachment: A psychological study of the Strange Situation.* Hillsdale, NJ: Erlbaum.

Alberto, P. A., & Troutman, A. C. (1999). *Applied behavior analysis for teachers* (5th ed.). Upper Saddle River, NJ: Prentice-Hall.

Allen, K. E., Hart, B., Buell, J. S., Harris, F. R., & Wolf, M. M. (1964). Effects of social reinforcement on isolate behavior of a nursery school child. *Child Development, 35,* 511-518.

Atwater, J., Montagna, D., Creighton, M., Williams, R., & Hou, S. (1993). *Code for interactive recording of caregiver and learning environments-2.* Kansas City, KS: Early Childhood Institute on Substance Abuse.

Bagnato, S. J., & Neisworth, J. T. (1991). *Assessment for early intervention: Best practices for professionals.* New York: Guilford.

Bandura, A. (1977). *Social learning theory.* Englewood Cliffs, NJ: Prentice-Hall.

Belchic, J. K., & Harris, S. L. (1994). The use of multiple peer exemplars to enhance the generalization of play skills to the siblings of children with autism. *Child & Family Behavior Therapy, 16*(2), 1-25.

Bell, R. Q. (1968). A reinterpretation of the direction of effects in studies of socialization. *Psychological Review, 75*(2), 81-95.

Bjorkland, D. J. (1989). *Children's thinking: Developmental function and individual differences* (pp. 174-197). Pacific Grove, CA: Brooks/Cole.

Bricker, D. (1995). The challenge of inclusion. *Journal of Early Intervention, 19,* 179-194.

Bronfenbrenner, U. (1979). *The ecology of human development: Experiments by nature and design.* Cambridge, MA: Harvard University Press.

Brown, W. H., Ragland, E. U., & Fox, J. J. (1988). Effects of group socialization procedures on the social interactions of preschool children. *Research in Developmental Disabilities, 9,* 359-376.

Bursuck, W. D., & Asher, S. R. (1986). The relationship between social competence and achievement in elementary school children. *Journal of Clinical Child Psychology, 15*(1), 41-49.

Cairns, R. B., Green, J. A., & MacConbie, D. J. (1980). The Dynamics of Social Development. In E. C. Simmel (Ed.), *Early experiences and early behavior: Implications for social development* (pp. 79-105). New York: Academic.

Carr, E. G., & Durand, V. M. (1985). Reducing behavior problems through functional communication training. *Journal of Applied Behavior Analysis, 18,* 111-126.

Charlebois, P., LeBlanc, M., Gagnon, C., & Larivee, S. (1994). Methodological issues in multiple-gating screening procedures for antisocial behaviors in elementary students. *Redial and Special Education, 15*(1), 44-54.

Davis, C. A., Brady, M. P., Hamilton, R., McEvoy, M. A., & Williams, R. E. (1994). Effects of high-probability requests on the social interactions of young children with severe disabilities. *Journal of Applied Behavior Analysis, 27,* 619-637.

De Kleyn, M., & Odom, S. L. (1989). Activity structure and social interactions with peers in developmentally integrated play groups. *Journal of Early Intervention, 13,* 342-352.

Deno, S. L. (1989). Curriculum-Based Measurement and special education services: A fundamental and direct relationship. In M. R. Shinn (Ed), *Curriculum-Based Measurement: Assessing special children* (pp. 1-18). New York: Guilford.

Deno, S. L. (1997). Whether thou goest ... Perspectives on progress monitoring. In J. W. Lloyd, E. J. Kame'enui, & D. Chard (Eds.), *Issues in educating students with disabilities* (pp. 77-99). Malwah, NJ: Erlbaum.

Deno, S. L., Mirkin, P. K., Robinson, S., and Evans, P. (1980). *Relationships among classroom observations of social adjustment and sociometric rating scales* (Research Report No. 24). Minneapolis, MN: University of Minnesota, Institute for Research on Learning Disabilities.

Doyle, W. (1986). Classroom organization and management. In M. C. Wittrock (Ed.), *Handbook of research on teaching* (pp. 392-431). New York: Macmillan.

Early Childhood Research Institute on Measuring Growth and Development. (2000). *Longitudinal study of individual growth and development indicators of social interaction* (Technical Report). Minneapolis, MN: University of Minnesota.

Elliott, S. N., & Gresham, F. M. (1993). Social skills interventions for children. *Behavior Modification, 17*(3), 287-313.

English, K., Goldstein, H., Shafer, K., & Kaczmarek, L. (1997). Promoting interactions among preschoolers with and without disabilities: Effects of a buddy skills-training program. *Exceptional Children, 63,* 229-243.

Foulks, B., & Morrow, R. D. (1989). Academic survival skills for the young child at risk for school failure. *Journal of Educational Research, 82*(3), 158-165.

Fox, J. J., McEvoy, M. A., Leech, R. L., & Moroney, J. J. (1990, May). Generaliza-tion, maintenance, and social interaction with exceptional children: Ten years after Stokes and Baer. Paper presented at the 16th annual convention of the Association for Behavior Analysis, Nashville, TN.

Fox, J., Shores, R., Lindeman, D., & Strain, P. (1987). Maintaining social initiations of withdrawn handicapped and nonhandicapped preschoolers through a response-dependent fading tactic. *Journal of Abnormal Child Psychology, 14*(3), 387-396.

Frea, W., Craig-Unkefer, L., Odom, S. L., & Johnson, D. (1999). Differential effects of structured social integration and group friendship activities for promoting social interaction with peers. *Journal of Early Intervention, 23,* 243-256.

Fuchs, L. S., & Deno, S. L. (1991). Paradigmatic distinctions between instructionally relevant measurement models. *Exceptional Children, 57*(6), 488-500.

Gallagher, T. M. (1991). Language and social skills: Implications for clinical assessment and intervention with school-age children. In T. M. Gallagher (Ed.), *Pragmatics of language: Clinical practice issues* (pp. 11-41). San Diego: Singular.

Gilbert, T. F. (1978). *Human competence.* New York: McGraw-Hill.

Goldstein, H., Kaczmarek, L., & Hepting, N. (1994). Communication interventions: The challenges of across-the-day implementation. In I. R. Gardner & D. M. Sainato (Eds.), *Behavior analysis in education: Focus on measurably superior instruction* (pp. 101-113). Pacific Grove, CA: Brooks/Cole.

Goldstein, H., Kaczmarek, L., Pennington, R., & Shafer, K. (1992). Peer-mediated intervention: Attending to, commenting on, and acknowledging the behavior of preschoolers with autism. *Journal of Applied Behavior Analysis, 25*(2), 289-305.

Gonzalez-Lopez, A., & Kamps, D. M. (1997). Social skills training to increase social interactions between children with autism and their typical peers. *Focus on Autism & Other Developmental Disabilities, 12*(1), 2-14.

Greenwood, C. R., Carta, J. J., Kamps, D., & Delquadri, J. (1997). *Ecobehavioral assessment systems software: EBASS.* Lawrence, KS: University of Kansas, Juniper Gardens Children's Project.

Greenwood, C. R., Walker, H. M., Todd, N. M., & Hops, H. (1981). Normative and descriptive analysis of preschool free play social interaction rates. *Journal of Pediatric Psychology, 6*(4), 343-367.

Gresham, F. M. (1985). Utility of cognitive-behavioral procedures for social skills training: A review. *Journal of Abnormal Child Psychology, 13,* 411-423.

Gresham, F. M. (1997). Social skills. In G. Bear, K. Minke, & A. Thomas (Eds.), *Children's needs II: Development, problems and alternatives* (pp. 39-50). Bethesda, MD: National Association of School Psychologists.

Guralnick, M. J. (1992). A hierarchical model for understanding children's peer-related social competence. In S. L. Odom, S. R. McConnell, & M. A. McEvoy (Eds.), *Social competence of young children with disabilities* (pp. 73-64). Baltimore: Brookes.

Guralnick, M. J., & Groom, J. M. (1988). Peer interactions in mainstreamed and specialized classrooms: A comparative analysis. *Exceptional Children, 54*(5), 415-425.

Hadley, P. A., & Rice, M. L. (1991). Conversational responsiveness of speech- and language-impaired preschoolers. *Journal of Speech and Hearing Research, 34,* 1308-1317.

Harper, G. F., Guidubaldi, J., & Kehle, T. J. (1978). Is academic achievement related to classroom behavior? *Elementary School Journal, 78,* 203-207.

Hart, B., & Risley, T. (1996). *Meaningful differences in the everyday experiences of young American children.* Baltimore, MD: Brookes.

Hartup, W. W. (1983). Peer relations. In E. M. Hetherington (Ed.), *Handbook of child psychology: Vol. IV: Socialization, personality, and social development* (pp. 103-196). New York: Wiley.

Hazen, N. L., & Black, B. (1989). Preschool peer communication skills: The role of social status and interaction context. *Child Development, 60,* 867-876.

Hendrickson, J. M., Gardner, N., Kaiser, A. P., & Riley, A. (1993). Evaluation of a social interaction coaching program in an integrated day-care setting. *Journal of Applied Behavior Analysis, 26*(2), 213-225.

Hendrickson, J. M., Strain, P. S., Tremblay, A., & Shores, R. E. (1981). Relationship between toy and material use and the occurrence of social interaction behaviors by normally developing preschool children. *Psychology in the Schools, 18,* 50-55.

Hinshaw, S. P. (1992). Externalizing behavior problems and academic underachievement in childhood and adolescence: Causal relationships and underlying mechanisms. *Psychological Bulletin, 3,* 127-155.

Hops, H. (1983). Children's social competence and skill: Current research practices and future directions. *Behavior Therapy, 14,* 3-18.

Hunt, P., Alwell, M., Goetz, L., & Sailor, W. (1990). Generalized effects of conversation skill training. *Journal of the Association for Persons with Severe Handicaps, 15,* 250-260.

Kamps, D. M., Leonard, B. R., Vernon, S., Dugan, E. P., Delquadri, J. C., Gershon, B., Wade, L., & Folk, L. (1992). Teaching social skills to students with autism to increase peer interactions in an integrated first-grade classroom. *Journal of Applied Behavior Analysis, 25*(2), 281-288.

Katz, L. G. (1987). What should young children be doing? *American Educator: The Professional Journal of the American Federation of Teachers, 12*(2), 28-33, 44-45.

Kohler, F. W., Strain, P. S., Maretsky, S., & DeCesare, L. (1990). Promoting positive and supportive interactions between preschoolers: An analysis of group-oriented contingencies. *Journal of Early Intervention, 14*(4), 327-341.

Krumboltz, J., Ford, M., Nichols, C., & Wentzel, K. (1987). The goals of education. In R. C. Calfee (Ed.), *The study of Stanford and the schools: Views from the inside: Part II.* San Jose, CA: School of Education, Stanford University.

Ladd, G. W. (1981). Effectiveness of a social learning method for enhancing children's social interaction and peer acceptance. *Child Development, 52,* 171-178.

Ladd, G. W., & Coleman, C. C. (1997). Children's classroom peer relationships and early school attitudes: Concurrent and longitudinal associations. *Early Education and Development, 8*(1), 51-66.

LaFreniere, P. J., & Sroufe, L. A. (1985). Profiles of peer competence in the preschool: Interrelations between measures, influence of social ecology, and relation to attachment history. *Developmental Psychology, 21*(1), 56-69.

Lefebvre, D., & Strain, P. S. (1989). Effects of a group contingency on the frequency of social interactions among autistic and nonhandicapped preschool children: Making LRE efficacious. *Journal of Early Intervention, 13*(4), 329-341.

Loeber, R. (1990). Development and risk factors of juvenile antisocial and delinquency. *Clinical Psychology Review, 10,* 1-41.

Lord, C. (1993). Early social development in autism. In E. Schopler & M. E. Van Bourgondien (Eds.), *Preschool issues in autism. Current issues in autism* (pp. 61-94). New York: Plenum.

Lord, C., & Magill-Evans, J. (1995). Peer interactions of autistic children and adolescents. *Development and Psychopathology, 7,* 611-626.

Masten, A. S., & Coatsworth, J. D. (1995). Competence, resilience, and psychopathology. In D. Cicchetti & D. J. Cohen (Eds.), *Developmental psychopathology: Vol. 2. Risk, disorder, and adaptation* (pp. 715-752). New York: Wiley.

Masten, A. S., Coatsworth, J. D., Neemann, J., Gest, S. D., Tellegen, A., & Garmezy, N. (1995). The structure and coherence of competence from childhood through adolescence. *Child Development, 66,* 1635-1659.

Mayer, G. R. (1995). Preventing antisocial behavior in the schools. *Journal of Applied Behavior Analysis, 28,* 467–478.

McCabe, J. R., Jenkins, J. R., Mills, P. E., Dale, P. S., & Cole, K. N. (1999). Effects of group composition, materials, and developmental level on play in preschool children with disabilities. *Journal of Early Intervention, 22,* 164-178.

McCabe, J. R., Jenkins, J. R., Mills, P. E., Dale, P. S., Cole, K. N., & Pepler, L. (1996). Effects of play group variables on language use by preschool children with disabilities. *Journal of Early Intervention, 20,* 329-340.

McConnell, S. R. (1987). Entrapment effects and the generalization and maintenance of social skills training for elementary school students with behavioral disorders. *Behavioral Disorders, 12*(4), 252-263.

McConnell, S. R. (2000). Assessment in early intervention and early childhood special education: Building on the past to project into our future. *Topics in Early Childhood Special Education, 20*(1), 43-48.

McConnell, S. R., McEvoy, M. A., & Odom, S. L. (1992). Implementation of social competence interventions in early childhood special education classes: Current practices and future directions. In S. L. Odom, S. R. McConnell, & M. A. McEvoy (Eds.), *Social competence of young children with disabilities: Issues and strategies for intervention* (pp. 277-306). Baltimore: Brookes.

McConnell, S. R., & Odom, S. L. (1986). *Sociometrics: Peer-referenced measures and the assessment of social competence* (pp. 215-284): New York: Academic.

McConnell, S. R., & Odom, S. L. (1999). A multimeasure performance-based assessment of social competence in young children with disabilities. *Topics in Early Childhood Special Education, 19,* 67-74.

McConnell, S. R., Sisson, L. A., Cort, C. A., & Strain, P. S. (1991). Effect of social skills training and contingency management on reciprocal interaction of preschool children with behavioral handicaps. *Journal of Special Education, 24*(4), 473-495.

McEvoy, M. A., Nordquist, V. M., Twardosz, S., Heckaman, K. A., Wehby, J. H., Denny, R. K. (1988). Promoting autistic children's peer interaction in an integrated setting using affection activities. *Journal of Applied Behavior Analysis, 21,* 193-200.

McEvoy, M. A., Odom, S. L., & McConnell, S. R. (1992). Peer social competence intervention for young children with disabilities. In S. L. Odom, S. R. McConnell, & M. A. McEvoy (Eds.), *Social competence of young children with disabilities: Issues and strategies for intervention* (pp. 113-133). Baltimore: Brookes.

McEvoy, M. A., Silberglitt, B., Novack, M., & Priest, J. S. (2000, December). *Follow that trend! Measuring social interaction of preschool children.* Paper presented at the annual meeting of the Division of Early Childhood, Council for Exceptional Children, Albuquerque, NM.

McFall, R. M. (1982). A review and reformulation of the concept of social skills. *Behavioral Assessment, 4,* 1-33.

Missall, K. N. (2000). *Reconceptualizing school adjustment: A search for intervening variables.* Unpublished manuscript, University of Minnesota.

Moore, C., & Dunham, P. J. (Eds.). (1995). *Joint attention: Its origins and role in development*. Hillsdale, NJ: Erlbaum.

Neisworth, J. T., & Bagnato, S. J. (1996). Assessment for early intervention: Emerging themes and practices. In S. L. Odom and M. E. McClean (Eds.), *Early intervention/early childhood special education: Recommended practices* (pp. 23-57). Austin, TX: PRO-ED.

O'Connor, R. D. (1969). Modification of social withdrawal through symbolic modeling. *Journal of Applied Behavior Analysis, 2*(1), 15-22

Oden, S. L., & Asher, S. R. (1977). Coaching children in social skills for friendship making. *Child Development, 48,* 495-506.

Odom, S. L., & Brown, W. H. (1993). Social interaction skills interventions for young children with disabilities in integrated settings. In C. A. Peck, S. L. Odom, and D. D. Bricker (eds.), *Integrating young children with disabilities into community programs* (pp.39-64). Baltimore: Brookes.

Odom, S. L., Chandler, L. K., Ostrosky, M., McConnell, S. R., & Reaney, S. (1992). Fading teacher prompts from peer-initiation interventions for young children with disabilities. *Journal of Applied Behavior Analysis, 25*(2), 307-317.

Odom, S. L., Hoyson, M., Jamieson, B., & Strain, P. S. (1985). Increasing handicapped preschoolers' peer social interactions: Cross-setting and component analysis. *Journal of Applied Behavior Analysis, 18*(1), 3-16.

Odom, S. L., & McConnell, S. R. (1985). A performance-based conceptualization of social competence of handicapped preschool children: Implications for assessment. *Topics in Early Childhood Special Education, 4*(4), 1-19.

Odom, S. L., & McConnell, S. R. (1992). Improving social competence: An applied behavior analysis perspective. *Journal of Applied Behavior Analysis, 25*(2), 239-244.

Odom, S. L., McConnell, S. R., & Chandler, L. K. (1994). Acceptability and feasibility of classroom-based social interaction interventions for young children with disabilities. *Exceptional Children, 60*(3), 226-236.

Odom, S. L., McConnell, S. R., & McEvoy, M. A. (1992). Peer-related social competence and its significance for young children with disabilities. In S. L. Odom, S. R. McConnell, & M. A. McEvoy (Eds.), *Social competence of young children with disabilities* (pp. 37-42). Baltimore: Brookes.

Odom, S. L., McConnell, S. R., McEvoy, M. A., Peterson, C., Ostrosky, M., Chandler, L. K., Spicuzza, R. J., Skellinger, A., Creighton, M., & Favazza, P. C. (1999). Relative effects of interventions supporting the social competence of young children with disabilities. *Topics in Early Childhood Special Education, 19,* 75-91.

Odom, S. L., McEvoy, M. A. (1988). Integration of young children with handicaps and normally developing children. In S. L. Odom & M. B. Karnes (Eds.), *Early intervention for infants and children with handicaps: An empirical base* (pp. 241-267). Baltimore: Brookes.

Odom, S. L., Peterson, C., McConnell, S. R., & Ostrosky, M. (1990). Ecobehavioral analysis of early education/specialized classroom settings and peer social interaction. *Education and Treatment of Children, 13*(4), 316-330.

Odom, S. L., & Strain, P. S. (1986). A comparison of peer-initiation and teacher-antecedent interventions for promoting reciprocal social interaction of autistic preschoolers. *Journal of Applied Behavior Analysis, 19*(1), 59-71.

Odom, S. L., & Watts, E. (1991). Reducing teacher prompts in peer-mediated interventions for young children with autism. *Journal of Special Education, 25*(1), 26-43.

O'Neill, R. & Reichle, J. (1993). Addressing social motivated challenging behaviors by establishing communicative alternatives: Basics of a general-case approach. In J. Reichle & D. P. Wacker (Eds.)., *Communicative alternatives to challenging behavior: Integrating functional assessment and intervention strategies* (pp. 205-235). Baltimore: Brookes.

Osnes, P. G., Guevremont, D. C., & Stokes, T. R. (1986). If I say I'll talk more, then I will: Correspondence training to increase peer-directed talk by socially withdrawn children. *Behavior Modification, 10,* 287-299.

Patterson, G. R., DeBaryshe, B. D., & Ramsey, E. (1989). A developmental perspective on antisocial behavior. *American Psychologist, 44,* 329-335.

Patterson, G. R., Reid, J. B., & Dishion, T. J. (1992). *Antisocial boys.* Eugene, OR: Castalia.

Pellegrini, A. D., & Glickman, C. D. (1990, May). Measuring kindergartners' social competence. *Young Children,* 40-44.

Peterson, C. A., & McConnell, S. R. (1993). Factors affecting the impact of social interaction skills interventions in early childhood special education. *Topics in Early Childhood Special Education, 13*(1), 38-56.

Peterson, C. A., & McConnell, S. R. (1996). Factors related to intervention integrity and child outcome in social skills interventions. *Journal of Early Intervention, 20,* 146-164.

Piaget, J. (1926). *The language and thought of the child.* London: Routledge & Kegan Paul.

Priest, J. S., McConnell, S. R., Walker, D., Carta, J. J., Kaminski, R. A., McEvoy, M. A., Good, R. H., Greenwood, C. R., & Shinn, M. R. (in press). General growth outcomes for children between birth and age eight: Where do you want young children to go today and tomorrow? *Journal of Early Intervention.*

Quillitch, H. R., & Risley, T. R. (1973). The effects of play materials on social play. *Journal of Applied Behavior Analysis, 6,* 573-578.

Rice, M. L. (1993). "Don't talk to him; he's weird": A social consequences account of language and social interaction. In A. P. Kaiser & D. B. Gray (Eds.), *Communication and language interventions series: Vol. 2. Enhancing children's communication: Research foundations for intervention* (pp. 139-158). Baltimore: Brookes.

Richardson, C. A., McConnell, S. R., McEvoy, M. A., & Creighton, M. M. (1992). *Ecobehavioral Assessment of Social Interaction (EASI): An observational code. Training Manual.* Unpublished manuscript, University of Minnesota.

Risley, T. R., & Hart, B. (1968). Developing correspondence between the nonverbal and verbal behavior of preschool children. *Journal of Applied Behavior Analysis, 1,* 267-281.

Rogers-Warren, A., & Baer, D. M. (1976). Correspondence between saying and doing: Teaching children to share and praise. *Journal of Applied Behavior Analysis, 9,* 335-354.

Ross, D. D. & Rogers, D. L. (1990). Social competence of kindergarten: Analysis of social negotiations during peer play. *Early Child Development and Care, 64,* 15-26.

Sainato, D. M., Goldstein, H., & Strain, P. S. (1992). Effects of self-evaluation on preschool children's use of social interaction strategies with their classmates with autism. *Journal of Applied Behavior Analysis, 25*(1), 127-141.

Saunders, S. A., & Green V. (1993). Evaluating the social competence of young children: A review of the literature. *Early Child Development and Care, 87,* 39-46.

Schroeder, S. (1990). *Ecobehavioral analysis and developmental disabilities.* New York: Springer-Verlag.

Shafer, M. S., Egel, A. L., & Neef, N. A. (1984). Training mildly handicapped peers to facilitate changes in the social interactions skills of autistic children. *Journal of Applied Behavior Analysis, 17,* 461-476.

Shearer, D. D., Kohler, F. W., Buchan, K. A., & McCullough, K. M. (1996). Promoting independent interactions between preschoolers with autism and their nondisabled peers: An analysis of self-monitoring. *Early Education and Development, 7*(3), 205-220.

Sigman, M. (1994). What are the core deficits in autism? In S. H. Broman & J. Grafman (Eds.), *Atypical cognitive deficits in developmental disorders: Implications for brain function* (pp. 139-157). Hillsdale, NJ: Erlbaum.

Sigman, M., & Ruskin, E. (1999). Continuity and change in the social competence of children with autism, Down Syndrome, and developmental delays. *Monographs of the Society for Research in Child Development, 64,* 1-130.

Smith, P. K., & Connolly, K. J. (1976). Social and aggressive behavior as a function of crowding. *Social Science Information, 16,* 601-620.

Stokes, T. F., & Baer, D. M. (1977). An implicit technology of generalization. *Journal of Applied Behavior Analysis, 10,* 349-367.

Strain, P. S., Kerr, M. M., & Ragland, E. U. (1979). Effects of peer-mediated social initiations and prompting/reinforcement procedures on the social behavior of autistic children. *Journal of Autism & Developmental Disorders, 9*(1), 41-54.

Strain, P. S., Kohler, F. W., Storey, K., & Danko, C. (1994). Teaching preschoolers with autism to self-monitor their social interactions: An analysis of results in home and school settings. *Journal of the Association for Persons with Severe Handicaps, 2,* 78-88.

Strain, P. S., & Odom, S. L. (1986). Peer social initiations: Effective intervention for social skills development of exceptional children. *Exceptional Children, 52*(6), 543-551.

Strain, P. S., Odom, S. L., & McConnell, S. (1984). Promoting social reciprocity of exceptional children: Identification, target behavior selection, and intervention. *Rase: Remedial & Special Education, 5*(1), 21-28.

Taylor, A. R. & Machida, S. (1994). The contribution of parent and peer support to Head Start children's early school adjustment. *Early Childhood Research Quarterly, 9,* 387–405.

Taylor, A. R., & Trickett, P. K. (1989). Teacher preference and children's sociometric status in the classroom. *Merrill-Palmer Quarterly, 35,* 343–361.

Timm, M. A., Strain, P. S., & Eller, P. H. (1979). Effects of systematic, response-dependent fading and thinning procedures on the maintenance of child-child interaction. *Journal of Applied Behavior Analysis, 12,* 308.

Tremblay, A., Strain, P. S., Hendrickson, J. M., & Shores, R. E. (1981). Social interactions of normal preschool children. *Behavior Modification, 5*(2), 237–253.

Vandell, D. L., & Mueller, E. C. (1977, March). The effects of group size on toddler's social intervention with peers. Paper presented at the biennial meeting of the Society for Research on Child Development, New Orleans.

Vanderbilt-Minnesota Social Interaction Project. (1993). *Play time/social time: Organizing your classroom to build interaction skills. Institute on Community Integration, University of Minnesota.* Minneapolis MN: Institute on Community Integration, University of Minnesota.

Walker, H. M., Colvin, G., & Ramsey, E. (1995). *Antisocial behavior in school: Strategies and best practices.* Pacific Grove, CA: Brooks/Cole.

Walker, H. M., Greenwood, C. R., Hops, H., & Todd, N. M. (1979). Differential effects of reinforcing topographic components of social interaction. *Behavior Modification, 3*(3), 291–321.

Walker, H. M., Hops, H., & Greenwood, C. (1993). *RECESS: A program for reducing negative-aggressive behavior.* Seattle: Educational Achievement Systems.

Walker, H. M., & McConnell, S. R. (1995). *The Walker-McConnell scale of social competence and school adjustment-elementary version: A social skills rating scale for teachers.* Belmont, CA: Wadsworth/Thomson Learning, Inc.

Walker, H. M, McConnell, S. R., Walker, J. L., Clarke, J. Y., Todis, B., Cohen, G., & Rankin, R. (1983). Initial analysis of the ACCEPTS curriculum: Efficacy of instructional and behavior management procedures for improving the social adjustment of handicapped children. *Analysis and Intervention in Developmental Disabilties, 3,* 103–127.

Walker, H. M., Severson, H. H., Feil, E. G., Stiller, B., & Golly, A. (1998). First step to success: Intervening at the point of school entry to prevent antisocial behavior patterns. *Psychology in the Schools, 35*(3), 259–269.

Walker, H. M., Shinn, M. R., O'Neill, R. E., & Ramsey, E. (1987). A longitudinal assessment of the development of antisocial behavior in boys: Rationale, methodology and first year results. *Remedial and Special Education, 8*(4), 7–16, 27.

Wandless, R. L., & Prinz, R. J. (1982). Methodological issues in conceptualizing and treating childhood social isolation. *Psychological Bulletin, 92,* 39–55.

Wentzel, K. R. (1991). Social competence at school: Relation between social responsibility and academic achievement. *Review of Educational Research, 61*(1), 1–24.

Windsor, J. (1995). Language impairment and social competence. In M. E. Fey, J. Windsor, & S. F. Warren (Eds.), *Language intervention: Preschool through the elementary years* (pp. 213-238). Baltimore: Brookes.

Wolfe, V. V., Boyd, L. A., & Wolfe, D. A. (1983). Teaching cooperative play to behavior-problem preschool children. *Education and Treatment of Children, 6*(1), 1-9.

Wright, M. J. (1980). Measuring the social competence of preschool children. *Canadian Journal of Behavioral Science, 12*(1), 17-32.

Zanolli, K., & Daggett, J. (1998). The effects of reinforcement rate on the spontaneous social interactions of socially withdrawn preschoolers. *Journal of Applied Behavior Analysis, 31,* 117-125.

AUTHORS' NOTE

Preparation of this chapter was supported in part by the U.S. Department of Education, Office of Special Education Programs, as part of the Early Childhood Research Institute on Measuring Growth and Development (grant H024S600010). The authors thank our colleagues at the University of Minnesota site who have worked on the research reported here, and our colleagues at Juniper Gardens Children's Project of the University of Kansas and the School Psychology Program at the University of Oregon. We also thank Dr. Samuel L. Odom of Indiana University, who has been a long-time colleague to Drs. McConnell and McEvoy in the work reported here.

CHAPTER 20

Building, Implementing, and Sustaining a Beginning Reading Improvement Model: Lessons Learned School by School

Deborah C. Simmons, Edward J. Kame'enui, and Roland H. Good III
University of Oregon

Beth A. Harn
California State University-Fresno

Carl Cole and Drew Braun
Bethel School District, Bethel, Oregon

INTRODUCTION

The goal of having all children read at or above grade level by the end of Grade 3 appears closer to reality than at any point in educational history. The scientific knowledge base of the causes and correlates of reading success and reading difficulty has never been more mature or convergent. Syntheses of reading research conducted by the National Research Council (1998) and more recently by the congressionally commissioned National Reading Panel (2000) provide ample and compelling evidence of the skills, experience, and knowledge children need to become successful readers in our alphabetic writing system. This research makes clear that children must develop and demonstrate proficiency in the "big ideas" (See Kame'enui & Simmons, 1998) of phonemic awareness, alphabetic understanding, and automaticity with the code. Equally important is the scientific evidence that early reading proficiency is best developed through early, systematic, explicit instruction (National Reading Panel, 2000). Unfortunately, less understood is how to translate this scientific knowledge of early reading into the schools and classrooms charged with the monumental task of teaching all children to read.

An estimated 20% of students will encounter serious reading difficulty or reading disability (Lyon, 1997); another 20% will have reading difficulties so severe as to hinder their enjoyment of reading (Grossen, 1997). The magnitude of reading difficulties among America's children compels us to rethink our system of reading education. Knowledge of effective, research-based practice is necessary but insufficient. The goal must, therefore, be to increase the probability that research-based effective practices (a) *find* their way into schools, (b) *are implemented* at sufficient levels to effect significant improvement, and (c) *are sustained* over time. Achieving this goal requires that we identify the essential curricular and instructional components in schools that interact with the scientific knowledge base of beginning reading to create an effective and efficient improvement model of reading for the full range of learners. In this chapter, we examine the intricacies of teaching beginning reading in schools and describe a prevention model of schoolwide beginning reading improvement.

Schools are complex educational environments that are made even more complex by social, political, economic, pedagogical, legal, cultural, demographic, and historical forces of the times. Although some of these forces are dynamic (e.g., cultural, social) and others coercive (e.g., legal, economic), they unwittingly shape the very nature and function of schools. Of course, as complex environments, schools come in all sizes, and the cultural, linguistic, and developmental variation of the student populations that occupy each of the more than 85,000 public elementary and secondary schools in the United States (National Center for Education Statistics, 1995) is also great. Given this complexity and diversity, schools have a formidable responsibility to improve the academic and social outcomes of all students. This covenant is perhaps most significant to those students who are at serious academic risk and who present the biggest challenge for public schools every day of the school week. In addressing this challenge, it is imperative to identify those factors that matter most.

DO SIZE AND PLACE MATTER TO SUSTAINING EFFECTIVE EDUCATIONAL PRACTICE IN READING?

In many cases, school size and location matter (Lee & Loeb, 2000). Not surprisingly, large, urban schools are likely to have more complicated administration and organization than small, rural schools. For example, the Los Angeles Unified School District (LAUSD) is the second largest school district in the country. LAUSD has 420 elementary schools, 72 middle schools, 49 high schools, an enrollment of 697,143 students who speak more than 88 different languages and dialects, a certified staff of more than 41,000, and a total district budget of $6.5 *billion*. In fact, the budget for the LAUSD is bigger than the *state budgets* of, for example, Alaska, Colorado, Delaware, Hawaii, New Hampshire, or Wyoming.

In contrast to LAUSD is Bethel School District (BSD) in Eugene, Oregon. Bethel has six elementary schools, two middle schools, and one high school, with a total enrollment of 5,246, a certified staff of 272, and a total district budget of $30 million. The numerical differences between these districts are staggering. LAUSD has *70 times more schools, 133 times more students, 150 times more certified staff, and a budget that is 220 times greater* than BSD. In light of these manifest quantitative differences in the administrative and fiscal profiles of the Los Angeles and Bethel school districts, it would be reasonable to pose several questions about what these differences mean for reading instruction. For example:

1. Should the classroom instructional practices and interventions be very different in design, scale, and impact for schools in large school districts compared to those in small school districts?

2. Does the extant research direct teachers and administrators to employ a very different curriculum and technology to address the instructional demands of large, urban schools in contrast to small, rural, or suburban schools?

3. Is there reliable evidence from the extant research about "scaling up" for large urban schools in ways that will lead to significant increases in students' academic achievement?

A reasonable response to each of the questions is an unequivocal "Yes." After all, large urban schools are the gargantuans of the educational enterprise and are different in almost every aspect from small, rural schools. Yet, with respect to instructional factors, there are critical features that are essential and generalizable irrespective of school size. In fact, there is substantial persuasive literature on scaling up for the implementation of curriculum innovations in such complex environments as LAUSD (Elmore, 1996). An organizing principle of this literature is that solving the problem of scaling up actually requires "scaling down," which suggests that large, urban districts must behave organizationally, administratively, and pedagogically like small districts. They must recognize that the instructional variables (e.g., core curricular materials, time allocated for instruction) within school jurisdictions that account for differences in learner performance *are the same* across districts. Though organizational factors such as district and school size clearly impact *how* things operate, the common and essential elements of effective schoolwide beginning reading improvement are fundamentally the same irrespective of size. We advance three principles to guide schools' approach to improving reading achievement:

1. Although school districts vary greatly in size and resources, the principles and strategies for conceptualizing, designing, implementing, and sustaining instructional and behavioral change are *fundamentally* the same for all *individual schools,* whether they are in Los Angeles or Bethel.

2. If effective curriculum programs, instructional and assessment strategies, staff development support, and organizational structures are to be sustained for extended periods of time, they must be anchored, implemented, monitored, and supported at the *school-building level* where the instructional complexities unfold daily.

3. Implementing instructional, behavioral, and organizational change *at the building level* is a *necessary, but insufficient* condition for increasing and sustaining student performance. District-level support and commitment are imperative for long-term sustainability.

The fundamental sameness about beginning reading improvement is that within every school's jurisdiction are alterable variables (e.g., time, group size, curricular goals, instructional materials) (Carroll, 1963) that when carefully understood, strategically managed, and faithfully implemented, are capable of producing positive and sustainable results for the full range of learners.

ADDRESSING THE COMPLEXITIES OF SYMBOLS AND SCHOOLS

Schoolwide beginning reading improvement involves the integration of two complex systems: (a) the declarative knowledge of reading in an alphabetic writing system, and (b) the procedural knowledge of how to organize and implement what we know about reading in a complex host environment known as a school and, which is composed of people, practices, pedagogy, and policy. The elements of both systems and the need for strategic integration to assist schools in attaining the goal of *all children reading* by Grade 3 are detailed in Figure 1.

Figure 1 is simple by necessity and does not suggest the complexity of the process. Action plans for individual schools, however, are similar, regardless of school size, site, or socioeconomic status. In the following section, we (a) describe a set of tenets to guide schoolwide beginning reading improvement initiatives and (b) discuss a schoolwide improvement model of reading improvement for translating research into practice. The model and its decision-making processes draw extensively on the work in reading assessment of Kaminski and Good (1996), (e.g., Deno, 1985; L. S. Fuchs & Deno, 1991; Shinn, 1989, 1998 with respect to Curriculum-Based Measurement [CBM]), and M. R. Shinn, M. M. Shinn, Hamilton, and Clarke, this volume. These researchers' procedures for identifying, grouping, problem solving, and performance monitoring are combined with Kame'enui and Simmons' (1998) components of contextual interventions to build an integrated and comprehensive beginning reading improvement intervention model. This model represents an evolution of guidelines and procedures based on lessons we've learned from our work with schools throughout the United States (e.g., Alabama, California, Hawaii, Minnesota, and Texas) and from three years of systematic and sustained implementation in a local school district of Eugene.

SCHOOLWIDE BEGINNING READING IMPROVEMENT MODEL: TENETS AND STAGES

As emphasized earlier in the chapter, our perspective is that the individual school must be the fundamental unit of change if significant and sustainable reading improvement is to occur. Our model of beginning reading improvement adheres to eight research-based tenets listed in Figure 2, on page 542.

FIGURE 1

Two Complex Systems in a Schoolwide Beginning Reading Improvement Model

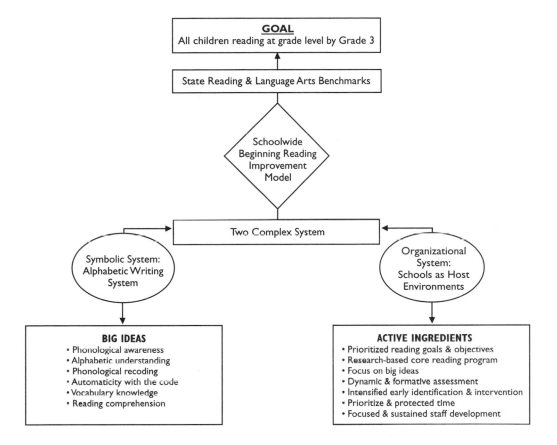

Collectively, these eight tenets characterize a philosophy of beginning reading improvement that is proactive, intensive, and effective for the full range of learners in schools. In the sections that follow, we illustrate how each of these tenets is implemented in a schoolwide model and the actions and decisions involved in K–3 beginning reading improvement.

Stages and Levels of a Schoolwide Beginning Reading Improvement Model

The architectural blueprint of the model is framed by five successive stages (see Figure 3, on page 543). Within each stage are two distinct levels (school and individual student) that operate concurrently. The premise of the two levels is that school-level decisions have consequences for individual students, for a schoolwide model that employs school-level procedures also must provide for the needs of individual students.

FIGURE 2

Tenets of the Schoolwide Beginning Reading Improvement Model

Schoolwide reading improvement:

1. Addresses reading success and reading failure from a schoolwide *systemic* perspective;

2. Embraces a *prevention framework* by intervening early and strategically during the critical window of instructional opportunity (National Research Council, 1998);

3. Recognizes and responds to the *multiple contexts of reading achievement* and includes carefully articulated goals, research-based programs, dynamic assessment, adequate and protected instructional time, quality instructional delivery, differentiated instruction, and effective organization and grouping (Editor, *American Educator,* 1998);

4. Develops and promotes a *comprehensive system of instruction* based on a research-based core curriculum and enhancement programs (Editor, *American Educator,* 1998);

5. Anchors instruction and practices to the *converging knowledge* base of effective reading practice (National Research Council, 1998);

6. Builds capacity in the school by *using school-based teams* to customize interventions to the host environment;

7. Relies on and fosters the *ability of the school principal* to serve as the instructional leader; and

8. Uses ongoing tests sensitive to changes of student performance to identify students at risk, plan instructional groups, and modify instruction according to levels and rates of learning (Good, Simmons, & Smith, 1998).

Stage I: Conduct School Audit and Assess Student Performance K–3

Activities and actions in Stage I focus on two critical levels—the *school* and the *individual* student. As illustrated in Figure 4, on page 544, the primary functions in Stage I are for the school to (a) conduct a thorough and instructionally focused audit of cur-

FIGURE 3

Stages and Levels of a Schoolwide Beginning Reading Improvement Model

STAGE I: Conduct Schol Audit and Assess Student Performance	STAGE II: Analyze School and Student Performance	STAGE III: Design Instructional Interventions	STAGE IV: Set Goals and Monitor Progress Formatively	STAGE V: Evaluate Intervention Efficacy and Adjust Instruction
School Level ◇ Conduct School Audit • Use *Planning and Evaluation Tool* (Kame'enui & Simmons, 2000).	**Identify Reading Priorities and Develop Action Plan** • Review Audit • Identify strengths and areas of development based on audit summary scores • Identify and develop three priorities • Establish Action Plan	**Design Core Instructional Interventions** • Specify the following: Goals Core Curriculum Program Time for Reading Instructional Grouping and Scheduling Instructional Implementation Progress-Monitoring System	**Establish and Implement Progress-Monitoring System** • Identity valid and reliable dynamic reading indicators • Establish absolute and relative goals • Commit resources • Determine schedule • Interpret and communicate results	**Evaluate School-Level Performance** • Evaluate effectiveness three times per year • Examine components of interventions in Stage III • Make instructional adjustments • Determine whether and for whom to maintain or adjust intervention
Student Level ◇ Assess Student Performance • Use *Dynamic Indicators of Basic Early Literacy Skills* (Kaminski & Good, 1998). (CBM) (Deno, 1985; L. S. Fuchs & Deno, 1997; Shinn, 1998)	**Analyze Individual Performance and Plan Instructional Groups** • Identify students who require: Benchmark Intervention Strategic Intervention Intensive Intervention	**Customize Intensive and Strategic Interventions** • Specify the following: Goals Core or Specialized Curriculum Materials Time for Reading Instructional Grouping and Scheduling Instruction Progress-Monitoring System	**Customize Progress-Monitoring System for Intensive and Strategic Interventions** • Intensive: Monitor progress every 2 weeks • Strategic: Monitor progress every month • Benchmark: Monitor progress three times per year	**Intensify Intervention** • Determine students who are and are not "learning enough" • Chart instructional profiles for students making little or no progress • Adjust components of interventions in Stage III

rent reading practices, and (b) assess each student's reading performance on a set of grade-appropriate and instructionally relevant measures.

Conduct school audit. The first goal for a school is to determine what is currently in place with respect to (a) instructional priorities, (b) reading assessment, (c) instructional practices and materials, (d) time allocated to reading instruction, (e) grouping and organizational strategies, (f) administrative involvement and decision making, and (g) professional development. To obtain this information, schools conduct an internal audit using the *Planning and Evaluation Tool for Effective Schoolwide Reading Programs* (Kame'enui & Simmons, 2000). The audit uses a 100-point scale divided across seven areas (e.g., goals and priorities, assessment) to quantify a school's current state of practice, and the resulting data provides a first step in identifying areas of improvement. The tool's purpose is to quantify and develop awareness of a school's current policies and practices in beginning reading. Figure 5, on page 545, presents items from the Administration, Organization, Communication element of the tool. As indicated, respondents complete six items in this area using a 0–2 scale (i.e., 0 = not in place, 1 =

FIGURE 4

STAGE 1:
Conduct School Audit
and Assess Student
Performance

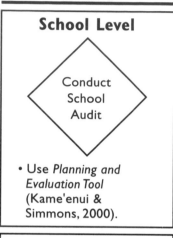

School Level

Conduct
School
Audit

• Use *Planning and
Evaluation Tool*
(Kame'enui &
Simmons, 2000).

School Level

Assess
Student
Performace

• Use *Dynamic Indicators
of Basic Early Literacy
Skills* (Kaminski &
Good, 1998).

partially in place, and 2 = fully in place) and document evidence to support the rating. Schools work in grade-level teams or representative teams to evaluate prevailing practices and complete the seven components. The process can be unifying and instructive as teachers and administrators work together to take inventory of their schools' reading disposition. For example, from the items illustrated, schools may realize that while they have a principal who is highly knowledgeable of state standards and priorities and works effectively with staff to create a coherent plan for reading instruction, the coordination of instruction across Title I, special education, and general education may not be complementary—and insufficient to realize schoolwide performance goals. A discussion on how to use this tool follows (see Stage II).

FIGURE 5

Example Items From Planning and Evaluation Tool for Effective Schoolwide Reading Programs (Kame'enui & Simmons, 2000)

0	1	2
Not in place	Partially in place	Fully in place

EVALUATION CRITERIA	DOCUMENTATION OF EVIDENCE
VI. *Administration/Organization/Communication* - Strong instructional leadership maintains a focus on high-quality instruction, organizes and allocates resources to support reading, and establishes mechanisms to communicate reading progress and practices.	
2 1. Administrators are knowledgeable of state standards, priority reading skills and strategies, assessment measures and practices, and instructional programs and materials.	
2 2. Administrators work with staff to create a coherent plan for reading instruction and institute practices to attain school reading goals.	
2 3. Administrators maximize and protect instructional time and organize resources and personnel to support reading instruction, practice, and assessment.	
2 4. Grade-level teams are established and supported to analyze reading performance and plan instruction.	
1 5. Concurrent instruction (e.g., Title I, special education) is coordinated with and complementary to general education reading instruction.	
1 6. A communication plan for reporting and sharing student performance with teachers, parents, and other stakeholders is in place.	

10/12 **Total Points**   80%

Percent of Implementation:

6 = 50%   10 = 80%   12 = 100%

Assess student performance. As shown in Figure 4, the second goal of Stage I is to identify children who may be at risk of reading failure and to determine the need for early intervention (Kaminski & Good, 1996). All children, kindergarten through Grade 3, are screened on 1-minute measures that correspond to the big ideas in beginning reading: (a) phonological awareness, (b) alphabetic understanding, and (c) automaticity with the code (Simmons & Kame'enui, 1998). The tests are used as screening measures; Dynamic Indicators of Basic Early Literacy Skills (DIBELS) and Reading CBM (R-CBM) are not intended to tell us everything about each student's reading skills. Rather, they serve as valid and reliable *indicators* or predictors of skills highly associated with later reading achievement.

In the area of early literacy, DIBELS (Kaminski & Good, 1998) are used to identify children whose performance differs significantly from their same-age peers and who may need early intervention in kindergarten and first grade. DIBELS measures align with the big ideas in early reading and include (a) Letter-Naming Fluency, (b) Onset-Recognition Fluency, (c) Phonemic-Segmentation Fluency, and (c) Nonsense-Word Fluency. Once students are able to read words in connected text (typically mid-first grade) 1-minute measures of oral reading fluency from R-CBM passages are used as indicators of general reading achievement. R-CBM is then used as the primary indicator of reading progress through Grade 5. These measures provide "vital signs of growth in basic skills comparable to the vital signs of health used by physicians" (Deno, 1992, p. 6). In addition, they provide fast and efficient indications of a student's reading well-being on skills that are essential to success in the general education curriculum (Kaminski & Good, 1998). For more information on these practices, see M. R. Shinn, M. M. Shinn, Hamilton, and Clarke, this volume.

A word of caution: reliance on vital-sign indicators does not dismiss or discount the importance of other reading dimensions such as vocabulary and comprehension. Rather, 1-minute R-CBM, fluency-based measures allow educators to identify potential prereading and reading difficulties early and to monitor progress more frequently. The purpose of assessment in Stage I is not to label, but to identify children at risk of reading difficulty to provide levels of intervention necessary to alter and increase early learning trajectories. Figure 6 indicates the administration schedule of early literacy and reading tests by grade. We refer to these tests as big-idea indicators as they align with the critical skills necessary for early reading success (i.e., big ideas).

In Stage I, a centralized system for managing student performance data is established and maintained at the school level to enable timely and informed decisions. In the project described in this school, schoolwide data were collected three times per year, entered into a Web-based template, and forwarded to the Institute for the Development of Educational Achievement (IDEA), College of Education, University of Oregon.

FIGURE 6

Administration Schedule of Early Literacy and Reading Tests by Grade

	Fall	Winter	Spring
Kindergarten			
Letter-Naming Fluency	◆	◆	◆
Onset Recognition	◆	◆	
Phonemic-Segmentation Fluency		◆	◆
Nonsense-Word Reading Fluency		◆	◆
First Grade			
Letter-Naming Fluency	◆		
Phonemic-Segmentation Fluency	◆	◆	◆
Nonsense-Word Reading Fluency	◆	◆	◆
R-CBM		◆	◆
Second–Fifth Grades			
R-CBM	◆	◆	◆

Stage II: Analyze School and Student Performance

Identify reading priorities and develop an action plan. In Stage II, schools review results of the schoolwide audit conducted in Stage I (See Figure 7, on page 548). Audit results quantify what is *in place,* what is *partially in place,* and what is *not in place* along a range of critical dimensions (e.g., reading goals and objectives, assessment tools and strategies, instructional programs). The audit provides information at three levels: (a) an overall score based on a total of 100 points that indicates relative ranking toward a standard, (b) dimension scores (i.e., curriculum programs and instruction, professional development), and (c) individual item scores (e.g., Is there a commonly articulated and understood set of goals in reading for each grade?). After reviewing and completing all items in the audit, schools summarize their overall level of reading implementation quantitatively (see Figure 8, on page 549), prioritize areas of improvement, and develop an "Action Plan" to direct schoolwide beginning reading improvement.

As the percentile scores reflect, this school rated itself high in administration (88%) and goals (81%) and low in differentiated grouping (55%) and assessment (59%). The resulting priorities from this audit included (a) using assessment data to establish flexible grouping to provide differentiated instruction, (b) allowing time to share this information and inservice all teachers regarding the assessment system and instruction-

FIGURE 7

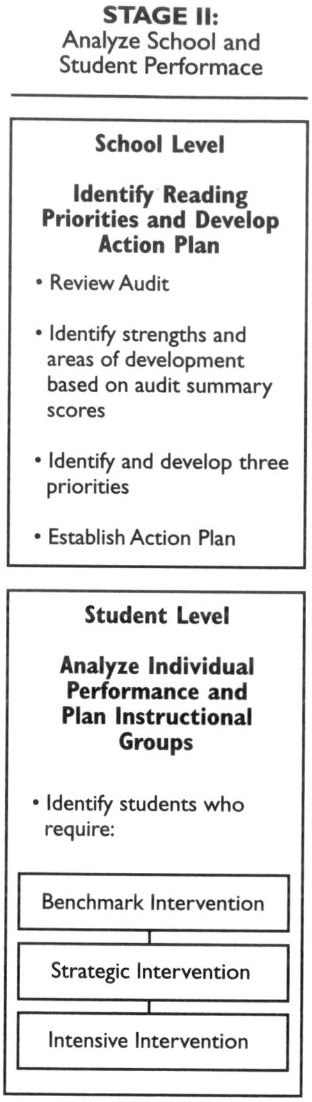

STAGE II:
Analyze School and
Student Performace

School Level

**Identify Reading
Priorities and Develop
Action Plan**

- Review Audit

- Identify strengths and
  areas of development
  based on audit summary
  scores

- Identify and develop three
  priorities

- Establish Action Plan

Student Level

**Analyze Individual
Performance and
Plan Instructional
Groups**

- Identify students who
  require:

Benchmark Intervention

Strategic Intervention

Intensive Intervention

---

al implications, and (c) implementing assessments three times per year to assess progress and determine instructional needs. These priorities are documented in an action plan (see Figure 9, on page 550) and are used to guide reading improvement for the academic year.

Analyze individual performance and plan instructional groups. In Stage II, schools examine *each* learner's performance on critical prereading and reading skills to determine the scope and scale of instructional needs. Grade-level summary data are provided in the form of histograms that indicate the number of children by level of proficiency on a specific measure (See Figure 10, on page 551). For example, in the fall of 2000, all children enrolled in first grade were administered the Nonsense-Word Fluency meas-

FIGURE 8

Summary of Level of Reading Improvement from School Audit

Element	Score	Percent
I. Goals/Objectives/Priorities	11.5/14	81.4%
II. Assessment	11.8/20	59.0%
III. Instructional Practices and Materials	15.0/22	68.0%
IV. Instructional Time	8.0/14	57.0%
V. Differentiated Instruction/Grouping	5.5/10	55.0%
VI. Administration/Organization/Communication	10.6/12	88.0%
VII. Professional Development	4.5/8	56.0%
Total Score	**66.9/100**	**67.0%**

ure. Results indicated that eight children identified fewer than four correct letter sounds in one minute and six identified more than 75. The distribution of performance on this measure informs the school about the magnitude of need and how to allocate resources. In this school, 25% of students identified less than 20 correct letter sounds, 22% identified 20–39, and 52% identified 40 or more correct letter sounds. The benchmark goal is 40 correct letter sounds by January. From this information, schools determine children who have already reached benchmark goals and those who have not (See Figure 11, on page 552). Moreover, grade-level teams and teachers can identify children who are at risk of not meeting benchmark goals. Benchmark goals indicate a level of performance on a particular measure that (a) establishes a solid, fluent proficiency on the particular measure, and (b) forecasts future performance on higher-order skills. For example, reading 60 correct words per minute in the spring of first grade strongly correlates with reading 90 correct words per minute in the spring of second grade (Good, Simmons, & Kame'enui, in press).

Individual student performance on DIBELS and R-CBM is compared to the benchmark goals to identify children who may be at risk of reading disability or delay (see Figure 8). Performance expectations are derived from research-based criterion levels of performance (Hasbrouck & Tindal, 1992; Good et al., 2000), and students are identified as potentially at risk relative to how other students in their school and district perform and in comparison to research-based criteria. For example, a child entering first grade scoring less than 20 letter sounds per minute on the Nonsense-Word Fluency measure may be at risk, as the target criterion for the mid-first-grade

FIGURE 9

An Action Plan of Instructional Priorities

Planning and Evaluation Tool for Effective Schoolwide
Beginning Reading Programs

Prioritization and Action

Based on the previous listing of areas to improve, rank order three areas. The areas may include one element or items from several different elements.

Priority #1	**Action Plan**	**Who & When?**
To use our assessment data to establish flexible grouping to provide differentiated instruction to benchmark, strategic, and intensive groups.	Teachers review data to establish instructional groups.	Classroom teachers 8/9/01
Priority #2	**Action Plan**	**Who & When?**
To allow time to share this information and inservice with others regarding DIBELS and the reading big ideas. To continuously analyze our program and make changes as needed.	Review information in first faculty meeting.	Classroom teachers 8/9/01
Priority #3	**Action Plan**	**Who & When?**
To implement assessment timelines and measurements to determine instructional needs and interventions.	Develop schedule and assessment team. 8/9/01	Classroom, resource, and grade-level teachers

---

Support Team Members and Schedule

Identify the date, time, and place for the next schoolwide reading meeting.

---

benchmark of 40 correct letter sounds per minute. Likewise, a student exiting second grade reading 40 words correct per minute may be identified for more intensive intervention and follow-up, as the end-of-year target for correct words per minute is 90.

Teachers perform "instructional triage" on students by using a process developed by M. R. Shinn, M. M. Shinn, Hamilton, and Clarke (this volume) and elaborated by Kaminski and Good (1998), by assessing student performance on the critical reading skills using DIBELS, and by assimilating other information from teachers. Children

FIGURE 10

First-Grade Fall 2000 DIBELS Nonsense-Word Fluency Histogram Summary

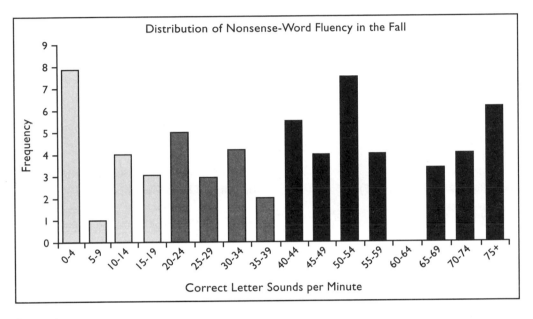

Legend
Solid black = identified 40 or more correct letter sounds in 1 minute (75%)
Diagonal = identified 20–39 correct letter sounds in 1 minute (20%)
Cross hatch = identified fewer than 20 correct letter sounds correct in 1 minute (5%)

who are at greatest risk are identified from those at less risk. To operationalize this process, we use the following criteria.

Students benefiting from benchmark reading intervention. In the following discussion, we assign a label to the type of intervention that is indicated by a student's performance rather than assign a label to the learner. This may appear to be a subtle shift, but it is one we consider important. Our focus is to use the student's performance on indicator measures to help design the type of intervention necessary to change learning outcomes. Therefore we focus on the factor of intervention opposed to learner. Further, we use the term *intervention,* rather than *instruction program* or *practice,* as *intervention* consists of multiple components. These dimensions will be discussed further in Stage III.

Benchmark interventions are those *core* instructional practices and programs provided in general education that position students to meet or exceed commonly agreed-upon reading goals and priorities. By design, they are intended to ensure that the majority of students in a given school achieve adequate (i.e., benchmark) levels of performance. The elements of benchmark intervention vary across schools, but the

FIGURE 11

Dynamic Indicators of Basic Early Literacy Skills and R–CBM Benchmark Levels and Goals

MEASURE	BENCHMARK GOAL
Onset-Recognition Fluency Measure (OnRF)	• 25–35 Correct Onsets per minute by *winter* of Kindergarten
Phonemic-Segmentation Fluency Measure (PSF)	• 35–45 Correct Phonemes per minute by *spring* of Kindergarten
Nonsense-Word Fluency Measure (NWF)	• 40–50 Correct Letter Sounds per minute by *winter* of First Grade
R-CBM Measure (ORF)	• 40–60 Words read correct per minute by *end* of First Grade
	• 90 Words read correct per minute by *end* of Second Grade

common factor is that the majority of students derive adequate benefit to pass school-, district-, and state-level assessments of reading. As a general rule, we suggest that benchmark intervention should prepare 80% or more of the students in a school to read at grade level. The 80% criterion is a logical cut off point. If more than 20% of the students fail to reach benchmarks at designated intervals (see Figure 11), then the core reading program and practices are not adequately addressing the schools' needs. Recent studies synthesized by Lyon and colleagues at the National Institute of Child, Health, and Human Development indicate that 20% of children in schools will experience significant reading difficulties.

Students who attain benchmark performance on critical literacy skills (e.g., 35–45 phonemes per minute by the end of kindergarten) are on track to attain later reading outcomes (Good, Simmons, & Kame'enui, 2001). Students receiving benchmark intervention are monitored three times a year in the fall, winter, and spring to evaluate growth toward common goals. If a child's performance does not maintain adequate growth toward benchmark goals, appropriate interventions are provided.

Students in need of strategic intervention. Students who receive strategic intervention typically are not acquiring and demonstrating foundational reading skills at high levels and rates of success. They may begin moderately below their average-achieving peers in critical areas or may start at adequate levels but fail to progress over time. For students who are not grasping and applying grade-level reading skills and strategies proficiently and fluently, we recommend more explicit, systematic, and timely intervention and monitoring. In general, strategic intervention is for students who need more than what is typical of the general education curriculum and instruction. Of the 20% of children who are likely to have difficulty in beginning reading, we reason that approximately 15% of students may need additional, strategic instructional support. Students in the strategic intervention group may exhibit mixed performance patterns; that is, some may perform well on one measure but low on another, while others may perform moderately below average on a range of measures. In some schools, students requiring strategic intervention may constitute a large number of students, while in other schools they may be a small number. The goal of strategic intervention is to identify children who are potentially at risk of serious reading difficulty and to provide sufficient systematic instruction so that their performance rapidly reaches and exceeds benchmark levels. Shinn (1997) recommends frequent monitoring for students who are failing to demonstrate adequate rates of progress. In the schoolwide beginning reading improvement model, we monitor students who are receiving strategic intervention monthly.

Students in need of intensive intervention. Intensive intervention is recommended for students who are significantly at risk based on their extremely low performance on one or more big idea performance indicators. The greater the number of measures and the lower the performance across measures, the greater the risk. The need for immediate intensive intervention is even more urgent when students display continued low rates of progress even when provided with strategic intervention. With effective benchmark and strategic instruction in place in the primary grades, it is estimated that approximately 5% of students would need intensive intervention (Torgesen, 2000).

Much like children with serious medical conditions, children in need of intensive intervention in reading are in acute need of early identification, the most effective interventions available, and frequent monitoring to ensure that their reading performance does not remain seriously low. Educators must intervene with a sense of urgency and with the most effective tools and strategies available. Moreover, the intensive interventions should be short-term and temporary, rather like an intensive care unit in a hospital.

As illustrated in Stage II, Student Level of the model, children with similar performance profiles are grouped according to intervention needs (i.e., benchmark, strategic, intensive). The purpose of grouping is to ensure that children are given ample *opportunities* to receive instruction and increased opportunities to respond at their instructional level. As a rule, the number of students who receive intensive instruction should be smaller than that in either the strategic or benchmark groups. Groups should be dynamic rather than static. Strategic, ongoing, and frequent monitoring of performance when students are grouped homogeneously has been demonstrated to contribute to overall achievement effects (Guitiérrez & Slavin, 1992) and is critical for adjusting groups in response to instruction and assessment.

As a rule, approximately 20% of students in the fall would require strategic or intensive intervention. Identifying 20% of children in the fall for intensive intervention may constitute "overidentification;" however, the consequences of providing extra intervention are considered far less risky than a *wait-and-see* position that withholds opportunity for additional instruction until students are seriously discrepant compared to their peers. In addition to the 20% criterion, we employ research-based guidelines on selected measures that predict success. For instance, a first-grade student who can identify 40 or more letter sounds correctly on the Nonsense-Word Fluency measure in the winter is highly likely to read 40 correct words per minute on R-CBM (Good et al., 2000) in the Spring of Grade 1. The correlational nature of the early indicator measures allows schools and teachers to make high-probability predictions of success and risk. For example, a mid-year first-grader who identifies only nine correct letter sounds on the Nonsense-Word Fluency measure is at serious risk of not attaining the end-of-year first-grade R-CBM benchmark of 40–60 correct words per minute and would warrant more instructional support than students performing in the benchmark range.

Stage III: Design Instructional Interventions

In Figure 12, we summarize the critical features of Stage III, which is arguably the most critical and complex component of the schoolwide beginning reading model—intervention. Of foremost importance to the model is the instructional fit of the instructional reading intervention within the school's host environment; therefore, schools invest serious and sustained energy at this stage. Stage III decisions focus on (a) specifying and implementing core instructional interventions, and (b) customizing strategic and intensive interventions for students who are not benefiting adequately from the core curriculum or are at high risk of reading difficulty.

Designing a core instructional intervention. Two principles guide decisions in Stage III: (a) intervention is bigger than program alone, and (b) identification and implementation of a research-based core intervention provides the highest probability of success in the host environment. A common misperception is that once a commercial program is identified and adopted, the reading intervention is "determined." Commercial programs constitute a critical component of a schoolwide model, but as documented in the Stage III figure, core intervention encompasses far more than the adoption of an instructional program. The entire core intervention begins with the review and adoption of grade-level goals. These goals may be state- or locally mandated standards; in some cases they may be school-determined. Specifying grade-level expectations for all students is fundamental to core intervention and provides the basis for other decisions. For example, if a kindergarten content standard is that students will be able to segment 2- and 3-phoneme words, core instructional programs should address this standard adequately and fully. Moreover, standards should specify the level of performance students should achieve. An example first-grade performance goal is for students to be able to read orally 60 correct words per minute on grade-level text. Goals specification is a critical dimension of the schoolwide inventory conducted in Stage I and many schools in which we work allocate significant time specifying expectations for K–3 reading.

FIGURE 12

STAGE III:
Design Instructional
Interventions

School Level

**Design Core Instructional
Interventions**

• Specify the following:

Goals
Core Curriculum Program
Time for Reading
Instructional Grouping and Scheduling
Instructional Implementation
Progress-Monitoring System

Student Level

**Customize Intensive
and Strategic
Interventions**

Goals
Core or Specialized Curriculum Materials
Time for Reading
Instructional Grouping and Scheduling
Instruction
Progress-Monitoring System

Once goals are specified and the magnitude of the school's need is evaluated in relation to the goals, school teams design the optimal school-level intervention that fits their host environment. School teams consist ideally of all professionals in the school who are responsible for reading achievement, including the general education teachers, school administrators, school psychologist, speech and language specialist, Title I or reading support teacher, etc. In Stage III, school teams essentially move beyond the question of "What does reading instruction look like in our school?" to "What should reading instruction look like in our school?" Critical decisions such as time allocations for reading, instructional grouping procedures, who delivers instruction, where it is delivered, and so on are considered and specified explicitly. Schools invest considerable time designing this intervention map, document their plan of action in writing, and review this map at critical decision points throughout the year. In essence, the outcome of Stage III is an intervention map that specifies what core instruction looks like for students in Kindergarten, Grade 1, Grade 2, and beyond.

Central to the instructional map is the selection of the research-based core program that fits the host environment. From the outset, schools are encouraged to review commercial programs that have solid, scientific evidence and that produce strong and positive results for children when implemented faithfully. A short list of research-based commercial programs is currently available (Editor, *American Educator*, 1998); however, the new generation of programs holds great promise because of their attention to research-based findings documented in NICHD research, summarized and synthesized by the National Research Council (1998) and the National Reading Panel (2000), and mandated by populous states such as California and Texas. From the short list, we encourage schools to (a) review scope and sequences; (b) conduct a discrepancy analysis with school-adopted expectations; (c) compare programs within the list to identify the one that aligns most closely with the needs of students, the instructional priorities, and the school environment; (d) pilot the program with faithful implementation; (e) monitor student performance; and (f) evaluate performance toward key early reading outcomes.

Through our work in schools and districts, we find that a site-based reading coordinator (e.g., a Title I teacher, school psychologist) greatly facilitates schoolwide beginning reading improvement coupled with strong administrative leadership. The site coordinator and principal work with collaborative grade-level intervention teams in initial intervention development and adaptation. Throughout the intervention process, collaborative intervention teams construct or customize the intervention from a menu of validated options. It is this "fit" within the school that further distinguishes this model from more traditional reading models.

Customize intensive and strategic interventions. With the core reading intervention specified, the next set of decisions involves how to *customize* interventions for students who are not benefiting adequately from that core intervention or for children who enter with high levels of risk on the big idea early reading indicators. Questions such as "Can the core commercial program be used, but in smaller groups?" "Could the student benefit from more instruction either through a longer period or an extra period of instruction, but with a different program?", "Could preteaching critical lesson components such as new phonic elements or story vocabulary result in adequate progress?" These questions relate to customization. In some cases, students may require a specialized and intensified program that focuses prominently on the big ideas of early reading. In other cases, customization may involve adding a second reading period. The degree and kind of customization must be determined at the school level and governed by school resources of time, programs, and personnel.

Stage IV: Set Goals and Monitor Progress Formatively

The efficacy of the schoolwide model hinges largely on the ability of a school to document whether students are learning enough (Carnine, 1997). In Stage IV, schools assess *all* students' reading progress and evaluate *each* student's progress. A school's ability to document and act upon individual student performance dynamically, reliably, and formatively distinguishes it from the majority of schools in the traditional educational system. Although norm-referenced, commercially published measures of reading achievement do an adequate job of documenting groups of learners' performance at a given point in time (e.g., spring), the purpose of these measures was never to inform instruction for individual learners or to monitor performance. Moreover, these measures were never intended to monitor progress frequently and formatively over time.

Establish and implement a progress-monitoring system. A key feature of the Schoolwide Beginning Reading Improvement Model is the essential linkage between assessment and instruction. This linkage is predicated on a simple but vital proposition: We have valid, reliable, and efficient (one minute to administer) measures that, when given early in a child's beginning literacy experience, serve as powerful predictors of later reading success or risk. Moreover, when these measures are administered frequently, they can document student progress or lack thereof. For any school seriously interested in serving *all* students, which requires serving *each* and every student, this is a powerful proposition with practical implications.

An effective and efficient progress-monitoring system consists of five critical factors: (a) reliable and valid measures with alternate forms that can be administered frequently, (b) established *absolute* and *relative* learning targets to evaluate whether the rate and slope of learning is adequate, (c) resources and personnel to prepare assessment materials, administer and score measures, and enter data, (d) a confirmed and commonly agreed-upon schedule for collecting data, and (e) an efficient process for analyzing, summarizing, and reporting data to constituencies and for using student performance to inform instruction. Integrating assessment and instruction is not a novel concept and has long been a signature of effective special education (Deno, 1992; D. Fuchs & L. Fuchs, 1994). What is innovative and effective about this process is that the technology can be applied at the school level in time to catch children before they fail (Torgesen, 1998). At the present time, Good, Kame'enui, and Simmons are building and refining a website through which schools enter DIBELS and R-CBM data and immediately receive reports of student performance at classroom, school, and district levels. Information from these reports includes the percentage of students at benchmark, strategic, and intensive intervention levels and class profiles delineating the individual performance of each learner across measures.

In summary, in the upper box of Figure 13, on page 558, we highlight the schoolwide system of monitoring student performance as an essential element in a beginning reading improvement model. In the bottom box of Figure 13, we outline how to use the formative assessment system for students who are at greater risk of reading failure than the majority of children in the school.

FIGURE 13

STAGE IV:
Set Goals and Monitor
Progress Formatively

School Level

**Establish and Implement
Progress-Monitoring
System**

- Identify valid and reliable
dynamic indicators

- Establish absolute and
relative goals

- Commit resources

- Determine schedule

- Interpret and
communicate results

Student Level

**Customizing Progress-
Monitoring System for
Intensive and Strategic
Interventions**

- Intensive: Monitor
progress every two weeks

- Strategic: Monitor
progress every month

- Benchmark: Monitor
progress three times per
year

Customize progress-monitoring system for intensive and strategic interventions. For children who are at risk of reading difficulty or for those whose reading performance is not within "acceptable" zones of proficiency, we recommend frequent progress monitoring. For frequent progress monitoring, we use the same measures used in schoolwide assessment. The primary difference between the schoolwide and customized progress monitoring is the frequency of administration and analysis. At the school level, all students are assessed quarterly on critical performance indicators to

FIGURE 14

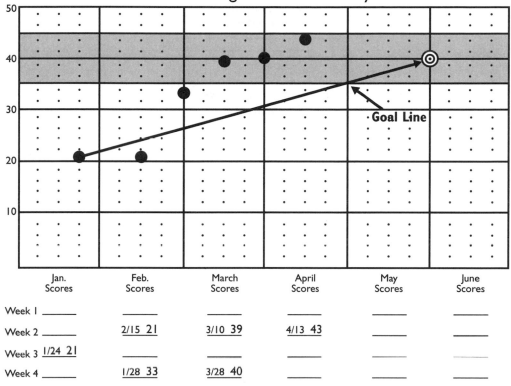

Kindergarten Example of Progress Monitoring
on the Phonemic Segmentation Fluency Measure

	Jan. Scores	Feb. Scores	March Scores	April Scores	May Scores	June Scores
Week 1	_____	_____	_____	_____	_____	_____
Week 2	_____	2/15 21	3/10 39	4/13 43	_____	_____
Week 3	1/24 21	_____	_____	_____	_____	_____
Week 4	_____	1/28 33	3/28 40	_____	_____	_____

determine their progress toward goals. Students in strategic interventions are monitored monthly, and students in intensive interventions are monitored more frequently (e.g., every 2–4 weeks). Learning targets are established, and each learner's performance on target goals is documented. Figure 14 depicts one kindergarten student's monthly progress on the Phonemic-Segmentation Fluency measure. The student whose performance is reflected in Figure 14 was identified at the beginning of the year as needing intensive intervention based on his performance on Onset-Recognition and Letter-Naming Fluency measures. As indicated in the graph, he met the end-of-kindergarten goal of 35–45 phonemes per minute in March and continued to make progress through April. Through monthly monitoring, teachers can evaluate each child's progress precisely and adjust instruction as needed.

Stage V: Evaluate Intervention Efficacy and Adjust Instruction

In the final stage of the model (see Figure 15, on page 560), the effects of intervention conducted in Stages I–IV are evaluated directly and interventions are

FIGURE 15

STAGE V:
Evaluate Intervention
Efficacy and Adjust
Instruction

School Level

Evaluate School-Level Performance

• Evaluate effectiveness three times per year

• Examine components of interventions in Stage III

• Make instructional adjustments

• Determine whether and for whom to maintain or adjust intervention

Student Level

Intensify Intervention

• Determine students who are and are not "learning enough"

• Chart instructional profiles for students making little or no progress

• Adjust components of interventions in Stage III

intensified as indicated by student performance. In this stage, schools address the following questions: "Are the instructional interventions working for the full range of learners? Are students learning enough? What instructional adjustments must be made to enhance beginning reading performance?"

Evaluate school–level performance. In the Bethel Reading Project, each school evaluates the performance of all students three times a year on big idea early reading

FIGURE 16

The Number of Correct Letter Sounds Correctly Identified by 54 First-Grade Students in January 2000

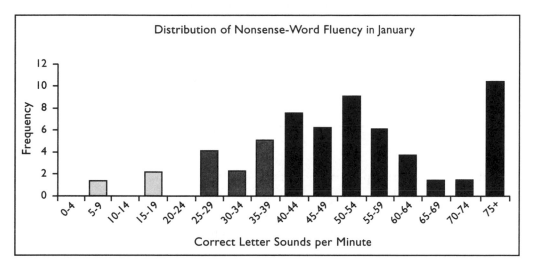

Legend
Solid black = identified 40 or more correct letter sounds in 1 minute (75%)
Diagonal = identified 20–39 correct letter sounds in 1 minute (20%)
Cross hatch = identified fewer than 20 correct letter sounds correct in 1 minute (5%)

indicators. Progress is reviewed at each grade to evaluate the efficacy of the instructional intervention in the respective grades. Classroom teachers also receive summaries of students in their classrooms to identify specific children who need more effective instructional interventions.

The histogram in Figure 16 displays the performance distribution of all first-grade students in one school (N = 54) on the Nonsense-Word Fluency measure. The target goal for first graders in January is 40–50 letter sounds per minute. As illustrated, 75% of students in the school met the target. Another 20% demonstrated emerging letter-sound knowledge (i.e., 20–39 letter sounds per minute). Five percent, or three children in this school, identified fewer than 20 correct letter sounds in one minute and are considered to have marked difficulty with the alphabetic principle.

This indicates that a relatively small percentage of children (i.e., cross-hatched bars) are at serious risk of difficulty as judged by students' ability to identify letter sounds. This is important information because it allows schools to reallocate instructional resources for children who have not made sufficient progress. The information from this performance period may also be compared to performance in the previous assessment period to determine how much growth has occurred. In essence, by comparing performance over time, schools can address the question, "Is the instructional intervention working?"

TABLE 1

Percent of Students in Each Level Based on Nonsense-Word Fluency (N = 387)

	At Risk—Deficit (0-19)	Emerging (20-39)	Established (40-60)
September 1999	47%	36%	17%
January 2000	5%	20%	75%

Table 1 compares the performance of first-grade students in the entire district (i.e., six elementary schools) on the Nonsense-Word Fluency measure at two points in the year: September 1999 and January 2000. Comparative performance data indicate that students in the district made significant progress, since 75% attained the benchmark. Moreover, the findings inform schools and teachers to concentrate energy on the 25% of students who did not reach the benchmark of 40 letter sounds per minute.

When a large number of students fail to reach target benchmarks (e.g., 40-50 letter sounds per minute), school teams return to the instructional interventions planned in Stage III. First, school teams evaluate critical dimensions of the core intervention to identify the source of the difficulty. First-order questions include:

1. Was the intervention implemented as planned or prescribed?

2. Did students receive the amount of intervention specified for the time allocated?

3. Were there high rates of absence for many learners?

4. Did the size of instructional groups permit adequate opportunities for students to respond?

5. Was progress monitored frequently to evaluate learning?

If a review of the core dimensions of intervention indicates one or more deviations from what was planned, procedures should be put in place to increase the fidelity of the planned intervention. If analysis reveals that all intervention components were implemented as planned, school teams should review the list of alterable variables to determine what and how much to intensify. If performance trends are positive and adequate for all but a few children, then large-scale intervention adjustment is not warranted. Only if many students are failing to progress adequately is full review and adjustment of the core intervention components necessary.

Intensify intervention. In Stage V, each classroom teacher reviews performance data at each of the three assessment periods to determine whether specific children have an inadequate rate of reading growth to attain targeted proficiency goals on critical measures of early reading. From this information, teachers assess each child's performance on multiple measures to determine whether the student's performance is deficit, emerging, or established. Instructional recommendations are then based on the number of essential skills on which the student is experiencing difficulty and the magnitude of their educational need. The following winter report for a first-grade class illustrates a mid-first-grade goal of 35–45 phonemes per minute on the Phonemic Segmentation Fluency measures and 40–50 letter sounds per minute on the Nonsense-Word Fluency measure (see Figure 17, on page 564). In this class, nine children (e.g., John, Gillian, Beth) are benefiting from benchmark instruction. Benchmark instruction is the instructional recommendation for all children who score (a) 35 or more on phonemic segmentation, *and* (b) 40 or more on nonsense word fluency. Four children require strategic intervention. The criteria for recommending strategic intervention are (a) 11–34 on phonemic segmentation fluency, or (b) 20–39 on nonsense word fluency, or (c) less than 10 words correct per minute on oral reading fluency, or (d) any combination of a, b, or c. Four children are recommended for intensive intervention. The criteria for intensive intervention include scores of (a) less than 10 on phonemic segmentation fluency, (b) less than 20 on nonsense word fluency, or (c) less than 10 on oral reading fluency.

In addition to evaluating absolute performance (i.e., where a student scores at one point in time), it is important to evaluate growth and the nature of performance differences. For example, although Suzy and Mandy both are recommended for intensive intervention, Suzy made enormous growth on phonemic segmentation from fall (0) to winter (58) and on nonsense words (from 0 to 39). Yet, she read only four words correct in the Oral Reading Fluency passage; hence, the reason for the intensive intervention recommendation. Mandy, however, grew from 10 to 19 on phonemic segmentation and from 4 to 15 on nonsense words. Though the intervention recommendation is for both children, the type of instructional focus would differ.

As indicated in the Student Level component of Figure 17, determining how to intensify intervention is essential in Stage V of the Schoolwide Beginning Reading Improvement Model. A first-order question for students identified as being in need of intensive and strategic intervention is, "Have these children been enrolled in the school and received instruction?" or are there obvious attendance and enrollment issues that shed light on their low progress or performance levels? Answers to these questions may explain the differential progress rates of children such as Suzy and Mandy. If low performance cannot be explained by attendance factors, teachers then review and intensify levels of intervention to increase the probability that students will attain adequate levels of proficiency. Common adjustments used to intensify intervention are (a) increasing the amount of time by providing double doses of reading instruction, (b) reducing the size of the instructional group, (c) using a more specialized and explicit instructional program, and (d) monitoring progress more frequently. A table of alterable components and specific adjustments is shown in Table 2, on page 565.

FIGURE 17

First-Grade Winter DIBELS and R-CBM Benchmark Teacher Report

Teacher: Mrs. Smith   District: Oregon School District   Grade: 1   School: Anywhere Elementary

Student	Letter Naming Fall	Phonemic-Segmentation Fluency Fall	Winter	Status	Nonsense-Word Fluency Fall	Winter	Status	Oral Reading Fluency Winter	Status	Instructional Recommendation Based Primarily on Nonsense Word Fluency
Andy	22	16	50	Established	33	38	Emerging	11	Emerging	Strategic instruction
John	31	13	62	Established	42	66	Established	42	Established	Benchmark instruction
Suzy	6	0	58	Established	0	39	Emerging	4	Nonreader	Intensive instruction
Erin	42	0	23	Emerging	29	37	Emerging	18	Emerging	Strategic instruction
Gillian	44	28	56	Established	47	52	Established	23	Emerging	Benchmark instruction
Beth	57	25	49	Established	27	56	Established	46	Established	Benchmark instruction
Joe	16	1	47	Established	32	50	Established	7	Nonreader	Strategic instruction
Mandy	20	10	19	Emerging	4	15	Deficit	7	Nonreader	Intensive instruction
Sarah	55	55	47	Established	59	70	Established	36	Emerging	Benchmark instruction
Fred	46	22	42	Established	45	62	Established	74	Established	Benchmark instruction
Neil	39	31	40	Established	35	53	Established	27	Emerging	Benchmark instruction
Stewart	40	14	40	Established	13	14	Deficit	13	Emerging	Intensive instruction
Deborah	24	17	24	Emerging	39	17	Deficit	13	Emerging	Intensive instruction
Edward	50	48	50	Established	49	48	Established	49	Established	Benchmark instruction
Katie	72	57	72	Established	40	57	Established	40	Established	Benchmark instruction
Josh	63	31	63	Established	50	31	Emerging	50	Established	Strategic instruction
Dave	36	24	50	Established	35	49	Established	27	Emerging	Benchmark instruction

TABLE 2

Alterable Components and Specific Adjustments Used to Intensify Intervention

Alterable Components	Specific Adjustments				
Opportunities to Learn	Develop plan to increase attendance	Ensure instruction is provided daily	Increase number of opportunities for learner to respond	Increase teacher-directed instruction	Add another instructional period (double dose)
Program Efficacy	Preteach components of core program	Use materials that are extensions of the core	Supplement program with appropriate materials	Replace current core program	Implement specially designed program
Program Implementation	Model lesson delivery	Monitor implementation frequently	Provide coaching and ongoing support	Provide additional staff development	
Grouping for Instruction	Check to see students are appropriately placed	Reduce number of students in group	Provide individual instruction	Change instructor	
Coordination of Instruction	Clarify instructional priorities	Establish concurrent reading periods/ sessions	Provide complementary reading instruction across reading periods	Establish a communication system across instructors	

Summary of the Schoolwide Beginning Reading Improvement Model

Schoolwide beginning reading improvement involves the integration of two complex systems: (a) the scientific knowledge base of reading in an alphabetic writing system and (b) the design and implementation of the knowledge base in a complex host environment (i.e., schools) comprising people, practices, pedagogy, and policy.

We advocate that the *processes* and *procedures* required to effect and sustain reading improvement are fundamentally the same whether the school is in Los Angeles, California or Eugene, Oregon. The translation of the knowledge base of beginning reading from the research literature to practice in schools is built on and nurtured by a common set of components operationalized in the five stages of the Schoolwide Beginning Reading Improvement Model.

REFERENCES

Carnine, D. (1997). Instructional design in mathematics for students with learning disabilities. *Journal of Learning Disabilities, 30,* 130-131.

Carroll, J. B. (1963). A model of school learning. *Teachers College Record, 64,* 723-733.

Deno, S. L. (1985). Curriculum-based measurement: The emerging alternative. *Exceptional Children, 52,* 219-232.

Deno, S. L. (1992). The nature and development of curriculum-based measurement. *Preventing School Failure, 36*(2), 5-10.

Editor. (1998). Every child reading: An action plan of the Learning First Alliance. *American Educator, Spring/Summer,* 52-63.

Elmore, R. F. (1996). Getting to scale with good educational practice. Harvard *Educational Review, 66*(1), 1-26.

Fuchs, L. S., & Deno, S. L. (1991). Paradigmatic distinctions between instructionally relevant measurement models. *Exceptional Children, 58,* 232-243.

Fuchs, D., & Fuchs, L. (1994). Classwide curriculum-based measurement: Helping general educators meet the challenge of student diversity. *Exceptional Children, 60,* 518-537.

Good, R., Kaminski, R., Shinn, M., Bratten, J., Shinn, M., & Laimon, D. (2000). *Technical adequacy and decision making utility of DIBELS* (Tech. Rep. No. 7). Eugene, OR: University of Oregon, Early Childhood Research Institute.

Good, R. H., III, Simmons, D. C., & Kame'enui, E. J. (2001). The importance and decision-making utility of a continuum of fluency-based indicators of foundational reading skills for third-grade high-stakes outcomes. *Scientific Studies of Reading, 5*(3), 257-288.

Good, R., III, Simmons, D. C., & Smith, S. (1998). Effective academic interventions in the United States: Evaluating and enhancing the acquisition of early reading skills. *School Psychology Review, 27*(1), 45-56.

Grossen, B. (1997). *Thirty years of research: What we now know about how children learn to read.* Santa Cruz, CA: The Center for the Future of Teaching and Learning.

Guitiérrez, R., & Slavin, R. E. (1992). Achievement effects of the nongraded elementary school: A best evidence synthesis. *Review of Educational Research, 62*(4), 333-376.

Hasbrouck, J. E., & Tindal, G. (1992). Curriculum-based oral reading fluency norms for students in grades 2 through 5. *Teaching Exceptional Children, 24,* 41-44.

Kame'enui, E. J., & Simmons, D. C. (1998). Beyond effective practice to schools as host environments: Building and sustaining a school-wide intervention model in reading. *OSSC Bulletin, 41*(3), 3-24.

Kame'enui, E. J., & Simmons, D. C. (2000). *Planning and evaluation tool for effective schoolwide reading programs.* Unpublished manuscript.

Kaminski, R. A., & Good, R. H., III. (1996). Toward a technology for assessing basic early literacy skills. *School Psychology Review, 25*(2), 215-227.

Kaminski, R. A., & Good, R. H., III. (1998). Assessing early literacy skills in a problem-solving model: Dynamic indicators of basic early literacy skills. In M. R. Shinn (Ed.), *Advanced applications of curriculum-based measurement*. New York: Guilford.

Lee, V. E., & Loeb, S. (2000). School size in Chicago elementary schools: Effects on teachers' attitudes and students' achievement. *American Educational Research Journal, 37*(1), 3-31.

Lyon, G. R. (1997, July 10). *How do children learn to read?: Statement before the Committee on Education and the Workforce, U.S. House of Representatives,* Washington, DC.

National Center for Education Statistics. (1995). *Digest of Education Statistics.* Washington DC: U.S. Dept. of Education.

National Reading Panel. (2000). *Teaching children to read: An evidence-based assessment of the scientific research literature on reading and its implications for reading instruction* [online]. Available Internet: *www.nichd.nih.gov/publications/nrp/smallbook.htm*.

National Research Council. (1998). *Preventing reading difficulties in young children.* Washington, DC: National Academy Press.

Shinn, M. R. (Ed.). (1989). Curriculum-based measurement: Assessing special children. New York: Guilford Press.

Shinn, M. (1997). *Instructional decision making using curriculum-based measurement.* Unpublished workshop materials.

Shinn, M. R. (1998). Advanced applications of curriculum-based measurement. New York: Guilford Press.

Simmons, D. C., & Kame'enui, E. J. (Eds.). (1998). *What reading research tells us about children with diverse learning needs: Bases and basics.* Mahwah, NJ: Lawrence Erlbaum Associates.

Torgesen, J. K. (1998). Catch them before they fall: Identification and assessment to prevent reading failure in young children. *American Educator, 22*(1), 32-39.

Torgesen, J. K. (2000). Individual differences in response to early interventions in reading: The lingering problem of treatment resisters. *Learning Disabilities Research & Practice, 15*(1), 55-64.

AUTHORS' NOTE

The contents of this document were developed in part for the Office of Special Education Programs, U.S. Department of Education under Contract Number H324M980127. This material does not necessarily represent the policy of the U.S. Department of Education, nor is the material necessarily endorsed by the federal government.

We gratefully acknowledge and warmly thank the dedicated, hard-working, and enthusiastic Bethel District elementary administrators, teachers, and educational assistants who so expertly implemented the Schoolwide Beginning Reading Model. We extend a special thanks to the reading coordinators for their leadership and perseverance. Their collective sustained efforts are realized in the reading growth of children in the Bethel School District. We further acknowledge the contributions of Katie Tate in her expert preparation of this manuscript.

Chapter 21

Promoting Mathematics Achievement

Mark K. Harniss and Marcy Stein
University of Washington, Tacoma

Douglas Carnine
University of Oregon

INTRODUCTION

One of the most intense debates in the field of education currently is over mathematics instruction. Participation in this debate is not limited to educators, but includes many others interested in the mathematics performance of American students. The debate has drawn the attention of mathematicians, scientists, four Nobel laureates (Riley, 1999), as well as legislators and parents (Colvin, 1999). Questions of how best to teach mathematics have become so prevalent, in fact, that they are receiving attention in local, national, and international arenas. Student achievement in mathematics is discussed at Parent-Teacher Association (PTA) meetings, at universities, in state legislatures, and over the Internet. Furthermore, as countries of the world interact more, the relative effectiveness of American mathematics instruction, in comparison to instruction common in other countries, continues to be questioned (Bracey, 2000).

The debate has been fueled at least partially by the poor mathematics performance of American students. Students struggle to perform satisfactorily in math at all grade levels. According to the 1996 National Assessment of Educational Progress Mathematics Report Card, only 21% of fourth-grade students perform well enough in math to be labeled "Proficient" in the subject. This percentage drops to 16% for high school seniors (Reese, 1996). Ultimately, most American students graduate from high school without the mathematics competencies required for many career options.

In order to understand the seriousness of the problem in the United States, researchers have compared the mathematics performance of American students to that of students from other countries. The results of the Third International Mathematics and Science Study (TIMSS), a comprehensive educational survey based on participating students from 40 countries, revealed that significant performance gaps exist between

American students and students in other countries (e.g., gaps of 1.5 standard deviations between American students and students in Singapore) (Loveless & Diperna, (2000).

To help explain the TIMSS results, researchers examined the curricula used by mathematics teachers in various countries. First, TIMSS researchers found that American mathematics textbooks are *longer* than most and cover a greater number of topics. For example, a typical fourth-grade American mathematics textbook contains an average of 530 pages. In contrast, the average length of international mathematics textbooks is only 170 pages. One explanation for the differences is that most U.S. states have standards that guide the development and production of textbooks. Because the standards are not identical in each state, publishers are compelled to include the greatest number of topics to meet the greatest number of standards so that their textbooks will sell to the greatest number of teachers. However, because of the large number of topics included at any given grade level, textbooks often allocate the same amount of space for simple skills as they do for more complex skills. Moreover, the textbooks place little emphasis on systematic skill progression or skill mastery. According to the study, most American textbooks sacrifice depth for breadth (Valverde & Schmidt, 1998).

In addition to curricular issues regarding mathematics instruction, researchers are finding that many American teachers are simply underprepared to teach mathematics. According to Wu (1999), American teacher preparation courses are notably lacking in the area of mathematics instruction. This study also revealed that some American elementary teachers themselves had difficulties performing certain mathematical calculations, such as dividing fractions. Furthermore, none of the teachers in the study could adequately explain the mathematical reasoning in the algorithms of the problems they were given, nor could they devise real world applications or offer proofs. This problem has also been highlighted in Ma's (1999) comparison of Chinese and American educators.

Given that the curriculum materials teachers are given may not be adequately designed and that some teachers may not be adequately prepared to teach mathematics, especially to students with disabilities or those at risk for academic failure, we propose two options for the role of the school psychologist. First, at the school or district level, school psychologists can help teachers and administrators *identify evidenced-based models* of mathematics instruction that have documented academic success with diverse student populations. Depending on availability of resources, administrators may explore the possibility of implementing one of these evidenced-based schoolwide models at a school or throughout an entire district. Second, at the classroom level, school psychologists may be able to *provide support to individual teachers* by helping them modify their curriculum materials to best meet the needs of their low-performing students.

To assist school psychologists in pursuing either of the options mentioned above, we have divided this chapter into two major parts. First, we examine several models of mathematics instructional interventions that are based on a strong body of research. Next, we outline general principles of curriculum modification that are derived from examining the instruction in those models. We conclude with recommendations on how school psychologists can contribute to the mathematics achievement of diverse student populations.

MATHEMATICS INSTRUCTIONAL INTERVENTIONS

We have identified four different instructional intervention models, all of which have been supported by empirical research, to describe briefly in this section: The Missouri Mathematics Effectiveness Project, Cooperative Learning, Classwide Peer-Tutoring, and Direct Instruction. Each of these models was designed as a developmental (i.e., not remedial) model to meet the needs of students representing a wide range of abilities, especially those who may be at risk for academic failure. In fact, much of the research on each model was conducted with students from economically disadvantaged communities.

The Missouri Mathematics Effectiveness Project

This project is among the first experimental studies to demonstrate the relationship between specific teaching activities and student achievement in the area of mathematics (Good & Grouws, 1979). Previous to this study, the teacher effectiveness literature consisted largely of process-product studies that yielded correlations between specific teaching behaviors and student performance. In fact, Good and Grouws based their instructional intervention on the results of a naturalistic observation study of mathematics teachers from which they were able to identify a set of factors that discriminated the highly effective teachers from those who were less effective. After integrating their findings with variables suggested by other teacher effectiveness studies, they derived five key instructional features to include in their model of mathematics instruction: Daily Review, Development, Seatwork, Homework Assignment, and Special Reviews. (See Good, Grouws, & Ebmeier, 1983, for a more complete description of these variables.)

Good and Grouws then tested the effectiveness of providing staff development in the form of inservice training on this model by comparing the mathematics performance of students in the treatment classrooms to that of students in the control classrooms where teachers were encouraged to maintain their own teaching style. Importantly, they first determined that the level of implementation of their model was quite high. Only 2 of the 21 treatment teachers scored low on measures of implementation, and the treatment teachers did exhibit more of the treatment teaching behaviors than did the control teachers. The results of this study provided evidence that the Missouri Mathematics Effectiveness Model was effective in increasing mathematics achievement as measured by both standardized and criterion-referenced mathematics tests.

This study is significant for several reasons. First, the researchers demonstrated under experimental conditions that *how* students are taught mathematics has a significant impact on what students learn about mathematics. Perhaps even more significantly, the researchers demonstrated that teachers using this instructional system could increase the achievement of low-income, inner city students, and overcome the risk of low expectations. Another relevant finding from this study is that the "development" component of the instructional system (i.e., the explanations and initial teaching of new concepts) was the most difficult component for teachers to implement. The implications that this finding has for the evaluation, selection, and use of instructional material are discussed in the section on designing effective mathematics instruction.

Cooperative Learning

Cooperative learning is an instructional model characterized by the use of student teams to enhance learning. In his analysis of cooperative learning, Slavin (1983) found that the interdependence of two features, (a) group goals and (b) individual accountability, was critical for student success in any cooperative learning model. The Team-Assisted Instruction (TAI) program for mathematics instruction is an example of the application of cooperative learning to the teaching of mathematics (Slavin, Leavey, & Madden, 1984). In TAI, students work in heterogeneous teams but on mathematics materials designed to meet their individual needs. Members of the team help each other with problems as well as check work and perform other "managerial" duties. In addition to the team work, teachers work with homogeneous groups drawn from each team at specified times delivering direct instruction on important mathematics concepts and skills. At the end of each week, all team members are assessed using criterion-referenced measures and group points are allocated according to team performance. TAI has been described as integrating both individualized instruction and direct instruction with cooperative learning teams and cooperative incentives (Slavin & Karweit, 1984). It should be noted that other generic models of cooperative learning such as Student Teams-Achievement Division (STAD) also have been applied to the teaching of mathematics (Nattiv, 1994).

Several studies have demonstrated that students taught mathematics using TAI have outperformed students in control conditions (Slavin et al., 1984; Slavin & Karweit, 1984; Stevens & Slavin, 1995). A particularly interesting study, involving two experiments, investigated the effects of three different instructional models commonly used to teach mathematics: (a) individualized instruction as exemplified by TAI, (b) whole-class instruction, using the Missouri Mathematics Program (MMP), and (c) within-class ability grouping using the principles of the MMP applied to two homogeneous groups of students. In both experiments, TAI and the ability-grouped instruction increased achievement in mathematics computation more than the MMP and traditional whole class instruction. The latter was present in Experiment 2 only. No differences were found in both experiments for TAI and ability-grouped instruction.

In Experiment 2, students taught using the MMP significantly outperformed those who were taught using traditional instruction, thereby replicating earlier research on the MMP. No treatment effects were found in either experiment on measures of mathematics concepts and applications. Finally, in both experiments, students' attitudes toward math class were more positive for TAI groups. In addition, more teachers reportedly chose TAI when given the opportunity to choose any method, other than the one they had used before, for training and materials.

ClassWide Peer Tutoring

ClassWide Peer Tutoring (CWPT) is an instructional system that employs simultaneous tutoring throughout the entire class. The tutor-tutee pairing is established at the beginning of each week along with assignments of tutoring pairs to teams. All students are both tutors and tutees and as such all students are taught to provide feedback through appropriate error correction. CWPT is similar to TAI in its use of interdependent social reward structures for both individual and team performance. However, CWPT differs from TAI in that mathematics instruction and practice are organized for an entire class and not completely individualized. CWPT was designed to maximize academic engaged time in the classroom, promote high levels of mastery, and ensure sufficient content coverage. For more detail on CWPT, see Greenwood, Maheady, and Delquadri in this volume.

While CWPT is not restricted to use with economically disadvantaged students, this instructional model has been effective in producing achievement gains for these students commensurate with their more advantaged peers. In a longitudinal study of first- through fourth-grade students (Greenwood, Delquadri, & Hall, 1989), the experimental low socioeconomic status (SES) group using CWPT achieved greater gains in mathematics (and language and reading) than did the low SES control group. At the same time, no differences in academic performance were evident between the low SES experimental group, using CWPT, and a high SES comparison group, using traditional instruction. Notably, in this study, student satisfaction with tutoring was quite high.

In a follow-up study 2 years later at the end of sixth grade, Greenwood, Terry, Utley, Montagna, and Walker (1993) examined the achievement outcomes for the low SES experimental group, the low SES control group and the nonrisk group. They found that the CWPT students maintained their advantage over their low SES peers on the mathematics subtest of a standardized achievement test, produced significantly higher scores on tests of science and social studies not previously measured, and were referred less often for special education services and for less restrictive services. Findings from this study also demonstrated that the CWPT students performed similarly to the nonrisk students in the area of mathematics.

A substantial amount of research has been conducted on different models of classwide peer tutoring (Fantuzzo, Polite, & Grayson, 1990), the effects of supplemental peer practice (Good, Reys, Grouws, & Mulryan, 1989/1990; Kohler, Ezell, Hoel, & Strain, 1994), and teachers' perceptions of classwide peer tutoring and curriculum-based measurement (Phillips, L. S. Fuchs, & D. Fuchs, 1994). Findings from both short-term and longitudinal studies support the continued use of CWPT and suggest that this model is an exemplary preventive and prereferral intervention strategy for those students most at risk for academic failure.

Direct Instruction

The term *direct instruction* has appeared in the literature in various contexts, often referring to systematic instruction. The *Direct Instruction* model (DI), described in this section, refers to a comprehensive instructional model involving many of the features of the previously discussed models including (a) organizational structure, in this case, small group instruction; (b) systematic teacher preparation; (c) the use of guided and frequent practice with feedback; as well as (d) a system for monitoring student and teacher performance.

However, a defining feature of the Direct Instruction model is the use of a carefully designed curriculum based on the text *Theory of Instruction* (Engelmann & Carnine, 1991), that explicitly teaches not only algorithms for computation but also *generalizable rules and strategies* for solving problems. The nature of the DI curriculum differs from those used in other instructional models primarily in the specificity of the major instructional strategies. DI emphasizes the identification of, and instruction in, (a) background knowledge, (b) a carefully designed sequence of instruction, and (c) the use of cumulative introduction and review to integrate new and previously introduced skills and concepts (Carnine, Grossen, & Silbert, 1995; Gersten, Woodward, & Darch, 1986).

In 1968, the Direct Instruction Model was selected as one of the nine major instructional models to be evaluated as part of Project Follow Through, a federally funded project designed originally for the development and implementation of innovative teaching practices in schools serving low-income student populations. Over 180 school districts have been involved in the Follow Through Project. The major models it has used reflect a range of educational philosophies including Piagetian approaches and models based on discovery learning, in addition to three models based on behavioral principles. The Direct Instruction Model was implemented in communities throughout the United States including Flippin, Arkansas; the Rosebud Sioux Reservation in South Dakota; inner city schools in New York and Washington, D.C.; rural schools in Williamsburg County, North Carolina; as well as in Hispanic communities such as East Las Vegas, New Mexico.

ABT Associates conducted an independent evaluation of Follow Through for the U.S. Office of Education (Stebbins, St. Pierre, Proper, Anderson, & Cerva, 1977). The measures used to determine mathematics achievement were the math problem-solving and math computation subtests of the *Metropolitan Achievement Test* and the mathematics subtest of the *Wide Range Achievement Test*. Data from the Follow Through evaluation were quite revealing. The results indicated that low-income primary-grade students who received the full 3- to 4-year Direct Instruction mathematics program outperformed students who were taught using other approaches on all *Metropolitan Achievement Test* mathematics subtests. The Direct Instruction students achieved a level higher than was expected for students of similar demographic characteristics, a level that was commensurate with that of their middle-income peers (Gersten & Carnine, 1984).

Results from a follow-up study of fifth- and sixth-grade students who had been taught using DI mathematics programs in the primary grades but were no longer in the programs indicated consistent positive findings in the area of mathematics problem solving, weaker but significant effects in mathematics concepts, and null effects in computation (Becker & Gersten, 1982). The results from the follow-up study seem to suggest that the DI students maintained those skills that were most generalizable—for example, problem-solving skills. Once the students left third grade, they were taught multiplication and division computation skills by use of more traditional instruction and no longer demonstrated significant achievement in the area of computation. Notably, evidence on the effectiveness of Direct Instruction is not limited to data from the Follow Through program but comprises a rich literature that has been summarized recently by Adams and Engelmann (1996).

Summary

The four instructional models discussed in this chapter share many features including teacher-directed instruction, high levels of academic engagement, continuous progress monitoring, and frequent feedback to students. More importantly, they all have been evaluated experimentally to determine their relative effectiveness in improving the mathematics performance of students, especially those at risk for academic failure. Notably, most of the features of the instructional models outlined above are related to either what is taught or how it is being taught.

CURRICULUM MODIFICATION

Not all school psychologists will have the opportunity to implement the school-wide programs previously described. As an alternative, school psychologists can provide support to individual teachers by helping them modify their existing mathematics curriculum. Three areas of a curriculum should be addressed in this modification: (a) instructional goals, (b) instructional strategies, and (c) formative assessment. These three areas are discussed in more detail in the following sections.

Instructional Goals

All teachers have learning goals for their students, but some goals may be more important than others. When evaluating mathematics instruction in the classroom, school psychologists can assist teachers in determining the *relative importance* of these goals. Relative importance is determined by examining two factors. First, learning goals should focus on skills that are most frequently used. Second, learning goals should address the foundational concepts or "big ideas" in mathematics.

The first factor in determining the importance of student learning goals is frequency of use. Given a limited amount of instructional time, teachers must select goals that address important concepts and skills. For example, teaching students to write numbers in the billions is less important than teaching a strategy for solving ratio and proportion word problems. One means of determining importance is by examining district grade-level expectations often found in curriculum guides.

A second and related means of determining importance is by ensuring that student learning goals focus on *big ideas*. Big ideas are major organizing principles that have rich explanatory and predictive power and are applicable in many situations and contexts

(Kame'enui & Carnine, 1998). Guidelines written by The National Council of Teachers of Mathematics (NCTM, 2000) suggest that, "Foundational ideas like place value, equivalence, proportionality, function, and rate of change should have a prominent place in the mathematics curriculum because they enable students to understand other mathematical ideas and connect ideas across different areas of mathematics" (p. 15).

Davis (1990) points out that too often teachers focus their instruction on "small ideas." For example, arbitrary procedures such as cross-multiplying to solve problems like x/a = b/c. Such procedures frequently rely only on rote recall, preempting the possibility that students *will infer* the important mathematical principles underlying them. In addition, many mathematics textbooks are not designed using the concept of big ideas. For example, in most textbooks students are expected to learn different formulas to calculate the volume of seven three-dimensional figures:

- Rectangular prism: $l \cdot w \cdot h = v$

- Wedge: $1/2 \cdot l \cdot w \cdot h = v$

- Triangular pyramid: $1/6 \cdot l \cdot w \cdot h = v$

- Cylinder: $p \cdot r^2 \cdot h = v$

- Rectangular pyramid: $1/3 \cdot l \cdot w \cdot h = v$

- Cone: $1/3 \cdot p \cdot r^2 \cdot h = v$

- Sphere: $4/3 \cdot p \cdot r^3 = v$

These equations emphasize rote formulas rather than big ideas. An analysis based on big ideas reduces the number of formulas students must learn from seven to slight variations of a single formula, that is, the area of the base times the height ($B \cdot h$). This approach enhances understanding while simultaneously reducing the quantity of content to be learned, remembered, and applied.

Big ideas are found throughout mathematics. For example, the four operations of addition, subtraction, multiplication, and division rest upon a limited set of big ideas. These ideas include place value; the distributive, commutative and associative principles; equivalence; and number sense (i.e., primarily the concept of composition and decomposition of numbers in a base 10 system [Ma, 1999]). Figure 1 provides a detailed description and examples of these big ideas for operations. These big ideas interweave throughout the teaching and learning of the operations. When they are clearly understood by teachers and students, they serve as the conceptual underpinnings for understanding the operations. (See Carnine, Dixon, & Silbert, 1998, for a lengthier discussion of big ideas in mathematics.)

FIGURE 1

Big Ideas in Operations

Big Idea	Example
Place value is the understanding that in our number system, the "place" a number holds in a sequence of numbers gives information about that number.	In the number 324, the 3 at the beginning of the number is a one hundreds number. We know that the placement of the 3 tells us that there are three units of 100, or three 100s, in that number. Similarly, the location of the 2 tells us that there are 2 units of 10 in the number.
Expanded notation is simply the awareness by learners that you can reduce a number to its constituent units.	The number 432 is composed of four 100s, three 10s, and two ones which can be represented in an equation as $100 + 100 + 100 + 100 + 10 + 10 + 10 + 1 + 1 = 432$ or conversely as $400 + 30 + 2 = 432$.
Commutative property: The order in which numbers are placed in the equation can be changed without affecting the outcome. $a + b = b + a$	Addition and multiplication are commutative: In addition, $5 + 6 = 11$ and $6 + 5 = 11$ In multiplication, $4 \times 5 = 20$ and $5 \times 4 = 20$ Subtraction and division are not commutative: In subtraction, $6 - 1 = 5$ and $1 - 6 = -5$ In division, $8 \div 4 = 2$ and $4 \div 8 = 0.5$
Associative property: The groupings in which numbers are placed in the equation can be changed without affecting the outcome. $(a + b) + c = a + (b + c)$	Addition and multiplication are associative: In addition, $(6 + 3) + 3 = 12$ and $6 + (3 + 3) = 12$ In multiplication, $(3 \times 2) \times 5 = 30$ and $3 \times (2 \times 5) = 30$ Subtraction and division are not associative: In subtraction, $(15 - 5) - 3 = 7$ and $15 - (5 - 3) = 13$ In division, $(32 \div 8) \div 2 = 2$ and $32 \div (8 \div 2) = 8$
Distributive property: You can distribute numbers in a problem that includes multiplication and addition. $a \times (b + c) = (a \times b) + (a \times c)$ You can also distribute numbers in an equation that includes division and subtraction or addition. $(a + b) \div c = (a \div c) + (b \div c)$	$5 \times (3 + 2) = (5 \times 3) + (5 \times 2)$ $(8 + 4) \div 2 = (8 \div 2) + (4 \div 2)$
Equivalence: The quantity to the left of the equal sign (=) is the same as the quantity to the right.	$32 + 15 = 47$ $16 + 16 + 15 = 47$ $8 + 8 + 8 + 8 + (5 \times 3) = 20 + 20 + 7$ Note: Many students interpret the equal sign as an operation (e.g., "when I see the equal sign I add, subtract, etc.") rather than as a relationship (e.g., "when I see the equal sign I know that the quantity on one side must be the same as the other side").
The *"rate of composition/decomposition of numbers"* (Ma, 1999) is a form of number sense. The rate of composition (or decomposition) of sets of numbers in our base 10 system is simply 10.	When you have accumulated 10 ones you have one 10. When you have accumulated 10 tens you have one 100 and so on. This concept is sometimes referred to as unitizing, that is, creating a tens unit from ten ones. Similarly, when you remove a one from a 10 you have nine ones, that is you have decomposed the ten.

Instructional Strategies

School psychologists can help teachers evaluate the quality of the instructional strategies available to them in their mathematics textbooks by considering four factors: (a) clarity of instructional strategies, (b) prerequisite knowledge, (c) scaffolding, and (d) review and integration.

Clarity of instructional strategies. Any routine that leads to both the acquisition and utilization of knowledge can be considered a strategy (Prawat, 1989). Prawat recommends that efficient strategy interventions be of intermediate generality. That is, efficient strategies fall somewhere between the extremes of being narrow in application and consistently reliable and being broad but not necessarily reliable.

An example of a narrow strategy would be teaching students to "carry the one" when solving addition problems with renaming to the 10s column. Using this strategy, students may not recognize the role of place value in renaming and may apply the strategy inappropriately. At the other extreme, an instructional strategy may be so general that it is little more than a broad set of guidelines. For instance, a broad problem-solving strategy such as "draw a picture" or "read, analyze, plan, and solve" will not help students who do not already have the component skills necessary for solving the problem.

A major challenge of instruction is to identify or modify strategies to assist students who do not develop these strategies on their own. Once teachers identify these strategies, they need to *teach them explicitly.* The support for explicitly teaching strategies is quite strong (Cardelle-Elawar, 1995; Carnine & Stein, 1981; Charles, 1980; Gleason, Carnine, & Boriero, 1990 Leinhardt, 1987; Moore & Carnine, 1989; Resnick, Cauzinille-Marmeche, & Mathieu, 1987; Resnick & Omanson, 1987; Woodward, Baxter, & Robinson, 1999). It should be noted that some educators confuse explicit instruction with rote instruction. With explicit instruction students do not memorize the answers to a set of examples; they learn a *set of procedures* that when successfully applied to the examples will result in greater accuracy and deeper understanding.

Prerequisite knowledge. School psychologists and teachers also should be aware of the need to identify important background knowledge critical to the strategies being taught. If students lack this knowledge, teachers must provide appropriate background instruction. If students have been taught this knowledge previously, they may still need to be "primed." That is, students will need to be reminded of what they know and shown how and when their previous knowledge supports their learning of new knowledge. This explicit linking of old to new knowledge is critical in helping students develop rich conceptual networks of mathematical knowledge.

Instruction on prerequisite skills should ideally occur prior to the introduction of a strategy requiring those skills. An example of critical prerequisite knowledge can be seen with an example from instruction on fractions. Students must know how to find the least common multiple of a set of numbers before they can successfully solve addition problems with fractions having unlike denominators. Thus, teachers would be wise to ensure that students are competent in finding the least common multiple before moving into teaching addition with unlike denominators.

Scaffolding. Scaffolding is a means by which students receive support from teachers in various forms as they are learning new content or strategies. More support is provided during initial instruction with a reduction of support as students become more proficient. (See Kame'enui & Carnine, 1998, for more information on scaffolding.)

Scaffolding in mathematics can include teacher prompting through focused questions, graphic support (e.g., the use of grids to assist students in column alignment), and peer collaboration in problem solving. Eventually all forms of support should be unnecessary as students demonstrate content or skill mastery.

An important part of scaffolding a task appropriately is to determine students' prerequisite knowledge accurately and target the task toward their instructional level. Vygotsky (1978) used the term *zone of proximal development* to describe situations in which students' cognitive ability matches the cognitive requirements demanded by an instructional activity.

Review. Most teachers would agree that review is important. However, all review is not the same. Sometimes review can be punishing in its repetitiveness or the amount can be aversive. Other times, review can be disconnected or out of sync with student learning. Too often, review is used only immediately after learning a new concept and then is dropped before students firmly attain a skill or concept. Developing good cycles of review takes careful thought and attention to detail.

Research strongly supports certain types of review (e.g., Dempster, 1991). Teachers should plan review that is sufficient (i.e., adequate to initially learn the content information), distributed (i.e., integrated over time so students do not forget what they have learned), cumulative (i.e., built upon previously learned information), and varied (i.e., applied in a variety of contexts) (Kame'enui & Carnine, 1998).

When review is planned appropriately, students not only understand individual strategies, but also learn how different instructional strategies are related to one another (Nickerson, 1985; Prawat, 1989; Van Patten, Chao, & Reigeluth, 1986). When scheduling review, it is also critical that only important information be placed into the review cycle. If instructional content has been identified as important to teach, then that content is worth the time spent reviewing.

Formative assessment. Teachers need to understand clearly how they know if and when their students have learned mathematical content. Many teachers are not taught in their teacher preparation programs how to use objective measures to evaluate student learning over time for the purpose of deciding whether students are benefiting from instruction. Moreover, teachers often are not taught how to link assessment data to instructional decision making.

Traditionally, school psychologists are trained to use published norm-referenced tests to identify students with disabilities and subsequently make placement recommendations. However, school psychologists can be of great assistance to teachers in identifying more functional measures of student mathematics performance as well as in helping teachers use data on student performance to modify classroom instruction.

Two types of assessment are critical in mathematics: (a) criterion-referenced assessment with error analysis, and (b) formative evaluation of student progress over time.

Ideally, teachers should integrate *both* criterion-referenced measures and formative evaluation over time into their mathematics instruction. Because school psychologists are familiar with these types of assessment, we will spend limited time describing each type.

In short, criterion-referenced measures help teachers know whether the instructional strategies they taught allowed students to achieve mastery on the goals they have established. Most mathematics programs provide a wide variety of criterion-referenced (i.e., mastery-oriented) assessment options from which teachers can choose. School psychologists need to become familiar with the advantages and disadvantages of the available options in order to help teachers make decisions about the most useful type of assessment.

In addition, school psychologists might assist teachers in conducting error analyses. An error analysis of the mistakes made on a criterion-referenced assessment helps teachers identify specific content for which students need additional instruction to help move students toward mastery. When examining student errors in mathematics, teachers should note whether the error appeared to be caused by (a) lack of knowledge of basic facts, (b) lack of a reliable problem-solving strategy, (c) lack of prerequisite knowledge, or (d) lack of motivation. If a student consistently misses problems requiring knowledge of basic facts, remediation will need to include independent work on facts. (See Stein, Silbert, & Carnine, 1997, for recommendations about setting up a fact mastery program.) If students lack the appropriate strategy to solve a certain type of problem, teachers need to reteach that strategy to the students using scaffolded instruction until students can demonstrate mastery.

As we noted earlier, some students may lack prerequisite knowledge for mastery of a given strategy. For example, students must know how to add a single column of one-digit numbers (e.g., $4 + 3 + 2$) if they are going to be successful in renaming in column addition (e.g., $24 + 13 + 42$). As teachers conduct an error analysis, they must be able to determine whether the student errors were attributable to lack of knowledge of the appropriate strategy or lack of prerequisite knowledge.

Finally, teachers must be able to determine whether student errors are caused by a lack of motivation rather than a lack of knowledge. One way for teachers to explore motivation as a cause of poor performance is by providing incentives to students for good work (e.g., stickers, stamps, points toward extra recess). If motivation is an issue, teachers should see a difference in student work when incentives are provided. If students are making errors owing to lack of knowledge rather than lack of motivation, they will not be able to improve their work in mathematics regardless of the nature of the incentive.

Formative evaluation techniques, such as Curriculum-Based Measurement (CBM), help teachers know whether students are progressing at an acceptable rate toward mastery of their annual learning goals. For more detail on formative evaluation see Deno, Espin, and Fuchs; and Shinn, Shinn, Hamilton and Clarke, both in this volume. Many mathematics programs do not contain provisions or materials for this type of formative evaluation. This situation is unfortunate since research suggests that teachers who monitor growth over time (a) use more specific, acceptable achievement goals; (b) are more realistic and less optimistic about goal attainment; (c) cite more objective and frequent data sources; (d) modify student programs more frequently; and (e) use more effective instructional variables (L. S. Fuchs & D. Fuchs, 1991; Shinn, 1989). In other words, teachers who use CBM to monitor growth are more aware of students' actual performance, and with this awareness, they are able to modify their instruction more rapidly and effectively (e.g., L. S. Fuchs, D. Fuchs, Hamlett, Phillips, & Bentz, 1994). School psychologists might explore the possibility of helping to develop probes from the curriculum for teachers. School psychologists could also do a great service by helping to establish school or district norms for purposes of setting annual mathematics goals.

Summary

School psychologists can help teachers navigate through their mathematics programs by helping them establish reasonable goals, evaluate the quality of the instructional strategies recommended in the programs, and assist teachers in choosing and implementing assessment procedures that will help them make important instructional decisions. To summarize our recommendations and assist school psychologists in helping teachers analyze and modify their mathematics programs, we have included Curriculum Analysis Guidelines in Figure 2, on page 584. These guidelines are derived from the three curricular areas of instructional goals, instructional strategies and informal assessment discussed in previous sections of this chapter. School psychologists can use these guidelines with classroom teachers as a framework for helping teachers examine their current instructional practice.

CONCLUSION

In this chapter we have suggested that the role of the school psychologist in helping schools, districts, or individual classroom teachers improve the mathematics performance of their low-achieving students is twofold. First, school psychologists can serve as an important resource providing information to administrators and teachers regarding research-based schoolwide mathematics interventions. Many school psychologists serve on committees charged with generating solutions to problems of poor school performance. When they are consulted about possible options for improving mathematics performance, school psychologists need to be knowledgeable about those interventions that have demonstrated success in improving the mathematics performance of a diverse group of students.

The second role we have proposed for the school psychologist is that of consultant to individual classroom teachers. Given the lack of preparation of most teachers in the area of mathematics and the questionable quality of mathematics curricula, school psychologists can serve as critical collaborators with teachers searching for ways to improve their mathematics instruction. The mathematics achievement of low-achieving students can be increased with the coordinated efforts of teachers, administrators, and school psychologists. Most effective interventions include a well-designed or modified mathematics

FIGURE 2

Curriculum Analysis Guidelines

Curriculum Analysis Guidelines

I   Instructional Goals
   - A. Are student learning goals focused on skills that are frequently used?
   - B. Are student learning goals focused on "big ideas?"

II   Instructional Strategies
   - A. Are the recommended strategies of intermediate generality – not too narrow or too broad?
   - B. Are the recommended strategies generalizable or do they involve rote instruction?
   - C. Has the teacher identified the prerequisite knowledge required by the instructional strategy?
   - D. Has the teacher scaffolded the strategy instruction by providing the greatest amount of support initially and gradually reducing that support?
   - E. Has the teacher provided adequate opportunities for review of newly introduced concepts or skills?

III   Informal Assessment
   - A. Does the teacher include both criterion-referenced and progress monitoring assessment options?
   - B. Does the teacher conduct an analysis of student errors to examine the cause of the errors? Has the teacher determined whether the errors are caused by lack of fact mastery, lack of strategy knowledge, lack of prerequisite knowledge, or lack of motivation?

program that includes a systematic means of assessing student performance. School psychologists can have a significant role in identifying effective programs or helping teachers modify programs so that more students will experience success.

REFERENCES

Adams, G. L., & Engelmann, S. (1996). *Research on Direct Instruction: Twenty-five years beyond Distar.* Seattle, WA: Educational Achievement Systems.

Becker, W. C., & Gersten, R. (1982). A follow-up of Follow Through: The later effects of the Direct Instruction Model on children in fifth and sixth grades. *American Education Research Journal, 19*(1), 75-92.

Bracey, G. (2000). Trying to understand teaching math for understanding. *Phi Delta Kappan, 81*(6), 473-474.

Cardelle-Elawar, M. (1995). Effects of metacognitive instruction on low achievers in mathematics problems. *Teaching and Teacher Education, 11,* 81-95.

Carnine, D., Dixon, R., & Silbert, J. (1998) Effective strategies for teaching mathematics. In D. Carnine & E. Kame'enui (Eds.), *Effective teaching strategies that accommodate diverse learners.* Upper Saddle River, NJ: Merrill.

Carnine, D., Grossen, B., & Silbert, J. (1995). Direct Instruction to accelerate cognitive growth. In J. Block, S. Everson, & T. Guskey (Eds.), *Choosing research-based school improvement programs* (pp. 129-152). New York: Scholastic.

Carnine, D. W., & Stein, M. (1981). Organizational strategies and practice procedures for teaching basic facts. *Journal for Research in Mathematics Education, 12*(1), 65-69.

Charles, R. I. (1980). Exemplification and characterization moves in the classroom teaching of geometry concepts. *Journal for Research in Mathematics Education, 11*(1), 10-21.

Colvin, R. (1999). Math wars: Tradition vs. real-world applications. *School Administrator, 56*(12), 26-31.

Davis, R. B. (1990). Discovery learning and constructivism. In R. B. Davis, C. A. Maher, & N. Noddings (Eds.), *Constructivist views on the teaching and learning of mathematics.* Reston, VA: National Council of Teachers of Mathematics.

Dempster, F. N. (1991). Synthesis of research on reviews and tests. *Educational Leadership, 48*(7), 71-76.

Engelmann, S. & Carnine, D. (1991). *Theory of instruction: Principles and applications.* Eugene, OR: ADI Press.

Fantuzzo, J. W., Polite, K., & Grayson, N. (1990). An evaluation of reciprocal peer tutoring across elementary school settings. *Journal of School Psychology, 28,* 309-323.

Fuchs, L. S., & Fuchs, D. (1991). Curriculum-Based Measurements: Current applications and future directions. *Preventing School Failure, 35*(3), 6-11.

Fuchs, L. S., Fuchs, D., Hamlett, C. L., Phillips, N. B., & Bentz, J. (1994). Classwide curriculum-based measurement: Helping general educators meet the challenge of student diversity. *Exceptional Children, 60*(6), 518-37.

Gersten, R., & Carnine, D. (1984). Direct instruction mathematics: A longitudinal evaluation of low SES elementary students. *Elementary School Journal, 84*(4), 395-407.

Gersten, R., Woodward, J., and Darch, C. (1986). Direct Instruction: A research-based approach to curriculum design and teaching. *Exceptional Children, 53*(1), 17-31.

Gleason, M., Carnine, D., & Boriero, D. (1990). Improving CAI effectiveness with attention to instructional design in teaching story problems to mildly handicapped students. *Journal of Special Education Technology, 10*(3), 129-136.

Good, T. L., & Grouws, D. A. (1979). The Missouri Mathematics Effectiveness Project: An experimental study in fourth-grade classrooms. *Journal of Educational Psychology, 71,* 355-362.

Good, T. L., Grouws, D. A., & Ebmeier, H. (1983). *Active mathematics teaching.* New York: Longman.

Good, T. L., Reys, B. J., Grouws, D. A., & Mulryan, C. M. (1989/1990). Using work-groups in mathematics instruction. *Educational Leadership,* 56-62.

Greenwood, C. R., Delquadri, J. C., & Hall, R. V. (1989). Longitudinal effects of class-wide peer tutoring. *Journal of Educational Psychology, 81*(3), 371-383.

Greenwood, C. R., Terry, B., Utley, C. A., Montagna, D., & Walker, D. (1993). Achievement, placement, and services: Middle school benefits of classwide peer tutoring used at the elementary school. *School Psychology Review, 22*(3), 497-516.

Kame'enui, E., & Carnine, D. (1998). *Effective teaching strategies that accommodate diverse learners.* Upper Saddle River, NJ: Merrill.

Kohler, F. W., Ezell, H., Hoel, K., & Strain, P. S. (1994). Supplemental peer practice in a first grade math class: Effects on teacher behavior and five low achievers' responding and acquisition of content. *The Elementary School Journal, 94*(4), 389-403.

Leinhardt, G. (1987). Development of an expert explanation: An analysis of a sequence of subtraction lessons. *Cognition and Instruction, 4*(4), 225-282.

Loveless, T. & Diperna, P. (2000). How well are American students learning: Focus on math achievement. *The Brown Center Report on American Education, 1*(1), 1-36.

Ma, L. (1999). *Knowing and teaching elementary mathematics: Teachers' understanding of fundamental mathematics in China and the United States.* Mahwah, NJ: Erlbaum.

Moore, L. J., & Carnine, D. W. (1989). A comparison of two approaches to teaching ratio and proportions to remedial and learning disabled students: Active teaching with either basal or empirically validated curriculum design material. *Remedial and Special Education, 10*(4), 28-37.

National Council of Teachers of Mathematics. (2000). *Principles and standards for school mathematics.* Available Internet: *http://standards.nctm.org/index.htm.*

Nattiv, A. (1994). Helping behaviors and math achievement gain of students using cooperative learning. *The Elementary School Journal, 94*(3), 285-297.

Nickerson, R. S. (1985). Understanding. *American Journal of Education, 93,* 201-239.

Phillips, N. B., Fuchs, L. S., & Fuchs, D. (1994). Effects of classwide curriculum-based measurement and peer tutoring: A collaborative researcher-practitioner interview study. *Journal of Learning Disabilities, 27*(7), 420-434.

Prawat, R. S. (1989). Promoting access to knowledge, strategy, and disposition in students: A research synthesis. *Review of Educational Research, 59*(1), 1-41.

Reese, C. M. (1996). *NAEP's 1996 Mathematics Report Card for the Nation and the States. Executive summary.* National Center for Education Statistics. Available Internet: *http://nces.ed.gov/nationsreportcard/96report/97488.pdf.*

Resnick, L. B., Cauzinille-Marmeche, E., & Mathieu, J. (1987). Understanding algebra. In J. A. Sloboda & D. Rogers (Eds.), *Cognitive processes in mathematics* (pp. 169-203). Oxford: Clarendon Press.

Resnick, L. B., & Omanson, S. F. (1987). Learning to understand arithmetic. In R. Glaser (Ed.), *Advances in instructional psychology* (pp. 41-95). Hillsdale, NJ: Erlbaum.

Riley, R. (1999). Scholars object to education department endorsement of 10 math programs for children. *The Chronicle of Higher Education, 46*(15), 37-38.

Shinn, M. R. (1989). *Curriculum-Based Measurement: Assessing special children.* New York: Guilford Press.

Slavin, R. E. (1983). *Cooperative learning.* New York: Longman.

Slavin, R., & Karweit, N. (1984). Mastery learning and student teams: A factorial experiment in urban general mathematics classes. *American Education Research Journal, 21,* 725-736.

Slavin, R., Leavey, M., & Madden, N. (1984). Combining cooperative learning and individualized instruction: Effects on student mathematics achievement, attitudes, and behaviors. *Elementary School Journal, 84,* 409-422.

Stebbins, L. B., St. Pierre, R. G., Proper, E. C., Anderson, R. B., & Cerva, T. R. (1977). Education as experimentation: A planned variation model (Vols. IVA, IVC). An Evaluation of Follow Through. Cambridge, MA: ABT Associates.

Stein, M., Silbert, J., & Carnine, C. (1997). *Designing effective mathematics instruction: A direct instruction approach* (3rd ed.). Upper Saddle River, NJ: Merrill.

Stevens, R. J., & Slavin, R. E. (1995). The cooperative elementary school: Effects on students' achievement, attitudes, and social relations. *American Education Research Journal, 32*(2), 321-351.

Valverde, G., & Schmidt, W. (1998). Refocusing U.S. math and science education. *Issues in Science and Technology, 14,* 60-66.

Van Patten, J., Chao, C., & Reigeluth, C. M. (1986). A review of strategies for v14 n2 sequencing and synthesizing instruction. *Review of Educational Research, 56*(4), 437-471.

Vygotsky, L. S. (1978). *Mind in society: The development of higher psychological processes* (M. Cole, V. John-Steiner, S. Scribner, & E. Souberman, Eds. & Trans.). Cambridge, MA: Harvard University Press.

Woodward, J., Baxter, J., & Robinson, R. (1999). Rules and reasons: Decimal instruction for academically low achieving students. *Learning Disabilities Research & Practice, 14,* 15-24.

Wu, H. (1999). Pre-service professional development of mathematics teachers. Unpublished manuscript. Available Internet: *www.math.berkeley.edu/~wu.*

CHAPTER 22

Prevention and Intervention for Struggling Writers

Steve Graham and Karen R. Harris
University of Maryland

INTRODUCTION

A long, but not always distinguished, writing career began in July 1965, when a typewriter was placed on the roof of a house, and the immortal line, "It was a dark and stormy night," was typed for the first, but not the last, time by an aspiring novelist. Although this author never published a single work, his writing entertained millions over the course of the next 25 years. As you have probably guessed, this paragon of literature was none other than Snoopy, the beloved dog from the comic strip Peanuts.

Although Snoopy enjoyed a rich fantasy life, involving many careers and personas, ranging from lawyer to World War I flying ace, the writing career of this unusual beagle was especially interesting to us, as it provided a comic reflection of the types of problems faced by many school-age children who experience difficulty learning to write. Drawing on cartoons involving Snoopy and his most ardent critic, Lucy, we identify below five factors that often limit the performance of struggling writers.

FACTORS THAT INFLUENCE THE PERFORMANCE OF STRUGGLING WRITERS

Planning

> **While writing his life history, Snoopy indicates that soon after he was born, he was adopted by that round-headed kid (i.e., Charlie Brown). When Lucy tells him that he needs to use peoples' names, he shrugs it off because he hates doing all of that research.**

Like Snoopy, many students who find writing difficult do little planning in advance of writing (MacArthur & Graham, 1987). Instead, they typically plan as they write, drawing any information from memory that is somewhat appropriate, writing it down, and using each preceding idea to stimulate the generation of the next one (Graham, 1990; Thomas, Englert, & Gregg, 1987). This retrieve-and-write process functions much like an encapsulated program, operating largely without self-monitoring or evaluation (McCutchen, 1988). As a result, little attention is directed by the writer to the development of rhetorical goals, the organization of text, the constraints imposed by the topic, or the needs of the reader.

Generating Ideas

While completing another section of his memoirs, Snoopy writes that his "life has been one of constant struggle." Lucy's predictable response is, "That's a laugh," whereupon Snoopy writes, "Ha, Ha, Ha, Ha!" Even though this addition to his text is ill-advised, it is not surprising, as Snoopy is constantly perplexed by what to say next.

Similar to Snoopy, children with writing problems frequently encounter difficulty generating or getting ideas for their writing. One of the most striking characteristics of their writing is that they produce so little of it, as their papers are inordinately short, containing little elaboration or detail (Graham, Harris, MacArthur, & Schwartz, 1991). One reason why poor writers may generate so little content when writing is that they terminate the composing process too soon, before accessing all that they know. For example, Graham (1990) found that poor writers in the upper elementary grades spent only about 6 or 7 minutes composing persuasive essays, but when they were prompted to write more, they produced two to four times more text, with one half of the new material being new and useful.

Transcribing Words Into Print

After reading one of Snoopy's papers, Lucy complains that she doesn't know which is worse, his writing, typing, or spelling. Snoopy wisely responds that they are all in this together, implying that several factors, including the mechanics of writing, are equally responsible.

Just like Snoopy in this cartoon, many children who experience writing difficulties struggle with the mechanics of writing. Their papers are full of capitalization, punctuation, and spelling errors (Graham et al., 1991), and their handwriting is often slow and laborious (Graham & Weintraub, 1996). In addition to making their writing hard to read, these mechanical difficulties can impede the process of writing in three ways (Graham, 1990; Scardamalia, Bereiter, & Goleman, 1982). One, having to switch attention during composing to mechanical demands, such as figuring out how to spell a word, may lead the writer to forget ideas or plans already held in working memory.

Two, if students' transcription skills are not fast enough to keep up with their thoughts, they are likely to forget possible writing ideas, as they slip from working memory. Three, if their attention is occupied with mechanical concerns, there may be fewer opportunities for writers to plan while writing or make their expressions more precisely fit intentions at the point of translation.

Revising

> **After Snoopy writes, "It was a dark and stormy night," an exasperated Lucy exclaims, "All of your stories are alike." Snoopy subsequently revises the story to read: "It was a dark and stormy noon." This is a common interaction between Snoopy the writer and Lucy the editor, with Lucy critiquing some aspect of his writing, and Snoopy responding with either an inconsequential or inane revision in his text.**

Snoopy's approach to revising is similar to the one adopted by many children who experience writing difficulties. They employ a "thesaurus" approach to revising, focusing most of their efforts on making word substitutions, correcting mechanical errors, and producing a neater product (Graham, 1997), rather than making substantive or meaningful changes in their text. This thesaurus approach is generally ineffective, as it has little effect on the overall quality of their writing (MacArthur & Graham, 1987).

Why do poor writers focus so much of their revising efforts on word changes and the mechanical features of text? Once again a Snoopy cartoon provides a critical clue. Snoopy has followed Charlie Brown to school, and is sitting at a desk behind him. He has only one worry, noting, "If she asks me to spell 'Mississippi' I'm in trouble." Snoopy's concern about spelling reflects the overemphasis that many struggling writers place on the importance of transcription skills, such as spelling, handwriting, capitalization, and punctuation. In comparison to their classmates who write well, they are more likely to stress the mechanics of writing (e.g., "letters are all the same size" or "all words are spelled correctly"), rather than substance or meaning, when defining good writing and describing what good writers do (Graham, Schwartz, & MacArthur, 1993; Wong, Wong, & Blenkinsop, 1989). It is not surprising, therefore, that poor writers place so much emphasis on correcting spelling, handwriting, and other mechanical errors, as this is consistent with their conceptualization of what good writing is all about.

This is not the only reason why these children's revising skills are so limited, however. Several studies have found that such children are not particularly adept at activating and coordinating the separate skills involved in revising, such as (a) locating a problem, (b) diagnosing its cause, (c) determining the type of change needed, or (d) executing it (Graham, 1997; De La Paz, Swanson, & Graham, 1998). Furthermore, they are often indifferent to, or perhaps unaware of, the possible concerns and needs of their audience (Graham, 1997).

Knowledge of Writing

> **After reading another one of Snoopy's papers Lucy comments, "This isn't very romantic," and encourages him to write something more romantic. As is often the case, he doesn't quite get it, writing: "When he said he loved her it was a dark and stormy night." Clearly, Snoopy's understanding of romantic writing can use some work.**

Like Snoopy, many children who find writing challenging generate text that fails to conform fully to the attributes and expectations found in different types of discourse (Englert, Raphael, Fear, & Anderson, 1988; Thomas et al., 1987). For instance, they often omit basic parts of a story such as the story problem, ending, or moral. Although it is not clear whether such lapses are attributable to an incomplete knowledge about how stories are constructed or to difficulties accessing or generating ideas for these story parts, they are common in the narrative as well as the expository writing of these children (Graham, 1990; Graham & Harris, 1989).

Implications for Instruction

When Snoopy first got his typewriter in position back in 1965, probably no one, not even his creator Charles Schulz, envisioned a 35-year career that would personify the pitfalls and difficulties faced by struggling writers. Although the consequences of Snoopy's writing difficulties were mainly limited to sarcastic rejection slips from various publishing houses, the results of poor writing in the real world are usually much more pervasive. Among its many functions, writing is used as a mechanism for assessing knowledge, as a vehicle for learning, an instrument for communication, and a medium for self-expression (e.g., artistic, spiritual, or political). Writing can even have therapeutic effects, as writing about one's feelings can lower blood pressure, reduce depression, and boost the immune system (Swerdlow, 1999). Poor writing can limit the utility and/or the power of each of these functions. Consider, for instance, the use of writing as a means for assessing students' knowledge. Many poor writers have difficulties with the skills involved in transcribing ideas into written language (Juel, 1988). It takes some of these students almost twice as long to write down their ideas as it does their better-writing counterparts (Weintraub & Graham, 1998). For these slower writers, timed tests that require a considerable amount of composing place them at a distinct disadvantage, and any resulting evaluation may seriously underestimate how much they actually know. Similarly, the use of writing to support learning, promote communication, and facilitate self-expression is likely to be undermined with struggling writers, as they often avoid writing whenever they can (Berninger et al., 1997).

In this chapter, we examine how schools can help struggling writers become skilled writers.

The construction of writing programs that support these children's development is challenging, as it cannot be limited to a single teacher or grade. Instead, it requires a coherent, coordinated, and extended effort by schools, as writing problems are not transitory difficulties that are easily fixed (Graham & Harris, in press a). Effective writing programs for struggling writers also must emphasize the processes that play a vital role in shaping and transforming a writer's capabilities. Although writing development is a complex and somewhat uncertain process, it depends upon changes that occur in the learner's motivation, knowledge about writing, and strategic behaviors (Alexander, Graham, & Harris, 1998). Thus, an effective program must include methods and procedures that amplify these students' writing knowledge, skill, will, and self-regulation. We further believe that writing instruction for these students must emphasize both prevention and intervention; respond to the specific needs of each student; maintain a healthy balance between meaning, process, and form; and employ both formal and informal learning methods (Graham & Harris, 1997). Principles for actualizing these beliefs are presented next.[1] To help us present each principle, in the following section we draw upon another cartoon character that could easily serve as the poster boy for struggling writers, Calvin from the Calvin and Hobbes comic strip, written and drawn by Bill Watterson.

WRITING IS THE FOUNDATION OF AN EFFECTIVE WRITING PROGRAM

Calvin excitedly informs his imaginary tiger friend, Hobbes, that he has figured out how *not* to write an assigned story. They will jump into their time machine constructed earlier out of a paper box and go a few hours into the future. Because Calvin will surely have written his story by then, they will simply collect it and return to the present; thus, avoiding having to write it at all! Hobbes wryly notes that something doesn't make sense here, but is told to relax as they will be back as soon as they go!

Like Calvin, many students who find writing difficult avoid writing whenever they can. Students who do not write frequently and for extended periods of time, however, are unlikely to develop the knowledge, skill, will, and self-regulation underlying effective composing (Graham & Harris, 1997). William Hazlitt, the 19th century novelist, acknowledged this when he observed, "The more a man writes, the more he can write" (Burnham, 1994, p.114). This simple homily recognized that the *opportunity to write* is the foundation on which an effective writing program is built. In other words, children are not likely to make much progress as writers if they are not given plenty of opportunities to apply and develop their craft.

Despite the obvious importance of the opportunity to write as part of the process of learning to write, children in some schools spend very little time actually writing. In a study of 10 elementary schools by Christenson, Thurlow, Ysseldyke, and McVicar (1989), for example, students with special needs only averaged 25 minutes of any type of writing a day. What's more, very little of this time was spent composing text. Most of it involved writing numbers during math, handwriting, and spelling practice, filling out worksheets during social studies, and so forth. Although students without disabilities in these same schools averaged a slightly better 33 minutes of writing a day, they also spent little time composing text, as the bulk of what they wrote resembled the writing of their counterparts with special needs.

How much time should students spend composing each day? A good rule of thumb is that they should spend at least an hour or more each day in the process of writing—either planning, revising, or authoring text. Moreover, writing should not be limited just to the "language arts" period for younger children or English for the older ones, but should occur in content area classes as well. For example, students can maintain a log or journal during science, recording their observations and reflections on experiments or classroom activities.

It is important to note that the beneficial effect of frequent and extended opportunities to write may be undermined if students do not *value* the topics or tasks they write about. This was aptly illustrated in another Calvin and Hobbes cartoon, where Calvin complains that because of grades, deadlines, and all of the rules, writing assignments don't teach you how to write, but how to hate writing. Hobbes provides one solution to Calvin's complaint, suggesting that he not concentrate so much on the end result, but just enjoy the process of creating—even though Calvin had to visit the school psychologist the last time he did that!

Means of increasing writing interest include allowing children to work on projects of their own choosing and modifying assignments so that they meet personal goals. Writing is also more engaging and interesting when it serves a real purpose and is aimed at a real audience. For instance, when our daughter was in fourth grade, her class set a goal to clean a local stream. As part of this effort, they wrote letters to the city council, mayor, and local newspapers. They also wrote a grant to obtain funds for cleaning the stream and placards for a "save the stream" rally. With only minimal guidance from the teacher, the students took responsibility for planning and completing all of these writing activities, enjoying the fact that they were doing something that would, in their words, "make a difference."

PROVIDE EXEMPLARY WRITING INSTRUCTION

Worrying about the quality of his education, Calvin asks his teacher why she isn't teaching them the gender of nouns. He argues that foreign kids know them, complaining that it is not surprising the U.S. can't compete in a global market. He ends his argument by demanding sex education!

Although Calvin's demand for sex education is misplaced, his underlying issue, the importance of a quality education, is not. A critical tactic in preventing writing difficulties is to provide exemplary writing instruction right from the start, beginning in first grade and continuing through high school. Providing *consistent* quality instruction in writing is advantageous for three reasons. One, it serves to maximize the writing development of children in general. Two, it minimizes the number of students who experience writing problems as a result of poor instruction. Three, it helps to ameliorate the severity of writing difficulties experienced by children whose primary problems are not instructional, such as children with special needs.

What does quality writing instruction look like? Although it will clearly differ somewhat from grade to grade, common processes that play a vital role in shaping and transforming writing competence should be emphasized, including methods and procedures for increasing students' writing knowledge, skill, will, and self-regulation. Just as important, an exemplary writing program should be based on the empirical analysis of effective writing practices. This includes research on practices that are effective with both good (see, e.g., Hillocks, 1986) and struggling writers (see, e.g., Graham & Harris, 1998) as well as the practices of highly effective writing teachers (see, e.g., Wray, Medwell, Fox, & Poulson, 2000). Finally, research-based practices should be combined with knowledge that teachers gain through clinical and practical experience (e.g., Scott, 1989). We recently completed such an analysis (Graham & Harris, in press a) and developed a list of features for an exemplary writing program. The results of our analysis are presented as a checklist in Table 1, on page 596. The checklist provides an instrument for assessing the general quality of classroom writing instruction.

An example of a program that incorporates many of the principles listed in Table 1 is the Early Literacy Project (ELP) designed by Englert and her colleagues (Englert et al., 1995). With this program, writing and reading instruction occurs within the confines of thematic units. In such a unit, reading and writing activities operate together to promote students' learning about a specific theme. For a thematic unit on wolves, for example, students read expository and narrative material about these animals and then use writing as a means for responding to the text. They also use writing as a mechanism for gathering additional information about wolves. Both skill (e.g., spelling) and strategy instruction (e.g., planning and revising processes) occur within the context of these units and are supported by teacher modeling, discussion, and guided practice. Opportunities to engage in meaningful writing are plentiful, as children not only respond in writing to their reading materials, but keep a journal, generate personal-experience stories, and write reports that are shared with others.

Teachers further assist students' efforts by providing scaffolding or temporary and adjusted support as needed. For instance, word banks, pictionaries, and planning sheets are often used as temporary aids to support students' writing efforts. A positive classroom environment is also created by encouraging children to share and collaborate. Students work together to apply strategies taught by their teacher, frequently talk with each other about what they are doing, and share their writing with the class. Furthermore, the ELP program is supplemented by more conventional systematic instruction, as students are explicitly and systematically taught skills such as phonemic awareness, spelling, and phonics skills.

Research on the effectiveness of the ELP program demonstrates that it can have a positive impact on the writing performance of children who are among the most dif-

TABLE 1

Checklist for Classroom Writing Instruction

My students...

___ Write daily and work on a wide range of writing tasks for multiple audiences, including writing at home.

___ Help each other plan, draft, revise, edit, or publish their written work.

___ Share their work with each other, receiving praise and critical feedback on their efforts.

___ Use writing as a tool to explore, organize, and express their thoughts across the curriculum.

___ Assess their progress as writers.

I make sure that I...

___ Develop a literate classroom environment where students' written work is prominently displayed and the room is packed with writing and reading material.

___ Establish a predictable writing routine where students are encouraged to think, reflect, and revise.

___ Hold individual conferences with students about their current writing efforts, helping them establish goals or criteria to guide their writing and revising efforts.

___ Make writing motivating by setting an exciting mood, creating a risk-free environment, allowing students to select their own writing topics or modify teacher assignments, developing assigned topics compatible with students' interests, reinforcing children's accomplishments, specifying the goal for each lesson, and promoting an "I can do" attitude.

___ Provide frequent opportunities for students to self-regulate their behavior during writing, including working independently, arranging their own space, and seeking help from one another.

___ Conduct periodic conferences with parents, soliciting their advice and communicating the goals of the program as well as their child's progress as a writer.

To help students progress as writers I...

___ Model the process of writing as well as positive attitudes toward writing.

___ Provide instruction on a broad range of skills, knowledge, and strategies, including phonological awareness, handwriting and spelling, writing conventions, sentence-level skills, text structure, the functions of writing, and planning and revising.

___ Deliver follow-up instruction to ensure mastery of targeted writing skills, knowledge, and strategies.

___ Monitor students' progress as writers as well as their strengths and needs.

___ Adjust my teaching style and learning pace as needed, conduct minilessons that are responsive to current student needs, and provide individually guided assistance with writing assignments.

Note
Place a check next to each item that describes a feature of writing instruction in your classroom. Determine whether the actualization of any **unchecked items** would improve the quality of writing instruction in your class.

ficult to teach. Over the course of a year, Englert et al. (1995) examined whether the program improved the writing of children with special needs in Grades 1 through 4. In comparison to similar children in special education classes, the researchers found that students taught by experienced ELP teachers made greater gains in writing than students in control classrooms, as their papers contained fewer spelling miscues, were longer, and better organized. In addition, Mariage (1993) reported that 2 to 3 years of such instruction, starting in the primary grades, was enough to bring some students with special needs up to grade-level performance.

TAILOR INSTRUCTION TO MEET THE NEEDS OF INDIVIDUAL STUDENTS

Calvin describes his new system, Effective Time Management (ETM), for doing homework. He draws up a schedule for each subject and uses a kitchen timer to monitor his pace. According to Calvin, he is now more efficient and his work goes faster. Just then the timer goes off, and Calvin exclaims, "There, my math minute is up!"

Although outstanding teachers are not likely to stress Calvin's version of ETM, they recognize the importance of tailoring writing instruction to meet the needs of children experiencing difficulty learning to write (Graham & Harris, in press a). For example, Pressley et al. (1996) found that outstanding literacy teachers in the primary grades provided *qualitatively similar* instruction for all students, but that children experiencing difficulty with literacy learning received *extra* teacher support. This included extra help learning critical skills, more explicit teaching of these skills, and more individually guided assistance.

A Survey of Adaptations Made by Teachers

A recent nationwide survey by Graham, Harris, Fink, and MacArthur (2000) revealed that primary-grade teachers use a variety of adaptations to tailor instruction to meet the needs of struggling writers. When teachers were asked to identify the types of adaptations made for weaker writers, responses ranged from procedures for circumventing writing problems (e.g., dictation and spelling words for students) to extra encouragement and praise. The most frequent adaptations involved additional one-on-one help, including individual assistance from the teacher, adult tutors or volunteers, or older and same-age peers (including collaborative planning, writing, or revising with a peer).

Adaptations to meet the spelling and handwriting difficulties experienced by many struggling writers were also quite common. To address difficulties with spelling, for instance, teachers created personalized spelling lists for weaker writers, directly helped them spell unknown words, or employed word banks and other aids to facilitate correct spelling. In contrast, some teachers sought to bypass handwriting difficulties by allowing weaker writers to dictate their compositions or write with a keyboard (e.g., Alpha Smart).

A third set of adaptations focused on procedures for supporting the thinking and creative processes involved in writing. For example, teachers facilitated the planning of weaker writers by having them talk out their ideas in advance of writing, using webs or graphic organizers to generate and sequence ideas, or drawing what they planned to write about. Children's revising efforts were supported through the use of revising checklists or via direct help from the teacher or a peer during revising. Other adaptations included helping weaker writers select writing topics, making writing assignments shorter or easier, assigning additional writing homework, and extra instruction on grammar and sentence writing skills.

Finally, when teachers were asked to indicate how often they employed specific activities or instructional procedures, they indicated that they devoted more attention to teaching handwriting, phonics for spelling, and punctuation and capitalization skills to weaker writers than to average writers. In addition, they were more likely to reteach writing skills to weaker writers, provide minilessons that are responsive to their needs, and conference with these children about their writing.

It is important to note that almost 20% of the teachers who participated in the Graham, Harris, Fink, & MacArthur (2000) study made *no* adaptations for struggling writers. Another 24% made only one or two adaptations, and some of the adaptations made by teachers were not necessarily positive ones. In comparison to average writers, for example, weaker writers were *less* likely to share their writing with peers, help others, select their own writing topics, or complete writing assignments at their own pace. Teachers are unlikely to maximize the success of struggling writers, however, if they make no adjustments or their modifications limit children's participation or decision making.

Effective and Extra Help With Handwriting and Spelling

A critical issue in tailoring instruction to meet children's individual needs involves identifying *which* writing skills and strategies require additional attention. This will vary depending upon the student. In a study by Juel (1988), for instance, some children who were poor writers had difficulties with transcription skills (i.e., spelling) as well as planning processes (i.e., content generation), whereas others had difficulties in just one area. As a result, some students would have benefited from extra help in both areas, whereas other students needed help in only one.

Two of the areas where we know a lot about teaching and adapting instruction to meet the needs of struggling writers are handwriting and spelling. Tables 2 and 3 present checklists for evaluating the quality of handwriting and spelling instruction, respectively. Both checklists are based on the findings from comprehensive reviews of the empirical literature (Graham, 1983, 1999; Graham & Miller, 1979; Graham & Weintraub, 1996) and emphasize effective instructional procedures and productive adaptations for struggling writers.

TABLE 2

Checklist for Handwriting Instruction

I teach children how to write each letter by...
__ Showing them how it is formed.
__ Describing how it is similar to and different from other letters.
__ Using visual cues, such as numbered arrows, as a guide to letter formation.
__ Providing practice tracing, copying, and writing the letter from memory.
__ Keeping instructional sessions short, with frequent reviews and practice.
__ Asking children to identify or circle their best formed letter or letters.
__ Encouraging them to correct or rewrite poorly formed letters.
__ Monitoring their practice to ensure that letters are formed correctly.
__ Reinforcing their successful efforts and providing corrective feedback as needed.

I help children become more fluent in handwriting by...
__ Providing them with plenty of opportunities to write.
__ Eliminating interfering habits that may reduce handwriting fluency.
__ Having them copy a short passage several times, trying to write it a little faster each time.

I promote handwriting development by...
__ Making sure that each child develops a comfortable and efficient pencil grip.
__ Encouraging children to sit in an upright position, leaning slightly forward, as they write.
__ Showing them how to place or position their paper when writing.
__ Teaching children to identify and name the letters of the alphabet.
__ Teaching them how to write both upper- and lowercase letters.
__ Allotting 75 to 100 minutes per week to handwriting instruction (grades 1 through 4).
__ Providing children with plenty of opportunities to use different types of writing instruments and paper.
__ Asking children to set goals for improving specific aspects of their handwriting.
__ Implementing appropriate procedures for left-handed writers, such as how to properly place or position their paper when writing.
__ Monitoring students' handwriting, paying special attention to their instructional needs in letter formation, spacing, slant, alignment, size, and line quality.
__ Dramatizing children's progress in handwriting through the use of charts or graphs, praise, or posting neatly written papers

I assist students who are experiencing difficulty by...
__ Organizing my class so that I can provide additional handwriting instruction to children who need it.
__ Coordinating my handwriting instruction with the efforts of other professionals, such as an occupational therapist.
__ Placing special emphasis on the teaching of difficult letters, such as *a, j, k, n, q, u,* and *z,* as well as reversals.
__ Ensuring that they master one style of handwriting before a second style is introduced.
__ Considering whether an alternative to handwriting, such as an Alpha Smart keyboard, is warranted.
__ Helping them develop a positive attitude about handwriting.
__ Talking with their parents about my handwriting program and soliciting advice.

I make sure that I...
__ Encourage students to make all final drafts of papers neat and legible.
__ Maintain a balanced perspective on the role of handwriting in learning to write.

Note
Place a check next to each item that describes a feature of handwriting instruction in your classroom. Determine whether the actualization of any **unchecked items** would improve the quality of handwriting instruction in your class.

TABLE 3

Checklist for Spelling Instruction

I help children learn new spellings by...
___ Teaching them how to spell words they are likely to use when writing.
___ Providing them with plenty of opportunities to read and write.
___ Encouraging them to use spell checkers, dictionaries, and so forth to determine the correct spelling of unknown words.
___ Modeling correct spelling when I write.
___ Having them build words from letters or letters and phonograms (e.g., c - at).

I help children learn their spelling list words by...
___ Administering a pretest to identify which words need to be studied.
___ Teaching them an effective strategy for studying words.
___ Having them practice their words together.
___ Keeping instructional sessions short, with frequent practice and review.
___ Administering a posttest to determine which words were mastered.
___ Asking that words misspelled during testing are corrected.
___ Monitoring to see whether they continue to correctly spell mastered words over time.
___ Providing additional study for words that were not mastered or maintained over time.
___ Reinforcing the correct spelling of taught words in their writing.

I promote spelling development by...
___ Making sure that each child can segment words into sounds as well as add, delete, and substitute one sound for another in a word.
___ Showing students how the sounds in a word are related to print.
___ Teaching them common sound/symbol associations, spelling patterns, and helpful spelling rules.
___ Teaching them strategies for determining the spelling of unknown words.
___ Providing instruction and practice in proofreading.
___ Allotting at least 60 to 75 minutes per week to spelling instruction.

I assist students who are experiencing difficulty by...
___ Organizing my class so that I can provide additional spelling instruction to those who need it.
___ Adjusting the number of words that they have to study each week.
___ Providing them with a personalized list of words to study.
___ Asking them to set goals for how many new words they will learn to spell each week.
___ Setting aside time for them to study their spelling words at school.
___ Presenting only a few words to be studied at a time.
___ Testing their daily progress on the words they are studying.
___ Encouraging them to monitor their study behavior and subsequent spelling performance.
___ Using spelling games and computer programs to reinforce the learning of spelling words and skills.
___ Teaching them spelling mnemonics for words that are especially difficult to spell.
___ Providing them with a personalized dictionary that contains an alphabetical listing of the correct spellings of words they are likely to misspell.
___ Placing spelling demons and other difficult words on wall charts.
___ Dramatizing their progress in spelling through the use of charts or graphs, praise, or posting papers with little or no misspellings.
___ Reteaching skills and strategies that they did not master.
___ Helping them develop a positive attitude about spelling.
___ Talking with their parents about my spelling program and soliciting advice.

I make sure that I...
___ Encourage students to correct misspellings in all final drafts of papers.
___ Maintain a balanced perspective on the role of spelling in learning to write.

Note
Place a check next to each item that describes a feature of spelling instruction in your classroom. Determine whether the actualization of any **unchecked items** would improve the quality of spelling instruction in your class.

Extra instruction in handwriting and spelling may be especially beneficial for students who experience difficulty mastering these skills during the primary grades. The results of four recent studies indicate that such supplemental instruction can improve not only these children's transcription skills, but their writing performance as well (Berninger et al., 1997, 1998; Graham, Harris, & Fink, 2000; Jones & Christensen, 1999). For example, Graham, Harris, and Fink (2000) provided first-grade children with slow handwriting and generally poor writing skills with approximately 7 hours of additional handwriting instruction. Three times a week, each child met with a specially trained tutor for 15 minutes of instruction. Each 15-minute lesson involved four activities. For the first activity, Alphabet Warm-up, the students learned to name and identify the letters of the alphabet. With the second activity, Alphabet Practice, three lowercase letters, sharing common formational characteristics (e.g., **l**, **i**, and **t**) were introduced and practiced. The instructor modeled how to form the letters, followed by the student practicing each letter by tracing it three times, writing it three times inside an outline of the letter, copying it three times, and circling the best formed letter. Three lessons were devoted to mastering each letter set, with the second and third sessions primarily involving letter practice in the context of single words (e.g., lit) or hinky-pinks (rhyming word such as itty-bitty). The third activity, Alphabet Rockets, involved asking the child to copy a short sentence quickly and accurately for a period of 3 minutes. The sentence contained multiple instances of the letters that were emphasized in Alphabet Practice during that lesson (e.g., "**Litt**le kids **l**ike **t**o ge**t** le**tt**ers"). The number of letters written was recorded on an alphabet rocket chart and during the next two lessons, students tried to beat their previous score by writing at least three more letters during the specified time period. With the fourth activity, Alphabet Fun, the student was taught how to write one of the letters from Alphabet Practice in an unusual way (e.g., as long and tall or short and fat) or use it as part of a picture (e.g., turning an **i** into a butterfly or an **s** into a snake). Students who received this extra handwriting instruction became quicker and better handwriters than their peers assigned to a contact control group receiving instruction in phonological awareness. They also showed evidence of greater gains in their ability to craft sentences and generate text when writing a story.

Similarly, a study by Berninger et al. (1998) demonstrated that extra spelling instruction can have a positive effect on compositional fluency. Poor spellers in second grade were provided with approximately 8 hours of supplemental spelling instruction. Instruction was delivered by specially trained tutors during 24 sessions, each 20 minutes long. Children who were taught common phoneme-spelling associations for consonants, blends, and digraphs practiced new spellings by pointing to each letter in a left-to-right order while simultaneously saying the sound. They also used their spelling words when writing a short composition, demonstrating greater gains in spelling than their peers in a contact control condition, who had received instruction in phonological and orthographic awareness skills. Finally, they wrote longer compositions. Although additional replication is needed, these studies indicate that an important ingredient in preventing writing problems is to provide early and extra help to address children's *handwriting* and *spelling* difficulties.

Effective and Extra Help in Teaching Planning and Revising

Two other areas where we know a lot about teaching and adapting instruction to meet the needs of struggling writers are *planning* and *revising*. Undoubtedly, the use of traditional procedures, such as a *predictable writing routine* where these processes are expected and encouraged (see the checklist in Table 1, on page 596, for other examples), increases the likelihood that struggling writers will plan and revise when writing. For many struggling writers, however, these procedures alone are not powerful enough to ensure that they learn to plan and revise skillfully. Numerous studies have shown that weaker writers benefit from *extended and explicit instruction* in both of these processes (Englert et al., 1991; Harris & Graham, 1999; Wong, 1997).

In our own research, for example, we have successfully taught struggling writers to use the same kinds of planning and revising strategies that more skilled writers use when they compose (Harris & Graham, 1996, 1999). With this approach (Self-Regulated Strategy Development), the teacher first models how to use a planning or revising strategy, and then provides students with scaffolding or temporary and adjusted support as they learn to apply it. Support ranges from the teacher helping students apply the strategy, to peers helping each other apply it, to simple reminders to use part or all of the strategy. Students also learn any background knowledge needed to use the strategy, develop a thorough understanding of how it can support their writing, and systematically investigate when, where, and how to apply it in the future. Learning and application of the strategy is further supported through the use of goal setting, self-monitoring, self-evaluation, and self-instructions. For instance, students may develop and use a specific self-statement to help them manage some aspect of their behavior (e.g., impulsiveness) that interferes with using the strategy. Likewise, they may evaluate how the strategy helped them improve their writing or set goals for applying the strategy in new situations. Throughout instruction, the importance of effort and students' role as collaborators is stressed. Finally, instruction is criterion- rather than time-based, as students do not move to later stages of instruction (e.g., from supported-use to independent-use of the strategy) until they have met at least initial criteria for doing so.

The Self-Regulated Strategy Model has been used to teach a variety of planning and revising strategies to children with learning disabilities, including brainstorming, semantic webbing, generating and organizing writing content using text structure (e.g., story grammar), reading to locate information, goal setting, revising using peer feedback, and revising for both mechanics and substance (see Harris & Graham, 1996). Instruction in these strategies has led to improvements in four aspects of students' performance: quality of writing, approach to writing, knowledge of writing, and self-efficacy (Graham & Harris, 1993). Readers interested in a more detailed presentation of the model or these strategies may consult Harris and Graham (1996).

Balanced Instruction

A critical aspect of tailoring writing instruction to meet the needs of struggling writers is finding the right balance between formal and informal instruction (Graham & Harris,

1997). For instance, consider the writing skill of spelling. Research shows that students learn to spell some words incidentally or informally as they read or write, but that students who are good spellers learn many more words via informal methods than do poor spellers (Graham, 2000). There is also a considerable body of research demonstrating that formal or direct instruction improves the spelling performance of both good and poor spellers (e.g., Gordon, Vaughn, & Schumm, 1993; Graham, 1983). It is unlikely, however, that direct instruction is typically complete or extensive enough to account for all of the growth needed to become a skilled speller (Graham, 2000). To illustrate, most adults can spell 10,000 or more words correctly, but are only taught about 3,000 spelling words while in school. As a result, both informal and formal methods must be stressed, as neither by itself is powerful enough to ensure the attainment of spelling competence by struggling writers. It should be noted that the level of informal and formal instruction needed by individual students will vary and should be adjusted accordingly. With balanced instruction, the fulcrum is the student, and balance depends on the needs of the student.

The principle of balanced instruction also applies to considerations about the role of meaning, process, and form in writing instruction. All three of these are important components in the development of skilled writing (Graham & Harris, 1997). Teachers do students no favor when they suggest, even implicitly, that one or more of these three aspects of writing are unimportant. Likewise, the amount of emphasis teachers place on either meaning, process, or form should be adjusted so that it is consistent with students' needs.

IDENTIFY AND ADDRESS ROADBLOCKS TO LEARNING

> **While taking a test, Calvin's attention has wandered and he imagines that he is about to fly a spaceship into battle. Not aware of Calvin's inattention, one of the other children whispers to him, "What was the capital of Poland until 1600?" Calvin responds, "KRAKOW!" A few seconds later, Calvin again responds, yelling: "KRAKOW! KRAKOW! Two direct hits."**

Like Calvin's problems with inattentiveness, many students who experience writing difficulties encounter obstacles that impede their success in school. It is not uncommon for these students to exhibit one or more interfering behaviors, such as a low tolerance for frustration, maladaptive beliefs, or difficulty activating and orchestrating the elements involved in learning (Harris, 1982). Teachers at the Benchmark School, for example, identified 32 academic and nonacademic roadblocks experienced by students with learning problems. Roadblocks included a lack of persistence, impulsivity, inflexibility, disorganization, frequent absences, poor home support, and so forth (Gaskin, 1998). Ninety percent of the students had two or more roadblocks to learning, with some having as many as 10 roadblocks.

Teachers need to address any roadblocks struggling writers experience that might impede their writing development. For example, students who have difficulties activating and organizing cognitive and motivational resources when writing can learn how to modify this situation through the application of self-regulatory strategies, such as goal setting, self-monitoring, self-instructions, and self-reinforcement (Harris & Graham, 1996). To illustrate, inattentive struggling writers who were taught to count and graph daily the number of words they wrote evidenced a 50% increase in on-task behavior and wrote compositions that were two to three times longer (Harris, Graham, Reid, McElroy, & Hamby, 1994). Likewise, we can enhance the performance of struggling writers who attribute their failures to uncontrollable factors such as lack of ability or luck and hence are unwilling to exert much academic effort. These maladaptive attributes can be shifted by teaching them to use strategies to accomplish writing tasks while persuading them that their successes and failures on these tasks are tied to their efforts in using these strategies. In a study by Sexton, Harris, and Graham (1998), for example, struggling writers with maladaptive beliefs about the cause of success and failure were taught a planning strategy for improving their work and to attribute their successes in writing to effort and use of the planning strategy. Following instruction, the students' compositions became longer and qualitatively better, and there was a positive change in their attributions for writing.

EXPECT THAT EACH CHILD WILL LEARN TO WRITE

> **While playing with a ouija board, Calvin asks whether he will grow up to be the President. As the answer comes letter by letter, Hobbes repeats each leader: "G ... O ... D ... F ... O ... R ... B ... I ... D." Calvin reacts by knocking the ouija board over, declaring that he did not ask for an editorial.**

Like Calvin's ouija board, teachers often view children with writing difficulties negatively, setting low expectations for their performance and limiting their exchanges with them (Graham & Harris, in press a). Such negative views may take the form of less attention and praise, more criticism, and briefer and less informative feedback (Johnston & Winograd, 1985). Children with writing difficulties may be viewed as so challenging that a form of pedagogical paralysis occurs for some teachers, as they are uncertain about what to do with these students—or they lack confidence in their own capabilities to teach them (Kame'enui, 1993). Teachers are not powerless, however, as the findings from the Englert et al. (1995) study reviewed earlier showed. These children, including those with special needs, *can* be taught to write.

Just as teachers need to believe that they are capable of succeeding, so do struggling writers. Teachers can foster these students' sense of competence by treating them as capable learners. One of the outstanding first-grade teachers interviewed in a study by Pressley and his colleagues (Pressley et al., 1996), for instance, noted that she approaches each child as a competent learner, one who can learn to work productively and independently in the classroom. Another vital ingredient was captured by a second exceptional teacher (Pressley, 1998) who indicated that the weaker students in his classroom are never shown disrespect. Instead, he constantly seeks to support their partici-pation in class without stigmatizing them. He has made sitting next to him a special honor, for example, so that no stigma is attached to getting extra help from the teacher. It is also important to ignore negative expectations (e.g., "Students with special needs cannot learn to write well"), help struggling writers develop a "can do" attitude, set high but realistic expectations for the students' writing performance, and build a posi-tive relationship with them.

TAKE ADVANTAGE OF TECHNOLOGICAL TOOLS FOR WRITING

While working on a writing assignment, our comic strip pro-tagonist, Calvin, constructs a "thinking cap" from a kitchen colander, attaching a grounding string designed to act like a lightning rod for brainstorms so that his ideas would be firm-ly grounded in reality!

Although we will never be able to "boost" brain power through the use of a kitchen colander, some pretty incredible writing tools have been developed in recent years. For instance, scientists in Germany were able to develop a writing machine for Hans-Peter Balzmann, a victim of Lou Gehrig's disease, who has spent the last 4 years locked in a paralyzed body. Using the "thought translation device," Balzman is able to amplify and dampen his brainwave patterns in a way that allows him to select letters from a video screen to spell out his messages (Begley, 1999).

Another impressive account of how technology can be used to support writing is provided by Erickson and Koppenhaver (1995). Erica, a 6-year-old with cerebral palsy who was unable to speak, learned to use a Touch Talker, a dedicated communication device that provides speech output, using a programmable system with a keyboard com-posed of icons and letters. This technological tool allowed her to participate successfully in calendar time, a writing activity in which students were directed to produce short statements about the date, weather, or anything else they thought was important.

An expanding array of more familiar technological devices, many of them elec-tronic, provide teachers with new options for minimizing writing difficulties. These technological tools can make the process of writing easier as well as more motivating for struggling writers, providing them with support to overcome some problems while allowing them to circumvent others (MacArthur, 1996). Word processing, for example, provides at least three possible advantages to these students: (a) revising can be done eas-ily, (b) the resulting paper can be presented in a variety of professional-looking formats, and (c) typing provides an easier means for producing text for many children with fine motor difficulties (MacArthur, 1999). Text production processes also can be facilitated by using a spell checker, speech synthesis, word prediction program, or a grammar and style checker. Planning and revising processes can be prompted and directed through outlining and semantic mapping software as well as multimedia applications. Finally, communication and collaboration with diverse audiences can be promoted through the use of computer networks.

CONCLUDING COMMENTS

> **Recognizing that he needs some help with the concept of relativity, Calvin asks his Dad why "time goes slower at great speed." His Dad provides a concrete explanation, indicating that when you fly to California you gain 3 hours on a 5-hour flight, and that if you go at the speed of light, you gain even more time because you get there faster. He adds, however, that the theory of relativity only works if you are going west.**

Just as Calvin recognized the need for additional assistance from his father, there is a growing recognition that there is no quick or easy fix that will make writing difficulties disappear. Although an individual teacher can make a difference, the prevention of writing problems and intervening successfully when such problems occur requires a sustained and coherent effort on the part of *school*. One of the most basic options available to schools for eliminating writing difficulties is to provide exemplary writing instruction to *all* children beginning in first grade and continuing through high school. This includes providing students with plenty of opportunities to write on topics that are engaging and aimed at a real audience. These efforts can be enhanced by tailoring classroom instruction so that it is responsive to the needs of struggling writers. For example, teachers can provide these students with extra help, modify writing assignments so that they are more appropriate, increase the intensity of their writing instruction, and so forth. Opportunities for individualized attention in writing can be increased by reducing the number of students in a class; having a trained specialist, such as a special education teacher, provide in-class or pull-out assistance to struggling writers; and enrolling these students in programs that provide supplemental writing instruction either during or after school.

The success of struggling writers can further be maximized by identifying and addressing roadblocks, such as attentional and motivational difficulties, that contribute to students' writing problems. It is also critical that teachers maintain a "can do" attitude when working with struggling writers, while treating these students as capable and competent learners. The success of a writing program can be seriously undermined if teachers have little confidence in their own capabilities or those of their students. Technological tools provide an additional resource that should be employed with struggling writers, as they can make the process of writing easier as well as more motivating for many of these students.

The six principles presented in this chapter should be viewed as necessary, but not sufficient, components of an overall response to the needs of struggling writers for two reasons. One, individual schools or school systems will undoubtedly need to add additional principles that are responsive to their specific situations. Two, we focused only on what the school can do and not on other critical constituencies such as the family or the community. By working closely with parents and the community, schools can enhance their overall efforts to prevent writing difficulties and intervene successfully when such problems do occur.

REFERENCES

Alexander, P., Graham, S., & Harris, K. R. (1998). A perspective on strategy research: Progress and prospects. *Educational Psychology Review, 10,* 129-154.

Begley, S. (1999, April 5). Thinking will make it so. *Newsweek,* p. 64.

Berninger, V., Vaughn, K., Abbott, R., Abbott, S., Rogan, L., Brooks, A., Reed, E., & Graham, S. (1997). Treatment of handwriting problems in beginning writers: Transfer from handwriting to composition. *Journal of Educational Psychology, 89,* 652-666.

Berninger, V., Vaughn, K., Abbott, R., Brooks, A., Abbott, S., Rogan, L., Reed, E., & Graham, S. (1998). Early intervention for spelling problems: Teaching functional spelling units of varying size with a multiple-connections framework. *Journal of Educational Psychology, 90,* 587-605.

Burnham, S. (1994). *For writers only.* New York: Ballantine Books.

Christenson, S., Thurlow, M., Ysseldyke, J., & McVicar, R. (1989). Written language instruction for students with mild handicaps: Is there enough quantity to ensure quality? *Learning Disability Quarterly, 12,* 219-229.

De La Paz, S., Swanson, P., & Graham, S. (1998). The contribution of executive control to the revising of students with writing and learning difficulties. *Journal of Educational Psychology, 90,* 448-460.

Englert, C., Garmon, A., Mariage, T., Rozendal, M., Tarrant, K., & Urba, J. (1995). The Early Literacy Project: Connecting across the literacy curriculum. *Learning Disability Quarterly, 18,* 253-275.

Englert, C., Raphael, T., Anderson, L., Anthony, H., Steven, D., & Fear, K. (1991). Making writing and self-talk visible: Cognitive strategy instruction writing in regular and special education classrooms. *American Educational Research Journal, 28,* 337-373.

Englert, C., Raphael, T., Fear, K., & Anderson, L. (1988). Students' metacognitive knowledge about how to write informational text. *Learning Disability Quarterly, 11,* 18-46.

Erickson, K., & Koppenhaver, D. (1995). Developing a literacy program for children with severe disabilities. *The Reading Teacher, 48,* 676-684.

Gaskin, I. (1998). There's more to teaching at-risk and delayed readers than good reading instruction. *The Reading Teacher, 51,* 534-547.

Gordon, J., Vaughn, S., & Schumm, S. (1993). Spelling interventions: A review of literature and implications for instruction for students with learning disabilities. *Learning Disability Research & Practice, 8,* 175-181.

Graham, S. (1983). Effective spelling instruction. *Elementary School Journal, 83,* 560-567.

Graham, S. (1990). The role of production factors in learning disabled students' compositions. *Journal of Educational Psychology, 82,* 781-791.

Graham, S. (1997). Executive control in the revising of students with learning and writing difficulties. *Journal of Educational Psychology, 89,* 223-234.

Graham, S. (1999). Handwriting and spelling instruction for students with learning disabilities: A review. *Learning Disability Quarterly, 22,* 78-98.

Graham, S. (2000). Should the natural learning approach replace spelling instruction? *Journal of Educational Psychology, 92,* 235-247.

Graham, S., & Harris, K. R. (1989). A component analysis of cognitive strategy instruction: Effects on learning disabled students' compositions and self-efficacy. *Journal of Educational Psychology, 81,* 353-361.

Graham, S., & Harris, K. R. (1993). Self-Regulated Strategy Development: Helping students with learning problems develop as writers. *Elementary School Journal, 94,* 169-181.

Graham, S., & Harris, K. R. (1997). It can be taught, but it does not develop naturally: Myths and realities in writing instruction. *School Psychology Review, 26,* 414-424.

Graham, S., & Harris, K. R. (1998). Writing instruction. In B. Wong (Ed.), *Learning about learning disabilities* (pp. 391-423). San Diego, CA: Academic Press.

Graham, S., & Harris, K. R. (in press a). The road less traveled: Prevention and intervention in written language. In K. Butler & E. Silliman (Eds.), *The language learning disabilities continuum: Integration of research, technology, and education.* Mahwah, NJ: Erlbaum.

Graham, S., & Harris, K. R. (in press b). Prevention and intervention of writing difficulties for students with learning disabilities. *Learning Disabilities Research and Practice.*

Graham, S., Harris, K. R., & Fink, B. (2000). Is handwriting causally related to learning to write? Treatment of handwriting problems in beginning writers. *Journal of Educational Psychology, 92,* 620-633.

Graham, S., Harris, K. R., Fink, B., & MacArthur, C. (2000). *How do primary grade teachers adapt instruction to meet individual needs in writing?* Manuscript submitted for publication.

Graham, S., Harris, K. R., MacArthur, C., & Schwartz, S. (1991). Writing and writing instruction with students with learning disabilities: A review of a program of research. *Learning Disability Quarterly, 14,* 89-114.

Graham, S., & Miller, L. (1979). Spelling research and practice: A unified approach. *Focus on Exceptional Children, 12,* 1-16.

Graham, S., Schwartz, S., & MacArthur, C. (1993). Knowledge of writing and the composing process, attitude toward writing, and self-efficacy for students with and without learning disabilities. *Journal of Learning Disabilities, 26,* 237-249.

Graham, S., & Weintraub, N. (1996). A review of handwriting research: Progress and prospects from 1980 to 1994. *Educational Psychology Review, 8,* 7-87.

Harris, K. R. (1982). Cognitive-behavior modification: Application with exceptional children. *Focus on Exceptional Children, 15,* 1-16.

Harris, K. R., & Graham, S. (1996). *Making the writing process work: Strategies for composition and self-regulation.* Cambridge, MA: Brookline.

Harris, K. R., & Graham, S. (1999). Programmatic intervention research: Illustrations from the evolution of Self-Regulated Strategy Development. *Learning Disability Quarterly, 22,* 251-262.

Harris, K. R., Graham, S., Reid, R., McElroy, K., & Hamby, R. (1994). Self-monitoring of attention versus self-monitoring of performance: Replication and cross-task comparison studies. *Learning Disability Quarterly, 17,* 121–139.

Hillocks, G. (1986). *Research on written composition: New directions for teaching.* Urbana, IL: National Conference on Research in English.

Johnston, P., & Winograd, P. (1985). Passive failure in reading. *Journal of Reading Behavior, 17,* 279–301.

Jones, D., & Christensen, C. (1999). The relationship between automaticity in handwriting and students' ability to generate written text. *Journal of Educational Psychology, 91,* 44–49.

Juel, C. (1988). Learning to read and write: A longitudinal study of 54 children from first through fourth grade. *Journal of Educational Psychology, 80,* 437–447.

Kame'enui, E. (1993). Diverse learners and the tyranny of time: Don't fix blame; fix the leaky roof. *The Reading Teacher, 46,* 376–383.

MacArthur, C. (1996). Using technology to enhance the writing performance of students with learning disabilities. *Journal of Learning Disabilities, 29,* 344–354.

MacArthur, C. (1999). Overcoming barriers to writing: Computer support for basic writing skills. *Reading and Writing Quarterly, 15,* 169–192.

MacArthur, C., & Graham, S. (1987). Learning disabled students' composing with three methods: Handwriting, dictation, and word processing. *Journal of Special Education, 21,* 22–42.

Mariage, T. (1993, December). *The systemic influence of the Early Literacy Project curriculum: A four-year longitudinal study of student achievement from first to fourth grade.* Paper presented at the Annual Meeting of the National Reading Conference, Charleston, SC.

McCutchen, D. (1988). "Functional automaticity" in children's writing: A problem of metacognitive control. *Written Communication, 5,* 306–324.

Pressley, M. (1998). *Reading instruction that works: The case for balanced teaching.* New York: Guilford.

Pressley, M., Wharton-McDonald, R., Rankin, J., Mistretta, J., Yokoi, L., & Etterberg, J. (1996). The nature of outstanding primary-grades literacy instruction. In E. McIntyre & M. Pressley (Eds.), *Balanced instruction: Strategies and skills in whole language* (pp. 251–276). Norwood, MA: Christopher-Gordon.

Scardamalia, M., Bereiter, C., & Goleman, H. (1982). The role of production factors in writing ability. In M. Nystrand (Ed.), *What writers know: The language, process, and structure of written discourse* (pp. 173–210). New York: Academic Press.

Scott, C. (1989). Problem writers: Nature, assessment, and intervention. In A. Kamhi & H. Catts (Eds.), *Reading disabilities: A developmental language perspective* (pp. 303–344). Boston: Allyn and Bacon.

Sexton, M., Harris, K. R., & Graham, S. (1998). Self-regulated strategy development and the writing process: Effects on essay writing and attributions. *Exceptional Children, 64,* 295–311.

Swerdlow, J. (1999). The power of writing. *National Geographic, 196,* 110–132.

Thomas, C., Englert, C., & Gregg, S. (1987). An analysis of errors and strategies in the expository writing of learning disabled students. *Remedial and Special Education, 8,* 21–30.

Weintraub, N., & Graham, S. (1998). Writing legibly and quickly: A study of children's ability to adjust their handwriting to meet common classroom demands. *Learning Disability Research and Practice, 13,* 146–152.

Wong, B. (1997). Research on genre-specific strategies for enhancing writing in adolescents with learning disabilities, *Learning Disability Quarterly, 20,* 140–159.

Wong, B., Wong, R., & Blenkinsop, J. (1989). Cognitive and metacognitive aspects of learning disabled adolescents' composing problems. *Learning Disability Quarterly, 12,* 310–323.

Wray, D., Medwell, J., Fox, R., & Poulson, L. (2000). The teaching practices of effective teachers of literacy. *Educational Review, 52,* 75–84.

AUTHORS' NOTES

Correspondence should be directed to Steve Graham, University of Maryland, Department of Special Education, College Park, MD 20742. E-mail: *sg23@umail.umd.edu*. The preparation of this chapter was supported by the Center to Accelerate Student Learning, funded by the U.S. Department of Education's Office of Special Education Programs (Grant # H324V980001).

[1]This chapter incorporates and expands on principles presented in Graham and Harris (in press a, in press b).

CHAPTER 23

Classwide Peer Tutoring Programs

Charles R. Greenwood
University of Kansas

Larry Maheady
SUNY College at Fredonia

Joseph Delquadri
University of Kansas

INTRODUCTION

We face a continuing national crisis of poor learning outcomes in reading, mathematics, and other core academic subjects. We know that these poor outcomes are the product of wide variability in children's developmental assets and attainment of essential skills in preschool, and the relatively weak instructional interventions they encounter in elementary school. In young children, the failure to acquire literacy skills puts them on a trajectory leading to early school failure (e.g., Federal Interagency Forum on Child and Family Statistics, 1997; Greenwood, Delquadri, & Hall, 1989; Greenwood, Hart, Walker, & Risley, 1994; McKinney, Osborne, & Schulte, 1993). We use the term literacy to mean learning to communicate; to decode and comprehend print; and to spell, write, and compute. For example, the majority of child referrals to special education services are linked to slow reading progress (Snow, Burns, & Griffin, 1998) and most qualify for learning disabilities services because of slow progress learning to read (Council for Exceptional Children, 1994). Failure to attain literacy is a factor in the development of disruptive behavior and school violence (e.g., Walker, Colvin, & Ramsey, 1995).

> Children who are particularly likely to have difficulty with learning to read in the primary grades are those who begin school with less prior knowledge and skill in relevant domains, most notably general verbal abilities, the ability to attend to the sounds of language as distinct from meaning, familiarity with the basic purposes and mechanisms of read-

ing, and letter knowledge. Children from poor neighborhoods, children with limited proficiency in English, children with hearing impairments, children with preschool language impairments, and children whose parents had difficulty learning to read are particularly at risk of arriving at school with weakness in these areas and hence fall behind from the outset. (Snow et al., 1998, p. 5)

It is widely recognized that students who experience continuing failed remedial efforts to accelerate their basic academic skills past the primary grades are deprived of the opportunity to learn advanced subject matter (e.g., math and science; U.S. Department of Education, 1997—the 19th Annual IDEA Report to Congress). Early failure *compounds* and potentially limits an individual's future access to additional education, employment, independent living, and contribution to society (Heal, Khoju, & Rusch, 1997; Wagner, D'Amico, Marder, Newman, & Blackorby, 1992). In too many cases, these early problems are attributable to less than optimal experiences at home and weak instruction strategies used at school during the elementary years (Greenberg, 1998). "Each child presents the teacher with a unique history of earlier literacy experiences that underlie subsequent achievement" (Snow et al., 1998).

The *combined* effects of each student's unique history contribute to the problem of limited literacy outcomes. The extent and diversity of this uniqueness represents extreme classroom skill variability for the teacher. It is estimated that the academic skills of individual students span 5 or more grade levels in the typical American elementary classroom of 22–29 students (Jenkins, Jewell, Leceister, Jenkins, & Troutner, 1990). Rightly or wrongly, this diversity is rooted in policies and socioeconomic conditions that have led to increased numbers of students reared in poverty; the placement of low-, medium-, and high-ability students in the same classrooms with the end of student tracking policies (i.e., skill grouping); and the inclusion of students with disabilities (Brooks-Gunn & Duncan, 1997; L. S. Fuchs & D. Fuchs, 1998). Unfortunately, the majority of mandated general education reading and mathematics programs used in local schools are rarely designed to accommodate this range of diversity. In addition, student literacy problems may never be addressed in the general education classroom because effective instructional practices have yet to bridge the gap between research and practice.

A basic learning principle of educational psychology is that individual differences among diverse learners can only be accommodated if future instruction is adapted based on judgments about the success of prior teaching (e.g., Corno & Snow, 1986). In spite of this widely accepted fact, the majority of elementary-level general educators by training and local policy teach using whole-class, undifferentiated routines (i.e., curriculum, pacing, and classroom organization), which structure instruction uniformly for all students (e.g., Moody, Vaughn, & Schumm, 1997). Just one example is placing all students in the same reading text level and moving ahead based on mandated policy rather than evidence of student progress in the curriculum (Slavin, Dolan, & Madden, 1996).

In addition to misguided local policies, violation of the principle that future instruction be based on the success (or failure) of prior teaching may be further explained by the fact that the majority of general education teachers have been taught and believe that organic factors within the student (e.g., intelligence), and outside teachers' control, determine most of what students can and will learn (e.g., Simmons, Kame'enui, & Chard, 1998). This is startling when educational research has debunked this myth time and again and affirmed the powerful impact that teaching has on student learning (Brophy & Good, 1989). Thus, we offer this chapter to school psychologists to help them enable classroom teachers, special educators, teacher trainers, and policy makers reach the understanding that use of research-validated teaching strategies, such as peer tutoring, will produce measurably superior results for their students.

In a chapter devoted to this topic 10 years ago (Greenwood, Maheady, & Carta, 1991) we concluded that evidence from both research and practice had demonstrated peer tutoring to be an effective, acceptable, and sustainable means of "orchestrating the classroom processes" responsible for student learning. Furthermore, we reported that peer tutoring strategies represented the kind of instructional technology that would be "necessary to address the commonly encountered problems of diverse student populations" in the general education classroom. With the hindsight of an additional 10 years of experience with classwide peer tutoring research and practice, we are happy to state that these conclusions remain true, and even more convincing today. In this new chapter, we are able to discuss several classwide peer tutoring programs now supported by strong evidence in student learning, as compared to conventional teaching methods. The new programs are also supported by materials and training that make them accessible and usable by school psychologists and classroom teachers. As well, we discuss recent and future developments in these programs that promise to extend and expand their use across students, age groups, and subject matter content.

PURPOSE OF THIS CHAPTER

Classwide peer tutoring is a class of instructional strategies wherein students are taught by their peers who have been *trained* and are *supervised* by the classroom teacher. We have restricted our review to just those interventions whose goal it is to use peers to directly teach each other academic content. Thus, we are excluding many of the well-known peer-mediation and peer-influence strategies in the literature—e.g., cooperative learning (Greenwood, Carta, & Hall, 1988; Utley, Mortweet, & Greenwood, 1997). In this chapter, the focus is on *classwide direct peer teaching*.

First, we provide a background perspective on our own interest in peer teaching methods for systematic use in general education instruction. Next, we summarize the advantages and disadvantages of peer tutoring compared to whole-class, teacher-led instruction. We discuss design issues that impact the development and improvement of classwide peer tutoring programs. We discuss four classwide peer-tutoring programs in depth—these should be seriously considered for implementation by school psychologists because of their well-defined procedures, documented effects on student learning, and the materials/training available to access and use them. We then look into the knowledge/skills school psychologists need to acquire and training they have to undergo to be able to implement—and train others to implement—these programs. We conclude with a discussion of the implications of the programs.

CLASSWIDE PEER TUTORING AS A VIABLE INSTRUCTIONAL OPTION FOR THE REGULAR CLASSROOM

Historically, peer tutoring has been an approach used by teachers to repair the inadequacies of traditional, whole-class, teacher-led instruction. One of many examples involves helping to individualize the instruction of several students who have fallen behind the class academically and who are now unsuccessful in the regular curriculum. Our own interest in children unable to function successfully in the classroom curriculum and the movement toward peer tutoring is reflected in this bit of personal history.

In the early 1980s, general education teachers were seeking effective strategies for "mainstreaming" students with mild disabilities into general education instruction. In Kansas City, Kansas, Kathleen Stretton, a third-grade teacher at Fairfax Elementary School, was seeking a method of integrating students with learning disabilities (LD) into instruction with her other students in response to the new "least restrictive environment" provisions of Public Law (P.L.) 94-142. Her goal was integrating these students in a way that did not create separate "LD" or "EMR" student groupings. At the same time, a local group of researchers at the Juniper Gardens Children's Project (JGCP) were concerned because classroom observational research findings indicated that too many area students in local Title 1 elementary school classrooms were not actively engaged during whole-class, teacher-led instruction (Greenwood, Delquadri, & Hall, 1984). Consequently, Kathleen Stretton and Joseph Delquadri, a researcher at the JGCP, collaborated in an effort that became Classwide Peer Tutoring (CWPT; Arreaga-Mayer, Terry, & Greenwood, 1998; Delquadri, Greenwood, Stretton, & Hall, 1983). Both Stretton and Delquadri brought important elements to this collaboration that, when combined, led to an acceptable instructional solution.

Delquadri had just completed a doctoral dissertation on the effects of pullout, one-on-one tutoring, and he had been able to successfully engage even the most challenging students—all made measurable progress on the material he had taught them (Delquadri, 1978). Stretton was seeking a method that would enable students to master the classroom curriculum, accommodate diversity in academic skill levels, and enable all students to play roles that would not label or stigmatize. She also used a classwide mastery monitoring system (e.g., Deno, 1997) that employed a posted wall chart where she recorded weekly test results. One benefit of Stretton's mastery monitoring approach was that it did not require complicated graphing in order for her or her students to see trends in individual and group progress.

The CWPT Spelling Game emerged from their collaboration (Delquadri et al., 1983). Its design sought the benefits of Delquadri's one-on-one tutoring applied classwide, where all students were involved simultaneously in peer tutoring, and Stretton's goals to instructionally integrate all students and her mastery monitoring approach. Thus, CWPT became a form of intraclass, reciprocal, classwide peer tutoring.

In CWPT, the tutor and tutee roles were *reciprocal;* each student functioned as the tutor and tutee during *each* CWPT session, thereby avoiding the stigmatizing effects of a student always being the tutee and never the tutor. A critical factor was that CWPT was not just two students "teaching each other" informally. Other instructional components were important, including a curriculum, tutor training, and motivational strategies.

For example, in the CWPT spelling game, the teacher selected the spelling curricula from within the reading program. Each week, tutors used a new list of 20 spelling words. Tutors used a *scripted teaching strategy* because earlier research had demonstrated that better results were obtained by trained rather than untrained peer tutors (Niedermeyer, 1970). Scripting what the tutor was to say and do while teaching captured an effective teaching strategy and made the strategy easy to teach to all students while adhering to high standards of fidelity. In support of motivation, an individual point system with competing teams was used, similar to the game of basketball. Students earned two points for their team for each correctly spelled word. They earned one point for correcting an error after respelling it correctly three times. Like basketball, students' points were summed to form a team total and a winning team was declared after each daily session and each week.

Compared to other tutoring programs, tutors in this program were only those students normally present in the general education classroom. Because dependence on upper-grade students had previously proven to be an unreliable source of tutors, it was considered an advantage that CWPT did not require the use of older/upper-grade, cross-age students.

Students' learning with the CWPT spelling game, compared to baseline and reversal measurements when they were taught using conventional teacher-led instruction, was accelerated. Most notable was reduction in spelling errors on weekly posttests—often to the point where students with LD spelled as accurately as did students without LD (Delquadri et al., 1983). These results were sustained one week to the next as Stretton continued to use CWPT.

Stretton noticed, without having to see an analysis of data, that CWPT produced better spelling performance than did her conventional teaching. Her conventional spelling instruction consisted of a combination of chalkboard discussion followed by seatwork with students assigned to complete workbook exercises designed to build vocabulary and spelling skills. Many students were not nearly as engaged in academic responding during this instruction in the absence of peer tutors. Students made twice as many errors on average using this form of spelling instruction. During CWPT, Stretton busily supervised the work of the peer tutors, checking to make sure that they followed the scripted procedure, and providing help when questions arose about the pronunciation of some words or their spelling—instead of lecturing, discussing, or questioning students as she had done in her conventional teacher-led instruction. During CWPT, it was observed that tutors tended to present new material as fast as the tutee could respond by writing the word and spelling it aloud, or made the necessary corrections. Similarly, if the tutors drifted off-task, tutees quickly prompted them for the next item (e.g., "Give me the next one!"). *Engaged, high-paced, partner-regulated instructional interactions* became the signature characteristic of CWPT.

This bit of history illustrates the successful collaboration between a general education teacher and special education researcher around a significant instructional problem and its solution through a classwide peer tutoring game. Because CWPT was effective for students with and without LD, because it included design elements contributed by the classroom teacher, and because it included design elements of effective instruction and principles of motivation, students' engagement and content learning improved. The program was sustained and the teacher and students preferred participating in CWPT compared to teacher-led instruction.

These core features, when joined with new curriculum designs in subsequent work, made CWPT an increasingly viable instructional alternative for teaching a range of subject matter. Heron, Heward, Cooke, and Hill (1983) used CWPT procedures to teach students sight words in Columbus, Ohio. Maheady and Harper (1987) replicated spelling CWPT in an elementary school in Fredonia, New York. Because students' learning improved and they liked CWPT, teachers found it useful.

RELATIVE ADVANTAGES OF PEER TUTORING COMPARED TO TRADITIONAL TEACHER-LED INSTRUCTION

The relative advantages of peer tutoring reported in the literature, versus traditional whole-class, teacher-led instruction, are profiled in Table 1. As can be seen, peer tutoring was rated superior to teacher-led instruction across 14 procedural and student learning factors ranging from pupil/teacher ratio to reading fluency. With respect to seven disadvantages, ranging from training requirements to ethical costs, peer tutoring was rated behind teacher-led instruction. The advantages reflect aspects of instruction known to promote and accelerate learning. With peer tutoring, teachers can arrange, for at least a portion of the instructional time, one teacher for every student—a pupil-teacher ratio of 1:1 (King-Sears & Cummings, 1996). Research indicates that with peer tutoring, students are more engaged; are afforded more opportunities to respond to the curriculum; receive more frequent error correction, help, and encouragement; and experience both competitive and cooperative learning (Greenwood, 1991; Simmons, Fuchs, Fuchs, Hodge, & Mathes, 1994). Because of a range of possible reward structures and contingencies of reinforcement, students in peer tutoring are more motivated and satisfied with their experiences (Kohler & Greenwood, 1986; 1990; Kohler, Richardson, Mina, Dinwiddie, & Greenwood, 1985). In peer tutoring compared to traditional instruction, students learn to teach others and the social skills necessary to do so (Strayhorn, Strain, & Walker, 1993). Research also reports that peer tutoring promotes consistently greater learning across a range of subject matter and ages of students (Greenwood, 1996).

TABLE 1

Teacher-Led Instruction Versus Peer Tutoring

Factors	Instructor Teacher	Peer
Advantages		
Pupil/teacher ratio	High	Low
Engaged time	Variable	High
Opportunities to respond	Low	High
Opportunities for error correction	Low	High
Immediacy of error correction	Delayed	Immediate
Opportunities for help and encouragement	Few	Many
Opportunities for both competitive and cooperative learning experiences	Few	Many
Motivation	Teacher	Teacher & Peer
Learn to teach others	No	Yes
Learn peer social skills	No	Yes
Increased engagement	No	Yes
Skill mastery	Good	Better
Achievement test tesults	Good	Better
Reading fluency	Good	Better
Disadvantages		
Tutor training requirements	Few	Many
Quality control requirement	Few	Many
Content coverage	Good	Variable
Tutor selection	None	Required
Curriculum adaptations	Few	Many
Costs	High	Low
Ethical concerns	Few	Increased

Note
Adapted from Greenwood, Carta, and Kamps (1990, p. 191).

The disadvantages compared to traditional instruction reflect an increased cost in time and effort to establish and sustain peer tutoring programs. Added to the effort is the need to train teachers and peer tutors and monitor the quality of their implementation. To the extent that peer tutoring is not planned to integrate with the existing curriculum, what is taught in peer tutoring may be misaligned with mandated goals and standards tested. Furthermore, tutor selection and partner-pairing options may be exhausted as soon as the tutor has taught the tutee what he or she knows (e.g., tutor obsolescence). Because there are few "out the box" curricula ready made for use by peer tutors, teacher-developed curriculum adaptations are necessary. Thus, start-up costs of peer tutoring programs may be initially higher than for teacher-led instruction given that extra planning time, teacher training, material development, and monitoring of implementation are significant issues. However, once underway, costs may approach the same levels as—or even fall below—those of teacher-led programs (Armstrong, Conlon, Pierson, & Stahlbrand, 1979; Levin, Glass, & Meister, 1984).

Peer tutoring raises ethical concerns as well, when questions about the effectiveness of peer tutoring programs are not adequately addressed and sufficiently documented (Greenwood, 1981). For example, it is not ethical to assign peer tutors to students in the absence of convincing evidence that the tutoring procedures to be followed are effective—or if there is no progress monitoring in place that can demonstrate that these procedures are working and should be continued.

DESIGN ISSUES IN PEER TUTORING PROGRAMS

Effective peer tutoring programs vary across a number of design factors that affect utility, scale, outcomes, sustainability, and participant satisfaction. Among these factors are the (a) handling of tutor obsolescence, (b) use of naturalistic versus structured instructional procedures, (c) content, tasks, and materials employed, (d) training of tutors, (e) secondary or side effects, (f) peer pairing strategies used, (g) arrangement of tutoring pairs on teams, (h) use of contingencies and consequences, (i) formative evaluation measures, and (j) administrative support.

Tutor Obsolescence

All tutoring programs must address the fact that any single tutor-tutee partnership becomes "obsolete" as soon as the tutee has mastered the skill(s) the tutor originally was assigned to teach. This problem is particularly true in programs that rely extensively on the superior knowledge of the peer tutor, and relatively less on materials and systematic curricula. A traditional design point in peer tutoring programs is achieving a "good fit" between tutor and tutee. In traditional forms of peer tutoring, it is believed that assigning a tutor with the knowledge to teach a student who is deficient on some particular skill is all that is needed. This position is ill founded, however, because the supply of knowledgeable tutors is always too short and the teacher's workload associated with continually assessing and reassigning matched pairs is too high. The tutor obsolescence problem has frequently limited the duration and scale of peer tutoring use to fewer than several students in one single classroom for only a few weeks at a time. Thus, peer tutoring has always been considered by many teachers as just a patch, to be used only in those few cases until a student was "caught up" and/or ready to learn in conventional instructional methods.

We know now that obsolescence may be eliminated using designs that anticipate this problem. For example, providing tutors with tools that support accurate error correction and that regularly refresh the material to be learned prevents obsolescence and promotes content coverage on a greater scale. This approach also sustains the material's use over time. Similarly, employing procedures that introduce tutors and tutees to new material by calling on their background knowledge—that is, guiding them through the process with examples and preliminary experiences prior to tutoring sessions—also obviates tutor obsolescence.

Who May Tutor Whom

Traditionally, the "ideal" tutor has been considered to be a student with both the social and academic skills necessary to instruct a tutee with a minimum of training, teacher planning, and teacher assistance. In this top-down approach, tutors have been upper-grade and/or higher-skilled students who spend a portion of the day working one-on-one in a lower-grade or special education classroom (e.g., Jenkins & Jenkins, 1988). As mentioned previously, tutor selection based on finding the "ideal tutor" usually produces only a limited number of tutors that meet the ideal criteria. Thus, higher-skilled tutors are always in short supply. We now know, however, that short of this ideal, in well-designed peer tutoring programs that provide certain conditions of training, materials, and monitoring, peers of equal or even less academic skill are clearly able to provide effective tutoring services (e.g., Osguthorpe & Scruggs, 1986).

In classwide peer tutoring programs, all students can legitimately serve as a tutor and, in fact, are required to serve as *both* tutor and tutee in the course of a single tutoring session (Delquadri et al., 1983). For example, in Delquadri et al. tutor/tutee pairs were formed randomly each week. Students formed partnerships simply by drawing names from a box. Each student then served as the tutor for half the session and then switched roles in the second half of the session. Using answer sheets and assistance from the teacher, all students were able to present task trials and to make adequate corrections when in the tutor's role.

Naturalistic Versus Structured, Explicit Teaching Procedures

Tutoring programs differ in the extent to which peer teaching strategies are left to the discretion of the tutor versus conforming to accepted principles of effective instruction. Traditional tutoring methods typically have not sought to equip tutors with formal teaching procedures. Rather, tutors have had responsibility for determining how to work with their tutees. As early as 1970, Niedermeyer (1970) reported that *training* tutors in specific, instructional techniques (e.g., using task presentation with response feedback) resulted in better achievement outcomes than no training at all. Thus, most classwide tutoring programs today teach tutors the use of explicit peer teaching strategies, including routines for task presentation, error correction, and provision of feedback and reinforcement. Once determined, peer teaching procedures can be taught to many or most of the students in a classroom with the performance of individual tutors monitored for fidelity in implementation. Consequently, use of structured peer teaching procedures supports quality, scale, and sustainability.

Arrangements: Pairs, Triads, and Teams

Although pairs are the typical tutoring unit, some tutoring programs accommodate triads (i.e., one tutor and two tutees) and small group or team arrangements (Maheady & Harper, 1987; Maheady, Harper, & Sacca, 1988; Pigott et al., 1986). Either by design or in cases involving an uneven number of students present in class, one tutor can teach two tutees simultaneously (e.g., Greenwood, et al., 1987). Other programs may employ teams composed of small student groups in which any team member may tutor any other member. For example, in Classwide Student Tutoring Teams (CSTT), the tutoring role is rotated among the four to six students of heterogeneous ability on each of four to five teams (Maheady, Sacca, & Harper, 1988). Other programs (e.g., Heron et al., 1983) employ *both* pairs and teams within a classwide peer tutoring program (Heward, Heron, Ellis, & Cooke, 1986). As in CSTT, tutor/tutee pairs are assigned to heterogeneous teams. Teams meet together before and after tutoring sessions to introduce new material and correct completed work. The teams or "tutor huddles" are supervised by students with the highest skill level—these students introduce new material, clarify instructions, supervise, and correct. During tutoring sessions, the tutoring pairs work independently through the material to be learned (Heron et al., 1983).

Contingencies, Rewards, and Consequences

Because of their motivational properties, reinforcement contingencies may be employed to improve each student's performance as a tutor and as a tutee, and to maintain enthusiasm and participation of groups of students (Greenwood & Hops, 1981). Examples of reinforcement contingencies used in peer tutoring are points earned for correctly spelled words and error corrections—these points may be traded for pencils, note paper, or other desired objects, or special activities awarded to a team of tutor-tutee partners because of their winning point total. However, tutoring procedures vary in the extent to which contingencies of reinforcement are employed and the extent that their beneficial effects are fully exploited. When behavior management or behavior problems are of concern, combining reinforcement with peer tutoring is often highly effective (Bell, Young, Blair, & Nelson, 1990).

In traditional applications of tutoring, individual contingencies of social reinforcement and punishment (e.g., praise vs. criticism) are thought to operate naturally in the context of the moment-to-moment "give and take" between tutor and tutee. These contingencies are determined by the tutor and tutee while they work together. In this process of tutoring, tutors and tutees may or may not provide one another prompts for responses, feedback, and forms of approval or disapproval as they work together with the subject matter.

In most effective peer tutoring programs, however, a tutor's use of prompts, feedback, and approval is designed according to principles of effective teaching and monitored for occurrence by the classroom teacher. These interactions often consist of the presentation of discrete task trials by the tutor and task responses by the tutee (e.g.,

Kohler et al., 1985), or presentations of conceptual mathematics rules and principles (L. S. Fuchs, D. Fuchs, Hamlett, et al., 1997). For example, tutors may be taught to award points and approval for correct tutee responses and/or to remove points based on off-task or slow responses.

Individual reinforcement contingencies are those in which the behavior of the individual student results in individual consequences—either positive or negative. *Group-oriented contingencies* of reinforcement are those in which the collective behavior of the group determines a group member's consequences—again, either positive or negative. Group reinforcement contingencies in peer tutoring programs are those that are focused on the collective performance of teams or the entire class in which tutoring partners, tutor and tutee belong. For example, Delquadri and his colleagues (Delquadri et al., 1983) employed a point system implemented by the tutors. At the individual level, tutees earned points for responding to the tutor and/or the tutoring materials and reported these point scores to the teacher for public posting. Additionally, each tutor-tutee pair was a member of one of two teams competing for the highest point total. At the group reinforcement level, each pair contributed their individual point totals toward a team total. At the end of each session, individuals' points were summed for each team and the team with the highest point total was announced the winner.

Academic Content and Tasks

The subject matter content and the learning tasks used in classwide peer tutoring, when compared to those in conventional teacher-led instruction, often require specialized designs and materials to guide learners and to ensure that their success rate and satisfaction remains high. For example, if the tutoring program is based on a mastery learning approach, as is often the case, learning tasks need to be organized into short units sequenced hierarchically by difficulty level. When students with moderate to severe disabilities are included in the general education classroom, separate curricula linked to their Individualized Education Programs (IEPs) may be necessary. For example, while the majority of the class is engaged in tutoring on grade-level reading passages, lower-skilled students may be engaged in tutoring on color discrimination or survival/safety vocabulary tasks (e.g., Reddy et al., 1999). Additionally, when students with severe disabilities have a paraprofessional assigned to assist them, it is possible to include the paraprofessional in the peer tutoring framework. For example, children with significant hearing loss may participate directly in peer tutoring when the paraprofessional translates their tutor-tutee interactions from sign language to English. The peer tutor may present a word to be spelled; the paraprofessional may then sign the word, and then say the tutee's signed spelling of the word to the tutor in the typical tutor-tutee scripted interaction.

If peer tutoring is organized around developing a class product or completing a project, task individualization based on skill levels can be accomplished by differentiating students' contributions. For example, when painting a picture depicting the Western movement in the 1870s, the tutee with fine motor disabilities might paint the sky and the tutor without a disability might sketch in the covered wagons.

Tutoring materials are often designed to fit interactive formats of tutor presentation and tutee response (e.g., Heron et al., 1983). For example, flashcards are often used in a format in which the tutor presents a word written on a card to the tutee and says, "Read this word." If the word is read correctly, it is stacked in a pile of correct cards; if read incorrectly it is corrected by the tutor who might say, "No, its Cat, What is it?" to which the tutee responds "Cat." The card is then placed back in the deck for an additional trial (Heward, 1996, p. 66). Or, in a slightly different example, from a list of spelling words the tutor may ask the tutee to spell the word cat. The tutee then attempts to spell it orally while also writing it on a response sheet. When the tutee is finished, the tutor then checks the word against the list and awards points for corrrectness or provides a correction when an error is made. Similarly, peer teaching materials may include vocabulary words or even sentences read orally from text passages. In the latter, each sentence can be counted as a response opportunity. Alternatively, in a paragraph-shrinking task in which students learn to identify the main ideas in what they read (D. Fuchs, L. S. Fuchs, Mathes, & Simmons, 1996), tutors ask tutees to identify the main idea by using such prompts as "identify the 'who or what' in this story" and "what was the most important thing about the 'who or what.'" Thus, peer teaching materials and tasks are quite different from the often open-ended study tasks or the worksheets used during independent study or seatwork activities.

Spelling and vocabulary materials for use with English Language Learners (ELL) have been developed with special attention placed on components addressing students' active engagement in learning tasks, extended discourse in English, and respect for cultural diversity. For example, first graders are taught sight words because they are not ready to read and need a base in English vocabulary to support additional enrichment activities designed to foster their language and literacy skills (Greenwood, Arreaga-Mayer, Utley, Gavin, & Terry, 2001). Prior to the week's session, the teacher introduces new sight vocabulary words (i.e., the Dolch word list) using bilingual flashcards and modeling procedures within a whole-class discussion format. First, the teacher pronounces each word in Spanish and the students repeat the word in Spanish. Second, the teacher pronounces each word in English and the students repeat the word in English. Third, the teacher verbally spells each word in English and the students spell the words aloud in English. In addition, the teacher uses scaffolding strategies and mediation/feedback techniques to expand the students' understanding of the vocabulary words.

In the peer tutoring process, sight-recognition word flashcards are placed in the center of an 8 1/2" x 11" place mat with a smiley face on the left side and a question mark on the right side. Students are paired depending on their level of English proficiency such that each student with little proficiency is matched with one who is much more fluent in English. Once the students are paired into tutor and tutee roles, the tutor is instructed to show the flashcard to the tutee and ask the tutee to say the word. If the word is pronounced correctly, the tutor places the flashcard on the smiley face. For every correct response, the tutor awards the tutee 2 points. If the tutee does not pronounce the word correctly, the tutor corrects the tutee by supplying the correct response. The tutee pronounces the word once. Following this response, the tutee is awarded 1 point. The flashcard is then placed on the question mark. If either the tutor or tutee does not know the word, the tutor raises his or her hand holding up the help card for teacher assistance.

Effective peer tutoring materials frequently incorporate *explicit* instructional scripts and tutors are taught to use these scripts in their teaching. Compared to implicit instruction in which the student is left to discover and *learn on his or her own,* explicit instruction is designed to *guide* a student's learning using prompting, scaffolding, and feedback. For example, the explicit instructional designs and materials in Direct Instruction have been successfully adapted for use in classwide peer tutoring for teaching phonemic segmentation in beginning reading (Mathes, Howard, Allen, & Fuchs, 1998).

Conventional curriculum materials also may be employed directly in classwide peer tutoring programs. One example is using basal textbook stories in each day's tutoring sessions. When divided into 100-word passages—which are short enough to be read and reread several times during peer tutoring—the basal text may be used in peer tutoring to build students' reading accuracy and fluency (e.g., Greenwood et al., 1989). Based on reading these passages, tutors may also ask comprehension questions framed around "who, what, where, when, and why," providing formal opportunities for students to recall, apply, and extend the knowledge acquired through their reading. A prediction-relay task, in which tutees are prompted by their tutor through the task of predicting (before reading) and then confirming actual outcomes (after reading) in a passage, is another example (D. Fuchs et al., 2001). During this task, students use what they have learned in reading earlier paragraphs to predict what may happen next. Then, by confirming predictions after reading, the students' use and understanding of what they are reading is improved.

Materials and procedure that enable *accurate correction* by the tutor of the tutee's responses are a highly desired component of effective peer tutoring materials. These may include answer lists, words spelled phonetically to prompt correct pronunciation by tutors, correction routines, etc. Additionally, procedures that make it possible to chart and monitor tutees' performance over time frequently are employed. Sheets designed for recording points earned or graphing the number of correctly spelled words also are typical components in effective peer tutoring programs.

Tutor Training

The amount of training, follow-up, and retraining provided to tutors and their tutees varies widely, depending on the complexity of the program and the social skills of the tutors. If tutors need to learn specific methods of task presentation and error correction and the uses of consequences (e.g., points, tokens, praise), tutor training requires advance planning. Typically, several sessions (ranging from 4 to 8 sessions) are needed to sufficiently train tutors. In applications in which tutors will be working with children with special needs, it also may be desirable that tutors learn about the nature of their disability, what to reasonably expect, how to access help from the teacher, and how to deal effectively with responses that may fall outside of the usual range of conventional classroom behavior (e.g., Whorton, Rotholz, Walker, McGrale, & Locke, 1987).

In some classwide peer tutoring programs with very young students or students with disabilities, it may be necessary to teach tutors the academic responses that they then must teach to their tutees. For example, Kohler (1987) reported that tutors of preschoolers had to be trained in color names prior to tutoring their peers in the same skills. Brown, Fenrick, and Klemme (1971) used similar preteaching procedure with students with moderate-to-severe disabilities.

Secondary (Side) Effects of Peer Tutoring

The secondary effects of peer tutoring, those beyond improved academic learning for tutees, range across a number of domains. An often-reported side effect is that tutors benefit academically as much as or more than their tutees (e.g., Polirstok & Greer, 1986). However, this outcome has not always been the case and likely depends on the learning requirements of tutors in the program. For example, tutors who are required to teach skills that they have mastered only recently may have the opportunity to "firm up" these skills as a product of tutoring others. While tutoring, peer teachers may have new opportunities to review or generalize uses of academic skills that they acquired previously during teacher-led teacher instruction.

Tutoring programs implemented primarily to improve students' academic skills also have been linked to increases in the sociometric status of tutored students (Maheady & Sainato, 1985), increases in peer social interactions between students with and without disabilities (Kamps, Barbetta, Leonard, & Delquadri, 1994), and improved relationships between minority group and majority group students (Greenwood et al., 1989).

Negative side effects also are possible. For example, being a tutor in some programs may mean time away from one's conventional classroom program. The trade-off between time away and time tutoring others is a consideration that should be made based on the potential benefits for both tutor and tutee (e.g., Greenwood, 1981). Whenever possible, the design of the tutoring program should protect tutors from this problem. In classwide peer tutoring, for example, because the program can accommodate varied instructional needs from student to student and is designed around all students in the class, as opposed to cross-age or cross-grade-level tutors, this problem is less of a concern.

Another negative side effect can emerge in tutoring programs when one student is always the tutee and never the tutor. The potential exists in these programs for some students to be stigmatized as low achievers or as slow learners if they are deprived of the opportunity to tutor others, or if they are not afforded the opportunity to work with other tutors. These tutees have a higher risk of becoming reluctant participants, sometimes even refusing to engage in tutoring activities (e.g., Greenwood et al., 1988).

Formative Evaluation

Tutoring programs vary in the extent to which data on student learning are collected and used to monitor progress, adapt instruction, and improve the quality of the program. Those reviewed in this chapter employ either unit mastery monitoring and/or Curriculum-Based Measurement (CBM) in a general outcome measurement approach. For more detail on these approaches see the Chapter by Deno, Espin, and L. S. Fuchs in this volume.

An example of mastery monitoring is the use of weekly pretest to posttest gains in spelling accuracy after peer tutoring. An example of general outcome measurement is assessing the rate of weekly growth in the number of correctly written digits on a CBM math test. Unit pre- and posttesting is helpful in establishing growth in specific skills taught using peer tutoring and identifying the skills that need to be taught. CBM is also helpful in establishing the rate of growth in the grade-level curriculum and identifying the need to adapt instruction to accelerate the learning of individual children in order to reach grade-level progress norms (Deno, 1997). Most tutoring programs advocate collecting and analyzing information concerning the *errors* made during tutoring sessions or CBM probes (e.g., Delquadri, Greenwood, Whorton, Carta, & Hall, 1986), in order to identify skills learned and needing to be taught. A recent development is the use of computer software in peer tutoring programs for this purpose (L. S. Fuchs, D. Fuchs, & Hamlett, 1994; L. S. Fuchs, Hamlett, & D. Fuchs, 1999; L. S. Fuchs, D. Fuchs, Hamlett, & Bentz, 1994; Greenwood, Finney, et al., 1993; Greenwood, Hou, Delquadri, Terry, & Arreaga-Mayer, 2001; Greenwood, Delquadri, Hou, Terry, & Arreaga-Mayer, 2001).

Peer tutoring programs also vary in the extent that measures are available for assessing *fidelity of implementation*. For example, Maheady and Harper (1987) and Greenwood, Dinwiddie, et al., (1987) employed observational checklists to assess the presence of the necessary materials, the correct sequence of teacher behaviors, and student tutoring behaviors. Similarly, Greenwood, Dinwiddie, et al., (1987) used implementation data to certify teachers as trained in a classwide tutoring program and to monitor the quality of their continued use of it over time. Programs that employ point systems to reinforce tutoring behaviors may use point earning data to track tutees' academic responding in the daily tutoring sessions (e.g., Maheady & Harper, 1987). If academic responding is low based on the number of points earned relative to the number earned the day before or compared to peers' scores, adaptations in the program can be made to improve students' responding in terms of the number of spelling words attempted or sentences read by the tutee. Analysis and advice provided by computer software are increasingly available, enabling the implementers to assess the quality of their peer tutoring program (e.g., Greenwood, Hou, et al., 2001).

Building and District Administrative Supports

Tutoring programs vary in the extent to which they are initiated by individual teachers or district policy (Greenwood, Delquadri, & Bulgren, 1993). In either case, support for the adoption of classwide peer tutoring programs is a major factor in scale and sustainability—and therefore is crucial. Evidence of formal adoption can be found if classwide peer tutoring appears in a district's published curriculum guide for teachers or as an approved procedure for use in the IEPs of students receiving special education services. A second compelling form of evidence is formal descriptions of the tutoring procedures and standards used for assessing their implementation. A third form of evidence is formal training experiences provided to teachers and district staff in these procedures.

A fourth indication of administrative support is the extent to which professionals other than the regular classroom teacher (e.g., special education teachers, school psychologists, school principals, grade-level curriculum coordinators, and district executive officers) are knowledgeable of the rationale for classwide peer tutoring and the particular procedures.

Clearly the greatest potential for impact is when both administrative and program personnel have specific roles to play in the implementation and evaluation of classwide peer tutoring programs. In schools where the curriculum coordinators, school psychologists, and lead teachers serve as trainers and coaches for a tutoring program, sustained use of tutoring programs is likely to occur. In schools where the principal plays a role in objectively evaluating a teacher's implementation of a tutoring program—for example, by office postings of weekly summaries of data produced in all classrooms where tutoring is occurring—tutoring programs likely will be implemented broadly and will be maintained over time. In contrast, where teachers employ peer tutoring at their own initiative and the principal plays no direct role, the program probably will not be employed schoolwide—nor will it persist from one year to the next.

INSTRUCTIONAL SYSTEMS BUILT AROUND CLASSWIDE PEER TUTORING COMPONENTS

Since our chapter on this topic appeared in 1991, several classwide peer tutoring programs have emerged with well-defined procedures for teachers and compelling research evidence that students' learning is accelerated in these programs. These include Classwide Peer Tutoring (CWPT), Peer-Assisted Learning Strategies (PALS), Classwide Student Tutoring Teams (CSTT), and Reciprocal Peer Tutoring (RPT). These programs have been used to improve the effectiveness of pullout instructional programs (i.e., RPT) for at-risk students in urban elementary schools and to improve the effectiveness of general classroom instruction in which students with disabilities have been included (e.g., CWPT, PALS, and CSTT). In Tables 2 and 3, we compare them across a range of procedural and evidence-based factors.

Classwide Peer Tutoring (CWPT)

As previously described, CWPT originated in the 1980s as a means of improving the spelling accuracy of students who were low achieving and/or who were categorized as LD. Because the teacher did not want to teach students in different ability groups, she used CWPT as a way of including *all* students in classroom spelling instruction at the same time. To include all students in instruction, the subsequent design of

TABLE 2

Procedural Comparison Among Methods

Core Procedures	CWPT	PALS	CSTT	RTP
Teacher-led introductions of new material	yes	yes	yes	yes
Materials preparation/selection	yes	no	yes	yes
New content	weekly	weekly	weekly	as mastered
Study guides	no	no	yes	no
Teacher trains student tutors and tutees	yes	yes	yes	yes
Weekly tutoring sessions	3–4 days	3 days	3 days	2 days
Session duration	30–40 min	30–40 min	30–40 min	45 min
Pairing of students	yes	yes	no	yes
Matched ability pairing	yes	no	no	yes
Random pairing	yes	no	no	no
Pairing of low- and high-performing students	no	yes	no	no
Teacher overide for specific reasons	yes	yes	yes	yes
Reciprocal student roles	yes	yes	yes	yes
Higher-performing student tutors first as a model	no	yes	no	no
Pairs assigned to teams	yes	yes	no	yes
More than two teams	no	no	yes	yes
Tutors correct errors	yes	yes	yes	yes
Heterogeneous teams	no	yes	yes	no
Points earned for responding	yes	yes	yes	yes
Bonus points for tutors	yes	yes	no	no
Game/sports theme	yes	yes	yes	yes
Winning teams	weekly	weekly	yes	yes
Back-up rewards (e.g., privileges)	no	no	no	yes
Public posting of individual and/or team points	yes	yes	yes	yes
New pairs and/or teams	weekly	monthly	4–6 weeks	no
Mastery/fluency monitoring formative evaluation	yes	no	yes	yes
General outcome measurement	no	yes	no	no
Elementary and secondary applications	yes	yes	yes	no
Reading	yes	yes	no	no
Beginning reading applications	yes	yes	no	no
Spelling	yes	no	no	no
Mathematics	yes	yes	no	no
Subject matter curricula	yes	no	yes	no
Custom computer software tools	yes	yes	no	no

CWPT sought to take full advantage of a number of effective components, including one-on-one peer tutoring and group contingencies of reinforcement (see Table 2). Other components included were the tutor's modeling of the correct response as an error correction strategy, tutor task presentations and response opportunities, tutor monitoring of tutee performance, and recording of points earned by the tutee. Additional instructional components taken from research on effective instruction

TABLE 3

Some Additional Curriculum Features

	CWPT	PALS	CSTT	RTP
Elementary Reading Activities				
Partner reading with error correction	yes	yes	no	no
What, why, when, where comprehension	yes	no	no	no
Paragraph shrinking	no	yes	no	no
Prediction relay	no	yes	no	no
Secondary Extensions/Adaptions				
Work rather than sports/game theme	no	yes	no	no
Backup reinforcement	yes	yes	no	yes
Expository rather than narrative reading material	no	yes	no	no
Subject matter study guides	yes	no	yes	no

included (a) frequent opportunities to respond and practice, (b) reciprocal tutor-tutee roles, (c) immediate error correction, (d) frequent (weekly) testing, (e) posting of performance, and (f) feedback on progress, mastery and content coverage (Greenwood, Terry, Delquadri, Elliot, & Arreaga-Mayer, 1995).

A manual of procedures guides teachers' implementation of CWPT (Greenwood, Delquadri, & Carta, 1997). The core procedures include the following:

- Review and introduction of new material to be learned;

- Unit content materials to be tutored (e.g., reading passages, spelling word lists, or math fact lists);

- New partners each week;

- Partner pairing strategies;

- Reciprocal roles in each session;

- Teams competing for the highest team point total;

- Contingent individual tutee point earning;

- Tutors providing immediate error correction;

- Public posting of individual and team scores; and

- Social reward for the winning team.

Added to these core procedures are *subject-matter-specific procedures* that support peer teaching. At the *elementary school level,* CWPT is designed to supplement traditional instruction in the basic academic skills and to replace seatwork, lecture, and oral reading group activities. The *teacher's role* during CWPT sessions is to supervise and monitor both tutors' and tutees' responding. Teachers are concerned with the *quality* of tutoring, and they award bonus points to tutors for using correct teaching behaviors. The teacher ensures that tutees are working quickly and that they are spelling words aloud as they write them. Teachers evaluate the general outcomes of the program, such as oral reading fluency and mastery of content tutored.

At the *secondary level,* CWPT is focused on practice, skill building, application, and review of content subject matter (e.g., science, social studies, history). Following the work of Maheady, Sacca, and Harper (1988), teacher-developed study guides are used to structure tutor-tutee interactions around details of the subject matter in the CWPT format. Like traditional study guides that help students locate important information, CWPT study guides organize the interaction between the tutor and tutee in ways that teach the content. The interaction between tutors and tutees is similar to that described earlier for spelling, math, and for reading at the elementary level, as can be seen in this interaction focused on Ancient Greece.

Tutor: "On what continent is Greece located?"
Tutee: (Saying and then writing) "Europe."
Tutor: "Correct! 2 points."
Tutor: "What two effects did the mountainous geography of Greece have during ancient times?"
Tutee: "Travel and communication were difficult and they protected Greece from invasion."
Tutor: "Yes, two points."

Based on the study guide, the tutor reads a question. The tutee responds orally and in writing, the tutor checks for accuracy, and the tutor awards points to the tutee. Questions and tutees' responding continue until time is up, earning as many points as possible for the team.

A week's tutoring around a study guide is organized as follows:

- DAY 1: Monday.   INTRODUCTION

- DAY 2: Tuesday.   TUTORING

- DAY 3: Wednesday.   TUTORING

- DAY 4: Thursday.   TUTORING REVIEW

- DAY 5: Friday.   POST/PRETESTING

The teacher introduces new content on Monday using a lecture format. Tutoring occurs on Tuesday and Wednesday over new material. A tutoring review is conducted on Thursday, and testing of progress is completed on Friday along with a pretest of the following week's planned material. Week study guides are organized as smaller units within larger units or chapters from textbooks (Greenwood, Delquadri, et al., 2001).

Perhaps the most pervasive outcomes supporting CWPT have come from a 12-year experimental, longitudinal study (Greenwood & Delquadri, 1995). Results indicated that CWPT, compared to at-risk and a nonrisk comparison groups that did not receive CWPT, (a) increased students' engagement during instruction, grades 1 to 3 (Greenwood, 1991); (b) increased growth in student achievement at grades 2, 3, 4, and 6 (Greenwood, 1996; Greenwood et al., 1989; Greenwood, Terry, Utley, Montagna, & Walker, 1993); (c) reduced the number of CWPT group students needing special education services by seventh grade (Greenwood, Terry, Utley, Montagna, & Walker, 1993), and (d) reduced the number of CWPT students dropping out of school by the end of 11th grade (Greenwood & Delquadri, 1995).

EFFECTS FOR ELEMENTARY-AGED STUDENTS WITH DISABILITIES AND AT RISK FOR SCHOOL FAILURE

CWPT has successfully been used to integrate students with disabilities into the general education curriculum (Mathes, Fuchs, & Fuchs, 1998; Mortweet et al., 1999; Sideridis et al., 1997). For example, Kamps et al. (1994) reported that CWPT improved the reading skills and peer interactions of students with autism and general education peers in an integrated setting. These students were a subgroup of high-functioning students with autism. They were children of normal intelligence but with serious deficits in social competence (e.g., rigid adherence to structure and schedules; a general disinterest in others, especially peers; and perseveration on objects or topics, or both). CWPT has been effective in teaching children with mental retardation health and safety information (Reddy et al., 1999). DuPaul and Henningson (1993) and Fiore and Becker (1994) reported that CWPT was effective for students with attention deficit/hyperactivity disorder (ADHD) in general education classrooms. Harper, Mallette, Maheady, Bentley, and Moore (1995) demonstrated improvements in spelling for students with mild disabilities including their retention and generalization of the words learned during CWPT to writing tasks in the absence of specific training (Harper, Mallette, Maheady, & Brennan, 1993; Mallette, Harper, Maheady, & Dempsey, 1991). Wright, Cavanaugh, Sainato, and Heward (1995) reported improvements in the academic, language learning, and social outcomes of English Language Learners (ELL). Similar findings have been reported by Arreaga-Mayer (1998a;1998b) and Greenwood, Arreaga-Mayer, et al. (2001).

EFFECTS FOR SECONDARY-AGED STUDENTS WITH DISABILITIES AND AT RISK FOR SCHOOL FAILURE

Bell et al. (1990) reported improvements in the behavior and achievement of secondary-level students with behavior disorders (BD) in a history class. Similar findings were reported for secondary-level applications by Maheady, Harper, and Sacca (1988), and Maheady, Sacca, and Harper (1987, 1988). It is noteworthy that CWPT has been extended to physical education settings with positive results (Block, Oberweiser, & Bain, 1995; Ward, Crouch, & Patrick, 1998) and, compared to alternative teaching practice, it has produced superior results in the teaching of cardiopulmonary resuscitation to physical education majors (Ward & Ward, 1996).

Peer-Assisted Learning Strategies (PALS)

Developed in the early 1990s (Simmons et al., 1994), PALS like CWPT was an effort to provide second- to sixth-grade teachers an effective, feasible, and acceptable intervention for the entire class in which students with LD were included. PALS was built around CWPT, but it includes a number of different effective peer teaching strategies, and it can be linked to computerized formative evaluation systems using CBM (L. S. Fuchs, D. Fuchs, Phillips, & Karns, 1994). Thus, like CWPT, PALS joins effective classwide peer tutoring components to specific instructional tasks and peer teaching strategies. PALS math, for example, provides teachers with group and individual CBM reports on students' learning of specific math skills. This enables teachers to gear instruction to the group as well as the needs of specific students.

PALS math instruction sessions typically last 40 minutes and may be implemented at least twice a week. Higher-performing students are paired with lower-performing students by rank-ordering class members on math performance, splitting the list at the median, and then pairing the first student in the upper half with the first student in the lower half, etc. This step may be performed by the teacher or by the computer program accompanying the program. This pairing creates 13 to 15 unique pairings capable of working together all at the same time on individually tailored learning tasks instead of a single, whole-class, teacher-directed activity that may address the instructional needs of only a few students. PALS math tutoring is reciprocal, like CWPT. Each student serves in the role as a "player" and a "coach" during the session. The "strongest" student is identified as a coach first in the session, and the lower-performing student is identified as a player. The stronger student serves as tutor first as a model and accuracy checker, followed by the weaker student. Student pairings are changed every two weeks.

General PALS math strategy consists of skill "coaching" followed by practice. During coaching, the player solves a sheet of assigned problems. The coach guides the player's responding by presenting a series of questions read from a prompt card. The questions break down the problem into its component parts (e.g., "Look at the sign. What kind of problem is it?"). The coach corrects responses and awards points much like tutors in CWPT. Midway through the sheet, they trade roles and continue. Practice follows after 15–20 minutes of coaching. During practice, each student completes a problem sheet that contains easier problems combined with the problem type just coached. After 10–15 minutes, students exchange papers and correct the answers. The pair of students with the highest point total wins applause and the opportunity to collect the PALS folder from their classmates, ending the session.

PALS reading is designed to be implemented 2 to 3 times per week during 35-minute sessions (Fuchs, Mathes, & Fuchs, 1996). Sessions are divided into classwide activities, including (a) partner reading, (b) story retelling after partner reading, (c) paragraph shrinking, and (d) prediction relays for 10 minutes each. The remaining few minutes are devoted to clean-up and transitional activities. Like *PALS math,* partners are formed to include heterogeneous pairs of high-performing and low-performing readers. Classroom textbook materials are used and teachers may individualize the difficulty of the reading materials for each pair, with a specific emphasis on the needs of the weaker reader. As is the case in CWPT, both coaches and players read the assigned material.

During Partner Reading/Story Retelling the strongest student reads first, as a model, for 4 minutes; the lower-performing student then reads the same material for 4 minutes. The lower-performing student then sequences major events from the material read for about 1–2 minutes. During Paragraph Shrinking, the higher-performing student resumes reading new text and stops after each paragraph to summarize the material for the next 4 minutes. The lower-performing student continues reading with new material and summarizes each paragraph. Prompt cards are used to direct readers to answer comprehension questions (e.g., who, what, where, when, and why) in 10 or fewer words. During Prediction Relay, students continue reading new textbook material with the stronger student reading aloud for 5 minutes and stopping after each page to summarize information and make a prediction about what will happen next. The lower-performing student then follows the same procedure for the next 5 minutes. Students earn points from the coaches for reading each sentence correctly, for summarizing what they read, for making reasonable predictions, and for working cooperatively with their partner.

Research on the effectiveness of PALS provides convincing support for its superiority compared to conventional general education instruction in reading and math. Results indicate that all students (with and without LD) made measurably greater progress on test scores in the same amount of time. Teachers and students both reported high levels of satisfaction with PALS instruction (Mathes, Fuchs, Fuchs, Henley, & Sanders, 1994). In addition, these authors reported that students with LD were better liked, made friends better, and were better known by peers during PALS instruction than in conventional teacher-led instruction.

As in CWPT, these findings have also been extended to students with behavior disorders (Locke & Fuchs, 1995). PALS reading and math have won approval by the Program Effectiveness Panel, National Diffusion Network, and the U.S. Department of Education. Work has been completed and is underway on extensions of PALS to kindergarten and first-grade reading and early literacy instruction (Mathes, Howard, et al., 1998;

Mathes, Howard, Torgesen, Edwards, & Allen, 1997–1998), as has worked at the secondary level with reading and subject matter instruction (D. Fuchs et al., 2001).

Classwide Student Tutoring Teams (CSTT)

CSTT is another variation of CWPT designed specifically to support content-area instruction at the secondary level (Harper & Maheady, 1999; Maheady, Harper, Sacca, & Mallette, 1991). CSTT activities incorporate content-related discussions and review to supplement teacher-led mathematics, social studies, science, and history instruction. It has been used as a means of improving students' mastery of skills and concepts that the teacher has previously introduced. Developed during the late 1980s (Maheady, Sacca, & Harper, 1988), CSTT combined the peer-teaching procedures of CWPT with specific facets of Teams-Games-Tournaments (TGT; DeVries & Slavin, 1978; Harper, Mallette, Maheady, & Brennan, 1993). TGT combines heterogeneously skilled teams of students in a classroom with competition among teams. In contrast to CWPT and PALS, CSTT uses four to five heterogeneous learning teams consisting of at least one high-, one average-, and one low-performing student to increase the probability and accuracy of peer teaching, help, and correction.

As noted in the CSTT instructor's manual, a major antecedent requirement of CSTT is the development of study guides for use by the student teams (Maheady et al., 1991). Development of these study guides involves identifying important units of instruction that correspond to weekly subject matter. Each study guide consists of questions that evoke student responses of practice, recall, and application and that reflect content instructional goals. Tutors use the study guides to prompt their teaching. Short exams also are developed based on the guides and administered as pre-post indicators of unit learning outcomes. It is essential that CSTT be used in the context of clear classroom behavior rules and that students be fully taught how to work and fill the roles of a CSTT team member.

In most secondary classrooms, CSTT is relatively easy to implement. After new subject matter is introduced, CSTT is used. CSTT is typically incorporated into a teacher's instructional program twice a week with 30 minutes per session (Harper, Mallette, Maheady, & Brennan, 1993). The peer teachers on each team use study guides to focus student attention and eliminate the guesswork about what must be learned.

During a CSTT session, each team is given a folder containing the study guide for the week, paper and pencils, and a small deck of cards. The cards are numbered in correspondence to items in the study guide. Students rotate taking turns as the teacher. The teacher draws a card from the deck of cards and reads the corresponding item to the teams (e.g., "What does empiricism mean?"). Each student writes his or her answer. The peer teacher then checks each teammate's response against the answer guide, awarding five points if the response is correct or supplying the correct answer if the response is in error. A student may receive two points if he or she corrects the error and successfully writes the correct response three times. When all answers have been corrected, the study guide is passed to the next student to the left and the top card is selected, thereby designating the next study question for the group's tutor to read. The team continues working. If time remains after completing 30 items, they reshuffle the deck and continue the activity to earn additional points.

Like CWPT and PALS, the teacher's role in CSTT is one of (a) monitoring team teaching, and (b) awarding bonus points for teaching steps, good manners, and constructive, supporting comments between and among team members. The teacher times the sessions, answers questions, collects team points, and posts winning point totals on the board. The noncompetitive reward system in CSTT ensures that (a) all teams that meet a minimum standard are recognized by the teacher, (b) the most improved team is recognized, and (c) the most outstanding team members are recognized.

Maheady, Sacca, and Harper (1988) compared the effects of CSTT to conventional teacher-led instruction on the math performance of six classes of low-achieving 9th- and 10th-grade pupils enrolled in a program for potential high school dropouts. These classrooms contained 28 students with mild disabilities and 63 typical peers. During CSTT instruction, all students' weekly math quiz scores increased by approximately 20 percentage points. The academic gains of the students with mild disabilities closely paralleled those of their typical peers. Students with and without disabilities were able to identify important content material and become better listeners. Furthermore, the students reported that because of CSTT they had developed new friends and increased their self-esteem.

Reciprocal Peer Tutoring (RPT)

Developed in the late 1980s, RPT has been used as a pullout program for serving low-achieving, high-risk students in urban elementary schools. RPT has compiled an impressive record of measurably superior results improving the math achievement of students who typically tested within the 20th and 50th percentile range prior to RPT. RPT also was designed to take advantage of effective components including peer teaching and the interdependence of pairs of learners produced by group reward systems. In RPT, as in CWPT, PALS, and CSTT, students serve as both teachers and students during tutoring sessions, and they follow a structured format of interacting with and teaching each other. Like PALS math, in RPT an initial 20-minute session of reciprocal coaching is followed by a 7-minute worksheet-testing session. Peers select rewards and performance goals from a list prepared by the teacher. Peers monitor and evaluate their own performance (Fantuzzo, King, & Heller, 1992). Unlike PALS, students are paired randomly in same-age dyads.

Students' responding in RPT is structured by four standard response opportunities for each problem: Try 1, Try 2, Help, and Try 3 (Fantuzzo & Ginsburg-Block, 1998). The peer teacher presents his or her student with a problem to solve using a flashcard with the answer on its back. The student computes the problem in writing on a structured worksheet similar to that used in CWPT math/spelling. If the first try is correct, the teacher praises the student and presents the next problem. If incorrect, the peer teacher provides structured help, as described on the answer side of the flashcard, and coaching. The student then attempts the problem at Try 2. If the answer is still wrong, a teacher aide is called to coach the student in the correct-solution model, followed by a final effort by the student to solve it (i.e., Help). The student is given an additional opportunity to solve the problem independently in Try 3. Following 10 minutes of RPT, the pair switches roles and continues for another 10 minutes. Finally, as an assessment of learning, 20 minutes of RPT is followed by a 16-problem quiz covering the material taught. Following this session, the individual accomplishments of each student are combined and compared to the student's predetermined goal. If the student exceeds that goal, he or she scores a "win" for the day. After five "wins," the pair is permitted to obtain a previously selected reward.

The early evaluations of RPT demonstrated significant academic gains in achievement, better social interactions, and less disruptive behavior for participating students (Pigott, Fantuzzo, & Clement, 1986). Subsequent replications and applications also indicated significantly improved math achievement with RPT students for low-income minority and nonminority groups in urban schools (Fantuzzo, Polite, & Grayson, 1990). In an investigation of the component procedures of RPT, Fantuzzo et al. (1992) reported that students did best when the RPT program combined structured peer tutoring with the group reward components. The structured peer-tutoring component provided tutors with training in the use of a script defining their instructional interactions with each other. The group reward component provided students with rewards contingent on the combined average performance of each partner pair rather than individual performance (Ginsburg-Block & Fantuzzo, 1997). Students significantly increased their academic gains compared to students in structure-only, group-reward-only, and no-structure and no-reward comparison groups.

These component research findings confirmed the importance of using an explicit, well-designed peer teaching procedure (script) and not relying on the tutor's own unique method of teaching (L. S. Fuchs, D. Fuchs, Hamlett, & Bentz, 1994). Furthermore, it has been shown that creating interdependence through the group reward system makes an important contribution to the overall effects of RPT in terms of increasing the concern, help, and support for partner's progress during tutoring.

Recent studies have combined RPT at school with parent home tutoring. Heller and Fantuzzo (1993) and Fantuzzo, Davis, and Ginsburg (1995) reported that superior mathematics resulted on math CBM measures and standardized achievement tests of a group of African-American fourth- and fifth-grade students receiving both components compared to results for those receiving either a one-component or a no-treatment control. Students receiving RPT rated themselves as more socially confident with peers than did students in the control group, and students and teachers in the RPT conditions gave their experiences high ratings.

KNOWLEDGE AND TRAINING REQUIRED OF THE SCHOOL PSYCHOLOGIST

School psychologists are able to play a substantial role in bringing peer tutoring strategies to scale in local schools in their roles as policy makers, trainers, interventionists, supervisors, and evaluators. Peer tutoring programs are excellent options for prevention and prereferral interventions. They are a logical first step in problem solving with students with special needs. In many circumstances, evidence indicates that use of peer tutoring interventions may preclude the need for special education referral. Early use with students at risk for learning and behavior problems in the elementary grades may promote resiliency in the secondary grades (Greenwood & Delquadri, 1995; Greenwood, Terry, Utley, Montagna, & Walker, 1993). The school psychologist's background knowledge related to conducting classroom instructional interventions and skills as a consultant-trainer for teaching and coaching teachers through implementation contributes significantly to bringing peer tutoring strategies to scale in local schools.

Interventionist Background Knowledge

A prerequisite skill for school psychologists is first-hand experience establishing and maintaining classroom interventions that can be successfully carried on by others, including classroom teachers. Intervention knowledge and skill is clearly different from that needed to make diagnostic recommendations or advising teachers on alternative approaches to solving a particular, troublesome problem. Because peer tutoring programs such as CWPT, PALS, CSTT, and RPT are specific practices, they must be established with a high degree of fidelity in order to replicate and not dilute their beneficial effects on student learning. School psychologists must know how to directly provide one-on-one classroom assistance or, alternatively, prepare a cadre of peer tutoring coaches/mentors to assist new teachers through their first implementation. School psychologists also should be experienced in the use of formative assessment (e.g., CBM, mastery monitoring) because all these peer tutoring methods use them for tracking student progress and planning changes in future lessons. This knowledge is particularly useful in demonstrating the effects of peer tutoring interventions and in understanding the direct relationship between, for example, the PALS program and increased student engagement and accelerating rates of growth in CBM reading measures.

Consultant-Trainer Role

School psychologists are in a unique position to recommend and advocate for classwide and schoolwide uses of peer tutoring programs. Because school psychologists have a strong background in educational measurement and standards of evidence for educational decision making, they are in a critical position to recommend and defend peer tutoring programs based on the programs' research record of producing measurably superior effects in student learning and satisfaction. Thus, school psychologists may find themselves in an excellent position to serve as a primary disseminator of CWPT-type programs throughout entire school buildings and school districts.

Introducing tutoring procedures early in the school year is a recommended strategy for preventing subsequent academic or behavioral problems. School psychologists must therefore engage in systematic staff development efforts, preferably in the prior year leading up to training and technical support. Short awareness sessions can be conducted to acquaint teachers with the major components and principles underlying the use of CWPT. Subsequent in-class assistance then can be provided using existing materials, paper and electronic media, for interested teachers.

School psychologists also can use peer tutoring programs as a selected strategy for teachers having problems with or who have a number of students who could benefit. These are also particularly attractive intervention options in that (a) powerful effects are almost immediately obvious, (b) they are feasible to implement, and (c) teachers and students usually prefer using them. Moreover, the intervention target in this case can be the entire class as well as a single target student. Classwide peer tutoring programs also support access to the general education curricula because students with disabilities can be readily included.

School psychologists may function well as direct teacher trainers in CWPT. This role may include the training of related school personnel, including principals and regular and special education teachers, in the roles of CWPT users and CWPT support personnel. The school psychologist can provide the designs for summarizing and correctly interpreting these results. They can assist teachers in solving problems in the program. The psychologist also provides checks on teachers' implementation and the feedback necessary to maintain a high level of program fidelity.

IMPLICATIONS AND CONCLUSION

We began this chapter with mention of the national crisis in poor learning outcomes and the daunting challenges faced by teachers serving groups of students in the general education classroom that vary widely in ability. Teachers require effective and sustainable strategies for meeting the *range* of needs presented by diverse students. The classwide peer tutoring programs discussed in our chapter are reasonable means to this end. Unfortunately, these programs are underutilized, much to the detriment of the vast numbers of students who could benefit from them.

We reviewed four classwide peer tutoring programs, with evidence in student learning, recommended for use by school psychologists and classroom teachers. Ten years ago CWPT, PALS, CSTT, and RPT were just on the horizon. Today they are increasingly sophisticated instructional systems, supported and improved by research studies and evaluations over more than a decade of work. These programs today should be considered as major research-based components in comprehensive curricula. However, they are not yet comprehensive programs in their own right—as is a curriculum such as *Success for All* (Slavin, Madden, Dolan, & Waski, 1996), for example.

Peer tutoring programs are a means of accelerating the learning of students with and without learning risks and disabilities. Peer tutoring also provides the opportunity for sufficient practice, high levels of student engagement, immediate error correction with feedback, and the integration of students with heterogeneous abilities including disabilities.

Arranging general education instruction to incorporate CWPT components provides a major assist in terms of better behavior management and individualizing teaching and learning. For example, high teacher-pupil ratios have remained a major roadblock to individualization, and teachers consider it a keystone in the effort to increase effectiveness for students with special needs. Peer tutoring formats offer efficient alternatives for providing one-on-one, tailored instructional interventions in the general education classroom at a reasonable cost and effort. In the evaluation studies that others and we have conducted and reviewed, these procedures have been reasonable and acceptable to teachers, sustainable over time, and cost efficient relative to alternate practices.

Peer tutoring provides an efficient and effective method of correction and providing feedback to students, and of managing the paperwork involved in general education instruction. The extra time necessary to develop children's social skills has traditionally been a stumbling block in making general education more effective. Peer tutoring strategies address academic and social goals at the same time. And they have academic as well as social outcome benefits. The difficulty in individualizing and adapting instruction to all students' needs has been another barrier to instructing students with special needs in the general education classroom. Peer tutoring components enable individualization of instruction commensurate with the needs of many students who are at risk and/or have specific disabilities. Programs of instruction and intervention that today are CWPT, PALS, CSTT, and RPT need to be brought to a higher scale of use in local schools. School psychologists can play a major role to bring about this change.

PEER TUTORING PROGRAM MATERIALS AND RESOURCES LIST

Books/Special Issues

Foot, H., Morgan, M. J., & Shute (Eds.). (1990), *Children helping children*. Chichester, England: Wiley.

Topping, K., & Ehly (Eds.). (1998). *Peer-assisted learning*. Mahwah, NJ: Erlbaum.

Utley, C. A. (Ed.). (2001). Peer-mediated instruction and interventions (Part 1). *Remedial and Special Education, 22*(1), 1-34.

Utley, C. A., Mortweet, S. L., & Greenwood, C. R. (1997). Peer-mediated instruction and interventions. *Focus on Exceptional Children, 29*(5), 1-23.

Whorton, D., Rotholz, D., Walker, D., McGrale, J., & Locke, P. (1987). *Alternative instructional strategies for students with autism and other developmental disabilities: Peer tutoring and group teaching procedures*. Austin, TX: Pro-Ed.

CWPT

Arreaga-Mayer, C. (1998). Increasing active student responding and improving academic performance through class-wide peer tutoring. *Intervention in School and Clinic, 34*(2), 89-94.

Arreaga-Mayer, C., Terry, B., & Greenwood, C. R. (1998). Class-wide peer tutoring. In K. Topping & S. Ehly (Eds.), *Peer-mediated instruction* (pp. 105–119). Mahwah, NY: Erlbaum.

Cooke, N. L., Heron, T. E., & Heward, W. L. (1983). *Peer tutoring: Implementing classwide programs in the primary grades*. Columbus, OH: Special Press.

Greenwood, C. R., Delquadri, J., & Carta, J. J. (1997). *Together we can! ClassWide Peer Tutoring for basic academic skills*. Longmont, CO: Sopris West.

Greenwood, C. R., Delquadri, J., & Terry, B. (1998). *ClassWide Peer Tutoring: CD-Interactive*. Kansas City, KS: Juniper Gardens Children's Project, University of Kansas.

Greenwood, C. R., & Hou, S. (1997). *The Classwide Peer Tutoring Learning Management System (CWPT-LMS): User's guide*. Kansas City, KS: Juniper Gardens Children's Project, University of Kansas.

Greenwood, C. R., & Hou, S. (2001). *The Classwide Peer Tutoring Learning Management System (CWPT-LMS): Manual for teachers*. Kansas City, KS: Juniper Gardens Children's Project, University of Kansas (Available Internet: *http://www.lsi.ukans.edu/jg/cwpt-lms/*).

Greenwood, C. R., Hou, L. S., Delquadri, J., Terry, B. J., & Arreaga-Mayer, C. (2001). ClassWide Peer Tutoring Program: A learning management system. In J. Woodward & L. Cuban (Eds.), *Technology, curriculum, and professional development: Adapting schools to meet the needs of students with disabilities* (pp. 61-86). Thousand Oaks, CA: Corwin.

Greenwood, C. R., Terry, B., Delquadri, J., Elliott, M., & Arreaga–Mayer, C. (1995). *Class Wide Peer Tutoring (CWPT): Effective teaching and research review.* Kansas City, KS: Juniper Gardens Children's Project, University of Kansas.

Greenwood, C. R., Terry, B., & Sparks, C. (1997). *Accommodating students with special needs: Classwide Peer Tutoring (Satellite Broadcast and Video Tape).* Athens, GA: University of Georgia, The Interactive Teaching Network (ITN).

PALS

Fuchs, D., Fuchs, L. S., Mathes, P. G., & Simmons, D. C. (1996). *Peer-assisted learning strategies in reading (PALS): A manual.* (Available from Box 328, Peabody College, Vanderbilt University, Nashville, TN 37203.)

Fuchs, D., Fuchs, L. S., Thompson, A., Svenson, E., Yen, L., Al Otaiba, S., Yang, N., & Nyman, K. (2001). Peer-assisted learning strategies: Extensions downward into kingergarten/first grade and upward into high school. *Remedial and Special Education, 22*(1), 15-21.

Fuchs, D., Mathes, P. G., & Fuchs, L. S., (1996). *Peabody Peer-Assisted Learning Strategies (PALS): Reading methods* (Rev. ed.). (Available from Douglas Fuchs, Box 328, Peabody College, Vanderbilt University, Nashville, TN 37203.)

Fuchs, L. S., Fuchs, D., Phillips, N. B., & Karns, K. (1994). *Peer-mediated mathematics instruction: A manual.* Nashville, TN: Peabody College of Vanderbilt University.

Fuchs, L. S., Hamlett, C. L., & Fuchs, D. (1999). *Monitoring basic skills progress* (MBSP) (2nd ed.). Austin, TX: ProEd.

Mathes, P. G., Fuchs, D., & Fuchs, L. S. (1998). Enhancing teachers' ability to accommodate diversity through Peabody Classwide Peer Tutoring. *Interventions in School and Clinic, 31,* 46-50.

Mathes, P., Fuchs, D., Fuchs, L. S., Henley, A. M., & Sanders, A. (1994). Increasing strategic reading practice with Peabody Classwide Peer Tutoring. *Learning Disabilities Research and Practice, 8*(4), 233-243.

Mathes, P., Howard, J., Torgesen, J., Edwards, B., & Allen, S. (1997–1998). *Peer-assisted learning strategies for beginning readers.* Tallahassee, FL: Florida State University.

CSTT

Harper, G. F. & Maheady, L. (1999). Classwide Student Tutoring Teams: Aligning course objectives, student practice, and testing. *Proven Practice: Prevention and Remediation of School Problems, 1,* 55-59.

Maheady. L., Harper, G. F., & Mallette, B. (in press). Peer-mediated instruction and interventions and students with mild disabilities. *Remedial and Special Education.*

Maheady, L., Harper, G. F., Sacca, M. K., & Mallette, B. (1991). *Classwide Student Tutoring Teams (CSTT): Instructor's manual and video package.* Fredonia, NY: School of Education, SUNY College at Fredonia.

RPT

Fantuzzo, J., & Ginsburg-Block, M. (1998). Reciprocal peer tutoring: Developing and testing effect peer collaborations for elementary school students. In K. Topping & S. Ehly (Eds.), *Peer assisted learning* (pp. 121–144). Mahwah, NY: Elbaum.

REFERENCES

Armstrong, S. B., Conlon, M. F., Pierson, P. M., & Stahlbrand, K. (1979). *The cost effectiveness of peer and cross-age tutoring.* Paper presented at the Annual Meeting of the Council for Exceptional Children, Dallas, TX.

Arreaga-Mayer, C. (1998a). Increasing active student responding and improving academic performance through class-wide peer tutoring. *Intervention in School and Clinic, 34*(2), 89–94.

Arreaga-Mayer, C. (1998b). Language sensitive peer-mediated instruction for culturally and linguistically diverse learners in the intermediate elementary grades. In R. M. Gersten & R. T. Jimenez (Eds.), *Promoting learning for culturally and linguistically diverse students* (pp. 73–90). Belmont, CA: Wadsworth.

Arreaga-Mayer, C., Terry, B., & Greenwood, C. R. (1998). Class-wide peer tutoring. In K. Topping & S. Ehly (Eds.), *Peer-mediated instruction* (pp. 105–119). Mahwah, NY: Erlbaum.

Bell, K., Young, K. R., Blair, M., & Nelson, R. (1990). Facilitating mainstreaming of students with behavior disorders using classwide peer tutoring. *School Psychology Review, 19,* 564–573.

Block, M. E., Oberweiser, B., & Bain, M. (1995). Using classwide peer tutoring to facilitate inclusion of students with disabilities in regular physical education. *Physical Educator, 52,* 47–56.

Brooks-Gunn, J., & Duncan, G. J. (1997). The effects of poverty on children. *The Future of Children, 7*(2), 55–71 [Center for the Future of Children, The David and Lucile Packard Foundation, Los Altos, CA].

Brophy, J. E., & Good, T. L. (1989). Teacher behavior and student achievement. In M. C. Wittrock (Ed.), *Handbook of research on teaching* (3rd ed., pp. 328–375). New York: Macmillan.

Brown, L., Fenrick, N., & Klemme, H. (1971). Trainable pupils learn to teach each other. *Teaching Exceptional Children, 4,* 18–24.

Cooke, N. L., Heron, T. E., & Heward, W. L. (1983). *Peer tutoring: Implementing classwide programs in the primary grades.* Columbus, OH: Special Press.

Corno, L., & Snow, R. W. (1986). Adapting teaching to differences among individual learners. In M. Wittrock (Ed.), *Third handbook of research on teaching* (pp. 605–629). New York: McMillan.

Council for Exceptional Children. (1994). Statistics profile of special education in the United States, 1994. *TEACHING Exceptional Children, 26,* Supplement.

Delquadri, J. (1978). *An analysis of the generalization effects of four tutoring procedures on the oral reading responses of eight learning disability children.* Unpublished doctoral dissertation. University of Kansas, Department of Human Development and Family Life.

Delquadri, J., Greenwood, C. R., Stretton, K., & Hall, R. V. (1983). The peer tutoring game: A classroom procedure for increasing opportunity to respond and spelling performance. *Education and Treatment of Children, 6,* 225–239.

Delquadri, J., Greenwood, C. R., Whorton, D., Carta, J. J., & Hall, R. V. (1986). Classwide peer tutoring. *Exceptional Children, 52,* 535-542.

Deno, S. L. (1997). Whether thou goest... Perspectives on progress monitoring. In J. W., Lloyd, E. J., Kame'enui, & D. Chard (Eds.), *Issues in educating students with disabilities* (pp. 77-99). Mahwah, NJ: Erlbaum.

DeVries, D., & Slavin, R. (1978). Teams-games-tournaments (TGT). Review of ten classroom experiments. *Journal of Research and Development in Education, 12,* 28-38.

DuPaul, G. J., & Henningson, P. N. (1993). Peer tutoring effects on the classroom performance of children with attention deficit hyperactivity disorder. *School Psychology Review, 22*(1), 134-143.

Fantuzzo, J. W., Davis, T., & Ginsburg, W. (1995). Effects of parent involvement in isolation or in combination with peer tutoring on student self-concept and mathematics achievement. *Journal of Educational Psychology, 87*(2), 272-281.

Fantuzzo, J. W., & Ginsburg-Block, M. (1998). Reciprocal peer tutoring: Developing and testing effect peer collaborations for elementary school students. In K. Topping & S. Ehly (Eds.), *Peer assisted learning* (pp. 121-144). Mahwah, NJ: Erlbaum.

Fantuzzo, J. W., King, J. A., & Heller, L. R. (1992). Effects of reciprocal peer tutoring on mathematics and school adjustment: A component analysis. *Journal of Educational Psychology, 84,* 331-339.

Fantuzzo, J. W., Polite, K., & Grayson, N. (1990). An evaluation of reciprocal peer tutoring across elementary school settings. *Journal of School Psychology, 21,* 255-263.

Federal Interagency Forum on Child and Family Statistics. (1997). *America's children: Key national indicators of well-being.* Washington, DC: Author.

Fiore, T. A., & Becker, E. A. (1994). *Promising classroom interventions for students with attention deficit disorder.* Research Triangle Park, NC: Center for Research in Education.

Fuchs, D., Fuchs, L. S., Mathes, P. G., & Simmons, D. C. (1996). *Peer-assisted learning strategies in reading: A manual.* (Available from Box 328, Peabody College, Vanderbilt University, Nashville, TN 37203.)

Fuchs, D., Fuchs, L. S., Thompson, A., Svenson, E., Yen, L., Al Otaiba, S., Yang, N., & Nyman, K. (2001). Peer-assisted learning strategies: Extensions downward into kindergarten/first grade and upward into high school. *Remedial and Special Education, 22*(1), 15-21.

Fuchs, D., Mathes, P. G., & Fuchs, L. S., (1996). *Peabody Peer-Assisted Learning Strategies (PALS): Reading methods* (Rev. ed.). (Available from Douglas Fuchs, Box 328, Peabody College, Vanderbilt University, Nashville, TN 37203.)

Fuchs, L. S., & Fuchs, D. (1998). General educators' instructional adaptation for students with learning disabilities. *Learning Disability Quarterly, 21,* 23-33.

Fuchs, L. S., Fuchs, D., & Hamlett, C. L. (1994). Strengthening the connection between assessment and instructional planning with expert systems. *Exceptional Children, 61*(2), 138-147.

Fuchs, L. S., Fuchs, D., Hamlett, C. L., & Bentz, J. (1994). Classwide curriculum-based measurement: Helping general educators meet the challenge of student diversity. *Exceptional Children, 60,* 518-537.

Fuchs, L. S., Fuchs, D., Hamlett, C. L., Phillips, N. B., Karns, K., & Dutka, S. (1997). Enhancing students' helping behavior during peer-mediated instruction with conceptual mathematical explanations. *The Elementary School Journal, 97,* 223-229.

Fuchs, L. S., Fuchs, D., Phillips, N. B., & Karns, K. (1994). *Peer-mediated mathematics instruction: A manual.* Nashville, TN: Peabody College of Vanderbilt University.

Fuchs, L. S., Hamlett, C. L., & Fuchs, D. (1999). *Monitoring basic skills progress* (MBSP) (2nd ed.). Austin, TX: ProEd.

Ginsburg-Block, M., & Fantuzzo, J. (1997). Reciprocal Peer Tutoring: An analysis of "teacher" and "student" interaction as a function of training and experience. *School Psychology Quarterly, 12*(2), 134-149.

Greenberg, P. (1998). Warmly and calmly teaching young children to read, write, and spell: Thoughts about the first four of twelve well-known principles: Part 2. *Young Children, 53*(5), 68-82.

Greenwood, C. R. (1981). Peer-oriented behavioral technology and ethical issues. In P. Strain (Ed.), *The utilization of peers as behavior change agents* (pp. 327-360). New York: Plenum.

Greenwood, C. R. (1991). A longitudinal analysis of time to learn, engagement, and academic achievement in urban versus suburban schools. *Exceptional Children, 57*(6), 521-535.

Greenwood, C. R. (1996). Research on the practices and behavior of effective teachers at the Juniper Gardens Children's Project: Implications for diverse learners. In D. L. Speece & B. K. Keogh (Eds.), *Research on classroom ecologies: Implications for inclusion of children with learning disabilities* (pp. 39-68). Mahwah, NJ: Erlbaum.

Greenwood, C. R., Arreaga-Mayer, C., Utley, C. A., Gavin, K., & Terry, B. J. (2001). ClassWide Peer Tutoring Learning Management System: Applications with elementary-level English language learners. *Remedial and Special Education, 22*(1), 34-47.

Greenwood, C. R., Carta, J. J., & Hall, R. V. (1988). The use of tutoring strategies in classroom management and educational instruction. *School Psychology Review,* 258-275.

Greenwood, C. R., Carta, J. J., & Kamps, D. (1990). Teacher- versus peer-mediated instruction. A review of educational advantages and disadvantages. In H. Foot, M. Morgan, & R. Shute (Eds.), *Children helping children* (pp. 177-205). Chichester, England: Wiley.

Greenwood, C. R., & Delquadri, J. (1995). ClassWide Peer Tutoring and the prevention of school failure. *Preventing School Failure, 39*(4), 21-25.

Greenwood, C. R., Delquadri, J., & Bulgren, J. (1993). Current challenges to behavioral technology in the reform of schooling: Large-scale, high-quality implementation and sustained use of effective educational practices. *Education and Treatment of Children, 16,* 401-440.

Greenwood, C. R., Delquadri, J., & Carta, J. J. (1997). *Together we can! ClassWide Peer Tutoring for basic academic skills. Longmont,* CO: Sopris West.

Greenwood, C. R., Delquadri, J., & Hall, R. V. (1984). Opportunity to respond and student academic performance. In W. L. Heward, T. E. Heron, J. Trap-Porter, & D. S. Hill (Eds.), *Focus on behavior analysis in education* (pp. 58-88). Columbus, OH: Merrill.

Greenwood, C. R., Delquadri, J., & Hall, R. V. (1989). Longitudinal analysis of the effects of classwide peer tutoring. *Journal of Educational Psychology, 81,* 371-383.

Greenwood, C. R., Delquadri, J., Hou, L. I., Terry, B. & Arreaga-Mayer, C. (2001). *Together We Can! ClassWide Peer Tutoring Learning Management System* (CWPT-LMS): Teacher's Manual. Juniper Gardens Children's Project, University of Kansas, Kansas City, KS.

Greenwood, C. R., Dinwiddie, G., Bailey, V., Carta, J. J., Dorsey, D., Kohler, F. W., Nelson, C., Rotholz, D., & Schulte, D. (1987). Field replication of classwide peer tutoring. *Journal of Applied Behavior Analysis, 20,* 151-160.

Greenwood, C. R., Finney, R., Terry, B., Arreaga-Mayer, C., Carta, J. J., Delquadri, J., Walker, D., Innocenti, M., Lignugaris-Kraft, J., Harper, G. F., & Clifton, R. (1993). Monitoring, improving, and maintaining quality implementation of the ClassWide Peer Tutoring Program using behavioral and computer technology. *Education and Treatment of Children, 16,* 19-47.

Greenwood, C. R., Hart, B., Walker, D., & Risley, T. R. (1994). The opportunity to respond revisited: A behavioral theory of developmental retardation and its prevention. In R. Gardner, III, D. M. Sainato, J. O. Cooper, T. E. Heron, W. L. Heward, J. W. Eshleman, & T. A. Grossi (Eds.), *Behavior analysis in education: Focus on measurably superior instruction* (pp. 213-223). Pacific Grove, CA: Brooks/Cole.

Greenwood, C. R., & Hops, H. (1981). Group contingencies and peer behavior change. In P. Strain (Ed.), *The utilization of classroom peers as behavior change agents* (pp. 189-259). New York: Plenum.

Greenwood, C. R., Hou, L. S., Delquadri, J., Terry, B. J., & Arreaga-Mayer, C. (2001). ClassWide Peer Tutoring Program: A learning management system. In J. Woodward & L. Cuban (Eds.), *Technology, curriculum, and professional development: Adapting schools to meet the needs of students with disabilities* (pp. 61-86). Thousand Oaks, CA: Corwin.

Greenwood, C. R., Maheady, L., & Carta, J. J. (1991). Peer tutoring programs in the regular education classroom. In G. Stoner, M. R. Shinn, & H. M. Walker (Eds.), *Interventions for achievement and behavior problems* (1st ed., pp. 179-200). Washington, DC: National Association for School Psychologists.

Greenwood, C. R., Terry, B., Delquadri, J., Elliott, M., & Arreaga-Mayer, C. (1995). *ClassWide Peer Tutoring (CWPT): Effective teaching and research review.* Kansas City, KS: Juniper Gardens Children's Project, University of Kansas.

Greenwood, C. R., Terry, B., Utley, C. A., Montagna, D., & Walker, D. (1993). Achievement, placement, and services: Middle school benefits of ClassWide Peer Tutoring used at the elementary school. *School Psychology Review, 22,* 497-516.

Harper, G. F., & Maheady, L. (1999). Classwide Student Tutoring Teams: Aligning course objectives, student practice, and testing. *Proven Practice: Prevention and Remediation of School Problems, 1,* 55-59.

Harper, G. F., Mallette, B., Maheady, L., Bentley, A. E., & Moore, J. (1995). Retention and treatment failure in ClassWide Peer Tutoring: Implications for further research. *Journal of Behavioral Education, 5,* 399-414.

Harper, G. F., Mallette, B., Maheady, L., & Brennan, G. (1993). Classwide Student Tutoring Teams and Direct Instruction as combined instructional program to teacher generalizable strategies for mathematics word problems. *Education and Treatment of Children, 16,* 115-134.

Heal, L. W., Khoju, M., & Rusch, F. R. (1997). Predicting quality of life of youth after they leave special education high school programs. *Journal of Special Education, 31*(3), 279-299.

Heller, L. R., & Fantuzzo, J. W. (1993). Reciprocal peer tutoring and parent partnership: Does parent involvement make a difference? *School Psychology Review, 22*(3), 517-534.

Heron, T. E., Heward, W. L., Cooke, N. L., & Hill, D. S. (1983). Evaluation of classwide peer tutoring systems: First graders teach each other sight words. *Education and Treatment of Children, 6,* 137-152.

Heward, W. L. (1996). *Exceptional children: An introduction to special education* (5th ed.). Columbus, OH: Merrill.

Heward, W. L., Heron, T. E., & Cooke, N. L. (1982). Tutor huddle: Key element in a classwide peer tutoring system. *Elementary Education Journal, 82,* 115-123.

Heward, W. L., Heron, T. E., Ellis, D. E., & Cooke, N. L. (1986). Teaching first-grade peer tutors to use verbal praise on an intermittent schedule. *Education and Treatment of Children, 9,* 5-15.

Jenkins, J. R., & Jenkins, L. M. (1988). Peer tutoring in elementary and secondary programs. *Focus on Exceptional Children, 17,* 1-12.

Jenkins, J. R., Jewell, M., Leceister, H., Jenkins, L., & Troutner, N. (1990, April). *Development of a school building model for educating handicapped and at-risk students in general education classrooms.* Paper presented at the annual meeting of the American Educational Research Association, Boston.

Kamps, D. M., Barbetta, P. M., Leonard, B. R., & Delquadri, J. (1994). Classwide peer tutoring: An integration strategy to improve and promote peer interactions among students with autism and general education peers. *Journal of Applied Behavior Analysis, 27*(1), 49-61.

King-Sears, M. E., & Cummings, C. S. (1996). Inclusive practices for classroom teachers. *Remedial and Special Education, 17*(4), 217-225.

Kohler, F. W. (1987). *Peer-mediation in the integrated classroom: A presentation of research at the LEAP preschool.* Symposium presented at the Thirteenth Annual Convention of the Association for Behavior Analysis, Nashville, TN.

Kohler, F. W., & Greenwood, C. R. (1986). Toward a technology of generalization: The identification of natural contingencies of reinforcement. *The Behavior Analyst, 9,* 19-26.

Kohler, F. W., & Greenwood, C. R. (1990). Effects of collateral peer supportive behaviors within the classwide peer tutoring program. *Journal of Applied Behavior Analysis, 23*(3), 307–322.

Kohler, F. W., Richardson, T., Mina, C., Dinwiddie, G., & Greenwood, C. R. (1985). Establishing cooperative peer relations in the classroom. *The Pointer, 29,* 12–16.

Levin, H., Glass, G., & Meister, G. (1984). *Cost effectiveness of four educational interventions* (Report No. 84–A11). Stanford, CA: Institute for Research in Educational Finance and Governance, Stanford University.

Locke, W. R., & Fuchs, L. S. (1995). Effects of peer-mediated reading instruction on the on-task and social interaction of children with behavior disorders. *Journal of Emotional and Behavioral Disorders, 3,* 92–99.

Maheady, L., & Harper, G. (1987). A classwide peer tutoring program to improve the spelling test performance of low-income, third- and fourth-grade students. *Education and Treatment of Children, 10,* 120–133.

Maheady, L., Harper, G. F., & Sacca, M. K. (1988). Classwide peer tutoring programs in secondary self-contained programs for the mildly handicapped. *Journal of Research and Development in Education, 21*(3), 76–83.

Maheady, L., Harper, G. F., Sacca, M. K., & Mallette, B. (1991). *Classwide Student Tutoring Teams (CSTT): Instructor's manual and video package.* Fredonia, NY: School of Education, SUNY College at Fredonia.

Maheady, L., Sacca, M. K., & Harper, G. F. (1987). Classwide peer tutoring teams: Effects on the academic performance of secondary students. *Journal of Special Education, 21*(3), 107–121.

Maheady, L., Sacca, M. K., & Harper, G. F. (1988). The effects of a classwide peer tutoring program on the academic performance of mildly handicapped students enrolled in 10th grade social studies classes. *Exceptional Children, 55,* 52–59.

Maheady, L., & Sainato, D. (1985). The effects of peer tutoring upon the social status and social interaction patterns of high and low status elementary students. *Education and Treatment of Children, 8,* 51–65.

Mallette, B., Harper, G. F., Maheady, L., & Dempsey, M. (1991). Retention of spelling words acquired using a peer-mediated instructional strategy. *Education and Training in Mental Retardation, 26*(2), 156–164.

Mathes, P. G., Fuchs, D., & Fuchs, L. S. (1998). Enhancing teachers' ability to accommodate diversity through Peabody Classwide Peer Tutoring. *Interventions in School and Clinic, 31,* 46–50.

Mathes, P. G., Fuchs, D., Fuchs, L. S., Henley, A. M., & Sanders, A. (1994). Increasing strategic reading practice with Peabody Classwide Peer Tutoring. *Learning Disabilities Research and Practice, 8*(4), 233–243.

Mathes, P. G., Howard, J. K., Allen, S. H., & Fuchs, D. (1998). Peer-assisted learning strategies for first-grade readers: Responding to the needs of diverse learners. *Reading Research Quarterly, 33,* 62–94.

Mathes, P. G., Howard, J., Torgesen, J., Edwards, B., & Allen, S. (1997-1998). *Peer-assisted learning strategies for beginning readers.* Tallahassee, FL: Florida State University.

McKinney, J. D., Osborne, S. S., & Schulte, A. C. (1993). Academic consequences of learning disability: Longitudinal prediction of results at 11 years of age. *Learning Disabilities Research and Practice, 8*(1), 19-27.

Moody, S. W., Vaughn, S., & Schumm, J. S. (1997). Instructional grouping for reading: Teachers' views. *Remedial and Special Education, 18*(6), 347-356

Mortweet, S. L., Utley, C. A., Walker, D., Dawson, H. L., Delquadri, J. C., Reddy, S. S., Greenwood, C. R., Hamilton, S., & Ledford, D. (1999). Classwide peer tutoring: Teaching students with mild mental retardation in inclusive classrooms. *Exceptional Children, 65*(4), 425-536.

Niedermeyer, F. C. (1970). Effects of training on the instructional behaviors of student tutors. *Journal of Educational Research, 64,* 119-123.

Osguthorpe, R. T., & Scruggs, T. E. (1986). Special education students as tutors: A review and analysis. *Remedial and Special Education, 7,* 15-26.

Pigott, H. E., Fantuzzo, J. W., & Clement, P. W. (1986). The effects of reciprocal peer tutoring and group contingencies on the academic performance of elementary school children. *Journal of Applied Behavior Analysis, 19,* 93-98.

Polirstok, S. R., & Greer, R. D. (1986). A replication of collateral effects and a component analysis of a successful tutoring package for inner-city adolescents. *Education and Treatment of Children, 9,* 101-121.

Reddy, S. S., Utley, C. A., Delquadri, J. C., Mortweet, S. L., Greenwood, C. R., & Bowman, V. (1999). Peer tutoring for health and safety. *TEACHING Exceptional Children, 31*(3), 44-52.

Sideridis, G. D., Utley, C., Greenwood, C. R., Delquadri, J., Dawson, H., Palmer, P., & Reddy, S. (1997). Classwide Peer Tutoring: Effects on the spelling performance and social interactions of students with mild disabilities and their typical peers in an integrated instructional setting. *Journal of Behavioral Education, 7*(4), 435-462.

Simmons, D. C., Fuchs, D., Fuchs, L. S., Hodge, J. P., & Mathes, P. G. (1994). Importance of instructional complexity and role reciprocity to Classwide Peer Tutoring. *Learning Disabilities Research and Practice, 9*(4), 203-212.

Simmons, D. C., Kame'enui, E. J., & Chard, D. J. (1998). General education teachers' assumptions about learning and students with learning disabilities: Design of instruction analysis. *Journal of Learning Disabilities, 21,* 6-21.

Slavin, R. E., Dolan, L. J., & Madden, N. A. (1996, February). *Scaling up: Lessons learned in the dissemination of Success for All.* Baltimore: Johns Hopkins University, Center for Research on the Education of Students Place at Risk.

Slavin, R. E., Madden, N. A., Dolan, L. J., & Waski, B. A. (1996). *Every child, every school: Success for All.* Newbury Park, CA: Corwin.

Snow, C. E., Burns, M. S., & Griffin, P. (1998). *Preventing reading difficulties in young children.* Committee on the Prevention of Reading Difficulties in Young Children, Commission on Behavioral and Social Sciences and Education, National Research Council. Washington DC: National Academy Press.

Strayhorn, J. M., Strain, P. S., & Walker, H. M. (1993). The case for interaction skills training in the context of tutoring as a preventive mental health intervention in schools. *Behavior Disorders, 19*(1), 11-26.

U.S. Department of Education. (1997). *19th Annual IDEA Report to Congress.* Washington, DC: Office of Special Education and Rehabilitation Services.

Utley, C. A., Mortweet, S. L., & Greenwood, C. R. (1997). Peer-mediated instruction and interventions. *Focus on Exceptional Children, 29*(5), 1-23.

Wagner, M., D'Amico, R., Marder, C., Newman, L., & Blackorby, J. (1992). *What happens next? Trends in post-school outcomes of youth with disabilities.* Menlo Park, CA: SRI International.

Walker, H. M., Colvin, G., & Ramsey, E. (1995). *Antisocial behavior in school: Strategies and best practices.* Pacific Grove, CA: Brooks/Cole.

Ward, P., Crouch, D. W., & Patrick, C. A. (1998). Effects of peer-mediated accountability on opportunities to respond and correct skill performance by elementary school children in physical education. *Journal of Behavioral Education, 8,* 103-114.

Ward, P., & Ward, M. C. (1996). The effects of Classwide Peer Tutoring on correct cardiopulmonary resuscitation performance in physical education majors. *Journal of Behavioral Education, 6*(3), 331-342.

Whorton, D., Rotholz, D., Walker, D., McGrale, J., & Locke, P. (1987). *Alternative instructional strategies for students with autism and other developmental disabilities: Peer tutoring and group teaching procedures.* Austin, TX: Pro-Ed.

Wright, J. E., Cavanaugh, R. A., Sainato, D. M., & Heward, W. L. (1995). Somos Todos Ayudantes y Estudiantes: A demonstration of a classwide peer tutoring program for modified Spanish class for secondary students identified as learning disabled and academically at risk. *Education and Treatment of Children, 18*(1), 33-52.

CHAPTER 24

Interventions for Improving Study Skills

Mary M. Gleason
Educational Consultant, Eugene, Oregon

Anita L. Archer
Educational Consultant, Portland, Oregon

Geoff Colvin
Educational Consultant, Eugene, Oregon

INTRODUCTION

Currently, many millions of students receive remedial services for academic deficits. The academic difficulties experienced by these students could be ameliorated with a variety of approaches, including (a) *teaching these students basic skills,* such as reading, writing, and mathematics; (b) *modifying instructional delivery* to make it easier for those students to learn, thus lessening the instructional demands; and (c) *teaching students how to learn better.* Many suggestions are presented elsewhere in this monograph for ways that the general education teacher could teach basic skills effectively and/or modify the instructional demands presented to students with disabilities. Both are critical interventions for students faced with academic challenges. However, as students with disabilities progress and become more proficient with basic skills, they need more help in meeting academic demands. In order to be successful in general education classes, these students need to learn *specific learning strategies* that will assist them to meet the demands of the complex tasks required in content area classes. Derry and Murphy (1986) defined strategies as "the collection of mental tactics employed by an individual in a particular learning situation to facilitate acquisition of knowledge or skill" (p. 2). Most work in the area of learning strategies has been conducted at junior high school, high school, or college level, most notably by Schumaker, Deshler, and their colleagues at the University of Kansas (this volume).

SPECIFIC LEARNING STRATEGIES

For 9 years, Archer and Gleason field-tested and revised strategies for the elementary level (grades 3–6) so that study behaviors might be firmly established by the time students reach the challenges of junior high or high school. These strategies have been used nationally for the past 12 years and revised yet again (Archer & Gleason, 2002), and are the basis for this chapter. These specific learning strategies include skimming through textbook material to find information needed for answering a particular question, reading textbook material and deciding which information is important and which is not, using the identified relevant information to take notes and study the material, and many more.

Many students with problems learning and/or with learning disabilities are passive in their approach to the use of strategies to accomplish classroom tasks (Newman & Hagen, 1981; Torgesen, 1982). Teachers face the challenge of transforming these passive learners into learners who are involved more actively and who are more successful in meeting classroom expectations. We will accomplish this task by teaching students effective specific learning strategies for gaining information, responding to information, and organizing information.

Gaining Information From Content-Area Textbooks

A major goal in content-area classes is that of gaining information from content-area textbooks. Using study skills to gain information from textbooks can be difficult if students are left to devise their own strategies. Archer and Gleason (1993, 2002) determined that for students to gain information from textbooks they must be taught directly the following five strategies: (a) decoding of longer words, (b) surveying the chapter and forming a general impression of the important information to be emphasized in the chapter, (c) reading the text and attending to the main ideas and important details, (d) attending to the content of maps and graphics that accompany the text, and (e) verbally rehearsing the main ideas and details and/or completing written notes on the main ideas and details. Archer and Gleason (2002) use teacher-directed instruction to teach all five component strategies. In addition, other researchers have studied one or more of these strategies in isolation. Each strategy will be described with enough detail that a school psychologist could implement the strategy or facilitate implementation with a classroom teacher. Further information on content area reading strategies can be found in reviews by Boyle and Yeager (1997); Bryant, Ugel, Thompson, & Hamff (1999); De La Paz (1999); Deshler, Schumaker, Harris, & Graham (1999); Gersten (1998); Mastropieri and Scruggs (1997); Munk, Bruckert, Call, Stoehrmann, and Radandt (1998); Swanson and De La Paz (1998); Vaughn, Gersten, and Chard (1999); and Vaughn, Klingner, and Bryant (2001).

Decoding longer words. One of the major challenges that students face when reading content area textbooks is the number of long words. Poor readers tend to skip or guess at these words. Nagy and Andersen (1984) determined that from fifth grade on average students encounter approximately 10,000 words each year that they have never encountered in print before. Most of these new words are longer words having two or more syllables (Cunningham, 1998). In content-area passages, multisyllabic words such as *evaporation, precipitation,* and *transpiration* generally carry most of the passage's meaning. Unfortunately, poor decoders, even those who can read single syllable words, have a difficult time with multisyllabic words (Just & Carpenter, 1987; Samuels, LaBerge, & Bremer, 1978). Perfetti (1986) concluded that the ability to decode long words increases the qualitative differences between good and poor readers.

A number of studies have shown that teaching students strategies for decoding longer words improves their decoding ability. Shefelbine (1990) taught fourth and sixth graders having difficulty decoding multisyllabic words to use affixes (e.g., *dis* and *tion*) and vowels (e.g., *ea* and *ow*) to pronounce longer words. When compared to a control group, significant gains were made in ability to pronounce long words. Similarly, Lenz and Hughes (1990) were able to reduce the oral reading errors and increase students' comprehension at reading level by teaching seventh, eighth, and ninth graders a decoding strategy.

Students taught a research-validated decoding strategy that was later incorporated into the *REWARDS* program (Archer, Gleason, & Vachon, 2000) made significant gains in decoding longer words presented in isolation and within passages (Archer, Gleason, Vachon, & Hollenbeck, 2002). The *REWARDS* strategy reflects two important patterns in multisyllabic words: (a) the presence of affixes in about 80% of multisyllabic words and (b) the presence of vowel grapheme (i.e., letter or letters that map a vowel sound) in all decodable "chunks." By using this strategy, the student does not need to segment the word into perfect dictionary syllables, but rather into manageable chunks that can be decoded. For example, once students have learned to recognize the affix *ism* at the end of words, the word *astigmatism* can be divided into the chunks *a stig mat ism* rather than *a stig ma tism* as it would be found in the dictionary. Similarly, the student also does not need to emerge with the exact pronunciation of the word on the first attempt. Instead, the student gets a close approximation of the word's pronunciation and corrects it using his or her knowledge of language and the context in which the word appears. Thus, a flexible strategy rather than a rule-bound strategy is taught to students. As seen in Figure 1, on page 654, students are first taught an overt strategy in which they physically circle word parts at the beginning and end of words and underline vowel sounds in the rest of the word. Eventually, students transition to a covert strategy where they look for word parts and vowel sounds and note them mentally before saying the word parts and then the whole word.

Surveying the chapter. Many students, especially those with achievement problems, read a textbook chapter without a framework for sorting the important from the less important information. This lack of discrimination frequently leads to poor comprehension of the chapter. To facilitate more successful comprehension of content area chapters, students benefit from surveying or previewing the chapter before reading. During the survey or preview, they examine chapter headings and subheadings, key graphics, chapter summaries, questions at the end of the chapter, and any other features that might help them focus their attention on certain aspects of the chapter. The pur-

FIGURE 1

Strategies
for Reading Long Words

Overt Strategy

1. Circle the word parts (prefixes) at the beginning of the word.

2. Cirlce the word parts (suffixes) at the end of the word.

3. Underline the letters representing vowel sounds in the rest of the word.

4. Say the parts of the word.

5. Say the parts fast.

6. Make it a real word.

EXAMPLE

Covert Strategy

1. Look for word parts at the beginning and end of the word, and vowel sounds in the rest of the word.

2. Say the parts of the word.

3. Say the parts fast.

4. Make it a real word.

Note

From *REWARDS* (p. 314), by A. L. Archer, M. M. Gleason, and V. Vachon, 2000, Longmont, CO: Sopris West Educational Services, www.sopriswest.com. Copyright 2000 by Sopris West. Reprinted with permission.

poses of the preview are to (a) learn as much as possible in a brief amount of time, (b) to activate their background knowledge concerning the subjects covered, (c) and to make predictions about the content (Klingner & Vaughn, 1998). Additionally, students learn how the chapter is organized, which will facilitate their reading of the chapter and selecting an appropriate strategy for reading the chapter.

In a strategy called *Warm-up,* Archer and Gleason (2002) taught students previewing skills for content area chapters to determine the important information to be emphasized and to develop an organizational framework for the information. Before showing students the strategy, they discussed the rationale for the strategy, telling students that "warming up" for reading is just like warming up for an athletic event. They warm up for reading by accomplishing two goals: (a) finding out what the chapter is about and (b) making predictions about what is to be learned from the chapter.

To teach the warm-up strategy, the teacher asks students to examine the *beginning* of the chapter (the title of the chapter and the introduction), the *middle* (the headings and subheadings), and the *end* (the summary and the questions at the end of the chapter). As students examine different parts of the chapter they practice making predictions about what is to be learned from the chapter. The steps for warming up are written out on a poster for all students to see, and the teacher covers the poster and provides students an opportunity for verbal rehearsal of the steps in the Warm-up strategy. Students then practice the Warm-up strategy with several textbook chapters, verbally reporting their predictions to the teacher or to a peer. Students then complete a written worksheet that demonstrates their predictions about the chapter content and share the content with the teacher.

There are a number of similar research-validated preview strategies. As part of *Collaborative Strategic Reading* (Klingner & Vaughn, 1998; Vaughn & Klingner, 1999; Vaughn, Klingner, & Bryant, 2001) students quickly preview passages by looking at the chapter headings, words that are bolded or underlined, and pictures, tables, graphs, and other key information to help them brainstorm what they already know about the topic and to predict what they will learn. The students are then given about 6 minutes to discuss among themselves what they have learned, predictions they have formulated, and any connections they can make between what they already know and what they will read.

The *KWL* strategy is also used to activate students' background knowledge (Ogle, 1986, 1992). Using the KWL strategy, students record what they *K*now, and what they *W*ant to learn before reading a selection. After reading of the selection, the students record what they have *L*earned.

Reading the text. After students have previewed the chapter sufficiently, they must read the chapter and attend to the main ideas and important details that are worth remembering and that will assist students in answering questions at the end of the chapter. The strategy that will work best for a particular group of students depends on their reading level and their experience with reading content area material. Many study strategies for reading expository materials have been developed and tested with elementary and secondary students (e.g., Archer & Gleason, 2002; Bakken, Mastropieri, & Scruggs, 1997; Chan & Cole, 1986; Englert & Mariage, 1991; Englert, Tarrant, Mariage, & Oxer, 1994; Graves, 1986; Jenkins, Heliotis, Stein, & Haynes, 1987; Scanlon, Duran,

Reyes, & Gallego, 1992; Schumaker, Denton, & Deshler, 1984; Wong, Wong, Perry, & Sawatsky, 1986). These strategies have several similarities (Archer & Gleason, 1997). First, they all attempt to *engage students more actively* in the reading process. Students are asked to formulate questions, take notes on content, or verbally paraphrase the critical information. Second, all strategies attempt to *direct students' attention to the most important ideas and details.* Third, the strategies *engage the students in rehearsal* by asking them to recite or write down critical information. Four strategies that appear to exemplify these key steps are outlined here.

The first strategy, a *self-questioning summarization strategy* developed by Wong et al. (1986), teaches students to ask themselves a series of six questions as they proceed paragraph by paragraph and section by section to read and summarize a chapter.

1. In this paragraph, is there anything I don't understand?

2. In this paragraph, what's the most important sentence (main idea sentence)? Let me underline it.

3. Let me summarize the paragraph. To summarize, I rewrite the main idea sentence and add important details.

4. Now, does my summary sentence link up with the subheading?

5. When I have written summary statements for the whole subsection:

    a. Let me review my summary statements for the whole subsection. (A subsection is one with several paragraphs under the same subheading).

    b. Do my summary statements link up with one another?

    c. Do they all link up with the subheading?

6. At the end of the assigned reading section: Can I see all the themes here? If yes, let me predict the teacher's test question on this section. If no, let me go back to Step 4. (Wong et al., 1986, pp. 24–26.)

The second strategy, a verbal rehearsal strategy developed by Archer and Gleason (2002), is called *Active Reading.* The Active Reading strategy is based on a strategy for memorizing material called *RCRC* (Archer & Gleason, 2002) that was learned earlier in the curriculum material. RCRC assists students in memorizing by having them Read, Cover, Recite, and Check material such as spelling words, math facts, or vocabulary meanings. Active Reading uses the same read, cover, recite, and check steps but with connected text, one paragraph at a time.

First, the teacher discusses the rationale for the strategy. Students are told that using this strategy will help them remember more information from a chapter. Then, the steps of the Active Reading strategy are modeled, guided practice is provided, and then independent practice is expected. First the teacher and then the students *read* (R) a paragraph and tell themselves the topic and details. They *cover* (C) the paragraph and *recite* (R) the important information in their own words. Then they uncover the paragraph and *check* (C) their recitation by examining the paragraph again.

Students verbally rehearse the RCRC steps used in the Active Reading strategy and practice the Active Reading strategy with several paragraphs, verbally reporting their topics and details to a teacher or peer. Finally, they complete a written worksheet in which the peer checks on a checklist whether the recital included topic and details and was in the student's own words.

Before learning the Active Reading strategy, students first are taught some component preparatory skills. With several short paragraphs the teacher demonstrates *naming the topic of the paragraph,* then asks students to practice naming the topics of several more paragraphs. Once students can say a word or phrase to name the topic of a paragraph, students are taught to *identify critical details in the paragraph* and to *retell the topic and details in their own words.* During additional practice, with either the teacher or peers, students practice saying and checking off on a checklist that they have (a) said the topic, (b) noted the important details, and (c) used their own words. When students can retell paragraph content fluently , the teacher shows how to put all the steps of the Active Reading strategy together (see Figure 2, on page 658, for the steps).

The third way to engage students actively in reading content area textbooks is to enlist them in *taking notes on the important information.* A critical error made in many classrooms is to allow students to take notes haphazardly. Many students do not differentiate important information from unimportant nor show relationships between levels of information. Once students learn to take notes in a more systemic way, the notes can be used in studying for tests, writing summaries of what was read, answering chapter questions, or writing a report.

Archer and Gleason (2002) developed a system of note taking, Indentation Notes, appropriate for upper elementary students and lower-performing junior high or high school students. As with the Active Reading strategy, the note taking depends on the single paragraph as the unit for reading and writing notes and requires students to attend to the topic and important details. Students should demonstrate mastery of the Active Reading strategy before attempting the note-taking strategy. As with all teacher-directed strategies, the teacher provides a rationale, demonstrates use of the strategy, and guides students through the steps. Students are told that taking notes will help them concentrate better on what the author is saying and that their notes can be used for other purposes, such as studying for tests. The teacher tells students why notes should be written briefly and in their own words. Students record headings or subheadings in the center of the paper followed by the corresponding page numbers. Then they take notes on each paragraph, using an *indenting style* (see Figure 3, on page 659, for an example).

To produce notes such as those in Figure 3 students read each paragraph and record the topic for the paragraph. Then they indent and record the important details, using abbreviations and symbols when possible and indenting again when recording subordinate details. When notes have been completed, the students check them for clarity.

FIGURE 2

A Verbal Rehearsal Strategy Referred to as ACTIVE READING

ACTIVE READING

R = READ

Read a paragraph.

Think about the topic and the important details.

C = COVER

Cover the paragraph with your hand.

R = RECITE

Tell yourself what you have read.
- Say the topic.
- Say the important details.
- Say it in your own words.

C = CHECK

Lift your hand and check.

If you forget something important, begin again.

Note
From *Advanced Skills for School Success: Module 3* (p. 61), by A. Archer and M. Gleason, 1993, North Billerica, MA: Curriculum Associates. Copyright 1993 by Curriculum Associates. Reprinted with permission.

Next to each paragraph section of notes the students write a question in the left-hand margin that could be asked about those notes.

Any note-taking strategy will benefit students *only* if they are provided with opportunities to use the notes. If students take notes but do not look at them again, then they

FIGURE 3

INDENTATION NOTES

	Internal Structure of Earth (p 25)
How many layers	*Model of earth*
does the earth have?	*-developed by scientists from bits of info.*
	-3 layers
What is the	*Crust*
crust like?	*-thin layer of solid rock*
	-covered w/rock, soil, sand,
	oceans, seas
How does the	*Thickness of crust*
thickness of the	*-different thicknesses*
crust vary?	*-thinner under oceans and seas*

Hints for Taking Good Notes
1. Write your notes in your own words.
2. Make your notes brief.
3. Use abbreviations and symbols.
4. Be sure you understood your notes.

Note

From *Advanced Skills for School Success: Module 3* (p. 83), by A. Archer and M. Gleason, 1993, North Billerica, MA: Curriculum Associates. Copyright 1993 by Curriculum Associates. Reprinted with permission.

will likely remember less information than if they review the notes to remember the information for class discussions or for written tests. To remember the information contained in the notes, students can use a verbal rehearsal strategy such as RCRC (read the question, cover, recite the answer, check the answer). They can participate in a class study session, in which the teacher asks questions about the content and the students answer the questions, then quickly show where the information can be located in their notes. Students also can conduct similar sessions with their peers, thus giving them practice in the use of their notes, feedback on the adequacy of their notes, and participation in study teams.

As an alternative to indentation notes, students can *map* the topics and important details. When teaching students the process of designing self-generated organizers, Archer and Gleason (2002) taught students to first prepare a preliminary map by drawing circles and recording the title headings and subheadings. Next, they read a paragraph, drawing another circle for each new topic and recording important details on lines extending from the topic circle. As they worked, students linked headings, subheadings, topics, and details to show the semantic relationships between the ideas (see Figure 4 for an example of mapping).

To assist students in creating maps, which they called cognitive maps, Boyle and Yeager (1997, p. 30) taught students the following steps using the acronym *TRAVEL:*

1. *T*opic: Students write down the topic and circle it.

2. *R*ead: Students carefully read the first paragraph.

3. *A*sk: Students covertly ask themselves what the main idea and three details are and then write them down in as few words as possible.

4. *V*erify: Students verify the written main idea by placing a circle around it and then draw a line from the main idea to each detail.

5. *E*xamine: Students repeat the Read, Ask, and Verify steps on each successive paragraph.

6. *L*ink: Students link together all of the main ideas that are related to one another.

Attending to content of maps and graphics that accompany text. The strategies described so far have concentrated on reading the text portion of content-area textbooks. But most content-area textbooks also provide students with a lot of information by using graphics, pictures, and maps that accompany the text. The information contained in these visual aids is not necessarily described or repeated in the text itself. Frequently, the questions at the end of a social studies chapter or the questions on tests require answers that can be found only in the aids. However, explicit instruction in the interpretation of these aids typically is lacking. Again, the presumption of most classroom teachers is that students would know how to read and use the graphics.

When a student is experiencing difficulty in a content area class, the school psychologist should examine that student's textbooks and determine the types of visual aids that student is failing to use and interpret correctly. Archer and Gleason (2002) found direct teaching of interpretation of tables and graphics, such as pie graphs, pictographs, bar graphs, and line graphs, to be particularly efficient. In a few short days a student could answer questions above a 90% level. They taught their strategy by *demonstrating* and *guiding* students through a series of steps. First, the teacher and students determined the topic

FIGURE 4

Example of a Chapter Map

MAPPING WRITTEN MATERIAL

1. Draw circles for the heading and subheadings.

2. Take notes on each paragraph.
   a. Write the topic in the circle.
   b. Write an important detail on each line.

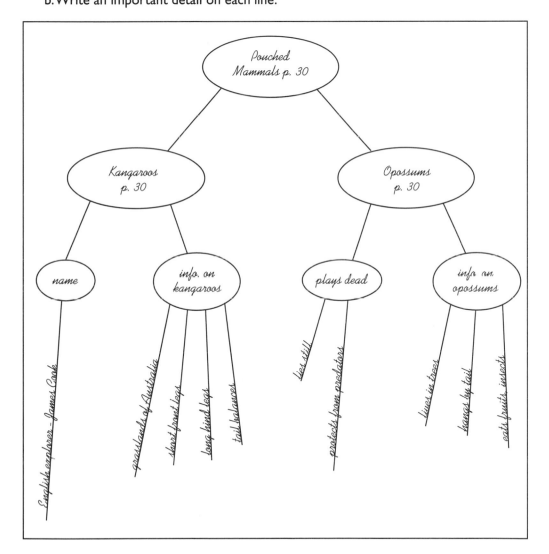

Note
From *Advanced Skills for School Success: Module 3* (p. 84), by A. Archer and M. Gleason, 1993, North Billerica, MA: Curriculum Associates. Copyright 1993 by Curriculum Associates. Reprinted with permission.

of the graphic material by interpreting the title or caption. Then they looked at the numbers or words across the bottom or top and up and down the left side to understand the organization of the graphic. The students located information in the graphic and answered literal questions about the information. Comparisons were made by using the non-numerical information in the graph (e.g., size of the pie pieces, height of the bars) as well as the numerical information. The teacher guided the students in calculating answers to questions by adding, subtracting, or multiplying information in the graphs. Finally, students made inferences based on the information. The teacher guided the students in calculating answers to questions by adding, subtracting, or multiplying information in the graphs. Finally, students made inferences based on the information.

In some lessons, students learned to compare information from two graphs. The teacher provided relevant information, demonstrated how the comparison of two graphs works, and asked a set of structured questions about a particular set of graphs. The series of questions might sound like this:

- What are the titles of the two graphs we're going to compare?

- Notice how the numbers of miners in Virginia and Utah have declined over the years.

- Why might the number of miners have declined?

- What do the numbers across the bottom of each graph refer to?

- What do the numbers on the left side of each graph refer to?

- In which year were the most miners employed in Virginia?

- In which year were the fewest number of miners employed in Virginia?

- How many more miners worked in Utah than in Virginia in 1925?

- Figure out the difference between the number of miners in the two states in 1945.

- What was the total number of people employed in the mines for the two highest employment years in Virginia?

In addition to learning how to interpret visual aids, students also must be taught *when* to refer to the visual aids and *how* to move from reading the text to the aid and back again. Typically, various cues are embedded in text to let the reader know when to refer to a visual aid. Some cues may take the form of explicit directions (such as "see diagram"), but text often has cues that are only implicit, such as a general discussion of a subject that is supplemented with a visual aid but includes no explicit reference to the visual. Students should be taught to read in the text up to the point where a proximate visual aid is referred to (e.g., "See Table 12"), place a finger at that place in the text, refer to the visual aid, examine the information, then resume reading where the finger was keeping the place. Teachers must emphasize to students that they must not neglect the visual aids while reading a content area textbook.

Responding to Information Learned From Content-Area Textbooks

The previous section presented strategies that students could use to gain information from content-area textbooks. A second major goal in content-area classes is to lead students to respond to information learned from their content-area textbooks. Using study skills to respond to information learned is difficult for students who must "create" their own strategies without direct help from the teacher. It is possible for students to design their own strategies, but they are at best time consuming or, worse, ineffective. For example, a student might decide that to do well on content area tests he or she must memorize every sentence of an assigned chapter. Clearly, the student must be introduced to a more efficient strategy. In many classrooms, students are asked to respond to information by using a variety of strategies: (a) answering questions at the end of a chapter or on worksheets, (b) performing well on tests and quizzes, and (c) writing summaries of what they read.

Answering questions about assigned chapters. To respond to information learned from their reading, students typically must answer questions at the end of chapters in texts or on worksheets prepared by teachers. To be able to accomplish these activities successfully, students must be taught directly to turn the question into part of the answer, find the answer in the text material, and write the complete answer to the question. Archer and Gleason (2002) embed these in a strategy for *Answering Chapter Questions.*

Before learning the Answering Chapter Questions strategy, students must be taught to read the question carefully, turn the question into part of the answer, and then write that part down. This initial step is beneficial to students because it gives them a way to focus on the content of the question and a written referent *while* they are looking back in the chapter for the answer. It also helps the students write a complete sentence for the answer and ensures that they will answer the question that was asked. For example, when students are answering the question *What are three ways to recycle natural resources?,* if they first write down "Three ways to recycle natural resources are" then they are much more likely to look back in the chapter and find three ways to recycle and write a complete answer to the question.

Working on the preparatory skill of turning the question into part of the answer may take many practice sessions before students are ready to learn the Answering Chapter Questions strategy. When they have mastered this skill, the teacher demonstrates and guides the students through the whole strategy. The teacher begins by having students preview, then read a chapter or part of a chapter. Then, on their own, students read a question carefully, and change the question into part of the answer and write that part down. After writing down part of the answer, students locate headings or subheadings in the section of the chapter that treats the topic indicated by the question. They read that section until they find the answer, then write the rest of the answer in a complete sentence that answers the question. After repeated practice with the teacher, students use this strategy independently, by following the steps contained in Figure 5.

Another strategy for answering questions on expository and narrative material is referred to as the *QAR* (Question-Answer-Relationship) strategy (Raphael, 1986; Raphael & Pearson, 1985). This strategy stresses the relationships among the question, the text to which it refers, and the background knowledge of the reader. When using this strategy, the student reads the question and determines if the source of the answer is the text material ("In the Text") or the students' own background knowledge ("In My Head").

Writing summaries of materials read. Writing a summary of what has been read can help students remember and comprehend text material (Gajria & Salvia, 1992; Murrell & Surber, 1987) as well as provide the type of writing practice that will be needed for writing reports or research papers. Despite its benefits, summarizing is a difficult skill to develop to proficiency (Brown & Day, 1983; Hare & Borchardt, 1984). Students must determine what information should be included and excluded and how the information should be reorganized and reworded into a concise summary.

Although there are numerous summarization strategies (Rinehart, Stahl, & Erickson, 1986; Taylor & Beach, 1984), one of the most explicit strategies found in the literature was developed by Sheinker and Sheinker (1989). Their strategy guided students in summarizing content-area material by teaching students to first skim a passage and list key points, then to combine related points into single statements, cross out the least important points, reread the list, and combine and cross out some statements to condense the points. Finally, the remaining points are numbered in a logical order and written into a paragraph in numbered order (p. 135).

Taking tests. When studying for and taking tests, students must be taught a strategy for anticipating what will be on the test, a strategy for studying and memorizing the necessary information, and a strategy for responding to specific test formats (e.g., multiple-choice, true-false). The first strategy can be taught through the self-questioning summarization strategy developed by Wong et al. (1986) and in the note-taking strategy designed by Archer and Gleason (2002), which have been described previously in this chapter.

The second part of test taking, studying and memorizing the necessary information, can be accomplished with the RCRC strategy also described earlier (Archer & Gleason, 2002) or with any number of *mnemonic* strategies reported in the literature (e.g., Mastropieri, Sweda, & Scruggs, 2000; Bulgren, Schumaker, & Deshler, 1994).

The third part of the test-taking strategy, responding to specific formats (e.g., multiple-choice, true-false), should be taught in several forms. Students should be taught one form for each testing format that they will be faced with. What follows is an example of a teaching procedure for teaching students how to take a multiple-choice test (Archer & Gleason, 2002).

FIGURE 5

Answering Written Questions

(Note: Read the textbook material <u>before</u> attempting to answer the questions.)

Step 1: Read the question carefully.

Step 2: Change the question into part of the answer and write it down.

Step 3: Locate the section of the chapter that talks about the topic.

Use the headings and subheadings.

Step 4: Read the section until you find the answer.

Step 5: Complete your answer.

Note
From *Advanced Skills for School Success: Module 2* (p. 70), by A. Archer and M. Gleason, 1993, North Billerica, MA: Curriculum Associates. Copyright 1993 by Curriculum Associates. Reprinted with permission.

The teacher guides the students in applying the test-taking steps to several multiple-choice items, some with *all of the above* and some with *none of the above* as one of the choices. Students complete some items independently, then check answers with the teacher. The teacher provides several opportunities for practice, and students use the strategy each time they complete a multiple-choice test.

Scruggs, Mastropieri, and Tolfa-Veit (1986) found that fourth-, fifth-, and sixth-grade students with mild disabilities who received training on test-taking skills like those required for the Stanford Achievement Test (SAT) scored significantly higher on tests of reading decoding and math concepts. They concluded that results of this and previous investigations suggest that students with mild handicaps know more than they are able to demonstrate on published tests. Furthermore, training in test-taking skills should be undertaken not only to add to the strategy repertoire of these students but also to promote generalization and transfer of learned information.

Organizing Information

Managing the use of time for school tasks and managing materials used in completion of school tasks are important parts of being successful students. These management skills become more critical to students' success around grade 3 and continue to increase in importance as students move from one grade level to the next. Students with learning problems and disabilities, in particular, have difficulty (a) locating homework, (b) coming to class with materials, and (c) tracking when assignments are due.

To help resolve these major problems, three general organizational skills must be modeled directly by teachers, practiced by the students, and reinforced on a daily basis. The first skill is the organization of materials in a notebook or set of folders for easy retrieval and for study. The second skill is the organization of time through the use of an assignment calendar that helps students record assignments, determine nightly homework activities, and remember important events. The third skill is the completion of neat, well-organized papers so that the appearance meets the standards usually expected of successful students.

Notebook organization. Students must be taught very early in their academic careers to build an organizational system that allows them to store papers, retrieve necessary materials, and transport materials between classroom and home (Archer & Gleason, 2002). When working with students with learning disabilities, Lobay (1993) found a strong relation between their use of notebooks and grade point averages. Intermediate and secondary students can use a three-ring notebook that contains a pen and pencil pouch, pocket dividers for each subject area, and notebook paper. Younger students might be taught to use two folders: one for in-class use and one for taking things home. The pockets of the in-class folder might be labeled "Paper" and "Work," and the take-home folder labeled "Leave at Home" and "Bring Back to School." Students with notebooks should label each divider with the name of a subject area, then label one divider "Extra Paper" for blank notebook paper and one divider with the word "Take Home" for finished work or notices to parents to take home. The pen and pencil pouch is placed at the front of the notebook.

Regardless of the system used, notebook or folders, the teacher must demonstrate *how* to use the system, then provide daily opportunities for students to *practice* storing and retrieving materials and keeping materials organized, or reorganizing materials if they have become unorganized. Teachers can encourage maintenance of organization systems through a variety of activities. They can tell students how organized materials will help them be better students, just as remembering their work materials would help them be a good employee. They might assist students in placing papers behind the correct pocket divider in the notebook each time a paper is handed back. Frequent feedback regarding notebook organization can be given, and students can learn to use a checklist to give themselves feedback about their organization. Teachers can praise students who remember to take notebooks home, bring them back, and take them to other classes, and they can invite students to show their organized notebooks to significant school personnel (e.g., the principal). The teacher can use any activity that promotes the notebook as integral to the daily successes of students.

Assignment calendars. As students begin to assume responsibility for longer assignments and for bringing various materials home, typically in grades 3 and above, they must be taught basic time management skills. One of these skills involves keeping a monthly assignment calendar on which students record when assignments are due or when special events will occur (Archer & Gleason, 2002). Students also can learn to use their calendars to determine nightly study activities, such as reading several pages in their content-area textbook, studying notes for a test on Friday, or beginning to collect samples of objects that demonstrate earth science principles.

Teaching the assignment calendar skills requires teaching a number of component skills first. Students must learn to locate today's date on a monthly calendar, locate a due date given a variety of directions, write abbreviations for subject areas and for assignments, and record appropriate calendar entries. Although many of these component skills seem obvious, the fact that they are seen as such leaves many teachers with the idea that they do not need to be taught. Failing to teach these component skills has serious consequences for many students. However, once they have learned these component skills for assignment calendars, they will the foundation for using calendars to plan for nightly homework activities (i.e., breaking homework assignments into small parts and using calendar entries to determine homework assignments that should be completed). The teacher should teach each of the component skills separately and provide many opportunities for practice.

After the preskills have been demonstrated and practiced, the teacher can give assignments and ask students to record them on their calendars, then follow through by asking students to turn in their assignments on the date due. Teaching students to maintain the use of the assignment calendars throughout the school year is a challenging task. A large class calendar located in front of the room can be made each month, on which are recorded the assignments that should have been included in individual calendars. The teacher can assist students in *daily* use of the calendars by providing time each day for them to consult their calendars and prepare materials to take home that will help them with their homework. In addition, students can be encouraged to show their assignment calendars to their parents and tell them about homework assignments and special events.

Neat papers. A third organizational skill is that of organizing and creating a neat appearance for written papers. Students frequently hear teachers ask them to make their papers neater but most students do not know the attributes of a neat, well-organized paper. In a strategy called *HOW,* Archer & Gleason (2002) define these features as *H*eading, *O*rganized, and *W*ritten neatly. Each feature is broken down into specific attributes and introduced to students. The specific attributes are presented in Figure 6, on page 669.

The attributes for neat, well-organized papers with a heading are again are best taught through demonstration and guided practice. The teacher should present *positive examples* that show *what is wanted* in a neat paper and *negative examples* that illustrate what is *not* desired in a student paper. The purpose for showing both positive and negative examples is to demonstrate the difference to the students, so that they can determine for themselves when their papers have achieved a neat appearance and when they do not look acceptable. Students should practice evaluating other people's papers until they understand what makes a paper attractive, and then they should begin evaluating their own papers.

Teachers can assist students in maintaining use of this skill by following up with a number of activities. For example, teachers might make a large poster that displays the attributes and one that shows an example of an attractive paper, posting them in the front of the room. They might provide a checklist to students so they can evaluate their papers' appearance. Papers that are well done can be displayed publicly on a bulletin board or in the hallway. Alternately, excellent papers can be shared with parents at conference time. To encourage constant attention to producing neat papers, teachers can ask students to redo papers if they do not meet the teacher's standards.

GENERAL PROCEDURES FOR TEACHING STRATEGIES

To ensure that students attain independent use of study strategies, teachers must systematically engage in an effective instructional *cycle* (e.g. Ellis, Deshler, Lenz, Schumaker, & Clark, 1991; Gleason, 1988; Hudson, Lignugaris-Kraft, & Miller, 1993). When teaching a new strategy teachers should first discuss the rationale for the strategy. In part, this rationale should center on how the new strategy will contribute to success in school and how it will make learning easier for the students (Dye & Elksnin, 1994). Next, the teacher should use all the design principles that would be used to teach any new cognitive skill, for example, long division (Engelmann & Carnine, 1982), as well as those shown to enhance strategy instruction (Swanson, 1999). Swanson's meta-analysis determined that combining direct instruction and strategy instruction was more effective than either type of instruction alone.

In general, the teacher overtly and explicitly demonstrates or models the strategy, prompts or guides students in use of the strategy, and, finally, checks the students' use of the strategy without the teacher's assistance. Across these three steps the teacher provides many examples. The examples should be varied and cognitively complex (Vaughn, Gersten, & Chard, 2000). In addition, the practice opportunities should require self-questioning (e.g. Harris & Graham, 1996; Graham & Wong, 1993; Wong & Jones, 1982) or other types of thinking aloud (Kukan & Beck, 1997).

For some study strategies, the teacher must break the strategy down into its component parts and provide model, prompt, and check on separate components of the strategy before incorporating them into an entire strategy. For example, for writing answers to questions at the end of a textbook chapter, students must be taught separate strategies for turning the question into part of the answer, for finding the answer in the text material, for writing the complete answer to the question, and for proofreading their answers. Likewise, when studying for and taking tests, students must be taught a strategy for anticipating what will be on the test, a strategy for studying and memorizing the necessary information, and a strategy for responding to specific formats (e.g., multiple-choice, true-false). Learning to perform each step in the strategy before attempting to use the entire strategy will provide students with more immediate success and will result in more efficient learning of the strategy. The model, prompt, and check series of steps will be explained below as they apply to instruction in study strategies.

FIGURE 6

Checklist Indicating the Standards to be Applied in the HOW Strategy

HOW Should Your Papers Look?

H = Heading

1. First and last name
2. Today's date
3. Subject/Period
4. Page number if needed

O = Organized

1. On the front side of the paper
2. Left margin
3. Right margin
4. At least one blank line at the top
5. At least one blank line at the bottom
6. Uniform spacing

W = Written neatly

1. Words and numbers on the lines
2. Words and numbers written neatly
3. Neat erasing or crossing out

Note

From *Advanced Skills for School Success: Module 2* (p. 52), by A. Archer and M. Gleason, 1993, North Billerica, MA: Curriculum Associates. Copyright 1993 by Curriculum Associates. Reprinted with permission.

Modeling the Strategy

Teaching any strategy requires teachers to present an initial demonstration of it. While they are demonstrating, teachers should *exaggerate* the critical steps in the strategy and, at the same time, describe exactly what they are doing. Stating explicitly what they are thinking (i.e., "thinking aloud") is an instructional component associated with positive achievement outcomes (Swanson, Hoskyn, & Lee, 1999). For example, when teaching students how to use an index, the instructors should open a book to the index and demonstrate how to run a finger down the page until the correct letter of the alphabet is located and then until the desired topic is located. At the same time, they should talk about what they are doing and what they are looking for. Then they should demonstrate and talk about how to determine the pages to look at within the textbook to find the desired information.

Guiding Students Through the Strategy

Using a new example, the teacher then guides students through the strategy, at the same time continuing to think aloud and model the questions students should be asking themselves. This time, however, the teacher has the students answer the questions and listens to see if they are learning to use the strategy. If errors are made or misunderstandings become apparent, then the teacher provides feedback to students. Ongoing and systematic feedback is a critical component of effective interventions (Vaughn, Gersten, & Chard, 2000; Wong, 1999). Several practice opportunities (at least three) should be provided. For each practice opportunity a new example is used. By providing a range of examples, the teacher is showing the students that the steps in the strategy remain the same across a wide range of examples. For example, when teaching students to use an index for locating particular information, the teacher provides several different textbooks, each with an index that looks different and is organized a little differently from the others. Students are shown that the purpose for an index, and the way an index is used, remains the same. By the third guided-practice opportunity, the teacher lessens the cueing or prompting, allowing students to employ more of the strategy on their own. If students continue to be successful even when receiving less prompting, then the teacher moves on to testing whether they can use the strategy independently.

Checking Student Performance of the Strategy

After three or four sessions of guided practice, the teacher should monitor whether students can use the strategy independently. Only when students are independent users of the strategy in a particular context or content area with a range of examples will they be ready to transfer (using what has been learned in a new setting or with a new set of materials) and/or generalize (using what has been learned in a new way but could be in the same setting). The importance of teaching students to *transfer* and *generalize* cannot be overstated. In a meta-analysis of intervention studies involving adolescents with learning disabilities, Swanson (1999) found that extended practice with feedback was the *only* instructional component that contributed independently to the variance of the effect sizes when teaching complex material and skills.

TRANSFER AND GENERALIZATION

One of the major assumptions underlying special education services for students with disabilities at all grade levels is that eventually students will be able to transfer the skills and behaviors as learned in one setting into another setting. The transfer setting might be a regular classroom, a social situation, or an employment situation. However, transfer is not at all easy to accomplish. In many cases, students with disabilities do not automatically transfer the skills they learn from one setting to another (e.g. Borkowski & Muthukrishna, 1992; Ellis, Lenz, & Sabornie, 1987; Garner, 1990; Wong, 1994). Teachers must tell students to use their newly learned skills in another setting, make sure the way the strategy was taught matches how it will be used in the new setting, and make sure students have mastered and maintained the strategy in the original setting.

Generalization is even more difficult to achieve than transfer of what was learned from one setting to another. In order to use a strategy in a new way, students must have had the opportunity to use the strategy on a range of examples. To understand why this is true, consider a situation in which students were taught in a special education resource center to identify the main idea in a paragraph. The examples used in the original teaching set were from worksheets, were composed of three or four sentences, and the main idea statement matched several key words presented in the first sentence of the paragraph. Students did not have to glean the overall gist of the paragraph in order to state the main idea. These students then are presented in the general education classroom with a textbook chapter and asked to identify the main idea in the third paragraph, which happens to be seven sentences long. In addition, the students must pull out the main idea by considering all seven sentences at once and determining the main thing the paragraph was about. The main idea was not stated in the first sentence. It would not be surprising to find that most students were not able to complete the task, for the very particular reason that they were not taught to work from a range of examples that included the type they are now encountering (Engelmann & Carnine, 1982; Horner, Bellamy, & Colvin, 1984).

Although generalization is difficult to accomplish, it is not impossible. Unfortunately, teachers frequently do not prioritize generalization techniques until after instruction has been completed. This is not surprising in that the research literature provides far less assistance on *how* to achieve generalization than it does on how to teach strategies initially (Vaughn, Gersten, & Chard, 2000). However, in order for the possibility of generalization and transfer of study strategies to other settings and untrained examples, teachers must systematically plan to do so before instruction occurs. Ellis and his colleagues found that students of various abilities learned to generalize Strategies Intervention Model (SIM) strategies when generalization was included as a phase of strategy teaching (e.g., Lenz, Ellis, & Scanlon, 1996).

Teachers can organize generalization planning around three time frames: before, during, and after strategy instruction. Not all suggestions in the following section need to be utilized for each strategy taught, but the listing can serve as an outline for teacher's planning.

Generalization Planning Before Instruction

Two major procedures used before instruction will increase the probability that students will generalize skills to other settings and environment. Teachers must carefully select relevant study skills to teach to their students and then must follow at least two basic rules in choosing the examples to be used for instruction.

Carefully select relevant study skills. Because the major purpose for teaching study skills is to empower students for success and promote independent learning, the strategies taught must be of particular relevance to the students (e.g. Harris & Graham, 1996; Pressley et al., 1995). For example, if students attend three classes in which the teacher lectures, learning a strategy for taking notes from lectures would meet an immediate need. In addition, teachers must select skills that can be applied in a variety of settings, have proven effectiveness, and have a specific outcome that can be observed by the teacher. If the study skills taught are relevant to the students' success in school, students are more likely to use the skills (Lenz, Ellis, & Scanlon, 1996).

Follow two basic rules. To promote generalization, teachers should apply the following two rules in choosing examples for instruction.

1. First rule. Select teaching examples that sample the range of examples likely to be encountered. When a particular skill is targeted for instruction, the teachers should examine the contexts in which that particular skill is likely to be needed or applied. For example, suppose the teacher decides to teach comprehension strategies, and specifically, to teach the rule that a paragraph has one main idea. The first step would be to identify the various contexts in which the students are likely to be required to read paragraphs at school. These contexts could include worksheets, overheads, workbooks, textbooks, novels, periodicals, newspapers, letters, and magazines of various lengths and various levels of explicitness in stating the main idea. Teaching examples should then be selected to adequately represent the *range* of examples included in these contexts (Horner, Bellamy, & Colvin, 1984).

Instruction is more likely to be effective if the teaching examples are sequenced so that successive examples are maximally different and cover a range of examples that communicate a breadth of application to students (Engelmann & Carnine, 1982). The assumption is that by teaching the paragraph using these *representative* examples the student would be able to apply the skill to all examples. For example, the first example used in teaching the paragraph rule could be on an overhead transparency. The successive examples could be paragraphs from a textbook, a worksheet, and a newspaper. Similarly, examples could be sequenced on the basis of length of the paragraph (e.g., overhead, three sentences; textbook, seven sentences; worksheet, two sentences; newspaper, five sentences). In addition, the explicitness of the main idea could be varied, from paragraphs in which the main idea is matched by key words in the first sentence to paragraphs where the main idea is gleaned from the gist of all sentences in the paragraph taken together. In effect these successive examples are sequenced to show maximum variation across the possible variables.

2. Second rule. Because students may apply skills only to the specific examples used in initial instruction, the teacher should produce a second set of examples, which were not part of the initial teaching set, in order to test for the possibility of generalization (Engelmann & Carnine, 1982). For example, let us suppose that a student has met criteria on the skill of identifying the main idea in a paragraph. It is assumed that the teaching examples were representative of the contexts likely to be encountered by the student and the examples were sequenced so that successive examples were maximally different. Test examples (e.g., text on an Internet site or paragraphs of 10 or more sentences) should now be introduced that were *not used* in the initial teaching. Other variations that were not used in initial training also could be used, such as a paragraph in a periodical that utilizes three columns of print.

Generalization Planning During Instruction

While the teacher is demonstrating and guiding students through a new study strategy, several steps can be taken to promote generalization and transfer.

Provide rationale for use of the strategy. As was discussed earlier in the chapter, the teacher can assist students in understanding the relevance of learning a particular strategy by explaining what is to be gained by its use. In particular, the teacher should emphasize the increased success that students will experience after learning a new study skill. Presenting the benefits of strategy use has been found to be one of the instructional components that predicts greater treatment outcomes (Swanson, 1999).

Discuss when and where the strategy can be used. In addition to discussing why students should learn the strategy, teachers should discuss when and where students might use the strategy (Swanson & De La Paz, 1998). Teachers also might ask students to name other settings and other sets of materials in which they could use their new study strategy.

Ensure that students achieve mastery of the new strategy. In all cases, systematic instruction must be provided that ensures that students become proficient in the use of a particular study skill. If students cannot perform the skill at a high level of success in the training setting, then they probably will not generalize use of the skill to another setting.

Teach students effective self-monitoring or self-evaluation procedures. While receiving instruction on using a strategy independently, students will benefit from learning self-management skills such as self-questioning, self-monitoring, self-evaluation, or self-recording skills (e.g. Chan, 1991; Harris & Graham, 1996; Swanson, 1999; Wong & Jones, 1982). A meta-analysis of the effects of teaching students to use self-questioning strategies found such interventions to be successful (Huang, 1992). Later, students can use these skills to monitor their progress in other settings.

Generalization Planning After Instruction

Although it is important to address generalization before and during instruction, teachers also must attend to it after instruction. Typically, students in the initial stages of learning, students at risk for failure, and students with disabilities forget what they have learned if it is no longer reviewed or maintained.

Inform others of new strategies. Although it would be ideal if all teachers encountered by a group of students would teach and require use of learning strategies, occasionally they are taught in one setting (e.g., resource room) with the expectation of generalization to another setting (e.g., general education classroom). In this case, general education classroom teachers should be encouraged to review a new strategy in their classes, display a poster listing the steps in the strategy, and reinforce use of the strategy on a consistent basis. Teachers might teach the steps in the strategy to everyone in the general education class and then pair more successful students with less successful students until they are independently using the new strategy in the transfer setting. Review of strategies and reminders to use strategies have been found to be important instructional components for achieving high strategy use (Swanson, 1999).

Tell students to use the strategy in other settings. While this procedure may seem obvious, many teachers do not routinely tell students to use new skills in other settings. At the end of a lesson or at the end of the day, teachers should remind students that new strategies are to be used in other classes throughout the school day.

Ask students to verbalize their success with strategies in other settings. Many students with learning disabilities experience difficulty in associating their skills and knowledge with their success in school. To strengthen this association, teachers should encourage students to report their use of new strategies in other settings. Teachers should show particular interest in students' reports of increased success in other settings that can be attributed directly to the use of study strategies. If students do not make this association, then teachers should tell students that increased success is connected to their use of their new study strategies. In a series of experiments, Schunk and Rice (1992) found that students who received strategy-value feedback demonstrated higher skill and higher self-efficacy than students in strategy-only or control conditions. Subsequently, students in the strategy-value feedback condition also maintained strategy use.

Discuss cues in other settings that signal use of the strategy. Generalization of study skills is particularly difficult when they are content-free and not associated with certain subjects or classroom tasks. For this reason, it is important to discuss the similarities and differences between the response demands and cues of the training setting and those of the transfer setting (e.g., Deshler & Schumaker, 1986; Gelzheiser, Sheperd, & Wozniak, 1986). For example, the cue for taking notes in the training setting may be the teachers' announcing that students should take out notebook paper and begin taking notes. In the transfer setting, the cue might be the teacher's announcement that students are going to have a test on Friday or the teacher's writing an outline on the blackboard while talking about a particular topic.

Use role-playing to practice transfer to other settings. Assisting students in role-playing transfer of skills to other settings is especially beneficial if the response demands and cues of the other settings are considerably different from those used during the training. For example, students could practice responding to various cues that indicate "it is time to listen to the teacher and take notes." The teacher who is presenting study strategies to the students might mix up a variety of cues to see if the students can choose which study strategy to use. Students need many opportunities to practice and review all the strategies they have learned.

ROLE OF THE SCHOOL PSYCHOLOGIST WITH REGARD TO STUDY SKILLS

Although direct teaching of study skills would not be practical, school psychologists could serve as an advocate for all students to learn study skills as early as possible and sustain their use throughout their school years. The literature continues to document the struggles of students with learning problems and identified disabilities to learn in whole-class settings (e.g., Baker & Zigmond, 1990; McIntosh, Vaughn, Schumm, Haager, & Lee, 1994; Scanlon, Deshler, & Schumaker, 1996; Vaughn, Klingner, & Bryant, 2001).

1. School psychologists could create an awareness of the need for study skills interventions as part of school improvement and better preparation of students for school success.

2. If classroom observations and/or assessments reveal weaknesses in the area of study skills, then the school psychologist should advocate that the Individual Education Plan reflect study skills among the necessary interventions.

3. School psychologists also could advocate the need to teach study skills across settings and across grade levels as a preventative measure to reduce the need for individualized services. If these skills were taught to all students, then the support structure would exist for teaching individual students.

4. School psychologists could help provide resources for instruction in study skills.

Finally, school psychologists could advocate for presentations on study skills to be offered at national and state conferences for school psychologists, and assist in soliciting articles on study skill interventions for the school psychology journals such as *School Psychology Review.*

SUMMARY

Many students struggle in content area classes because they lack the specific learning strategies that would help them be more successful. In particular, students need to learn strategies for gaining information, responding to information, and organizing information. To ensure that students attain independent use of study skill strategies, teachers must systematically engage in an effective instructional *cycle* that includes modeling the strategy, guiding students in its use, and providing opportunities for independent practice and use of the strategy. In addition, care must be taken to design instruction so that students will transfer and generalize their newly learned strategies to other settings, other sets of materials, and novel situations. Attention must be paid to generalization before, during, and after instruction. School psychologists can play an important role in advocating for interventions that improve study skills, and simultaneously, students' school success.

REFERENCES

Archer, A., & Gleason, M. (1993). *Advanced skills for school success, Module 3: Effective reading of textbooks.* North Billerica, MA: Curriculum Associates.

Archer, A., & Gleason, M. (1997). Direct instruction in content area reading. In D. Carnine, J. Silbert, & E. Kame'enui (Eds.), *Direct instruction reading* (3rd. ed.). Columbus, OH: Merrill.

Archer, A., & Gleason, M. (2002). *Skills for school success* (teacher guides and student workbooks, grades 3-6). North Billerica, MA: Curriculum Associates.

Archer, A. L., Gleason, M. M., & Vachon, V. (2000). *REWARDS Reading excellence: Word attack and rate development strategies.* Longmont, CO: Sopris West.

Archer, A. L., Gleason, M. M., Vachon, V., & Hollenbeck, K. (2002). *Effects of teaching multisyllabic word reading to skill-deficient fourth and fifth graders.* Unpublished manuscript.

Baker, J. M., & Zigmond, N. (1990). Are regular education classes equipped to accommodate students with learning disabilities? *Exceptional Children, 56,* 515-526.

Bakken, J. P., Mastropieri, M. A., & Scruggs, T. E. (1997). Reading comprehension of expository science material and students with learning disabilities: A comparison of strategies. *The Journal of Special Education, 31*(3), 300-324.

Borkowski, J. G., & Muthukrishna, N. (1992). Moving metacognition into the classroom: "Working models" and effective strategy teaching. In M. Pressley, K. R. Harris, & J. T. Guthrie (Eds.), *Promoting academic competence and literacy in schools* (pp. 477-501). San Diego, CA: Academic.

Boyle, J. R., & Yeager, N. (1997). Blueprints for learning: Using cognitive frameworks for understanding. *Teaching Exceptional Children, 29*(4), 26-31.

Brown, A. L., & Day, J. D. (1983) Macro-rules for summarizing texts: The development of expertise. *Journal of Verbal Learning and Verbal Behavior, 22,* 1-14.

Bryant, D. P., Ugel, N., Thompson, S., & Hamff, A. (1999). Instructional strategies for content-area reading instruction. *Intervention in School and Clinic, 34,* 293-302.

Bulgren, J. A., Schumaker, J. B., & Deshler, D. D. (1994). The effects of a recall enhancement routine on the test performance of secondary students with and without learning disabilities. *Learning Disabilities Research & Practice, 9*(1), 2-11.

Chan, L. K. S. (1991). Promoting strategy generalization through self-instructional training in students with reading disabilities. *Journal of Learning Disabilities, 24,* 427-433.

Chan, L. K. S., & Cole, P. G. (1986). The effects of comprehension monitoring training on the reading competence of learning disabled and regular class students. *Remedial and Special Education, 7*(4), 33-40.

Cunningham, P. (1998). The multisyllabic word dilemma: Helping students build meaning, spell, and read "big" words. *Reading and Writing Quarterly: Overcoming Learning Disabilities, 14,* 189-219.

De La Paz, S. (1999). Teaching writing strategies and self-regulation procedures to middle school students with learning disabilities. *Focus on Exceptional Children, 31*(5), 1-16.

Derry, S. J., & Murphy, D. A. (1986). Designing systems that train learning ability: From theory to practice. *Review of Educational Research, 56,* 1-39.

Deshler, D. D., & Schumaker, J. B. (1986). Learning strategies: An instructional alternative for low-achieving adolescents. *Exceptional Children, 52*(6), 583-590.

Deshler, D. D., Schumaker, J., Harris, K. R., & Graham, S. (1999). *Teaching every adolescent every day.* Cambridge, MA: Brookline Books.

Dye, V. P., & Elksnin, L. K. (1994). Promoting strategic learning. *Intervention in School and Clinic, 29,* 262-270.

Ellis, E. S., Deshler, D. D., Lenz, K., Schumaker, J. B., & Clark, F. L. (1991). An instructional model for teaching learning strategies. *Focus on Exceptional Children, 23*(6), 1-24.

Ellis, E. S., Lenz, B. K., & Sabornie, E. J. (1987). Generalization and adaptation of learning strategies to natural environments: Part 2. Research into practice. *Remedial and Special Education, 8*(2), 6-23.

Engelmann, S., & Carnine, D. (1982). *Theory of instruction: Principles and applications.* New York: Irvington.

Englert, C. S., & Mariage, T. V. (1991). Making students partners in the comprehension process: Organizing the reading "POSSE". *Learning Disability Quarterly, 14,* 123-138.

Englert, C. S., Tarrant, K. L., Mariage, T. V., & Oxer, T. (1994). Lesson talk as the work of reading groups: The effectiveness of two interventions. *Journal of Learning Disabilities, 27,* 165-185.

Gajiria, M., & Salvia, J. (1992). The effects of summarization instruction on text comprehension of students with learning disabilities. *Exceptional Children, 58*(6), 508-516.

Garner, R. (1990). When children and adults do not use learning strategies: Toward a theory of settings. *Review of Educational Research, 60,* 517-529.

Gelzheiser, L. M., Shepherd, M. J., & Wozniak, R. H. (1986). The development of instruction to induce skill transfer. *Exceptional Children, 53,* 125-129.

Gersten, R. (1998). Recent advances in instructional research for students with learning disabilities: An overview. *Learning Disabilities Research & Practice, 13*(3), 162-170.

Gleason, M. M. (1988). Teaching study strategies. *Teaching Exceptional Children, 20*(3), 52-53.

Graham, L., & Wong, B. Y. L. (1993). Comparing two modes of teaching a question-answering strategy for enhancing reading comprehension: Didactic and self-instructional training. *Journal of Learning Disabilities, 26,* 270-279.

Graves, A. W. (1986). Effects of direct instruction and metacomprehension training on finding main ideas. *Learning Disabilities Research, 1,* 90-100.

Hare, V. C., & Borchardt, K. M. (1984). Direct instruction of summarization skills. *Reading Research Quarterly, 21,* 62-78.

Harris, K. R., & Graham, S. (1996). *Making the writing process work: Strategies for composition and self-regulation.* Cambridge, MA: Brookline Books.

Horner, R. H., Bellamy, G. T., & Colvin, G. T. (1984). Responding in the presence of nontrained stimuli: Implications of generalization error patterns. *Journal of the Association for Persons with Severe Handicaps, 9*(4), 287-295.

Huang, Z. (1992). A meta-analysis of student self-questioning strategies. *Dissertation Abstracts International, 52*(11), 3874A.

Hudson, P., Lignugaris-Kraft, B., & Miller, T. (1993). Using content enhancements to improve the performance of adolescents with learning disabilities in content classes. *Learning Disabilities Research & Practice, 8*(2), 106-126.

Jenkins, J. R., Heliotis, J. D., Stein, M. L., & Hayes, M. C. (1987). Improving reading comprehension by using paragraph restatement. *Exceptional Children, 54,* 54-59.

Just, M. A., & Carpenter, P. A. (1987). *The psychology of reading and language comprehension.* Boston: Allyn & Bacon.

Klingner, J. K., & Vaughn, S. (1998). Using collaborative strategic reading. *Teaching Exceptional Children, 30*(6), 32-37.

Kukan, L., & Beck, I. L. (1997). Thinking aloud and reading comprehension research: Inquiry, instruction, and social interaction. *Review of Educational Research, 67,* 271-299.

Lenz, B. K, Ellis, E. S., & Scanlon, D. (1996). *Teaching learning strategies to adolescents and adults with learning disabilities.* Austin, TX: PRO-ED.

Lenz, B. K., & Hughes, C. A. (1990). A word identification strategy for adolescents with learning disabilities. *Journal of Learning Disabilities, 23,* 149-163.

Lobay, E. E. (1993). *Middle school study skills: The correlation between binder skills and academic achievement.* Unpublished Master's thesis. San Jose State University.

Mastropieri, M. A., & Scruggs, T. E. (1997). Best practices in promoting reading comprehension in students with learning disabilities 1976–1996. *Remedial and Special Education, 18*(4), 197-213.

Mastropieri, M. A., Sweda, J., & Scruggs, T. E. (2000). Putting mnemonic strategies to work in an inclusive classroom. *Learning Disabilities Research & Practice, 15*(2), 69-74.

McIntosh, R., Vaughn, S., Schumm, J. S., Haager, D., & Lee, O. (1994). Observations of students with learning disabilities in general education classrooms. *Exceptional Children, 60,* 249-261.

Munk, D. D., Bruckert, J., Call, D. T., Stoehrmann, T., & Radandt, E. (1998). Strategies for enhancing the performance of students with LD in inclusive science classes. *Intervention in School and Clinic, 34*(2), 73-78.

Murrell, P.C., Jr., & Surber, J. R. (1987, April). *The effect of generative summarization on the comprehension of main ideas from lengthy expository text.* Paper presented at the annual meeting of the American Educational Research Association, Washington, DC.

Nagy, W., & Anderson, R. C. (1984). How many words are there in printed school English? *Reading Research Quarterly, 19,* 304-330.

Newman, R. S., & Hagen, J. W. (1981). Memory strategies in children with learning disabilities. *Journal of Applied Developmental Psychology, 1,* 297-312.

Ogle, D. M. (1986). K-W-L: A teaching model that develops active reading of expository text. *The Reading Teacher, 39,* 564-570.

Ogle, D. M. (1992). KWL in action: Secondary teachers find applications that work. In E. K. Dishner, T. W. Bean, J. E. Readence, & D. W. Moore (Eds.), *Content area reading: Improving classroom instruction* (3rd ed., pp. 270-282). Dubuque, IA: Kendall/Hunt.

Perfetti, C. A. (1986). Continuities in reading acquisition, reading skill, and reading disability. *Remedial and Special Education, 7,* 11-21.

Pressley, M., Woloshyn, V., Burkell, J., Cariglia-Bull, T., Lysynchuk, L., McGoldrick, J. A., Schneider, B., Snyder, B., & Symons, S. (1995). *Cognitive strategy instruction that really improves children's academic performance* (2nd ed.). Cambridge, MA: Brookline Books.

Raphael, T. E. (1986). Teaching question answer relationships, revisited. *The Reading Teacher, 39,* 516-522.

Raphael, T. E., & Pearson, P. D. (1985). Increasing students' awareness of sources of information for answering questions. *American Educational Research Journal, 22,* 217-235.

Rinehart, S. D., Stahl, S. A., & Erickson, L. G. (1986). Some effects of summarization training on reading and studying. *Reading Research Quarterly, 21,* 422-438.

Samuels, S. J., LaBerge, D., & Bremer, C. D. (1978). Units of word recognition: 715-720.

Scanlon, D. J., Deshler, D. D., & Schumaker, J. B. (1996). Can a strategy be taught and learned in secondary inclusive classrooms? *Learning Disabilities Research & Practice, 11*(1), 41-57.

Scanlon, D. J., Duran, G. Z., Reyes, E I., & Gallego, M. A. (1992). Interactive semantic mapping: An interactive approach to enhancing LD students' content area comprehension. *Learning Disabilities Research & Practice, 7*(3), 142-146.

Schumaker, J. B., Denton, P. H., & Deshler, D. D. (1984). *The paraphrasing strategy.* Lawrence, KS: The University of Kansas.

Schunk, D. H., & Rice, J. M. (1992). Influence of reading-comprehension strategy information on children's achievement outcomes. *Learning Disability Quarterly, 15,* 51-64.

Scruggs, T. E., Mastropieri, M. A., & Tolfa-Veit, D. (1986). The effects of coaching on the standardized test performance of learning disabled and behaviorally disordered students. *Remedial and Special Education, 7*(5), 37-41.

Shefelbine, J. (1990). A syllabic-unit approach to teaching decoding of polysyllabic words to fourth- and sixth-grade disabled readers. In J. Zutell & S. McCormick (Eds.), *Literacy theory and research: Analysis from multiple paradigms. Thirty-ninth yearbook of the National Reading Conference* (pp. 223-229). Fort Worth, TX: Texas Christian University Press.

Sheinker, J., & Sheinker, A. (1989). *Metacognitive approach to study strategies.* Rockville, MD: Aspen.

Swanson, H. L. (1999). Instructional components that predict treatment outcomes for students with learning disabilities: Support for a combined strategy and direct instruction model. *Learning Disabilities Research and Practice, 14*(3), 129-140.

Swanson, H. L., Hoskyn, M., & Lee, C. (1999). *Interventions for students with learning disabilities: A meta-analysis of treatment outcomes.* New York: Guilford.

Swanson, P. N., & De La Paz, S. (1998). Teaching effective comprehension strategies to students with learning and reading disabilities. *Intervention in School and Clinic, 33,* 209-218.

Taylor, B. M., & Beach, R. W. (1984). The effects of text structure instruction on middle-grade students' comprehension and production of expository. *Reading Research Quarterly, 19,* 134-146.

Torgesen, J. K. (1982). The learning-disabled child as an inactive learner: Educational implications. *Topics in Learning and Learning Disabilities, 2,* 45-52.

Vaughn, S., Gersten, R., & Chard, D.J. (2000). The underlying message in LD intervention research: Findings from research syntheses. *Exceptional Children, 67*(1), 99-114.

Vaughn, S., & Klingner, J. K. (1999). Teaching reading comprehension through collaborative strategic reading. *Intervention in School and Clinic, 34,* 284-292.

Vaughn, S., Klingner, J. K., & Bryant, D. P. (2001). Collaborative strategic reading as a means to enhance peer-mediated instruction for reading comprehension and content-area learning. *Remedial and Special Education, 22*(2), 66-74.

Wong, B.Y. L. (1994). Instructional parameters promoting transfer of learned strategies in students with LD. *Learning Disability Quarterly, 7,* 229-236.

Wong, B.Y. L. (1999). Metacognition in writing. In R. Gallimore, L. P. Bernheimer, D. L. MacMillan, D. L. Speece, & S. Vaughn (Eds.), *Developmental perspectives on children with high-incidence disabilities* (pp. 183-198). Mahwah, NJ: Erlbaum.

Wong, B.Y. L., & Jones, W. (1982). Increasing metacomprehension in learning disabled and normally achieving students through self-questioning training. *Learning Disability Quarterly, 5,* 228-240.

Wong, B.Y. L., Wong, R., Perry, N., & Sawatsky, D. (1986). The efficacy of a self-questioning summarization strategy for use by underachievers and learning disabled adolescents in social studies. *Learning Disabilities Focus, 2,* 20-35.

CHAPTER 25

Prevention and Early Interventions for Addictive Behaviors: Health Promotion in the Schools

Herbert H. Severson and Lisa James
Oregon Research Institute
Eugene, Oregon

INTRODUCTION

Drug, alcohol, and tobacco use by adolescents has become a major social problem. Despite growing efforts to curb the use of these substances among teens, there has been little change in prevalence over the years and, in some cases, use has actually increased. The proportion of eighth-graders reporting use of any illicit drug in the last 12 months has almost doubled since 1991, from 11% to 21%. Since 1992, the proportion reporting use of any illicit drugs in the past year has risen by nearly two thirds among tenth-graders, from 20% to 39% (Johnston, O'Malley, & Bachmann, 1995). Rates of tobacco and alcohol use among youth are also exceedingly high. According to the most recently published results of the Youth Risk Behavior Survey (YRBS), nationwide, 70.4% of students had tried cigarette smoking (including those who had taken only one or two puffs), and in 1999, 34.8% of high school students had smoked cigarettes during the past 30 days (Centers for Disease Control and Prevention [CDC], 2000). Additionally, 50% had drunk alcohol during the past 30 days (CDC, 2000). These figures, already alarming, probably do not accurately reflect the scope of the problem since they fail to assess alcohol, tobacco, and drug use among teenagers not attending school, a population in which these behaviors are significantly higher. Clearly, this shows that teenagers' drug involvement is not merely a passing experimental phase; for many, drug use has become part of a daily lifestyle.

While public interest tends to focus on curtailing the use of illicit drugs such as marijuana, cocaine, and heroin, common popular drugs such as cigarettes and alcohol may pose a greater threat to public health. Use of tobacco products appears to be a very robust habit, as evidenced by stable use rates through the high school years. Tobacco use initiation also appears to follow an increasing pattern as teenagers enter high school. Female students in grades 10, 11, and 12 (75.1%, 71.8%, and 75.5%, respectively) were significantly more likely than female students in ninth grade (60.3%) to have ever tried cigarette smoking. Male students in 12th grade (80.5%) were significantly more likely than male students in 9th and 11th grades (63.1% and 68.1%, respectively) to report this behavior (CDC, 2000). According to the 1999 Youth Risk Behavior Survey (YRBS), nationwide, 81.0% of students had consumed more than one drink (one beer, glass of wine, shot of liquor, or its equivalent) of alcohol during their lifetime and half of all students (50.0%) nationwide had consumed more than one drink of alcohol on more than one of the 30 days preceding the survey. Additionally, 31.5% of students had consumed more than five drinks of alcohol on more than one occasion during the 30 days preceding the survey (CDC, 2000). The 1999 YRBS also reports that lifetime marijuana use for school-age children ranges from 24.1% to 57.1% (median: 44.6%) across state surveys and from 30.6% to 48.6% (median: 41.3%) across local surveys. More than one fourth (26.7%) of the surveyed students had used marijuana more than one time during the 30 days preceding the survey (CDC, 2000).

Given the ongoing use patterns reported above, and the fact that smoking has been linked to more deaths than all other lifestyle factors including the use of "hard" drugs, it is imperative that any efforts to prevent drug use target tobacco as well as illicit substances (Lynch & Bonnie, 1994). Prevention efforts should include the most prevalent drugs used by teens: tobacco (cigarettes and chew), alcohol, and marijuana.

Early Substance Use Initiation

The leading causes of mortality and morbidity among youth can be traced to a relatively small number of preventable health-risk behaviors that are often initiated during youth and may extend into adulthood (Kolbe, Kann, & Collins, 1993). Surveys of drug use confirm not only that drugs are being used, but also that the age of initial use for most drugs is at the elementary school level. Studies of cigarette, chewing tobacco, and marijuana use report experimentation in fourth and fifth grades. This early experience with drug use is related to subsequent regular use and abuse (Severson, 1984). It has been shown repeatedly that initiation of alcohol and drug use at an early age is one of the strongest predictors of later substance abuse (Grant & Dawson, 1997; Robins & Przybeck, 1985). Early drug use has been shown to be related to a wide range of antisocial behaviors and subsequent school failure (Donovan & Jessor, 1978). Substance use by adolescents often occurs in the context of other behaviors, such as delinquency (Donovan & Jessor), school failure (Hundleby, Carpenter, Ross, & Mercer, 1982), high-risk sexual behavior (Biglan et al., 1990), and low self-esteem (Bry, McKeon, & Padina, 1982). Indeed, the number of problems a youth experiences (e.g., poor relationships with parents or peers, psychopathology, low grade point average) increases the risk of concurrent and later drug use (Newcomb, Maddahian, & Bentler, 1986). In a related context, risk behaviors vary by age, suggesting that interventions must be sensitive to developmental changes and appropriately timed to have maximum effects (Brener & Collins, 1998).

While many factors, such as substance use by parents and substance accessibility, are beyond the scope of a school-based intervention, there is increasing evidence showing the efficacy of early interventions to reduce tobacco, alcohol, and drug use and abuse. Teachers, school personnel, and the community at large have the obligation to establish prevention and treatment programs for children and adolescents in order to avoid the negative health outcomes associated with substance use.

IMPORTANCE OF PREVENTION AND EARLY INTERVENTION

Although substance abuse recently has achieved widespread public attention, illicit drug use has been of major concern to schools, communities, and health professionals for decades. Not only does substance use remain high, but the average age of onset for most substances also has decreased (CDC, 2000). Young people typically experiment with a wide range of behaviors and lifestyles as they seek to define a personal identity and declare independence from their parents. Social pressures from peers and family, positive depictions of substance use (especially tobacco) in the popular media, perceptions of use as normative behavior, personality factors such as low self-esteem, confidence, or self-efficacy, and antisocial behavior patterns all contribute to an adolescent's choice to begin experimenting with drugs. Once substance use is initiated, the physiological addictive process encourages continued use despite harmful effects. Adolescence is a time of great developmental change. Physical addiction can occur more quickly, and cessation is more difficult, among youth than among adults.

Relationships Between Substance Use and Depression

Youths with substance use and abuse problems have high rates of comorbidity with conduct disorders and depression. For example, Clark et al. (1997) report that, in a sample of alcohol-dependent adolescents seeking treatment, 89% also had Conduct Disorder, Major Depressive Disorder, or both. Miller-Johnson and her colleagues (Miller-Johnson, Lochman, Cole, Terry, & Hyman, 1998) report that both depression and conduct disorders have been linked to an increased risk for substance use, and that co-occurrence of the two disorders elevates this risk. Compared with other groups, the comorbid group reported the most frequent use of tobacco at grade 6, alcohol at grade 8, and marijuana at grades 6 and 8. Adolescents with high levels of conduct disorders in early adolescence were at increased risk for high rates of tobacco, alcohol, and marijuana use over time, with this effect more pronounced for males than for females. Their findings suggest that preventive efforts designed to increase resistance to substance use would be useful for youngsters exhibiting early conduct disorders.

It is clear that the most favorable approach to reducing substance abuse among youth is prevention. School personnel have the responsibility, as well as the opportunity, to be the first line of defense against negative health outcomes and to intervene early to interrupt the cycle of initiation and addiction. In order for school-based prevention to be effective, however, the intervention programs need to be introduced before the behavior has escalated into a regular use pattern. For example, in the case of smoking, over 90% of adult smokers report they were regular users before leaving high school;

62% report that they had at least tried cigarettes by the ninth grade. Our own research shows that, among seventh-graders, 10% report having used cigarettes, 14% of the boys report having used chewing tobacco, and 23% report having used alcohol in the previous week. Of more serious concern is the fact that 11% of seventh-graders report that in the previous week they have had five or more drinks on a single occasion, a standard used to measure inebriation.

If we want to change substance use patterns, we must identify users at the early stages of use and apply effective prevention tactics to reduce the number of adolescents who go on to regular use. Researchers have striven to identify the most effective means of prevention for the past 30 years.

History of Prevention

Prevention efforts can be viewed as either primary or secondary. As has been the theme of this volume, **primary prevention** is designed to prevent a target person (or population) from engaging in a particular behavior, and occurs before the behavior. **Secondary prevention** aims to inhibit the person (or population) from continuing a behavior that already has been initiated. The distinction between these two types of prevention may become blurred when we attempt to study drug use. For example, if one were to intervene in the sixth grade and focus on smoking prevention, such an intervention could be considered primary prevention because most sixth-grade students are not smokers. However, because some students of that age report having experimented with tobacco, and the age of onset is decreasing over time, the intervention must include secondary prevention components as well.

Ineffective prevention strategies. In the early 1970s, school-based prevention models traditionally focused on providing factual information about the harmful effects of using drugs. Many programs attempted to deter the behavior by using "scare tactics" aimed at instilling fear of the physical and punitive consequences of using substances. Empirical evaluation of such programs, however, indicated that they were *not* effective in achieving reductions in youth drug use (Botvin, Baker, Filazzola, & Botvin, 1990); in fact, in some cases, evidence showed that these strategies actually led to increased use (e.g., Swisher, Crawford, Goldstein, & Yura, 1971). While educating youth about the harmful effects of drug use may increase their knowledge about such consequences, and in some cases also may change their attitudes toward drug use, education alone has no impact on subsequent drug use behavior (e.g., Kearney & Hines, 1980; Kim, 1988).

More effective prevention strategies. In more recent years, a number of prevention strategies have been empirically shown to be effective. These include (a) the social influence approach, (b) community interventions, (c) efforts to change perceived social norms, and (d) approaches to affect policy change. Social influence strategies involve teaching young people not only the skills to resist pressures to use tobacco and other drugs, but also the general problem-solving, decision-making, social, and assertiveness skills that contribute to the child's overall life success. Community interventions support youth nonuse of substances by enlisting the help of a wide cross section of community representatives to work toward altering community knowledge, attitudes, and practices related to drug use. Social norms approaches seek to decrease the social acceptability of substance use and correct the common misconception that most young people use drugs. Clear, fair, and consistently enforced policies at the school and community levels also can help adolescents decide not to use tobacco and other drugs.

CONCEPTUAL MODEL FOR PREVENTION

Those who seek to develop effective prevention programs can find guidance among many theoretical frameworks for explaining tobacco use behavior and specifying ways to prevent that behavior. The conceptual model described in this chapter is based in *social contextualist theory*. This theory advocates analyzing the environmental context within which a given behavior occurs and adopting the goal of predicting and influencing the cultural practices that encourage or discourage that behavior.

Researchers in the behavioral sciences have come to realize that addressing problem behaviors that are highly prevalent, such as drug use, requires efforts that go beyond interventions targeted at the individual (Biglan, 1995). The value of such interventions is limited when the target behavior is influenced by variables in the context of the individual that cannot be addressed in a one-on-one setting. For example, treating an adolescent's smoking addiction may be difficult when that adolescent's peer group comprises many smokers, or when the young person is repeatedly exposed to powerful tobacco marketing messages. In addition, while school-based prevention curricula have proven effective, those effects are often modest and short term (Rooney & Murray, 1996; U. S. Department of Health and Human Services [U.S. DHHS], 1994). Evidence now illustrates a need to enhance school-based prevention with community-wide programs that target other elements in the social environment surrounding youth peers, parents, community organizations, and the media.

TOBACCO PREVENTION AS A MODEL FOR OTHER DRUG USE PREVENTION

For several reasons, we suggest that currently recognized best practices for tobacco use prevention provide a satisfactory model for strategies to prevent the use of alcohol, marijuana, and other drugs. First, although public interest may place primary focus on the problem of illicit drug use, tobacco use kills more people in the U.S. each year than do alcohol, drug abuse, AIDS, car accidents, homicides, suicides, and fires *combined*. Every day, 3,000 adolescents in this country smoke their first cigarettes on the way to becoming regular smokers as adults. More than five million children living today will die prematurely because of a decision they will make in adolescence—the decision to smoke cigarettes (CDC, 2000). Clearly, efforts to prevent *any* drug use should target tobacco use as a central theme. In many states, school-level tobacco prevention education is mandated.

Second, a body of research evidence now points to the role of tobacco as a "gateway" drug, that is, a pattern of progression in which a young person's use of a legal, or more easily attainable, drug precedes the use of illicit substances (e.g., Baily, 1992; Henningfield, Clayton, & Pollin, 1990; Kandel & Yamaguchi, 1993; Kandel, 2000). Some researchers have postulated that the effects of nicotine on the brain may predispose one to experimentation with other drugs; others have hypothesized that the behavioral patterns learned by youth who obtain tobacco products then translate into behaviors that facilitate experimentation with other drugs. Thus preventive efforts targeting tobacco use can help prevent the likelihood that an adolescent will go on to illicit substance use behavior.

Third, findings from some studies have indicated that programs aimed at preventing tobacco use may contribute to discouraging other substance use (e.g., Biglan, Ary, Smolkowski, Duncan, & Black, 2000; Flay, 1985; Johnson, Pentz, & Weber, 1992). Given that tobacco use can be viewed as one facet of a more global syndrome of adolescent problem behaviors (Biglan et al., 1990; Duncan, Duncan, Biglan, & Ary, 1998), and the evidence that smoking is frequently the first of these behaviors to emerge (Kandel, 2000), these studies strengthen the notion that effective tobacco use prevention programs can serve as models for preventing other substance use.

Relationship Between Smoking and Other Problem Behaviors

An enormous amount of research shows that smoking behavior is correlated with engagement in other problem behaviors, including all forms of substance use, antisocial behavior, and high-risk sexual behavior, as well as academic failure (e.g., Biglan & Smolkowski, 1999; Jessor, 1991; Arnett, 1992). Most of these studies correlate rates of engagement among behaviors, which makes it difficult to gauge the size of subgroups engaging in one, two, three, or more of the behaviors. Moreover, the correlational approach does not address "problemicity," or the degree to which youth engage in the behaviors at a level that could be considered problematic. For some behaviors, such as smoking, failure to address problemicity may not be a serious limitation, because any level of regular smoking puts a person at greater risk for disease. However, for a behavior such as alcohol use, which is normative among adolescents (Holder, 1998), it may be important to distinguish between levels of use that are predictive of concurrent health risks or later alcoholism and levels that are unlikely to lead to such problems.

Willard and Schoenborn (1995) present data on the co-occurrence of cigarette smoking and other behaviors from the 1992 National Health Interview Survey of Youth Risk Behavior (NHIS-YRBS). The survey is "a continuous, nationwide, household interview survey of the civilian noninstitutionalized population of the United States ..." conducted by the National Center for Health Statistics. There were 10,645 persons, aged 12 to 21 years, who were interviewed. Respondents reported the proportion of current smokers (one or more cigarettes in the last month) who engaged in each of a range of problem behaviors. Behaviors that significantly co-occurred with smoking are presented in Table 1. Smoking was not significantly related to cocaine use, owing to the unreliability of the reports for respondents who said they had never smoked. However, 3.5% of current smokers reported cocaine use, and only 0.2% of respondents in the Never Smoked category reported using cocaine.

TABLE 1

The Co-Occurrence of Smoking and Other Problem Behaviors

Problem Behavior	Currently smoking (SE)	Never smoked (SE)
Drank alcohol in past month	74.4% (1.11)	23.0% (1.02)
Five or more drinks in row	50.3% (1.22)	9.5% (.69)
Used marijuana in past month	26.5% (1.02)	1.5% (.025)
Used smokeless tobacco in past month (boys only)	28.1% (1.76)	4.1% (0.52)
Carried a weapon	25.6% (1.12)	9.5% (0.59)
Physical fight in past year	54.7% (1.09)	29.0% (0.86)
Ever had sexual intercourse	80.0% (0.99)	41.4% (1.40)

The comorbidity of cigarette smoking and major depressive disorder (MDD) among adolescents has received considerable attention in recent literature. Brown, Lewinsohn, Seeley, and Wagner (1996) report that adolescent smokers were more than twice as likely to exhibit a Major Depressive Disorder (Odds Ratio = 2.28). The finding that smoking is a risk for MDD in adolescents is consistent with adult findings by Breslau, Kilbey, and Andreski (1991), who found that nicotine dependence predicted episodes of MDD during their 14-month follow-up.

It is possible that the onset of smoking makes engagement in other problem behaviors more likely and the relationships among smoking and other problems have often been cited as another justification for efforts to prevent adolescent smoking. The evidence on this point is equivocal. Perhaps smoking changes adolescents in ways that make them more susceptible to the reinforcement of other substances. It also could be that the behavior of smoking is associated for the young smoker with rule violation so that initiation of smoking desensitizes the young person to other forms of rule violation. In any case, it is possible that preventing smoking could help to prevent other problem behaviors, but even if this is not the case, there is ample justification for major efforts to prevent tobacco use as a health promotion strategy.

PEER AND PARENT INFLUENCES ON YOUTH TOBACCO USE

The addictive nature of cigarettes and smokeless tobacco is now well established. The 1988 Surgeon General's report states the addictive quality of tobacco and identifies nicotine as the drug in tobacco that leads to addiction U.S. DHHS, 1988). However, nicotine addiction does not explain a person's choice to begin experimenting with tobacco; that choice must be motivated by other factors. While many factors may influence the onset of tobacco use in youth, two variables have emerged as most clearly influential: peer influences and parent influences.

Peer Influences on Tobacco Use

Peers are the single greatest influence on young people to begin using tobacco. The substantial evidence of peer influence on adolescent tobacco use is summarized in the 1994 Surgeon General's report (U.S. DHHS, 1994). Most tobacco use initiation is motivated by peers who also use tobacco, and most cigarette experimentation episodes occur in the presence of other adolescents who are smoking (Friedman, Lichtenstein, & Biglan, 1985; Bauman, Foshee, & Haley, 1991).

Longitudinal studies also point to the crucial influence of peer smoking. In one study, 60% of 11- to 17-year-olds reported that they had first smoked with close friends (Hahn et al., 1990). In their 1992 review of the recent prospective research in the field, Conrad, Flay, and Hill found that friends' smoking predicted some phase of adolescent smoking in 88% of the longitudinal studies reviewed.

As described above, all empirically validated school-based tobacco prevention programs contain components that target peer influences. However, trying to address those influences within the classroom setting has inherent limits. Students who are at highest risk to begin using tobacco may be frequently absent from school and may be less engaged in classroom activity than other students. Anti-tobacco messages will have more impact on high-risk youth when placed in the context of groups to which those youth already belong (Glynn, Anderson, & Schwarz, 1991), and those groups are likely to exist outside of the school environment.

In recent efforts, youth anti-tobacco activities taking place outside the classroom have shown promise (Biglan et al., 2000; Pentz et al., 1992). For example, adolescents have been involved in creative activities (such as designing anti-tobacco posters or T-shirts), planning activities (such as sponsoring an anti-tobacco dance, sports tournament, or other event), and policy activities (such as advocating for clean indoor air policies in the community). Identifying youth at highest risk to begin use, and finding ways to involve them in such activities, is key to the success of those activities in targeting peer influences on adolescent tobacco use.

Parent Influences on Tobacco Use

The influence of parents on a child's tobacco use initiation has been extensively studied, but most studies have focused on parental modeling of smoking behavior as a predictor of youth smoking. While evidence shows that parents who smoke are more likely to have children who take up the behavior (U.S. DHHS, 1994), this relationship often is modest and sometimes has not been found (Ary & Biglan, 1988). Bauman,

Foshee, Linzer, and Koch's (1990) study showed that youth smoking is more strongly related to whether a parent has ever smoked than to a parent's current smoking status, suggesting that parent influences on youth smoking behavior may be attributable to factors other than modeling. Positive or neutral parental attitudes toward tobacco use and easy youth access to cigarettes when parents are smokers are examples of such factors.

Even if parent tobacco use has a powerful influence on an adolescent's decision to begin using tobacco, the modeling process is contingent on the nature of the parent-child relationship (Andrews, Hops, & Duncan, 1997). High levels of family conflict contribute to the development of diverse youth problem behaviors, including tobacco use (Ary et al., 1999; Ary, Duncan, Duncan, & Hops, 1997; Patterson, Reid, & Dishion, 1992). When parental attempts to influence their children's behavior result in conflict, development of the necessary systems to ensure a positive growth process is threatened. Finding ways for parents to set and enforce effective rules about their children's association with peers who engage in problem behavior, to express their desire that their children decide to remain tobacco-free, and to communicate these concepts with minimal conflict appears to have compelling potential as a prevention strategy.

Other, more general, parenting practices also influence whether children initiate tobacco use. A growing body of evidence consistently identifies two ways in which parents can effectively prevent their children from drifting toward problem behaviors: by curtailing their association with deviant peers, and by making and enforcing rules about where and with whom children spend their free time (Ary et al., 1999; Ary et al., 1997; Irvine, Biglan, Smolkowski, Metzler, & Ary, 1999). Effective limit setting can contribute directly to preventing experimentation with tobacco and other problem behaviors.

WHAT CAN WE DO AND HOW CAN WE DO IT?

As discussed previously in this chapter, analysis of the social context within which young people decide whether to initiate tobacco use delineates schools, parents, peers, and the community as key components influencing that decision. Evidence clearly supports five strategies for tobacco prevention targeting these influences: (a) presenting a school-based prevention curriculum, (b) linking youth with cessation programs, (c) developing appropriate school policies, (d) involving parents in delivering prevention messages, and (e) community-wide programs. The school psychologist need not be a prevention expert to make a difference, but can serve as a resource to the school, an advocate for the importance of tobacco prevention and cessation, as well as a facilitator between school and community resources in tobacco control.

School-Based Curricula

School-based prevention programs are a crucial element in substance abuse prevention because most regular users of tobacco and other drugs have already initiated use before they leave high school. Schools provide a unique access to adolescents, and the prevention of smoking and other addictive behaviors fits well within the mission of schools' current health curriculum and community values for health promotion. Several studies have shown that school-based tobacco prevention programs that identify the social influences promoting tobacco use among youth and teach skills to resist such influences can significantly reduce or delay adolescent smoking (Lynch & Bonnie, 1994; CDC, 1994; Glynn, 1989). Programs that vary in format, scope, delivery methods, and community setting have produced differences in smoking prevalence between intervention and nonintervention groups ranging from 25% to 60% and persisting for 1 to 5 years after completion of the programs (Bruvold, 1990). Because many students begin using tobacco before high school and because impressions about tobacco use are formed even earlier, tobacco use prevention education must be provided in elementary school and continued through middle and high school grades (CDC, 1994).

Although long-term follow-ups of programs have indicated that the effect may dissipate over time (Murray, Pirie, Luepker, & Pallonen, 1989), other studies have shown that the effectiveness of school-based tobacco prevention programs can be significantly strengthened by booster sessions and community-wide programs involving parents and community organizations and including school policies, mass media, and restrictions on youth access (U.S. DHHS, 1994). Booster sessions refer to additional classroom interventions in subsequent years to support the training or instruction that occurred in the primary intervention. For example, if peer refusal skills were taught as an integral part of the seventh-grade intervention, booster sessions in the eighth and ninth grades would reinforce these skills and provide additional opportunity for behavioral rehearsal and peer feedback. Similarly, the additional measure of involving both parents and community organizations in tobacco prevention or getting students to become active in community antitobacco activities, such as working on tobacco-free workplace ordinances, can significantly enhance the modest effects of a classroom-only program.

The school-based tobacco prevention program forms the essential core element to successful prevention of teen tobacco use. School-based programs with as few as five lessons have been successful in delaying tobacco use onset, and daily program delivery appears superior to delivery separated by wider time spaces. However, providing all lessons from the program, even if presented over several weeks, is more important than daily presentation and much preferable to delivering only a part of the program (Sussman, Dent, Burton, Stacy, & Flay, 1995; Elder et al., 1993). Glynn (1989) identified eight essential elements of successful school-based tobacco prevention programs:

1. Classroom sessions should be delivered at least five times per year in each of 2 years in the sixth through eighth grades.

2. The program should emphasize the social factors that influence smoking onset, short-term consequences, and refusal skills.

3. The program should be incorporated into the existing school curricula.

4. The program should be introduced during the transition from elementary school to junior high or middle school (sixth or seventh grades).

5. Students should be involved in the presentation and delivery of the program.

6. Parental involvement should be encouraged.

7. Teachers should be adequately trained.

8. The program should be socially and culturally acceptable to each community.

In addition to the guidelines suggested by Glynn, the CDC Office on Smoking and Health has published *Guidelines for School Health Programs to Prevent Tobacco Use and Addiction* (CDC, 2000). These guidelines suggest specific tobacco-free policies for schools, cite specific evidence-based curricula, and describe recommended teacher training, procedures for parental involvement, and procedures for implementing cessation services.

One exemplary program that has demonstrated consistent impact is the LifeSkills Training program, developed by Botvin and colleagues (Botvin & Dusenbury, 1989). LifeSkills consists of 15–20 sessions for seventh-grade students and booster sessions in the eighth and ninth grades. The specific objectives of the program are to teach skills that help students resist direct pressures to smoke; to enhance students' self-esteem, self-mastery, and self-confidence in order to decrease their susceptibility to indirect social pressures to smoke; to prepare students to cope with anxiety induced by social situations; to enhance students' knowledge of the actual prevalence of smoking among adolescents and adults; and to promote attitudes and beliefs consistent with nonsmoking.

This program has been evaluated extensively in progressively larger studies with encouraging results that have ranged from 40% to 80% reductions in smoking prevalence and with long-term effects lasting up to four years (Botvin & Dusenbury, 1989). In the most comprehensive evaluation of the LifeSkills Training program to date, 56 schools in three different geographic regions were randomly assigned to three study conditions: LifeSkills plus one-day teacher training, LifeSkills plus video training for teachers, and a control condition. Significant positive effects were reported for cigarette use and for smoking-related knowledge, attitudes, and normative expectations. In most cases, the two treatment conditions had similar results: students in both groups demonstrated more positive effects than students in the control group (Botvin et al., 1990). The effects of the LifeSkills Training program have been demonstrated regardless of whether the program is delivered by project staff, older peers, or regular classroom teachers (Botvin, Baker, Dusenbury, Botvin, & Diaz, 1995).

Another program with credible evidence of sustained impact on youth smoking rates, and identified by the CDC as a program that works, is Project Towards No Tobacco Use (Project TNT; Dent et al., 1995). The TNT program, which is described in detail in *Developing School-Based Tobacco Use Prevention and Cessation Programs*

(Sussman et al., 1995) focuses on activities that attempt to alter the social influences thought to impact adolescent smoking. They identify "normative social influence," where a group wants its members to act in ways consistent with the group, and "informational influence," where social groups provide information to socialize others. An example of normative influence is when children accept offers of cigarettes or chew to gain acceptance in a group. Teaching children to identify social pressure to smoke and learn refusal skills would be important elements in reducing negative influences. Informational influences can be translated into prevention activities by identifying social images to which students aspire, such as independence, maturity, and gregariousness, and counter the advertising used to create these images of smokers.

Sussman and colleagues at USC have conducted a number of longitudinal studies and have reported positive preventive effects for this curriculum program (Sussman et al., 1993; Sussman et al., 1995). These programs generally have targeted seventh-grade students and involve 10 class periods to fully present the intervention.

The school psychologist can support school-based tobacco prevention programs by identifying efficacious school-based prevention programs that have been empirically validated and are being promoted by the National Cancer Institute and CDC Office on Smoking and Health. The publication by the CDC of *The Best Practices for Comprehensive Tobacco Control Programs* (CDC, 1999) is a good source of information on proven school-based intervention programs.

Cessation Programs

Any comprehensive program to reduce tobacco use must include assistance in quitting, as many young people are already dependent on cigarettes or moist snuff at the time they come in contact with the program. Unfortunately, school-based programs to help adolescent smokers and chewers quit have shown limited effectiveness. Few studies have been conducted on adolescent cessation of tobacco use, and those vary considerably in scientific quality, with many being anecdotal. There is encouragement, however, from several sources. First, national probability samples indicate that adolescents express an interest in quitting and have made attempts to quit (CDC, 1998). Second, studies of prevention of tobacco use report treatment effects on youth who were smoking at baseline (Sussman et al., 1995). Third, programs that try explicitly to recruit adolescent smokers and chewers into cessation programs report positive response to the offer of a program in school (Sussman, 2001).

One model program of a school-based cessation study recruited students to attend four sessions on immediate physiological effects of smoking (e.g., high levels of carbon monoxide in their expired air after smoking just a couple of puffs on a cigarette) and social cues that influence adoption of the smoking habit. The program was implemented in 10th-grade health classes in three California high schools (n = 477) and resulted in a significantly greater percentage of subjects reporting abstinence than in the control group (Perry, Killen, Telch, Slinkard, & Danaher, 1980).

Adolescents may be reluctant to participate in multisession quit programs for several reasons. Young smokers may worry that teachers or parents will learn that they smoke (since parental permission is required for participation), and long-term health consequences such as cancer may not be salient to young people who are healthy. As schools have gone "tobacco free," many students get referred for disciplinary action when they are caught smoking on school property. While cessation rates among students attending mandatory cessation meetings owing to rule infractions could be expected to be low, these programs can have some success in helping smokers quit if they are well organized and structured to promote cessation (Lynch & Bonnie, 1994).

One program that shows promise is a "diversion" program in which students caught using tobacco on campus are required to attend multiple sessions of an educational exercise developed by the American Lung Association. While a nonvoluntary program may result in low rates of cessation, such as the 14% in the evaluation trial (CDC, 1994), a diversion program provides school administrators with a way to deal with violation of school tobacco use policies and promotes enforcement of those rules while supporting teen cessation. A structured curriculum for high-risk youth shows promise and could be used in conjunction with student referral to a diversion program (Sussman et al., 1995).

The National Cancer Institute has recently funded several randomized clinical trials to test innovative strategies to encourage cessation of tobacco use among teens, but the results of these trials are not yet known. Recent programs that use interactive computer-based cessation in a game-like format show promise in helping adolescent smokers and chewers quit (Fisher, Severson, Christiansen, & Williams, 2001).

The school psychologist can become involved in setting up diversion or cessation programs for students already using tobacco on high school or middle school campuses. School administrators and teachers are more likely to enforce tobacco-free policies or act in response to violations of rules when they believe that the consequences for violating these rules are consistent and appropriate and that a reasonable diversion or treatment program is in place to assist users in quitting. Even if users do not quit smoking or chewing immediately, their attendance and participation in an after-school diversion program may move them toward quitting by educating them about the risks of using tobacco and benefits of quitting.

School Policy

Outside of the home, the school constitutes an adolescent's principal environment. The school environment prescribes social norms—directly or indirectly—via policy, teacher expectations and behavior, and peer group action. Schools have the opportunity to promote tobacco-free norms, counter pro-tobacco messages, and provide an environment that supports healthy choices.

Pentz et al. (1989) examined the impact of school smoking policies on more than 4,000 adolescents in 23 schools in California. The schools' written smoking policies were evaluated on whether they banned smoking on school grounds, restricted students leaving school grounds, banned smoking near school, and mandated tobacco prevention education. Schools with policies in all these areas, and which also emphasized prevention and cessation, had significantly lower smoking rates than schools with fewer policies.

Elder et al., (1993) reported that, in their evaluation of 96 schools in four states, implementation and enforcement of school policies appear crucial to school-based interventions, and must be tailored to political and regional factors affecting a specific school district.

Schools can create powerful environments for promoting nonsmoking norms, and school policy development is recommended as an integral part of a tobacco prevention program (Glynn, 1993).

Involvement of Parents

Another element of reducing tobacco use is the involvement of parents, since parental smoking and attitudes toward tobacco use have been shown to be related to a teen's use of tobacco (U.S. DHHS, 1994). The school psychologist could help motivate parents to become involved in the school's efforts toward youth tobacco prevention.

Biglan et al. (1996) found that school-prompted parent-child interactions about tobacco use could influence adolescents' perceptions that their parents do not want them to use tobacco. Middle school students took quizzes about tobacco use home to their parents as homework assignments. The students were instructed to ask their parents the questions on the quiz, and give immediate feedback as to the correct answers. Students then brought the quizzes back to school, signed by the parents to indicate that they had completed the quiz in exchange for a small incentive (i.e., a granola bar, candy, or a coupon). In some cases, students returning the assignments also were entered into a competition for a larger incentive (i.e., a class party for the classroom with the highest return rate). This activity increased both youth and parental knowledge about the harmful effects of tobacco use and induced more attitudes that were negative toward tobacco use. These findings suggest that parents can be encouraged to communicate with their children that they do not want them to use tobacco and to set limits on activities that would put their children at risk to experiment with tobacco.

The school psychologist can aid in getting parents involved in prevention. Most parents, even parents who smoke, would say that they do not want their children to become addicted to tobacco. Presentations to parents that focus on how to talk to their children about tobacco and drug use can be facilitated by the school psychologist. Student take-home assignments can be used to encourage students to engage their parents in discussions about rules and consequences for tobacco use. We are currently developing videotapes that will be used as part of homework assignments for sixth-graders, in which students are asked to watch the video with their parents, discuss and problem-solve issues presented on the video, and complete brief homework assignments signed by the parent. The prime objective is to promote parent-child communication around rules, expectations, and consequences related to the child's use of tobacco.

Community Programs

Community-based strategies to prevent youth tobacco use are now recognized as important adjuncts to school-based and educational programs (U.S. DHHS, 1994). A youth's social environment may contain strong prompts to initiate tobacco use behavior, such as industry marketing ploys or the presence of adult role models who smoke. Thus, the mobilization of facets of that social environment—i.e., parents, the media, policy makers, the religious community, social services, and business leaders—can enhance the effects of concerted prevention efforts.

The Centers for Disease Control and Prevention has identified four best practices for community programs aimed at tobacco prevention: (1) building community coalitions that maximize the number of organizations and individuals who plan and conduct community-level education programs; (2) counter-marketing campaigns that support local tobacco control initiatives and policies with pro-health messages; (3) promoting the adoption of public and private tobacco control policies; and (4) measuring outcomes using validated evaluative tools (CDC, 1999). These practices can work to change community norms, thus changing the perceived acceptability of tobacco use for a community's young people.

An example of practices aimed at changing community norms about youth tobacco use can be found in efforts to reduce illegal sales of tobacco to minors. Biglan et al., (1995, 1996) developed a program that rewarded clerks for not selling tobacco products to underage youth, and reminding them of the law when they were willing to sell (Reward and Reminder). This program was found to significantly reduce levels of illegal tobacco sales. In addition to clerk rewards and reminders, the program includes three other components: (a) obtaining endorsement and support from community leaders, (b) generating media coverage for the campaign, and (c) providing feedback to merchants about their rates of sales to minors. After completing the study, these researchers launched wide-scale efforts to disseminate the program around the state of Oregon (Biglan & James, in preparation). The results of the research were successfully replicated in 11 Oregon counties. Undertaking the Reward and Reminder campaign in a community can provide a vehicle for involving youth and the community in tobacco prevention efforts.

As school psychologists we can aid a community-level program in several ways. First, we can become involved in a local tobacco-free coalition, or provide a link between the school and a community coalition. Second, we can help parents to form a local network that would support parenting skills education, community norms about monitoring and behavioral programs for parents and children, and social support for parents. Third, we can offer support to local initiatives for policy change—for example, helping to identify a student group willing to participate in the Reward and Reminder program, or to advocate for smoke-free environments in the community.

TRAINING IMPLICATIONS

The current training of pre-service school psychologists may be inadequate in the area of promoting prevention of tobacco and drug use in the schools. We would suggest that a course covering preventive models and how prevention programs can be implemented would be a useful component of professional training when combined with the consultation and intervention skills that are already part of a school psychologist's repertoire.

A clear training need for school psychologists to become effective proponents of substance use prevention is to incorporate what we call the "public health perspective." This perspective involves the understanding and acceptance of the primary role of prevention in the amelioration of problems. Most psychologists have lots of practice promoting and setting up interventions for students already identified as having a problem, but a prevention approach couples a psychologist's experience and practical knowledge about the process of early screening and problem identification with advocating for preventive programs in the schools. A brief course in prevention might cover the behavioral epidemiology of problems most likely to confront psychologists in the schools, preventive interventions that have been tried, and their relative levels of success.

For school psychologists in practice there are many research-based and public health workshops and in-service training opportunities available in tobacco and other substance use prevention. One good example is the Tobacco Use Prevention Training Institute run by the Center for Health Promotion and Disease Prevention at the University of North Carolina. This institute is sponsored in large measure by the Centers for Disease Control (CDC) Office on Smoking and Health in Atlanta, Georgia. The institute's annual weeklong series of workshops provides in-depth practical training in prevention and cessation of tobacco use among youth through both school and community interventions. Other examples of training opportunities include the annual meetings of the Society for Prevention Research (SPR) and the American Public Health Association (APHA), and conferences hosted by state-level alcohol, tobacco, and other drug prevention and treatment groups.

Prevention is not easy work. In many ways it can be frustrating, because it involves coordinating more people and components than does the "diagnose and remediate" model. Screening, as well as intervention, must be done in the context of general education. Working to educate teachers about student behaviors to look for, and developing cost-effective ways to screen for problem behaviors, may put school psychologists in an uncomfortable or unfamiliar position. On the other hand, prevention helps put the school psychologist in the mainstream of education and promotes participation in the education process. Although this change may constitute new territory, it also can be quite rewarding and can visibly broaden the impact of our work. Changing perspective to encompass prevention is not intended to replace those activities that require our skills in working with problems that require assessment and treatment; it provides a valuable adjunct to those efforts. Training in prevention, screening, early classroom intervention, and linkage to community programs can promote our participation in all levels of school programming and, in the end, ensure a broader context for our role.

REFERENCES

Andrews, J. A., Hops, H., & Duncan, S. C. (1997). Adolescent modeling of parent substance use: The moderating effect of the relationship with the parent. *Journal of Family Psychology, 11,* 259-270.

Arnett, J. (1992). Reckless behaviour in adolescence: A developmental perspective. *Developmental Review, 12,* 339-373.

Ary, D. V., & Biglan, A. (1988). Longitudinal changes in adolescent cigarette smoking behavior: Onset and cessation. *Journal of Behavioral Medicine, 11,* 361-382.

Ary, D. V., Duncan, T. E., Biglan, A., Metzler, C. W., Noell, J. W., & Smolkowski, K. (1999). Development of adolescent problem behavior. *Journal of Abnormal Child Psychology, 27*(2), 141-150.

Ary, D. V., Duncan, T. E., Duncan, S. C., & Hops, H. (1997). Adolescent problem behavior: The influence of parents and peers. *Behaviour Research and Therapy, 37,* 217-230.

Baily, S. L. (1992). Adolescents' multi-substance use patterns: The role of heavy alcohol and cigarette use. *American Journal of Public Health, 82,* 1220-1224.

Bauman, K. E., Foshee, V. A., & Haley, N. J. (1991). *The interaction of sociological and biological factors in the onset of cigarette smoking.* Chapel Hill, NC: University of North Carolina Press.

Bauman, K. E., Foshee, V. A., Linzer, M. A., & Koch, G. G. (1990). Effect of parental smoking classification on the association between parental and adolescent smoking. *Addictive Behaviors, 15*(5), 413-422.

Biglan, A. (1995). *Changing cultural practices: A contextualist framework for intervention research.* Reno, NV: Context Press.

Biglan, A., Ary, D. V., Koehn, V., Levings, D., Smith, S., Wright, Z., James, L., & Henderson, J. (1996). Mobilizing positive reinforcement in communities to reduce youth access to tobacco. *American Journal of Community Psychology, 24*(5), 625-638.

Biglan, A., Ary, D. V., Smolkowski, K., Duncan, T., & Black, C. (2000). A randomized controlled trial of a community intervention to prevent adolescent tobacco use. *Tobacco Control, 9,* 24-32.

Biglan, A., Henderson, J., Humphreys, D., Yasui, M., Whisman, R., Black, C., & James, L. (1995). Mobilizing positive reinforcement to reduce youth access to tobacco. *Tobacco Control, 4,* 42-48.

Biglan, A., & James, L. (in preparation). Assessment of the effectiveness of a positive reinforcement approach to reducing illegal sales of tobacco to young people.

Biglan, A., Metzler, C. A., Wirt, R., Ary, D., Noell, J., Ochs, L., French, C., & Hood, D. (1990). Social and behavioral factors associated with high-risk sexual behavior among adolescents. *Journal of Behavioral Medicine, 13*(3), 245-261.

Biglan, A., & Smolkowski, K. (1999). Critical influences on the development of adolescent problem behavior. In D. B. Kandel (Ed.)., *Stages and pathways of drug involvement: Examining the gateway hypothesis.* Los Angeles: UCLA Youth Enhancement Service.

Botvin, G. J., Baker, E., Dusenbury, L., Botvin, E. M., Diaz, T. (1995). Long-term follow-up results of a randomized drug abuse prevention trial in a white middle-class population. *Journal of the American Medical Association (JAMA), 273*(14), 1106-1112.

Botvin, G. J., Baker, E., Filazzola, A. D., & Botvin, E. M. (1990). A cognitive-behavioral approach to substance abuse prevention: One-year follow-up. *Addictive Behaviors, 15,* 47-63.

Botvin, G. J., & Dusenbury, L. (1989). Primary prevention and promotion in the schools. In L. A. Bond & Compas, B. E. (Ed), *Primary prevention of psychopathology, Vol. 12* (pp. 146-178). Thousand Oaks, CA: Sage.

Brener, N. D., & Collins, J. L. (1998). Co-occurrence of health-risk behaviors among adolescents in the United States. *Journal of Adolescent Health, 22,* 209-213.

Breslau, N., Kilbey, M., & Andreski, P. (1991). Nicotine dependence, major depression, and anxiety in young adults. *Archives of General Psychiatry, 48,* 1069-1074.

Brown, R. A., Lewinsohn, P. M., Seeley, J. R., & Wagner, E. F. (1996). Cigarette smoking, major depression, and other psychiatric disorders among adolescents. *Journal of the American Academy of Child and Adolescent Psychiatry, 35*(12), 1602-1610.

Bruvold, W. H. (1990). A meta-analysis of the California school-based risk reduction program. *Journal of Drug Education, 20*(2), 139-152.

Bry, B. H., McKeon, P., & Padina, R. J. (1982). Extent of drug use as a function of number of risk factors. *Journal of Abnormal Psychology, 91,* 237-279.

Centers for Disease Control and Prevention (CDC). (1994). *Preventing tobacco use among young people: A report of the Surgeon General* (pp. 209-292). Washington, DC: U.S. Department of Health and Human Services. Available Internet: *www.cdc.gov/tobacco/sgryth2.htm.*

Centers for Disease Control and Prevention (CDC). (1998). Tobacco use continues to rise among U.S. high school students. *Public Health Reports, 113*(July/August), 300.

Centers for Disease Control and Prevention (CDC). (1999). *Best practices for comprehensive tobacco control programs—August 1999.* Atlanta, GA: U.S. Department of Health and Human Services, Centers for Disease Control and Prevention, National Center for Chronic Disease Prevention and Health Promotion, Office on Smoking and Health.

Centers for Disease Control and Prevention (CDC). (2000). CDC Surveillance Summaries. *MMWR 2000;* 49(No. SS-5).

Clark, D. B., Pollock, N., Bromberger, J. T., Bukstein, O. G., Mezzick, A. C., Bromberger, J. T., & Donovan, J. E. (1997). Gender and co-morbid psychopathology in adolescents with alcohol dependence. *Journal of the American Academy of Child and Adolescent Psychiatry, 36*(9), 1195-1203.

Conrad, K. M., Flay, B. R., & Hill, D. (1992). Why children start smoking cigarettes: Predictors of onset. *British Journal of Addiction, 87*(12), 1711-1724.

Dent, C. W., Sussman, S., Stacy, A. W., Craig, S., Burton, D., & Flay, B. R. (1995). Two-year behavior outcomes of Project Towards No Tobacco Use. *Journal of Consulting and Clinical Psychology, 63,* 676-677.

Donovan, J. E., & Jessor, R. (1978). Adolescent problem drinking: Psychosocial correlates in a national sample study. *Journal of Studies on Alcohol, 39,* 1506-1524.

Duncan, S. C., Duncan, T. E., Biglan, A., Ary, D. (1998). Contributions of the social context to the development of adolescent substance use: A multivariate latent growth modeling approach. *Drug and Alcohol Dependence, 50*(1), 57-71.

Elder, J. P., Wildey, M., deMoor, C., Sallis, J. F., Eckhardt, L., Edwards, C., Erickson, A., Golbeck, A., Hovell, M., Johnston, D., Levitz, M. D., Molgaard, C., Young, R., Vito, D., & Woodruff, S. I. (1993). The long-term prevention of tobacco use among junior high school students: Classroom and telephone interventions. *American Journal of Public Health, 83*(9), 1239-1244.

Fisher, K. J., Severson, H. H., Christiansen, S. J., & Williams, C. (2001). *Using interactive technology to aid smokeless tobacco cessation: A pilot study. American Journal of Health Education,* in press.

Flay, B. R. (1985). Psychosocial approaches to smoking prevention: A review of findings. *Health Psychology, 4*(5), 449-488.

Friedman, L. S., Lichtenstein, E., & Biglan, A. (1985). Smoking onset among teens: An empirical analysis of initial situations. *Addictive Behaviors, 10,* 1-13.

Glynn, T. J., (1989). Essential elements of school-based smoking prevention programs. *Journal of School Health, 59*(5), 181-188.

Glynn, T. J. (1993). Improving the health of U.S. children: The need for early interventions in tobacco use. *Preventive Medicine, 22,* 513-519.

Glynn, T. J., Anderson, D. M., & Schwarz, L. (1991). Tobacco-use reduction among high-risk youth: Recommendations of a National Cancer Institute Expert Advisory Panel. *Preventive Medicine, 20*(2), 279-291.

Grant, B. F., & Dawson, D. A. (1997). Age of onset of alcohol use and its association with DSM-IV alcohol abuse and dependence: Results from the National Longitudinal Alcohol Epidemiologic Survey. *Journal of Substance Abuse, 9,* 103-110.

Hahn, G., Charlin, V. L., Sussman, S. Y., Dent, C. W., Manzi, J., Stacy, A. W., Flay, B., Hansen, W. B., & Burton, D. (1990). Adolescents' first and most recent use situations of smokeless tobacco and cigarettes: Similarities and differences. *Addictive Behaviors, 15,* 439-448.

Henningfield, J. E., Clayton, R., & Pollin, W. (1990). Involvement of tobacco in alcoholism and illicit drug use. *British Journal of Addiction, 85,* 279-292.

Holder, H. (1998). *Alcohol and the community: A systems approach to prevention.* Cambridge, United Kingdom: Cambridge University Press.

Hundleby, J. D., Carpenter, R. A., Ross, R. A., & Mercer, G. W. (1982). Adolescent drug use and other behaviors. *Journal of Child Psychology and Psychiatry, 23,* 61-68.

Irvine, A. B., Biglan, A., Smolkowski, K., Metzler, C. W., & Ary, D. V. (1999). The effectiveness of a parenting skills program for parents of middle school students in small communities. *Journal of Consulting and Clinical Psychology, 67*(6), 811-825.

Jessor, R. (1991). Risk behavior in adolescence: A psychosocial framework for understanding and action. *Journal of Adolescent Health, 12*(8), 597-605.

Johnson, C. A., Pentz., M. A., & Weber, M. D. (1992). Relative effectiveness of comprehensive community programming for drug abuse prevention with high risk and low risk adolescents. *Journal of Consulting and Clinical Psychology, 58,* 447-456.

Johnston, L., O'Malley, P., & Bachmann, J. (1995). *Drug use among American high school seniors, college students, and young adults, 1975-1995.* Rockville, MD: National Institute on Drug Abuse. (DHSS publication No. ADM91-1813.)

Kandel, D. B. (2000). Examining the gateway hypothesis: Stages and pathways of drug involvement. In D. B. Kandel (Ed.), *Examining the Gateway Hypothesis.* New York: Cambridge University Press.

Kandel, D. B., & Yamaguchi, R. (1993). From beer to crack: Developmental patterns of drug involvement. *American Journal of Public Health, 83,* 851-855.

Kearney, A. L., & Hines, M. H. (1980). Evaluation of the effectiveness of a drug prevention education program. *Journal of Drug Education, 10,* 127-134.

Kim, S. (1988). A short- and long-term evaluation of "Here's Looking at You" alcohol education program. *Journal of Drug Education, 18*(3), 235-242.

Kolbe, L. J., Kann, L. & Collins, J. L. (1993). Overview of the Youth Risk Behavior Surveillance System. *Public Health Reports, 108* (Suppl. 1), 2-10.

Lynch, B. S., & Bonnie, R. J. (Eds.). (1994). *Growing up tobacco free: Preventing nicotine addiction in children and youth.* Washington, DC: Institute of Medicine.

Miller-Johnson, S., Lochman, J. E., Cole, J. D., Terry, R., & Hyman, C. (1998). Co-morbidity of conduct and depressive problems at sixth grade: Substance use outcomes across adolescence. *Journal of Abnormal Child Psychology, 26*(3), 221-232.

Murray, D. M., Pirie, P. Luepker, R.V., & Pallonen, U. (1989). Five- and six-year follow-up results from four seventh-grade smoking prevention strategies. *Journal of Behavioral Medicine, 12*(2), 207-218.

Newcomb, M. D., Maddahian, E., & Bentler, P. M. (1986). Risk factors for drug use among adolescents: Concurrent and longitudinal analyses. *American Journal of Public Health, 76,* 525-531.

Patterson, G. R., Reid, J. B., & Dishion, T. J. (1992). *Antisocial boys: A social interactional approach, Volume 4.* Eugene, OR: Castalia.

Pentz, M. A., Dwyer, J. H., MacKinnon, D. P., Flay, B. R., Hansen, W. B., Wang, E., & Johnson, C. A. (1989). A multicommunity trial for primary prevention of adolescent drug abuse. *Journal of American Medical Association, 261,* 3259-3266.

Pentz, M. A., Johnson, C. A., Dwyer, J. H., MacKinnon, D. M., Hansen, W. B., & Flay, B. R. (1992). A comprehensive community approach to adolescent drug abuse prevention: Effects on cardiovascular disease risk behaviors. *Annals of Medicine, 21,* 219-222.

Perry, C. L., Killen, J. D., Telch, M. J., Slinkard, L. A., & Danaher, B. G. (1980). Modifying smoking behavior of teenagers: A school-based intervention. *American Journal of Public Health, 70,* 722-725.

Robins, L. N., & Przybeck, T. R. (1985). Age of onset of drug use as a factor in drug and other disorders. In C. I. Jones & R. J. Battjes (Eds.), *Etiology of drug abuse: Implications for prevention* (pp. 178-192). Rockville, MD: National Institute on Drug Abuse.

Rooney, B. L., & Murray, D. M. (1996). A meta-analysis of smoking prevention programs after adjustment for errors in the unit of analysis. *Health Education Quarterly, 23*(1), 48-64.

Severson, H. H. (1984). Adolescent social drug use: School prevention programs. *School Psychology Review, 13*(2), 150-160.

Sussman, S. (2001). School-based tobacco use prevention and cessation: Where are we going? *American Journal of Health Behavior, 25*(3), 191-199.

Sussman, S. Dent, C. W. Burton, D., Stacy, A. W., & Flay, B. R. (1995). *Developing school-based tobacco use prevention and cessation programs.* Thousand Oaks, CA: Sage.

Sussman, S. Y., Dent, C. W., Simon, T. R., Stacy, A. W., Burton, D., & Flay, B. R. (1993). Identification of which high-risk youth smoke cigarettes regularly. *Health Values, 17,* 42-53.

Swisher, J. D., Crawford, J. L., Goldstein, R., & Yura, M. (1971). Drug Education: Pushing or preventing? *Peabody Journal of Education, 49,* 68-75.

U.S. Department of Health and Human Services (DHHS). (1988). *The health consequences of smoking: Nicotine addiction: A report of the Surgeon General.* Washington, DC: U.S. Department of Health and Human Services (publication no. CDC88-8406).

U.S. Department of Health and Human Services (DHHS). (1994). *Preventing tobacco use among young people: A report of the Surgeon General.* Atlanta, GA: U.S. Department of Health and Human Services, Public Health Service, Centers for Disease Control and Prevention, National Center for Chronic Disease Prevention and Health Promotion, Office on Smoking and Health.

Willard, J. C., & Schoenborn, C. A. (1995). Relationship between cigarette smoking and other unhealthy behaviors among our nation's youth: United States, 1992. *Advance Data,* Number 263. National Center for Health Statistics.

CHAPTER 26

Remedial Interventions for Students
With Reading Decoding Problems

Paul T. Sindelar and Holly B. Lane
University of Florida

Paige C. Pullen
University of Virginia

Roxanne F. Hudson
University of Florida

INTRODUCTION

A decade ago, when the first edition of this text appeared, it included two chapters on reading, one focused on classroom instruction and the second on remediation. In the former, Grossen and Carnine (1991) covered decoding and comprehension instruction, with greater emphasis on comprehension, as befits a chapter on classroom instruction. In the latter, Sindelar and Stoddard (1991) discussed fluency, vocabulary, and comprehension strategies. Thus, coverage of decoding was limited, and neither chapter alluded to skills that are prerequisites for decoding. Of course, these prerequisite skills phonological awareness, print awareness, and the alphabetic principle—were to become preeminent in remedial reading research in the 1990s, as phonological awareness training became the most thoroughly investigated remedial intervention. As a result, this chapter on remediation will bear little resemblance to the one that preceded it.

We begin with a review of research on phonological awareness. We discuss what it is, how it develops, and what teachers can do to promote it. We go on to discuss the alphabetic principle and decoding, including what teachers can do to promote young children's understanding of the relationship between letters and sounds. We conclude this chapter with a brief consideration of strategies for developing fluent reading of narrative text, with particular attention to the method of repeated readings. It is our purpose to provide sufficient background for practitioners to understand the rationale for the interventions we describe and enough detail to create a sense of how to implement them in the classroom. In an appendix, we also list commercially available materials designed to develop phonological awareness, understanding of the alphabetic principle, and/or reading fluency.

PHONOLOGICAL AWARENESS AND DECODING

Phonological awareness is the conscious awareness of the sound structure of language. It includes the ability to detect, manipulate, and think about the various sound units in spoken language (e.g., syllables, phonemes) separate from meaning. Phonological awareness has received enormous attention in the research literature during the past two decades. Because as many as 90% of children and adults with serious reading problems display a core deficit in phonological processing (Blachman, 1994), the attention is warranted. To illustrate how phonological awareness contributes to skilled reading, we begin this section by presenting a model of the reading process.

Adams (1990) proposed that skilled reading is a product of the orchestration of four distinct, but linked processors: (a) the phonological processor, (b) the orthographic processor, (c) the context processor, and (d) the meaning processor. The meaning processor is central to the model, just as obtaining meaning from print is the central purpose of reading. Through the context processor, the reader accesses prior knowledge and the context of the reading material to construct an ongoing, coherent understanding of the text. None of this is possible, however, if the reader is unable to read the words on the page. Because humans have a limited capacity for sight word memory, the ability to access the meaning of text by decoding the words is essential.

According to Adams' model, as a skilled reader notices a word on a page, that word is perceived through both orthographic and phonological processing channels. While the orthographic processor takes in the visual or graphic information on the page, it simultaneously excites the phonological processor, which produces a subvocalization of the sounds in the word. The phonological processor, which gets auditory information from speech, works with the orthographic processor to decode the word. Only through this connection between the orthographic and phonological processors can decoding— and, therefore, skilled reading—occur.

Findings From the Phonological Awareness Research

The value of phonological awareness as a predictor of later reading success or failure has been demonstrated repeatedly (e.g., Alegria & Morais, 1991; Blachman, 1984, 1989, 1994; Catts, 1989, 1991; Ehri, 1979; Lenchner, Gerber, & Routh, 1990; Lundberg, Olofsson, & Wall, 1980; Mann, 1991a, 1991b; Perfetti, 1991; Perfetti, Beck, Bell, & Hughes, 1987; Stanovich, 1992). That is, children who have strong phonological awareness typically become strong readers, and children who have weak phonological awareness typically become poor readers.

Unlike other reliable predictors of later reading success or failure (e.g., socioeconomic status, mother's level of education), phonological awareness improves with instruction (Blachman, 1994; Busink, 1997; Lundberg, Frost, & Petersen, 1988; O'Connor, Jenkins, Leicester, & Slocum, 1993; Pratt & Brady, 1988; Stanovich, 1992). Moreover, increases in phonological awareness can and usually do result in improved reading outcomes (Adams, Foorman, Lundberg, & Beeler, 1998; Cornwall, 1992;

Elkonin, 1963; Griffith & Olson, 1992; Torgesen, Morgan, & Davis, 1992; Torgesen, Wagner, & Rashotte, 1994; Uhry & Shepherd, 1997). Although most children acquire adequate phonological awareness without explicit instruction, researchers have consistently demonstrated the importance of explicit instruction for children who fail to develop it well on their own (Lane, 1994; Lundberg et al., 1988; Torgesen et al., 1992; Torgesen et al., 1994).

Development of Phonological Awareness

Adams (1990) emphasized the importance of early reading and language experiences to the development of phonological awareness and reading skill. She argued that many children come to school at a significant disadvantage owing to severely limited early experiences with print. The development of phonological awareness requires experience with language activities, many of them informal and game-like, that promote linguistic awareness. Many children develop some level of phonological awareness through frequent engagement in spoken language and language play with caregivers.

Phonological awareness comprises at least four developmental levels: word, syllable, onset/rime, and phoneme (see Figure 1, on page 706). Very young children exhibit a developing awareness of the sounds in language as they attempt to form their own words. This can be considered the *word* level of phonological awareness. By the time most children are 3 years old, they are able to notice the "beat" of spoken language and to clap or march to the parts of multisyllable words—*syllable* awareness. As children get a little older, they develop a curiosity about language and become interested in language games that manipulate the sounds in words, particularly rhyming games. Children who are able to identify, match, and generate rhyming words have developed *onset/rime* awareness. The onset is the part of a syllable that precedes the vowel, and the rime includes the vowel and any sounds that follow the vowel (i.e., the rime is the part of a syllable that rhymes). For example, the /s/ in *sat* is the onset, and the /at/ in *sat* is the rime. This intrasyllabic level of phonological awareness is important for assessment and instruction.

The most sophisticated level of phonological awareness is the *phoneme* level, which includes the abilities to detect, match, and blend phonemes, the smallest units of sound in language, and segment words and syllables into phonemes. By the end of kindergarten, most children who will go on to become skilled readers have the capacity to perform each of these tasks with some success. Children who are unable to segment and blend sounds have difficulty with phonics instruction, which teaches children the correspondences between sounds and letters. Success in phonics instruction and, ultimately, success in independent decoding require the ability to segment and blend the sounds of letters. The terms *phonological awareness* and *phonemic awareness* are frequently—and incorrectly—used interchangeably. The term phonemic awareness refers simply to the phoneme level of phonological awareness.

For children who have not developed sufficient levels of phonological awareness to experience early success in reading, explicit instruction in phonological skills is necessary. In describing the relationship between phonological deficits and difficulties with

FIGURE 1

Developmental Levels of Phonological Awareness

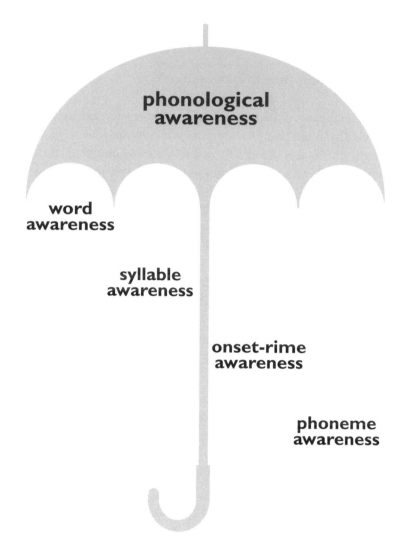

Note
From "Preventing reading failure: Phonological awareness assessment and instruction," by H. B. Lane, P. C. Pullen, M. R. Eisele, and L. Jordan, (2002). *Preventing School Failure, 46*(2). Reprinted with the author's permission of the Helen Dwight Reid Educational Foundation. Published by Heldref Publications, 1319 18th Street, Washington, DC 20036-1802.

decoding, Shankweiler (1989) explained that poor readers cannot successfully analyze orthographic information through phonological channels to access the meaning in text. A lack of phonological awareness can prevent a reader from decoding, thus limiting access to meaning. Therefore, according to Shankweiler, phonological awareness is linked to reading comprehension through its effect on decoding ability. The following sections provide an overview of classroom activities that promote children's development of phonological awareness at each level.

Instructional Activities That Promote the Development of Phonological Awareness

The activities we describe are useful for practicing and developing phonological skills. The tasks are sequenced by level, in an order that approximates the developmental sequence. However, it should be noted that the sequence and rate of skill development varies from child to child, and skills overlap during development. It should also be noted that these instructional tasks are *auditory* and *interactive* in nature. Each activity requires the teacher and students to be engaged in interactive oral communication, because children do not develop phonological skills by doing indepen-dent written work.

Word-Level Activities

The awareness that speech flow is a compilation of individual words is typically achieved at a very young age. For example, although a young child may have heard the word "bottle" used only in the context of spoken language (e.g., "I'll get your bottle for you" or "Oops, you dropped your bottle on the floor!"), eventually he or she will utter the word (or some approximation of the word) in isolation. This utterance demonstrates that the child has segmented an individual word from the speech flow. The linguistic play of young children, including rhyming and the generation of nonsense words, provides additional evidence of this early awareness (Bradley, 1988).

Word-level activities are designed to increase the student's sensitivity to individual words within the speech flow. This level of activity is most appropriate for children in preschool and kindergarten, although older children with severe language deficits also may have difficulty at this level and need instruction and practice. Appropriate activities for increasing word-level phonological awareness include clapping or marching to each word in a sentence or phrase, counting the number of words in a sentence, or adding single-word descriptors to a list of words that describe a given object (see Table 1, on page 708, for sample activities at the word level).

Syllable-Level Activities

Syllables are the most easily distinguishable units within words. Most children acquire the ability to segment words into syllables with minimal instruction (Liberman, Shankweiler, & Liberman, 1989; Lundberg, 1988). This level of phonological awareness is useful for initial instruction in detection, segmentation, blending, and manipulation of phonological components of language. The abilities to detect and count syllables and to segment words into syllables are more important to reading acquisition than the ability to manipulate and transpose them (Adams, 1990). Even very young children can enjoy and benefit from activities at the syllable level. Teaching students to segment multisyllable words into individual syllables can begin in kindergarten or preschool. This process can be made into a game in which children separate their names or the names

TABLE 1

Activities to Develop Phonological Awareness at the Word Level

Tapping Words	Children can be taught to tap out words in a sentence or phrase with a rhythm stick or finger. Most children acquire this skill with minimal instruction. Teacher modeling and guidance are useful for those children who have difficulty with this task. Drums, sandpaper blocks, or other percussion instruments provide fun variations of this activity.
Connecting Words	Provide each student with a set of connecting blocks or cubes (e.g., Unifix Cubes). Read a sentence aloud and have the child add a cube or block for each word read.
Tallying Words	Provide each student with a sponge tip moistener (as used to moisten envelopes) and a sheet of colored construction paper. As the teacher reads a sentence, the students will tap their moistener one time for each word. The children can then go back and count the number of spots to determine the number of words in the sentence. The spots will dry quickly and the same sheet of construction paper can be used for the next sentence.

Note

These activities can be modified for use at the syllable or phoneme level. From Lane and Pullen (1998).

of familiar objects into syllables. Children also may be taught to count the number of syllables in other long but familiar words (e.g., alligator, motorcycle). Using objects or picture cards, children may sort words by the number of syllables (see Table 2 for sample activities at the syllable level).

Onset/Rime-Level Activities

Treiman (1985, 1991, 1992) promotes the use of instruction at the onset and rime, or intrasyllabic, level. Because tasks that require onset and rime analysis require the segmentation of syllables, they are more sophisticated than syllable-level tasks. Yet, these same tasks are easier than phoneme-level tasks because they do not require discrimination among all of the individual phonemes in a syllable. Onset–rime tasks could, therefore, be considered an intermediate step in the development of phonological awareness. The difficulty that many children experience when progressing from syllabic analysis to phonemic analysis may arise because the intermediate step, the

TABLE 2

Activities to Develop Phonological Awareness at the Syllable Level

Junk Box Rock	Fill a box with common objects and toys that have multisyllable names. Call on a child to pull an item from the box. The child should name the item and do the "Junk Box Rock" by rocking his/her hips back and forth for each syllable.
Bean Bag Toss	With children seated in a circle, the teacher begins the game by tossing the bean bag to student 1. This student claps out the syllables in the teacher's name. Student 1 tosses the bean bag to student 2, and student 2 claps out the syllables in student 1's name. The game continues until each child has had a turn.
Hopscotch	For this activity, a set of picture cards is required. Draw a standard hopscotch board with sidewalk chalk. The teacher or a student pulls a picture card from the deck. The first player counts the syllables in the selected word and tosses a beanbag or other marker to the corresponding square on the hopscotch pattern. The player hops the squares as in a traditional hopscotch game.

Note

From Lane and Pullen (1998).

intrasyllabic unit, is often omitted from early reading instruction. Providing experience working with onsets and rimes may alleviate this difficulty. The most common onset- and rime-level activities are those involving rhyming or word families. Learning nursery rhymes and rhyming songs and poems helps develop this level of phonological awareness (see Table 3, on page 710, for sample activities at the onset/rime level).

Phoneme-Level Activities

Phonemes, the smallest sound units of spoken language, are usually represented in print by single letters (e.g., pet has three phonemes, /p/, /ɛ/, and /t/) or by digraphs (e.g., *faith* has three phonemes, /f/, /e/, /Θ/). The term *phonemic awareness* is frequently—but incorrectly—used interchangeably with phonological awareness, a much broader construct. Phonemic awareness is different from phonological awareness in that it applies specifically to the ability to manipulate sounds at the phoneme level. Phonemic awareness skills include the ability to detect, segment, and blend phonemes and to manipulate their position in words (Adams, 1990; Lenchner et al., 1990).

TABLE 3

Activities to Develop Phonological Awareness at the Onset–Rime Level

Oddity Detection	This task requires children to indicate which in a list of three or four words does not rhyme with the other words in the list. The familiar song from the television show *Sesame Street* does this well. "Which of these words is not like the others? Which of these words just doesn't belong?" (e.g., fat, hat, sun, mat)
ABC Sponging	Materials: lowercase-alphabet-shaped sponges, construction paper, plastic storage bags
	This activity combines phonological awareness and the alphabetic principle. Select a word family and gather the appropriate sponges needed to make words. For example, if you are working on the word family *at*, use the following sponges: *a, t, b, c, f, h, m, p,* and *r.* Moisten the sponges with water and place them in a plastic storage bag. Students will use the sponges to create words on construction paper. Store different word families in different storage bags. When the first word family dries, students can trade bags and create a new set of words.
Rhyme Matching with Picture Cards	For these activities, children are asked to look at pictures and generate the sounds themselves by naming the word the picture represents. Students match pictures illustrating words that share a common rhyme. This activity is somewhat more advanced (demanding) than activities that begin with the teacher generating the sounds, because some students find it more difficult to detect individual phonemes when they do not hear someone else say the word.

Note

From Lane and Pullen (1998).

In speech, it is impossible to segment words into phonemes. In the speech flow, phonemes are formed and blended in such a way that one phoneme's production is influenced by the surrounding phonemes. For example, the /k/ is formed differently in the words *cat* and *coop* because of the vowels that follow it. (Try saying these words and notice the difference in the position of your mouth when you produce the /k/ sound). Because phonemic analysis requires the reader to detect and manipulate individual phonemes, it is a much more sophisticated and, thus, much more difficult task than either syllabic or intrasyllabic analysis (Treiman, 1991, 1992).

Phoneme-level activities include sound detection, matching, deletion, blending, segmenting, and manipulation. Skills in blending phonemes into words and segmenting words into phonemes are the most sophisticated associated with phonological awareness and the most important for application to decoding. Blending and segmenting may be taught in a variety of ways.

As early as the 1950s, educators speculated that children must be able to hear, distinguish, and analyze the separate sounds in words to be able to learn to read, and Elkonin (1963) created a training method that would develop these necessary skills. He provided counters and pictures of objects with squares drawn beneath each picture representing the number of separate sounds in the word. The child was asked to segment the phonemes in the word while placing one counter in a square for each sound. This training resulted in increased abilities in phonemic segmentation and increased decoding skills (see Figure 2, on page 712, for an example).

One of the most useful methods for helping young children to understand the concepts of phonemic blending and segmentation is teaching them to "converse" with a puppet or toy robot in a "secret language." Torgesen and Bryant (1994) described a complete sequence of lessons using this approach in *Phonological Awareness Training for Reading,* but the method is easy to adapt to informal instruction. The teacher explains that the puppet or robot can only say words or can only understand words when they are said one sound at a time. Young children seem to accept and understand this explanation quite readily and are eager to try communicating in this unusual fashion. Table 4, on page 713, provides additional examples of activities at the phoneme level.

When teaching or assessing blending and segmentation skills, the teacher should be careful to segment phonemes completely before blending them. Many teachers have the tendency simply to say a word slowly, drawing out the phonemes. When children learn to decode, it is necessary for them to identify the sounds of separate letters and then to blend those letter sounds together. Previous oral blending practice is helpful for students when they are ready to become more fluent with decoding skills.

Another important caution for teachers is that individual phonemes must be pronounced in a manner that will make them blendable. In other words, teachers should be very careful to model *correct* letter sound pronunciation. Many teachers, in an effort to make stop consonant sounds (e.g., /b/, /d/, /k/) more audible, add a vowel sound to the consonant. This additional sound, usually a schwa or short /u/ sound, distorts the consonant sound, making it very difficult to blend with other phonemes. For example, a *b* may be incorrectly pronounced "buh," and a *t* may be incorrectly pronounced "tuh." Blending the letters *b, a,* and *t* then produces "buh-a-tuh," and most children have difficulty identifying the word *bat* pronounced this way. It is important to pronounce stop consonants as quickly as possible, without the confusing "uh." Because it is impossible to pronounce a voiced stop consonant such as /b/ or /d/ in isolation with no vowel sound attached, the teacher should model saying the sound with an extremely brief short /i/ sound following it. The place in the vocal anatomy where the short /i/ is pro-

FIGURE 2

Elkonin Boxes

Elkonin (1963) introduced a method of developing phonemic segmentation skills that has become quite popular in recent years. This method involves the use of Elkonin boxes—picture cards with boxes under each picture representing the number of phonemes in that word. While saying the word slowly—sound by sound—the student moves a marker into each box to represent each sound in the word. This activity may be modified to allow the teacher and student to practice the skill orally. The teacher demonstrates using fingers to count phonemes, raising one finger as each phoneme is pronounced. With teacher guidance, the student should be able to learn how to count phonemes independently.

Materials: Picture cards, counters

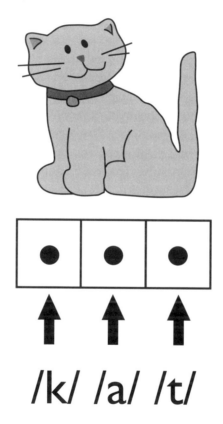

/k/ /a/ /t/

The teacher models moving one chip into a square for each sound in *cat*. The student then moves the ships into the squares with help from the teacher. Finally, the student can move the ships into the squares independently.

duced has more sounds close to it than does the short /u/. Teaching children to use this strategy helps them blend stop consonants more readily.

To assist children in the development of blending skills, teachers should begin instruction in blending and segmenting using only words with continuous consonant sounds (e.g., s, v, z, f, m, n, sh, th) at the beginning position. These sounds are much easier to blend than the stop consonants, and their use in early instruction makes the skill of blending more accessible for children. As children are introduced to blending skills,

TABLE 4

Activities to Develop Phonological Awareness at the Phoneme Level

Bead Strings	String 6 beads on a string and knot at each end. Provide each student with a bead string. Use the bead strings to teach students to segment words at the phoneme level. Give students a word and have them move a bead for each phoneme in the word. The students can then hold up their bead strings and the teacher can conduct a quick survey to see which students segmented the word correctly. This activity can be implemented in large groups, small groups, or one-on-one.
Sound Detection	Given a target phoneme, students determine which words on a list begin or end with that sound. This activity can be used during story or passage reading, as well. While reading connected text, students find all words that contain the target phoneme. As students become comfortable with beginning and ending sounds, activities that include detection of a target medial sound should be added.

Note

From Lane and Pullen (1998).

stop consonants may be used at the end of words. In the final position, stop consonants are easier to pronounce quickly and with little distortion. When students become competent with pronunciation of stop consonants at the end of a word, the introduction of stops at the initial position becomes less troublesome.

THE ALPHABETIC PRINCIPLE AND DECODING

Although phonological awareness is a necessary foundational skill, it is not sufficient for acquiring decoding ability. The ability to manipulate the sounds in language alone does not guarantee the smooth transition to automatic word recognition skills. Several understandings related to print concepts and the alphabetic principle are also necessary for skilled decoding. For example, understanding that (a) words can be spoken or written, (b) print corresponds to speech, (c) words are composed of individual sounds (i.e., phonemes), and (d) words are composed of letters (i.e., graphemes) that map to phonemes is necessary for the facilitation of word recognition and decoding skills (Juel, 1991). In particular, understanding of the alphabetic principle—the fundamental insight that letters and sounds work together in systematic ways to form words—prepares the emergent reader to process print and decode words.

Development of Word Reading

Phonological awareness, print awareness, and an understanding of the alphabetic principle are necessary to progress through the phases of word recognition ability. Ehri (1991, 1995, 1998) describes the four phases through which a reader moves from immature forms of word reading to reading words by sight. It is learning to read words that is the "major hurdle in gaining reading skill" (Ehri, 1998, p. 101).

During the first phase of development in word reading, which is often referred to as the *logographic, visual cue,* or *prealphabetic phase,* young children read words using salient but nonalphabetic cues (Ehri, 1991, 1992, 1995, 1998; Gough, Juel, & Roper/Schneider, 1983). Instead of using letter-sound relationships to read words, young children associate visual cues—such as word shape or a logo paired with the word (e.g., McDonald's arches)—that correspond with a word in their memory. However, this logographic strategy has obvious limitations. Without a working knowledge of the alphabetic principle, individuals are unable to move on to other phases of word reading.

When readers move from the logographic phase, they do not automatically get to complete phonological recoding (i.e., translating print into speech). Instead, they may begin noticing boundary letters (i.e., first letters, or first and last letters in a word). Ehri (1991) distinguishes this second phase of word reading development as *phonetic cue reading.* The beginning reader notices partial, rather than complete, letter-sound relations. However, some knowledge of the alphabetic principle and phonological awareness are necessary to move into phonetic cue reading.

The third phase of word reading—the *full alphabetic phase*—is characterized by the use of phonemic segmentation and *phonological recoding.* In this third phase, word recognition occurs through the process of phonological recoding. A reader phonologically recodes when print is converted into speech (Foorman, Francis, Beeler, Winikates, & Fletcher, 1997; Hoover & Tunmer, 1993). The ability to make use of these systematic grapheme-phoneme matches is the only means of becoming a proficient reader.

In the fourth or *consolidated alphabetic* phase, readers access complete spellings of words from lexical memory, their system for remembering words (Ehri, 1998). They also store sequences of phonemes that occur frequently in words (e.g., syllables, onsets and rimes, or morphemes). Readers can access the units from memory when learning words never before encountered, allowing the reader's lexicon—the reader's personal store of words in memory—to grow rapidly. When the reader reaches the consolidated alphabetic phase, less attention is devoted to deciphering each word, and more attention may be focused on interpretation of the text.

Instructional Activities That Promote the Alphabetic Principle

To become fully literate, a reader must be able to decode unknown words, mapping graphemes to phonemes for linguistic comprehension. It is the goal of beginning reading instruction to move students through the phases of sight word learning so they may attend to building fluency and accessing the meaning of the text. In this section, we discuss interventions that are appropriate for each phase of word reading.

The Prealphabetic Phase

As described earlier in this chapter, in the prealphabetic phase, instruction should focus on the development of phonological awareness and concepts about print. Children should be actively engaged in literacy activities that encourage the development of these skills. Shared stories with big books can help children develop understanding of how books and print work. For example, when the teacher points to words during shared reading, children may learn that (a) print is read from left to right, top to bottom; (b) one word in speech matches one word in print; (c) when one page of text is read, the story continues on the following page; (d) the white spaces between groups of letters represent breaks between spoken words or word boundaries; and (e) the print in books tells the story (Clay, 1993). Children's active engagement in pointing to words should also be encouraged to promote independence.

Shared book reading need not be limited to fiction picture books. Children can learn the many forms and functions of print while reading various genres during shared stories. Students' familiarity with text structure may be increased through activities with nonfiction topic books or children's magazines. In addition, phonological awareness activities may be integrated into reading poetry books.

In the prealphabetic phase, phonological awareness activities such as those described earlier in this chapter should be a routine part of every school day. Foorman et al. (1997) reported that with 15 minutes of phonological awareness training in their daily routine, kindergarten students were able to develop early literacy skills—phonemic and orthographic processing and rapid letter naming—at a faster rate than students who did not receive phonological awareness training. For students who received direct instruction in sound-symbol relationships, reading achievement benefits persisted through first and second grade.

The Partial Alphabetic Phase

During the partial alphabetic phase, the teacher should develop children's understanding of the alphabetic principle. To promote this understanding, instruction in decoding skill should be systematic and explicit and include a multisensory component. The following sections provide a rationale for explicit, systematic, and multisensory instruction and suggestions for effective implementation of these methods.

Explicit and systematic instruction. Students may not automatically make the connection between graphemes (print) and phonemes (speech). According to Mercer, Lane, Jordan, Allsopp, and Eisele (1996), an explicit approach to instruction is warranted for skills or concepts about which students have little or no background knowledge, or for students who have demonstrated weaknesses. They characterize explicit instruction as teacher-directed, as opposed to implicit instruction, which they characterize as student regulated. Explicit instruction in the alphabetic principle and decoding leaves little to chance and ensures almost all students successful skill acquisition (Moats, 1998). Further, explicit instruction provides students with a real relationship between printed letters and phonemes (Beck & Juel, 1992).

In addition to being explicit, instruction in the alphabetic principle and decoding should be systematic. Instruction should follow a logical sequence from simple to more complex (Moats, 1998). In developing a sequence, the teacher should consider the frequency of letters and letter patterns. That is, instruction should begin with common, high-frequency spelling patterns (e.g., *at, ing*) before moving to less common ones (e.g., *ough, sch*) (Beck & Juel, 1992).

The sequence of the instruction also should ensure that students have the opportunity to apply their newly acquired knowledge and skills. Therefore, a few consonants and a vowel should be taught in the early lessons so that students can then practice blending those sounds to make words (Chard & Osborn, 1999). Teachers must avoid teaching all the consonants first, before vowels. Instruction in the alphabetic principle and decoding is pointless if students cannot apply that knowledge to read words (Beck & Juel, 1992). Teachers also should provide students opportunities to apply the alphabetic principle and decoding skills to reading the meaningful context of real books (Beck & Juel; Chard & Osborn).

Multisensory instruction in the alphabetic principle and decoding. Multisensory instruction incorporates input from more than one sensory channel (i.e., auditory, visual, tactile, kinesthetic) to promote skill acquisition. Multisensory instruction at the partial alphabetic phase can help students develop an understanding of the alphabetic principle. Multisensory instruction should be systematic, explicit, and integrated with instruction in meaningful connected text.

The results of a recent study of an intervention using the multisensory techniques indicated improved decoding ability for struggling first-grade readers (Pullen, 2000). The intervention combined multisensory instruction in the alphabetic principle with reading in context. This strategy involved selecting appropriate-level books and decodable words. After the targeted words were selected, teachers created new words and nonwords to form with manipulative letters. The word sets began with a target word such as *hot*; one phoneme was changed at a time to create new words and nonwords (e.g., *hot, jot, lot, cot,* and *vot*). Initially, only onsets were changed, beginning with continuous sounds and moving to stop sounds. Eventually, new words were created by substituting final phonemes (e.g., changing *fan* to *fat* to *fap*) and medial phonemes (e.g., changing *sat* to *sit* to *sut*). The use of nonwords in these activities ensured that students attended to letters and sounds rather than relying on their sight word memory.

During manipulative letter activities, teachers demonstrated how letters came together to form words and modeled the segmentation and blending of phonemes, focusing on the onset-rime and phoneme levels. Teachers pointed out similarities and differences between new words and words the students already knew or had been practicing. Teachers prompted students to practice words and nonwords, and talked explicitly about the difference between them. Students were prompted to locate words they made in the book they read.

The Full Alphabetic Phase

Instruction in this phase should continue to be explicit and systematic, and should begin to focus on various orthographic or spelling patterns. Multisensory activities should be continued, with emphasis on multisyllable words, word chunks, and word endings. For example, as a child moves from the partial alphabetic to the full alphabetic phase, they become ready to work on words in which a phoneme is represented by more than one grapheme (e.g., *sh, ai, ea*). To provide ample opportunities for independent practice, students should have access to decodable text.

Experiences that incorporate writing serve to enhance the student's development through the full alphabetic phase. The process of encoding (i.e., writing words) is closely linked to the process of decoding (i.e., reading words). Teachers should encourage students at this phase of development to use invented spellings in their writing. In invented spellings, children use their knowledge of letter-sound correspondences to represent sounds in print. Pointing out the similarities and differences between invented and conventional spellings may alert students to new orthographic patterns. Elkonin boxes may be used with letters to promote students' understanding of and familiarity with orthographic patterns (see Figure 3, on page 718).

The Consolidated Alphabetic Phase

In this phase, students are learning to put together skills into competent and flexible reading and are entering into the most mature form of reading. They begin to consolidate multiletter patterns in memory in larger chunks (e.g., syllables, common rime patterns, or morphemes). During this stage, providing enough practice to build fluency and automaticity in word recognition is of paramount importance. Most students have reached the consolidated alphabetic phase by the end of first grade and continue to develop throughout their schooling. Poor readers, even those in upper grades, may never fully develop in this phase without targeted intervention.

Selecting Appropriate Text

The choice of text in which to practice decoding skills is an important one. Fountas and Pinnell (1999) note the importance of carefully matching readers and books. Matching ensures that text is neither too easy nor too hard and that it provides the right amount of challenge to promote reading growth. Some researchers advocate using only decodable text with beginning readers; others discourage the use of decodable text in favor of books with predictable language patterns. Hiebert (1999) points out that beginning readers require texts that allow them to become proficient with multiple aspects of written English. She advocates using a variety of books to provide exposure to decodable words, high-frequency words, predictable language patterns, and books of literary merit. She also suggests that some books—Dr. Seuss's *Green Eggs and Ham* (1960) being a case in point—fulfill all of these criteria. Hiebert calls on children's book authors and publishers to model their books after this type of text.

FIGURE 3

Developing Understanding of the Alphabetic Principle Through Elkonin Boxes

Help students write words by drawing Elkonin boxes. In early experiences, select only words that have few sounds and that have regular spellings. Begin by having the student push markers into the boxes as described previously. Then ask him/her to identify the letter that makes the first sound and prompt him/her to write that letter in the first box. Help the student identify the letter that corresponds to each sound and write it in the appropriate box. If the student needs a model of how to write the letter, show him/her a magnetic letter or a letter card with the letter. At first, do not emphasize the order of the sounds. Let the student enter the letters he knows, and provide the other letters for him. As he becomes more confident with this procedure, begin to require that he enter the letters in the correct order from beginning to end.

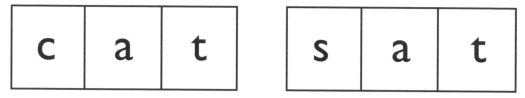

As you move from words with regular, simple spellings to words with more difficult spellings, you may need to put more than one letter in a box to represent a single sound. Use this opportunity to point out to the student that, often, several letters work together to make one sound (eg., *sh* in shop) and some letters are silent (eg., e in hope).

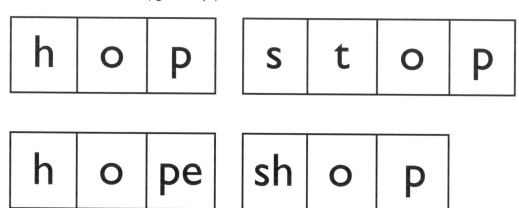

To help the student progress to spelling more difficult words independently, use dotted lines to split those boxes in which two letters are required to make one sound. After sufficient practice with each of these activities, the student should be able to make his or her own boxes when needed. Eventually, the student should be able to spell the words using the sounding-out techniques without the Elkonin boxes.

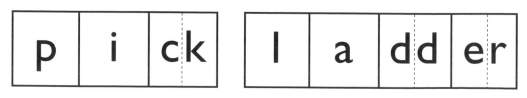

Without access to appropriate and engaging text, poor readers are likely to spend little time reading. Of course, avoiding reading and receiving less practice limit improvement, a phenomenon Stanovich (1986) has called the Matthew Effect in reading. In contrast, good readers tend to enjoy reading, get more reading practice, and continue to improve. The Matthew Effect contributes to an ever-widening gap between poor readers and good readers. One way to narrow the gap is to ensure that poor readers have sufficient access to books they are able to and want to read. Extended practice in a meaningful context—using appropriate text—helps children develop automaticity in their decoding skills, which leads to fluent reading.

READING FLUENCY AND DECODING

As we use the term, fluent reading is rapid, accurate, and expressive; it is seemingly effortless, except that it requires extensive training to achieve. Fluent reading is important for several reasons, most fundamentally because good readers read faster and more accurately than poor readers and fluency is a major component of reading proficiency (Adams, 1990; Allington, 1983; Binder, 1993; Hasbrouk & Tindal, 1992; Samuels, Schermer, & Reinking, 1992). Moreover, lack of reading fluency is a reliable predictor of reading comprehension problems (Lyon, 1998; Stanovich, 1991). Fluent decoding permits "multitasking" (National Institute of Child Health and Human Development, 2000), so that fluent readers have cognitive resources available to access meaning (LaBerge & Samuels, 1974). Furthermore, in a recent analysis of National Assessment of Educational Progress (NAEP) data, Pinnell et al. (1995) showed that 44% of a representative national sample of fourth-graders were not fluent in grade-level material.

Instructional Activities to Increase Reading Fluency

Conventional wisdom (cf. Rayner & Pollatsek, 1989) has it that isolated word training does little to enhance comprehension of text. Indeed, in our first version of this chapter (Sindelar & Stoddard, 1991), we recommended word practice as an error correction procedure only. More recently, word practice has been shown to benefit not only passage reading but also comprehension, at least in some cases (Levy, Abello, & Lysynchuk, 1997; Tan & Nicholson, 1997; van den Bosch, van Bon, & Schreuder, 1995). In these studies, participants were 7 to 11 year olds, and word drills emphasized speed of recognition. In fact, Levy et al. conducted two studies that differed only by the duration of word presentations during training. They found that students read passages faster and more accurately if they had been trained on novel words, regardless of presentation speed. Comprehension, on the other hand, was improved only after short exposure training.

In their first study, Levy et al. (1997) trained 72 words—about 80% of the words that occurred in the passages—and training occurred 6 times a day for 4 days. In the second, all 90 words were practiced for 20 trials each, 5 times a day for 4 days. In both studies, readers were monitored for the purpose of error correction. Of course, the intensity of these interventions—individual monitoring of 24 trials with 72 words—is not feasible in classrooms. It is unlikely that reading specialists or special education resource room teachers—no less classroom teachers—would have time to use this procedure with sufficient fidelity to guarantee effects. The same point may be argued about the interventions in the other two studies. Although Tan and Nicholson (1997) trained only 7–8% of passage words, their sessions were 20 minutes long and individualized; van den Bosch et al. (1995) used pseudowords, on which participants received nearly 8 hours of training. Clearly, for teachers, such interventions are impossibly long and complex.

Consequently, we focus our discussion of improving reading fluency on techniques that involve practice on reading narrative passages. The National Reading Panel (NRP; NICHHD, 2000) recently compared two methods, the method of repeated readings and the more general strategy of increasing independent and recreational reading. Because the NRP concluded that the former worked and the latter did not, we focus on the method of repeated readings.

Repeated Readings

Repeated readings procedures are simple to use and require no special materials. The NRP recommends that sessions be brief (15 to 30 minutes) and that repeated readings be used as part of a larger program of reading instruction. The method of repeated readings was initially developed by Samuels (1979). His procedure involved (a) selecting a short passage at a student's instructional level, (b) setting a rate criterion at 85 words per minute (wpm), and (c) having the student read and reread the passage until the rate criterion is reached. Errors and hesitations typically are corrected by providing the unknown or misread word. Oral reading rate is determined by timing students for 1 minute, then counting how many words they read correctly. Charting fluency performance is recommended for keeping records and motivating students. As former classroom teachers, we have found that charting students' progress was particularly powerful with students with reading disabilities, who often were proud of their progress.

There have been many modifications to this original method, all with positive effect. Most modifications have involved determining the optimal number of readings. Researchers have had children read passages a predetermined number of times, commonly three (e.g., O'Shea, Sindelar, & O'Shea, 1987), or until they have achieved three consecutive improvements (Weinstein & Cooke, 1992). Simmons, Fuchs, Fuchs, Mathes, and Pate (1995) had children read passages three times, but for only 1 minute per reading. Also, researchers have recommended a range of fluency criteria from 45 wpm in first grade to 200 wpm in fifth grade (e.g., Carnine & Silbert, 1979; Dowhower, 1991; Howell, Kaplan, & O'Connell, 1979; Samuels, 1979).

These various repeated reading methods have been shown to improve reading fluency, expression, and comprehension (e.g., Dowhower, 1987; Meyer & Felton, 1999), although these effects seem to be limited to practiced passages or untrained passages with many of the same words as practiced passages (Rashotte & Torgesen, 1985). This limitation notwithstanding, repeated readings have been shown to benefit young, normally developing readers and struggling readers, including students with disabilities. In fact, Sindelar, Monda, and O'Shea (1990) demonstrated that the effects of repeated readings were the same for elementary students with learning disabilities and younger, typically developing readers of the same reading age.

In its meta-analysis of 16 empirical studies of 752 elementary/secondary students using repeated readings, the NRP reported an overall effect size (ES) of .41 (weighted for sample size). A .41 ES means that the average experimental group participant scored .41 standard deviations higher than the average control group participant, a moderate effect. Participants in these studies were second- to ninth-graders, with younger competent readers and older struggling readers benefiting most. The ES for struggling readers from the upper middle grades was .50. Repeated readings had an impact on word recognition (ES = .55), fluency (ES = .42), and comprehension (ES = .35).

Researchers, teachers, paraprofessionals, peers, and parents have implemented repeated readings successfully, although some exceptions have been reported in the literature. Notably, Mathes and Fuchs (1993) reported no effects for repeated readings when implemented in a special education resource room using students with learning disabilities as tutors. This finding suggests that practitioners intending to implement repeated readings in a peer tutoring arrangement should pair struggling readers with competent readers. Many other variations of the repeated reading procedure have been studied, including simultaneous reading and listening, listening and delayed reading, and previewing. Several error correction and feedback procedures also have been tried. In these studies, word supply—that is, the procedure wherein tutors provide words after errors or hesitations—has proven as effective as any.

CONCLUSION

An effective reading program consists of explicit and systematic instruction in (a) phonological awareness, (b) concepts about print, (c) the alphabetic principle, (d) decoding strategies, (e) fluency training, and (f) comprehension strategies. That is, it should be balanced, and grounded in meaningful context across a variety of literary genres (Adams, 1990; Chard & Osborn, 1999; Lyon, 1998; Snow, Burns, & Griffin, 1998). We have focused on the areas of phonological awareness, the alphabetic principle, and reading fluency because these areas are critical for developing skilled decoding, and because deficits in these skill areas are typical of most struggling readers.

As our review reflects, phonological awareness, the alphabetic principle, and fluency work together to create skilled decoding that permits full access to text meaning. The phonological and orthographic processors work in reciprocal fashion as young readers encounter oral and written language patterns and establish strong connections between the sounds of speech and symbols on paper. Daily activities to develop phonological awareness, to build concepts about print and understanding of the alphabetic principle, and to build fluent reading in narrative text represent the best of what reading research currently has to offer teachers.

REFERENCES

Adams, M. J. (1990). *Beginning to read: Thinking and learning about print.* Cambridge, MA: MIT Press.

Adams, M. J., Foorman, B. R., Lundberg, I., & Beeler, T. (1998). The elusive phoneme: Why phonemic awareness is so important and how to help children develop it. *American Educator, 22,* 18–29.

Alegria, J., & Morais, J. (1991). Segmental analysis and reading acquisition. In L. Rieben & C. A. Perfetti (Eds.), *Learning to read: Basic research and its implications* (pp. 135–148). Hillsdale, NJ: Erlbaum.

Allington, R. L. (1983). Fluency: The neglected reading goal. *The Reading Teacher, 36,* 556–561.

Beck, I., & Juel, C. (1992). The role of decoding in learning to read. In S. J. Samuels & A. E. Farstrup (Eds.), *What research has to say about reading instruction* (2nd ed., pp. 101–123). Newark, DE: International Reading Association.

Binder, C. (1993). Behavioral fluency: A new paradigm. *Educational Technology, 33*(10), 8–14.

Blachman, B. A. (1984). Language analysis skills and early reading acquisition. In G. P. Wallach & K. G. Butler (Eds.), *Language learning disabilities in school-age children* (pp. 271–287). Baltimore: Williams and Wilkins.

Blachman, B. A. (1989). Phonological awareness and word recognition: Assessment and intervention. In A. G. Kamhi & H. W. Catts (Eds.), *Reading disabilities: A developmental language perspective* (pp. 133–158). Austin, TX: Pro-ed.

Blachman, B. A. (1994). What we have learned from longitudinal studies of phonological processing and reading, and some unanswered questions: A response to Torgesen, Wagner, and Rashotte. *Journal of Learning Disabilities, 27,* 287–291.

Bradley, L. (1988). Rhyme recognition and reading and spelling in young children. In R. L. Masland & M. W. Masland (Eds.), *Preschool prevention of reading failure* (pp. 143–162). Parkton, MD: York Press.

Busink, R. (1997). Reading and phonological awareness: What we have learned and how we can use it. *Research and Instruction, 36,* 199–215.

Carnine, D., & Silbert, J. (1979). *Direct instruction reading.* Columbus, OH: Merrill.

Catts, H. W. (1989). Phonological processing deficits and reading disabilities. In A. G. Kamhi & H. W. Catts (Eds.), *Reading disabilities: A developmental language perspective* (pp. 101–132). Austin, TX: Pro-ed.

Catts, H. W. (1991). Early identification of reading disabilities. *Topics in Language Disorders, 12*(1), 1–16.

Chard, D. J., & Osborn, J. (1999). Phonics and word recognition instruction in early reading programs: Guidelines for accessibility. *Learning Disabilities Research and Practice, 14,* 107–117.

Clay, M. (1993). *Reading Recovery: A guidebook for teachers in training.* Portsmouth, NH: Heinemann.

Cornwall, A. (1992). The relationship of phonological awareness, rapid naming, and verbal memory to severe reading and spelling disability. *Journal of Learning Disabilities, 25,* 532-538.

Dowhower, S. L. (1987). Effects of repeated reading on second-grade transitional readers' fluency and comprehension. *Reading Research Quarterly, 22,* 389-406.

Dowhower, S. L. (1991). Speaking of prosody: Fluency's unattended bedfellow. *Theory into Practice, 30,* 165-175.

Ehri, L. C. (1979). Linguistic insight: Threshold of reading acquisition. In T. G. Waller & G. E. MacKinnon (Eds.), *Reading research: Advances in theory and practice* (Vol. 1, pp. 63-114). New York: Academic Press.

Ehri, L. C. (1991). Development of the ability to read words. In R. Barr, M. L. Kamil, P. B. Mosenthal, & P. D. Pearson (Eds.), *Handbook of reading research* (Vol. 2, pp. 383-417). New York: Longman.

Ehri, L. C. (1992). Reconceptualizing the development of sight word reading and its relationship to recoding. In P. Gough, L. C. Ehri, & R. Treiman (Eds.), *Reading acquisition* (pp. 107-143). Hillsdale, NJ: Erlbaum.

Ehri, L. C. (1995). Phases of development in learning to read words by sight. *Journal of Research in Reading, 18,* 116-125.

Ehri, L. C. (1998). Grapheme-phoneme knowledge is essential for learning to read words in English. In J. L. Metsala & L. C. Ehri (Eds.), *Word recognition in beginning literacy* (pp. 3-40). Mahwah, NJ: Erlbaum.

Elkonin, D. B. (1963). The psychology of mastering the elements of reading. In B. Simon & J. Simon (Eds.), *Educational psychology in the U.S.S.R.* (pp. 165-179). Stanford, CA: Stanford University Press.

Foorman, B., Francis, D., Beeler, T., Winikates, D., & Fletcher, J. (1997). Early interventions for children with reading problems: Study designs and preliminary findings. *Learning Disabilities: A Multi-Disciplinary Journal, 8*(1), 63-72.

Fountas, I. C., & Pinnell, G. S. (1999). *Matching books to readers: Using leveled books in guided reading, K-3.* Portsmouth, NH: Heinemann.

Gough, P., Juel, C., & Roper/Schneider, D. (1983). Code and cipher: A two-stage conception of initial reading acquisition. In J. A. Niles & L. A. Harris (Eds.), *Searches for meaning in reading/language processing and instruction* (32nd Yearbook of the National Reading Conference, pp. 207-211). Rochester, NY: National Reading Conference.

Griffith, P. L., & Olson, M. W. (1992). Phonemic awareness helps beginning readers break the code. *The Reading Teacher, 45,* 516-523.

Grossen, B., & Carnine, D. (1991). Strategies for maximizing reading success in the regular classroom. In G. Stoner, M. R. Shinn, & H. M. Walker (Eds.), *Interventions for achievement and behavior problems* (1st ed., pp. 333-355). Silver Spring, MD: National Association of School Psychologists (NASP).

Hasbrouk, J. E., & Tindal, G. (1992). Curriculum-based oral reading fluency norms for students in grades 2 through 5. *TEACHING Exceptional Children, 24*(3), 41-44.

Hiebert, E. H. (1999). Text matters in learning to read. *Reading Teacher, 52,* 552-566.

Hoover, W. A., & Tunmer, W. E. (1993). The components of reading. In G. B. Thompson, W. E. Tunmer, & T. Nicholson (Eds.), *Reading acquisition processes* (pp. 1–14). Clevedon, PA: Multilingual Matters.

Howell, K. W., Kaplan, J. S., & O'Connell, C. Y. (1979). *Evaluating exceptional children: A task analysis approach.* Columbus, OH: Merrill.

Juel, C. (1991). Beginning reading. In R. Barr, M. L. Kamil, P. B. Mosenthal, & P. D. Pearson (Eds.), *Handbook of reading research* (Vol. 2, pp. 759–788). New York: Longman.

LaBerge, D., & Samuels, S. J. (1974). Toward a theory of automatic information processing in reading. *Cognitive Psychologist, 6,* 293–323.

Lane, H. B. (1994). *The effects of explicit instruction in contextual application of phonological awareness on the reading skills of first-grade students.* Unpublished doctoral dissertation, University of Florida, Gainesville.

Lane, H. B., & Pullen, P. C. (1998). *Jump start in reading: Assessment and instruction in phonological awareness.* Gainesville, FL: Author.

Lane, H. B., Pullen, P. C., Eisele, M. R., & Jordan, L. (2002). Preventing reading failure: Phonological awareness assessment and instruction. *Preventing School Failure, 46*(2).

Lenchner, O., Gerber, M. M., & Routh, D. K. (1990). Phonological awareness tasks as predictors of decoding ability: Beyond segmentation. *Journal of Learning Disabilities, 23,* 240–247.

Levy, B. A., Abello, B., & Lysynchuk, L. (1997). Transfer from word training to reading in context: Gains in reading fluency and comprehension. *Learning Disabilities Quarterly, 20,* 173–188.

Liberman, I. Y., Shankweiler, D., & Liberman, A. M. (1989). The alphabetic principle and learning to read. In D. Shankweiler & I. Y. Liberman (Eds.), *Phonology and reading disability: Solving the reading puzzle* (pp. 1–33). Ann Arbor: The University of Michigan Press.

Lundberg, I. (1988). Preschool prevention of reading failure: Does training in phonological awareness work? In R. L. Masland & M. W. Masland (Eds.), *Preschool prevention of reading failure* (pp. 163–176). Parkton, MD: York Press.

Lundberg, I., Frost, J., & Petersen, O. (1988). Effects of an extensive program for stimulating phonological awareness in preschool children. *Reading Research Quarterly, 23,* 263–284.

Lundberg, I., Olofsson, A., & Wall, S. (1980). Reading and spelling skills in the first school years, predicted from phonemic awareness skills in kindergarten. *Scandinavian Journal of Psychology, 21,* 59–173.

Lyon, G. R. (1998). Why reading is not a natural process. *Educational Leadership, 55*(6), 14–18.

Mann, V. A. (1991a). Language problems: A key to early reading problems. In B. Y. L. Wong (Ed.), *Learning about learning disabilities* (pp. 130–162). San Diego, CA: Academic Press.

Mann, V. A. (1991b). Phonological abilities: Effective predictors of future reading ability. In L. Rieben & C. A. Perfetti (Eds.), *Learning to read: Basic research and its implications* (pp. 121–133). Hillsdale, NJ: Erlbaum.

Mathes, P. G., & Fuchs, L. S. (1993). Peer-mediated reading instruction in special education resource rooms. *Learning Disabilities Research and Practice, 8,* 233-243.

Mercer, C. D., Lane, H. B., Jordan, L., Allsopp, D. H., & Eisele, M. R. (1996). Empowering students and teachers with instructional choices in inclusive settings. *Remedial and Special Education, 17,* 226-236.

Meyer, M. S., & Felton, R. H. (1999). Repeated reading to enhance fluency: Old approaches and new directions. *Annals of Dyslexia, 49,* 283-306.

Moats, L.C. (1998). Teaching decoding. *American Educator, 22,* 42-96.

National Institute of Child Health and Human Development (NICHHD). (2000). *Report of the National Reading Panel: Reports of the subgroups.* Washington, DC: U.S. Department of Health and Human Services, National Institutes of Health.

O'Connor, R. E., Jenkins, J. R., Leicester, N., & Slocum, T. A. (1993). Teaching phonological awareness to young children with learning disabilities. *Exceptional Children, 59,* 532-546.

O'Shea, L. J., Sindelar, P. T., & O'Shea, D. J. (1987). The effects of repeated readings and attentional cues on the reading fluency and comprehension of learning disabled readers. *Learning Disabilities Research, 2,* 103-109.

Perfetti, C. A. (1991). Representations and awareness in the acquisition of reading competence. In L. Rieben & C. A. Perfetti (Eds.), *Learning to read: Basic research and its implications* (pp. 33-44). Hillsdale, NJ: Erlbaum.

Perfetti, C. A., Beck, I., Bell, L. C., & Hughes, C. (1987). Phonemic knowledge and learning to read are reciprocal: A longitudinal study of first grade children. *Merrill-Palmer Quarterly, 33,* 283-319.

Pinnell, G. S., Pikulski, J. J., Wixson, K. K., Campbell, J. R., Gough, P. B., & Beatty, A. S. (1995). *Listening to children read aloud.* Washington, DC: U.S. Department of Education, National Center for Educational Statistics.

Pratt, A. C., & Brady, S. (1988). Relation of phonological awareness to reading disability in children and adults. *Journal of Educational Psychology, 80,* 319-323.

Pullen, P. C. (2000). *The effects of alphabetic word work with manipulative letters on the reading skills of struggling first-grade students.* Unpublished dissertation, University of Florida, Gainesville.

Rashotte, C. A., & Torgesen, J. K. (1985). Repeated reading and reading fluency in learning disabled children. *Reading Research Quarterly, 20,* 180-188.

Rayner, K., & Pollatsek, A. (1989). *The psychology of reading.* Mahwah, NJ: Erlbaum.

Samuels, S. J. (1979). The method of repeated readings. *The Reading Teacher, 32,* 403-408.

Samuels, S. J., Schermer, N., & Reinking, D. (1992). Reading fluency: Techniques for making decoding automatic. In S. J. Samuels & A. E. Fartrup (Eds.), *What research has to say about reading instruction* (2nd ed., pp. 124-144). Newark, DE: International Reading Association.

Seuss, Dr. (1960). *Green eggs and ham.* New York: Random House.

Shankweiler, D. (1989). How problems of comprehension are related to difficulties in decoding. In D. Shankweiler & I. Y. Liberman (Eds.), *Phonology and reading disability: Solving the reading puzzle* (pp. 35-68). Ann Arbor: The University of Michigan Press.

Simmons, D. C., Fuchs, L. S., Fuchs, D., Mathes, P., & Pate, J. P. (1995). Effects of explicit teaching and peer tutoring on the reading achievement of learning-disabled and low-performing students in regular classrooms. *Elementary School Journal, 95,* 387-408.

Sindelar, P. T., & Stoddard, K. (1991). Teaching reading to mildly disabled students in regular classes. In G. Stoner, M. R. Shinn, & H. M. Walker (Eds.), *Interventions for achievement and behavior problems* (1st ed., pp. 357-378). Silver Spring, MD: National Association of School Psychologists.

Sindelar, P. T., Monda, L. E., & O'Shea, L. J. (1990). The effects of repeated readings on instructional and mastery level readers. *Journal of Educational Research, 83,* 220-226.

Snow, C., Burns, S., & Griffin, P. (1998). *Preventing reading difficulties in young children.* Washington, DC: National Academy Press.

Stanovich, K. E. (1986). Matthew effects in reading: Some consequences of individual differences in the acquisition of literacy. *Reading Research Quarterly, 21,* 360-406.

Stanovich, K. E. (1991). Word recognition: Changing perspectives. In R. Barr, M. L. Kamil, P. Mosenthal, & P. D. Pearson (Eds.), *Handbook of reading research* (Vol. 2, pp. 418-452). New York: Longman.

Stanovich, K. E. (1992). Speculations on the causes and consequences of individual differences in early reading acquisition. In P. B. Gough, L. C. Ehri, & R. Treiman (Eds.), *Reading acquisition* (pp. 307-342). Hillsdale, NJ: Erlbaum.

Tan, A., & Nicholson, T. (1997). Flashcards revisited: Training poor readers to read words faster improves their comprehension of text. *Journal of Educational Psychology, 89,* 276-288.

Torgesen, J. K., & Bryant, B. R. (1994). *Phonological awareness training for reading.* Austin, TX: Pro-ed.

Torgesen, J. K., Morgan, S. T., & Davis, C. (1992). Effects of two types of phonological awareness training on word learning in kindergarten children. *Journal of Educational Psychology, 84,* 364-370.

Torgesen, J. K., Wagner, R. K., & Rashotte, C. A. (1994). Longitudinal studies of phonological processing in reading. *Journal of Learning Disabilities, 27,* 276-286.

Treiman, R. (1985). Onsets and rimes as units of spoken syllables: Evidence from children. *Journal of Experimental Child Psychology, 39,* 161-181.

Treiman, R. (1991). The role of intrasyllabic units in learning to read. In L. Rieben & C. A. Perfetti (Eds.), *Learning to read: Basic research and its implications* (pp. 149-160). Hillsdale, NJ: Erlbaum.

Treiman, R. (1992). The role of intrasyllabic units in learning to read and spell. In P. B. Gough, L. C. Ehri, & R. Treiman (Eds.), *Reading acquisition* (pp. 65-106). Hillsdale, NJ: Erlbaum.

Uhry, J. K., & Shepherd, M. J. (1997). Teaching phonological recoding to young children with phonological processing deficits: The effect on sight vocabulary acquisition. *Learning Disability Quarterly, 20,* 104-125.

van den bosch, K., van Bon, W. H. J., & Schreuder, R. (1995). Poor readers' decoding skills: Effects of training with limited exposure duration. *Reading Research Quarterly, 30,* 110-125.

Weinstein, G., & Cooke, N. L. (1992). The effects of two repeated reading interventions on generalization of fluency. *Learning Disability Quarterly, 15,* 21-28.

APPENDIX

The following are examples of effective materials that can be used to develop students' phonological awareness, understanding of the alphabetic principle, and reading fluency. This list, although by no means exhaustive, provides a range of choices for teachers and other professionals.

Phonological Awareness

Road to the Code: A Phonological Awareness Program for Young Children (by Blachman, Ball, Black, & Tangel, 2000; available from Brookes Publishing) is designed for use with children in kindergarten and first grade. The program has been extensively field-tested and is the result of numerous studies of phonological awareness development.

Phonological Awareness in Young Children (by Adams, Foorman, Lundberg, & Beeler, 1998; available from Brookes Publishing) is a collection of activities designed to promote phonological awareness. This program is based on a Scandinavian program and has been field-tested in this country as well.

Ladders to Literacy (by O'Connor, Notari-Syverson, & Vadasy, 1998; available from Brookes Publishing) is a kindergarten activity book designed to promote print awareness, phonological awareness, and oral language. The program has been field-tested with more than 700 children, and a preschool companion program is also available.

DaisyQuest and Daisy's Castle (available from Great Wave Software) are computer programs that provide opportunities to develop phonological awareness through motivating games. These programs have been demonstrated effective in several studies.

Earobics (available from Cognitive Concepts) is another software program designed to develop phonemic awareness and letter-sound knowledge. This program has been tested in a variety of settings with promising results.

Alphabetic Principle

Making Words, Making Big Words, and Making More Words (by Cunningham & Hall; available from Good Apple) are phonics and spelling activity books that teachers use to guide students in making words with letter cards. These effective activities are motivating for children and the approach has been field-tested.

Reading Mastery (by Engelmann & Bruner; available from SRA) is a systematic, explicit reading curriculum that uses the Direct Instruction approach to teach decoding skills. This program is probably the most thoroughly studied and validated decoding program available.

Open Court Reading (available from SRA) is a basal program that balances literature with explicit phonics skill instruction. This program has been successfully field-tested in several school districts.

Read, Write, and Type (1995; available from The Learning Company) is a computer software program that incorporates the development of decoding skills with written expression and keyboarding skills in an entertaining 40-lesson sequence. As a student types a key on the computer, he or she hears the sound that letter makes. This program has been demonstrated effective in several studies.

Word Matters: Teaching Phonics and Spelling in the Reading/Writing Classroom (by Pinnell & Fountas, 1998; available from Heinemann) is a resource book for teachers that includes descriptions of many methods for helping children engage in "word study" (the investigation of letters and words) and "word solving" (figuring out new words).

Fluency

Great Leaps Reading (by Campbell, 1997; available from Diarmuid) is a program designed specifically to enhance fluency through one-minute timings. The program is divided into sections on decoding, sight phrases, and passages, and is motivating for students. This program has been field-tested in several studies and is so easy to use that volunteer tutors and paraprofessionals have demonstrated excellent results.

Jamestown Timed Readers (available from Jamestown Publishers) are high-interest, low-level stories and expository passages. These selections are designed to be used for timed readings to improve reading rate and accuracy and have been tested successfully in several studies.

Carbo Recorded Books (available from the National Reading Styles Institute) are tape recordings that go along with popular children's books. Unlike other recorded books, these are recorded at a pace appropriate for a beginning reader and without background sounds.

CHAPTER 27

Interventions for Students With Reading Comprehension Problems

Scott Baker and Russell Gersten
Eugene Research Institute/
University of Oregon

Bonnie Grossen
University of Oregon

INTRODUCTION

An alarmingly high number of students go through school without learning to comprehend what they read beyond a very rudimentary level (National Reading Panel, 2000; Snow, Burns, & Griffin, 1998). The current version of the Individuals with Disabilities Education Act ensures access to "the general curriculum" for students with disabilities. Because so much of what students are able to access from the general curriculum depends on their ability to read and understand grade level textbooks, development of comprehension strategies is essential in order for them to adequately access the curriculum. Besides students with disabilities, however, there are also large numbers of students without disabilities who have serious reading comprehension problems.

It is possible to reduce the reading demands on some students by modifying or adapting reading materials, that is, making the content more accessible. There is a substantial body of research evaluating the effects of text adaptation or modification for students with learning disabilities (for those interested in this body of literature, see Higgins, Boone, & Louitt, this volume, and Gersten, Fuchs, Williams, & Baker, in press).

There are at least two limitations of reducing or modifying reading expectations as an overall approach to fundamentally address problems associated with reading comprehension difficulties. First, it conflicts with current reform efforts stipulating that *all* students should be held accountable for high learning standards, including the ability to read a variety of texts with comprehension. If the reading portion of the curriculum is "watered down," or extensively modified for some students, then the idea of universal high standards would seem to be compromised.

Another reason systematically decreasing reading demands for some students is undesirable as a large-scale option is that many effective reading interventions have been developed but are not yet typically implemented on a regular basis in most general education or special education classrooms. If these techniques *were* used correctly and consistently, the comprehension of many students would improve substantially. In fact these approaches would also benefit students who are already proficient readers, increasing their feasibility in both general and remedial education settings.

School psychologists and administrators who regularly work with teachers on classroom instructional approaches are in a strong position to advocate the importance of quality reading comprehension instruction. One key to understanding effective instruction is understanding some of the difficulties that lead to comprehensions breakdowns.

SOURCES OF READING COMPREHENSION DIFFICULTIES

Many students have serious difficulties comprehending what they read even when they have adequate decoding skills (Englert & Thomas, 1987; Gersten, et al., in press; Taylor & Williams, 1983). For example, when text is read aloud to students with comprehension problems to eliminate the possibility that decoding difficulties are causing the comprehension breakdowns, their struggles with comprehension persist. In many cases, students with comprehension problems seem unaware of their comprehension difficulties. We describe some of the most important sources of comprehension difficulties in the next section (Gersten et al., in press).

Vocabulary Development and Background Knowledge

Limitations in vocabulary and background knowledge are a primary cause of comprehension failure, especially after the third grade (Baker, Simmons, & Kame'enui, 1998a, 1998b; Baumann & Kame'enui, 1991; Becker, 1977; Graves & Cooke, 1983; Graves, Cooke, & LaBerge, 1983; Graves & Palmer, 1981; Stanovich, 1986a). Compared with their peers, students with reading comprehension problems know less about most topics they are expected to read about and understand. Knowledge gaps in history, geography, and science interfere with how well these students adequately understand their assigned reading material. Most contemporary approaches to reading comprehension instruction (e.g., Bos & Anders, 1990; Klingner & Vaughn, 1996; Palincsar & Brown, 1984) attempt to assess students' background knowledge about a given topic before they read about it, and encourage students to ask their peers or the teacher when their background knowledge is limited (Klingner & Vaughn, 1996).

The relationship between reading comprehension and vocabulary knowledge also is strong and unequivocal (Baker, et al., 1998a, 1998b; Baumann & Kame'enui, 1991; Paul & O'Rourke, 1988; Stanovich, 1986b). Although the precise causal nature of the relationship is not completely understood, it does seem to be largely reciprocal. In other words, it appears vocabulary knowledge contributes to reading comprehension (Stanovich, 1986b), but also that knowledge of word meanings grows through reading experiences (Cunningham & Stanovich, 1998). The reciprocal nature of the relationship seems to hold true for readers at all skill and age levels. Even weak readers' vocabulary knowledge is strongly correlated with the amount of reading they do (Cunningham & Stanovich, 1998), and increased reading increases their vocabulary.

Directly teaching students word meanings to increase their vocabulary knowledge can do no more than explicitly deal with a small fraction of the words that students need to learn during their K–12 years (Baker, et al., 1998a, 1998b). Despite the limitations of explicit, teacher-directed vocabulary instruction, there appears to be a beneficial snowballing effect to at least some explicit vocabulary instruction. Directly teaching a small, select number of word meanings can have a significant impact not only on comprehension of passages containing those words but also on comprehension in general, and *on the ability to learn new words in context*. For example, Beck, Perfetti, and McKeown (1982) found that students who were given direct instruction in word meanings were better able to discern meanings of untaught words than other students. Stahl and Fairbanks (1986) suggest that teaching 350 words each year may augment learning from context by 10–30%, a significant amount.

On their own, students do learn word meanings in the course of reading connected text, but the process is not particularly efficient (Beck & McKeown, 1991). Beck and McKeown noted that research spanning several decades "failed to uncover strong evidence that word meanings are routinely acquired from context" (p. 799). Jenkins, Stein, and Wysocki (1984) found that students needed up to 6 or 10 exposures to words in context before they learned their meanings. If students were told their definitions prior to passage reading, however, then only two encounters were necessary to produce positive effects. This difference represents a significant increase in efficiency and a feasible approach for teachers in the classroom. Jenkins et al.'s research has direct classroom applications.

Strategic Processing of Text

Breakdowns in strategic processing of text and how well students monitor their understanding of what they are reading (i.e., metacognition) contribute to comprehension difficulties (Gersten et al., in press). Students may lack appropriate reading strategies or they many not know *when* to use strategies they, in fact, do possess. Students may not realize, or they may ignore, the importance of actively monitoring their comprehension by rereading passages that are confusing, for example.

Williams (1993) proposed that some students with comprehension problems have difficulty "getting the point," most likely because they are unable to create effective representations of the text being read. She found, for example, that students with learning disabilities had more trouble identifying important information when they summarized or discussed what they read than students without disabilities. Williams (1991) also found that students who tended to idiosyncratically introduce into stories inaccurate or irrelevant information also had more difficulty making accurate predictions based on story content.

Torgesen (1977) described students who had difficulty strategically processing text as "inactive learners." In one study he conducted, students were taught specific techniques to increase retention of material read, such as how to underline. Even with a seemingly simple technique such as underlining, students with comprehension problems displayed improvements in reading performance, albeit erratic, unlike their peers without comprehension problems whose improvements were much more consistent (Torgesen, 1982).

Text Structures

Descriptive research indicates that students with comprehension problems frequently possess limited knowledge of how various types of texts are *organized* and *structured*. Texts are commonly divided into two types of basic structures. Narrative texts are fictional stories and are typically structured to contain elements associated with a plot, setting, characters, a central problem or problems, and efforts by principle characters to solve problems. Usually there is some type of resolution at the conclusion of the story.

Expository texts are nonfiction, and their structure is more complex because it is more varied. Some purposes of expository texts are to inform, explain how to do something, make a persuasive argument in favor of a controversial issue, or describe a place or person. Each of these expository styles is structured differently, and different expository styles are typically interwoven into the same source. In other words, in the same textbook chapter an author might describe ancient Egyptians, explain how they lived, and argue their position as an advanced early civilization.

Many students are unaware of even very broad distinctions between the standard organization of narrative texts versus the organization of expository texts. Children with good comprehension skills typically have developed an understanding of how stories are structured even before they are taught to read. Once they begin reading on their own, they expect stories to unfold in certain ways. As they make the transition to reading expository text, they develop expectations for how this text might be organized. Knowledge of text structures leads students to ask relevant questions about the material they are reading as they are reading it, and to form internal predictions about the content, which produces considerable benefits in terms of reading comprehension.

Research has shown that the more students know about how narrative texts are structured—that is, that stories have a beginning, middle, and end, and typically include a plot, setting, and characters—the more information they are able to recall related specifically to these major narrative categories compared to other information in the story (Hansen, 1978; Weaver & Dickinson, 1982; Williams, 1993). Students with this "story-grammar" knowledge also are better able to recognize which story events are closely related to the basic causal chain in a story (Wolman, 1991). Students with comprehension problems are less able to distinguish between essential and nonessential material (Taylor & Williams, 1983). They are also less adept at formulating hypotheses about upcoming details in the text.

The way expository texts are structured is more troublesome for students with comprehension problems than narrative texts, in part because there are so many different types of structures. The number of expository structures varies depending on the source of the information. Essentially one type of structure fits the vast majority of narrative texts. As is the case with narrative texts, skill at discerning expository structures—and using them—facilitates reading comprehension (Hiebert, Englert, & Brennan, 1983; Taylor & Beach, 1984).

Students' awareness of text structure is acquired in a predictable pattern over time (Brown & Smiley, 1977; Englert & Hiebert, 1984), and some expository text structures are more obvious and easier to comprehend than others (Englert & Hiebert, 1984). Some commonly identified expository structures include (a) description, (b) temporal sequence of events, (c) explanation (of concepts or terminology), (d) compare/contrast, and (e) problem-solution-effect (Anderson & Armbruster, 1984). In reality, few texts are written solely according to any one of these formats. Most chapters in content-area texts, for example, are a hybrid of several of these structures (Armbruster, Anderson, & Meyer, 1991; Dimino & Kolar, 1990).

Readers who are unaware of how expository texts are structured do not approach text reading with any particular "plan of action," appearing, instead, to retrieve information in a seemingly random way (Meyer, Brandt, & Bluth 1980). Students with more sophisticated knowledge of text structures, on the other hand, tend to "chunk" and organize the text as they are reading it.

When researchers have examined these chunks of information from proficient readers, the underlying structures used to organize the text are revealed. And when some type of prompt is provided that helps students chunk information, their comprehension increases. For example, Wong (1980) demonstrated that students with comprehension problems could recall as many main ideas as their peers when questions were used to prompt responses, but performed significantly less well when prompting questions were not provided.

Reading Fluency

The importance of fluent reading, reading with a combination of speed and accuracy, in successful comprehension is undeniable. Studies have demonstrated that correlations between measures of reading fluency and comprehension are consistently robust, usually on the order of .70 to .90 (Deno, Mirkin, & Chiang, 1982; Fuchs, Fuchs, & Maxwell, 1988; Jenkins & Jewell, 1993). Cunningham and Stanovich (1998) present a rationale for the link that researchers always find between reading fluency and comprehension this way:

> Slow, capacity-draining word recognition processes require cognition resources that should be allocated to comprehension. Thus *reading for meaning is hindered;* unrewarding reading experiences multiply; and practice is avoided or merely tolerated without real cognitive involvement (italics added, p. 8).

In other words, when too much attention is allocated to low-level processes such as word recognition, not enough attentional resources are available to accomplish the higher-order processing involved in comprehension (LaBerge & Samuels, 1974). Furthermore, reading becomes an unpleasant task, one that students tend to avoid.

One promising technique for improving reading fluency is called *repeated readings* (Samuels, 1979; Sindelar, Monda, & O'Shea, 1990), and as its name implies, the technique involves having students reread passages and stories as a way to improve fluency. Repeated readings clearly improve students' overall reading fluency and comprehension on the passages they read multiple times, which itself is important because it gives students a tangible sense of what successful fluent reading is like. Whether the strategy generalizes to improvements in reading fluency and comprehension when students read unfamiliar stories has not been established empirically, however. A reasonable intervention approach would be to use repeated readings as a supplement to direct reading comprehension instruction.

Encouraging Task Persistence

Early academic experiences that consistently end in failure can easily decrease students' motivation to engage in the hard work reading requires. The consequence is that many unsuccessful readers learn to avoid settings and activities that require reading skills, both at school and at home (Stanovich, 1986b). Many adults can relate to this pattern in their own lives. In an academic environment, for example, many beginning graduate students have a very negative experience in their first statistics class. They quickly learn to avoid all but the requirement statistics classes and frequently go to great lengths to avoid other types of classes as well, such as those having to do with more conceptual approaches to research design.

Research increasingly stresses that task persistence is a major source of variability in comprehension among students, especially when it comes to expository text (DeWitz, 1997). As reading material becomes more complex and involved, all readers must expend more effort deriving meaning, and layers of meaning, from the text. The persistence they demonstrate in working out text meaning increases as the difficulty of the material increases. Beginning readers may struggle quite a bit to determine the meaning of even seemingly simple narrative or expository passages. Many students with serious reading problems seem to have limited reserves of task persistence when compared with their peers. This finding was highlighted in a large observational study by McKinney, Osborne, and Schulte (1993).

A major movement in the field of comprehension research has been to develop teaching approaches that actively encourage students *to persist* in "figuring out" what the text is saying (e.g., Beck, McKeown, Sandora, Kucan, & Worthy, 1996). In the next two major sections of the chapter we discuss ways to improve the comprehension of narrative and expository text.

IMPROVING COMPREHENSION OF NARRATIVE TEXT

Students are expected to read narrative text in school, and the stories are generally structured similarly. Characters have goals that are either stated directly or can be inferred. The key characters are placed in settings, and they make plans and undertake actions to achieve these goals. Actions unfold in an orderly sequence. Ultimately, there is an outcome, which constitutes success or failure in reaching important goals.

Students who grasp the basic text structure for narratives (often called story grammar) recall more of the key story elements than other information in the story (Hansen, 1978; Weaver & Dickinson, 1982; Williams, 1993). They also recognize which events are closely related to the basic causal chain in a story (Wolman, 1991). In other words, knowledge of story grammar helps students discern what is likely to be most relevant for understanding the story.

Many studies devoted to improving comprehension of stories utilize story grammar as a basis for the strategy (Singer & Donlan, 1982). Students are taught to identify the principal components of a story and then to use this knowledge as an organizational guide when reading. Teaching this structure explicitly is effective for students with comprehension problems as well as students without comprehension problems (Gersten et al., in press).

A useful way to think about interventions for students with and without reading comprehension problems centers on the concept of *procedural facilitators* (Gersten, Baker, Pugach, Scanlon & Chard, 2001). Procedural facilitators are questions, prompts, simple outlines, or other graphic organizers that target important structures critical in reading the text with comprehension (Scardamalia & Bereiter, 1986). Common story grammar procedural facilitators provide a way for students to approach reading difficult text. It is important to realize they are not a summary of the text developed by the teacher but a type of scaffold designed to help students organize their thoughts about a story.

A seminal study on the use of procedural facilitators was conducted by Idol (1987), who used a story mapping technique to enhance the reading comprehension of students with comprehension problems and peers who were average and above average readers. The story map was designed to "draw the readers' attention to the common elements among stories," which she thought would foster the "possibility of the reader searching his or her mind for possible information" related to the text (p. 197). In other words, the story map was to serve as a framework for integrating story elements from the text with the reader's own experiences.

On the story map, students recorded information about 10 story grammar questions, having to do with important elements of the story. Examples of the questions used throughout the intervention include: *Where* did the story take place? *When* did the story take place? *How* did [*main character*] try to solve the problem? Was it hard to solve the problem? (*Explain in your own words*) (Gersten et al., 2001).

As concrete supports, procedural facilitators highlight in an overt fashion what expert readers do more or less intuitively as they read. Many different types of procedural facilitators exist, but their goal is the same—to provide a "plan of action" for readers, and a system for teachers or peers to use to provide ongoing feedback and support. A plan of action is derived from the learners' need for help with text organization and structure (Kolligian & Sternberg, 1987) and their need for a road map or guide to successfully negotiate the comprehension process.

Procedural facilitators are essentially tools providing a *common language* between teachers and students to help guide dialogue and interactions between teachers and students and between readers and authors. During teacher-student interactions, teachers can verbally model patterns of thinking about and comprehending text. Students can display their attempts to comprehend text—either verbally or in writing—and get feedback from teachers.

In the study by Idol (1987), use of the story map procedural facilitator resulted in improved comprehension of all students in the study. It seemed to be particularly effective for students with learning disabilities and for the other students with serious reading comprehension problems. Idol found that when given the option students almost unanimously preferred to use the story maps *after* reading a story rather than during reading.

One of the most important findings was that when formal use of the story maps was discontinued the comprehension of students on average remained high, indicating that students had begun to internalize the strategies. The comprehension of some students decreased significantly, however, indicating that for them internalization had not occurred and that the removal of the facilitator was premature.

Another finding in Idol's study was entirely unexpected. Idol analyzed students' writing before and after the intervention. Prior to the intervention, students with comprehension problems included fewer story grammar components in their journal entries than other students. After the intervention, these students significant increased the number of elements they included. In fact, 80% of these students began to write stories that included all of the story grammar elements that were taught.

Idol's study lead to a series of related studies confirming that when teachers explicitly taught narrative text structures using story maps there was an increase in students' reading comprehension, especially for students with comprehension problems (Dimino, Gersten, Carnine, & Blake, 1990; Gurney, Gersten, Dimino, & Carnine, 1990; Williams, Brown, Silverstein, & deCani, 1994). Explicitly teaching narrative text structures has had a consistent positive impact on reading comprehension.

Explicit teaching. In teaching students comprehension strategies related to story grammar dimensions, initial instruction might focus on (a) who the story is about, (b) the main problem, (c) attempts to solve the problem, and (d) how the story ends. As students read stories during this instructional phase the teacher should pause to ask questions related to these dimensions, and make sure that all students comprehend the story. This is particularly important, of course, for students with comprehension problems. At the end of the story, students should try to summarize the story using the four questions to guide them.

Guided practice. In the guided practice phase, story grammar questions and maps are central to reading. The maps should have enough room on them for students to take notes as they read or after. At the end of the story, students should try to summarize the story by using the story grammar questions. Teachers should have frequent class discussions centered on answering the story grammar questions. Students should learn to support their answers by indicating specific parts of the story. This can be particularly effective if students answer a question incorrectly. Rather than telling the student the answer is incorrect, it can be more beneficial when teachers have students find the sentence or paragraph that supports their answer. It is critical, however, that teachers make sure students understand what the correct answer is and why. If there are frequent errors at this level, then it may be necessary to return to an earlier, more explicit level where teachers more carefully monitor and model the use of the story grammar questions.

Independent use. As students become adept at reading stories by using story maps and questions as a guide, teachers should continue to monitor students' use and begin to prompt students to provide analyses of stories that probe deeper levels of meaning. In some cases pursuing deeper levels of comprehension can stem directly from the original story grammar categories. In other cases additional categories can be integrated with existing ones. This is important because continued improvement in comprehension requires that readers pay attention to key details that change from story to story and are not easily categorized in maps and questioning facilitators. Frequently, it is possible to link these important details to the ideas represented in the story grammar framework, and teachers should do this explicitly to make sure students see the connection.

Teacher Questioning During Reading

Teacher questioning during reading can support students becoming active readers. Ongoing questioning is more effective when it is structured and follows a specific pattern because students are more likely to internalize self-questioning strategies and use them independently after instruction.

Essentially, interspersed questions model for children how good readers actively question the text as they read. Questions posed before reading can improve comprehension if they are general and focus on the most salient information in the text (Rickards, 1976). They help orient beginning readers to the idea that it is important to have thought about what the content of the text might be before reading it.

It is important to stress that during the reading of the text these same questions should be addressed (White, 1981) so that readers get to see how their expectations and predictions about the story held up. Discrepancies should be noted and discussed. For example, in H. G. Wells' story, *The Star,* questions might include: What made the new star? Where was the star heading? Why did the star become brighter and brighter? After reading, the same three questions could be asked, plus some additional ones, such as What was the school girl worried about?

Asking the same questions before and after reading is especially effective if the reading material is difficult to comprehend (Hartley & Davies, 1976; Levin & Pressley, 1981), and the more precise the questions are, the more students can focus their attention on specific information (Anderson & Biddle, 1975). Asking additional questions after reading helps students not become preoccupied with reading the text just to answer the orienting questions.

Recent research has shown that *teacher questioning* is also an effective way to help students understand how stories are structured. Answering predictable, repeated patterns of questions helps students focus their attention on the crucial structure of the story and results in better comprehension than asking unpredictable, uniquely relevant questions (Carnine & Kinder, 1985; Dimino et al., 1990; Gurney et al., 1990; Idol, 1987; Short & Ryan, 1984; Singer & Donlan, 1982; Williams et al., 1994). In other words, interspersed questions should be aligned with the story maps students use to depict the structure of the stories (Idol, 1987).

As stories become more complex the mapping and questioning procedures teachers use to facilitate comprehension can also increase in complexity to include more elements, require greater elaboration, and so forth. The important point about story maps and related teacher questioning strategies is that a consistent pattern be used and that the stories used during instruction should lend themselves to this pattern. In the next section we outline a general sequence of instruction for expository text.

IMPROVING COMPREHENSION OF EXPOSITORY TEXT

By the time children enter the fourth grade the demand for them to read and understand expository material (i.e., history, science, geography, social studies, and other disciplines) is substantial (Wilson & Rupley, 1997). In fact, most reading beyond the primary grades involves expository text, as does most reading that adults find necessary for work and in everyday life (Stanovich, 1994).

Comprehending expository text is typically more difficult than comprehending narrative text for four reasons (Hidi & Hildyard, 1983; McCutchen & Perfetti, 1982). Expository text is more likely to be "information dense," with unfamiliar technical vocabulary and content (Lapp, Flood, & Ranck-Buhr, 1995). A second reason, which has generated a great deal of attention, is that expository texts use more complicated and varied structures than do narrative texts (Kucan & Beck, 1997).

The third challenge of expository texts is that they involve reading long passages without prompts from a "conversational partner" (Bereiter & Scardamalia, 1987). In narrative texts, dialogues are typically interspersed throughout the text, and conversations per se are an everyday part of children's oral language experiences. Fourth, as Stein and Trabasso (1981) have suggested, the logical-causal arguments typical of expository text structure are more abstract, and therefore less familiar, than the goal-directed events that characterize narrative texts.

Single-Strategy Instruction

The major method for enhancing student comprehension of expository text is "strategy instruction," which is intended to improve how readers "attack" expository material, in order to become more deliberate and active in processing it. Examples of strategies to improve the comprehension of expository text include passage organization training, self-questioning procedures, mapping organizers, and summary skills training (Gersten et al., in press). Research on strategy instruction in reading comprehension has tended to investigate one strategy in isolation or the effect of multiple strategies together.

One study with a high degree of classroom utility examined the *Question Answer Relationships* strategy (QARs) (Simmonds, 1992). Students were taught to categorize comprehension questions as *Right There* (text explicit), *Think and Search* (text implicit), and *On My Own* (script implicit). Twenty-four special education teachers teaching more than 400 students with significant reading comprehension problems used the QARs strategy to teach students to categorize the three types of questions.

Students in the experimental group performed better than students in comparison groups on question-answering and maze tasks constructed by the teachers using actual classroom social studies material. The effects were consistent across measures, which were not closely aligned with the treatment, making the findings more convincing.

Overall, research on single-strategy instruction suggests that careful teacher mediation is important. Unfortunately, students do not easily internalize the use of single-strategy methods or use them in reading *different* types of texts. Consequently, teachers should be very systematic about teaching the process of applying a strategy and provide students with carefully structured practice opportunities. Support should be faded slowly, and close monitoring of students' application and understanding should continue for an extended period of time.

Multiple Strategy Instruction

Studies evaluating the simultaneous use of more than one strategy have been conducted in laboratory-like and real classroom settings. They also vary in terms of the explicitness of the instruction provided. Some studies have investigated the use of two strategies, frequently combining (a) summarization of main ideas with (b) self-monitoring. Other studies have investigated the use of more than two strategies at a time.

In one study, Graves (1986) compared direct instruction on identifying main ideas with direct instruction combined with self-questioning and self-monitoring. In self-questioning and self-monitoring, students recorded their progress as they read, repeatedly asking themselves, "Do I understand what the whole passage is about?" Results were assessed under three different conditions:

1. Students read outcome passages under a reading aloud condition (as they had been trained to do, with materials cueing students to self-monitor).

2. Students read outcome passages silently, again with materials designed to prompt students to self-monitor.

3. Students read passages silently or aloud (student's choice) 1 week later, with no cues. Each reading required the students to identify main ideas in the passages.

In all three conditions students in the direct instruction with self-questioning and monitoring group performed better than students in the direct instruction alone group, who themselves did better than students in the comparison group. This finding suggests that careful teacher mediation of summarization (i.e., direct instruction on identifying main ideas) combined with a self-monitoring strategy can significantly improve the reading comprehension of expository text.

One of the most thorough approaches to teaching comprehension of expository text was conducted by Englert and Mariage (1991). A generic graphic organizer was developed to support the use of *multiple* strategies by fourth-, fifth-, and sixth-grade students with significant reading comprehension problems. The "POSSE" intervention used the graphic organizer in combination with the following set of strategies: *P*redicting ideas, *O*rganizing predicted ideas and background knowledge based on text structure, *S*earching for the text structure, *S*ummarizing the main ideas, and *E*valuating comprehension.

Teachers modeled the use of these strategies with the graphic organizer and gradually transferred responsibility of the dialogue supporting use of these strategies to the students. An important part of the intervention was students learning to work together on explaining what they read using the graphic organizer as a guide. Although some students had not fully internalized the strategies during the 2-month training, they did increase their strategy knowledge more than comparison students. This was particularly true in the classrooms where teachers did a good job of transferring control of the dialogue to the students. Overall, however, the intervention produced substantial effects, and demonstrated that students with reading comprehension problems could learn to use a relatively sophisticated combination of strategies to improve their reading comprehension.

Graphic Displays

Visual organizers of expository text can also be used to help students comprehend what they are reading (Raphael, Englert, & Kirschner, 1986; Sinatra, 1984; Sinatra, Stahl-Gemake, & Berg, 1984; Sinatra, Stahl-Gemake, & Morgan, 1986). Visual depictions of text structure should be integrated with instruction in other reading comprehension strategies (e.g., identifying main ideas, summarizing) to help students hone in on the central features of comprehension.

Graphic displays of expository text can be helpful in providing a visual picture of the content and showing key linkages. We have synthesized the work of Meyer and Rice (1984) and of Sinatra et al. (1986) into a model of four text structure maps that may be used in conjunction with strategy instruction to improve comprehension in a variety of content areas. The maps illustrated here include important *signal words* that help indicate specific types of text structure.

In the model that follows, pupils learn to identify the text structure of passages by identifying a possible "map" of the structure. In doing this, students are taught to read the text, searching for ways it might be mapped using familiar terminology such as "wheels" for a descriptive/thematic map and "steps" for a sequential episodic map.

FIGURE 1

Descriptive or Thematic Map

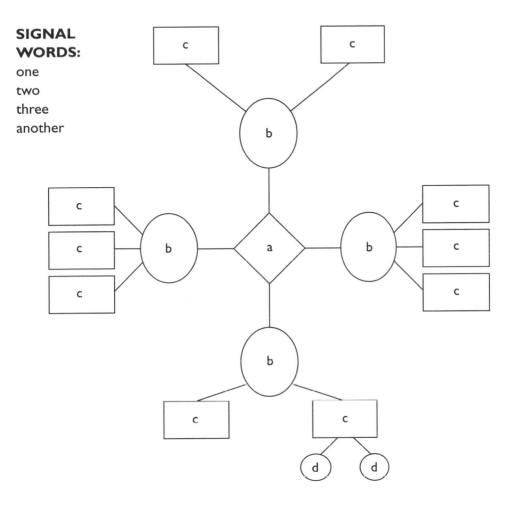

SIGNAL WORDS:
one
two
three
another

Descriptive/Thematic maps. This type of map, represented in Figure 1, has broad application in many subject areas in which ideas are subsumed by other superordinate ideas. For example, it can be used for describing systems (e.g., body systems) or for illustrating the relationship between ideas in persuasive essays, in which evidence is used to support each point. This map is most comparable to a traditional "outline" pattern. Cell *a* corresponds to the main idea or system (e.g., body systems). At the next level, the four *b* cells list the components of the main system (e.g., nervous, circulatory, skeletal, and digestive systems). The *c* cells each contain a subordinate point to each of the components (e.g., heart, veins, and arteries under circulatory system). Additional breakdown of points can be accommodated by adding additional subordinate levels of cells, as the *d* cells illustrate.

FIGURE 2

Comparative/Contrastive Map

SIGNAL WORDS:
on the other hand
however
in contrast
but

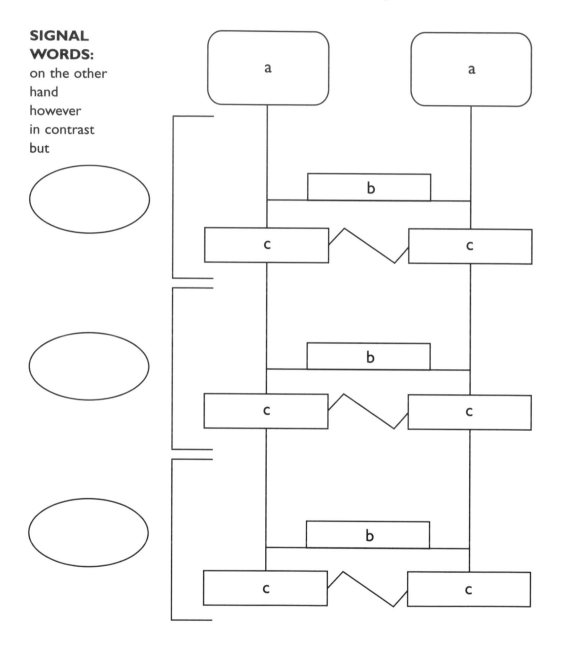

Comparison/Contrast map. Being able to compare and contrast events, people, ideas, places, etc., is important in learning to read with understanding. Figure 2 can be used when students read expository material and should compare two concepts. The parallel structure in the map is critical in how it is used. Simply listing features of one concept and then listing the features of the other concept is a common error made in

FIGURE 3

Problem Solution Map

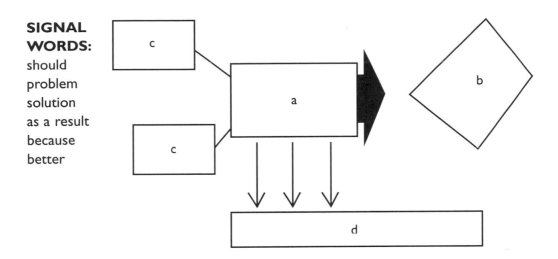

SIGNAL WORDS:
should
problem
solution
as a result
because
better

comparison/contrast tasks and is likely to result in shallow levels of comprehension. The top boxes, labeled *a,* display the concepts being compared and contrasted. The map has boxes for features that the concepts share, labeled *b,* and room for features that are unique to each concept, labeled *c.* The circles to the left are very important and require higher level processing skills. Having teachers spend time teaching students to work on accurate labels for those circles can result in rich opportunities for comprehension processing. The circles require the naming of the dimensions on which the two concepts are being compared. For example, a comparison between the North and the South before the Civil War might list the dimensions of economics, politics, and social order.

Problem/Solution map. In expository text that has a clear identifiable problem, it can facilitate comprehension to try and understand fundamental *causes,* and consider *solutions,* in the context of specific causal factors. For example, understanding how to solve cancer problems requires understanding factors that cause cancer. To illustrate cause-and-effect relationships (Figure 3), the large arrow, labeled *a,* is used to show a cause, resulting in a problem, labeled *b.* The boxes labeled *c* are used to define the cause, or to list critical features of the cause. Describing attributes of the cause is an important level of analysis. The vertical arrows indicate that the cause of a problem, and how it is defined, implies or leads to possible solutions.

In some content, a better understanding of solutions may result from the careful *analysis* of the problem rather than from a direct understanding of the cause. For example, in dealing with a personal problem identified as the problem, it may be too late or impossible to change the specific events that caused the problem. A better way to target possible solutions may be to deal directly with specific dimensions of the problem.

FIGURE 4

Sequential Episodic Map

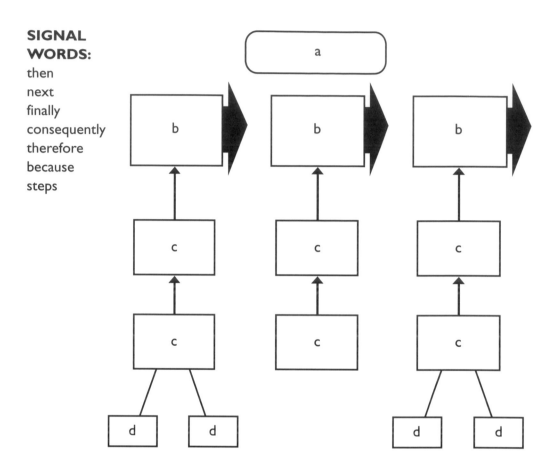

SIGNAL WORDS:
then
next
finally
consequently
therefore
because
steps

Sequential episodic map. Sequential episodic maps can be particularly useful for students reading history texts. Figure 4 is an example of a map that could be used to depict the causes of a major historical event. The major event is labeled *a* in the figure. The second level *b* boxes illustrate the relevant causes and consequences of the major event. The first *b* level event results in a consequence, which would be recorded in the second *b* level box. The series of *c* level boxes indicates that each event recorded in the *b* boxes is also associated with one or more causes. The series of *d* boxes shows that *c* level events are also associated with specific causes.

Peer-Mediated Instruction in Reading Comprehension

Procedures to build reading fluency, the use of procedural facilitators, teaching single or multiple reading comprehension strategies, and graphic organizers of text are all ways to get students to process and understand what they are reading more effectively.

The most recent research on reading comprehension incorporates more flexibility in how these techniques are used by students because the variations in the types of text students have to learn are extensive, and long-term effectiveness requires that students internalize these approaches if they are going to be used over time. Researchers increasingly believe that ongoing dialogue about the meaning of text is a critical component in boosting comprehension levels, especially for students with comprehension problems. One popular technique for increasing dialogue and active processing is through the use of peer tutors. As with most intervention approaches, there are benefits and drawbacks of using peers to "teach" or foster comprehension (Fuchs, Fuchs, Mathes, & Simmons, 1997; Vadasy, Jenkins, Antil, Phillips, & Pool, 1997).

Peer tutoring has the potential to provide ongoing interactive dialogue in a system in which students have the opportunity to work cooperatively and provide feedback to each other (see Greenwood et al., this volume, and Fuchs et al., 1997; Greenwood et al., 1992; Simmons, Fuchs, Fuchs, Hodge, & Mathes, 1994). Studies have begun to provide empirical support for the impact elaborated dialogue has on the comprehension of students with serious comprehension problems. In contemporary models of peer tutoring and contemporary approaches to explicit teaching of comprehension it is possible to conceptualize a system in which feedback is truly tailored to the unique abilities of each student. Another potential advantage is that having peers working together is a very feasible configuration. If actual benefits in comprehension are derived, then the amount of time devoted to this type of instructional arrangement is much less limited by resource considerations or logistic factors than many other types of reading instruction, such as one-to-one tutoring with an adult.

A potential limitation of peers is that they may not have the verbal skill to adequately assist other students, even if they themselves have strong reading skills. On the other hand, it is also possible that peers might actually use language that is more easily understood by other students than the more formal language of adults.

Studies demonstrate the potential for strategy instruction with students with learning disabilities, but few have focused on teacher delivery within naturally occurring classroom settings. An exception is the work of Fuchs, Fuchs, Mathes, and Simmons (1997), which has addressed how a peer-tutoring system focused on comprehension can be achieved in the context of real classroom conditions. Peer-Assisted Learning Strategies, or PALS, is a class-wide one-to-one peer-tutoring program involving partner reading, paragraph summary, prediction, and other activities that have been demonstrated to strengthen reading comprehension. The truly innovative feature of the system is that students work with each other on sophisticated reading comprehension strategies but do so in a very structured format.

In one important study (Fuchs et al., 1997), 20 teachers implemented PALS for 15 weeks. Students in the PALS classrooms demonstrated greater reading progress on all measures of reading achievement than students in comparison classrooms. Measures included words read correctly during a read-aloud, comprehension questions answered correctly, and missing words identified correctly in a *cloze* (maze) test. The intervention was effective for students with learning disabilities and for students without disabilities, including low and average achievers.

SUMMARY

Research has consistently demonstrated the possibility of teaching methods and strategies that significantly improve reading comprehension skills of students with serious reading difficulties. Many studies have been conducted in real classroom settings, and the approaches are eminently feasible for classroom application. There are a number of important aspects about the knowledge base that school psychologists and others who work with teachers on effective implementation of these approaches should bear in mind.

Research studies have made an important distinction between comprehension approaches that target narrative text versus expository text. Change agents, such as school psychologists, and classroom teachers can improve student performance by using this distinction as they target ways to improve comprehension instruction. The commonality that ultimately bridges narrative and expository instruction is that both genres can be read with deeper understanding by accessing the underlying text structures on which they are developed.

In general, narrative texts are easier to understand because a single underlying story grammar structure supports the vast majority of narrative texts. Expository texts tend to be more challenging to read with understanding because, in part, there are many different types of structures that underlie how they are written. Expository texts also are more challenging because the content and vocabulary may be entirely unfamiliar to many students.

Because text structures do serve as an organizer for the material students are expected to read and understand, however, instruction should address providing access to those structures for the purpose of improving comprehension. Deciphering text structures becomes even more important as reading demands increase, and as the shift to reading primarily expository material occurs, usually around grade 4.

Research is clear on the benefits of teachers explicitly teaching students reading comprehension strategies. This instruction includes early explicit instruction on text structures, beginning with narrative texts and moving to different types of expository texts. Building on text structures is instruction that demonstrates that comprehension during actual reading is an entirely active process rather than a passive one. Teachers can model this, for example, by using think aloud techniques and other explicit approaches. Question asking before, during, and after reading should be an integral part of comprehension instruction. Predictions about content could be confirmed, and students should be required to find evidence supporting their answers to questions by finding relevant content in the text.

It is crucial that students begin to internalize the reading comprehension techniques and approaches they have been taught. Extended practice fosters internalization, but this is best accomplished under the careful guidance of the teacher, who can provide support and feedback. The goal is for students to personalize comprehension strategies, to use them independently to the point where they become more and more automatic, as they are for good readers.

Constructive classroom dialogues can help students internalize their use of formal reading strategies. Interactive dialogue—either with the teacher or proficient peers—is certainly one of the key areas of contemporary research on reading comprehension instruction. The growing evidence, in particular, that peers can work together to improve comprehension has tremendous potential for classroom application because there are many peers but only one teacher, and opportunities for extensive work and practice are abundant.

One final consideration is that the development of strong reading comprehension skills should begin early. There is every reason to expect that in first and second grade students should be well on their way toward becoming fluent readers of grade level text (i.e., automaticity with decoding). During that development, reading comprehension strategies should be a consistent part of reading instruction. As decoding improves and becomes less and less a barrier to successful reading, the emphasis on comprehension strategies can continue to increase. Of real assistance in this scenario is that basal reading programs have started to change quite substantially to reflect more research-based approaches. More empirically validated and explicit techniques for teaching phonemic awareness, alphabetic understanding, and reading fluency are being included and integrated. Approaches for teaching comprehension strategies are also infused in these lessons and become a more substantial part of the program over time.

REFERENCES

Anderson, R. C., & Biddle, W. B. (1975). On asking people questions about what they are reading. In G. Bower (Ed.), *Psychology of learning and motivation.* New York: Academic.

Anderson, T. H., & Armbruster, B. B. (1984). Content area textbooks. In R. C. Anderson & J. Osborn & R. J. Tierney (Eds.), *Learning to read in American schools* (pp. 193-226). Hillsdale, NJ: Erlbaum.

Armbruster, B. B., Anderson, T. H., & Meyer, J. L. (1991). Improving content area reading using instructional graphics. *Reading Research Quarterly, 26,* 393-441.

Baker, S. K., Simmons, D. C., & Kame'enui, E. J. (1998a). Vocabulary acquisition: Research bases. In D. C. Simmons & E. J. Kame'enui (Eds.), *What reading research tells us about children with diverse learning needs* (pp. 183-218). Mahwah, NJ: Earlbaum.

Baker, S. K., Simmons, D. C., & Kame'enui, E. J. (1998b). Vocabulary acquisition: Research bases. In D. C. Simmons & E. J. Kame'enui (Eds.), *What reading research tells us about children with diverse learning needs* (pp. 183-218). Mahwah, NJ: Lawrence Erlbaum Associates.

Baumann, J. F., & Kame'enui, E. J. (1991). Research on vocabulary instruction: Ode to Voltaire. In J. Flood, D. Lapp & J. R. Squire (Eds.), *Handbook of research on teaching the English language arts* (pp. 604-632). Upper Saddle River, NJ: Merrill/Prentice-Hall.

Beck, I., & McKeown, M. (1991). Conditions of vocabulary acquisition. In R. Barr, M. Kamil, P. Mosenthal & P. D. Pearson (Eds.), *Handbook of reading research* (Vol. 2, pp. 789-814). New York: Longman.

Beck, I. L., McKeown, M. G., Sandora, C., Kucan, L., & Worthy, J. (1996). Questioning the author: A yearlong classroom implementation to engage students with text. *Elementary School Journal, 96,* 385-414.

Beck, I. L., Perfetti, C. A., & McKeown, M. G. (1982). Effects of long-term vocabulary instruction on lexical access and reading comprehension. *Journal of Educational Psychology, 74,* 506-521.

Becker, W. C. (1977). Teaching reading and language to the disadvantaged—What we have learned from field research. *Harvard Educational Review, 47,* 518-543.

Bereiter, C., & Scardamalia, M. (1987). *The psychology of written composition.* New York: Erlbaum.

Bos, C. S., & Anders, P. L. (1990). Effects of interactive vocabulary instruction on the vocabulary learning and reading comprehension of junior-high learning disabled students. *Learning Disability Quarterly, 13,* 31-42.

Brown, A. L., & Smiley, S. S. (1977). Rating the importance of structural units of prose passages: A problem of metacognitive development. *Child Development, 48,* 1-8.

Carnine, D., & Kinder, B. D. (1985). Teaching low-performing students to apply generative and schema strategies to narrative and expository material. *Remedial and Special Education, 6*(1), 20-30.

Cunningham, A. E., & Stanovich, K. E. (1998). What reading does for the mind. *American Educator, 22*(1, 2), 8-15.

Deno, S., Mirkin, P. K., & Chiang, B. (1982). Identifying valid measures of reading. *Exceptional Children, 49*(1), 36-45.

DeWitz, P. (1997). *Comprehension instruction: A research agenda for the 21st century: Understanding expository texts.* Paper presented at the annual meeting of the American Educational Research Association, Chicago, IL.

Dimino, J., Gersten, R., Carnine, D., & Blake, G. (1990). Story grammar: An approach for promoting at-risk secondary students' comprehension of literature. *Elementary School Journal, 91*(1), 19-32.

Dimino, J., & Kolar, C. (1990). Using frames to improve at-risk students' comprehension in the content areas. In G. Tindal (Ed.), *Proceedings from the Oregon Conference.* Eugene, OR: The University of Oregon.

Englert, C. S., & Hiebert, E. H. (1984). Children's developing awareness of text structures in expository materials. *Journal of Educational Psychology, 76,* 65-75.

Englert, C. S., & Mariage, T. V. (1991). Making students partners in the comprehension process: Organizing the reading "POSSE." *Learning Disability Quarterly, 14,* 123-138.

Englert, C. S., & Thomas, C. C. (1987). Sensitivity to text structure in reading and writing: A comparison between learning disabled and non-learning disabled students. *Learning Disability Quarterly, 10,* 93-105.

Fuchs, D., Fuchs, L. S., Mathes, P. H., & Simmons, D. C. (1997). Peer-assisted strategies: Making classrooms more responsive to diversity. *American Educational Research Journal, 34*(1), 174-206.

Fuchs, L. S., Fuchs, D., & Maxwell, L. (1988). The validity of informal reading comprehension measures. *Remedial and Special Education, 9,* 20-28.

Gersten, R., Baker, S., Pugach, M., Scanlon, D., & Chard, D. (2001). Contemporary special education teaching. In V. Richardson, (Ed.), *Handbook of Research on Teaching* (4th ed., pp. 695-722). Washington, DC: American Educational Research Association.

Gersten, R., Fuchs, D., Williams, J., & Baker, S. (in press). Teaching reading comprehension strategies to students with learning disabilities. *Review of Educational Research.*

Graves, A. W. (1986). Effects of direct instruction and metacomprehension training on finding main ideas. *Learning Disabilities Research, 1*(2), 90-100.

Graves, M. F., & Cooke, C. L. (1983). Effects of previewing difficult short stories for high school students. *Research on Reading in Secondary Schools, 6,* 38-54.

Graves, M. F., Cooke, C. L., & LaBerge, M. J. (1983). Effects of previewing difficult short stories on low ability junior high school students' comprehension, recall, and attitudes. *Reading Research Quarterly, 18,* 262-276.

Graves, M. F., & Palmer, R. J. (1981). Validating previewing as a method of improving fifth and sixth grade students' comprehension of short stories. *Michigan Reading Journal,* 1-3.

Greenwood, C. R., Carta, J. J., Hart, B., Kamps, D., Terry, B., Arreaga-Mayer, C., Atwater, J., Walke, R. D., Risley, T., & Delquadri, J. (1992). Out of the laboratory and into the community: 26 years of applied behavioral analysis at the Juniper Gardens Children's Project. *American Psychologist, 47,* 1464-1474.

Gurney, D., Gersten, R., Dimino, J., & Carnine, D. (1990). Story grammar: Effective literature instruction for high school students with learning disabilities. *Journal of Learning Disabilities, 23,* 335-342.

Hansen, C. L. (1978). Story retelling used with average and learning disabled readers as a measure of reading comprehension. *Learning Disability Quarterly, 1,* 62-69.

Hartley, J., & Davies, I. K. (1976). Preinstructional strategies: The role of pretests, behavioral objectives, overviews and advance organizers. *Review of Educational Research, 46,* 239-265.

Hidi, S. W., & Hildyard, A. (1983). The comparison of oral and written productions in two discourse types. *Discourse Processes, 6,* 91-105.

Hiebert, E. H., Englert, C. S., & Brennan, S. (1983). Awareness of text structure in recognizing and producing expository discourse. *Journal of Reading Behavior, 15,* 63-80.

Idol, L. (1987). Group story mapping: A comprehension strategy for both skilled and unskilled readers. *Journal of Learning Disabilities, 20*(4), 196-205.

Jenkins, J. R., & Jewell, M. (1993). Examining the validity of two measures for formative teaching: Reading aloud and maze. *Exceptional Children, 59,* 421-432.

Jenkins, J. R., Stein, M., & Wysocki, K. (1984). Learning vocabulary through reading. *American Educational Research Journal, 21,* 767-787.

Klingner, J. K., & Vaughn, S. (1996). Reciprocal teaching of reading comprehension strategies for students with learning disabilities who use English as a second language. *Elementary School Journal, 96,* 275-293.

Kolligian, J., & Sternberg, R. J. (1987). Intelligence, information processing, and specific learning disabilities: A triarchic synthesis. *Journal of Learning Disabilities, 20,* 8-17.

Kucan, L., & Beck, I. L. (1997). Thinking aloud and reading comprehension research: Inquiry, instruction, and social interaction. *Review of Educational Research, 67,* 271-299.

LaBerge, D., & Samuels, S. J. (1974). Toward a theory of automatic processing in reading. *Cognitive Psychology, 6,* 293-323.

Lapp, D., Flood, J., & Ranck-Buhr, W. (1995). Using multiple text formats to explore scientific phenomena in middle school classrooms. *Reading and Writing Quarterly: Overcoming Learning Difficulties, 11,* 173-186.

Levin, J., & Pressley, M. (1981). Improving children's prose comprehension: Selected strategies that seem to succeed. In C. M. Santa & B. L. Hayes (Eds.), *Children's prose comprehension: Research and practice.* Newark, DE: International Reading Association.

McCutchen, D., & Perfetti, C. A. (1982). Coherence and connectedness in the development of discourse production. *Text, 2,* 113-119.

McKinney, J. D., Osborne, S. S., & Schulte, A. C. (1993). Academic consequences of learning disability: Longitudinal prediction of outcomes at 11 years of age. *Learning Disabilities Research and Practice, 8,* 19-27.

Meyer, B. J. F., Brandt, D. M., & Bluth, G. J. (1980). Use of top-level structure in text: Key for reading comprehension of ninth-grade students. *Reading Research Quarterly, 16,* 72-103.

Meyer, B. J. F., & Rice, G. E. (1984). The structure of text. In P. D. Pearson (Ed.), *Handbook of reading research* (pp. 319-351). New York: Longman.

National Reading Panel. (2000). *Report of the national reading panel: Teaching children to read: An evidence-based assessment of the scientific research literature on reading and its implications for reading instruction.* Washington, DC: National Institute of Child Health and Human Development.

Palincsar, A. S., & Brown, A. L. (1984). Reciprocal teaching of comprehension-fostering and comprehension-monitoring activities. *Cognition and Instruction, 1,* 117-175.

Paul, P. V., & O'Rourke, J. P. (1988). Multimeaning words and reading comprehension: Implications for special education students. *Remedial and Special Education, 9*(3), 42–51.

Raphael, T. E., Englert, C. S., & Kirschner, B. W. (1986). *The impact of text structure instruction and social context on students' comprehension and production of expository text* (Research Series No. 177). East Lansing: Michigan State University, Institute for Research on Teaching.

Rickards, J. P. (1976). Type of verbatim question interspersed in text: A new look at the position effect. *Journal of Reading Behavior, 8,* 37–45.

Samuels, S. J. (1979). The method of repeated readings. *The Reading Teacher, 32,* 403–408.

Scardamalia, M., & Bereiter, C. (1986). Written composition. In M. Wittrock (Ed.), *Handbook on research on teaching* (3rd ed., pp. 778–803). New York: Macmillan.

Short, E. J., & Ryan, E. B. (1984). Metacognitive differences between skilled and less skilled readers: Remediating deficits through story grammar and attrition training. *Journal of Educational Psychology, 76,* 225–235.

Simmonds, E. P. M. (1992). The effects of teacher training and implementation of two methods of improving the comprehension skills of students with learning disabilities. *Learning Disabilities Research and Practice, 7,* 194–198.

Simmons, D. C., Fuchs, D., Fuchs, L. S., Hodge, J. P., & Mathes, P. G. (1994). Importance of instructional complexity and role reciprocity to class-wide peer tutoring. *Learning Disabilities Research and Practice, 9,* 203–212.

Sinatra, R. (1984). Visual/spatial strategies for writing and reading improvement. In A. Walker, R. Braden, & L. Dunker (Eds.), *Enhancing human potential* (pp. 101–122). Blacksburg, VA: Virginia Polytechnic Institute and State University.

Sinatra, R., Stahl-Gemake, J., & Berg, D. (1984). Improving reading comprehension of disabled readers through semantic mapping. *Reading Teacher, 38,* 22–29.

Sinatra, R., Stahl-Gemake, J., & Morgan, N. W. (1986). Using semantic mapping after reading to organize and write original discourse. *Journal of Reading, 30,* 4–13.

Sindelar, P. T., Monda, L. E., & O'Shea, L. J. (1990). Effects of repeated readings on instructional- and mastery-level readers. *Journal of Educational Research, 8*(4), 220–226.

Singer, H., & Donlan, D. (1982). Active comprehension: Problem solving schema with question generation for comprehension of complex short stories. *Reading Research Quarterly, 17*(2), 166–185.

Snow, C. E., Burns, M. S., & Griffin, P. (Eds.). (1998). *Preventing reading difficulties in young children.* Washington, DC: National Academy Press.

Stahl, S. A., & Fairbanks, M. M. (1986). The effects of vocabulary instruction: A model-based meta-analysis. *Review of Educational Research, 56,* 72–110.

Stanovich, K. E. (1986a). Cognitive processes and the reading problems of learning-disabled children: Evaluating the assumption of specificity. In J. K. Torgesen & B. Y. L. Wong (Eds.), *Psychological and educational perspectives on LD* (pp. 87–131). Orlando, FL: Academic.

Stanovich, K. E. (1986b). Matthew effects in reading: Some consequences of individual differences in the acquisition of literacy. *Reading Research Quarterly, 21*(3), 360–406.

Stanovich, K. E. (1994). Romance and reality. *The Reading Teacher, 47,* 280-291.

Stein, N. L., & Trabasso, T. (1981). What's in a story: An approach to comprehension and instruction. In R. Glaser (Ed.), *Advances in instructional psychology* (Vol. 2). Hillsdale, NJ: Erlbaum.

Taylor, B. M., & Beach, R. W. (1984). The effects of text structure instruction on middle grade students' comprehension and production of expository text. *Reading Research Quarterly, 19,* 134-146.

Taylor, M. B., & Williams, J. P. (1983). Comprehension of learning-disabled readers: Task and text variations. *Journal of Educational Psychology, 75,* 743-751.

Torgesen, J. (1977). The role of nonspecific factors in the task performance of learning disabled children: A theoretical assessment. *Journal of Learning Disabilities, 10*(1), 33-39.

Torgesen, J. (1982). The learning-disabled child as an inactive learner: Educational implications. *Topics in Learning and Learning Disabilities, 2*(1), 45-52.

Vadasy, P. F., Jenkins, J. R., Antil, L. R., Phillips, N. B., & Pool, K. (1997). The research-to-practice ball game: Class-wide peer tutoring and teacher interest, implementation, and modifications. *Remedial and Special Education, 18*(3), 143-156.

Weaver, P. A., & Dickinson, D. K. (1982). Scratching below the surface structure: Exploring the usefulness of story grammar. *Discourse Processes, 5,* 225-243.

White, R. (1981). Tight spot. In G. R. Duffy & L. R. Roehler (Eds.), *Basic reading skills* (pp. Level 2, Red, pp. 12-17). Evanston, IL: McDougal, Litell.

Williams, J. P. (1991). Comprehension by learning disabled and nondisabled adolescents of personal/social problems presented in text. *American Journal of Psychology, 104,* 563-586.

Williams, J. P. (1993). Comprehension of students with and without learning disabilities: Identification of narrative themes and idiosyncratic text representations. *Journal of Educational Psychology, 85,* 631-641.

Williams, J. P., Brown, L. G., Silverstein, A. K., & deCani, J. S. (1994). An instructional program in comprehension of narrative themes for adolescents with learning disabilities. *Learning Disability Quarterly, 17,* 205-221.

Wilson, V. L., & Rupley, W. H. (1997). A structural equation model for reading comprehension based on background, phonemic, and strategy knowledge. *Scientific Studies of Reading, 1,* 45-63.

Wolman, C. (1991). Sensitivity to causal cohesion in stories by children with mild mental retardation, children with learning disabilities, and children without disabilities. *Journal of Special Education, 30,* 439-455.

Wong, B. Y. L. (1980). Activating the inactive learner: Use of questions/prompts to enhance comprehension and retention of implied information in learning disabled children. *Learning Disability Quarterly, 3,* 29-37.

AUTHORS' NOTES

Sections of this chapter are adapted from Gersten, Fuchs, Williams, and Baker (in press).

CHAPTER 28

Adapting Challenging Textbooks
to Improve Content Area Learning

Kyle Higgins and Randall Boone
University of Nevada, Las Vegas
Department of Special Education
College of Education

Thomas C. Lovitt
University of Washington

INTRODUCTION

The ability to read is the most fundamental skill one needs to succeed in society today, and has been identified as a necessary skill for competitive involvement in our technological society (National Research Council [NRC], 1998). As a society and as educators we have recognized the importance of successful reading; however, only recently have we begun to understand the profound and enduring consequence of not learning to read or extract meaning from the printed word (Juel, 1988; Lyon & Chhabra, 1996). The lack of proficient reading skills has been identified as a risk factor associated not only with academic failure and school dropout but with unemployment and adjudication (Cornwall & Bawden, 1992; Werner, 1993). Whitman (1995) found that individuals who test in the least proficient literacy levels are often unemployable, since even low-skilled jobs demand adequate reading abilities. Thus a vicious cycle begins; if you cannot read, you do not practice reading; if you do not practice reading, you do not become automatic and fluent in your ability to recognize words; and, if you do not read, you do not succeed in today's modern world.

Although experts do not agree on the exact number of poor readers caught in this cycle, a report from the U.S. Department of Education (National Center for Education Statistics, 1993) indicated that 90 million of America's 191 million adults either are illiterate or can perform only simple literacy tasks. Focusing these data on school-age students, national longitudinal studies indicate that one in six children will encounter a problem in learning to read (National Center to Improve the Tools of Educators, 1996).

Particularly affected are students with disabilities. These children are given a variety of labels by the educational system—students with learning disabilities, students with mental retardation, students with communication disorders, or students at risk. Regardless of the label, most of these students have one characteristic in common—they struggle to read. Among the millions of Americans who have learning disabilities, at least 75% have been identified as having a reading disability (National Institute of Child Health and Human Development [NICHD], 1994). The viciousness of this cycle is exemplified by recent research indicating that this problem emerges during the first 3 years of school (National Center to Improve the Tools of Educators, 1996) and that 74% of the readers who are unsuccessful readers in the third grade are still unsuccessful readers in the ninth grade (Lyon, 1995).

As students with disabilities and students considered at-risk progress through school, reading expectations begin to change. In the primary grades, reading skills and literal reading comprehension are usually the major areas of focus in school. By the upper elementary grades, students are asked to *apply* their reading skills by drawing conclusions and formulating principles in their content area subjects such as science and social studies. It is during this time that the main format of reading materials used in the classroom begins to shift from narrative text to expository text. Thus, what was once familiar in the early grades (e.g., narrative story lines) is replaced by unfamiliar facts, concepts, and material that is expressed in new and more abstract form (Jordan, 1994). In middle school and high school the emphasis changes again for students. Content area teachers believe that students already have, or should have, the reading, writing, and thinking skills necessary to process the required readings (Hollander, 1991). Thus, students are expected to (a) read independently, (b) process information, (c) analyze what they have read, and (d) synthesize multiple points of view. Literacy is now considered a tool used to *extract information* from expository texts in content area subjects such as history, science, social studies, and literature.

In secondary school, the instruction of students with disabilities becomes particularly difficult because of the discrepancy between the students' performance levels and these curriculum demands in their content classes (Schumaker & Deshler, 1984). These students begin to experience failure in their content area coursework. For example, Donahoe and Zigmond (1988) found that 69% of the grades received by ninth-grade science students with learning disabilities were D or below.

Thus, Stanovich's (1986) application of the "Matthew Effect" concept—the rich get richer and the poor get poorer—is very true for students who struggle to read as they progress through school. If a student reads well, he or she will in all likelihood be successful in school; if not, he or she will be unsuccessful and/or decide to leave school. Because these students perform poorly in school owing to their inability to meet the increasingly high demands for literacy present in today's high schools (Donahoe & Zigmond, 1990), they often drop out of school (deBettencourt, Zigmond, & Thornton, 1989; Rumberger, 1987; Zigmond & Thornton, 1985). In the end, the ramifications of struggling to read have profound effects on the lives of these students. Not only are the paths to content area material blocked, but ultimately their lives are affected socially and personally. We live in a society that places great value on literacy—a person who does not learn to read or to apply literacy skills in a variety of situations suffers greatly in this environment (Lerner, 1997).

INCLUSION OF STUDENTS WITH DISABILITIES

Over the past 15 years, the movement in special education has been to provide educational services for students with disabilities in the general education classroom to the greatest extent possible. This trend to serve students with disabilities in more inclusive programs comes from a number of sources, the primary source being the least restrictive environment clause (LRE) of the Individuals with Disabilities Act of 1997 (IDEA '97) (U. S. Department of Education, 1998). In fact, the passage of IDEA '97 mandates that the placement of students with disabilities in settings other than general education classes must be justified specifically. The law also states that placement in a setting other than the general education classroom may occur *only* after intensive supports have been provided to keep the child in the general education classroom.

The impact of IDEA '97 is reflected in the 20th Annual Report to Congress (U.S. Department of Education, 1998), which indicates that in the 1995–96 school year more than 95% of students with disabilities ages 6–21 attended schools with their peers without disabilities. These data indicate a gradual increase in the percentage of students with disabilities who are educated in general education for 80% or more of the school day. Approximately 46% of all students with disabilities are removed from their general education classes for less than 21% of the school day. These data also reflect a decrease in the number of students who are removed from general education for 21–60% of the school day. Overall, there has been a decrease in special education resource room use for students with disabilities and an increase in the use of the general education classroom as the primary educational placement. As a result, general education teachers are responsible for the academic instruction of students with mild disabilities for the majority of the academic day (Parmar & Cawley, 1993; Passe & Beattie, 1994).

The movement to provide special education services in the inclusive community of the general education classroom has its roots in the philosophical ideology of the normalization of children with disabilities and the elimination of labels for these children (Lerner, 1997). The belief is that all students have the basic human right to attend school with their typical peers in their neighborhood school (Edgar, 1987; Ferguson, 1996; Sawyer, McLaughlin & Winglee, 1994). This philosophy holds that moving students with disabilities away from their typical peers highlights their disabilities, disrupts or fragments their education, and teaches them to be dependent (Friend & Bursuck, 1999). The goal is to provide education in a setting that more approximates the real world in which the students will live and function when they leave school.

The emphasis on including students with disabilities in the general education classroom also reflects the growing knowledge that many students with disabilities do not complete high school with the knowledge and skills necessary for adult independence (U.S. Department of Education, 1997; Wagner, D'Amico, Marder, Newman, & Blackorby, 1992). For all students with disabilities the major factor predicting successful high school graduation is the ability to read at a fourth-grade level (U.S. Department of Education, 1998). Yet data collected by the National Longitudinal Transition Study (NLTS) (Wagner et al., 1992) indicate that 3–5 years after leaving high school fewer than 25% of youth with disabilities were enrolled in postsecondary education, those who were employed were engaged in low-wage jobs with few opportunities for promotion, and more than half continued to live with their parents—all factors that have been correlated with the lack of reading proficiency (Cornwall & Bawden, 1992; Werner, 1993; Whitman, 1995).

CONTENT AREA INSTRUCTION

Typical general education secondary content area instruction is constructed around a teacher-directed lecture concerning information contained in a textbook, followed by students reading independently in their textbooks (Kinder & Bursuck, 1991; Ravitch & Finn, 1987). Often, this type of reading involves answering questions at the end of a chapter, defining vocabulary words, or studying for a weekly test—all activities based around extracting information from the textbook. It appears that in content area classrooms, the most predominant instructional tool is the textbook (Goodlad, 1976). The literature indicates that in elementary and secondary schools, science, social studies, and history are primarily taught through the use of a textbook by general and special educators (Armento, 1986; Patton, Polloway, & Cronin, 1990; Raizen, 1988; Woodward, Elliot, & Nagel, 1986) with 91% of teachers reporting that they use a single content area text as the primary resource for planning instruction (Bean, Zigmond, & Hartman, 1994). With 75–90% of teachers organizing their content area instruction around a textbook (Mullis & Jenkins, 1988; Tyson & Woodward, 1989), the estimate is that between second grade and 12th grade, a student will read at least 33,000 pages from content area materials (May, 1994). Estimates of the amount of time students actually spend on reading and doing exercises from these textbooks range from 55% to 95% of their classroom instructional time (Zahorik, 1991).

Although textbooks are the primary instructional tool in content area classrooms at the secondary level (Woodward et al., 1986), there is a great deal of criticism targeting these books in terms of their suitability for both students with disabilities and students in general education. This criticism ranges from their content (Beck, McKeown, & Gromoll, 1989), instructional design (Armbruster, & Gudbrandsen, 1986; McKeown, Beck, Sinatra, & Loxterman, 1992), and level of difficulty (Chall & Conrad, 1991; Lovitt, Horton, & Bergerud, 1987) to the irrelevancy of the text (Estes, 1982), overall considerateness of the text (Armbruster, 1984; Anderson & Armbruster, 1984), and the ability of the text to cooperate with the reader during the reading process (Boone, Higgins, Falba, & Langley, 1993). It is important for educators to consider these criticisms when working with or selecting a content area text. General criticisms leveled by researchers concerning content area textbooks are contained in Table 1. Specific concerns relating to social studies and history textbooks are found in Table 2, on page 760, while science textbook criticisms are shown in Table 3, on page 761.

TABLE 1

Overall Criticisms of Content Area Textbooks

1. Content area textbooks are often organized around misleading titles and subtitles (Estes, 1982).

2. Many content area textbooks assume unrealistic levels of students' background knowledge (McKeown & Beck, 1990).

3. Fifty-seven percent of the best-selling content area textbooks are above the grade level for which they were written (e.g., on the fourth-grade level, the average social studies textbook is written for Grade 5 or 6, and the average science textbook for Grade 7 or 8) (Conrad, 1990).

4. Often, supplemental materials (e.g., workbooks) that accompany content area textbooks contain poorly sequenced tasks that provide poor directions for completing the activities (Osborn, 1984).

5. Content area textbooks often only represent mainstream society (Pace, 1992) and sometimes do not include certain cultures (King, 1992).

6. Textbooks often include highly interesting, but trivial or unimportant details designed to heighten the interest of the reader. Often this intriguing information actually distracts the reader from the content that is important (Garner, Gillingham, & White, 1989) and is assigned main idea status, which disrupts the comprehension of the reader (Garner, Alexander, Gillingham, Kulikowich, & Brown, 1991; Graves et al., 1991).

7. Textbook writing tends to be loosely organized and does not focus the reader's attention on important content (Chambliss & Calfee, 1989) and does not provide explicit signals to the reader that certain information is important (Hare, Rabinowitz, & Schieble, 1989).

STUDENTS WITH DISABILITIES IN THE CONTENT AREA CLASSROOM

Overall, the research appears to indicate that textbooks are not designed for the *typical reader* much less for a student who struggles with reading. Kantor, Anderson, and Armbruster (1983) indicated that textbooks are suitable for only the top half of the students in a general education classroom on measure of organizational structure and audience appropriateness. With more and more students with disabilities being included in the general education classroom, particularly for science and social studies instruction (U.S. Department of Education, 1998) and the high reliance of content area teachers on textbooks (Bean et al., 1994), educators must begin to focus on the char-

TABLE 2

Criticisms of Social Studies and History Textbooks

1. Social studies textbooks have four problem areas: unclear content goals, assumed background knowledge of the reader, inadequate explanations of material presented, and poor presentation of content (Beck, McKeown, & Gromoll, 1989).

2. Social studies textbooks tend to focus on learning names, definitions, and facts— rather than meaningful "big ideas" (Armbruster & Ostertag, 1987).

3. There is a discrepancy among the difficulty levels of social studies textbooks when compared to basal reading texts for the same grade, and the lower the grade level the more difficult the text in relation to the reading ability of the students (Chall & Conrad, 1991).

4. Main ideas are not explicitly stated in most social studies texts, which results in a text that does little to help build understanding for students with little background knowledge of the material being covered (Baumann & Serra, 1984; Tyson & Woodward, 1989).

5. The writing style found in social studies/history textbooks lacks coherence (Beck, McKeown, & Gromoll, 1989; May, 1994).

6. Historical facts often are not presented as a coherent whole in American history textbooks and students are often overwhelmed by the quantity of material presented to them (Kinder & Bursuck, 1991).

acteristics of these students as content area learners and consider textbook modifications to facilitate their learning.

Characteristics of Students

The increase in diverse learners in the general education classroom has been problematic for teachers who continue to use traditional curricula, conventional instructional methods and materials, and standard textbooks and workbooks. Content area textbooks and expository reading places heavy demands on the student with a disability or the student who struggles with reading (see Table 4, on page 762). With readability assessments of upper elementary content area texts indicating that over half of all students assessed were at their frustration reading level (Wait, 1987) and 92% of the students at the high school level were at the frustration reading level in their assigned textbooks (Sellers, 1987), it is no wonder that general education teachers are quickly discovering that traditional methods do not meet the needs of increasingly heterogeneous classrooms (Ciborowski, 1992).

TABLE 3

Criticisms of Science Textbooks

1. Science textbooks are usually written at reading levels higher than the grade for which they are recommended (Wood & Wood, 1988).

2. Most science textbooks are designed around the focus of acquiring scientific facts, with the predominant activity being the memorization of vocabulary terms (Horizon Research, 1989; Stinner, 1992).

3. In science textbooks students are deluged with new terms and concepts at the rate of approximately 300 new words per text in the sixth grade (Armbruster & Valencia, 1989), to over 3,000 new terms and symbols per text in the 10th grade (Hurd, 1986).

4. Science textbooks fail to incorporate sound instructional design principles (e.g., activating prior knowledge, previewing concepts and vocabulary, presenting metacognitive strategies) (Mastropieri & Scruggs, 1994).

Educators who seek solutions in the teacher's guides provided by textbook publishers often encounter prescriptions that are not applicable to the specific population of students they find in their classroom. Parmar and Cawley (1993), in a study that examined the efforts of textbook publishers to provide educators with teaching manuals outlining strategies specifically designed for students with disabilities, found impractical recommendations, inconsistencies across grade levels, and a poor correspondence between actual student needs and publisher recommendations.

Determining Textbook User-Friendliness for Students With Disabilities

Because of the criticisms leveled against content area textbooks and the knowledge we have concerning the interactions of students with disabilities and other students who experience reading difficulties with these texts, it is prudent that teachers assess the quality of the instructional design, or *user-friendliness,* of a textbook for supporting a wide variety of learning needs. Through this evaluation the teacher will have a clearer idea of the obstacles that may prevent certain students from being successful with a particular textbook. This evaluation of the textbook also will provide a road map for teachers to follow as they design modifications or adaptations of the textbook to match the specific learning needs of the students. Since there is a wide range of abilities within each class, teachers should not attempt to implement a "one size fits all" modification or adaptation of the textbook.

Therefore, the first step in making the textbook more user-friendly is to assess the interaction of individual students with the text in question. This involves assessing (a)

TABLE 4

Students With Disabilities and Content Area Learning

1. The expository text found in content area textbooks is more complex and varied than the narrative text read in elementary school. Students with disabilities often are unaware of the organizational structure of text and consequently overlook main ideas and important details (Englert & Thomas, 1987).

2. Ninety-one percent of content area teachers express concerns about the "readability" of the textbooks they use for instruction (Bean, Zigmond, & Hartman, 1994) and indicate that the vocabulary is too difficult for students with reading problems (Friend & Bursuck, 1999).

3. Students with disabilities often lack much of the prior knowledge of concepts necessary to extract meaning from the expository text contained in content area texts (Bos & Anders, 1987; Lenz & Alley, 1983).

4. When reading content area textbooks, students with disabilities do not use efficient skills and strategies for learning and remembering information, unless specifically cued to do so (Dole, Valencia, Greer, & Wardrop, 1991).

5. Students with disabilities have a difficult time understanding which ideas are important in expository text (Kinder & Bursuck, 1991) and how the ideas relate to one another in social studies (Lawton, 1995) and in science (Scruggs & Mastropieri, 1994).

6. Often the reading rate of secondary students with disabilities is substantially lower than that of their peers in science, social studies, and health classes (Lovitt & Horton, 1988). This often results in the students scoring lower on written tests (Lovitt, Horton, & Bergerud, 1987).

7. Students with disabilities often expect to perform poorly in content area classes (e.g., science, history, social studies) and thus simply go through the motions of learning, dispensing only minimal effort (Readence, Bean, & Baldwin, 1998).

8. The science reading comprehension scores for students with disabilities are minimal, with performance scores on tests hovering around the 33% correct level (Cawley, Miller, & Carr, 1989; Lovitt & Horton, 1994). Low scores are also found in social studies classrooms, with 66% of students with disabilities scoring below average on work completed (Passe & Beattie, 1994).

9. Prior to their inclusion in the content area classroom, students with disabilities receive limited instruction in the use of higher-level cognitive skills (Morsink, Soar, Soar, & Thomas, 1986). This limited exposure could severely impede their ability to function in a situation that requires them to read and generalize information (Passe & Beattie, 1994).

10. Many secondary students with disabilities continue to struggle with simple word identification skills, which severely impacts their ability to read fluently and comprehend text (Moats, 1998) and identify words that are multisyllabic (Lenz & Hughes, 1990). Because they often lack automatic word recognition skills and decoding skills, these students are unable to focus on reading for meaning in their secondary-level content area text (Snider, 1989).

11. When reading content area textbooks, students with disabilities spend an inordinate amount of time focusing on specific words and as a result experience difficulty with comprehension (Horton, Lovitt, & Bergerud, 1990). Because of their concentration on individual components of the reading material to the exclusion of the whole or big idea, they are often easily distracted by trivial, yet captivating, bits of unimportant information (Winograd, 1984).

the students, (b) the textbook, and (c) the students as they interact with or read the textbook. In this manner, the teacher will have a greater understanding of the "goodness of fit" between the academic needs of the students, the textbook in question, and what occurs when the students attempt to use the textbook to learn.

Schumm and Stickler (1991) suggest that the teacher begin by validating the reading skills of each individual student by reviewing standardized test scores or Individual Educational Plans (IEPs), administering an informal reading inventory to the students, and inquiring of the special educator and/or other content area teachers concerning the reading characteristics of individual students. In this manner, the teacher builds an individual reading profile of each student in the class. This knowledge is beneficial to understanding why some students may not be extracting meaning from the text.

The assessment of the textbook first involves ascertaining the readability level of the text. Even though the problems with readability formulas are well documented (Lovitt & Horton, 1991), they do provide a *one*-dimensional view of the text that, with other information, can contribute to the decision-making process. Ascertaining the readability level of the text provides educators with information concerning specific areas in which modifications must be made (e.g., vocabulary, comprehension strategies).

The second step in the assessment of the textbook involves the actual determination of the degree of user-friendliness of the textbook. Singer (1992) suggests that teachers review the text for (a) text organization (e.g., uniform style of writing, consistent method of material presentation, and cohesiveness of the way the information ties together); (b) explication of ideas (e.g., information is stated directly, new terms are defined as they are introduced, text relates new information to information students may already possess or information already presented in the text); (c) conceptual density (e.g., the presentation of new information is spaced out in the text); (d) metadiscourse (e.g., the author talks directly to the reader about the information contained in the text by explicitly stating the purpose or goal of the text, advising students on how to learn from the text, or telling the students how to apply text information in other situations); and (e) instructional devices (e.g., text includes organizational aids such as headings, subheadings, an index, chapter overviews, diagrams, tables, annotations in margins, summaries, and conclusions). Several checklists have been created to assist teachers in this evaluation (Readence, Bean, & Baldwin, 1998; Singer, 1992; Steinley, 1987).

The last step in evaluating the user-friendliness of the textbook involves assessing the student/text interaction. This process involves previewing the textbook with the students to determine their knowledge of the particular text in terms of organization, instructional devices, conceptual density, metadiscourse, and explication of ideas. Irwin and Baker (1989) suggest constructing a textbook "scavenger hunt" to ascertain the students' awareness of these components (e.g., ask the student to indicate headings, annotations, summaries, or overviews). Schumm and Stickler (1991) suggest a cloze reading test and a content reading inventory be used to assess the student's ability to interact and construct meaning from the textbook. Readence et al. (1998) provide a comprehensive description of how to construct and administer a cloze test and create a content reading inventory.

Other characteristics of user-friendly textbooks for teachers to consider are presented in Table 5. These characteristics should be viewed in reference to the audience with whom the textbook will be used. Probably the most important characteristic of a textbook is whether or not it is appropriate for a specific audience. That is, does the text truly consider the prior knowledge and background of the readers who are targeted? If a text does not consider its audience, it is possible that no amount of modification or adaptation will make it user-friendly.

Determining a textbook's user-friendliness is only the first step in adapting challenging textbooks to improve content area learning. The second step to facilitate learning is for the teacher to enhance the textbook to increase the interactions of the reader with the text.

Traditional Content Area Textbook Modifications

There are four reasons to consider modifying or adapting content area reading for students with disabilities and students who struggle with reading in order to make the text more user-friendly.

1. The majority of these students are unable to read their textbooks with the proficiency required to gain enough information from them to assimilate and integrate the information with previously learned material (Lovitt & Horton, 1991, 1998).

2. The textbooks lack the structure, coherence, unity, and audience appropriateness necessary for learning in an efficient manner (Lovitt & Horton, 1991, 1998).

3. Secondary students are very sensitive to changes in their textbooks that result in their having a different textbook than the other students in the class (Vaughn, Schumm, Niarhos, & Daugherty, 1993).

TABLE 5

Components of User-Friendly Textbooks

Characteristic	Components
Text Organization	• The text contains a uniform style of writing (e.g., text frames are used to provide consistent structure to the writing). • Information is presented in a consistent and predictable manner. • The writing style is cohesive, the relationship among concepts is clear, and information is tied together for the reader. • There is logical connection and flow of meaning from one idea or concept to the next. • The text provides the reader with information concerning the organization of the text (e.g., through the use of a variety of instructional devices embedded in the text). • Overall, the text is well written (e.g., clear references, explicit quantifiers, definite pronoun phrases, easy to follow chronological sequences, and appropriate transitions from one topic to another).
Metadiscourse	• The author talks directly to the reader about the information contained in the text by explicitly stating the purpose or goal of the text. • The text advises students on how to best learn from the text. • The text explicitly tells students how to apply text information in other situations and provides examples of how to do so.
Explication of Ideas	• Information is stated directly. • New terms are defined as they are introduced. • The text, directly and explicitly, relates new information to information that students may already possess or to information previously presented in the text. • Complete explanations of concepts are provided. • The text provides enough examples and nonexamples of concepts to provide readers with adequate information to relate to their background knowledge. • The text considers the limited background knowledge of some readers and provides clear descriptions of information that may be necessary to interpret facts or data presented. • Relationships among key pieces of information are provided.
Conceptual Density	• The presentation of new information is spaced out in the text so that concept overload does not occur in one chapter or recommended reading assignment. • The text considers the amount of vocabulary and concepts introduced in a lesson. • The text considers the number of new concepts or vocabulary introduced in a single sentence. • The text does not include irrelevant or distracting information. • Information that is only peripherally related to the purpose of a chapter (e.g., excerpts from a diary or a letter) is set aside in a boxed-in area. • The text balances breadth with depth by addressing a limited number of powerful ideas or big ideas.
Instructional Devices Incorporated	• The headings and subheadings are appropriate and are accurate indications of the information that follows.

Table 5 continued on page 766

Table 5 continued

Characteristic	Components
	• The textbook contains an index. • Each chapter or section contains an overview of the new information to be introduced. • Each chapter or section contains a summary of the information presented. • Appropriate diagrams, tables, and illustrations are included to clarify concepts or information introduced rather than distract or present nonessential information. • Annotations of important information or concepts are provided in the margin. • Important information is highlighted (e.g., color coded, in italics, boldface). • The text makes use of appropriate signaling words (e.g., first, second, then, therefore). • Semantic maps, concept maps, or graphic organizers are use to highlight important information or to depict relationships. • Typographical cuing is used appropriately (e.g., varied print size, items enumerated with bullets). • Topic sentences or main ideas are highlighted to increase comprehension.

4. The textbooks are not "cooperative" in that they do not have scaffolds built into them by the publisher and/or author to provide support and assistance for a wide variety of readers (Boone & Higgins, 1993; Boone et al., 1993; Higgins & Boone, 1994; Higgins, Boone, & Lovitt, 1996).

Regardless of the criticism leveled against them, textbooks continue to be a pervasive feature of education in secondary schools (Tyson & Woodward, 1989) and as such are considered to be a legitimate source of content knowledge by teachers and students. Because teachers often find themselves with only one textbook to use with all students in the classroom—from the student who is able to work totally indepen-dently to the student who needs one-on-one instruction—modifications and adaptations to the text appear to be the best option to address the diversity of the classroom.

Educators in the field of reading (Armbruster & Gudbrandsen, 1986; Dishner, Bean, Readence, & Moore, 1992; Readence et al., 1998) and in special education (Boone & Higgins, 1992, Higgins & Boone, 1992; Higgins et al., 1996; Lovitt & Horton, 1991, 1998; MacArthur & Haynes, 1995; Schumm & Stickler, 1991) have suggested a variety of methods by which teachers can modify textbooks. These modifications provide the basis by which the texts become more effective learning tools so that all students are better able to meet the demands in content area classrooms. These suggestions range along a continuum from more traditional techniques designed to help students use the text more efficiently, to ideas for supplementing the use of the text, to the more radical ideas of recreating the text as a digital study guide or digital textbook.

We should remember that experts continue to stress the importance of the teacher's willingness to make adaptations to accommodate individual differences among learners and that the success of including students with disabilities in general education classrooms will rest upon the teacher's ability and willingness to make these changes (Stainback, Stainback, Courtnage, & Jaben, 1985). Because the population of a typical general education classroom is a heterogeneous group of students, modifications made will benefit many of the general education students in the classroom as well. Recent research has indicated that teachers view textbooks and their accompanying material as important instructional resources that they do not want to do without (Bean et al., 1994). This research also reveals that teachers do not often suggest any methods by which they modify the text to make it more "user-friendly" or considerate for students. Thus, it is prudent for all educators to review suggested methods for modifying and supplementing content area textbooks so that students with disabilities and other students who struggle with reading are better able to participate more successfully in the secondary content area classroom. Table 6, on page 768, delineates a number of paper/pencil methods for modifying and/or supplementing content area textbooks. The modifications presented here are by no means the only modifications that may be used to increase the user-friendliness of a text. However, they are the modifications found most often in the research literature to be effective for students with disabilities and other students at risk for reading failure.

DIGITAL TEXTBOOKS AS COOPERATIVE INSTRUCTIONAL TOOLS

Technology use in education has grown exponentially over the last 15 years. A recent survey of special educators indicated that 85% use technology in literacy instruction, 97% believe that technology can help students acquire literacy skills, and 91% expect to increase their use of technology in the future (Burton-Radzely, 1998). Although not a panacea for all of the problems students encounter when they read content area material, adapting a textbook to the digital format can provide a tool with which to assist students who struggle to read and learn from the text. The most important consideration is that the digital text provides the learning strategies in an individualized, learner-centered situation (Boone et al., 1993) that does not conflict radically with the traditional organization of the content area classroom or the instructional strategies typically used by the content area teacher (Loucks & Zacchei, 1983).

Adjusting a textbook to a digital format does not mean "dumbing down" or "watering down" instruction. Cooperative digital textbooks offer great potential for students with disabilities by providing *alternate access* to the standard textbook. The textbook can be customized to meet the unique needs of each individual student (e.g., style and pace). When students read from a traditional content area textbook, they are limited to the information contained in that particular volume, with any additional facts, details, or clarification being obtained from supplementary reference sources (e.g., a dictionary, thesaurus, encyclopedia, or another person). A cooperative digital textbook, on the other hand, provides immediate access to supplemental data through its computer format without the interruptions of having to seek additional help outside of the immediate reading environment. A digital cooperative textbook can include extra information in the form of additional text, computer-generated speech or sound, graphics, animated sequences, digital video clips, access to the Internet, or combinations of these various media.

TABLE 6

Traditional Modifications to Content Area Textbooks

Modification	Explanation
Advance Organizers	Advance organizers are presented to students before the actual lesson or reading assignment to activate prior knowledge and to provide a cognitive road map for students as they progress through the lesson or reading material. They may be written on the board, passed out to students on a worksheet, or given verbally. Typically the components in an advance organizer are as follows: (a) the tasks involved in the lesson, (b) topics and concepts to be covered in the lesson, (c) pertinent background information to understand the lesson, (d) the rationale for the lesson (e.g., why the lesson or information is important), (e) key vocabulary contained in the lesson, and (f) expected student outcomes. The goal is to get students to think about what they already know about a topic, direct their attention to the reason(s) they will be reading, and to activate their interest and curiosity.
Vocabulary Development	Vocabulary development is the foundation on which students will place the information collected in their reading (e.g., facts, ideas, concepts). Vocabulary selected for instruction should be words that the student is likely to encounter again, or only those words that pertain to the main concepts/ideas of the lesson. Students who have a working knowledge of the vocabulary to be encountered in an assignment stand a better chance of comprehending the material read. Vocabulary development typically occurs prior to reading the assigned material and may take several forms: (a) a series of timed drills in which students write terms that match definitions; (b) lessons designed to develop an understanding not only of the word definition, but also of how the term may be used in different contexts; (c) assessment of student knowledge of content vocabulary to ascertain the level of understanding a student has for a particular word (e.g., "I've never seen that word before," "I've heard that word, but I don't know what it means," "I can read that word and I think it has something to do with ..." (Nagy, 1998); and (d) opportunities to learn the relationships of words.
Study Guides	Study guides usually are incorporated into a worksheet and take the form of questions or statements designed to help students learn content information. They may be used before, during, or after reading the assigned material and serve as a supplement to teacher-led instruction. Study guides attempt to abstract or isolate important pieces of information, thereby guiding student comprehension. Study guides should be constructed around the three levels of comprehension: applied (e.g., helps students understand how this information can be used), interpretive (e.g., helps students understand what the author means), and factual (e.g., helps students understand what the author said). Study guide formats that have been effective with students with disabilities and remedial students in content area classrooms include short-answer questions, framed outlines, and matching. It is suggested that study guides cover an approximately 1,500-word passage (Lovitt & Horton, 1994) and include no more than 10 questions (Readence et al., 1998). The goal is to design a study guide that helps students organize information and reflect upon the information they collect.

Modification	Explanation
Graphic Organizers	Graphic organizers are visual representations of key vocabulary or content information in which subordinate categories branch off from superordinate categories in the form of tree diagrams. Information contained in the graphic organizer is connected graphically into a meaningful whole to provide organization to a series of related terms, facts, or concepts. Other terms used to refer to graphic organizers are tree diagrams, structured overviews, semantic maps, concept maps, and flowcharts. Graphic organizers are beneficial learning tools used prior to reading, during reading, and as a follow-up to reading assignments. It appears that graphic organizers help students learn the interrelatedness of meaningful concepts and principles (Novak, 1990). Well-developed graphic organizers can communicate complex relationships (e.g., comparison, contrast, cause, effect, superordination, and subordination) and have been found to facilitate not only the initial learning of concepts, but the subsequent retention and retrieval of information learned (Carnine, Silbert, & Kame'enui, 1990).
Visual Displays	Visual displays are illustrations or line drawings combined with words to convey facts, concepts, or to illustrate relationships among pieces of information. The types of enhancements found in visual displays may include hierarchical, comparative, directional, and representative information. A visual display may be a diagram, a concrete model that students label, or an illustration that portrays relationships to be learned. The visual display may be used in any part of the lesson in combination with effective teaching practices.
Interspersed Questions	A common instructional tool used by content area teachers is to stop periodically during reading or direct instruction and ask questions. Interspersing questions is a technique that positively influences test performance (Tobias, 1987; Wong, 1980) in that the teacher has the opportunity to immediately provide corrective feedback to students. It is important that the questions be planned in advance and require the students to identify critical pieces of information and associations in the text (Kame'enui & Simmons, 1990). In this manner, the interspersed questions focus the students' attention on critical concepts and principles contained in the content area textbook.
Mnemonic Devices	Mnemonic strategies are verbal or pictorial memory-facilitating strategies designed to help low-achieving students learn factual information. Mnemonic strategies facilitate the acquisition of content material by training students in specific memory strategies to apply to unfamiliar information. Typically, students must be trained in the use and application of mnemonic strategies with the teacher monitoring their use over time. Five types of mnemonic devices have been explored in the literature: (a) first-letter mnemonics (e.g., students are taught to use the first letter of a word, phrase, or sentence as a cue to recall information); (b) keyword mnemonics (e.g., students are presented with an illustration that is phonetically similar to the unfamiliar term to be learned—a picture of a box to remember the mineral bauxite [Mastropieri, Scruggs, & Levin, 1986]); (c) pegword mnemonics (e.g., students are taught to connect a series of numbers to familiar objects that rhyme with the numbers—1 equals bun, 2 equals shoe; the association between the number and pegword helps the student to remember sequential information [Mastropieri et al., 1986]); (d) mimetic mnemonics (e.g., exercises that involve the actual pictorial representation of the information to be learned—if the students need to learn the chambers of the heart, they are presented with an illustration of the heart with the chambers identified); and (e) symbolic mnemonics (e.g., common symbols are used to represent information to be learned—a donkey to represent the Democratic Party, a coin to represent money).

FIGURE 1

A Sample Page of Digital Text Illustrating Additional Information Accessible by the Student

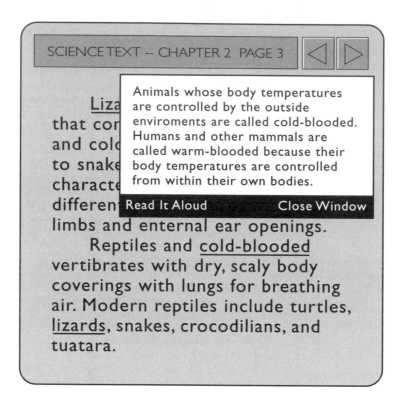

Note
A new window of text is linked to the vocabulary word "cold-blooded" from a digital science text and is available when the student requests it with a simple click of the mouse.

For example, in a digital science textbook, a student may begin reading about reptiles. Some words are underlined, indicating to the student that extra, related information is available either as text, pictures, or sound. The student selects the underlined text, "cold-blooded," and a text window appears partially overlaying the original text (see Figure 1). The student reads the information or selects to have the information read to her and when finished closes the window. The student then selects the word "lizard" and a picture of a common lizard is displayed in a graphic window (see Figure 2). Digitized voice, music, or sound effects can accompany both the graphic and text windows for further help or clarification.

Although these adaptations to the text seem relatively simple, they mimic the types of strategies that teachers traditionally employ with students when reading in a group situation. For example, monitoring for new and unusual words with which the student may have difficulty, providing definitions, suggesting that students define key words, and drawing relationships between pictures and text elements are all successful strategies for

FIGURE 2

Another Example of Additional Information About a Topic That Can Be Selected by a Student Using a Digital Text

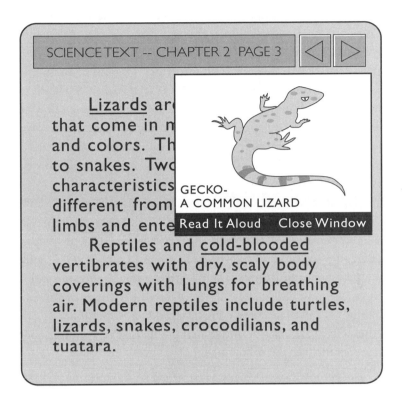

Note
A graphic window is linked to the word "lizard" and depicts a gecko, a common lizard.

improving comprehension. For students who struggle with reading, the benefit to the digital textbook is that it provides these strategies in the private learning environment of the computer screen, thus individualizing the instruction for each student. Students who are hesitant to ask questions can review the material over and over without the stress of speaking up in class.

Digital textbooks can be constructed in a variety of formats, from a textbook designed for nonlinear browsing to a more specific, directed teaching tool. Research has shown that digital texts and study guides, designed as directed teaching tools, can be powerful instructional interventions (Anderson-Inman, Horney, Chen, & Lewin, 1994; Anderson-Inman, Knox-Quinn, Horney, 1996; Boone & Higgins, 1993; Higgins & Boone, 1990a, 1990b; Higgins et al., 1996; Horton, Boone, & Lovitt, 1990; MacArthur & Haynes, 1995).

Successful Adaptations to a Digital Text

A plethora of research indicates that when teachers make traditional modifications and adaptations to content area material for students with disabilities and for students who struggle with reading, the students achieve at a higher level (Horton & Lovitt, 1989; Lenz & Hughes, 1990; Lovitt & Horton, 1991, 1994, 1998; Mastropieri, Scruggs, & Levin, 1986; Wong, 1980). This higher achievement level also is the outcome when technological modifications and adaptations are implemented (Anderson-Inman et al., 1994; Anderson-Inman et al., 1996; Boone & Higgins, 1993; Higgins & Boone, 1990a, 1990b; Higgins et al., 1996; Horton, Boone, & Lovitt, 1990; MacArthur & Haynes, 1995).

The capacity for the individualization of the digital textbook allows for each student's disability and learning style to be taken into consideration when the digital text is designed by the teacher(s). Further individualization occurs when the student works with the digital textbook and "elects" to interact (or not) with the various modifications made by the teacher(s).

Textbook adaptations that have shown positive results in the research include (a) reading text aloud to students; (b) using related pictures, recordings, or video; (c) constructing abridged versions of the text; (d) providing students with outlines or summaries; (e) using a multilevel approach in difficulty of text; (f) introducing key vocabulary in a prereading situation; (g) summarizing textbook information; (h) reducing the length of assignments; (i) slowing the pace of the instruction; and (j) teaching students to take notes and record key concepts and terms (Schumm & Stickler, 1991).

Most of these strategies can be implemented successfully in a cooperative digital textbook. Examples include the following:

1. Provide Talking Text. Text can be "read aloud" from the digital textbook as a digitally recorded voice.

2. Use related pictures, recordings, or video. These three types of media are easily incorporated into a digital textbook. The capability also exists to connect students to the Internet from within a digital textbook.

3–5. Construct abridged material. Many students need an abridged version of the content contained in the text. This can be done by providing chapter outlines, summaries, graphic organizers, or study guides. The construction of the abridged material takes a multilevel approach in that the extra information is available through information windows (e.g., text, graphic, and video) as well as text rewritten at a lower reading level. It is important to remember not to sacrifice the content to be learned when making these modifications. When in doubt, consider formatively evaluating the modification with students and use their suggestions to make the modification. It is best to build in supports that provide clarification of material to be learned, thus "watering up" the curriculum rather than taking out important material.

6. Introduce key vocabulary. Boldface words can be used to introduce the important new vocabulary before reading takes place. Students can highlight key words and the digital text can either display a "talking" printed definition of the word, provide a picture of the word, or provide a video clip of the vocabulary word. For example, if the vocabulary word was "photosynthesis," the student could hear the word pronounced, hear or read the definition, view a diagram of the process of photosynthesis and hear it explained, or watch a video of the process of photosynthesis.

7–8. Summarize content. Reworking the text into the page-by-page chunks for the digital textbook, the teacher(s) can select the amount of text necessary to fill each page by changing the font and size of the text, reducing the length of the text, or rewriting the content to more approximate the reading level and/or background knowledge of the audience.

9. Modify the pace. Working with the digital textbook allows each student to work at his or her own pace. The student has the opportunity to read and reread the material, access the supporting material in any order to aid comprehension, move about in the text, and determine how fast or slow the information is presented. The textbook can also be designed so that students must proceed through certain instruction routines that teachers want all students to access. Teachers can also put the digital textbook up on the Internet for students to access from home, thus increasing the opportunity to interact with the text in a variety of settings.

10. Encourage study skills. Built-in, easy-to-use, note-taking functions can be built into the digital textbook that provide students with the option of writing their own notes or selecting text from the text to be included in their notes. Teachers also can include study guides to direct the students in extracting information from the textbook, embed questions into the text read as a comprehension strategy, include quizzes that pertain to material read, and incorporate other traditional content area modifications into the digital textbook.

Incorporating Empirical Research Into the Design of the Digital Textbook

The ultimate goal in the creation of a cooperative digital textbook is to make use of the "best practices" research concerning content area instruction for students with disabilities and the components of user-friendly textbooks and to incorporate those findings into the design of the software. Teachers who develop digital textbooks should make every effort to reflect current research on the learning characteristics of the students with whom they work. The digital textbook should be designed around explicit instructional methods for learning so that clear expectations are communicated to the students.

Tables 1–6 provide a research base from which to begin to design and create cooperative digital textbooks. The research contained in these tables is provided to assist educators in the development of the basic digital textbook so that the text offers systematic instruction to the students. The information is by no means exhaustive of the research in the field. It is offered merely to stimulate development. The goal is to take the empirical research and use it in the design of a cooperative textbook that is tailored to the learning strengths and needs of students in content area classrooms. The ability to customize a digital content area textbook for a particular group of students, to reinforce certain learning behaviors, or to provide controlled practice on a skill is limited only by the educator's imagination.

Systematic Design of the Digital Textbook

Instructional components to incorporate into the design of a digital textbook include (a) the empirical research in the field of content area learning as well as the field of special education in regard to the content area learning of students with disabilities, (b) the educator's knowledge concerning the learning characteristics of the students, (c) the educator's knowledge concerning the components of user-friendly textbooks, and (d) the educator's knowledge concerning the use of the particular authoring software being used. Current authoring systems have reduced drastically the amount of time needed to create digital reading material, but educators should be warned that the estimates for creating interactive computer-based instructional materials can vary widely depending on the complexity of the design (Sampath & Quaine, 1990). MacArthur and Haynes (1995) found that by using an authoring system, 3 to 4 hours were required to convert a typical textbook chapter that included speech synthesis, access to a glossary, highlighted main ideas, questions embedded within the text, and summaries of important points. Currently it is possible to create digital, hypermedia texts directly from just about any modern word processing or desktop publishing program simply by saving an existing document file as hypertext markup language (HTML), thus drawing on skills that many people have already. And with many documents that might be utilized in a digital textbook already extant in a word processing or desktop publishing file, many of the more time-consuming obstacles are eliminated.

Although the creation of a digital cooperative text is a labor-intensive task, it can be managed if members of a department, a school district that has adopted the same text for a particular grade level, or a curriculum committee of a school or school district divide the task into manageable units. If educators are willing to pool their resources and talents to collaborate in creating a digital modification of the content area textbook, the benefits will provide support for a variety of students in the content area classroom.

Much of the time involved in the creation of a digital textbook is in the preplanning stage, when content is targeted, skills are targeted, goals are written, proper reinforcement is selected, research is consulted, and student characteristics are considered (see Figure 3). In the preplanning stage, it is important to ask the following questions:

FIGURE 3

Identifying Critical Information for Use in a Digital Text in the Planning Process

Chapter 3	Page 234

The **vaqueros** were America's first cowboys. They came to Mexico from Spain with the first cattle herds that were brought to the New World. With them came new skills, games, and songs that will always be a part of our country. The vaqueros came north from Mexico to the land that is now the state of New Mexico. They drove the thousands of cattle that came with the wealthy **Dons**. The vaqueros lived with their families at the **haciendas**. There they tended the cattle herds that belonged to the wealthy Dons.

The tough little companies of the vaqueros were well trained and skillful. They knew when to run and when to make sharp turns or sudden stops. The lasso rope that the vaqueros used was eighty feet long and made of tightly woven sea grass, horse hair, or leather. The vaqueros used these long ropes as a tool for herding cattle, a plaything for performing rope tricks, and sometimes even as a weapon. Some vaqueros boasted that they had used their lassos to catch mountain lions and bears.

Identify important vocabulary for new imformation "pop up" windows in digital textbook.

Identify important information for questions or extension of ideas.

Delete unwanted sections.

Note
This page from a history textbook is marked up during the preplanning stage in transforming a text on paper to digital format.

1. Is there a piece of commercial software available to meet the learning needs of the students (e.g., does the read-aloud part of a "talking storybook" CD-ROM provide adequate help for students who need to hear the words spoken)?

2. Would traditional instructional methods be just as effective as the digital textbook?

3. What are the prerequisite computer skills students will need to work with the digital text?

4. What is the background knowledge the student will need prior to working with the digital text?

5. Are there any learning or behavioral idiosyncrasies that might preclude a student using the digital text appropriately?

Once preplanning has occurred, those involved in the creation of the digital textbook need to consider the actual design of the text (see Figure 4, on page 776). The

FIGURE 4

Translating the Critical Information
Into a Draft of a Page of Digital Text

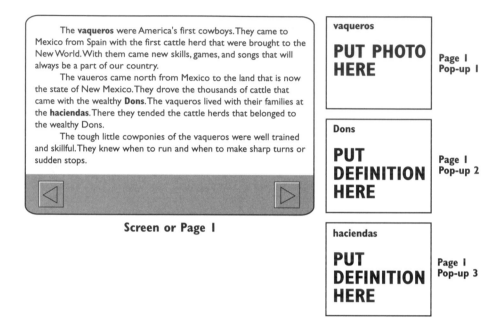

The **vaqueros** were America's first cowboys. They came to Mexico from Spain with the first cattle herd that were brought to the New World. With them came new skills, games, and songs that will always be a part of our country.

The vaueros came north from Mexico to the land that is now the state of New Mexico. They drove the thousands of cattle that came with the wealthy **Dons**. The vaqueros lived with their families at the **haciendas**. There they tended the cattle herds that belonged to the wealthy Dons.

The tough little cowponies of the vaqueros were well trained and skillful. They knew when to run and when to make sharp turns or sudden stops.

Screen or Page 1

vaqueros
PUT PHOTO HERE
Page 1
Pop-up 1

Dons
PUT DEFINITION HERE
Page 1
Pop-up 2

haciendas
PUT DEFINITION HERE
Page 1
Pop-up 3

Note
A storyboard or flowchart of each page in a digital text is created to determine both design and content.

more work done here, the fewer the problems encountered in the actual creation of the digital textbook. In fact, if the work done in this stage is thorough and complete, an educational assistant or parent can be taught to use the authoring software and simply follow the educator's design instructions to create the actual digital textbook. A storyboard or flowchart is very helpful for visualizing the work to be done in this stage (Fitzgerald, Bauder, & Werner, 1992). The ability to "see" what will be incorporated into the design of the digital textbook helps clarify where problems may arise or where errors of logic have occurred. The starting point should be a review of the chapters to be transferred into a digital format, the order in which teachers cover these chapters, the time during the school year the chapters are taught, and the depth of coverage that the teachers provide when teaching a particular chapter. Suggested considerations at this stage are:

1. Make sure that all skills and subskills included in the content area text are also included in the digital textbook—ask both a content area expert and a special educator to review the logic of the instruction.

2. Decide on the level of interactivity to be incorporated into the digital textbook (e.g., simple to complex).

3. Decide whether the student will be "branched" to easier or more difficult tasks depending on his or her responses.

4. Decide whether the digital textbook will keep track of student responses or selections.

5. Decide whether the digital textbook will provide the teacher with data to analyze concerning the student's interaction with the text.

6. Review the language demands of the textbook and decide how to modify or support the language in the digital textbook.

7. Identify the prompts and cues to be used in the digital textbook.

8. Decide whether the digital textbook will contain time constraints or whether students will be allowed to interact freely with the text with no time constraints.

9. Design the digital textbook to be as flexible as possible so that it can be changed as the student needs change.

It is important to remember as one begins to create cooperative digital textbooks that the possibilities for the textbook design depend on the authoring software selected and what the software will and will not allow the educator to do. It is not unusual for educators to begin with the easiest-to-learn authoring software and progress to more powerful and complicated software as they become more skilled. It is also not unusual for digital textbooks designed and created by educators to become more sophisticated as the educators become more proficient in using the software selected. In fact, one of the main benefits of a digital textbook is that it can be modified as the learning needs of the students change, as the teacher finds interesting supportive items to include in the text, and as the structure of the learning environment changes.

As each chapter of the content area textbook is created, it should be field-tested and piloted with the students and/or other content area educators. The goal here is to ascertain whether the digital chapter "works" as intended with students and meets with the satisfaction of the content area experts (the teachers). Often there are errors in the programming that need to be corrected, and sometimes there are logic errors in the design of the digital textbook so that it is unclear to the students what they are being asked to do. Sometimes the students simply do not respond to the software in the anticipated manner and revisions are needed. It is also at this point that the experts (teachers) often find items they want to add (e.g., a video clip), emphasize (e.g., a learning sequence), or delete.

Once completed, the digital textbook and its use by students should continue to be periodically evaluated, both formatively and summatively, and updated as necessary.

As the students become more familiar with the technology and more sophisticated in their use of the digital textbook, they may even begin to make suggestions for enhancements. Continuous evaluation allows the educator to make revisions to the digital textbook so that continued student interaction is assured.

Digital Content Delivery

With the overwhelming popularity of the Internet, few people still think of computers in terms of programs such as spreadsheets, databases, and word processors. The commercialization and popularization of the World Wide Web (WWW), with its non-linear, multimedia interface, has transformed many computer users' ideas of what it means to use a computer. It has also brought about a new avenue of multimedia content delivery not only for school settings, but anywhere one can connect a computer to a phone line or cable TV outlet. Online journals, multimedia encyclopedias, and electronic books and novels are a very real part of current technology. With this "pipeline" for digital content delivery, and the ever-increasing speeds for computer processing units and Internet access (e.g., cable modems and digital phone service—digital subscriber line, or DSL—offer Internet access at 100 times the speed of a typical 56K phone modem), little stands in the way of *access* to digital content. But equating *access to information* and *access to learning* is a misreading of the terms (Rose & Meyer, 2000). Using the technology of digital content simply to make information more accessible is not enough. Differentiating learning from access is an important feature in determining instructional design for digital content.

It is very easy to be distracted by the variety of presentation tools (i.e., bells and whistles) available in many of the digital content-delivery software programs now available. The structure of the software tool that is chosen for digital content delivery can likewise influence the look and feel or instructional design of the product. For example, there are several computer programs such as PowerPoint (1998) that allow easy creation of slides for presentation purposes. Most of these programs, because of the way in which they are designed, promote the creation of linear presentations of ideas, not very different from transparencies on an overhead projector. This is just one example of improving access without necessarily improving learning.

Creating Digital Content

The World Wide Web is overwhelmingly the most readily available and most affordable delivery system for digital content. Internet browser software, the programs that read the multimedia files that make up the Web, are generally free (especially to educators and schools) and almost without exception come installed on most new computer systems. The hypertext markup language (HTML) that serves as the principal programming language for the Web is not specific to any one type of computer (e.g., both Macintosh and Windows computers can read it) and is relatively easy to employ using new Web authoring tools such as PageMill (1999), DreamWeaver (1997), and FrontPage (1998). And with most word processing programs now having

FIGURE 5

A Finished Page of Digital Text as It Appears to the Student

Cold-Blooded

Animals whose body temperatures are controlled by the outside environment are called cold-blooded. Human and other mammals are called warm-blooded because their body temperatures are controlled from within their own bodies.

Go Back

Gecko — A common lizard

Go Back

Note
A single-document digital text was created on a typical word processing program and saved as HTML. The main text at the top contains links to the information in the middle and at the bottom of the page. This file can be viewed by any Web browser such as Internet Explorer, Netscape, or Opera.

HTML as an alternate file format for saving, teachers easily can design a Web document using their familiar word processor and then save it in a file format that is compatible with the Web (see Figure 5 above and Table 7, on page 780, for a detailed description of creating a digital text using a word processor). Even with these improvements in access and development of digital content, the most important issue remains—developing instructional goals and translating those into an instructional design that works.

Practical Issues to Consider in Creating a Digital Textbook

There are some practical issues to consider when educators make the decision to create digital textbooks from content area texts. The first is the level of collaboration that will be necessary between the general educator and the special educator. With the inclusion of students with disabilities into the general education classroom for content

TABLE 7

Using a Typical Word Processor to Create a Single-Document, Digital Text for the World Wide Web

The example used here is AppleWorks 6.0 (formerly ClarisWorks), available for both Windows and Macintosh computers)

Basic Task	Specific Instructions
Type in or scan main text.	Be sure to include a title word at the top. This word will serve as an "anchor" or reference spot for creating links.
Format the main text.	This is the initial text that the student will read. It should be at the top of the document.
Insert a page break.	The page break will show up as a horizontal rule or line when saved as HTML.
Type in or scan text for definition pop-up window.	Be sure to include a title word at the top. This word will serve as an "anchor" or reference spot for creating links.
Format the pop-up window text.	Use a different font or text style to indicate to the user that a definition section is being viewed.
Include the words Go Back to be used as a navigation button.	Put this at the bottom left corner of the page.
Insert a page break.	The page break will show up as a horizontal rule or line when saved as HTML.
Type in text title for graphic pop-up window.	This word will serve as an "anchor" or reference spot for creating links.
Paste or insert graphic onto page.	
Include the words Go Back to be used as a navigation button.	Put this at the bottom left corner of the page.
Spell-check the entire document.	
Save the document as a Word Processing File. Saving as HTML will come later.	Use the Save command usually found under the File menu.
Make the word "LIZARDS" in the Title of the Main Text section an Anchor.	Select the word LIZARDS. Then choose Create an Anchor Link from the Format menu.
Make the word "Cold-blooded" in the Definition pop-up window an Anchor.	Select the word Cold-blooded. Then choose Create an Anchor Link from the Format menu.
Make the word "Gecko" in the Graphic pop-up window an Anchor.	Select the word Gecko. Then choose Create an Anchor Link from the Format menu.
Make the word "Lizards" in the Main Text section a Document Link to the Anchor "Gecko."	Select the word Lizards. Then choose Create a Document Link from the Format menu. Choose Gecko as the appropriate Anchor from the pop-up dialog box that appears.

Basic Task	Specific Instructions
Make the word "cold-blooded" in the Main Text section a Document Link to the Anchor "Cold-blooded."	Select the word Cold-blooded. Then choose Create a Document Link from the Format menu. Choose Cold-blooded as the appropriate Anchor from the pop-up dialog box that appears.
Make the words "Go Back" in both pop-up Window sections as Document Links to the Anchor "LIZARDS."	Select the words Go Back. Then choose Create a Document Link from the Format menu. Choose LIZARDS as the appropriate Anchor from the pop-up dialog box that appears.
Save file again as a word processor document.	Use the Save command.
Save file as HTML with the .html suffix.	Use the Save As command. Select HTML and the file type and add ".html" as a suffix to the name of the file (i.e., myfile.html).

area instruction, more and more collaboration between general educators and special educators is occurring. Educators now meet more often in grade-level or department-level teams to share, solve problems, and create interdisciplinary teams to work on curricula (Friend & Bursuck, 1999). These interdisciplinary teams work together to support one another, develop appropriate instructional plans for students, modify and adapt instructional materials for students, and work to ensure the success of students with disabilities within the general education content area classroom. Because general education teachers often have not been trained to make adaptations for students with disabilities (Schumm & Vaughn, 1991), it is important that the special educators and general educators work together to assess the students, review the content area textbook, and evaluate the interaction between the student and the textbook. From this initial assessment and subsequent collaboration will evolve the appropriate adaptation and modifications to create the digital textbook. An exciting element in the development of a digital textbook is that it allows for the creation of an adaptation or modification that, depending on the enhancements built into the digital text, can meet the learning needs of a wide variety of students—both those with disabilities and those who are at risk for school failure.

The second issue that educators should consider is the physical makeup of the content area classroom as well as the instructional routine of the classroom. Each classroom is different and each teacher has a different instructional style. Thus, educators need to decide upon the placement of the computers in the classroom or if the students will travel to a computer lab, when the students access the digital text (e.g., before a teacher-led lesson as an advance organizer or following a teacher-led lesson for reinforcement), and the Internet access that students will have to the digital textbook from home. It is important to note that an abundance of computers is not necessary to incorporate a digital textbook into the instructional routine of a classroom. Boone and Higgins (1993) found that with as few as two computers in a classroom, a digital textbook could become a regular feature of reading instruction.

The third consideration educators must keep in mind as they create digital content area textbooks is that the power of the digital textbook lies in its ability to mimic the paper textbook, yet become a dynamic interactive learning tool. The technology allows for the creation of a digital textbook that looks just like the paper textbook but contains access to study guides, graphic organizers, speech, video, vocabulary, scenarios that create background knowledge, etc.—all available with a click of the mouse. Thus, the textbook becomes a multidimensional learning tool. When the full power of the technology is considered, a truly cooperative digital text is created that works along with the reader in the reading process.

The final practical consideration is that students must be trained concerning the use of the digital textbook. It is not enough to create the digital textbook and simply allow students access to it. Students must be directly trained in accessing all the enhancements (e.g., vocabulary definitions, embedded questions, video clips) of the digital textbook and a thorough explanation provided as to how each enhancement can facilitate their learning. Initial use of the digital textbook should be monitored to ascertain whether or not students are making full use of the enhancements and periodic retraining scheduled to emphasize to the students the power of the digital textbook to act as a tool to connect reading, thinking, and learning of content.

Copyright Rules

The question of copyright always comes up when digital media are discussed; unfortunately no one ever seems to have clear-cut answers to the questions asked. Until the regulations of copyright and the digital modification of instructional materials by educators are clarified, it seems reasonable to follow the rules outlined for paper reproduction via copy machines that educators have been using for several years. The following two scenarios illustrate situations that probably fall on either side of copyright infringement.

1. An educator wants to create digital text based on a chapter contained in the American History text she is using in her classroom. The classroom contains at least one copy of the textbook for each student in the class. Creating a digital text based on this chapter for use within this classroom probably does not involve infringement of any copyright.

2. Another educator wants to create a digital text based on a chapter out of a historical novel as part of an instructional unit. The teacher buys one copy of the book to read aloud to the class and then creates a digital text of the one chapter for students to use. He makes copies of the digital text for every student in his class to work with independently. This is very likely an infringement of copyright. Purchasing a copy of the book for every student, however, would probably alleviate the problem.

These are not hard-and-fast rules, of course. Educators should obtain copies of copyright policies at their schools and follow those policies as stringently as possible.

CONCLUSION

The use of technology for content area learning purposes within special education and general education to facilitate the inclusion of students with disabilities is just beginning. Initial research into the use of technology to adapt content area textbooks in both environments indicates that digital textbooks are as effective as teacher-led instruction and/or a traditional content area textbook (Anderson-Inman et al., 1994; Anderson-Inman et al., 1996; Boone & Higgins, 1993; Higgins & Boone, 1990a, 1990b; Higgins et al., 1996; Horton, Boone, & Lovitt, 1990; MacArthur & Haynes, 1995). Whether the content to be learned comes from a basal reader or a content area textbook, the digital adaptation of the text has proven to be an effective instructional modification for students of varying ages and ability levels.

The technology of today has already eclipsed the technology used in these early studies concerning digital textbooks in terms of power, speed, ease of use, adaptability, capacity to include a variety of enhancements, and availability—and as a result today's educators can create more sophisticated and cooperative text than was created in the past. As educators begin to visualize their content area classrooms, the inclusion of students with disabilities into those classrooms, and the unique learning needs of those students, it would appear that the creation of a digital content area textbook should be considered a viable alternative to the traditional content area textbook with which these students so often struggle.

REFERENCES

Anderson, T. H., & Armbruster, B. B. (1984). Content area textbooks. In R. C. Anderson, J. Osborn, & R. J. Tierney (Eds.), *Learning to read in American schools: Basal readers and content texts* (pp. 193-226). Hillsdale, NJ: Erlbaum.

Anderson-Inman, L., Horney, M. A., Chen, D., & Lewin, L. (1994). Hypertext literacy: Observations from the ElectroText project. *Language Arts, 71*(4), 37-45.

Anderson-Inman, L., Knox-Quinn, C., & Horney, M. A. (1996). Computer-based study strategies for students with learning disabilities: Individual differences associated with adoption level. *Journal of Learning Disabilities, 29,* 461-484.

Armbruster, B. B. (1984). The problem of "inconsiderate text." In G. G. Duffy, L. R. Roehler, & J. Masson (Eds.), *Comprehension instruction* (pp. 202-217). New York: Longman.

Armbruster, B. B., & Gudbrandsen, B. (1986). Reading comprehension in social studies programs. *Reading Research Quarterly, 21,* 36-48.

Armbruster, B. B., & Ostertag, J. (1987, April). *Questions in elementary science and social studies textbooks.* Paper presented at the American Educational Research Association, Washington, DC.

Armbruster, B. B., & Valencia, S. W. (1989, March). *Do basal reading programs prepare children for reading science textbooks?* Paper presented at the annual meeting of the American Educational Research Association, San Francisco.

Armento, B. (1986). Research on teaching social studies. In M. Witrock (Ed.), *Handbook of research on teaching* (3rd ed., pp. 942-951). New York: Macmillan.

Baumann, J. F., & Serra, J. K. (1984). The frequency and placement of main ideas in children's social studies textbooks: A modified replication of Braddock's research on topic sentences. *Journal of Reading Behavior, 16,* 27-40.

Bean, R. M., Zigmond, N., & Hartman, D. K. (1994). Adapted use of social studies textbooks in elementary classrooms. *Remedial and Special Education, 15*(4), 216-226.

Beck, I. L., McKeown, M., & Gromoll, E. W. (1989). Learning from social studies texts. *Cognition and Instruction, 6*(2), 99-153.

Boone, R., & Higgins, K. (1992). Hypermedia applications for content area study guides. *Reading and Writing Quarterly: Overcoming Learning Difficulties, 8*(4), 379-393.

Boone, R., & Higgins, K. (1993). Hypermedia basal readers: Three years of school-based research. *Journal of Special Education Technology, 12*(3), 86-106.

Boone, R., Higgins, K., Falba, C., & Langley, W. (1993). Cooperative text: Reading and writing in a hypermedia environment. *LD Forum, 18*(3), 28-37.

Bos, C. S., & Anders, P. L. (1987). Semantic feature analysis: An interactive teaching strategy for facilitating learning from text. *Learning Disability Focus, 3*(1), 55-59.

Burton-Radzely, L. (Ed.). (1998). *A national perspective on special educators' use of technology to promote literacy: Technical report.* Washington, DC: MACRO International and the Council for Exceptional Children.

Carnine, D., Silbert, J., & Kame'enui, E. J. (1990). *Direct instruction reading* (2nd ed.). Columbus, OH: Merrill.

Cawley, J., Miller, J., & Carr, S. (1989). An examination of the reading performance of students with mild educational handicaps or learning disabilities. *Journal of Learning Disabilities, 23,* 630-634.

Chall, J. S., & Conrad, S. S. (1991). *Should textbooks challenge students?* New York: Teachers College Press.

Chambliss, M. J., & Calfee, R. C. (1989). Designing science textbooks to enhance student understanding. *Educational Psychologist, 24,* 307-322.

Ciborowski, J. (1992). *Textbooks and the students who can't read them: A guide to teaching content.* Cambridge, MA: Brooklyn Books.

Conrad, S. S. (1990, May). *Change and challenge in content textbooks.* Paper presented at the annual conference of the International Reading Association, New Orleans.

Cornwall, A., & Bawden, H. (1992). Reading disabilities and aggression: A critical review. *Journal of Learning Disabilities, 25,* 281-299.

deBettencourt, L. U., Zigmond, N., & Thornton, H. S. (1989). Follow-up of postsecondary age rural learning disabled graduates and dropouts. *Exceptional Children, 56,* 40-49.

Dishner, E. K., Bean, T. W., Readence, J. E., & Moore, D. W. (1992). *Reading in the content areas: Improving classroom instruction* (3rd ed.). Dubuque, IA: Kendall/Hunt.

Dole, J. A., Valencia, S. W., Greer, S. W., & Waldrop, J. L. (1991). Effects of two types of prereading instruction on the comprehension of narrative and expository text. *Reading Research Quarterly, 26,* 142-159.

Donahoe, K., & Zigmond, N. (1988). *High school grades of urban LD students and low-achieving peers.* Paper presented at the annual meeting of the American Educational Research Association, San Francisco.

Donahoe, K., & Zigmond, N. (1990). Academic grades of ninth-grade urban learning disabled students and low-achieving peers. *Exceptionality, 1*(1), 17-27.

DreamWeaver [Computer software]. (1997). San Francisco, CA: Macromedia, Inc.

Edgar, E. (1987). Secondary programs in special education: Are many of them justifiable? *Exceptional Children, 53,* 555-561.

Englert, C. S., & Thomas, C. C. (1987). Sensitivity to text structure in reading and writing: A comparison of learning disabled and nonhandicapped students. *Learning Disability Quarterly, 10,* 93-105.

Estes, T. (1982). The nature and structure of text. In A. Berger & H. A. Robinson (Eds.), *Secondary school reading: What research reveals for classroom practice* (pp. 85-96). Urbana, IL: ERIC Clearinghouse on Reading and Communication Skills.

Ferguson, D. L. (1996). The real challenge of inclusion: Confessions of a "rabid inclusionist." *Phi Delta Kappan, 77,* 281-287.

Fitzgerald, G. E., Bauder, D. K., & Werner, J. G. (1992). Authoring CAI lessons: Teachers as developers. *Teaching Exceptional Children, 21*(2), 15-21.

Friend, M., & Bursuck, W. (1999). *Including students with special needs: A practical guide for classroom teachers.* Boston: Allyn and Bacon.

FrontPage [Computer software]. (1998). Redmond, WA: Microsoft.

Garner, R., Alexander, P. A., Gillingham, M. G., Kulikowich, J. M., & Brown, R. (1991). Interest and learning from text. *American Educational Research Journal, 28,* 643-659.

Garner, R., Gillingham, M., & White, C. S. (1989). Effects of "seductive details" on macroprocessing and microprocessing in adults and children. *Cognition and Instruction, 6,* 41-57.

Goodlad, J. I. (1976). *Facing the future: Issues in education and schooling.* New York: McGraw-Hill.

Graves, M. F., Prenn, M. C., Earle, J., Thompson, M., Johnson, V., & Slater, W. H. (1991). Commentary: Improving instructional text: Some lessons learned. *Reading Research Quarterly, 26,* 110-122.

Hare, V. C., Rabinowitz, M., & Schieble, K. M. (1989). Text effects on main idea comprehension. *Reading Research Quarterly, 24,* 72-88.

Higgins, K., & Boone, R. (1990a). Hypertext: A new vehicle for computer use in reading instruction. *Intervention in School and Clinic, 26*(1), 26-31.

Higgins, K., & Boone, R. (1990b). Hypertext computer study guides and the social studies achievement of students with learning disabilities, remedial students, and regular education students. *Journal of Learning Disabilities, 23*(9), 529-540.

Higgins, K., & Boone, R. (1992). Hypermedia computer study guides for social studies: Adapting a Canadian history text. *Social Education, 56*(3), 168-173.

Higgins, K., & Boone, R. (1994). Site-based software: Hypermedia instructional applications. *Technology and Disability, 3*(2), 137-147.

Higgins, K., Boone, R., & Lovitt, T. C. (1996). Hypermedia text-only information support for students with learning disabilities and remedial students. *Journal of Learning Disabilities, 29*(4), 402-412.

Hollander, S. K. (1991). Introduction. *Reading, Writing, and Learning Disabilities, 7,* 291-295.

Horizon Research. (1989). *Science and mathematics education briefing book.* Chapel Hill, NC: Author.

Horton, S., Boone, R., & Lovitt, T. (1990). Teaching social studies to learning disabled high school students: Effects of a hypertext study guide. *The British Journal of Educational Technology, 21*(2), 118-131.

Horton, S. V., & Lovitt, T. C. (1989). Construction and implementation of graphic organizers for academically handicapped and regular secondary students. *Academic Therapy, 24,* 625-640.

Horton, S. V., Lovitt, T. C., & Bergerud, C. (1990). The effectiveness of graphic organizers for three classifications of secondary students in content area classes. *Journal of Learning Disabilities, 23,* 12-22, 29.

Hurd, P. (1986). *Analysis of biology texts.* Unpublished manuscript.

Irwin, J. W., & Baker, I. (1989). Promoting active reading comprehension strategies: A resource book for teachers. Englewood Cliffs, NJ: Prentice-Hall.

Jordan, N. C. (1994). Developmental perspectives on reading disabilities. *Reading and Writing Quarterly: Overcoming Learning Difficulties, 10,* 297-311.

Juel, C. (1988). Learning to read and write: A longitudinal study of fifty-four children from first through fourth grade. *Journal of Educational Psychology, 80,* 437–447.

Kame'enui, E., & Simmons, D. (1990). *Designing instructional strategies: The prevention of academic learning problems.* Columbus, OH: Merrill.

Kantor, R. N., Anderson, T. H., & Armbruster, B. B. (1983). How inconsiderate are children's textbooks? *Journal of Curriculum Studies, 15,* 6–72.

Kinder, D., & Bursuck, W. (1991). The search for a unified social studies curriculum: Does history really repeat itself? *Journal of Learning Disabilities, 24*(5), 270–275, 320.

King, J. (1992). Diaspora literacy and consciousness in the struggle against miseducation in the black community. *Journal of Negro Education, 61,* 317–340.

Lawton, M. (1995, Nov. 8). Students post dismal results on history test. *Education Week, 1,* 12.

Lenz, B. K., & Alley, G. R. (1983). *The effects of advance organizers on the learning and retention of learning disabled adolescents within the context of a cooperative planning model.* Final research report submitted to the U. S. Department of Education, Office of Special Education.

Lenz, B. K., & Hughes, C. A. (1990). A word identification strategy for adolescents with learning disabilities. *Journal of Learning Disabilities, 23,* 149–163.

Lerner, J. W. (1997). *Learning disabilities: Theories, diagnosis, and teaching strategies.* Boston: Houghton Mifflin.

Loucks, S. F., & Zacchei, D. A. (1983). Applying our findings to today's innovations. *Educational Leadership, 41* (3), 28–31.

Lovitt, T. C., & Horton, S. V. (1988). [Oral reading rates of learning-disabled adolescents]. Unpublished raw data.

Lovitt, T. C., & Horton, S. V. (1991). Adapting textbooks for mildly handicapped adolescents. In G. Stoner, M. R. Shinn, & H. M. Walker (Eds.), *Interventions for achievement and behavior problems* (pp. 439–471). Silver Spring, MD: National Association of School Psychologists (NASP).

Lovitt, T. C., & Horton, S. V. (1994). Strategies for adapting science textbooks for youth with learning disabilities. *Remedial and Special Education, 15*(2), 105–116.

Lovitt, T. C., & Horton, S. V. (1998). Strategies for adapting science textbooks for youth with learning disabilities. In E. L. Meyen, G. A. Vergason, & R. J. Whelan (Eds.), *Educating students with mild disabilities: Strategies and methods* (pp. 163–176). Denver, CO: Love Publishing.

Lovitt, T. C., Horton, S. V., & Bergerud, D. (1987). Matching students with textbooks: An alternative to readability formulas and standardized tests. *B. C. Journal of Special Education, 2*(1), 49–55.

Lyon, G. R. (1995). Research initiatives and discoveries in learning disabilities: Contributions from scientists supported by the National Institute of Child Health and Human Development. *Journal of Child Neurology, 10* (Suppl. 1), S120–S126.

Lyon, G. R., & Chhabra, V. (1996). The current state of science and the future of specific reading disability. *Mental Retardation and Development Disabilities Research and Reviews, 2,* 2–9.

MacArthur, C. A., & Haynes, J. B. (1995). Student Assistant for Learning from Text (SALT): A hypermedia reading aid. *Journal of Learning Disabilities, 28*(3), 150–159.

Mastropieri, M. A., & Scruggs, T. E. (1994). Text versus hands-on science curriculum. *Remedial and Special Education, 15*(2), 72–85.

Mastropieri, M. A., Scruggs, T. E., & Levin, J. R. (1986). Direct vs. mnemonic instruction: Relative benefits for exceptional learners. *The Journal of Special Education, 20,* 199–308.

May, F. B. (1994). *Reading as communication.* New York: Merrill.

McKeown, M. G., & Beck, I. S. (1990). The assessment and characterization of young learners' knowledge of a topic in history. *American Educational Research Journal, 27*(4), 688–726.

McKeown, M. G., Beck, I. S., Sinatra, G. M., & Loxterman, J. A. (1992). The contribution of prior knowledge and coherent text to comprehension. *Reading Research Quarterly, 27,* 78–93.

Moats, L. C. (1998). Reading, spelling, and writing disabilities in the middle grades. In B. Wong (Ed.), *Learning about learning disabilities* (2nd ed.). San Diego, CA: Academic Press.

Morsink, C. V., Soar, R. S., Soar, R. M., & Thomas, R. (1986). Research in teaching: Opening the door to special education classrooms. *Exceptional Children, 53,* 32–40.

Mullis, I. V., & Jenkins, L. B. (1988). *The science report card: Elements of risk and recovery.* Princeton, NJ: Educational Testing Service.

Nagy, W. E. (1998). *Teaching vocabulary to improve reading comprehension.* Newark, DE: International Reading Association.

National Center for Education Statistics. (1993). *Adult literacy in America: A first look at the results of the National Adult Literacy Survey* (Survey No. 065-000-00588-3). Washington, DC: U.S. Government Printing Office.

National Center to Improve the Tools of Educators. (1996). *Learning to read/reading to learn information kit.* Reston, VA: Council for Exceptional Children.

National Institute of Child Health and Human Development (NICHD). (1994, August). National Institute of Child Health and Human Development Conference on Intervention Programs for Children with Reading and Related Language Disorders, Washington, DC.

National Research Council (NRC). (1998). *Preventing reading difficulties in young children.* Washington, DC: National Academy Press.

Novak, J. D. (1990). Concept maps and Venn diagrams: Two metacognitive tools to facilitate meaningful learning. *Instructional Science, 19*(1), 29–52.

Osborn, J. (1984). The purposes, uses, and contents of workbooks and some guidelines for publishers. In R. C. Anderson, J. Osborn, & R. Tierney (Eds.), *Learning to read in American schools: Basal readers and content texts* (pp. 45–111). Hillsdale, NJ: Erlbaum.

Pace, B. (1992). The textbook canon: Genre, gender, and race in U. S. literature anthologies. *English Journal, 81,* 33–38.

PageMill [Computer software]. (1999). San Jose, CA: Adobe Systems.

Parmar, R. S., & Cawley, J. F. (1993). Analysis of science textbook recommendations provided for students with disabilities. *Exceptional Children, 59*(6), 518-531.

Passe, J., & Beattie, J. (1994). Social studies instruction for students with mild disabilities: A progress report. *Remedial and Special Education, 15*(4), 227-233.

Patton, J., Polloway, E., & Cronin, M. (1990). *A survey of special education teachers relative to science for the handicapped.* Unpublished manuscript.

PowerPoint [Computer software]. (1998). Redmond, WA: Microsoft.

Raizen, S. (1988). *Increasing educational productivity through improving the science curriculum.* New Brunswick, NJ: Center for Policy Research in Education.

Ravitch, D., & Finn, C. (1987). *What do our 17-year-olds know?* New York: Harper and Row.

Readence, J. E., Bean, T. W., & Baldwin, R. S. (1998). *Content area literacy: An integrated approach.* Dubuque, IA: Kendall/Hunt.

Rose, D. & Meyer, A. (2000). Universal Design for Learning. [Associate editor column]. *Journal of Special Education Technology, 15*(1), 67-70.

Rumberger, R. (1987). High school dropouts: A review of issues and evidence. *Review of Educational Research, 57*(2), 101-121.

Sampath, S., & Quaine, A. (1990). Effective interface tools for CAI authors. *Journal of Computer-Based Instruction, 17*(1), 31-34.

Sawyer, R. J., McLaughlin, M. J., & Winglee, M. (1994). Is integration of students with disabilities happening? *Remedial and Special Education, 15,* 204-215.

Schumaker, J. B., & Deshler, D. D. (1984). Setting demand variables: A major factor in program planning for LD adolescents. *Topics in Language Disorders, 4*(2), 22-44.

Schumm, J. S., & Stickler, K. (1991). Guidelines for adapting content area textbooks: Keeping teachers and students content. *Intervention in School and Clinic, 27,* 79-84.

Schumm, J. S., & Vaughn, S. (1991). Making adaptations for mainstreamed students: General classroom teachers' perspectives. *Remedial and Special Education, 12*(4), 18-27.

Scruggs, T., & Mastropieri, M. (1994). The construction of scientific knowledge by students with mild disabilities. *Journal of Special Education, 28,* 307-321.

Sellers, G. B. (1987). A comparison of the readability of selected high school social studies, science, and literature books (Doctoral dissertation, Florida State University, 1987). *Dissertation Abstracts International, 48,* 3085A.

Singer, H. (1992). Friendly texts: Description criteria. In E. K. Dishner, T. W. Bean, J. E. Readence, & D. W. Moore (Eds.), *Reading in the content areas: Improving classroom instruction* (pp. 155-170). Dubuque, IA: Kendall/Hunt.

Snider, V. E. (1989). Reading comprehension performance of adolescents with learning disabilities. *Learning Disability Quarterly, 12,* 87-96.

Stainback, W., Stainback, S., Courtnage, L., & Jaben, T. (1985). Facilitating mainstreaming by modifying the mainstream. *Exceptional Children, 52,* 144-152.

Stanovich, K. E. (1986). Matthew effect in reading: Some consequences of individual difference in the acquisition of literacy. *Reading Research Quarterly, 21,* 360-407.

Steinley, G. L. (1987). A framework for evaluating textbooks. *Clearing House, 61,* 114-118.

Stinner, A. (1992). Science textbooks and science teaching: From logic to evidence. *Science Education 76*(1), 1–16.

Tobias, S. (1987). Mandatory text review and interaction with student characteristics. *Journal of Educational Psychology, 79*(2), 154–161.

Tyson, H., & Woodward, A. (1989). Why students aren't learning very much from textbooks. *Educational Leadership, 47,* 14–17.

U.S. Department of Education. (1997). *Nineteenth annual report to Congress on the implementation of the Education of the Handicapped Children's Educational Act.* Washington, DC: Author.

U.S. Department of Education. (1998). *Twentieth annual report to Congress on the implementation of the Education of the Handicapped Children's Educational Act.* Washington, DC: Author.

Vaughn, S., Schumm, J. S., Niarhos, F., & Daugherty, T. (1993). What do students think when teachers make adaptations? *Teaching and Teacher Education, 9,* 107–118.

Wagner, M., D'Amico, R., Marder, C., Newman, L., & Blackorby, J. (1992). What happens next? *Trends in postschool outcomes of youth with disabilities.* Menlo Park, CA: SRI International.

Wait, S. S. (1987). Textbook readability and the predictive value of the Dale-Chall, comprehensive assessment program, and cloze procedure (Doctoral dissertation, Florida State University, 1987). *Dissertation Abstracts International, 48,* 357A.

Werner, E. (1993). Risk, resilience, and recovery: Perspectives from the Kauai longitudinal study. *Development and Psychopathology, 5,* 503–515.

Whitman, D. (1995, January 16). Welfare: The myth of reform. *U.S. News & World Report, 118,* 30–33, 36–39.

Winograd, P. N. (1984). Strategic difficulties in summarizing texts. *Reading Research Quarterly, 19,* 404–425.

Wong, B. Y. L. (1980). Activating the inactive learner: Use of questions/prompts to enhance comprehension and retention of implied information in learning disabled children. *Learning Disabilities Quarterly, 3,* 29–37.

Wood, T. L., & Wood, W. L. (1988). Assessing potential difficulties in comprehending fourth grade science textbooks. *Science Education, 72,* 561–574.

Woodward, A., Elliot, D., & Nagel, K. (1986, April). *Scientific illiteracy in elementary science textbook programs.* Paper presented at the annual meeting of the American Educational Research Association, San Francisco.

Zahorik, J. A. (1991). Teaching style and textbooks. *Teaching and Teacher Education, 7,* 185–196.

Zigmond, N., & Thornton, H. S. (1985). Follow-up of post secondary age LD graduates and dropouts. *Learning Disabilities Research, 1*(1), 50–55.

CHAPTER 29

Ensuring Success in the Secondary General Education Curriculum Through the Use of Teaching Routines

Jean B. Schumaker, Donald D. Deshler, and Philip McKnight
The University of Kansas

INTRODUCTION

Several trends within the education field and our society today are presenting new challenges to educators who work with students with learning problems. First, the amount and complexity of information that is now available to be taught is expanding rapidly. As a result, textbooks are getting thicker and more and more difficult to digest, and students are expected to learn more and more each year (Kame'enui & Carnine, 1998). Second, the standards-based education movement, which is based on the notion that students must meet certain academic standards and is predicated on the national goal of increasing student achievement throughout the country, permeates education today. Indeed, *all* learners, including those with disabilities, are expected to meet curriculum standards adopted by states and professional organizations (Erickson, Ysseldyke, Thurlow, & Elliot, 1998). Third, many students with disabilities are included in general education classes for a majority of the school day (Wagner, Blackorby, & Hebbeler, 1993), and federal law (P.L. 105-17) dictates that these students be given *real* access to the curriculum in those classes.

These trends have resulted in an increasingly difficult task for educators who work with secondary students with learning problems. Unfortunately, the academic failure of this group is well documented (e.g., Boyer, 1983; Deshler & Schumaker, 1988; Goodlad, 1984; Powell, Farrar, & Cohen, 1985), and the reasons for this failure are often varied, exceedingly complex, and highly interrelated (Sinclair & Ghory, 1987). Recent research on low-achieving adolescents has indicated that these students' problems are related primarily to three major factors that appear singly or in combination: (a) learning inefficiencies or disabilities inherent in the student, (b) complex curricular and setting demands in secondary schools, and (c) ineffective teaching practices (Deshler, Schumaker, Lenz, & Ellis, 1984).

The first factor, the learning deficiencies evidenced by at-risk adolescents, has received significant attention from researchers, resulting in a profile of these youths that reflects a reduced probability of success for this population in secondary general education classes. First, these students' performance on reading, writing, and math achievement tests plateaus at approximately the fourth- or fifth-grade level when they reach the tenth grade in school (Warner, Schumaker, Alley, & Deshler, 1980). Thus, the "performance gap" between their skill levels and their grade level in school continues to grow as they move from one high school grade level to the next and as curricular demands escalate (Schumaker & Deshler, 1988). Second, these students often lack much of the prior knowledge of facts and concepts necessary for benefiting from the secondary curriculum (Bos & Anders, 1987). Third, they tend not to use effective strategies for coping with specific academic demands (Carlson, 1985) and often fail to invent strategies when approaching novel tasks (Ellis, Deshler, & Schumaker, 1989; Warner, Schumaker, Alley & Deshler, 1989). Fourth, these students often have difficulty when taking notes from lectures (Carlson & Alley, 1981), tending only to write what the teacher writes on the board (Bulgren, Schumaker, & Deshler, 1988). Fifth, when asked to write a paragraph or theme, these students generally write incomplete sentences or poorly structured complete sentences containing many spelling and grammatical errors. In addition, their written products suffer from lack of organization (Deshler, Kass, & Ferrell, 1978; Moran, Schumaker, & Vetter, 1981; Schmidt, Deshler, Schumaker, & Alley, 1989; Schumaker, Deshler, Alley, et al., 1982). Sixth, the majority of these students are concrete thinkers (Skrtic, 1980) and have difficulty making complex discriminations between main ideas and details as well as important versus unimportant information (Carlson & Alley, 1981; Lenz, 1984). Seventh, some of these students do not spontaneously generalize newly learned skills across settings, conditions, and time unless they are specifically taught to do so (Ellis, Lenz, & Sabornie, 1987; Schmidt et al., 1989). Finally, they tend not to be motivated to learn (Seabaugh & Schumaker, 1981a, 1981b). In essence, research has shown that these students are severely deficient in the critical skills required for coping with the rigors of the secondary curriculum and associated higher-order learning tasks.

The second factor that often precipitates the failure of low-achieving adolescents relates to the complex curricular and setting demands in secondary schools. Putnam (1988), for example, found that success in secondary grades depends upon students' ability to gain information from textbooks that are often both poorly organized and written, typically at an eleventh-grade reading level. In addition, the classroom lectures and discussions from which they are expected to gain information (Schumaker, Wildgen, Sherman, 1980) often are characterized as lacking: (a) advance organizers and postorganizers, (b) appropriate pacing to permit notetaking, (c) adequate instruction on prerequisite vocabulary, and (d) sufficient repetition of information (Lenz, Alley, & Schumaker, 1987; Moran, 1980). Grades in secondary content courses are largely dependent on the students' ability to succeed on tests that contain primarily objective-type questions and require about 40 responses about factual information (Putnam, 1988). Grades on written products depend mainly on students' ability to write correctly spelled words and grammatically error-free, long sentences (Moran & DeLoach, 1982). In short, success in secondary schools is, in large measure, directly related to a student's ability to acquire, manipulate, store, and express or use large amounts of information that can be obtained only from sources that do not allow for learning inefficiencies in key areas.

A third factor that may contribute to student failure in secondary schools is the application of ineffective or inappropriate teaching practices by many teachers responsible for content instruction (e.g., chemistry, social studies, English literature) (Cuban, 1984; Cusick, 1983). Secondary teachers often report that their primary role is to serve as "content experts" who have major responsibility for delivering accurate and current content information to students; in addition, they do not feel responsible for spoon-feeding students who are ill prepared to learn (Lieberman & Miller, 1978). Consequently, secondary teachers do not exhibit much variation in the pedagogical approaches they employ, and the predominant instructional method used by these teachers is the lecture (Goodlad, 1984; Moran, 1980; Schumaker et al., 1980). Although lecturing, per se, is not an ineffective format, Moran's (1980) and Lenz's (1984) research studies have underscored the failure of many secondary teachers to incorporate effective teaching skills within their lectures (e.g., organizing statements, clarifying questions).

Secondary content teachers' reliance on the lecture format may be the result of the fact that many preservice curricula offered by schools of education prepare secondary teachers to be primarily content rather than instructional experts. Specifically, the overwhelming majority of course hours taken by secondary trainees are in the content areas; relatively few deal with instructional methods (Scanlon, 1982). In short, many secondary teachers lack the technical teaching skills required to facilitate learning for all students, especially students with disabilities (McKnight, 1980).

Any combination of these three major factors in the learning situation can result in several potentially negative ramifications for student achievement and school adjustment. For example, suppose that one of the factors causes an increased number of students to be referred for special education services (Mellard & Deshler, 1984). Once students are placed in special education classes, much of the responsibility for their total educational program is shifted from general education teachers to the special class teacher, including delivery of content information (Alley & Deshler, 1979). Allington (1984) strongly questioned the ability of special class teachers to teach all content subjects when they are not certified to do so. Furthermore, when the policy of readily referring students with learning problems to special education is followed over time within a given school building, the accepted norm is that the special class teacher carries the major responsibility for educating low-achieving students. Such a mind set might preclude the introduction of instructional changes in the regular classroom to accommodate students with learning problems. Additionally, unless the majority of teachers within a given school building assume some responsibility for low student achievement and unless their instructional practices are modified accordingly, the reintegration of at-risk students who have been receiving services in the special classroom into the general education curriculum becomes difficult (Licopoli, 1984). Not surprisingly, the high dropout rate among high-risk populations is reported to be, in part, due to the existing environment in secondary schools that is predominately unfriendly to learners with problems (Howe & Edelman, 1985).

The challenges related to educating at-risk students certainly must be addressed. While the solution to these challenges will be multifaceted, a significant part of the solution will be providing secondary teachers the instructional methods that they need to teach these students as well as providing at-risk students the skills they need to succeed in mainstream learning environments. Improving the technical skills with which teachers teach content will go a long way toward enabling at-risk learners to benefit from the information taught in the content classroom. As the needs of low-achievers are better met in general education classrooms, there will be less need to refer large numbers of students for special services. Equally important, students who are referred to special classes can be taught specific strategies for enabling them to cope independently with general class instruction instead of becoming dependent on tutoring from the special education teacher. The probability of school success will be greatly improved because of more accommodating learning environments in general education classes.

A NEW INSTRUCTIONAL MODEL FOR AT-RISK STUDENTS

Staff members of the University of Kansas Center for Research on Learning (KU-CRL) have designed a new instructional model for at-risk secondary students that takes into account these students' need to learn how to independently succeed in mainstream environments as well as their instructional needs within these environments (Deshler & Schumaker, 1988). In this model, hereinafter referred to as the Strategic Instruction Model (SIM), special education teachers and general education teachers maintain different roles as they work cooperatively to improve the performance of low-achieving students in general education classes. In this model, the special education teacher's major role is that of the "learning specialist," one who teaches students how to learn and how to succeed in response to academic demands in general education classes. In turn, the major role of the general education teacher is to deliver content to the students in such a way that they can understand and remember it. The partnership between the two types of teachers comes through their communication about: (a) the demands related to succeeding in general education classes, (b) the skills needed by particular students, (c) students' progress, and (d) techniques that can be used to help at-risk students within general education classes.

Other persons also play critical roles in this model. The students must not only be willing and motivated participants, they must take major responsibility for their learning and performance. Administrators, school psychologists, other support staff, family members, and personnel in other community agencies also can play an important part in a SIM program.

How teachers, students, and others interact to promote successful participation of at-risk adolescents within the general education curriculum as well as facilitate their successful transition to post-secondary life has been the subject of a programmatic line of research for 23 years at the KU-CRL. The products of this research have served as building blocks for the comprehensive SIM program. As the roles of participants in a SIM program are described in the following sections, the components of the model are clarified.

The Role of the Learning Specialist

The learning specialist's major responsibility in a SIM program is to teach students specific strategies by using a validated instructional methodology. Usually, this instruction takes place in a support class (e.g., a special education classroom, a strategies course, a remedial course) or in a general education class in which the curriculum is tightly aligned with the strategy being taught (e.g., teaching a paragraph writing strategy in a co-teaching arrangement in an English class in which students are learning to write paragraphs). The strategies to be taught include: *learning strategies,* which enable students to learn and perform academic tasks (Deshler & Schumaker, 1988); *social skills strategies,* which enable students to interact effectively with others (Schumaker, 1992); *motivational strategies,* which enable students to motivate themselves and exercise self-control (Seabaugh & Schumaker, 1981a, 1981b; VanReusen, 1998); *transition strategies,* which enable students to solve their own problems and plan for the future (Crank, Deshler, & Schumaker, 1995; Vernon, Deshler, & Schumaker, 1999); and *executive strategies,* which enable students to analyze a task, then select, adapt, or invent a strategy for use, and evaluate the results of applying the strategy (Ellis et al., 1989).

The instructional methodology used in teaching these strategies comprises eight major instructional stages to: (a) obtain a pretraining measure of the students' skills and gain the students' commitment for learning; (b) make the students aware of the strategy steps, where the strategy can be applied, and how the strategy will benefit them; (c) demonstrate for students how to use the strategy; (d) ensure that students understand and can name the strategy steps: (e) ensure that students master the use of the strategy in simplified materials/situations; (f) ensure that students master the use of the strategy in materials and situations similar to those encountered in general education classes ; (g) obtain a post-training measure of the students' skills; and (h) ensure that the students generalize the use of the strategy to general education classes (Ellis, Deshler, Lenz, Schumaker, & Clark, 1991). The materials and procedures to be used by the learning specialist in these undertakings have been empirically validated in a series of studies (e.g., Clark, Deshler, Schumaker, Alley, & Warner, 1984; Hughes, Deshler, Ruhl, & Schumaker, 1993; Hughes & Schumaker, 1991; Lenz & Hughes, 1990; Robbins, 1982; Schmidt et al., 1989; Schumaker, Deshler, Alley, et al., 1982; Schumaker, Deshler, Denton, et al., 1982). Some of the materials have been published for teachers' use (e.g., Hazel, Schumaker, Sherman, & Sheldon-Wildgen, 1981; Hughes, Schumaker, Deshler, & Mercer, 1988; Lenz, Schumaker, Deshler, & Beals, 1984; Nagel, Schumaker, &

Deshler, 1986; Schumaker, Denton, & Deshler, 1984; Schumaker, Hazel, Pederson, 1988; Schumaker, Nolan, & Deshler, 1985; Schumaker & Sheldon, 1985; and Van Reusen, Bos, Schumaker, & Deshler, 1994); others currently are being prepared for publication. (Some of these materials [i.e., those associated with the *Learning Strategies Curriculum* and the *Content Enhancement Series*] are available only through training sessions led by trainers associated with the KU-CRL. For more information, contact the Coordinator of Professional Development , KU-CRL, 517 J. R. Pearson Hall, 1122 West Campus Road, Lawrence, KS 66045.).

In addition to fulfilling the major role of teaching students strategies by means of intensive instruction, the learning specialist also must perform other functions that ultimately facilitate this major role. One function is to create a strategic environment within the support service setting. The strategic environment serves as the context in which specific strategies can be learned and generalized most effectively. In other words, if strategies are taught in an isolated fashion, unrelated to the solution of day-to-day problems within a broader context, students will have difficulty generalizing mastered strategies. Therefore, the learning specialist must model the use of strategic approaches to new problems and engage the students in strategic activities whenever possible in order to teach the students the generality of the approach to life situations.

Additionally, the learning specialist must promote students' independent functioning in academic and social realms. In partial fulfillment of this goal, the learning specialist must refrain from tutoring students in content subjects to avoid encouraging the dependence that typically results from such tutoring (Carlson, 1985; Hock, Deshler, & Schumaker, 1999). Also, the learning specialist must deliberately involve students in planning their instructional programs, setting their own learning goals, and advocating for themselves in instructional planning sessions (Van Reusen et al., 1994). Finally, the learning specialist must require students to think and act on their own rather than performing tasks for the students. For example, when asked a question by a student, the teacher should redirect the question in a way that students can answer it themselves. Materials and equipment should be accessible to students so they can obtain needed resources and start work on their own. Academic work should never be done "for" students. They should be given the tools to complete the work independently.

Besides fulfilling these complex responsibilities within the support setting, the learning specialist also must perform a leadership role outside the support setting to promote a cooperative partnership with general education teachers. A set of "Teaming Strategies" has been developed and validated for use in this partnership. These strategies allow learning specialists and mainstream teachers to work together to identify mainstream setting demands, discuss and solve problems, negotiate conflicts, and encourage the use of validated instructional techniques in general education classrooms (Knackendoffel, 1989; Knackendoffel, Robinson, Deshler, & Schumaker, 1992).

To summarize, the learning specialist must create a strategic environment in which a specialized set of curriculum materials is used in conjunction with a validated instructional methodology designed to promote students' independent functioning in general education classes. Additionally, this teacher must work cooperatively with general education teachers to ensure that the goal of independent student functioning is met.

The Role of the General Education Teacher

The major role of the general education teacher is straightforward; it involves the delivery of content to students so as to promote (a) their application of the strategies they have learned, (b) their understanding of the content information, and (c) their recall of that information. Occasionally (e.g., in the case of an English teacher who needs to teach students how to write complete sentences), the general education teacher also may be responsible for teaching a particular strategy—for example, the Sentence Writing Strategy (Schumaker & Sheldon, 1985).

To promote the use of strategies learned in the support setting, general education teachers can rely on a variety of cueing devices to remind students to use the strategies when appropriate; they can also structure their delivery of content so that strategies can be applied easily. For example, a teacher can organize a lecture into four major sections, orally cue students to use the Listening and Notetaking Strategy (Berry, 1999) before the lecture begins, and cue students when a transition is being made during the lecture to each of the four major sections.

To teach strategies in large classes, which are so prevalent in the mainstream at the secondary level, general education teachers can use a variety of instructional arrangements and techniques. To promote students' understanding and retention of the content of lectures and other lessons, these teachers can use teaching routines and devices designed specifically to be integrated into the class routine while promoting gains in student performance. These routines and devices, as well as the cueing techniques and instructional arrangements that can be used by general education teachers, are described in detail later in this chapter.

The Role of Students

Two types of students have been served successfully in SIM programs: students who qualify for special services in support classes and other at-risk students. Normally, students with disabilities have been served both in support classes and in general education classrooms. Other at-risk students (i.e., low-achievers, those at-risk for dropping out of school) traditionally have been served in general education classrooms, but some educators now are designing support-class settings (e.g., courses in learning strategies) for these students as well. Thus, students typically enrolled in a SIM program have roles to fulfill in both settings. In the support service setting, students are responsible for (a) planning their instructional programs, (b) specifying what they will learn and how fast they will learn it, (c) learning specific strategies to mastery, (d) recording their own progress, (e) evaluating their own progress, and (f) changing goals accordingly. In general education classes, they are responsible for applying, adapting, and inventing strategies where they are needed and for monitoring and evaluating their own progress. They are also responsible for learning the content and meeting the demands of their courses. Thus, students within a SIM program assume an active role in their learning; they are viewed by educators as persons who can learn to succeed independently instead of being dependent entities whose lives must be arranged for them.

The Role of Others

As the SIM has evolved, the roles that administrators, school psychologists, other support staff, family members, and community agency personnel can play in promoting at-risk students' success within the general education curriculum have become clearer. School administrators, for example, can play a critical role in ensuring that the program operates as specified. Not only must they provide the necessary financial and other support, they must voice the necessary expectations so that learning specialists and general education teachers, in turn, can fulfill their roles and can work together productively. They must arrange appropriate and ongoing professional development experiences for their staff. They must require accountability in the form of reports of student progress.

Support staff also can be helpful in promoting the program's success. School psychologists, for example, can help identify general education class demands (e.g., the readability level of textbooks, the types and length of assignments, the types of tests given) and ensure that all participants in educational planning meetings (including students and parents) have a voice in making decisions about students' learning. Likewise, scheduling officers can contribute by hand-scheduling (versus computer-scheduling) students' programs so that they can be grouped for appropriate instruction in certain general education classes and in the support setting as needed. Furthermore, parents can participate by offering support and encouragement in the home and by promoting the generalization of strategies to homework and other situations encountered in the home and community.

Finally, personnel in community agencies can aid the transition of graduates of SIM programs into adult life. For example, personnel in one community mental health center worked with school district staff to match each SIM student with a community volunteer who served as the youth's mentor through the transition process. Agency staff recruited and trained mentors, had regular contact with mentors, and monitored a youth's progress through a series of goal-setting and evaluation sessions with mentor-youth pairs. This type of program has proved very successful in getting youths involved in postsecondary education and training and employed in meaningful jobs (Moccia, Schumaker, Hazel, Vernon, & Deshler, 1989; Schumaker, Hazel, & Deshler, 1985).

An Example of the Strategic Instruction Model

An example of how a SIM program might work for a student under certain circumstances illustrates some of the processes that have been activated in school districts across the nation. Suppose that in a school in which teachers, support staff, and administrators have worked together to promote a SIM program, the school psychologist has determined that students have to be able to memorize lists of items and learn the meaning of vocabulary terms to succeed on a particular biology teacher's tests. A student enrolled in the learning specialist's support class also is enrolled in the targeted biology class. The school psychologist informs the learning specialist of this class demand. The learning specialist then works with the student to determine whether he or she wants to learn strategies that will help meet this class demand. First, pretests are given to determine how well the student can organize and memorize lists as well as learn the definitions of vocabulary. Next, the results of the pretest are shared with the student. If the results indicate that the student needs to learn one or both strategies, the student decides whether he/she wants to learn a strategy and, if necessary, which strategy to learn first. Upon deciding to learn a strategy, the student writes a goal to that effect. Then the learning specialist teaches the student (and others who have written a similar goal) the chosen strategy. For example, the learning specialist might teach the student the FIRST-Letter Mnemonic Strategy (Nagel et al., 1986), a strategy for (a) organizing information into list form, (b) memorizing the information, and (c) utilizing the information to answer test questions. After working hard over a period of about 3 weeks, the student masters the strategy and applies it to the textbook used in the biology class and the notes taken in that class.

Meanwhile, the learning specialist and the biology teacher work together to ensure that the biology teacher understands the strategy the student (and other students in the class) is learning in order to be better able to facilitate the student's use of the strategy. Whenever possible, the biology teacher presents lecture information in list form and, in addition to writing lists on the board, cues students when information in the lists must be learned for tests. When time permits, the teacher helps design a mnemonic device for a given list or asks students to work cooperatively to design the devices themselves. When the biology teacher reviews information the day before a test or when he or she gives students a study guide, the necessary information is provided in list form. The day before the test, the students who have learned the strategy are reminded to use the FIRST-Letter Mnemonic Strategy as they study for the test.

Throughout instruction on each new biology unit, the target student builds up a file of 3" x 5" cards containing important lists. The night before a test, in a study session supported by the student's parents, the student applies the FIRST-Letter Mnemonic Strategy to the lists taken from lectures as well as other lists derived from the assigned textbook chapter to ensure that he or she has memorized the necessary information. As the student takes each test, the student recalls information through the use of the memory devices he or she has designed.

This student receives grades of As and Bs on the tests. After learning and integrating several strategies like this and applying them to several courses, the student graduates from high school. By working with a mentor, the student later enrolls in junior college courses, taking biology and other courses at the local junior college and continuing to apply the strategies learned in high school. The student has become an independent learner and performer.

CONTENT ENHANCEMENT ROUTINES FOR IMPROVING PERFORMANCE IN GENERAL EDUCATION CLASSES

As described earlier, the role of the content teacher in a SIM program is not only to teach a prescribed body of subject matter to students but to do so in a way that facilitates students' understanding and recall of that content. This additional aspect of the role of content teachers is particularly pertinent in light of the increasingly heavy challenge that they are expected to meet with respect to teaching not only more content but also more advanced and complex content (Powell et al., 1985). These increased pressures have surfaced in recent years as a result of the Excellence in Education movement (Spady & Marx, 1984) and the adoption of high-stakes assessment tests (Erickson et al., 1998) as mentioned above.

To fulfill these aspects of their role, general education teachers must use a variety of routines, devices, and instructional arrangements to promote performance gains by students. Researchers at the KU-CRL have applied five criteria when designing and researching instructional routines or devices. First, such routines and devices must be straightforward and easy to master in a relatively short time. Second, they must be perceived by teachers as practical and easy to use. Third, teachers must be able to teach similar amounts of content through the use of these routines and devices versus having to sacrifice large amounts of their content because they are using the routines. Fourth, they must be perceived by teachers as being effective for normal-achieving and high-achieving students as well as for at-risk students and students with disabilities. Similarly, normal-achieving and high-achieving students must perceive the teacher's use of the routines and devices as facilitative, not as "extra baggage" that gets in the way of learning. Fifth, the routines and devices must be sufficiently powerful to improve the performance of students with disabilities and other at-risk learners in required general education classes in which heterogeneous groupings of students are enrolled. Further, their performance must be improved to a level where they are at least passing classes and hopefully to a level where they can feel good about their progress (i.e., they earn grades of C and above). Finally, the routines must lend themselves to easy integration with current teaching practices. The following sections describe a variety of routines and devices that have been developed by KU-CRL researchers and associates and that fulfill these criteria. All have been validated experimentally.

Routines for Teaching Strategies in General Education Environments

In some instances, instructional routines can be used to teach learning in general education classes, as detailed earlier. For example, learning strategies in the written expression strand of the *Learning Strategies Curriculum*—for example, the Sentence Writing Strategy (Schumaker & Sheldon, 1985), the Paragraph Writing Strategy (Schumaker & Lyerla, 1991), the Error Monitoring Strategy (Schumaker, Nolan, & Deshler, 1985), the InSPECT Strategy (a strategy for using computerized spellcheckers) (McNaughtin & Hughes, 2000), and the Theme Writing Strategy (Schumaker, in preparation)—can be taught in English and language arts classes. Strategies that enable students to study for tests (Bulgren, & Schumaker, 1996; Ellis, 1993; Nagel, et al., 1986) and take tests (Hughes et al., 1988) can be taught in content classes such as history and science. Alternatively, learning strategies classes or study skills classes can become a standard part of the curriculum, as has happened in many school districts across the nation.

Large numbers of students and heterogeneous groupings of students usually characterize these classes. Such characteristics create especially heavy demands on learning-strategies instructors because (a) students must practice using a strategy several times before mastering it; (b) they master the use of a strategy after varying numbers of practice attempts in relation to their skills and abilities; and (c) they must receive specific, individual feedback about each of their practice attempts to make progress toward mastery. Ensuring mastery and providing individual feedback in large classes is often problematic. Thus, teaching strategies to large numbers of students with a variety of learning characteristics requires special methods. Recently, a number of methods have been validated experimentally for accomplishing this type of instruction, including the use of special feedback systems, cooperative group instruction, and peer tutoring.

Special feedback systems. One method that has proved useful is a special way of giving individualized feedback to students. Typically, this involves a feedback sheet on which the teacher can indicate the type of error(s) the student made on the last practice attempt. This sheet is given back to the student along with the student's product. The teacher allows the students a couple of minutes to review the feedback sheet and then gives feedback to the class. For example, the teacher asks students whose feedback sheets indicated that they failed to include a transition sentence between paragraphs to pay attention to her feedback. After giving feedback to those students, she asks those students who failed to use a logical sequence across paragraphs to pay attention to her feedback, and so forth.

This method has been shown to be effective by Howell (1986), who used it while teaching the Theme Writing Strategy (Schumaker, in preparation) in her five general education English classes to a total of 150 students. In addition to following the instructions for teaching her students to acquire and generalize the strategy just as a support class teacher would, she provided specific written individual feedback to all 150 students after each attempt via a specially designed Feedback Sheet. The Feedback Sheet contained a list of descriptions of areas in which students could do well and a list of descriptions of possible errors. After reading and scoring a theme, Howell simply checked those items that had been done well and those that needed improvement. She also wrote brief comments on the sheet as needed. The Feedback Sheet allowed the teacher to give the majority of her feedback in written form so that class time could be spent on additional instructional activities, reviewing common trouble spots for the class, and providing oral feedback and help to individual students having major difficulties. Students were told to review their Feedback Sheets, listen to the oral whole-class feedback, ask the teacher for help with items that were unclear, and pay particular attention to the Feedback Sheets as they wrote their subsequent papers. Howell found that her students mastered the strategy at levels comparable to those of students who had received individual instruction and individual feedback.

Cooperative group instruction. Another method that has been validated experimentally for teaching strategies within general education classes is cooperative group instruction. In essence, with this method, the teacher introduces the strategy to the whole class, and then students work in cooperative groups during the practice activities to help each other master the strategy. Beals (1983) used this method in a study in which two strategies, the Sentence Writing Strategy (Schumaker & Sheldon, 1985) and the Paraphrasing Strategy (Schumaker et al., 1984), were taught in general education English classes. After the strategy was introduced to each class, the students were divided into small heterogeneous groups, and practice assignments were given to the groups. At the end of a given lesson, one group member was selected randomly from each group to perform the target skill for the lesson. The group's grade for the day was contingent on that person's performance. Individual grades also were given for individual performance on the lesson. At the beginning of each subsequent lesson, group members were required to review and discuss the feedback received by each member on individual work and to help each other understand relevant concepts. Beals (1983) found that all the students (high-achievers, normal-achievers, low-achievers, and students with learning disabilities) showed improvement in their skills and mastered the use of the strategy. The students with learning disabilities achieved at levels comparable to levels attained when similar students were taught the strategies in resource room programs.

Peer tutoring. Peer tutoring also can be used when teaching strategies to large groups of students in heterogeneous general education classes. This method has been validated as effective in resource classes; thus, its use in general education classes seems to be a logical extension. Keimig (in preparation) developed a method by which learning disabled (LD) students who had mastered the Error Monitoring Strategy (Schumaker et al., 1985) taught this strategy to other students with learning disabilities (LD) in a resource room. Simple instructions were written on cards for the student tutors to follow as they taught each lesson. The student tutors were responsible for providing instruction, answering questions, scoring lessons according to answer keys, giving individual feedback after each practice attempt, and stating that mastery of the skills would be required. The tutors were taught how to perform these teaching tasks in 1 1/2 hours of instruction. Keimig found that the students with LD in his study learned to use the strategy at levels comparable to levels exhibited by students with LD who had been taught the strategy by a teacher. They had mastered the strategy after comparable amounts of instruction. Keimig's study shows that, given some training, students with LD who have mastered a learning strategy can serve as effective instructors of those strategies to other dysfunctional learners.

A logical extension of Keimig's work includes teaching learning strategies to small groups of students enrolled in general education classes by student tutors who have mastered these strategies and the necessary instructional procedures. Such an arrangement would allow students with disabilities or other learning problems to "shine" in their general education classes and conceivably could enhance their self-esteem. Additionally, if supposed "dysfunctional" learners can be successful instructors of learning strategies, other, more functional learners might be recruited as "student aides" to perform some of the teaching tasks that must be carried out in settings with large numbers of students. For example, they might lead verbal rehearsal exercises, check off verbal mastery of the concepts and steps of a strategy, and provide explanations and/or additional feedback on graded work.

Routines for Cueing Use of Strategies

When students with disabilities are taught strategies to mastery levels in support classes, they sometimes fail to generalize the use of those strategies to other classrooms. Several methods involving cueing (i.e., prompting the student to use strategies) in the general education classroom have been found to help ensure generalization.

Visual cueing methods. The first type of method involves visually cueing students to use a given strategy. One effective format for visual cueing (Schmidt, 1983) involves the use of cue cards. The student writes the steps of a strategy on a 3" x 5" or 4" x 6" card that is affixed to the appropriate textbook or notebook. For example, students who have learned a strategy for extracting important facts from textbook chapters would make cue cards that list the steps of the strategy and attach them to the cover of each of their textbooks or use them as bookmarks. Students who have learned a strategy for taking notes during lectures would make cue cards listing the steps of the strategy and affix them to each of their notebooks for classes in which notetaking is appropriate. In the case of writing strategies, students make a set of cue cards of formulas and rules to which they can refer as they write. They keep these aids in their notebooks for classes in which they are asked to write. The cards must be colorful and assigned a visually prominent place so that the student will see them as the textbook or notebook is opened.

Another type of visual cueing technique was built into one of the strategies, the Test Taking Strategy (Hughes et al., 1988). To perform the first step of the Test Taking Strategy, students must write a cue word on their test papers before they begin taking the test and applying the strategy. Each letter of the cue word represents something the students must do or attend to as they take the test. Thus, in effect, by writing the cue word in a visually prominent place, the students cue themselves to use the strategy.

The general education teacher's role with respect to these visual cueing systems is to encourage their use; that is, general education teachers must be aware of the rationale for using these visual cueing devices and must allow their use. They also must be sensitive to adolescent students' need to "be like" other students and, therefore, avoid drawing attention to the fact that they are different because they use these visual cueing devices.

Verbal cueing devices. Another type of cueing that has been found effective in encouraging generalized use of a learning strategy is verbal cueing. For one verbal cueing technique, the general education teacher is designated as the person who supplies the cues. For example, if the student has mastered the Sentence Writing Strategy (called "PENS" by the students), the teacher surreptitiously says to the student, "Be sure to use 'PENS' on today's assignment," after giving the class an assignment to write a paragraph. Specifically, the general education teacher's role with verbal cueing consists of being aware of the strategies a student has mastered, matching those strategies appropriately to given assignments, and remembering to cue the student before she or he begins a task.

The other verbal cueing technique that has been found to be effective (Keimig, in preparation) involves student peers. Here, students who have learned a strategy in the special class also learn to cue each other to use the strategy in other classes and to help each other when needed. For example, two students who have learned the Error Monitoring Strategy (Schumaker et al., 1985), a strategy for detecting and correcting errors in written work, can learn to become responsible for cueing each other to use the strategy any time written work is assigned in their shared classes. That is, the students can be responsible for discriminating the conditions for which the use of the strategy is appropriate; in addition, they can be responsible for briefly communicating to each other about those conditions (e.g., "We should use the Error Monitoring Strategy on this assignment."). The general education teacher must allow the students to be seated close enough to each other so that they can cue each other without disturbing others and let them briefly chat at the beginning of an assignment so that they can determine which strategies are most applicable and whether certain adjustments need to be made in the strategies.

Routines for Teaching Content

As emphasized earlier, the primary role of most secondary teachers is to convey information in such a way as to ensure that students understand it and remember it. When students with disabilities and other at-risk students are enrolled in content courses, the teacher's role becomes more complex. Thus, in classrooms where these types of students are being educated, effective techniques or teaching routines that correspond to these students' particular characteristics are needed. Over the past 15 years, a number of specifically designed routines have been proved effective for helping at-risk students learn in general education classes (Table 1). These routines are called Content Enhancement Routines (Lenz & Bulgren, 1995) because they enable teachers to enhance the learning of content by all the students in their classes. In general, through the use of Content Enhancement Routines, teachers think deeply about the content that students need to learn, organize and manipulate that content in a way that makes the content "learner friendly," and deliver that content to students in a way that keeps them active in the learning process and enhances their retention of the content. The design of the routines is based on several principles, such as: (a) students learn more when they are actively involved, (b) students learn abstract content easier if it is presented in concrete form, (c) students learn more information when the structure or organization of that information is presented to them first and when relationships among pieces of information are explicitly taught, (d) students are more likely to learn new information if it is tied to information they already know, and (e) students learn more important information if that information is distinguished from unimportant information. Teachers use the Content Enhancement Routines to create a learning apprenticeship (Bulgren & Lenz, 1996; Hock, Deshler, & Schumaker, 1993; Hock, Schumaker, & Deshler, 1999) in their classrooms whereby they show students how to learn information through modeling the processes involved in manipulating and transforming it.

Four types of Content Enhancement Routines have been developed and validated: Organizing Routines, Understanding Routines, Recall Routines, and Application

TABLE 1

Content Enhancement Routines

Routine	When Used	Purpose	Teacher Materials	Student Materials
Course Organizer Routine	At the beginning of a course and between units	To introduce the course, to keep students informed of progress through the course, to review the course	Textbook, course notes, other resources, Course Organizer	Course Organizer and pencil
Unit Organizer Routine	At the beginning of a unit, during the unit, at the end of the unit	To introduce a unit and to keep students informed of progress through the unit, to review the unit	Textbook, unit notes, other resources, Unit Organizer	Unit Organizer and pencil
Lesson Organizer Routine	At the beginning of a lesson (or group of lessons), during a lesson, at the end of the lesson	To introduce a lesson and to keep students informed of progress through the lesson, to review the lesson	Textbook, lesson notes, other resources, Lesson Organizer	Lesson Organizer and pencil
Survey Routine	When students are given an assignment to read a chapter	To provide an overview of a chapter and the information to be learned	Textbook, "TRIMS" Worksheet	Textbook, "TRIMS" Worksheet, pencil
Framing Routine	During a lesson	To depict relationships among main ideas and details in a lesson	Textbook, resources, The Frame	The Frame and pencil
Concept Mastery Routine	During a unit of study	To introduce a major concept in the unit	Textbook, resources, Concept Diagram	Concept Diagram and pencil
Concept Anchoring Routine	During a unit of study	To connect a major concept to students' background knowledge	Textbook, resources, Concept Anchoring Table	Concept Anchoring Table and pencil
Concept Comparison Routine	During a unit of study	To compare and contrast two or more concepts	Textbook, resources, Concept Comparison Table	Concept Comparison Table and pencil
Recall Enhancement Routine	During a lesson	To help students remember information	Lesson notes, textbook, chalkboard	Paper and pencils
Clarifying Routine	During a lesson	To introduce a new term and help students remember it	Lesson notes, textbook, Clarifying Table	Clarifying Table and pencil
Quality Assignment Routine	When an assignment is to be given	To plan, present, and evaluate an assignment	Quality Assignment Planning Worksheet, Assignment Window or Handout	Assignment notebook and pencil

Routines. Organizing Routines are used to show students how the information related to a course is organized and related. Understanding Routines are used to teach students about major concepts and main ideas in a course. Recall Routines are used to help students understand and remember important details related to a course. Application Routines are used to set up situations in which students can practice with new information and apply what they have learned.

Organizing Routines. Several Organizing Routines have been developed. Teachers can use the Course Organizer Routine (Lenz with Schumaker, Deshler, & Bulgren, 1998) to introduce a whole course to students and to review progress through the course. They can use the Unit Organizer Routine (Lenz with Bulgren, Schumaker, Deshler, & Boudah, 1994) to introduce and review progress through a unit of study. They can use the Lesson Organizer Routine (Lenz, Marrs, Schumaker, & Deshler, 1993) to present a prescribed set of information as an advance organizer for a lesson.

Indeed, all three of these routines serve as advance organizers. An advance organizer has been defined as information that is delivered "in advance of and at a higher level of generality, inclusiveness, and abstraction than the learning task itself" (Ausubel & Robinson, 1969, p. 606). The purpose of an advance organizer is to strengthen a student's cognitive structures, which are defined by Ausubel (1963) as the student's knowledge of a given subject matter at a given time with regard to its organization, clarity, and stability. For students with a paucity of background knowledge or an inability to organize information such that it can be easily retrieved, and for those with poor motivational and/or inactive learning styles, advance organizers take on special roles. They can serve as vehicles for presenting background knowledge that is required for understanding a lesson, for highlighting organizational patterns about which the students should be aware, for motivating students to learn, and for communicating to students expectations about what they should be doing during instructional activities.

In one of the studies that has been conducted on the Organizing Routines, Lenz, Alley, and Schumaker (1987) designed a lesson organizer routine consisting of 12 components and evaluated its effectiveness in terms of students' learning in general education classrooms. These 12 components can be used to inform the learner about (a) the purpose of the advance organizer for the lesson, (b) the actions to be taken by the teacher and the students during the lesson, (c) the topic and subtopics to be covered in the lesson, (d) background knowledge related to the lesson, (e) concepts to be learned, (f) reasons for learning the information, (g) new vocabulary, (h) organizational frameworks, and (i) desired lesson outcomes.

Teachers were trained to design and deliver lesson organizers containing the 12 components in their secondary content classes (e.g., history, English, physical science) at the beginning of each class period. Lenz et al. monitored the effects of the routine on students' acquisition of the information presented in the class period by interviewing the students after each class. They found that teachers who used few of the lesson organizer components at the start of their lessons could be trained in less than an hour to use them at mastery levels in the classroom. When students with disabilities were specifically taught to attend to the teacher's use of the routine, the number of relevant statements they made about the content of the lesson after the lesson increased substantially compared to the number of statements they made after lessons when they had not been informed about how to attend to the lesson organizer.

Lenz (1984) also conducted another study to determine the effects of a lesson organizer on students' learning and retention of written information. Basically, the same format was used for the lesson organizer as described for the Lenz et al. (1987) study; a few adjustments were necessitated by the reading task as opposed to the lecture/discussion task. In addition, the usefulness of the lesson organizer was explained specifically to the students, who were instructed to take advantage of it before reading the assigned passage. Lenz found substantial differences between the recall performance of students with LD when they received an organizer before reading a passage and their performance when they did not receive the organizer. Students with LD who had not received an organizer correctly answered more questions about unimportant information than questions about important information in the passage. In contrast, students with LD who had received an organizer answered more questions correctly about important information than about unimportant information. In fact, they correctly answered about the same number of questions correctly about important information (an average of 19 out of 30 questions) as a group of normal achievers who had not received an organizer (an average of 21 out of 30 questions). The use of the organizer only slightly improved the typical achievers' recall of important information (from an average of 21 to 22 answers correct), but it substantially improved the performance of the students with LD (from an average of 13 to 19 answers correct).

These data indicate that the use of organizers by a teacher helps students with disabilities discriminate important information from unimportant information. In addition, organizers help them store that information so that it can be recalled later for a test over the information. The result of this more efficient storage is that their performance on a test covering important information is not substantially different from the performance of non-handicapped learners. These findings suggest that an organizing routine that precede a classroom lesson or a reading assignment can be a beneficial tool for enhancing the performance of low-performing students. Although the research conducted to date has not identified the effects of an organizing routine used on a daily basis on students' grades in general education courses, one logically might assume that the effects noted in the tests in Lenz's study (1984) would be reflected in higher scores on unit tests. Since a large percentage of a student's grade is based on test scores in secondary classrooms (Putnam, 1988), one also might suppose that course grades would be improved.

In a study in which unit test scores were used as a measure of the effects of teacher use of a routine, Lenz and his colleagues found that the unit test performance of students with and without learning disabilities increased an average of 10 points above baseline when the Unit Organizer Routine (Lenz, with Bulgren, Schumaker, Deshler, & Boudah, 1994) was used to introduce each unit of study in secondary general education science and history courses and to continue to inform students about relationships among information during each. Seven of the eight students with LD who participated in the study and who were earning failing scores on unit tests during the baseline condition earned average scores of 72% or higher on unit tests after their teachers started using the Unit Organizer Routine unit (Joint Committee on Teacher Planning for Students with Disabilities, 1995).

Another Organizing Routine that appears to hold promise for enhancing the achievement of low-achieving students is the Survey Routine (Deshler, Schumaker, & McKnight, 1997). This routine was designed to enable general education teachers to provide an overview of a new textbook chapter to their students before initiating instruction related to that chapter. Low-achieving students frequently have difficulty reading textbooks written at grade level (Schumaker & Deshler, 1984), often demonstrate limited background knowledge related to lessons and assignments (Graff, 1987), and have difficulty discriminating important from unimportant written information (Lenz, 1984). In addition, textbooks often are written in a way that is "inconsiderate" (Armbruster, 1984) for the reader.

The Survey Routine was designed to help students compensate for these problems; it is an interactive routine in which the teacher leads students through a step-by-step process of analyzing the content of the new chapter while taking notes on a specially constructed worksheet. There are places on this worksheet for the students to record information derived from each step. In the first step, students read and paraphrase the chapter's title. Next, the relationship of the new chapter to previous and subsequent chapters is discussed by reference to the table of contents in the textbook. Third, the introduction of the chapter (or the first paragraph) is read aloud and paraphrased by the students. Fourth, the major sections of the chapter are delineated. Here, the teacher draws a diagram of the chapter on the board, using boxes to represent each part of the chapter. The title of a major section is paraphrased and written at the top of each box. The most important items to which the students should attend within each section (e.g., new vocabulary, a diagram, a map, or an important explanation) then are listed within each box by the teacher. Finally, the summary of the chapter is read and paraphrased.

The results achieved through the use of this routine have been promising but inconsistent. For some teachers who used the routine, students' test scores on regularly scheduled chapter tests increased an average of 10 percentage points above baseline levels. All students, including normally achieving students, realized some improvement, with the students with LD achieving the largest gains; when the teachers stopped using the routine, all students' test scores returned to baseline levels. Other teachers did not achieve the same positive results. The reasons for these differences remain unclear. Perhaps the way in which the overall organization of the chapter is described and the ways in which important details are highlighted are factors. Perhaps the kinds of details that are highlighted or the enthusiasm with which the teacher delivers the information influences the results. Clearly, additional research is needed on this routine.

One more Organizing Routine that can be used to facilitate subject-matter learning is the Framing Routine (Ellis, 1998). Teachers use this routine to organize information in a lesson or series of lessons and to portray the relationships among information. The routine is used in conjunction with a graphic organizer called the "Frame." The Frame helps students see the relationships among abstract pieces of information because it is a concrete representation of the structure of the information. It also helps them to see the relationship between main ideas and details within a lesson. The teacher prepares a draft of the Frame before class and then uses the routine to interactively discuss the information with students in class. Both the teacher and the students fill in blank Frames as the class proceeds. Thus, the final Frame is a joint product created by the teacher and students working together.

In one study by Ellis, Raines, & Hansford (in preparation), the Framing Routine was used for some lessons and not for other lessons in a fourth and fifth-grade multi-age social studies class. The results indicated that essay test scores were an average of 21 percentage points higher when the routine had been used as opposed to when it was not used. Similar gains were achieved by students with and without disabilities.

Another study focused on the writing performance of eighth graders who received Framing Routine instruction versus the writing performance of students who did not receive the instruction. Results showed that the performance of the experimental students was significantly higher than that of the comparison students on every writing measure. For example, the experimental students wrote an average of 102 words more than the comparison students (Ellis & Feldman, 1994).

Understanding Routines. Other routines that have had positive effects on the test performance of students with disabilities and other students in secondary general education courses are the Understanding Routines. The purpose of these routines is to deliver information about complex, abstract concepts (e.g., democracy, thesis, equation) in such a way that students' understanding and memory of the information will be enhanced. The Concept Mastery Routine (Bulgren, Deshler, & Schumaker, 1993), for example, entails the use of a Concept Diagram, which serves to organize the information related to the concept into categories of information that (a) name and define the concept; (b) are related to the characteristics that are always, sometimes, and never present in the concept; and (c) are related to examples and nonexamples of the concept. Symbols and shapes are used on the diagram to make the differences between information categories distinct and concrete for the students. A rough draft of the Concept Diagram is prepared by the teacher before class. Through an interactive discussion, which comprises the Concept Mastery Routine, the teacher and students fill in blank Concept Diagrams about the concept in class. The final diagram, then, is a product that is co-constructed by the teacher and students working together.

Bulgren, Schumaker, & Deshler (1988) evaluated whether teachers could learn to use the Concept Teaching Routine and the subsequent effects of its use on students' performance in general education courses. They found that content teachers readily learned to use the routine at mastery levels in less than 3 hours of instructional time. When the teachers settled into a routine of presenting one major concept during each unit of study, students' performances were enhanced in a variety of ways. For example, both students with LD and other students wrote three times more items of concept-related information in their notes than before the Concept Teaching Routine was used. When the students took a test over the concept information covered in a given unit, mean test scores also increased above baseline levels for all students. Test scores improved even further when the concept information was reviewed the day prior to the test along with other material in the regularly scheduled review session. Test scores on regularly scheduled unit tests also showed a significant improvement when the concept information was reviewed as a part of the regular review. During baseline, only 57% of the students with learning disabilities were passing the regularly scheduled unit tests. During the concept training and review condition, however, 75% of the students with learning disabilities were passing the tests. Thus, the learning and retention of conceptual knowledge enhanced students' performance on unit tests, all of which were publisher-made tests designed to measure factual knowledge.

Similar results have been achieved through the use of the Concept Anchoring Routine (Bulgren, Schumaker & Deshler, 1994a), a routine for helping students connect new knowledge about a concept to their prior knowledge, and the use of the Concept Comparison Routine (Bulgren, Lenz, Deshler, & Schumaker, 1995), a routine for helping students compare and contrast two or more concepts. When students with LD participated in the Concept Anchoring Routine along with other students in their general education classes, they earned an average test score of 69%; other students with LD who participated in traditional instruction about the same concept earned average test scores of 40%. Comparable differences were found for other low-achieving students and for normally achieving students in the same classes (Bulgren, Lenz, Schumaker, Deshler, & Marquis, in press).

Similarly, when the Concept Comparison Routine was used, students recalled more information than when it was not used. Control students with LD earned a mean test score of 57%, whereas experimental students with LD earned a mean test score of 71%. Other low-achieving students in the control group earned a mean test score of 63% and in the experimental group earned a mean test score of 86%. Similarly, normally achieving students in the control group earned a mean test score of 76% and in the experimental group earned a mean test score of 84% (Bulgren, Schumaker, Deshler, & Lenz, in preparation).

Recall Routines. A third type of routine that has been used by general education teachers and that produces gains in the performance of students with learning problems is the Recall Routines. One of these routines, the Recall Enhancement Routine (Schumaker, Bulgren, & Deshler, & Lenz, 1998) has been the focus of two experimental studies. This routine involves the co-construction of mnemonic devices (memory tools) by the teacher and students to help the students remember information. For example, if students are required to remember that Joseph Swan developed an early form of the lightbulb, they might make a mental picture of a swan holding a lightbulb that shines weakly. To use the routine, the teacher cues students that certain information is important to remember and explains why, helps the students construct a mnemonic device for remembering the information, and supervises student review of the information. One experimental study showed that students with LD scored significantly higher on content tests when this routine was used (their mean score was 71%) as opposed to when it was not used (their mean score was 42%) (Bulgren, Schumaker, & Deshler, 1994b). Another experimental study showed that students whose teachers used the routine scored significantly higher on a test that measured their ability to construct mnemonic devices than students of teachers who did not use the routine (Bulgren, Deshler, & Schumaker, 1997).

Another Recall Routine is called the Clarifying Routine (Ellis, 1997). It is used by teachers to help students understand and master the meaning of important words or phrases (e.g., vocabulary, names of historical figures, events, ideas) within the context of subject-matter instruction. The Clarifying Routine is used to reveal (a) the name of the term to be explored, (b) important information or facts related to the term, (c) examples of how the term might be used correctly and incorrectly, (d) the core idea behind the term, (e) a connection between the term and something within the students' lives, and (f) the correct usage of the term in a sentence. A graphic device called the Clarifying Table is completed by the teacher and students as they discuss the term and information related to the term. One of the instructional principles on which this routine is based is that students must encounter a term a minimum of 14–20 times within meaningful contexts if they are to master its meaning and significance. Other principles on which it is based are that students must have opportunities to use a term several times and to connect the term to their personal lives if they are to learn it. Thus, during the routine, students hear the term spoken by the teacher and other students many times, use it and write it themselves, and are asked to connect the term to their own lives.

In a study focused on the effects of the Clarifying Routine, Ellis, Raines, Farmer, and Tyree (1997) found that students in general education classes answered substantially more test questions related to information that had been presented through the use of the Clarifying Routine than questions that were related to information that had been presented through traditional instruction. For example, students answered 63% of the questions on the traditionally presented information and 83% of the questions on information presented with the Clarifying Routine.

Application Routines. Through the use of Application Routines, the teacher dramatically shifts control of learning to the students and sets up conditions in which students can demonstrate their competence with regard to using or manipulating information. One Application Routine that has been developed is called the Quality Assignment Routine (Rademacher, Deshler, Schumaker, & Lenz, 1998). Teachers use this routine to plan assignments for and with students, present assignments, evaluate assignment products, and give feedback to students about the quality of their work. This routine is based on several principles that were derived by working with students and teachers in focus groups. For example, students are more likely to complete assignments which they have created themselves and within which they have choices. Additionally, students must understand the purpose of the assignment, what they are to do, and how they can do well. They must see the assignment as personally relevant and optimally challenging (i.e., not too difficult or too easy).

Research related to this routine has focused on its implementation by teachers. Before instruction in the routine, teachers used an average of 51% of the planning behaviors, 33% of the presentation behaviors, and 8% of the evaluation behaviors specified by focus groups of students and teachers. After instruction, the teachers used an average of 96% of the planning behaviors, 89% of the presentation behaviors, and 94% of the evaluation behaviors that had been specified. A comparison group of teachers used only 45% of the planning behaviors, 26% of the presentation behaviors, and 10% of the evaluation behaviors at the end of the study. The students of the experimental teachers and the teachers themselves were significantly more satisfied with various aspects of their assignments than the students of the comparison teachers and the comparison teachers (Rademacher, 1993).

Integration of routines. Certainly, additional research is required to study further the usefulness of the notion that general education teachers can enhance the understanding and recall of information by students with disabilities and other low-achieving students. Some of the routines (e.g., the Survey Routine) need further study in isolation to determine under what conditions they are most effective. Additionally, the effects of the integration of the routines should be studied as well. For example, the Course Organizer Routine might be used to introduce a course, the Unit Organizer Routine might be used to introduce each unit in the course, the Survey Routine might be used to introduce especially difficult chapters in the textbook, the Concept Teaching Routine might be used to present information related to a major concept in each unit, the Lesson Organizer and Framing Routines might be used to enhance difficult lessons, the Recall Enhancement Routine and the Clarifying Routine might be used to highlight information as it is presented in each lesson, and the Quality Assignment Routine might be used to plan, present, and evaluate assignments. Conceivably, such an integrated sequence might have an even greater effect on students' performance than can be created when the routines or devices are used in isolation.

TRANSLATING RESEARCH INTO PRACTICE

The instructional devices and routines described in this chapter for use by general education teachers as well as those developed by other researchers (e.g., Brophy & Good, 1985; Weinstein, Goetz, & Alexander, 1988) provide reasons to be optimistic about being able to address effectively the learning and academic achievement problems of low-achieving adolescents in today's secondary schools. Regardless of the nature or magnitude of the results achieved through recent research efforts, however, little change in school practices will occur unless appropriate steps are taken to ensure effective translation of these instructional procedures into usable teaching products and ongoing staff-development and teacher-training efforts.

The task of translating research prototypes into usable teaching products is a critical one if educational change is to occur. The literature is replete with research studies reporting that positive learning effects have been achieved as a result of using specific teaching procedures. Unfortunately, in the vast majority of cases, practitioners must extrapolate the procedures for implementing the instructional practice from the methodology section of a journal article. If they request additional information from the researcher, they often get a lengthy field-test protocol of the instructional procedures used during data collection, or they receive an abbreviated synopsis of the procedure. In either case, the teacher still lacks the information needed to translate the instructional routine accurately, and with relative ease, into classroom practice. Researchers must rethink their responsibility to the educational community with regard to translating validated teaching routines into usable, teacher-friendly instructional packets or materials. The gap between research and practice that has existed historically in education may, in large part, be accounted for by the failure of researchers to view the research process as including the extra steps of translating the field-test versions of innovative procedures into instructional materials conducive to use in the classroom.

When KU-CRL staff members completed the first phases of intervention research on the SIM, they thought that the magnitude of the reported improvement would be sufficiently powerful to encourage teachers to use the procedures. Only after discovering that classroom implementation rates were abysmally low did they realize that, as researchers, they needed to make a significant commitment to the translation process. Since then, KU-CRL staff members have committed themselves to going the extra step of translating validated instructional routines or devices into teachers' manuals (and, where appropriate, student materials) that are available to educators. To do so has required a significant investment of time and resources. In addition, staff members have had to make trade-offs between doing new research and translating completed research into usable products. In the process of making this translation, staff members have found that working very closely with the ultimate consumers of the instructional packages is imperative to ensure that the packages are designed in a way that meets their instructional and classroom organization and management needs.

A second area to consider when attempting to optimize the translation of research into practice has to do with professional staff development. Each year, school districts pour millions of dollars into efforts to upgrade the instructional effectiveness of their teachers through inservice training programs. The majority of these efforts tend to be one-shot programs (e.g., a 1- to 2-hour training session on a new teaching routine) with no follow-up included as a part of the overall professional development design. Research findings on the efficacy of such training efforts are clear. Very little, if any, permanent change in instructional practice results (Fullan, 1982; Hord, Rutherford, Huling-Austin, & Hall, 1987).

Thus, as a profession, educators must stop ignoring documented principles of staff development and system change. The current course of action will have little or no effect on bringing about significant changes in educating students and will lead to inappropriate conclusions about the efficacy of new teaching procedures. In other words, teachers may conclude that new procedures lack power when the real reason for their failure may be that teachers were not given enough exposure to and practice with the procedure under controlled conditions with sufficient feedback from others to enable them to reach a level of comfort and fluency.

The following principles of effective staff development should be applied to facilitate translation of any new teaching routine into the instructional practices of general education teachers. First, key stakeholders in a school district (e.g., administrators, teachers, and school psychologists) must be involved in deciding whether to adopt and receive instruction in a given procedure. In short, this step in a system's adoption of an educational innovation is evaluative. Questions as to whether the innovation is consistent with the district's philosophy, goals, and other current teaching practices must be addressed.

Second, the issue of trade-offs must be resolved. That is, the incorporation of any innovation usually adds significantly to teachers' planning and/or instructional load initially; hence, decisions must be made regarding the elimination or reduction of current programs or practices. Since such decisions are often difficult to make in education, educators often follow the course of least resistance and simply view the new procedure as an add-on. In turn, they often elect to keep using practices with which they feel most comfortable (the old practices); thus, the probability of adopting a new practice is greatly minimized. Strong administrative support and endorsement (including permission to make necessary trade-offs) are very important.

Third, to ensure the adoption of complex educational innovations, a professional development sequence must be offered over a sustained period of time rather than as a one-shot event. Sustained efforts allow time for modeling, practice, feedback, and questions. In addition, teachers need the opportunity to try out the new procedure (or portions of the new procedure if it consists of many steps or is complex) in their classroom and to debrief with the instructor on problems encountered. Finally, following the formal professional development session(s), teachers must have the opportunity to receive ongoing support in their efforts to implement the new procedure. Initial support can be provided through the use of support teams (i.e., small groups of teachers who meet to discuss implementation problems and other issues) (Huberman & Miles, 1984) and peer coaching (Joyce & Showers, 1982).

Another area that must be considered in an effort to increase the likelihood of innovative adoptions is the role of pre-service teacher-training programs. The current teaching corps in the United States will be undergoing significant changes in the next decade (Ingersoll, 1999). There will be a large turnover in the nation's teaching staff owing to retirements and decisions to leave the teaching profession for another career (Ingersoll, 2001). Filling this void represents not only a tremendous challenge, but also a significant opportunity to affect the types of skills new teachers should possess in respect to the instruction of low-achieving students. The first step toward meeting this challenge requires careful review of the content of current teacher preparation programs. Especially in the preparation of secondary teachers, additional time is needed to train teacher trainees in specific procedures for effectively delivering their content. Prospective teachers not only need to be made aware of specific teaching routines and devices for enhancing the delivery of curriculum content but also need ample opportunities to practice such procedures to mastery in practicum and field experiences. Many authors who have written about the educational crisis confronting our nation's schools have argued that meaningful solutions will mean having to make dramatic departures from traditional practices (National Commission on Teaching and America's Future, 1997). As dropout and low-achievement problems escalate in magnitude (524,000 students dropped out in 1999; another 700,000 were barely functionally literate), steps must be taken to equip teachers with skills that will enable them to organize and present content information more effectively to at-risk students. This process should begin most logically in the formative years of teacher preparation. The climate for such reform is right in the light of current efforts to raise the quality of teacher preparation (e.g., Wise, 1999).

Finally, the important role that school psychologists can play in effective translation and utilization of the teaching procedures discussed in this chapter must be underscored. To fulfill this role, school psychologists must expand the focus of their assessment efforts to include a profile of the different setting demands (e.g., the types of tests, the readability and "considerate" nature of the textbooks, the format of assignments) that students encounter in their regular classrooms. If teachers are informed about the setting demands that particular students will have difficulty in meeting, then they will be better able to work with school psychologists and other personnel to adapt instruction to correspond with particular students' needs. Teachers will understand more fully how teaching practices and curriculum materials can precipitate failure as much as specific student deficits, and they will be more able to accommodate special learners in their classes.

Additionally, as contributors to Individual Education Planning meetings and other educational planning meetings, school psychologists must recognize the importance of having all members of the committee (teachers, parents, and students) actively participate in the decision-making process (VanReusen, Deshler, & Schumaker, 1989; Van Reusen et al., 1994). Providing opportunities for participation in such meetings is central to obtaining the necessary commitment and support of key participants (general education and support service teachers, parents, and the student). The school psychologist should view his or her role in such meetings as a conveyor of information, problem solver, and advocate of change in teaching practices on the part of teachers as well as change on the part of the student.

Also, the school psychologist can do much to promote cooperative planning and other interactions among teaching staff. Cooperative planning between special class teachers and general education teachers is particularly challenging because of the schedule conflicts that arise during a typical school day (e.g., planning periods or lunch periods that do not match). Because of school psychologists' relatively more flexible schedules, they can facilitate the efforts of different staff members in cooperative planning by being mediators or by encouraging a reluctant staff member to interact with other teachers on behalf of targeted students. Finally, school psychologists can play a valuable role by making staff aware of newly validated teaching routines and by modeling their use. They also can team with general education teachers in efforts to increase the effectiveness of their presentations of subject matter. This teaming relationship can be established, for example, in the form of a peer-coaching arrangement (Joyce & Showers, 1982). In brief, school psychologists can do a great deal to support and facilitate the processes that are critical to bringing about instructional improvements in school settings.

In summary, research has shown that to bring about a strong impact on the academic success and life adjustment of at-risk students requires the use of a broad array of instructional strategies and techniques in a coordinated fashion by several teaching and support personnel (Hock, Deshler, & Schumaker, 1993; Deshler & Schumaker, 1988). The major components of an innovative model for providing such services have been summarized in this chapter. A key element of that model is the effective use, by general education teachers, of a host of validated teaching routines and devices that can facilitate students' understanding and retention of content information presented in the general education class. Given the results presented here, general education teachers clearly possess the means of significantly halting the decline in school achievement of many at-risk students as well as reducing the escalation of referral rates of these students to special education. Research data suggest that teachers who manipulate, organize, and present their content information in such a way that it becomes easy to understand and remember produce greater learning in their students. Thus, ensuring teachers learn these new methods becomes a priority for all educators interested in the achievement of students.

REFERENCES

Alley, G. R., & Deshler, D. D. (1979). *Teaching the learning disabled adolescent.* Denver: Love.

Allington, R. L. (1984). So what is the problem? Whose problem is it? *Topics in Learning and Learning Disabilities, 3*(4), 91–99.

Armbruster, B. B. (1984). The problem of "inconsiderate text." In G. Duffy, L. Roehler, & J. Mason (Eds.), *Comprehension instruction: Perspectives and suggestions.* New York: Longman.

Ausubel, P. (1963). *The psychology of meaningful verbal learning.* New York: Grune & Stratton.

Ausubel, D. P., & Robinson, F. G. (1969). *School learning: An introduction to educational psychology.* New York: Holt, Rinehart & Winston.

Beals, V. L. (1983). *The effects of large group instruction on the acquisition of specific learning strategies by learning disabled adolescents.* Unpublished doctoral dissertation, University of Kansas.

Berry, G. C. (1999). *Development and validation of an instructional program for teaching post-secondary students with learning disabilities to take and study notes.* Unpublished doctoral dissertation. University of Kansas.

Bos, C. S., & Anders, P. L. (1987). Semantic feature analysis: An interactive teaching strategy for facilitating learning from text. *Learning Disability Focus, 3*(1), 55–59.

Boyer, E. L. (1983). *High school: A report on secondary education in America.* New York: Harper & Row.

Brophy, J., & Good, T. L. (1985). Teaching behavior and student achievement. In M. Wittrock (Ed.), *Handbook of research on teaching.* New York: Longman.

Bulgren, J. A., Deshler, D. D., & Schumaker, J. B. (1993). *The Concept Mastery Routine.* Lawrence, KS: Edge Enterprises.

Bulgren, J. A., Deshler, D. D., & Schumaker, J. B. (1997). Use of a recall enhancement routine and strategies in inclusive secondary classes. *Learning Disabilities Research & Practice, 12*(4), 198–208.

Bulgren, J. A., Deshler, D. D., Schumaker, J. B., & Lenz, B. K. (2000). The use and effectiveness of analogical instruction in diverse secondary content classrooms. *Journal of Educational Psychology.*

Bulgren, J. A., & Lenz, B. K. (1996). Strategic instruction in the content areas. In D. D. Deshler, E. S. Ellis, & B. K. Lenz (Eds.), *Teaching adolescents with learning disabilities: Strategies and methods* (2nd ed., pp. 409–473). Denver: Love.

Bulgren, J. A., Lenz, B. K., Deshler, D. D., & Schumaker, J. B. (1995). *The Concept Comparison Routine.* Lawrence, KS: Edge Enterprises.

Bulgren, J. A., & Schumaker, J. B. (1996). *The Paired-Associates Strategy.* Lawrence: The University of Kansas Center for Research on Learning.

Bulgren, J. A., Schumaker, J. B., & Deshler, D. D. (1988). Effectiveness of a concept teaching routine in enhancing the performance of LD students in secondary level mainstream classes. *Learning Disability Quarterly, 11*(1), 319–331.

Bulgren, J. A., Schumaker, J. B., & Deshler, D. D. (1994a). *The Concept Anchoring Routine.* Lawrence, KS: Edge Enterprises.

Bulgren, J. A., Schumaker, J. B., & Deshler, D. D. (1994b). The effects of a recall enhancement routine on the test performance of secondary students with and without learning disabilities. *Learning Disabilities Research & Practice, 9*(1), 2-11.

Bulgren, J. A., Lenz, B. K., Schumaker, J. B., Deshler, D. D., & Marquis, J. (in press). *The use and effectiveness of a comparison routine in diverse secondary content classrooms. Journal of Educational Psychology.*

Carlson, S. A. (1985). The ethical appropriateness of subject-matter tutoring of learning disabled adolescents. *Learning Disability Quarterly, 8,* 310-314.

Carlson, S. A., & Alley, G. R. (1981). *Performance and competence of learning disabled and high achieving high school students on essential cognitive skills* (Research Report 53). Lawrence, KS: University of Kansas Institute for Research in Learning Disabilities.

Clark, F. L., Deshler, D. D., Schumaker, J. B., Alley, G. R., & Warner, M. M. (1984). Visual imagery and self-questioning: Strategies to improve comprehension of written material. *Journal of Learning Disabilities, 17,* 145-149.

Crank, J. N., Deshler, D. D., & Schumaker, J. B. (1995). *Surface counseling.* Lawrence, KS: Edge Enterprises.

Cuban, L. (1984). *How teachers taught: Constancy and change in American classrooms, 1890-1980.* New York: Longman.

Cusick, P. A. (1983). *The equalitarian ideal and the American high school.* New York: Longman.

Deshler, D. D., Kass, C. E., & Ferrell, W. R. (1978). Monitoring of schoolwork errors by LD adolescents. *Journal of Learning Disabilities, 11*(7), 10-23.

Deshler, D. D., & Schumaker, J. B. (1988). An instructional model for teaching students how to learn. In J. L. Graden, J. E. Zins, & M. J. Curtis, (Eds.), *Alternative education delivery systems: Enhancing instructional options for all students* (pp. 391-411). Washington, DC: National Association of School Psychologists.

Deshler, D. D., Schumaker, J. B., Lenz, B. K., & Ellis, E. S. (1984). Academic and cognitive interventions for LD adolescents: Part II. *Journal of Learning Disabilities, 17*(3), 170-187.

Deshler, D. D., Schumaker, J. B., & McKnight, P. C. (1997). *The Survey Routine.* Lawrence, KS: Edge Enterprises.

Ellis, E. S. (1993). The LINCS Vocabulary Learning Strategy. Lawrence, KS: Edge Enterprises.

Ellis, E. S. (1997). *The Clarifying Routine.* Lawrence, KS: Edge Enterprises.

Ellis, E. S. (1998). *The Framing Routine.* Lawrence, KS: Edge Enterprises

Ellis, E. S., Deshler, D. D., Lenz, B. K., Schumaker, J. B., & Clark, F. L. (1991). An instructional model for teaching learning strategies. *Focus on Exceptional Children, 23*(6), 1-24

Ellis, E. S., Deshler, D. D., & Schumaker, J. B. (1989). Teaching adolescents with learning disabilities to generate and use task-specific strategies. *Journal of Learning Disabilities, 22*(2), 108-119, 130.

Ellis, E. S., & Feldman, K. (1994). Creating "thoughtful" classrooms: Fostering cognitive literacy via cooperative learning and integrated strategy instruction. In S. Sharan (Ed.), *Handbook of cooperative learning methods* (pp. 157-176). New York: Praeger.

Ellis, E. S., Lenz, B. K., & Sabornie, E. J. (1987). Generalization and adaptation of learning strategies to natural environments: Part I: Critical agents. *Remedial and Special Education, 8*(1), 6-20.

Ellis, E. S., Raines, C., Farmer, T., & Tyree, A. (1997). *Effectiveness of a concept clarifying routine in upper-elementary and middle-school mainstream classes.* Tuscaloosa: The University of Alabama Multiple Abilities Program.

Ellis, E. S., Raines, C., & Hansford, C. (in preparation). *Evaluation of a hierarchical graphic organizer on written expression of conceptual knowledge of students in a fourth-fifth grade multiage inclusive inner-city classroom.* Tuscaloosa: The University of Alabama.

Erickson, R. N., Ysseldyke, J. E., Thurlow, M. L., & Elliott, J. L. (1998). Inclusive assessment and accountability systems: Tools of the trade in educational reform. *Teaching Exceptional Children, 31*(2), 4-9.

Fullan, M. (1982). *The meaning of educational change.* New York: Teachers College Press.

Goodlad, J. L. (1984). *A place called school.* New York: McGraw-Hill.

Graff, H. J. (1987). *The legacies of literacy: Continuities and contradictions in Western culture and society.* Bloomington, IN: Indiana University Press.

Hazel, J. S., Schumaker, J. B., Sherman, J. A., & Sheldon-Wildgen, J. (1981). *ASSET: A social skills program for adolescents.* Champaign, IL: Research Press.

Hock, M. F., Deshler, D. D., & Schumaker, J. B. (1993). Learning strategy instruction for at-risk and learning-disabled adults: The development of strategic learners through apprenticeship. *Preventing School Failure, 38*(1), 43-49.

Hock, M. F., Deshler, D. D., & Schumaker, J. B. (1999). Tutoring programs for academically underprepared college students: A review of the literature. *Journal of College Reading and Learning, 29*(2), 101-122.

Hock, M. F., Schumaker, J. B., & Deshler, D. D. (1999). Closing the gap to success in secondary schools: A model for cognitive apprenticeship. In D. D. Deshler, J. B. Schumaker, K. R. Harris, & S. Graham (Eds.), *Advances in teaching and learning: Teaching every child every day: Learning in diverse middle and high school classrooms* (pp. 1-52). Cambridge, MA: Brookline Books.

Hord, S. M., Rutherford, W. L., Huling-Austin, L., & Hall, G. (1987). *Taking charge of change.* Alexandria, VA: Association of Supervision and Curriculum Development.

Howe, H., & Edelman, M. W. (1985). *Barriers to excellence: Our children at risk.* Boston: National Coalition of Advocates for Students.

Howell, S. B. (1986). *A study of the effectiveness of TOWER: A theme writing strategy.* Unpublished master's thesis. University of Kansas.

Huberman, A. M., & Miles, M. B. (1984). *Innovation up close: How school improvement works.* New York: Plenum.

Hughes, C. A., Deshler, D. D., Ruhl, K. L., & Schumaker, J. B. (1993). Test-taking strategy instruction for adolescents with emotional and behavioral disorders. *Journal of Emotional and Behavioral Disorders, 1*(3), 188-199.

Hughes, C. A., & Schumaker, J. B. (1991). Test-taking strategy instruction for adolescents with learning disabilities. *Exceptionality, 2,* 205-221.

Hughes, C., Schumaker, J. B., Deshler, D. D., & Mercer, C. (1988). *The Test Taking Strategy: Instructor's manual.* Lawrence, KS: Edge Enterprises.

Ingersoll, R. (1999). The problem of under qualified teachers in American Secondary schools. *Educational Researcher, 28*(2), 26-37.

Ingersoll, R. (2001). *Teacher turnover, teacher shortages and the organization of schools.* Seattle, WA: University of Washington Center for the Stdy of Teaching and policy.

Joint Committee on Teacher Planning for Students with Disabilities (1995). *Planning for academic diversity in America's classrooms: Windows on reality, research, change, and practice.* Lawrence: The University of Kansas Center for Research on Learning.

Joyce, B. R., & Showers, B. (1982). The coaching of teaching. *Educational Leadership, 40,* 4-10.

Kame'enui, E. J., & Carnine, D. W. (Eds.). (1998). *Effective strategies for accommodating students with diverse learning and curricular needs.* Columbus, OH: Merrill.

Keimig, J. (in preparation). *The effects of peer tutoring in the acquisition and generalization of learning strategies* (Research Report). Lawrence: University of Kansas Institute for Research in Learning Disabilities.

Knackendoffel, A. (1989). *Development and validation of a set of teaming strategies for enhancing collaboration between secondary resource and content teachers.* Unpublished doctoral dissertation. University of Kansas.

Knackendoffel, E. A., Robinson, S. M., Deshler, D. D., & Schumaker, J. B. (1992). *Collaborative problem solving.* Lawrence, KS: Edge Enterprises.

Lenz, B. K. (1984). *The effect of advance organizers on the learning and retention of LD adolescents within the contexts of a cooperative planning model.* Final research report. Washington, DC: U.S. Department of Education, Special Education Services.

Lenz, B. K., Alley, G. R., & Schumaker, J. B. (1987). Activating the inactive learner through the presentation of advance organizers. *Learning Disability Quarterly, 10*(1), 53-67.

Lenz, B. K., & Bulgren, J. A. (1995). Promoting learning in content classes. In P. T. Cegelka & W. H. Berdine (Eds.), *Effective instruction for students with learning disabilities* (pp. 385-417). Boston: Allyn & Bacon.

Lenz, B. K., with Bulgren, J. A., Schumaker, J. B., Deshler, D. D., & Boudah, D. A. (1994). *The Unit Organizer Routine.* Lawrence: Edge Enterprises.

Lenz, B. K., & Hughes, C. A. (1990). A word identification strategy for adolescents with disabilities. *Journal of Learning Disabilities, 23*(3), 149-158, 163.

Lenz, B. K., Marrs, R. W., Schumaker, J. B., & Deshler, D. D. (1993). *The Lesson Organizer Routine.* Lawrence, KS: Edge Enterprises.

Lenz, B. K., Schumaker, J. B., Deshler, D. D., & Beals, V. L. (1984). *The Word Identification Strategy: Instructor's manual.* Lawrence: The University of Kansas Center for Research on Learning.

Lenz, B. K., with Schumaker, J. B., Deshler, D. D., & Bulgren, J. A. (1998). *The Course Organizer Routine.* Lawrence: Edge Enterprises.

Licopoli, L. (1984). The resource room and mainstreaming secondary handicapped students: A case history. *Topics in Learning and Learning Disabilities, 3*(4), 1-16.

Lieberman, A., & Miller, L. (1978). The social realities of teaching. *Teachers College Record, 80,* 55-61.

McKnight, P. C. (1980). Microteaching: Development 1968 to 1978. *British Journal of Teaching Education, 6*(3), 214-226.

McNaughtin, D. B., & Hughes, C. A. (2000). *InSPECT: A strategy for finding and correcting spelling errors.* Lawrence, KS: Edge Enterprises.

Mellard, D. F., & Deshler, D. D. (1984). Modeling the condition of learning disabilities on post-secondary populations. *Educational Psychologist, 19,* 188-197.

Moccia, R. E., Schumaker, J. B., Hazel, J. S., Vernon, D. S., & Deshler, D. D. (1989). A mentor program for facilitating the transitions of individuals with learning disabilities. *Journal of Reading, Writing, and Learning Disabilities, 5*(2), 177-195.

Moran, M. R. (1980). *An investigation of the demands on oral language skills of learning disabled students in secondary classrooms* (Research Report 1). Lawrence: University of Kansas Institute for Research in Learning Disabilities.

Moran, M. R., & DeLoach, T. F. (1982). *Mainstream teachers' responses to formal features of writing by secondary learning disabled students* (Research Report 61), Lawrence: University of Kansas Institute for Research in Learning Disabilities.

Moran, M. R., Schumaker, J. B., & Vetter, A. F. (1981). *Teaching a paragraph organization strategy to learning disabled adolescents* (Research Report 54). Lawrence: University of Kansas Institute for Research in Learning Disabilities.

Nagel, D., Schumaker, J. B., & Deshler, D. D. (1986). *The FIRST-Letter Mnemonic Strategy: Instructor's manual.* Lawrence, KS: Edge Enterprises.

National Commission on Teaching and America's Future (1997). *Doing what matters most: Investing in quality teaching.* New York: National Commission on Teaching and America's Future.

Powell, A. G., Farrar, E., & Cohen, D. K. (1985). *The shopping mall high school: Winners and losers in the educational marketplace.* Boston: Houghton Mifflin.

Putnam, M. L. (1988). *An investigation of the curricular demands in secondary mainstream classrooms containing mildly handicapped students.* Unpublished doctoral dissertation. University of Kansas.

Rademacher, J. A. (1993). *The development and validation of a classroom assignment routine for mainstream settings.* Unpublished doctoral dissertation. University of Kansas.

Rademacher, J. A., Deshler, D. D., Schumaker, J. B., & Lenz, B. K. (1998). *The Quality Assignment Routine.* Lawrence, KS: Edge Enterprises.

Robbins, D. (1982). *The FIRST-Letter Mnemonic Strategy: A memorization technique for learning disabled high school students.* Unpublished master's thesis. University of Kansas.

Scanlon, R. G. (1982). *Report of the Council of Chief State School Officers and Ad Hoc Committee on Teacher Certification Preparation and Accreditation.* Washington, DC: Council of Chief State School Officers and Ad Hoc Committee on Teacher Certification Preparation and Accreditation.

Schmidt, J. (1983). *The effects of four generalizations conditions on learning disabled adolescents' written language performance in the regular classroom.* Unpublished doctoral dissertation. University of Kansas.

Schmidt, J. L., Deshler, D. D., Schumaker, J. B., & Alley, G. R. (1989). Effects of generalization instruction on the written language performance of adolescents with learning disabilities in the mainstream classroom. *Reading, Writing, & Learning Disabilities, 4*(4), 291–309.

Schumaker, J. B. (1992). Social performance of individuals with learning disabilities: Through the looking glass of KU-IRLD research. *School Psychology Review, 21*(3), 387–399.

Schumaker, J. B. (in preparation). *The Theme Writing Strategy: Instructor's manual.* Lawrence: University of Kansas Institute for Research in Learning Disabilities.

Schumaker, J. B., Bulgren, J. A., Deshler, D. D., & Lenz, B. K. (1998). *The Recall Enhancement Routine.* Lawrence, KS: Edge Enterprises.

Schumaker, J. B., Denton, P. H., & Deshler, D. D. (1984). *The Paraphrasing Strategy: Instructor's manual.* Lawrence: University of Kansas Center for Research on Learning.

Schumaker, J. B., & Deshler, D. D. (1984). Setting demand variables: A major factor in program planning for LD adolescents. *Topics in Language Disorders, 4*(2), 22–40.

Schumaker, J. B., & Deshler, D. D. (1988). Implementing the regular education initiative in secondary schools: A different ball game. *Journal of Learning Disabilities, 21*(1), 36–42.

Schumaker, J. B., Deshler, D. D., Alley, G. R., Warner, M. M., Clark, F. L., & Nolan, S. (1982). Error monitoring: A learning strategy for improving adolescent's academic performance. In W. M. Cruickshank & J. W. Lerner (Eds.), *Coming of age: Vol. 3. The best of ACLD.* Syracuse, NY: Syracuse University Press.

Schumaker, J. B., Deshler, D. D., Denton, P. M., Alley, G. R., Clark, F. L., & Warner, M. M. (1982). Multipass: A learning strategy for improving reading comprehension. *Learning Disability Quarterly, 5,* 195–304.

Schumaker, J. B., Hazel, J. S., & Deshler, D. D. (1985). A model for facilitating post-secondary transitions. *Techniques: A Journal for Remedial Education and Counseling, 1,* 437–446.

Schumaker, J. B., Hazel, J. S., & Pederson, C. (1988). *Social skills for daily living.* Circle Pines, MN: American Guidance Service.

Schumaker, J. B., & Lyerla, K. (1991). *The Paragraph Writing Strategy: Instructor's manual.* Lawrence: University of Kansas Center for Research on Learning.

Schumaker, J. B., Nolan, S. M., & Deshler, D. D. (1985). *The Error Monitoring Strategy: Instructor's manual.* Lawrence: University of Kansas Center for Research on Learning.

Schumaker, J. B., & Sheldon, J. (1985). *The Sentence Writing Strategy: Instructor's manual.* Lawrence: University of Kansas Center for Research on Learning.

Schumaker, J. B., Wildgen, J., & Sherman, J. (1980). *An observational study of the academic and social behaviors of LD adolescents in the regular classroom (Research Report 22).* Lawrence: University of Kansas Institute for Research in Learning Disabilities.

Seabaugh, G. O., & Schumaker, J. B. (1981a). *The effects of three conferencing procedures on the academic productivity of LD and NLD adolescents (Research Report 36).* Lawrence: University of Kansas Institute for Research in Learning Disabilities.

Seabaugh, G. O., & Schumaker, J. B. (1981b). *The effects of self-regulation training in the academic productivity of LD and NLD adolescents (Research Report 37).* Lawrence: University of Kansas Institute for Research in Learning Disabilities.

Sinclair, R. L., & Ghory, W. J. (1987). *Reaching marginal students: A primary concern for school renewal.* Chicago: McCutchan.

Skrtic, T. (1980). *Formal reasoning abilities of learning disabilities adolescents (Research Report 7).* Lawrence: University of Kansas Institute for Research in Learning Disabilities.

Spady, W. G., & Marx, G. (1984). *Excellence in our schools: Making it happen.* San Francisco: Far West Laboratory.

VanReusen, A. K. (1998). Self-Advocacy Strategy instruction: Enhancing student motivation, self-determination, and responsibility in the learning process. In M. Wehmeyer & D. Sands (Eds.), *Making it happen: Student involvement in education planning, decision-making, and instruction* (pp. 131-152). Baltimore: Brookes.

Van Reusen, A. K., Bos, C., Schumaker, J. B., & Deshler, D. D. (1994). *The Self-Advocacy Strategy for Education and Transition Planning.* Lawrence, KS: Edge Enterprises.

Van Reusen, A. K., Deshler, D. D., & Schumaker, J. B. (1989). Effects of a student participation strategy in facilitating the involvement of adolescents with learning disabilities in the individualized education program planning process. *Learning Disabilities, 1*(2), 23-34.

Vernon, D. S., Deshler, D. D., & Schumaker, J. B. (1999). *The THINK Strategy.* Lawrence, KS: Edge Enterprises.

Wagner, M., Blackorby, J., & Hebbeler, K. (1993). *Beyond the report card: The multiple dimensions of secondary school performance of students with disabilities. A report from the National Longitudinal Study of Special Education Students.* Menlo Park, CA: SRI International.

Warner, M. M., Schumaker, J. B., Alley, G. R., & Deshler, D. D. (1980). Learning disabled adolescents in the public schools: Are they different from other low achievers? *Exceptional Education Quarterly, 1*(2), 27-36.

Warner, M. M., Schumaker, J. B., Alley, G. R., & Deshler, D. D. (1989). An epidemiological study of school identified LD and low-achieving adolescents on a serial recall task: The role of executive control. *Learning Disabilities Research, 4*(2), 107-118.

Weinstein, C. E., Goetz, E. T., & Alexander, P. A. (1988). *Learning and study strategies: Issues in assessment, instruction, and evaluation.* New York: Harcourt Brace Jovanovich.

Wise, A. E. (1999). Effective teachers … or warm bodies. *Quality Teaching.* Washington, DC: National Council for Accreditation of Teacher Education.

CHAPTER 30

Curriculum–Based Collaboration in Secondary Schools

Lindy Crawford and Gerald Tindal
University of Oregon

INTRODUCTION

In the original chapter written in the previous edition of this volume (Tindal & Germann, 1991), mainstream consultation agreements (MCAs) were described with three essential components: (a) minimum essential learner outcomes, (b) roles and responsibilities for teachers and consultants, and (c) measurement systems for documenting outcomes. MCAs were implemented in this way because of the belief that few contingencies were thought to exist for keeping students in mainstream classrooms. MCAs were "procedures for maintaining the focus of decision-making on instruction rather than placement" (p. 497).

In the past decade, however, with a new emphasis on standards, teachers have had to focus their curriculum and instruction on critical student learning outcomes. For example, while the previous chapter emphasized grades and all the behaviors needed to be successful in classrooms (e.g., complete assignments, pass tests, etc.), this current version is oriented toward specific mastery of secondary content. Only with such concentrated attention to learning the declarative, conditional, and procedural knowledge of the arts, sciences, and social sciences can students with disabilities be given appropriate access to the general education curriculum. The system we propose is highly structured and, similar to the previous chapter, provides school psychologists and special educators with an important role to play in working with general education content teachers.

With our specific focus on educational supports that help students learn content, we emphasize instructional consultation rather than other approaches described in the educational literature. At some level, mental health (Caplan, 1970) or organizational (Maher, Illback, & Zins, 1984) models of consultation may be important for special educators and school psychologists to use in other aspects of their jobs, while the behavioral model (Bergan, 1977) of consultation is the most researched (Martens, 1993) and the most widely practiced (Costenbader, Swartz, & Petrix, 1992.)

The behavioral model (Bergan, 1977), demonstrated to be effective in many contexts (Sheridan, Welch, & Orme, 1996), relies on a problem-solving approach to improving academic and behavioral outcomes for students (Bergan & Kratochwill, 1990). Unfortunately, it is largely reactive, employed *after* a student encounters difficulties in the general education environment. The behavioral model also is inefficient in its single case-study approach to solving classroom-based problems. For example, in this model teachers contact a consultant (often a school psychologist or special education teacher) for assistance if a particular student is having academic or behavioral problems. Interventions in the form of instructional strategies, behavior modification programs, or adjusted academic expectations are designed to change the teacher's behavior with the goal of changing the student's behavior. Ecological variables are taken into account, but often only at a surface level—and more substantive issues are sometimes overlooked.

Although the behavioral model of consultation is designed to be efficient in that the consultant provides services to teachers rather than individual students, it is still very time-consuming for teachers. Individual students remain the focus of a teacher's efforts, resulting in different plans for different students. Even when an effective plan is developed, it constantly needs modification because human behavior (especially the behavior of adolescents) is dynamic. In secondary schools, where teachers are responsible for teaching 100–180 students per day, time and resources are typically insufficient to successfully maintain several different interventions for several different students.

Placing the student at the center of the model also encourages professionals to attribute lack of progress in the general education curriculum to problems with the student. The practice of blaming the student for his or her lack of success in the classroom is overused and outdated. Instead, "If the learner fails, the failure must be framed in terms of the instruction the teacher controls. This allows the teacher to be an active agent of change" (Kame'enui & Simmons, 1990, pp. 12–13). Teachers and other education professionals need to design and deliver instruction that meets the needs of a diverse student body. With current knowledge about the process of human learning, as well as increased access to technology in the schools, teachers can no longer design and deliver instruction using a "one format fits all" approach.

Sailor (1989) highlights our primary concern with traditional models of consultation:

> We are a nation of plumbers. As a people, we Americans tend to approach life as if it were a complicated hydraulic structure that constantly springs leaks all over the place which must be fixed. Seldom do we question the adequacy, let alone the function, of the structure itself (p. vii).

In this chapter we outline a collaborative approach to consultation characterized as proactive rather than reactive, focusing on the initial "structure" rather than the eventual "leaks." This approach, curriculum-based collaboration (CBC); (Nolet & Tindal, 1994), attempts to ensure progress in the general education curriculum for ALL students. We propose that education professionals place the curriculum, not the child, at the center of any model of consultation, and that teachers and consultants engage in advance planning to increase opportunities for student success. This focus has been made even sharper and more compelling with the reauthorization of the Individuals with Disabilities Education Act, Amendments of 1997 (IDEA-97). This mandate is clearly results oriented and promotes inclusion: Students with disabilities must participate in programs rooted in the general education curriculum.

In their model of "collaborative consultation," Idol, Nevin, and Paolucci-Whitcomb (1994) combine attributes of consultation and collaboration and define it as "an interactive process that enables teams of people with diverse expertise to generate creative solutions to mutually defined problems" (p. xi). The model outlined in this chapter, CBC, is similar to Idol et. al.'s model in that it constitutes an interactive process among a diversity of education professionals. In curriculum-based collaboration, however, professionals work together to identify core curriculum concepts and design instruction that is accessible to all students—as opposed to solving problems caused by students' lack of progress in a curriculum that may be poorly defined and rigidly delivered. Furthermore, the focus is on "formative assessments—ongoing assessments designed to make students' thinking visible to both teachers and students ... In the assessment-centered classroom environments, formative assessments help both teachers and students monitor progress" (Bransford, Brown, & Cocking, 2000, p. 24). The key to integrating the core concepts into the design of instruction, providing access to all students, and formatively evaluating student progress, however, requires teachers to think of universal designs in the beginning, rather than differentiating instruction after students have failed.

UNIVERSAL DESIGN

The concept of universal design provides a theoretical foundation for curriculum-based collaboration. Universal design is a product of federal legislation passed in 1990, titled the Americans with Disabilities Act (ADA). One of the requirements of this piece of legislation is that public buildings be physically accessible to all people. The passage of ADA resulted in the retrofitting of many public places with devices such as wheelchair ramps, elevators, and curb cuts in sidewalks. Although many viewed it as an expensive process, in the end, expense was only part of the reason why architectural designers became committed to universal designs for new buildings and other public places. Soon, many realized that accommodations made for people with disabilities actually benefited other people as well. For example, ramps have become useful in moving heavy furniture in and out of buildings, elevators have helped elderly people who are challenged by steep stairs, and curb cuts in sidewalks have benefited all pedestrians, not just those using wheelchairs. Universal design of buildings and other public places has become the rule, not the exception, as architects have realized the effectiveness and efficiency of designing physical structures accessible by all.

The effectiveness and efficiency of universal design have recently been applied in the field of education (CAST, 2001). Researchers have been studying the benefits of proactive design of curriculum and instruction in a way that meets the needs of students with disabilities, as well as other students who have not always excelled under traditional models of instruction. Similar to the concept of physical access, cognitive access has been made easier and more efficient when the concepts of universal design have been included in the design of learning and delivery of instruction.

In a universal design for learning, curriculum is diversified and instruction is designed and delivered to accommodate a multitude of student differences through four fundamental assumptions about teaching and learning (CAST, 2001):

1. A continuum of learner differences exists.

2. Teaching is designed to accommodate the learning needs of ALL students.

3. Curriculum materials are diverse and rely on various presentation formats, including technological delivery.

4. Student problems are not "fixed" in response to their lack of progress in a set curriculum. Instead, the curriculum is made more flexible.

Using these four assumptions, we propose that the design of curriculum and instruction take into account the unique learning needs of all students before they become involved in a classroom learning experience, thus minimizing the need for instructional interventions. Rather than assume that students with diverse learning needs pose problems requiring solutions, in curriculum-based collaboration, the assumption is made that diversity is inherent in the classroom. Furthermore, thoughtful curriculum planning and instructional design create an engaging learning environment that is relatively free of "problems" requiring interventions.

This is not a new concept. Educators have been utilizing curriculum modifications and instructional accommodations for decades. The difference lies in the view that these behaviors were seen as add-ons that teachers employed for "special kids." Teachers modified what worked for most in an attempt to create a system that would work for all. Despite teachers' best intentions, however, adding modifications to an already defined curriculum and narrowly designed instructional plan still reflected a reactive approach to teaching. A more proactive approach has been expressed most effectively in the principles of universal design, providing a framework for teachers to preplan in ways that promote all students' progress in the general education curriculum.

ATTRIBUTES OF CURRICULUM-BASED COLLABORATION

Curriculum-based collaboration (CBC) consists of three critical attributes: (a) collaboration focused on the curriculum, (b) a proactive approach to supporting students in the general education curriculum, and (c) formative evaluation to ensure program effectiveness.

The first and most important attribute of CBC is that curriculum planning is the focal point for collaborative activities. Collaboration focuses on alignment of curriculum content (articulated by content area teachers) with instructional strategies (suggested by school psychologists or special education teachers) and assessment formats. In this way, the curriculum provides a context in which professionals with diverse training, philosophies, and responsibilities engage in collaborative activities, empowering participants to become involved in thoughtful, creative, and preventative curriculum planning. Focusing on the curriculum avoids placing blame on students or teachers, making the collaborative process less threatening and more productive. We also believe that instructional strategies and assessment procedures designed with the curriculum in mind, as opposed to individual students, are more generalizable, more efficient, and arguably more ethical.

The second attribute of CBC is a proactive focus on supporting students and preventing academic failure through universal design. Teachers cannot wait for students to fail before requesting help from the school psychologist or special education teacher. Instead, the collaborative team meets well in advance of beginning a unit of study and develops concept-based curriculum goals and multidimensional means of instructional delivery. Teachers, working in collaborative teams, develop menus of student response opportunities in the form of learning activities and performance-based assessments that are comprehensive enough to provide all students with an opportunity to demonstrate their knowledge and skills in the general curriculum. Instruction is differentiated from the beginning so all students have access.

The third and final attribute of CBC is formative evaluation to develop effective programs that ensure progress in the general education curriculum. Programs, rather than being assumed guaranteed to be effective, are continuously evaluated and assessed. Outcome data are generated in an ongoing manner, with time-series data providing timely information on program effectiveness. In this process, student learning becomes the driving force for making changes when they are needed, with appropriate justification. Relying on research in the field of curriculum and instructional design, we have established six critical components of CBC that can, and should, be monitored. At times these six attributes need to be manipulated to ensure their positive effect on student learning. In the remainder of this chapter, we delineate the six components.

SIX INTERACTIVE COMPONENTS OF CURRICULUM-BASED COLLABORATION

Curriculum-based collaboration is premised on the importance of curriculum and instruction delivered by content area experts in a style that is designed to meet the needs of all students. To accomplish this, a number of variables in the classroom environment should be considered within the teaching and learning process, including curriculum materials, teacher expertise, student prior knowledge and motivation, instructional technology, learning strategies, and assessment formats. Clear, effective translation of content information and subsequent assessment of learning outcomes depend on the alignment of these components with one another. When they are not aligned, learning is impeded and ineffective programs are promulgated. However, when they are aligned, learning is facilitated and programs are vindicated.

FIGURE 1

A View of Learning When Alignment Is Lacking

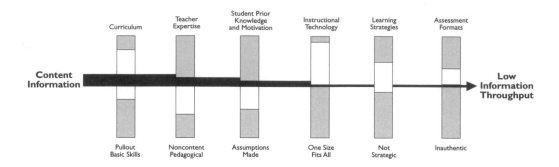

We consider the alignment of these components and the facilitation of learning in terms of signal strength (of information) and filtering. We display two figures to compare a traditional model of educational programming for students with diverse learning needs with a dynamic model based on curriculum-based collaboration. These two figures depict the components as filters that interactively and sequentially have an impact on the amount of learning that occurs (i.e., strength of the signal). When these components are not aligned, the strength of this (information) signal is reduced. In contrast, when the components are aligned, learning is enhanced, as illustrated by the strength of the information signal noted in the outcome.

In the situation depicted in Figure 1, the filters are not aligned. Information transmitted through the curriculum represents part of the broader domain of content knowledge, but this information is dissipated when it is filtered through a tutorial or special education program, and often is less robust when delivered by a teacher without expertise in the content area. Furthermore, students who do not have adequate prior knowledge, whether it is a basic skill, strategic knowledge, or content-related knowledge, may be unable to make efficient use of the information they do receive. Similarly, student motivation may further diffuse the message if preexisting attitudes and behaviors are not addressed. Next, instruction focused on the basic skills of reading or writing to a greater extent than key information in the content area exacerbates lack of alignment across the filters. Even more degradation of learning occurs when instruction fails to provide students with strategic responses, in which they learn metacognitive and strategy-based skills. Finally, assessment procedures focusing on a very narrow dimension of content area knowledge, such as specific facts, may result in a very distorted view of the learning that has occurred. In the end, much of the learning process has been lost through the misalignment of these filters.

Contrast the scenario above with the following one in which the school psychologist or special education teacher collaborates with the content area teacher to provide optimal learning opportunities for all students. In this situation (Figure 2), the content area teacher delivers information that is less affected by a poorly articulated curriculum

FIGURE 2

A View of Learning When Alignment Is Present

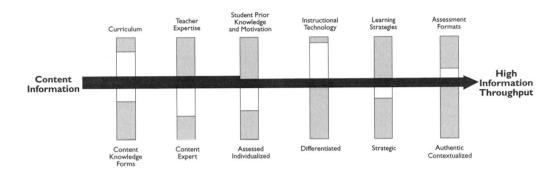

or lack of teacher expertise, often inherent in tutorial models or pullout programs. Student perceptions, in the form of background knowledge and motivation, are effectively utilized and incorporated into instructional planning and delivery. Furthermore, because the school psychologist or special education teacher is consulting with the classroom teacher on pedagogical issues, instruction in the general education classroom becomes more universal in design and results in greater student learning. Finally, students are taught strategies for accessing content-based information, while assessment formats encourage students to manipulate information and demonstrate their knowledge and skills through one of many higher-order processes such as prediction, explanation, or evaluation. Although some filters may continue to exist to diffuse the message (for example, students' lack of prior knowledge) the path from content domain to learning outcomes is much more direct than in the previous scenario. The result is that the signal strength of information coming through the teaching-learning cycle is very strong.

The important role these filters play in curriculum-based collaboration is detailed in the remainder of this chapter. In each of the next six sections, we first describe critical and empirical issues from the professional literature and then proceed to explain how each filter fits into the CBC model.

Curriculum

We view the curriculum broadly to include not only a course of study with consequent activities but also as educative experiences within a field of inquiry (Carter, 1992). The content area information presented within any field of inquiry can be classified into different knowledge forms: facts, concepts, principles, and procedures. Each classification denotes a particular kind of knowledge with facts being the lowest level of knowledge and principles and procedures arguably the most complicated. At the heart of any classification of knowledge forms, however, are concepts that help bridge the factual content of a discipline to the use of principles and procedures within problem-solving situations. Klausmeier (1990) describes concepts as having attributes and examples/nonexamples. "The defining attributes of a concept are those invariant intrinsic, functional, and/or relational attributes that together differentiate the examples of any given concept from examples of all other concepts" (p. 96).

CBC begins with an analysis of the types of knowledge forms that are most present in the curriculum materials with specific attention to critical concepts. If materials are not organized around critical concepts, they should be reconceptualized so that students are able to discern patterns in the information presented, while connecting it with previously learned concepts and principles. Research on learning has demonstrated that students do not retain information presented in isolation; by focusing on the interrelationship, or "sameness" (Carnine, 1991), of concepts and principles, they are better able to integrate and generalize information.

The content area teacher identifies and prioritizes the most critical conceptual information to be learned by students. One tool for organizing curriculum around critical concepts is a Content Planning Form, originally developed by Tindal, Nolet, and Blake (1992), and modified in Figure 3. Using this form, teachers clearly identify the key concepts to be taught and learned and create a document that can be used over time and across various situations. The Content Planning Form is effective in its focus on only the critical concepts to be learned by students, and efficient in its brevity, ease of completion, and applicability across various settings. Once the content area teacher has articulated the information students are expected to acquire during a unit of study, the collaborative team meets to discuss curriculum goals, generate instructional plans, and develop assessment techniques focused on students' application of knowledge and skills.

Teacher Expertise

Increasingly, professionalism in education has followed the same path as in other occupations, with specializations being carved into both training and practice. Teacher knowledge and expertise can be viewed from several vantages: planning and decision making, classroom knowledge, and command of content information (Carter, 1990). In secondary settings, it is the last type of expertise that is so crucial, particularly in representing the complexities of subject matter information. "Representation involves thinking through the key ideas in the text or lesson and identifying the alternative ways of representing them to students. What analogies, metaphors, examples, demonstrations, simulations, and the like can help to build a bridge between the teacher's comprehension and that desired for the students?" (Shulman, 1987, p. 16).

The general education teacher at the middle or high school brings command of content knowledge to the collaborative activities. He or she is viewed as the content area expert and understands the curriculum goals as well as the progression of learning that needs to occur for students to master curriculum content. The collaborative team relies on the content area teacher's subject matter knowledge to focus discussions on how to organize and present key concepts and principles to students.

The specific role of the school psychologist or special education teacher, in contrast, may vary as a function of school contexts and variables, but primarily focuses on

FIGURE 3

Content Planning Form

Date: _____ Class: _____

Teacher(s): _____

Textbook: _____ Unit #: _____

Other Curriculum Materials: _____

Approximate Schedule of Content To Be Delivered

Week	Dates		Textbook Chapters	Assignments To Be Completed	Due Dates	Test Dates
1	From:	To:				
2	From:	To:				

Key Concepts

Concept	Attributes		Examples/Nonexamples	
1		Page		Page
2				
3				

Note
Adapted from Tindal et al. (1992, p. 31) with permission.

pedagogical issues. In CBC, the school psychologist or special education teacher brings an understanding of the principles of instructional design and delivery to the collaborative meetings. He or she also is versed on how to accommodate students with varying skill levels during instruction and how to design assessments that truly capture students' knowledge and skills. With the emphasis we place on formative evaluation, a need exists to render and interpret data so that the content curriculum expert can make informed instructional decisions.

Capitalizing on the expertise of different educational professionals is an efficient and effective use of time. It is not realistic to assume that educational professionals have expert knowledge in every area of curriculum and instruction. We do not agree that learning specialists at the secondary level should have an in-depth knowledge of the subject matter as well as pedagogical expertise (Jorgensen, 1998). Instead, in our model of collaboration, the roles of each collaborative partner are clarified during curriculum planning and responsibilities are divided between instructional specialists (school psychologists and special education teachers) and content area teachers (see Figure 4). In the end, each member contributes his or her own expert knowledge and distinct set of skills to the process, resulting in powerful collaborative partnerships.

Student Prior Knowledge and Motivation

As important as teacher expertise is, however, teaching cannot begin until students' prior knowledge and levels of motivation are evaluated and incorporated into a design of instruction. An integral filter in the implementation of CBC is consideration of these necessary access skills as they influence the breadth and depth of curriculum coverage as well as the model of instructional delivery. In our model, the content area teacher identifies the type and level of skills students need to access the general curriculum, and collaborates with the school psychologist or special education teacher to identify students who may not have these skills. Identified students then complete assessments, designed by the school psychologist or special education teacher, to provide information about their levels of prior knowledge, as well as their motivation for learning.

Prior knowledge. After critical concepts have been delineated and before instruction begins, the collaborative team must take into account students' prior knowledge—"a logical extension of the view that new knowledge must be considered from existing knowledge is that teachers need to pay attention to the incomplete understandings, the false beliefs, and the naïve renditions of concepts that learners bring with them to a given subject" (Bransford et al., 2000, p. 10).

Teachers' awareness of students' prior knowledge in the form of basic academic skills is essential if they want to design instruction and activities that are accessible by all. In the context of today's classroom, progress in the general education curriculum is often measured by student gains in conceptual understanding, problem solving, and ability to apply knowledge and skills in novel situations. Theory and practice have contributed to an expansion of curriculum goals to include more than rote memorization of factual information and fluency in basic skills to include the importance of conceptual knowledge and skill application. We believe that all students deserve opportunities

FIGURE 4

Responsibilities of Education Professionals

Content Area Teacher	Learning Specialist
Identify curriculum materials.	Adapt curriculum materials in advance of instruction.
Complete Content Planning Form by identifying critical concepts to be taught and learned.	Assist in designing instruction using research-based principles.
Plan lessons according to a universal design for learning, proactively considering student needs and skills.	Encourage content area teachers to consider various models of instructional delivery.
Use computer technology to present information, provide practice opportunities, and assess learning.	Brainstorm uses of multimedia for instruction and assessment that promote learning for all students.
Provide large group instruction in content area classroom.	Provide small group or individualized instruction in or out of the classroom.
Create an inclusive learning environment by enlisting support of assistants, parents, and cross-age tutors.	Supervise assistants in the content area classroom.
Assess students' knowledge and skills through use of authentic performance tasks.	Assist students in developing appropriate exhibitions, portfolios, and/or demonstrations.
Employ accommodations when necessary to allow students opportunity to demonstrate what they know.	Facilitate use of specialists from outside agencies.
Attend collaborative team meetings.	Attend collaborative team meetings.

to engage in higher-order thinking, and do not believe that "The best procedure to follow is to remediate basic skills first and then work on content area performance" (Idol, 1992, p. 181). We believe that even if a student has not mastered basic skills, he or she should be given opportunities to engage in higher-level thinking and problem-solving tasks that are now central to most state and local curricula.

Students still should continue to work toward achieving fluency in basic skill areas, but they also should be offered an opportunity to engage in higher-order conceptual tasks. Students may learn how to utilize technology and manipulate information in ways that compensate for their lack of fluency in basic academic skills. For example, word processing programs provide students with immediate feedback related to basic conventions of writing, interactive encyclopedias make it possible for students to research a topic without needing exact spelling, and graphics or drawing software provides students with alternate means of communicating knowledge. In the end, the collaborative team needs to assess and discuss student levels of basic skills, as possible obstacles to accessing the general curriculum as well as important instructional goals. If students cannot access the material because of weak basic skills, the collaborative team needs to preplan instructional and assessment techniques (e.g., use of technology, or allowing assessments to be completed orally) that will provide students with full access to the general curriculum.

In curriculum-based collaboration, all students are seen as moving toward the same outcome—acquiring knowledge and skills reflected in the general curriculum and displaying their proficiencies on authentic problem-solving activities. Some students will reach this outcome fairly effortlessly, while others will progress at a more laborious pace, requiring outside resources and comprehensive collaborative efforts. Yet our goals for students are similar. We want students to apply information that they have learned in real-life situations; we want them to solve complex problems and write meaningful compositions. We want them to transfer what they have learned to novel but similar situations in the future (Norris, 1992).

Realistically, students progress toward these comprehensive goals at a different pace. Even those with fully individualized goals continually make progress toward attaining higher-level learning goals in the general curriculum. For example, if the end goal is that a student will learn to read a variety of texts with understanding, and a high-school student, receiving instruction in the resource room, is learning how to decode, he or she is still making progress in the general education curriculum. This student's end goal is not to learn how to decode, yet decoding is an access skill needed to read a variety of texts with understanding.

In the same way that basic skills are important, strategic, or procedural knowledge, is critical for student retention and generalization of newly acquired content knowledge. Content knowledge is more easily retained when students are able to pair new information with information already learned. "Schemata represent knowledge that we experience—interrelationships between objects, situations, events, and sequences of events that normally occur ... Schema theory assumes that the memory structures for recurrent situations have a major function in the construction of and interpretation of a new situation" (Gagne & Glaser, 1987, p. 70). In the same way, content knowledge is more easily generalized when students have strategies for applying and using newly acquired content area information in novel settings. Succinctly stated, students must be able to access, organize, and display their understanding of content area information.

An understanding of students' declarative knowledge also is an essential ingredient of instructional planning. In Figure 5, we illustrate one method for gaining insight into students' level of prior knowledge related to the content area of interest. First conceptualized as a semantic relatedness measure (Valencia, Stallman, Commeyras, Pearson, & Hartman, 1991) and later reconceptualized as a bull's-eye chart (Sugai & Tindal, 1993), this measure provides basic information about students' prior vocabulary knowledge. Students complete the chart by writing down key vocabulary words that relate to one of the primary concepts to be learned. (Teachers supply the vocabulary words.) Once students have recorded one vocabulary word for each numbered blank they are asked to circle the corresponding number for each word within the bull's-eye chart. Students circle the number within the ring that best illustrates the relationship of the vocabulary word to the critical concept. Such a chart can provide teachers with information related to students' understanding of critical content area vocabulary, providing a maximum

FIGURE 5

Bull's-Eye Chart for Assessing Student Vocabulary

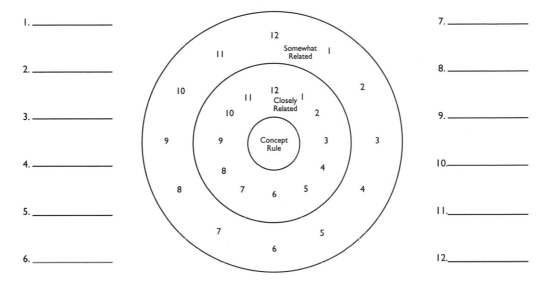

Note

Adapted from Valencia et al. (1991, p. 216) with permission.

amount of information in a minimum amount of time. Other tools for assessing students' declarative knowledge include brainstorming activities undertaken with whole groups of students, a 3-minute write completed individually, or graphic orga-nizers completed individually. All of these activities are designed to elicit what students know about a particular topic in a fairly limited amount of time.

Such assessments need to be developed and administered if the team is concerned about low levels of prior knowledge demonstrated by some students. Then, the possible impact on learning of content area information can be hypothesized and curriculum goals planned accordingly, including the breadth and depth of content to be taught, as well as methods of instructional delivery to be used. It is important to note, however, that measuring prior knowledge is only a first step. If a student does not have adequate prior knowledge, the collaborative team needs to provide instructional support until adequate knowledge is attained.

Numerous supports for students who lack prior knowledge of content area information have been described in the educational literature. One type of teacher support is scaffolding, first described by Wood, Bruner, and Ross (as cited in Grigorenko, 1998). Scaffolding provides students with enough cues to complete assignments while gradually withdrawing support as students' prior knowledge increases. Teachers may also use graphic organizers (Jones, Pierce, & Hunter, 1998–1999) to provide students with critical content area information that they might not otherwise possess. Models of instructional delivery also can be employed to provide support for students who lack prior knowledge (e.g., using differentiated questioning strategies or verbal prompts). Effective use of peers also can be incorporated into supported classroom instruction, such as peer tutoring (Greenwood & Delquadri, 1995) or cooperative learning (Johnson & Johnson, 1975), both of which rely on grade-level peers to supply students with needed content area knowledge. Finally, the use of technological supports can be very effective. For example, students might work on interactive computer programs designed to correct student errors and provide them with the accurate information needed to complete the task. Or students may use a graphics program to assist them in organizing the prior knowledge that they do possess.

Motivation for learning. The perception that motivation exists independent of context may be misconstrued. Students are not born with differing amounts of motivation; instead motivation for learning is largely influenced by teacher expectations (Brophy, 1984) and peer relationships (Johnson, 1980). Motivation for learning may best be described as a combination of intrinsic student factors, teacher variables (expectations and efficacy), and the social structure of the classroom (Good & Tom, 1984). Therefore, if the collaborative team is concerned about a student's level of motivation, team members should collect information through direct observation procedures in various content area classes.

Functional analyses of students' academic behavior can be conducted in order to pinpoint specific antecedents and reinforcements that help maintain academic or nonacademic behaviors. Again assuming that these steps are proactive as opposed to reactive, observations are even more objective in that the observer does not have a "problem" in mind. Instead student behaviors, teacher behaviors, and the behaviors of peers in the classroom are observed and recorded. Patterns of human behavior, as well as environmental antecedents, may become obvious during the observation and may be seen as contributing to a student's level of motivation. The collaborative team then uses this to identify how to best engage students in learning.

Direct observations also can be conducted on students' level of academic learning time or degree of academic engagement (Ysseldyke, Thurlow, Mecklenburg, Graden, & Algozzine, 1984). These observation systems do not systematically record antecedents and other environmental barriers but instead focus primarily on the frequency or duration of time that students remain engaged in the academic instruction or activity. Information derived from direct observations also can be used during the content planning sessions, especially to generate hypotheses related to what may be the most effective models of instructional delivery.

Student motivation can be measured through use of other techniques such as student interviews or attitudinal surveys. However, these forms of data collection may result in less reliable information than direct observations of student behavior, and the collaborative team would benefit from conducting direct observations as well.

Instructional Technology

Although CBC places the curriculum at the center, we also realize the importance of research-based instructional practices designed and delivered to accommodate the needs of a wide range of learners. Instructional technology emphasizes the importance of instructional design and delivery in its aim to improve student learning. Instructional technology may or may not include the use of multimedia, although technology use probably increases the accessibility of information for all students (Gagne, 1987). Collaborative efforts at the secondary level may result in increased student learning when a technology of instruction is employed that incorporates the following three elements: (a) principles of instructional design, (b) methods of instructional delivery, and (c) use of multimedia.

We distinguish between the design of instruction and its delivery. "Instructional design models describe the process for designing and developing instruction. As such they contain no predetermined delivery model" (Gustafson & Tillman, 1991, p. 9). Principles of instructional design attempt to align current knowledge about human learning with instructional planning for student success. For example, many instructional designers rely on Gagne's principles, or the "nine events of instruction," when planning instructional units or lessons (Gagne, 1985). These nine events are as follows: (a) gain attention, (b) share objectives, (c) stimulate recall of prerequisite knowledge, (d) present instruction, (e) provide practice opportunities, (f) elicit performance, (g) provide feedback, (h) assess performance, and (i) enhance retention and generalization. In Figure 6, on page 840, we show Gagne's nine instructional design principles to organize a list of research-based instructional design practices (Kame'enui & Simmons, 1999; Nolet & McLaughlin, 2000). In curriculum-based collaboration, educational professionals rely on these principles to plan instruction.

During collaborative planning, the team decides upon models of instructional delivery and menus of student response formats. Variables such as the type of content area information, teacher knowledge and style, student characteristics, and ecological conditions are taken into account. As noted earlier, the concept of a universal design for learning is used to provide the team with a foundational framework for collaborative planning.

In Figure 7, on page 841, we illustrate various instructional delivery models using a modified version of Gustafson & Tillman's Planning Matrix (1991, p. 185). As is obvious in this figure, some models are more suited for small group or individualized instruction, while other models are designed for large group instruction. Although limited teacher support is involved in many large group formats (the delivery model often employed in content area classrooms), there still may be times when the teacher has to accommodate instructional delivery to meet the needs of a small, diverse group of learners. In theory, these accommodations should not be necessary because collaborative teams have relied on a universal design for learning to plan curriculum and instruction. In practice, as teachers are acquiring skills in universal design, there still may exist a need to make accommodations for certain individuals.

FIGURE 6

Gagne's Nine Events of Instruction and Research-Based Instructional Practices

1. <u>Gain attention</u> before beginning instruction.
   use signals and various cues
   pace presentation of information

2. <u>Share objectives</u> with students.
   share concepts to be learned with students
   illustrate attributes within concepts and connections across concepts

3. <u>Stimulate recall of prerequisite knowledge</u>/learning.
   use scaffolding to supplement low levels of prior knowledge
   ask students to paraphrase information learned
   use graphic organizers to show connection between old and new information

4. <u>Present instruction.</u>
   use clear and concise directions
   focus on one task at a time
   present information in more than one format
   use graphic displays and advance organizers
   incorporate multimedia into presentations
   use a variety of examples and sequence their complexity

5. <u>Provide practice opportunities</u> and guidance.
   teach using rich and varied models
   share examples and nonexamples of concepts
   provide varied and cumulative practice
   use computer programs to encourage individualized practice opportunities

6. <u>Elicit performance.</u>
   use a variety of questioning strategies to aid students' recognition of information.
   provide frequent response opportunities
   encourage students to use technology (audiotapes; electronic devices; Web-based projects)
   allow adequate think time

7. <u>Provide feedback</u> about student performance.
   regularly check for understanding
   correct misinformation immediately
   reinforce students for improving individual performances even if outcome has not been met

8. <u>Assess performance.</u>
   use formative assessments to monitor students' understanding and adjust instruction accordingly
   design open-ended performance tasks to assess various levels of understanding

9. <u>Enhance retention and generalization</u> of newly acquired knowledge/skills.
   teach students metacognitive strategies for retention and recall of information
   require students to apply content area knowledge and skills in authentic settings

Even after the collaborative team has proactively designed a unit of study through use of curriculum planning and application of sound instructional design principles, including the use of technology when possible, some students still may require accommodations to acquire information or demonstrate what they know. Not providing these accommodations is unfair to students who may know information but are unable to access or demonstrate it. Therefore, the collaborative team needs to be aware of various

FIGURE 7

Levels of Teacher Support

	Significant	Some	Little
Individual	Individual Instruction 1:1 Tutorials	Independent Research Problem-Solving Simulations Web-Based Instruction	Textbook Reading Computer-Assisted Instruction
Group	Whole-Group Lecture Discovery Learning	Student Debates Role Playing Interactive Slide Discussions Brainstorming	Student Presentations Peer Tutoring Cooperative Learning Jigsaw Activities

Note

Adapted from Gustafson and Tillman (1991) with permission.

instructional accommodations. A menu of accommodations is included in Figure 8, on page 842. This list is not comprehensive, and for a more thorough discussion of accommodations the reader is directed to the Web site for the National Center on Educational Outcomes (*www.coled.umn.edu/NCEO/*).

The final element of an instructional technology that supports curriculum-based collaboration is the use of multimedia. "Inventions in communication hardware and associated use procedures (often collectively termed media), while they may be primarily designed for other applications, often make possible new opportunities for means of delivering instruction. Instructional technology seeks to investigate, develop, evaluate, and promote the application of such techniques" (Gagne, 1987, p. 5). Possible uses of multimedia to support instruction are growing exponentially and are partially responsible for the new concept of universal design for learning. Teaching behaviors that once were not possible because of time and task constraints are now made possible through the use of computer technology. Delivery of instruction is enhanced through use of Web-based learning, audio and visual supports, computer simulation programs, and hypertext (textbook information presented in an interactive, electronic format).

In summary, student learning is increased when collaborative teams rely on the principles of instructional design to plan instruction that incorporates situational use of multimedia. This universal design for learning allows all students an opportunity to

FIGURE 8

Menu of Accommodations

Acquiring Information	Demonstrating Knowledge and Skills
Large print texts	Extended time for completion of assignments or tests
Cooperative research projects	Use of technology (e.g. word processors, spell checkers)
Multimedia access to information (e.g., audio books; video clips)	Use of a scribe
Framed outlines	Oral vs. written responses
Peer note-takers	Graphics or illustrations instead of words
Oral as well as written directions	Changing format of assessment
Pairing with a classmate to complete assignments	Study carrel or quiet space to complete tests

progress in the general education curriculum. As stated by Good and Brophy (cited in Janney & Snell, 2000), "It seems most appropriate to use principles of instructional design and pedagogy to develop high quality instructional materials and methods intended to be effective for all students rather than to set out from the beginning to develop different materials and methods for various students" (p. 10).

Learning Strategies

We view the inclusion of learning strategies in the design and delivery of instruction as critical. Learning strategies make it possible for students to access, organize, and display their understanding of recently acquired knowledge and skills. "An individual's approach to a task is called a strategy when it includes how a person thinks and acts when planning, executing, and evaluating performance on a task and its outcomes" (Lenz, Ellis, & Scanlon, 1996, p. 5). Teachers need to provide students with explicit instruction on strategy use, then they need to model it, and finally they must create conditions that encourage it. Three conditions may increase the likelihood that students will use learning strategies. First, if the strategy addresses a key problem that students encounter in authentic settings, its usefulness is obvious and students are motivated to learn and apply it. Second, when the strategy relates to frequently required demands, students will have more opportunities to apply it and will see the success in choosing to use it. Third, if the strategy is not subject specific, students will generalize its use to multiple content area classes (Lenz et al., p. 5).

Teachers can increase the likelihood of students' generalizing learning strategies by creating authentic learning situations in secondary classrooms that encourage students to apply and adapt content area information. Mastropieri and Scruggs (1987) emphasize the importance of knowing when and how to apply strategies to ensure generalization: (a) knowing when a particular strategy is needed (conditional knowledge), (b) recalling how to apply a specific strategy (declarative knowledge), and (c) using the strategy (procedural knowledge).

Types of learning strategies. A number of different strategies have been developed to help students acquire, process, and demonstrate knowledge and information. We already have discussed many of these strategies within previous components of our conceptual model (e.g., advance organizers, bull's-eye charts, and cooperative learning). However, one important body of research related to the importance of learning strategies in secondary content classes is that of reading comprehension. Many strategies to facilitate reading comprehension have been validated through multiple lines of research, much of it at the secondary level, including (a) paraphrasing (Schumaker, Denton, & Deshler, 1984), (b) keyword mnemonics (Mastropieri, Scruggs, Levin, Gaffney, & McLoone, 1985), (c) semantic maps (e.g., Bos & Anders, 1990), (d) think sheets (Englert, Raphael, Anderson, Anthony, & Stevens, 1991), (e) advance organizers (Ausubel & Robinson, 1969), and (f) concept diagrams (e.g., Bulgren & Scanlon, 1997–1998). In the following sections we share the practical application of three research-based reading comprehension strategies.

Summarization and main idea strategies. Retelling the main idea of passages read or summarizing content area information is a powerful learning strategy for students in middle and high school. Teaching students to summarize information presented in content area textbooks encourages them to read for meaning and retell what they have learned in their own words. Furthermore, students with learning disabilities who are taught summarization strategies have been shown to outperform their peers, who have not been taught the strategies, on tests of reading comprehension (Gajria & Salvia, 1992; Malone & Mastropieri, 1992). Content area teachers benefit by explicitly teaching students how to use summarization strategies. Teachers can ask students to orally retell or complete a written retelling of what was read. Students who have problems comprehending large chunks of textual information can be taught to pause and summarize small sections of text and gradually increase the amount of text as their level of comprehension increases.

Text-structure-based strategies. Some researchers report that strategies based on the structure of expository texts are even more powerful than summarization strategies (Bakken, Mastropieri, & Scruggs, 1997). In text-structure-based strategies, students learn to identify and apply specific reading strategies to three different types of passages (main idea, list, and order). Main idea passages are those that focus on one central idea. List passages are those that include a compilation of factual information concerning one central topic, while order passages generally describe a sequence of events. Students use the keywords and structure contained in the first paragraph of a passage to identify the type of text and then apply specific strategies to aid in comprehension. Students also have been shown to transfer these strategies from textual information in one content area (science) to a different content area (social studies) without any additional training. Students' ability to generalize the steps of this strategy makes it an extremely powerful skill to teach at the secondary level.

Mnemonic illustrations. The third and final learning strategy with a strong research base is the use of mnemonic illustrations that are "thought to promote recall by enhancing the concreteness and meaningfulness of the information to be remembered and connecting it to the learner's prior knowledge" (Mastropieri & Scruggs, 1997, p. 202). Owing to the effectiveness of mnemonic strategies, Scruggs and Mastropieri (1993) state, "we have come to think of mnemonic instruction as (although not a panacea) an essential component of effective content area instruction for students with learning disabilities" (pp. 393–394).

Mnemonics are strategies for enhancing students' memory. Keyword mnemonics can be developed that trigger a student's recall of newly learned vocabulary. Furthermore, teaching students to pair keywords with imagery results in a powerful learning strategy for remembering novel information. An example of a mnemonic illustration strategy is provided by Mastropieri and Scruggs (1997) when describing one of their earlier research studies: When studying expository passages about North American minerals "a mineral name was recoded to a keyword (e.g., wolframite = wolf) and associated with other descriptions found in the text (e.g., soft minerals included a baby in the picture and hard minerals included an old man as symbolic codes)" (p. 202).

Mnemonic illustration strategies are designed to encourage recall and comprehension of content area information, including recall of science and social studies textbook information. It is important for teachers, however, to explicitly model and teach mnemonic strategies to students instead of allowing them to develop their own mnemonics, as their pace through content area information may be slower than when strategies are explicitly taught by teachers (Scruggs & Mastropieri, 1992). In the end, it may be more important for students with learning challenges in content area classrooms to be taught a strategy directly so that they do not lose important instructional time developing their own.

Assessment Formats

The sixth and final filter in curriculum-based collaboration is student assessment. In the CBC model the focus of the assessment is to provide students with multiple opportunities to apply what they have learned in novel situations. Assessment activities are aligned with curriculum and instruction and therefore result in more valid information concerning the quality of student learning.

Before assessing students' progress in the general education curriculum, the collaborative team should clarify its definition of "progress." Our conceptualization of learning or progress centers around an ability to apply information and skills learned in authentic situations. We use a model first described by Roid and Haladyna (1982) and later adapted by Nolet, Tindal, and Blake (1993) to describe different ways of demonstrating "progress" or knowledge of content area information. These different ways of knowing (or intellectual operations) are outlined in Figure 9 and are cross-referenced with three basic knowledge forms. As is obvious in Figure 9, when information is

FIGURE 9

Knowledge Forms Cross-Referenced to Intellectual Operations

		Knowledge Forms		
		Facts	Concepts	Principles
	Reiteration	Yes	Yes	Yes
	Summarization	Yes	Yes	Yes
Intellectual Operations	Illustration	No	Yes	Yes
	Prediction	No	Yes	Yes
	Evaluation	No	(Yes)	Yes
	Application	No	(Yes)	Yes

Note

Adapted from Nolet et al. (1993, p. 16). Reprinted with permission.

taught using concepts, assessment of students' progress focuses on synthesis, application, or evaluation of conceptual information. Assessing conceptual knowledge is most easily, and we argue, most validly conducted through the use of authentic problem-solving performance tasks.

Students' progress in the general education curriculum should be assessed often using a variety of formats. Formative assessments such as brief curriculum-based measures of student progress or perception probes allow teachers to continually measure effects of their instruction. Summative assessments, on the other hand, provide end-of-the-unit information related to the level of understanding attained by students. Summative assessments exist in the form of extended performance tasks that require students to apply what they have learned to "real-life" scenarios. In the following section we provide examples of formative and summative assessments.

Formative assessments. The first, and possibly most important, measure for assessing students' progress is the use of brief formative measures. Because of their brevity, these measures can be administered frequently and student progress can be closely monitored. Well-designed formative measures are sensitive to slight increases in student learning and provide collaborative teams with quantitative information that can be compared over time. A visual display of this quantitative data is useful in illustrating students' growth in the general curriculum over time. One approach to formative assessment is Curriculum-Based Measurement (CBM) in content area instruction (Tindal & Nolet, 1995). Skills related to problem solving and higher-level thinking can be assessed using curriculum-based measures such as content area retells (student is awarded points for quantity of concepts shared about a particular subject) and graphic organizers (students use graphic organizers to map out primary concepts and their relationships). Finally, CBM's efficiency and use of graphs to chart progress are attributes that make it appealing to teachers.

A second type of formative assessment is the use of perception probes (Tindal et al., 1992). An example of a perception probe is provided in Figure 10. Students complete perception probes in 15 minutes or less at the conclusion of a lesson or miniunit. These assessments provide teachers with information related to the concepts that students believe to be the most important. Oftentimes, student perceptions of critical information and teachers' perceptions of critical information do not align. Perception probes provide teachers with a glimpse into students' understanding of content area information and assist them in making decisions related to future instruction.

Summative assessments. Extended performance tasks are most often used as summative assessments. Content area performance tasks are drawn from curriculum materials and created by the collaborative team. Assessments are concept based and linked to instruction in that key information presented during instruction is later manipulated by students using one of many response formats. Students are given a range of opportunities in which to illustrate their level of understanding, and all students, regardless of skill level, are asked to complete open-ended performance tasks. Finally, well-designed performance tasks require students to generalize what they have learned during content area instruction by applying their knowledge and skills to authentic scenarios.

The increasing sophistication of computer-based technology makes it possible for students to engage in authentic performance tasks designed to meet a full range of knowledge and skills. For example, computer simulation programs such as The Oregon Trail (2001) or SimCity 3000 (2001) require students to manipulate key information to arrive, eventually, at a solution to a complex problem. But, as is true in real life, a single correct solution does not exist. Instead, students make decisions, receive feedback, and make new decisions until one of many possible solutions is reached (Provenzo, Brett, & McCloskey, 1999). Simulation programs often are used as instructional supports, but with appropriate dependent measures, they can be used as content area performance tasks as well, to evaluate students' problem-solving skills.

There are two important considerations to keep in mind when involving students with diverse knowledge and skills in content area performance tasks. First, students need to be tested using the same format in which they were taught (i.e., if a student's instruction was accommodated to address his or her diverse needs, the assessment should be accommodated in the same way). Second, the impact of access skills on student performance needs to be considered. Students may be unable to access the test for reasons discussed earlier (e.g., poor basic skills, lack of content knowledge, or weak motivation). If this is the case, teachers need to plan assessments to ensure that all stu-

FIGURE 10

Perception Probe

Pretend you are telling a friend what you learned in class today. You would want to tell your friend about the most important words and ideas discussed. You also would want to tell your friend why these words and ideas are important to remember

---

IMPORTANT WORDS

List the <u>words</u> you think are most important to help your friend understand the material discussed in class today. You may list new words you learned for the first time in this chapter or unit or you may list words we have talked about in previous classes. List as many <u>important</u> words as you can remember.

1. _____   5. _____   9. _____

2. _____   6. _____   10. _____

3. _____   7. _____   11. _____

4. _____   8. _____   12. _____

IMPORTANT IDEAS

Tell three important ideas that were discussed today. You may write a phrase or a complete sentence, but be sure to provide your friend with enough information for him or her to know what you mean.

1. _____

   _____

2. _____

   _____

3. _____

   _____

PUTTING IT ALL TOGETHER

Tell how the words and ideas you listed above are related to one another. You may write a short paragraph or you may draw a sketch that shows how these ideas and words are connected. Use as many words and ideas from your lists as you like. If you need more room, use the back of this page.

Note

Adapted from Tindal et al. (1992, p. 77). Reprinted with permission.

dents are guaranteed an opportunity to demonstrate what they know or can do. For example, if a small group of students do not have adequate basic skills in writing, teachers should allow them to demonstrate their knowledge about specific content area information in a mode other than writing. In this scenario, teachers would assess students' progress in content area information, not their skills in written expression.

CONCLUSION

Curriculum-based collaboration is a proactive and multidimensional system for ensuring the success of students with disabilities in content area classrooms. It is premised on the assumption that educational support needs to be planned before problems appear. Although behavioral in nature, it is different from traditional models in that student behavior is not viewed as the impetus for problem solving. Rather, CBC begins with the curriculum and remains focused on the teaching-learning cycle. It also is systemic in that all professionals are brought together with a focus on teaching and learning for ALL students. Finally, principles of universal design are used as a framework for integrating all of the components of the model. These principles help operationalize our attention to being collaborative, proactive, and formative.

We presented the model using a signal strength metaphor in which six specific filters were viewed as potential barriers in teaching and learning content information. We began with the *curriculum* as an important influence on learning. For CBC to be effective in supporting students, content information needs to be effectively framed and accessible. This curriculum, however, also needs to be enacted by content experts so that information is not just transmitted but also transformed. We asserted that *teacher expertise* needs to be considered—both content experts who knit together the meaning of the content, and learning specialists (special education teachers and school psychologists) who help with pedagogical planning. Clearly, however, students do not arrive in classrooms tabula rasa. Rather, they come with *prior knowledge and motivation,* preconceptions, misconceptions, and incomplete conceptions, which provided yet another filter to be considered in our model. As teachers interact with students, we believe they gain better insights about what and how students think about the content. Thus, teachers can rely on *instructional technology,* and more effectively incorporate *learning strategies* into their instruction to improve learning outcomes for all students. We rarely, however, want students simply to become more knowledgeable about a fixed content. Rather, we want them to learn how information is organized in general and how it can be accessed—as well as how they can solve more general-case problems beyond those presented in schools. Therefore, to ascertain student improvement, we then turned to *assessments* as the final filter in our model. Teachers need to both formatively and summatively evaluate students' performance and progress. This last filter of assessment then interacts with all of the other filters in a reciprocal manner. Through CBC and its accompanying filters, the learning needs of all students are made explicit, thus improving their chances for success in the general education curriculum."

REFERENCES

Ausubel, D. P., & Robinson, F. G. (1969). *School learning: An introduction to educational psychology.* New York: Holt, Rinehart & Winston.

Bakken, J. P., Mastropieri, M. A., & Scruggs, T. E. (1997). Reading comprehension of expository science material and students with learning disabilities: A comparison of strategies. *Journal of Special Education, 31*(3), 300-324.

Bergan, J. R. (1977). *Behavioral consultation.* Columbus, OH: Merrill.

Bergan, J. R., & Kratochwill, T. R. (1990). *Behavioral consultation and therapy.* New York: Plenum.

Bos, C. S., & Anders, P. L. (1990). Effects of interactive vocabulary instruction on the vocabulary learning and reading comprehension of junior high learning disabled students. *Learning Disability Quarterly, 13,* 31-42.

Bransford, J. D., Brown, A. L., & Cocking, R. R. (2000). *How people learn: Brain, mind, experience and school.* Washington, DC: National Academy Press.

Brophy, J. (1984). Teachers' expectations, motives, and goals for working with problem students. In C. Ames & R. Ames (Eds.), *Research on motivation in education: Vol. 2* (pp. 175-212). Orlando, FL: Academic Press.

Bulgren, J., & Scanlon, D. (1997–1998). Instructional routines and learning strategies that promote understanding of content area concepts. *Journal of Adolescent and Adult Literacy, 41*(4), 292-302.

Caplan, G. (1970). *The theory and practice of mental health consultation.* New York: Basic Books.

Carnine, D. (1991). Curricular interventions for teaching higher order thinking to all students: Introduction to the special series. *Journal of Learning Disabilities, 24*(5), 261-269.

Carter, K. (1990). Teachers' knowledge and learning to teach. In W. R. Houston (Ed.), *Handbook of research on teacher education* (pp. 291-310). New York: Macmillan.

Carter, K. (1992). Conceptions of curriculum and curriculum specialists. In P. W. Jackson (Ed.), *Handbook of research on curriculum* (pp. 3-24). New York: Macmillan.

CAST. (2001). *Summary of universal design for learning concepts.* [Online]. Available Internet: *www.cast.org/udl/index.cfm?i=7.* Peabody, MA: Center for Applied Special Technology.

Costenbader, V., Swartz, J., & Petrix, L. (1992). Consultation in the schools: The relationship between preservice training, perception of consultative skills, and actual time spent in consultation. *School Psychology Review, 21,* 95-108.

Englert, C. S., Raphael, T. E., Anderson, L. M., Anthony, H. M., & Stevens, D. D. (1991). Making strategies and self-talk visible: Writing instruction in regular and special education classrooms. *American Educational Research Journal, 28*(2), 337-372.

Gagne, R. (1985). The conditions of learning (4th ed.). New York: Holt, Rinehart, & Winston.

Gagne, R. M. (1987). Introduction. In R. M. Gagne (Ed.), *Instructional technology: Foundations* (pp. 1-9). Hillsdale, NJ: Erlbaum.

Gagne, R. M., & Glaser, R. (1987). Foundations in learning research. In R. M. Gagne (Ed.). *Instructional technology: Foundations* (pp. 49-83). Hillsdale, NJ: Erlbaum.

Gajria, M., & Salvia, J. (1992). The effects of summarization instruction on text comprehension of students with learning disabilities. *Exceptional Children, 58,* 508-516.

Good, T. L., & Tom, D. Y. H. (1984). Self-regulation, efficacy, expectation, and social orientation: Teacher and classroom perspectives. In C. Ames & R. Ames (Eds.), *Research on motivation in education: Vol. 2* (pp. 307-325). Orlando, FL: Academic Press.

Greenwood, C. R., & Delquadri, J. (1995). Classwide peer tutoring and the prevention of school failure. *Preventing School Failure, 39*(4), 21-25.

Grigorenko, E. L. (1998). Mastering tools of the mind in school. In R. J. Sternberg, & W. M. Williams (Eds.), *Intelligence, instruction, and assessment: Theory into practice* (pp. 201-231). Mahwah, NJ: Erlbaum.

Gustafson, K. L., & Tillman, M. H. (1991). Introduction. In L. J. Briggs, K. L. Gustafson, & M. H. Tillman (Eds.), *Instructional design: Principles and applications* (pp. 3-16). Englewood Cliffs, NJ: Educational Technology Publications.

Idol, L. (1992). *Special educator's consultation handbook* (2nd ed.). Austin, TX: PRO-ED.

Idol, L., Nevin, A., & Paolucci-Whitcomb, P. (1994). *Collaborative consultation* (2nd ed.). Austin, TX: PRO-ED.

Janney, R., & Snell, M. E. (2000). *Modifying schoolwork.* Baltimore: Brookes.

Johnson, D. W. (1980). Group processes: Influences of student-student interactions on school outcomes. In J. McMillan (Ed.), *Social psychology of school learning* (pp. 123-157). New York: Academic Press.

Johnson, D. W., & Johnson, R. T. (1975). *Learning together and alone: Cooperation, competition, and individualization.* Englewood Cliffs, NJ: Prentice-Hall.

Jones, B. F., Pierce, J., & Hunter, B. (1998-1999). Teaching students to construct graphic representations. *Educational Leadership, 46*(4), 20-25.

Jorgensen, C. M. (1998). *Restructuring high schools for all students: Taking inclusion to the next level.* Baltimore: Brookes.

Kame'enui, E. J., & Simmons, D. C. (1990). *Designing instructional strategies: The prevention of academic learning problems.* Englewood Cliffs, NJ: Macmillan.

Kame'enui, E. J., & Simmons, D. C. (1999). *Toward successful inclusion of students with disabilities: The architecture of instruction.* Reston, VA: The Council for Exceptional Children.

Klausmeier, H. J. (1990). Conceptualizing. In B. F. Jones and L. Idol (Eds.), *Dimensions of thinking and cognitive instruction* (pp. 93-138). Hillsdale, NJ: Erlbaum.

Lenz, B. K., Ellis, E. S., & Scanlon, D. (1996). *Teaching learning strategies to adolescents and adults with learning disabilities.* Austin, TX: PRO-ED.

Maher, C. A., Illback, J. R., & Zins, J. E. (1984). *Organizational psychology in the schools: A handbook for professionals.* Springfield, IL: C. C. Thomas.

Malone, L. D., & Mastropieri, M. A. (1992). Reading comprehension instruction: Summarization and self-monitoring training for students with learning disabilities. *Exceptional Children, 58,* 270-279.

Martens, B. K. (1993). A behavioral approach to consultation. In J. E. Zins, T. R. Kratochwill, & S. N. Elliott (Eds.), *Handbook of consultation services for children* (pp. 65-86). San Francisco: Jossey-Bass.

Mastropieri, M. A., & Scruggs, T. E. (1987). *Effective instruction for special education.* Austin, TX: PRO-ED.

Mastropieri, M. A., & Scruggs, T. E. (1997). Best practices in promoting reading comprehension in students with learning disabilities: 1976 to 1996. *Remedial and Special Education, 18*(4), 297-314.

Mastropieri, M. A., Scruggs, T. E., Levin, J. R., Gaffney, J., & McLoone, B. (1985). Mnemonic vocabulary instruction for learning disabled students. *Learning Disability Quarterly, 8,* 299-309.

National Center on Educational Outcomes. Available Internet: *http://www.coled.umn.edu/NCEO/.* University of Minnesota, Minneapolis.

Nolet, V., & McLaughlin, M. J. (2000). *Accessing the general curriculum: Including students with disabilities in standards-based reform.* Thousand Oaks, CA: Corwin Press.

Nolet, V., & Tindal, G. (1994). Curriculum-based collaboration. *Focus on Exceptional Children, 27*(3), 1-12.

Nolet, V., Tindal, G., & Blake, G. (1993). *Focus on assessment and learning in content classes* (Training Module No. 4). Eugene: University of Oregon, Resource Consultant Training Program.

Norris, S. P. (1992). *The generalizability of critical thinking.* New York: Teachers College Press.

Oregon Trail (4th ed.) [Computer software]. (2001). Fremont, CA: Learning Company. Available Internet: *http://www.learningco.com/company/.*

Provenzo, E. F., Jr., Brett, A., & McCloskey, G. N. (1999). *Computers, curriculum, and cultural change: An introduction for teachers.* Mahwah, NJ: Erlbaum.

Roid, G. H., & Haladyna, T. M. (1982). *A technology of test item writing.* New York: Academic Press.

Sailor, W. (1989). Foreword. In C. Murray-Seegert, *Nasty girls, thugs, and humans like us: Social relations between severely disabled and nondisabled students in high school* (pp. vii-ix). Baltimore: Brookes.

Schumaker, J., Denton, P. H., & Deshler, D. D. (1984). *The paraphrasing strategy.* Lawrence: University of Kansas.

Scruggs, T. E., & Mastropieri, M. A. (1992). Classroom applications of mnemonic instruction: Acquisition, maintenance, and generalization. *Exceptional Children, 58,* 219-229.

Scruggs, T. E., & Mastropieri, M. A. (1993). Special education for the twenty-first century: Integrating learning strategies and thinking skills. *Journal of Learning Disabilities, 26*(6), 392-398.

Sheridan, S. M., Welch, M., & Orme, S. F. (1996). Is consultation effective? A review of the outcome research. *Remedial and Special Education, 17*(3), 341-354.

Shulman, L. S. (1987). Knowledge and teaching: Foundations of the new reform. *Harvard Educational Review, 57,* 1-22.

SimCity 3000 [Computer software]. (2001). Redwood City, CA: Maxis Corporation. Available Internet: *http://simcity.ea.com/us/guide.*

Sugai, G., & Tindal, G. (1993). *Effective school consultation: An interactive approach.* Pacific Grove, CA: Brooks/Cole.

Tindal, G., & Germann, G. (1991). Mainstream consultation agreements in secondary settings. In M. Shinn, G. Stoner, & H. Walker (Eds.), *Interventions for achievement and behavior problems* (pp. 495–517). Silver Spring, MD: National Association of School Psychologists.

Tindal, G., & Nolet, V. (1995). Curriculum-based measurement in middle and high schools: Critical thinking skills in content areas. *Focus on Exceptional Children, 27*(1), 1–22.

Tindal, G., Nolet, V., & Blake, G. (1992). *Focus on teaching and learning in content classes* (Training Module No. 3). Eugene: University of Oregon, Resource Consultant Training Program.

Valencia, S. W., Stallman, A. C., Commeyras, M., Pearson, P. D., & Hartman, K. (1991). Four measures of topical knowledge: A study of construct validity. *Reading Research Quarterly, 26*(3), 204–233.

Ysseldyke, J. E., Thurlow, M. L., Mecklenburg, C., Graden, J., & Algozzine, B. (1984). Changes in academic engaged time as a function of assessment and special education intervention. *Special Services in the Schools, 1*(2), 31–44.

CHAPTER 31

Interventions for Vandalism and Aggression

G. Roy Mayer
California State University, Los Angeles

Beth Sulzer-Azaroff
University of Massachusetts Amherst

INTRODUCTION

Antisocial behavior, including school vandalism, is a complex area of extreme social importance. It is a continual problem affecting all areas of the United States and all socioeconomic levels. Although rates of crime are dropping overall, reports show that young children are increasingly involved in deadlier crime, such as murder, rape, robbery, and aggravated assault (Butts & Snyder, 1997; Snyder & Sickmund, 1995). More juveniles are locked up in secure detention centers, training schools, jails, and prisons than ever before, partially because many states are now emphasizing longer and more punitive sanctions rather than treatment or prevention (Puritz & Shang, 1998). Ingersoll and LeBoeuf (1997) also have noted that there have been increases in student suspensions and expulsions.

During the 1998–1999 school year, Los Angeles City schools experienced close to 3,700 incidents of vandalism, and over 4% of their students were victimized (*www.laspd.com/crimstat/burglary.html*). Nationally, during 1996–1997, 98,490 acts of vandalism, 10,950 fights with weapons, 115,500 thefts, and 187,890 fights occurred in our public schools (*nces.ed.gov/pubs98/violence/98030003.html*). Such violence is typically responded to by new security devices and the addition of school guards, which increases the cost of education considerably. Los Angeles Unified, for example, has 398 full-time and 229 part-time security staff (personal correspondence, Office of the Chief at LAUSD, 3/27/00).

FACTORS CONTRIBUTING TO ANTISOCIAL BEHAVIOR

From the basic research on behavior, we have learned that a few types of circumstances predictably set the stage for antisocial behavior, including aggression, destruction of property, and escape. One is extinction, another punishment. Another is receiving reinforcement for antisocial behavior or observing models who receive such reinforcement.

Extinction is defined as non-delivery of reinforcement following a previously reinforced response. Students who are accustomed to obtaining praise or attention and suddenly fail to receive praise or attention because their classroom assignments are too difficult may be provoked to various forms of antisocial behavior including aggression or vandalism. Their behavior under these extinction conditions is similar to many people's behavior when the vending machine fails to deliver after consuming your coins.

Punishment, the presentation of an aversive stimulus that reduces the rate of a behavior, also can promote antisocial behavior. For example, when a small child gets spanked by a parent, he or she often goes off and sulks alone or responds by hitting a younger sibling, the parents, or any other handy person or object. A parent who has been punished (e.g., criticized) at work may take it out on his or her family or may seek isolation for a while. A student, after being punished verbally or physically by a teacher, may fight back by destroying school property or fighting with others. Of course, not all students respond to a punitive environment with aggression or retaliation. Some attempt to escape by being tardy or truant, by tuning out in a class, or by dropping out of school. Thus, because overly punitive environments promote vandalism, violence, and attendance problems, the use of punitive consequences must be minimized.

Students who are reprimanded for failing to meet unusually demanding academic standards, or who consistently fail, may react aggressively. That is why knowing and adjusting to students' repertoires of skills and abilities is so important.

Youngsters may receive reinforcement in the form of peer approval for being antisocial or destructive or they may successfully use those tactics to attain positions of social leadership. Alternatively, they may see others obtain those enviable consequences. In these two instances every effort should be made, when possible, to remove such sources of reinforcement. Yet being able to remove peer approval is often beyond the capacities of most schools, so we must turn elsewhere: making antisocial behavior less likely by using such strategies as are available and focusing on factors within the school that are under our control.

Factors within the school that contribute to antisocial behavior have been difficult to identify because most are temporally remote from the acts of vandalism. However, by taking some of our research (Mayer, 1995; Mayer & Butterworth, 1979, 1981; Mayer, Butterworth, Nafpaktitis, & Sulzer-Azaroff, 1983b; Mayer, Nafpaktitis, Butterworth, & Hollingsworth, 1987) as a point of departure, and by extrapolating from our knowledge of behavioral principles, we are beginning to identify some of the factors that appear to serve as *setting events* for various antisocial behaviors. Setting events are occurrences, or stimuli, that may be temporally remote, yet overlap with, and in any case influence current stimulus-response interactions. Much evidence now points to an overly punitive school environment as a general setting event for aggression, violence, and property destruction. Such a milieu is characterized by (a) an over-use of punitive methods of control; (b) a lack of clarity of both school and classroom rules and disciplinary policies; (c) weak or inconsistent administrative support and follow-through; and (d) few or no allowances made for individual differences in respect to the selection of academic materials, reinforcers, and punishers. These factors are similar to those that have been identified in the home that likely contribute to antisocial behavior: a coercive and punitive environment and inconsistencies in setting rules and applying consequences (see Mayer, 1995, for a review).

Overuse of Punitive Methods of Control

Research indicates that schools too often emphasize punitive measures to manage student behavior. This overemphasis occurs with many students, but especially among males, minority, and developmentally delayed students, and those from low-income homes (McFadden, Marsh, Price, & Hwang, 1992; Shaw & Braden, 1990; Shores et al., 1993). Teachers' disapproval statements directed at students with disabilities have been observed to outnumber approval statements by a ratio of 15 to 1 (Shores et al., 1993). Teachers in low-income areas and/or in schools containing a low percentage of whites more frequently endorse the use of punishment and the removal of students (Moore & Cooper, 1984). Similarly, adolescents from low-income homes report a greater number and variety of school-imposed penalties that tend to be both disproportionately harsh in relation to the offenses committed and humiliating in nature (Brantlinger, 1991). Finally, Larson's (1994) findings illustrate how punitive some school environments are. He reports that learning disabled and emotionally disturbed students experience an even more aversive, punitive environment in public schools than in the youth prisons in which they were incarcerated. Thus, the school environment is very punitive for some students, and certain groups appear to be singled out for punishment.

Disapproval is used more frequently than approval as a consequence of child behavior not only in high-risk homes (Hart & Risley, 1995) but also by many teachers (Heller & White, 1975; Shores et al., 1993; Thomas, Presland, Grant, & Glenn, 1978; Van Acker, Grant, & Henry, 1996; White, 1975), though certainly not all (Nafpaktitis, Mayer, & Butterworth, 1985; Wyatt & Hawkins, 1987). Unfortunately teacher disapproval or "reprimands appear to exacerbate student negative behavior and non-compliance" (Van Acker et al., 1996, pp. 330-331).

Repeated failure experiences also function as punishment, resulting in aggression. For example, Munk and Repp (1994) have pointed out that when a series of teacher instructions is followed by several student errors, the next teacher instruction can result in an aggressive response by the student. Another problem is that many teachers have a tendency not to attend positively to the desired *social* behavior of any of their students, nor to praise the *academic* behavior of those of their students who often misbehave (Shores et al., 1993; Van Acker et al., 1996). Such extinction conditions for positive, prosocial, and academic behaviors are likely to promote additional student aggression (Wehby, Symons, & Shores, 1995).

Sometimes the total school environment is overly punitive. This type of school climate has a long tradition. Results from a survey by the American Association of School

Administrators (Brodinsky, 1980) indicated that school personnel spent more time and energy in implementing punitive than positive or preventive measures. Additionally, as several investigators point out (Greenberg, 1974; Mayer & Leone, 1999), a reliance on heavy security arrangements (e.g., security guards, metal detectors, locked doors) and school-adopted punitive discipline strategies appears to promote, not reduce, vandalism, aggression, and disorder. In fact, "creating an unwelcoming, almost jail-like, heavily scrutinized environment, may foster just the violence and disorder school administrators hope to avoid" (Mayer & Leone, 1999). Thus, it appears that schools, particularly urban schools, are indeed punitive for many students.

Similarly, Mayer and his colleagues (1979, 1981, 1983a, 1993, 1995) have gathered evidence to suggest that a heavy reliance on punishment as a school-wide and classroom management procedure can actually promote vandalism as well as other forms of disruptions. For example, the cost and frequency of vandalism were found to be higher in schools that emphasized punitive school disciplinary methods than those in which more positive methods were applied (Mayer et al., 1987). More compelling is the evidence, also presented by Mayer and his colleagues, as to the impact of making the school environment more reinforcing for students and staff:

1. Antisocial behaviors and vandalism costs diminish

2. Attendance improves

3. Dropouts and suspensions decrease

4. More students increase the time they spend on assigned tasks

5. Cooperation and positive feelings among students and staff increase

Others have observed informally (Flaherty, 1987; Krause, 1985) that vandalism decreases as a result of making the school environment less aversive and more reinforcing. Berkowitz (1983) also pointed to the "mounting evidence that aversive stimulation generates an instigation to aggression in our species as well as lower orders" (p. 1139). Such aggression can be against school facilities, teachers, and other students. It seems reasonable to conclude, from the above evidence, then, that at least some proportion of the aggression and destruction that takes place in our schools is tied to punitive school environments.

Absence of Clearly Stated Rules, Vague Discipline, and Inconsistently Administered Policies

It is difficult to develop appropriate "stimulus control," or promote uniform rule-following, unless discipline policies and rules are clearly communicated (Mayer, 1999, 2000; Sulzer-Azaroff & Mayer, 1991, 1994a). Furthermore, because many youngsters simply do not know what behavior is expected of them, students may fail to follow rules. This in turn tends to increase teachers' use of punishment—a vicious cycle. When disciplinary policies are unclear to the staff or are inconsistently supported by their supervisors, both positive and negative consequences tend to be dispensed arbitrarily. Under such circumstances, youngsters have a difficult time knowing what to do, because the result of any particular behavior is unpredictable. Anticipated reinforcement may fail to be attained or punishment received unexpectedly. Obviously, inappropriate student behaviors are much more likely to occur under such confusing conditions, again resulting in increased uses of punishment by staff. It should come as no surprise, then, that Mayer et al. (1987) found this lack of clarity of rules and policies about conduct to be one factor that relates significantly to vandalism cost and frequency. (For more detail on this topic, see Sugai, Horner, & Gresham, this volume.)

Weak or Inconsistent Administrative Support and Follow-Through

Weak or inconsistent administrative support limits the reinforcement staff receive for consistently and cooperatively implementing disciplinary programs (Mayer, et al., 1983a). A lack of support can also be aversive for staff, which, in turn, may well foster aggression on their part. This readily transfers to resorting to punitive methods of control in managing student behavior (Mayer et al., 1987; Mayer, 1995). "In the same way that social support from a spouse or family member increases the effectiveness of the interventions used in the home, support from other teachers and administrators appears critical for effective program implementation by a teacher at school" (Mayer, 2000). In any event, vandalism tends to be higher in schools where administrative support and follow-through are lacking or weak, rules are unclear, and insufficient allowances are made for individual student differences (Mayer et al., 1987).

Allowances Made for Individual Differences

It is hard to believe that in this age of enlightenment many educators fail to provide for individual social or academic differences. You can still walk into a high school history class and find all the students required to read from a text written at or beyond the twelfth-grade level of difficulty even though many of the students' reading skills are considerably lower. As Mayer et al. (1983b) has pointed out,

> ... many students, particularly those whose reading ability does not permit them to complete their assignments successfully, are more apt to experience defeat, reproach, ridicule, and other probable aversive consequences. This combination of extinction and punishment may also serve to imbue scholastic activities and materials with conditioned aversive properties. (p. 356).

Whether because of insufficient time for tailoring assignments to individual students' abilities, school policy, failure to detect the difficulty, inadequate instructional resources, or a combination of these factors, teachers often assign material that is either too difficult or too easy for their students. (For more detail, see Higgins, Boone, & Lovitt, this volume.) As Sulzer-Azaroff and Mayer (1994c) have stated, "The result can be failure (i.e., punishment) or boredom (i.e., extinction). Many students respond to such situations by acting aggressively against their classmates, their teachers, or their physical surroundings" (p. 331). Similarly, Greenberg (1974) has shown a strong relation between delinquency and reading ability; Center, Deitz, and Kaufman (1982) have found that "failure level academic tasks resulted in significant increases in inappropriate behavior from some students" (p. 355); and Berkowitz (1983) has pointed out that even frustrations and failure to attain a desired goal "can produce aggressive inclinations because of their aversive nature" (p. 1143). Mayer (2000) and Sulzer-Azaroff and Mayer (1994b) identify several features of effective instruction that can help reduce the likelihood that scholastic activities and materials are imbued with aversive properties.

Failure to individualize consequences, for example, by meting out common punishers and rewards, can result in an increase, rather than a decrease, of vandalism and other aggressive behavior (Mayer, 1995). This is because individuals have distinctive learning histories that cause particular consequences to be more or less effective for them. In our work, we have attempted to allow for individual differences by assigning reading materials appropriately matched to student performance levels and by individualizing behavioral consequences. As a result, we have found that, compared to control schools and each school's previous approaches, vandalism decreased, fewer discipline problems were reported, and cooperation and positive feelings among students and staff increased (Mayer & Butterworth, 1979, 1981; Mayer et al., 1983b). These findings are similar to those of Gold and Mann (1982), who concluded that "poor scholastic experiences are significant causes of delinquent and disruptive behavior' (p.313). They found that when curriculum was more closely tailored to the individual and the environment made more reinforcing, students' behavior and scholastic performance improved.

Based upon the above review of literature it should come as no surprise that in a recent federal publication (U.S. Department of Education, 2000) it was stated:

> Studies indicate that approximately four of every five disruptive students can be traced to some dysfunction in the way schools are orga-nized, staff members are trained, or schools are run. The development of sound policies, staff and professional development, and consistent and proven management practices are essential (p. 10).

For the school psychologist who is concerned with various antisocial behaviors, including vandalism, we recommend a formal program to allay the situation. It consists of assessing the situation, designing and conducting the intervention program, maintaining it, and evaluating the program's effectiveness.

FIGURE 1

Recording Sheet for Occurrence and Cost of Vandalism

	CLASSROOM BUILDING		CAFETERIA		WASHROOM		OTHER (please specify, e.g., library, playground, administration building, bus)	
	Date of Occurrence(s)	Cost*	Date of Occurrence(s)	Cost*	Date of Occurrence(s)	Cost*	Date of Occurrence(s)	Cost*
BROKEN GLASS								
EQUIPMENT THEFT								
FIRE DAMAGE								
PROPERTY DAMAGE (Graffiti, smashed furniture, fixtures torn off wall, carved desks, miscellaneous ruination)								

*Be sure to include labor cost. If precise dollar figures are not immediately available, estimate cost in pencil. When accurate figures are available, indicate in ink.

ASSESSING THE SITUATION

Assessing the Need and School Climate

An assessment should be undertaken initially to verify the need to undertake a program to reduce various antisocial behaviors like vandalism. To illustrate with vandalism, the costs and number of episodes of vandalism should be determined. Figure 1 displays a form used by Mayer et al. (1983b) to collect monthly vandalism data. The date of each incident and the cost of repairing and replacing vandalized property are recorded in the appropriate space. Note that the form also helps to determine the location of the episodes. This kind of information can help determine if there is a need for a program throughout the school or only in a specific area. Also, should you subsequently decide to implement a program, you can use the data gathered to constitute a baseline against which to measure future change.

Referrals to the office also appear to be a good basis for determining the need to undertake a program to reduce aggression and other highly disruptive antisocial behavior (Metzler, Biglan, Rusby, & Sprague, in press; Taylor-Greene et al., 1997; Tobin, Sugai, & Colvin, 1996).

FIGURE 2

The School Discipline Survey

DISCIPLINE SURVEY

The growing problems of school violence, vandalism, and absenteeism are serious concerns of the Office of the Los Angeles County Superintendent of Schools. We are asking your help in a research project related to these problems. We need to know how student discipline is handled at your school. Most items in this survey pertain to what is actually being practiced in your school, except for specific questions that request your personal opinion.

Responses will be grouped to give an overall picture of your school, but your independent judgment is essential. The form should not take longer than fifteen minutes to complete.

Part I

Please read each item and place an "X" on the line corresponding to your answer.

	Yes	No
1. Our school has a written discipline policy. (If answered "no," proceed directly to item 2).		
a. I have read or referred to the school discipline policy within the past year.		
b. A copy of the discipline policy is given at least on an annual basis to each student.		
c. A copy of the discipline policy is given at least on an annual basis to the parents of each student.		
2. I have a written set of standards for classroom discipline that I use. (If answered "no," proceed directly to Part II.)		
a. I have read or referred to my written classroom standards within the past year.		
b. A copy of my classroom standards is given at least on an annual basis to each student in my class.		
c. A copy of my classroom standards is given at least on an annual basis to the parents of each student in my class.		

Part II

Following is a series of statements describing student discipline and staff relationships. Place a check in the column below the word or phrase which best indicates how closely the statement describes your school or your opinion.

	Rarely	Sometimes	More Often Than Not	Consistently
3. Instructional materials to meet individual student differences are provided when I request them.				
4. Action is taken promptly by school authorities when I make a disciplinary referral.				
5. In my opinion, disciplinary action taken by school authorities is appropriate.				
6. Good teaching is recognized and appreciated by the administration.				
7. I confer with other teachers regarding instructional activities occurring in my classroom.				
8. I confer with other teachers regarding how I maintain discipline in my classroom.				
9. Faculty requests and suggestions regarding discipline policy are acted upon promptly.				
10. When disciplining students, it is easy for me to follow the school-wide discipline policy.				

	Rarely	Sometimes	More Often Than Not	Consistently
11. When I follow the discipline policy, I receive administrative support for my actions.				
12. When I follow my own judgment in administering discipline, I receive support for my actions.				
13. As far as I know, other teachers follow the school discipline policy.				
14. I am in agreement with the discipline practices of counselors and administrators.				

	Disagree	Somewhat Disagree	Somewhat Agree	Agree
15. In my opinion, the school discipline policy is effective.				
16. In my opinion, the school discipline policy is overly punitive.				
17. Every student who engages in a suspendible offense should be suspended.				
18. Every student who engages in an offense for which expulsion can be applied should be expelled.				

	Rarely	Sometimes	More Often Than Not	Consistently
19. I start to formulate an individual plan for improving a student's behavior when the usual methods of classroom discipline fail.				
20. An individual plan for improving a student's behavior is formulated when the usual methods of school discipline fail.				
21. Students who have not been attending school regularly are rewarded for improved attendance.				
22. Students receive school-wide recognition for behaving as they should.				
23. Students receive recognition in my classroom for behaving as they should.				
24. I consider using positive incentives to assist students who need to improve their behavior in my classroom.				
25. I consider using changes in assignments and materials to assist students who need to improve their behavior in my classroom.				
26. School authorities consider using positive incentives to assist students who need to improve their school behavior.				
27. School authorities consider using program or class changes to assist students who need to improve their school behavior.				
28. I make allowances for specific students when applying the school discipline policy.				

The relevant aspects of the school climate can be assessed by using the School Discipline Survey (SDS) (Mayer et al., 1987) as illustrated in Figure 2, on page 860. Completed by the teaching staff, the SDS attempts to measure how punitive the school environment is, particularly in their disciplinary practices. We have found that the higher the scores obtained on the SDS the lower the costs and frequency of vandalism tend to be and vice versa (Mayer et al., 1987). The survey is divided into the three major sections: Clarity (items 1–2), Administrative Support (items 3-16), and Individual Differences (items 17–28). Maximum possible scores are the following: Clarity, 32, Administrative Support, 56, Individual Differences, 48, for a total possible of 136 points. Such a score would indicate a highly reinforcing environment with clear discipline policies, good administrative support, and maximum allowance for individual differences (see Mayer et al., 1987, for scoring procedures).

Determining Environmental Support and Resources

Considering the total system is critical in order to obtain the kind of ongoing support that is certain to be needed to implement almost any program of change. Additionally, such an analysis can help to identify organizational factors that may influence the effectiveness of the program.

The school environmental analysis should be conducted at several levels, including supervisory, instructional, support staff, and students. Their cooperation is crucial, as these people control many important contingencies and may possess important data that could be made available for the assessment. Similarly, at the district level, those in charge, such as the superintendent and the head of security, need to be contacted for their approval and support. Their administrative roles must be clarified, along with a determination of the extent of the help they will provide and the data (such as aggression, vandalism costs, and incidence rates) they will make available. Currently operating programs and policies related to vandalism and aggression need to be described. Such information should permit those initiating the behavioral interventions to decide on the feasibility of incorporating their program within these current structures. Otherwise, it is best to negotiate a mechanism for collaboratively modifying those policies and procedures.

Local and state laws governing acts of school aggression, vandalism, and prevailing standards for administering such legislation among juveniles in your community also need to be investigated. Contacting juvenile authorities is often helpful, as is soliciting the cooperation of parents and community leaders. Often these people are willing to help by supplying prizes, gift certificates, admission passes, funds, time, and other rewards that can be used as incentives. For example, in Burlington, Vermont, the operator of a video game arcade permitted children to earn tokens to operate his machines by accomplishing academic tasks (Barrera, 1984). When community leaders, businesses, and parents are informed about how they will all benefit when violence and vandalism diminish, they probably will become active supporters of the program.

Sulzer-Azaroff and Mayer (1994a) have described an environmental analysis form that can be used as a guide to obtain most of the information described above (see Table 1, on page 864). If used appropriately, this analysis of the system should yield valuable information that increases the likelihood of a successful operation.

Measuring Vandalism and Its Setting Events

Measuring vandalism. Because acts of vandalism usually are impossible to directly observe at the time of their occurrence, we must use indirect measures, such as the results or repair costs of acts of vandalism, or count each day during which new damage was done as a separate instance. We have used the Vandalism Cost and Occurrence form illustrated earlier in Figure 1 (Mayer & Butterworth, 1979; Mayer et al., 1983b; Mayer et al., 1987) as the basis for estimating rates of vandalism. The form asks for the date of each occurrence and the monthly costs of repairing or replacing property (per 100 students, to account for differences in school size).

Measuring possible setting events. As previously noted, several temporally remote factors (e.g., history of punishment) appear to be related to aggression and vandalism. These factors could be assessed not only by means of the School Discipline Survey (Mayer et al., 1987) but also by collecting other data, such as tabulating positive notes sent to teachers by administrators or by directly observing many of the items listed in the School Discipline Survey. Collecting such observational data provides reasonably objective measures of factors that appear most relevant to preventing violence, but because such an activity does involve personnel time, the extent to which this information will contribute to the potential effectiveness of the program must be considered. Whatever setting event, aggressive act, or vandalism data are collected, they need to be collected repeatedly over a period of several months in order to obtain a representative baseline providing a measure of the severity of the problem.

DESIGNING AND CONDUCTING THE INTERVENTION PROGRAM

Once the scope of the problem, the anticipated degree of support and cooperation, acceptable objectives, and the severity of the problem have been determined by means of a baseline measure, the stage is set for designing and implementing the intervention strategy. At the onset, though, we must recognize that no single intervention program has been totally effective in preventing vandalism or any other antisocial behavior. Thus, we will discuss a variety of approaches for reducing and preventing this problem.

Selecting Deterrents and Punishment Strategies

Generally when faced with excessive violence and vandalism, administrators turn to deterrents or methods of detection or punishment as their first option (Brodinsky, 1980; Mayer & Leone, 1999). Frequently, these methods are designed to inhibit or immediately suppress such acts. They include hiring security personnel, installing alarm systems, posting punitive consequences, and involving community members in various school watch programs.

TABLE 1

Suggested Activities for Assessing Environmental Support and Resources

I. District Level
    A. Inform and request support from each of the following.
        1. Superintendent.
        2. Person(s) with the major responsibility for overseeing data and programs in the area on which you plan to work (e.g., vandalism, attendance, discipline, etc.).
        3. Director of special services and/or others recommended by the superintendent.
    B. Locate supplemental resources such as the instructional materials center or other repository of extra books and materials.
    C. Familiarize yourself with any district-wide programs and policies that have been or are operating in your targeted area.

II. School Level
    A. Inform, request support, and discover information about each of the following:
        1. *Principal.* The principal's leadership role; his or her view of instructional and professional staff and school's strengths and weaknesses; programs supported; years in school; related background information; how principal is viewed by staff; degree to which he or she uses praise; behaviors; particular staff member he or she reinforces or recognizes more than others; availability to staff; and degree of rapport and interaction with students.
        2. *Vice-Principal* (when applicable). Obtain same information as for the principal, plus how that role differs from the principal's.
        3. *Secretary.* Attitude toward principal, instructional, and professional staff; years at school; attitude of staff toward secretary; strengths and weaknesses; interests; control over communications; and nature and degree of administrative responsibilities held.
        4. *Psychologist/Counselor.* Attitude toward staff and project; knowledge of behavioral approach; days per week at school; role; and background.
        5. *Custodian.* Role and attitude of staff and students toward custodian and vice versa.
        6. *School Staff.* Are there cliques? Views of psychologist, principal, and faculty leaders, gathering places for breaks, lunch, etc.; and current philosophical orientation.
        7. *Special Staff and Services.*
            a. *Remedial Reading Teachers.* Time spent at school; approach used in remediation; materials available; relation to staff; and willingness to cooperate.
            b. *Librarian.* Level of training; time available; relation to staff; and availability of high interest/low vocabulary materials.
            c. *Resource Specialist.* Level of training; number of days or time spent at school; relation to staff; any behavioral approaches used; and available materials.
            d. *Available Aids/Volunteers.* Degree of responsibility and training.
            e. *Student Council and Student Officers.* Degree of leadership and responsibility.
            f. *School Security Personnel.* Responsibilities; relation to students; number; and visibility.
            g. *School Nurse and Attendance Clerk.* Responsibilities and available information.
    B. Any school-wide programs and policies that have been or are operating in your targeted area.

III. Community Resources
    A. Inform, request support, and discover information about each of the following:
        1. *PTA.* Size; involvement; support funds; chairperson's telephone number; degree to which members are interested in supporting a project in your targeted area; and other leaders in the group.
        2. *Library.* Location and availability of films, records, tapes, etc.
        3. *Community Recreation.* Local programs; involvement; size; time; and location.
        4. *Description of Immediate Neighborhood.* Perception of school; socioeconomic status; and neighborhood service organizations that may be willing to help.
        5. *Local Educational Supply Stores.* Those available.
        6. *School Advisory Council.* Role.

Note
This table is an adaptation of one developed by Mayer et al. (1983c).

Security personnel. Security personnel should be trained when they are hired, and expected to perform a role beyond that of just enforcers of the law. Because they serve not only to protect facilities but also to provide students and staff with a safe environment, security officers must be able to relate effectively with those people. Scrimger and Elder (1981) pointed out that the more successful security personnel programs provide a balance of security *and* educational functions. Security personnel need adequate training and supervision if this balance is to be accomplished. Training should include not only technical preparation for the job but also a familiarity with local gangs, behavior management problems, skill in the use of reinforcement, effective modeling, and other interpersonal expertise.

Alarm systems. A variety of alarm systems have been used for the purpose of deterring vandalism. They range from a bell, horn, siren, or light activated by intruders to systems that notify protection or security agencies. However, because of the assortment of systems and the diversity of needs among schools, the help of an independent security consultant should be sought to design the best system for your school, instead of depending upon the advice of a commercial alarm manufacturer or distributor. It should be noted that some alarms limit access to the building by staff during non-school hours or require someone to be available on a 24-hour basis to allow legitimate access to the buildings.

Community watch programs. These programs are designed to alert local residents to the problems that the school is having with vandalism and solicit their support in reporting anything suspicious, such as the presence of vehicles on or near the school grounds during non-school hours, people on roofs of buildings, unusual odors, lights, noises, smoke coming from the school, or individuals observed stealing or destroying school property. Local resident support has been obtained in several ways. Students have disseminated written letters to residents that explained the problem and requested that they call enclosed phone numbers if they should observe anything suspicious at the school. Teachers, uniformed peace officers from the school district's security department, and school administrators have all been involved in contacting persons living within view of the school. Regardless of who informs community members, Mullendore (1981) wisely suggests that the information distributed should describe useful items that the school could purchase with money saved by not needing to repair the effects of vandalism.

Another type of school watch program involves live-in "school sitters." In return for watching the school and reporting vandals to the police, school sitters receive a rent-free trailer site. Others have tried parent patrols, consisting of interested parents who patrol the school grounds whenever possible. For example, some parents may walk their dogs around a school building instead of around the block. Others may offer to drive by the school slowly on an evening out.

When the community shows concern about its schools, the climate becomes more conducive to reducing violence and vandalism. Also, such parental involvement may not only boost school morale but also foster more parental awareness and involvement in other aspects of school life.

Posting punitive consequences. Punitive deterrents, of course, rely on the administration of aversive consequences. Typically a list of penalties is posted and one or more applied when a student has been caught aggressing or vandalizing. These might include requiring students and their parents to pay for the damage (restitution), suspension, expulsion, or criminal charges.

Problems With Deterrents and Punishment

In addition to the obvious cost involved in hiring security agents and purchasing alarm systems, an over-reliance on deterrent and punishment methods tends to result in several problems. First, the more these aversive control methods are used, the less effective they become, often requiring increasingly harsh methods to achieve similar results. Second, they do not address the factors that may be promoting the antisocial behavior in the first place, such as an overly punitive school environment. In fact, these measures can add to the image of the school as punitive. Perhaps this is why, according to Greenberg (1974), Mayer and Leone (1999), and Scrimger and Elder (1981), campus security forces often have appeared to aggravate rather than to deter violence and vandalism.

Sometimes a crisis situation mandates a crash program to deter vandalism and provide safety for students and staff. However, if the effects are to be enduring, then these short-range deterrents must be combined with long-range preventive programs that will make the school a more reinforcing place for everyone. Deterrents like these must be viewed as temporary expedients to augment your long-term strategies of prevention.

Preventing Vandalism

Mayer and his colleagues (Mayer, 1995, 1999; Mayer & Butterworth, 1979; Mayer et al., 1983b) have devised a model to prevent antisocial behavior in the school. One of the first steps is to implement a school-wide antisocial prevention team. This is followed by implementing, maintaining, and evaluating various programs for preventing antisocial behavior.

Antisocial behavior prevention team. Our research has indicated that the total school climate can be improved by collaborating initially with the most influential members of a school staff, including designated and natural leaders. We formed a team within each school that consisted of the principal, school counselor or psychologist, three or four teachers, and two or three students to lead in the selection and implementation of programs to reduce vandalism. The teachers on the team pilot-tested the classroom programs before recommending the programs to the entire staff, permitting us to observe, supervise closely, and provide feedback frequently. Once programs were working effectively in their classes, the teachers on the team then served as models and resource persons for other staff interested in conducting similar programs. With teachers serving such a key modeling role, selecting the best candidates was of critical import. We chose participants who (a) demonstrated willingness to try and share new ideas; (b) were respected by their fellow staff members; and (c) consented to commit the time to work with administrators and others involved with the project, including having observers in their classrooms.

We have found that the membership of school principals on the team is of critical importance, for without their support our efforts have failed (Mayer et al., 1983a). In particular, the extent of the principal's support of teachers and programs has influenced the degree to which other teachers followed their colleagues in implementing similar programs. Clearly, the principal's support, encouragement, and participation are essential if the program is to succeed.

The counselors and psychologists provided valuable expertise in methods of modifying social behaviors. They consulted with team teachers and other staff members, helping the teachers and other staff members design and implement constructive discipline programs (Mayer, 1999, 2000) to meet the unique needs of individual students or classes.

Students were included on the team to represent their peers' perspectives, and because research (Fixsen, Phillips, & Wolf, 1973; Lovitt & Curtiss, 1969) has shown that programs tend to be better accepted, understood, supported, and enforced by students when they have been involved in the program planning. We selected students to serve on the team who were highly respected by their peers and committed to providing the time and energy required for team activities.

While forming a vandalism prevention team obviously takes organization and planning, the investment pays off in the form of broadened acceptance of and enthusiasm for the program and in its ultimate effectiveness. A well-constituted team is in a position to assess the needs of the school, and collaborate toward solving vandalism problems by participating in designing and carrying out selected strategies.

Preventive programs. Once the team is operational, it begins to select and conduct various programs of intervention. When the situation is of crisis proportion, the team may begin by choosing a deterrent strategy to protect property and make conditions safer for students and staff as a temporary expedient. However, in the schools in which we have worked, deterrents were not implemented unless long-term preventive strategies also were initiated. Now let us look at some of the features of these preventive strategies.

If assessments have revealed the circumstances that tend to promote misconduct (e.g., assignment of inappropriate academic materials, failure to individualize consequences, and so on) then we try to alter or remove those circumstances (Touchette, MacDonald, & Langer, 1985). Academic materials need to be adjusted continually to the students' level of functioning while still capturing their interests. Use of the materials also needs to be paired with considerable positive reinforcement if learning is to be encouraged (Mayer, 2000; Sulzer-Azaroff & Mayer, 1994b) and if aggression and vandalism are to be reduced. Also, we look carefully to see if a particular sequence of acts can be detected that culminate in serious misbehavior (O'Leary & Dubey, 1979). For example, students who are known to start by muttering and then swearing aloud, and subsequently to move on to pushing their own and then their neighbors' papers and books off the desk, may well start throwing large objects at the other children.

Having observed this sequence several times, the experienced teacher will redirect such students to a preferred activity at the first mutter. Alternatively, redirecting toward the end of the sequence is not a good idea, because it can serve a reinforcing function. It is better to interrupt the sequence, if necessary with a simple sharp reprimand or some other punisher that is effective with the individual.

Our most successful preventive strategies have been based on what Goldiamond (1974) refers to as a *constructional approach* or what Mayer (1999) has called *constructive discipline.* The emphasis is on *teaching* or *building* rather than reducing or eliminating behavior and involves: (a) selecting behaviors to be established or strengthened, rather than those to be reduced or eliminated; (b) identifying academic and social repertoires upon which to build; (c) matching procedures of change to those repertoires; and (d) selecting reinforcing contingencies to increase and maintain the goal behaviors. Using reinforcers natural to the environment, such as those that previously reinforced the problem behavior, is emphasized.

Constructive discipline contrasts, then, with traditional discipline approaches, which have tended to rely much more heavily on punishment of misconduct, combined only to a minor extent with reinforcement of preferred alternatives. Such a heavy reliance on punishment again contributes to an overly punitive school climate. Furthermore, when punishment is applied frequently over extended periods, its effectiveness begins to diminish. For example, when parents spank a child for every major and minor infraction, spanking begins to lose its reductive power, unless the blows become more intense and the parent is on the road to physically abusing the child. The same can be said about school suspensions. Also, as we mentioned before, punitive consequences can provoke aggression and destruction of property. Therefore, the use of punishment must be minimized. It should be delivered only for extremely serious or dangerous acts. See Sulzer-Azaroff and Mayer (1991, 1994a) for a more extensive discussion on the pros and cons of using punishment as a management procedure.

Over-dependence upon punishment poses additional difficulties. We have already indicated that individuals may respond to the same consequences in different ways. For example, some students have been known to misbehave to be kept after school rather than return to an empty house or unpleasant home atmosphere. In other cases, teachers who rely heavily on punishment and use isolation as a management device actually may be teaching some of their students to misbehave by removing them from a classroom milieu that the students find unpleasant. For instance, a pupil who has a history of failure in math might learn that he can avoid an onerous math session with a single sortie of spitwads if such a misbehavior will lead to his being ejected from class. Although isolation may work to reduce the misbehavior of some, its influence upon behavior is particular to the individual student.

Built into the constructive discipline approach, then, is the recognition that uniform consequences, whether reinforcing or punitive, will not affect each student in the same way. Instead, to allow for individual differences, educators choose from a variety of jointly selected consequences. If a student should ask, "Why did you send me to the office for marking on my desk, but you only fined Jim five points for doing the same thing?" the teacher should be honest and explain, "I didn't fine you five points because fines don't work for you, but they do work to stop Jim's misbehavior. Similarly, to reward you, I allowed you to work with Jane on that project, but I allowed Jim to work on his homework. Would you prefer to work on your homework rather than with Jane? You see, the point is that you and Jim are different people, so how can I treat you the same?"

Too heavy a reliance on punishment carries other disadvantages. Teachers who punish model the very class of behavior they are trying to reduce: use of aversive methods. Youngsters who are punished appear to learn by example to deliver punishment to others (Conger, 1982; Sulzer-Azaroff & Mayer, 1994a). Additionally, when punishment is applied inconsistently as often is the case, students learn to risk misbehaving because they succeed in getting away with it sufficiently often. As mentioned earlier, punishment predictably promotes aggression, the acts we are hoping to eradicate. Effective punishment is intense, and is administered immediately, every single time the unwanted behavior occurs; and these standards are difficult to meet in most schools and are questionable ethically when applied following minor infractions. So, as we can see, punishment is not the management strategy of choice in schools. (For further discussion of these issues, also see Sugai, Horner, & Gresham, this volume.)

An alternative and even more effective method to apply is the triadic behavioral model illustrated in Figure 3, on page 870. We have successfully used this constructional approach as a basis for designing our vandalism and other antisocial behavior prevention/reduction programs. Reinforcing consequences, such as praise, privileges, and rewards, are used to increase or maintain the occurrence of rule-following and other appropriate behaviors; and punitive consequences, such as isolation, penalties, scolding, referral, suspension, restitution, and expulsion, are reserved for major or serious infractions. However, for the most commonly occurring minor infractions, constructive alternatives, or positive behavioral interventions, are selected.

Developing and communicating rules. Before specific consequences are selected and administered, rules of deportment need to be established and communicated clearly. Not only does this step make sense, but it is frequently required by law. For example, Section 35291 of the California Education Code requires that the principal of each school "take steps to insure that all rules pertaining to the discipline of pupils are communicated to continuing students at the beginning of each school year, and to transfer students at the time of their enrollment in the school." Too often we assume that school discipline standards are understood or that students already know or should know how to behave. Furthermore, we frequently communicate standards indirectly, requiring that students learn the rules through trial and error, which necessarily entails using punishment.

Several steps will increase the likelihood that rules will be communicated clearly. First, all relevant parties, including students, should be represented when school-wide rules are being developed. Rules tend to be better understood, accepted, supported, and enforced when all concerned parties, or their representatives, have been included in drawing up a conduct code. Once an initial draft of the rules and consequences has

FIGURE 3

A Triadic Approach to Discipline

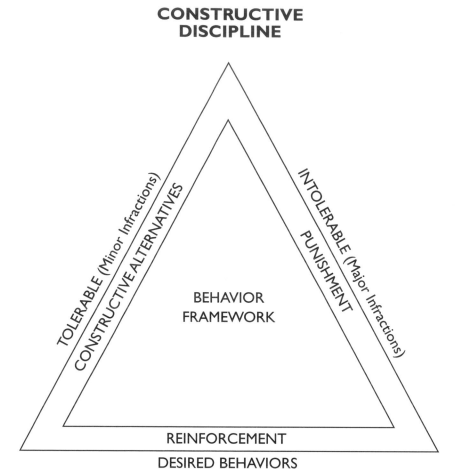

been developed, broadly based community input should be solicited. A draft, including formulated consequences, can be circulated to all staff, students, and parents for additional comments. A legal review of the document may be necessary before a final draft is drawn up for administrative approval.

As with the school-wide rules, students should be involved in developing classroom rules. We suggest that the resultant classroom behavior code include no more than six or eight rules, be simple and to the point, stated positively, and coordinated with school-wide policies. Rather than stating, "Don't be late to class" or 'Don't talk without raising your hand," you could say, "Be in your seat before the tardy bell rings" and "Raise your hand before asking questions." An illustrative set includes:

1. Bring books, pencil, and paper

2. Be in your seat when tardy bell rings

3. Listen carefully

4. Follow directions

5. Complete assignments

6. Show courtesy and respect to others

7. We will try to include *all* students in activities

8. We will help others who are being bullied by getting adult help and/or speaking out

A positive list will guide students in how to behave in preference to how not to behave, which will be more instructive and less suppressive. Once developed, the classroom rules, like the school-wide rules, should be shared with and approved by the responsible administrator(s).

Once approval has been obtained, it is important to teach the behavior code to all involved parties, specifically to staff and students. The rules can be presented to staff during meetings and workshops, and follow-up consultation should be provided (Sulzer-Azaroff & Mayer, 1994c). For students, presenting classroom and school-wide rules both in writing and pictorially helps to assure understanding. Classroom rules can be displayed prominently on a poster, printed in handout form, and copied by students in their notebooks. For preschool and primary pupils, and for students with learning difficulties, it is helpful to role-play each rule as part of the explanatory process. School-wide rules for older students can be printed in a student handbook and discussed in class. Both classroom and school-wide rules should be reviewed orally at regular intervals and constructive changes made when necessary. In summary, students and staff must be helped to actively learn the code of conduct, not just presented with a paper or booklet and left to their own devices.

Ongoing parental support is important if classroom and school-wide rules are to function successfully, so the code must be communicated to parents. This can be accomplished by sending a letter home with students. We have also found it helpful to request that the parents sign the letter to indicate that they agree to the rules and have discussed them with their youngsters. Using this form of communication gives evidence that parents have seen and support the code of conduct.

Selecting positive consequences for following rules. After the rules have been jointly established and posted, students must receive reinforcement for adhering to those rules, because *rules will only be followed when differential consequences are applied for compliance and noncompliance.*

People learn to behave differently in different contexts because they have experienced the distinctive consequences for acts that they have performed in those contexts. For example, students learn to raise their hands in Ms. Smith's classroom because she only recognizes students who have their hands up, but they learn to speak out freely in Ms. Freebee's classroom because she sometimes recognizes students who speak out. Discriminating how to behave often stems from students' experiences with their teachers. When rule-following is reinforced, the students learn which behaviors are acceptable under what circumstances. However, if rule following is not reinforced, it eventually will cease. If Ms. Freebee fails to call on those who raise their hands, then hand raising will probably not occur in her classroom.

In the early stages of instruction in rule-following, reinforcement for adherence to school-wide rules needs to be delivered very frequently, perhaps daily or weekly, and possibly as often as every hour or following every period for classroom rules. The teacher might, for instance, plan to terminate instruction 5 minutes early for each class period in which the students, or those who complied with the code, are permitted a special event, such as a song, a dance, free time, or something similar. Later on, once adherence to rules reaches a high and steady rate for several weeks, praise and recognition can be substituted gradually for the special events, without eliminating them altogether.

Raising the general level of reinforcement. Beyond the differential reinforcement that teaches students to follow rules, schools that are seeking to reduce vandalism need to provide reinforcement in many other forms. High-density reinforcement will imbue the school's atmosphere with a positive environment and make it a place that students like and respect; and vandalism, aggression, and attendance problems should diminish as a result. We have accomplished reductions in vandalism by providing lots of praise and recognition, special rewards and activities as consequences of academic progress and also as noncontingent benefits by providing students access to many intrinsically reinforcing educational events, such as entertainment, arts, music, dance, handicrafts, trips, and audio-visual presentations. (See Mayer, 2000; Sulzer-Azaroff & Mayer, 1991, 1994a for reinforcing programs and lists of reinforcers for students. Also see Mayer et al., 1983c, for a variety of practical reinforcing programs that were used as part of an overall strategy to reduce vandalism, aggression, and attendance problems.) As Nevin (1988) has demonstrated, dense reinforcement helps maintain pro-social behavior.

Selecting consequences for minor infractions. As we mentioned previously, individually effective punitive procedures are selected for major infractions, and reinforcement is withheld from minor infractions while constructive alternatives, or positive behavioral interventions, are selected and applied to diminish them. Constructive alternatives might include (a) providing reinforcement when target students engage in desirable alternatives to infractions, such as cleaning up messes on the campus and in the classroom, raising their hands, and acceptably completing assigned work (technically, this procedure is DRA (differential reinforcement of alternative responses)); (b) reinforcing students' engagement in appropriate rule-following behavior to permit their actions to serve as models for those engaged in minor infractions (technically, this procedure is modeling); (c) providing reinforcement for reduced rates of the undesirable behavior, such as diminished rates of absenteeism, vandalism, littering, or blurting out (technically, this procedure is DRD [differential reinforcement of diminishing rates]); and (d) providing reinforcement when students stop engaging in specific misbehaviors for a period of time, such as fighting during break time, being tardy or committing vandalism for a month, or blurting out for a similar period (technically this procedure is DRO [differential reinforcement of the zero-occurrence of a behavior]). We have elaborated on and illustrated these strategies elsewhere (Mayer, 2000; Sulzer-Azaroff & Mayer, 1991, 1994a). Finally, assuming that rules are familiar to all and that punishment is called for, we recommend that warnings are not given after observing a serious infraction, because such warnings can serve as an invitation to further misbehave. Instead, it is important to deliver the selected consequence immediately after the infraction occurs.

The triadic model appears especially effective for several reasons. First, by using constructive alternatives, instead of punishment for minor infractions, school and classroom climates become less punitive and more positive. In turn, this produces higher rates of reinforcement and a more positive learning climate, resulting in less vandalism and violence (Mayer & Butterworth, 1979; Mayer et al., 1983b). Also, on the rare occasions when we must use punishment, it is more likely to work effectively because it has not been overused.

MAINTAINING PREVENTION PROGRAMS

Phasing Out Reminders and Consequences

Students soon will learn the rules if they were involved in their development, the conduct code is posted in a prominent place and reviewed periodically, and if consequences consistently are provided both for violating and for abiding by the rules. After students have been adhering consistently to the rules for a long time, the frequency of delivering the positive consequences can gradually be reduced, so that rule-following behavior will become more habitual and not overly dependent on rewards. This is particularly important if tangible incentives have been used because more natural reinforcers were not effective or meaningful to the youngster involved. These contrived reinforcers can be replaced gradually by the reinforcers indigenous to the situation or the learning activity. For example, if tickets, ice cream, certificates, or award assemblies are provided once a week initially, they should be paired with and slowly replaced by more natural reinforcers, such as praise and recognition, while the more intrusive reinforcers are phased back to twice a week for a couple of times, then to once a month several times, then perhaps to once every other month. *It is important, however, that the incentives are not stopped abruptly,* because a sharp cutoff may cause the desired behavior to disintegrate. If adherence to the rules begins to fade, we recommend that you back up a bit and offer the incentives more frequently again and then phase them out more gradually than before.

Similarly, as students learn to abide by the rules, fewer reminders will be needed. Review of rules also can be phased out gradually. Rules may also be combined or made more general, perhaps as simple as "Bring supplies, pay attention, and behave according to the rules."

Fostering Continued Environmental Support

We have shown how aggression and vandalism can relate to the management strategies used by educators; thus, continuing environmental support of these strategies is essential. Beyond assurances, we need actively to promote continuation of effective behavior management strategies if change is to be sustained. What measures can *you* take?

We believe that several measures need to be taken. First, every educator must realize that staff, like each of us, needs to receive very frequent reinforcement for their initial efforts to make school more reinforcing and less punitive. As we discussed previously in regard to students, this reinforcement of staff performance can become less frequent with time (Holden & Sulzer-Azaroff, 1972; MacDonald, Gallimore, & MacDonald, 1970; Sulzer-Azaroff & Mayer, 1994c). These efforts can take the form of specific feedback, recognition, praise, or even special privileges or rewards. If abrupt termination of reinforcement occurs, then changes or new programs are not likely to continue. Dustin (1974) stressed this point when he wrote:

> One reason that institutions change superficially has to do with ineffective behaviors on the part of the change agent. These proponents of change "burn out," or move on, before the change is fully implemented. It is necessary that a change agent possess tenacity to follow through and to return to the same tasks and the same individuals time and again (pp. 423-424).

Often, reinforcing feedback is done in person, but we have found that adequate support can be attained by providing charts, telephone calls, and notes (Fox & Sulzer-Azaroff, 1982; Hunt & Sulzer-Azaroff, 1974) and also by encouraging colleagues to provide positive recognition for the newly acquired skills. The advantage of involving colleagues or peers in delivering reinforcement is that the natural social environment begins to assume discriminative control to prompt and support the desired behaviors. For example, such a positive outcome was shown with students by Jones, Young, and Friman (2000) at Flanagans Boys' Home. When peers were taught to focus on the *star of the week* and "… look at the person, smile, report something positive the person said or did during the day and saying something like 'good job' or 'way to go,'" (p. 34), three formerly low social status students with extensive records of antisocial activities became more cooperative.

We strongly recommend that programs not be started until it is certain that staff will be provided with reinforcement at least twice a week during the early phase of program implementation. This immediate and frequent reinforcement is necessary until the new behaviors are well established; otherwise they are likely to disintegrate. The resultant failure will then punish attempts to implement the approach. Later on, the frequency of praise, phone calls, and so forth can be reduced gradually. As Sulzer-Azaroff and Mayer

(1994c) noted, "this occasional intermittent reinforcement and the support provided by the consultees' peers, enables you to reduce the amount of time you need to devote to any one consultee while supporting the durability of change" (p. 92).

The importance of sustained reinforcement must be stressed. This is especially true in attempting to implement preventive programs, because unlike the very discernible immediate reinforcement provided by deterrents and punishment, the reinforcing consequences for prevention are delayed and difficult to detect. Consequently, staff frequently requires supplementary positive reinforcement, from one another, consultants, administrators, their students, and community members, if they are to continue conducting their preventive programs until the programs become embedded in the school's natural environment. Intermittent praise, though, may be sufficient. For example, Cossairt, Hall, and Hopkins (1973) found that teachers use of praise was maintained and even increased when it was in turn praised intermittently by their principals. They concluded that:

> This would seem to indicate that the excuse that principals and supportive staff do not have time for the social reinforcement of teacher behavior is invalid. Operant principles of reinforcement systematically applied would therefore seem to be functional in helping principals and consultants accomplish their primary goals, which should be improved instruction. It would also seem that this could be done with a minimal amount of time and effort (p. 100).

Goal setting is another way to promote initial and enduring improvement in staff performance. This strategy, used in all types of organizations (Fellner & Sulzer-Azaroff, 1984) assists people to progress in increments toward their ultimate objectives (e.g., tailoring instruction to individual student skills and interests; developing and rehearsing classroom rules; planning and conducting reinforcing activities for students; suppressing reprimands, sarcasm, and other forms of punishment). After discovering their current levels of functioning by constructing a baseline composed of repeated measures of the performance of concern, the performer sets a level to be attained during the next few days or weeks that is challenging yet attainable. Achieving a level set as a goal becomes an occasion for feedback and reinforcement. Then a new goal is set and so on until the ultimate objective is accomplished. Reinforcement and feedback are then continued as the newly acquired routine becomes habitual and incorporated into the staff members' daily routine (see Gillat & Sulzer-Azaroff, 1994, for an illustrative example).

EVALUATING THE PROGRAM'S EFFECTIVENESS

Every school is different, just as each student and staff member is unique. Consequently, the only way to determine whether a given prevention program is successful is to conduct a formal evaluation.

As was stated earlier, for aggression we might use office referrals. Another more direct measure would be to observe and record aggressive incidents on the grounds (e.g., hitting). With vandalism we generally have to rely on indirect measures, such as the cost and frequency of damage, which can be misleading. For example, one frequently used method for evaluating the effectiveness of a vandalism program is to compare the cost and frequency of various types of vandalism (i.e., property damage, fire, theft) each month while the program is in effect against cost and frequency figures from previous years (Mayer & Butterworth, 1979). Another method that can be used for evaluating the impact of an intervention to reduce aggression and vandalism is to use a multiple-baseline design across schools (Mayer et al., 1983b). This would involve collecting as accurate as possible baseline data in several schools on episodes of aggression and vandalism and on the severity of vandalism acts, and then implementing the selected intervention first in one, then in another, and perhaps later in yet another of the schools. If the antisocial behavior changes maximally in each school only after intervention is applied, then the evidence favors the intervention rather than some other influence.

We prefer the multiple baseline tactic (Sulzer-Azaroff & Mayer, 1991, 1994a) for evaluating the effectiveness of a vandalism and aggression reduction program. It is a natural way to approach the issue because an evaluator would first want to find out if the problem decreases in one school after the program has been carried out but before proceeding to the next implementation. The most logical approach would be to replicate the presumably successful program in another school to see if similar positive results could be achieved.

One problem we have encountered following program implementation is that people involved tend to scrutinize the occurrences of vandalism more closely than previously, resulting in more accurate reporting (i.e., reporting more episodes of vandalism) than during baseline. Obviously, this can obscure actual improvement to an unknown extent. Two independent reporters are more likely to obtain accurate data throughout baseline and intervention, enhancing the believability of the data (Mayer et al., 1983b). Disagreements can be discussed and resolved following observational recording sessions, and inter-reporter agreement indexes can be calculated. To help reduce errors in reporting school crimes like vandalism, California Assembly Bill 2583 (Chapter 78), which became law on January 1, 1989, stipulated that districts can be fined if a crime report is not submitted or contains intentionally misleading data.

Reducing antisocial behavior is the *outcome* (long range) objective. Intermediary (process) objectives can be evaluated similarly. For example, a small number of teachers can be involved initially in a program designed to increase their use of positive reinforcement, and other teachers added after longer baseline periods. Other evidence of change in performance can also be collected. For example, you might want to record and graph the number of positive notes sent to teachers by administrators, comparing baseline to program rates. Detailed descriptive data of staff training and disciplinary policy changes might also prove helpful in permitting later replication of the program.

IMPLICATIONS FOR THE ROLE AND TRAINING OF THE SCHOOL PSYCHOLOGIST

The factors contributing to antisocial behavior, such as aggression and vandalism, obviously are complex and require a comprehensive approach to evaluation and to intervention and prevention. There are a variety of skills, then, that school psychologists need to possess if they are to work effectively in the area of preventing and reducing antisocial behavior. These include skills in consulting, observing, recording, graphing, selecting and using behavioral strategies, ecobehavioral assessment, and leadership skills, such as being able to persuade, make decisions, take risks, and amass support. The school psychologist must be able to examine behavior both in the school and in the class-rooms, not only in relation to its immediate antecedents and consequences but also in relation to more temporally remote stimuli, such as setting events, the general context of ongoing and prior events, and elements of the physical environment that might contribute to problem behavior. The purpose of doing such an extensive ecobehavioral or functional assessment (Mayer, 1996, 1999) is to help the psychologist to better plan, intervene, and evaluate and to provide more effective support services.

Not only do school psychologists often assess ability, academic skills, learning styles, and interests, but they must be able to provide consultation with teachers, helping the teachers to match assignments and curricula with students' skills, abilities, and interests. School psychologists need to be specialized in individual and group behavior management and goal setting strategies, and to consult, teach, and provide supervision and feedback regarding their use. School psychologists need to know how to analyze the school as an organization within the community. As a result, school psychologists will be able to identify and capitalize on potential support, and will be able to detect and manage potential impediments to change. Finally, their skills must extend to consulting with and actively involving administrators and other specialists, as well as managing their own time, setting their own priorities, and devising a system to reinforce their own behavior.

SUMMARY

Antisocial behavior, such as aggression against others and facilities, is a major problem in many of our schools. Recent research, though, is beginning to give us some answers: Emphasize and implement prevention programs that address the key factors related to promoting antisocial behavior, such as punishment, extinction, and reinforcement. Many of these factors occur within the school and appear to contribute to most of the problem behaviors that occur therein. In other words, as Mayer (in press) has stated, *the school environment appears to be a major contributor to the antisocial behavior that occurs on our school campuses.*

Most school programs that address aggression/vandalism have relied on deterrents and punitive measures. The paradox is that such measures can sometimes inadvertently exacerbate the situation by making the environment more punitive, thereby setting the occasion for increased aggression and vandalism. Thus, deterrents and punitive measures should not be used unless implemented as a temporary expedient and combined with positive practices designed to prevent, reduce, or eliminate the factors within our schools that evoke acts of aggression/vandalism.

A constructive approach to school discipline has been described that is aimed at reducing punitiveness and presumably, as a consequence, aggression/vandalism. Assignments are adjusted to promote individual success and sense of accomplishment, and school is made a more reinforcing place. Constructive discipline (Mayer, 1999) contrasts with traditional discipline approaches in several ways; that is, its reliance on primarily positive consequences, and its clarity and specificity. The first step involves determining a set of specific rules, using student input and administrative approval at the classroom level and including student, staff, and parental input at the school level. Then these rules are to be stated positively, posted in a prominent place, and periodically reviewed. Students are most likely to follow the rules when consequences are applied immediately and consistently for adherence to and violation of the rules. Punitive consequences for rule violations, however, are kept to a minimum, because too many punitive consequences may cause the punishment to lose its effectiveness, as well as provoke the very behavior you seek to reduce.

A triadic framework has been presented that categorized behaviors to be (a) reinforced, (b) dealt with by constructive alternatives to punishment, or (c) punished. This triadic model restricts the use of punishment to major infractions. As a result, punishment will be minimized, resulting in a more positive school environment, less vandalism, and aggression. Similarly, because constructive alternatives, or positive behavioral interventions, are used for minor infractions, students are taught how to behave, not just how not to behave, and student attitudes toward themselves and schools are likely to become more positive.

As with the specification of rules, selection of the actual consequences to be used in the classroom and at the school level should involve both student and teacher input and administrative approval. Educators must be able to choose from a variety of jointly selected reinforcing and punitive consequences to allow for individual student differences. Once a punishing consequence is selected for a student's major infraction, it should be applied immediately and consistently.

Any code of conduct should be viewed as a living document. Because of student, staff, and environmental changes, it needs to be reviewed, and revised as necessary, at least yearly. As the context of the school changes, the conduct code must adjust also, to allow for individual differences.

As Mayer (in press) has stated:

> This approach implies that our efforts should no longer emphasize "treating" students as the source of the problem. Rather, we must be child advocates as we focus on helping teachers and administrators identify and correct the factors within the school that promote antisocial behavior. In other words, as Ysseldyke et al. (1997) point out, *problem behaviors,* rather than being located within the student, *are often due to a "mismatch between*

the characteristics of the learner and those of the instructional environment or the broader home/school contest" (p. 5). Accepting this approach will require a paradigm shift for many educators, who for years have been told that behavior problems originate from within their students.

We now know that school psychologists and other educators can do more than just punish or design deterrents in response to antisocial behavior, and we are in a good position to ensure that a more constructive approach to discipline is applied in our schools. Educators, pupil personnel specialists, students, and society all stand to benefit.

REFERENCES

Barrera, R. D. (1984, August). *Programmed supplemental grammar instruction in the video arcade.* Paper presented at the annual Meeting of the American Psychological Association, Toronto.

Berkowitz, L. (1983). Aversively stimulated aggression: Some parallels and differences in research with animals and humans. *American Psychologist, 38,* 1136-1144.

Brantlinger, E. (1991). Social class distinctions in adolescents' reports of problems and punishment in school. *Behavioral Disorders, 17,* 36-46.

Brodinsky, B. (1980). *AASA critical issues report: Student discipline, problems, and solutions* (Report No. 021-00334). Arlington, VA: American Association of School Administrators.

Butts, J. A., & Snyder, H. N. (1997). *The youngest delinquents: Offenders under age 15.* U.S. Department of Justice, Office of Juvenile Justice and Delinquency Prevention.

Center, D. B., Deitz, S. M., & Kaufman, M. E. (1982). Student ability, task difficulty, and inappropriate classroom behavior: A study of children with behavior disorders. *Behavior Modification, 6,* 355-374.

Conger, R. D. (1982). Behavioral intervention for child abuse. *Behavior Therapist, 5,* 49-53.

Cossairt, A., Hall, R. V., & Hopkins, B. L. (1973). The effects of experimenter's instructions, feedback, and praise on teacher praise and student attending behavior. *Journal of Applied Behavior Analysis, 6,* 89-100.

Dustin, R. (1974). Training for instructional change. *Personnel and Guidance Journal, 52,* 422-427.

Fellner, D. J., & Sulzer-Azaroff, B. (1984). A behavioral analysis of goal setting. *Journal of Organizational Behavior Management, 6,* 33-51.

Fixsen, D. L., Phillips, E. L., & Wolf, M. M. (1973). Achievement place: Experiments in self-government with pre-delinquents. *Journal of Applied Behavior Analysis, 6,* 31-47.

Flaherty, G. (1987). Reducing vandalism by changing the school community. *Thrust for Educational Leadership, 16*(5), 28-30.

Fox, C. J., & Sulzer-Azaroff, B. (1982). *A program to supervise geographically dispersed foster parents' teaching of retarded youth.* Unpublished manuscript.

Gillat, A., & Sulzer-Azaroff, B. (1994). Promoting principals, managerial involvement in institutional improvement. *Journal of Applied Behavior Analysis, 27,* 115-129.

Gold, M., & Mann, D. W. (1982). Alternative schools for troublesome secondary students. *Urban Review, 14,* 305-316.

Goldiamond, I. (1974). Toward a constructional approach to social problems: Ethical and constitutional issues raised by applied behavior analysis. *Behaviorism, 2,* 1-85.

Greenberg, B. (1974). School vandalism: Its effects and paradoxical solutions. *Crime Prevention 1,* 105.

Hart, B., & Risley, T. (1995). *Meaningful differences in the everyday experience of young American children.* Baltimore: Brookes.

Heller, M. C., & White, M. A. (1975). Rates of teacher verbal approval and disapproval to higher and lower ability classes. *Journal of Educational Psychology, 67,* 796–800.

Holden, B., & Sulzer-Azaroff, B. (1972). Schedules of follow-up and their effect upon the maintenance of a prescriptive teaching program. In G. Semb, D. P. Green, R. P. Hawkins, J. Michael, E. L. Phillips, J. A. Sherman, H. Sloane, & D. R. Thomas (Eds.), *Behavior analysis and education—1972.* Lawrence: University of Kansas.

Hunt, S., & Sulzer-Azaroff, B. (1974, September). *Motivating parent participation in home training sessions with pretrainable retardates.* Paper presented at the American Psychological Association, New Orleans.

Ingersoll, S., & LeBoeuf, K. (1997, February). Reaching out to youth out of the education mainstream. *Juvenile Justice Bulletin,* 1–11.

Jones, K. M., Young, M. M., & Friman, P. C. (2000). Increasing peer praise of socially rejected delinquent youth: Effects on cooperation and acceptance. *School Psychology Quarterly, 15,* 30–39.

Krause, D. (1985). Our school C.A.R.E.S. for good behavior. *Principal, 65,* 44–45.

Larson, K. (1994). *Negative school culture.* Office of Special Education Programs, Spring Leadership Conference Executive Report, May, 9–12, p. 8. (Available: Mountain Plains Regional Resource Center, Utah State University, Logan, Utah, 84341.)

Lovitt, T. C., & Curtiss, K. (1969). Academic response rate as a function of teacher- and self-imposed contingencies. *Journal of Applied Behavior Analysis, 2,* 49–53.

MacDonald, W. S., Gallimore, R., & MacDonald, G. (1970). Contingency counseling by school personnel: An economical model of intervention. *Journal of Applied Behavior Analysis, 3,* 175–182.

Mayer, G. R. (1995). Preventing antisocial behavior in the schools. *Journal of Applied Behavior Analysis, 28,* 467–478.

Mayer, G. R. (1996). Conducting a functional assessment and its relevance to intervention. *California School Psychologist, 1,* 29–34.

Mayer, G. R. (1999). Constructive discipline for school personnel. *Education and Treatment of Children, 22,* 36–54.

Mayer, G. R. (2000). *Classroom management: A California resource guide.* Los Angeles: County Office of Education, Division of Student Support Services, Safe Schools Center.

Mayer, G. R. (in press). Antisocial behavior: Its causes and prevention in our schools. *Education and Treatment of Children, 24*(4).

Mayer, G. R., & Butterworth, T. (1979). A preventive approach to school violence and vandalism: An experimental study. *Personnel and Guidance Journal, 57,* 436–441.

Mayer, G. R., & Butterworth, T. (1981). Evaluating a preventive approach to reducing school vandalism. *Phi Delta Kappan, 62,* 498–499.

Mayer, G. B., Butterworth, T., Komoto, T., & Benoit, R. (1983a). The influence of the school principal on the consultant's effectiveness. *Elementary School Guidance & Counseling, 17,* 274–279.

Mayer, G. R., Butterworth, T., Nafpaktitis, M., & Sulzer-Azaroff, B. (1983b). Preventing school vandalism and improving discipline: A three-year study. *Journal of Applied Behavior Analysis, 16,* 355–369.

Mayer, G. R., Butterworth, T., Spaulding, H. L., Hollingsworth, P., Amorim, M., Caldwell-McElroy, C., Nafpaktitis, M., & Perez-Osorio, X. (1983c). *Constructive discipline: Building a climate for learning. A resource manual of programs and strategies.* Downey, CA: Office of the Los Angeles County Superintendent of Schools.

Mayer, G. R., Mitchell, L., Clementi, T., Clement-Robertson, E., Myatt, R., & Bullara, D. T. (1993). A dropout prevention program for at-risk high school students: Emphasizing consulting to promote positive classroom climates. *Education and Treatment of Children, 16,* 135-146.

Mayer, G. R., Nafpaktitis, M., Butterworth, T., & Hollingsworth, P. (1987). A search for the elusive setting events of school vandalism: A correlational study. *Education and Treatment of Children, 10,* 259-270.

Mayer, M. J., & Leone, P. E. (1999). A structural analysis of school violence and disruption: Implications for creating safer schools. *Education and Treatment of Children, 22,* 333-356.

McFadden, A. C., Marsh, G. E., Price, B. J., & Hwang, Y. (1992). A study of race and gender bias in the punishment of school children. *Education and Treatment of Children, 15,* 140-146.

Metzler, C. W., Biglan, A., Rusby, J. C., & Sprague, J. R. (in press). Evaluation of a comprehensive behavior management program to improve school-wide positive behavior support. *Education and Treatment of Children.*

Moore, W. L., & Cooper, H. (1984). Correlations between teacher and student backgrounds and teacher perceptions of discipline problems and disciplinary techniques. *Discipline, 5,* 1-7.

Mullendore, P. (1981). Program to divert dollars lost to crime. *Campus Strife, 2,* 4-5.

Munk, D. D., & Repp, A. C. (1994). The relationship between instructional variables and problem behavior: A review. *Exceptional Children, 60,* 390-401.

Nafpaktitis, M., Mayer, G. R., & Butterworth, T. (1985). Natural rates of teacher approval and disapproval and their relation to student behavior in intermediate school classrooms. *Journal of Educational Psychology, 77,* 362-367.

Nevin, J. A. (1988). Behavioral momentum and the partial reinforcement effect. *Psychological Bulletin, 103,* 44-56.

O'Leary, S. G., & Dubey, D. R. (1979). Applications of self-control procedures by children: A review. *Journal of Applied Behavior Analysis, 12,* 449-465.

Puritz, P., & Shang, W. W. L. (1998, December). Innovative approaches to juvenile indigent defense. *OJJDP Juvenile Justice Bulletin* 1-8.

Scrimger, G. C., & Elder, R. (1981). *Alternatives to vandalism: Cooperation or wreckreation.* Sacramento, CA: School Safety Center, California Department of Justice.

Shaw, S. R., & Braden, J. P. (1990). Race and gender bias in the administration of corporal punishment. *School Psychology Review, 19,* 378-383.

Shores, R. E., Jack, S. L., Gunter, P. L., Ellis, D. N., DeBriere, J. J., & Wehby, J. H. (1993). Classroom interactions of children with behavior disorders. *Journal of Emotional and Behavioral Disorders, 1,* 27-29.

Snyder, H. N., & Sickmund, M. (1995). *Juvenile offenders and victims: A focus on violence. Statistics summary.* Washington, DC: U.S. Office of Justice, Office of Juvenile Justice and Delinquency Prevention.

Sulzer-Azaroff, B., & Mayer, G. R. (1991). *Behavioral analysis for lasting change.* New York: Harcourt Brace.

Sulzer-Azaroff, B., & Mayer, G. R. (1994a). *Achieving educational excellence: Behavior analysis for school personnel.* San Marcos, CA: Western Image.

Sulzer-Azaroff, B., & Mayer, G. R. (1994b). *Achieving educational excellence: Behavior analysis for improving instruction.* San Marcos, CA: Western Image.

Sulzer-Azaroff, B., & Mayer, G. R. (1994c). *Achieving educational excellence: Behavior analysis for achieving classroom and school-wide behavior change.* San Marcos, CA: Western Image.

Taylor-Greene, S., Brown, K., Nelson, L., Longton, J., Gassman, T., Cohen, J., Swartz, J. Horner, R. H., Sugai, G., & Hall, S. (1997). School-wide behavioral support: Starting the year off right. *Journal of Behavioral Education, 7,* 99-112.

Thomas, J. D., Presland, I. E., Grant, M. D., & Glynn, T. (1978). Natural rates of teacher approval and disapproval in grade-7 classrooms. *Journal of Applied Behavior Analysis, 11,* 91-94.

Tobin, T., Sugai, G., & Colvin, G. (1996). Patterns in middle school discipline records. *Journal of Emotional and Behavioral Disorders, 4,* 82-94.

Touchette, P. E., MacDonald, R. F., & Langer, S. N. (1985). A scatter plot for identifying stimulus control of problem behavior. *Journal of Applied Behavior Analysis, 18,* 343-351.

U.S. Department of Education. (2000). *Effective alternative strategies: Grant competition to reduce student suspensions and expulsions and ensure educational progress of suspended and expelled students.* Washington, DC: Safe and drug-free schools program.

Van Acker, R., Grant, S. H., & Henry, D. (1996). Teacher and student behavior as a function of risk for aggression. *Education and Treatment of Children, 19,* 316-334.

Wehby, J. H., Symons, F. J., & Shores, R. E. (1995). A descriptive analysis of aggressive behavior in classrooms for children with emotional and behavioral disorders. *Behavioral Disorders, 20,* 87-105.

White, M. A. (1975). Natural rates of teacher approval and disapproval in the classroom. *Journal of Applied Behavior Analysis, 8,* 367-372.

Wyatt, W. J., & Hawkins, R. P. (1987). Rates of teachers' verbal approval and disapproval: Relationship to grade level, classroom activity, student behavior, and teacher characteristics. *Behavior Modification, 11,* 27-51.

Ysseldyke, J., Dawson, P., Lehr, C., Reschly, D., Reynolds, M., & Telzrow, C. (1997). *School psychology: A blueprint for training and practice II.* Bethesda, MD: National Association of School Psychologists.

CHAPTER 32

Depression in Youth: Epidemiology, Identification, and Intervention

John R. Seeley, Paul Rohde, and Peter M. Lewinsohn
Oregon Research Institute

Gregory N. Clarke
Kaiser Permanente Center for Health Research, Portland, Oregon

INTRODUCTION

Depression is among the most common of psychiatric disorders in adults (cf. Kessler, McGonagle, Swartz, Blazer, & Nelson, 1993) and in adolescents (Lewinsohn, Hops, Roberts, Seeley, & Andrews, 1993). Recent findings based on adults indicate that for a large proportion of individuals, depression first begins in adolescence (for review, see Essau & Petermann, 1999). Depression seriously impacts the functioning of adolescents and adults (e.g., in school, work, family, and social domains). Indeed, the World Health Organization (2000) projects that depression will become the leading cause of disability and the second leading contributor to the global burden of disease by the year 2020. Given the high prevalence and associated impairment of youth depression, research on epidemiology, etiology, and intervention within this age group has increased dramatically over the past two decades. Unfortunately, despite recent efforts, a large proportion of youths who suffer from depression go undetected and do not receive adequate treatment.

In this chapter, we describe a program of research on adolescent depression that has been conducted since the mid-1980s at the Oregon Research Institute, the Oregon Health Sciences University, and the Kaiser Permanente Center for Health Research. Our program of research is based on Lewinsohn's earlier work with adult depression (Lewinsohn, Antonuccio, Steinmetz, & Teri, 1984; Lewinsohn, Hoberman, Teri, & Hautzinger, 1985; Lewinsohn, Muñoz, Youngren, & Zeiss, 1986) and is consistent with the Institute of Medicine's (IOM) paradigm on the development of successful preventive interventions for mental disorders (Mrazek & Haggerty, 1994). The IOM paradigm consists of the following five stages: (1) identify the problem or disorder and review information to determine its extent; (2) determine the risk and protective factors that may be amenable to intervention, (3) conduct pilot studies and efficacy trials aimed at reducing the risk factors and promoting the protective factors, (4) conduct effectiveness trials of the intervention in real-world conditions, and (5) implement the preventive intervention in large-scale community campaigns. In the following sections, we present our progress to date in addressing the various stages of the IOM prevention paradigm. In the last section, we point to future directions for research in order to reach the final stage of the IOM prevention paradigm.

SCOPE OF THE PROBLEM

Since 1985, we have been conducting a large, prospective, epidemiologic study on adolescent depression and other mental disorders, entitled the Oregon Adolescent Depression Project (OADP). Participants were randomly selected in three cohorts from nine senior high schools representative of urban and rural districts in western Oregon. Sampling was proportional to the size of the school, grade within the school, and gender within the grade. A total of 1,709 adolescents completed the initial assessment (T1), which included a diagnostic interview and a questionnaire assessment. Approximately one year later (T2), 1,507 (88%) of the participants returned for a second diagnostic interview and questionnaire assessment. Participants were assessed on a comprehensive array of psychosocial constructs either known to be associated with depression in adults or hypothesized to be important with respect to depression in adolescents. We recently completed a third diagnostic assessment (T3) with a randomly selected subset of OADP participants ($n = 941$) near the time of their 24th birthday and are currently in the process of collecting a fourth diagnostic assessment (T4) from the participants around their 30th birthday.

Average age of the OADP sample at T1 was 16.6 ($SD = 1.2$, range = 14–18). Slightly over half of the participants (53%) were female; 91% were White; 12% had repeated a grade in school; 53% were living with both biological parents at the time of the T1 interview, and an additional 18% were living with a biological parent and a step-parent. Most participants resided in households in which one or both parents worked as a minor professional or professional (for more detail, see Lewinsohn et al., 1993).

Diagnostic information regarding current and past disorders as per the Diagnostic and Statistical Manual of Mental Disorders (DSM-III-R; American Psychiatric Association, 1987; DSM-IV; American Psychiatric Association, 1994) was collected using the adolescent report on the Schedule for Affective Disorders and Schizophrenia for School-Age Children (K-SADS; Orvaschel, Puig-Antich, Chambers, Tabrizi, & Johnson, 1982) at the point of entry into the study, and in conjunction with the Longitudinal Interval Follow-up Evaluation (LIFE; Keller et al., 1987) at subsequent observation points. Interrater reliability of the interviews was high and comparable to what has been found in other studies (e.g., kappas generally greater than .80).

Epidemiology of Depression

Based on the DSM-IV classification system, depressive disorders include major depressive disorder (MDD) and dysthymia. MDD among children and adolescents has the same symptoms and criteria for diagnosis as adults. To meet criteria for MDD, an individual must have experienced five or more symptoms during the same two-week period. At least one of the symptoms must be either a depressed mood (or irritable mood for children and adolescents) or loss of interest or pleasure. The other symptoms include changes in weight or failure to make necessary weight gains during childhood; sleep problems; psychomotor agitation or retardation; fatigue or loss of energy; feelings of worthlessness or excessive guilt; difficulty concentrating or indecisiveness; and repeated suicidal ideation or plans for suicide, as well as attempts. The essential feature of dysthymia in children and adolescents is a chronically depressed mood that occurs for most of the day, for more days than not, and for at least one year (two years for adults). In addition, while depressed, two or more of the following six symptoms must be present: poor appetite or overeating, insomnia or hypersomnia, low energy or fatigue, low self-esteem, poor concentration or difficulty making decisions, and feelings of hopelessness.

Data from the OADP provide estimates of the basic parameters of epidemiology including *point prevalence* (i.e., percentage in an episode of disorder at the time of the assessment), *lifetime prevalence* (i.e., percentage who have experienced an episode during their lifetime), and *incidence* (i.e., percentage who are not depressed at the beginning of an observation period but who develop an episode during a specified period of time). Incidence rates are customarily divided into *first incidence* (i.e., percentage who develop an episode for the first time during the observation interval) and *recurrence* (i.e., percentage with a previous episode who develop another episode during the interval). From a public health perspective, the total incidence rate is important for planning the delivery of mental health services because it indicates how many individuals in the population will become depressed during a certain time period.

Epidemiologic data from the OADP are shown in Table 1, on page 888. As can be seen, depression is surprisingly common in adolescence. The lifetime prevalence rates of MDD for the OADP participants are especially high. Conversely, the lifetime prevalence of dysthymia was only 3% during adolescence. It should be noted that our prevalence rates for adolescent MDD are comparable to the rates that have been reported for adults in more recent studies, such as the National Comorbidity Study (Kessler et al., 1993). Our tentative conclusion is that the prevalence of depression in older adolescents is at adult levels. Previous research reporting much lower rates of depression in younger children (e.g., Rutter, 1976) suggests a substantial increase in the prevalence of depression from childhood to adolescence.

Gender differences in the rate of depression among adults have been reported many times, with a typical ratio of 2:1 (e.g., Nolen-Hoeksema, 1990). Conversely, most studies of preadolescent children find no gender difference in rates of depression or a slight elevation in boys compared to girls (e.g., Garrison et al., 1997). Gender differences in

TABLE 1

Prevalence and Incidence of Major Depressive Disorder (MDD) and Dysthymia From the Oregon Adolescent Depression Project

	Total Sample		Female Sample		Male Sample	
	MDD	Dysthymia	MDD	Dysthymia	MDD	Dysthymia
Point Prevalence						
T1	2.9	0.5	3.4	0.6	2.0	0.5
T2	3.1	0.1	3.6	0.3	2.6	0.0
Lifetime Prevalence						
T1	18.5	3.2	24.8	4.0	11.6	2.3
T2	24.0	3.0	31.6	4.1	15.2	1.7
One-Year Incidence						
T1-T2						
Total incidence	7.8	0.1	10.4	0.1	4.8	0.0
First incidence	5.7	0.1	7.1	0.1	4.4	0.0
Recurrence	17.9	0.0	21.1	0.0	9.1	0.0

the onset of MDD are shown in Figure 1, with girls being twice as likely as boys to become depressed. Prorating our results, we estimate that approximately 28% of adolescents will have experienced an episode of MDD by age 19. Comparing our results with other studies suggests that the gender difference in MDD levels probably emerges in the relatively small window between the ages of 12 and 14 (e.g., Nolen-Hoeksema & Girgus, 1994).

The mean age of MDD onset was 14.9 years (SD = 2.8); median onset was 15.5. The rates of depression onset in childhood are low, doubling from an annual incidence rate of 1% to 2% at age 13 and from 3% to 7% at age 15. Figure 1 also shows that the onset of depression begins to escalate around the age of 12 for girls and 14 for boys. The mean duration of episodes of MDD was 26 weeks, with a range of 2 to 520 weeks (Lewinsohn, Clarke, Seeley, & Rohde, 1994). The duration was highly skewed, with a median duration of 8.0 weeks. Longer MDD episodes were associated with earlier onset, suicidal ideation, and seeking mental health treatment.

Of the adolescents who recovered from the depressive episode, 5% experienced another episode within six months, 12% within one year, and approximately 33% within four years. Shorter time to MDD recurrence was associated with prior suicidal ideation, attempts, and with later first onset. Formerly depressed female adolescents were more likely to have another episode between the two assessment points, although the mean time to recurrence for female and male adolescents who relapsed did not significantly differ. Among 26 OADP participants who experienced three episodes of

FIGURE 1

Cumulative Proportion Experiencing an Episode of Major Depressive Disorder as a Function of Age and Gender

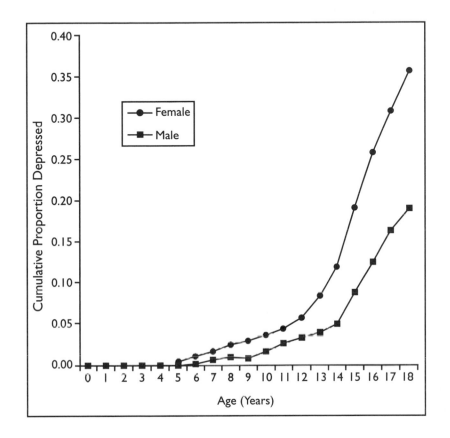

MDD by T2, the amount of well-time from second to third episode was significantly less than from first to second episode (13 versus 27 weeks, $p < .05$).

Risk Factors for Depression

We have presented findings regarding risk factors for adolescent depression previously (Lewinsohn, Roberts, et al., 1994; Lewinsohn, Gotlib, & Seeley, 1995). In addition, Lewinsohn and Essau (in press) provide a recent review of the risk and protective factors for adolescent depression. Risk factors include female gender; family history of depression; pubertal timing; elevated depressive symptomatology; depressotypic cognitive style; poor physical health; major life events; daily hassles; poor academic functioning; conflict with parents; low social support from family; poor coping skills; low self-esteem; low self-rated social competence; emotional reliance on others; externalizing behavior problems; cigarette smoking; internalizing behavior problems; and a previous history of depression, anxiety disorders, or suicide attempts. To summarize our risk factor research, the prototypical adolescent most likely to become depressed is a 16-year-old girl who had an early or later puberty. She is experiencing low self-esteem, poor body image, feelings of worthlessness, pessimism, and self-blame. She is self-conscious and overly dependent on others, although she feels that she is receiving little support from her family. She is experiencing both major and minor stressors, such as conflicts with parents, physical illness, poor school performance, and relationship breakups; she is coping poorly with the ramifications of these events. Other manifestations of psychopathology—including anxiety disorders, smoking, and past suicidality—are probably present. In addition, it is likely that she has family members who have a history of depression.

Comorbidity of Depression

Interest in the co-occurrence, or comorbidity, of psychiatric disorders is a rather recent phenomenon. First introduced into the medical literature by Feinstein (1970), comorbidity refers to the fact that individuals with one disorder may be at elevated risk for a second disorder and this co-occurrence may affect the course of the two disorders. Comorbidity is said to exist either when persons with a current disorder have an elevated prevalence of other current disorders (concurrent comorbidity), or when persons with a history of a disorder have an elevated prevalence of other disorders (lifetime comorbidity). The study of comorbidity has been an active area of our research and some selected findings regarding lifetime comorbidity with depression are presented next.

Among adolescents with unipolar depression, approximately 80% experienced MDD by itself or in conjunction with nonmood disorders, 10% experienced dysthymia without MDD, and the remaining 10% experienced MDD with lifetime comorbid dysthymia (Lewinsohn, Rohde, Seeley, & Hops, 1991), a condition that has been termed "double depression." Gender differences in the patterns of MDD-dysthymia comorbidity were nonsignificant. Almost half (43%) of adolescents with MDD also had a lifetime occurrence of a nonmood disorder at T1. Rates of comorbidity in depressed adults are roughly comparable or slightly higher, estimated to be approximately 60% (e.g., Blazer, Kessler, McGonagle, & Swartz, 1994). Depression during adolescence was significantly comorbid with eating disorders (odds ratio [OR] = 9.0), alcohol and drug abuse/dependence (OR = 4.5), anxiety disorders (OR = 4.4), and disruptive behavior disorders (OR = 2.2). Among comorbid cases, 80% of the youth developed the MDD episode *after* the other disorder.

Given the high degree of comorbidity, further study of the risk factors for "pure" and comorbid depressive episodes is needed. Many variables thought to be associated with depression may in fact only be risk factors for the comorbid disorder, as opposed to depression per se (Lewinsohn, Gotlib, & Seeley, 1997). Although the occurrence of other disorders given an episode of MDD is much greater than expected by chance, the degree of comorbidity with depression appears to be lower than comorbidity of some other mental disorders. Comorbidity rates for anxiety, attention–deficit/hyperactivity disorder (ADHD), conduct disorder, oppositional defiant disorder, alcohol abuse/dependence, drug abuse/dependence, and eating disorders are substantially higher (60–90%). Given adolescent psychopathology, psychiatric comorbidity appears to be the rule rather than the exception.

Most combinations of psychiatric disorders have serious negative consequences on functioning (Lewinsohn, Rohde, & Seeley, 1995; Seeley, Lewinsohn, & Rohde, 1997). Areas of functioning that are especially impacted by psychiatric comorbidity in adolescents include academic problems, mental health treatment utilization, and suicide attempts, followed by impaired role functioning and increased conflict with parents. Regarding specific patterns of comorbidity with depression, the co-occurrence of MDD and alcohol or drug abuse/dependence appears to be the most deleterious combination, increasing the likelihood of treatment utilization, suicide attempts, impaired role functioning, and academic problems. The occurrence of a comorbid anxiety disorder has the smallest impact on MDD, increasing only the likelihood of treatment utilization. It may be confidently assumed that depressed adolescents with multiple diagnoses are overrepresented in clinical practice.

Suicidal Behavior

Given our focus on depression, the occurrence of suicidal ideation and suicide attempts has been an area of particular interest and we have previously summarized our research on suicidal behavior in this age group (Lewinsohn, Rohde, & Seeley, 1996). Consistent with other studies, we found that suicide attempts almost always occur in the context of significant psychopathology. For example, 96% of the adolescents who made a suicide attempt between the T1 and T2 assessment points had a concurrent diagnosis. Suicide attempts were most highly associated with MDD, alcohol and drug use disorders, disruptive behavior disorders, and, to a lesser extent, anxiety disorders. The likelihood of a suicide attempt in adolescence increases greatly given the presence of multiple psychiatric disorders. Among the depressed adolescents, 41% reported suicidal ideation. Suicidal ideation was associated with chronic, long-lasting and recurrent MDD episodes. Twenty-one percent of the adolescents with MDD reported a past suicide attempt.

Treatment Utilization

Although 61% of the OADP adolescents with MDD reported receiving some type of treatment (Lewinsohn, Rohde, & Seeley, 1998), most of these treatments were relatively unsystematic and brief, and did not make use of recent research developments in the cognitive-behavioral treatment of depression (Hibbs & Jensen, 1996). Treatment in this population has typically been quite brief; we found that 22% of the treated adolescents received one or two sessions, and 27% received three to seven sessions. Unfortunately, those who received treatment were as likely to relapse into another episode of depression during young adulthood as those who had not received treatment

(Lewinsohn et al., 1998). We believe that this nonsignificant difference is probably due to greater depression severity in youth who sought treatment compared to that in depressed youth who did not.

ASSESSMENT AND IDENTIFICATION

Several questions remain regarding the assessment of depression and other psychopathology in youth. One important issue concerns the necessary sources of information. There is longstanding and widespread agreement that the assessment of child psychopathology should be based on multiple sources of information, generally including the child and the parent and, if possible, a teacher. Multiple informants are thought to be useful for several reasons: (a) young children may be developmentally unable to provide certain kinds of information in a reliable and valid way, (b) children may deny or minimize undesirable symptoms, (c) children and adults may have different thresholds for considering deviant behaviors to be problematic, and (d) parents may have limited knowledge of the full range of situations in which the problematic behavior occurs. Because parents of the first 281 OADP participants at T1 also were interviewed as part of the assessments, we had an opportunity to contribute to this issue (Cantwell, Lewinsohn, Rohde, & Seeley, 1997). We found that parent-adolescent agreement varies widely as a function of disorder. Most importantly, parent-adolescent agreement for a diagnosis of MDD was poor (kappa = .31) because of lower rates reported by parents. Adolescents reported 54 cases of MDD, of which the parents were aware of only 16 (in other words, 30% cases). Conversely, 26 parents reported that their son or daughter had met lifetime criteria for MDD; 16 (62%) of the cases were corroborated by the adolescent. In addition, interviewers tended to have less confidence in diagnoses of MDD via only parent-report compared to diagnoses of MDD based only on adolescent report. Because of the low number of dysthymic cases, we were unable to address this issue regarding dysthymia.

In general, adolescents appear to be the primary source of valid information regarding MDD, other internalizing disorders, and drug and alcohol abuse. Gathering data from parents on these disorders would have generated relatively few additional cases. On the other hand, parents appear to be the primary source of valid information for diagnosing ADHD and oppositional defiant disorder. Our research suggests that multiple informants are valuable but the diagnostician should seldom rely exclusively on parental report. If one is forced to rely on a single source of information, assessing the adolescent will detect the greatest number of cases of depression.

Diagnostic Interviews

Standardized and comprehensive interviews for children and adolescents include the K-SADS, the Diagnostic Interview Schedule for Children (DISC; Costello, Edelbrock, & Costello, 1985; Piacentini et al., 1993), the Diagnostic Interview for Children and Adolescents (DICA; Herjanic & Reich, 1982), and the Child and

Adolescent Psychiatric Assessment (CAPA; Angold et al., 1995). A review of these interviews is provided by Essau, Hakim-Larson, Crocker, and Petermann (1999). We encourage a comprehensive assessment of all MDD criteria as per the DSM-IV as a way of gauging the severity of the depressive disorder. In addition, given the frequent occurrence of comorbid psychopathology in depressed adolescents, we strongly advise the use of semi-structured interviews to consistently and systematically assess a broad range of mental disorders, including alcohol/drug abuse and dependence, post-traumatic stress disorder and other anxiety disorders, conduct and oppositional defiant disorders, and ADHD.

Self-Report Depression Questionnaires

In addition to semistructured interviews, several questionnaires are available to assess for the presence of depressive symptoms. These instruments focus on current depressive symptomatology and may be particularly valuable for tracking change over time. In addition to monitoring change, self-report questionnaires are useful for screening and for therapeutic purposes as they identify specific problem areas that need attention. Screening for depression is especially important because adolescents may not readily volunteer that they are severely depressed or suicidal, although they do appear willing to admit these difficulties if asked directly (Reynolds, 1986).

For older adolescents, we recommend the Center for Epidemiological Studies' Depression Scale (CES-D; Radloff, 1977), which is in the public domain, and the Beck Depression Inventory (BDI; Beck, Ward, Mendelson, Mock, & Erbaugh, 1961). The BDI was recently revised to correspond to DSM-IV symptom criteria (BDI-II; Beck, Steer, & Brown, 1996) and is appropriate for adolescents aged 13 years or older. Although the CES-D and BDI were developed for use with adults, they are easy to administer and have been shown to be reliable and valid screeners for depression in adolescent samples (Roberts, Lewinsohn, & Seeley, 1991). Other youth self-report measures include the Dimensions of Depression Profile for Children and Adolescents (Harter & Nowakowski, 1987), the Reynolds Adolescent Depression Scale (RADS; Reynolds, 1987a), the Children's Depression Inventory (Kovacs, 1985), and the Mood and Feelings Questionnaire (Angold et al., 1987). Detailed descriptions and summaries of the psychometric properties of these instruments have been presented by Reynolds (1994) and Essau et al. (1999).

Multistage Identification

Depression screening tests are usually employed as the first stage of a multistage process (Reynolds, 1991) in which those who score above a prespecified cutoff are identified as putative cases. Screening can serve as an efficient and effective first step in large settings, such as schools. The identified youth may be given another screening at a later date using a serial screening strategy. In the final stage, a semistructured diagnostic interview (e.g., K-SADS) is administered and from that a definitive diagnosis is established. The screener should represent a fast, economical, and valid way of identifying as many cases in the population as possible, without diagnostically interviewing everyone. Screeners are usually evaluated in terms of sensitivity (proportion of cases who meet criteria for depression identified by the screener), specificity (proportion who do *not* meet criteria for depression identified by the screener), positive predictive value (PPV, proportion of true cases among those identified by the screener as cases), and negative predictive value (NPV, proportion of true noncases among those identified by the screener as noncases). Optimal CES-D cutpoints for identifying current MDD were 24 for female adolescents and 22 for male adolescents; comparable BDI cutpoints were 11 and 15 for female and male adolescents, respectively (Roberts et al., 1991). Sensitivity for identifying clinical depression was 84% for both the CES-D and BDI, with a specificity of 75% or greater. Large-scale screening procedures that have been developed for adults, such as the National Depression Screening Day, should be expanded to include school-aged children, especially adolescents.

Assessment of Suicidal Behavior

We strongly recommend that the assessment of past and current suicidal behavior (ideation and attempts) be a routine component of assessment procedures with distressed adolescents. Schools would be an ideal setting for conducting such assessments. A review of the suicide assessment measures for adolescents is available (Garrison, Lewinsohn, Marsteller, Langhinrichsen, & Lann, 1991). Recommended self-report measures of suicidal ideation include the Suicidal Ideation Questionnaire (Reynolds, 1987b), which has two forms specifically developed for adolescents (grades 7–9 and 10–12), and the Beck Scale for Suicide Ideation (Beck & Steer, 1991). In addition, we have developed a very brief, four-item screener that is answered using the CES-D format: (1) I had thoughts about death; (2) I thought about killing myself; (3) I felt that my family and friends would be better off if I was dead; and (4) I felt that I would kill myself (Lewinsohn et al., 1996). To be rated positive on the screener, the item had to be endorsed as occurring on the two higher scale points (i.e., 2 = occasionally/a moderate amount of time; 3 = most/all of the time during the past week) rather than on the two lower scale points (i.e., 0 = rarely/none of the time; 1 = some/a little of the time).

Based on a review of the suicide assessment literature, we wanted to develop an assessment tool that would test the hypothesis that suicidal behaviors could be broadly defined along a continuum from positive life-enhancing to negative life-threatening behaviors. The questionnaire we developed, entitled the Life Attitudes Schedule (LAS; Lewinsohn, Langhinrichsen-Rohling, et al., 1995), deals with suicidal behavior at the most general level. The LAS assesses a broad range of suicidal behaviors that are categorized into death-related, health-related, injury-related, and self-related content areas. The 96-item LAS measures actions, thoughts, and feelings on a continuum ranging from positive (life-enhancing) to negative (life-threatening) behaviors. The LAS is a psychometrically sound instrument with robust internal consistency and test–retest reliability. A 24-item LAS Short Form also has been developed (Rohde, Lewinsohn, Seeley,

& Langhinrichsen-Rohling, 1996). Versions of the LAS, along with psychometric data and sample norms, are available from the authors upon request.

THEORETICAL MODEL OF DEPRESSION

Our research has been guided by a social learning conceptualization that was developed on the basis of findings with adults (Lewinsohn, Hoberman, et al., 1985). In this framework, depression is conceptualized as the end result of environmentally initiated changes in behavior, affect, and cognitions. Antecedent risk factors (e.g., macro- and microstressors) are assumed to trigger the depressogenic process by disrupting important adaptive behavior patterns. If such disruptions lead to increased levels of aversive experiences, they shift the quality of a person's life in the direction of more negative and fewer positive interactions. The person's inability to reverse this trend is hypothesized to lead to increased dysphoria, which in turn leads to the many negative cognitive and behavioral changes associated with clinical depression. Individual differences may moderate the impact of antecedent events in setting off the events that lead to depression. These characteristics, which can be divided into vulnerabilities and protective factors, are hypothesized to act additively and interactively with each other and with other stages in the cycle. The model allows for many points of entry into the chain of events leading to depression and thus allows for a multiplicity of "causes," each of which is contributory but not essential. The model also allows for many points of intervention such as changing (a) depressogenic cognitions and behaviors, (b) mood state, and (c) parent-child interactions.

Other theoretical models of depression include self-control theory (Rehm, 1977), learned helplessness theory (Seligman, 1975), cognitive theory (Beck, 1967), and family theory (Beardslee, 1990). These theoretical models of depression have been reviewed previously (e.g., Gladstone & Beardslee, 2000; Reynolds, 1991; Stark, 1990).

INTERVENTIONS FOR YOUTH DEPRESSION

The study of psychosocial treatments for depression in adolescents has become an active area of research and clinical attention, with over a dozen treatment studies for adolescent depression generally indicating positive results (reviewed by Birmaher et al., 1996a; Birmaher, Ryan, Williamson, Brent, & Kaufman, 1996b; Lewinsohn & Clarke, 1999; Reinecke, Ryan, & DuBois, 1998; Weisz, Valeri, McCarty, & Moore, 1999). Cognitive-behavioral therapy (CBT) has been shown to be superior to no treatment or wait-list control conditions (Brent et al., 1997; Kahn, Kehle, Jenson, & Clark, 1990; Kroll, Harrington, Jayson, Fraser, & Gowers, 1996; Reynolds & Coats, 1986; Stark, Reynolds, & Kaslow, 1987; Vostanis, Feehan, Grattan, & Bickerton, 1996; Wood, Harrington, & Moore, 1996). However, the results have been equivocal when CBT is compared to nonspecific alternative treatments such as relaxation training. Individual CBT was found to be comparable to interpersonal psychotherapy for adolescents and superior to wait-list control in a sample of 71 depressed Puerto Rican adolescents

(Rosselló & Bernal, 1999). Brent et al. (1997) contrasted individual CBT, systemic behavior family therapy, and individual nondirective supportive therapy in 107 clinically referred depressed adolescents. CBT showed a lower rate of MDD posttreatment compared to supportive therapy, and higher remission (no MDD and consecutively low BDI scores) compared to both of the other two treatments. However, by the end of a two-year follow-up period, no differential effects for the three treatments were found (Birmaher et al., 2000), with 80% of patients in all treatments recovering and 30% experiencing depression recurrence. CBT in the form of bibliotherapy also has been shown to be effective, in comparison to wait-list controls, for adolescents with mild and moderate depressive symptomatology (Ackerson, Scogin, McKendree-Smith, & Lyman, 1998). As summarized next in this chapter, our own program of research has shown the Adolescent Coping with Depression (CWD-A) course to be efficacious in treating depression in older (ages 14–18) community-residing adolescents.

The Adolescent Coping With Depression Course

Our intervention approach is rooted in behavioral (e.g., Ferster, 1966; Lewinsohn, Weinstein, & Shaw, 1969) as well as cognitive formulations of depression (e.g., Beck, 1967; Ellis & Harper, 1961; Seligman, 1975). The primary goal of cognitive therapy is to help the depressed individual become aware of pessimistic and negative thoughts, depressotypic beliefs, and causal attributions in which the person blames himself or herself for failures but does not take credit for successes. Once these depressotypic patterns are recognized, the individual is taught how to substitute more constructive cognitions for these destructive ones. The primary goal of behavior therapy for depression is to increase engagement in behaviors that elicit positive reinforcement and that avoid negative reinforcement from the environment. The CWD-A course combines cognitive and behavioral strategies aimed at ameliorating the types of problems that have been shown to be troublesome for depressed individuals (e.g., pessimism; internal, global, and stable attributions for failure; low self-esteem; low engagement in pleasant activities; social withdrawal; anxiety and tension; low social support; and increased conflict). The treatment incorporates other elements shared by cognitive-behavioral treatments, such as the focus on specific and current actions and cognitions as targets for change, structured intervention sessions, repeated practice of skills, use of rewards and contracts, homework assignments, and a relatively small number of therapy sessions.

Our approach rests on an underlying theoretical model of depression presented earlier, which assumes that multiple causal factors can contribute to the outcome of depression, none of which by themselves are necessary or sufficient preconditions. The CWD-A course is based on the premise that teaching adolescents a variety of coping skills and strategies will allow them to counteract the diverse putative causal factors that contribute to their depressive episode and deal more effectively with the problems posed by their environment.

The CWD-A was originally adapted from the adult version of the CWD course (Lewinsohn et al., 1984). In modifying the course for use with adolescents, in-session material and homework assignments were simplified, experiential learning opportunities (e.g., role plays) were enhanced, and problem-solving skills were added to the curriculum. The CWD-A course materials are available for free via the Internet (*www.kpchr.org/acwd/acwd.html*).

The CWD-A course consists of 16 two-hour sessions conducted over an eight-week period for mixed-gender groups of up to 10 adolescents. Each participant receives a workbook that provides structured learning tasks, short quizzes, and homework forms. To encourage generalization of skills to everyday situations, adolescents are given homework assignments, which are reviewed at the beginning of the subsequent session.

Given that parents are an integral part of the adolescent's social system and may contribute to the onset and maintenance of depression, a parallel group intervention for the parents of depressed adolescents was developed (Lewinsohn, Rohde, Hops, & Clarke, 1991). The parent course has two primary goals: (a) inform parents of the CWD-A material in order to encourage support and reinforcement of the adolescent's use of skills, and (b) teach parents the communication and problem-solving skills being taught to their son or daughter. Parents meet with a separate therapist weekly for 2-hour sessions conducted at the same time as the teen group. Two joint sessions are held in the seventh week during which the adolescents and the parents practice these skills on issues that are salient to each family. Workbooks have been developed for the parents to guide them through the sessions.

Components of the CWD-A Course

Guidelines for the group, the rationale for treatment, and the "social learning" view of depression (Lewinsohn, Steinmetz-Breckenridge, Antonuccio, & Teri, 1985) are presented in the first session. From the very beginning, participants are taught to monitor their mood to provide baseline data and a method for demonstrating changes in mood as a result of learning new skills and engaging in activities. As shown in Figure 2, on page 898, the remaining sessions focus on teaching the various skills.

Increasing social skills. Depressed individuals are often deficient in social skills. To remedy this problem, training in basic conversation techniques, planning social activities, and strategies for making friends is spread throughout the course and provides a foundation upon which to build other essential skills (e.g., communication).

Increasing pleasant activities. Sessions designed to increase pleasant activities are based on the assumption that relatively low rates of positive reinforcement are critical antecedents of depressive episodes (Lewinsohn, Biglan, & Zeiss, 1976). To increase pleasant activities, adolescents are taught basic self-change skills: (a) self-monitoring to establish a baseline, (b) setting realistic goals, (c) developing a plan for behavior change, and (d) self-reinforcement for achieving the goals of their plan. The Pleasant Events Schedule (MacPhillamy & Lewinsohn, 1982), a comprehensive list of potentially pleasant activities which has been adapted for use with adolescents, provides each participant with an individualized list of activities to be targeted for increase.

FIGURE 2

Overview of the Adolescent Coping With Depression (CWD) Course

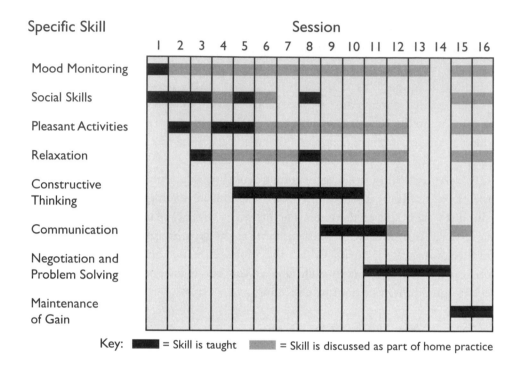

Key: ■■■ = Skill is taught   ▓▓▓ = Skill is discussed as part of home practice

Decreasing anxiety. Relaxation training with the Jacobson (1929) progressive muscle relaxation procedure is provided. A less conspicuous deep-breathing method (Benson, 1975) is subsequently taught for use in more public settings. Relaxation training is provided because many depressed individuals also are anxious, which may reduce the potential enjoyability of many pleasant, especially social, activities.

Reducing depressogenic cognitions. Elements of interventions developed by Beck and his colleagues (e.g., Beck, Rush, Shaw, & Emery, 1979) for identifying, challenging, and changing negative thoughts and irrational beliefs have been adapted and simplified. Cartoon strips with popular characters that appeal to adolescents (e.g., Garfield the cat) are used to illustrate depressotypic thoughts and alternative positive thoughts that may be used to counter them.

Communication and problem solving. Six sessions provide training in communication, negotiation, and conflict-resolution skills for use with parents and peers. The specific techniques were derived from techniques used in behavioral marital therapy (e.g., Gottman, 1979) and their adaptations for use with parents and children (e.g., Forgatch, 1989). Communication training focuses on the acquisition of positive behaviors (e.g., active listening) and the inhibition or correction of nonproductive behaviors (e.g., accusations). The adolescents are taught four steps for problem solving: (a) defining the problem without criticism, (b) brainstorming alternative solutions, (c) evaluating and mutually agreeing on a solution, and (d) specifying the agreement, including positive and negative consequences for compliance and noncompliance, respectively.

Planning for the future. The final two sessions focus on the integration of skills, anticipation of future problems, and developing a life plan and goals. Aided by the group leader, each adolescent develops a written, personalized "emergency plan" detailing the steps he or she will take to counteract renewed feelings of depression, should they occur in the future.

Booster Sessions

Recurrence following treatment-mediated recovery occurs in up to 50% of depressed adults within two years after initial recovery (Belsher & Costello, 1988). Our initial assumption was that the high rate of relapse noted in adults also would characterize depressed adolescents. Therefore, for the second clinical trial we adapted relapse prevention procedures from the addictive disorder treatment literature (e.g., Marlatt & Gordon, 1985) to develop a protocol in which individualized "booster" sessions were offered at 4-month intervals for a 2-year posttreatment period. Although manualized, booster sessions address specific concerns of individual adolescents. After the follow-up assessment, the therapist works with the family and/or adolescent to determine which of the six booster protocols (pleasant events, social skills and communication, relaxation, cognitions, negotiation and problem solving, and maintaining gains and setting goals) would be most appropriate for them. The booster sessions (1–2 meetings) focus on how specific skills learned in CWD-A could be used to cope with the specific problematic situations that have emerged since the group ended. Because of staff turnover, booster sessions were generally not conducted by the therapist who had led the CWD-A group.

Efficacy of the CWD-A Course

Clinical trial #1. Our first controlled clinical trial (Lewinsohn, Clarke, Hops, & Andrews, 1990) involved 59 adolescents meeting DSM-III (American Psychiatric Association, 1980) criteria for MDD or dysthymia, or Research Diagnostic Criteria for minor depression. They were randomly assigned to one of three treatment conditions: (a) a group for adolescents only (Condition A; $n = 21$); (b) an identical group for adolescents but with their parents enrolled in a separate parent group (Condition A+P; $n = 19$); and (c) a wait-list condition (WL; $n = 19$). Participants and their parents completed extensive diagnostic and psychosocial measures at intake, posttreatment, and at 1, 6, 12, and 24 months posttreatment. Multivariate analyses demonstrated significant pre- to posttreatment change on all dependent variables across treatment conditions. Planned comparisons indicated that all significant improvement was accounted for by the two active treatment conditions (mean scores on the BDI for the two active treatments dropped from 21.5 to 8.3; Cohen's $h = 1.18$, which indicates a large effect size). Contrary to expectation, with only one exception, differences between Conditions A and A+P on diagnostic and other outcome variables failed to attain statistical significance. The one exception was that parents assigned to Condition A+P reported fewer problems on the Child Behavior Checklist (Achenbach & Edelbrock, 1983) at the end of treatment. Forty-six percent of the treated adolescents no longer met DSM-III criteria for depression by the end of treatment (compared with 5% in the wait-list condition). By 6 months posttreatment, the rate of recovery for the treated adolescents had increased to 83%. Two-year follow-up data indicated that treatment gains were maintained for the adolescents in the two active interventions, with very few teenagers experiencing recurrence.

Clinical trial #2. Our second clinical trial (Clarke, Rohde, Lewinsohn, Hops, & Seeley, 1999) involved 96 adolescents meeting DSM-III-R criteria for MDD or dysthymia who were assigned randomly to one of the following conditions: (a) adolescents only (Condition A; $n = 37$); (b) adolescent plus parent groups (Condition A+P; $n = 32$); or (c) wait-list control (WL; $n = 27$). Our primary purpose in this study was to conduct a direct replication of our initial findings with a larger sample. Our second purpose was to evaluate the previously described "booster" protocol in the maintenance of treatment gains. At the end of treatment, patients in the two active treatment conditions were randomly assigned to one of three 24-month follow-up conditions: (a) "Booster," consisting of treatment sessions and independent assessments every four months ($n = 24$); (b) "Frequent Assessment," consisting only of assessments every four months ($n = 16$); or (c) "Annual Assessment," consisting only of assessments every 12 months ($n = 24$). The latter two assessment-only conditions evaluated whether more frequent assessment contacts posttreatment had a therapeutic effect independent of booster therapy.

As in the first clinical trial, posttreatment diagnostic recovery rates in the two treatments were superior to the wait-list control (67% vs. 48%; Cohen's h = .38, a small-to-medium effect size). Likewise, recovery in the two active treatments did not significantly differ (65% in Condition A vs. 69% in Condition A+P). Regarding continuous measures, the two active treatments (which did not differ) were associated with significantly greater reductions in both BDI scores (change score effect size = .61) and Global Assessment of Functioning (GAF) scores (change score effect size = .54). The two active treatments also did not significantly differ in recovery rates across the two-year follow-up.

This replication study confirmed our previous finding that parent involvement in the CWD-A course was not associated with significantly enhanced improvement. As before, we recognize that these results are contrary to widely held clinical beliefs concerning the importance of parental involvement in adolescent treatment. We acknowledge that parental attendance, especially for fathers, was not perfect and that both of our studies examined only one method of involving parents in treatment. It may be that other modalities, such as an integrated family therapy approach (e.g., Beardslee, 1990), would yield better outcomes. However, our results are consistent with the findings of Brent et al. (1997), who also found no advantage to family therapy relative to individual CBT for adolescent depression.

The primary impact of the Booster condition was to significantly accelerate the recovery of adolescents who were still depressed at the end of acute treatment. By 12-

month follow-up, 100% (5/5) of depressed adolescents randomized to the Booster condition had recovered, versus 50% (6/12) of participants in the two assessment-only conditions—a significant ($p < .05$) difference. However, by 24-month follow-up, these rates had converged, with 100% (5/5) of participants in the Booster condition recovered versus 90% (9/10) of participants in the two assessment-only conditions. The mean time to recovery for "still depressed" adolescents in the Booster condition was 23.5 weeks (SE = 3.8), compared to 67.0 weeks (SE = 8.4) for adolescents in the two assessment-only conditions ($p < .001$). Although comparable proportions of adolescents eventually recovered in the two assessment-only conditions, we believe that the shorter time to recovery in the booster condition (a mean reduction of almost 44 weeks) is clinically meaningful. In light of the present findings, our booster intervention may be better described as a "continuation" treatment aimed to improve on the gains of the acute intervention, rather than a "prophylactic" treatment focused on preventing future depressive episodes. Regarding depression recurrence, at two-year follow-up, differences in recurrence rates for the three follow-up conditions were nonsignificant (22% overall).

Beginning to Evaluate the Effectiveness of the CWD-A Course

Given the high rate of psychiatric comorbidity with depression in adolescents, treatment interventions shown to be efficacious with "pure" samples of depressed adolescents need to be evaluated with adolescents who have comorbid conditions. We are currently evaluating the effectiveness of the CWD-A intervention for adolescents whose depression is comorbid with conduct disorder (NIMH MH56238, Paul Rohde, Principal Investigator). Adolescents age 13–17 were referred by staff at a county department of juvenile corrections. A total of 181 adolescents, 94 of whom had current MDD/dysthymia and conduct disorder, were randomly assigned to either a modification of the CWD-A course or academic tutoring. Adolescents are assessed pre- and posttreatment and at 6 and 12 months posttreatment. Posttreatment data collection, which includes academic and criminal arrest records, will be completed in 2002. Preliminary results indicate that the CWD-A is effective in reducing depressive symptomatology posttreatment compared to the academic tutoring condition. In a related study, the CWD-A intervention is being modified to serve as a more general prosocial coping skills group beneficial to youths incarcerated in state youth correctional facilities.

Modifying the CWD-A Course for Use as a Secondary Prevention Intervention

School-based prevention. Based on the success of the CWD-A as an intervention for currently depressed adolescents, we conducted a randomized trial to examine whether a school-based group cognitive therapy prevention program would significantly reduce the incidence of unipolar affective disorders in high school adolescents at risk for future depression (Clarke et al., 1995). Ninth-grade adolescents in three high schools were identified as potentially at risk for depression through a schoolwide administration ($n = 1,652$) of the CES-D scale, followed by a structured diagnostic interview (the K-SADS) for the 222 adolescents with CES-D scores of 24 or greater. The 172 adolescents identified as not currently depressed but with elevated CES-D scores were invited to participate in the prevention study; 150 accepted and were randomly assigned to either (a) a 15-session, after-school, cognitive-behavioral preventive intervention ($n = 76$); or (b) a "usual care" control condition ($n = 74$). The intervention, entitled the Adolescent Coping With Stress course (CWS-A; Clarke & Lewinsohn, 1991) consisted of fifteen 45-minute sessions in which participants are taught cognitive therapy techniques to identify and challenge negative or irrational thoughts that may contribute to the development of future affective disorder. Survival analysis results indicated significantly fewer of the at-risk youth in the CWS-A group developed either MDD or dysthymia during the 12-month follow-up period compared to the control group (14% vs. 26%, respectively; Mantel-Cox$\chi^2 = 2.72, p < .05$).

HMO-based prevention. Clarke et al. (in press) recently completed a randomized trial of a cognitive-behavioral prevention program for adolescents with subsyndromal levels of depressive symptoms who were offspring of parents receiving treatment for depression in a Health Maintenance Organization (HMO). Adults in treatment for depression who had children between the ages of 13 and 18 were sent letters from their health care providers inviting them to participate in the study. Interested parents were interviewed to confirm their diagnosis of a mood disorder, and the children were evaluated with regard to their history and current level of depressive symptoms and disorders. A "demoralized" group at high risk for future depression was identified that had current subdiagnostic levels of depressive symptoms (i.e., a CES-D score >24) or a previous episode of MDD. These 123 adolescents were randomly assigned to either a "usual care" control condition or the CWS-A course. Survival analyses revealed significantly fewer new episodes of affective disorder in the CWS-A group (9%) versus the treatment-as-usual group (29%) at the 15-month follow-up. The odds ratio of depression at 12 months was 5.6 (95% CI = 1.6 - 20.4) when adjusted for gender, age, CES-D score, and previous depression history.

FUTURE DIRECTIONS

The program of research developed by Lewinsohn and colleagues has documented the extent of the problem of youth depression. By developmentally adapting psychosocial interventions originally designed for adults, the CWD-A tertiary treatment program and the CWS-A secondary prevention program have proven to be effective interventions for adolescent depression. Despite recent advancements toward intervening on youth depression by our group and others, much work is still needed to reach the final stage of the IOM prevention paradigm of large-scale community prevention campaigns.

Based on longitudinal studies such as the OADP, the putative early risk and protective factors for youth depression need to be clearly established in order to refine models of etiology and guide prevention efforts. Factors that contribute to the onset of depression need to be distinguished from those that maintain depression or predict depression recurrence. Furthermore, risk and protective factors that are specific to certain developmental periods, or that are gender-specific, should be determined. To this end, current efforts are underway to cross-validate risk and protective factors from the OADP, the Great Smokey Mountains Study (Costello et al., 1996), and the Simmons Longitudinal Study (Reinherz et al., 1993) based on a multisite secondary analysis project funded by the National Institute of Mental Health.

Although results for the CWD-A/CWS-A intervention are highly encouraging, several issues still need to be addressed. For example, this intervention approach needs to be adapted and evaluated for use with ethnic minorities and preadolescent youth. Research also needs to determine whether the intervention can be effectively used in conjunction with other modes of therapy (e.g., family therapy, pharmacotherapy). Additional research might examine alternative approaches for prophylactic treatment, including "reunion" meetings of the acute treatment groups. Our experience indicates that many adolescents are very enthusiastic about seeing their former group members and the group leader. Other possible recurrence prevention interventions include telephone boosters, or boosters only for those youth with the highest risk for recurrence (e.g., those with previous recurrent episodes or with a family history of depression).

Group treatment is one of the most preferred and cost-efficient methods of intervening with depressed or at-risk adolescents (Weisz et al., 1999). However, programs based on CBT that teach multiple components assume that all youth with depression or who were at risk for depression require similar skills training (e.g., cognition or self-talk training, pleasant activity scheduling, relaxation techniques, or social skills training). Individualized programs that specifically target skills deficits may be less demanding for the participant and, therefore, may result in better program adherence. Furthermore, whereas group interventions require several youth to be identified at the same time, it may be logistically easier to intervene on an individual basis in some settings.

As presented earlier in Figure 1, on page 889, the risk for depressive disorders begins to sharply increase at age 12 for girls and age 14 for boys. Thus, preadolescence represents an important age period in which to target preventive interventions for reducing the incidence of depression. Although there have been no school-based studies that focus on the prevention of depressive disorders in at-risk preadolescent youth to date, there have been encouraging results reported on the prevention of depressive symptoms. For example, The Penn Prevention Program (Jaycox, Reivich, Gillham, & Seligman, 1994) developed and evaluated a districtwide, school-based prevention program aimed at children aged 10–13 who were at risk for depression based on elevated self-reported depressive symptomatology and/or parental conflict. By teaching cognitive and problem-solving techniques, the intervention targeted depressive symptoms and related difficulties such as conduct problems, low academic achievement, low social competence, and poor peer relations. Pre-post analyses indicated that depressive symptomatology was significantly reduced and classroom behavior was significantly improved in the intervention condition compared to the control condition. In addition, the 6-month follow-up showed continued reduction in depressive symptomatology and significantly fewer conduct problems. Clearly, further research is needed to extend these promising findings and to assess the long-term impact of preventive interventions for preadolescent youth who are at risk for depression.

Schools are an ideal setting for identifying, remediating, and preventing depression among at-risk youth. It is our hope that by promoting protective factors and ameliorating modifiable risk factors via school-based interventions, the longstanding difficulties associated with youth depression may be averted.

REFERENCES

Achenbach, T. M., & Edelbrock, C. S. (1983). *Manual for the Child Behavior Checklist and Revised Child Behavior Profile.* Burlington, VT: University of Vermont, Department of Psychiatry.

Ackerson, J., Scogin, F., McKendree-Smith, N., & Lyman, R. D. (1998). Cognitive bibliotherapy for mild and moderate adolescent depressive symptomatology. *Journal of Consulting and Clinical Psychology, 66,* 685-690.

American Psychiatric Association. (1980). *Diagnostic and statistical manual of mental disorders* (3rd ed.). Washington, DC: American Psychiatric Association.

American Psychiatric Association. (1987). *Diagnostic and statistical manual of mental disorders* (3rd ed., rev.). Washington, DC: American Psychiatric Association.

American Psychiatric Association (1994). *Diagnostic and statistical manual of mental disorders* (4th ed.). Washington, DC: American Psychiatric Association.

Angold, A., Prendergast, M., Cox, A., Rutter, M., Harrington, R., & Simonoff, E. (1995). The Child and Adolescent Psychiatric Assessment: CAPA. *Psychological Medicine, 25,* 739-754.

Angold, A., Weissman, M. M., John, K., Merikangas, K. R., Prusoff, B. A., Wickramaratne, P., Gammon, G. D., & Warner, V. (1987). Parent and child reports of depressive symptoms in children at low and high risk of depression. *Journal of Child Psychology and Psychiatry, 28,* 901-915.

Beardslee, W. R. (1990). Development of a clinician-based preventive intervention for families with affective disorders. *Journal of Preventive Psychiatry and Allied Disciplines, 4,* 39-61.

Beck, A. T. (1967). *Depression: Clinical, experimental, and theoretical aspects.* New York: Harper & Row.

Beck, A. T., Rush, A. J., Shaw, B. F., & Emery, G. (1979). *Cognitive theory of depression.* New York: Guilford Press.

Beck, A. T., & Steer, R. A. (1991). *Beck scale for suicide ideation.* St. Antonio, TX: Harcourt Brace Educational Measurement.

Beck, A. T., Steer, R. A., & Brown, G. K. (1996). *Beck Depression Inventory* (2nd ed.). St. Antonio, TX: Harcourt Brace Educational Measurement.

Beck, A. T., Ward, C. H., Mendelson, M., Mock, J., & Erbaugh, J. (1961). An inventory for measuring depression. *Archives of General Psychiatry, 4,* 561-571.

Belsher, G., & Costello, C. G. (1988). Relapse after recovery from unipolar depression: A critical review. *Psychological Bulletin, 104,* 84-96.

Benson, H. (1975). *The relaxation response.* New York: William Morrow.

Birmaher, B., Brent, D. A., Kolko, D., Baugher, M., Bridge, J., Holder, D., Iyengar, S., & Ulloa, R. E. (2000). Clinical outcome after short-term psychotherapy for adolescents with major depressive disorder. *Archives of General Psychiatry, 57,* 29-36.

Birmaher, B., Ryan, N. D., Williamson, D. E., Brent, D. A., Kaufman, J., Dahl, R. E., Perel, J., & Nelson, B. (1996a). Childhood and adolescent depression: A review of the past 10 years. Part 1. *Journal of the American Academy of Child and Adolescent Psychiatry, 35,* 1427-1439.

Birmaher, B., Ryan, N. D., Williamson, D. E., Brent, D. A., & Kaufman, J. (1996b). Childhood and adolescent depression: A review of the past 10 years. Part II. *Journal of the American Academy of Child and Adolescent Psychiatry, 35,* 1575-1583.

Blazer, D. G., Kessler, R. C., McGonagle, K. A., & Swartz, M. S. (1994). The prevalence and distribution of major depression in a national community sample: The national comorbidity survey. *American Journal of Psychiatry, 151,* 979-986.

Brent, D. A., Holder, D., Kolko, D., Birmaher, B., Baugher, M., Roth, C., & Johnson, B. (1997). A clinical psychotherapy trial for adolescent depression comparing cognitive, family, and supportive therapy. *Archives of General Psychiatry, 54,* 877-885.

Cantwell, D. P., Lewinsohn, P. M., Rohde, P., & Seeley, J. R. (1997). Correspondence between adolescent report and parent report of psychiatric diagnostic data. *Journal of the American Academy of Child and Adolescent Psychiatry, 36,* 610-619.

Clarke, G. N., Hawkins, W., Murphy, M., Sheeber, L. B., Lewinsohn, P. M., & Seeley, J. R. (1995). Targeted prevention of unipolar depressive disorder in an at-risk sample of high school adolescents: A randomized trial of a group cognitive interview. *Journal of American Academy of Child and Adolescent Psychiatry, 34,* 312-321.

Clarke, G. N., Hornbrook, M. C., Lynch, F., Polen, M., Gale, J., Beardslee, W., O'Connor, E., & Seeley, J. (in press). Offspring of depressed parents in a HMO: A randomized trial of a group cognitive intervention for preventing adolescent depressive disorder. *Archives of General Psychiatry.*

Clarke, G. N., & Lewinsohn, P. M. (1991). *The coping with stress course adolescent workbook.* Unpublished work.

Clarke, G. N., Rohde, P., Lewinsohn, P. M., Hops, H., & Seeley, J. R. (1999). Cognitive-behavioral treatment of adolescent depression: Efficacy of acute group treatment and booster sessions. *Journal of the American Academy of Child and Adolescent Psychiatry, 38,* 272-279.

Costello, E. J., Angold, A., Burns, B. J., Stangl, D. K., Tweed, D. L., Erkanli, A., & Worthman, C. M. (1996). The Great Smoky Mountains study of youth: Goals, design, methods, and the prevalence of DSM-III-R disorders. *Archives of General Psychiatry, 53,* 1129-1136.

Costello, E. J., Edelbrock, C. S., & Costello, A. J. (1985). Validity of the NIMH Diagnostic Interview Schedule for Children: A comparison between psychiatric and pediatric referrals. *Journal of Abnormal Child Psychology, 13,* 579-595.

Ellis, A., & Harper, R. A. (1961). *A guide to rational living.* Hollywood, CA: Wilshire.

Essau, C. A., Hakim-Larson, J., Crocker, A., & Petermann, F. (1999). Assessment of depressive disorders in children and adolescents. In C. A. Essau & F. Petermann (Eds.), *Depressive disorders in children and adolescents: Epidemiology, risk factors, and treatment* (pp. 27-67). Northvale, NJ: Jason Aronson.

Essau, C. A., & Petermann, F. (Eds.). (1999). *Depressive disorders in children and adolescents.* Northvale, NJ: Jason Aronson.

Feinstein, A. R. (1970). The pretherapeutic classification of comorbidity in chronic disease. *Journal of Chronic Diseases, 23,* 455-468.

Ferster, C. B. (1966). Animal behavior and mental illness. *Psychological Record, 16,* 345-356.

Forgatch, M. S. (1989). Patterns and outcome in family problem solving: The disrupting effect of negative emotion. *Journal of Marriage and the Family, 51,* 115-124.

Garrison, C. Z., Lewinsohn, P. M., Marsteller, F., Langhinrichsen, J., & Lann, I. (1991). The assessment of suicidal behavior in adolescents. *Suicide and Life-Threatening Behavior, 21,* 217-230.

Garrison, C. Z., Waller, J. L., Cuffe, S. P., McKeown, R. E., Addy, C. L., & Jackson, K. L. (1997). Incidence of major depressive disorder and dysthymia in young adolescents. *Journal of the American Academy of Child and Adolescent Psychiatry, 36,* 458-465.

Gladstone, T. R. G., & Beardslee, W. R. (2000). The prevention of depression in at-risk adolescents: Current and future directions. *Journal of Cognitive Psychotherapy: An International Quarterly, 14,* 9-23.

Gottman, J. M. (1979). *Marital interaction: Empirical investigations.* New York: Academic Press.

Harter, S., & Nowakowski, M. (1987). *Manual for the Dimensions of Depression Profile for Children and Adolescents.* Denver, CO: University of Denver Press.

Herjanic, B., & Reich, W. (1982). Development of a structured psychiatric interview for children: Agreement between child and parent on individual symptoms. *Journal of Abnormal Child Psychology, 10,* 307-324.

Hibbs, E. D., & Jensen, P. S. (1996). *Psychosocial treatments for child and adolescent disorders: Empirically based strategies for clinical practice.* Washington, D.C.: American Psychological Association.

Jacobson, E. (1929). *Progressive relaxation.* Chicago: University of Chicago Press.

Jaycox, L. H., Reivich, K. J., Gillham, J., & Seligman, M. E. P. (1994). Prevention of depressive symptoms in school children. *Behavior Research Therapy, 32,* 801-816.

Kahn, J. S., Kehle, T. J., Jenson, W. R., & Clark, E. (1990). Comparison of cognitive-behavioral, relaxation, and self-modeling interventions for depression among middle-school students. *School Psychology Review, 19,* 196-210.

Keller, M. B., Lavori, P. W., Friedman, B., Nielsen, E., Endicott, J., & McDonald-Scott, P. A. (1987). The Longitudinal Interval Follow-up Evaluation: A comprehensive method for assessing outcome in prospective longitudinal studies. *Archives of General Psychiatry, 44,* 540-548.

Kessler, R. C., McGonagle, K. A., Swartz, M., Blazer, D. G., & Nelson, C. B. (1993). Sex and depression in the National Comorbidity Survey I: Lifetime prevalence, chronicity, and recurrence. *Journal of Affective Disorders, 29,* 85-96.

Kovacs, M. (1985). The Children's Depression Inventory. *Psychopharmacology Bulletin, 21,* 995-998.

Kroll, L., Harrington, R., Jayson, D., Fraser, J., & Gowers, S. (1996). Pilot study of continuation cognitive-behavioral therapy for major depression in adolescent psychiatric patients. *Journal of the American Academy of Child and Adolescent Psychiatry, 35,* 1156-1161.

Lewinsohn, P. M., Antonuccio, D. O., Steinmetz, J. L., & Teri, L. (1984). *The coping with depression course: A psychoeducational intervention for unipolar depression.* Eugene, OR: Castalia.

Lewinsohn, P. M., Biglan, A., & Zeiss, A. M. (1976). Behavioral treatment of depression. In P. O. Davidson (Ed.), *The behavioral management of anxiety, depression and pain* (pp. 91–146). New York: Brunner/Mazel.

Lewinsohn, P. M., & Clarke, G. N. (1999). Psychosocial treatments for adolescent depression. *Clinical Psychology Review, 19,* 329–343.

Lewinsohn, P. M., Clarke, G. N., Hops, H., & Andrews, J. A. (1990). Cognitive-behavioral treatment for depressed adolescents. *Behavior Therapy, 21,* 385–401.

Lewinsohn, P. M., Clarke, G. N., Seeley, J. R., & Rohde, P. (1994). Major depression in community adolescents: Age at onset, episode duration, and time to recurrence. *Journal of the American Academy of Child and Adolescent Psychiatry, 33,* 809–818.

Lewinsohn, P. M., & Essau, C. (in press). Depression in adolescents. In I. H. Gotlib & C. Hammen (Eds.), *Handbook of depression.* New York: Guilford Press.

Lewinsohn, P. M., Gotlib, I. H., & Seeley, J. R. (1995). Adolescent psychopathology: IV. Specificity of psychosocial risk factors for depression and substance abuse in older adolescents. *Journal of the American Academy of Child and Adolescent Psychiatry, 34,* 1221–1229.

Lewinsohn, P. M., Gotlib, I. H., & Seeley, J. R. (1997). Depression-related psychosocial variables in adolescence: Are they specific to depression? *Journal of Abnormal Psychology, 106,* 365–375.

Lewinsohn, P. M., Hoberman, H., Teri, L., & Hautzinger, M. (1985). An integrative theory of depression. In S. Reiss & R. Bootzin (Eds.), *Theoretical issues in behavior therapy* (pp. 331–359). San Diego, CA: Academic Press.

Lewinsohn, P. M., Hops, H., Roberts, R. E., Seeley, J. R., & Andrews, J. A. (1993). Adolescent psychopathology: I. Prevalence and incidence of depression and other DSM-III-R disorders in high school students. *Journal of Abnormal Psychology, 102,* 133–144.

Lewinsohn, P. M., Langhinrichsen-Rohling, J., Langford, R., Rohde, P., Seeley, J. R., & Chapman, J. (1995). The Life Attitudes Interview Schedule: A scale to assess adolescent life-enhancing and life-threatening behaviors. *Suicide and Life Threatening Behavior, 25,* 458–474.

Lewinsohn, P. M., Muñoz, R. F., Youngren, M. A., & Zeiss, A. M. (1986). *Control your depression.* Englewood Cliffs, NJ: Prentice-Hall.

Lewinsohn, P. M., Roberts, R. E., Seeley, J. R., Rohde, P., Gotlib, I. H., & Hops, H. (1994). Adolescent psychopathology: II. Psychosocial risk factors for depression. *Journal of Abnormal Psychology, 103,* 302–315.

Lewinsohn, P. M., Rohde, P., Hops, H., & Clarke, G. N. (1991). *Leaders's manual for parent groups: Adolescent coping with depression course.* Eugene, OR: Castalia Publishing Company.

Lewinsohn, P. M., Rohde, P., & Seeley, J. R. (1995). Adolescent psychopathology: III. The clinical consequences of comorbidity. *Journal of the American Academy of Child and Adolescent Psychiatry, 34,* 510–519.

Lewinsohn, P. M., Rohde, P., & Seeley, J. R. (1996). Adolescent suicidal ideation and attempts: Prevalence, risk factors and clinical implications. *Clinical Psychology: Science and Practice, 3,* 25–46.

Lewinsohn, P. M., Rohde, P., & Seeley, J. R. (1998). Treatment of adolescent depression: Frequency of services and impact on functioning in young adulthood. *Depression and Anxiety, 7,* 47–52.

Lewinsohn, P. M., Rohde, P., Seeley, J. R., & Hops, H. (1991). Comorbidity of unipolar depression: I. Major depression with dysthymia. *Journal of Abnormal Psychology, 100,* 205–213.

Lewinsohn, P. M., Steinmetz-Breckenridge, J., Antonuccio, D. O., & Teri, L. (1985). Group therapy for depression: The coping with depression course. *International Journal of Mental Health, 13,* 8–33.

Lewinsohn, P. M., Weinstein, M., & Shaw, D. (1969). Depression: A clinical-research approach. In R. D. Rubin & C. M. Frank (Eds.), *Advances in behavior therapy, 1968* (pp. 231–240). New York: Academic Press.

MacPhillamy, D. J., & Lewinsohn, P. M. (1982). The Pleasant Events Schedule: Studies on reliability, validity, and scale intercorrelations. *Journal of Consulting and Clinical Psychology, 50,* 363–380.

Marlatt, G. A., & Gordon, J. R. (1985). *Relapse prevention: Maintenance strategies in the treatment of addictive behaviors.* New York: Guilford Press.

Mrazek, P. J., & Haggerty, R. J. (1994). *Reducing risks for mental disorders: Frontiers for preventive intervention research.* Washington, DC: National Academy Press.

Nolen-Hoeksema, S. (1990). *Sex differences in depression.* Stanford, CA: Stanford University Press.

Nolen-Hoeksema, S., & Girgus, J. S. (1994). The emergence of gender differences in depression during adolescence. *Psychological Bulletin, 115,* 424–443.

Orvaschel, H., Puig-Antich, J., Chambers, W. J., Tabrizi, M. A., & Johnson, R. (1982). Retrospective assessment of prepubertal major depression with the Kiddie-SADS-E. *Journal of the American Academy of Child Psychiatry, 21,* 392–397.

Piacentini, J., Shaffer, D., Fisher, P., Schwab-Stone, M., Davies, M., & Gioia, P. (1993). The Diagnostic Interview Schedule for Children—Revised Version (DISC-R): III. Concurrent criterion validity. *Journal of the American Academy of Child and Adolescent Psychiatry, 32,* 658–665.

Radloff, L. S. (1977). The CES-D Scale: A self-report depression scale for research in the general population. *Applied Psychological Measurement, 1,* 385–401.

Rehm, L. P. (1977). A self-control model of depression. *Behavior Therapy, 8,* 787–804.

Reinecke, M. A., Ryan, N. E., & DuBois, D. L. (1998). Cognitive-behavioral therapy of depression and depressive symptoms during adolescence: A review and meta-analysis. *Journal of the American Academy of Child and Adolescent Psychiatry, 37,* 26–34.

Reinherz, H. Z., Giaconia, R. M., Pakiz, B., Silverman, A. B., Frost, A. K., & Lefkowitz, E. S. (1993). Psychosocial risks for major depression in late adolescence: A longitudinal community study. *Journal of the American Academy of Child and Adolescent Psychiatry, 32,* 1155–1163.

Reynolds, W. M. (1986). A model for the screening and identification of depressed children and adolescents in school settings. *Professional School Psychology, 1,* 117–129.

Reynolds, W. M. (1987a). *Reynolds Adolescent Depression Scale.* Odessa, FL: Psychological Assessment Resources.

Reynolds, W. M. (1987b). *Suicidal Ideation Questionnaire: Professional manual.* Odessa, FL: Psychological Assessment Resources.

Reynolds, W. M. (1991). Psychological intervention for depression in children and adolescents. In G. Stoner, M. R. Shinn, & H. M. Walker (Eds.), *Interventions for achievement and behavior problems* (pp. 649-683). Silver Spring, MD: National Association of School Psychologists.

Reynolds, W. M. (1994). Assessment of depression in children and adolescents by self-report questionnaires. In W. M. Reynolds & H. F. Johnston (Eds.), *Handbook of depression in children and adolescents* (pp. 209-234). New York: Plenum.

Reynolds, W. M., & Coats, K. I. (1986). A comparison of cognitive-behavioral therapy and relaxation training for the treatment of depression in adolescents. *Journal of Consulting and Clinical Psychology, 54,* 653-660.

Roberts, R. E., Lewinsohn, P. M., & Seeley, J. R. (1991). Screening for adolescent depression: A comparison of depression scales. *Journal of the American Academy of Child and Adolescent Psychiatry, 30,* 58-66.

Rohde, P., Lewinsohn, P. M., Seeley, J. R., & Langhinrichsen-Rohling, J. (1996). The Life-Attitudes Schedule Short Form: An abbreviated measure of life-enhancing and life-threatening behaviors in adolescents. *Suicide and Life-Threatening Behavior, 26,* 272-281.

Rosselló, J., & Bernal, G. (1999). The efficacy of cognitive-behavioral and interpersonal treatments for depression in Puerto Rican adolescents. *Journal of Consulting and Clinical Psychology, 67,* 734-745.

Rutter, M. (1976). Isle of Wight studies, 1964-1974. *Psychological Medicine, 6,* 313-332.

Seeley, J. R., Lewinsohn, P. M., & Rohde, P. (1997). *Comorbidity between conduct disorder and major depression during adolescence: Impact on phenomenology, associated clinical characteristics, and continuity into young adulthood.* Poster presented at the International Society for Research in Child and Adolescent Psychopathology Eighth Scientific Meeting, Paris, France.

Seligman, M. E. P. (1975). *Helplessness: On depression, development, and death.* San Francisco: Freeman.

Stark, K. D. (1990). *Childhood depression: School-based intervention.* New York: Guilford Press.

Stark, K. D., Reynolds, W. M., & Kaslow, N. J. (1987). A comparison of the relative efficacy of self-control therapy and a behavioral problem-solving therapy for depression in children. *Journal of Abnormal Child Psychology, 15,* 91-113.

Vostanis, P., Feehan, C., Grattan, E., & Bickerton, W. (1996). A randomised controlled outpatient trial of cognitive-behavioural treatment for children and adolescents with depression: 9-month follow-up. *Journal of Affective Disorders, 40,* 105-116.

Weisz, J. R., Valeri, S. M., McCarty, C. A., & Moore, P. S. (1999). Interventions for child and adolescent depression: Features, effects, and future directions. In C. A. Essau &

F. P. Petermann (Eds.), *Depressive disorders in children and adolescents*. Northvale, NJ: Jason Aronson.

Wood, A., Harrington, R., & Moore, A. (1996). Controlled trial of a brief cognitive-behavioural intervention in adolescent patients with depressive disorders. *Journal of Child Psychology and Psychiatry, 37,* 737-746.

World Health Organization. (2000). Mental health and brain disorders: What is depression? Available Internet:

www.who.int/mental_health/Topic_Depression/depression1.htm.

AUTHORS' NOTES

This research was supported by National Institute of Mental Health Grants MH41278, MH40501, and MH56238 (Dr. Lewinsohn). Correspondence concerning this article should be addressed to John R. Seeley, Oregon Research Institute, 1715 Franklin Boulevard, Eugene, Oregon, 97403-1983, USA.

CHAPTER 33

Interventions for Attention Problems

George J. DuPaul
Lehigh University

Gary Stoner
University of Massachusetts Amherst

INTRODUCTION

Problems with attention, impulse control, and activity level are among the most frequent behavior difficulties exhibited by children in classroom settings (Barkley, 1998). In fact, approximately 3–5% of elementary school-age children in the United States are diagnosed with Attention-Deficit/Hyperactivity Disorder (ADHD), a psychiatric condition applied to individuals who exhibit developmentally inappropriate levels of inattention and/or impulsivity/overactivity (American Psychiatric Associa-tion, 1994). Boys with ADHD outnumber girls with this disorder at about a 2:1 to 5:1 ratio (Barkley, 1998). Given that most public school classrooms include 20–30 students, teachers will likely address the needs of at least one student with ADHD per school year. Further, ADHD symptoms typically persist from early childhood through at least adolescence for a majority of individuals (Barkley, 1998; Weiss & Hechtman, 1993). Thus, attention and behavioral difficulties are likely to affect a children's school functioning throughout their educational career.

Children with attention problems related to ADHD are at higher than average risk for a variety of behavioral difficulties, including defiance toward authority figures, poor relationships with peers, and antisocial acts such as lying, stealing, and fighting (American Psychiatric Association, 1994; Barkley, 1998). In addition to these behavioral risks, students with ADHD frequently struggle scholastically, presumably owing to their low academic engagement rates and inconsistent work productivity (DuPaul & Stoner, 1994). The results of prospective follow-up studies of children with ADHD into adolescence and adulthood indicate significantly higher rates of grade retention, placement in special education classrooms, and school drop-out relative to their peers as well as significantly lower high school grade point average, enrollment in college degree programs, and socioeconomic status (e.g., Barkley, Fischer, Edelbrock, & Smallish, 1990; Mannuzza, Gittleman-Klein, Bessler, Malloy, & LaPadulla, 1993; Weiss & Hechtman, 1993). Lower than expected rates of work completion may, in part, account for the association of ADHD with academic underachievement, because up to 80% of students with this disorder have been found to exhibit academic performance problems (Cantwell & Baker, 1991). Further, a significant minority (i.e., 20–30%) of children with ADHD are classified as "learning disabled" because of deficits in the acquisition of specific academic skills (DuPaul & Stoner, 1994; Knivsberg, Reichelt, & Nodland, 1999; Semrud-Clikeman et al., 1992). Additional students with ADHD may receive special education services as a function of being classified as "other health impaired." In fact, "other health impaired" is the fastest growing special education category, increasing 280% over the past 10 years, presumably owing to an increased identification of students with ADHD (U.S. Department of Education, 1999).

Given the risk for poor academic outcomes, school professionals must design and implement interventions to address not only the attention problems and behavioral difficulties associated with ADHD but also the academic achievement problems associated with this disorder. The two primary interventions for ADHD are psychostimulant medication (e.g., methylphenidate) and contingency management programming (e.g., token reinforcement and response cost). These intervention strategies have been found to enhance rates of academic productivity and accuracy for most study participants (for review see Barkley, 1998; DuPaul & Eckert, 1997; Pelham, & Waschbusch, 1999; Swanson, 1992). The most comprehensive, large-scale treatment outcome study to date, referred to as the Multimodal Treatment Study of Children with ADHD, found that pharmacotherapy was superior to behavioral interventions in reducing ADHD symptoms and related disruptive behaviors (The MTA Cooperative Group, 1999). However, these two treatments did not differ with respect to their effects on academic achievement. Further, some children may require the combination of stimulant medication and behavioral intervention to show improvements in academic functioning. Nevertheless, despite their positive effects, these interventions do not comprehensively address all of the academic deficits (i.e., beyond productivity on independent seatwork) that may be exhibited by students with ADHD. For example, approximately 47% of children treated with methylphenidate will either show no change or decrements in academic performance relative to placebo conditions (Rapport, Denney, DuPaul, & Gardner, 1994). Effect sizes for academic outcome measures typically are lower than for measures of behavioral outcome for both stimulant medication (Forness, Kavale, Sweeney, & Crenshaw, 1999) and behavioral interventions (DuPaul & Eckert, 1997). Thus, although necessary for many students with ADHD, these interventions *are not sufficient* for ameliorating academic performance problems.

The purpose of this chapter is to describe empirically supported, school-based interventions that address the attention problems, behavior difficulties, and academic performance of children exhibiting behaviors related to ADHD. Conceptual issues underlying intervention design and implementation will be reviewed. Also, interventions that are useful for preschool, elementary, and secondary school students will be discussed.

Throughout this chapter, we emphasize three overarching points. First, for interventions to be effective, they must be linked to baseline and ongoing assessment data. Second, children with attention problems related to ADHD are a heterogeneous group. Therefore, intervention strategies for each student must be individually tailored to meet both student needs and the specific environmental context. Finally, a balanced approach to treatment planning should be adopted wherein both proactive (i.e., antecedent-based) and reactive (i.e., consequent-based) intervention strategies are implemented.

CONCEPTUAL FOUNDATIONS OF INTERVENTION

School psychologists and other professionals are guided by numerous approaches to intervention design, implementation, and evaluation (e.g., intervention strategies linked to functional analysis of problem behavior). In designing interventions for students with ADHD, we suggest a focus on five guiding principles. Intervention effectiveness can be enhanced by attending to these five principles, which involve the use of (a) assessment data, (b) multiple intervention agents or mediators, (c) both proactive and reactive intervention strategies, (d) individualized strategies, and (e) interventions in close proximity to the behavior of concern. In the following sections we briefly describe each principle, and throughout the remainder of the chapter the principles are illustrated by examples of intervention strategies.

Link Assessment Data to Interventions

Intervention effectiveness will be enhanced when interventions are designed using assessment data (e.g., baseline data, functional assessment data). Assessment data can be used in many ways to guide interventions. For example, functional assessment data can inform professionals as to when and under what conditions problem behavior is both most (e.g., during math instruction) and least likely (e.g., during non–academic times) to occur (Touchette, MacDonald, & Langer, 1985). In addition, these data can help in the generation of hypotheses as to what function a behavior of concern might be serving for a student (e.g., produce social attention) (Nelson, Roberts, & Smith, 1998; O'Neill et al., 1997). These data, then, can help guide decisions pertaining to, for example, when and where interventions are most needed. In addition, these data might suggest what could be done to prevent problem behavior through re-arrangement of environments and instruction, and what strategies are likely to be effective in managing the behavior(s) of concern (e.g., teaching and/or strengthening appropriate behaviors for obtaining social attention).

In addition, once interventions are put into place, treatment integrity data (Gresham, 1989) can be useful both for guiding the refinement of intervention strategies so as to be feasible for individual teachers as well as for contributing to the evaluation of treatment outcomes. That is, given a "weak" treatment effect, can we say the treatment was implemented well and should be considered a failure in this instance? Or, rather, should we conclude the intervention was not implemented with enough integrity to produce an effect, therefore guiding us to re-design the intervention so as to be feasible for the intervention agent?

Finally, outcome data need to be collected to guide conclusions regarding overall intervention effectiveness, consumer satisfaction with treatment outcomes, and the magnitude of treatment effects relative to baseline data and treatment goals. These conclusions, then, will guide decisions about continuing, discontinuing, and/or supplementing the intervention strategy at hand.

These uses of assessment data thus yield conceptual assessment-intervention linkages, improvements in understanding treatment integrity and feasibility, and improvements in accountability systems around interventions. Ultimately, these data can contribute to enhanced treatment effectiveness by guiding the continuance of effective strategies and the discontinuance of ineffective ones.

Use Multiple Intervention Agents

For students with ADHD, intervention effectiveness will be enhanced when multiple intervention agents or mediators are employed. This guiding principle is consistent, for example, with the notion that when psychotropic medication is used to treat students with ADHD, the medication should not be the sole intervention strategy used. Rather, it is most often recommended that medication be accompanied by other individualized behavioral and academic support strategies. In these instances the multiple intervention agents involved would likely be a physician, teacher, and parents.

Further consideration of this principle could be guided by the information in Table 1, consisting of a grid of intervention agents and mediators, and the different types of interventions they could be responsible for depending on the age level of the focus student(s). In general, involvement of multiple intervention agents, using more than one intervention strategy, will preclude over-reliance on one particular strategy.

Combine Proactive and Reactive Strategies

A third guiding principle for designing effect interventions for students with ADHD is that interventions should be designed to combine both proactive and reactive support strategies. Proactive strategies are those instructional and/or behavior management strategies designed to prevent problem behavior from occurring in the first place. For example, reviews of classroom rules and expectations at the start of an activity could reduce the likelihood of problem behavior occurrence. Also, reviewing and clarifying assignment directions prior to beginning an academic task would be considered a proactive management strategy.

Reactive strategies, on the other hand, are designed to effectively manage problem behavior when it does occur. For example, a response cost component of a token economy, whereby a student might be "fined" contingent on problem behavior, could serve to call a student's attention to both expectations and contingencies as well as to reduce the likelihood of future problems. In our experience with students with ADHD, com-

TABLE 1

Academic and Behavior Support Strategies for Students With ADHD Organized by Intervention Agent and Student's Level of Schooling

Intervention agent	Preschool	Elementary	Secondary
Teacher-mediated	• Behavior management • Instructional strategies	• Behavior management • Instructional strategies	• Study skills • Contracting
Parent-mediated	• Behavior management • Communication with teachers	• Goal-setting • Contracting • Home-based reinforcement • Parent tutoring	• Negotiating • Contracting • Home-based reinforcement
Peer-mediated		Peer tutoring	• Peer coaching • Peer mediation
Computer-assisted		• Instruction • Drill and practice	• Instruction • Word processing
Self-directed		Self-monitoring	• Self-monitoring • Self-evaluation
Other-directed (e.g., physician or counselor)	Medication and monitoring (behavioral outcomes)	Medication and monitoring (academic and behavioral outcomes)	Medication and monitoring (including self-report)

binations of proactive and reactive strategies are more effective at engendering well-regulated behavior, as compared to either approach alone.

Individualize Interventions

Students with ADHD are a heterogeneous group, varying widely with respect to the types of presenting difficulty, the magnitude of problems, and the etiological and maintaining variables related to the problems. As such, intervention effectiveness will be enhanced when interventions are designed so as to be individualized. While this principle may seem self-evident, it is not uncommon for professionals to approach all students with ADHD in a similar manner in our schools and communities.

To avoid a "one size fits all" approach, interventions need to be individually tailored to meet the needs of each student despite the fact that students may share a common diagnosis (DuPaul, Eckert, & McGoey, 1997). Planning for such individualization will need to take into account: (a) the child's current level of academic functioning, (b) current presenting problem behaviors, (c) the possible environmental functions of presenting inattentive behavior, (d) the target behaviors of greatest concern to the teacher and/or student, and (d) elements of the classroom environment and/or teaching approach that might limit the effectiveness of some interventions. Individualized interventions should be developed through a consultative problem–solving process using assessment data and collaborative interactions among teachers, parents, and other school professionals.

Deliver Interventions at the "Point of Performance"

A final guiding principle in designing effective interventions for students with ADHD is to intervene at the point of performance (Goldstein & Goldstein, 1998). This principle suggests that to be optimally effective strategies must be implemented as close in time and place as possible to the target behavior(s) of concern. For example, if the behavior of concern is attention to and completion of math work, then those strategies used in math class at the time when the student is expected to complete math work will be more effective than those removed in time/place. The further removed in time and place the intervention is from the occurrence of the behavior of interest, the less effective that strategy will be. This guiding principle is based on growing evidence that impulsivity is the primary deficit underlying the attention difficulties and other symptoms of ADHD (Barkley, 1998). Thus, to be effective at changing and managing impulsive behavior, interventions need to be implemented at the point of performance of those behaviors.

INTERVENTIONS FOR PRESCHOOL-AGE STUDENTS

Children with attention problems and/or ADHD typically begin exhibiting difficulties prior to the age of 7 years (American Psychiatric Association, 1994). Further, young children exhibiting ADHD–related behaviors are at higher than average risk for the development of oppositional and defiant behavior as well as academic difficulties upon school entry (Campbell & Ewing, 1990; Lahey et al., 1998). Thus, it is important to intervene early not only to address current behavior difficulties but also to prevent or reduce the severity of aggression, defiance, and academic skills deficits. The three major intervention approaches taken with this age group are parent–mediated behavioral strategies, modifications to preschool programming, and prescription of stimulant medication (McGoey, Eckert, & DuPaul, in press).

Parent–Mediated Interventions

A number of research studies have provided evidence that parent training interventions improve parent–child interactions assessed under analog conditions (e.g.,

Erhardt & Baker, 1990; Strayhorn & Weidman, 1989). Positive treatment effects have included increases in child compliance, use of appropriate parental commands, knowledge of appropriate parenting techniques, and positive parental statements. In addition, some preliminary research evidence suggests that once parenting patterns are established, positive effects in the behavior of preschool-age children with ADHD may be observed in settings other than the home (e.g., school setting) and over a long time period (Strayhorn & Wiedman, 1991).

Home-based intervention strategies that have been found effective include (a) use of brief, direct commands; (b) positive parent attention to appropriate child behavior; (c) implementation of contingency management strategies wherein children earn token reinforcers (e.g., poker chips) for compliance with parent directives; (d) use of response cost and time-out from positive reinforcement strategies to reduce noncompliant and aggressive behavior; and (e) discussion of methods to promote maintenance of behavior change over time. Typically, training is delivered to parents in the context of weekly, 60- to 120-minute sessions over the course of several months. Training can be provided on an individual basis to parents or in a more cost-effective manner by working with small groups of parents. Further, there is evidence that a videotape-based discussion approach may be preferable to a didactic approach to training (Webster-Stratton, 1993).

It is clear that parent-mediated behavioral strategies lead to positive outcomes for young children with ADHD, at least at the group level. Because most studies have employed multi-component treatment packages, it is unclear which component or combination of components is the active ingredient for successful behavior change. Stated differently, no existing study of parent training has employed a dismantling strategy to discern which treatment procedures are effective and which procedures are superfluous. This is not merely an academic question, given that treatment in a managed-care environment must be as streamlined as possible.

Most of the existing research on parent-mediated interventions for young children exhibiting symptoms of ADHD has focused on increasing compliance to parent directives. Clearly, a more comprehensive approach to altering the trajectory of academic and behavioral problems of these children is needed. For example, parents might be trained to assist in the instruction of pre-academic skills, to provide support in communicating effectively with teachers, and to help focus on injury prevention in parenting highly active and aggressive youngsters. Unfortunately, no empirical data are available regarding the efficacy of more comprehensive home-based strategies applied over a long time period.

Preschool Intervention Strategies

Although surprisingly few studies have been conducted on preschool interventions with this population, contingency management interventions have been found to be effective in reducing disruptive behavior and enhancing attention to classroom activities among young children exhibiting behaviors related to ADHD (e.g., McCain & Kelley, 1993; McGoey & DuPaul, 2000). Studies have documented the effects of two variants of contingency management. One approach is for the preschool teacher to provide positive reinforcement (i.e., praise and token reinforcement) for appropriate classroom behavior while also employing response cost (i.e., removal of tokens) following disruptive behavior. McGoey and DuPaul found that this intervention combination led to noticeable reductions in the inattentive, disruptive behavior of several young children diagnosed with ADHD. Another option is to use a school-home note system wherein home-based reinforcement (e.g., preferred activities) is provided contingent on appropriate behavior at school. McCain and Kelley (1993) found that a daily note system led to demonstrable increases in on-task behavior and concomitant reductions in disruptive behavior in a 5-year-old boy diagnosed with ADHD.

In order for classroom interventions to be successful for this age group, several procedures must be used by school professionals. First, a consultative problem-solving process should be followed wherein a preschool teacher and a consultant jointly identify target behaviors and generate potential intervention strategies (Kratochwill & Bergan, 1990). Following this process helps to ensure that interventions are individualized, are appropriate for the specific environmental context, and are acceptable to the teacher. Second, contingency management interventions should directly address the function of the challenging behavior being reduced. For example, Boyajian, DuPaul, Handler, Eckert, and McGoey (2001) demonstrated that aggressive behavior exhibited by young children with ADHD can serve a variety of functions and that incorporating the latter into intervention design leads to effective outcomes. Finally, preschool interventions should go beyond attempts to reduce inattentive and disruptive behavior. Given the risk for academic difficulties in this population, preschool teachers should be encouraged to incorporate strategies that enhance the early literacy and numeracy skills of young children with attention problems. For example, the *Ladders to Literacy* program (Notari-Syverson, O'Connor, & Vadasy, 1998) has been found to enhance the early language and literacy development of children with disabilities, children at-risk for learning difficulties, and typically developing children. Although this literacy development program has not been directly field-tested with children exhibiting ADHD-related behaviors, it is imperative that strategies designed to prevent academic difficulties in these children be implemented prior to school entry. Unfortunately, even when contingency management interventions are effective in reducing disruptive behavior, we cannot assume that academic skills are enhanced as a result.

Pharmacological Interventions

A growing number of young children are treated with medication to address attention and behavior difficulties. In fact, Zito et al. (2000) estimated that approximately 2–4% of preschool-age children are treated with psychotropic medication, with the majority receiving psychostimulant medication presumably to ameliorate ADHD symptoms. Fortunately, the results of several research studies suggest that methylphenidate (Ritalin®) can improve the compliance, on-task behaviors, and activity level of preschool-age children with ADHD. These positive behavioral effects have been observed with both low dosage levels (i.e., 0.3 mg/kg) and higher dosage levels (i.e., 10 mg/kg). Interestingly, although independent observations of child behaviors have been shown to improve at low dosage levels, parent and teacher ratings of child behaviors have not been affected in a unitary fashion. Only in high dosage conditions have significant changes in parent interactions been observed. Unfortunately, the likelihood of preschool-age children with ADHD experiencing medication side effects (e.g., loss of appetite and decreased social interaction) appears to increase with higher doses of methylphenidate.

Although research studies have documented significant behavioral improvements associated with methylphenidate, it is unclear whether this treatment is *necessary* for young children with this disorder. Stated differently, empirically based decision rules need to be developed to determine whether individual children exhibiting ADHD symptoms can profit from medication treatment beyond effects obtained with other interventions (e.g., home- and school-based contingency management programs). It is likely that some children will require medication while others will not. However, this decision must be made on an individual basis. Similarly, no investigation, to date, has examined possible individual differences in medication response with this age group. Numerous studies have delineated the idiosyncratic effects of methylphenidate for elementary school-age children with ADHD (e.g., Rapport et al., 1994). If we assume that individual differences in medication response also exist among younger children, then this would have important implications for clinical treatment of this disorder. Specifically, careful monitoring of medication effects must be conducted for each child treated with medication where baseline and ongoing assessment data are collected regarding changes in behavioral, academic, and social functioning. These data should include both parent and teacher perceptions of child behavior change to comprehensively document medication effects. Finally, potential side effects must be assessed, particularly if higher dosages are employed.

INTERVENTIONS FOR ELEMENTARY SCHOOL-AGE STUDENTS

Considerations of interventions for elementary school-age students with ADHD naturally begin with teacher-mediated strategies. Teachers, of course, are working with students at the "point of performance"—that is,—around academically and socially relevant issues throughout each school day. In addition to teachers, however, the classroom-based strategies described here can be used by other adults working in classrooms, such as teacher aides or parent and grandparent volunteers.

As was discussed earlier in this chapter, teacher-mediated strategies can be proactive or reactive. In our experience, a combination of the two generally provides the best results. Proactive strategies often will involve the entire class and are arranged to prevent academic and behavioral difficulties by altering the classroom conditions that allow problems to arise. By comparison, reactive strategies can be used to respond to both appropriate and problem behavior as part of an overall intervention program. Together, the goal of these strategies is to promote the monitoring and improvement of student performance through clearly communicated expectations and the provision of both positive and corrective feedback to students.

PROACTIVE INTERVENTIONS

Proactive intervention strategies typically involve arranging the conditions of the classroom environment prior to, and in the service of preventing, the occurrence of problem behavior. That is, if the teacher is able to accurately identify those situations and cues that are reliably followed by inattentive and disruptive behavior, then the most efficient manner of improving the situation is to do something before hand rather than waiting to react to the problem behavior. For many children with attention problems associated with ADHD, the two primary classroom situations that prompt inattentive behavior are teacher-directed instruction and the presentation of independent academic work. Further, inattentive behaviors can lead to academic difficulties, behavior problems, or both. Thus, in this section, examples of proactive strategies for preventing inattentive behavior associated with academic and behavioral problems are discussed. Proactive strategy selection for individual students should be guided by identifying antecedent conditions (i.e., variables related to task, person, time, or setting) that are associated with academic or behavioral difficulty.

Proactive Strategies to Improve Academic Performance

Several proactive interventions have been identified that can improve the academic performance of students with ADHD. These include adjusting academic expectations to match a student's current skills or instructional level, ClassWide Peer Tutoring (CWPT), computer-assisted instruction, arranging for students to have and make choices in their academic tasks, and providing for directed note-taking activities.

An initial consideration in support of the academic performance of students with attention difficulties is the degree to which curricular and instructional demands match a student's instructional level. This consideration is especially important in that some students, but certainly not all, may experience inattention and off-task behavior as a function of being asked to complete work beyond their current abilities. Curriculum-Based Measurement (CBM) data can help educators to avoid this situation by providing information to help in determining the proper placement of a student for instruction within the curriculum (Shinn, 1998). In addition to instructional placement considerations, children with attention problems related to ADHD will require additional interventions to address their academic and behavioral difficulties.

For example, students with ADHD have been shown to respond in a positive manner to peer-tutoring strategies. Peer tutoring can be defined as any instructional strategy in which two students work together on an academic activity with one student providing assistance, instruction, and/or feedback to the other (Greenwood, Maheady, & Carta, 1991). Various peer-tutoring models have been developed that differ as to instructional focus (acquisition versus practice), structure (reciprocal versus nonreciprocal), and procedural components (e.g., number of sessions per week, methods of pairing students, type of reward system used). However, the differing peer-tutoring models share a number of instructional characteristics that are known to enhance the task-related attention of students with ADHD including (a) working one-to-one with another individual; (b) instructional pace determined by learner; (c) continuous prompting of academic responses; and (d) frequent, immediate feedback about quality of performance (Barkley, 1998).

One widely used peer tutoring program is known as CWPT (see Greenwood, Maheady, & Carta, 1991). CWPT has been implemented in general-education classrooms to enhance the mathematics, reading, and spelling skills of students of all achievement levels. The primary procedures of CWPT include the following: (a) the class is divided into two groups identified as teams; (b) within each team, classmates form tutoring pairs; (c) students take turns tutoring each other; (d) tutors are provided with academic scripts (e.g., math problems with answers); (e) praise and points are available to students contingent on correct answers; (f) errors are corrected immediately by peers, along with an opportunity for practicing the correct answer; (g) the classroom teacher monitors the tutoring pairs and provides bonus points for pairs that are carefully following the CWPT procedures; and (h) points are tallied by each individual student at the conclusion of each session.

CWPT tutoring sessions typically last 20 minutes with an additional 5 minutes for charting progress and putting materials away. At week's end, the team with the most points is recognized by the other team through applause and praise. Earned points typically are not used in any other fashion. CWPT has been found to enhance the on-task behavior and academic performance of non-medicated students with ADHD in general education classrooms (DuPaul, Ervin, Hook, & McGoey, 1998). Also of interest was finding that typically achieving students also showed improvements in attention and academic performance when participating in CWPT activities. Thus, peer tutoring is an intervention that can help *all* students. As such, it has the potential to be seen by teachers as both a practical and a time-efficient strategy for meeting the needs of children with attention problems.

In addition to teachers and peers, computers also can mediate the delivery of instructional support for elementary school-age students. Specifically, computers can promote the initial acquisition of skills through the use of instructional technology and can enhance the mastery of already acquired skills through drill-and-practice software. For example, recent research by Ota and DuPaul (in press) has demonstrated increases in the on-task and work productivity of students with ADHD and learning disabilities by using computer-assisted instruction (CAI). It appears that the instructional features of CAI helped students to focus their attention on academic stimuli. Although not ever-present, the seemingly beneficial instructional design features of CAI are as follows: specific instructional objectives are readily presented alongside activities, highlighting of essential material (e.g., large print, and color) is provided for, multiple sensory modalities are used, content material is divided into manageable bits of information, and immediate feedback about response accuracy is provided. In addition, CAI can readily limit the presentation of nonessential features that may be distracting (e.g., sound effects, animation). More research is needed. It is clear that classroom use of CAI does hold promise for enhancing the academic behavior and performance of students with attention problems.

Another proactive strategy is choice making. Here, students are allowed to choose from two or more concurrently presented activities. Recent studies have demonstrated the value of providing task-related choices to students with behavior difficulties, including ADHD, in that on-task behavior and work productivity can increase under choice conditions (e.g., Dunlap et al., 1994). Choice making typically is implemented by providing a student with a menu of potential tasks in a particular academic subject area from which to choose. For example, if the student is having difficulty completing independent math assignments, then the child would be presented with several possible math assignments to choose from. The child would be expected to choose and complete one of the tasks listed on the menu during the allotted time period. Thus, while the teacher retains control over the general nature of the assigned work, the student is provided with some control over the specific assignment.

Proactive Strategies to Improve Social Behavior

Proactive strategies also can be used to enhance social behavior and to prevent problem behavior in classrooms. Examples of such strategies include active teaching of classroom or school rules and altering the structure of the classroom environment.

The degree to which teachers provide students with cues, prompts, or signals to follow classroom rules ultimately determines the effectiveness of those rules in maintaining appropriate student behavior (Paine, Radicchi, Rosellini, Deutchman, & Darch, 1983). Unfortunately, many elementary school-age children, including those with attention problems and ADHD, have difficulty following classroom rules—presumably because these rules have not been well learned.

Clearly, all teachers have classroom rules, ones that typically are taught specifically at the beginning of the school year. However, actively teaching these rules throughout the school year can be an effective deterrent for problem behavior as well as a support for appropriate behavior. Active teaching of classroom rules involves the following procedures: (a) developing four or five clearly stated rules(these should be "positively" stated, conveying information about what to do or how to behave rather than what not to do in the classroom), (b) initial teaching of those rules with examples and non-examples of rule-following, and (c) periodic (e.g., once per week) re-teaching or discussing of one or two of the classroom rules. This last procedure, for example, would involve the review of one rule via stating and discussing the rule with students and its importance for 2 minutes. This re-teaching might be arranged one or two times per week at the beginning of a class or day, followed by the acknowledgment of one or two examples of students following the rules each class period or three or four times throughout the day.

In addition to active teaching of classroom rules, teachers working with children who exhibit significant attention difficulties and ADHD-related behaviors should consider altering the classroom environment to allow for more careful monitoring of student activities. For example, placing a student's desk near the teacher's may allow easier observation of the student's behaviors and enhance the probability that the student will understand teacher directives (Paine et al., 1983). Teachers also should be encouraged to arrange the classroom so that students with attention problems are more likely to participate in class activities while not restricting opportunities to learn and benefit from instruction. For example, students with attention problems may sometimes be placed in isolated parts of the classroom to decrease potential distractions for the child. Although such environmental arrangements may be successful in some ways, it is important that the student remain accessible to teacher instruction, to appropriate peer interaction, and to important class activities.

REACTIVE INTERVENTIONS

Reactive intervention strategies typically focus on providing feedback to students and/or consequences for problem behavior. Typically, these strategies developed with a focus on individual students. Individually tailored strategies can help to minimize the impact of disruptive behavior on a classroom, reduce the frequency of negative interactions between a student and teacher, and teach the child a more appropriate way to get attention from the teacher. Thus, the goal of these strategies is to provide information and supports to enhance the student's ability to focus on learning and minimize the likelihood that disruptive behavior will be reinforced. This latter goal in particular will be facilitated by the use of functional assessment to assist in understanding what variables support the maintenance of problem behaviors among students with attention problems and ADHD.

Functional Assessment-Linked Strategies

Functional assessment strategies are interviews, observations, and environmental manipulations (e.g., changing a seating arrangement) intended to identify environmental variables that reliably precede or reliably follow problem behaviors of concern. Such variables are then hypothesized, in a behavior analytic formulation, to prompt or promote the occurrence of problem behavior in the case of preceding variables. And in the case of variables reliably following problem behavior, these are hypothesized to reinforce or maintain problem behavior (see Nelson et al., 1998).

Understanding the factors that maintain problem behaviors, along with the situations that appear to set the stage for those behaviors, is an essential first step in planning successful interventions (DuPaul et al., 1997). For example, consider a target student's disruptive classroom behavior (e.g., verbal disruptions, speaking out of turn) that is reliably occasioned by the teacher's instructional presentation of new math material. In this instance one potential intervention could involve provision of teacher assistance at the beginning of that activity to ensure that rules and expectations are understood, that the student has all materials needed to participate in the instruction, and that the student is able to clearly see and hear the teacher's presentation. This would be a preventive or proactive strategy.

Alternatively, consider the same student and behavior but a different formulation of the problem. In this instance, suppose the student's disruptive behavior reliably results in teacher attention (e.g., "Michael, please stop disrupting the lesson? Don't you remember the class rules?"). Here it might be hypothesized that Michael's disruptive behavior is being reinforced through teacher-delivered social attention. At least one component of a "functional" approach to intervention would include behavior management strategies intended to strengthen an alternative behavior that would produce the same type of reinforcement—in this case teacher attention. For example, the teacher might use a strategy that included providing attention contingent upon Michael's responding appropriately to a question posed by the teacher and/or otherwise maintaining appropriate attention to the lesson and withholding attention when disruptive behavior occurs.

Based on this type of functional formulation, Ervin, DuPaul, Kern, and Friman (1998) conducted a study using functional assessment strategies to guide the development of classroom-based interventions for four adolescents diagnosed with ADHD. For two of these students, the interventions used were linked to problems hypothesized to serve the functions of escape from written tasks for one student and access to peer attention for another student. The first student was allowed to complete written assignments using a computer rather than writing by hand: The problem behavior was hypothesized to be escape motivated. The second student was provided with peer attention contingent on the display of on-task behavior: The problem behavior was hypothesized to be maintained by peer attention. Results of this work suggested that the classroom interventions based on functional assessment strategies resulted in significant improvements in the behavior of both students.

Response Cost

One strategy that combines both proactive and reactive approaches to behavior management is known as response cost, a form of token economy. Token reinforcement is a commonly used strategy in which students earn points for meeting behavioral expectations, and the points can be exchanged for privileges. Response cost is a variation of a token economy wherein students earn tokens based on positive classroom behavior and lose them for inappropriate behavior. Response cost systems require planning and clear communication from the outset. The rules of the system should be taught and reviewed on an ongoing basis. The student should understand when the system will be used, how points may be gained or lost, what privileges are available in exchange for points, and when points may be turned in for privileges. It may be useful to check which privilege a student is working toward before beginning an activity and to intermittently change the available privileges in order to maintain student interest.

For these systems to be effective, it is imperative that students be involved in the creation of the menu of possible privileges, and that students be supported to gain privileges on a regular basis. Electronic versions of response cost, such as the Attention Training System (ATS; Rapport, 1987), allow the teacher to respond to inappropriate behavior on the part of one child while continuing to work with other children or the whole class. This electronic system is made up of a student module, which sits on the student's desk, and a teacher module. The student automatically accumulates points as the student works independently or in a group. When the teacher notices off-task or disruptive behavior, student points can be readily deducted by pushing a button on the teacher module. Thus, immediate feedback on student behavior is provided without interrupting classroom activities or instruction.

A manual version of response cost uses numbered cards held together by a binder ring. The teacher adds and subtracts points by changing the top card on his or her set of cards as the child demonstrates appropriate or inappropriate behavior. As the teacher changes cards, the student changes the number of points on his or her set of cards to match the teacher's set. These strategies provide the student with frequent and immediate feedback on performance, which is an important factor in helping children with ADHD meet the behavioral expectations of the classroom. This immediate communication of positive or corrective feedback helps to improve student outcomes in the areas of behavior and classroom achievement. Several studies have supported the use of response cost strategies for children with attention problems associated with ADHD (see Barkley, 1998).

Parents as Intervention Agents

Other effective strategies that can help improve student performance in the classroom are mediated by parents. Educators can provide an important service to parents of a child with ADHD by clearly communicating school expectations and by teaching strategies that can be used by parents to promote academic success. Systematic ongoing communication is needed between the parents and teachers in order for parents to effectively support their children's academic performance. Designing a system to support ongoing communication is important, whether it consists of notes sent home on a daily or weekly basis, weekly check-in phone calls or e-mail, brief conversations when a child is picked up after school, or some other system that fits the particular family and school. Maintaining communication allows parents to hear about their child's struggles and successes in school, to communicate about home issues that may be influencing classroom performance, and to build a partnership with teachers with a goal of improving children's ability to succeed in school.

Contingency Contracting

Home-based reinforcement programs can help to strengthen school-based behavior management systems by allowing the child to earn privileges at home based on positive school behavior. Effective home-based programs require ongoing communication between the teacher and parents, and this can be accomplished through the use of a daily note or report that is sent home with the student (Pelham & Waschbusch, 1999). Parents and teachers can negotiate a contingency contract, which specifies the academic performance and classroom behavior that is expected and the privileges that can be earned at home if the child successfully demonstrates the behaviors. This type of contract is most likely to be successful if privileges can be earned each day rather than on a week-ly basis. Long-term success is built on small successes right from the start, so choosing criteria that the child is easily able to meet at the beginning while slowly building up to more challenging goals is an important feature of the contingency contract.

One study of the use of school-home notes with a preschooler with ADHD showed that classroom on-task behavior increased contingent on home-based rein-forcement (McCain & Kelley, 1993). In this study, the preschooler was allowed to color in a happy face on his school-home note when he completed a predetermined amount of time engaged in a task. Eventually, the child was able to set his own timer, engage in the task, then color in the happy face if he had stayed on-task for the full time. In addi-tion, the preschool teacher circled happy, sad, or neutral faces on the school-home note at the end of various activities to provide feedback to the child and his parents about his success in meeting several target behaviors throughout the day. One drawback of home-school notes may be that the success of the system depends on the delivery of the notes, which is usually the responsibility of the child. In the case of a child with ADHD, home-school communication may be more consistent and accurate if it takes place directly between the teacher and parents. The most effective method of commu-nication should be determined on a case-by-case basis.

SELF-MANAGEMENT

A more advanced type of strategy to improve classroom behavior involves self-directed activities that require children to monitor and/or evaluate their own behavior over time. The aspects of a self-management system most likely to actually be managed by the student include observing and evaluating behavior whereas the task of identify-ing problem behaviors and goals is more likely to be done by adults (Fantuzzo & Polite, 1990). Further, interventions with a stronger self-management component may be more effective than those that are managed for the most part by the teacher. When developing interventions that include self-management components, it may be useful to clearly identify which aspects will be teacher-controlled and which will be managed by the student, and to make decisions about these based on the individual student's needs and abilities.

A self-evaluation system generally allows a student to earn points that can be exchanged for privileges (e.g., Rhode, Morgan, & Young, 1983). The teacher clearly identifies the target behaviors and academic performance expected and provides a writ-ten rating scale that states the performance criteria for each rating. The teacher and the student separately rate student behavior during an activity. At the end of the activity or time period, the teacher and student compare ratings. If they match exactly, then the student keeps all points and earns a bonus point. If the student rating is within one point of the teacher rating, then the student keeps his or her points. If the student rat-ing is more than one point away from the teacher ratings, then the student does not receive points for the activity. Eventually, the close teacher involvement is faded, and the student becomes responsible for monitoring his or her own behavior.

Children with ADHD often lack the skill to be accurate judges of their own behavior. Because they may have a tendency toward recalling their positive behaviors and not recognizing the problem behaviors that affect their ratings, a brief discussion or reminder of the behaviors that led to a lower rating may be useful (Hinshaw & Melnick, 1992). Designing a self-management system in a classroom involves teaching the child with ADHD to use the system, providing clear descriptions of the expected behaviors, and drawing up a list of privileges the student would like to earn. The goal of such a system is to eventually train the child to monitor his or her own behavior in the classroom without having constant feedback from the teacher.

Medication Treatment of Elementary School-Age Students With ADHD

Elementary school-age students with ADHD are considered good candidates for treatment with psychtropic medications—particularly psychostimulants—by pediatricians, psychologists, psychiatrists, and others. For thorough discussions of this topic, see Barkley (1998) and DuPaul and Stoner (1994). For our limited discussion here, though, a few points need to be made about the use of medications with these children. First, when students with ADHD are treated with psychostimulants, medication should be considered one component of a treatment package that also should include behavioral and educational supports. Second, school psychologists and other school personnel (e.g., school nurses, teachers) can play a crucial role in monitoring medication response, including the effects of medication dose on academic performance and behavior. Third, these professionals also can play a critical role in ongoing monitoring of medication effects, including the presence or absence of potentially harmful side effects. Finally, through careful and professional collaboration and communication regarding these issues with the medical professionals responsible for medication treatments, school-based personnel can enhance the experiences and functioning of children with ADHD and their parents and teachers.

INTERVENTIONS FOR SECONDARY SCHOOL-AGE STUDENTS

Many of the same interventions that are used with elementary school age students can be adapted for effective use with adolescents attending middle and high schools. The primary intervention approaches include teacher-mediated behavioral and organizational strategies, peer coaching, self-management, and vocational planning. Stimulant medication also can be an effective treatment for this age group. However, several factors unique to this age group must be considered in monitoring and managing pharmacotherapy.

Teacher-Mediated Interventions

Teachers continue to be a primary intervention agent for secondary school students with ADHD. Strategies include contingency contracts, support of student self-management (see self-management section, below), promoting study and organizational skills, and proactive communication with families.

Contingency contracting involves the negotiation of an agreement between a student and teacher that stipulates (a) what is expected of the student (i.e., responsibilities), (b) what will happen if responsibilities are fulfilled (i.e., privileges), and (c) what will happen if responsibilities are not met or if major rule violations are committed (i.e., penalties). This contract is a more abstract version of the token reinforcement approach used with younger children.

Several factors should be considered when designing a contract for a student with ADHD (DuPaul & Stoner, 1994). First, the length of time between the required behavior and the contingent reinforcement should be as brief as possible. Daily and weekly reinforcement is preferred over longer delays because students with ADHD often engage in impulsive actions that require relatively immediate consequences. Second, attainable goals should be set for the student so that immediate success can be achieved. The probability of success is further enhanced by the inclusion of a small number of goals or responsibilities at a time. Third, students should have a voice in determining the privileges that they will work for. This may necessitate including the parents in the negotiation process because home-based activities may be necessary to motivate secondary level students. Fourth, the contract should be re-negotiated on a regular basis (at least monthly) because a student's progress often will require changes to goals and privileges over time.

Teachers can implement a number of strategies to enhance the *study and organizational skills* of students with ADHD. For example, the Directed Note-Taking Activity (Spires & Stone, 1989) has been used successfully to teach students with ADHD organized and effective ways to take notes on classroom lectures (Evans, Pelham, & Grudberg, 1995). Specifically, the teacher instructs students on the note-taking process by illustrating how to outline notes based on main ideas and details. The number of teacher prompts is slowly faded until students are able to independently form an outline based on the presented lecture material. A similar, structured approach can be taken to help students prepare and study for tests and/or for the preparation of long-term projects (e.g., book reports). Teachers can help students by (a) breaking the studying or long-term project into a series of small steps that can be completed on a daily basis, (b) setting daily goals for completion of steps, (c) providing feedback to students about timely completion of short-term steps, and (d) providing reinforcement contingent upon completion of each daily step (this will necessitate the involvement of parents). Beyond the inherent structure of this approach, the key is making a long-term, more abstract assignment (e.g., studying for a test that is 2 weeks away) into a series of short-term, concrete, and brief tasks that are completed on a daily basis. Feedback and contingencies provide the motivation for students to complete these steps. Additional strategies for enhancing the study and organizational skills of students with ADHD can be obtained by consulting Gleason, Colvin, and Archer (1991, and this volume).

As students progress from elementary to middle school, parent-teacher contact typically lessens in intensity and frequency. Although this may not be detrimental to the educational progress of children without disabilities, the diminished frequency of home-school communication can exacerbate the problems experienced by adolescents with ADHD. Thus, a structured *home-school communication process* is necessary on an ongoing basis. This communication can take many forms. Perhaps the most common example is the use of daily or weekly school-home notes (see Kelley, 1990). These notes can be used to facilitate home-based reinforcement of school performance (as was discussed for elementary school-age students) or for communicating daily homework assignments. As is the case for younger students, home-school communication must be continuous (at least weekly), focused on the positive aspects of the student's performance, and should be tied to home-based consequences for motivational purposes. Further, the student should be directly involved in the design of this communication and in the negotiation of what consequences will be included. School-home communication should not occur solely when there are problems. Rather, it must be proactive and focused on growth.

Self-Management Interventions

In cases in which adolescents with ADHD have shown progress with externally managed interventions (e.g., contingency contract), self-management strategies can be used to promote the maintenance and generalization of obtained effects. Although self-control training procedures that embrace a cognitive therapy perspective have been minimally effective for the treatment of ADHD (see Abikoff, 1985), self-monitoring and self-evaluation strategies that include contingencies have greater potential for success (Shapiro & Cole, 1994).

Self-monitoring strategies involve training students to recognize and report whether they have demonstrated a specific behavior or sequence of behaviors during an identified time period. For example, Gureasko, DuPaul, and White (2000) investigated the effectiveness of a self-monitoring program in helping three middle school-age boys with ADHD to be better prepared for class. The boys received brief training from a school psychologist in how to monitor their classroom preparedness behaviors by using a checklist describing a range of student classroom behavior from very consistent with classroom rules and expectations to very inconsistent with them. Students also were taught to evaluate their performance in light of goals that they had set with the school psychologist (i.e., self-reinforcement). As they exhibited success with the procedures, the involvement of the school psychologist was faded so that procedures were eventually entirely self-managed. Each of the three students consistently improved in being prepared for class, and these improvements maintained over time even in the absence of external support.

Self-evaluation strategies incorporating a gradual shift from external to self-reinforcement have been found to enhance the attention and behavioral deportment of students with ADHD and related behavior disorders (Hoff & DuPaul, 1998; Rhode et al., 1983). Prior to the first stage of self-management, students are trained by teachers to recognize target behaviors associated with ratings from 0 to 5 (e.g., 5 = all work completed, of excellent quality; 0 = little or no work completed, quality of work is poor). These behaviors are modeled for children, and the latter also role-play target behaviors while stating the rating associated with the behavior. During the first stage of self-management, students and teachers independently rated student performance during one academic period. Ratings are then compared as follows: (a) if students' ratings are within one point of teacher's, then they keep the points they gave themselves; (b) if students ratings match teacher's exactly, then they receive the points they gave themselves plus one bonus point; and (c) if student and teacher ratings deviate by more than one point, then no points are awarded. As is the case in a token reinforcement system, points are exchanged for preferred activities on a daily or weekly basis.

During successive stages of the self-evaluation program, the frequency of teacher-student matches is gradually reduced to 0%. For example, during the 50% match stage, a coin is flipped following each rating period wherein the student is required to match the teacher an average of 50% of the time. Given that the outcome is random and unpredictable, students cannot assume prior to the coin flip that they do not have to match the teacher's rating. On the occasions where students do not have to match, they automatically keep the points they give to themselves. In the Hoff and DuPaul (1998) research, student behavior was evaluated across these self-management phases. Generalization across settings was programmed for and systematically evaluated. Obtained data showed that the student was able to maintain behavioral improvements initially elicited under token reinforcement despite the fading of teacher feedback. It is important to note that by the end of the study the student continued to provide written ratings of performance and continued to receive backup contingencies. The ideal outcome would be for written ratings to be faded to oral ratings while backup contingencies are phased out.

For some students exhibiting ADHD-related behaviors, the process of teaching self-management (i.e., achieving generalization across time and settings) will take several months while for others this will take several school years. Unfortunately, for some youngsters with more severe attention problems, this process may be a life-long affair. Nevertheless, a contingency-based, self-evaluation protocol may be a viable option for promoting the generalization of behavior change obtained under externally managed procedures.

Peer-Mediated Strategies

Positive peer influence can be a powerful motivator for children exhibiting behavior difficulties, particularly those with few friends. *Peer tutoring* interventions used for elementary school-age students (see above) can be adapted for use with older students. Clearly, tutoring strategies can be warranted when students are experiencing academic difficulties secondary to their attention or behavior problems, especially if the latter appear to be a function of peer attention.

Another promising strategy in this domain is the use of *peer coaching,* wherein the student with ADHD is paired with a classmate or older student who can provide ongoing support in the school setting. Dawson and Guare (1998) describe a model for coaching students with ADHD that has the potential for successful implementation by peers. The coaching process involves five steps: (a) identifying the need for a coach, (b) obtaining the target student's commitment to coaching, (c) matching the student with a coach, (d) setting up the first meeting with the coach, and (e) implementing daily coaching sessions. During daily sessions, the coach helps the student to set long-term goals, determine the steps to achieve these goals, identify potential obstacles, develop ways to circumvent obstacles, identify ways to enhance the probability of success, and ensure that the plan is realistic. Once goals and plans are formulated, daily sessions include a review of progress since the last session, an evaluation of the relative success of the plan, anticipation of what needs to be done next, and a plan for the time period before the next session. Dawson and Guare caution that selection of a peer coach must be done carefully because this is a considerable time commitment. Further, adult supervision (e.g., school psychologist or special educator) is necessary to ensure that potential conflict is handled in a proactive and effective fashion.

Medication Monitoring

As is the case for younger children, a variety of psychotropic medications (especially stimulants) can be helpful for adolescents with ADHD. Approximately 50–60% of teenagers with this disorder will respond positively to methylphenidate or other stimulants (Spencer et al., 1996). Care must be taken to monitor not only the behavioral effects of these medications but also their impact on academic performance at school and home. Further, students should participate in the evaluation of their response by reporting changes in their behavior and possible side effects (DuPaul, Anastopoulos, Kwasnik, Barkley, & McMurray, 1996). Because some of the side effects of stimulant medications may not be overt (e.g., dysphoric mood), students can report a greater number of these emergent effects than do teachers or parents. Finally, even when medication is effective, it should be supplemented with behavioral and educational interventions to optimize functioning in these areas.

Planning for School-School or School-Work Transition

Given the impulsivity associated with ADHD, many students exhibiting symptoms of this disorder do not systematically consider the long-term consequences or implications of their school performance. Thus, students with this disorder often require greater guidance in planning for post-secondary school activities (DuPaul & Stoner, 1994). Specifically, it is important that students receive ongoing and intensive advising as to educational and vocational options. Preferably, student interests and strengths should be identified at an earlier age than for other children to encourage the student to develop a focus or interest area that will maintain their motivation for schooling. One of the greatest risks for this population is poor scholastic performance and leaving school prematurely (e.g., Barkley et al., 1990). Beginning in middle school and continuing throughout high school, students with ADHD should meet regularly with their guidance counselor or related personnel to receive ongoing assessment and programming relevant to college or vocational aspirations. In some cases, colleges that have a strong track record for helping students with disabilities to achieve success should be explored with students. Unfortunately, there has been little empirical study of post-secondary planning with students who have ADHDADHD, and, therefore, there is little guidance that can be offered with respect to effective versus ineffective procedures. Nevertheless, it is important that all adolescents with ADHD be provided with this kind of support and planning so that their potential academic and occupational success is maximized.

SUMMARY AND CONCLUSIONS

Students identified with ADHD are likely to be difficult to teach and difficult to manage in classroom settings. In some cases these difficulties will be pervasive across time and settings, while in others these difficulties will be relatively confined to specific academic areas, or to particular phases or points in time. This, of course, is due to the heterogeneity that characterizes this like-diagnosed group of students. However, it also is the case that most of these students are capable of functioning quite well in school, behaving, performing academically, and achieving in ways that are similar to their typical peers. The strategies described in this chapter, mediated by teachers, parents, peers, computers, and the students themselves, hold great promise for providing the supports needed by individual students to succeed in school. To do so, however, the strategies, mediators, and specifics of intervention design and delivery will need to be individually tailored to each student and setting.

REFERENCES

Abikoff, H. (1985). Efficacy of cognitive training intervention in hyperactive children: A critical review. *Clinical Psychology Review, 5,* 479-512.

American Psychiatric Association. (1994). *Diagnostic and statistical manual of mental disorders* (4th ed.). Washington, DC: Author.

Barkley, R. A. (Ed.). (1998). *Attention-Deficit Hyperactivity Disorder: A handbook for diagnosis and treatment.* New York: Guilford.

Barkley, R. A., Fischer, M., Edelbrock, C. S., & Smallish, L. (1990). The adolescent outcome of hyperactive children diagnosed by research criteria: I. An 8-year prospective study. *Journal of the American Academy of Child and Adolescent Psychiatry, 29,* 546-557.

Boyajian, A. E., DuPaul, G. J., Handler, M. W., Eckert, T. L, & McGoey, K. E. (2001). The use of classroom-based brief functional analyses with preschoolers at-risk for Attention Deficit Hyperactivity Disorder. *School Psychology Review, 30,* 278-293.

Campbell, S. B., & Ewing, L. J. (1990). Follow-up of hard to manage preschoolers: Adjustment at age 9 and predictors of continuing symptoms. *Journal of Child Psychology and Psychiatry, 31,* 871-889.

Cantwell, D. P., & Baker, L. (1991). Association between Attention-Deficit Hyperactivity Disorder and learning disorders. *Journal of Learning Disabilities, 24,* 88-95.

Dawson, P., & Guare, R. (1998). *Coaching the ADHD student.* North Tonawanda, NY: Multi-Health Systems.

Dunlap, G., dePerczel, M., Clarke, S., Wilson, D., Wright, S., White, R., & Gomez, A. (1994). Choice making to promote adaptive behavior for students with emotional and behavioral challenges. *Journal of Applied Behavior Analysis, 27,* 505-518.

DuPaul, G. J., Anastopoulos, A. D., Kwasnik, D., Barkley, R. A., & McMurray, M. B. (1996). Methylphenidate effects on children with attention deficit hyperactivity disorder: Self-report of symptoms, side-effects, and self-esteem. *Journal of Attention Disorders, 1,* 3-15.

DuPaul, G. J., & Eckert, T. L. (1997). School-based interventions for children with Attention-Deficit/Hyperactivity Disorder: A meta-analysis. *School Psychology Review, 26,* 5-27.

DuPaul, G. J., Eckert, T. L., & McGoey, K. E. (1997). Interventions for students with Attention-Deficit/Hyperactivity Disorder: One size does not fit all. *School Psychology Review, 26,* 369-381.

DuPaul, G. J., Ervin, R. A., Hook, C. L., & McGoey, K. E. (1998). Peer tutoring for children with Attention Deficit Hyperactivity Disorder: Effects on classroom behavior and academic performance. *Journal of Applied Behavior Analysis, 31,* 579-592.

DuPaul, G. J., & Stoner, G. (1994). *ADHD in the schools: Assessment and intervention strategies.* New York: Guilford.

Erhardt, D., & Baker, B. L. (1990). The effects of behavioral parent training on families with young hyperactive children. *Journal of Behavior Therapy and Experimental Psychiatry, 21,* 121-132.

Ervin, R. A., DuPaul, G. J., Kern, L., & Friman, P. C. (1998). Classroom-based functional and adjunctive assessments: Proactive approaches to intervention selection for adolescents with attention deficit hyperactivity disorder. *Journal of Applied Behavior Analysis, 31,* 65-78.

Evans, S. W., Pelham, W., & Grudberg, M. V. (1995). The efficacy of notetaking to improve behavior and comprehension of adolescents with Attention Deficit Hyperactivity Disorder. *Exceptionality, 5,* 1-17.

Fantuzzo, J. W., & Polite, K. (1990). School-based, behavioral self-management: A review and analysis. *School Psychology Quarterly, 5,* 180-198.

Forness, S. R., Kavale, K. A., Sweeney, D. P., & Crenshaw, T. M. (1999). The future of research and practice in behavioral disorders: Psychopharmacology and its school implications. *Behavioral Disorders, 24,* 305-318.

Gleason, M. M., Colvin, G., & Archer, A. L. (1991). Interventions for improving study skills. In G. Stoner, M. R. Shinn, & H. M. Walker (Eds.), *Interventions for achievement and behavior problems* (pp. 137-160). Silver Spring, MD: National Association of School Psychologists.

Goldstein, S., & Goldstein, M. (1998). *Managing attention disorders in children.* New York: Wiley.

Greenwood, C. R., Maheady, L., & Carta, J. J. (1991). Peer tutoring programs in the regular education classroom. In G. Stoner, M. R. Shinn, & H. M. Walker (Eds.), *Interventions for achievement and behavior problems* (pp. 179-200). Silver Spring, MD: National Association of School Psychologists.

Gresham, F. M. (1989). Assessment of treatment integrity in school consultation and prereferral intervention. *School Psychology Review, 18,* 37-50.

Gureasko, S., DuPaul, G. J., & White, G. P. (2000). *The effects of self-monitoring of organizational skills on the classroom performance of adolescents with attention deficit hyperactivity disorder.* Paper presented at the annual convention of the National Association of School Psychologists, Washington DC.

Hinshaw, S. P., & Melnick, S. (1992). Self-management therapies and Attention-Deficit Hyperactivity Disorder. *Behavior Modification, 16,* 253-273.

Hoff, K., & DuPaul, G. J. (1998). Reducing disruptive behavior in general education classrooms: The use of self-management strategies. *School Psychology Review, 27,* 290-303.

Kelley, M. L. (1990). *School-home notes: Promoting children's classroom success.* New York: Guilford.

Knivsberg, A., Reichelt, K. L., & Nodland, M. (1999). Comorbidity, or coexistence, between dyslexia and Attention Deficit Hyperactivity Disorder. *British Journal of Special Education, 26,* 42-47.

Kratochwill, T. R., & Bergan, J. (1990). *Behavioral consultation in applied settings: An individual guide.* New York: Plenum.

Lahey, B. B., Pelham, W. E., Stein, M. A., Loney, J., Trapani, C., Nugent, K., Kipp, H., Schmidt, E., Lee, S., Cale, M., Gold, E., Hartung, C. M., Willcutt, E., & Baumann, B. (1998). Validity of DSM-IV Attention-Deficit/Hyperactivity Disorder for younger children. *Journal of the American Academy of Child and Adolescent Psychiatry, 37,* 695-702.

Mannuzza, S., Gittelman-Klein, R., Bessler, A., Malloy, P., & LaPadulla, M. (1993). Adult outcome of hyperactive boys: Educational achievement, occupational rank, and psychiatric status. *Archives of General Psychiatry, 50,* 565-576.

McCain, A. P., & Kelley, M. L. (1993). Managing the classroom behavior of an ADHD preschooler: The efficacy of a school-home note intervention. *Child & Family Behavior Therapy, 15,* 33-44.

McGoey, K. E., & DuPaul, G. J. (2000). Token reinforcement and response cost procedures: Reducing the disruptive behavior of preschool children. *School Psychology Quarterly, 15,* 330-343.

McGoey, K. E., Eckert, T. L., & DuPaul, G. J. (in press). Intervention for preschool-age children with ADHD: A literature review. *Journal of Emotion and Behavior Disorders.*

The MTA Cooperative Group. (1999). A 14-month randomized clinical trial of treatment strategies for Attention-Deficit/Hyperactivity Disorder. *Archives of General Psychiatry, 56,* 1073-1086.

Nelson, J. R., Roberts, M. L., & Smith, D. J. (1998). *Conducting functional behavioral assessments: A practical guide.* Longmont, CO: Sopris West.

Notari-Syverson, A., O'Connor, R. E., & Vadasy, P. F. (1998). *Ladders to Literacy: A preschool activity book.* Baltimore: Paul Brookes.

O'Neill, R. E., Horner, R. H., Albin, R. W., Sprague, J., Storey, K., & Newton, J. S. (1997). *Functional analysis and program development for problem behavior: A practical handbook.* Pacific Grove, CA: Brooks/Cole.

Ota, K. R., & DuPaul, G. J. (in press). Task engagement and mathematics performance in children with attention deficit hyperactivity disorder: Effects of supplemental computer instruction. *School Psychology Quarterly.*

Paine, S. C., Radicchi, J., Rosellini, L. C., Deutchman, L., & Darch, C. B. (1983). *Structuring your classroom for academic success.* Champaign, IL: Research Press.

Pelham, W. E., & Waschbusch, D. A. (1999). Behavioral intervention in attention-deficit hyperactivity disorder. In H. C. Quay & A. E. Hogan (Eds.), *Handbook of disruptive behavior disorders* (pp. 255-278). New York: Kluwer Academic/Plenum.

Rapport, M. D. (1987). *The Attention Training System: User's manual.* DeWitt, NY: Gordon Systems.

Rapport, M. D., Denney, C. B., DuPaul, G. J., & Gardner, M. J. (1994). Attention Deficit Disorder and methylphenidate: Normalization rates, clinical effectiveness, and response prediction in 76 children. *Journal of the American Academy of Child and Adolescent Psychiatry, 33,* 882-893.

Rhode, G., Morgan, D. P., & Young, K. R. (1983). Generalization and maintenance of treatment gains of behaviorally handicapped students from resource rooms to regular classrooms using self-evaluation procedures. *Journal of Applied Behavior Analysis, 16,* 171-188.

Semrud-Clikeman, M., Biederman, J., Sprich-Buckminster, S., Lehman, B. K., Faraone, S. V., & Norman, D. (1992). Comorbidity between ADHD and learning disability: A review and report in a clinically referred sample. *Journal of the American Academy of Child and Adolescent Psychiatry, 31,* 439-448.

Shapiro, E. S., & Cole, C. L. (1994). *Behavior change in the classroom: Self-management interventions.* New York: Guilford.

Shinn, M. R. (Ed.). (1998). *Advanced applications of Curriculum-Based Measurement.* New York: Guilford.

Spencer, T., Biederman, J., Wilens, T., Harding, M., O'Donnell, D., & Griffin, S. (1996). Pharmacotherapy of Attention-Deficit Hyperactivity Disorder across the life cycle. *Journal of the American Academy of Child and Adolescent Psychiatry, 35,* 409-432.

Spires, H. A., & Stone, D. P. (1989). The directed notetaking activity: A self-questioning approach. *Journal of Reading, 33,* 36-39.

Strayhorn, J. M., & Weidman, C. S. (1989). Reduction of attention deficit and internalizing symptoms through parent-child interaction training. *Journal of the American Academy of Child and Adolescent Psychiatry, 28,* 888-896.

Strayhorn, J. M., & Weidman, C. S. (1991). Follow-up one year after parent child interaction training: Effects on behavior of preschool children. *Journal of the American Academy of Child and Adolescent Psychiatry, 30,* 138-143.

Swanson, J. M. (1992). *School-based assessments and interventions for ADD students.* Irvine, CA: K.C. Publishing.

Touchette, P. E., MacDonald, R. F., & Langer, S. N. (1985). A scatter plot for identifying stimulus control of problem behavior. *Journal of Applied Behavior Analysis, 18,* 343-351.

U.S. Department of Education. (1999). *Twenty-first annual report to Congress on the implementation of the Individuals with Disabilities Education Act.* Washington, DC: Author.

Webster-Stratton, C. (1993). Strategies for helping early school-age children with Oppositional Defiant and Conduct Disorders: The importance of home-school partnerships. *School Psychology Review, 22,* 437-457.

Weiss, G., & Hechtman, L. (1993). *Hyperactive children grown up* (2nd ed.). New York: Guilford.

Zito J. M, Safer, D. J., dosReis, S., Gardner, J. F., Boles, M., & Lynch, F. (2000). Trends in the prescribing of psychotropic medications to preschoolers. *Journal of the American Medical Association, 283,* 1025-1030.

CHAPTER 34

Interventions for Fears and Anxiety Problems

John M. Hintze
University of Massachusetts Amherst

INTRODUCTION

Fear- and anxiety-provoking stimuli and manifestations of fears and anxiety change throughout childhood as a result of cognitive development and abilities to identify and understand threat across a variety of situations (Ollendick, Yule, & Ollier, 1991). As such, fears and anxieties can serve an adaptive function as they elicit protective responses to stimuli that may be threatening or harmful. However, when fear and anxiety persist, increase in intensity, and become more pervasive—causing unwanted psychological distress and significant negative interference with one's performance and adjustment—they are no longer considered adaptive (Kendall, Howard, & Epps, 1988; Kendall & Ronan, 1990).

Three popular models regarding the etiology and maintenance of fears and anxieties have been identified (Lick & Katkin, 1976). The most prominent in the behavioral assessment and treatment of fears and anxiety is the classical stimulus-response (S-R) model, which evolved from the work of Pavlov (1941), Hull (1943), and Wolpe (1958). This model assumes that maladaptive anxiety is formed by pairing a stimulus and a response. As such, previously unconditioned stimuli (i.e., stimuli that do not elicit an anxiety response) come to elicit anxious responses because of their pairing with conditioned stimuli that had previously elicited anxiety responses. For example, one of the most famous and earliest demonstrations of anxiety acquired through classical conditioning was reported in 1920 by Watson and Rayner. In this study, an 11-month-old infant boy named "Albert B" was conditioned to fear a white rat. During initial assessment, Watson and Rayner established that little Albert showed no fear of the rat (a neutral stimulus), but was startled and began to cry when a steel bar was struck against another metal object in the presence of the rat. Later on, he continued to show signs of anxiety when exposed to the rat and generalized the response to a rabbit, a dog, a fur coat, and a Santa Claus mask.

Another theory of anxiety discussed by Lick and Katkin (1976) is the response-reinforcement (R-R) model. This model holds that the consequences of anxious responses serve to reinforce and maintain the behavior. The consequences may be either positively or negatively reinforcing and often are socially mediated. For example, young children who exhibit separation anxiety disorder often refuse to be separated from a parent (most often the mother). When anticipating separation, a child may throw a tantrum, cry, or scream until the parent acquiesces and agrees to stay with the child. In this situation, the child's behavior is negatively reinforced in that separation from the parent is avoided. Likewise, the behavior of the parent (i.e., acquiescence) is negatively reinforced through escaping and/or avoiding the tantrum behavior of the child.

While these first two models assume that anxiety results from associative learning or reinforcement in conjunction with the environment, a third approach to anxiety—the cognitive mediation model—assumes that cognitive distortions associated with external stimuli play an influential role in producing and maintaining maladaptive levels of anxiety. For example, according to Beck's cognitive theory of anxiety (Beck, 1976) the thinking of the anxious individual is dominated by themes of danger. The individual anticipates threats to self and family, and those threats may be either physical, psychological, or social in nature. In generalized forms of anxiety, the individual anticipates danger in situations where the stimuli that arouse the anxiety are unspecific in nature. Thus, the thinking of the anxious individual is characterized by repetitive thoughts about danger that take the form of continuous verbal or pictorial cognition about the occurrence of harmful events.

Cognitive distortions that are particularly common with anxious individuals include: (a) *catastrophizing,* whereby the anxious individual tends to dwell on the most extreme negative consequences conceivable, assuming that any situation in which there is a possibility of harm constitutes a highly probable danger, (b) *personalization,* whereby the anxious individual reacts as though external events are personally relevant and are indications of a potential danger to him or her, (c) *magnification and minimization,* where the anxious individual focuses on signs of danger or potential threat to the exclusion of other aspects of the situation thereby minimizing or ignoring the non-threatening or rescue factors in the situation, (d) *selective abstraction,* where the anxious individual focuses on the threatening elements of a situation and ignores the context, (e) *arbitrary inference,* where the anxious individual jumps to dire conclusions on the basis of little or no data, and (f) *overgeneralization,* whereby the anxious individual views a time-limited situation as lasting forever (e.g., "these feelings of stress will never end"), or may assume that because a particular problem occurred previously it is bound to reoccur in the future.

Finally, a more recent theory of etiology and maintenance of anxiety postulates a neuro-evolutionary approach (Stein & Bouwer, 1997). The neuro-evolutionary approach rests on the assumption that general anxiety evolved to deal with threats whose nature could not be clearly defined, while subtypes of anxious behavior evolved to deal with specific types of danger. The subtypes of anxious behavior include: (a) escape or avoidance, aggressive defense, freezing/immobility, and submission/appeasement (Marks & Nesse, 1994). Equally important here is evidence that suggests that biological predispositions exist for anxiety responses toward specific types of stimuli

(Mineka, 1987). The neuro-evolutionary theory of anxiety helps to explain normal and maladaptive levels of anxiety depending on the individual. Evolutionary adaptation usually ensures an optimum level of anxiety—which may include some false alarms. However, in a suboptimal system, there may be too few or too many false alarms, which signal maladaptive levels of anxiety. Here, individual differences in anxiety are an inter-action of biological/genetic variations in the individual and his or her past experiences with threat.

Given these various theoretical foundations, it is not surprising that the majority of intervention approaches have relied heavily on behavioral and cognitive-behavioral prin-ciples for the treatment of fears and anxieties. The common link among most interventions lies in their ties to learning theory, with fundamentals of classical condi-tioning, operant conditioning, cognitive learning theory, and social learning theory serving as the basis for most treatment approaches. Nonetheless, while clinical descrip-tions and accounts of treatment protocols are extensive (e.g., case reports and single-case studies), definite conclusions regarding treatment efficacy are lacking (Francis & Beidel, 1995). Only recently has interest focused on childhood anxiety disorders (cf. March, 1995) with much of the literature focusing on classification and assessment. The balance of this chapter presents some of the most common intervention approaches used in the treatment of childhood fears and anxieties. Included are exposure-based strategies, sys-tematic desensitization, flooding, contingency management, modeling, and cognitive-behavioral approaches. Although presented in isolation, in practice these inter-ventions are often used in combination and share similar features across treatment methodologies.

PSYCHOTHERAPEUTIC STRATEGIES

Classical Conditioning Methods

Systematic Desensitization

Developed by Wolpe (1958, 1969), systematic desensitization involves the pairing of an incompatible response to anxiety, such as relaxation, with an anxiety-provoking stimulus. The process of systematic desensitization involves three steps: (a) relaxation training, (b) the construction of an anxiety hierarchy, and (c) the pairing of relaxation with the gradual presentation of anxiety-provoking stimuli or situations. Based on the principles of counterconditioning, the premise of this therapeutic technique rests on the assumption that if all skeletal muscles are deeply relaxed, it is impossible to experi-ence anxiety at the same time.

For example, a child may be experiencing anxiety related to specific stimulus situ-ations such as taking tests, interacting with other children, or performing in front of a group. Whatever the anxiety-producing situation, the first step in the process is to develop a hierarchy of mental images or scenes of the anxiety-producing situation, with mildly aversive scenes at the bottom of the hierarchy and progressively more aversive scenes at the top of the hierarchy. Second, the child is taught a deep muscle relaxation process. The relaxation exercises consist of successively tensing and relaxing various muscle groups beginning with the head and ending with the feet at varying intervals. For example, it is generally best to allow 5 to 10 seconds for the tensing of the muscles and 15 to 30 seconds for relaxing. Although a variety of muscle group progressions exist, a typical training sequence generally involves starting with the head and neck (e.g., pressing lips together, smiling as hard as one can, pressing head back against mat or pillow as hard as one can, turning head to right and left as far as one can); moving onto the shoulders, arms, and hands (e.g., lifting shoulders to head, clasping hands together and pushing one against the other as hard as one can, clasping fingers together and squeezing as hard as one can, and making fists in an alternating fashion as hard as one can); followed by the back, stomach, and hips (e.g., curling into a ball and holding legs with arms, pushing stomach as far out as possible, making stomach as tight as possible); and ending in the legs and feet (e.g., crossing legs at the ankles while pressing one leg against the other, lifting toes as far up as one can, curling toes tightly) (Gumaer, 1984). Finally, once the relaxation techniques are mastered, while relaxed, the child is asked to visualize the various scenes in the hierarchy. Beginning with the lowest anxiety-provoking stimulus on the hierarchy, the child is asked to visualize the scene and self-monitor any feelings of anxiety. When anxiety is felt, the child is asked to signal the therapist by raising one finger and the mental image is removed. The goal is to have the child progress through the images on the hierarchy without feeling anxiety. If during the process the child does signal anxiety, the therapist asks the child to revert back to a less anxiety-provoking scene on the hierarchy.

An example of systematic desensitization is reported by Rainwater et al. (1988), who used the technique with 25 youngsters (ages 7–20) who exhibited intense anxiety associated with the management of Type I diabetes mellitus. Each participant was treated individually and trained in the use of imaginal relaxation and deep breathing relaxation. Three separate hierarchies were developed for (a) self-injection, (b) finger sticks, and (c) blood drawing. The steps in each hierarchy ranged from nine (finger stick) to 20 (self-injection). Pre-post measures on a self-reported units of distress scale (SUDS) indicated significant decreases in levels of reported anxiety for all three hierarchies as a function of systematic desensitization. The number of systematic desensitization sessions required for beneficial change averaged around four. Follow-up data collected 1 year later indicated that 92% of the gains had been retained.

MacDonald (1975) used relaxation training and systematic desensitization to treat the intense anxiety and fear of an 11-year-old boy in response to dogs. A 37-item imaginal desensitization hierarchy was completed in 11 treatment sessions paired with relaxation training. Examples of the hierarchy included items ranging from "I'd like you to imagine that you are standing on the front porch in the late afternoon with your Dad, about ready to go inside, looking down the block and seeing a Beagle three houses away minding his own business and trotting toward you" (item 2) to "I'd like you to imagine that you are sitting in your back yard, alone with your G. I. Joe and looking up to see an unfamiliar collie running down your driveway and past the garage" (item

31). Once the boy was able to proceed through all 37 items without significant anxiety and arousal, programmed generalization was conducted—which included dog interaction skill training, modeling, and programmed outdoor activities. In doing so, the subject was taught to interpret dog body language such as tail-wagging and bristled neck fur. A model-prompt-reinforce sequence was used to shape back-petting, head-rubbing, and ear-scratching skills with a stuffed animal. Similar procedures were used to teach command skills. This was followed by viewing a terrier first through a one-way mirror and then through a chain-link fence. Once the subject was comfortable in the presence of the dog, a series of outdoor activities were scheduled (e.g., tennis lessons, walking to the comic book store) in which dogs might be present. At the end of treatment, the child reported staying outdoors without worry and anxiety about dogs for the first time in memory. Moreover, his parents reported appropriate reactions to benign as well as threatening dog encounters. Effects of treatment were maintained at follow-up 2 years later, at which time the subject continued to regularly play outdoors both alone and with friends and evidenced no avoidance of dogs.

In another example, Taylor (1972) used systematic desensitization to treat the excessive frequency of urination of a 15-year-old girl. In particular, the subject complained of an excessive need to urinate in connection with school and school-related activities. Specifically, the urgency would begin while waiting at home for the school bus and would intensify upon her arrival at school to the point that she would frequently have to leave a class several times during a single class period. As a result of her embarrassment, the subject reported increased attempts to avoid school and was withdrawing from social relationships and extracurricular activities. Treatment was carried out over summer vacation whereby the subject was seen weekly. Muscle relaxation was taught and three hierarchies were constructed upon the following themes: (a) riding the school bus, (b) being in school buildings and classrooms, and (c) actively participating in classroom activities. Desensitization to the three hierarchies was completed in five 1-hour sessions with the final sessions occurring on the last day of summer vacation. The subject returned to school the next day and reported no urinary urgency. A follow-up contact made 4 months later suggested that the frequency of urination was normal and that avoidance of school was nonexistent.

As can be seen from these examples, systematic desensitization can be effectively used to treat a variety of fears and anxieties. By pairing an incompatible response such as relaxation with an anxiety- or fear-producing stimulus, students learn to approach and overcome their fears in a safe, supportive environment. It is important to note, however, as with any type of indirect intervention the transfer of skills needs to be explicitly programmed so that students can generalize newly learned behaviors to more natural environments.

Flooding

Also referred to as reactive or internal inhibition, flooding (Francis & Beidel, 1995: Watson, Gaind, & Marks, 1972) involves the repeated and prolonged exposure to an anxiety-provoking stimulus with the goal of extinguishing the anxiety response. Like systematic desensitization, flooding can be presented imaginably; however, its typical usage involves in vivo exposure to the anxiety-provoking stimulus in analogue situations (Hintze, Stoner, & Bull, 2000a). As a key component of in vivo exposure, response prevention is used to extinguish avoidant or escape behaviors. That is, once placed within the situation all attempts to avoid or escape from the anxiety-provoking stimulus are suppressed or blocked by the therapist. Because of these procedures, it is absolutely essential that the child involved and guardian(s) be clear with respect to the rationale and procedures of the intervention and provide consent prior to its implementation. Once in the flooding situation, the child is asked to come in contact with the anxiety-provoking stimulus in a series of graduated steps. At each step in the graduated hierarchy, the child is asked to provide anxiety ratings and remain in the presence of the anxiety-provoking stimulus until his or her self-reported level of anxiety diminishes.

An example of in vivo flooding is presented by Houlihan, Schwartz, Miltenberger, and Heuton (1993) in the treatment of intense anxiety associated with the popping of balloons. Behavioral and self-report measures of a 21-year-old male college student suggested considerable anxiety and avoidance of all situations in which he might encounter balloons. Pretreatment behavioral assessment indicated that the subject could approach no closer than 4 feet from a balloon without experiencing intense fear and anxiety. Three sessions of flooding were conducted on 3 consecutive days, involving exposure to and participation in the popping of hundreds of balloons. Following the three flooding sessions, the subject showed no avoidance behavior and reported almost no subjective distress in the presence of balloons.

In another example, flooding was used to treat a past episode of sexual abuse in a 15-year-old girl by her father (Payne & Colletti, 1991). While being treated for chronic headaches the subject indicated persistent difficulties when interacting with her father, a reluctance to remain in close proximity to him, and feelings of irritation and disgust when touched by him. The abuse was confined to a single episode of caressing, and concluded with threats not to reveal the incident to the girl's mother. Implosive therapy was used targeting conditioned fears associated with the memory of the abuse. Implosive scenes emphasized sexual approaches by the subject's father and were presented for six sessions. Following implosive therapy, the subject reported diminished anxiety and increased feelings of control during the scenes, as well as greater comfort in actual interactions with her father. In addition, ratings of headaches also decreased substantially. Follow-up information collected nearly 2 years later indicated that the frequency of headaches continued to be low and the reduced level of discomfort was maintained regarding interactions with the girl's father. Not surprisingly the subject reported that the aspect of therapy she found most helpful was "making myself think about things I didn't want to."

While very common in the behavior therapy literature, school-based practitioners should be cautious with respect to the use of flooding in the treatment of fears and anxieties. The very nature of the technique requires the student to confront his or her fears in a manner that may be objectionable to parents and professionals. For this reason, consent should be obtained prior to implementing such techniques with children. Best practice should probably dictate that less aversive techniques (e.g., systematic desensitization) be attempted prior to the use of procedures such as flooding.

Operant Methods

Exposure-based strategies. Exposure-based treatment techniques involve placing the child in anxiety-provoking situations while providing both self- and externally delivered coping strategies. The anxiety-provoking situations may be either naturally occurring or artificially contrived enactments or role-plays (Hintze, Stoner, & Bull, 2000b). One of the most common exposure-based strategies involves the use of the Behavioral Avoidance Test (BAT; Hamilton & King, 1991; Van Hasselt, Hersen, Bellack, Rosenblum, & Lamparski, 1979). In its most typical usage, the BAT follows one of two variations in structure. In the first variation, a situational enactment is created whereby the child is brought into close proximity or contact with the anxiety-producing stimulus. Once the child is placed in the situational enactment, *in vivo desensitization* is provided and systematic direct observational data are recorded on preestablished criteria. Unlike systematic desensitization, which uses relaxation training as the counterconditioned response, in vivo desensitization capitalizes on the feelings of comfort, security, and trust that the child has developed for the therapist as the counterconditioning agent. In addition to direct desensitization, a critical component of treatment involves the collection of systematic direct performance data, which serve as a system of feedback and reinforcement for the child (cf. Hintze & Shapiro, 1995). For example, the amount of time spent within the enactment may be recorded (i.e., duration), frequency of engaging in the feared behavior can be noted (e.g., petting a dog), or proximity to the anxiety-producing stimulus may be measured (Hintze et al., 2000b). Guidelines for establishing the enactments and role-play and what to observe should be based on the most salient features of the child's anxious or fearful behavior. In addition to systematic direct observation, self-report measures also can be used, whereby the child reports on his or her own self-perceived level of discomfort. This procedure is usually conducted with some type of rating scale using a Likert-type response format.

In a second variation of exposure-based strategies, the child is requested to perform each step of a graded hierarchy of observable behaviors that bring him or her closer and closer to the anxiety-producing stimulus. Steps within the hierarchy are best formulated using the process of task analysis. In doing so, the therapist breaks down the desired behavior into its component parts by carefully observing the desired behavior and specifying the procedure that is presumed to be involved in performing the behavior. Each component is stated in order of its occurrence and should set the occasion or prompt the next component or behavior in the chain. At each step in the process, in vivo desensitization and social reinforcement are provided and progress through the chain of target behaviors is recorded.

An example of an exposure-based treatment using a BAT role-play analogue was presented by Esveldt-Dawson, Wisner, Unis, Matson, and Kazdin (1982), who treated a

12-year-old girl for anxieties and fears related to school and unfamiliar males. Responses to treatment outcomes were assessed with the use of a series of situational analogues. Five of the role-play analogues involved interactions with unfamiliar males: (1) asking an unfamiliar man for a donation to a children's hospital, (2) asking a salesman about trying on a new pair of shoes, (3) meeting a new male therapist, (4) welcoming a peer's father to the treatment session, and (5) sitting next to an usher at a wedding reception dinner. The five school-related role-play analogues consisted of (1) picking up a graded semester report with a poor mark, (2) being excluded by peers during an art project, (3) speaking in front of the class, (4) being accused of cheating by the teacher, and (5) being sent to the principal for being late. Treatment consisted of exposure to each of the situations with in vivo desensitization, instructions, social reinforcement, and modeling.

Each of the role-plays lasted approximately 15 minutes and data were collected on measures of avoidance (e.g., stiffness of body movements, nervous mannerisms, and self-rating of anxiety) and prosocial behaviors (e.g., eye contact, quality and amount of appropriate affect, overall social skills). Results showed a rapid reduction in the frequency and rate of avoidance behaviors and a concomitant increase in prosocial behaviors during all role-plays.

In another example Osborn (1986) used in vivo desensitization to reduce the anxiety associated with warm water bathing for a 6-year-old boy who had suffered severe burns as a result of hot water scalding. The desired goal for the boy was to have him remain in 100°F water up to his chest for 3 minutes. Increasing the boy's tolerance for warmer water was gradually increased over a 25-day period. On the first day, the boy's mother cradled him in her arms while standing in 2 inches of 70°F water. In graduated steps, she lowered and withdrew the boy until he could remain seated on the bottom and bathe or play for 3 minutes. The water temperature was increased by 1°F every 3 minutes thereafter. The maximum temperature that the boy would tolerate was recorded for each session. On day 6, the depth of the water was increased to 4 inches. Gradually increasing both the temperature and depth of the water continued until day 25, at which time the subject was able to tolerate water of 100°F and 33 inches deep. Results indicated that exposure-based in vivo desensitization could be effective in treating anxiety brought upon by warm water.

Contingency management. Contingency management procedures involve the manipulation of antecedent and consequent events that influence the acquisition and maintenance of anxiety (Francis & Beidel, 1995). These procedures include positive reinforcement, shaping, and extinction. Frequently, contingency management techniques are used as an adjunct to direct therapy with the child as the procedures can be easily taught to adults who are involved in the direct care of the child (e.g., parents and teachers). The involvement of parents and teachers can prove to be vital in facilitating the generalization and maintenance of therapeutic gains outside of therapy.

Positive reinforcement is defined as any event or activity following a behavior that results in an increase of frequency in the targeted behavior. Thus, in therapeutic settings behaviors targeted for positive reinforcement are generally those that are incompatible with anxious or fearful behaviors. For example, Leitenberg and Callahan (1973) demonstrated the use of contingent positive reinforcement in the reduction of anxiety induced by a fear of the dark in young children. Using a situational analogue, 7 matched pairs of children were assessed on pre- and posttest measures of avoidance of the dark. Specifically, the children were asked to enter a small photographic dark room and told to stay in the room as long as they could until they felt afraid. From each matched pair, one child was randomly assigned to the experimental group and one to the control group. Subjects in the experimental group were seen for 2 sessions per week, each consisting of 5 trials. At the beginning of each session, each experimental subject was allowed to select a prize (e.g., gum, trinkets, crayons, candies) each time he or she stayed in the dark room longer than his or her previous longest time. Since the concept of time was difficult for many of the children, a visual "thermometer-like" display was used. As such, after each trial, increases in elapsed time were indicated by shading in with a pencil the increased time in seconds on the indicator. In addition to the tangible reinforcement, social praise and encouragement were delivered contingent upon improved times. At the end of treatment, all children were assessed at posttest in the same manner as the pretest. Results indicated the children who had received contingent positive reinforcement were able to remain in the dark room for significantly longer time periods than those children who had not received contingent positive reinforcement. While the children in the control group were able to stay in the room on an average of 28 seconds, experimental group children were able to remain in the room for well over 3 minutes. Results of the experiment demonstrated quite clearly that contingent positive reinforcement can be a very powerful therapeutic tool in decreasing levels of anxiety and increasing adaptive behavior.

In another example, Ayllon, Smith, and Rogers (1970) used positive reinforcement in combination with other contingency management procedures to reduce the frequency of school refusal in an 8-year-old girl. Daily positive reinforcement in the form of soda, gum, and ice cream was delivered to the child contingent upon her going to school voluntarily. Weeks during which she achieved perfect attendance were positively reinforced further with a special treat or trip on the weekend. Results indicated that the use of contingency management procedures was effective in increasing the student's voluntary school attendance to 100% within one marking period. More specifically, prior to intervention the child voluntarily went to school on only about 20% of the school days. After intervention this increased to 100% and was maintained for four consecutive marking periods.

A second type of contingency management, shaping, involves the positive reinforcement of successive steps of desirable behaviors that are again incompatible with fearful or anxious responses. Common to the Behavioral Avoidance Tests (BAT) noted previously, shaping reinforces gradual steps toward the ultimate desired behavior. Shaping is particularly useful when performance of the desirable behavior, in its entirety, produces overwhelming anxiety to the point where the child can do little else but emit the anxious response (which is very often avoidance). Shaping was used by Luiselli (1978) in treating fears related to riding the school bus of a 7-year-old boy with autism.

On the first day of treatment, the boy's mother seated herself on the bus and the subject was brought on by the therapist. The subject, his mother, and the therapist sat on the bus for two minutes. During this time, the subject received verbal praise and edibles for "riding the bus." On the second day, the mother was again seated on the bus, but halfway through the session she left to stand outside directly beneath the subject's window. On day 3, the subject was placed on the bus by the therapist and his mother. Once he was seated, the mother left the bus and remained outside for the entire session. On day 4, the subject's mother remained in the car and he was taken on the bus by the therapist. Halfway through the session the therapist left the bus and stood outside the doorway of the bus. On the fifth treatment day, the bus went directly to the subject's house in the morning. The therapist waited in the doorway of the house with the subject while his mother seated herself on the bus. Both the subject and the therapist then walked onto the bus. The mother immediately presented the subject with an edible treat and together all three rode the bus to school. On the sixth day, the bus again picked up the subject at his house, but instead of riding the bus with him, his mother placed him on the bus with the therapist and then stood on the sidewalk as the bus drove away. The subject and the therapist then rode together to school. On the final treatment day, the subject was placed on the bus by his mother and he rode the entire distance to school alone. Several weeks after he was routinely boarding and traveling on the bus to school, treatment began for riding the bus home. Here, treatment consisted of two days of training. On day 1, the subject, his mother, and the therapist all rode the bus together. On day 2, the subject and the therapist rode on the bus. On day 3, and thereafter, the subject rode the bus home with no assistance or difficulty.

Finally, extinction involves the removal of reinforcing consequences that follow a child's anxious behavior. Extinction is particularly useful when the motivation behind a child's anxiety is social attention or escape/avoidance of an anxiety-provoking situation. In such cases, anxious responses on the part of the child are often inadvertently positively reinforced by adults involved in the child's care through such acts as affection, caressing, and other forms of positive social attention, or are negatively reinforced in that the anxious behavior leads to either removal or avoidance of the anxiety-producing stimuli. For example, a young child who is overly anxious and fearful of unfamiliar people may cling to an adult caregiver and cry in response to an adult stranger. In such a situation if the caregiver picks up the child, holds her closely, and offers soothing words of encouragement, the anxious behavior (i.e., clinging and crying) might be positively reinforced. If the caregiver took the child away from the stranger or had the stranger removed, the child's behavior might be negatively reinforced through escape or avoidance.

An example of an extinction-based intervention procedure is presented by Piersel and Kratochwill (1981) in increasing the number of words spoken by two siblings (ages 4 and 5) who were demonstrating selective mutism. Specifically, a contingency management program was developed that consisted of extinction of nonverbal communication behaviors and positive reinforcement of all verbal behavior. In doing so, the subjects' teachers were instructed not to respond to nonverbal communication and to require verbal responses in order to access desired tangibles or activities (e.g., asking for a snack, playing games, etc.). All verbalizations were immediately reinforced (e.g., "very good," "I like what you said," or "Yes, you may have another cookie"). Results at 3-month follow-up indicated that the frequency of verbalizations had increased and been maintained. Furthermore, social validation was evidenced by both teachers, who reported that the frequency of verbalizations by the children generally approximated that of the typical level for other children in their respective classes. In addition, both teachers also noted that the subjects were now talking to other teachers and peers outside the class.

Modeling. Widely researched by Bandura (1969, 1977), modeling involves learning that occurs by observing others and the imitative changes in a person's behavior that occur as a result of such observations. The modeling procedure involves an individual called a model (e.g., therapist, parent, teacher, sibling, or peer) and a person called the observer (e.g., the anxious child). As typically conducted, the observer observes the model (either live or symbolically through the use of videotape) while the model successfully and competently engages in a behavior that elicits a fearful or anxious response on the part of the observer. For modeling to be most successful the therapist should be certain that the child (a) can attend to the various salient aspects of the modeling situation, (b) can retain what has been learned from observing the modeling situation, (c) has the physical and cognitive ability to motorically reproduce what was observed in the modeling situation, and (d) when necessary has the motivation to perform the behavior that was observed (Morris & Kratochwill, 1998).

For example, Bandura and Menlove (1968) examined the effects of symbolic modeling on children's fearfulness and anxiety produced by dogs. Forty-eight children ranging in age from 3 to 5 years were randomly assigned to one of three groups. In the first group, children observed a graduated series of films in which a model displayed progressively more nonanxious and intimate interactions with a single dog. The second group observed a similar set of graded films; in this case, however, the models interacted nonanxiously with numerous dogs of varying size and fearsomeness. The third group served as a control and watched films that did not depict animals. Results indicated that children in the first two groups demonstrated significantly more approach behaviors to a live dog in a series of graduated steps ranging from walking up to a playpen and looking down at the dog to climbing into the playpen and petting and scratching the dog's stomach.

In another symbolic modeling study, Bray and Kehle (1998) reduced the severity of stuttering of four school-age children (ages 9 to 12) using an approach termed self-modeling. This procedure involves the repeated viewing of oneself on edited videotapes in which the desired behavior is performed. In this way, the targeted subject serves as both the model and the observer. In this particular application, the four students viewed two 5-minute edited videotapes of themselves speaking fluently (i.e., without stuttering) on 7 occasions during a period of 6 weeks. Using a multiple-baseline design, direct observations of the students in the natural school environment subsequent to intervention indicated a substantial decrease in the percentage of stuttered words per

_ :rvation as compared to baseline levels. Generalization and follow–up observations suggested that the effects generalized across a variety of school situations (e.g., academic time, lunch, recess, classroom party, field day, small group social gatherings) and time.

As with the classical conditioning methods discussed previously, operant-based strategies also should be considered in light of the range of intensity of treatment, with more mildly aversive techniques attempted prior to more restrictive or intense forms of therapy. For example, some of the exposure-based strategies may physically place a student in a situation that elicits high levels of fear or anxiety. Although effective, practitioners again may want to first consider the use of operantly based strategies that facilitate habilitation while minimizing perceived threat (e.g., contingency management, modeling).

Cognitive Strategies

Cognitive–Behavioral Interventions

Cognitive-behavioral interventions for fears and anxieties include a variety of techniques such as self–control techniques (Kanfer & Gaelick, 1986; Kanfer & Phillips, 1970), self–instructional training (Meichenbaum, 1974), problem solving (Kendall & Braswell, 1985), and rational–emotive therapy (Ellis, 1984). Although different in subtle ways, each of the techniques is based on a set of similar assumptions:

1. Human learning involves the use of cognitively mediated processes.

2. Thoughts, feelings, and behaviors are all causally interrelated.

3. Cognitive activities such as expectancy, self–statements, and attributions can predict maladaptive behavior and can be used in producing beneficial change.

4. Cognitive processes can be integrated into behavioral paradigms and be used as part of therapy.

5. Outcomes of therapy are directed at assessing distorted or deficient cognitive processes and behaviors, and designing learning activities that remediate and teach more adaptive cognitions, behaviors, and affective patterns (Kendall & Braswell, 1985).

In addition, each of the strategies typically incorporates features of modeling, exposure, and behavioral rehearsal as previously discussed. For example, a typical sequence of activities for self-instructional training would involve the following steps: (a) the therapist approaches the feared or anxiety-producing stimulus while talking aloud to himself or herself about coping, (b) the child performs the same task under the direction of the therapist, (c) the child approaches the feared or anxiety-producing stimulus by himself or herself while talking aloud about coping, (d) the child whispers the coping statements to himself or herself while approaching the feared or anxiety-producing stimulus, and (e) the child performs the task while guiding his or her performance using inaudible or private speech or nonverbal self-instructions (Meichenbaum, 1986).

Similarly, problem-solving training involves defining the problem, exploring and choosing an approach to solve the problem, evaluating the outcome, and self-reinforcement or coping statements (Kendall & Braswell, 1985). Typically, the child is taught to ask himself or herself a series of questions in order to solve a problem. For example, a child might be taught to go through the following sequence: (a) What is the problem? (i.e., defining the problem); (b) What are all the things I could do about it? (i.e., exploring solutions); (c) What will likely happen if I do those things? (d) Which solution do I think will work best? (i.e., choosing a solution); and (e) Now that I have tried that approach, how did I do? (i.e., evaluating the solution). It is important that during the process the child be taught to monitor and challenge the types of self-statements associated with anxiety and avoidance behaviors. This self-challenging is critical in the third step of the process, in which the child contemplates what is likely to happen if any one of the possible solutions is attempted. Once identified, negative self-statements are replaced with alternative adaptive self-statements that serve to decrease anxiety, improve coping, and facilitate adaptive behavioral functioning. In addition to these specific steps, the therapeutic process, can be fortified with a variety of process related activities. The Appendix provides some brief examples of the types of cognitive activities that can be integrated into cognitive-behavioral therapy or used as an adjunct to the therapeutic process.

CONSIDERATIONS FOR SCHOOL PSYCHOLOGISTS

In addition to the direct therapeutic intervention approaches noted above, school psychologists should also consider an integrated model of consultation (Erchul & Martens, 1997) that provides both education and training to those adults involved in the primary care of the child. Using aspects from both mental health (Caplan, 1970; Caplan & Caplan, 1999) and behavioral consultation (Bergan & Kratochwill, 1990), school psychologists can help parents and teachers (a) come to a better understanding of a child's anxiety and fear, and (b) enlist the support of primary caregivers in supporting any direct therapeutic interventions, as well as actively joining them in the therapeutic process by having them provide therapeutic assistance outside the direct therapy arrangement (e.g., home, classroom, school).

Specifically, from the mental health consultation approach, client-centered case consultation can be used in helping the parent or teacher develop a plan for dealing with the difficulties that excessive fears or an anxiety disorder may present in the home or school. Here, education and skill development are critical foci of the consultative process. The emphasis is on providing usable information for the parent or teacher and helping foster an understanding of how environmental variables interact with the child's difficulties. In doing so, the consultant must assess the resources and constraints that are operating in the child's environment, including role expectations, norms, financial and time constraints, and parent/teacher strengths and weaknesses that will affect the type of plan that is implemented. Of particular interest is the child/parent/teacher relationship and how this relationship might be strengthened or altered to improve the problem situation. Once these factors are better understood, the consultant can utilize these outside resources in an effort to promote the generalization of the types of skills being addressed in individual therapy and foster a systems-level focus to treatment.

Similarly, from a behavioral consultative approach, the school psychologist can extend many of the operantly based interventions used in individual therapy to other environments in which the child interacts (e.g., home, school). Using a four-step approach, the consultant would first identify the specific problems in the home or school that continue to be cause for concern as a result of the child's fear or anxiety. It is important that these concerns be defined in clear operational terms including the specification of the outcomes (i.e., changes) in measurable terms; the establishment of objective current levels of performance (i.e., baseline); and the identification of where, when, and with whom the outcome is expected to occur. For instance, while various forms of test anxiety might be able to be treated using many of the techniques noted above, eventually the child must be able to employ newly learned skills at the point of performance—notably, an actual test situation. Using a behavioral consultative approach, the consul-tant could help the child's teacher in identifying exactly what the test-anxious behavior looks like in the classroom. Once operationally defined, baseline-level measures of test-anxious behavior would be gathered, with a particular interest in specifying the conditions under which the behavior is noted. For example, does the behavior occur with all subject matters or with some but not others? Does the type of test (e.g., closed versus open-ended responses) seem to have some effect on behavior? And so on.

Once the problem and the conditions under which it occurs are specified, the second step of the behavioral consultative model would be an in-depth analysis of the problem situation with a particular focus on the identification of alterable variables and the generation of possible solutions that increase the likelihood of problem resolution. In the current example, plans for the generalization of direct therapeutic gains would be addressed, which might include teacher support (e.g., a brief enumeration of the skills learned in therapy and how they can be used in the current situation); self-monitoring (e.g., a "test taking" checklist, which might highlight key features of the process); or test modifications (e.g., change of testing format, extended time).

Once the problem has been completely analyzed, the third step of the model involves the systematic implementation of the intervention designed to deal with the problem. At this step, clear objectives and strategies must be established (i.e., exactly how the intervention is going to be delivered) with an eye toward a consideration for the practical constraints that might affect the utilization of the specific strategies, and how continued formative assessment information will be secured. Or more simply, what exactly is going to be done, how what is going to be done is to be implemented with a high degree of integrity, and what types of assessment data will be gathered that will inform those involved as to whether adequate changes in behavior are being observed.

Once the intervention is implemented, step four of the process consists of a series of meetings between the consultant and parent/teacher to determine (a) whether the goals established for the child have been attained, (b) the overall effectiveness of the plan that was established to attain the goals, and (c) whether the indirect form of treatment should be continued or terminated. Data to inform these decisions come primarily from systematic observations that began during the first step of the process (i.e., problem identification stage) and continue on throughout the consultation. If the goals and objectives of consultation have been met, plans for continued generalization and transfer should be made, which might include the fading of the intervention so that changes in the child's behavior will not regress to baseline levels of performance. On the other hand, the data might suggest the intervention was unsuccessful in effecting change in the child's behavior, at which time a new plan should be considered.

SUMMARY

This chapter has attempted to familiarize the practitioner with the various approaches commonly used in the amelioration of fears and anxieties commonly evidenced in children and youth. It should be evident from the review that the most common psychotherapeutic techniques have relied on either operant-based or cognitive-behavioral approaches to symptom reduction. Specifically, with respect to fear reduction, systematic desensitization and modeling approaches appear to be most efficacious, while anxiety disorders appear to profit most from a more cognitive-behavioral approach.

Nonetheless, practitioners must be cautioned that because of limited empirical data, few conclusions other than declaring that these strategies have substantial potential can be established at this time. Most notably, the current literature has failed to fully explore the conditions under which positive therapeutic changes have occurred and whether such changes could be expected across differing participants, behaviors, settings, times, or therapeutic change agents. Moreover, much of the literature has focused on case studies in which the fear or anxiety was mono-operative. That is, the fear or anxiety was fairly confined to one or a small series of interrelated stimulus events or activities. While this might be the case for specific fears, whether or not the approaches would be beneficial to more generalized types of fears or anxieties is not well understood. Although a single approach to treatment might make sense for those fears or anxieties that share a common functionality, more often than not multiple stimulus events serve as the source of discomfort and atypical response patterns.

Similarly, the extant literature has failed to fully explore changes in the participants from a variety of outcome perspectives. While the most common approach to outcome evaluation has been the gathering of systematic direct observation, few if any studies have included other measures that adequately assess cognitive/affective or physiologic correlates of fear and anxiety. A mono-method approach to data collection may obfuscate outcome findings, and at worst suggest that a clinical regimen is effective in the treatment of the disorder when in fact very little has been done to change cognitive/affective or physiologic features of the disorder. For example, while a flooding approach might be effective in changing the observable behavior of a child exhibiting social anxiety, the approach might be ineffective in reducing the cognitive/affective and physiological features of the problem. So, while the child might enter into and interact in what appears to be a socially appropriate manner, he or she might be doing so with continued high levels of cognitive/affective anxiety, sweating, and a rapid pulse.

Clearly, more research is needed in the treatment of such problems with children and youth. However, with proper caution and a hypothesis testing approach to problem solving, practitioners have a number of techniques derived from solid theoretical foundations that have been demonstrated effective in a wide variety of behavior change literature.

REFERENCES

Ayllon, T., Smith, D., & Rogers, M. (1970). Behavioral management of school phobia. *Journal of Behavior Therapy and Experimental Psychiatry, 1,* 125–138.

Bandura, A. (1969). *Principles of behavior modification.* New York: Holt, Rinehart, and Winston.

Bandura, A. (1977). *Social learning theory.* Englewood Cliffs, NJ: Prentice-Hall.

Bandura, A., & Menlove, F. L. (1968). Factors determining vicarious extinction of avoidance behavior through symbolic modeling. *Journal of Personality and Social Psychology, 8,* 99–108.

Beck, A. T. (1976). *Cognitive therapy and the emotional disorders.* New York: International Universities Press.

Bergan, J. R., & Kratochwill, T. R. (1990). *Behavioral consultation and therapy.* New York: Plenum Press.

Bray, M. A., & Kehle, T. J. (1998). Self-modeling as an intervention for stuttering. *School Psychology Review, 27,* 587–598.

Caplan, G. (1970). *The theory and practice of mental health consultation.* New York: Basic Books.

Caplan, G., & Caplan, R. B. (1999). *Mental health consultation and collaboration.* Prospect Heights, IL: Waveland.

Ellis, A. (1984). *Rational-emotive therapy and cognitive behavior therapy.* New York: Springer.

Erchul, W. P., & Martens, B. K. (1997). *School consultation: Conceptual and empirical bases of practice.* New York: Plenum Press.

Esveldt-Dawson, K., Wisner, K. L., Unis, A. S., Matson, J. L., & Kazdin, A. E. (1982). Treatment of phobias in a hospitalized child. *Journal of Behavior Therapy and Experimental Psychiatry, 13,* 77–83.

Francis, G., & Beidel, D. (1995). Cognitive-behavioral psychotherapy. In J. S. March (Ed.), *Anxiety disorders in children and adolescents* (pp. 321–340). New York: Guilford Press.

Gumaer, J. (1984). *Counseling and therapy for children.* New York: The Free Press.

Hamilton, D. I., & King, N. J. (1991). Reliability of a behavioral avoidance test for the assessment of dog phobic children. *Psychological Reports, 69,* 18.

Hintze, J. M., & Shapiro, E. S. (1995). Systematic observation of classroom behavior. In A. Thomas & J. Grimes (Eds.), *Best practices in school psychology III* (pp. 651–660). Washington, DC: National Association of School Psychologists.

Hintze, J. M., Stoner, G., & Bull, M. H. (2000a). Analogue assessment: Research and practice in evaluating emotional and behavioral problems. In E. S. Shapiro & T. R. Kratochwill (Eds.), *Behavioral assessment in schools: Theory, research, and clinical foundations* (2nd ed., pp. 104–138). New York: Guilford Press.

Hintze, J. M., Stoner, G., & Bull, M. H. (2000b). Analogue assessment: Emotional/behavioral problems. In E. S. Shapiro & T. R. Kratochwill (Eds.), *Conducting school-based assessments of child and adolescent behavior* (pp. 55–77). New York: Guilford Press.

Houlihan, D., Schwartz, C., Miltenberger, R., & Heuton, D. (1993). The rapid treatment of a young man's balloon (noise) phobia using in vivo flooding. *Journal of Behavior Therapy and Experimental Psychiatry, 24,* 233-240.

Hull, C. L. (1943). *Principles of behavior.* New York: Appleton-Century-Crofts.

Kanfer, F. H., & Gaelick, L. (1986). Self-management methods. In F. H. Kanfer and A. P. Goldstein (Eds.), *Helping people change* (3rd ed., pp. 283-345). Elmsford, NY: Pergamon Press.

Kanfer, F. H., & Phillips, J. S. (1970). *Learning foundations of behavior therapy.* New York: Wiley.

Kendall, P. C., & Braswell, L. (1985). *Cognitive-behavioral therapy for impulsive children.* New York: Guilford Press.

Kendall, P. C., Howard, B. L., & Epps, J. (1988). The anxious child: Cognitive-behavioral treatment strategies. *Behavior Modification, 12,* 281-310.

Kendall, P. C., & Ronan, K. R. (1990). Assessment of children's anxieties, fears, and phobias: Cognitive-behavioral models and methods. In C. R. Reynolds & R. W. Kamphaus (Eds.), *Handbook of psychological and educational assessment of children* (pp. 223-244). New York: Guilford Press.

Leitenberg, H., & Callahan, E. J. (1973). Reinforced practice and reduction of different kinds of fears in adults and children. *Behavior Research and Therapy, 11,* 19-30.

Lick, J. R., & Katkin, E. S. (1976). Assessment of anxiety and fear. In M. Hersen & A. S. Bellack (Eds.), *Behavioral assessment: A practical handbook* (pp. 175-206). New York: Pergamon Press.

Luiselli, J. (1978). Treatment of an autistic child's fear of riding a school bus through exposure and reinforcement. *Journal of Behavior Therapy and Experimental Psychiatry, 9,* 169-172.

MacDonald, M. L. (1975). Multiple impact behavior therapy in a child's dog phobia. *Journal of Behavior Therapy and Experimental Psychiatry, 6,* 317-322.

March, J. S. (Ed.). (1995). *Anxiety disorders in children and adolescents.* New York: Guilford Press.

Marks, I. M., & Nesse, R. M. (1994). Fear and fitness: An evolutionary analysis of anxiety disorders. *Ethology and Sociobiology, 15,* 247-261.

Meichenbaum, D. (1974). Self-instructional methods. In F. H. Kanfer & A. P. Goldstein (Eds.), *Helping people change* (pp. 357-392). Elmsford, NY: Pergamon Press.

Meichenbaum, D. (1986). Cognitive behavior-modification. In F. H. Kanfer & A. P. Goldstein (Eds.), *Helping people change* (3rd ed., pp. 346-380). Elmsford, NY: Pergamon Press.

Mineka, S. (1987). A primate model of phobic fears. In H. H. Eysenck & I. Martin (Eds.), *Theoretical foundations of behavior therapy* (pp. 81-111). New York: Plenum Press.

Morris, R. J., & Kratochwill, T. R. (1998). Childhood fears and phobias. In R. J. Morris & T. R. Kratochwill (Eds.), *The practice of child therapy* (3rd ed., pp. 91-131). Needham Heights, MA: Allyn and Bacon.

Ollendick, T. H., Yule, W., & Ollier, K. (1991). Fears in British children and their relationship to manifest anxiety and depression. *Journal of Child Psychology and Psychiatry and Allied Disciplines, 32,* 321-331.

Osborn, E. L. (1986). Effects of participant modeling and desensitization on childhood warm water phobia. *Journal of Behavior Therapy and Experimental Psychiatry, 17,* 117-119.

Pavlov, I. P. (1941). *Conditioned reflexes and psychiatry* (translated by W. H. Gantt). New York: International Publishers.

Payne, T. J., & Colletti, G. (1991). Treatment of a 15-year-old girl with chronic muscle-contraction headache using implosive therapy. *British Journal of Medical Psychology, 64,* 173-177.

Piersel, W. C., & Kratochwill, T. R. (1981). A teacher-implemented contingency management package to assess and treat selective mutism. *Behavioral Assessment, 3,* 371-382.

Rainwater, N., Sweet, A. A., Elliott, L., Bowers, M., McNeill, J., & Stump, N. (1988). Systematic desensitization in the treatment of needle phobias for children with diabetes. *Child and Family Behavior Therapy, 10,* 19-31.

Stein, D. J., & Bouwer, C. (1997). A neuro-evolutionary approach to the anxiety disorders. *Journal of the Anxiety Disorders, 11,* 409-429.

Taylor, D. W. (1972). Treatment of excessive frequency of urination by desensitization. *Journal of Behavior Therapy and Experimental Psychiatry, 3,* 311-313.

Van Hasselt, V. B., Hersen, M., Bellack, A. S., Rosenblum, N. D., & Lamparski, D. (1979). Tripartite assessment of the effects of systematic desensitization in a multi-phobic child: An experimental analysis. *Journal of Behavior Therapy and Experimental Psychiatry, 10,* 51-55.

Watson, J. B., & Rayner, R. (1920). Conditioned emotional reactions. *Journal of Experimental Psychology, 3,* 1-14.

Watson, J. P., Gaind, R., & Marks, I. M. (1972). Physiological habituation to continuous phobic stimulation. *Behaviour Research and Therapy, 10,* 269-278.

Wolpe, J. (1958). *Psychotherapy by reciprocal inhibition.* Stanford, CA: Stanford University Press.

Wolpe, J. (1969). *The practice of behavior therapy.* New York: Pergamon Press.

APPENDIX

Related Cognitive–Behavioral Activities

I.B.E.T.E.T.

A problem-solving technique that students can use to fine tune their problem-solving and decision-making skills. The acronym I.B.E.T.E.T. follows the following steps: (a) *I*dentify the problem, (b) *B*rainstorm options, (c) *E*valuate options, (d) *T*est one option, (e) *E*valuate again, and (f) *T*est another. As with other forms of cognitive-behavioral therapies, the therapist facilitates the child through the steps while teaching the use of appropriate self-statement and coping strategies.

Control/No Control Brainstorm

Start by discussing how worries can affect the way we feel (including emotionally and physically) and how they can affect our behavior. Then brainstorm all the worries the child (or the group or class) typically has. As the children share these, discuss each and list them in two columns. One column is for those that we have control over and can do something about and the other column is for those over which we have no control. Following this, discuss where the children should logically direct their limited energy.

Worry Cans

After writing the student's various worries on separate pieces of paper, place them into tow cans or jars marked as those belonging to them and those belonging to others. If possible, it helps for the child to distribute the "other" worries to those responsible for resolution.

S.T.O.P.

Another mnemonic that stands for *S*top, breathe, *T*hink, *O*ptions, and *P*lan.

Light Bulb/Thought Bubble

Draw a large bulb into which a child can write his or her worries, fears, or anxieties. Then draw an arrow to a blank oval face. Let the child complete the face with the feeling that he or she would have by having that thought. Then repeat the activity using a positive thought and the subsequent face/feeling. This same activity can also be done with a thought bubble.

Benefits/Cost

Identify a choice or decision about which the child is worried. List one choice in the left column. In the next column list the benefits of selecting the choice. In the last column list the costs of making that choice. Below the first choice list another, then the benefits of that one, the costs, and so on. Continue until all choices have been explored.

CHAPTER 35

Alternative Educational Programs: Accommodating Tertiary Level, At-Risk Students

Tary J. Tobin and Jeffrey R. Sprague
University of Oregon

INTRODUCTION

In this chapter, ideas from descriptive literature and findings from recent studies are organized in response to four major questions:

1. What is known about alternative programs for very at-risk students, some of whom are committing delinquent acts?

2. What are best practices for keeping these students engaged in schooling?

3. What are best practices for meeting their complex needs?

4. What are the essential features of proven programs for these students at *elementary* and *middle* school levels, respectively?

Before these questions are addressed, search strategies are explained, terms defined, the need for alternative programs described, and concerns about alternative programs discussed.

Search Strategies

Information was located by searches of electronic databases (e.g., ERIC, PsychINFO) using variations on, and combinations of, terms such as "alternative education, at-risk, antisocial, delinquency, dropout, expulsion, placement, prevention, school-based intervention, suspension." Hand searches of recent issues of journals that report studies related to behavior disorders and/or school-based interventions were conducted (e.g., *Behavioral Disorders, Career Development for Exceptional Children, Child and Family Behavior Therapy,*

Exceptional Children, Journal of Emotional and Behavioral Disorders, Journal of School Psychology, Proven Practice, Psychology in the Schools, School Psychology Review). Abstracts and/or introductions were read to determine if the material addressed the research questions listed above and, if so, which question was addressed most fully. Additional sources were identified from references of selected articles.

Terms Defined

Alternative. "Alternative education" can refer to any nontraditional educational service, but is often used to indicate a program provided for antisocial youth. We did not include for-profit or other private schools in this review.

At-Risk. "At-risk" can refer to being particularly vulnerable to any undesirable circumstance, but in the context of discussions of alternative education it means being likely to experience school failure and dropout, which in turn predict inadequate employment, health problems, criminal activities, dependence on welfare and other government programs (Rumberger, 1995), and substance abuse (Guagliardo, Huang, Hicks, & D'Angelo. (1998). In addition, the term suggests that the student may develop antisocial behavior patterns, emotional and behavioral disorders, or conduct disorder.

Tertiary. "Tertiary" refers to the third level of a continuum of prevention efforts, and is best understood in relation to primary and secondary levels of prevention. Primary prevention efforts are intended to keep the malady (in this case, school failure, and/or delinquency) from happening at all. Secondary prevention efforts are directed toward students who have minor behavior problems or a small number of risk factors, suggesting that greater difficulties are to be expected unless protective measures are taken. Tertiary prevention efforts are reactions to existing, serious behavior problems; these efforts are "preventive" in the sense of trying to prevent recurring or escalating difficulties of a very serious nature. Similarly, prevention interventions can be organized into the three levels of universal, selected, and indicated. *Universal* interventions are for all students in a school or classroom, *selected* interventions are targeted to students considered at-risk on the basis of general background factors or minor problem behaviors, and *indicated* interventions are for individuals with existing, serious problem behaviors and/or for whom universal and selected interventions have proved insufficient. Alternative education programs are at the indicated or tertiary level. As Leone and Drakeford (1999) have noted, "Rarely are [alternative] education programs available as a proactive choice to students or parents before serious problems develop."

"Best Practices" and "Proven Model Programs." We are using these terms to describe examples of practices that can be recommended with confidence because they are (a) supported by empirical evidence of their effectiveness and/or (b) based on principles supported by research with at-risk students in general or special education programs. However, ranking and comparing alternative education models in a linear fashion is inappropriate given the wide range of practices and programs in the field, the diverse array of needs they attempt to meet, and the very limited amount of rigorous research on outcomes. "Limited data on the efficacy of alternative education at the state

level ... and in the literature in general, ... makes it impossible to draw firm conclusions regarding the soundness of each educational practice" (Katsiyannis & Williams, 1998, p. 282). Nevertheless, after surveying the field, it is reasonable to highlight practices and programs that stand out as "state of the art" at this time.

The Need for Alternative Programs

Traditional education fails many students when measured by leaving school without a diploma and being unprepared to function as a productive adult (Dorn, 1996; Kasen, Cohen, & Brooks, 1998; U.S. Department of Education, 2000). Although dropouts are not likely to be able to earn a family wage in the United States if current economic conditions continue (Hamilton, 1999), they will start families and many may need welfare or other assistance to care for their children (Quinn et al., 1996). In addition to the problem of dropouts, students who experience academic difficulties are at-risk for becoming involved in juvenile crime (Chavez, Oetting, & Swaim, 1994; Gottfredson & Gottfredson, 1985) and for behavior problems at school. Negative consequences (e.g., suspension, expulsion) remain the standard approach to management of student behavior in traditional schools across the country (Bear, 1998).

Special education students who are suspended or expelled for weapons or drug offenses must be provided alternative educational services (Individuals with Disabilities Education Act Amendments of 1997, P.L. 105-17). In addition, in some states, and in some districts, alternative education may be provided for general education students facing long-term suspensions. For example, a "Youth Out of the Education Mainstream" initiative was implemented by the Center for the Prevention of School Violence in Raleigh, North Carolina, in response to concerns about disruption and crime. In 1995-1996, in North Carolina, 82,000 students (5.9% of all) were suspended out of school at least once; 1,614 received long-term suspensions (from 10 to 365 days), and 209 were expelled (Riley & McDaniel, 1999). With Office of Juvenile Justice and Delinquency Prevention (OJJDP) funding, the Center provided financial and technical support to alternative learning environments throughout the state; however, "there are not enough to handle the number of students who would potentially benefit from them" (Riley & McDaniel, 1999, p. 6).

The need for alternative education programs is aggravated by failure of traditional schools to identify and serve students with emotional and behavior disorders in a timely fashion, especially when these students also have discipline problems (Duncan, Forness, & Hartsough, 1995; Tobin & Sugai, 1999a; Walker, Zeller, Close, Webber, & Gresham, 1999). Inclusion of special education students in general education classes rather than providing a full continuum of placements and services has resulted in an increased need for interim and permanent alternative placements (Katsiyannis & Maag, 1998).

Financial costs associated with incarceration of juveniles and the rehabilitation of adolescents or adults may be a factor in the rising interest in alternative education. If alternative education and other dropout prevention programs, at all educational levels, were more widely used, and cost comparisons were based on all the programs that taxpayers support, "The benefits of dropout prevention would exceed the costs by a ratio of 9:1" (Altenbaugh, Engel, & Martin, 1995, p. 170). Even if students do not graduate, every year of schooling is valuable: "Each added year of secondary education reduces the probability of public welfare dependency in adulthood by 35% (National Research Council, 1993)" (Lerner & Galambos, 1998, p. 425).

A survey of state practices related to alternative education (Katsiyannis & Williams, 1998) indicated that although the number of students who need alternative education is increasing, funding is inadequate to meet the need. According to Susan Black, in discussing quality alternative schools with features such as "help from psychologists and social workers ... small student population, individualized instruction, flexible scheduling, peer counseling, caring and competent teachers and administrators, an interesting and relevant curriculum, and a home-like atmosphere" (Black, 1997, p. 41), the cost would be about double the standard per-pupil costs but "worth every penny" (Black, 1997, p. 40). According to Black (1997), citing an example of donations of almost $90,000 for Sobriety High in Providence, Rhode Island, alternative schools with clear missions may be able to combine school district money with special fund-raising efforts that bring in support from private sources. Although some federal and state funds are available, financing is primarily thorough local funds, which makes alternative programs vulnerable when school district budget cuts are needed or when the cost of the alternative program is underestimated (Merchant, 1999).

Alternative programs have been able to help some students remain in school; reduce delinquent activities; and develop academic, vocational, communication, and self-control skills (Katsiyannis & Williams, 1998). One advantage alternative schools have over traditional schools is the potential for providing greater flexibility in programming. Personalized and flexible approaches to classroom and individual behavior management are important elements of effective alternative education for many students (Gold & Mann, 1984).

Concerns About Alternative Programs

Trade-offs are involved in the provision of any special service. Alternative programs may be considered stigmatizing, although the behaviors that lead to the alternative placement, rather than the placement itself, may be the real reason for the stigma. If the goal of obtaining a satisfactory education is achieved, in the long run, the alternative placement may be seen as worthwhile in spite of any short-term discomfort. A more serious concern is that alternative programs may "serve as a catalyst in the formation of deviant groups" (Mahoney & Cairns, 1997, p. 248). Peers with similar behavior problems may have negative influences on each other (Arnold & Hughes, 1999; Cavell & Hughes, 2000; Dishion & Andrews, 1995; Kazdin, 1994). Another reason for concern about transferring an at-risk student from an integrated setting to a segregated setting is that such a transfer is a form of mobility and mobility is highly predictive of dropout: "Controlling for other predictors, students who made even one nonpromotional school change between the eighth and twelfth grades were twice as likely to not complete high school as students who did not change schools" (Rumberger & Larson, 1998, p. 1). However, segregated placements are sometimes required and, for high school age students with serious antisocial characteristics, may be beneficial and therapeutic, according to Gold and Mann (1984):

> Being in a separate building contributed a great deal to the flexibility of the programs. The more casual comings and going of alternative students, the occasionally higher noise level, the regular availability of coffee and a place to smoke, and other deliberate informalities that created the ambience of the alternative programs probably could not have been tolerated in the midst of a conventional comprehensive secondary school. (Gold & Mann, 1984, p. 156).

Teachers in alternative programs, especially correctional and other segregated settings, need specially designed pre-service training (Ashcroft, 1999), but such training is not widely available. In addition, teachers attempting to provide alternative programs for students who have already become involved with delinquency need to be supported by systems-level reforms that include (a) curricula designed to meet the needs of the at-risk students and (b) supported transitions back to general education (Cox, 1999).

In sum, alternative education is seen as beneficial but on the basis of limited evidence (Duke & Griesdorn, 1999; Gold & Mann, 1984; Guerin & Denti, 1999; Nichols & Utesch, 1998; Raywid, 1996, 1998). Program evaluations and research studies of alternative programs need to be conducted, proven models and their essential features identified, and then effects broadly replicated.

WHAT IS KNOWN ABOUT ALTERNATIVE PROGRAMS FOR VERY AT-RISK STUDENTS, SOME OF WHOM ARE COMMITTING DELINQUENT ACTS?

Perhaps the most striking known fact about alternative programs, for at-risk students, is that a *wide range* of alternative program models exist (Fizzell & Raywid, 1997). Examples to illustrate the range are described below.

Separate Schools for Students Who Have Been Expelled

Alternative education programs are characterized as "increasingly popular means of getting troublemakers out of the regular classroom" (Hill, 1998, p. 34). There is nothing specific to separate alternative schools that make them necessarily effective. Unfortunately, however, some of these programs provide very little allocated or engaged instructional time and no extracurricular activities or support services. For example, in the reform school described by Hill, the "troublemakers" could be on the streets by 11:40 a.m., because this alternative program offered only a half-day of schooling starting in the morning, with nothing "extraneous." Success with these students, expelled from their home schools because of violence, weapons, alcohol or drugs, or major disruptions, was measured by "recidivism" (a term usually associated with being incarcerated) or by the percentage of students who were sent back to the reform school after a temporary return to their home school. By that measure, 67% of the students were "successful" in that they were not sent to the reform school again. Unfortunately, the effectiveness of this specific intervention in terms of more meaningful outcomes achieved for the students (e.g., credentials earned, post-school employment) was not tracked. An afternoon session was added for *additional* students, who attend only in the afternoon, indicating that the number of students rejected as "troublemakers" increased in this area.

GED Preparation

The GAP program was for students (16–18 years old) who are sure they will not get a high school diploma but would like help in obtaining a GED (Craig, 1997). They were referred by their high school principal, and principals could not refer more than a total of 15 students to this program. The program served four high schools and had room for 60 students. If accepted, the students attended small classes for half of the day for 1 or 2 years. They took practice tests for the GED and learned entry-level job skills in a field they chose. This program insisted that the students (and their parents) understood that they were not going to go back to high school. They evaluated their program by the percent of students taking the practice GED tests and passing them. These are the reported results: In 1993–1994, 8 out of 13 passed (62%); in 1994–1995, 11 out of 19 (58%), and in 1995–1996, 10 out of 35 (29%). Although the percentage of students who passed dropped in 1995–1996, it was because more students attempted the practice tests. The actual number passing each year remained about the same. Students could attend more than 1 year.

Alternative Programs Offered in General Education Settings

"School within a school" programs. Stockard and Mayberry (1992) reported that students who were not able to cope with the variety and multiple transitions involved in a typical, large middle school, would do very well in a "school within a school" setting. The Multicultural Alternative Middle School Program for At-Risk Students (MLC) was a "school within a school" in the state of Washington (Weir, 1996). The host middle school's population was 45 percent Native American and about 55 percent Caucasian. MLC served 20 students with a staff consisting of one special education teacher, one full-time assistant, and one part-time assistant, with assistance from a county mental health worker. The mental health worker "relieved the program teacher/director from the difficult task of doing mental health work with students during class time (e.g., dealing with students who were fighting)" and with students who could not concentrate due to "abuse or drug/alcohol activities" (p. 50). Features of the program included (a) self-paced learning and flexibility to accommodate alternative

learning styles, (b) blended services with integration into some general school classes (e.g., physical education), (c) coordination with community agencies, (d) staff inservice and training, (e) interdisciplinary thematic units in academic areas, (f) daily journal writing, (g) cooperative learning and hands-on projects, and (h) efforts to evaluate the program and use data from surveys, interviews, attendance records, and classroom observations to plan for improving the program. An initial student survey of attitudes indicated that students felt they were trying harder and learning more in MLC than in traditional classes.

Preventing drug abuse by building social networks. An elective "Personal Growth Class" was offered for one semester to students in four high schools who were identified by school records and/or staff nominations as having risk factors related to dropout. The class met daily for 55 minutes and was designed to prevent drug abuse and high school dropout by providing information, developing skills related to solving personal problems, and improving interpersonal relationships by building social networks in a support group atmosphere. A 1:12 student-teacher ratio was maintained. Regular high school teachers attended a 3-day workshop on drug abuse prevention, therapeutic teacher-student relationships, small group-work, and skills training. Ongoing consultation (twice a month) provided additional support. The content of the specific skills training was based on four units: (a) self-esteem, (b) decision making, (c) personal control, and (d) interpersonal communication. The control group research design for the study indicated that the class "appeared effective in the short-term for reducing problems and consequences related to drug involvement and improving school achievement" (Eggert, Thompson, Herting, Nicholas, & Dicker, 1994, p. 212). The authors suggested that a longer program, follow-up booster sessions, alternative recreational experiences, and community activities could enhance the treatment effect. Gender differences were noticed in one of the outcomes (i.e., self-report bonds with deviant peers). There was no change in this measure for either gender in the control group and none for males in the experimental group. However, females in the experimental group had a decreasing trend, from pre-intervention to post-intervention and follow-up 5 months later, in charted data on deviant peer bonds. A refined version of this intervention, with increased attention to students' levels of depression, anger, and suicidal behaviors and more consistent teaching emphasis on content, produced stronger effects in reductions in both drug use and changes in attitudes about drugs (Thompson, Horn, Herting, & Eggert, 1997).

Computer-assisted instruction. The Advanced Achievement Academy (AAA) was a dropout prevention alternative program that relied heavily on computer-assisted instruction (Groth, 1998). Students earned credits toward graduation by working at their own pace on computer-assisted tutorials. A teacher was present to answer questions and monitor student progress. Twice a week a counselor led discussions about personal or community issues. Located in an urban setting, on the edge of a high school campus, the program served about 25 students per year. The ethnic composition was about half Hispanic and half white. The students needed to apply for program admittance and acceptance was considered a privilege. If accepted, students had access to the program for 1 year, provided they attended regularly. Hours were flexible. Many of the students were working and/or raising children and needed credits to graduate. Data about students' perspectives were collected using a "participant-observational approach" (Groth, 1998, p. 222). The consensus of the students was that without this program they would not be in school and that it was successful in helping them earn sufficient credits for graduation. The author, however, concluded that "it is unclear whether it can give students the educational experiences needed to successfully cope with their problematic circumstances" (p. 239).

Community-Based Learning

A magnet school developed an alternative program, called the Community-Based Learning Program, that featured service learning, career exploration, and civic education, in addition to academic development. Academic gains and improved attendance were reported as attributed to the program (Shumer, 1994). Participating students (ages 15–19) attributed their improved grades and school attendance to a curriculum, which connected them to their field experience within the community, and to the fact that they had a choice over what they studied. "Students in the program spend 2 days per week in self-selected field sites exploring occupations or interest areas and learning how basic skills and academic subjects are applied in real world settings" (Shumer, 1994, p. 358). At the end of the year the mean grade point average for students in this program was considerably higher that it had been the previous year (2.50 compared to 1.79). In contrast, the control group's mean grade point average was lower than it had been (2.37 compared to 2.53).

Student-adult interactions in the Community-Based Learning Program were an important aspect of the success of the program, as explained by Alice, one of the students. "'I always hated school—I never wanted to get up in the morning. Now I like school. I know how important it is and I go. The teachers here are open. They help you get things done. They don't just explain, they do it with you, and it helps'" (Shumer, 1994, p. 363). In the comparison group, the instruction generally consisted of individual seatwork or lectures but in the Community-Based Learning Program, in addition to the field experiences, students often worked in small groups with their teachers or with tutors. Students from local universities served as tutors.

Common Elements

Although great variation exists among alternative programs, common elements can be found. Housego (1999) reported the following features that were identified by students and teachers in successful alternative programs: low pupil-teacher ratio, participatory decision making, individualization, collaboration between school and community, and caring teachers. Gottfredson (1997) states that "In summary, programs which group high-risk students to create smaller, more tightly-knit units for instruction show promise for reducing delinquency, drug-use, and drop-out. These programs are risky in light of other research that shows negative effects of grouping high-risk youth for peer counseling or other therapeutic services ... but it may be beneficial ... in the context of 'schools-within-schools' which offer *strong academic programs, use effective instruction and classroom management strategies, and supportive staff*" (p. 19, emphasis added).

WHAT ARE BEST PRACTICES FOR KEEPING THESE STUDENTS ENGAGED IN SCHOOLING?

At-risk students often come to school with emotional and behavioral difficulties that interfere with their attempts to focus on academic instruction. Others may have interpersonal issues with other students or school staff that make concentrating on learning difficult. Best practice for these students begins with early identification of emotional, behavioral, and interpersonal needs, followed by interventions to reduce obstacles to successful school adjustment.

Early Identification and Intervention

In the wake of the recent series of incidents of violence at school, commentators with the clear 20/20 vision of hindsight discovered early warning signs of mental illness and other difficulties that teachers and parents either missed or inadequately addressed. Rather than wait for a crisis that distresses a teacher or parent sufficiently to prompt a request for a special education evaluation or other action, *universal screening* for emotional, behavioral, and interpersonal problems should be carried out when children first start school (Walker, Severson, & Feil, 1994) and at repeated regular intervals (e.g., October and March of each year) (Walker & McConnell, 1995; Walker & Severson, 1990). With this type of universal screening system, all students could be monitored for excessive internalizing or externalizing behaviors. A multiple gating system is recommended so that time-consuming assessments (e.g., direct observations by trained observers) are needed for only a few students, yet every student receives at least one rating by his or her teacher on key characteristics. Students who are identified as at-risk, yet are not qualified for special education, should be considered candidates for alternative educational practices.

Discipline referrals are warning signs of more serious problems likely to occur within the next few years (Tobin & Sugai, 1999b; Walker, Block-Pedego, Todis, & Severson, 1991; Walker, Stieber, Ramsey, & O'Neill, 1991, 1993). A referral for an act of aggression, or a threat, should not be ignored, even if the student does not have frequent referrals. School records of discipline referrals, grades, and attendance are increasingly being entered into computerized databases. This could help prevent a child from slipping through the cracks, as school staff sometimes become aware of an individual's need for support only when seeing this type of data charted. Although teachers generally know which students have behavior problems, we have seen classroom teachers express surprise when presented with charted data indicating that a "likable" or "quiet" student was among the top 5% of students in terms of frequency of discipline referrals, perhaps arising from incidents on the playground or in the hallways that classroom teachers had not observed. In this way, charted discipline referrals can function as an inexpensive monitoring-screening device to identify students for whom additional assessments and/or alternative programs may be beneficial.

Records of behavioral incidents also may be used to indicate the need for early intervention services for students who are victims of bullying or harassment. These students' needs are often neglected. Victims need "counseling, support, and protection so that the desire for revenge does not fuel more violence" (Day, 1996, p. 92). About 10% of schoolchildren are victimized frequently throughout their school years, suffer from depression, and often avoid school (Hodges & Perry, 1996). Hodges and Perry suggest providing social skills instruction in areas such as assertiveness and making friends. Doren, Bullis, and Benz (1996) also reported a need to teach ways to avoid victimization. Children who are frequently victimized by peers, if not helped, are likely to have lasting and serious adjustment problems (Crick and Grotpeter, 1996).

Effective Academic Instruction

Many at-risk students have learning disabilities (which may or may not have been identified) and may benefit from alternative instructional strategies. Swanson and Hoskyn (1998) conducted a meta-analysis of outcomes in 180 experimental studies and determined that the following instructional features are most successful for students with learning disabilities across all subject areas: (a) combining direct instruction and strategy instruction, (b) controlling task difficulty and number of steps, (c) using small interactive groups, and (d) directed responses and questioning of students.

The strategies that help students with learning disabilities also may benefit students with behavior disorders. Although research on effective academic practices with students with behavior disorders is limited, it seems likely that an extremely important aspect would be to design the instructional sequence(s) so that the student would be able to respond correctly (Gunter, Hummel, & Venn, 1998). Introducing new material at the child's level after teaching necessary pre-skills and modeling correct responses is important (Tobin & Sprague, 2000). In addition, working with the student, guiding initial attempts, and providing prompts as needed are important when a new task is attempted. The student should receive positive feedback quickly when he or she responds correctly. In addition, whenever possible, instructional tasks should be presented in a way that is interesting and meaningful to the student. In traditional school settings, students with behavior disorders often do not receive this type of instruction. Instead, as much as 70% of the school day may be spent in independent seatwork (Good & Brophy, 1997, cited in Gunter et al., 1998).

Katsiyannis and Archwamety (1999) found that for 12- to 18-year-old incarcerated male youths, *individualized* academic instruction was a valuable rehabilitation tool and concluded that "the results also support the need for intensive academic remediation for incarcerated youths, since academic improvement is associated with lower rates of recidivism" (p. 99). Instruction was provided on a year-round basis.

Positive Classroom Management

Lipsey and Wilson (1998) found that behavioral programs have "positive effects" and that the supporting evidence for non-institutionalized juvenile offenders is "consistent" (p. 332). One reason behavioral programs may be beneficial is that, when well implemented, the traditional use of punishment as a means of attempting to change behavior will be lessened. Punishment, as it is generally administered in traditional schools (e.g., detentions, suspensions), although intended to correct behavior problems, is generally not effective for students who have antisocial tendencies because they are likely to react to it in escalating and coercive ways (Patterson, Reid, & Dishion, 1992). The *Gateway Program* (Davis, 1994) is an example of a positive, non-punitive behavior management system in an alternative education for middle and high school students who have been suspended or expelled from traditional schools for carrying weapons, harassment, aggression, drugs, and other disciplinary problems. In addition to providing support through counseling, the school uses a level system in which students can earn privileges: "A student can earn *one point each hour for each rule* followed during that period. The rules are: (1.) Work for the entire period. (2.) Complete all assignments. (3.) Remain in your assigned area. (4.) Maintain a respectful attitude. (5.) Remain quiet." (Davis, 1994, p. 4, emphasis added). In traditional settings, when a student breaks one rule, generally the teacher's attention will be focused entirely on the broken rule. In the Gateway Program, although the student would not earn a point for the rule broken, he or she would still be given credit for the rules followed. In addition, every new *hour* brings a new start.

Informal Interactions and Low Pupil-Teacher Ratios

Teachers and other school staff often can strengthen school engagement by speaking to at-risk students informally and in a friendly way, greeting them by name, and sometimes asking about topics other than school work or problem behaviors (Altenbaugh et al., 1995; Walker, 1995). Although this type of "personalization" (Shore, 1996, p. 362) can reduce suspensions and dropout rates (Testerman, 1996) in general education settings, it is more likely to occur in alternative settings that have low pupil-teacher ratios. Descriptions of alternative programs often mention improved relationships between teachers and students as an advantage in comparison with traditional schools (e.g., Duggar & Duggar, 1998; Lange, 1998). Castleberry and Enger (1998) surveyed alternative education students and found that being able to work one-on-one with teachers was cited as a factor in decisions to try to graduate or receive a GED. Richardson and Griffin (1994) found similar results when they surveyed students about how their attitudes toward their alternative school differed from attitudes toward traditional schools. Students reported appreciating the following features of the alternative school: (a) teachers who genuinely cared about the students, (b) teachers who were not as authoritative as traditional teachers, and (c) the school policy of allowing student input in decision making (Richardson & Griffin, 1994).

Instruction in Interpersonal, Self-Control, and Social Skills

Social skill deficits are highly predictive of future delinquency (Bullis, Walker, & Stieber, 1998). Social skills instruction may help at-risk students establish positive relationships with adults and with other students, and this result, in turn, might help build resilience and lead to a more favorable future outcome. Planning for generalization is essential for effective social skill instruction (Doren et al., 1996; Walker, 1995). Effective generalization strategies include "teaching functional replacement behaviors, schedule thinning and involving peers (e.g., group contingencies, peer coaches)" (Scott & Nelson, 1998, p. 269).

Male and female at-risk students tend to have different needs in the area of social skills instruction, according to Hay (2000), who collected self-report data from 128 high school students placed in alternative settings due to frequent out-of-school suspensions: "Girls were in the low range for same-sex relationships and emotional stability, suggesting [being] rejected by their female peers and … more psychological stress. … The boys' antisocial behaviors were not associated with emotional instability or male peer rejection" (Hay, 2000, p. 348). Both boys and girls had low verbal ability scores, which Hays states indicates a need to facilitate interpersonal and social skills. Although boys were not low in same-sex relationships, Hays argues convincingly that "peer reputation enhancement is a motivational goal for *antisocial* behavior, as compensation for and an alternative to the negative feedback from parents and school" (p. 349, emphasis added). Suggestions for school-based interventions included providing positive feedback and rewards for prosocial behaviors, teaching "peer resistance" (e.g., refusal skills for coping with inappropriate requests), and individualized social skills instruction.

Results on the effectiveness of instruction in interpersonal skills are mixed. For example, Bennett and Gibbons (2000) conducted a meta-analysis of cognitive-behavioral interventions (i.e., behavioral rehearsal, coaching, modeling, assertiveness training, anger management, social problem solving or social skills instruction, cognitive restructuring, relaxation training) designed to reduce antisocial behavior. They found considerable variation but reported that, in general, two treatment sessions of about 50 minutes were held twice a week for about 9 weeks with moderately positive results and concluded such interventions "may be an effective part of a multimodal treatment of children, particularly older children, who exhibit antisocial behavior" (Bennett & Gibbons, 2000, p. 11). However, Cavell and Hughes (2000) found that social problem-solving classes focused on reducing aggression in children in grades 2 and 3 was not only not effective, but counter-productive in that it produced an increase in "positive beliefs about aggression" (p. 227) and "children's beliefs about aggression significantly predicted parents' ratings of [their child's] aggression at follow-up … [and] peer ratings" (p. 219). Cavell and Hughes concluded that instructional groups should not be made up entirely of aggressive children but should include an "equal or greater number of prosocial children" (p. 231).

Extracurricular Activities

Research supports the value of participation in extracurricular activities (e.g., athletics, drama, music) as a means of increasing school engagement, and with that engagement, improved academic achievement, for at-risk (and other) students (Holloway, 1999/2000; Mahoney & Cairns, 1997). However, school staff and community members may need to find creative ways to involve at-risk students in extracurricular activities, especially when parents are not able to pay extra fees or provide transportation. "Involvement in any extracurricular activity was significant such that if an individual was involved, ... he or she was 2.21 times more likely to be enrolled in school (p < .001). ... This positive effect is true for all individuals, regardless of ethnicity or gender" (Davalos, Chavez, & Guardiola, 1999, p. 69, p. 72).

"Check and Connect" Monitors

Check and Connect encourages at-risk students to stay in school by providing a "monitor" who regularly checks on students' engagement with school and helps the student and his or her family if problems arise. Even if the student changes schools, within the district, the same monitor works with the student. The program format follows the same pattern for the group of students who participate (i.e., the students are monitored in a similar way), but the service is delivered on a one-to-one basis. The monitor refers the student for additional services when necessary. An experimental study found that students in the treatment group were significantly more likely to be enrolled in school and attending regularly than were control group students (Sinclair, Christenson, Evelo, & Hurley, 1998). The monitors were credited with achieving a 50% reduction in the dropout rate.

Voluntary Service Learning

Moore and Allen (1996) reviewed research on eight programs that studied the effects of volunteer service learning. Most of the reports indicated positive changes in attitudes. Two provided strong evidence that dropout rates were reduced by offering structured opportunities for students to volunteer. Analysis of data for the Teen Outreach Program showed that the participating students, in the first 7 years of the program, had 50% lower dropout rates than comparison students, which was "statistically significant even after controlling for the student's race, gender, grade, living arrangements, mother's education, and pre-program levels of problem behaviors" (Moore & Allen, 1996, p. 235). This program also reduced teen pregnancy, course failure, and suspensions. However, the program combines community service with classroom discussions and the relative influence of each component is not known.

The Valued Youth Program resulted in a clear improvement in school engagement for middle school students with limited English proficiency who served as tutors to younger students. After 2 years, 12% of the students in the control group had dropped out of school in comparison with 1% of the students in the Valued Youth Program. Other components of the program that may have affected the results, in addition to the service learning component, included "weekly classes to improve tutoring skills ... [being] recognized throughout the year in a variety of events ... parental involvement ... in which a bilingual person visited parents' homes" (Moore & Allen, 1996, p. 249).

Flexibility

Gold and Mann (1984), in a study of alternative secondary schools using a longitudinal, experimental/control group design, found that flexibility was "critical to positive change" (p. 154). Interestingly, students who perceived the alternative school as flexible, and who changed their behavior in a positive way, were able to maintain gains even after returning to a less flexible traditional school, with an important exception. The exception was students who scored in the highest third on pre-test measures of anxiety and depression. These students were least likely to benefit from the alternative education program, perhaps being in need of additional mental health services or a more comprehensive intervention. Flexibility was defined as "taking into account the individual students' needs, fears, abilities, and mood in conducting the daily business of education" (p. 155). Flexibility stands in opposition to rigid enforcement of "one size fits all" rules and traditional expectations for formal (authoritarian) teacher–student social interactions. Flexibility affected continued engagement in schooling by making it possible for the students to be more optimistic about their chances for being academically successful.

WHAT ARE BEST PRACTICES FOR MEETING THEIR COMPLEX NEEDS?

The needs of at-risk students are complex and must be addressed if they are to succeed in their school careers. Effective alternative education programs for tertiary level students must do even more than provide creative academic instruction and build positive interpersonal relationships at school. Parental involvement, mentors, collaborative arrangements with community agencies, behavior support based on functional assessments, and professional technical education stand out as best practices for meeting the complex needs of at-risk students.

Involving Parents

Parent training is the most effective intervention for antisocial behavior in children and adolescents (Brestan & Eyberg, 1998, cited in Bennett & Gibbons, 2000), but it is an intervention that is not accessible to all families. Not only do parents often have constraints that prevent them from accessing training, but schools and agencies have financial and personal reasons for not developing programs for parents. Staffs in alternative programs for chronically disruptive youth are quite likely to feel that involving parents is too difficult to achieve. However, a recent study indicates that parental involvement is possible, and well worth the effort, even after students have been expelled from their home school for serious violations (e.g., fighting, alcohol or drugs, weapons, or threatening school personnel) and required to attend an alternative school for 45–180 school days (Aeby, Manning, Thyer, & Carpenter-Aeby, 1999). In one such school, 215 such students were divided randomly into two groups. The control group received the standard alternative program while an experimental group received the standard alternative program plus an intensive family involvement intervention. Dropout rates for the two groups were assessed over one school year. "At follow-up 180 days after their return to their home school, 1.7% of the experimental group and 10.5% of the control group students had dropped out of school, a statistically significant difference ($p < .05$)" (Aeby et al., 1999, p. 28). The intervention also was related to improved attendance and grade point averages. Family involvement consisted of approximately 8 hours of family therapy, at least one family-teacher conference, at least two meetings with the school administrator, and at least three family meetings that included training in how to work with the student at home (e.g., on academic assignments). Other types of parental involvement were (a) meeting with staff for 1 hour every 2 weeks, (b) individual counseling for family members, and (c) telephone conferences (average of one per week to discuss the student's progress).

Involving parents when their children are in elementary school is essential, and, although still requiring time, effort, and systems-level planning, it is less demanding than the model described above for parents of expelled students. At the elementary level, parental involvement interventions could start with improving the frequency and quality of communication between home and school about homework assignments (Epstein, Munk, Bursuck, Polloway, & Jayanthi, 1999). Ironically, although it is common for teachers who request assistance from a consultant in dealing with a student's behavior problems to state that the parents are largely responsible for the child's behavior, it is not common for schools to provide time for quality home-school communication or parent education programs. *Aware Parenting* (Bornstein et al., 1998) is a positive example of a school-based parent education program that benefits at-risk (and other) students. In this model, the parent trainer *first* addresses the parents' concerns and needs. Later, parents are asked to become more involved in their child's education and other tasks requiring effort on the part of the parent are suggested. The five components of the program are: (a) support, (b) attentiveness, (c) responsiveness, (d) guidance, and (e) receptivity to emotion. For example, "facilitators offered *support* by encouraging parents and complimenting them, both for sharing ideas and experiences and for trying out new approaches within the group and at home" (Bornstein et al., 1998, p. 138). In a controlled study, an 11-week intervention (meeting once a week for 2 hours) with parents of fifth-grade students produced lasting academic and behavioral gains for students that were evident when the students went to middle school. This model has been described in a manual, which could be used to enhance fidelity of implementation.

The Montreal Longitudinal Study reported on an alternative educational program, which was conducted in the general education setting. An essential feature was a program of parent training in behavior management for parents of disruptive and aggressive boys in the primary grades (Tremblay, Pagani-Kurtz, Mâsse, Vitaro, & Pihl, 1995). The boys also received social skill instruction in school. This study was impressive in that (a) it had both a no-treatment control group and a comparison group to control for the effects of contact, (b) participants were followed from kindergarten to high school, and (c) results were thoroughly analyzed and reported (e.g., Tremblay et al., 1995; Vitaro & Tremblay, 1994). The intervention was limited to the primary grades, and the researchers concluded that booster sessions in later years probably would have enhanced the effects. Nevertheless, the intervention was effective in helping students to remain in age-appropriate regular classrooms as opposed to being retained a grade or being placed in special classrooms or special schools, both related to school dropout. This favorable outcome was mediated by a reduction in overall disruptiveness. Parent training programs, of course, only reach cooperative parents who are willing and able to attend. When children come to school suffering from a lack of effective parenting and needing more attention from a caring adult than teachers can provide, mentors are especially relevant.

Mentors

An adult mentor *at school* (as opposed to in the community) can serve as a significant protective factor for youth with aggressive behavior or emotional and behavioral disturbance: "Promoting a school setting that emphasizes finding each high-risk child an adult mentor, who can reach out and take a special interest in that child, may go a long way toward enhancing educational progress" (Vance, Fernandes, & Biber, 1998, p. 220). According to Catalano and associates (1998), research supports mentoring *only* if mentors are trained to use behavior management and provide positive reinforcement for appropriate behavior, such as attending school. On the other hand, Cavell and Hughes (2000) report that, if the mentors are reasonably consistent in putting in the time promised (i.e., about 1 hour a week over a school year), even without extensive training for the mentor or having the intervention take place in the school, mentoring can result in significant decreases in teacher- and parent-rated aggression in children who were nominated and rated as aggressive by their teachers in grade 2 or 3.

Collaborative Arrangements

Students with significant behavioral challenges often require support and intervention across multiple life domains (Reid & Eddy, 1997). Walker et al. (1996) suggest that students who display at-risk and antisocial forms of behavior at an early age are deficient in many of the critically important behavioral competencies associated with schooling. These are the students who are most likely to be excluded from school through suspension or expulsion based on their behavior and/or major rule violations.

However, this behavior is rarely found in isolation from other major stresses in the lives of these students, such as family disruption, school failure, and negative peer associations. Thus, in addition to an emphasis on skill building of prosocial skills, these students need assistance with their family and community associations and with their ability to engage in and succeed in their academic endeavors (Furlong, Morrison, & Pavelski, 2000, p. 87).

Collaborative arrangements, such as "Wraparound" services, are needed. Wraparound was originally developed as a plan or model for integrating community mental health and school services. It has expanded to include other agencies and has been very effective in keeping students with multiple problems in school (Eber, 1996). "Wraparound" is a term used when school staff and personnel from other community agencies collaborate to provide services that "wrap around" the student and his or her family. This stands in contrast to situations without collaboration in which services are tied to, and limited by, narrow regulations designed for the convenience of specific agencies, often resulting in gaps, duplications, and inefficient delivery of services for an at-risk student with multiple needs. "Typically, wraparound planning results in a blend of nontraditional supports (e.g., community mentors, respite providers, parent partners) with traditional services, and it is a tool that can be used across the full continuum of services" (Eber & Nelson, 1997, pp. 387–388). Examples of services that might be coordinated in a comprehensive plan include (a) student services (e.g., behavior change program, medication management, after school tutoring); (b) school services (e.g., coverage for in-school respite to prevent out-of-school suspensions, technical assistance for staff, substitutes to assure teacher participation in meetings); (c) family services (e.g., trained advocates accompany parents and student to court, transportation to appointments provided, home behavior plans developed); and (d) community services (e.g., recreational coaching, partnerships with businesses, rent waivers and emergency funds to pay utilities, drug screening) (Eber, 1996). School staff collaborates with staff from community agencies and parents in the development of plans for coordinated individualized services (Eber, Nelson, & Miles, 1997).

Wraparound services were part of an intensive program developed to serve a small group of students in a public school who "used drugs, engaged in criminal activity, had been placed in psychiatric hospitals or residential schools, at great expense to the district [and then] returned to school … no better prepared to cope than before [and] continued to be truant, made negligible academic progress, and caused behavioral disruptions that affected other students as well as themselves" (Wetzel, McNaboe, Schneidermeyer, Jones, & Nash, 1997, p. 180). Students of different ages learned together in this program. Each student had a support team, a committee of adults, called the *core group,* to seek out strategies that would help the student and to make decisions about his or her educational program and placement. The core group consisted of a behavior support specialist (hired by the school district from a private agency, "Camp Horizons"), a teacher, a guidance counselor, and sometimes other school staff members, students, family members, or parole officers or social workers. Core group meetings were held regularly, at 1- or 2-week intervals. Meetings followed a standard agenda: (a) accomplishments were listed and reviewed, (b) decisions were made about what was working and what was not, and (c) the next steps to take were specified. For activities and instruction, two rooms were used. One room was a basic classroom, and the second room was smaller and carpeted and was used for quiet study, time out, or meetings. Students also spent some time in general education classes and settings, using the second room as a "home room, study hall, and core group meeting place" (p. 180). A level system was in place for behavior management, in addition to individualized plans. In addition, family therapy might be provided. Busy-work was avoided. When possible, learning involved interesting tasks, such as working on computers or building picnic tables. An evaluation of the first 2 years of the program found that 16 students were served, 5 successfully completed middle school and transitioned to high school or to technical schools, 1 was unsuccessful in high school but continued to receive support from Camp Horizons, 5 continued in the program with most of their classes in the mainstream, and 5 moved out of the district and follow-up information for them was not available.

Behavior Support Based on Functional Assessments

Positive behavior support, based on functional assessments, can help resolve discipline and attendance problems (Sugai et al., 2000). Student interviews should be a part of the functional assessment process for students who are capable of reporting the environmental circumstances surrounding their challenging and preferred behaviors. Several standard forms for semi-structured student interviews are available for use in school settings (Kern, Dunlap, Clarke, & Childs, 1994; Reed, Thomas, Sprague, & Horner, 1997). Educators should be proactive about providing positive behavior support to students in general education who show signs of developing behavior problems that may later lead to situations in which special education alternative placement or expulsion is being considered (National Association of State Directors of Special Education, 1998). A variety of resources for practical applications of functional assessment in educational settings are now available (e.g., Liaupsin, Scott, & Nelson, 1999; O'Neill et al., 1997; Sugai, 1998; Witt, Daly, & Noell, 2000), and this field is growing rapidly so new materials will be forthcoming (see *http://pbis.org* and *http://darkwing.uoregon.edu/~ttobin*).

The use of functional assessment in resolving attendance problems holds particular promise for students who have frequent unexcused absences (Evans, 2000; Kearney & Tillitson, 1998). This tool should be explored in relationship to dropout prevention and inadequate "home schooling." Although some parents can and do provide adequate home schooling, others find it a convenient loophole in compulsory education laws and a way to avoid both the responsibility of making sure their child goes to school on a regular basis and any related sanctions.

Professional Technical Education

Strengthening professional technical education and vocational opportunities would benefit at-risk students, especially those with emotional and behavioral disabilities

(Rylance, 1997; Sitlington, Carson, & Frank, 1992). The School-to-Work Opportunities Act of 1994 made some funds available for programs with school-based learning, work-based learning, and meaningful connecting activities. The Carl D. Perkins Vocational-Technical Education Act of 1998 (Perkins III) may "increase collaboration between academic and vocational education teachers in meeting students' educational needs … states and localities [will be] more accountable for student achievement of vocational, technical, and academic proficiencies" (Finch, 1999, p. 17). If this goal is to be achieved for at-risk students, especially those with disabilities, more inservice training on inclusive practices and participation in the development of Individual Education Programs (IEPs) should be given to teachers of professional technical education classes and staff directing school-to-work programs (Lombard, Miller, & Hazelkorn, 1998). In addition, systems-level changes to enhance these programs should be promoted (Cobb & Johnson, 1997).

Alternative forms of learning that involve technology are particularly likely to provide meaningful and motivating experiences and can be developed for students at all age levels. Examples include classrooms set up like mini-communities where students create and run (with play money and practice activities) "a store, a travel agency, a garden center, a newspaper, and a construction company" (Hoffman, 1995, p. p.22). Some students who failed in traditional classrooms succeeded in alternative classrooms where they could use the AT&T Learning Network to communicate with students in other states and countries (Cardon & Christensen, 1998). Another example of a successful alternative program with an emphasis on technology comes from the Heuneme School District in California. This program utilized a "Smart Classroom," filled with technological tools. With a predominantly minority student body (17% African-American and 50% Hispanic), this district used its allotment of state lottery funds for modular, media-based instruction. The district also converted a drafting lab and a wood lab into a technology room where students could experiment with "computerized robotics, computer-aided manufacturing, computer publications, … the district observed tremendous improvement in the California Assessment Program (CAP) scores. These improvements coincided with the district's implementation of technology-based education in the classrooms. The average daily attendance of the 'futuristic science classroom' was 98% in 1990, *with very few referrals to the office for disciplinary concerns."* (Cardon & Christensen, 1998, pp. 52–53, emphasis added).

Computer-supported studying can facilitate successful transition to post-secondary education for high school students with learning disabilities, especially under the following conditions: (a) real-world tasks are involved, (b) computer-supported studying is an extra task but is functional as a part of the existing curriculum (although it also may lead to novel and interesting learning), and (c) the computer-supported studying is provided in a way that involves students in decision making and promotes independence so that they feel "in control of their learning" (Anderson-Inman, Knox-Quinn, & Szymanski, 1999, p. 209).

Coping With Transitions and Mobility

Many students in alternative programs need assistance in coping with transitions and mobility. Assistance could take several forms, beginning with facilitating adjustment to the current placement. Assessments that will enable "wise placement decisions *from the beginning* ease the transition" (Beck, Kratzer, & Isken, 1997, p. 354, emphasis in the original). Taking time to carefully assess the students' academic and personal needs initially makes it possible to maximize the value of instruction and services provided as soon as possible, even if records from the previous school are delayed or the child's situation has changed. Tutoring, even when provided in a "pull out" model, is an effective strategy for many transfer students, who, even if capable learners, often have missed essential elements of instruction due to moving from school to school (Jason et al., 1992).

All students are likely to benefit from planned preparation for transition to the next environment, whether it is another school, a more restrictive placement, or a post-school work situation. Depending on the student's level and needs, preparation might vary from instruction in self-management and other skills that the student will use on his or her own in the future to formal intervention and services provided by adult professionals who facilitate transitions by working with the student and with adults in both the new and the old environment. An example of a formal transition plan from one school to another is given in a report on the Inverness Center (Lloyd, 1997a, 1997b), which is an alternative program for middle-school-level students who have been expelled or had to transfer because of behavior problems. Features of the program included (a) individualized remedial instruction in academic areas, (b) environmental projects (e.g., building sailboats), (c) service learning in partnership with Meals on Wheels and volunteering as tutors for special needs elementary students, (d) a level system for behavior management, (e) daily meetings with a mentor to review progress toward individual behavior goals, (f) peer mediation, and (g) regular home-school communication. When the student was ready to return to the home school, a transition plan was developed and monitored by a counselor.

Trans-environment programming (Walker, 1995) is sorely needed by at-risk students in our fragmented educational system, in which the differences from one school to the next may be huge, especially for students with emotional and behavioral disorders (Tobin & Sugai, 1999a) but also for others. Unfortunately, the school culture currently tends to make teachers' focus entirely on the current situation, and the lack of planning for transfer of training, or generalization, sets the stage for future problems. The more the current environment provides structure and special services that will not be continued in the future, the greater the risk that long-term goals will not be achieved without systematic planning for transition. Planning for any type of transition involves understanding the similar and dissimilar elements and demands of the new and the old school environment(s), with a view toward enabling continued use of known skills that will be valuable in the new environment but may require some modifications, as well as teaching new skills that will be needed in the future but have not yet been developed. In addition, practice in using a problem-solving approach in making decisions, sufficient to assure fluency when used independently, is essential because it will serve the student well when unexpected events occur.

WHAT ARE THE KEY FEATURES OF PROVEN MODEL PROGRAMS FOR STUDENTS AT ELEMENTARY AND MIDDLE SCHOOL LEVELS?

Although most alternative programs are for high school students, some alternative education programs exist for younger students, and it seems likely that there will be more in the future. Recent research demonstrates that at-risk students can be identified early (Loeber & Farrington, 1998; Patterson, Reid, & Dishion, 1992; Roderick, 1993). The increase in the use of weapons in acts of violence by children and young adolescents (Butts & Snyder, 1997; Declining violence, 1998), and especially the recent increase in highly publicized school shootings, have led to pressures to provide alternative education to younger students. However, alternative programs for younger, high-risk, antisocial students have not been studied as extensively as programs for older students. Although some of the findings on what is effective in alternative programming for older students may apply to students of any age, clearly age differences must be considered. We conclude this chapter with brief explanations of essential features of effective alternative programs for younger students.

Elementary School Example

Although the need for alternative programs for students at the elementary level is not as great as it is for older students in terms of the number of tertiary level, at-risk students in the adolescent range, when a young child has such serious behavior problems that he or she cannot be accommodated in traditional classrooms, the importance of providing a high-quality alternative program cannot be overestimated. The 1997 amendments to the Individuals with Disabilities Education Act call for interim placements of up to 45 days for students with disabilities (including elementary school students) who bring weapons to school (Katsiyannis & Maag, 1998; Yell, 1998). Many would say that such a child needs much more than a 45-day placement in an alternative program. Be that as it may, the key question remains: How can a short-term, alternative program for elementary students with serious behavior problems be structured to provide educational benefit? We recommend it be structured in a way similar to the *Engineered Learning Program* (Walker, 1995, see Chapter 9), which will be described below. It was provided to a total of 67 students (about 8 at a time) over a 4-year period.

In the Engineered Learning Program (ELP), a brief (8 weeks) alternative placement students who were seriously disruptive in their home school learned to follow directions and improved academically at a much greater rate, as shown by impressive gains in reading and arithmetic, than would be expected in typical general education classrooms. Key features of the ELP program included (a) small class size with a "staging" procedure (Walker, 1995, p. 359) such that students were enrolled in pairs rather than all at once, thereby allowing resident students to orient the new students to the classroom rules and facilitating teacher attention to individual needs; (b) an emphasis on basic academic skills, which were well below the student's frustration level as established initially by diagnostic tests of reading and arithmetic skills; (c) daily individualized assignments provided with clear, step-by-step directions; (d) prompt feedback on academic performance with any errors corrected before going on to the next task; (e) a token economy point system with points earned via group and individual contingencies with options for exchanging points for reinforcers (tangible items or activity privileges) provided regularly; (f) systems for providing immediate feedback on appropriate and inappropriate behaviors, positively reinforcing appropriate behavior, and providing mild response costs for inappropriate behavior; (g) recess and physical education time earned by appropriate behavior for the group as a whole; (h) self-recording as needed for individual students learning to control unique problem behaviors; and (i) instruction and reinforcement for working as independently as possible and for using a standard procedure for requesting teacher assistance (with a red tag) but continuing to work—going on to an easier task—while waiting. The routines for the school were taught, and the day was highly structured. Immediate feedback on behavior was provided silently, using an electronic device somewhat like an athletic scoreboard, designed so that each child could look at it and see how he or she was doing. A somewhat similar technological intervention, although serving only 1–4 children at a time and also functioning as a timer, is the Attention Training System (Gordon, Thomason, Cooper, & Ives, 1990), which has recently been reported as being especially helpful for increasing on-task behavior among students with Attention Deficit Hyperactivity Disorder (Polaha & Allen, 2000).

A close replication of the ELP alternative program was studied using an experimental/control group design and a half-day resource room arrangement (O'Connor, Stuck, & Wyne, 1979, cited in Walker, 1995). The ELP model was modified for use in a resource room where acting-out elementary school students were taught in the mornings but attended regular classes in the afternoon. Students in the experimental group were found to be superior to control students in percent of time on-task and reading and arithmetic achievement on posttest measures.

Middle School Example

Skills for Success (Sprague et al., 2000) is an alternative program for middle school students at risk for, or demonstrating, delinquent and other maladaptive behaviors in school, family, and community settings. Skills for Success is an alternative classroom within a traditional middle school setting designed to enhance and sustain participation in the regular life of the school. The alternative intervention is a package that includes academic support in the general education classroom, study skills training, alternatives to suspension and expulsion, service learning, social/behavioral skills training (e.g., conflict and anger management, empathy, impulse control, limit setting, and choosing appropriate peers), school-based adult mentors, personal issues counseling, positive behavior support plans, life skills instruction, and trans-environmental programming (based on Chapter 10 in Walker, 1995).

The direct service staff for Skills for Success consists of two half-time, certified teachers and one full-time Educational Assistant (EA). Students are served primarily in the regular school environment, except one classroom is used for additional academic or social skill instruction not appropriate for the regular classroom. In addition, a student who is suspended for problem behavior is supervised in this classroom rather than being sent home with no supervision or academic support. The intervention school also has a school discipline team that coordinates implementation of the Effective Behavioral Support (Sugai & Horner, 1994; Sugai, Horner, & Sprague, 1999) school-wide discipline model and the Second Step Violence Prevention Curriculum (Committee for Children, 1990) and other activities germane to operation of the school.

Four components make up the main services of the intervention program in its initial phase. First, students check in at the beginning of the day with the EA, receiving individual attention and a form to use in self-monitoring behavior and recruiting teacher attention appropriately, from *Check and Connect* (Evelo, Sinclair, Hurley, Christenson, & Thurlow, 1996). For students who follow this behavior support plan and check back with the EA at the end of the day, positive reinforcement, in the form of brief adult attention and edibles, is provided. In addition, the information gathered in this program is a source of data for the research. Second, a period of the school day is dedicated to individualized academic assessment and assistance in a class for participants called the Structured Learning Center. Third, as the program students are integrated into general education classes most of the day, teachers provide instructional assistance during academic classes in math, language arts, and science. Skills for Success teachers are well accepted in the general education classrooms, in part because they provide leadership for the universal *Second Step* (Committee for Children, 1990) intervention. A fourth component uses an additional period of the school day for more in-depth social skills (including more concentrated *Second Step* activities) and study skills instruction. Personal issues counseling, student and family case management, and service learning activities are applied individually based on student need.

The intended outcomes of this intervention include reduction of delinquent and other high-risk, antisocial behavior; successful retention of targeted students in school programs (i.e., dropout prevention, alternatives to suspension and expulsion); and successful transition to, or participation in, regular school activities. In addition, by meeting the needs of high-risk students, who might otherwise have had a negative effect on the school climate, the entire school benefits. In fact, outcome data from the first year of the project revealed a statistically significant improvement in school climate in terms of students' perceptions of safety and attitudes toward violence. For the treatment students, improvements (indicated by reductions in violence or victimization) were noted regarding reasons to fight, perception of fighting skill, ways to avoid violence, and weapon carrying. Victimization and perpetration experiences were reported as increasing, but this is likely an artifact of students having spent almost the entire year in school by the time of the posttest (Sprague et al., 2000).

CONCLUSION

Alternative educational programs exist that can benefit tertiary level, antisocial students who are at high risk for dropout and delinquency if no support is provided. A wide range of models for secondary age level students are available, and some appear to be more successful than others. Recommended features at the high school level include low pupil-teacher ratio, participatory decision making and individualization, collaboration between school and community, and caring teachers. Keeping students engaged in school can be facilitated by (a) early identification and intervention; (b) effective academic instruction; (c) positive classroom management; (d) informal interactions and low pupil-teacher ratios; (e) instruction in interpersonal problem solving, self-control, and social skills; (f) extracurricular activities; (g) an adult at school who monitors an at-risk student's engagement daily and develops a relationship that is maintained even if the child changes schools within the district; (h) voluntary service learning; and (i) flexibility, defined as taking into account the individual student's needs on a daily basis. At-risk students have complex needs, but these can be met by (a) involving parents, (b) providing mentors, (c) collaborating with community agencies to provide services, (d) function-based behavioral support, and (e) professional technical education.

Although alternative programs for high school students are often successfully provided in locations separate from the traditional school, and that may also be necessary sometimes for younger children, whenever possible alternative programs for younger children should be incorporated into the traditional school setting. At any age level, if a separate placement is needed for an alternative program, it is essential for lasting effectiveness that transitions back to the traditional school, or into the next environment if it is different, be carefully planned and implemented. The student should be prepared to cope with and to meet the demands of the next environment. Although the problems that lead to the need for alternative educational programs are great, many strategies for meeting the need are known.

REFERENCES

Aeby, V. G., Manning, B. H., Thyer, B. A., & Carpenter-Aeby, T. (1999). Comparing outcomes of an alternative school program offered with and without intensive family involvement. *The School Community Journal, 9*(1), 17–32.

Altenbaugh, R. J., Engel, D. E., & Martin, D. T. (1995). *Caring for kids: A critical study of urban school leavers.* Washington, DC: Falmer.

Anderson-Inman, L., Knox-Quinn, C., & Szymanski, M. (1999). Computer-supported studying: Stories of successful transition to postsecondary education. *Career Development for Exceptional Individuals, 22*(2), 185–211.

Arnold, M. E., & Hughes, J. N. (1999). First do no harm: Adverse effects of grouping deviant youth for skills training. *Journal of School Psychology, 37*(1), 99–115.

Ashcroft, R. (1999). Training and professional identity for educators in alternative education settings. *The Clearing House, 73*(2), 82–89.

Bear, G. G. (1998). School discipline in the United States: Prevention, correction, and long-term social development. *School Psychology Review, 27*(1), 14–32.

Beck, L. G., Kratzer, C. C., & Isken, J. A. (1997). Caring for transient students in one urban elementary school. *Journal for a Just and Caring Education, 3*(3), 343–369.

Bennett D. S., & Gibbons, T. A. (2000). Efficacy of child cognitive-behavioral interventions for antisocial behavior: A meta-analysis. *Child and Family Behavior Therapy, 22*(1), 1–15.

Black, S. (1997, May). One last chance. *The American School Board Journal,* 40–42.

Bornstein, P., Duncan, P., Clauson, J., Abrams, C., Yannett, N., Ginsburg, G., & Milne, M. (1998). Preventing middle school adjustment problems for children from lower-income families: A program for aware parenting. *Journal of Applied Developmental Psychology, 19*(1), 129–151.

Brestan, E. V., & Eyberg, S. M. (1998). Effective psychosocial treatments of conduct-disordered children and adolescents. *Journal of Clinical Child Psychology, 27,* 180–189.

Bullis, M., Walker, H. M., & Stieber, S. (1998). The influence of peer and educational variables on arrest status among at-risk males. *Journal of Emotional and Behavioral Disorders, 6*(3), 141–152.

Butts, J. A., & Snyder, H. N. (1997, September). The youngest delinquents: Offenders under age 15. *Juvenile Justice Bulletin,* 1–12.

Cardon, P. L., & Christensen, K. W. (1998). Technology-based programs and drop-out prevention. *The Journal of Technology Studies, 24*(1), 50–54.

Castleberry, S. E., & Enger, J. M. (1998). Alternative students' concepts of success. *NASSP Bulletin, 82*(602), 105–111.

Catalano, R. F., Arthur, M. W., Hawkins, J. D., Berglund, L., & Olson, J. J. (1998). In R. Loeber & D. P. Farrington (Eds.), *Serious and violent juvenile offenders: Risk factors and successful interventions* (pp. 248–283). Thousand Oaks, CA: Sage.

Cavell, T. A., & Hughes, J. N. (2000). Secondary prevention as context for assessing change processes in aggressive children. *Journal of School Psychology, 38*(3), 199–235.

Chavez, E. L., Oetting, E. R., & Swaim, R. C. (1994). Dropout and delinquency: Mexican-American and Caucasian non-Hispanic youth. *Journal of Clinical Child Psychology, 23*(10), 47-55.

Cobb, B., & Johnson, D. R. (1997). The statewide systems change initiative as a federal policy mechanism for promoting educational reform. *Career Development for Exceptional Individuals, 20*(2), 179-190.

Committee for Children. (1990). *Violence prevention: Second step.* Seattle, WA: Author.

Cox, S. M. (1999). An assessment of an alternative education program for at-risk delinquent youth. *Journal of Research in Crime and Delinquency, 36*(3), 323.

Craig, R. M. (1997). The graduation alternative program: A model for dropout prevention. *The Delta Kappa Gamma Bulletin, 63*(2), 50-55.

Crick, J. R. & Grotpeter, J. K. (1996). Children's treatment by peers: Victims of relational and overt aggression. *Development and Psychopathology, 8,* 367-380.

Davalos, D. B., Chavez, E. L, & Guardiola, R. J. (1999). The effects of extracurricular activity, ethnic identification, and perceptions of school on student dropout rates. *Hispanic Journal of Behavioral Sciences, 21*(1), 61-77.

Davis, S. M. (1994). How the Gateway Program helps troubled teens. *Educational Leadership, 52*(1), 17-19.

Day, N. (1996). *Violence in schools: Learning in fear.* Springfield, NJ: Enslow.

Declining violence. (1998). *The CQ researcher, 8*(38), 892.

Dishion, T. J., & Andrews, D. W. (1995). Preventing escalation of problem behaviors in high risk young adolescents: Immediate and 1-year outcomes. *Journal of Consulting and Clinical Psychology, 63*(4), 538-548.

Doren, B., Bullis, M., & Benz, M. R. (1996). Predicting the arrest status of adolescents with disabilities in transition. *The Journal of Special Education, 29*(4), 363-370.

Dorn, S. (1996). *Creating the dropout: An institutional and social history of school failure.* Westport, CT: Praeger.

Duggar, J. M., & Duggar, C. W. (1998). An evaluation of a successful alternative high school. *High School Journal, 81,* 218-228.

Duke, D. L., & Griesdorn, J. (1999). Considerations in the design of alternative schools. *The Clearing House, 73*(2), 89.

Duncan, B. B., Forness, S. R., & Hartsough, C. (1995). Students identified as seriously emotionally disturbed in school-based day treatment: Cognitive, psychiatric, and special education characteristics. *Behavioral Disorders, 20*(4), 238-252.

Eber, L. (1996). Restructuring schools through the wraparound approach: The LADSE experience. *Special Services in the Schools, 11,* 135-149.

Eber, L., & Nelson, C. M. (1997). School-based wraparound planning: Integrating services for students with emotional and behavioral needs. *American Journal of Orthopsychiatry, 67,* 385-395.

Eber, L., Nelson, C. M., & Miles, P. (1997). School-based wraparound for students with emotional and behavioral challenges. *Exceptional Children, 63*(4), 539-555.

Eggert, L. L., Thompson, E. A., Herting, J. R., Nicholas, L. J., & Dicker, B. G. (1994). Preventing adolescent drug abuse and high school dropout through an intensive school-based social network development program. *American Journal of Health Promotion, 8,* 205-215.

Epstein, M. H., Munk, D. D., Bursuck, W. D., Polloway, E. A., & Jayanthi, M. (1999). Strategies for improving home-school communication about homework for students with disabilities. *Journal of Special Education, 33*(3), 166.

Evans, L. D. (2000). Functional school refusal subtypes: Anxiety, avoidance, and malingering. *Psychology in the Schools, 37*(2), 183-191.

Evelo, D., Sinclair, M., Hurley, C., Christenson, S., Thurlow, M. (1996). *Keeping kids in school: Using check and connect for dropout prevention.* Minneapolis, MN: College of Education and Human Development, Institute on Community Integration, University of Minnesota.

Finch, C. R. (1999). School-to-Work programs: Opportunities and issues. *School Business Affairs, 65*(5), 16-20.

Fizzell, R., & Raywid, M. A. (1997). If alternative schools are the answer ... What's the question? *Reaching Today's Youth: The Community Circle of Caring Journal,* 1(2), 7-9.

Furlong, M., Morrison, G., & Pavelski, R. (2000). Trends in school psychology for the 21st century: Influences of school violence on professional change. *Psychology in the Schools, 37*(1), 81-89.

Gold, M., & Mann, D. W. (1984). *Expelled to a friendlier place: A study of effective alternative schools.* Ann Arbor, MI: The University of Michigan Press.

Good, T. L., & Brophy, J. E. (1997). *Looking in classrooms* (7th ed.). New York: Addison Wesley Longman.

Gordon, M., Thomason, D., Cooper, S., & Ives, C. L. (1990). Nonmedical treatment of ADHD/Hyperactivity: The attention training system. *Journal of School Psychology, 29,* 151-159.

Gottfredson, D. C. (1997). School-based crime prevention. In L. W. Sherman, D. Gottfredson, D. MacKenzie, J. Eck, P. Reuter, & S. Bushway (Eds.), *Preventing crime: What works, what doesn't, what's promising* (pp. (3), 1-49). Washington, DC: U.S. Department of Justice, Office of Justice Programs.

Gottfredson, G. D., & Gottfredson, D. C. (1985). *Victimization in schools.* New York: Plenum.

Groth, C. (1998). Dumping ground or effective alternative: Dropout prevention programs in urban schools. *Urban Education, 33*(2), 218-242.

Guagliardo, M. F., Huang, Z., Hicks, J., & D'Angelo, L. (1998). Increased drug use among old-for-grade and dropout urban adolescents. *American Journal of Preventive Medicine, 15*(1), 42-48).

Guerin, G., & Denti, L. (1999). Alternative education support for youth at-risk. *The Clearing House, 73*(2), 76.

Gunter, P. L., Hummel, J. H., & Venn, M. L. (1998). Are effective academic instructional practices used to teach students with behavior disorders? *Beyond Behavior, 9*(3), 5-11.

Hamilton, S. F. (1999). Preparing youth for the work force. In A. J. Reynolds, H. J. Walberg, & R. P. Weissberg (Eds.), *Promoting positive outcomes: Issues in children's and families' lives* (pp. 297-325). Washington, DC: Child Welfare League of America Press.

Hay, I. (2000). Gender self-concept profiles of adolescents suspended from high school. *Journal of Child Psychiatry and Psychology, 41*(3), 345-352.

Hill, D. (1998). Reform school. *Teacher Magazine, 9*(8), 34-35, 38-41.

Hodges, E. V., & Perry, D. C. (1996). Victims of peer abuse: An overview. *Reclaiming Children and Youth: Journal of Emotional and Behavioral Problems, 5*(1), 23-28.

Hoffman, D. (1995). Learning for the real world. *Technology and Learning, 15*(6), 22-29.

Holloway, J. H. (1999/2000, December/January). Extracurricular activities: The path to academic success? *Educational Leadership,* 87-88.

Housego, B. E. J. (1999). Outreach schools: An educational innovation. *Alberta Journal of Research, 45*(1), 85-101.

Jason, L. A., Weine, A. M., Johnson, J. H., Warren-Sohlberg, L., Filippelli, L. A., Turner, E. Y., & Lardon, C. (1992). *Helping transfer students: Strategies for educational and social readjustment.* San Francisco: Jossey-Bass.

Kasen, S., Cohen, P. & Brooks, J. S. (1998). Adolescent school experiences and dropout, adolescent pregnancy, and young adult deviant behavior. *Journal of Adolescent Research, 13*(1), 49-72.

Katsiyannis, A., & Archwamety, T. (1999). Academic remediation/achievement and other factors related to recidivism rates among delinquent youths. *Behavioral Disorders, 24*(2), 93-101.

Katsiyannis, A., & Maag, J. W. (1998). Disciplining students with disabilities: Issues and considerations for implementing IDEA '97. *Behavioral Disorders, 23*(4), 276-289.

Katsiyannis, A., & Williams, B. (1998). A national survey of state initiatives on alternative education. *Remedial and Special Education, 19*(5), 276-284.

Kazdin, A. E. (1994). Interventions for aggressive and antisocial children. In L. D. Eron, J. H. Gentry, & P. Schlegel, (Eds.), *Reason to hope: A psychosocial perspective on violence and youth* (pp. 341-382). Washington, DC: American Psychological Association.

Kearney, C. A., & Tillotson, C. A. (1998). School attendance. In T. S. Watson & F. M. Gresham (Eds.), *Handbook of child behavior therapy* (pp. 143-161). New York: Plenum.

Kern, L., Dunlap, G., Clarke, S., & Childs, K. (1994). Student-assisted functional assessment interview. *Diagnostique, 19*(2/3), 29-39.

Lange, C. M. (1998). Characteristics of alternative schools and programs serving at-risk students. *High School Journal, 81,* 183-198.

Leone, P. E., & Drakeford, W. (1999). Alternative education: from a "last chance" to a proactive model. *The Clearing House, 73*(2), 86.

Lerner, R. M., & Galambos, N. L. (1998). Adolescent development: Challenges and opportunities for research, practice, and policies. *Annual Review of Psychology, 49,* 413-446.

Liaupsin, C. J., Scott, T. M., & Nelson, C. M. (2000). *Functional behavioral assessment: An interactive training module: User's manual and facilitator's guide* (2nd ed.) Longmont, CO: Sopris West.

Lloyd, D. L. (1997a). Alternative education: Stepping stone to success. *Schools in the Middle, 36-39.*

Lloyd, D. L. (1997b). From high school to middle school: An alternative school program for both. *Educational Digest, 62,* 32-35.

Lipsey, M. W., & Wilson, D. B. (1998). Effective intervention for serious juvenile offenders: A synthesis of research. In R. Loeber & D. P. Farrington (Eds.), *Serious and violent juvenile offenders: Risk factors and successful interventions* (pp. 313-345). Thousand Oaks, CA: Sage.

Loeber, R., & Farrington, D. P. (Eds.). (1998). *Serious and violent juvenile offenders: Risk factors and successful interventions.* Thousand Oaks, CA: Sage.

Lombard, R. C., Miller, R. J., & Hazelkorn, M. N. (1998). School-to-Work and technical preparation: Teacher attitudes and practices regarding the inclusion of students with disabilities. *Career Development for Exceptional Individuals, 21*(2), 161-172.

Mahoney, J. L., & Cairns, R. B. (1997). Do extracurricular activities protect against early school dropout? *Developmental Psychology, 33,* 241-253.

Merchant, B. (1999). Now you see it; now you don't: A district's short-lived commitment to an alternative high school for newly arrived immigrants. *Urban Education, 34*(1), 26-51.

Moore, C. W., & Allen, J. P. (1996). The effects of volunteering on the young volunteer. *The Journal of Primary Prevention, 17*(2), 231-258.

National Association of State Directors of Special Education. (1998). *Functional behavioral assessment: Policy development in light of emerging research and practice.* Alexandria, VA: Author.

Nichols, J. D., & Utesch, W. E. (1998). An alternative learning program: Effects on student motivation and self-esteem. *The Journal of Educational Research, 91*(5), 272-279.

O'Connor, P., Stuck, G., & Wyne, M. (1979). Effects of a short-term intervention resource-room program on task orientation and achievement. *Journal of Special Education, 13*(4), 375-385.

O'Neill, R. E., Horner, R. H., Albin, R. W., Storey, K., Sprague, J. R., & Newton, M. (1997). *Functional assessment and program development for problem behavior: A practical handbook* (2nd ed.). Pacific Grove, CA: Brooks/Cole.

Patterson, G. R., Reid, J. B., & Dishion, T. J. (1992). *Antisocial boys.* Eugene, OR: Castalia.

Polaha, J. A., & Allen, K. D. (2000). Using technology to automate off-task behavior: Classroom management made simple. *Proven Practice, 2*(2), 52-56.

Quinn, K. P., Epstein, M. H., Dennis, K., Potter, K., Sharma, J., McKelvey, J., & Cumblad, C. (1996). Personal, family, and service utilization characteristics of children served in an urban family preservation environment. *Journal of Child and Family Studies, 5*(4), 469-487.

Raywid, M. A. (1996). *Taking stock: The movement to create mini-schools, schools-within-schools, and separate small schools.* [Microform]. New York: ERIC Clearinghouse on Urban Education, Institute for Urban and Minority Education.

Raywid, M. A. (1998). Small schools: A reform that works. *Educational Leadership, 55*(4), 34-39.

Reed, H., Thomas, E., Sprague, J. R., & Horner, R. H. (1997). The student guided functional assessment interview: An analysis of student and teacher agreement. *Journal of Behavioral Education, 7,* 33-49.

Reid, J. B., & Eddy, J. M. (1997). The prevention of antisocial behavior: Some considerations in the search for effective interventions. In D. M. Stoff, J. Breiling, & J. D. Maser (Eds.), *Handbook of antisocial behavior* (pp. 343-356). New York: Wiley.

Richardson, M. D., & Griffin, B. L. (1994). Alternative schools: Research implications for principals. *NASSP Bulletin, 78,* 105-111.

Riley, P., & McDaniel, J. (1999, September). Youth out of the mainstream: A North Carolina profile. *OJJDP Juvenile Justice Bulletin,* 1-12.

Roderick, M. (1993). *The path to dropping out: Evidence for intervention.* Westport, CT: Auburn House.

Rumberger, R. W. (1995). Dropping out of middle school: A multilevel analysis of students and schools. *American Educational Research Journal, 32,* 583-625.

Rumberger, R. W., & Larson, K. A. (1998). Student mobility and the increased risk of high school dropout. *American Journal of Education, 107*(1), 1-35.

Rylance, B. J. (1997). Predictors of high school graduation or dropping out for youth with severe emotional disturbances. *Behavioral Disorders, 23,* 5-17.

Scott, T. M., & Nelson, C. M. (1998). Confusion and failure in facilitating generalized social responding in the school setting: Sometimes 2 + 2 = 5. *Behavioral Disorders, 23*(4), 264-275.

Shore, R. M. (1996). Personalization: Working to curb violence in an American high school. *Phi Delta Kappan, 77*(5), 362-363.

Shumer, R. (1994). Community-based learning: Humanizing education. *Journal of Adolescence, 17,* 357-367.

Sinclair, M. F., Christenson, S. L., Evelo, D. L., & Hurley, C. M. (1998). Dropout prevention for youth with disabilities: Efficacy of a sustained school engagement procedure. *Exceptional Children, 65,* 7-21.

Sitlington, P. L., Carson, R., & Frank, A. R. (1992). Adult adjustment among high school graduates with mild disabilities. *Exceptional Children, 59,* 221-233.

Sprague, J., Walker, H., Nishioka, V., Tobin, T., Bullis, M., & Eisert, D. C. (2000). *Skills for success: A violence prevention intervention for socially maladjusted middle school students.* Eugene, OR: University of Oregon, Institute on Violence and Destructive Behavior.

Stockard, J., & Mayberry, M. (1992). *Effective educational environments.* Newbury Park, CA: Corwin Press.

Sugai, G. (1998). The development of individualized behavior support plans. In M. M. Kerr & C. M. Nelson, *Strategies for managing behavior problems in the classroom* (3rd ed.; pp. 139-145). Upper Saddle River, NJ: Prentice-Hall.

Sugai, G., & Horner, R. (1994). Including students with severe behavior problems in general education settings: Assumptions, challenges, and solutions. In J. Marr, G. Sugai, & G. Tindal (Eds.), *The Oregon Conference monograph, vol. 6,* 102-120. Eugene, OR: University of Oregon.

Sugai, G., Horner, R. H., Dunlap, G., Hieneman, M., Nelson, C. M., Scott, T., Liaupsin, C., Sailor, W., Turnbull, A. P., Turnbull, H. R., Wickham, D., Wilcox, B., & Ruef, M. (2000). Applying positive behavior support and functional behavioral assessment in schools. *Journal of Positive Behavior Interventions, 2*(3), 131-143.

Sugai, G., Horner, R. H., & Sprague, J. (1999). Functional-Assessment-Based behavior support planning: Research to practice to research. *Behavioral Disorders, 24*(3), 253-257.

Swanson, H. L., & Hoskyn, M. (1998). Experimental intervention research on students with learning disabilities: A meta-analysis of treatment outcomes. *Review of Educational Research, 68*(3), 277-321.

Testerman, J. (1996). Holding at-risk students: The secret is one-on-one. *Phi Delta Kappan, 77*(5), 364-365.

Thompson, E. A., Horn, M., Herting, J. R., & Eggert, L. L. (1997). Enhancing outcomes in an indicated drug prevention program for high-risk youth. *Journal of Drug Education, 27*(1), 19-41.

Tobin, T., & Sprague, J. (2000, Fall). Alternative education strategies to reduce violence in school and community. *Journal of Emotional and Behavioral Disorders, 8*(3), 177-186.

Tobin, T. J., & Sugai, G. M. (1999a). Discipline problems, placements, and outcomes for students with serious emotional disturbance. *Behavioral Disorders, 24*(2), 109-121.

Tobin, T. J., & Sugai, G. M. (1999b). Using sixth-grade school records to predict violence, chronic discipline problems, and high school outcomes. *Journal of Emotional and Behavioral Disorders, 7*(1), 40-53.

Tremblay, R. E., Pagani-Kurtz, L., Mâsse, L. C., Vitaro, F., & Pihl, R. O. (1995). A bimodal preventive intervention for disruptive kindergarten boys: Its impact through mid-adolescence. *Journal of Consulting and Clinical Psychology, 63*(4), 560-568.

U.S. Department of Education. (2000). *To assure the free appropriate public education of all children with disabilities: Twenty-first annual report to Congress on the implementation of the Individuals with Disabilities Education Act.* Washington, DC: Author. [Available Internet: *http://www.ed.gov/offices/OSERS/OSEP/OSEP99AnlRpt/*].

Vance, J., Fernandez, G., & Biber, M. (1998). Educational progress in a population of youth with aggression and emotional disturbance: The role of risk and protective factors. *Journal of Emotional and Behavioral Disorders, 6*(4), 214-221.

Vitaro, F., & Tremblay, R. E. (1994). Impact of a prevention program on aggressive children's friendships and social adjustment. *Journal of Abnormal Child Psychology, 22*(4), 457-475.

Walker, H. M. (1995). *The acting-out child: Coping with classroom disruption* (2nd ed.). Longmont, CO: Sopris West.

Walker, H. M., Block-Pedego, A., Todis, B., & Severson, H. (1991). *School archival records search (SARS): User's guide and technical manual.* Longmont, CO: Sopris West.

Walker, H. M., Horner, R. H., Sugai, G., Bullis, M., Sprague, J. R., Bricker, D., & Kaufman, M. J. (1996). Integrated approaches to preventing anti-social behavior patterns among school-age children and youth. *Journal of Emotional and Behavioral Disorders, 4*(4), 194-209.

Walker, H. M., & McConnell, S. R. (1995). *The Walker-McConnell scale of social competence and school adjustment (SSCSA).* San Diego, CA: Singular.

Walker, H. M., & Severson, H. H. (1990). *The Systematic Screening for Behavior Disorders scale.* Longwood, CO: Sopris West.

Walker, H. M., Severson, H. H., & Feil, E. G. (1994). *The early screening project: A proven child-find process.* Longmont, CO: Sopris West.

Walker, H. M., Stieber, S. Ramsey, E., & O'Neill, R. E. (1991). Longitudinal prediction of the school achievement, adjustment, and delinquency of antisocial versus at-risk boys. *Remedial and Special Education, 12*(4), 43-51.

Walker, H. M., Stieber, S., Ramsey, E., & O'Neill, R. E. (1993). Fifth grade school adjustment and later arrest rate: A longitudinal study of middle school antisocial boys. *Journal of Child and Family Studies, 2*(4), 295-315.

Walker, H. M., Zeller, R. W., Close, E. W., Webber, J., & Gresham, F. (1999). The present unwrapped: Change and challenge in the field of behavioral disorders. *Behavioral Disorders, 24*(4), 293-304.

Weir, R. M. (1996). Lessons from a middle level at-risk program. *The Clearing House, 70,* 48-51.

Wetzel, M. C., McNaboe, K. A., Schneidermeyer, S. A., Jones, A. B., & Nash, P. N. (1997). Public and private partnership in an alternative middle school program. *Preventing School Failure, 41,* 179-184.

Witt, J. C., Daly, E. M., & Noell, G. (2000). *Functional assessments: A step-by-step guide to solving academic and behavior problems.* Longmont, CO: Sopris West.

Yell, M. (1998). *The law and special education.* Upper Saddle River, NJ: Prentice-Hall.

CHAPTER 36

Preparing for and Managing School Crises

Cathy Kennedy Paine
Springfield School District, Springfield, Oregon

INTRODUCTION

"I never thought it would happen here." The staff and students of Pearl, Mississippi; West Paducah, Kentucky; Jonesboro, Arkansas; Edinboro, Pennsylvania; Springfield, Oregon; Littleton, Colorado; and Santee, California all shared in the belief that a crisis would not happen in their school or school district. That belief in the fundamental safety and security of our schools has been shattered in these communities, and throughout the nation, as a result of a series of tragic school shootings involving multiple victims. When violence strikes at school, the impact can be devastating and the inevitable publicity widespread. Today's schools must be prepared for the unexpected. Cathy Danyluk, Safe School Consultant for the Indiana Department of Education, captured the importance of preparedness when she remarked, "The offenders in school shooting incidents came to school with a plan. So should educators" (Trump, 2000).

On May 21, 1998, the community of Springfield, Oregon experienced the most horrific school crisis imaginable. In a few short moments we were transformed from innocent, unsuspecting individuals engaged in our normal routines to traumatized victims of a school shooting spree. On that morning, 300 of Thurston High School's students gathered in the cafeteria, as always, eating breakfast and trading the tales of youthful innocence. That innocence was brutally shattered at 7:55 AM when a 15-year-old freshman entered the school grounds—a closed campus that had surveillance cameras, two campus monitors, a two-way communications system, cafeteria and campus supervision, and a confidential reporting system—with three concealed weapons. After shooting two students in a hallway, he pulled a .22 caliber semiautomatic rifle from beneath his trench coat and sprayed 50 rounds of ammunition throughout the cafeteria. This single act of violence left two students dead and 25 others seriously wounded. Although seemingly impossible, things would get worse. We soon learned that the parents of the shooter had been found dead in their home, each shot by their son the evening before the cafeteria rampage.

The effects of this tragedy spread immediately to every corner of our community. Throngs of frightened parents and neighbors rushed to the school. When I arrived, as part of the district crisis team, several local media stations were already broadcasting, a small contingent compared with what we would soon experience. In my 22 years as a school psychologist, I had never encountered anything like the trauma at Thurston High. Indelibly etched in my memory is the scene of police cars, yellow crime tape, ambulances, bloodstains, frantic faces, flashing lights, and panic-stricken crowds.

Inside the school, most students remained in their classrooms, while those who had been in the cafeteria waited in the library for police questioning. There had been many near misses and close calls. One student removed his backpack and discovered a bullet lodged in the middle of his history book. When the shots were fired on that spring morning our sense of safety and security was shattered along with our innocence. One fact is clear—if we had not had a crisis response plan and a trained crisis team we would not have been able to effectively respond to this tragedy.

In spite of these headline-grabbing events, it is a fact that the likelihood of a serious, violent incident occurring in a school remains extremely low. According to the report *Indicators of School Crime and Safety, 2000,* more children are victimized away from school than at school. For example, in 1998, students were twice as likely to be victims of serious violent crime away from school as at school (Kaufman et al., 2000). Beyond the high-profile incidents, schools must develop comprehensive crisis response plans that cover a range of possible events. Plans should be written to guide staff members in responding to a variety of crises including a natural disaster, extreme weather, the accidental death of a student or staff member, a suicide, or a threat of violence. In the Springfield, Oregon, School District, crisis response teams were formed in 1991, shortly after the accidental death of a middle school student. Over a period of 10 years in this moderate-sized district of 11,000 students, those teams have responded to the deaths of 24 students, 4 teachers, and 8 other staff members—not including the school shooting in May 1998. This chapter describes best practices in the development and implementation of crisis intervention plans for a variety of incidents.

The primary goal of a crisis response team is to assist a school to function effectively in the event of a crisis or tragedy that impacts members of the school building. There are two types of situations in which a crisis response is warranted: (a) an emergency such as a shooting, stabbing, natural disaster, or hostage situation occurs on the school campus and threatens the safety and security of the staff and students; and (b) a crisis such as a sudden student or staff death, chronic illness, house fire, or suicide occurs away from the campus, but affects the staff and students at school.

The members of the crisis response team should meet as soon as possible after learning of an event and implement the planned steps in the crisis plan. The crisis response team provides support to students, staff, and parents by responding to the event in a calm, compassionate, and timely manner. This results in a school climate that expedites the return of the school to "normal" as soon as is appropriate. Trained staff may be called in from the community if needed to provide immediate support to the school staff. These trained crisis response team members are less personally impacted and their special training enables them to give helpful assistance in emergencies.

During a crisis, one of three levels of intervention occurs, depending on the severity of the event (i.e., building-level, district-level, or trauma response). The length and type of the crisis response are different in each of these cases, with each succeeding level being more complex and requiring more trained crisis staff.

Building-level intervention: A response to a crisis event that is outside the normal operations of the school, but whose impact is limited to a single school building. Building team members are able to respond to the event without outside assistance (e.g., a student accident, low-level threat or non-threatening incendiary device on campus).

District-level intervention: A response that requires the assistance of team members from other buildings or districts. The event impacts people across several settings in the district (e.g., a teacher or staff member death, or the deaths of one or more students).

Trauma response: A response to an event when a portion, or all, of the students and staff are traumatized by a major disruption of normal events in the school or district. Outside resources are needed and grief is complicated by posttraumatic stress syndrome (e.g., a natural disaster, school shooting, stabbing or major accident).

Long before a crisis team is faced with the task of responding to a tragedy, it needs to do some planning and preparation. The planning and preparation elements that must be addressed prior to a crisis are described in the following section.

BEFORE A CRISIS: PLANNING AND PREPARATION

Before a crisis occurs, school staff members should engage in a process that prepares them to respond to a variety of incidents. The process should include the following steps: (a) form a building crisis response team, (b) develop a written crisis or emergency response plan, (c) coordinate the plan with the broader community, (d) conduct training for staff, and (e) integrate the crisis preparedness guidelines into a school safety plan.

Form a Building Crisis Response Team

The first step is to identify a group of individuals who can serve as members of a building crisis team. Using a team approach to crisis response provides three main benefits (Klicker, 1993). The team can (a) reduce the fear and anxiety that accompanies a crisis such as the death of a student or staff member, (b) educate staff and students in the dynamics of grief and prepare them for what they might experience, and (c) provide an opportunity for staff and students to express their feelings in an accepting environment.

Our experience in Springfield with a variety of crises has shown that in forming crisis response teams it is important to select people who think clearly, who remain focused and calm under stress, and who are able to quickly see alternative solutions to problems. In addition, they should communicate well, handle multiple tasks simultaneously, understand the dynamics of grief and loss in children, and work well as part of a team. The team's composition is important because the team members need to model effective coping strategies during a crisis. Following the shooting at Thurston High we needed to make decisions quickly, often with limited information. We had to be flexible, calm, and willing to work long hours.

TABLE 1

School Crisis Response Team Members and Suggested Roles

Principal:
Receive and verify information
Activate and oversee team functioning
Handle media calls
Contact district administration
Provide information and support to staff
Grant release time and hire substitutes
Write letter to parents/students

Crisis Team Coordinator:
Oversee logistics of implementing intervention
Activate phone tree
Work with principal to ensure smooth functioning and accurate flow of information
Keep log of intervention
Plan staff informational meeting
Schedule crisis team de-briefings

Care Coordinator:
Care room facilitator
Staff support and stabilization
Provide grief resources for teacher and families
Debrief with crisis team
Prioritize referrals for additional counseling

Teachers:
Relay plan information to other teachers
Distribute resources
Support students
Provide information to students
Give feedback to team regarding needs

Secretary:
Coordinate communications
Assist principal in disseminating information
Answer phone calls

Office Assistant:
Assist secretary
Relay information to classified staff
Copy and distribute memos and handouts

School Counselor:
Support and communicate with family
Coordinate remembrance activities
Assist in care room
Distribute suggestions for class discussion

School Psychologist:
Assist in care room
Contact other psychologists if needed
Prioritize referrals for counseling
Assist team with intervention

Note
Source: Springfield Public Schools. (2000). *Emergency response guide for administrators.* Springfield, OR: Author.

The composition of the team should be reviewed annually and commonly includes the principal (and assistant), school counselor, school psychologist, secretary, nurse, teacher(s), and school security or resource officer. In Springfield, the district psychologists are members of the building crisis teams where they are assigned and they also serve as a district-level team, assisting in schools across the district as needed. Following the shooting at Thurston, the school psychologists formed a core team that planned and implemented mental health services in response to the tragedy for the remainder of the school year. Table 1 summarizes the suggested roles and responsibilities of team members.

Develop a Written Crisis or Emergency Response Plan

Each school should have a written Crisis or Emergency Plan that describes the crisis intervention procedures. The plan should contain guidelines regarding the following topics: (a) board policy or goal statement regarding crisis management, (b) roles and responsibilities of building crisis team members, (c) phone tree directions for notifying staff, (d) responsibilities of district-level staff, and (e) emergency kit contents.

The plan should include procedures for the following: (a) lockdown, (b) evacuation, (c) communications, (d) incident command center, (e) family reunification, (f) traffic flow and transportation, (g) supporting special student populations, (h) dealing with media, and (i) counseling support for students and staff.

Reference information also should be available for the following situations: (a) memorials, (b) funerals and healing events, (c) evaluation of the crisis response, (d) long-term media issues, (e) anniversaries, (f) litigation preparedness and legal issues, (g) long-term mental health support, (h) care of caregivers, and (i) special situations (e.g., responding to a suicide, when the school is a crime scene, and supporting homicide survivors).

Procedures for handling specific emergencies such as bomb threats, natural disasters, or suicide should be contained in "flip chart" format that is easily accessed in an emergency. A sample table of contents for such a flip chart is contained in Table 2, on page 998.

Coordinate the Plan With the Broader Community

When a major crisis strikes a school, this quickly becomes a community event. Therefore, it is important to identify resources within the community during the planning stage. Some topics to be addressed in this regard include the availability of emergency service personnel, the availability of mental health professionals, communications capabilities across agencies, and integration with criminal justice procedures.

Once a rough draft of the crisis response plan is developed, engage the police, fire, emergency medical, clergy, media and community mental health personnel in reviewing the plan. Develop strategies to coordinate the efforts of each of these agencies in the event of a large-scale crisis. Make available maps of all school buildings to the law enforcement, fire department, and emergency responders, including the location of important switches and valves. In addition, conduct emergency drills to test the plan, including both lockdown and evacuation procedures. For example, in 1994, Springfield School District personnel and city officials collaborated in drafting the district's "Emergency Procedures Manual." A mock disaster drill was held (coincidentally) at Thurston High School just a year before the tragic shooting—a drill in which the hospital emergency responders were called to the high school to treat a large number of "injured" students.

Conduct Training for Staff

Training and preparation for handling a crisis is the only way to ensure rapid and sensitive handling of an otherwise chaotic situation. Training for staff on handling emergencies should be considered a necessity rather than a choice. Crisis preparedness is an ongoing process that requires testing crisis procedures and updating staff each school year.

TABLE 2

Emergency Procedures Manual: Sample Flip Chart Contents

General Emergency Procedures
- Direct Response
- Room clear
- Lockdown
- Evacuation

Immediate Threat of Injury of Death
- Violent incident with injuries
- Dangerous person on campus
- Suicide threat or attempt
- Kidnapping
- Child left at school and lost/runaway child
- Student or staff death, serious injury or medical condition on campus

Possible Threat of Injury or Death
- Fire or explosion
- Hazardous material spill
- Bomb or suspicious device
- Bomb threat
- Earthquake
- Civil disturbance

Possible Threat
- Severe weather while school is in session
- Power/telephone outage and suspected gas leak
- Bus or field trip emergency
- Spilled body fluids

Information and Resources
- Child abuse reporting
- Medication overdose and medical assessment procedure
- Communicating with the media
- School map and emergency information

Note
Source: *Emergency Procedures Manual,* Springfield Public Schools, 1999.

Integrate Crisis Preparedness Guidelines Into a School Safety Plan

Finally, integrate the crisis preparedness guidelines into the broader, comprehensive school safety plan. In addition to crisis response guidelines, this school safety plan should address community coordination, violence prevention curriculum, proactive student discipline policies, safe physical environment, school security, staff training, and the monitoring and evaluation of school safety (Paine and Sprague, 2000; Schneider, Walker and Sprague, 2000).

An important additional aspect of school safety has come to light just recently as educators and others have begun to examine the dynamics of school shooters. The United States Secret Service and the U.S. Department of Education recently completed a detailed analysis of 37 school shootings that have occurred in the United States since 1974. While there are varied and complex reasons for school shootings, one finding stands out among all the others: in over 3/4 of the cases, the attacker told someone before the incident about his interest in mounting an attack at the school (Vossekuil, Reddy, Fein, Borum, and Modzeleski, 2000). In over half of the incidents the attacker told more than one person. In almost all cases, peers did not believe the student would carry out his actions, or viewed reporting as "snitching"—and thus they did not report the threat to adults. This strongly suggests that a crisis preparedness plan should include a mechanism for students to anonymously report their concerns about a student who may pose a threat, so that those concerns can be thoroughly investigated.

Some resources for getting started in developing a comprehensive school safety plan include *Early Warning, Timely Response: A Guide to Safe Schools* (Dwyer, Osher, & Warger, 1998) and *Safeguarding Our Children: An Action Guide* (Dwyer & Osher, 2000), which were developed under the guidance of the U.S. Department of Education and the U.S. Department of Justice. They can be downloaded from the following websites: *www.ed.gov/offices/OSERS/OSEP/earlywrn.html* and *www.ed.gov/offices/OSERS/OSEP/ActionGuide.* In addition, the National Resource Center for Safe Schools has developed a safe schools planning process and has staff members who can assist a district in implementing a safe schools plan. The Resource Center can be accessed on the Web at *www.safetyzone.org* or at 1-800-268-2275. Additional resources regarding crisis response and school safety can be found in the Appendix, on page 1019.

DURING A CRISIS: THE ACTION PLAN

Intervention When a Crisis Occurs at School

No amount of planning and preparation can prevent all crises from happening. This section describes specific steps to take during a school crisis by applying a variety of emergency management guidelines to school settings. The section begins by dealing with a major on-campus crisis, then focuses on responding to other crisis incidents that affect students and staff members.

The most dreaded event for a school administrator or teacher is violence at school. In the wake of the sensational school shootings of the 1990s, we are now painfully aware of the devastating effects a violent event can have on a school and a community. When such a tragedy happens, the school is immediately flooded with three waves of humanity: emergency personnel, parents, and media, all of whom may arrive at approximately the same time, thereby creating chaos and confusion. The following section describes the actions that will maximize the response effectiveness in this situation.

Immediate Response

There are three priorities to address during the initial response to an on-campus school crisis (Trump, 2000). These priorities may operate simultaneously and they generally require attention immediately following the event. They involve literally hundreds of decisions that need to be made quickly; thus, it is essential to have a coordinated plan and trained staff.

Secure all students, staff, and legitimate visitors. This may involve a lockdown, evacuation, or both. When the Thurston shooting occurred, classrooms were placed in lockdown and non-critically injured students who were in the cafeteria were moved to the library.

Assist the injured. A quick response to the needs of the injured is critical. If school staff are prepared for a medical emergency the response will be timely and effective. At Thurston High, students in the Health Occupations class assisted the staff members in administering first aid in the cafeteria until emergency personnel arrived.

Request assistance. In a large-scale emergency, the 911 operator may receive hundreds of calls; thus, the staff member who phones emergency services has a critical role. This person should remain on the line as long as the emergency operator requests and should provide detailed information about the situation. At Thurston, the first police officer arrived 2 minutes after the first 911 call, and the first medic unit arrived within 5 minutes. Within 50 minutes all 25 wounded students were transported to two local hospitals.

Once the immediate safety and medical needs are addressed, the crisis team should ensure that the crisis guidelines of the established plan are implemented. Some of the most critical aspects of crisis response during an on-campus emergency include securing the crime scene, verifying facts, activating crisis communications, determining the status of the day, employing the incident command system, establishing a family reunification site, responding to the media, determining the need for outside help, providing counseling support, and aiding students and staff in returning to the scene of a trauma.

Managing the Crisis Day

Secure the crime scene and preserve evidence. If a crime has been committed on school grounds the staff should protect the area where the incident took place and prevent the contamination, destruction, or alteration of evidence. Trump (2000) advises restricting access to the area and prohibiting items from being moved, removed, or touched. He also notes that securing the area means not cleaning up crisis outcomes, such as blood on the floor or bullet holes in the wall. Once the police arrive they will take over the crime scene and assume responsibility for its protection. Trump (2000) further recommends that all school staff receive training by local law enforcement personnel on how to secure a crime scene and preserve evidence.

Verify facts and begin documentation. The school administrator in charge should verify the facts of the crisis as soon as feasible and designate someone to document the crisis and the response to it.

Activate the crisis communications plan. Trump (2000) notes that although school officials typically equate a communications plan with dealing with the media, there are many other essential facets of communications. Rapid, reliable, and frequent communication with parents and other staff members in the district is essential, as well as clear communication with the media. In a large-scale crisis, radios and cell phones may be needed when the district phone lines become overloaded. At Thurston High, for example, once word of the event spread to the community, all the school phone lines were jammed—no calls were possible either to or from the school for a period of time. Cell phones and two-way radios were invaluable in this instance. School and city personnel quickly set up additional phone lines and a central information number staffed by live operators 24 hours a day. In any crisis, staff should send frequent updates to other schools in the district and remember that members of the media can monitor radio frequencies.

Determine the status of the remaining school day. If the crisis occurs during the school day, the administrator must determine whether or not school will stay open for the remainder of the day. There are several factors to consider in determining whether to close school. If at all possible, it is beneficial to keep students at school so they can receive care and support in coping with the crisis. However, it was our experience that other priorities may supersede these considerations, as parents may wish to withdraw their children immediately following a crisis and the police may limit access to the school. In the case of Thurston High, the campus was declared a crime scene so all students were sent home shortly after the incident. Generally, when a traumatic event such as a shooting occurs, the school is closed for a day or two for repairs and investigations.

Manage the crisis with the incident command system. When a crisis of a major scope occurs, school personnel must know and understand their roles as well as those of the emergency service providers. It is important that school, police, fire, hospital, and city officials all work together to respond to the incident. The Incident Command System (ICS) is a recognized system for managing such a response and can be invaluable in managing an emergency. Many descriptions of this system exist; a brief summary follows as provided by Trump (2000).

The Incident Command System originated in the 1970s and has been adopted by the Federal Emergency Management Agency (FEMA, 1995) as a model for responding to all types of emergencies. The ICS is based on business management practices and includes the five functional areas of command, operations, planning, logistics, and finance. When school district personnel are involved in a major crisis response, their roles should be coordinated with the public safety incident commanders. While school officials need to evaluate their own organizational structure and personnel resources, Trump (2000) suggests the following roles for school personnel:

> *Command:* The incident commander for the school district would likely be the superintendent. A risk management official and a public/community relations official should support the incident commander. Depending on the size of the district a security director or school resource officer could serve as a liaison with other public safety agencies.

Operations: The building principal would typically lead the actual response to the crisis, supported by the school crisis team members.

Planning: The school administrator in charge of student services (counselors, school psychologists, social workers, and nurses) would fulfill the planning role. This includes the collection of information on the incident and status of resources.

Logistics: The school administrator in charge of the district facilities, services, grounds, food services, and transportation would serve this function.

Finance: A school business manager or financial director would handle financial decisions. In a major crisis there can be many financial implications from overtime pay to the dispersal of special funds.

Establish a family reunification site. Immediately following a crisis at a school, parents and family members usually rush to the site to find their children. The arrival of hundreds or thousands of people can overwhelm and interfere with the emergency responders and school staff members who are providing immediate assistance. School officials should move students to a "family reunification" site near the school and direct parents to meet their students there.

Michael Dorn, school safety specialist for the Georgia Emergency Management Agency, has described these key elements of an effective reunification strategy: (a) never plan to use a school for a reunification center as this results in two schools being in crisis; (b) do not announce the location of a family reunification center to the public in advance as this could lead to explosives being planted at the site; (c) plan every detail of the family reunification protocol carefully; (d) develop a solid system of accountability for students; (e) arrange for adequate law enforcement presence at the reunification site; (f) designate a media staging area and provide the media with regular updates; (g) develop a system to encourage people to leave once they have picked up students; (h) provide a specific area for mental health workers to provide assistance; (i) publicize the location with local media to quickly divert people to the site; and (j) test the reunification system with local emergency management personnel (Dorn, 2001).

Manage the media. Reporters have a job, and that is to get a story. They will do this with or without the cooperation of school personnel. The district communications officer or designee should handle all media communications during and after a crisis. The spokesperson should update information frequently and control rumors during a crisis through scheduled press conferences, preferably held away from the site of the event. In a large-scale crisis, it is helpful to provide a united front by holding press conferences in conjunction with law enforcement, city managers, and hospital staff. Springfield School District Communications Director Cherie Kistner noted, "The advantage in working together on our response is that we ensure that the information given is factual and credible, and perhaps most importantly, consistent" (*Emergency*

Response Guide for Administrators, Springfield Public Schools, 2000). In our experience, it is best not to allow the media on school grounds in a crisis, or if necessary, only when students are not present. However, it is also important to work with the media during a crisis, as they can assist in relaying important information to the public. For example, our local media broadcast the conditions of victims, times and locations of memorial services, and information on how people could help. Table 3, on page 1004, contains suggestions for communicating with media.

Following the shooting at Thurston, our community was flooded with reporters both on the ground and in the air. Reporters from as far away as Japan, England, and Australia quickly took on a larger-than-life presence in our normally quiet community. Representatives from ABC, NBC, CBS, CNN, PBS, NPR, *Inside Edition, Hard Copy, USA Today, Time, Life, Newsweek, People, Rolling Stone,* and *Psychology Today* all appeared at the school. A surrealistic scene developed as the normally wide street in front of the high school was reduced to a one-lane road, with cars forced to crawl between the constantly humming generators and blazing lights of 20 satellite vans. Then, as quickly as they had appeared, one week after the shooting, they all abruptly disappeared.

Determine whether to ask for outside help. During the first hour, the crisis team members should assess whether they need additional assistance in responding to the event. This assistance may come from other school districts, local community mental health providers, or from the national level. The Springfield School District is part of the *Lane County Tragedy Response Network,* which provides immediate help from other school districts. In addition to these local resources, we discovered that both the National Organization for Victim Assistance (NOVA) and the National Emergency Assistance Team (NEAT) were excellent resources for community support in a large-scale crisis. The first NOVA volunteers were on the scene the afternoon of the shooting, and more arrived the following day. NOVA and NEAT also provided support to the school districts in West Paducah, Kentucky and Jonesboro, Arkansas, following their school tragedies. For a description of the role played by NOVA and NEAT in these responses, see Poland and McCormick (1999).

Provide counseling support through critical incident stress debriefing. When students and staff have witnessed a traumatic event, specially trained counselors may be needed to aid the survivors in dealing with the trauma. Jeffrey Mitchell of the Department of Emergency Health Services, University of Maryland, described a group crisis intervention model for use with traumatized emergency teams (Mitchell, 1983). Critical Incident Stress Debriefing (CISD) has relevant application in school crises as well. Among others, Kendall Johnson (1998) has applied the CISD model to classroom debriefings and he suggested that school counselors and psychologists can be trained to facilitate these discussions. CISD is a process that normalizes reactions and provides information and referral sources to victims. Critical Incident Stress Debriefings should be held during the first few days following an on-campus crisis to aid students and staff members in coping with the event. Members of NOVA and NEAT are trained in CISD and can provide additional resources if the event has a large impact on the community.

Aid students and staff in returning to the scene of a trauma. It is often difficult for students and staff to return to a school where a crisis has just occurred. In most cases,

TABLE 3

Suggestions for Media Communication During a Crisis

1. **USE KEY STAFF** and community communicators to dispel rumors.

2. **CONTROL THE GRAPEVINE.** Check rumors at the source and establish the facts.

3. **MAINTAIN AN ATMOSPHERE OF OPENNESS AND TRUST.** Be honest about mistakes. Provide plans for correcting weaknesses. Enlist aid. Fill requests for comments, interviews, photos, and statistics. The approach of a school staff member is, "We can use all the help we can get to solve this problem—together."

4. **SWIFTLY SUPPLY APPROPRIATE, KNOWN INFORMATION.** *Expect "officials" not to be believed,* which is why a key communicators meeting works. Community or staff people are the ones reporters talk to—the ones people believe—the ones who are "close" to the problem.

5. **SET UP AVENUES OF COMMUNICATION** before you see the likelihood of using them. Reap benefits of having already developed a cooperative relationship with the media over the long term.

6. **DISCUSS WITH STAFF** their role in crisis situations. Identify a line of spokespersons—an order of who will speak when the first spokesperson is not available. Outline and assign administrative duties.

7. **MAKE SURE ADULT STAFF** members answer phones during and immediately after a crisis.

8. **DO NOT SAY WHAT YOU THINK**—only what you *know* to be true.

9. **REIN IN EMOTIONAL INVOLVEMENT**—yours—and be aware of its predominance in others.

10. **PROVIDE A PRESS ROOM** (crisis communication center). If possible, locate a room with phones separate from the office of the person in charge (i.e., the principal's office) but near the scene of the crisis. Assign a staff member to remain there who knows what is going on and is in touch with both the principal and the media. (The Administrative Assistant to the Superintendent can help here.)

11. **TAKE THE INITIATIVE** with media where possible. You're better off informing them than reacting to them.

12. **BE WILLING TO SHARE** information, but do not speculate when all the facts are not in. Emphasize what is NOT yet known as well as what is known (see **8** above).

13. **EMPHASIZE WITH THE MEDIA AND STAFF YOUR UNDERSTANDING** of their ability to help handle the crisis by informing them. Thank them for their cooperation and resist the temptation of rapping publicly the ones who are not helpful.

14. **ANNOUNCE A SCHEDULE** of times when District spokespersons will meet the media—on the hour, on the half hour, etc.—but if you get new information that they are seeking, do not wait until the scheduled time to provide it.

15. **USE A P.A. SYSTEM** or bullhorn to address crowds if one is available.

16. **REMEMBER THAT ANYTHING YOU SAY WILL BE FOR THE RECORD.** Phone conversations probably will be taped—a good idea, when possible, also to tape from your end.

17. **EXPLAIN TO REPORTERS WHY** you cannot provide certain information (because of privacy rights of anyone involved, the possibility of hindering investigations, etc.).

18. **IF A REPORTER BECOMES A PROBLEM,** explain why you are having trouble communicating. (I cannot answer that now, but, if you can let me get back to you in 3 minutes, I can.).

19. **CONSIDER USE OF ALL CONCEIVABLE** communication tools: telephone trees, bulletins, hotline phones, paid advertising, posted notices, district-wide mailings.

20. **DECISIONS NOT TO COOPERATE** with the media should be made only as a last resort—and then by the Superintendent or designee. Since public education is public sector, non-cooperation should be rare indeed.

Note
Source: Springfield Public Schools. (2000). *Emergency response guide for administrators.* Springfield, OR: Author.

students and staff should return to the school as soon as possible, although law enforcement constraints may delay reentry to a crime scene. The crisis team will need to design a plan that makes it easier for victims to adjust and return to the school. For example, following the Thurston tragedy, an open house was held on Memorial Day (prior to the reopening of school) to allow students and staff the opportunity to reenter the campus with the support of their families and friends, as well as trauma specialists. Over 2,000 people sat or stood in the repaired cafeteria that day, though many could not enter the room in which such terrible violence had occurred.

Intervention When a Crisis Occurs Away From School

The majority of events that require a school-based crisis team response are crises occurring away from school that affect students and staff (for example, the accidental death of a student or staff member, a house fire, or a car accident with multiple student injuries). In these situations, the key priorities are slightly different from those for an on-campus emergency.

Immediate Response

There are three priorities for a school administrator to address upon hearing of a crisis event that has occurred off campus:

Receive and verify information. The administrator in charge should verify the facts of the event. Rumors frequently spread faster than truth, so finding reliable sources is important.

Notify district office personnel, staff, students, and parents. Once the facts are known the administrator should contact the key individuals in the school and district. If appropriate, a media contact also may be made at this time.

Convene crisis team members. The crisis team members should meet with the administrator as soon as possible after learning of the tragedy to make plans for student and staff support at the school.

Managing the School Day

When a student death or other tragedy occurs, school generally remains in session, although the students and staff may be impacted to the extent that proceeding with a normal school day is not possible. Campbell (1999) recommended steps for managing the day in her training manual, *Tragedy Response Team Training.* We have used these procedures numerous times in the Springfield School District with good results. This section will illustrate the crisis day steps using one example of a student death. This is a good framework; however, flexibility is the key to the success of a crisis intervention.

In this incident, a middle school principal received a call from a parent that a student had died suddenly and unexpectedly. A second call from another source verified the information. In this case, the principal notified the superintendent, the Director of Secondary Education, the nearby elementary school where the student's siblings attended, and the district media spokesperson. At the student's middle school, the building crisis team met during the afternoon and members reviewed their roles and responsibilities. They planned a staff meeting to occur immediately after school to notify the teachers. After the immediate response, the administrator and crisis team members planned for the events of the next school day by following the procedures described below.

Extent of the impact assessment: At the staff meeting after school, the team attempted to determine how much support would be needed the following day by soliciting input from teachers as to who would be affected. They notified other district counselors and psychologists of the need for their additional assistance.

Emergency morning staff meeting: The principal held an emergency staff meeting before school the following day to update the staff on current information, answer questions, and prepare them for the day. Team members reviewed logistics regarding the access and location of counseling services and other procedures for the day. After the meeting, staff members began greeting students as they arrived on campus.

Student support at arrival: Teachers discussed the tragedy, giving the information provided by the principal at the staff meeting. In this case, many students were aware of the death upon arriving at school so discussions began immediately. Here is where one major problem occurred in this intervention. Many more students than anticipated arrived at school distraught, angry, and upset. This resulted in a period of time where more students needed assistance than was available, creating confusion and tension. Counselors immediately called for more assistance. The lesson learned was to plan for more counselors than anticipated. It is better to send some counselors away than not to have enough help.

A counselor met with the first period class the deceased student had attended. Some students were sent to the "safe room" for assistance (description follows). Two substitute teachers were available to relieve teachers throughout the day as needed. The principal prepared and sent home a letter to all parents describing the incident, the supports available at the school, and some of the normal reactions of students. Figure 1, on page 1008, contains a sample of this type of letter.

Counseling support in the "safe room": Providing mental health support for the staff and students is essential following any crisis. When an event such as the death of a student or staff member occurs, many students can be impacted to the point where their functioning within normal school routines is impossible. The "safe room" or "care room" is a location (it can be one or more rooms) in the school where students can receive counseling support for their grief. Counselors trained in the dynamics of child and adolescent grief and loss should staff the room. In a district-level or trauma response, these counselors will likely come from either outside the building or outside the district because of the large number of counselors needed.

Campbell (1999) has described the rationale and operations of the safe room. According to Campbell, students generally grieve a school-related loss in the community of the school. It is most helpful for students to be able to discuss the death or tragedy in their classrooms with their peers. Usually the whole class will take some time to talk about the loss. The function of the safe room is to provide support and a safe environment for any student who is not ready to return to the academic routine when the class does so. Sometimes small groups of students who knew the deceased well also benefit from having a special meeting place. A staff-to-student ratio in the safe room of 1:3 is recommended for elementary students, 1:5 for secondary students.

The safe room is a place for students to deal with their anger, confusion, fear, and other normal emotions that arise in times of grief or trauma. It is also a place where staff can identify those students who may be at risk for depression or suicide, or in need of counseling. Students who experience "secondary" loss (re-experiencing a prior loss triggered by the current event) also benefit from the support services of a safe room. An important point made by Campbell (1999) is that this is not therapy or counseling, but rather it is a way to provide a witness to grief. Staff members ask questions and make comments that normalize the experience for the students and help them deal with their grief. Students often engage in activities such as drawing or writing to mitigate their feelings of helplessness or hopelessness.

After-school staff meeting: It is important to check in with the staff at the end of the day. In the middle school example, the principal held a staff meeting after school to debrief the day. Teachers reviewed the status of referred students, prioritized needs for the next day, and began to consider follow-up activities.

AFTER A CRISIS: FOLLOW-UP

The degree of impact of a crisis event will determine the length of the recovery period for the school and community; in general, most crisis events will be resolved

FIGURE 1

Sample Letter to Send Home Regarding a Tragedy

Date

Dear Parents:

All of us at _____ School are deeply saddened by the death of _____, who was a student here. Our condolences go out to _____ family and friends.

During the day today, numerous counselors and psychologists were available to meet and talk with students, assisting them in dealing with their grief. Support from counselors and psychologists will continue to be available for students as needed.

Some of the reactions or behaviors you might see as a result of this sudden loss include shock, fatigue, anger, depression and sleeping problems. These reactions are normal, but if you are concerned, contact our school counselors, _____.

We would like to thank parents for their support during this difficult time. Please contact me if the school staff can be of further assistance to you.

Sincerely,

Principal

Note
Source: Springfield Public Schools. (2000). *Emergency response guide for administrators.* Springfield, OR: Author.

within one to two weeks. Following the death of a student, for example, the school's normal activities generally resume after a day or two. After a major crisis, such as a school shooting, the follow-up activities may need to continue for weeks, months, or even years. Following a crisis, planning for continued mental health support should occur. School staff will also need to consider memorials, funerals and healing events, evaluating the crisis response, anniversaries, ongoing media issues, litigation preparedness and legal issues, long-term mental health support, and taking care of the caregivers.

Mental Health Support

After any crisis, mental health counseling should be provided through on-site support groups or referrals to community counseling agencies. Identify individual students who need counseling and establish drop-in support groups or more formal grief support groups if appropriate. Introduce grief and loss materials into the curriculum. Help parents understand their children's reaction to the crisis by sending information to them. Provide debriefing and grief counseling for adults as well as students. Just as students can have reactive symptoms, so can adults. The ability to teach may be affected. It is recommended that a trained facilitator conduct at least one session with the entire staff to review grief dynamics and allow staff to share their feelings. In addition, convene a meeting of all persons who participated in the crisis intervention, including outside building counselors who assisted in the safe room, so that the team members can discuss their reactions to the events.

In Springfield, our approach to follow-up of the Thurston shooting was twofold: to recapture the school's normal activities, and at the same time, to support the 1,500 students and staff members in achieving a healthy recovery. Immediate follow-up activities included critical incident debriefings, grant writing to obtain funding for trauma counselors at Thurston High, staff training in the dynamics of post-trauma reactions, and summer activities for students at Thurston High. The Thurston Assistance Center was established to provide counseling support and information to Springfield students and families affected by the shooting. The Thurston Healing Fund collected more than $400,000 for the support of the victims' families.

Memorials

Remembering a deceased student through some form of school ceremony or observance is a meaningful way for all students and staff to become actively involved and contribute to honoring the memory of a friend (see *Emergency Response Guide for Administrators,* Springfield Public Schools, 2000). A memorial promotes the healing process by providing an opportunity for students to join together and participate in a grieving ritual. The memorial may take many forms and is limited only by the creativity of those planning it. Activities may range from a simple tree planting to a more traditional "service." In addition, a school memorial brings closure to a period of grieving and serves as a clear statement that it is time to move on with regular school activities. One of our most creative memorials happened following the death of a middle school boy who was killed while riding a bike without a helmet. The school staff and students raised money and received donations so that every student in the school could have a bike helmet.

Examples of school memorials include a tree or flower planting; dedication of a plaque or picture; fundraising for a scholarship or charity; assembly of interested students including music, readings, stories, or poems written by students and staff; reflections on the life of the deceased student; or a collection of memorabilia that reflects the life of the student. Refer to Figure 2, on page 1010, for a sample memorial program.

FIGURE 2

Sample School Remembrance Program

ANY SCHOOL   OFFICE OF THE PRINCIPAL

CELEBRATION OF LIFE
IN REMEMBRANCE OF

ORDER OF THE PROGRAM
FRIDAY, APRIL 17, 19--
1:40 PM, MAIN GYM

QUIET MUSIC - as teachers enter with their classes in the main gym a designated student should place the class project on the front of the stage.

MUSIC – "It's So Hard To Say Goodbye" - Choir

OPENING COMMENTS - Mr._____

STUDENT SPEAKERS - Ms._____will introduce each student speaker in the following order:

    1._____   4._____
    2._____   5._____
    3._____   6._____

MUSIC – "Wind Beneath My Wings" - Special student ensemble

COMMENTS - Mr._____.

MUSIC – "Amazing Grace" - Choir

STAFF SPEAKERS - Mr._____ will speak and introduce the staff members who are speaking.

MUSIC – "Blowin' In The Wind" - Choir

BALLOON RELEASE - In remembrance of _____we will have a balloon release in the field, south of C wing. Please observe the following directions, while quiet music is being played:

    1. Volleyball and wrestling coaches will come to the stage and get balloons.
    2. 8th grade volleyball team and wrestling team will come forward and receive a balloon and move quietly to the field.
    3. After all balloon carriers are out, the students will be dismissed by classes to walk quietly out to the field. Teachers form a ring around the balloon carriers and students will stay around their teacher.
    4. Mr._____ will announce the release of the balloons when all students are assembled.
    5. Students will be released to return to their 2nd period class.

A special edition of the Newsletter should be handed out to your students when you get back to the classroom. These will be available to you at noon in your boxes. Be sure and pick them up.

Note

Source: Springfield Public Schools. (2000). *Emergency response guide for administrators.* Springfield, OR: Author.

Establishing a permanent memorial is important following tragedies and can require considerable time and emotional energy. Do not rush into the completion of a permanent memorial, as time and emotional distance from the incident often bring insight into the design (Robert Pynoos, advice to Springfield staff, 1998). It is important to involve students in the planning and design of a memorial and to establish who will make the final decisions. Define the roles of students, staff, administrators, family, and community members in the process. Carefully consider the location of any permanent memorial. Following the Thurston shooting, a group of students, representatives of the victims, parents, and school staff all worked together to plan a permanent memorial with input from the community at large regarding the design.

Funerals and Healing Events

To the extent possible, coordinate plans between the school and the families regarding funerals and other healing events. In a large-scale crisis it is often necessary to dismiss school to allow students and staff to attend a funeral or a memorial event. Community healing events such as the community candlelight vigil held in Springfield in May 1998 serve an important function in the healing process.

Crisis Response Evaluation

Within three to four weeks of a crisis intervention it is helpful for the Crisis Response Team to evaluate the overall response. This can be done through a staff questionnaire and/or group discussion. A facilitator who is not a member of the crisis team is a good person to direct the discussion.

Anniversaries

The anniversary of a death of a student or staff member is a time for reflection and remembrance. It is appropriate and helpful to remember the deceased at the anniversary. Students who participated in grief groups may meet briefly to share this special time. Following a large-scale tragedy, the anniversary often generates a renewed interest in the event by the community as well as by the media.

The days leading up to the one-year anniversary of the Thurston shooting were filled with anticipation, anxiety, rumors of copycat violence, and daily doses of media coverage (all intensified by the Columbine incident one month prior to the anniversary). The day of the anniversary began with bomb-sniffing dogs searching the campus and dozens of parents patrolling the area, and continued with counselors and police officers supporting and reassuring those who attended classes. The day ended as over a thousand people gathered to remember the families of the victims in a "Community Gathering for Remembrance and Renewal" at Thurston High School.

Media Issues During Follow-Up

After a tragedy, school officials can count on the media to continue its coverage for as long as there is a story. This may last for days, weeks, or months following the event. After the shooting at Thurston High School the (local) Eugene *Register-Guard* newspaper printed continuous coverage of the event and its follow-up for 31 days; related stories appeared in each of the 36 months following the tragedy; and in all, over 600 associated stories have been published to date in that newspaper alone.

On the basis of his experience as a school security supervisor and director, Kenneth Trump identified seven stages of the media coverage of a school crisis (Trump, 2000): (a) breaking news stage, (b) investigation stage, (c) analysis stage, (d) grief stage, (e) recovery and return-to-normal stage, (f) future predictions and positive angle stage, and (g) anniversary stage. We experienced all of these stages following the shooting in Springfield. The following section describes each stage.

Breaking news stage. This stage involves the first level of coverage as a crisis breaks; the media focuses on getting information out to the public about the crisis as quickly as possible. There are generally few facts known at this stage, but competition by the various media outlets to get the first facts is fierce.

Investigation stage. The focus at this stage is on securing as many details as possible about what exactly happened. Media representatives also begin seeking information on how the crisis is affecting people and school operations.

Analysis stage. As the facts of the crisis begin to emerge, media personnel attempt to provide an analysis, typically through the "expert opinions" of professionals regarding exactly what occurred, why it occurred as it did, and its impact on students, staff, and school operations. Because of media helicopters, the availability of 24-hour-a-day news programs, and other technology, this stage may actually occur at the same time as stages 1 and 2.

Grief stage. The media focus shifts to the impact of the crisis on the injured, their families, and friends of deceased individuals. The length of this stage of coverage depends on the size and severity of the crisis, and generally includes coverage of funerals and memorials.

Recovery and return-to-normal stage. Once funerals and memorials have occurred, the attention typically shifts to the recovery stage. The focus is on how school officials, students, and the community are returning to normalcy.

Future predictions and positive angle stage. As schools and communities return to normal, the media coverage focuses on what people can expect in the future. The media may also temporarily close out coverage with a positive story about some aspect of the schools.

Anniversary stage. The media may return to the crisis story anywhere from one month to six months—or even one year—after the incident to acknowledge the anniversary of the crisis event. Following large-scale incidents, such as Columbine, we have seen this anniversary coverage continue for several years.

Litigation Preparedness and Legal Issues

Unfortunately, the probability of a school district being sued following a school crisis seems to be increasing. Therefore, district legal counsel and risk managers should be involved in the planning process and should review all crisis plans. During a crisis, school officials should document details of their response to the situation. As noted by Kenneth Trump, "Although litigation concerns are legitimate, those concerns must also be balanced with caring and compassion in responding to the crisis aftermath" (Trump, 2000).

If the tragedy involves a crime, the follow-up should include support for victims and survivors during the legal proceedings. While victim's assistance workers in the district attorney's office provide most of this support, school counselors and psychologists may provide support as well. The legal proceedings following the Thurston shooting attracted the attention of the world, just as the school shooting had. In preparation for the trial we sought the advice of experts and held planning meetings involving staff of the school district, the City of Springfield, and the Lane County District Attorney's office; victim's assistance workers; public information directors; and trauma counselors.

Sixteen months after the shooting, we were ready to face the suspect's trial. Then suddenly, just four days before jury selection was to begin, he pleaded guilty to the charges, thus avoiding a trial. Subsequently, during a seven-day sentencing hearing, the attorneys for both the defense and prosecution presented witness testimony to the judge. Many of the victims spoke of the impact of this tragedy in emotional, heart-wrenching testimony reflecting anger, hate, sadness and sorrow. On November 10, 1999, the perpetrator was sentenced to 112 years in prison, with no parole, and our community breathed a sigh of relief.

Long-Term Mental Health Support

Following a crisis, school staff, students, and team members are often emotionally and physically exhausted and wish things could just return to "normal." The community of the school, however, is usually permanently affected both by the loss and the experience of witnessing the grief of the students. For example, the accidental death of one of our middle school teachers profoundly affected many staff members and students for weeks, months, and even years. It is critical that school personnel recognize the long-term impact of a death or other tragedy and provide support for both staff and students.

Although the majority of Thurston High students and teachers were able to move on with life and learning, it was not so simple for the 300 people who were in the cafeteria that day. Twenty of the 25 injured students returned to Thurston High the following fall, some with physical scars, and others with bullets still within them; still others faced surgeries and lengthy rehabilitation. Bereavement was complicated by traumatic grief. Then, some months later, we were shocked and saddened once again when one of the shooting survivors was accidentally shot and killed while hunting.

Moving through the school years following the Thurston tragedy we have seen a variety of reactions from students. Many have been able to go through the school years without noticeable effects and without outside help. However, for some, their beliefs about the safety and security of school were affected permanently and some experienced posttraumatic stress reactions. The citizens of Springfield cannot go back to the way they were before the shooting. We no longer are unsuspecting individuals marginally affected by youth violence. This event forced us to deal with a large-scale tragedy that even now demands our attention and our strength.

If a crisis involves a traumatic event, the healing may take longer and the educational process can be disrupted by posttraumatic stress in a variety of ways (Eth & Pynoos, 1985). Posttraumatic symptoms specific to children and adolescents include (a) withdrawal and subdued and muted behavior; (b) participation in reenactments and plans involving traumatic themes; (c) anxious attachment behaviors including greater separation or stranger anxiety, clinging to a cherished object, whining, crying, clinging and tantrums; (d) regression to previous levels of functioning; (e) denial of permanence of change; (f) lowered intellectual functioning and decline in school performance; (g) obsessive talking about the incident; (h) constant anxious arousal; (i) problems relating to peers; (j) psychosomatic complaints resulting in absences; (k) acting-out behavior (truancy, substance abuse, sexual behavior); (l) self-criticism; and (m) fear of repetition of the event in the future.

Care of the Caregivers

Do not overlook the need to take care of those who provide the immediate and long-term support services for students and families. The aftermath of a crisis is exhausting, not only for the victims but also for those who provide care and support. Crisis responders may experience fatigue, depression, vicarious victimization, burnout, and even long-term stress reactions. "Caregivers are faced with constantly giving of themselves to others. They are compelled by an ethical imperative to sacrifice themselves for the needs of victims" (Young, 1998). The NOVA manual goes on to note that "if the counselors are members of the community that has been affected by the disaster, they, too, are victims and survivors in spite of the fact that they often see themselves primarily in the role of a responder" (Young, 1998). This fact creates special stresses for responders. In all situations, caregivers must receive information, training, support, and debriefing following a crisis event. See Table 4 regarding suggestions for care of caregivers.

SPECIAL SITUATIONS

There are certain circumstances that require special crisis response procedures. These situations are rare and do not follow the typical response pattern. They include responding to a suicide, handling the school as a crime scene, and supporting homicide survivors.

TABLE 4

Care for Caregivers

Drink water.
Write poetry.
Get lots of sleep.
Enjoy a bubble bath.
Draw pictures. Get into art.
Listen to raucous music & dance!
Care for your pets and houseplants.
Snack on healthy foods. Take vitamins.
Write your thoughts and feelings in a journal.
Collect a favor from someone who owes you one.
Talk to family or friends about how you are feeling/doing.
Write letters of regret and appreciation about anything in life.
Laugh. Rent a great, hilarious video. See a fun flick.
Ask someone who loves you to read you a story.
Take a favorite stuffed animal to bed with you.
Play a game or sport. Get lots of exercise.
Ask for a hug. Ask for another hug!
Spend time in prayer or meditation.
Treat yourself to a massage.
Listen to soothing music.
Read a favorite story.
Let yourself cry.
Light a candle.
Sing loud.

Note
Source: Campbell, N. (1999). *Tragedy response team training*. Eugene, OR: Neila Campbell and Associates.

Responding to a Suicide

The suicide of a student or staff member presents unique challenges to school administrators and crisis responders owing to the nature of the event and the danger of "copycat" suicides or contagion among the student's peers. The following recommendations, made in the Los Angeles Unified School District's *Quick Reference Guide for School Crisis Management* (1998) provides guidance in this area. The guide recommends that staff keep the school open in order to provide services to students, staff, and parents. It is helpful to provide fact sheets acknowledging that the death was a suicide; however, the information released should avoid details. Following a suicide, determine intervention groups—particularly for friends of the deceased—and provide grief counseling in small groups, avoiding large assemblies. In addition, it is critical to communicate with the media. Finally, do not have a memorial, dedication, or plaque; instead, encourage donations to a charity or to the family.

When the School Is a Crime Scene

When a crime is committed on a school campus, the school administrator must relinquish his or her authority to law enforcement for a period of time. Law enforcement will establish a crime scene under circumstances involving the following: (a) murder or suicide, (b) death due to suspicious circumstances, (c) a person who is the victim of a crime and may possibly die, or (d) serious crime. In such cases only authorized personnel will be allowed to enter the crime scene and an officer will be in charge of serving as the liaison with the school's administration. It is imperative that all school employees and community members not interfere with or contaminate any identified crime scene (Los Angeles Unified School District, 1998). As with suicide, an additional challenge related to school crime is the potential for copycat events. This copycat phenomenon was particularly widespread following the shooting at Columbine High School, and was repeated again after the recent shootings in Santee and El Cajon, California.

Supporting Homicide Survivors

Providing assistance to homicide survivors is a great challenge because the issues are extremely complex and multifaceted. Trauma counselor Debra Alexander states, "Grieving the loss of someone who has been killed suddenly, violently, and senselessly is different from any other form of grieving" (Alexander, 1999). Alexander, a trauma survivor herself, notes that in these situations "sometimes the pain is too deep for words. Images of the death or knowledge of a loved one's last moments may be overwhelming. Criminal justice systems, insurance companies, settlements, and media can present a multitude of frustrations for families and their children and often repeatedly cause a return to initial trauma reactions" (Alexander, 1999). Professional mental health assistance is often recommended for students, staff, or families in these circumstances.

CONCLUSION

Tragedy can strike any school, any time, anywhere. No longer can we afford to think, "It can't happen here." We were recently reminded of the ever-present danger of school violence in America. For a long period following Columbine there were few incidents in our nation of large-scale school violence. Then, ironically, during the writing of this chapter, two school shootings occurred in California. The first, at Santana High School in Santee, California, resulted in 2 student deaths and 13 injuries. The second shooting, which happened in the same school district less than three weeks later, thankfully resulted in no fatalities, although 5 students and teachers were injured. Once again we observed the physical and emotional damage that a troubled youth could cause by a single act lasting mere minutes—damage that will take months and years to repair. Fortunately, the Grossmont Union High School District had a good crisis response plan in place, security officers and others intervened promptly, and trained crisis workers responded skillfully. In addition, the National Emergency Assistance Team provided posttrauma support for both communities.

As schools struggle to recover from violence, they face a task described by Marleen Wong, Director of District Crisis Teams for the Los Angeles Unified School District. She told the Springfield School District teachers, "Work hard to find that balance between mourning the past, treasuring the present, and keeping hope for the future." It is that future we now must focus on. Although there are increasing efforts to predict and prevent school violence, it appears that violent incidents will continue to occur on school campuses for the foreseeable future.

Responding effectively to a school crisis is a complex responsibility that must be a priority for school districts today. A comprehensive plan that includes crisis preparedness and crisis response procedures is the foundation of a safe school. Schools must form a crisis response team, develop a comprehensive written crisis response plan that covers a range of possible events, coordinate the plan with local emergency responders, conduct training of all school staff, and integrate the plan into a comprehensive school safety plan. It is no longer a question of *whether* a crisis will strike, it is a matter of *when*. The time to assess your district's preparedness is now.

REFERENCES

Alexander, D. W. (1999). *Children changed by trauma: A healing guide.* Oakland, CA: New Harbinger.

Campbell, N. (1999). *Tragedy response team training.* Eugene, OR: Neila Campbell and Associates.

Dorn, M. (2001, March). Key elements of effective family reunification strategy. *Practical Strategies for Maintaining Safe Schools, 7*(3): 3.

Dwyer, K., & Osher, D. (2000). *Safeguarding our children: An action guide.* Washington, DC: U.S. Departments of Education and Justice, American Institutes for Research.

Dwyer, K., Osher, D., & Warger, C. (1998). *Early warning, timely response: A guide to safe schools.* Washington, DC: U.S. Department of Education.

Eth, S., & Pynoos, R. S. (1985). *Post-traumatic stress disorder in children.* Washington, DC: American Psychiatric Press.

Federal Emergency Management Agency. (1995, November). *Incident command system self-study unit.* Jessup, MD.

Johnson, K. (1998). *Trauma in the lives of children.* Alameda, CA: Hunter House.

Kaufman, P., Chen, X., Choy, S. P., Ruddy, S. A., Miller, A. K., Fleury, J. K., Chandler, K. A., Rand, M. R., Klaus, P., & Planty, M. G. (2000). *Indicators of school crime and safety, 2000.* Washington, DC: U.S. Departments of Education and Justice.

Klicker, R. (1993). *A student dies, a school mourns. Are you prepared?* Bristol, PA: Hemisphere.

Los Angeles Unified School District. (1998). *A quick reference guide for school crisis management.* Los Angeles, CA: Author.

Mitchell, J. (1983). When disaster strikes: The critical incident stress debriefing process. *Journal of Emergency Medical Services, 8:* 36–39.

Paine, C., & Sprague, J. (2000). "Crisis prevention and response: Is your school prepared?" *Oregon School Study Council Bulletin, 43*(2) (Winter 2000).

Poland, S., & McCormick, J. S. (1999). *Coping with crisis: Lessons learned.* Longmont, CA: Sopris West.

Schneider, T., Walker, H., & Sprague, J. (2000). *Safe school design: A handbook for educational leaders.* Eugene, OR: ERIC Clearinghouse on Educational Management.

Springfield Public Schools. (1999). *Emergency procedures manual.* Springfield, OR: Author.

Springfield Public Schools. (2000). *Emergency response guide for administrators.* Springfield, OR: Author.

Trump, K. S. (2000). *Classroom killers? Hallway hostages? How schools can prevent and manage school crises.* Thousand Oaks, CA: Corwin Press.

Vossekuil, B., Reddy, M., Fein, R., Borum, R., & Modzeleski, W. (2000). *U.S.S.S. Safe School Initiative: An interim report on the prevention of targeted violence in schools.* Washington, DC: U.S. Secret Service, National Threat Assessment Center.

Young, M. (1998). *The community crisis response team training manual.* Washington, DC: National Organization for Victim Assistance.

APPENDIX

Crisis Response Resources

Crisis Management Institute
PO Box 331, Salem, OR 97308; (503) 364-0403
www.cmionline.org

Federal Emergency Management Agency (FEMA)
FEMA Publications, PO Box 70274, Washington, DC 20027; (202) 646-3484

National Association of School Psychologists/National Emergency Assistance Team
4340 East West Highway, Suite 402, Bethesda, MD 20814; (301) 657-0270
www.nasponline.org

National Organization for Victim's Assistance
1–800–TRY-NOVA
www.try-nova.org

National Resource Center for Safe Schools
101 SW Main Street, Portland, OR 97204; 1–800–268–2275
www.safetyzone.org

National School Boards Association
www.nsba.org

National School Public Relations Association
www.nspra.org/entry.htm

National School Safety Center
4165 Thousand Oaks Blvd., Suite 290, Westlake Village, CA 91362
www.nssc.org

U.S. Department of Education
www.ed.gov/

U.S. Department of Justice
www.usdoj.gov/

CHAPTER 37

Preparing School Psychologists for Early Intervention Settings

David W. Barnett, Kendra Hamler, Linda Conway-Hensley,
Kelly Maples, Amy Murdoch, Karin Nelson,
Julie Sand-Niehaus, and Sheryl Siemoens
University of Cincinnati

INTRODUCTION

A child's early developmental years, encompassing approximately birth through age 5, are pivotal for the professional preparation of school psychologists in several ways. First, early intervention research provides school psychology students with one of the best opportunities for understanding theory and practice related to the nature of risk. Some children are born "at risk," other children move in and out of risk situations throughout their developmental period, and for others, risk has strong cumulative effects (Hart & Risley, 1995). Many converging lines of investigation point to the significant potential of early developmental experiences for reducing risk and improving subsequent social and academic outcomes. Second, students learn constructs related to intervention design, which is significant for early intervention preparation in school psychology. As an example, the construct of intervention *strength* is defined as the likelihood of bringing about desired changes in the most natural and least intrusive way (Lentz, Allen, & Ehrhardt, 1996; Yeaton & Sechrest, 1981). Third, school psychology students also learn about professional "risks." Among the *risks* of early intervention are selecting weak or unreliable targets for change, and placing children, through inappropriate interventions, on trajectories that lead further away from typical peers and beneficial natural environments.

Professional training experiences should have clear links to evidence demonstrating benefits to children (e.g., Kratochwill & Stoiber, 2000). There are two major sources for early intervention efficacy data that guide training experiences. Most prominently, outcomes are generalized from experimental programs (Guralnick, 1997; Karoly et al., 1998). Generally, infants or young children and families are assigned to control or experimental groups. Children and parents in the experimental group receive a multifaceted intervention over a substantial period of time, developmental measures are repeated, and outcomes are summarized. The interventions typically have complex "mixes" of programs for parents, such as job training and parenting skills, and for children, early childhood education and specialized therapies. The locus of intervention may be center- or home-based. The literature is valuable because it describes the foundations, promises, as well as questions related to early intervention (Ramey & Ramey, 1998). Positive findings are associated with high quality early intervention programs; early intervention for children described as high risk has been associated with relatively immediate but uneven gains in development and achievement, and long-term social advantages such as fewer bouts with social services and the law (e.g., Guralnick, 1997; Karoly et al., 1998).

While experimental early intervention programs are significant sources for professional preparation and practice, flexible service delivery systems are called for by the profession of school psychology (e.g., Gutkin & Curtis, 1999; Sheridan & Kratochwill, 1992). Other important sources for early intervention training may be generalized from thousands of single case studies since the 1960s targeting the developmental and behavioral challenges of young children (Baer, Wolf, & Risley, 1968). In order to "translate" these research studies and methods into professional practices, we use the term *intervention-based service delivery* and the context of consultation (Barnett, Bell, & Carey, 1999). As an overview, intervention-based service delivery is guided by problem solving, functional and contextual assessments, intervention design principles including positive behavioral support (Koegel, Koegel, & Dunlap, 1996), and strong accountability methods (e.g., Flugum & Reschly,1994). Intervention-based research has been carried out in diverse settings including home, schools, and communities. This is of critical importance in training professionals since early intervention settings are wherever parents, teachers, and young children are "found." Professional preparation in intervention-based service delivery stresses basic behavioral change skills and accountability methods to document individual child outcomes (Barnett, Daly, et al., 1999).

Support for intervention-based service delivery also comes from the shift occurring in school psychology training as evidenced by the APA's and NASP's professional training standards (American Psychological Association, 1996; National Association of School Psychologists, 1995). In the past, professionals may have described their preparation in early intervention by citing courses taken, techniques mastered, or by hours accumulated in specialized settings. In the future, training in school psychology is more likely to focus on professional skills directly related to improving *educational outcomes*. This emphasis may be referred to as *performance-based* (Barnett, Daly, et al., 1999; NASP, 1995) or, here, *intervention-based* preparation.

This chapter describes early intervention training in school psychology at the University of Cincinnati. We use intervention-based service delivery as a foundation for professional preparation because it (a) can be used within diverse early intervention settings; (b) shows substantial evidence of service delivery benefits to young children, parents, and teachers; (c) fits with school psychology training reforms emphasizing outcomes (Reschly & Ysseldyke, 1995); and (d) links to Ohio's *intervention-based assessment* reform initiative for improving child evaluation.

First, we discuss content associated with successful outcomes in providing early intervention-based services. Second, we review themes related to professional roles in early intervention. Third, we characterize aspects of professional training for second-year preinternship students and fourth-year doctoral students emphasizing intervention-based field experiences.

PREPARATION FOR INTERVENTION-BASED PRACTICE

Our training context is an intervention-based service delivery system, guided by strong accountability methods for evaluating outcomes. Intervention-based theory and research has been well developed since the late 1960s and 1970s (i.e., Baer et al., 1968). The basics include (a) iterative problem solving; (b) target variable selection and measurement; (c) intervention selection including acceptability of intervention plans; (d) measurement of intervention integrity; and (e) intervention outcome measurement and follow-up. While the basics have been well described, attempts to integrate intervention-based *practice* into early intervention service delivery have been rare (e.g., Strain et al., 1992). In the next section, guidelines for organizing intervention-based service delivery training experiences are presented.

Training in Functional Assessment and Naturalistic Intervention Design

To introduce students to early intervention practice and have them participate meaningfully as soon as possible, we stress functional assessment and naturalistic intervention design. *Functional assessments* are based on a contextual analysis of children's development and behavior in activities that allow for identifying skills necessary to adapt to beneficial environments. A functional assessment has the following outcomes: (a) description of behaviors targeted for change; (b) description of sequences of times, activities, events, and behaviors that occur together; (c) description of activities and times when targeted behavior is not of concern; (d) description and measurement of consequences that maintain targeted behaviors; and (e) ongoing observations that show relationships among activities, behaviors, and outcomes or consequences (e.g., O'Neill et al., 1997). Functional assessments include the important ideas of planning environments to accelerate learning and to reduce the need for common "reactive" interventions, where parents or teachers "wait" for the behavior to occur, then "give" reinforcement or "punish" behavior (Luiselli & Cameron, 1998).

Naturalistic intervention design applies problem-solving steps toward identifying in order of possibility or caregiver preference: (a) naturally occurring parent or teacher intervention strategies likely to be successful either as implemented or with minor changes developed through consultation and feedback, (b) research-based interventions adaptable to evident styles of parenting or teaching within a problem context and setting, or (c) other positive interventions that may be acceptable to parents and teachers as well as effective (Barnett, Bell, & Carey, 1999). Strong intervention plans have natural as well as empirical support in that they are based on actual observations of behavior in context and on research.

A major "checkpoint" in professional preparation is intervention plan development. Students develop intervention plans by responding to "who, what, where, when, why, and how" questions in sufficient detail that (a) instructors and supervisors can inspect plans for soundness and opportunities for student feedback; (b) parents and teachers can approve the final plans to make sure that their ideas are represented, and that the plans are acceptable and believed likely to bring about desired changes; and (c) the person or persons responsible for the plans can carry them out effectively. Students submit a "conceptual and technical adequacy" section along with the report of consultations that includes (a) specific links between the intervention plans and early intervention research, and (b) empirical support for each step in problem solving. These points are explored further in the section below titled *Technical adequacy for the individual case.*

Passkey Procedural Guidelines

An important consideration for consumers and school psychology students is clarifying how services are to be provided. First we describe our model and then present the steps that school psychology students follow. The professional practice steps are described in the form of procedural guidelines that outline key service delivery functions to help with informed consent and monitoring of school psychology student progress throughout the consultation process.

Functional assessment and naturalistic intervention design components for early intervention settings—including school, home, and community—have been organized into procedural guidelines under the acronym PASSKey, which stands for *P*lanned *A*ctivity, *S*trategic *S*ampling, and *Key*stone variable. The PASSKey model was developed to bring intervention-based service delivery in line with developmentally appropriate practices serving as guidelines for early education programs (Bredekamp & Copple, 1997; Carta, 1995; Neuman, Copple, & Bredekamp, 1999). *Planned activities* are socially valid ecological units identified and prioritized by care providers, such as dressing, transportation to school, shopping, learning activities, or free play. The defining characteristic of a *Keystone variable* is the selection of a relatively narrow target variable that has widespread positive consequences. Keystone variables are individually determined, but they frequently involve language and social competence. Examples of intervening with keystone behaviors are given later in the chapter. *Strategic sampling* refers to collaboratively derived plans to acquire sufficient data about significant planned activities, or behavior in context, for intervention decisions. An example would be combining brief student observations of specific activities such as free play and transitions, and teacher observations of activities including entering the classroom in the morning and lunch, into a coherent sampling plan for the ongoing recording of targeted behaviors within specific planned activities to help make intervention decisions. For more detail about the origins of the three concepts and associated techniques, as well as evidence for positive outcomes associated with use of the procedures, see other sources (Barnett, Bell, et al., 1997; Barnett, Pepiton, et al., 1999).

PASSKey is used to structure problem solving. The first step is to complete a record review and relevant developmental/educational history to help identify family and health issues that may be contributing to the reason for the referral. Important concerns often include continuity of care, family stressors, medication effects, and hearing. Other core assessment and intervention planning techniques include (a) interviews with parents and teachers to help identify planned activities, keystone variables, and a sampling plan; (b) observations carried out by students, supervisors, and care providers; (c) possibly a functional analysis that involves manipulating specific antecedents or consequences based on hypotheses about variables that maintain behaviors of concern (e.g., Luiselli & Cameron, 1998); (d) curriculum-based assessment; and (e) a specific review of the empirical intervention literature based on the referral concern and problem-solving outcomes.

When the problem-solving team is ready to begin intervention planning, team members consider the least intrusive/most naturalistic interventions that will support the child's learning goals. Intervention plans are developed within the consultation relationship. PASSKey uses *scripts* that detail intervention plans as "steps" that fit the natural context of the problem situation and help parents, teachers, and other care providers perform the intervention skills (Ehrhardt, Barnett, Lentz, Stollar, & Reifen 1996). Scripts are tried out and refined as necessary. Scripting intervention plans benefits school psychology students because they learn to critically appraise intervention research and consider the realities of settings in helping parents and teachers develop workable and acceptable plans. The PASSKey procedural guidelines are available from the first author of this chapter.

Training in Accountability Methods for Evaluating Change

Providing accountability as a core professional role is carried out by evaluating evidence that intervention plans are actually helping as intended. That is, intervention plans are carefully developed, tried out, and evaluated with regard to outcomes for children, parents, and teachers. Accountability efforts are shared in that early intervention teams monitor children's progress toward goals using direct measures of performance (Ehrhardt et al., 1996).

Students' preparation in accountability methods at the University of Cincinnati includes the following topics: (a) the Scientist-Practitioner model (e.g., Stoner & Green, 1992); (b) practical sampling theory and tactics, including participant, time, behavior, and setting, and stimulus or conditions sampling (Barnett, Lentz, et al., 1997; Bell & Barnett, 1999); (c) technical adequacy for the individual case (Macmann et al., 1996); (d) accountability designs and data analysis (e.g., Barlow, Hayes, & Nelson, 1984; Parsonson & Baer, 1992); and (e) methods of program accountability or "summing up" closely related intervention series (Barnett, Daly, et al., 1999; Barnett, Pepiton, et al., 1999). We highlight some of the "less traveled" content that receives emphasis in our training.

Technical adequacy for the individual case. Students need to apply fundamental technical adequacy concepts to designing and carrying out interventions. The major objective is that students would know how to marshal and examine evidence for sound decision-making practices in problem solving. Parallel to other discussions of technical adequacy (Barnett, Lentz, & Macmann, 2000), key organizers are the reliability and validity of the variables targeted for change, and the reliability and validity of intervention design and outcome determination (Macmann et al., 1996). For an example pertaining to the reliability of problem solving, data collection methods, such as interviews with parents and teachers and direct observations, may or may not "converge" on variables targeted for intervention or there may be disagreements on how they are grouped or measured (e.g., Lentz, 1988). Students use methods for understanding variability in judgments such as examining research, continuing observations, and clarifying differences through consultation and problem solving. The validity of the targeted variable is based on research, direct empirical evidence such as a functional analysis, as well as parent and teacher judgments (Wolf, 1978). Similarly, evidence may or may not converge "reliably" on decisions related to intervention selection, implementation (e.g., Gresham, 1996), or outcome (e.g., Parsonson & Baer, 1992; Wolf, 1978). An example of an emerging practical and empirical approach to intervention selection validity can be found in brief intervention trials (Daly, Martens, Hamler, Dool, & Eckert, 1999; Harding, Wacker, Cooper, Millard, & Jensen-Kovalan, 1994; Martens, Eckert, Bradley, & Ardoin, 1999).

The major difference between traditional technical adequacy concepts of reliability and validity and those pertaining to the individual case is that the psychometric qualities of much of the intervention-based data are collected and examined during problem solving rather than by referring to test or instrument manuals. Students are required to know both traditional and intervention-based domains of technical adequacy.

Accountability designs. Students receive substantial preparation in single-case experimental designs consistent with the above discussions of scientist-practitioner methods and technical adequacy for the individual case. While experimental designs are sometimes used by students to examine referral questions (Wacker, Steege, & Berg, 1988), we have been examining outcomes of training experiences using data organized by a single case accountability or "A-B" design, a baseline followed by intervention, as the "building block" for individual students as well as school psychology program accountability (Barlow et al., 1984). The A-B design allows for brief intervention trials as necessary (Martens et al., 1999) as well as accountability for individual student consultations. In addition, students participate in analyzing the results of A-B designs for their cohorts as program-level accountability data, or "summing up," using techniques from the visual analysis of data and those borrowed from meta-analysis (Barnett, Daly, et al., 1999; Barnett, Pepiton, et al., 1999).

Professional practices portfolios. All school psychology students build portfolios consisting of descriptions of their training experiences that reflect program themes—for example, the scientist-practitioner model, leadership, child and family advocacy, and others. The descriptions include documentation of their performance in carrying out the competency area. Students build early intervention sections of the portfolios at entry or advanced levels by displaying the outcomes of consultations, parent groups, and staff development experiences. Consultations are organized into entries consisting of individual case data such as technical adequacy of key measured variables, scripts, intervention adherence data, graphs of outcomes, and social validity data. The portfolio entries also include outcomes associated with other service delivery functions such as parent groups and staff development. Portfolios serve essential functions in assessing, monitoring, and demonstrating school psychology student progress and performance with regard to early intervention as well as other training objectives. They also are used for comprehensive examinations to satisfy university requirements. In addition, students use their portfolios for interviews to obtain internships and professional positions. Portfolios are analyzed by faculty for each student cohort with regard to evidence of performance across program themes.

PREPARATION FOR EARLY INTERVENTION PROFESSIONAL ROLES

In this section we review themes and key content areas for training early intervention professionals. Topics have been selected for entry-level and advanced preparation based on likely agency referrals in early intervention settings, generalizations from research, and discussions of personnel preparation for early childhood settings (e.g., Hemmeter, 2000; McConnell, 2000; Winton, 2000).

Problem Solving and Team Building

A major objective in school psychology training is accomplished by practice in problem solving and teaming (Gutkin & Curtis, 1999). Students apply a collaborative problem-solving process to parents' and teachers' referrals in a general sequence: (a) problem identification, (b) problem analysis, (c) plan development and implementation, and (d) evaluation (e.g., Allen & Graden, 1995). Although complicated, perhaps the most important premise of problem solving and collaboration as a foundation of intervention-based service delivery is that interventions are "built" from the "raw materials" of environments controlled or influenced by adults other than school psychologists. Problem solving and collaboration with key adults in children's lives are well-established means to help promote environmental changes to benefit children (Gutkin & Curtis, 1999; Wolery, 1994a, 1994b).

Another major training objective is accomplished by considering the roles of specialized disciplines and community agencies. Students are guided through the development of an appropriate team for children's referrals that will collaboratively address the problem situation. Students consider the multiple systems—such as family, school, day care, church, and community—that are part of a child's life and also hold potential resources for intervention. Students and their supervisors agree on procedures for contacting caregivers and other potential team members, and review actions they might take for establishing and maintaining rapport. A plan also is developed for making the consultation process explicit to team members, describing roles related to participation, and explaining necessary legal requirements such as informed consent and confidentiality. This is the beginning of a collaborative plan for communication, which is revisited as necessary. Although team composition is idiosyncratic and based on need established through problem solving, it is typically composed of the child's parents and teachers, as well as school psychology students and doctoral supervisor, other agency personnel, and, often, specialized service providers.

Parent Groups

A major training objective strongly related to early intervention is accomplished by having students practice diverse ways to establish partnerships with parents (Christenson & Buerkle, 1999; Winton, 2000). In addition to problem solving with individual parents and teachers for child referrals, all students participate in the design and facilitation of parent groups at a local Head Start. One purpose of these groups has been to provide a supportive atmosphere to discuss effective parenting techniques. Consistent with our service delivery model and research, parents choose the topics; they are taught the problem-solving model; and topics, mostly related to child behavior, are organized by planned activities to help promote problem solving (Sanders & Dadds, 1993). A second parent group has been developed to promote early literacy skills (Neuman et al., 1999). Students help with planning activities, recruiting parents, advertising the group meetings, establishing positive contingencies for participation, and arranging for other logistics such as child care.

Students are helped by Head Start personnel and doctoral supervisors with group planning and processing skills. They consider group structure and composition, environmental arrangement, and the use of supplementary materials. Training in using effective listening techniques and facilitating active participation by group members are areas that often require modeling in addition to prompts and feedback. Other critical points of conducting parent groups involve establishing an atmosphere that conveys acceptance among participants and facilitators, dealing with challenging questions and comments, applying principles of learning to skill-focused group sessions, and being responsive to individual participant needs. The last point includes making referrals to community agencies, providing additional resources, or following up on individual concerns.

Effective Classrooms and Classwide Interventions

Considering research for classroom change variables provides important opportunities for expanding students' experiences as well as intervention plans (Gettinger & Stoiber, 1999; Martens & Kelly, 1993; McEvoy, Fox, & Rosenberg, 1991; Nordquist & Twardosz, 1990; Paine, Radicchi, Rosellini, Deutchman, & Darch, 1983). As examples, ways in which effective teachers manage their classrooms include the following: (a) creating engaging activities; (b) arranging the physical environment to help avoid disruptions, developing predictable schedules, and planning transitions; (c) establishing clear rules as positive guides to actions and self-regulated behaviors (or limits; see Bredekamp & Copple, 1997, p. 19); and (d) effectively scanning groups and attending to appropriate behaviors. Other potential key variables for intervention-based training include the use of effective requests (Atwater & Morris, 1988); group contingency programs; peer-mediated interventions (e.g., English, Shafer, Goldstein, & Kaczmarek, 1997); the pacing, difficulty, and format of learning activities (e.g., McKee & Witt, 1990); and the language and listening environment (e.g., Kaiser & Hester, 1996).

Another key area for students to have experience with is classwide interventions. Classrooms often have several children with challenging behaviors. Through the development of effective classwide interventions, students learn to become more effective in meeting service delivery needs (e.g., Gutkin & Curtis, 1999). Fewer individualized interventions may be needed—and the capacity of classrooms to support individual children with challenging behaviors should increase (Koegel et al., 1996). *Classwide interventions* refer to modifications of social or physical environments to target educationally related variables that affect the entire class or a subgroup of children (Siemoens, 2001). Classwide interventions frequently include various combinations of planned changes in activities and routines; teachers' monitoring activities; specific responses to children such as attention, consequences, or requests for assistance; and additional support. Variables targeted for change usually include increasing active engagement or reducing disruptive behaviors. Classwide interventions also can be an integral component of a plan for an individual child. Closely related, interventions to help with challenging educational goals may be embedded in ongoing classroom routines and activities (Hemmeter, 2000). Examples of embedded interventions for individuals or groups of children may include creating more opportunities to practice language or social skills or modifying entry and transition routines.

Staff Development

Planning and carrying out staff development programs helps meet our School Psychology Program's training objectives in leadership and system change. It also provides ways of improving classroom effectiveness beyond individual consultations. Within the context of effective classrooms and classwide interventions, advanced doctoral students use an observation-based ecobehavioral checklist with pertinent domains, such as qualities of activity centers, classroom management, language/listening environment, and others, in each classroom (Storer, 1997). Teachers self-rate on a similar checklist (Stollar, 1994). Following class observations and consultation sessions with teachers to prioritize classroom goals, a needs assessment also is carried out by students to help identify objectives for agencywide staff development. With the database that includes advanced doctoral student observations and teacher self-ratings, students work in collaboration with each other in small groups and with agency personnel on the selection, presentation, and facilitation of staff development activities for teachers (e.g., Sexton, Snyder, Wolfe, Lobman, Stricklin, & Akers, 1996). Generally the process begins by helping students consider high-impact topics based on commonalities among teachers' concerns. Through planning meetings, student teams facilitate problem solving related to (a) completing literature reviews for instructional, management, or related topics; (b) creating a presentation format for making the session interactive; (c) determining how to structure opportunities for practice and application/generalization of skills; and (d) planning for evaluation. Feedback sessions between the students and supervisors are held after staff development programs.

High–Incidence Intervention Preparation

Students need to be well prepared for the most likely questions raised by parents and teachers in field settings. "High incidence" refers to the relatively high base rates for referral questions and intervention plans that students are expected to address in problem solving. Based on a review of early intervention research (Barnett, Bell, & Carey, 1999), interventions for language and early literacy, and for disruptive behaviors, are of significant importance in preparing professionals for entry-level positions in many early intervention settings.

Interventions for language and literacy. To adequately prepare for future roles, school psychology students should have substantial experiences in academic interventions. Significant foundations for later academic success are language and emergent literacy skills (Adams, 1990; National Research Council, 1998). Moreover, students' field experiences with language and literacy skills can help meet dual training objectives since they may include individual child, teacher, and parent consultations, and also contribute to students' preparation for leadership roles through efforts to improve literacy skills programmatically (Neuman et al., 1999). Longitudinal research has shown that language differences emerge early, many children who begin first grade with lower language and early literacy/prereading skills continue struggling to "catch up" with their peers, and children from lower socioeconomic classes often begin school with lower preacademic skills than their middle and upper class peers (i.e., Hart & Risley, 1995; Juel, 1988). Without effective early intervention programs, these initial skill gaps widen dramatically (Greenwood, Hart, Walker, & Risley, 1994).

Students are expected to be able to help plan and implement *milieu language interventions*. Milieu language intervention refers to several naturalistic and research-based teaching strategies (Hart, 1985; Wolery, 1994a). Common examples include incidental teaching (e.g., Warren, 1992), mand modeling, naturalistic time-delay (e.g., Halle, Marshall, & Spradlin, 1979), and missing-item format (e.g., Tirapelle & Cipani, 1992). These interventions embed teaching opportunities within typical classroom/home activities. In incidental learning, the environment is structured so that it encourages the child to seek adult interactions. The child picks the teaching moment by initiating an interaction with an adult. Once initiated, the adult uses this time to request the child to use more elaborate language and to model the use of language. The components of strong intervention design—including providing frequent opportunities to practice, modeling and prompting performances, correcting errors, and providing positive feedback—are incorporated into brief teaching sessions. Successfully targeted children's performances have shown an increase in the number of words used, specific types of words or labels (e.g., polite, descriptive), compound sentences, novel words, and words to make a request.

Students also learn and practice basic interventions for improving early literacy skills. Research on young prereaders indicates the importance of skills that include (a) understanding the function of printed material such as "letters make up words," "print is different from pictures," "words tell us stories and information," and "we read from left to right"; (b) building "phonemic awareness" skills such as rhyming, isolating beginning, ending, and middle sounds, segmenting, and blending sounds through oral activities; and (c) learning letter recognition and letter-sound correspondence (Adams, 1990; Carnine, Silbert, & Kame'enui, 1997; National Research Council, 1998). These skills can be taught through incidental teaching described earlier as well as individual and small group direct instruction activities and practice (National Research Council, 1998). The amount of reading opportunities, materials slightly above the child's linguistic level, and the active engagement of the child revealed by asking/answering questions have a significant impact on later vocabulary and reading achievement (Adams, 1990). One of the most important activities that parents and teachers can engage in to help young children become strong readers is to read aloud to them interactively (e.g., Dale, Crain-Thoreson, Notari-Syverson, & Cole, 1986).

Professional competencies in early intervention also must address situations in which children require more explicit and directed teaching opportunities for language and literacy or preacademic skills. In identifying specific target skills for intervention, it is important to consider children's skill performance within their natural environment while engaged in tasks that they are expected to perform in their preschool curriculum. This analysis can be done through the use of direct measures of language and preacademic skills via observation and the basics of Curriculum-Based Measurement (CBM; Shinn, 1998).

Once intervention targets are identified, an examination of why the problem situation is occurring should be conducted. During *problem analysis,* the child's behavior/skills and their environmental determinants are considered. The focus is on examining how the environment might support learning—as opposed to looking for within-child deficits. Specific intervention components to consider in order to design strong language and preliteracy/preacademic interventions include (a) creating literacy-rich environments that promote natural skill development; (b) ensuring frequent opportunities to respond and practice using the skill targeted for intervention (e.g., Wolery, Anthony, & Heckathorn, 1998); (c) providing positive contingencies for accurate performance; (d) delivering immediate feedback regarding performance/progress; (e) using effective instruction principles during teaching sessions such as appropriate pace, modeling and/or prompting of correct responding, and plans for the eventual fading of these components; (f) applying the "instructional hierarchy" by focusing, in order, on accuracy, fluency, generalization, and application/adaptation; (g) monitoring the intervention as carried out; and (h) using direct assessment procedures for student progress such as direct observation and CBM (Haring & Eaton, 1978; Lentz et al., 1996).

Interventions for disruptive and dangerous behaviors. Our referrals have often been dominated by parents' and teachers' concerns about disruptive and dangerous behaviors. Therefore this is definitely a high-impact area of professional preparation for early intervention (Walker, Colvin, & Ramsey, 1995). Critical components of training include many of the steps already outlined such as building an appropriate team and evaluating family and health-related concerns that could impact the behavior.

Students are expected to articulate a data-based hypothesis about the function of a disruptive behavior and evaluate the hypothesis, ending with intervention plans that are subsequently refined, carried out, and evaluated. Students help determine whether the child's challenging behavior stems from (a) a need to teach or build skills, such as how to enter a play group or ask for help (e.g., Carr & Durand, 1985), or (b) a performance deficit whereby the child has the necessary skills, and a closer analysis of antecedents and contingencies is used to promote the demonstration of more appropriate behavior. Based on data from a descriptive antecedent-behavior-consequence (ABC) or experimental functional analysis (e.g., Umbreit, 1995), students then are required to examine environmental variables that could be restructured to prevent the disruptive behaviors.

The training objective of having students skilled in guiding teams toward the concept of "least intrusive and effective intervention plan" benefits from a relatively new literature and thus is "less traveled." Components of strong interventions for disruptive behaviors may include (a) sequential and hierarchical plans whereby the easiest, most natural, and promising interventions are tried first and they become progressively more intensive as necessary (e.g., Harding et al., 1994); (b) the analysis of appropriate replacement behaviors for the disruptive behavior; (c) a plan for teaching and prompting the replacement behavior; (d) the development of increased opportunities for the child to practice new responses; (e) choices for events and positive contingencies for desirable behaviors (Peck et al., 1996); and (f) planned responses for inappropriate behaviors. From the data collected in a functional assessment, information would be used to establish positive intervention components and antecedent control to the extent possible (e.g., Luiselli & Cameron, 1998). As examples, students' intervention plans for disruptive behaviors have often included functional communication training (Carr & Durand, 1985), "timed positives" known as fixed interval schedules or noncontingent reinforcement (Tucker, Sigafoos, & Bushell, 1998), and high-probability request sequences or the structuring of adult requests into a sequence that the child is likely to follow (Davis & Reichle, 1996). The "least intrusive intervention plan" also includes sound plans for fading effective interventions that involve the transfer of behavioral control from the intervention to the natural setting (i.e., Lentz et al., 1996).

Another significant skill in preparing school psychologists for intervention roles is the ability to evaluate plans when interventions appear ineffective. This type of situation presents opportunities for students to develop strategies for working with team members who do not carry through with previously agreed upon plans in order to look more closely at barriers to intervention adherence. These barriers are approached through teaming and problem solving. Steps may include (a) consulting further on the feasibility of plans, such as ensuring the adequacy of teacher and parent support or finding ways to make plans more acceptable without losing effectiveness; (b) adding practice steps to promote fluency with the intervention; (c) noting the influence of interfering classroom or outside events on the team member attempting to carry out intervention scripts; and (d) recycling back through the problem-solving process, checking hypotheses, and possibly redoing a functional analysis to examine the validity of the intervention plan.

Students learn how to identify a wide range of possible influences on young children's behaviors. A *setting event search* is used to examine challenging behaviors when the analysis of "close" antecedents and consequences, described above, proves to be inconclusive, ineffective, or impossible. Setting events are specific but indirect antecedent events related to the likelihood of occurrence of a challenging behavior (e.g., Wahler & Fox, 1981). Examples common in our preschool experiences have been health factors such as hunger, hearing, or medication that may be related to a wide range of challenging classroom behaviors. Other examples include the presence or absence of a specific person, such as a teacher or child, special classroom circumstances, or home situations that may include abuse. A setting event search may be carried out by using the PASSKey model.

In rare instances, dangerous behaviors may continue despite reanalysis of plans and a setting event search. In such situations, students learn how to construct a crisis management and safety plan. Such plans may include expanding the mental health team, intensifying agency and professional supervision, and adding support such as more planning time and trained personnel. Likely steps include much of the above, emphasizing positive classroom routines and teaching opportunities for children, and *adding* other steps and safeguards for more intensive interventions and dangerous behaviors (Lohrmann-O'Rourke & Zirkel, 1998).

Cross-Cultural Practice

An essential component of a student's early intervention training involves the development of *cross-cultural competency*—the awareness, knowledge, and skills required to work effectively with students and families from cultural backgrounds that differ from one's own (e.g., Harry, Reuda & Kalyanpur, 1999; Lynch & Hanson, 1998). The development of cross-cultural competency includes many issues. We highlight several related to preparing students for early intervention roles.

Students' training in cross-cultural intervention is built on competencies in problem solving, teaming, and naturalistic intervention design described earlier. Two potential challenges stand out with regard to the complexities of cross-cultural competency in designing interventions. These are *developing partnerships* with parents and *ensuring the acceptability* of problem solving and intervention plans. A concept that can help guide intervention training is *ethnic validity,* the degree to which problem identification and problem solving are acceptable to parents in respect of the parents' and child's ethnic/cultural group (Barnett et al., 1995). There are many examples of strategies that students may consider to help anchor the problem-solving process to the cultural community of the child. They include having students help identify a "cultural mediator" or "guide" (Lynch & Hanson, 1998, p. 500) for (a) understanding parent preferences for involvement, (b) considering culturally specific information that may influence problem solving, and (c) having language representation on the problem-solving team. Students may conduct observations of teacher and peer interactions as well as children's engagement to help clarify the appropriateness of the instructional and social environments for children of different cultures (e.g., Arreaga-Mayer & Perdomo-Rivera, 1996). Another example that meets training objectives in leadership as well as cross-cultural practice is having students consult with teachers and staff members programmatically about supporting children and families of different cultures (U.S. Department of Health and Human Services, 1996). Steps may include assisting teachers in learning key words in children's home languages, adding culturally diverse classroom materials and books, and planning agency and classroom cultural activities.

Services for Infants and Toddlers

A major early intervention theme is that *earlier* intervention is better for many educational risk conditions (Guralnick, 1997; Hart & Risley, 1995). Infants and toddlers have not often been served by school psychologists. However, such services can be a valuable training experience and opportunities for school psychology roles are likely to increase. Training includes intervention skills discussed earlier, such as teaming, problem solving, and naturalistic intervention design. We highlight some shifts in emphasis that occur in training.

For infants and toddlers, training efforts usually are focused on the family in the context of the family's daily functioning and teaming with community agencies. Students prepare for relatively common referral concerns including communication, troublesome sleep patterns, feeding, and difficulties with behaviors such as persistent crying; elimination problems; aggressive behaviors toward themselves and others; stereotypic behaviors such as rocking or hand-flapping; and compliance with therapeutic exercises (e.g., Florian, 1995; Zeanah, Larrieu, & Zeanah, 2000). Often families receive support services from multiple agencies such as local hospitals or physicians, private therapists, community-based child care agencies, churches, children's protective services, and social security agencies.

There are several factors complicating students' roles. Parents may be faced with *first-time* challenges of a child requiring health-related and social services. Also, in comparison to preschool services, there may be considerable variability in the frequency of contact with children and families typically participating in services to infants and toddlers, since families are usually given the opportunity to define the amount of time spent in the agency or other aspects of services depending on their needs. Services often require frequent home visits or visits with the family to other agencies requiring nontraditional, more flexible contacts. Another training challenge is the issue of maintaining appropriate professional relationships despite the more intimate nature of providing support to the whole family during emotionally pivotal moments in family members' lives.

Intervention-Based Preparation in Eligibility Determination

One of most controversial training roles is "testing" for special services eligibility for infants and young children (Public Law [PL] 105-17) (e.g., Neisworth & Bagnato, 1992; Shepard, Kagan, & Wurtz, 1998). This is one of the reasons for our training emphasis on intervention-based preparation.

Intervention-based training emphasizes the collaborative problem-solving approach described earlier in order to derive a sound *ecological* context for analyzing developmental delays and making eligibility decisions (Barnett, Bell, Gilkey, et al., 1999). Methods for eligibility determination may be operationalized by applying appropriate measurement tactics that focus on "child *and* environment" and examining differences in the instructional, environmental, or related classroom strategies that are required to meet children's needs (Hardman, McDonnell, & Welch, 1997). As an example, a successful intervention for a child may be based on a teacher significantly modifying classroom routines and embedding individualized interventions throughout the day. Through appropriate measurement tactics and procedures, discussed next, a team may use this information to help determine eligibility for special services (PL 105-17) as a source of appropriate and specific support for the child and teacher.

Based on a review of intervention research, the following measurement tactics were identified that serve as important targets for student preparation in observation skills when questions are raised about eligibility determination: (a) teacher monitoring, or the amount of time required in close proximity or supervision, and quality of interaction; (b) activity engagement, or children's participation in classroom activities; (c) levels of assistance, or prompting strategies facilitating learning and adapting to routines; (d) trials to criterion, or rate of learning measured by learning trials and practice time; (e) behavioral fluency, or children's accuracy and rate of specific skills; (f) modifying classroom activities, or activities and instruction that involve unique or more complex interventions; and (g) curricular adaptations, or domains, skill sequences, and instructional techniques that need to be modified (Barnett, Bell, et al., 1999).

Eligibility decision making for young children is based both on (a) a discrepancy between *educational performance* in a critical or significant curriculum area of the referred child in comparison to expectancies for the performance of typical peers (Bell & Barnett, 1999), *and* (b) a *desired change* in performance that is resistant to planned intervention efforts that are naturally sustainable within the educational service unit. At least three patterns or combinations of patterns derived from direct measurement of "intensity of the need for special support" are used for making decisions (Hardman et al., 1997, p. 64):

1. An intervention may be successful but requires extraordinary effort to be sustained.

2. An intervention may need to be in place extensively or throughout the school day for appropriate inclusion.

3. Interventions carried out by a teacher may be unsuccessful, requiring replanning and special resources to be added to a situation.

The performance discrepancy and intervention data are used to clarify the special education services or supports needed for a child in the present environment or to establish needed environmental modifications to do so. One advantage of a functional approach to eligibility determination is that the outcomes are immediately useful for determining positive behavioral support and needed specialized services in natural environments or regular classrooms entitled through federal law (PL 105-17). For young children, this information is then readily linked to the individual plans—the Individualized Family Services Plan (IFSP) for infants and toddlers and the Individualized Education Program (IEP) for older children.

Transition Planning

Another important early intervention training objective is having students assist teams with transition plans for children who have received consultation services. *Transitions* refer to children entering early intervention settings or moving to the next settings (e.g., Rous, Hemmeter, & Schuster, 1994). Our students help children and parents transition from Head Start to kindergartens in local schools. Depending on parent preferences, strategies may include visiting schools with parents and meeting with teachers and administrators. Students help parents with understanding legal rights and determining whether intervention scripts might be useful in subsequent settings.

FIELD SETTINGS AND SUPERVISION FOR INTERVENTION-BASED TRAINING

At the center of early intervention preparation is an *integrative* field experience with an emphasis on designing and evaluating empirically based interventions in natural settings (Stoner & Green, 1992). We review the structure of field experiences and supervision in this section. As an overview, training experiences are built into the entry level and advanced levels of the program. They occur over a full academic year, allowing for a minimum of two academic years of preparation for advanced levels. The experiences include parent and teacher referrals for child-related concerns, parent groups, and staff development.

Instructor's Role in Preparing for Practicum

Early intervention training for school psychologists requires three components: (a) finding a setting with young children, and parents and teachers perplexed by challenging behaviors; (b) clarifying the service delivery model in terms of professional steps; and (c) providing appropriate instruction and feedback for students to carry out the services. For second-year students, skill sequencing builds on applied courses during the first year that include Legal and Ethical Issues, Applied Behavior Analysis, Assessment and Intervention for Early Childhood, as well as other basic courses (see Barnett, Daly, et al., 1999). In addition, the practicum is designed to integrate concurrent course work in Consultation, Family Interventions, Functional Assessment, and Behavioral Research and Accountability Methods.

Following a general problem-solving model and intervention-based service delivery, the instructor identifies the knowledge and skills students need that are specific to the field setting where the practicum will occur. This process is simplified at the University of Cincinnati by having students placed in a local Head Start. Common referral questions have included language-related concerns and literacy or preacademic skill attainment and aggressive/disruptive behaviors. The skills required to assist with less common referrals, such as those that are medically related, are addressed as they arise, but the same model still is applied.

Year-Long Practicum and Advanced Internship Sequences

The entry-level practicum combines early intervention with school-age experiences. It occurs during the second year of full-time study before the internship year and is carried out for 3 quarters for a total of 14 quarter hours or about 400 hours of total supervised experiences. Approximately 30% of the experiences occur in an early intervention setting. A typical pattern for early intervention practicum students includes two intensive referrals from parents or teachers with responsibilities that may continue for the academic year, two parent groups, and two staff development programs. Weekly supervision classes for early intervention practicum students are held at the Head Start center.

Advanced doctoral students have completed a 1,500-hour internship and are credentialed school psychologists in their fourth year of training. Capitalizing on the same field placements, advanced doctoral students acquire supervisory skills and advanced internship hours that can be applied to an early intervention or other intervention-related specialization. A typical pattern for advanced students includes 500 hours of advanced internship and 9 quarter hours of credit in supervision for the academic year. Advanced students may split placements with other field settings.

Peer and Hierarchical Supervision

Behavioral principles are applied to supervising students who are assigned to child-related consultations (Kratochwill, Bergan, & Mace, 1981). As a part of the training experience, supervision comes in two approaches, *peer supervision* and *hierarchical supervision*. In the former, second-year practicum students work in teams of two, sharing responsibilities in meeting service delivery objectives and providing each other with peer supervision and support. Teaming also helps maintain the continuity of effort required by intervention-based service delivery by facilitating more frequent checks on children's progress. In hierarchical supervision, advanced students work closely with the practicum students on their cases and provide direct supervision of activities. Both practicum and advanced students are supervised at the university level in ongoing meetings with a professor.

To aid supervision, and to provide training in professional judgment and "case notes," practicum students submit their analysis of key events following methods of retrospective protocol analysis (Barnett, 1988; Ericsson & Simon, 1996). Organized chronologically, and with headings describing key events such as "Parent interview," "Class observation," "Intervention script development," or "Supervisory session," students record their thoughts, actions, and next steps. Entries are succinct, objective, descriptive; focus on problem solving; and are written in a manner that would not offend others who may have reason to read them. Typically, they are read only by the instructor, who provides written feedback.

CONCLUSIONS

One of the most exciting areas of professional preparation is enabling school psychology students to learn and practice skills that may help fulfill the promise of early intervention programs. Our training context is an intervention-based service delivery system guided by strong accountability methods for evaluating outcomes consistent with calls for reform. We reviewed a subset of key early intervention themes and content associated with successful outcomes based on the likelihood of referrals and empirical support for practices. Evidence for successful preparation is accumulated in students' professional practice portfolios, which include data-based entries for critical practice areas.

Student preparation involves consulting with parents and teachers under appropriate supervision to practice key professional skills, as well as helping to develop, try out, and evaluate intervention plans in field settings. Early intervention roles also include diverse ways of providing parent and staff support. Effective instruction and supervision are characterized by preparing students for field placements; communicating expectations, roles, and procedures; guiding practice; providing feedback and support; and evaluating outcomes.

REFERENCES

Adams, M. J. (1990). *Beginning to read: Thinking and learning about print.* Cambridge, MA: MIT Press.

Allen, S. J., & Graden, J. L. (1995). Best practices in collaborative problem solving for intervention design. In A. Thomas & J. Grimes (Eds.), *Best Practices in School Psychology III* (pp. 667-678). Washington, DC: National Association of School Psychologists.

American Psychological Association. (1996). *Guidelines and principles for accreditation of programs in professional psychology.* Washington, DC: Author.

Arreaga-Mayer, C., & Perdomo-Rivera, C. (1996). Ecobehavioral analysis of instruction for at-risk language minority students. *The Elementary School Journal, 96,* 245-258.

Atwater, J. B., & Morris, E. K. (1988). Teachers' instructions and children's compliance in preschool classrooms: A descriptive analysis. *Journal of Applied Behavior Analysis, 21,* 157-167.

Baer, D. M., Wolf, M. M., & Risley, T. R. (1968). Some current dimensions of applied behavior analysis. *Journal of Applied Behavior Analysis, 1,* 91-97.

Barlow, D. H., Hayes, S. C., & Nelson, R. O. (1984). *The scientist-practitioner: Research and accountability in clinical and educational settings.* New York: Pergamon Press.

Barnett, D. W. (1988). Professional judgment: A critical appraisal. *School Psychology Review, 17,* 656-670.

Barnett, D. W., Bell, S. H., Bauer, A., Lentz, F. E., Jr., Petrelli, S., Air, A., Hannum, L., Ehrhardt, K. E., Peters, C. A., Barnhouse, L., Reifen, L. H., & Stollar, S. (1997). The Early Childhood Intervention Project: Building capacity for service delivery. *School Psychology Quarterly, 12,* 293-315.

Barnett, D. W., Bell, S. H., & Carey, K. T. (1999). *Designing preschool interventions: A practitioner's guide.* New York: Guilford Press.

Barnett, D. W., Bell, S. H., Gilkey, C. M., Lentz, F. E., Jr., Graden, J. L., Stone, C. M., Smith, J. J., & Macmann, G. M. (1999). The promise of meaningful eligibility determination: Functional intervention-based multifactored preschool evaluation. *The Journal of Special Education, 33,* 112-124.

Barnett, D. W., Collins, R., Coulter, C., Curtis, M. J., Ehrhardt, K., Glaser, A., Reyes, C., Stollar, S., & Winston, M. (1995). Ethnic validity and school psychology: Concepts and practices associated with cross-cultural professional competence. *Journal of School Psychology, 33,* 219-233.

Barnett, D. W., Daly, E. J., III, Hampshire, E. M., Hines, N. R., Maples, K. A., Ostrom, J. K., & Van Buren, A. E. (1999). Meeting performance-based training demands: Accountability in an intervention-based practicum. *School Psychology Quarterly, 14,* 357-379.

Barnett, D. W., Lentz, F. E., Jr., Bauer, A. M., Macmann, G., Stollar, S., & Ehrhardt, K. (1997). Ecological foundations of early intervention: Planned activities and strategic sampling. *The Journal of Special Education, 30,* 471-490.

Barnett, D. W., Lentz, F. E., Jr., & Macmann, G. (2000). Psychometric qualities of professional practice. In E. S. Shapiro & T. R. Kratochwill (Eds.), *Behavioral assessment in schools* (2nd ed., pp. 355–386). New York: Guilford Press.

Barnett, D. W., Pepiton, A. E., Bell, S. H., Gilkey, C. M., Smith, J. J., Stone, C. M., Nelson, K. I., Maples, K. A., Helenbrook, K., & Vogel, L. H. (1999). Evaluating early intervention: Accountability methods for service delivery innovations. *The Journal of Special Education, 33,* 117–188.

Bell, S. H., & Barnett, D. W. (1999). Peer micronorms in the assessment of young children: Methodological review and examples. *Topics in Early Childhood Special Education, 19,* 112–122.

Bredekamp, S., & Copple, C. (Eds.). (1997). *Developmentally appropriate practice in early childhood programs* (rev. ed.). Washington, DC: National Association for the Education of Young Children.

Carnine, D. W., Silbert, J., & Kame'enui, E. J. (1997). *Direct instruction reading* (3rd ed.). Upper Saddle River, NJ: Prentice-Hall.

Carr, E. G., & Durand, V. M. (1985). Reducing behavior problems through functional communication training. *Journal of Applied Behavior Analysis, 18,* 111–126.

Carta, J. (1995). Developmentally appropriate practice: A critical analysis as applied to young children with disabilities. *Focus on Exceptional Children, 27*(8), 1–14.

Christenson, S. L., & Buerkle, K. (1999). Families as educational partners for children's school success: Suggestions for school psychologists. In C. R. Reynolds & T. B. Gutkin (Eds.), *The handbook of school psychology* (3rd ed., pp. 709–744). New York: Wiley.

Dale, P. S., Crain-Thoreson, C., Notari-Syverson, A., & Cole, K. (1986). Parent-child book reading as an intervention technique for young children with language delays. *Topics in Early Childhood Special Education, 16,* 213–235.

Daly, E. J., III, Martens, B. K., Hamler, K. R., Dool, E. J., & Eckert, T. L. (1999). A brief experimental analysis for identifying instructional components needed to improve oral reading fluency. *Journal of Applied Behavior Analysis, 32,* 83–94.

Davis, C. A., & Reichle, J. (1996). Variant and invariant high-probability requests: Increasing appropriate behaviors in children with emotional-behavior disorders. *Journal of Applied Behavior Analysis, 29,* 471–482.

Ehrhardt, K. E., Barnett, D. W., Lentz, F. E., Jr., Stollar, S. E., & Reifen, L. (1996). Innovative methodology in ecological consultation: Use of scripts to promote treatment acceptability and integrity. *School Psychology Quarterly, 11,* 149–168.

English, K., Shafer, K., Goldstein, H., & Kaczmarek, L. (1997). *Teaching buddy skills to preschoolers.* Washington, DC: American Association on Mental Retardation.

Ericsson, K. A. & Simon, H. A. (1996). *Protocol analysis: Verbal reports as data* (rev. ed.). Cambridge, MA: MIT Press.

Florian, L. (1995). Part H early intervention program: Legislative history and intent of the law. *Topics in Early Childhood Special Education, 15,* 247–262.

Flugum, K. R., & Reschly, D. J. (1994). Prereferral interventions: Quality indices and outcomes. *Journal of School Psychology, 32,* 1–14.

Gettinger, M., & Stoiber, K. C. (1999). Excellence in teaching: Review of instructional and environmental variables. In C. R. Reynolds & T. B. Gutkin (Eds.), *The handbook of school psychology* (3rd ed., pp. 933-958). New York: Wiley.

Greenwood, C. R., Hart, B., Walker, D., & Risley, T. (1994). The opportunity to respond and academic performance revisited: A behavioral theory of developmental retardation and its prevention. In R. Gardner, III, D. M. Sainato, J. O. Cooper, T. E. Heron, W. L. Heward, J. W. Eshleman, & T. A. Grossi (Eds.), *Behavioral analysis in education: Focus on measurably superior instruction* (pp. 213-224). Pacific Grove, CA: Brooks/Cole.

Gresham, F. M. (1996). Treatment integrity in single subject research. In R. D. Franklin, D. B. Allison, & B. S. Gorman (Eds.), *Design and analysis of single-case research* (pp. 93-117). Mahwah, NJ: Erlbaum.

Guralnick, M. J. (1997). Second-generation research in the field of early intervention. In M. J. Guralnick (Ed.), *The effectiveness of early intervention* (pp. 3-20). Baltimore: Brookes.

Gutkin, T. B., & Curtis, M. J. (1999). School-based consultation theory and practice: The art and science of indirect service delivery. In C. R. Reynolds & T. B. Gutkin (Eds.), *The handbook of school psychology* (3rd ed., pp. 598-637). New York: Wiley.

Halle, J. W., Marshall, A. M., & Spradlin, J. E. (1979). Time delay: A technique to increase language use and facilitate generalization in retarded children. *Journal of Applied Behavior Analysis, 12,* 431-439.

Harding, J., Wacker, D. P., Cooper, L. J., Millard, T., & Jensen-Kovalan, P. (1994). Brief hierarchical assessment of potential treatment components with children in an outpatient clinic. *Journal of Applied Behavior Analysis, 27,* 291-300.

Hardman, M. L., McDonnell, J., & Welch, M. (1997). Perspectives on the future of IDEA. *Journal of the Association for Persons with Severe Handicaps, 22,* 61-77.

Haring, N. G., & Eaton, M. D. (1978). Systematic instructional procedures: An instructional hierarchy. In N. G. Haring, T. C. Lovitt, M. D. Eaton, & C. L. Hansen (Eds.). *The fourth R: Research in the classroom* (pp. 23-40). Columbus, OH: Merrill.

Harry, B., Reuda, R., & Kalyanpur, M. (1999). Cultural reciprocity in sociocultural perspective: Adapting the normalization principle for family collaboration. *Exceptional Children, 66,* 123-136.

Hart, B. (1985). Naturalistic language training techniques. In S. F. Warren & A. K. Rogers-Warren (Eds.), *Teaching functional language* (pp. 63-88). Baltimore: University Park.

Hart, B., & Risley, T. R. (1995). *Meaningful differences in the everyday experiences of young American children.* Baltimore: Brookes.

Hemmeter, M. L. (2000). Classroom-based interventions: Evaluating the past and looking toward the future. *Topics in Early Childhood Special Education, 20,* 56-61.

Juel, C. (1988). Learning to read and write: A longitudinal study of 54 children from first through fourth grades. *Journal of Educational Psychology, 80,* 306-327.

Kaiser, A. P., & Hester, P. P. (1996). How everyday environments support children's communication. In L. K. Koegel, R. L. Koegel, & G. Dunlap (Eds.). *Positive behavioral support: Including people with difficult behavior in the community* (pp. 145-162). Baltimore: Brookes.

Karoly, L. A., Greenwood, P. W., Everingham, S. S., Hoube, J., Kilburn, M. R., Rydell, C. P., Sanders, M., & Chisea, J. (1998). *Investing in our children: What we know and don't know about the costs and benefits of early childhood interventions.* Santa Monica, CA: Rand.

Koegel, L. K., Koegel, R. L., & Dunlap, G. (Eds.). (1996). *Positive behavioral support: Including people with difficult behavior in the community.* Baltimore: Brookes.

Kratochwill, T. R., Bergan, J. R., & Mace, F. C. (1981). Practitioner competencies needed for implementation of behavioral psychology in the schools: Issues in supervision. *School Psychology Review, 10,* 433-444.

Kratochwill, T. R., & Stoiber, K. C. (2000). Empirically supported interventions and school psychology: Conceptual and practice issues: Part II. *School Psychology Quarterly, 15,* 233-253.

Lentz, F. E., Jr. (1988). On-task behavior, academic performance, and classroom disruptions: Untangling the target selection problem in classroom interventions. *School Psychology Review, 17,* 243-257.

Lentz, F. E., Jr., Allen, S. J., & Ehrhardt, K. E. (1996). The conceptual elements of strong interventions in school settings. *School Psychology Quarterly, 11,* 118-136.

Lohrmann-O'Rourke, S., & Zirkel, P. (1998). The case law on aversive interventions for students with disabilities. *Exceptional Children, 65,* 101-123.

Luiselli, J. K. & Cameron, M. J. (Eds.). (1998). *Antecedent control.* Baltimore: Brookes.

Lynch, E. W., & Hanson, M. J. (1998). *Developing crosscultural competency: A guide for working with children and their families* (2nd ed.). Baltimore: Brookes.

Macmann, G. M., Barnett, D. W., Allen, S. J., Bramlett, R. K., Hall, J. D., & Ehrhardt, K. E. (1996). Problem solving and intervention design: Guidelines for the evaluation of technical adequacy. *School Psychology Quarterly, 11,* 137-148.

Martens, B. K., Eckert, T. L., Bradley, T. A., & Ardoin, S. P. (1999). Identifying effective treatments from a brief experimental analysis: Using single-case design elements to aid decision making. *School Psychology Quarterly, 14,* 163-181.

Martens, B. K., & Kelly, S. Q. (1993). A behavioral analysis of effective teaching. *School Psychology Quarterly, 8,* 10-26.

McConnell, S. R. (2000). Assessment in early intervention and early childhood special education: Building on our past to project into our future. *Topics in Early Childhood Special Education, 20,* 43-48.

McEvoy, M. A., Fox, J. J., & Rosenberg, M. S. (1991). Organizing preschool environments: Suggestions for enhancing the development/learning of preschool children with handicaps. *Topics in Early Childhood Special Education, 11,* 18-28.

McKee, W. T., & Witt, J. C. (1990). Effective teaching: A review of instructional, and environmental variables. In T. B. Gutkin & C. R. Reynolds (Eds.), *The handbook of school psychology* (2nd ed., pp. 823-846). New York: Wiley.

National Association of School Psychologists (NASP). (1995). Standards for training and field placement programs in school psychology (1994). In A. Thomas & J. Grimes (Eds.), *Best practices in school psychology III* (pp. 1173-1177). Washington, DC: Author.

National Research Council. (1998). *Preventing reading difficulties in young children.* Washington, DC: National Academy Press.

Neisworth J. T., & Bagnato, S. J. (1992). The case against intelligence testing in early intervention. *Topics in Early Childhood Special Education, 12,* 1-20.

Neuman, S. B., Copple, C., & Bredekamp, S. (1999). *Learning to read and write: Developmentally appropriate practices for young children.* Washington, DC: National Association for the Education of Young Children.

Nordquist, V. M., & Twardosz, S. (1990). Preventing behavior problems in early childhood special education classrooms through environmental organization. *Education and Treatment of Children, 13,* 274-287.

O'Neill, R. E., Horner, R. H., Albin, R. W., Sprague, J. R., Storey, K., & Newton, J. S. (1997). *Functional assessment and program development for problem behavior: A practical handbook* (2nd ed.). Pacific Grove, CA: Brooks/Cole.

Paine, S. C., Radicchi, J., Rosellini, L. C., Deutchman, L., & Darch, C. B. (1983). *Structuring your classroom for academic success.* Champaign, IL: Research Press Company.

Parsonson, B., & Baer, D. (1992). The visual analysis of data, and current research into the stimuli controlling it. In T. R. Kratochwill & J. R. Levin (Eds.), *Single-case research design and analysis: New directions for psychology and education* (pp. 15-40). Mahwah, NJ: Erlbaum.

Peck, S. M., Wacker, D. P., Berg, W. K., Cooper, L. J., Brown, K. A., Richman, D., McComas, J. J., Frischmeyer, P., & Millard, T. (1996). Choice-making treatment of young children's severe behavior problems. *Journal of Applied Behavior Analysis, 29,* 263-290.

Ramey, C. T., & Ramey, S. L. (1998). Early intervention and early experience. *American Psychologist, 53,* 109-120.

Reschly, D. J., & Ysseldyke, J. E. (1995). School psychology paradigm shift. In A. Thomas & J. Grimes (Eds.), *Best practices in school psychology III* (pp. 17-31). Washington, DC: National Association of School Psychologists.

Rous, B., Hemmeter, M. L., & Schuster, J. (1994). Sequenced transition to education in the public schools: A systems approach to transition planning. *Topics in Early Childhood Special Education, 14,* 374-393.

Sanders, M. R., & Dadds, M. R. (1993). *Behavioral family intervention.* Boston: Allyn and Bacon.

Sexton, D., Snyder, P., Wolfe, B., Lobman, M., Stricklin, S., & Akers, P. (1996). Early intervention inservice training strategies: Perceptions and suggestions from the field. *Exceptional Children, 62,* 485-495.

Shepard, L., Kagan, S. L., & Wurtz, E. (Eds.). (1998). *Principles and recommendations for early childhood assessments.* Washington, DC: National Educational Goals Panel.

Sheridan, S. M., & Kratochwill, T. R. (1992). Behavioral parent-teacher consultation: Conceptual and research considerations. *Journal of School Psychology, 30,* 117–139.

Shinn, M. R. (Ed.). (1998). *Advanced applications of curriculum-based measurement.* New York: Guilford Press.

Siemoens, S. (2001). *Class-wide interventions for challenging behaviors: An extension of PASSKey procedures.* Unpublished doctoral dissertation, University of Cincinnati, Ohio.

Stollar, S. A. (1994). *The development of the ecobehavioral preschool classroom environment checklist: Preliminary technical characteristics.* Unpublished doctoral dissertation, University of Cincinnati, Ohio.

Stoner, G., & Green, S. K. (1992). Reconsidering the scientist-practitioner model for school psychology practice. *School Psychology Review, 21,* 155–166.

Storer, A. L. (1997). *The ecobehavioral preschool classroom environment checklist-observation form: Further development and investigation of technical characteristics.* Unpublished doctoral dissertation, University of Cincinnati, Ohio.

Strain, P. S., McConnell, S. R., Carta, J. J., Fowler, S. A., Neisworth, J. T., & Wolery, M. (1992). Behaviorism in early intervention. *Topics in Early Childhood Special Education, 12,* 121–141.

Tirapelle, L., & Cipani, E. (1992). Developing functional requesting: Acquisition, durability, and generalization of effects. *Exceptional Children, 58,* 260–269.

Tucker, M., Sigafoos, J., & Bushell, H. (1998). Use of noncontingent reinforcement in the treatment of challenging behavior. *Behavior Modification, 22,* 529–547.

Umbreit, J. (1995). Functional analysis of disruptive behavior in an inclusive classroom. *Journal of Early Intervention, 20,* 18–29.

U.S. Department of Health and Human Services. (1996). *Head Start program performance standards.* Washington, DC: Author.

Wacker, D. P., Steege, M., & Berg, W. (1988). Use of single-case designs to evaluate manipulable influences on school performance. *School Psychology Review, 17,* 651–657.

Wahler, R. G., & Fox, J. J. (1981). Setting events in applied behavior analysis: Towards a conceptual and methodological expansion. *Journal of Applied Behavior Analysis, 14,* 327–338.

Walker, H. M., Colvin, G., & Ramsey, E. (1995). *Antisocial behaviors in schools: Strategies and best practices.* Pacific Grove, CA: Brookes/Cole.

Warren, S. F. (1992). Facilitating basic vocabulary acquisition with milieu teaching procedures. *Journal of Early Intervention, 16,* 325–251.

Winton, P. J. (2000). Early childhood intervention personnel preparation: Backward mapping for future planning. *Topics in Early Childhood Special Education, 20,* 87–94.

Wolery, M. (1994a). Instructional strategies for teaching young children with special needs. In M. Wolery & J. S. Wilbers (Eds.), *Including children with special needs in early childhood programs* (pp. 119–150). Washington, DC: National Association for the Education of Young Children.

Wolery, M. (1994b). Designing inclusive environments for young children with special needs. In M. Wolery & J. S. Wilbers (Eds.), *Including children with special needs in early childhood programs* (pp. 97–118). Washington, DC: National Association for the Education of Young Children.

Wolery, M., Anthony, L., & Heckathorn, J. (1998). Transition-based teaching: Effects on transitions, teachers' behaviors, and children's learning. *Journal of Early Intervention, 21,* 117–131.

Wolf, M. M. (1978). Social validity: The case for subjective measurement or how applied behavior analysis is finding its heart. *Journal of Applied Behavior Analysis, 11,* 203–214.

Yeaton, W. H., & Sechrest, L. (1981). Critical dimensions in the choice and maintenance of successful treatments: Strength, integrity, and effectiveness. *Journal of Consulting and Clinical Psychology, 49,* 156–167.

Zeanah, P. D., Larrieu, J. A., & Zeanah, C. H. Jr. (2000). Training in infant mental health. In C. H. Zeanah Jr. (Ed.), *Handbook of infant mental health* (2nd ed., pp. 548–558). New York: Guilford Press.

CHAPTER 38

Preparing School Psychologists as Interventionists and Preventionists

Thomas J. Power
The Children's Hospital of Philadelphia
University of Pennsylvania

INTRODUCTION

In the early 1980s, the field of school psychology assembled many of its leaders for two major conferences at Spring Hill and Olympia to discuss the prevailing and preferred roles of school psychologists (Ysseldyke, 1982). A consensus was reached that a paradigm shift in school psychology was required for the field to have a major impact on outcomes for children, families, and schools. Historically, school psychologists had used their assessment information primarily for the purposes of making decisions about special education eligibility. The paradigm shift emphasized the critical importance of linking assessment to effective intervention, designing empirically supported intervention plans, implementing instructional and behavioral change strategies, and evaluating the effectiveness of intervention approaches (Reschly, 1988; Reschly & Ysseldyke, 1995). Guidelines for professional practice and training were derived in response to the pressing need to shift priorities and roles for school psychologists (Ysseldyke, Reynolds, & Weinberg, 1984).

Several concurrent events have underscored the need for a paradigm shift from disability determination to intervention design and outcome evaluation. An extensive body of research conducted since 1980 has seriously challenged the validity of the 13 special education disability categories delineated under federal law. There is essentially no compelling evidence to support the usefulness of classifying children into one of the disability categories or denying students services because they do not meet disability eligibility criteria (Heller, Holtzman, & Messick, 1982; Reynolds & Lakin, 1987; Ysseldyke, Thurlow, Christenson, & Weiss, 1987).

Research has seriously challenged the practice of using discrepancy scores reflecting differences in performance on cognitive ability tests and achievement measures as a method of determining the presence of learning disabilities (Lyon, 1996). The use of a discrepancy score approach to disability diagnosis may fail to identify accurately students with significant learning problems, and it may deny services to students in need (Fletcher et al., 1994; Shaywitz, Fletcher, Holahan, & Shaywitz, 1992).

As described in other chapters in this volume, school psychologists' use of norm-referenced cognitive testing has been defended because of the useful information it contributes to intervention planning. Historically, school psychologists have analyzed data acquired from measures of broad-band constructs, such as intelligence or verbal and visual-spatial abilities, to identify underlying patterns and processes that may be suggestive of specific intervention strategies. Unfortunately, the idea that knowing how students perform on these types of tests can lead to the prescription of effective interventions generally has not been supported (Braden & Kratochwill, 1997).

Given that special education has placed so much emphasis on eligibility testing and that intervention planning historically has been based on assessment information with questionable treatment utility, it is not surprising that there is little evidence to support the effectiveness of special education (Fuchs & Fuchs, 1986; Kavale, 1990). However, just as research in school psychology has highlighted approaches that are not effective, the literature clearly documents methods that can be effective in improving the academic and social functioning of students. It has become evident that positive student outcomes are related to the type and intensity of instructional and behavioral strategy applied as opposed to the special education classification and placement assigned to the child (Shinn, 1995; Ysseldyke et al., 1987).

The paradigm shift in school psychology has highlighted the importance of (a) developing methods of assessment that are linked with intervention (McComas & Mace, 2000; Shapiro, 1996); (b) selecting and implementing intervention strategies that are supported by empirical research (Stoiber & Kratochwill, 2000); and (c) designing strategies to monitor progress and evaluate outcomes in response to intervention (Reschly & Ysseldyke, 1995). Alternative models of practice (Shinn & Bamonto, 1998; Tilly & Grimes, 1998; Ysseldyke et al., 1997) have been developed to respond to the pressing need for reform in school psychology.

Even more recently, reforms in education and health care beginning in the late 1980s have led to the creation of roles for school psychologists that extend beyond the domain of special education. Increasingly, psychologists working in the schools are being enlisted to link community systems to provide coordinated health and mental health services for children and their families (Kolbe, Collins, & Cortese, 1997; Short & Talley, 1997). By addressing the health and mental health needs of children, school psychologists can assist in the removal of barriers to effective instruction (Adelman & Taylor, 1998) and contribute to the prevention of tragic outcomes for youth, such as suicide, violence, and drug and alcohol abuse (Talley & Short, 1995). In addition, school psychologists can serve important roles in developing programs of health promotion for all children (Power, 2000; Power, Heathfield, McGoey, & Blum, 1999).

The paradigm shift in school psychology in the 1980s and recent reforms in education and health care have important implications for the training of school psychologists. The most recent *Blueprint for School Psychology Training and Practice* (Ysseldyke et al., 1997) was highly responsive to these major developments and highlighted the critical need to train school psychologists in data-based decision making, intervention and prevention strategies, and approaches to facilitate collaboration among systems of care. Given that training programs in school psychology have traditionally emphasized preparation in the domain of assessment, it is important that the focus of preservice training shift to include preparation in the domains of intervention, prevention, and intersystemic collaboration. The purposes of this chapter are to (a) describe essential components in the training of school psychologists as interventionists and preventionists, and (b) outline a set of integrated didactic and practicum experiences needed to prepare school psychologists to be effective in the domains of intervention, prevention, and community collaboration.

COMPONENTS OF TRAINING IN INTERVENTION AND PREVENTION

The preparation of school psychologists as interventionists and preventionists requires training in linking assessment to intervention, selecting and implementing empirically supported interventions, and evaluating intervention effectiveness. In addition, there is an increasing need for school psychologists to be trained in strategies of risk prevention and health promotion and in approaches to link community-based agencies to provide integrated care to children and their families.

Linking Assessment to Intervention

Research conducted in the fields of school psychology, special education, and behavioral psychology, in particular, have contributed greatly to the development of assessment procedures that are useful in intervention planning. Curriculum-based assessment (CBA) techniques have been demonstrated to be highly useful in developing effective instructional interventions. Through the assessment of a child's accuracy and fluency in performing academic tasks that closely correspond with curricular demands, it is possible to delineate the optimal level of instruction for the student in critical domains of educational functioning (Shapiro, 1996). Achieving the proper instructional match has been shown to improve academic engaged time and productivity and to lead to accelerated rates of academic skill attainment (Gickling & Rosenfield, 1995; Roberts & Shapiro, 1996).

Curriculum-based measurement (CBM), a set of techniques that apply curriculum-based assessment approaches (Shinn, Rosenfield, & Knutson, 1989), has been incorporated into a problem-solving model (Deno, 1995) to provide a comprehensive set of strategies to address the instructional needs of students. CBM techniques have been demonstrated to be very useful in identifying problems in academic functioning related to local normative standards and describing the extent of the discrepancy between expected and actual performance. This measurement tool provides a methodology for targeting goals for academic instruction, evaluating progress in meeting goals, and determining whether the proposed solutions have been sufficient in enabling the student to achieve targeted goals and perform at a level similar to peers' (Fuchs &

Shinn, 1989; Shinn, 1995). A clear advantage of CBM is that it provides a methodology for making decisions about eligibility for special services in a manner that is reasonable and fair for students from diverse ethnic and socioeconomic backgrounds (Shinn, Collins, & Gallagher, 1998).

Behavioral consultation is another methodology that has had substantial utility in designing effective instructional and behavioral interventions. Through the careful delineation of specific target behaviors and an in-depth problem analysis using functional assessment methods, the school psychologist is able to delineate an intervention plan that is highly likely to be successful (Bergan & Kratochwill, 1990; Kratochwill & Bergan, 1990). A critical component of most behavioral consultation approaches is the functional assessment of behavior. By using interview and observation methods to identify antecedent conditions and setting events as well as contingencies related to specified target behaviors, the provider is in a position to develop hypotheses about one or more possible functions of a child's problems. Potential functions of challenging behaviors may include task avoidance, adult attention, peer attention, concrete reinforcement, and sensory stimulation (Nelson, Roberts, & Smith, 1998). The delineation of potential functions of problem behavior is highly useful in developing interventions to address instructional, behavioral, and emotional needs (DuPaul & Ervin, 1996).

Selecting Empirically Supported and Socially Valid Interventions

A hallmark of effective intervention is the selection of empirically supported treatments. Given the existing gap between research and practice in psychology, it is important that guidelines be established for delineating efficacious treatments and that intervention procedures used by practitioners be evaluated with regard to whether they meet standards for being efficacious (Weisz & Hawley, 1998). Recently, Division 12 (Clinical Psychology) of the American Psychological Association (APA) established guidelines for differentiating intervention approaches into those that are efficacious and possibly efficacious (Chambless & Hollon, 1998). Even more recently, APA's Division 16 (School Psychology) and the Society for the Study of School Psychology have collaborated in the development of a Task Force on Empirically Supported Interventions in Schools. The purposes of this task force are to (a) examine the research literature and disseminate reports about intervention and prevention programs that are empirically supported for application in school and community settings, and (b) expand the knowledge base about empirically supported interventions by promoting the design and implementation of research using rigorous research methods and technologies (Stoiber & Kratochwill, 2000).

A wide range of efficacious and promising intervention strategies are available to solve the problems presented by children in school, at home, and in the community. These strategies can be classified as a function of the primary agents of change (DuPaul & Power, 2000). For example, interventions can be differentiated into those that are teacher-mediated (e.g., positive reinforcement and response cost techniques; Pfiffner, Rosen, & O'Leary, 1985; Rapport, Murphy, & Bailey, 1982), parent-mediated (e.g., homework interventions, school-home notes; Kelley, 1990; Power, Karustis, &

Habboushe, 2001), peer-mediated (e.g., peer tutoring and social problem solving; DuPaul, Ervin, Hook, & McGoey, 1998; Fantuzzo, King, & Heller, 1992), self-managed (e.g., self-evaluation and self-monitoring; Rhode, Morgan, & Young, 1983; Shapiro & Cole, 1994), and pharmacological (MTA Cooperative Group, 1999; Phelps, Brown, & Power, 2001).

To increase the likelihood that treatment will be effective, intervention approaches ought to be applied systematically, albeit in a manner that is responsive to the needs of participants. Outlining intervention procedures in treatment manuals facilitates the training of practitioners and promotes systemic implementation (Kratochwill & Stoiber, 2000). Further, manualized intervention programs permit the monitoring of procedural integrity—that is, an assessment of the extent to which interventions are being applied as indicated (Gresham, 1989).

An essential element of effective intervention is social validity, which refers to the extent to which the goals, methods, and outcomes of intervention are viewed as reasonable and fair by participants, including teachers, children, and parents (Kazdin, 1980). Social validity can be assessed by interviewing participants or by having them respond to brief questionnaires (Witt & Elliott, 1985), but recently researchers have emphasized the importance of observing and coding behaviors that may be markers for social validity (e.g., adherence to intervention procedures; Gresham & Lopez, 1996). Researchers generally agree that success in initiating and maintaining an intervention program requires ongoing affirmation by caregivers, children, and educators that the program is appropriate, fair, and reasonable (Eckert & Hintze, 2000). Including key participants in all phases of intervention, including problem identification, intervention planning and implementation, and outcome evaluation, is a highly useful strategy to ensure the social validity of intervention programs (Fantuzzo, Coolahan, & Weiss, 1997; Nastasi et al., 2000).

Linking Systems to Provide Integrated Care for Children

Research has strongly affirmed the importance of involving participants from multiple systems in designing and implementing interventions for children. Given the strong relationship between parental involvement and academic success, collaboration between the family and school systems is extremely useful in solving children's problems and promoting academic achievement (Christenson & Sheridan, 2001; Sheridan, Kratochwill, & Bergan, 1996). At a broader level, a strong working relationship between the school and the community in which it is embedded is critical to promoting educational success and emotional resiliency (Comer, Haynes, Joyner, & Ben-Avie, 1996). When the culture of the school is discontinuous with the culture of the surrounding neighborhoods, which often arises in urban, ethnically diverse settings, students may have problems forming strong attachments with school professionals and family-school relationships may be distant or strained. In contrast, when the school is responsive to the values and priorities of the community in which it is embedded, children are more likely to receive the mentoring they need and families become more involved in their children's education (Pianta & Walsh, 1998; Power & Bartholomew, 1987). Because of the importance of providing services to students in a culturally relevant and community-responsive manner, the involvement of community leaders and residents along with school professionals in planning, implementing, and evaluating educational programs is extremely useful (Dowrick et al., 2001).

Close collaboration between the educational and health systems is also critical, particularly in addressing the complex school issues that can arise among children with neuro-developmental disorders, such as attention-deficit/hyperactivity disorder (ADHD), autistic spectrum disorders, tic disorders (DuPaul & Stoner, 1994; Power & Mercugliano, 1997; Shriver, Allen, 1999), and chronic medical conditions, such as HIV/AIDS, traumatic brain injury, and sickle cell disease (Bonner, Gustafson, Schmacher, & Thompson, 1999; Clark, Russman, & Orme, 1999; Mangione, Landau, & Pryor, 1999). Caregivers are often placed in the untenable position of coordinating communications between the school and health systems. With effective collaboration between these agencies, children and families can receive the support and advocacy they need and intervention plans are more likely to account for the complex biopsychosocial needs of these students (Power, Atkins, Osborne, & Blum, 1994). Although school psychologists traditionally have not focused on the interface of the school and health systems, recent reforms in education and health care have signaled the need for school psychologists to coordinate these systems to provide integrated services for children and their families (Power, DuPaul, Shapiro, & Parrish, 1995).

Evaluating Outcomes

Using assessment methods that are closely linked with intervention increases the likelihood of treatment effectiveness, but it does not guarantee success. Programs of intervention designed on the basis of functional assessment methods need to be evaluated to determine their effects on participants (Stoner & Green, 1992).

Both summative and formative methods can be useful in evaluating intervention effects. Summative evaluation generally includes the use of pre- and post-treatment measures, yielding data about changes in level of functioning over time. The inclusion of control groups, such as a wait-list group or a group that is administered an alternative treatment, can improve the internal validity of the research. A limitation of summative approaches to evaluating intervention effectiveness is that they fail to provide information about treatment response during the course of intervention. Further, summative evaluation does not yield data pertaining to slope or rate of skill acquisition. In contrast, formative methods of evaluation provide feedback during the course of intervention and may yield information that is useful in evaluating changes in rate of skill acquisition (Deno, 1986).

Single-subject research technologies provide a systematic set of methods for conducting a formative evaluation of intervention effectiveness. Through the serial assessment of instructional and/or behavioral functioning during intervention and control conditions, it is possible to determine the effectiveness of an intervention for a child. In particular, multiple-baseline, withdrawal, and multi-element designs have been demonstrated to have an acceptable level of methodological rigor and to be very useful in determining the effects of instructional and behavioral treatments applied in school settings.

Curriculum-based measurement (CBM) procedures typically incorporate single-subject research methods and provide a highly useful methodology for conducting a formative evaluation of instructional interventions (Shinn & Bamonto, 1998). The serial assessment of fluency in performing academic tasks across multiple domains of functioning (e.g., reading, spelling, written expression, and math computation) has been demonstrated to be highly sensitive to the effects of instructional change strategies over short intervals of time as well as over relatively long intervals (Good & Jefferson, 1998). A real advantage to CBM is that it indexes variations in academic functioning with regard to changes in level as well as slope of performance (Fuchs, Fuchs, Hamlett, Walz, & Germann, 1993).

For the evaluation of program outcomes, participatory action research methods are particularly well suited. With participatory action research, members of the research or clinical team partner with the stakeholders of the program (e.g., school personnel, families, youth, community members) at every step in the process, including problem identification, needs assessment, program development, implementation, and evaluation (Nastasi & Berg, 1999). Involving key stakeholders in the process helps to ensure that programs are socially valid and that the research addresses issues that are meaningful and important to schools, families, and communities (Nastasi et al., 2000).

Moving Beyond Service Delivery: Risk Prevention and Health Promotion

The paradigm shift in school psychology that started in the 1980s highlighted the importance of training practitioners in the development, implementation, and evaluation of intervention approaches. More recently, in the 1990s, reforms in education and health care have underscored the importance of preventing academic failure, antisocial behavior, and health problems and promoting healthy patterns of behavior. Increasingly, psychologists have been urged to expand their role to include prevention and health promotion (Kolbe et al., 1997; Power et al., 1999). An emerging paradigm change in the field of school psychology is a shift in emphasis from an exclusive focus on service provision to a focus that includes a public health orientation in addition to a service provision orientation (Short & Talley, 1997). Whereas the focus of a service provision orientation is on designing, implementing, and evaluating interventions for a child or small group of children with identified problems or risk factors, the focus of a public health orientation is to establish a classwide or schoolwide program to promote health for a large group of children who may not have identified needs (Power, 2000).

A hallmark of prevention programming is to use a balanced approach that identifies and addresses both risk and resilience factors (Doll & Lyon, 1998). Promoting the development of resilience entails strategies that prevent the emergence of risk factors and approaches that build the assets of children and the systems in which they operate (Masten, 2001).

INTEGRATED TRAINING EXPERIENCES

Given current and emerging directions in the field, as reflected in the *Blueprint for School Psychology Training and Practice,* the preparation of school psychologists needs to include intensive training in intervention and prevention at both the doctoral and specialist levels. We propose that a four-course core sequence with accompanying practicum experiences be offered to trainees in their first 2 years of study. These core courses in intervention and prevention should be embedded in a training program that includes a foundational course in professional issues and practices in school psychology that covers the history of school psychology, critical issues in school psychology research and practice, school ecology, and legal and ethical issues. Additional foundational courses in developmental psychology, learning theory, research methods, and data analysis are also required. Subsequently, students can be guided to select additional courses and practicum experiences that would enable them to learn advanced skills in intervention, prevention, and intersystem collaboration. The following is a brief description of the core learning experiences. Table 1 outlines the primary themes and *Blueprint* domains addressed in each of the core courses.

Year 1

Course I: Linking Assessment to Intervention. This course provides instruction in methods of data collection and interpretation that are highly useful in designing instructional and behavioral interventions and that are likely to result in effective treatment approaches. Major topics addressed in the course are the following: (a) using CBA to determine the instructional levels of students across multiple domains of academic functioning (Shapiro, 1996); (b) integrating CBM with a problem-solving orientation to determine eligibility for specialized instruction, to identify targets for intervention, and to delineate intervention goals (Shinn, 1995); (c) applying a behavioral consultation model to address challenging instructional and behavioral problems (Bergan & Kratochwill, 1990); (d) promoting family-school collaboration in the application of a behavioral consultation model (Sheridan et al., 1996); and (e) conducting a functional assessment of behavior to determine the functions of challenging behaviors and to design comprehensive intervention plans (McComas & Mace, 2000). In addition, this course challenges students to consider the merits and limitations of functional methods of assessment in relation to standardized, norm-referenced methods of assessing cognitive and behavioral functioning (Braden & Kratochwill, 1997; Power & Eiraldi, 2000).

Course II: Empirically Supported and Culturally Sensitive Intervention Strategies. This course provides a review of the literature on intervention strategies that have been demonstrated to be effective in addressing children's instructional and behavioral problems, with particular emphasis on school-related concerns. Intervention strategies are presented with regard to the manner in which they address each function of behavior, as determined through a functional assessment of behavior (DuPaul & Ervin, 1996). Also, interventions are differentiated according to the primary agents of change (e.g.,

TABLE 1

Summary of Topics Addressed in Core Courses Related to Intervention and Prevention and the *Blueprint* Domains Addressed by Each Course

Course	Topics Addressed	*Blueprint* Domains Addressed[a]
I. Linking Assessment to Intervention	Curriculum-based assessment Curriculum-based measurement and Problem-solving model Behavioral consultation Conjoint behavioral consultation Functional assessment of behavior	1, 2, 3, 8
II. Empirically Supported Interventions	Interventions for each function of behavior Teacher-mediated strategies Parent-mediated strategies Family-school intervention approaches Peer-mediated strategies Self-management strategies Psychopharmacological methods Culturally competent intervention Social validity Intervention integrity Ethical and legal issues related to intervention	3, 4, 5, 8, 10
III. Health Promotion and Risk Prevention	Rationale for developing prevention and health promotion programs in schools Factors that promote resilience Exemplars of universal prevention programs Exemplars of selective prevention programs Exemplars of indicated prevention programs Principles of organizational change Strategies for changing school structure and climate Developing grant writing skills Challenges and proposed solutions for developing health promotion programs	6, 7
IV. Program Evaluation	Differentiating formative from summative methods Single-subject designs Within-subjects group designs Between-subjects group designs CBM in single-subject designs Determining effect sizes Participatory action research methods Conducting research with diverse students Ethical issues in conducting research	5, 9, 10

[a] The following is the key for identifying domains of training and practice as indicated in *School Psychology: A Blueprint for Training and Practice II* (Ysseldyke et al., 1997):

1 — Data-based decision making and accountability
2 — Interpersonal communication, collaboration, and consultation
3 — Effective instruction and development of cognitive/academic skills
4 — Socialization and development of life competencies
5 — Student diversity in development and learning
6 — School structure, organization, and climate
7 — Prevention, wellness promotion, and crisis intervention
8 — Home/school/community collaboration
9 — Research and program evaluation
10 — Legal and ethical practice and professional development

teacher, parent, peer, self, computer, pharmacological). Intervention approaches that involve multiple systems and promote a coordinated approach among agencies will be highlighted. In this course students learn about the rationale for the movement to identify and disseminate information about empirically supported intervention and prevention strategies in school psychology and related disciplines (Stoiber & Kratochwill, 2000). Also, students are encouraged to examine the advantages and limitations of this movement (Hughes, 2000).

The course emphasizes the importance of designing and implementing interventions in a culturally sensitive and socially valid manner by involving participants at every step in the process (Nastasi & Truscott, 2000). Further, strategies for ensuring that interventions are applied with integrity are discussed (Gresham & Lopez, 1996).

Practicum experiences. To assist students in learning about intervention strategies and to provide them with guidance in linking research with practice, it is important that students engage in practicum experiences that are directly linked with their instruction in the classroom. The integration of coursework with practicum experiences does not happen magically; it requires the selection of well-trained, committed supervisors who are highly knowledgeable about the concepts discussed in the courses and who routinely apply recommended strategies in their practice. Field supervisors and university faculty need to collaborate regarding the goals of the practicum and primary methods of practice to be utilized, and ongoing collaboration between them is needed to ensure integration. In the first year, students should have the opportunity to utilize CBA, CBM, problem-solving strategies, behavioral consultation techniques, and functional assessment procedures in this practicum. Typically, we recommend 200 hours of practicum experience directly related to intervention in the first year.

Year 2

Course III: Health Promotion and Risk Prevention. This course provides instruction to students in the rationale for conducting prevention and health promotion programming in schools. It introduces students to the various types of prevention programming, including universal prevention (i.e., programs for all students), selected prevention (i.e., programs for youngsters who have characteristics that place them at risk), and indicated prevention (i.e., programs for students who already display signs of risk; Institute of Medicine, 1994). Multiple illustrations of each type of prevention program are provided. An emphasis is placed on developing programs that promote healthy outcomes and resilience (e.g., a balanced diet, a reasonable amount of exercise, literacy, prosocial behavior, and strong mentoring relationships), although programs designed to prevent challenging problems and risk factors from emerging (violence, drug and alcohol abuse, sexually transmitted diseases, depression) also are addressed (Doll & Lyon, 1998). The course emphasizes the importance of designing programs in partnership with educational professionals and community members to ensure social validity and to promote community-school collaboration (Nastasi et al., 2000). Further, the course stresses the importance of grant writing to acquire the support necessary to develop health promotion programs and to evaluate their effectiveness (Power et al., 1999), and it provides instruction in writing grants to public agencies and private foundations. A potentially useful learning exercise is to have students prepare a grant proposal for a school-based health promotion or risk prevention program.

Course IV: Progress Monitoring and Program Evaluation. This course challenges students to consider the limitations of assessment and pre-intervention planning, including rigorously designed functional assessment regimens, and highlights the importance of investigating systematically the effectiveness of intervention and prevention programs (Johnson, Stoner, & Green, 1996; Stoner & Green, 1992). Trainees are instructed in both formative and summative strategies for evaluating the effects of intervention and prevention strategies (Deno, 1986). Students are instructed in single-subject research designs as well as group methods, including within-subjects and between-subjects designs. The strengths and limitations of each design with regard to internal validity, external validity, feasibility, and social validity are considered. Methods for monitoring academic progress by evaluating changes in level and slope in relation to baseline performance and realistic goals for performance using CBM methodologies are addressed (Fuchs, Fuchs, Hamlett, & Stecker, 1991). In addition, the course provides instruction in methods of analyzing data collected using single-subject, within-subjects, and between-subjects designs. Procedures for determining intervention effect sizes are examined.

This course also includes the study of participatory action research methods in which the investigator serves as a participant-observer in research. Students receive instruction in methods to partner with school professionals, family members, and community residents in designing research investigations, developing socially valid and potentially efficacious interventions, selecting developmentally appropriate and culturally sensitive measures, collecting data, and interpreting the results of research projects (Nastasi et al., 2000). The challenges intrinsic to action research are considered and potential solutions for overcoming barriers to conducting methodologically rigorous research are discussed. The advantages to conducting action research in ethnically diverse settings serving families from lower socioeconomic backgrounds are emphasized (Dowrick et al., 2001). A potentially useful independent learning activity is for students to design an intervention or prevention program using action research methods and to conduct a preliminary investigation of its effectiveness.

Practicum Experiences. In order to learn about prevention strategies and methods of progress monitoring and outcome evaluation, students need to be involved in meaningful practicum experiences that are closely linked with classroom instruction in these areas. Students ought to be placed in settings in which they can observe effective health promotion and risk prevention programs and have opportunities to collaborate in the design of these programs. The practicum should be designed in a way that enables them to conduct independent projects assigned to them in their course (e.g., grant writing to develop a health promotion program, or action research to design and evaluate an intervention or prevention program). Field supervisors and university faculty need to collaborate closely regarding the goals of the practicum and primary methods of practice that will be emphasized. Ongoing collaboration between them is essential to meet

TABLE 2

Examples of Advanced Seminars Related
to Intervention and Prevention

Psychopharmacology

Pediatric School Psychology

Family-School Collaboration and Intervention

Participatory Action Research in Urban Schools

Advanced Methods in Applied Behavior Analysis

Advanced Methods in Curriculum-Based Measurement

Advanced Methods in Prevention Programming

Advanced Strategies in Early Intervention Programming

Advanced Strategies in Literacy Development

Advanced Strategies in Program Development and Evaluation

Advanced Strategies for Grant Writing

the goals of the training program. Typically, we recommend 400 hours of practicum experience related to prevention, progress monitoring, and program evaluation, in addition to practicum experiences pertaining to other types of methods.

Additional Coursework, Practicum Experiences, and Internship

The four courses and 600 hours of practicum experience described above provide the core training in intervention and prevention for school psychology trainees in specialist-level or doctoral-level training programs. For students in doctoral-level programs, additional coursework related to intervention and prevention is needed. The focus and sequence of these advanced courses can be determined by faculty in accordance with the mission and goals of the training program. Table 2 includes suggestions for additional coursework that can enable students to achieve an advanced understanding of issues related to intervention, prevention, intersystem collaboration, and program evaluation.

Training programs that specialize in preparing leaders to link the school, family, and health systems can include advanced courses in psychopharmacology intervention strategies for children with chronic illnesses, and prevention strategies to promote healthy outcomes (Power et al., 1995; Power et al., 1999). Programs preparing students for leadership in family-school collaboration can offer advanced courses in community-school relationships, family involvement in education, and conjoint behavioral consultation (Christenson & Sheridan, 2001; Sheridan et al., 1996). As a final example, programs specializing in developing leaders in early childhood education can offer courses in early intervention programming, family involvement in literacy, and strategies to promote literacy development.

Doctoral students continue to need practicum experiences in the 3rd and 4th doctoral years to further develop their skills in intervention, prevention, intersystem collaboration, progress monitoring, and program evaluation. Gaining experience in alternative settings, such as primary care pediatric clinics, community-based mental health centers, and community-based early education centers, can be very useful in learning about the interface of systems of care in the community. Once again, it is important that the goals and methods of field experiences are congruent with models of intervention and prevention being recommended in coursework, and that practicum supervisors and university faculty pursue similar training goals.

The predoctoral internship can be completed in a variety of settings, although it is important that students have opportunities to work closely with schools, families, health systems, and mental health systems. Further, it is important that students select internships that recognize the unique contributions of school psychologists as interventionists and preventionists, that provide training rotations related to intervention and prevention, and that provide mentoring in strategies to evaluate the effectiveness of intervention and prevention strategies.

CONCLUSIONS

Advancements in the field of school psychology and reforms in health care and education have highlighted the need for new models of training that emphasize the importance of (a) linking assessment with intervention, (b) using empirically supported intervention strategies, (c) connecting systems of care in the community for children and families, and (d) investing in the development and evaluation of prevention initiatives. The *Blueprint for School Psychology Training and Practice II* provides an excellent framework for guiding reforms in the training of school psychologists. This chapter described a four-core course sequence, based on training and practice domains outlined in the *Blueprint,* that can serve as the foundation for training related to intervention and prevention. Practicum experiences that are closely linked with coursework were also described. Training programs can address core requirements related to intervention and prevention and still have considerable latitude to address areas of specialty training that are unique to the program, such as pediatric school psychology, family-school collaboration, early literacy development, and programming for children with severe developmental disabilities.

REFERENCES

Adelman, H. S., & Taylor, L. (1998). Mental health in schools: Moving forward. *School Psychology Review, 27,* 175–190.

Bergan, J. R., & Kratochwill, T. R. (1990). *Behavioral consultation and therapy.* New York: Plenum Press.

Bonner, M. J., Gustafson, K. E., Schmacher, E., & Thompson, R. T. (1999). The impact of sickle cell disease on cognitive functioning and learning. *School Psychology Review, 28,* 182–193.

Braden, J. P., & Kratochwill, T. R. (1997). Treatment utility of assessment: Myths and realities. *School Psychology Review, 26,* 475–485.

Chambless, D. L., & Hollon, S. D. (1998). Defining empirically supported therapies. *Journal of Consulting and Clinical Psychology, 66,* 7–18.

Christenson, S. L., & Sheridan, S. M. (2001). *Schools and families: Creating essential connections for learning.* New York: Guilford Press.

Clark, E., Russman, S., & Orme, S. (1999). Traumatic brain injury: Effects on school functioning and intervention strategies. *School Psychology Review, 28,* 242–250.

Comer, J. P., Haynes, N. M., Joyner, E. T., & Ben-Avie, M. (1996). *Rallying the whole village: The Comer process for reforming education.* New York: Teachers College Press.

Deno, S. L. (1986). Formative evaluation of individual student programs: A new role for school psychologists. *School Psychology Review, 15,* 358–374.

Deno, S. L. (1995). School psychologist as problem solver. In A. Thomas & J. Grimes (Eds.), *Best practices in school psychology III* (pp. 471-484). Washington, DC: National Association of School Psychologists.

Doll, B., & Lyon, M. A. (1998). Risk and resilience: Implications for the delivery of mental health services in the schools. *School Psychology Review, 27,* 348–363.

Dowrick, P. W., Power, T. J., Manz, P. H., Ginsburg-Block, M., Leff, S. S., & Kim-Rupnow, S. (2001). Community responsiveness: Examples from under-resourced urban schools. *Journal of Prevention and Intervention in the Community, 21,* 71–90.

DuPaul, G. J., & Ervin, R. A. (1996). Functional assessment of behaviors related to attention-deficit hyperactivity disorder: Linking assessment to intervention design. *Behavior Therapy, 27,* 601–622.

DuPaul, G. J., Ervin, R. A., Hook, C. L., & McGoey, K. E. (1998). Peer tutoring for attention deficit hyperactivity disorder: Effects on classroom behavior and academic performance. *Journal of Applied Behavior Analysis, 31,* 579–592.

DuPaul, G. J., & Power, T. J. (2000). Educational interventions for students with attention-deficit disorders. In T. E. Brown (Ed.), *Attention-deficit disorders and comorbidities in children, adolescents, and adults* (pp. 607-636). Washington, DC: American Psychiatric Press.

DuPaul, G. J., & Stoner, G. (1994). *ADHD in the schools: Assessment and intervention strategies.* New York: Guilford Press.

Eckert, T. L., & Hintze, J. M. (2000). Behavioral conceptions and applications of acceptability: Issues related to service delivery and research methodology. *School Psychology Quarterly, 15,* 123-148.

Fantuzzo, J. W., Coolahan, K., & Weiss, A. (1997). Resiliency partnership-directed research: Enhancing the social competencies of preschool victims of physical abuse by developing peer resources and community strengths. In D. Cicchetti & S. Toth (Eds.), *Developmental perspective on trauma: Theory, research and intervention* (pp. 463-514). Rochester, NY: University of Rochester Press.

Fantuzzo, J. W., King, J. A., & Heller, L. R. (1992). Effects of reciprocal peer tutoring on mathematics and school adjustment: A component analysis. *Journal of Educational Psychology, 84,* 331-339.

Fletcher, J. M., Shaywitz, S. E., Shankweiler, D. P., Katz, L., Liberman, I. Y., Stuebing, K. K., Francis, D. J., Fowler, A. E., & Shaywitz, B. A. (1994). Cognitive profiles of reading disability: Comparisons of discrepancy and low achievement definitions. *Journal of Educational Psychology, 86,* 6-23.

Fuchs, L. S., & Fuchs, D. (1986). Effects of systematic formative evaluation on student achievement: A meta-analysis. *Exceptional Children, 53,* 199-208.

Fuchs, L. S., Fuchs, D., Hamlett, C. L., & Stecker, P. M. (1991). Effects of curriculum-based measurement and consultation on teacher planning and student achievement in mathematics operations. *American Educational Research Journal, 28,* 617-641.

Fuchs, L. S., Fuchs, D., Hamlett, C. L., Walz, L., & Germann, G. (1993). Formative evaluation of academic progress: How much growth can we expect? *School Psychology Review, 22,* 27-48.

Fuchs, L. S., & Shinn, M. R. (1989). Writing CBM IEP objectives. In M. R. Shinn (Ed.), *Curriculum-based measurement: Assessing special children* (pp. 132-154). New York: Guilford Press.

Gickling, E. E., & Rosenfield, S. (1995). Best practices in curriculum-based assessment. In A. Thomas & J. Grimes (Eds.), *Best practices in school psychology III* (pp. 587-595). Washington, DC: National Association of School Psychologists.

Good, R. H., & Jefferson, G. (1998). Contemporary perspectives on curriculum-based measurement validity. In M. R. Shinn (Ed.), *Advanced applications of curriculum-based measurement* (pp. 61-88). New York: Guilford Press.

Gresham, F. M. (1989). Assessment of treatment integrity in school consultation and prereferral intervention. *School Psychology Review, 18,* 37-50.

Gresham, F. M, & Lopez, M. F. (1996). Social validation: A unifying concept for school-based consultation research and practice. *School Psychology Quarterly, 11,* 204-227.

Heller, K., Holtzman, W., & Messick, S. (Eds.). (1982). *Placing children in special education: A strategy for equity.* Washington, DC: National Academy Press.

Hughes, J. N. (2000). The essential role of theory in the science of teaching children: Beyond empirically supported treatments. *Journal of School Psychology, 38,* 301-330.

Institute of Medicine. (1994). *Reducing risks for mental disorders: Frontiers for preventive intervention research.* Washington, DC: National Academy Press.

Johnson, T. C., Stoner, G., & Green, S. K. (1996). Demonstrating the experimenting society model with classwide behavior management. *School Psychology Review, 25,* 199-214.

Kavale, K. (1990). The effectiveness of special education. In T. B. Gutkin & C. R. Reynolds (Eds.), *The handbook of school psychology* (2nd ed., pp. 868-898). New York: Wiley.

Kazdin, A. E. (1980). Acceptability of alternative treatments for deviant child behavior. *Journal of Applied Behavior Analysis, 13,* 259-273.

Kelley, M. L. (1990). *School-home notes: Promoting children's classroom success.* New York: Guilford.

Kolbe, L. J., Collins, J., & Cortese, P. (1997). Building the capacity of schools to improve the health of the nation: A call for assistance from psychologists. *American Psychologist, 52,* 256-265.

Kratochwill, T. R., & Bergan, J. R. (1990). *Behavioral consultation in applied settings: An individual guide.* New York: Plenum Press.

Kratochwill, T. R., & Stoiber, K. C. (2000). Empirically supported interventions and school psychology: Rationale and methodological issues—Part II. *School Psychology Quarterly, 15,* 233-253.

Lyon, G. R. (1996). Learning disabilities. *The Future of Children: Special Education for Students with Disabilities, 6,* 56-76.

Mangione, C., Landau, S., & Pryor, J. B. (1998). HIV/AIDS (pediatric and adolescent). In L. Phelps (Ed.), *Health-related disorders in children and adolescents* (pp. 328-336). Washington, DC: American Psychological Association.

Masten, A. S. (2001). Ordinary magic: Resilience processes in development. *American Psychologist, 56,* 227-238.

McComas, J. J., & Mace, F. C. (2000). Theory and practice in conducting functional analysis. In E. S. Shapiro & T. R. Kratochwill (Eds.), *Behavioral assessment in schools: Theory, research, and clinical foundations.* New York: Guilford Press.

MTA Cooperative Group. (1999). Mediators and moderators of treatment response for children with attention–deficit/hyperactivity disorder: The Multimodal Treatment Study of Children with Attention Deficit Hyperactivity Disorder Study. *Archives of General Psychiatry, 56,* 1088-1096.

Nastasi, B. K., & Berg, M. (1999). Using ethnography to strengthen and evaluate intervention programs. In J. J. Schensul & M. D. LeCompte (Eds.), *The ethnographer's toolkit: Using ethnographic data: Interventions, public programming, and public policy* (Vol. 9, pp. 1-56). Walnut Creek, CA: AltaMira Press.

Nastasi, B. K., & Truscott, S. D. (2000). Acceptability research in school psychology: Current trends and future directions. *School Psychology Quarterly, 15,* 117-122.

Nastasi, B. K., Varjas, K., Schensul, S. L., Silva, K. T., Schensul, J. J., & Ratnayake, P. (2000). The participatory intervention model: A framework for conceptualizing and promoting intervention acceptability. *School Psychology Quarterly, 15,* 207-232.

Nelson, R., Roberts, M., & Smith, D. (1998). *Conducting functional behavioral assessments: A practical guide.* Longmont, CO: Sopris West.

Pfiffner, L. J., Rosen, L. A., & O'Leary, S. G. (1985). The efficacy of an all-positive approach to classroom management. *Journal of Applied Behavior Analysis, 18,* 257-261.

Phelps, L., Brown, R. T., Power, T. J. (2001). *Pediatric psychopharmacology: Facilitating collaborative practices.* Washington, DC: American Psychological Association.

Pianta, R. C., & Walsh, D. J. (1998). Applying the construct of resilience in schools: Cautions from a developmental systems perspective. *School Psychology Review, 27,* 407-417.

Power, T. J. (2000). Commentary: The school psychologist as community-focused, public health professional: Emerging challenges and implications for training. *School Psychology Review, 29,* 557-559.

Power, T. J., Atkins, M. S., Osborne, M. L., & Blum, N. J. (1994). The school psychologist as manager of programming for ADHD. *School Psychology Review, 23,* 279-291.

Power, T. J., & Bartholomew, K. L. (1987). Family-school relationship patterns: An ecological assessment. *School Psychology Review, 14,* 222-229.

Power, T. J., DuPaul, G. J., Shapiro, E. S., & Parrish, J. M. (1995). Pediatric school psychology: The emergence of a subspecialty. *School Psychology Review, 24,* 244-257.

Power, T. J., & Eiraldi, R. B. (2000). Educational and psychiatric classification systems. In E. S. Shapiro & T. R. Kratochwill (Eds.), *Behavioral assessment in schools: Theory, research, and clinical foundations.* New York: Guilford Press.

Power, T. J., Heathfield, L., McGoey, K., & Blum, N. J. (1999). Managing and preventing chronic health problems: School psychology's role. *School Psychology Review, 28,* 251-263.

Power, T. J., Karustis, J. L., & Habboushe, D. F. (2001). *Homework success for children with ADHD: A family-school intervention program.* New York: Guilford Press.

Power, T. J., & Mercugliano, M. (1997). Tic disorders. In G. G. Bear, K. M. Minke, & A. Thomas (Eds.), *Children's needs II: Development, problems, and alternatives* (pp. 887-896). Bethesda, MD: National Association of School Psychologists.

Rapport, M. D., Murphy, A., & Bailey, J. S. (1982). Ritalin vs. response cost in the control of hyperactive children: A within subject comparison. *Journal of Applied Behavior Analysis, 15,* 205-216.

Reschly, D. J. (1988). Special education reform: School psychology revolution. *School Psychology Review, 17,* 459-475.

Reschly, D. J., & Ysseldyke, J. E. (1995). School psychology paradigm shift. In A. Thomas & J. Grimes (Eds.), *Best practices in school psychology III* (pp. 17-31). Washington, DC: National Association of School Psychologists.

Reynolds, M. C., & Lakin, K. C. (1987). Noncategorical special education for mildly handicapped students. A system for the future. In M. C. Wang, M. C. Reynolds, & H. J. Walberg (Eds.), *The handbook of special education: Research and practice* (Vol. I, pp. 331-356). Oxford, UK: Pergamon Press.

Rhode, G., Morgan, D. P., & Young, K. R. (1983). Generalization and maintenance of treatment gains of behaviorally handicapped students from resource rooms to regular classrooms using self-evaluation procedures. *Journal of Applied Behavior Analysis, 16,* 171–188.

Roberts, M. L., & Shapiro, E. S. (1996). Effects of instructional ratios on students' reading performance in a regular education program. *Journal of School Psychology, 34,* 73–91.

Shapiro, E. S. (1996). *Academic skills problems: Direct assessment and intervention* (2nd ed.). New York: Guilford Press.

Shapiro, E. S., & Cole, C. L. (1994). *Behavioral change in the classroom: Self-management interventions.* New York: Guilford Press.

Shaywitz, B. A., Fletcher, J. M., Holahan, J. M., & Shaywitz, S. E. (1992). Discrepancy compared to low achievement definitions of reading disability: Results from the Connecticut longitudinal study. *Journal of Learning Disabilities, 25,* 639–648.

Sheridan, S. M., Kratochwill, T. R., & Bergan, J. R. (1996). *Conjoint behavioral consultation: A procedural manual.* New York: Plenum Press.

Shinn, M. R. (1995). Best practices in curriculum-based measurement and its use in a problem-solving model. In A. Thomas & J. Grimes (Eds.), *Best practices in school psychology III* (pp. 547–567). Washington, DC: National Association of School Psychologists.

Shinn, M. R., & Bamonto, S. (1998). Advanced application of curriculum-based measurement: "Big ideas" and avoiding confusion. In M. R. Shinn (Ed.), *Advanced applications of curriculum-based measurement* (pp. 1–31). New York: Guilford Press.

Shinn, M. R., Collins, V. L., & Gallagher, S. (1998). Curriculum-based measurement and its use in a problem-solving model with students from minority backgrounds. In M. R. Shinn (Ed.), *Advanced applications of curriculum-based measurement* (pp. 143–174). New York: Guilford Press.

Shinn, M. R., Rosenfield, S., & Knutson, N. (1989). Curriculum-based assessment: A comparison and integration of models. *School Psychology Review, 18,* 299–316.

Short, R. J., & Talley, R. C. (1997). Rethinking psychology in the schools: Implications of recent national policy. *American Psychologist, 52,* 234–240.

Shriver, M. D., Allen, K. D., & Matthews, J. R. (1999). Effective assessment of the shared and unique characteristics of children with autism. *School Psychology Review, 28,* 538–558.

Stoiber, R. C., & Kratochwill, T. R. (2000). Empirically supported interventions and school psychology: Rationale and methodological issues—Part I. *School Psychology Quarterly, 15,* 75–105.

Stoner, G., & Green, S. K. (1992). Reconsidering the scientist-practitioner model for school psychology practice. *School Psychology Review, 25,* 199–213.

Talley, R. C., & Short, R. J. (1995). *School health: Psychology's role. A report to the nation.* Washington, DC: American Psychological Association.

Tilley, W. D., & Grimes, J. (1998). Curriculum-based measurement: One vehicle for systemic educational reform. In M. R. Shinn (Ed.), *Advanced applications of curriculum-based measurement* (pp. 32–60). New York: Guilford Press.

Weisz, J. R., & Hawley, K. M. (1998). Finding, evaluating, refining, and applying empirically supported treatments for children and adolescents. *Journal of Clinical Child Psychology, 27,* 206-216.

Witt, J. C., & Elliott, S. N. (1985). Acceptability of classroom intervention strategies. In T. R. Kratochwill (Ed.), *Advances in school psychology* (Vol. 4). Hillsdale, NJ: Erlbaum.

Ysseldyke, J. E. (1982). The Spring Hill Symposium on the future of psychology in the schools. *American Psychologist, 37,* 547-552.

Ysseldyke, J., Dawson, P., Lehr, C., Reschly, D., Reynolds, M., & Telzrow, C. (1997). *School psychology: A blueprint for training and practice II.* Bethesda, MD: National Association of School Psychologists.

Ysseldyke, J. E., Reynolds, M. C., & Weinberg, R. A. (1984). School psychology: A blueprint for training and practice. Minneapolis: National School Psychology Inservice Training Network, University of Minnesota.

Ysseldyke, J. E., Thurlow, M., Christenson, S. L., & Weiss, J. (1987). Time allocated to instruction of mentally retarded, learning disabled, emotionally disturbed, and nonhandicapped students. *Journal of Special Education, 21,* 43-55.

INDEX

D